THIRD EDITION

THE HUMAN VENTURE

A World History
from Prehistory to the Present

Anthony Esler
College of William and Mary

Prentice Hall, Upper Saddle River, New Jersey 07458

Library of Congress Cataloging-in-Publication Data

Esler, Anthony.
    The human venture: a world history from prehistory to the present
    / Anthony Esler.—3rd ed.
       p.   cm.
    Includes bibliographical references and index.
    ISBN 0-13-190695-X
    1. World history.   I. Title
D21.E755   1996
909—dc20
                                      95-31665
                                      CIP

*For my father, Jamie Arthur Esle,r
who wrote the history of the world
on one page many years ago.*

Editorial director: *Charlyce Jones Owen*
Acquisitions editor: *Sally Constable*
Editorial assistant: *Justin Belinski*
Editorial/production supervision: *Linda Pawelchak*
Interior design: *Christine Gehring Wolf*
Cover design: *Thomas Nery*
Photo research: *Rona Tucillo*
Manufacturing buyer: *Nick Sklitsis*
Design director: *Anne Bonanno Nieglos*
Marketing manager: *Alison Pendergast*
Line art coordinator: *Michele Guisti*
Illustrator: *Maryland Cartographics*
Electronic Art Production: *Maria Piper, Mirella Signoretto*
Cover photo: *Scala / Art Resource*
Electronic page makeup: *Lori Kane*

© 1996, 1992, 1986 by Prentice-Hall, Inc.
Simon & Schuster / A Viacom Company
Upper Saddle River, New Jersey 07458

Printed in the United States of America
10 9 8 7 6 5 4 3 2 1

ISBN 0-13-190695-X

PRENTICE-HALL INTERNATIONAL (UK) LIMITED, *London*
PRENTICE-HALL OF AUSTRALIA PTY. LIMITED, *Sydney*
PRENTICE-HALL CANADA INC., *Toronto*
PRENTICE-HALL HISPANOAMERICANA, S.A., *Mexico*
PRENTICE-HALL OF INDIA PRIVATE LIMITED, *New Delhi*
PRENTICE-HALL OF JAPAN, INC., *Tokyo*
SIMON & SCHUSTER ASIA PTE. LTD., *Singapore*
EDITORA PRENTICE-HALL DO BRASIL, LTDA., *Rio de Janeiro*

ONTENTS

PREFACE   XV

THE GREAT ENTERPRISE: A WORLD HISTORY TO 1500

OVERVIEW III

ZONE OF CULTURE AROUND THE WORLD   235

Chapter 18

THE MUSLIM CENTER 261

Chapter 19

GHANA AND MALI, ETHIOPIA AND ZANJ 276

Chapter 20

INDIA AND SOUTHEAST ASIA 287

Chapter 21

CHINA AND EAST ASIA 299

Chapter 22

THE MONGOL EMPIRE 316

THE GLOBE ENCOMPASED: A WORLD HISTORY SINCE 1500

OVERVIEW IV

THE WORLD IN BALANCE   353

*O*VERVIEW VI

THE WORLD TORN BY WAR AND REVOLUTION   559

OVERVIEW VII

THE GLOBALIZATION OF HISTORY   661

PREFACE

The world today seems to have entered a twilight zone between historic ages. The third edition of this book appears at a moment in history that is most commonly defined by what it is not—the *post*–cold war world, the *post*modern age, the *end* of the millennium. The New World Order so eagerly expected just a few years ago appears to be turning into a chaotic time of global *dis*order. Ours, in short, is a period between clearly defined periods.

Such in-between ages play a crucial part in human history. These transition periods reject the past, as our postmodern age is clearly doing. But they also establish new directions, new agendas that will shape our history for generations to come. Such periods are turning points, and it seems very likely that we are living through one now.

It is a fascinating time to study world history, to try to figure out how we got where we are—and where we are going from here.

As in earlier editions, the goals of this book include global perspective, breadth of coverage, a human dimension, and a strong narrative line.

Global perspective means in the first instance a book that is not Western or Europe-centered. This is *not* a history of Western civilization with chapters on "other cultures" pasted in here and there. In addition, this book tries to avoid the temptation to slip into a Eurasian-centered mode. While emphatically recognizing the remarkable contributions of both Asia and Europe to world history, *The Human Venture* tries to give due attention to early African and American civilizations as well.

Breadth of coverage means more than geographical sweep, however. Breadth means recognizing the many roles played by the female half of humankind, both as outstanding individuals and in terms of the many parts played by women in all human societies. In this book, breadth also means sometimes venturing beyond the frontiers of civilization altogether to spend some time with preurban

peoples, from Native American societies to the Aboriginal peoples of Australia. And breadth means an enthusiastic emphasis on "high culture," the art and ideas of each age and people—a cultural legacy that constitutes our most enduring inheritance from the global past.

The part played by *people*—both outstanding individuals and typical types—in history is easy to neglect when dealing with so big a picture as the whole human story. But a history that is entirely given over to trends and movements, classes, institutions, statistics, and other abstractions is, for many readers, no history at all. Writing human beings back into global history also emphasizes the human qualities we all share—an awareness we could all use more of in these troubled times.

Finally, the *strong narrative line* that the book attempts to maintain reflects two convictions. The first is that history is by its very nature a matter of change, of development or degeneration, of human affairs on the move through time. The second and perhaps more controversial assumption is that global history is going somewhere—that world history is the story of the coming together of all the peoples of Planet Earth—of a long, slow, but inexorable drift toward one world. To what final end, only the future can say.

In reviewing this book to try to keep pace with such kaleidoscopically changing times as ours, I have gone over the entire text as carefully as I could. I have introduced corrections, clarifications, and amplifications in almost every chapter.

In particular, this third edition adds considerably to the coverage of earlier African and pre-Columbian American civilizations, expanding three chapters on those areas into six. The last two chapters, on twentieth-century culture and on the problems and prospects of our own times, have also been substantially rewritten. There is more material throughout on women in history, and several chapters now draw upon "world systems" analysis of modern and premodern times.

In line with past policy, I have also introduced some new glimpses of both the ruins of the past and the changing world we live in, collected on a number of overseas journeys—this past year alone to Western Europe, Russia, China, and South Africa, among other places. I hope that these brief vignettes will both enliven the book and bring us all closer to the global past and to the world we live in today.

This daunting task has depended heavily on the editorial help and critical insights of many people.

My first thanks still go to Dan Pellow of Prentice Hall's sales department for asking what my next writing plans were—and for taking the outlandish answer seriously. I am grateful to Steve Dalphin, the former Prentice Hall editor who accepted my proposal for a single-author world history text a dozen years ago. My thanks to Sally Constable, the present History Editor under whom this edition was completed, for miraculously transforming what I feared might be seen as costly "extra pages" into "features"—a marketing plus! Thanks also to Production Editors Tony VenGraitis and Linda Pawelchak, who somehow turned hundreds of marked-up pages and typed inserts into a book.

I cannot adequately thank the scholarly readers commissioned by the publisher for their hard work, insights, objections, and advice. The finished product owes much to their criticisms.

My thanks, then, to Joe Gowaskie, Rider College; John Voll, University of New Hampshire; Penny S. Gold, Knox College; Walter S. Hanchett, SUNY/Cortland; Donald L. Layton, Indiana State University; Melvin E. Page, Murray State University; Susan Fitzpatrick, Lindenwood College; Curtis Anderson, Oakland Community College; Dorothy Zeisler-Vralsted, University of Wisconsin, La Crosse; Ed Balog and James Hood, Lindenwood College; James Weland and Nancy R. Northrup, Bentley College; Thomas Anderson, Eastern Connecticut State University; Howard A. Barnes, Winston Salem University; Olwyn M. Blouet, Virginia State University; Robert Garfield, De Paul University; W. Scott Jessee, Appalachian State University; Gerald Newman, Kent State University; and John A. Phillips, University of California–Riverside.

Special thanks must go to those who listened, argued, answered my endless questions, and generally made this book possible. For discussing the problems of writing and teaching various aspects of world history, and in some cases for letting me solicit responses from their students, I would like to thank Marjorie W. Bingham, of Women in World Area Studies; Mario D. Mazzarella and the Department of History at Christopher Newport College; J. F. Watts and the faculty of the trailblazing World Civilization course at City College of New York; Richard Snyder, William Pemberton, and the landmark World History program at the University of Wisconsin, La Crosse; and Bill Alexander, Cassandra Newby, and the students at Norfolk State University.

As always, my thanks must go to friends and colleagues here at William and Mary, who do their best to correct the sweeping generalizations I bring to the acid test of their expertise. For many years of help, my thanks to Ismail Abdalla, Berhanu Abegaz, Jim Axtell, Craig Canning, Ed Crapol, Judy Ewell, A. Z. Freeman, Phil Funigiello, Dale Hoak, Ward Jones, Gil McArthur, Jim McCord, Ed Pratt, Abdul Karim Rafeq, Ernie Schwintzer, John Selby, Tom Sheppard, Rich Sigwalt, George Strong, Cam Walker, Jim Whittenburg, and Jeanne Zeidler.

For introductions to some fascinating corners of the world, my thanks to Steve and Peggy Brush, for Peru when things were much too exciting to be saddled with a guest as well; to Professor Dong Leshan, of the Chinese Academy of Social Sciences; to Chris Drake, for showing me how to look at the African land; to Carol Clemeau Esler, for all the village-level sojourns in Europe; to Marcia Davidson Field, for her insights into Latin America over many years; to Richard Goff, for caustic comments and sage council along the Atlantic; to Professor Isaria N. Kimambo, of the University of Dar es Salaam, for insights into African historiography; to Ross Kreamer for Java and Sumatra; to Chris Mullen Kreamer, for sharing her remarkable "African destiny"; to Steve and Ann Marlowe, for expat Europe and much more; to Don Meyer, for Benares, the Ganges, and the border roads of India; and to Jerry Weiner, for running a tight ship from Abidjan to Zanzibar.

Thanks above all to my wife, Professor Cam Walker, an intrepid traveler who always sees more than I do and who agrees with me that getting altitude-sick in Lhasa or assaulted on the streets of Jo'burg is well worth what you bring back—the living memories of prayer flags fluttering above Tibetan villages, or of the sun-drenched silences that hover today over the ruins of Great Zimbabwe.

Anthony Esler

VENTURE INTO HISTORY

AN UNDERTAKING OF UNCERTAIN OUTCOME   THE HUMAN COMMITMENT TO HISTORY

HISTORY AND CIVILIZATION

AN UNDERTAKING
OF UNCERTAIN OUTCOME

History does not happen—it is made by human beings. It is made by people of differing opinions, of varied degrees of knowledge and control, of more or less good will. It is the work of all the peoples of this world, down all the human centuries. History is, has been, and will continue to be the common venture of us all.

The word *venture* derives from an old word for *adventure*—and history is surely that.

It is too easy in writing (or reading) a textbook to lose sight of the great adventure that is the human story. The long wanderings of our prehistoric predecessors over land and sea, peopling the continents, are epics of adventure that will never be written. The struggles of our ancestors with each other, sometimes savage and often tragic, are nonetheless tales of human heroism too. Even the silent inner struggles of the poet or the philosopher may be great adventures of the human spirit.

Nor are all the historic adventurers famous names in history books. The cabin boy who signed on to sail with Ferdinand Magellan and returned alive—one of seventeen to do so, the first human beings to circumnavigate the globe—was as much an adventurer as Magellan himself, whose bones whitened on a far Pacific shore. The peasant girl who never traveled ten miles from her medieval village but heard the voices of angels in the church bells ringing was as much an adventurer of the spirit as Joan of Arc, who rallied armies and left her name to history.

We are all of us part of the human venture. Bantus trekking across Africa, Amerindians descending the length of the Americas, builders of the ancient cultures of Egypt or India or China—we are all adventurers in history. The future may well look back upon our own endless sweep of four-lane, six-lane, eight-lane roads, our towers of steel and glass and concrete, our miles-high jets and rockets drifting among the stars, and see all of us today as a race of heroes.

A *venture*, according to *Webster's* dictionary, is "an undertaking involving chance, risk, or danger," an attempt fraught with "peril" and "jeopardy." We who have lived in the shadow of the mushroom cloud for two generations scarcely need to be told that history is dangerous. We may be spared the great plagues, the long hungers, the slowly descending ice that pressed inexorably upon our ancestors. But thickening air and darkening water, swollen populations, atomic power, and atomic weapons may be every bit as dangerous. And the threat of political oppression, economic collapse, war and civil war, and even of famine in some parts of the world are clearly with us as much today as they ever were.

Webster's further defines a venture as "an undertaking of uncertain outcome." Here, too, history clearly qualifies. Even the most clear-sighted historian would hesitate to say much about where we are all going—let alone whether we will ever get there. There have been those who thought they saw the outcome. Chinese scholars saw history following a pattern of endless cycles. Medieval Christians and medieval Muslims sought meaning in history as the will of God. Enlightenment philosophers and the ideologues of the last two centuries have offered various versions of the gospel of progress, of social and material improvement as the road to utopia. But we do not know that any of these patterns imposed upon the human story accurately describes the primary direction in which history is moving. We do not know for certain that history is moving in any particular direction at all!

What does seem evident from the historical record is that we are trying. The outcome may be unsure, but human beings have been laboring for many centuries to give direction to the human story. In this sense, at least, our human venture into history is a purposeful one. We may frequently be blind to our true destination. We may often be operating at vigorous cross-purposes with one another, one nation or one people against another. We may fail of our endeavors; some of the most promising historic drives have broken down in the end, collapsing from internal rot or overwhelmed by external enemies. But they have been conscious drives. Launched in the names of whatever false gods or faltering causes, group follies or individual egotism, every great movement, every great civilization has nonetheless been a deliberate effort to impose human will upon the world.

THE HUMAN COMMITMENT TO HISTORY

The perilous course of human history is thus something more than an adventure. It is a great commitment.

To our ancestors several centuries ago, the word *venture* could mean simply an investment, a risking of capital in hopes of a golden return. The human venture into history may also be seen as such an investment—a commitment of energy, purpose, and generations of human lives to the great undertaking called civilization. If history is the unending human venture as a whole, civilization may be history's greatest enterprise.

Civilization as it is usually defined began more than five thousand years ago in the Near East. From small beginnings in a river valley in ancient Mesopotamia, it has since spread round the earth.

The pattern has looked much the same everywhere and ever since. Civilization means cities and larger states, centralized and bureaucratic governments, classes and castes, technological advance and the growth of trade, the magical craft of writing, and increasingly sophisticated arts and sciences, religions and philosophies. Not all of these are found in all cases, but the overall picture is similar and clearly recognizable wherever it appears.

All civilizations also have in common a higher degree of social complexity than the societies they replace. By comparison with such nonhuman societies as those of ants or mountain gorillas, even the simplest preurban culture is a marvel of social integration. But the developed culture of Confucian China, medieval Byzantium, or the modern Western industrial state is another quantum leap ahead in complexity, intricacy, and elaborateness of social institutions.

All civilizations also make possible larger and more impressive human endeavors than would be possible otherwise. Great buildings, marvelous engineering works, and the integration of large numbers of people into a single system of administration and law are made possible by the larger resources and shared cultural assumptions of a great civilization. So are elaborate systems of thought, art of unexcelled subtlety and grandeur, and longer, healthier, less circumscribed lives for millions of people. Major civilizations, in short, substantially enhance the human capacity for achieving human goals.

Yet there are those who regard this entire enterprise as pointless, illusory, or even downright dangerous, and their objections are not to be lightly dismissed by the serious student of history.

As far back as ancient times, for instance, some students of the human past saw civilization as a pointless exercise. In their view, the fundamental pattern of the histories of all nations was a meaningless trajectory of rise and fall. Rome and Babylon, mighty once, are ruins today. What purpose, then, in laboring to build anew, if such desolation is the end of all constructive labor? Even those who see much virtue in our efforts at building civilization must admit that many—though not all—civilizations have followed this path from hopeful beginnings to an apogee of greatness and then down once more into oblivion.

Another school of critical thought, also going back to ancient times, rejects civilization as an illusory attempt to improve human welfare, hailing instead the easy round of life among preurban peoples as a happier and more natural mode of existence. This glorification of the noble savage finds its most recent embodiment in the uncritical admiration of hunter-gatherer societies or of self-sufficient agricultural village life today. Again, it may well be that the lives of such peoples in the distant past were healthier, less authoritarian, and even less dangerous than we once believed.

It is true, finally, that the increased capacity for working our human will upon the world, which comes with civilization, has not always been utilized to advance the common good. Great crimes have been committed in the name of civilization. Narrow definitions of good and evil have led highly civilized peoples to deal savagely with others whose definitions differed from their own. Ignorance, self-interest, and perhaps even darker instincts in the human psyche have led high cultures to devastate their neighbors. Twentieth-century industrial civilization has doubled the human life span and provided cradle-to-grave security for whole populations. It has also applied its unparalleled technological ingenuity to such unhappy inventions as total war and totalitarian politics, widespread economic exploitation and unprecedented destruction of our natural environment.

Heavy charges, then, may be laid against the human enterprise we call civilization.

Perhaps the best response to all these criticisms lies in the historical record itself—in the long record of human commitment to the rearing of complex and far-reaching civilized societies. At least as striking as the pattern of rise and fall in the history of cultures is the eternal recurrence of the drive to build and build again, to raise civilization once more from its own ruins. Earlier styles of life, like the hunting band and the pastoral nomadic style, are rapidly nearing extinction today. Even the once widespread autonomous agricultural village is undergoing rapid assimilation into an urban-dominated order as peoples the world around rush to join the latest wave of civilized societies, those built on the culture of the machine.

On the whole, then, human beings seem to value what more sizable and complex societies can give them more than they fear the abuses of power that go with civilization. From the nomadic Germans and Mongols who begged admittance into the empires of ancient Rome and Han China to the Africans and Asians who swarm into the cities of those continents today, people have been voting for civilization with their lives for many hundreds of years.

HISTORY AND CIVILIZATION

This millennial drift toward larger and more complex cultures will be one of the main themes of this book. Before beginning the story, however, let us look at least briefly at this positive side of the ledger, at some of the splendid achievements of human civilization over the centuries.

Of course, not everyone chose that most difficult game, the building of civilization. In what is now Cameroon, at the inner angle of West Africa, they say that the forest peoples who are traditionally imagined to have "retreated" into the jungle under "pressure" from the great West African kingdoms to the north in fact withdrew deliberately into the freedom of the rain forest. They turned their backs on the substantial burdens that would accompany what their more powerful northern neighbors thought of as a higher culture.

Others followed this same road. The nomads of the Eurasian steppes and the clans of the Celtic hills *chose* their wastelands, as we shall learn. The adventures they had there and the genuine achievements of their variety of the human venture will have their honored place in this chronicle too.

In the beginning, indeed, they had it all their own way, these peoples of deserts and grasslands, rain forests, and the sea. The city-based cultures were few and isolated, and they frequently fell before the onslaught of the perfectly adapted neighbors they called "barbarians." We shall see a good deal of the accomplishments of these earlier forms of the human venture. Long voyagers like the Vikings and the Polynesians, far wanderers like the African Bantu or the mongoloid first Americans who in a few thousand years colonized two whole continents—all have performed wonders well worth recording. The victories of the great "barbarian" conquerors, from the ancient Indo-Europeans to Genghis Khan and Tamerlane, will get as much attention here as the triumphs of Alexander the Great or Chandragupta.

But in the end the mainstream of this history must be the story of the city builders, the empire builders. The peoples who undertook the greatest of human enterprises appeared in all corners of the earth, on almost every habitable continent. Isolated at first, they slowly expanded the areas of their domination at the expense of their neighbors who did not know how to build great walls or make the magic signs that spoke on stone or clay or paper. By A.D. 1500, as we shall see, the tide was turning decisively against other forms of the human venture. At the beginning of modern history, the road was open to the final victory of the city-based civilizations.

Victory justifies much, and history, as we are often told, is always written by the winners. But there is more than simply victory to justify our focus on what this book calls the great enterprise of civilization building. The builders of great civilizations have, after all, been constructing something of value.

The ruins of vanished civilizations strew the earth—evidence not so much of the inevitability of human failure as of the grandeur of the great enterprise at its best. Chinese archaeologists are still exhuming the buried army of Huangdi, thousands of life-size statues of men, horses, even chariots that tell us much about that driven man and the laboring generations who built the Great Wall of China. The glooms and glimmers of St. Peter's in Rome, aglow with marble and pigment and bronze—room after room, acre after acre of art—remind us at every visit of what splendid things the Western spirit has been capable. The great gold Buddha at Bodh Gaya in northern India and the temples of all nations grouped around it still draw pilgrims today, as they have ever since Prince Gautama found enlightenment here twenty-five centuries ago. The pitted stones of Machu Picchu, heaved high on a mountain peak above the Peruvian jungles, stir a vague feeling of awe and respect for the vanished Incas in even the most jaded tourist.

These and many other monuments, reared to the honor of forgotten kings and debatable mythologies, testify still to the strength of the backs that labored and the hands that wrought. They bear witness to the good side of the great enterprise.

There was, no doubt, an easy camaraderie in the primal band of hunters and gatherers, perhaps a certain closeness and warmth in the Neolithic village that is harder to find in civilized society. Such earlier peoples may have approximated more closely the daily, yearly round of feeding, fun, and reproduction that humans share with other animals. It was a life closer to nature than our own. And it has no history.

But one may also ask, has human life no more meaning, no more point than the life of a rabbit or an ant? Poets whisper, great faiths thunder that human life is more than that.

Socrates and Muhammad in their market squares, Christ and Buddha wandering the dusty roads of Galilee or the banks of the Ganges, Confucius preaching common decency to a war-torn world—all had, at one level, a single message. It was the message of all the storytellers and praise singers, the shapers and singers of dreams, who have immortalized human heroism and human love, great leaders and great souls. It was a word the preachers and the poets shared: We can do better. We can be more.

The builders of pyramids and skyscrapers, the human eyes and hands that painted the cave walls at Lascaux and aim rockets at distant planets today bear witness to the things humanity alone can do. With all the crimes and follies on our consciences, we are thinkers, doers, builders. And the great enterprise continues. If the past is any guide at all to what lies ahead, we will probably go on constructing ever more elaborate attempts at civilization, as we have done for the past fifty centuries and more. The good society may still elude us, but we will not stop trying.

The crimes and follies, the labors, exploits, and achievements of those first fifty centuries of the human venture are the subject of this book.

SUGGESTED READING

BARRACLOUGH, G. "The Prospects of World History," *Main Trends in History*. New York: UNESCO, 1979. Problems and possibilities of the global approach.

_____ , ed. *The Times Atlas of World History*. London: Times Books, 1978. An essential guide, with clear, colorful maps tracing major trends, from migration and trade to religious conversion and invasions.

BRONOWSKI, J. *The Ascent of Man*. Boston: Little, Brown, 1973. A topical account, with emphasis on science and technology. Lavishly illustrated.

LANGER, W. L., ed. *An Encyclopedia of World History*. Boston: Houghton Mifflin, 1972. The standard chronological reference.

MCNEILL, W.H. "A Defense of World History," *World History Bulletin*, 1 (1983), 1, 3–7. A more positive assessment than Barraclough's.

_____ , *A World History*, 2nd ed. New York: Oxford University Press, 1971. A pioneering one-volume overview by a leading proponent of the global approach.

ROBERTS, J. M. *The Pelican History of the World*. New York: Penguin Books, 1980. A reflective look at the global past; especially good on available sources for each culture and period.

STAVRIANOS, L. S. *Lifelines from Our Past: A New World History*. New York: Pantheon Books, 1989. Links past and present in a new periodization of global history.

THOMAS, H. *A History of the World*. New York: Harper Collins, 1979. Valuable study, with emphasis on technology and material culture.

TOYNBEE, A. *A Study of History* (12 vols.). New York: Oxford University Press, 1934–1961. Controversial but erudite multivolume study of past civilizations, with emphasis on culture and on the historical process itself. A two-volume abridgment by D. C. Somervell (New York: Dell Books) gives the gist of Toynbee's work.

UNESCO History of Mankind (6 vols.). New York: Harper & Row, Pub., 1963. One of a number of useful multivolume and multiauthor series on world history, this one reflecting the views of many non-Western as well as Western historians.

CHAPTER 1

Before Civilization

HUMAN DEVELOPMENT

BEGINNINGS

Perhaps the most familiar version of the beginning of human life on earth is that given in the Judeo-Christian Old Testament:

> But there went up a mist from the earth, and watered the whole face of the ground.
> And the Lord God formed man of the dust of the ground, and breathed into his nostrils the breath of life; and man became a living soul. (*Genesis* 2:6–7)

And more familiar still:

> So God created man in his own image, in the image of God created he him; male and female created he them. (*Genesis* 1:27)

One of the most vivid modern Western representations of the creation is surely the series of pictures painted by Michelangelo on the ceiling of the Sistine Chapel in the Vatican at Rome. Thousands of tourists daily crane their necks to gaze up at the magnificently muscled, hugely bearded figure of Jehovah dividing light from darkness with a gesture, rolling the sun and the moon into being, extending his powerful right hand to bestow upon Adam the ultimate gift of life.

An African version of the creation says that Doondari made humankind out of the "five elements"—fire, water, air, iron, and stone. The oldest of all creation stories, that of the "Memnite theology" carved in stone at Memphis on the Nile almost five thousand years ago, calls the creator Ptah and says that he made the first sentient beings with weapons in their hands! Down the centuries and around the world, "first things" have thus been matters of profound concern for many peoples.

Our own modern version of the beginnings of things is as exotic as any, though it seems (to us, at least) rather more likely to be true.

In the beginning, modern science tells us, the solid earth beneath our feet was not solid at all, but a ring of glowing, superheated gases swirling around the searing core of our sun. There was a cooling and a condensing, and where only the gaseous outreach of a spinning star had been, there were separate whirling chunks of slowly cooling matter. Several billions of years in the future people would call these "planets."

The cooling and settling continued, with dramatic changes in what became our world. This third planet out from the sun cooled and hardened on the surface, though the core has remained molten and seething. Water spread over much of the globe, and an atmosphere that we would find breathable slowly formed to a height of several miles above the surface. In this strange world of exploding volcanoes, flickering lightning, and bombarding cosmic rays, matter miraculously quickened into life in the primal seas.

From single-celled bacteria and "blue-greens" to shapeless jellies and shelled creatures in the sea, from shellfish to insects, from backboned fish to reptiles, birds, and beasts, animal life evolved. Vegetable life developed also over the uncountable hundreds of millions of years, from moss and horsetails to conifers and broad-leafed trees, from ferns to fruits and flowers. Long before the first identifiable hominid squinted into the sun, our Eden was prepared.

Change continued in the world around us even after the human race had begun to take shape. Shifts in the surface structures of the earth caused the continental masses to drift slowly apart. The oceans grew and shrank, rose and fell. The climate changed drastically from one geological epoch to the next, caking the northern zone with ice, turning forests into grasslands, grasslands into deserts. Nevertheless, by the time history began, a recognizable geography had taken shape. Since, with some continuing changes, this was to be the stage for all our subsequent adventures, we should survey it briefly before going on to the actors and the story.

More than two thirds of the earth—the oceans, seas, lakes, and rivers of the world—was covered with water. The large expanses of dry land that protruded from this world-ocean formed seven continents. One of these, Antarctica, the frozen land around the South Pole, was all but uninhabitable. Of the other six, two were actually a single land mass, the great world island of Eurasia, divided for historical reasons into Europe in the west and the far larger expanse of Asia to the east. South of Europe, Africa, the largest continent after Asia, stretched southward across the equator and on toward the southern pole.

The other three continents lay farther away, cut off by seas and oceans from Eurasia and Africa. Australia lay at the far edge of Southeast Asia, in the western Pacific. North and South America, linked by the narrow isthmus of Central America, were isolated even more thoroughly from the rest of the world by the ocean barriers of the Atlantic and the Pacific.

Each of these continental land masses, and many of the islands that lay between them, had a range of climate and topography that provided a great variety of environments for human beings. These varying niches would in turn foster a variety of styles of life and help shape a number of historic societies, as we shall see.

Many factors, of course, have had a hand in shaping human cultures in history. For the time being, the fact of regional and cultural differences and the fact that geography helped determine them need only be noted here. There were, however, many ways in which our common humanity also determined our destiny as a species on this planet. It is to the emergence of that common human nature that we must now turn.

THE BONE HUNTERS

Almost all we know about the earliest stages of human life on hearth has been uncovered during the last century and a half. The first Neanderthal bones clearly identified as belonging to prehistoric "cave men" were found by workers building a railway in the Neander Valley of Germany in 1856. Since then, archaeologists, antropologists, and other professional "bone hunters" have dug up whole races of our human and prehuman ancestors. They have also stirred up considerable controversy in so doing.

Their discoveries have pushed the human story back far into the prehistoric past. In Olduvai Gorge in Tanzania, East Africa, Mary and Louis Leakey uncovered the skull that established the African origins of the human species. The skeleton of Don Johanson's "Lucy," found scattered over a hillside in Ethiopia, pushed prehuman origins back several million years. Hominid or human-like bones from more recent times include those of the Cro-Magnon and Neanderthal types first found in France and Germany and their kin Peking Man and Java Man discovered at the other end of Asia. With many of these finds, rude stone tools and later pots, pictures, and bits of clothing have been unearthed.

Experts in many fields have contributed to our understanding of these remains. Geologists and laboratory scientists have learned to date the finds by analyzing the rock strata in which they are found or by carbon dating, which measures the dwindling carbon radiation of the finds themselves. Biologists link the surviving bits of bone to ourselves by comparing anatomical structures, blood groups, and chromosome patterns. Ethologists and anthropologists make more controversial comparisons with the behavior of other animals and of surviving food-

gathering peoples like the Khoi-San of Africa or the Australian Aborigines.

Though they usually consist only of bones and stones, these discoveries have sometimes been much more sensational. The famous "Ice Man," an intact human corpse discovered frozen in the Alpine ice in 1991, came complete with deerskin coat, fur hat, stone dagger, bow and arrows, and a crude copper ax. Scientific theories can also be astonishing. Comparisons of genetic material from contemporary humans around the world, for instance, have led some scientists to claim that all of us can trace our ancestry to an "African Eve." This single early hominid—if the theory proves correct—lived in Africa 200,000 years ago.

The experts have come up with many such theories to explain the connections between these prehistoric remains, and between prehistoric people and ourselves. The pattern of evolutionary development favored by most scientists is outlined very generally below. But how many earlier human-related species there were, how they related to each other, whether we have a "family tree" or a confusing evolutionary bush with many branches rather than a single central stem—all these questions await final answers.

BIOLOGICAL EVOLUTION

A few simple numbers may help to put the story that begins here in at least rough chronological perspective. Dates have that value, at least, in history. And these dates are easy enough to remember, since all of them begin with five.

What is usually taught in school as modern history—from the world of Christopher Columbus and Leonardo da Vinci, Babur the Great and Suleiman the Magnificent, to the present age of Einstein and atomic power—covers a span of some five hundred years. The entire history of civilized humanity, from the first clay cities in ancient Sumer to the present, goes back more than five thousand years. The prehistoric line of human evolutionary development extends at least five million years into the past. It is this immense span of time with which we shall be primarily concerned in the present chapter.

Our most ancient detectable ancestors actually go considerably farther back than that. Scarcely recognizable as our kin to any but the informed scientific imagination, these small, furry creatures had huge nocturnal eyes and long tails. They balanced on high branches and snatched at insects in the primeval rain forests of the earliest age of mammals, not long after the passing of the dinosaurs. From these *prosimian* ancestors who lived tens of millions of years ago, there evolved several lines of mammals called *primates*: lemurs and their kin, Old and New World monkeys, and apes, the family to which the human race belongs. Among these ancient apes—whose other descendants today include orangutans, chimpanzees, and gorillas—there emerged as long as five million years ago the line of devel-

PROBING THE PAST

"The gully in question was just over the crest of the rise where we had been working all morning. . . . But as we turned to leave, I noticed something lying on the ground partway up the slope.

"That's a bit of a hominid arm," I said.

"Can't be. It's too small. Has to be a monkey of some kind."

We knelt to examine it.

"Much too small," said Gray again.

I shook my head. "Hominid."

"What makes you so sure?" he said.

"That piece right next to your hand. That's hominid too."

"Jesus Christ," said Gray. He picked it up. It was the back of a small skull. A few feet away was part of a femur: a thighbone. "Jesus Christ," he said again. We stood up, and began to see other bits of bone on the slope: a couple of vertebrae, part of a pelvis—all of them hominid. An unbelievable, impermissible thought flickered through my mind. Suppose all these fitted together? Could they be parts of a single, extremely primitive skeleton? No such skeleton had ever been found—anywhere.

"Look at that," said Gray. "Ribs."

A single individual?

"I can't believe it," I said. "I just can't believe it."

"By God, you'd better believe it!" shouted Gray. "Here it is. Right here!" His voice went up into a howl. I joined him. In that 110-degree heat we began jumping up and down. With nobody to share our feelings, we hugged each other, sweaty and smelly, howling and hugging in the heat-shimmering gravel, the small brown remains of what now seemed almost certain to be parts of a single hominid skeleton lying all around us."

---◆─◆─◆---

The excitement of digging up the past is vividly illustrated by this first-hand account of the 1974 discovery by paleo-anthropologist Donald Johanson and his colleague Tom Gray of the skeleton of a prehuman hominid, Lucy, believed to have lived three and a half million years ago.

What problems of identifying such bones are indicated by Gray's remarks? What can you deduce about the particular importance of the find from Johanson's thoughts? Maitland Edey, Johanson's co-author, is a distinguished writer on scientific subjects for nonscientific readers. What do you think he may have contributed to this dramatic account? (Assume Johanson and Gray did not happen to have a tape recorder running when they made their discovery.)

Donald Johanson and Maitland Edey. Lucy: The Beginnings of Humankind (New York: Warner Books, 1981), pp. 16–17.

opment known as *hominids*, of which the humans of our own time are the only surviving descendants.

Over this vast tract of time, from the first prosimian to the most developed hominid, the ancestors of humanity changed both biologically and culturally. These changes first enabled them to survive and then gave them increasing mastery of their environment. For biological evolution, a few paragraphs will suffice; for the story of our cultural evolution, the rest of the chapter will be required.

The biological changes over tens of millions of years were certainly striking. The eyes of that first tree dweller, for instance, evolved dramatically, developing both stereoscopic (depth) vision and color sightedness, very useful capacities for leaping from branch to branch or distinguishing brightly colored fruit from the green canopy that was the prosimian's world.

When our progenitors abandoned the shrinking primeval forest for the open grasslands five million years ago, more changes followed. Their legs and feet changed to permit erect bipedal walking on the African savannas. This in turn freed the hands for carrying game and foraged nuts and berries back to the family circle. The hands developed too, producing the most efficient opposable thumb for fine manipulation of any primate's. Most important, the hominid brain grew, doubling and tripling in size and evolving a neural capacity that gave human beings their most valuable biological advantage: the capacity to go beyond biology to culture.

Down the long evolutionary road, a number of hominid species developed, flourished for a time, and then died out. The earliest Australopithecines, of three and a half million years ago, were perhaps four feet tall and had brains about a third the size of a modern human's. Hominids of the Neanderthal line, who appeared perhaps 125,000 years ago, were close enough to ourselves, it is sometimes said, to pass for modern people in the New York subway.

These species left their bones on the African grasslands, in the caves of North China, or among the glaciers of ice-age Europe. But those hominids who survived were making delicate stone tools, burying their dead with ceremony, and decorating the walls of their caves with paintings of the animals they hunted as the last glaciers withdrew to the north. These survivors, who emerged approximately thirty-five thousand years ago, were the Cro-Magnon people, a subspecies of the hominid family called *Homo sapiens sapiens* ("wise people"). They were in fact the last of the hominid line. Biologically, they were indistinguishable from ourselves.

The Prehistoric Migrations

While it evolved physically, the human race was also spreading to almost every corner of the earth.

The earliest hominid species first evolved toward humanity in southern and eastern Africa. Fossil bones going back several million years testify to our long residence on that continent. Then, perhaps half a million years ago, human beings began to move northward. Both the motive for this greatest of human migrations and the means to make these journeys were provided by the most disturbing natural phenomenon of the period: the ice age.

A rather modest drop in average temperatures in the Northern Hemisphere—no more than a few degrees—was enough to prevent the winter's snows from melting the following summer, so that next winter's snows piled on top of them. By 500,000 B.C., the ice stood thick over northern Europe and had intruded deep into North America. In time, however—forty thousand to sixty thousand years—the cooling trend reversed itself, and warmer weather pushed the edge of the ice cap back into the Arctic. This advance and retreat of the ice took place several times over the last half million years of the Old Stone Age.

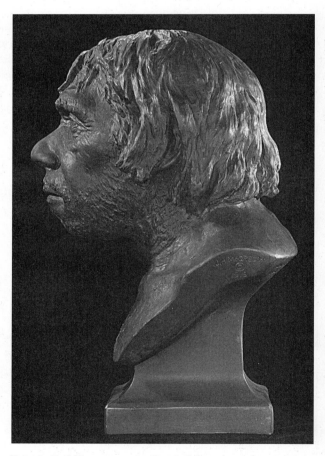

Neanderthal Man—as reconstructed from bone fragments by a modern researcher—squints into an uncertain future. Some authorities now suspect that the Neanderthal subdivision of the hominid family did not die out before breeding with <u>Homo sapiens sapiens</u>. Modern people may thus carry some of the genes of this long-vanished race. (American Museum of Natural History)

The descent and withdrawal of the glacier turned Europe and other parts of the Northern Hemisphere from relatively barren areas to well-watered comparatively lush forests and grasslands, the latter especially capable of supporting deer, bison, hairy elephants, and other large game for hominid hunters. The freezing over of the north had a second great effect, however; by locking up a significant percentage of the earth's surface water in colossal ice sheets, the glaciers lowered the level of the world's oceans, creating temporary land bridges between large land areas that were otherwise cut off from each other by sea.

Perhaps two million years ago, then, our hominid forebears moved north out of Africa and up through the Near East into Eurasia. From the Near East, some drifted west into Europe, others eastward across Asia. A skull recently found in China indicates that our ancestors reached East Asia two hundred thousand years ago.

Migration beyond the Old World—Africa, Europe, and Asia—had to wait for the land bridges. Between 70,000 and 40,000 B.C., however, human beings reached Australia, going most of the way by land and improvising some sort of boats for perhaps only fifty miles or so. Between 40,000 and 20,000 B.C., other groups of humans followed their prey across another land bridge at what is today the Bering Strait to the Americas. Canadian glaciation may have held them up for a considerable time, but once a corridor had opened southward, hunting and gathering humanity flooded south to feed upon whole new species of food plants and game. In a short time, perhaps no more than a few thousand years, the human race had colonized North and South America too.

The great migrations were neither as purposive nor as direct as this schematic account may sound. Quite likely, humans advanced and retreated as the glaciers did, hunting and gathering in the shadow of the ice. Whole branches of the evolving half-human race were caught in culs-de-sac and became extinct, along with the plants and animals they fed on. Others adapted to new conditions and drifted on, reacting to shifts in climate and vegetation, following the herds.

We should not imagine anything like the picturesque migrations of historic nomads, whole tribes and peoples trundling across the steppes with beasts and baggage. It might take a tiny hunting band several lifetimes to decide to move on to the next valley. But then, even at an average pace of no more than ten miles a generation, it would have taken early hominids only fifteen thousand years to travel from East Africa to North China.[1] Even with endless backtracking and aimless wandering—since after all they had no plans for reaching North China, or anywhere else in particular—it is not surprising that

our prehistoric ancestors were able to spread around the world in half a million years.

THE HUMAN RACES

Closely related to these primal folk wanderings is another often-noticed aspect of our humanness: the racial differences that distinguish some groups of human beings from others.

They are very modest differences. No human type differs as strikingly from another as a St. Bernard does from a Chihuahua, or a tiger from an alley cat. But there are detectable physical differences among the three major racial groups—caucasoid, mongoloid, and negroid—and among such surviving racial remnants as the bushmanoid and pygmoid peoples of Africa and the australoids who were the original inhabitants of Australia. And these differences do go back to the great migrations of prehistoric times.

Racial differences seem to have evolved like other human adaptations, in order that subdivisions of the species might survive under the drastically differing conditions humanity encountered in various parts of the world. For instance, Eskimos tended toward stocky builds, which retain body heat in the arctic cold. Equatorial peoples developed high concentrations of skin-darkening melanin, which protect them from the sun's heat.

We thus became hardy and versatile animals indeed. Some of us developed immunities to the ever-present infectious parasites of tropical rain forests. Others built lungs capable of breathing the thin air of the Andes and the Himalayas. We have adapted physically as well as culturally to deserts where only a few spiny growths of vegetation and a handful of insects and reptiles can survive, and to arctic wastelands where houses must be built of snow and the sun does not rise above the horizon for half the year. We have learned to live in a wider range of physical environments than any other species on the face of the planet—and some of this versatility is due to racial variations.

Two or three other points should be briefly made about the racial diversity that is part of our heritage from prehistory.

First and most important, we are in fact not many but one single human race. Only one branch of the hominid line has survived—*Homo sapiens sapiens*—and we are all members of that species. Beneath all minor differences of lip thickness, inner eyefold, texture of hair, skin pigmentation, and proportion of leg length to length of trunk, we remain one breeding group, one people biologically.

Second, the various subdivisions of the species we have come to call *races* have historically become inextricably mixed almost everywhere—with generally excellent results. The exchange of cultural know-how that comes

[1] Richard E. Leakey and Roger Lewin, *Origins* (New York: E. P. Dutton, 1977), pp. 120–121.

GLOBAL DISTRIBUTION OF HOMINIDS AND HOMO SAPIENS

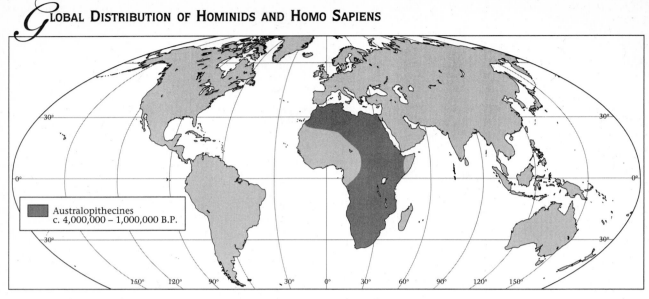

Australopithecines
c. 4,000,000 – 1,000,000 B.P.

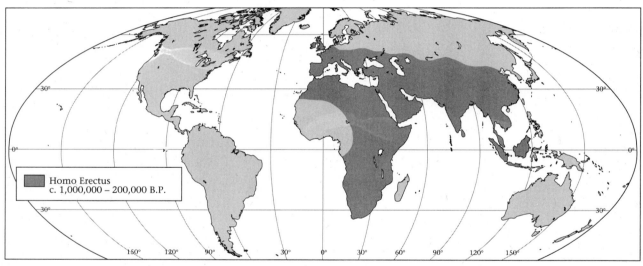

Homo Erectus
c. 1,000,000 – 200,000 B.P.

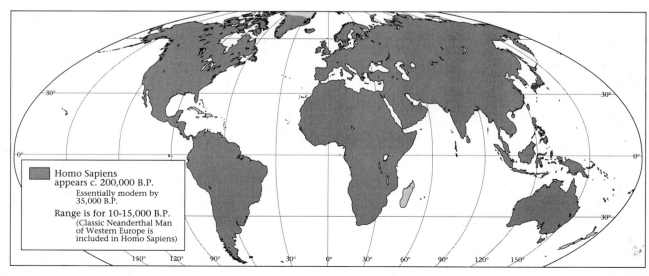

Homo Sapiens
appears c. 200,000 B.P.

Essentially modern by
35,000 B.P.

Range is for 10-15,000 B.P.
(Classic Neanderthal Man
of Western Europe is
included in Homo Sapiens)

with the mixing of peoples made the polyglot, often turbulent Near East perhaps the most culturally productive corner of the globe. The historic isolation of a place such as Australia, by contrast, produced little in the way of social change and cultural development.

Finally, it scarcely needs to be mentioned that no one of the world's peoples has shown any intrinsic superiority to any other. There have been barbarians of every color, and enviable civilizations have been built by people of all racial stocks. In the end, it is the course of cultural evolution that distinguishes one people from another historically—not biological evolution. And it is to that cultural evolution that we must turn now.

PALEOLITHIC FOOD GATHERERS

THE FOOD-GATHERING BAND

In terms of cultural development, the evolving lifeways of the species, almost all of this first five million years is called the *Paleolithic period*, or Old Stone Age. For it was with stone tools that our human and prehuman ancestors survived on the land.

Like their prehuman ancestors, early hominids were both vegetarian and carnivorous. They were gatherers of nuts, roots, berries, and other vegetable food. They were also hunters of all sorts and sizes of game—from the huge, hairy mammoth and vast herds of deer to a wide range of smaller animals, birds and fish. Their style of living and the whole course of their cultural evolution were significantly shaped by this fundamental activity of prehistoric people: the collection of sufficient food to keep them alive.

Humans seem to have learned quite far back that survival is a cooperative venture. Food gathering alone, the collection of primarily vegetable food, can be undertaken on an individual basis. Hunting, however, particularly the hunting of large animals, is practiced most efficiently by groups working in close cooperation. Prehistoric hominids, like wolves or lions, worked together to pull down animals as large as the giant sloth or the elephant-sized mammoth. Almost uniquely even among hunting animals, furthermore, hominids seem to have shared their food on a regular basis, dividing up game and vegetable food among all the members of the group.

From very early times, then, human beings were social animals, living and working together in the tight-knit community of a band of hunters and gatherers. In prehistoric times, as among Pygmies, Bushmen, or Eskimos today, a typical band probably numbered five or six nuclear families—no more than two or three dozen individuals altogether. These small groups developed some ingenious hunting techniques, inventing pits and other traps or using brush fires to drive whole herds of game over cliffs or into swamps where they might be easily killed. At certain seasons of the year, when major herds were due in the neighborhood, a number of such bands, adding up to several hundred hunters, might come together for a large-scale cooperative hunting expedition and a great gorge afterwards.

The technology that accompanied this social evolution—and made much of it possible—included a large "kit" of tools and weapons. Rudely split rocks were apparently being used for cutting and scraping by prehuman creatures a couple of million years ago. During the hundreds of thousands of years that followed, hand axes and knives, scrapers and spears, and finally spear-throwers and bows and arrows were chipped out of flint or carved from wood all over Africa, Europe, and Asia. Long after Europeans with more complex metallurgical skills had landed in the New World, stone arrowheads, some exquisitely shaped, were still serving American Indians as well as they had all our ancestors.

Fire, clothing, and rude shelters also appeared well before history began. Our forebears met the millennial cold of recurring ages of ice, first by wrapping themselves in animal hides, then by sewing the hides into sleeves and pantlegs, coats and hoods. They took shelter in caves and under rocky outcroppings, then in tents and shelters made primarily of bone. They tamed fire perhaps half a million years ago, first using it where they found it, then learning to kindle it through friction. The warm yellow-orange flame, used for both heating and cooking, became the center of the developing group life of the prehistoric band.

It was a simple society, rude and dangerous. For several millions of years, from the African savannas to glacier-prone Eurasia, this was the lifestyle of all our ancestors. Around such fires, it has been suggested, the monkey jabber of earlier hominids may have become speech as hunters and gatherers laid plans for the next day's labors or tried to explain more clearly than grunts and gestures could about the one that got away.

Social relations within the hunter-gatherer community may also be deduced from what we know about surviving preagricultural peoples and from some basic facts of all human life. Thus it has been suggested that these small prehistoric bands, like hunter-gatherer societies of our own time, were probably roughly egalitarian. They had little of the division into castes and classes, the powerful sense of hierarchy that was to come with organization into larger social units.

Like today's Pygmies, Bushmen, and others, prehistoric hominids probably recognized degrees of family kinship. They perhaps shared the meat of a large kill on the basis of elaborate social categories of their own, as hunting peoples still do. But in groups as small as two or three dozen, possessing so little in the way of material things, class divisions on the basis of power or wealth seem exceedingly unlikely.

STONE AGE WOMEN

Sexual distinctions probably did exist among our earlier prehistoric ancestors; but there is no reason to assume that prehistoric sex roles resembled those of any particular historic people, including our own. The female half of the human race has played many roles in a wide variety of societies down the centuries. This is quite likely to have been true in prehistoric times also.

There is some general agreement that among Stone Age hunter-gatherers, as among such peoples today,

A Venus figurine, found in Austria, of the sort that made earlier researchers see these cult objects as fertility symbols. What reasons can you think of for the omission of the individualizing face entirely? (Museum of Natural History, Vienna)

women were almost always the gatherers. Whereas hunting might involve more teamwork, gathering probably provided a more reliable source of food most of the time. Fruit, berries, nuts, roots, grubs, and shellfish were more stable and dependable sources of nutriment than the large or middle-sized game that might or might not show up at the water hole. Except in the depths of winter, then, Stone Age women—again, like hunter-gatherer women today—probably brought in most of the Paleolithic family's steady diet.

A few more generalizations may be risked about the role of women in prehistoric societies—some obvious, some rather more debatable. Women were, of course, the producers of new Paleolithic people and therefore essential to the survival of the band, indeed of the species. In addition, it seems likely that roughly monogamous pair bonding—close personal and social relations between individual men and women that provided a stable environment for rearing children—goes far back into our human and prehuman past. Women may also have been early recognized as custodians of the camp, the band's home base, while men and boys predominated in the hunting terrain.

Overall, women probably enjoyed more freedom and more influence in hunting and gathering societies than they often have in later civilizations. In surviving food-gathering cultures, at least, domestic chores and child-rearing duties are more equally shared between women and men. Within the band, women as foragers often have as much mobility and initiative as the male hunters do.

It is also possible, finally, that women were considered to have mysterious powers, perhaps on the order of those attributed to witches, prophetesses, and priestesses in later times. Almost all the sculptured figures that survive from Paleolithic times—the so-called Venus figurines—are of women. The figurines are by no means all of pregnant women, as was once thought, but range from virginal maidens to full-breasted mothers and withered crones.[2] Why these tiny figures were carved we do not know, but cult or religious purposes seem likely. In any event, these carved figures do seem to reflect the crucial place of women in the Stone Age world.

BEGINNINGS OF RELIGION AND ART

If it is difficult to reconstruct the social life of the Old Stone Age, it would seem downright foolhardy to try to guess what went on inside the skulls of our hominid ancestors. Yet even here we can do some conjecturing,

[2]Patricia C. Rice, "Prehistoric Venuses: Symbols of Motherhood or Womanhood?" *Journal of Anthropological Research*, 37 (1981), 402–414.

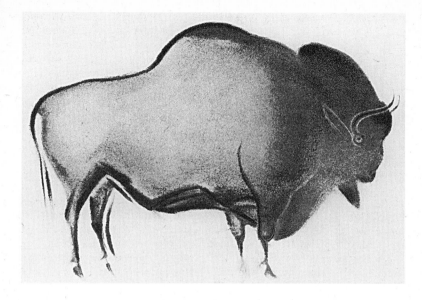

Vivid impression of a bison—huge shoulders, shaggy chest, and jutting horns—as it looked to prehistoric hunters. If you doubt the skill of the prehistoric artist who produced this cave painting, try to reproduce it with a freehand drawing of your own. (American Museum of Natural History)

at least about our more recent forebears of later Paleolithic times.

There is at least some evidence that some sort of supernatural belief—the seeds of religion—existed as far back as 100,000 B.C. At that time prehistoric hunters appear to have set up the skulls of cave bears, early humans' fiercest challengers for the rock shelters they both needed, as though to worship these huge rivals. By 50,000 B.C., Neanderthal people were burying their dead with a care and ceremony that points to a belief in some sort of life after death. Corpses were painted with red ocher, positioned carefully with the knees drawn up, provided with flint weapons, and in one famous case—at Shanidar in Iraq—strewn with fresh flowers from the surrounding hills. Finally, Cro-Magnon cave paintings of game animals indicate the possibility, by 30,000 B.C., of magical rites aimed at controlling the game supply. It is about this time also that the Venus figurines appear, quite possibly indicating not only respect for womanhood but special reverence for female divinities.

Bear skulls and burial customs, hunting rites, and rude statuettes are clues rather than proof. Still, they point to religion as one of the earliest detectable achievements of human abstract thought.

There is no question, however, about the early emergence of another basic impulse toward higher cultural expression: the invention of art.

As we noted above, Cro-Magnon people—our own direct forebears—seem to have been the inventors of the arts. They engraved recognizable animals on bone. They produced the small stone Venus figures, rudely made, armless, but clearly representational and clearly intended to be feminine. Prehistoric musical instruments have been discovered, including bone drums, rattles, whistles, pipes, and "bull roarers." Still used by aboriginal Australians on ceremonial occasions, bull roarers are attached to a string and swung around the head to produce a terrifying booming sound.

The most celebrated examples of prehistoric art are the paintings of bulls, bison, deer, horses, and other animals on the walls of caves. The most famous of them, including the dazzling painted caves at Lascaux in southern France, have been closed to the hordes of visitors whose very breath damaged pigments tens of thousands of years old. But you can go into the dark, cold caverns at nearby Les Eyzies for a glimpse of the leaping animals that filled the imaginations—and the lives—of Europe's prehistoric hunters. Thousands of miles to the south, you can see other prehistoric creatures, including some very realistic red giraffes, marching around the walls of caves in the sunny Motopo hills of southern Zimbabwe.

These prehistoric cave paintings have been interpreted in a number of ways: as hunting-cult ritual objects, as tribal totems, and even as art for art's sake. Whatever the artists' motive for making them, these naturalistic renderings of the game animals that were life itself to our ancestors certainly reveal a startling level of artistic skill.

What totems these people believed in, what taboos they practiced must remain largely objects of speculation. But we know from their graves that they talked seriously about life and death around their glowing fires. We know that bone music echoed from those painted caves tens of thousands of years before civilization as we know it was born.

NEOTHOLIC FARMERS

THE DISCOVERY OF AGRICULTURE

Group life, rudimentary technology, and the beginnings of high culture thus flourished by the end of the Paleolithic period, or Old Stone Age, the immensely long period of human development that began several million years in the past and ended no more than ten thousand years ago. The Neolithic period, or New Stone Age, that followed provides the final link in the long chain of cultural evolution that led to history proper.

The common designation of the period from 8000 to perhaps 3500 B.C. as the New Stone Age refers to the new, even more expertly crafted stone implements produced during this period. Metalworking remained undiscovered, but the polished stone tools and weapons of these last centuries of prehistory are a notable step beyond the flaked flints of earlier generations, and many steps beyond the split pebbles of our earliest precursors. The great event of the Neolithic period, however, was not the advance in stoneworking but a much more fundamental step forward in the material culture of the human race: the discovery of agriculture.

The original Agricultural Revolution was in fact the climax of prehistory—and the essential foundation upon which civilization itself would be built.

This great change from the moving life of hunting and gathering to the settled life of the farmer may have been made independently in a number of places, including several parts of Eurasia, West Africa, and Mesoamerica, but it was in the Near East that the best documented and historically most significant shift from following game to growing crops came first. It was a crucial change in the life of the race. Nothing as sweeping would occur again until the Industrial Revolution of the last two centuries.

Because the Agricultural Revolution was primarily a change in human methods of exploiting vegetable food, it is likely that this breakthrough was the work of women. As the primary gatherers of vegetable food, women would have been most likely to understand the cycle of growth, to see how human ingenuity might seize control of this natural cycle from seed to edible plant.

A number of explanations have been offered for this basic shift from hunting and gathering to agriculture. One likely cause may have been the simple exhaustion of game animals in a particular region, forcing humanity to seek other means of subsistence. Another factor may have been the evolutionary development of more readily cultivated annual forms of cereal grains in the hot, arid climate of postglacial times.

Whatever the underlying causes, this fundamental transformation in the basic human economy almost cer-

tainly came about gradually, in stages. Recent archaeological finds reveal transitional phases. Some Paleolithic peoples developed some of the social and technological skills usually associated with the Agricultural Revolution while still living primarily by hunting and gathering. Thus Old Stone Age Russian hunters built semipermanent shelters of mammoth bone twenty thousand years ago, and the Natufian food-gathering people of what is today Israel lived in rude stone huts thirteen thousand years back. On such foundations, then, the first agricultural villages rose in the Near East some ten thousand years ago.

CROPS AND FLOCKS

Agriculture most likely began with the simple practice of harvesting edible grains found growing wild, part of the normal food-gathering procedures of Old Stone Age people. Alert gatherers might sometimes encourage the ripening of the crop by extra care—for instance, by watering plants at the end of a dry summer. But the great breakthrough came when bands of *Homo sapiens sapiens* learned to plant some of the grain in order to guarantee a harvest the following year. Wherever this occurred—with wheat and barley in the Near East, millet in North China, corn in Central America—the wandering days of the hunting band were numbered and a new way of life was set in train.

Besides the growing of crops, another important aspect of the Agricultural Revolution was the domestication of animals. Again, transition stages have been hypothesized, including perhaps the herding and riding of reindeer, a comparatively docile game animal that is both ridden and herded in northern Asia today. From this success, Neolithic people could have moved naturally to herding other animals or to keeping them in pens and enclosed fields. Cattle, sheep, goats, and pigs were early domesticated in this way, horses only much later.

For some early peoples, the herding of animals became the center of their posthunting cultures. These peoples became pastoralists rather than cultivators of the soil. They did not settle, but followed their herds of deer, cattle, or horses from summer to winter pasturage, sometimes migrating across hundreds of miles of savanna, steppe, or even less attractive desert land in search of water and grass. Pastoral peoples remained closer to the lives of their hunting ancestors than farmers did. In historical times, at least, nomadic pastoralists came to covet the material goods accumulating among more settled peoples, with sometimes violent results.

Life thus grew in complexity as the Neolithic centuries rolled on. The settled agricultural peoples of the Near East, like their fellows in many parts of the globe, learned to cultivate their crops with care, to weed and irrigate, to use the manure produced by their stock to fertilize their croplands. They discovered how to breed stock for meat or for strength, how to use milk, milk products, and other animal and vegetable products seldom utilized

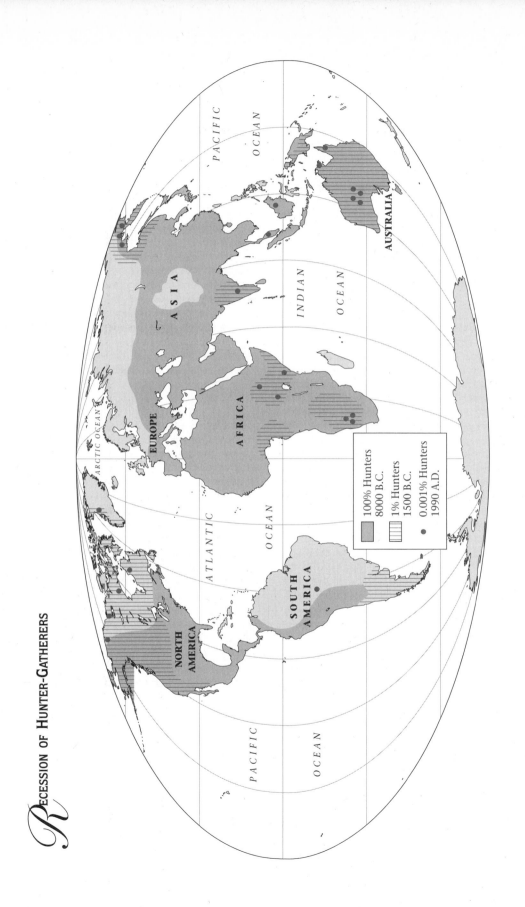

RECESSION OF HUNTER-GATHERERS

Legend:
100% Hunters 8000 B.C.
1% Hunters 1500 B.C.
0.001% Hunters 1990 A.D.

by their hunting-and-gathering predecessors. First in the rain-watered hills, then in the river valleys that provided the most fertile land, these prehistoric farmers reaped a greater bounty than nature had normally provided for their Paleolithic ancestors.

Above, all, they grew in numbers. Farming was hard work, probably more demanding than hunting and gathering had been. But agriculture had the great advantage of feeding many more people from the same tract of land than could be fed by hunting and gathering. One estimate suggests that whereas the foraging economy could support one person per square kilometer, even primitive farming could feed 50 persons from a single square kilometer. From this population growth came the Neolithic agricultural village and—in time—the city, the political state, and all their history.

LIFE IN THE NEOLITHIC VILLAGE

Handicraft technology also improved noticeably during the five millennia of the New Stone Age. As we noted above, Neolithic people learned to make polished stone tools and weapons that eclipsed even the most impressive chipped flints of their forebears. They also developed such basic agricultural equipment as a simple stick plow, pulled first by a man and later by an animal, and a flint-bladed sickle with which they harvested grain.

Other crafts also flourished. Ceramics was born, and pots made of coiled clay were decorated and glazed in a primitive kiln. Neolithic clothing progressed from animal hides to woven fabrics, first of all wool from the backs of newly domesticated sheep. And there is increasing evidence of trade, or perhaps of ritual exchanges of gifts, between one agricultural community and another.

Most striking, the New Stone Age produced the Neolithic village, and with it a revolution in the life ways of the race.

About ten thousand years ago the caves and tent shelters of roving hunters were replaced by permanent collections of huts. These were simple structures, usually made of sun-dried mud, clay brick, or stone. You can visit a stone-age village at Skara Brae in the Orkney Islands north of Scotland. Walking among the now roofless stone huts, you will find each equipped with a central cooking area, roughly partitioned sleeping spaces, and even stone shelves. Fish hooks and stone-edged scythes give clues to an economy that still included fishing even while the people learned to plant and harvest grain.

At Jericho on the west bank of the Jordan River, you can look down into the excavated site of an even older— and considerably larger—Neolithic town. Jericho, which existed as early as 7800 B.C., was at that time a cluster of round, beehive-shaped huts. Like many such communities, the town was walled and even moated—clear evidence that there was danger in the Neolithic world. There appears to have been a temple of sorts in the center of Jeri-

cho—an indication of the considerable elaboration of the simple cults and sympathetic magic of Paleolithic people into true religions.

The population of Jericho was about twenty-five hundred people, much larger than Skara Brae. But the overall pattern of settled life must have been much the same wherever it evolved, whether in the Near East thousands of years before Christ or in the Americas much later. It was to be the basic pattern of farm life throughout history—the basic pattern, to this day, of the lives of most of the world's people.

Life in the agricultural villages that sprang up around the world meant pigs and goats in the house and out, chickens under foot, and long days for a boy or girl alone in far pastures, watching the sheep or following the cattle. It was lambing or calving, milking and shearing, spinning and weaving wool from a sheep's back into rough woolen clothing. It was a close-knit community of a few hundred people whose families had lived on the same land, in the shadow of the same blue hills, as far back as the most distant memory reached, worshiping the same gods of the natural world around them, accepting the same immemorial taboos and customs.

ALTERNATE LIFESTYLES

The human venture into history has taken many forms. Its most amazing enterprise, as we shall see, has been the series of essays in civilization that began in various parts of the world more than five thousand years ago. But 99 percent of the human story thus far was played out before civilization began. And even during the historical period, most of the world remained in the hands of people who were neither literate nor urban, who did not build states or litter the earth with massive ruins; people who, though they lived in historic times, lived pretty much as their prehistoric ancestors had.

Some of this continuing precivilized majority of the human race were village agriculturalists, living in many ways as Neolithic farmers did. Some would become pastoralists, nomads following their herds of sheep or cattle in an unending search for grass and water. Some would remain hunters and gatherers, living off game and fish, fruits, roots, and vegetables, as their Paleolithic forebears did before civilization began.

Today, these are the people of the agricultural villages of Asia, Africa, and Latin America whose way of life is being slowly transformed by the encroachments of modern industrial society. They are the few surviving true nomads, whose old life is being drastically curtailed by closed frontiers and the deliberate policies of governments. They are the handful of hunter-gatherers who remain in shrinking rain forests or unoccupied polar reaches, in the Kalahari Desert of Africa or the Australian Outback.

Today, they are a dwindling portion of humankind.

EXPANSION OF AGRICULTURALISTS

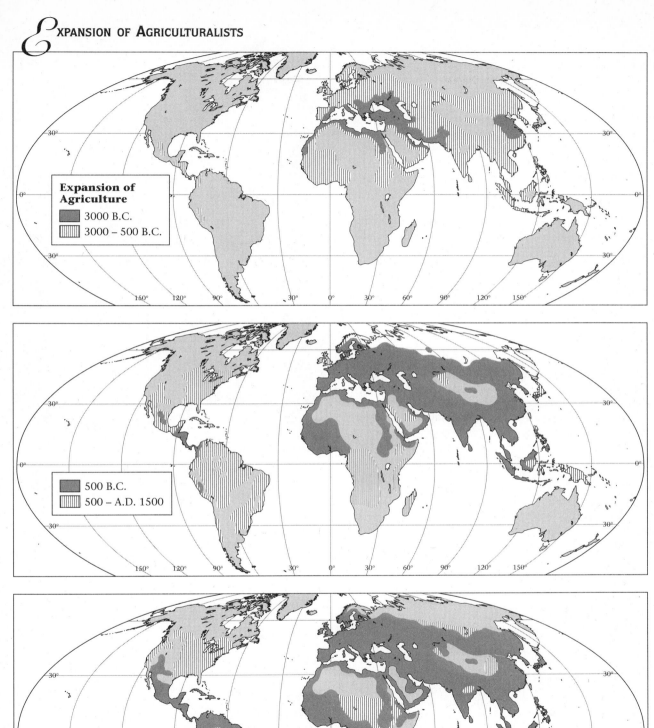

**Expansion of
Agriculture**

3000 B.C.

3000 – 500 B.C.

500 B.C.

500 – A.D. 1500

A.D. 1500

A.D. 1500 – 1990

Five and a half thousand years ago, when civilization had just begun, they were still the masters of most of the earth.

Climate and geography tended to determine the distribution of these basic styles of life—agricultural, pastoral, hunter-gatherer—around the globe during the first three thousand years of history. Thus, cultivators of such cereal crops as maize, wheat, millet, and rice were concentrated in the world's temperate zones. They flourished across central Eurasia—in Europe, the Middle East, China, and India—and in the middle parts of the Americas, from the southern reaches of North America to the northern highlands of South America. The cultivation of root crops, such as yams and manioc, was most common in the tropics, including the rain forests of South America, Central Africa, and Southeast Asia. In all these areas, agricultural villages were scattered over the land. But it was only in the temperate grain-growing regions that urban power centers eventually emerged.

Pastoral nomads wandered the steppes of Eurasia and the savannas of Africa. Their flocks of sheep and cattle were here one month and gone the next. In their journeyings they not infrequently brushed—often violently—against the new city-based civilizations of the Old World.

Finally, surviving hunter-gatherers were increasingly limited to the northern and southern extremities of the world's landmasses and the most arid corners of the earth. Hunting tribes as vigorous as their ice-age ancestors still stalked deer and other large game in the arctic regions of both the Old and New worlds. Thinning populations of hunters and gatherers scraped a living out of much smaller game and meager vegetation in the desiccated southern reaches of South America and Africa and in Australia. There were hunters on North American plains and gatherers in the deserts of the American Southwest. Living thus primarily on the last frontiers, far from the fertile temperate zones, primordial hunters and food gatherers were unlikely to have any knowledge that such a thing as civilization existed in the world.

THE TRANSITION TO CIVILIZATION

FROM CLAN TO KINGDOM

Recent work on the evolution of preurban cultures suggests that some of these early societies developed more complex political institutions as well as evolving economically, technologically, and socially. The leap from small face-to-face groups to large urban communities and empires with populations of millions is simply too great to have happened without intermediate steps. From anthropologists who have studied preurban peoples surviving

The world view of one early civilization. This Mesopotamian clay map shows the inhabited earth ringed by the Bitter Sea, with islands and perhaps a Celestial Sea beyond, the home of banished gods. Would such a schematic map be of use to travelers? What purpose could it serve? (Culver Pictures, Inc.)

into recent centuries come three possible stages of prehistoric political development: the rule of a "headman," the chiefdom, and finally the birth of monarchy in still preurban societies.

As we have seen, political institutions scarcely existed in the simplest food-gathering bands or early agricultural villages. Kinship relations, traditions and taboos, and family vengeance for offenses against a family member seem to have taken the place of governments and laws. Group allegiance focused on the family and the clan. Family members lived and worked together, forming the fundamental social unit in preurban societies. Clan members shared real or mythic ancestors, traditions, customs, and territory. But there was no political organization, no recognized leadership beyond the authority of heads of families and the influence of prestigious families within a clan.

Some such societies, however, may have produced clan or village *heads* of the sort found in such communities today. "Headmen," as they are commonly called, presided in a personal, face-to-face way over members of a clan or residents of a village, who were of course also likely to be related by blood. Often simply the senior member of a respected family, the headman exercised influence on the basis of family prestige, lavish entertainment, distribution of favors, and personal ascendancy, but this person had no prescribed powers or legal position.

Here and there, however, some headship systems may have evolved further, producing a *chiefdom*. A chief may be defined as a leader who rules, not through personal contact with members of a clan or a village community, but through *other people* who are heads of villages or clans. Chiefs could claim mythic ancestors and even supernatural powers; they were ritually installed in recognized political office; and they often passed on their exalted positions through inheritance. They exercised legal authority, served as war leaders, and surrounded themselves with pomp and circumstance. Not merely personal influence, then, but formal political power and a modest hierarchy of headmen between the chief and his people distinguished the true chiefdom.

Finally, a chiefdom on occasion might develop into a *monarchy*, or kingdom. Again, the distinction is a technical anthropological one: These kings were still leaders of preurban, preliterate peoples, not the crowned heads of the city-states and empires that would emerge with the beginnings of civilization. A kingdom among these earlier cultures, then, would be a state in which a single ruler presided over a number of chiefdoms. In later historic times, this new level of power was often generated by the raw ambition of a particular chief who imposed his will upon neighboring chiefdoms and succeeded in institutionalizing his paramount power by establishing the royal office. Claiming divine sanction for his authority, surrounding himself with ritual and taboo, appointing royal officials to speak and act for him, and ruthlessly suppressing all rivals, such a monarch might reign as "paramount chief" over thousands of people scattered over many villages. Such a preurban monarchy had clearly advanced to the brink of state organization, the emergence of cities, nations, and empires.

The Emergence of Civilization

For a period as long as all recorded history since, the agricultural village was the most complex form of human social organization, and the chiefdom and the primitive monarchy the most elaborate political structure. Then, sometime around 3500 B.C., small segments of the human family stumbled into a new and even more elaborate way of life. This new stage of human group life was achieved in the city-states and empires of ancient times. It is frequently described as the birth of civilization.

Like the Neolithic village, cities and empires emerged in different places over a span of several thousand years. Beginning not much more than five thousand years ago, civilization appeared first in Mesopotamia, Egypt, northern India, and northeastern China. Later still, urban life and imperial structures evolved in Europe, parts of Africa and the Americas, Southeast Asia, Japan, and elsewhere.

These unprecedented developments in the cultural evolution of the race have been explained in a number of ways. Some attribute the rise of larger political units to climatic change; the gradual drying out of marshes along major rivers left firm but extremely fertile land capable of supporting much larger populations. Others describe the early states as "hydraulic empires," emphasizing the need for a central political authority to tame great rivers such as the Nile, the Tigris and Euphrates, the Indus, and the Huanghe (Yellow River) of China.[3] Imperial power, according to this view, was needed to maintain the elaborate systems of dams, canals, and rules for water use that were necessary if agriculture was to realize its immense productive potential along these waterways. Still others see the expansion of political power as fundamentally a matter of greed for dominion, wealth, and glory leading to military conquest. Certainly "conquest empires" arose in many parts of the world as a result of self-aggrandizing wars—the winners absorbing the lands of the losers in larger and larger imperial domains.

Whatever the origins of these ancient cities and empires, they became the birthplaces of civilization. *Civilization* is a much debated term, one that may mean different things to different people. Here, I will define civilization as a form of society based on particular political and economic structures and generating particular social and cultural forms. Not all civilizations exhibit all these features. But all reveal a scale and complexity that distinguish them from hunter-gatherer bands, pastoral nomads, or agricultural villages. *Civilization* may be hard to define, but you will know one when you see one—whether it is in ancient Egypt or ancient Greece, China before Confucius or pre-Columbian Mexico.

Monarchy, Hierarchy, and Patriarchy

Three organizational principles dominated most early civilizations. We may call them monarchy, hierarchy, and patriarchy.

Monarchy was a form of government in which political power was exercised by monarchs—kings, queens, emperors, or other powerful individual rulers. Monarchs passed on their power through hereditary succession, so that a single family might govern for generations, even centuries. Almost everywhere monarchs ruled in close alliance with gods and the priests who

---

[3]Karl A. Wittfogel, *Oriental Despotism* (New Haven: Yale University Press, 1957).

tended them. This divinely sanctioned political authority was commonly exercised through proliferating bodies of officials. These early scribal bureaucrats collected royal taxes, administered royal justice, kept the irrigation ditches in repair or the armies in the field, and ruled in the sovereign's name as far as his cohorts could reach or his justice prevail.

The society over which monarchs ruled was increasingly organized according to the principle of *hierarchy*. Society was divided up into groups based on the function they performed, on the prestige they enjoyed, or simply on how many material things they possessed. Those with highly valued functions, traditional prestige, or material wealth were ranked higher than other people. Thus, a priest, an aristrocratic landowner, or a wealthy merchant would outrank an artisan, a peasant, or a slave in the new social hierarchy. This system of classes, castes, or social orders, which originated at the beginning of our history, is with us still today.

The term *patriarchy* refers to a family structure in which husbands and fathers exercise authority over other members. In a more general sense, patriarchy means male dominance of society as a whole. As we will see, women have always played a variety of roles in civilized societies. Nevertheless, it does seem to be true that the rough gender equality of food-gathering bands faded in early villages and cities. Men emerged as heads of the family, plowers of fields, soldiers, priests. Women were increasingly identified with household responsibilities and child rearing, with the "private sphere" of life, while men dominated the "public sphere"—the palace, the temple, and the battlefield.[4]

City Life

Crucial economic and cultural changes also characterized early civilizations. The city emerged as a uniquely powerful economic unit, the home of vast public buildings, specialized crafts, organized systems of religion, and elaborate fine arts.

_____

[4]On this complex subject, see Gerda Lerner, *The Creation of Patriarchy* (New York: Oxford University Press, 1986).

The economic foundations of city-based civilizations that emerged about 3500 B.C. were broader and more complex than at any earlier stage. Urban centers were the focus of economic innovation as well as political development during the first two or three millennia of civilization—the Bronze and Iron Ages. It was in the cities that metallurgy and other advanced crafts developed, and from these centers of wealth and population that long-distance trade reached out to similar urban areas, some of them hundreds of miles away. The hinterland, by contrast, was typically composed of agricultural villages much like those of Neolithic times, though their methods of cultivation were now more efficient and they were now firmly integrated into the larger city-centered economic unit.

In the earliest historic centuries, ancient artisans—builders, carvers of stone, workers in precious metals—joined painters, poets, philosophers, and prophets of many faiths in producing a high culture that still has the power to amaze and move us today. Vast structures such as the pyramids of Egypt or Mexico, the palace at Knossos, and the white temples on the Athenian Acropolis still draw tourists in the thousands. Jades and bronzes from the earliest periods of Chinese history have been treasured by collectors for hundreds of years.

Literature was highly developed as an art form long before any of our modern languages even existed. Early systems of writing, including Mesopotamian cuneiform, Egyptian hieroglyphics, Indian Sanskrit, Chinese characters, the Phoenician alphabet, and the Greek and Roman scripts derived from it, made it possible to preserve at least some of the wisdom and belief, the legend and poetry, of these dawn ages of human civilization.

We have not been "civilized" very long. Historic humans and their prehistoric ancestors have existed for several million years; the new life of city-dwelling, state-building, literate humanity goes back only a few thousand years. Nevertheless, that step into history was a momentous one. For better or for worse, it has made us what we are today. It has opened up an almost limitless future for the human race—if continue the pattern of development laid down so long ago, from local to larger cultures, from isolated communities toward the interdependence and even integration of the world's great civilizations.

Summary _____

The human venture actually began several million years before history did. Humankind passed through a complex development long before city life, civilization—and with them, history—finally emerged. Crucial aspects of these first five million years included evolution, migration, and racial differentiation. The human species evolved biologically from prehuman forms to *Homo sapiens sapiens*, its present incarnation. At the same time, humankind evolved culturally, adapting to its changing environment with an ingenious series of technological and social inventions. During prehistoric times also, human beings migrated from their original home in Africa to all the other habitable continents: Europe and Asia, the Americas, and Australia. Racial differences developed as additional biological adaptations to these varied habitats.

The first stage of human cultural evolution was the Paleolithic or Old Stone Age, the hunting and gathering phase of human cultural evolution, which began several million years ago. The Paleolithic era brought such fundamental discoveries as fire, clothing, basic techniques of hunting game and gathering vegetable food, and the simple social organization of the hunting band. Women played an important role in Old Stone Age society. Forms of art and religious beliefs also took shape, probably toward the end of this period.

The second stage of human social development was the Neolithic agricultural phase, which began only ten thousand years ago. Having perhaps exhausted the game in a given area, some humans settled down to cultivate crops and domesticate animals. Over a few thousand years their stone tools improved drastically, and they learned to make textiles and pottery. They also lived a more settled life in small villages, with women, the probable discoverers of agriculture, playing an important part.

A third stage of human social evolution—and the beginning of *civilization*—was reached when villages evolved into cities. This happened for the first time more than five thousand years ago, around 3500 B.C., in the Middle East. The same transition occurred over the next two or three thousand years elsewhere in Eurasia, in northern Africa, and in Middle and South America. The more complex urban-imperial cultures that resulted were distinguished by such skills and trends as city- and empire-building, metalworking, monumental architecture, literacy, bureaucratic centralized government, class structure, and a possible tendency toward patriarchy. The unfolding of this final stage over the past fifty-five hundred years will be the central concern of this book.

SUGGESTED READING

BETTINGER, P. L. *Hunter-Gatherers*. New York: Plenum Press, 1991. Contributions of archaeology and biology to our understanding of early human society. See also G. Clark's older but expert evaluation, *Stone Age Hunters* (New York: McGraw-Hill, 1967).

BORENHULT, G., ed. *The First Humans*. San Francisco: Harper, 1993. Authoritative coverage of the Old Stone Age. See also the archaeological perspectives in P. Mellars, ed., *The Emergence of Modern Humans* (Ithaca: Cornell University Press, 1990), and essays in G. L. Isaac's *The Archaeology of Human Origins* (New York: Cambridge University Press, 1989).

CAMPBELL, B. *Humankind Emerging*. Boston: Little, Brown, 1979. Highly recommended treatment of human evolutionary development. See also R. Foley, ed., *Hominid Evolution and Human Ecology* (London: Academic Press, 1984) for biological perspectives on human adaptation to a changing environment.

CHAMBERS, F. M., ed. *Climate Change and Human Impact on the Landscape*. London: Chapman and Hall, 1993. Studies of the complex relationship between humans and their environment. See also K. W. Butzer's monumental and scholarly *Environment and Archaeology: An Ecological Approach to Prehistory*, 2nd ed. (Chicago: Aldine-Atherton, 1971).

CLIVE, G. *Timewalkers: The Prehistory of Global Colonization*. Cambridge, Mass.: Harvard, 1994. Valuable account of prehistoric human migration.

COHEN, M. N. *The Food Crisis in Prehistory: Overpopulation and the Origins of Agriculture*. New Haven, Conn.: Yale University Press, 1977. Useful look at a key problem.

COON, C. *The Origin of Races*. New York: Knopf, 1963. Widely cited treatment.

EHRENBERG, M. *Women in Prehistory*. Norman: University of Oklahoma Press, 1989. Women in prehistoric Europe. See also J. M. Gero and M. W. Conkey, eds., *Engendering Archaeology: Women and Prehistory* (Oxford: Blackwell, 1991), for papers on women in preurban societies in both the Old and New Worlds; and F. Dahlberg, ed., *Woman, the Gatherer* (New Haven, Conn.: Yale University Press, 1983), for essays on women in paleolithic times. Older studies include R. Briffault's controversial theory of a "matriarchal stage" of human cultural development, *The Mothers* (New York: Atheneum, 1977). For a broader analysis, see Lerner, below.

GOUDSBLOM, J. *Fire and Civilization*. London: Allan Lane, 1992. Sees human control of fire as our first major transformation of global ecology.

HARRIS, M. *Cannibals and Kings: The Origins of Cultures*. London: Collins, 1978. Argues the advantages of earlier stages of human cultural evolution from an anthropological perspective.

HENRY, D. O. *From Foraging to Agriculture: The Levant at the End of the Iron Age*. Philadelphia: University of Pennsylvania Press, 1989. A detailed study of the first such transition. See also B. Bender,

Farming in Prehistory: From Hunter-Gatherer to Food Producer (London: J. Baker, 1975).

JOHANSON, D., and M. EDEY. *Lucy: The Beginnings of Humankind.* New York: Warner Books, 1981. Highly readable account of an important discovery. See also D. Johanson, D. L. Johanson, and B. Edgar, *Ancestors: In Search of Human Origins* (New York: Villard Books, 1994).

LERNER, G. *The Creation of Patriarchy.* New York: Oxford University Press, 1986. A classic on the interaction of class and gender in the shaping of early society.

MELKO, M., and L. R. SCOTT. *The Boundaries of Civilizations in Space and Time.* Lanham, Md.: University Press of America, 1987. The concept of "civilization" defined by historians, social scientists, philosophers and others. See also R. J. Wenke, *Patterns in Prehistory*, 3rd ed. (New York: Oxford University Press, 1990).

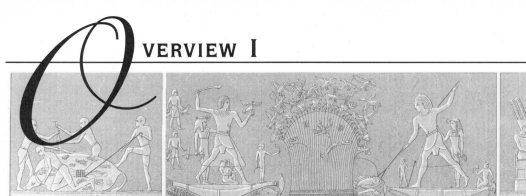

THE DAWN AGE

Civilization was born not once, but many times.

For millions of years, the sun that rose red each morning looked down on slowly evolving human species that were probably not readily distinguishable from foraging baboons or chimpanzees. A little interesting teamwork, a bit of chipped stone fitting with increasing comfort into a slowly evolving hand, was not much difference to notice. Scavenging the African grasslands where the human race was born or stalking hairy elephants amid the northern ice, Paleolithic people left little but their bones and a few chipped flints as evidence of their passing.

Then suddenly, startlingly, there was a difference. Clusters of huts appeared, with small plots of plowed and planted land and other, less clever animals penned up or grazing docilely under the watchful eyes of human herders. Here and there around the globe these clusters of settled human beings took shape and multiplied. In a scant few thousand years they were found on every continent and on many islands in the sea, as Neolithic agriculture began to change the world.

Then came another change—the great change. Less than five thousand years after the emergence of the agricultural village, vastly larger human anthills appeared, grew, and became the seedbeds of a still quite unimaginable future. The city was born—and with it, human civilization.

Like the earlier villages, the first cities cropped up in many places. At first under warm skies, close to the equator, and then in less obviously amenable environments—along northern rivers or in the high mountains—elaborate structures of stone and earth and clay brick heaved up above the surrounding landscape. There were towers and labyrinthine palaces, massive city walls, and tangled warrens of city streets. And scuttling through those mazes were human beings with a preoccupied look on their flat, relatively hairless faces. Their bobbing heads were full of most unusual questions—how to build a better brick, how to get a larger share of the irrigated fields beyond the gates, and what the great red disk that rose daily into view above the rim of the world might *mean* in the mystical cosmic scheme of things.

This moment was reached over and over again in a pell-mell rush over a few tens of centuries. It was a surge of civilizations flung up, flourishing, and tumbled down by alien hands or by the follies of their own builders. But once they had invented civilization, humans never abandoned it for long. For a few hundred years after a high culture fell, there might be only wandering herders or a scattering of villages where a city had briefly towered above the plain. But the ruins drew the eye, and the thoughtful look, the glimmer of ambition, would come once more into the naked faces of humankind. And then the walls would rise again, the labyrinths and towers.

The red sun rose on civilization's beginnings again and again around the world. Dawn rays lit up ziggurats in ancient Ur and cast long shadows from the pyramids along the Nile. Morning came over thronged cities in the jungles of the Ganges, along the Yellow River of northern China, and on the gray-green islands and narrow valleys of ancient Greece. It came in Africa among the furnaces of Meroë, and in the far Americas, where on some long forgotten day a rising sun must have shone for the first time on the colossal carved faces of the Olmecs and the first temples of Peru.

There were many differences between the civilizations that emerged around the world during the span of thirty centuries that began around 3500 B.C. Some were essentially differences of style. It is easy to distinguish between Egyptian pyramids and Indian *stupas* or shrines, between the two dozen letters of the Greek alphabet and the thousands of characters of the Chinese written language. There are more fundamental differences as well. The vast centralized empires of Persia and China contrast sharply with the small independent city-states of Mesopotamia and Greece. Some high civilizations even emerged without benefit of key elements in the standard definition of a civilization. Neither the Olmecs nor the Chavin culture of the ancient Americas developed the art of writing, and the pharaohs of Old Kingdom Egypt raised their awesome pyramids without having yet discovered the wheel.

The similarities, however, clearly outweigh the differences between these early civilizations. In a world still largely populated by agricultural villagers and wandering bands of nomads, such monumental achievements as the towering ziggurats of Babylon or the Great Wall of China, the temples of the Athenian Acropolis or the Persian palaces at Persepolis represented a great leap forward for the human race.

The dawn of civilization is a splendid phrase, conjuring up a new human day, new possibilities for the race. But civilization was many dawns, many red suns rising across the ancient world.

Each of the following chapters is such a beginning, such a new sun rising for the human race.

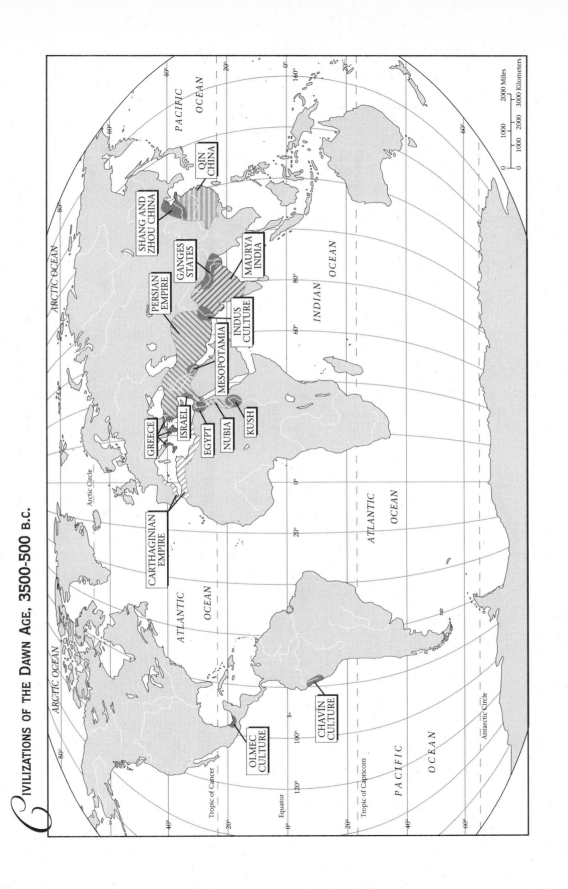

CIVILIZATIONS OF THE DAWN AGE, 3500-500 B.C.

CHAPTER 2

The Birth of the City

MESOPOTAMIAN SOCIETY

A LAND BETWEEN TWO RIVERS

Civilization was born where three worlds meet. It was southeast of the Mediteranean, where Asia, Africa, and Europe come together, that cities, literacy, the structure of the state, and other aspects of civilized living first took shape. The initial breakthrough came in the middle of the later fourth millennium B.C. in Sumeria, in the southeastern corner of Mesopotamia—present-day Iraq.

The Near East has been much in the news in recent decades, Iraq particularly so in the 1990s. But the world to which we must return now has little but geography in common with the morass of religious and national conflicts, oil, and imperialism, which have shaped the modern Middle East. The Muslim faith was not yet dreamed of, the Arabs who now rule the land had not yet come upon the scene, and the seas of oil slept untapped beneath the sands when civilization first emerged in this corner of the globe.

Mesopotamia means "Between the Rivers" in Greek, and "Land of the Two Rivers" is as adequate a label as we are likely to get for a place where so many political states have come and gone. Geographically speaking, it is the swath of alluvial plain and patches of bordering hills that run northwestward along the banks of the Tigris and Euphrates rivers from the head of the Persian Gulf to the edge of the Anatolian uplands of modern Turkey. It is an arid region now. Where the land once blew golden with grain in the palm-lined fields along the ancient canals, the earth cracks in the sun today or smoulders with the ruins of recent wars. Where the cities of Mesopotamia once stood, shapeless mounds called *tells* remain, from which the archaeologist's spade can bring forth no more than a rough sense of the shape and scale of the achievement of these first builders.

Over a span of some three thousand years, from perhaps 3500 to 539 B.C., the center of Mesopotamian civilization moved slowly up the two rivers. Cities and empires first emerged in Sumeria, or Sumer, in the marshy delta at the head of the Persian Gulf. Civilization flourished next in Akkadian Babylon, farther up the rivers, and came to a violent climax in the northwest, in Assyria, during the first millennium B.C.

The story of that three-thousand-year march of civilization is the subject of this chapter.

IRRIGATION, BUILDING, BRONZE AGE CRAFTS

It may have been the gradual drying out of the sea-covered delta at the mouths of the two rivers, producing marshy but highly fertile land, that first drew Neolithic farmers. They came down from the rain-watered hills, where they had already learned to cultivate the land, pasture animals, and live in villages, into Sumer. We do not really know. A pre-Sumerian people were there already; they have left us only a few stone tools and some non-Sumerian names on the land. We do know that during the fourth millennium before Christ, two groups met and merged along the lower Tigris and Euphrates. There was a Sumerian-speaking people from somewhere to the north, perhaps around the Caspian Sea, and the first of many waves of people who spoke Semitic languages, drifting in from Syria or Arabia to the west. From the fertile fusion of these two groups, a vastly productive little society emerged as early as 3500 B.C.

The members of this society built reed huts in the marshes of a sort that may still be seen in the delta of southern Iraq today. They hunted birds and speared fish from graceful canoes with high prows and sterns that glided through the marsh grass with scarcely a ripple. But they were farmers as well as hunters and gatherers, and the rich alluvial soil favored agriculture. Out of the reeds and the mud of the delta, then, the ancient Sumerians built over centuries a small prototype of all the larger civilizations that would follow.

Their first great discovery was how to tame the erratic rivers of Mesopotamia. The sluggish Euphrates and the faster-moving Tigris crested late for planting. They frequently brought unmanageable quantities of rainwater and melting snow down from the northern mountains to flood the land and sweep away homes and topsoil. Only with discipline and ingenuity did the Sumerians learn the proper combination of dikes, canals, and irrigation ditches for turning destructive floods into a source of ever more complex life.

By so doing they were able to raise enough food to support much larger populations than had been possible in the Neolithic villages of earlier times. The Sumerians grew barley as the staple grain of the south; wheat would

Ancient Civilizations of Eurasia, 3500–1500 b.c.

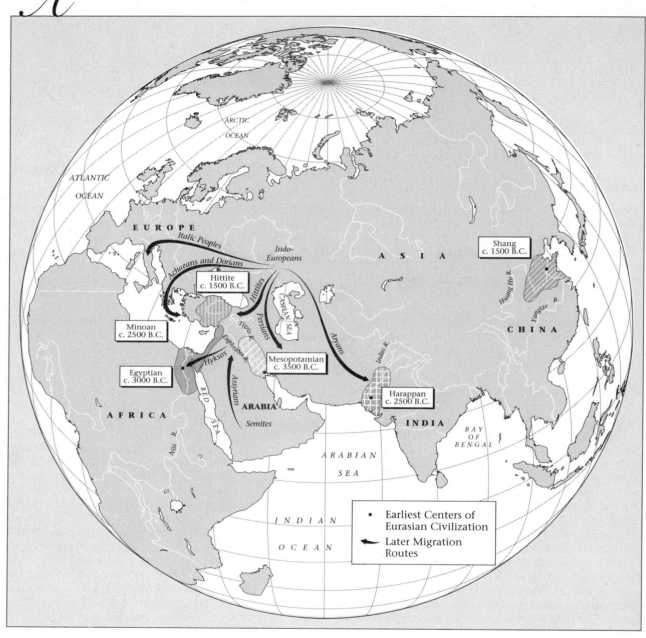

ARCTIC OCEAN

ATLANTIC OCEAN

EUROPE

Italic Peoples

Achaeans and Dorians

Indo-Europeans

A S I A

Shang
c. 1500 B.C.

Hittite
c. 1500 B.C.

Hittites

CASPIAN SEA

Huang Ho R.

Yangtze R.

CHINA

Minoan
c. 2500 B.C.

Persians

Tigris R.

Euphrates R.

Mesopotamian
c. 3500 B.C.

Aryans

Indus R.

Egyptian
c. 3000 B.C.

Hyksos

Assyrians

ARABIA

Harappan
c. 2500 B.C.

AFRICA

Semites

INDIA

Nile R.

RED SEA

BAY OF BENGAL

ARABIAN SEA

I N D I A N

O C E A N

• Earliest Centers of
Eurasian Civilization

◄── Later Migration
Routes

flourish later, in northern Mesopotamia. They cultivated the date palm for fruit and for palm wine. They grew onions and garlic and garnished meals of unleavened barley bread with the oil of the sesame seed. Sumerian shepherds watched flocks of sheep and goats, from whose wool and hair clothing was made. They learned to use oxen to pull their plows, and patient donkeys became their primary beasts of burden. Only later, when Mesopotamian kings went forth to make war upon their neighbors, were camels and horses brought home from foreign parts and domesticated along the two rivers.

There was little stone or wood for building on those flat, river-watered plains. Throughout Mesopotamia's history its primary building material would be the one developed first in ancient Sumer: mud brick, packed in molds and dried in the hot southern sun. With this rude material, compacted of the very reeds and mud that gave them life, the Sumerians, Babylonians, and Assyrians raised the fabled cities of Uruk and Lagash and Ur, Babylon, and Nineveh.

The Sumerians and their successors in the Land of the Two Rivers developed many crafts with great skill—textiles, pottery, and stone carving, the smelting of copper and the alloying of bronze. They even invented that archetype of human ingenuity, the wheel—solid and spoked—and the carts and wagons that went with it. Theirs is the first form of writing to come down to us. But their most important invention was the Mesopotamian city itself. The city became the center of this first of civilizations. And urban complexes, whatever their shortcomings as living spaces, have been the center of civilized society ever since.

THE CITY AND THE CITY-STATE

We cannot tell in any detail the steps by which the village became a city, and the city a city-state. But we can sketch the result, the unified complex of central city and agricultural hinterland, which will emerge again and again from one end of history to the other.

Walls, high and thick, pierced with monumental gateways, were the most prominent feature of Mesopotamian cities. Within the walls the typical large town was divided into four quarters by main streets that entered the city through four main gates, one in the middle of each wall. The developing power structure of the city and the city-state was architecturally embodied in the king's palace, the temples of the gods, and the large houses of the leading citizens. Palaces and houses tended to be built around a succession of courtyards, meandering labyrinths of cool, thick-walled rooms, some of which were elaborately decorated with painting or colored tiles. Temples were characterized most strikingly by *ziggurats*—pyramidal, terraced towers visible from far beyond the city walls. The streets were mostly narrow and winding, crowded with shopkeepers and artisans, jostling slaves and citizens, priests in fluted skirts, and the majestic sedan chairs of the wealthy.

The ruins of Babylon emerge from the earth as excavators' spades slowly separate the ancient clay brick from the alluvial plain along the Euphrates River in southern Iraq. The Iraqi government has attempted to develop the ruins as a tourist attraction and national shrine. Can you see how such an ancient site could encourage modern national pride? (Monkmeyer Press)

These first cities already contained a clear aristocracy and a detectable middle class. Handicraft industries, including the manufacture of textiles and metalwork in copper and bronze, produced a middle class of skilled artisans. Other bourgeois citizens included the merchants, especially the most wealthy among them, and the long-distance traders, whose caravans transported raw materials and luxury goods from one city to another. Above this stratum was a thin layer of aristocrats, royal officials, members of the royal family, and perhaps the chief priests of the major temples.

Few of the people who worked the fields outside the walls of these urban complexes were free peasants. Some were tenant farmers, holding their land in return for payment in kind to an absentee landlord who lived in the city. Others were serfs or even slaves, working the large tracts owned by the royal family and the chief gods of the city-state. All were subject to the rules laid down and the authority wielded by the officials who supervised the elaborate irrigation system that made the life of the city-state possible.

Originally, individual agricultural villages may have undertaken the control of stretches of the river for irrigation purposes. But the developed irrigation systems of these first Mesopotamian hydraulic empires involved massive dikes and levees that protected the croplands of large parts of the valley from the often destructive annual floods. Canals carried the runoff water, ditches distributed it to individual fields, and everywhere the *shaduf*—a long pivoted pole with a weight at one end and a bucket of some sort at the other—lifted the water from larger channels into the furrows where the seeds were planted. Levees had to be constantly strengthened, canals and ditches redredged to prevent silting up, and large-scale drainage efforts made in the south to slow the salinization of the soil by the salt water of the Persian Gulf. Elaborate regulations, rigid authority, and no doubt a good deal of cooperation were necessary if such elaborate group labors were to be successful.

Women enjoyed more personal rights and independent social status in Sumeria and later in Babylonia than they have in some other societies. They could become scribes, serve as legal witnesses, own property in their own names, and run their own businesses. The relatively high place of women in ancient Hebrew society may have been influenced by the long Jewish captivity in a Babylon that, two thousand years later, still followed the Sumerian custom of recognizing at least some rights for the female half of the human race.

THE PALACE AND THE TEMPLE

The central institutions of Sumerian society were the monarchies and the cults of the gods. The lofty temples and labyrinthine palaces of Sumerian and later Mesopotamian cities symbolized the primary place of divinity and royalty in the life of the Land of the Two Rivers.

The temple came first, at least in Sumerian times. The pyramidal ziggurats and broad temple complexes of the gods and goddesses—Anu and Enlil, Enki and Ninhursag and Innana (the last known later as Ishtar)—dominated the skyline of the Sumerian city. Each city had its own patron among the heavenly assembly, who was believed to bring rising rivers and rich harvests, to keep the barbarian from the gate, and to maintain order in the land.

Elaborate priesthoods served the major deities. Reverent hands dressed the cult statues daily, wafted food before their nostrils to feed them, played music to delight their ears. City dwellers could see their gods through the open doors of temple courtyards, dim and awesome in their niches. On great festival days such as the New Year, the gods and goddesses of the Land of the Two Rivers, gorgeously robed, their dark saucer-like eyes staring, were carried up the avenue in procession above the heads of their reveling worshipers.

Veneration of the gods predated the birth of the city; the power of the king grew more slowly in Sumer. Initially, the growing city was probably ruled by a city governor and war leader called the *ensi*, who governed in conjunction with an assembly of the city's free adult male citizens. As war leader, however, the *ensi* accumulated

emergency powers that he did not surrender. He thus emerged in time as a hereditary monarch, still general in wartime but responsible also for maintaining the irrigation system, regulating prices and wages, and implementing other welfare measures. The assemblies—no doubt legacies from earlier, smaller-scale social organizations—faded, and the power of the kings grew. In time, respect for royalty came to be seen as a mark of civilization in Mesopotamia; only less sophisticated peoples still kept to what we might call republics.

In Sumerian times, however, it was the power of the temple that predominated; kings governed only as stewards of the gods. The strength of the monarchy waxed only later, as Mesopotamian empires grew and more human power was required at the center. By the days of the Assyrian hegemony, the king had absorbed many religious functions, and the power of the palace clearly exceeded that of the temples of even the most ancient gods.

 MESOPOTAMIAN EMPIRES

IMPEDIMENTS TO EMPIRE

The political history of this oldest of civilizations is very scanty. Historical evidence is comparatively meager for events so old, and what evidence there is paints a confusing picture of a region torn by the squabbling of princes. Some generalizations about political events between the two rivers may be ventured, however, and three or four historic personalities may be plucked from the long list of Mesopotamian kings.

Successful efforts at empire building in the Tigris-Euphrates valley occurred less than half a dozen times over a period of nearly three thousand years. There was the Sumerian Empire of Sargon of Akkad in the twenty-third century B.C. There was the Old Babylonian Empire founded by Hammurabi in the eighteenth century before Christ. There was the fierce Assyrian predominance of the eighth and seventh centuries B.C. and the short-lived New Babylonian Kingdom of the sixth century B.C. After that, Cyrus the Persian swept down from the mountains, and Mesopotamia found unity at last—as a satrapy of the Persian Empire.

Many factors militated against unification in the Land of the Two Rivers during the three thousand years between the rise of the first Sumerian cities and the final fall of Babylon in the days of Belshazzar. Most obviously, the rich valley lay open to nomadic incursion from east, west, and north. Barbaric invaders such as the Akkadians, Gudians, Kassites, and Persians might in time be civilized by the enduring culture of Sumer. Nonetheless, such onslaughts from the deserts or the mountains repeatedly frustrated the best efforts of a Sargon or a Hammurabi to impose a single imperium on Mesopotamia.

A second challenge to larger unity was the appearance of a fragmented feudal order in much of Mesopotamia. As in medieval Europe many centuries later, feudalism in the Near East meant the division of a large measure of power among a landowning aristocracy. Such a divided socioeconomic structure evidently did not make for political unity.

A third force was what has been called *petty-statism*—a tendency of the region to break up into a number of middle-sized states, each enjoying local hegemony but none strong enough to overpower the others and impose a larger order on all of Mesopotamia.

A final roadblock to political unity was polarization. When one of the feuding Mesopotamian city-states did grow powerful enough to reach for supremacy, it was repeatedly confronted by the rise of a great rival. Polarization could clearly be as powerful an obstacle as barbarian invasions, feudalization, or petty-statism to unification in the Land of the Two Rivers.

When unity did come, albeit temporarily, it came as centralized political authority has normally come to disunited peoples. It was imposed by blood and violence and attended with toppling walls and corpses steaming in the roadways, with kings struck down and gods carried off into exile. Yet such a larger order, however imposed, could bring with it a better life for all the divided peoples of the wide valley.

SARGON OF AKKAD

The most celebrated of Sumerian kings was Sargon of Akkad, who founded a dynasty around 2300 B.C., which governed much of Mesopotamia for almost a hundred years.

Having begun his career as a Semitic royal official of one of the lesser Sumerian city-states, Sargon replaced his royal master on the throne, overthrew the mighty dynasty of neighboring Uruk, and subsequently conquered most of the Tigris and Euphrates valley. He garrisoned his conquests with Akkadian troops and built himself a new capital, the rich and powerful city of Agade. His son and grandson ruled after him. But volcanic ash from an eruption may have brought drought to the region. And then the violent Gutians swept down from the neighboring hills to destroy the city and its imperial Mesopotamian domain. The powerful bronze head traditionally identified as Sargon shows a strong, curly-bearded face with heavy lips and a hawklike nose—the face of the world's first empire builder.

Perhaps the most famous of all attempts at Mesopotamian unity, however, was that of Hammurabi, the lawgiver of Babylon.

HAMMURABI OF BABYLON

Few cities outside of Sodom and Gomorrah have enjoyed a worse—or a more glamorous—reputation in history than Babylon. To persecuted early Christians, Rome of the Cae-

Hammurabi, empire builder and codifier of the laws of Babylon, may be the subject of this carving in black granite from ancient Mesopotamia. The carving of a face in such hard stone is in itself evidence of the level of cultural achievement reached by the earliest human civilizations. (Hirmer Fotoarchiv)

sars was Babylon reborn, and the Antichrist himself was known as the Whore of Babylon. New York, Hollywood, and other modern metropolises famed for wealth and wickedness have been dubbed new Babylons in their turn.

At first glance, the real Babylon scarcely seems to deserve its reputation for wealth, worldliness, and power. The city on the Euphrates enjoyed only two periods of genuine supremacy in Mesopotamia: the period of the Old Babylonian Empire, roughly 1800 to 1600 B.C., beginning with the reign of Hammurabi, and the century beginning around 600 B.C., when Nebuchadnezzar created the New Babylonian Empire. But the wealth of the city was never denied, and its size and physical splendor grew over the centuries. In the fifth century B.C. the famous Greek historian Herodotus, who had traveled widely among the peoples of the civilized Near East, confidently described Babylon as the largest and most magnificent city in the world.

ᐱOICES FROM THE PAST

"*To the king, my lord (Assurbanipal), from your servant Adad-šumi-uṣur:*

Good health to Your Majesty! May the gods Nabû and Marduk give many, many blessings to Your Majesty.

When Aššur, the king of the gods, designated Your Majesty to rule Assyria as king, and when the gods Samaš and Adad confirmed by reliable oracles that Your Majesty should rule as king over all the countries, the great gods of the entire cosmos brought about during the reign of Your Majesty a happy rule with days and years in which law and order prevail: there are copious rains, abundant flooding of the rivers, favorable prices, and reconciliation of the gods; there is much piety and the temples of the gods are well provided. Old men dance with joy, young men sing happy songs, women and young girls happily learn to do what women do; they go into confinement and bring forth boys and girls, and the births are easy.

Why, then, since Your Majesty has pardoned persons condemned to death for their crimes, and has released those who for many years had been imprisoned, and since ... the hungry have been sated with food ... and those who had been destitute have been clad in sumptuous garments—why then should I and my son Arad-Gula, among all those happy people, remain restless and in low spirits? Only recently has Your Majesty shown his love for Nineveh by telling the prominent citizens: "Bring me your sons, they shall become servants at my court!" If this son of mine, Arad-Gula, could become a servant at the court of Your Majesty, serving together with these same people, then we too would be as happy as all other people are; we would dance and bless Your Majesty."

◆◆◆

This letter from an Assyrian courtier to Assurbanipal (668–627 B.C.) was written with a very practical purpose having little to do with historical interpretation. Yet his petition does offer an excellent brief summary of what good government and good times meant in ancient Mesopotamia.

What sanction for Assurbanipal's rule is stressed? What political and economic benefits has his rule conferred on his people? How does this courtier describe the "good life" for Mesopotamian women? Would a woman agree?

A. Leo Oppenheim, ed. and trans., Letters from Mesopotamia (Chicago and London: University of Chicago Press, 1967), pp. 149–150.

Hammurabi (c.1792–1750 B.C.) was born King of Babylon, the sixth in a line of otherwise undistinguished Amorite rulers of that city. He apparently governed his modest metropolis and its hinterland—at that time a city-state no more than fifty miles across—for some thirty years before he seized his chance to make Babylon great in the land. Then, late in his reign, he seems to have parlayed a combination of shrewd statecraft, brilliant timing, and military force into a far wider power than any of his predecessors had enjoyed. For a brief time, he and his heirs held supreme authority over all the peoples of Mesopotamia.

The reputation of Hammurabi as a ruler in peace, however, considerably outshines his claim to fame as an empire builder. In the chronicles of the Near East, he lived on not as Hammurabi the Conqueror but as Hammurabi the Lawgiver, the Moses and Solon of his people.

The three hundred Sumerian and Akkadian laws of the Code of Hammurabi cover a wide range of civil and criminal matters, from land law and business law to regulation of family relations, from personal injury to military service, from witchcraft to taxes. Many of the principles promulgated in the code seem harsh to the modern reader. The "Mosaic" principle of an eye for an eye, a life for a life, is here commonly invoked, centuries before Moses. Mutilation and death are repeatedly prescribed as fair and fitting punishments. And a clear sense of social hierarchy is reflected throughout; there is one law for slaves, another for their masters.

Yet the Code of Hammurabi does reveal a society with a highly developed belief in social justice. Even harsh punishment imposed by the state may be seen as an advance over the random retaliation of feuding clans that it replaced. And if the life of the slave is not rated as high in shekels of compensation as the life of a freeman, by the same token a nobleman may be punished more rigorously for the same offense than his social inferiors. Perhaps most important, there is a clear conviction that might does not make right, that the law has a fundamental obligation to protect the weak from the strong. It was not the worst foundation for this early attempt at a larger social order, which reached beyond the city-state to govern a whole people.

When the great king died, his heirs could not hold what he had won. New waves of preurban peoples appeared at the gates, most formidably the Kassites from the east, and within a century and a half, the brief Babylonian unification of Mesopotamia had crumbled away.

The next unifiers of the valley of the Tigris and Euphrates emerged still farther to the north, in the region that came to be known as Assyria.

THE ASSYRIAN WARFARE STATE

A bas-relief found in the ruins of the palace of Assurbanipal, the most famous of Assyrian kings, shows that monarch reclining at ease in his garden. His queen sits beside his couch, and the two are raising their wine cups, as though drinking a toast. Servants move gentle fly whisks among the palms, offer sweetmeats on trays, and play on musical instruments to entertain the King of Kings. The idyllic scene is marred by a single jarring detail. Just behind the harp player on the left, the severed head of Teumman, king of the Elamites, swings from a tree branch overhead.

The world has seen more than its share of frightfulness over the fifty-five hundred years since civilization was born in ancient Sumer. But the Assyrians were among the most savage of civilized peoples, even by modern standards of violence.

The source of the endless brutal military campaigns that are the very texture of Assyrian history has been sought in various aspects of this last great Mesopotamian culture. One approach is simply to point out that geographically, Assyria was highly vulnerable, more open even than southern Mesopotamia to foreign invasion. The Assyrians may thus have treated their foes more savagely than usual in order to replace nonexistent natural frontiers with a wall of fear.

There may also have been, at the royal palace and among the priesthood of their chief god, Assur, a sense of imperial and religious duty to impose and reimpose order on the chaos of the Near East in the second and first millennia B.C. There was, in addition, almost certainly a normal human lust for something for nothing, for the loot and tribute that made wars a paying proposition for the powerful Assyrian military machine. There may well have been, finally, more subtle economic motives at work. Some historians have detected behind Assyrian imperialism the need for copper and stone and timber, or the desire to control trade routes.

For whatever reason, the story of the rise and fall of the Assyrians is a story of almost unending war.

According to their own records, at least, they began to win wars with the barbarians in the fourteenth century B.C., during the Babylonian dark age that followed the decline of the heirs of Hammurabi. The bloody days of real Assyrian predominance did not begin, however, until sometime around the year 1000 B.C. During most of the next four centuries, they were the terror of the Near Eastern world.

The great raids began as early as the ninth century— long sweeps down the Tigris and back up the Euphrates, the Assyrians pillaging and exacting tribute as they went. By the latter part of the eighth century, they were incorporating their victims into a large and growing empire. Syria, the Phoenician trading cities of Lebanon, and the little kingdom of Israel collapsed under the repeated battering of Assyrian arms. In the seventh century, under Sennacherib and Assurbanipal, Assyrian power overwhelmed Egypt and most of Mesopotamia. In the reign of the redoubtable Assurbanipal, Assyria thus stood briefly as master of the band of civilized states that stretched from the Nile to the Persian Gulf.

Everywhere they went, they brought devastation. "I built a pillar over against his city gate," reported a ninth-century Assyrian ruler, "and I flayed all his chief men . . . and I covered the pillar with their skins. . . ."[1] Whole populations were deported, cities leveled, their gods—and sometimes their citizens—given over to the flames. And the tribute of a terrorized world rolled in.

But the lust for loot and victory of even the most martial people may be sated in time. Sennacherib built an aqueduct that pleased him perhaps as much as the looting of the land of the Hebrews. Assurbanipal in his garden may as easily have been lifting his wine cup to the completion of his famous library as to the head of the unfortunate Elamite king.

It was perhaps a softening. And it brought its reward. Chaos closed over the Assyrian Empire in the last years of the seventh century. In 612 B.C., an allied force of Chaldeans from Babylon and Medes from the eastern mountains broke into the heart of Assyria, ringed Nineveh, and crushed it.

The punishment imposed upon the erstwhile terror of the world was as thorough as any inflicted by the

---

[1]Samuel Noah Kramer, *Cradle of Civilization* (New York: Time-Life Books, 1967), p. 58.

Assyrian warriors in combat, vividly depicted on the walls of the royal palace at Nineveh. Charging troops, slaughtered foes, and severed heads all reflect the ferocity of the Assyrian war machine. (Art Resource)

Assyrians in their pride. Mighty Nineveh was leveled so efficiently that when the Greek general Xenophon passed that way two centuries later, no one could even identify the site for him. Sennacherib and Assurbanipal survived only as bogeymen of legend and biblical history until Lord Byron, a poet of the nineteenth century, used them to send a delightful shiver down Victorian spines:

> The Assyrian came down like the wolf on the fold,
> And his cohorts were gleaming in purple and gold. . . . [2]

[2]George Gordon, Lord Byron, "The Destruction of Sennacherib," *The Complete Poetical Works*, Vol III, ed. Jerome J. McGann (Oxford: Clarendon Press, 1981), p. 309.

The imagery is suitably barbaric, but the tone is perhaps a bit romantic. The poet makes no mention of severed heads, of the flames and the flaying knife.

NEBUCHADNEZZAR AND THE NEW BABYLONIAN EMPIRE

The New Babylonian Empire, which briefly succeeded Assyrian power in Mesopotamia, was very much the creation of one man: Nebuchadnezzar II (605–526 B.C.), notorious in Bible history as the Chaldean ruler who carried off the Hebrews into their Babylonian captivity. Nebuchadnezzar was a conqueror and an empire builder in the by now time-honored Mesopotamian tradition. Seven years after the fall of Nineveh, while still crown prince of Babylon, he commanded the Babylonian army that crushed the forces of the Egyptian pharaoh at Carchemish in 605 B.C. As king, he led repeated expeditions down into Palestine, destroying Jerusalem, and carrying much of the population of Judea off into exile. At its brief height, the New Babylonian Empire of the sixth century rivaled its Assyrian predecessor in size and splendor, governing once more from a single center all the land from the Persian Gulf to the Mediterranean.

Nebuchadnezzar built more than a mighty empire, however. He was celebrated in antiquity not as the man who took torch and crowbar to Solomon's Temple but as the rebuilder of the city of Babylon.

Just as Hammurabi was before him at Babylon, Nebuchadnezzar II was a great builder of canals and caravan roads, temples, and palaces. He raised huge new crenellated walls around his capital, eleven miles long and so wide that a chariot could turn around on the roadway that ran along the top. He opened the broad Processional Way through the heart of the city to the famous Ishtar Gate. He built the Hanging Gardens of Babylon—a towering ziggurat featuring terraces planted with trees and exotic plants—to please his Median wife, who missed the hills of her mountainous home.

The gardens and the city that housed them were hailed in their own day as one of the Seven Wonders of the World. "Babylon," said the prophet Jeremiah, "hath been a golden cup in the Lord's hand, that made all the earth drunken" (*Jeremiah*, 51:7). It was certainly the most famous of all the great cities of this oldest of city-based civilizations.

But the Babylon of Nebuchadnezzar—and of the Babylonian captivity of the Jews—was a brief, final flowering. Its conqueror was one of history's great empire builders—Cyrus the Great. This half-barbarian king, called Cyrus the Shepherd by his Persian and Median troops, had already overrun all the kingdoms of the north and east, from rich Lydia on the Mediterranean to the far frontiers of India. Then in 539 B.C., he turned his leather-clad horsemen toward the richest plum of all—Babylon.

He found the ancient city ripe for the plucking. Nebuchadnezzar's successors had not ruled well, and there were powerful men within the walls who felt that their interests would be better served by a change of dynasty than by a protracted struggle with as famous a soldier as Cyrus the Persian. So at least the historian tends to explain the famous night when, as every schoolchild once knew, Prince Belshazzar, the regent of Babylon, feasting in his arrogance and splendor, saw the handwriting on the wall. *Mene, mene, tekel, upharsin,* the moving finger wrote. "God hath numbered thy kingdom," translated Daniel the prophet, "and finished it. Thou art weighed in the balances, and art found wanting. Thy kingdom is divided, and given to the Medes and the Persians" (*Daniel,* 5:25–28).

And it was so.

Daniel's dramatic prophecy has an apocryphal ring to it and was apparently written long after the event. But Cyrus's troops, with the help of a quisling governor, actu-

ally did enter the city unresisted. And his victory did mark the beginning of a new era in the Near East.

The huge Persian Empire would stretch in time across all western Asia, dwarfing the intermittent empires of Mesopotamia. It would introduce a new scale of imperial government to this corner of the world.

But the valley of the Tigris and the Euphrates had been bringing its share of less ordered folk into that golden web of civilized living for some thirty centuries when Cyrus the Persian rode through the Ishtar Gate. If we want to assign firsts in history, Mesopotamia deserves its share. Civilization began in Sumer.

 # MESOPOTAMIAN CULTURE

POLYTHEISTIC RELIGIONS

The sources of religion have been sought in many places. Among them surely are the need our ancestors felt for supernatural help to ensure a supply of game, growing herds, rich harvest. Other sources no doubt include the desire of people for divine support when they deal with life transitions such as birth, initiation, and death and with such special afflictions as war, pestilence, famine, and oppression. Common human beliefs—in luck, charms, and fetishes, in ritual and taboo, in divination of the future, in life after death, in some sort of human spirit or soul—have probably all contributed to the rise of religions.

But a developed religion seems to require more than these. It requires an encounter with the numinous. The word comes from the Latin *numen*, meaning divine power. A numinous experience is defined by students of the history and nature of religion as a sense of the presence of something "wholly other," something totally different in kind from all the material realities of everyday living. One may have a sudden sense of the presence of divine power in nature itself—in running water, the whispering leaves of a giant tree, the knee-buckling immensity of the sky above. It may come in the lifting of the sun's disk above the horizon, in a circle of standing stones, in a carven idol, in an icon or a crucifix.

At this deepest level of experience, the origin of all religious belief is the same. As far as we can tell, the meditating Hindu, the Muslim Sufi, and the Christian saint all experience much the same thing at this transcendent moment: In their own minds, at least, they are all in the presence of the Lord.

This sense of the numinous—mysterious, tremendous, fascinating—intruding into the everyday world has, however, one crucial limitation. It is ineffable; that is, it cannot be described in words at all.

To express the inexpressible, religious leaders have therefore had to turn to metaphor. They have tried to say what that awesome encounter with the numinous was *like* in the everyday material world the prophet and his people all know. Inevitably, however, this expedient has brought religious discourse from the level of the universal down to the historically conditioned realities of a particular time and place. God is white and male in a white man's world; Shiva is a high-caste Indian; the sun god rides across the sky in a chariot in ancient Greece and sails down a celestial Nile in the mind of the Egyptian.

It is at this level that an essentially universal and ahistorical experience becomes part of history. From these efforts to express the inexpressible by giving it a local habitation and a name derive all the historic religions of humanity.

This process is nowhere better illustrated than among the Mesopotamians, where the first of human civilizations emerged. And if the religious vision that resulted seems strange to us, it is perhaps safer to attribute the differences to the civilization that shaped that vision, rather than to any crucial difference in the religious experience itself.

The peoples of ancient Sumeria, Babylonia, and Assyria, like most peoples in most times and places, felt themselves to be surrounded by spiritual presences. There were gods and goddesses associated with practically everything—gods of earth and sky, storm and bountiful harvest, brick mold and irrigation ditch. Most of these divinities were thoroughly anthropomorphic; they were depicted in sculpture as awesome figures with the long hair and square-cut beards of many Mesopotamian peoples and with the saucer-sized eyes that make them instantly recognizable in any museum. Confronted in spirit by true believers, they were terrifying presences, glowing with a luminosity that seems to have been a special source of dread.

In early Sumer the chief divinities in this numerous pantheon included Anu, the lord of heaven; Enlil, the water god; the earth mother, Ninhursag; the gods of the sun and moon, Utu and Sin; and the powerful goddess of love, Ishtar. Other leading divinities emerged over the centuries, notably Marduk, the chief god of imperial Babylon, and Assur, the sun god of the Assyrians.

Around these many divinities elaborate rites grew up. The great gods were believed to dwell within the ritually crafted and consecrated cult statues that the priests tended so carefully in the temples. Around these figures a year-round succession of ceremonies, processions, sacred drama, and other liturgical observances developed. Mythologies, sacred texts, and theological literature added to the richness of Mesopotamian religion.

There were also subtle changes in the religious conceptions held by the Mesopotamians over the three thousand years of their history. In the earliest times, gods and goddesses were conceived of as "indwelling wills and powers," divine presences *within* the natural forces, crops, and flocks necessary for human survival.[3] These early

divinities embodied the mysterious power that made the barley grow or the palm produce plentiful clusters of dates.

By the time of Sargon of Akkad, however, a political metaphor is increasingly used to describe the reality of the divine. Gods are *rulers* of humanity. They protect the citizens of a particular city-state, or they lead the people to imperial conquest of their neighbors. And as the monarchy grew among the Mesopotamians, so a single god came to be honored as the king of the divine assembly, just as the *ensi* governed on earth.

During the last Mesopotamian centuries, divinities seemed more and more like parents. The gods became as concerned about the behavior and the well-being of their worshipers as parents are for their children. In hard times, it was comforting to know that higher powers cared.

Toward the very last, in the days of the Assyrian terror and of unchecked barbarian incursions, religion seems to have degenerated into the rankest superstition. There was "a coarsening and barbarization of the idea of divinity . . . witchcraft and sorcery were suspected everywhere; demons and evil spirits threatened unceasingly."[4] In the worst of times, perhaps, it was hard to believe that there *were* any higher powers.

In a world directed by all these evolving divinities, human beings knew their place. "The service of the gods be their portion," the divine assembly decreed in a tablet of the first millennium B.C. The highest tasks of humankind were to build the temples and "to celebrate the festivals . . . in the great house of the gods."[5]

A narrow vision of the human condition. But at least the sun-darkened Mesopotamian farmer swinging the pail of the *shaduf* over a thirsty furrow and the woman feeding the sacred doves in the courtyard of the temple of Ishtar had no doubts about why they had been born.

WRITING, LEARNING, AND LITERATURE

The true inventors of writing were probably the nameless precursors of the Sumerians in the marshy delta of the two rivers. Sometime during the later fourth millennium B.C., however, Sumerian scribes were making lists of goods and produce, flocks and harvested grain. They did so by scratching crude *pictograms* (pictorial representations) of the items in question on a small clay tablet with a reed stylus. The strokes of the triangular reed came to be known as *cuneiform* (wedge-shaped) script. Over the centuries these signs began to be used simply to represent the *sounds* of the names of the original articles. Several of these sound-symbols, or *phonograms*, could then be combined to represent other words. The result was an exceedingly complicated system of writing that combined

[3]Thorkild Jacobsen, *The Treasures of Darkness: A History of Mesopotamian Religion* (New Haven: Yale University Press, 1976), p. 21.

[4]Ibid.

[5]Alexander Heidel, *The Babylonian Genesis: The Story of Creation* (Chicago: University of Chicago Press, 1951), pp. 70–71.

pictograms and phonograms and required a long course of specialized training in the scribal schools.

Only professional scribes could read, and the only "libraries"—collections of classic texts—were in the scribal schools and perhaps the temples. We know, however, that at least some of these mythological texts were read aloud to the populace as part of religious ceremonies. Some other tablets probably record oral literature that was sung or chanted by minstrels at royal palaces or in market squares. Such science and philosophy as there was, finally, is frequently closer to folk sayings and fortune-telling than to the complex systematic thought of later ages. Nevertheless, these early literary and theoretical labors deserve a brief glance here, if only for their antiquity and their originality.

The Mesopotamians left some mathematical insights and astronomical observations that still impress us. They based their number system on six rather than on ten; to them we owe the sixty-minute hour and the division of the circle into 360 degrees. The Babylonians charted the movements of the planets and predicted eclipses of the sun and the moon. Their knowledge of the night skies was so celebrated, in fact, that the word *Chaldean* became a synonym for *astronomer* in the ancient world.

The most famous literary product of ancient Mesopotamia is the *Epic of Gilgamesh*, the half-legendary Sumerian king who is sometimes called the Mesopotamian Hercules. The surviving fragments of this long poem tell how Gilgamesh and his friend Enkiddu, the wild man of the desert, killed the monster Huwawa and the Wild Bull of Heaven; how Gilgamesh scorned the advances of the goddess Ishtar; how he lost the faithful Enkiddu; and how he set out on his last and greatest adventure, the search for eternal life. His dreamlike journey to the twilight realm of Utnapishtim, sole survivor of the great flood that once destroyed humankind, climaxes with his discovery—and loss—of the plant that confers everlasting life, and with his final realization that death is the appointed end of every human life—even the life of a hero.

The poem as it has come down to us has little of the power or human feeling of Homer's epics, and none of the moral and metaphysical weight of the Hindu song of God, the *Bhagavadgita*. But it does bring us closer to the marvelous long-vanished people who created it and loved it on the plain between the rivers thousands of years ago.

THE ARTS: GOLD AND LAPIS LAZULI

Mesopotamian civilization is a remarkable example of what can be done by a people whose homeland has been endowed with almost no natural resources. They had water and clay, and with these they created a flourishing agriculture and raised humankind's first cities against the rainless southern sky. But they had almost no stone, no timber, no metals of any kind. These they had to do without or

import as trade goods, tribute, or booty before they could progress further in the civilized arts.

The Mesopotamian palaces and temples that have been excavated from the mounded earth have a simplicity of design and detail that could have produced an effect of monumental grandeur above the arid plain. Palaces, like private homes, were constructed around a series of courtyards. Monumental gateways, square towers, and crenellated walls provided some exterior variety, and glazed tile and wall paintings of animals and men enlivened cool, dim interiors. In Babylonian and Assyrian times, sculptured columns, stone reliefs on walls, and huge human-headed bulls and other creatures added an air of imperial magnificence to the Mesopotamian palace.

The temple, however, was the Mesopotamian city's dominant feature. The most striking element in the temple complex was the pyramidal terraced tower, or ziggurat. Wide stairways, much like those of the later pyramid temples of the Mayans and the Aztecs, led to the flat top of the ziggurat, where a special shrine to the god or goddess stood. A simple, open structure, it was nonetheless God's house to the ancient Mesopotamian, as surely as any church or temple since.

A winged, human-headed bull strides out of the mythic imagination of ancient Assyria in this monumental statue, fourteen feet high, carved from solid alabaster. What forms of stylization—symbolic rather than realistic representation— do you see here? (New York Public Library Picture Collection)

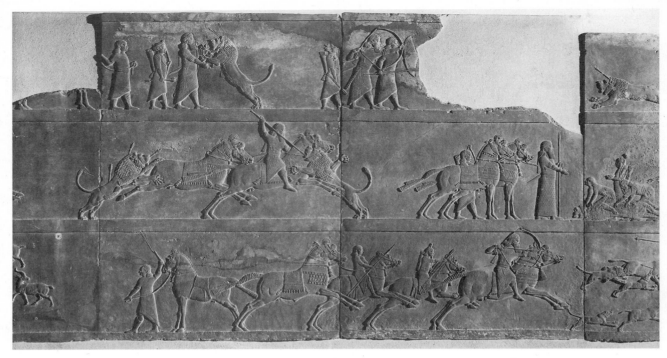

The Lion Hunt Frieze shows the mighty Assurbanipal mortally wounding a lion. The lions were actually kept in a game preserve for periodic royal hunts. (The British Museum)

The sculpture of ancient Mesopotamia does not catch the modern imagination as immediately as that of some other cultures. There is something cartoonlike about the ill-proportioned, saucer-eyed Sumerian gods and votive figures, something repetitious about the low reliefs of long-bearded, long-haired kings and soldiers in flowing robes, striding in hawklike profile across a wall.

Yet there is a convincing vitality in the smooth round face of a five-thousand-year-old Sumerian woman, bright-eyed and smiling still, her simple gown cut to leave the right arm and shoulder free for work. A rare wall painting of Assyrian officials brings these civilized savages to life, with their looped gold earrings, their black hair and beards oiled and dressed in ringlets. There is even a tense realism in the famous Lion Hunt Frieze: the horse of Assurbanipal charging with mouth open and tendons taut, and the dying lioness, arrows buried half their length in its flanks, dragging paralyzed hindquarters behind it, yet rearing up to roar in final defiance at the King of Kings.

Beyond all realism, however, there is a formal beauty to these excavated artifacts that reminds us that art, like the experience of religion, stands finally outside history.

The cylinder seal, the most distinctive of Mesopotamian art forms, was carved in intaglio on a small stone cylinder, then rolled over soft clay to leave a unique identifying mark on anything from a merchant's goods to a private letter. On these carved seals, animals, gods, and men mingle freely with symbolic objects, the owner's name in cuneiform script, and other sculptured space fillers. The endless ingenuity of the carvers as they fill these tiny friezes with gracefully balanced figures rearing up, wrestling, sometimes seeming almost to dance across the clay, can stir the sense of beauty in the observer still.

The same may be said of the gold of Ur. A treasure trove of necklaces, helmets, cups, and other artifacts exhumed from royal tombs, they are all as directly accessible to us in their intricate beauty as anything from Cartier's or Tiffany's. The smooth golden sheen of a bull's head or a dagger blade plays beautifully against the beard or the hilt, made of the blue stone called lapis lazuli of which Mesopotamians were so fond. The monumental power of the vastly winged, human-headed bulls that once guarded the palace of Khorasabad still stops museum visitors in their tracks and draws their eyes inevitably upward.

The lions, yellow tiles on blue, that still pace with gorgeous dignity up the Processional Way toward the Ishtar Gate of excavated Babylon are more than ancient artifacts. They are works of art. As such, they are as effective now as they were when their silent tread flanked the cheering crowds and the stately processions of Marduk and Ishtar, of Hammurabi and Nebuchadnezzar and Cyrus, into the heart of the city so many centuries ago.

SUMMARY

Civilization began in the Near East, first in Mesopotamia and then in surrounding regions, producing a network of cities, small empires, and high culture between 3500 and 500 B.C.

Mesopotamia—present-day Iraq—was the site of the first urban imperial cultures. Mesopotamian peoples built elaborate irrigation works and walled cities in the valley of the Tigris and Euphrates rivers. They also developed the city-state, a polity centered on the new urban complex but including the hinterland of villages around it. These city-states were dominated by priests in early times, later by kings.

A cycle of empires also evolved in ancient Mesopotamia. For most of its history, the Land of the Two Rivers remained divided between many feuding princes. Several times, however, a single power imposed imperial unity on the area for generations, or even centuries. The earliest such empire was that of the Sumerian ruler Sargon of Akkad in the twenty-third century B.C. The most famous was that of Hammurabi the Lawgiver of Babylon, founder of the Old Babylonian Empire in the eighteenth and seventeenth centuries B.C. The most oppressive was the Assyrian Empire (eighth and seventh centuries); the most admired in antiquity was the short-lived New Babylonian Empire of Nebuchadnezzar in the sixth century.

The culture of the ancient Near East was rooted in the polytheistic religion most common everywhere in the ancient world. Mesopotamians and their neighbors were also skilled at astronomy and mathematics, and they developed the first writing, cuneiform. They built truncated pyramidal temples called ziggurats and carved stone cylinder seals with which they left their mark on clay.

SUGGESTED READING

CRAWFORD, H. E. W. *Sumer and the Sumerians*. New York: Cambridge University Press, 1991. Good recent overview, with helpful illustrations. See also S. Kramer, *The Sumerians* (Chicago: University of Chicago Press, 1963), for a well-written and authoritative survey.

DIAKONOFF, H. E. W., ed. *Early Antiquity*. Chicago: University of Chicago Press, 1991. Essays on early civilizations from Sumer to China.

FRANKFORT, H. *Art and Architecture of the Ancient Orient*. Harmondsworth, England: Penguin Books, 1970. Near Eastern art in ancient times.

———, et al. *Before Philosophy*. Harmondsworth, England: Penguin Books, 1949. The best-known account of the myth-making mind of the Near East.

GORDON, C., ed. *Hammurabi's Code: Quaint or Forward Looking?* New York: Holt, Rinehart, & Winston, 1957. Collection of essays with a wide spectrum of evaluations of this early code of laws.

HAMLIN, D. J. *The First Cities*. New York: Time-Life Books, 1973. Vividly illustrated description of the emergence of urban culture in the Near East.

JACOBSEN, T. *The Treasures of Darkness: A History of Mesopotamian Religion*. New Haven: Yale University Press, 1976. Sums up a lifetime of research into this elusive subject.

LAESSOE, S. *The People of Ancient Assyria*. New York: Barnes & Noble, 1963. Older but widely cited overview of life in ancient Assyria.

LLOYD, S. *The Archaeology of Mesopotamia*. New York: Thames and Hudson, 1984. From prehistory to the Persian conquest.

OATES, J. *Babylon*. London: Thames and Hudson, 1979. Illustrated brief survey of Babylonian history. See also D. J. Wiseman, *Nebuchadnezzar and Babylon* (New York: Oxford University Press, 1985), for authoritative lectures on the builder of the New Babylonian Empire.

OPPENHEIM, A. L. *Ancient Mesopotamia: Portrait of a Dead Civilization*. Chicago: University of Chicago Press, 1964. Older but solid general account of the history of the region.

SAGGS, H. W. F. *The Encounter with the Divine in Mesopotamia and Israel*. London: Athlone Press, 1978. Interesting lectures comparing Mesopotamian religious ideas with those of the Old Testament.

SEIBERT, I. *Women in the Ancient Near East*. Leipzig: Edition Leipzig, 1974. Brief introduction, including representations of women in art. A useful comparative essay is B. Rohrlich-Leavitt, "Women in Transition: Crete and Sumer," in R. Bridenthal and C. Koontz, *Becoming Visible: Women in European History* (Boston: Houghton Mifflin, 1977).

SILVER, M. *Economic Structures in the Ancient Near East*. Totowa, N.J.: Barnes & Noble, 1985. Uses modern economic theory applied to Mesopotamian clay tablets to explain the economic organization of the region.

WALKER, C. B. F. *Reading the Past: Writing from Cuneiform to the Alphabet*. London: British Museum, 1990. Stimulating introduction to early forms of writing.

CHAPTER 3

The Kingdom of the Nile

THE PYRAMID AGE

EGYPT—THE GIFT OF THE NILE

Civilization apparently emerged a few centuries later in the Nile valley than it did on the banks of the Tigris and the Euphrates, perhaps around 3200 B.C. But the Egyptians very quickly moved ahead of their neighbors beyond the Arabian Desert, in one area at least. Egypt early developed a powerful centralized government, whereas Mesopotamia remained a land of city-states and short-lived empires throughout its long history. Egypt thus enjoyed a high degree of unity, stability, and cultural continuity through much of its almost three thousand years of independent life.

As is so frequently the case, the course of Egyptian historical development was in large part set by the geographical framework within which Egypt evolved. "Egypt," reported the ancient Greek historian Herodotus, "is the gift of the Nile." The river was clearly central to the daily life of the Egyptians. The heart of the land was that part of the river from the first cataract at Aswan to the fan-shaped delta where it flowed into the Mediterranean. (The Nile, incidentally, flows northward to the Mediterranean, so that *Upper* Egypt is in the south, *Lower* Egypt in the north.) The river winds six hundred miles from the cataracts to the delta, gouging out a valley that is seldom more than a few miles wide. Only over the last hundred miles or so does the valley open up into the flat, triangular delta spread along the sea. The traditional "two lands" of Egypt were defined by this difference: Upper Egypt, with its sacred city at Thebes, covered most of the river valley; Lower Egypt, with its even more ancient capital at Memphis, comprised mostly the delta.

The great river's annual rise and fall were crucial for the life of Egypt. The Nile has its sources far to the south, in the mountains of Ethiopia and the lake country of equatorial Africa. Each year spring rains in these far-off regions sent high water surging north across the Sudan and the lands of ancient Nubia, thrashing through the cataracts, and rolling on at a more majestic pace through the sandstone- and limestone-walled valley of Upper Egypt. Here the rising waters overflowed their banks and deposited over the narrow valley a layer of rich black mud,

alluvium picked up along all the hundreds of miles from central Africa. It was this rich gift of fertile soil and life-giving water that enabled the Nile valley to bloom and made Egypt the most favored land in the ancient world.

EGYPT AND AFRICA

The African location of Egypt brought the kingdom of the Nile more than fertile soil, however. Some cultural influences also flowed north from inner Africa into Egypt.

As we will see, scholars have long seen Mesopotamian influences at work in Egyptian civilization. More recently, historians like Cheikh Anta Diop have urged the importance of African influences on the shaping of Egyptian culture. Evidence of inner African influence on the emerging Egyptian kingdom includes political, social, and cultural similarities.

Culturally, Egyptians shared both myths and individual gods—including an important jackel-headed god of the dead—with other African peoples. Among similar artifacts, you can see wooden headrests like those used in ancient Egypt still in use in parts of rural Africa today. Social customs common to this ancient civilization and later African cultures include circumcision and totemic animals symbolizing a clan or people. There are also parallels between Egyptian and other African languages.

Similar political patterns also suggest closer ties than was once thought between Egypt and the rest of Africa. Matrilineal descent—the inheritance of property and power through the female side of the family—was common in Africa and crucial in Egypt, where even pharaohs often married their sisters to guarantee their hereditary power over the land. Specific forms and rituals of divine kingship also link the pharaohs with kings and chiefs from farther south.

We will see later contacts, often initiated by the Egyptians, in later centuries. For now, it will suffice to plant the kingdom of the pharaohs firmly in African soil before going on to survey Egypt's own development and its key role in the history of the Near East and the Eastern Mediterranean.

THE PHARAOHS UNIFY THE LAND

Efforts to assign periods to Egyptian history go back to the days of the ancient Egyptians. The priest Manetho divided the history of his country into thirty dynasties,

Ancient Egypt

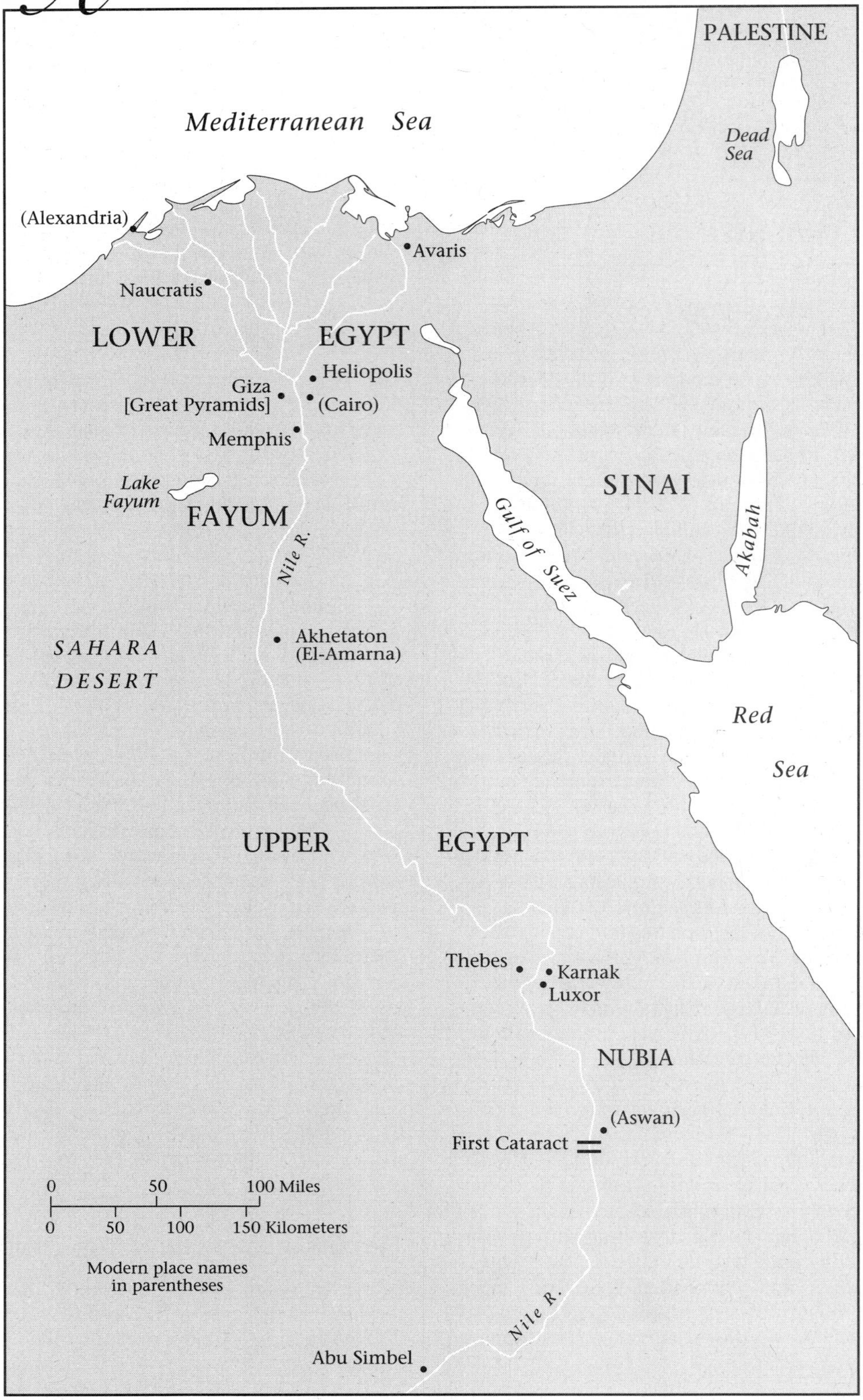

Mediterranean Sea

PALESTINE

Dead Sea

(Alexandria)

• Avaris

Naucratis •

LOWER   EGYPT

• Heliopolis

Giza •   • (Cairo)
[Great Pyramids]

Memphis •

Lake Fayum

FAYUM

SINAI

Gulf of Suez

Akabah

SAHARA DESERT

• Akhetaton
(El-Amarna)

Red Sea

UPPER   EGYPT

Thebes •   • Karnak
        • Luxor

NUBIA

(Aswan) •

First Cataract =

Nile R.

0	50	100 Miles

0	50	100	150 Kilometers

Modern place names
in parentheses

Nile R.

Abu Simbel •

beginning with the unification of Egypt under the first pharaoh, Menes, around 3000 B.C. Later historians subdivided the tangled chronicle of royal reigns into three periods—the Old Kingdom (ca. 2700–2200 B.C.), the Middle Kingdom (2050–1800 B.C.), and the New Kingdom (1550–1100 B.C.)—separated by social breakdowns called intermediate periods. Most recently, scholars concentrating on social, cultural, and institutional continuities have de-emphasized political periods altogether. This broader approach works particularly well with the earlier phases of Egyptian history, the predynastic Neolithic culture that preceded unification.

Perhaps as early as the fifth millennium B.C., the hunters and nomadic pastoralists who had gravitated to the well-watered river valley had discovered the agricultural potential of the endlessly replenished black earth along the Nile. Like their Neolithic fellows farther east, they settled into agricultural villages. There were differences, of course. The cereal on which Egyptian agriculture was based was wheat instead of barley, and the Egyptians grew flax for clothing instead of depending on sheep's wool. Like preurban peoples in many places, the Egyptians organized themselves into clans having animal totems, such as the crocodile or the hippopotamus. They probably worshiped these animals as well, since many of the gods of later Egyptian times were depicted with animal heads on their otherwise anthropomorphic bodies.

Along the Nile, as along the Tigris and Euphrates, it took slow centuries and many generations for village life to evolve into something more complex. Nevertheless, the outlines of a distinctly Egyptian culture were clear before the Old Kingdom ever began.

Sometime between 3500 and 3000 B.C., cooperative economic effort appeared as the Egyptians began to try to control the great river with dikes and catch basins. Copper was used more widely. The population grew. There was, however, less of the bustling urban life that had flourished in early Sumeria. Nor did trade play such an important part in Egypt; the Nile valley was so nearly self-sufficient that there was apparently little felt need for exotic foreign imports.

There were some influences from outside, even this early. Mesopotamian-style cylinder seals have been found in Egypt. Sumerian pictograms appear among the earliest Egyptian hieroglyphics. But there was one great difference: Because there was less urban commercial culture in Egypt, the city-state also failed to appear. Instead, Egypt seems to have moved relatively early directly into the centralized monarchical state.

There was one intermediate stage, however. After the villages along the river, there were the two lands of Upper and Lower Egypt. We do not know a great deal about these two lands before they became one. We know that the vulture of the goddess Nekhbet was sacred in Upper Egypt, the cobra of Wadjet in Lower Egypt. We know that the kings of the upper valley wore a white crown, the kings of the delta a red one. And we know that their two peoples fought each other.

We do not need to follow the struggle of the cobra and the vulture, the white crown and the red. After generations, maybe centuries, the warriors of Upper Egypt fought their way northward from inner Africa to the Mediterranean. A new capital was founded at Memphis, and the crowns of Upper and Lower Egypt were combined into the double crown of the pharaohs. By 3000 B.C., Egypt stood as a united land.

THE OLD KINGDOM: THE PYRAMID BUILDERS

Egypt was not a large nation by today's standards. It covered about the same area that Mesopotamia did—approximately ten thousand square miles—which made it about as large as a middle-sized American state. But in 3000 B.C. there was no nation in the world fully as large or half as centralized.

There was resistance, of course. Egyptians of the valley and Egyptians of the delta did not lose a sense of their differentness. The pharaoh was always officially "the King of Upper and Lower Egypt," "the Lord of the Two Ladies" (the vulture and the cobra), and as such was crowned and symbolically buried in each of the two lands. There were separate treasuries for the two halves of his kingdom and much duplication of officials.

More challenging still to the fundamental unity of the state was the tendency toward fragmentation embodied in the *nomes*, the provinces of pharaonic Egypt. Independent totemic tribes or clans prior to unification, the nomes could become centers of disunity under ambitious governors.

To hold the nation together, the early pharaohs, like the princes of Mesopotamia, forged a powerful alliance with the temples and the priests. Mesopotamian kings ruled as stewards or bailiffs of the gods; the pharaohs claimed that they themselves were incarnations of divinity.

Pharaoh was believed to be the son of the sun god Re. The reigning pharaoh was also Horus the sky god, symbolized by the falcon. On his death, "the falcon flew to the horizon," and the dead pharaoh became Osiris, king of the underworld. "What is the king of Upper and Lower Egypt?" a statesman of a later dynasty rhetorically inquired. "He is a god by whose dealings one lives, the father and mother of all men, alone by himself, without an equal."[1]

Above all, he was "the good god." Every year he performed religious ceremonies that guaranteed the rising of the river. He and his officials ruled the land in the spirit of *Ma'at*, a combination of truth, justice, and order that was for the Egyptians the highest of virtues. In the underworld,

---

[1]Milton Covensky, *The Ancient Near Eastern Tradition* (New York: Harper & Row, 1966), p. 51.

the souls of the dead were weighed against *Ma'at*. In this world, pharaoh himself was its living embodiment and the guarantee that the land would be ruled in its spirit.

To carry out the will of the god-king, the Egyptians developed an elaborate administrative system as early as the Old Kingdom. The chief administrative officer under the pharaoh was the vizier, whose roles included chief judge, superintendent of public works, and general right hand to the king. Under the vizier an impressive array of bureaus emerged, including the treasuries, the ministry of agriculture, the officials in charge of the irrigation system, and a secretariat that piled up an immense volume of public records.

There was also a provincial administration charged with governing the nomes. The rulers of these provinces, the *nomarchs*, exercised considerable local authority. In particular, they controlled the local militia, the source of most of the military strength of the kings of Upper and Lower Egypt.

The body of the Egyptian bureaucracy—and subsequently the top spots as well—was staffed by scribes, the masters of the sacred art of writing. If the records they left behind are any indication, Egyptian scribes were busy bureaucrats. They conducted censuses of land and people, estimated the size of the harvest, and collected taxes in kind. They supervised the vital irrigation system, organized the care and feeding of the pharaohs and the

building of the royal tombs. Next to the divinity of pharaoh himself, these scribal administrators were the glue that held ancient Egypt together in a genuine national state built many centuries before its time.

Old Kingdom Egypt was a thoroughly ordered state. Society was organized hierarchically, as it would be almost everywhere in the increasingly complex cultures of the civilized world. Peasant farmers were the backbone of the nation—and the bottom of the social pyramid. Many of them were serfs on royal or noble lands, required to labor on building projects as well as to till the soil. Above these peasant *fellahin* were the royal officials, the priesthoods of the temples, the nobles, the princes, and the incarnate god upon the throne.

This hierarchy was symbolized most massively by the pyramid tombs of the pharaohs of the famous fourth dynasty—the dynasty of Khufu (known to Western history as Cheops), builder of the great pyramid at Giza. Today the tombs of the pharaohs loom in splendid isolation above the sands. Originally the royal pyramids of Khufu, Khafre, Menkaure, and the rest stood not alone, but as centers of ordered necropolises, cities of the dead. Each pyramid was surrounded by the smaller pyramids of queens and princes of the blood and by row after row of the flat-roofed *mastaba* tombs of high officials. The total effect of these ranks of tombs laid out along straight-ruled streets must have been somberly impressive. It expressed to perfection

Egypt's most famous monuments, the pyramids at Giza outside Cairo, tombs of the Old Kingdom pharaohs. Thousands of visitors see these royal tombs every year. Many, however, are so busy being photographed riding a camel or distracted by souvenir sellers that it is only later, when they look at their slides, that they recognize the immensity of this ancient Egyptian achievement. (Hirmer Fotoarchiv)

the order of the living state. In death as in life, the "good god" ruled, and his people slept around him.

THE MIDDLE KINGDOM: A BRIDGE BETWEEN TWO WORLDS

The record of the early dynasties after unification around 3000 B.C. is, then, one of relative stability, prosperity, and order. The record of the Old Kingdom looks particularly good by comparison with what followed.

The Middle Kingdom and the intermediate periods before and after it may be seen as a historic transition, a bridge between two worlds. During these half-dozen centuries Egypt moved from the self-contained, intensely conservative land of the pyramid builders to the more dynamic—and more turbulent—New Kingdom. Therefore, this entire period, from the collapse of the Old Kingdom around 2200 B.C. to the emergence of the New Kingdom about 1550, will be considered here as a whole.

The initial phase of this great transition is what historians have called the First Intermediate. We do not know what triggered this great disruption. There may have been a series of low Niles, or a succession of weak rulers. There was clearly a good deal of political turbulence, particularly among the nomarchs. There was famine in the land of the bountiful Nile, and marauding desert bedouin appeared in the delta. The poor cried out for justice—so the scribes lamented—and all Egyptians longed for a return to the immemorial order of past centuries.

What they got, as frequently happens in history, was not a return to the past but a dynamic new direction in national life. Ambitious dynasts from the new city of Thebes in Upper Egypt wrested the kingdom from the last royal house to rule in Memphis. During the twentieth and nineteenth centuries before Christ, the powerful twelfth dynasty restored prosperity and order along the Nile.

The Middle Kingdom thus inaugurated brought what seems to many historians a new concern for the governed on the part of twelfth dynasty pharaohs. Contemporary scribes talked of a new sense of civic responsibility among the governed themselves during this briefest of the three Egyptian kingdoms.

But the most striking new dimension was the outward reach of the pharaohs of the twelfth dynasty. Trade expanded rapidly in the prosperous new era. Egyptian merchants traded with Palestine and Syria, satellite civilizations of ancient Mesopotamia, and even sailed to Minoan Crete, the island kingdom where the first European civilization was just emerging. Egyptian arms pushed south along the Nile into Nubia, the lands of the nearest black African people, and on into the Sudan.

Thus for the first time Egypt became involved on a large scale with the busy life of the Near East and northeastern Africa. From Middle Kingdom days on, the pharaohs were to play a key role in the history of both Africa and the Near East.

Contact with the outside world could flow two ways, however. The dynasties that followed the twelfth seem to have produced less capable rulers. Tendencies toward dissolution of the union, no longer restrained by a firm hand, reasserted themselves. And covetous strangers from overseas, attracted by the wealth and increasingly visible weakness of Egypt at the end of the Middle Kingdom, began to appear once more in the delta.

Shortly before 1700 B.C.—in the middle of the Second Intermediate—the gathering storm burst over Egypt in what ancient Egyptians regarded as their greatest catastrophe: the invasion of the Hyksos.

The priest Manetho described the onslaught of this mysterious Semitic-speaking people as "a blast of God." The seizure of power by the Hyksos may not have been quite that dramatic. The Hyksos influx was part of a general reshuffling of nomadic peoples during the second millennium B.C., to be discussed in the next chapter. These folk migrations were slow infiltrations as often as they were invasions. The invaders of Egypt actually spent several generations settling in the delta. Once they had seized power from the enfeebled pharaohs of the Second Intermediate, the Hyksos found nobles and nomarchs quite willing to collaborate with their leadership.

As often happens when a less sophisticated people overpowers a more developed culture, the newcomers soon became culturally assimilated, taking the names of the people they ruled, worshiping their gods, following all the traditional royal rites to the letter. For a century, perhaps a century and a half, they remained the predominant force in the Egypt of the Second Intermediate.

Governing the delta, dominating the valley, the Hyksos were also responsible for some valuable innovations. The use of bronze instead of the softer copper became widespread at this time. New weapons of war invented on the distant steppes were probably introduced by the intruders—notably the two-wheeled horse-drawn war chariot.

Then, as had happened twice already in Egyptian history, a powerful force surged out of the upper valley to restore the direction of that history to Egyptian hands once more.

 ## THE EGYPTIAN EMPIRE

THE NEW KINGDOM: THE TURN TOWARD EMPIRE

The spearhead of this northward drive was the princely house of Thebes and its current head, Ahmose I, founder of the eighteenth and most powerful of Egyptian dynasties. His father and his brother had rallied noble opposition to the Hyksos before him. Around 1550 B.C., Ahmose led an army up the Nile, mastered the delta, captured the

Hyksos capital, and harried the foreigner out of the land. He even pursued the Hyksos into Palestine, where they were conspiring with local chieftains for help, and destroyed their base there.

Returning to Egypt, the liberator crushed rebellions by some of the nobility and the Nubian princes who had collaborated with the Hyksos. He heaped the loot of all his victories at the feet of Amun, the sun god of Thebes. The priesthood of Amun thus became the most powerful in Egypt, and Thebes the new capital.

Thebes and the Theban princes were now at the head of an Egypt cleansed of foreign power. Egyptians had also had a taste of foreign conquest themselves, and of the loot and tribute that flowed from it. It was a heady experience, and it was to sweep Egypt into its last great age, the New Kingdom and the Empire (1550–1100 B.C.), when for four centuries Egyptian power would dominate the civilized people of the ancient Near East.

QUEEN HATSHEPSUT AND THUTMOSE THE CONQUEROR

The kings and queens of the New Kingdom seem to stand out in bold relief against the background of the centuries. These rulers of the last half of the second millennium B.C. were shapers of the history of their times. They also vividly illustrate those times, in all their strange ambitions and exotic grandeur. It will therefore be in order to slow the pace now and look into a royal lifetime or two as it was lived thirty-five hundred years ago.

Lying across the river from Thebes, the mortuary temple of Pharaoh Hatshepsut—wide and many-pillared, the cliffs of Deir el-Bahari looming dramatically behind it—is one of the most splendid sights in Egypt. And Hatshepsut was unique among pharaohs. She was a woman.

The daughter of one pharaoh and the widow of another, Hatshepsut began her reign as regent for the male heir to the throne. Soon, however, she went beyond this quite legal role. Unprecedentedly, she declared herself the child of Re and the god's designated ruler, had herself crowned with the double crown, and seated herself on the golden throne of the pharaohs.

Hatshepsut's most lifelike surviving statue shows an attractive, slightly built woman wearing the clothing and headdress of the King of Upper and Lower Egypt. She is known to have surrounded herself with brilliant and ambitious advisors, and to have lavished wealth on the powerful priesthood of Amun at Thebes. She trumpeted her deeds from temple wall and obelisk in true pharaonic fashion. It was a bravura performance, and we would like to know more about it.

The reign of Hatshepsut, however, is more than a startling historical anomaly. It illustrates a crucial aspect of New Kingdom history: the commercial development and widespread prosperity that made this one of the most pleasant times in Egypt's long history.

Queen and pharaoh, Hatshepsut wears the royal crown, collar, and short skirt of all her royal predecessors as she sits upon the throne of New Kingdom Egypt. What do such unchanging patterns in Egyptian life, institutions, and art tell you about Egyptian character? (Statue of Queen Hatshepsut Egyptian Antiquities–Sculpture [c. B.C. 1485], Dynasty xviii, Indurated limestone, The Metropolitan Museum of Art. Rogers Fund and Contributions from Edward S. Harkness, 1929.)

Under Hatshepsut, as under other pharaohs, high-prowed "Byblos travelers" plowed the gentle swells of the Mediterranean north to the cities of Phoenicia and beyond, while tinkling Egyptian caravans followed the great military roads north and east to Mesopotamia. Nubia and Sinai poured their copper and gold into the coffers of Egypt. Hatshepsut's most renowned commercial venture, however, was the expedition she dispatched down the Red Sea to the Terraces of Incense, the legendary land of Punt, where the natives had beards like Egyptian gods and lived in grass houses built on pilings. The Egyptian fleet returned laden with ebony

VOICES FROM THE PAST

"*[Long] live the female Horus . . . daughter of Amon-Re, his favorite, his only one. . . .*

"O ye people, who shall see my monument after years, those who shall speak of that which I have made, beware (lest) ye say, 'I know not, I know not why this was made, (and) a mountain fashioned entirely from gold. . . . I swear as Re loves me, as my father Amon favors me, as my nostrils are filled with satisfying life, as I wear the white crown, as I appear in the red crown, . . . as I rule this land like the son of Isis . . . as I have become strong like the son of Nut, as Re sets in the evening-barque, as he rises in the morning-barque, as he joins his two mothers in the divine barque, as heaven abides, as that which he hath made endures. . . .

"Let not him who shall hear this say it is a lie which I have said, but say, 'How like her it is! [who is] truth[ful] in the sight of her father!' The god knew it in me, Amon, lord of Thebes; he caused that I should reign. . . . I am his daughter of a truth, who glorifies him,—that which he exacted; my [—] is with my father; life, stability, and satisfaction, upon the Horus-throne of all the living, like Re, forever."

This inscription from Hatshepsut's obelisk at Karnak trumpets the glory of the builder as such monuments commonly do. At another level, however, the inscription may be seen to be making a case for the legitimacy of the only woman pharaoh in the history of New Kingdom Egypt.

What, for instance, do the "two crowns" she claims to wear represent? The "son of Isis" is Horus, and Amon and Re are of course names for the great sun god of Egypt's most powerful cult. What relationship does Hatshepsut claim to these divinities, and how does this strengthen her claim to the throne? From the tone of the inscription, would you guess that she enjoyed wielding power in Egypt?

James Henry Breasted, Ancient Records of Egypt: Historical Documents. Vol. II: The Eighteenth Dynasty (Chicago: University of Chicago Press, 1906), pp. 130, 132–134.

---

and ivory, perfumes and spices, apes, monkeys, leopard skins, slaves, and thirty-one live myrrh trees, which were ceremoniously replanted in front of the queen's temple at Deir el-Bahari.

She was a great ruler. But greatness sometimes kindles greatness in its rivals, and Hatshepsut had a great rival indeed. Prince Thutmose, the royal heir she had supplanted, grew into a restless young man. He was a skilled archer and charioteer, the darling of the militaristic elements among the aristocracy who longed for a more aggressive foreign policy. Thutmose himself seems to have chafed in his powerful aunt's leading strings, and to have resented the ambitious "new men" with whom she filled her court.

And then one year, as our meager records run, the young man had become Pharaoh Thutmose III, the new king of the two lands, and was preparing his chariots for war. Hatshepsut simply disappears from the records, and presumably from this world. It has been suggested—though there is no firm evidence—that the great queen did not "go gently into that good night."

Thutmose III, the "Napoleon of Egypt," embodied another and even more typical aspect of the history of the imperial New Kingdom: the unending military campaigns that fill the annals of the epoch. Thutmose himself fought seventeen campaigns, and he did more than anyone else to establish the bounds and form of Egypt's New Kingdom empire. From his time on, the pharaoh as god was complemented, if not replaced, by the pharaoh as hero and empire builder in the minds of the Egyptians.

Thutmose III was a short, thick-chested, bull-necked man with a large nose and immense physical strength and courage. His famous victories—the siege of Megiddo, the battle of Kadesh, the crossing of the Euphrates into the lands of the Mitanni—and the defeated princes who groveled in the dust before him to "beg breath for their nostrils" are long forgotten. But he did construct a genuine empire for Egypt that stretched over much of the ancient Fertile Crescent, from the Euphrates to the fourth cataract of the Nile. "I let you trample down the far corners of the lands," chanted the great god Amun on the granite of Karnak, "the circle of the ocean was caught in your fist."[2]

There was more to it, of course, than the favor of the gods. The soldiers of Thutmose III, battle-hardened veterans after a few campaigns, were equipped with the latest swords, bows, and armor of the late Bronze Age and led by the light, beautifully constructed chariots that the Hyksos had bequeathed to Egypt. Thutmose carefully established garrison towns, local governors, and a sophisticated system of puppet kings to control what he had conquered. Where he and his successors encountered really powerful rivals, such as the Hittites, the Egyptians soon turned from war to marriage alliances, from conquest to agreed-upon spheres of influence. This combination of force and diplomacy made Egypt the greatest power in the ancient Near East from the mid-fifteenth to the mid-twelfth century B.C.

Hatshepsut, queen and pharaoh, the living symbol of New Kingdom trade and affluence, crowned her towering obelisks with gold. The obelisks that Thutmose III scattered as far as the fourth cataract to thunder his imperial greatness to the world still stand today—in Istanbul, Rome, London, and New York's Central Park—loot of later empires larger by far than his. She was perhaps a vain queen, and he certainly a brutal conqueror, yet they were among the architects of Egyptian greatness.

AKHENATON, THE HERETIC PHARAOH

Perhaps the most fascinating of all the New Kingdom pharaohs was Akhenaton (c. 1379–1362 B.C.), described by later scholars as the heretic pharaoh, a religious visionary, or the doom of his dynasty. Akhenaton was in fact everything to intrigue the historian—and the romancer. He was abnormally ugly, but he had a beautiful wife, the swan-necked Nefertiti. He loved his family and his own version of religious truth. His unique contribution to Egyptian history consisted in his effort to impose monotheism upon the people of the Nile valley thirteen and a half centuries before Christ.

The son of one of the later pharaohs of the famous eighteenth dynasty, the prince apparently became fasci-

nated in his youth with one of the smaller solar cults, the worship of Aton, the sun disk itself. This fascination led the grown man to change his own name from Amenhotep IV (Amun Is Satisfied) to Akhenaton (Spirit of Aton). It drove him to move the capital of Egypt from Thebes, the stronghold of the priesthood of Amun, to a new city that he reared in the wilderness halfway between Thebes and Memphis, a city he christened Akhetaton ("Horizon of Aton"). His zealous faith, finally, apparently led him to launch a campaign to destroy all the other cults and replace them with the worship of the one true god, Aton the sun disk, throughout Egypt.

In this fantastic venture, Akhenaton shook up Egypt as it had not been shaken since the days of the Hyksos. The great Aton was represented not in human form, like the other gods, but simply by the solar disk. Rays spread down from it, and at the ends of the rays there were hands. Temples of Aton were built without roofs, so that the worshiper might commune directly with the god and feel in return the light and heat of the great creative force sailing majestically through the sky above. An Atonist hymn sometimes attributed to Akhenaton himself declares the glory of the one god, "beautiful, great, dazzling, and exalted over every land."[3]

The new city dedicated to the one god rose in a few years beneath the cliffs along the river near the present-day village of El-Amarna—hence the label Amarna Period for the whole unlikely adventure. Temples and palaces, fine homes for high officials, pleasure gardens and lovely courtyards grew up at the new cult center. Akhenaton may have been a fanatic, but there is an idyllic quality to those years at Horizon of Aton, cut off from the world and the gathering storm, that can scarcely fail to charm.

But it was not possible to transform the faiths of two thousand years in a single generation, and it took no more than the premature death of the pharaoh to destroy his new religion. The authority of the old cults was restored soon after Akhenaton's passing. Horizon of Aton was abandoned to the lizard and the jackal, and Akhenaton's very name was chiseled from the monuments and obliterated from the king list, as though he had never been. His youthful heir, Tutankhamun, returned to the faith of his ancestors and became a worshiper of Amun.

FINAL GLORIES AND A LONG DECLINE

Egypt had powerful pharaohs and pleasant times to come. But the tendency among historians has been to see all that came after the eighteenth dynasty, even the later centuries of the New Kingdom, as anticlimactic. The inner strength of these intensely conservative people seems to have weakened as the passing centuries carried them further from their roots. The empire grew harder to hold as its

[2]George Steindorff and Keith C. Seele, *When Egypt Ruled the East* (Chicago: University of Chicago Press, 1957), p. 55; Pierre Montet, *Lives of the Pharaohs* (Cleveland: World Pub. Co., 1968), p. 102.

[3]Steindorff and Seele, *When Egypt Ruled the East*, p. 214.

The heretic pharaoh Akhenaton, prophet of a lost religion. From the grotesquely exaggerated features and the encumbering royal regalia, an intensely human face looks out upon the world. Compare Akhenaton's face as depicted here with those of Hatshepsut and the gods Isis and Osiris. (Hirmer Fotoarchiv)

enemies grew more numerous and powerful. Despite intermittent high points, then, the last centuries of ancient Egypt are a story of long decline.

Pharaohs like Ramses II fought the Hittites to a standstill and watched the short-lived Hittite Empire crumble while life went on along the Nile. They repelled the attacks of the Sea People (the biblical Philistines), the greatest plague to descend upon the delta since the Hyksos. They built great temples and huge statues of themselves, and perhaps made Egyptians of the twelfth century B.C. think that the eternal life of Egypt would never end.

But weak kings, overmighty priests of Amun, and continuing waves of invaders undermined the state. During the thousand years that followed the end of the New Kingdom in the eleventh century, Theban priests, Libyan mercenaries, Nubian kings, Assyrians, Persians, Macedonians, and Romans ruled Egypt in turn. The notorious Cleopa-

tra, who welcomed Julius Caesar to Egypt, was as much Macedonian as she was Egyptian, and the most famous Egyptian city of her day was the hellenized metropolis of Alexandria. The Egypt of the Pyramid Age and the Empire had long since passed into history.

EGYPTIAN SOCIETY

The lives of ancient Egyptians, like those of many other peoples, depended very largely on their place in the social hierarchy. But images of enslaved masses toiling for the luxurious few owe more to the moralizing of their enemies and the romantic fiction of later ages than to historical realities. Egyptian peasants shared their mud-brick huts with farm animals and lived largely on wheat bread and barley beer. But even well-to-do Egyptians dined seated on grass mats, eating their elaborate meals mostly

The eternal fellahin labor for their masters in the fields along the Nile. Rich harvests like these earned Egypt the reputation of being the most favored of nations for many centuries. What rhythms, repetitions, and other elements of composition do you see in these pictures that make them as much works of art as records of Egyptian peasant life? (Wall painting: Harvest [c. 1415], copy in tempera. From Tomb of Menena, Scribe of the Fields of the Lord of Two Lands. The Metropolitan Museum of Art, Egyptian Expedition, Rogers Fund, 1930.)

with their fingers. It was by no means an egalitarian society, but neither was it one in which differences of class and caste completely undermined a certain shared satisfaction at being the most favored people of the gods.

We have many pictures of Egyptian *fellahin* hard at work in the fields, following a light plow or scattering seed in the furrows, harvesting wheat and barley, herding cattle in the delta, or fishing in the Nile. There was steady work also on the dikes and channels and basins that controlled the river, as well as compulsory labor on the tombs, temples, palaces, and public building projects of the pharaohs. But these projects depended for their success more on plenty of time and careful planning than on the flogged and sweated labor of the Hollywood epics. What records we have indicate a less than onerous work schedule: two four-hour work stints daily with a long noon siesta in between.

The condition of women was equally ambiguous among the Egyptians. Poor women worked as hard as their husbands, grinding grain at home and gleaning in the fields, with minimal time off to bear children. On the other hand, in contrast with many societies, Egyptians seem to have welcomed daughters as enthusiastically as they did sons.

The Greek historian Herodotus was struck by the freedom of Egyptian women to work and move freely in society. "The Egyptians," he wrote, "in their manners and customs, seem to have reversed the ordinary practices of mankind. For instance, women attend market and are employed in trade, while men stay at home and do the

weaving."[4] A woman was allowed to go into business for herself if she could demonstrate that she had had three children and could read and write. Among the professions filled by women were midwifery, mourning, dancing, music, some important priesthoods and—Herodotus to the contrary—weaving. The women of the royal harem in fact ran the state cloth manufactures and oversaw women weavers in the temples. Women are also recorded as running wig shops, dining halls, and other establishments.

As noted above, Egypt was a matrilineal society from top to bottom. All property was inherited in the female line. Even pharaoh frequently had to marry a sister in order to be sure of the crown. The leverage this gave the Egyptian woman must have been considerable.

The pictures we have of Egyptians at feasts seem to reveal a convivial people. They sat on reed mats with finger bowls and jars of wine at hand, while servants bore the festal meats around. The company was cheerfully mixed, men and women sitting easily together, crowned alike with garlands and entertained by the music of lutes and tambourines. Yet when the feast was over, a model mummy was carried through the company to remind them all of an old tune:

> Put song and music before thee
> Behind thee all evil things
> And remember thou only joy
> Till comes that day of mooring
> At the land that loveth silence.[5]

[4]B. Waterson, *Women in Ancient Egypt* (New York: St. Martin's Press, 1991), p. 25.

[5]W. M. Flinders Petrie, *Social Life in Ancient Egypt* (New York: Cooper Square Pub., 1970), p. 106.

The Wisdom of the Egyptians

Hieroglyphics, Science, and Literature

Among the Egyptians, as among the Mesopotamians, the discovery of the art of writing was one of the great civilizing inventions. It began quite literally as picture writing, as cuneiform had. But whereas the Mesopotamians soon reduced their little pictures to a collection of quick strokes of the stylus and went on to a system based entirely on signs that represented sounds, the official Egyptian hieroglyphic writing never completely abandoned the pictographic element. In the hands of conservative Egyptians, literacy remained to a considerable degree "picture writing" from one end of Egyptian history to the other.

Carved on stone monuments, this ancient priestly and official writing looked as impressive in the decadent days of Cleopatra as it had in the time of Khufu the pyramid builder. But it proved a bit cumbersome for busy scribes scrawling with reed pens on papyrus, the paper Egyptians made from the pith of the papyrus stem found along the Nile. As a working script, therefore, hieroglyphic writing evolved over centuries into a cursive script called *hieratic*, which looked more like modern Arabic than like pictograms.

Over the thirty-odd centuries of ancient Egypt, writing became a craft and a career ladder for government or temple scribes, a device for communicating at a distance and for keeping records. Like most early written languages, however, it was not originally intended as an instrument for literary self-expression.

Fragments of what we would call literature do exist, though. Hymns such as Akhenaton's song of praise to the sun and epic accounts of the victories of Thutmose III have the qualities of religious and patriotic literature from many times and lands. We have poetry too, especially from the New Kingdom, sad poems on the brevity of human life and happy poems of love. Perhaps the most impressive literary products of ancient Egypt, however, were to be found in the philosophical "wisdom literature" and the lively prose of Egyptian stories and tales.

Wisdom literature, common throughout the ancient Near East, includes collections of proverbs like those attributed to Solomon in the Old Testament. Here they are attributed to sages and pharaohs. These "instructions" urge youth to obey and respect their elders and betters and to sing the praises of old ways and ancient institutions. The famous wisdom of the Egyptians was thus profoundly— some would say crushingly—conservative. But perhaps we should wait until we have held our own world together for three thousand years before we dismiss the ancient Egyptians as unprogressive traditionalists.

If the Egyptians loved anything more than a good maxim for life, it was a good story. The most famous tale by far is the Middle Kingdom *Story of Sinuhe*, a first-person account of a noble Egyptian who, having been exiled from his native land, fights his way to fame and fortune among the bedouin of Syria. Yet Sinuhe's greatest joy—and no doubt the profoundest satisfaction of his readers—comes when he is summoned home to Egypt in his declining years by pharaoh himself. Egyptians loved to hear about wanderings in distant lands, but in the end they couldn't imagine anyone being happy far from the sound of the wind in the reeds along the Nile.

The ancient Egyptians have acquired a reputation for having esoteric knowledge of the nature of things. Actually, the mysterious Egyptians were in fact a thoroughly practical, pragmatic people having very little of the mystical in their makeup.

Their observation of nature could be remarkably precise. This was certainly the case in astronomy, one of the fields of scientific inquiry in which they were most successful. They divided the night sky into separate constellations, compiled detailed records of the nightly positions of some heavenly bodies, and constructed on this basis a calendar that is remarkably close to the solar one in use today. They used mathematics in a practical way—to survey and reestablish boundary lines after the annual inundation had washed out line markers up and down the Nile. They used measurement and calculation for architecture and engineering, for predicting harvests and totaling tax receipts. But their mathematics was not theoretical.

Egyptian medicine, which enjoyed great renown among other ancient peoples, also operated on the basis of experience and rules of thumb—plus a sizable dollop of magic. Nevertheless, Egyptian doctors did show genuine clinical concern with symptoms, diagnosis, and treatment. And some of the prescribed remedies include drugs, such as castor oil, that may even have done the patient some good.

Pyramids, Obelisks, and the Egyptian Canon

It is the immense age and the colossal size of the Old Kingdom pyramids that have awed posterity. The forty-five hundred years and the two and a half million cubic yards of solid stone in the great pyramid of Khufu add up to one of the most awesome of human engineering feats. Many of the gigantic masonry blocks had to be quarried at Aswan, five hundred miles up the Nile, floated down the river, and moved by sledge, levers, ropes, and straining human muscle across the desert and up immense temporary earthen ramps to their places in the rising structure. And all this without benefit of the wheel!

Obelisks were another Egyptian architectural specialty. These tall, thinly tapering stone spires cut in a single block sometimes stood almost a hundred feet high. Their hieroglyphic inscriptions described the achievements of the pharaohs who erected them, as the gold that gilded their pointed tips proclaimed the glory of Hatshepsut or Thutmose III. Temples to the gods also challenged the Egyptians to build greatly. Hordes of tourists gape daily at the eighty-foot columns at Karnak, raised by the celebrated New Kingdom warrior Ramses II, elaborately carved with hieroglyphics, and crowned with the characteristic papyrus-bud capitals of ancient Egypt. The facade of the temple at Abu Simbel, carved out of the living rock of the cliffs along the Nile, was flanked by four sixty-five-foot-tall statues of the militaristic New Kingdom pharaoh Ramses seated on his throne.

The gold of King Tut's tomb—the famous tomb of Tutankhamun, discovered practically intact in 1922—has shown us how dazzling the luxury art of the Egyptians could be. The golden sarcophagus of King Tut has symbolized the splendor of the pharaohs to generations of museum goers, though Tutankhamun himself, Akhenaton's unhappy successor, was a pharaoh of no particular distinction.

The conservative genius of the Egyptians is nowhere better revealed than in their representations of the human figure in paint and stone. In bas-relief sculpture and wall painting, the famous Egyptian "canon" prevailed for thousands of years. This set of academic rules for depicting the human form included such exotic requirements as representing the head and limbs in profile while showing the eyes and frequently the shoulders and torso in a full-face view. The pharaoh, moreover, was always to be painted or sculpted several times the size of his servants, soldiers, or defeated foes. There is also a powerful sense of artistic tradition at work in the three-dimensional, fully rounded sculpture of the Egyptians. Words such as *frontal* and even *cubical* are often used to characterize the seated or standing figures. The pharaohs all face the viewer directly, the shoulders square and broad, the waist narrow, the simple costume and headdress the same from Khafre and Menkaure, who built the second and third pyramids at Giza in the fourth dynasty, to the colossal statues of Ramses II in the nineteenth.

And yet from within this rigidly conventional art,

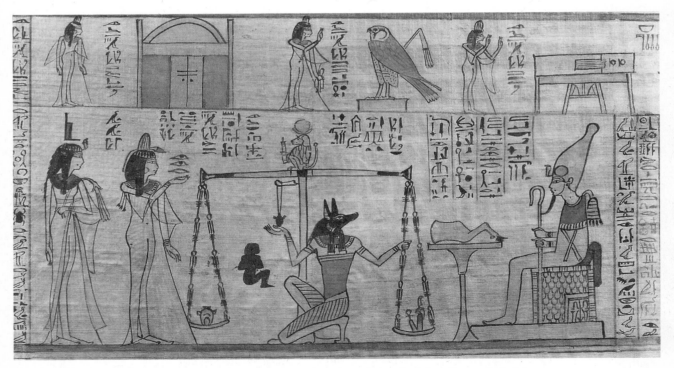

Isis on the left and Osiris on the right watch the weighing of a princess's heart against the symbol of *Ma'at*. This picture of a judgment in the underworld is from a New Kingdom papyrus copy of the *Book of the Dead* that was buried with a royal mummy. (Funerary Papyrus of the Princess Entiuny [c. 1025 B.C.]. From the tomb of Queen Meryet-Amun at Deir el Bahri, Thebes. The Metropolitan Museum of Art, Museum Excavations, 1928–1929, and Rogers fund, 1930.)

the living face of ancient Egypt manages from time to time to peer out at the modern viewer. Most striking is the brief interlude, lasting no more than a couple of generations, known as the Amarna Period.

The softer, more human style of this period, which was centered in Akhenaton's new city dedicated to Aton, depicted that unfortunate pharaoh not as the wide-shouldered, lean-hipped superman of yore but as the pot-bellied, long-headed, downright ugly figure he apparently was. The Amarna style also gave us the long-necked beauty of his queen, Nefertiti, much as she must have been in life, and painted their small daughters playing in their gardens, large-eyed and oddly sweet despite their shaved heads and thin, gracefully posed limbs.

It was the shortest of interludes in the stately march of Egyptian frontality, the briefest digression from the Egyptian canon. But it does give us a brief, warm glimpse of the living face of the builders of this great and vanished civilization.

Many Gods and Eternal Life

In Greek and Roman times, the Egyptians had the reputation of being the most religious and other-worldly of peoples. It is easy for moderns to imagine the Egyptians as a darkly superstitious race who worshiped monstrous animal-headed gods and were obsessed with mummies and tombs, with death and what comes after it. In fact, as we have seen, most Egyptians seem to have been thoroughly materialistic about most things, to have loved gardens and children and the hot African sun. But like their Near Eastern neighbors, they did worship many gods, some of whom retained more than a trace of their animal origins. And of all the earlier civilizations, the Egyptians seem to have been the most concerned with the universal fact of death and the dream of life eternal.

More than two thousand gods were worshiped by the people who lived along the Nile. The chief of these was always a god of the sun—first Re, the sun god of Memphis, later Amun of Thebes. There were other widely worshiped divinities, including Horus the sky god, represented as a falcon; Thoth the ibis-headed god of wisdom and of scribes; Hathor the cow, the Egyptian goddess of beauty; and Anubis the jackal-headed god of the tomb.

The most popular of Egyptian myths—particularly from the Middle Kingdom onward—was the sacred story of Isis the merciful and her husband Osiris, the god who rose from the dead. Many an Egyptian mother told her children how Osiris, son of the sky and the earth, married his sister Isis and ruled over all the gods, until their jealous brother Set murdered Osiris, tore him to pieces, and scattered the dismembered divinity up and down the land. But the story had a happy ending. Before mother put out the lamp she would tell how Isis, grieving but determined, hunted over the world to recover her hus-

band's body and bring it back to life, perhaps with a touch of the *ankh*, the looped cross that Egyptian mothers wore as amulets round their necks. Osiris lived still, as king of the underworld, with the loyal and compassionate Isis at his right hand. Egyptians fully expected to meet the divine pair when they too passed to the land of silence.

In the beginning only the pharaoh, who was himself a god, was sure of immortality. During the Middle Kingdom, however, when concern for the people rose, ordinary Egyptians began to believe that eternal life might be within their reach too. It might require expensive embalming and elaborate rituals for the dead. It might require a blameless life on earth. Osiris was known to weigh the souls of the departed and to cast those who were found wanting into the jaws of the crocodile god. But it was at least possible that the grave was not the end.

Mummification was a fine art in ancient Egypt. The corpse was washed with expensive oils, debrained through the nostrils, eviscerated through an incision in the abdomen, and dried for some weeks in a packing of natron, a crystalline substance with a special capacity to absorb moisture. It was then massaged and washed again, stuffed with amulets, more natron, and sometimes sand, sawdust, or other filling, wrapped carefully in endless strips of white linen, and returned at last to the mourning relatives for burial.

The spiritual parts, meanwhile, were believed to be undergoing their own transition from this life to the next.

To guide the soul through the underworld to its final judgment, the survivors inserted a collection of spells and ritual responses in the sarcophagus before interment. This so-called *Book of the Dead* depicts many aspects of the afterlife, climaxing in the final weighing of the soul against the principle of righteousness, *Ma'at*. This last judgment took place in the Hall of the Double Law under the eyes of twelve sceptered gods. The ape of Thoth crouched on the balance beam, jackal-headed Anubis adjusted the scale, and the hideous Devourer of the Dead crouched below, crocodile jaws agape for the soul found wanting. The soul that had not sinned against the gods, however, became "an Osiris," was led into the presence of the great king of the underworld, and was received into the company of the immortals.

Babylonian Arallu, the dim land of dust and shadows, was no place anyone could look forward to. The Elysian fields of the Greeks and the Roman underworld were closed to all but a few great heroes, and even these immortals testified through the poets that they would gladly trade an eternity below for one day of full-bodied life on earth. The Egyptians were perhaps the first to democratize the concept of immortality and to imagine an afterlife so glorious that one might aspire with joy to becoming an Osiris, one with Re, floating with the falcon Horus toward the sun.

SUMMARY

The history of ancient Egypt began before 3000 B.C. and lasted almost till the time of Christ, producing one of the most admired cultures of ancient times.

Egyptian civilization developed along the fertile banks of the Nile, as Mesopotamia had along the Tigris and Euphrates. Separate kingdoms first took shape in Upper and Lower Egypt but were unified by the first pharaohs around 3000 B.C. The Old Kingdom, or Pyramid Age (twenty-seventh to twenty-second centuries B.C.), was an extremely stable, strongly conservative society held together by pharaohs who were believed to be divine and by a busy scribal bureaucracy. The Middle Kingdom that followed (twentieth to eighteenth centuries) witnessed a transition to a more dynamic culture that interacted commercially and militarily with the rest of the Middle East.

The New Kingdom (sixteenth to twelfth centuries B.C.) saw the pharaohs of the powerful eighteenth dynasty building a large and impressive Egyptian Empire. The successful general Thutmose III and his successors conquered most of the crescent from Nubia (farther south up the Nile) around through Palestine to Mesopotamia. Under Hatshepsut, the only female pharaoh, Egypt grew rich in trade. Pharaoh Akhenaton, a religious zealot, attempted to impose a monotheistic religion on the nation, but his unique cult only lasted Akhenaton's lifetime.

From about 1100 B.C. on, Egypt underwent a long decline. During this period the ancient land was frequently ruled by foreigners, and after the first century B.C. it disappeared into the vastly larger empire of the Romans.

The Egyptians produced the best-known early form of writing, the system of pictograms known as hieroglyphics. Artistically a very conservative people, they painted and sculpted according to the same rules and formulas for thousands of years. They erected massive pillared temples to their animal-headed gods, proclaimed their pharaohs' achievements on gold-tipped obelisks, and left as their most famous monuments the huge pyramid tombs of the Old Kingdom. They were particularly concerned with life after death, as the pyramids, mummification, and the cult of Isis and Osiris all indicate.

SUGGESTED READING

ALDRED, C. *Akhenaton, Pharaoh of Egypt: A New Study.* London: Thames and Hudson, 1968. Expert evaluation of this much debated and romanticized monotheist pharaoh. On the pharaoh whose tomb revealed the splendor of royal Egypt, see C. Desroches-Noblecourt, *Tutankhamen: Life and Death of a Pharaoh* (New York: Viking Penguin, 1989).

BUTZER, K. W. *Early Hydraulic Civilization in Egypt.* Chicago: University of Chicago Press, 1976. Brief but illuminating introduction to the interaction of society and ecology in the Nile valley.

DIOP, C. A. *The African Origin of Civilization: Myth or Reality?* trans. Mercer Cook. New York: Lawrence Hill, 1974. Provocative study, including discussion of the influence of other African cultures on Egyptian civilization. More recent is M. Bernal's widely discussed multivolume study, *Black Athena: The Afroasiatic Roots of Classical Civilization* (New Brunswick, N.J.: Rutgers University Press, 1987–1991), which also emphasizes the African roots of Egyptian civilization.

EL MAHDY, C. *The World of the Pharaohs.* New York: Thames and Hudson, 1990. Illustrated guide to ancient Egypt.

FRANKFORT, H. *Ancient Egyptian Religion: An Interpretation.* New York: Harper & Row, 1961. Probably the best-known, comparatively recent study of this central aspect of Egyptian culture, by the leading authority on the mind of the ancient Near East. See also E. Hornung's more recent *Conceptions of God in Ancient Egypt: The One and the Many,* trans. John Baines (Ithaca: Cornell University Press, 1982) depicting the gods as powers thronging the universe and shaping human destinies.

JAMES, T. G. A. *Ancient Egypt: The Land and Its Legacy.* Austin: University of Texas Press, 1988. Scholarly overview. P. Jordan's *Egypt: The Black Land* (Oxford: Phaidon, 1976) is a lavishly illustrated look at the land along the Nile. Two good brief introductions to Egyptian civilization are A. R. David, *The Egyptian Kingdoms* (New York: Bedrick Books, 1988), and A. J. Spenser, *The Rise of Civilization in the Nile Valley* (London: British Museum Press, 1993).

LEPRE, J. P. *The Egyptian Pyramids.* Jefferson, N.C.: McFarland, 1990. Solid introduction to the tombs of the pharaohs. See also A. R. David, *The Pyramid Builders of Ancient Egypt* (London: Routledge and Kegan Paul, 1986), which focuses on "pharaoh's workforce," the people who physically built these monuments.

REDFORD, D. B. *Egypt, Canaan, and Israel in Ancient Times.* Princeton, N.J.: Princeton University Press,

1992. A scholarly, sometimes provocative study. For an introduction to disputes over the chronology of the ancient history of the region, see P. James, *Centuries of Darkness: A Challenge to the Conventional Chronology of Old World Archaeology* (New Brunswick, N.J.: Rutgers University Press, 1993).

ROBINS, G. *Women in Ancient Egypt.* Cambridge, Mass.: Harvard University Press, 1993. Scholarly discussion illustrated by well-chosen art. A good introduction to the subject is B. Waterson, *Women in Ancient Egypt* (New York: St. Martin's Press, 1991).

SIMPSON, W. K., ed. *The Literature of Ancient Egypt: An Anthology of Stories, Instructions, and Poetry.* Includes examples of all of the literary forms. See also A. E. and W. K. Simpson, eds., *The Ancient Egyptians: A Sourcebook of the Writings* (New York: Harper & Row, 1965).

SMITH, W. S., and W. K. SIMPSON, eds. *The Art and Architecture of Ancient Egypt,* rev. ed. Harmondsworth, England: Penguin Books, 1981. Small format but clear and well illustrated.

TAYLOR, J. H. *Egypt and Nubia.* Cambridge, Mass.: Harvard University Press, 1991. Illustrated guide to British Museum holdings on these two cultures.

TRIGGER, B. G., et al. *Ancient Egypt: A Social History.* New York: Cambridge University Press, 1983. Substantial survey. See also T. G. H. James, *Pharaoh's People: Scenes from Life in Imperial Egypt* (Chicago: University of Chicago Press, 1984), a social history enlivened by vignettes and citations from contemporary documents.

VAN SETERS, J. *The Hyksos: A New Investigation.* New Haven: Yale University Press, 1966. Sifts the evidence concerning these mysterious invaders.

WILSON, J. A. *The Culture of Ancient Egypt.* Chicago: University of Chicago Press, 1956. Old but excellent survey of the history, society, and culture of Egypt, with an anthropological slant.

CHAPTER 4

Nubia and Carthage

AFRICA SOUTH AND WEST

THE SECOND LARGEST CONTINENT

There was once a predisposition—rooted perhaps in too many old Tarzan movies—to imagine Africa as one vast jungle inhabited by "natives" who lived in grass huts and were constantly being devoured by tigers and crocodiles. Even people with some knowledge tended to fall in with this "dark continent" image, claiming that Africa had been cut off from progress through lack of intercourse with other peoples throughout its history. The reality, as usual, is a good deal more complex and interesting than the myth.

The world's second largest continent—only Asia is larger—covers a little less than twelve million square miles. More than two fifths of that vast area is covered with grassy plains. Another two fifths is arid-to-desert land. Less than one fifth is forested, and only a small part of that is genuine tropical rain forest, most of it in the Congo River basin and along the Guinea coast of West Africa.

The geography of the continent falls into a series of clearly definable bands: fertile Mediterranean coastal lands in the north, the wider swath of the barren Sahara, the sudannic belt of grasslands, the equatorial rain forests, then grassy plains again, the Kalahari Desert, and finally the fertile uplands of South Africa. This simplified pattern of east-to-west bands is complicated by a curving north-to-south trench composed of the Nile and the Great Rift Valley with its attendant lakes, running almost the length of East Africa.

The whole of Africa, finally, exists in a larger context of neighboring landmasses and seas. Thus the history of North Africa has traditionally been interwoven with that of the Near East, Europe, and the Mediterranean Sea. Africa's east coast, by contrast, has looked toward such regions as the Red Sea, the Indian Ocean, Arabia, and India.

Historically speaking, the peoples and cultures of Africa have been as varied as those of any other continent. Black Africans have apparently always been important, constituting 70 percent of the population today. But there are also Semitic-speaking Arabs and Berbers in large numbers in the north, Hamites in the Egyptian northeast, and in recent centuries influential immigrations from Europe and Asia. Even the "black" majority is normally subdivided into a variety of culturally diverse peoples and language groups, from the Bantu-speaking agricultural people of the central and southern portions of the continent to the food-gathering Khoi-San and Pygmies still to be found in the deserts and deep woods.

In the biblical book of *Isaiah*, inner Africa was "the land shadowing with wings," little known and almost untraveled by outsiders. For Western explorers and imperialists as recently as a century ago, Africa was the dark continent, a symbol of the unknown and the primitive.

In fact, Africa was making crucial contributions to the human story long before civilization was dreamed of. As the evidence now runs, the earliest hominids first evolved into human beings in Africa. Africa probably maintained a long lead in the production of basic stone tools throughout the Old Stone Age. One of the oldest civilizations, that of ancient Egypt, took shape in northeastern Africa, though as we saw in the last chapter, the history of the lower Nile was also closely bound up with the early history of the near East. Civilization, however, emerged, in parts of Africa besides Egypt, and it is with these historic beginnings that the following sections will be concerned.

The existence of these early African cultures argues strongly against the notion that Africa was cut off from progressive outside influences. Several of the early cultures to be considered here—Nubia and Kush on the upper Nile and Carthage on the western Mediterranean—developed in fruitful interchange with other areas. Their stories clearly illustrate the process of sociocultural development in the usual historical web of influences and interchange of goods and ideas.

Edgar Rice Burroughs, the creator of Tarzan and his fairy-tale Africa, once said that the best way to get ahead as a writer was to write about something you know absolutely nothing about. His vision of a dark continent thick with jungle, peopled by Hottentots, and stalked by man-eating tigers (who don't live in Africa at all) would seem to illustrate his theory to perfection. But that fictional vision does not tell us much about Africa. As a Swahili-speaking East African might put it, shaking his head over this Wild West legend of his own land: "More *Wazungu* lies!"

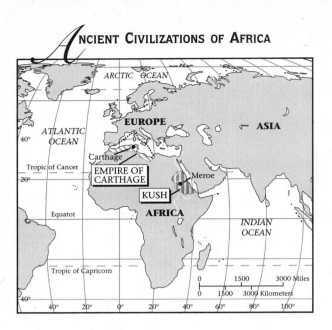

ANCIENT CIVILIZATIONS OF AFRICA

FARMERS AND GATHERERS SOUTH OF THE SAHARA

Africa in 3500 B.C., was in significant ways quite different from the Africa of today. Geographically, the most striking difference was that the Sahara was not a sun-bleached wasteland but a thoroughly habitable region of rivers and marshes, due to a generally wetter climate. The slow desiccation of the Sahara was one of the main features of African history over the millennia that followed.

The population of Africa more than five thousand years ago seems to have included the main groups present there today, but in very different proportions. The Khoi-San and the Pygmy, today constituting a tiny minority confined to wilderness areas in the south, were then widely scattered over sub-Saharan Africa. The negroid population seems to have inhabited the damp Saharan region of those times. And there were already caucasoid peoples along the Mediterranean coast.

Outside the Nile valley, all these peoples lived as their Neolithic or Paleolithic ancestors had at the beginning of this period. Neolithic agriculture was soon introduced to North Africa and the Sahara region, partly from Egypt, and perhaps partly through an independent evolution in West Africa. But the peoples of all the rest of Africa—Africa south of the Sahara, as it is commonly called—still hunted and gathered for subsistence, as their Paleolithic forebears had.

It was a dependable world to live in, particularly in the vast stretches of Africa south of the moist Sahara. There was game in the forest, fish in the rivers, easily built huts of wattle and daub for shelter, and the certainty that patient grinding and polishing would in the end produce

a serviceable stone tool. Only Africans of the far north-east would even have known that there was an Egypt, where people worked in long lines in fields, built artificial mountains out of stone blocks, and made tiny marks on reed paper that could talk.

The first great change was perhaps the most astonishing: the drying out of the Sahara, beginning about 2500 B.C. As the land parched and dried, the black population of the Sahara region retreated north and south. Those who reached the Mediterranean in the north may have mingled with the caucasoid population there to produce the Berbers of Carthaginian times. Those who migrated southward to the West African savannas—grasslands dotted with trees—and on to the rain forests beyond took with them the agricultural techniques they had developed along the rivers of the dying Sahara.

Agriculture thus spread further southward in Africa during these millennia. The new techniques included rice cultivation and the growth of certain kinds of yams that could prosper even in the deep forests of West and Central Africa. Pastoral herding developed on the arid Sahara, and the Berbers soon became the masters of the desert. Cattle were also herded in parts of East Africa about this time, as they are today.

But all these new skills were still limited to the northern parts of the continent. Further south, bushmanoid and Pygmy peoples continued to hunt and fish and gather vegetables and roots as they always had. Like most of the world's peoples, most Africans were still Stone Age toolmakers; and only a minority were using stone hoes and other agricultural tools to provide a more stable source of nutrients around their villages.

NUBIA, KUSH, AND INNER AFRICA

THE NUBIAN CORRIDOR

Out of the south they came, by river and by caravan into Egypt: gold, ivory, ebony, ostrich feathers, slaves. And more: cattle, grain, leopards (and their skins), giraffes (whose tails were used as fly whisks), oils and perfumes, "amazon stone," carnelian, gum and red ocher and ostrich eggs. Century after century the largesse of the mysterious lands beyond the cataracts of the Nile came north—in booty, in tribute, and in trade goods. Sometimes, especially during Egypt's long decline, African armies came down the Nile to smite Thebes and Memphis, and African kings from the south to sit on the throne of the pharaohs, to negotiate with the Greeks or fight the Romans.

For at least two thousand years there were rich lands south of Egypt, in that part of northeastern Africa once called Nubia, today straddling the border between Egypt and Sudan. For half that time, from the eighth century B.C. to the fourth century A.D., those southern lands coalesced into the powerful African state of Kush.

Nubia has become a catch-all geographical term for the area between the First Cataract of the Nile and the bifurcation of that immense river into the Blue and White Niles. On a map of modern Africa, it is the region of the cataracts and the enormous S-curve of the river between Egypt's Aswan High Dam and the Sudanese capital of Khartoum.

Before the beginning of history, the Nubians lived much as other Paleolithic or Neolithic peoples did along the banks of the Nile. From the Mediterranean in the north to the Ethiopian highlands and the Great Lakes of Central Africa, these early Africans hunted and fished and learned to grow crops and herd animals as other peoples did around the globe. Like other African peoples, they lived in small groups, in nomadic bands or agricultural villages. Some of the same tools and styles of pottery were produced in Nubia, south of the First Cataract, as in Egypt, north of it.

Then, around 3000 B.C. came the great change in Egypt. Led by the first pharaohs, centralized government mobilized the villages to bring the Nile under control. The resulting system of levees, catch basins, and irrigation ditches turned the Nile river north of the cataracts into one of the most productive agricultural zones in the world. Bureaucratic government, social classes, monumental building, and other elements of a developed civilization followed.

Life in Nubia, just south of the emerging Egyptian kingdom, could not help but be affected. In time, as we will see, many of the characteristics of Egyptian civilization would spread up the Nile into Nubia. Soon also, indigenous Nubian kingdoms—Kerma, Kush, and Meroe—would emerge in the south and begin to play a key part in the history of the Nile valley as a whole.

Perhaps most important, however, Nubia continued to serve as the most important link between Egypt and the Mediterranean world in the north and inner Africa to the south. Though the cataracts required that boats be transported overland around them, the long river remained the easiest north-south route across the desert.

It is not surprising, then, that Egyptian rulers, eager for ivory, ebony, incense, and other products, sent trading expeditions up the Nile toward the heart of Africa. Up and down the Nubian corridor, goods, ideas, and power thus flowed for many centuries. As early as the Egyptian Old Kingdom, a pharaoh gratefully accepted a Pygmy dancer from Central Africa, sent to him as a gift from Nubia. As late as Roman times, Kushite raiders carried off a carved head of Augustus Caesar from an attack on an Egypt that had become a Roman province. Nubia was thus a vital link in the chain that bound the civilizations of the Old World together.

THE RISE OF KERMA

The first step in the emergence of a distinctive Nubian civilization was the rise of the mysterious kingdom of Kerma shortly after 2000 B.C. The gigantic clay-brick ruins of Kerma in Upper Nubia represent a transition between the village culture of early Nubia and the kingdoms and empires to come.

Most Nubians of the second millennium B.C. continued to live by subsistence farming, measuring their wealth in cows and oxen. At the top of this simple society, however, powerful chiefs or kings had clearly emerged. The largest of the royal tombs at Kerma is nearly 300 feet in diameter and contains burial chambers larger than those of any Egyptian pyramid. The exquisite red-and-black Kerma ware pottery was treasured by a small elite at home and much valued up the Nile in Middle Kingdom Egypt. It was from Kerma that many of the exotic African goods so prized in Egypt flowed northward up the Nile.

Kerma's kings probably claimed divine descent and served as war leaders as well. But the foundation of their power was the state-organized trade with Egypt. With the help of Egyptian clerks, they produced and shipped north enough of the wealth of inner Africa to kindle the interest of Egypt's pharaohs. Kerma reached the height of its prosperity during the Hyksos period of foreign rule in Egypt. With the coming of the New Kingdom, however, the restored pharaohs marched south to impose an Egyptian hegemony on the peoples south of the First Cataract.

THE KINGDOM OF KUSH

From the beginning, Egyptian influences were of paramount importance in the development of these southern lands. The pharaohs of the Middle Kingdom went south of the first cataract and raided the region of the upper Nile. Around 1500 B.C., the aggressively expansionist pharaonic empire builders of the New Kingdom overran the area, and made the wealth—and the fearless bowmen—of the region prime resources in Egypt's most ambitious bid to master the Fertile Crescent.

During these centuries of northern domination, Egyptian governors and garrisons, priests, and artisans left an indelible mark on the lands and peoples of the upper Nile. The sons of Kushite kings were educated at the Egyptian royal court at Thebes. Egyptian temples and gods, Egyptian royal rituals, and Egyptian hieroglyphics were all transplanted to the Sudan. The Egyptian religious complex at Napata in particular became a center for the spread of Egyptian culture among the Africans beyond the cataracts.

When the long decline of Egypt began around 1100 B.C., Kush regained its independence. But the black kings of Kush still followed Egyptian ways and worshiped Egyptian gods. They glorified their own deeds

The "lion temple" at Naga in Kush reveals both Egyptian influences and the powerful new cult of the lion god. Guarded by the sacred rams of Egyptian Amun and decorated by images of the python, a symbol of spiritual potency all over Africa, this temple of the lion god Apedemak embodies both foreign influences and indigenous developments. Note the massive solidity of the building, the elaborate decoration, and the over-arching sense of splendor of this shrine built far up the Nile between 100 B.C. and A.D. 100. (Art Resource)

in hieroglyphic inscriptions and were buried under pyramids like those of the Old Kingdom. It was a new Egypt—upriver.

As old Egypt fell under foreign domination during the first millennium B.C., the Kushites may well have seen themselves as the true guardians of the old ways and ancient values they had shared with their neighbors down the river for so many centuries. Around 750 B.C., the Kushite kings Kashta and Piankhi marched north to liberate Egypt from its Libyan rulers, the mercenary North African princes who had seized the throne. For more than half a century thereafter, the Kushite pharaohs of the twenty-fifth Egyptian dynasty ruled a dual kingdom that stretched perhaps fourteen hundred miles from the Blue Nile to the shores of the Mediterranean.

But the future of Kush lay in the Sudan. Within sixty years the savage Assyrians had expelled the twenty-fifth dynasty and replaced the Kushite kings in Egypt. Assyrian predominance would be succeeded by that of other peoples, including the Greek Ptolemies and the Roman Caesars. Upriver, beyond the cataracts, Kush went its independent way.

THE FURNACES OF MEROE

The golden age of Kushite civilization was the period of the ascendancy of the city of Meroe, from the third to the first century B.C. Much of what follows will refer to these centuries.

The centers of Kushite civilization were populous cities, built from sun-dried brick, like those of Egypt and Mesopotamia, and garnished with palaces and temples. But there were differences too. The Kushite kings lived like Egyptian pharaohs, but the succession in Kush was decided by consensus among the royal princes, and the queen mother was uniquely powerful among the Kushites. Egyptian-style priesthoods, notably that of the sun god Amun, were extremely influential, but Amun's central place was later usurped by the Kushite lion god Apedemek, whose graven image is frequently found among the ruins of Kushite cities.

The wealth of Kush lay in its land, its location, and its energetic people. The Kushite capital of Meroe was watered not only by the Nile but by a significant annual rainfall. The result was a broad expanse of pasture and cropland, a green island in the desert where cattle grazed and grain stood tall. There were minerals of great value under the soil of Kush as well, including gold and iron. Kush was fortunate also in its locale, up the river from Egypt and on the trade routes that wound east through the Ethiopian uplands to the Red Sea. From these advantages a vigorous people—farmers and herders, soldiers, traders, builders—made a very good life indeed for several hundred years.

Kushite artisans in particular exploited the iron ore of southern Kush so industriously that Meroe became the greatest center for the production of iron in Africa. Its surviving heaps of slag have led some Africanists to see Meroe as the Birmingham—or Pittsburgh—of the continent.

Culture seems to have flourished too in the inner African world of Kush. Carved images of Kushite victories in nameless wars are still to be seen in low relief across ruined walls. There are long lines of prisoners and royal processions parading in Egyptian silhouette, though their royal figures are more solidly built than the leaner, more sinuous people downriver, and the jewelry they wear is of Kushite make. There are animal gods and royal beasts, the lion and the elephant soon replacing the Egyptian vulture and cobra.

The wars the Kushites fought remain for the most part nameless because just about the time that the independent greatness of Kush began, the Kushites evolved their own form of writing—and we cannot read it. They developed a true alphabet, like that of the Phoenicians or the Greeks. But there is no Rosetta stone for Kushite; we can pronounce the words, but we cannot tell their meanings.

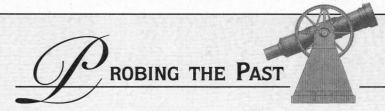

PROBING THE PAST

"Nubia appears to be closely akin to Egypt and the rest of Black Africa. It seems to be the starting point of both civilizations. . . . all the earliest scholars who studied Nubia, even those to whom we owe the discovery of Nubian archaeology (such as Cailliaud) conclude that Nubia had priority.

Their studies indicate that Egyptian civilization from that of Nubia, in other words, Sudan. As Pédrals observes, Cailliaud bases this argument on the fact that in Egypt all the objects of worship (thus, the essence of sacred tradition) are Nubian. Cailliaud assumes then that the roots of Egyptian civilization were in Nubia (the Sudan) and that it gradually descended the valley of the Nile. In this, he was merely rediscovering or conforming to some extent the unanimous opinion of the Ancients, philosophers and writers, who judged the anteriority of Nubia to be obvious. . . .

Egyptians themselves—who should surely be better qualified than anyone to speak of their origin— recognize without ambiguity that their ancestors came from Nubia and the heart of Africa. . . . [I]t is in Nubia that we find pyramids similar to those in Egypt, underground temples, and Meroitic writing, not yet deciphered, but closely related to Egyptian writing. Strangely enough, though this point is not emphasized, Nubian writing is more evolved than Egyptian. While Egyptian writing, even in its hieratic and demotic phases, has never completely eliminated its hieroglyphic essence, Nubian writing is alphabetical. . . ."

Cheikh Anta Diop, a distinguished twentieth-century Senegalese scholar, was French trained in a variety of disciplines, from history and archaeology to philosophy and languages. He became a leading exponent of the controversial view that Egypt belongs more to an African cultural zone than to a Near Eastern one, and that Egyptian influence was crucial to the emergence of Western civilization in later centuries.

What sort of evidence does Diop offer here to support his view of the crucial role of Nubia (Kush), further up the Nile toward the heart of Africa, in the development of Egyptian civilization? How does his view differ from that given in the text? Can you see how similarities between the two cultures could be read to support both the more orthodox interpretation presented in the text and Diop's revisionist thesis?

Cheikh Anta Diop. The African Origin of Civilization: Myth or Reality? Trans. Mercer Cook. (New York: Lawrence Hill and Co., 1974), pp. 147, 149–150.

Gradually over the centuries, Kush lost touch with the Mediterranean world to the north. Kings of Kush and later pharaohs of the Greek Ptolemy line built temples together. A bronze head of the emperor Augustus, apparently pillaged during a border raid on Roman Egypt, has been found buried under the doorsill of a Kushite temple. But for the most part, the land of Kush and the green island of Meroe at its heart lived out their long history in isolation, beyond the cataracts and the desert.

The passing of Kushite glory during the first cen-

turies of what was elsewhere the Christian era has been explained in various ways. The limited land was probably overgrazed and perhaps dried out by the slow southward creep of the Sahara. Kush's best customers in Egypt were ruined by Rome's insatiable demands upon this breadbasket of empire, and business in Meroe suffered as poverty spread along the Nile. Trade to the east was taken over by new Red Sea powers. And around A.D. 350 one of these East African States, the Kingdom of Axum, put an end to what had been the greatest early civilization of

Women of ancient Kush, illustrated in a black stone relief sculpture from Meroe. The figure on the left is a Kushite queen. Note the elaborate headdresses, necklaces, bracelets, and decorated skirts, as well as the impressive throne on which the sovereign sits. Archaeological investigation has added much to our appreciation of this ancient civilization in recent decades. (Art Resource)

inner Africa: "I made war on them [the Axumite king Ezana declared]. . . . I burnt their towns . . . and my army carried off their food and copper and iron . . . and destroyed the statues in their temples, their granaries and cotton trees and cast them into the [Nile]."[1]

The traveler approaching Meroe by train from Cairo today sees a scattering of ruined temples, huge broken pyramids, and heaps of slag from the famous ironworks. There is little left of the royal city at the center, the baths, the processional way running through row on row of rectangular roofs and courtyards up to the Kushite temple of the sun.

 # CARTHAGE: THE EMPIRE OF THE WESTERN SEAS

THE PHOENICIAN DIASPORA

At the other end of North Africa from Egypt, and facing the Mediterranean Sea rather than inner Africa, stood the great city of Carthage and its seaborne empire. Founded

by Near Eastern immigrants from Phoenicia—discussed in Chapter 5—Carthage became an independent African empire strong enough to challenge both the Greeks and the Romans for mastery of the western Mediterranean.

The founding of ancient Carthage is shrouded in myth and mystery. Legend has it that the imperial city of the western seas was built by a Near Eastern queen. Elissa—known to the Greeks and Romans as Dido—was the royal sister of the king of Tyre, a wealthy Phoenician trading city on the coast of Lebanon. Caught up in a bloody feud in her Phoenician home, Dido fled the city at the head of many Tyrian nobles. Gathering support from other Phoenician cities as they moved westward, Dido and her followers settled at last on the coast of what is today Tunisia, where she built her city.

Though political conflict and exile are certainly possible, modern historians have tended to see the founding of Carthage as part of a larger, primarily economic Phoenician diaspora. In this view, the far-trading Phoenicians first came ashore at the site of the future Carthage to establish a way station—one of many—on the road to Spain. On Spain's Atlantic coast, beyond the Pillars of Hercules—now called the Straits of Gibraltar—they had established a major base at Gades, modern Cadiz. There they traded with the indigenous Spanish population for silver mined nearby and for tin imported from France and England.

It was a profitable trade. But the Atlantic coast of Spain was 2000 miles from Lebanon, a long voyage even

---

[1] Robert W. July, *A History of the African People* (New York: Scribner's, 1970), p. 38.

for the intrepid Phoenicians. The merchants of Tyre needed way stations along the North African coast where they could get food and water and repair their ships. It was probably for this purpose that Phoenician ships first anchored in the sheltered harbor where Carthage would later rise.

Here in the ninth century B.C., Queen Dido may have come with her supporters. Here, certainly, Phoenicians began to build their "New City"—"Qart Hadasht" in their language, later Latinized as Carthage—around 800 B.C.

PEOPLES OF THE MAGHREB

The Tyrian immigrants built their city on land bought or leased from the African people who already lived there. The peoples of this part of North Africa, later known as the Maghreb, would play an important part in the history of this African commercial empire.

The ancient peoples of North Africa west of Egypt have traditionally been called Libyans. We have no way of knowing what they called themselves, and they may have had little sense of being one people at all. We know, however, that they spoke one language and shared a precarious living space between the scorching Sahara and the Mediterranean Sea. Ethnically, they were probably the ancestors of the modern Berber population who share the land today with the much later Arab conquerors of North Africa.

The Libyans were farmers and herders, growing grain and herding oxen, sheep, and goats. They rode horses and used them to pull carts and war chariots. They worked their land with stone tools, though some Libyans wore copper bracelets, anklets, and other metal items of personal adornment. Their religion, like that of ancient Egypt, seems to have focused on animal-headed gods and goddesses, especially on a ram-headed sun god called Ammon. Politically, they were originally organized into tribes and clans. In Carthaginian times, as we will see, some Libyan peoples developed hereditary kingdoms in the Maghreb.

These were the people, then, who agree to sell a strip of coastal land to a handful of immigrants from the east in the eighth century B.C. In the centuries that followed, the lives of both the indigenous population and the intruders would be transformed by this fertile fusion of cultures.

THE CARTHAGINIAN EMPIRE

From the eighth to the second century B.C., the naval and commercial power of Carthage grew till it dominated the western Mediterranean and the seas beyond.

The Phoenician cities from which Carthage sprang foundered and fell in the welter of near Eastern peoples. On its own, Carthage emerged by the sixth century as mistress of its own seaborne domain. Its power dominated all the other surviving Phoenician settlements of the west. The Carthaginian Empire included territories across the Mediterranean in southern Europe—parts of Spain and the islands of Sardinia, Corsica, and Sicily. In time it embraced trading centers on the Atlantic, from settlements in Britain and French Brittany through Cadiz in Spain down to the west coast of Africa. Sometime in the fifth century B.C., the Carthaginian navigator Hanno may even have sailed as

This artist's rendering of Carthage in the classic age owes more to imagination and analogy with other classical remains than to archaeology. Nevertheless, the picture captures something of the sense of grandeur and the subtropical Mediterranean locale of the capital of this powerful African empire. (unknown)

far around West Africa as the Guinea coast, though no permanent trade outlets were established so far south.

Closer to home, the nearby peoples of the Maghreb, including the sizable Berber states of Numidia and Mauritania, were subject to or allied with Carthage. Even desert tribes such as the Garamantes fed the insatiable hunger of the Carthaginians for trade, bringing goods by the Saharan ways only they could follow from the oases of Fezzan.

From this western, largely maritime empire the Carthaginians derived such valuable goods as pottery and glass, textiles and ivory, tin, silver, and gold. Much of this trade was by barter. The famous "silent trade" in African gold, described by the tireless Greek historian Herodotus, is perhaps not atypical of the trade that took place without money or a common language in these early times. The Greek explained how the Carthaginians, when trading with a certain African nation "beyond the pillars of Hercules," laid out their trade goods on the beach and then withdrew to their ships until the local people had brought forth sufficient gold to pay for what they wanted. No words were exchanged, only Mediterranean goods for West African gold. Herodotus added that "neither party deals unfairly with the other," as if it were rather an oddity in that world of shrewd horse traders.

THE VOYAGES OF HANNO

As a trading people, the Carthaginians were eager to discover new sources of potential profit. This dynamic aspect of Carthaginian history is well illustrated by the legendary African voyages of Hanno in the fifth century B.C.

There is evidence of earlier voyages down the coasts of Africa in the 500s and 400s B.C. In the early sixth century, the Egyptian pharaoh Necho is said to have dispatched an expedition down the Red Sea, which actually circumnavigated the continent over a period of two years. In the early fifth century, the Persian king Xerxes sent a nobleman west in an unsuccessful effort to go the other way around Africa. Shortly thereafter, the wealthy and respected Carthaginian Hanno set out with a large fleet on a similar voyage around West Africa.

Hanno's account of his adventures "beyond the Pillars of Hercules" so impressed the Carthaginians that they had it inscribed on stone in the great temple of Baal. The Greek version, which has come down to us, is clearly incomplete and much disputed by scholars. But it does at least give us a first-hand impression of what Africa looked like to these intrepid African explorers.

From Gibraltar, Hanno's ships slowly rounded the great bulge of West Africa, founding colonies, trading with the local people, and discovering strange lands. There were rivers filled with hippopotamuses and crocodiles and coasts lined with fires and drums in the night. There were people dressed in animal skins who pelted them with stones and hairy "savages" called Gorillas who resisted

capture by clawing, biting, and climbing up trees. There were mysterious islands and erupting volcanoes with lava flowing down into the sea.

How much of this really happened and how far down the African coast Hanno really sailed we will probably never know. Some scholars think he got as far as the modern country of Cameroon, at the inner angle of West Africa. If he did, it was a feat that would not be duplicated for almost two thousand years.

RIVALS OF THE GREEKS AND ROMANS

Carthage was governed by an oligarchy of increasingly wealthy commercial families. These plutocrats sat on the Carthaginian ruling councils and held the main magistracies, called *sufets*, which apparently were similar to the Roman consuls. These civilian authorities kept close watch over the military in particular, so that Carthaginian generals seldom challenged the civil government, as happened so often in Rome.

As seen by their rivals across the Mediterranean, these empire builders of northern Africa were a dour and grasping lot, possessing a streak of cruelty that even the Romans professed to be shocked by. And there does seem to be some substance to the charge that the lords of Carthage sacrificed even their children to the gods who brought the city its wealth and power. For human sacrifice was practiced among them, as among other Phoenician colonists, and the burned bones of children have been found in special tombs in the Carthaginian holy place, the *tophet*, close by the harbor.

Carthage in its prime in many ways resembled a Tunisian town of today. The whitewashed walls of the multistory tenements of the lower city must have been crammed with humanity, since estimates of the population run higher than half a million. Nicer homes and gardens lay in the northern suburbs. On the high city, or Byrsa, stood the temples of Baal the sun god, the even more popular goddess Tanit, and other divinities. A wall sixty feet high stretched across the neck of the peninsula on which the city stood, protecting Carthage from attack by land, while its fleet guarded it by sea.

To maintain its supremacy on the western seas, Carthage fought a long series of wars, particularly with the Greeks and the Romans on the other side of the Mediterranean. A brief glance at these conflicts may round out this overview of Africa's most celebrated early empire.

The Greeks were the great trade rivals first of the Phoenicians and later of the Carthaginians. Greek colonies in the western Mediterranean early ran afoul of Carthage's trade monopoly, and the two peoples fought intermittently through the fifth and fourth centuries B.C. Greeks even invaded the Maghreb and for a short time threatened the very survival of Carthage, only to be turned back in the end by Carthaginian forces.

During the third and second centuries, the rising power of Rome, almost due north of Carthage across the narrow waist of the Mediterranean, collided with this rich nation of traders. The results were the three Punic Wars, the most desperate struggles of Rome's own violent climb to mastery of the Mediterranean world.

The two empires first fell out with each other in the third century B.C. over rival claims in Sicily. Roman arms triumphed in the long run, but Carthage accepted only a temporary setback. The Second Punic War dealt the Romans a shock from which they did not recover for generations: the sudden descent of the Carthaginian general Hannibal's war elephants, come round by way of Spain, through the Alpine passes and into northern Italy. The armies of the great North African power ravaged the Roman heartland almost at will during the last years of the third century. But the Romans, fighting on their home ground, finally wore the invaders down once more. And fifty years later, in the middle of the second century, they launched the war of revenge that destroyed Carthaginian power forever.

It must have been a laborious as well as a bloody business to burn and topple into ruin a significant portion of a city that had once held half a million people. But the soldiers of Scipio the Younger managed it. Today the outer promontory of the double harbor is a dangerous underwater reef, and the line of the sixty-foot wall that once crossed the peninsula is detectable only from the air. The best that modern archaeology can muster has found very little of old Carthage in between.

SUMMARY

The early history of Africa focused along major waterways—down the Nile and along the Mediterranean. Food-gathering peoples and early agriculturalists roamed or settled into villages all across Africa south of the Sahara. But cities, kingdoms, and empires took shape in the north.

Egypt, discussed in the last chapter, was the oldest of these early African civilizations. Others were Kush, Meroe, and Carthage.

Both the Kingdom of Kush and the Carthaginian Empire were at their height during the later first millennium B.C. Kush evolved under Egyptian influence farther up the Nile, in what is today the Sudan. Kushite kings even ruled Egypt for a time in the eighth century B.C. During the golden age of Kush (third to the first centuries B.C.), the furnaces of Kushite Meroe spread iron and ironworking across much of Africa, enabling that continent to skip the Bronze Age entirely.

Carthage, a Phoenician colony in North Africa, established a commercial empire including most of the western Mediterranean, with trading posts beyond Gibraltar on the Atlantic coasts of Europe and Africa. At its height in the middle of the first millennium, Carthage repelled the Greeks, but it fell at last to the Romans in the middle of the second century B.C.

SUGGESTED READING

ADAMS, W. Y. *Nubia: Corridor to Africa*. Princeton, N.J.: Princeton University Press, 1984. Monographaic survey of evidence and conclusions on all phases of Nubian history and society.

Africa in Antiquity: The Arts of Ancient Nubia and the Sudan (2 vols.). New York: Brooklyn Museum, 1978. Essays illustrated by many photographs.

BEN KHADER, A. B. A., and D. SOREN, eds. *Carthage: A Mosaic of Ancient Tunisia*. New York: American Museum of Natural History and W. W. Norton, 1987. Western and North African perspectives, beautifully illustrated by many color photographs.

CHARLES-PICARD, G., and C. CHARLES-PICARD. *Daily Life in Carthage*, trans. A. E. Foster. New York: Macmillan, 1958. Older but readable account of society.

DAVIDSON, B. *Lost Cities of Africa*. Boston: Little, Brown, 1959. Vivid sketches by a journalist turned historian. See also his *Old Africa Rediscovered* (London: Gollancz, 1960) for a particularly lively reconstruction of ancient Kush.

DE BEER, G. R. *Hannibal*. New York: Viking, 1969. The life of Carthage's greatest hero.

FAIRSERVIS, W. *The Ancient Kingdoms of the Nile*. New York: Mentor Books, 1962. Good on Nubia and Kush.

HAGG, T. *Nubian Culture Past and Present*. Stockholm: Almbvist and Wiksell International, 1987. Scholarly papers on aspects of all periods of Nubian history.

HAKEM, A. A. "The Civilization of Napata and Meroe," in *Ancient Civilizations of Africa*, vol. 2 of the

UNESCO *General History of Africa*, G. Mokhtar, ed. London: Heinemann, 1981. With Leclant (see below), the best and most up-to-date studies available.

HANSBERRY, W. L. *Africa and Africans as Seen by Classical Writers*, ed. J. E. Harris. Washington, D.C.: Howard University Press, 1981. Discussion of references to Africa by Greek and Roman scholars, poets, and others.

JULY, R. W. *Precolonial Africa: An Economic and Social History*. New York: Scribner's, 1975. One of the best surveys available, with useful material on earlier periods.

LECLANT, J. "The Empire of Kush: Napata and Meroe," in *Ancient Civilizations of Africa*. See Hakem above.

OLIVER, R., ed. *The Dawn of African History*, 2nd ed. London: Oxford University Press, 1961. Excellent but brief introduction to the history and interpretation of each region of Africa in early times.

———— and B. FAGAN. *Africa in the Iron Age*. Cambridge, England: Cambridge University Press, 1975. Authoritative study that goes well beyond the period under consideration.

SHINNIE, M. *Ancient African Kingdoms*. New York: New American library, 1970. A quick overview by an authority.

———— *Meroe*. New York: Praeger, 1967. Thorough discussion by an archaeologist who worked in the Kushite capital for many years.

SOREN, D. *Carthage: Uncovering the Mysteries and Splendors of Ancient Tunisia*. New York: Simon & Schuster, 1990. Recent illustrated view.

TAYLOR, J. H. *Egypt and Nubia*. Cambridge, Mass.: Harvard University Press, 1991. The British Museum's excellent holdings illustrate many aspects of Nubian life.

WARMINGTON, B. H. *Carthage*. London: Hale, 1960. Overview with some emphasis on political and military matters.

CHAPTER 5

HEBREWS AND PERSIANS

TURBULENT CENTURIES

THE NEAR EAST IN TUMULT

When civilizations first emerged in Mesopotamia and Egypt in the fourth millennium B.C., they were solitary flowers blooming alone in a world of Paleolithic hunter-gatherers, Neolithic villages, and wandering pastoralists. By the second millennium B.C., however, when Hammurabi ruled in Babylon and the powerful twelfth dynasty in Egypt, a number of other islands of civilization had come into existence around the globe. In northwestern India, as we shall see, an impressive center of civilized living had emerged around the great cities of Harappa and Mohenjodaro. Still farther to the east, the states of north China were about to be drawn together into a loose-knit Bronze Age civilization dominated by the Shang dynasty. Minoan ships were sailing the blue Mediterranean from one bustling port city to another. And beyond the wide Atlantic, metals were being worked in Peru.

Civilization had also emerged among other Near Eastern peoples on the frontiers of the Mesopotamian world. The turbulent centuries between 2000 and 1000 B.C. were particularly fecund producers of new centers of civilized living, though others had predated these. During these centuries, nomadic peoples from the great Eurasian steppes or the deserts of Arabia and North Africa buffeted the city-based cultures of the Near East. In so doing, they helped bring about a fertile mixture of cultures and traditions. They brought skills with them from their earlier wandering lives, and they learned from the more settled peoples whom they frequently conquered. The invaders thus contributed largely to the emergence of a number of satellite cultures at the periphery of the cultural zone around Mesopotamia and Egypt. Several of these satellite civilizations will be examined here, including the Hittites, the Phoenicians, and the recently discovered society of ancient Ebla. Of greater historic importance than any of these, finally, the Hebrews and the Persians will get special attention in this chapter.

By the latter part of the first millennium B.C., then, the earliest civilizations had been joined by a number of other highly developed cultures. In the Near East, new skills had been added to civilization's store, iron joining bronze as a hard metal for weapons and tools, and the first alphabetical system of writing evolving among the Phoenicians. Geographically, the civilized zone in this part of the world expanded beyond the Near East to include the entire Middle East from the Mediterranean to the borders of India. And in Palestine, the Hebrews moved beyond polytheism to the worship of one God, the first successful monotheistic religion.

It was an impressive set of achievements for a turbulent time.

THE EBLA TABLETS

The oldest of these subsidiary cultures is that most recently uncovered by the excavator's pick. The society of ancient Ebla, which flourished between 2600 and 2240 B.C., was discovered by a team of Italian archaeologists in the 1960s and 1970s. The discovery in 1975 of the archives of Ebla—15,000 clay tablets inscribed in cuneiform—was a bonanza for students of the ancient Near East. These documents revealed the impressive achievements of this center of civilization, which flowered outside of the Egyptian and Mesopotamian river valleys, in what is today Syria, as far back as the days of Sargon of Akkad.

Economically, Ebla was highly advanced in agriculture, in handicrafts, and in commerce. The region produced a variety of crops, from cereals to grapes to olives. Ebla drew on neighboring peoples for timber and metals and made the working of silver, gold, copper, and tin major sources of revenue. Because of its location, finally, the city of Ebla was a prosperous center of trade, importing raw materials from the still undeveloped regions of Turkey and Iran and trading in textiles and other commodities with the older centers of civilization in Mesopotamia and Egypt.

The rulers of Ebla were kings who served for fixed terms and could not pass the throne on to their sons. Much real political authority actually seems to have remained in the hands of a council of elders, while the queens of Ebla enjoyed considerable economic power as traditional heads of the lucrative textile industry. On a day-to-day basis, thousands of scribal bureaucrats ran the kingdom, and more than a dozen tributary city-states accepted the overlordship of this ancient Syrian power.

Particularly revealing, finally, was the substantial cultural dependence of Ebla on the Sumerian civilization of early Mesopotamia. Eblaite writing, art, religion, and political structures all derived from those of the Land of the Two Rivers. In turn, Ebla passed on these cultural skills and practices to other peoples of the region. Sometimes, as in styles of art, Ebla even exercised a reciprocal influence on Mesopotamia itself.

The kingdom of Ebla was apparently crushed at last by Sumerian forces under Sargon's grandson, Naram-Sin, about 2240 B.C. The Ebla tablets, however, provide impressive evidence of the larger world of Near Eastern civilization that had begun to emerge as early as the third millennium B.C.

THE HITTITES AND THE IRON AGE

The Hittites were Indo-Europeans, speakers of languages ancestral to those of modern India, Iran, and most of Europe. The Hittite subdivision of this great steppe-dwelling people wandered down into Asia Minor, subdued the natives of the hill and mountain country north of Mesopotamia, and evolved a powerful empire in the second millennium B.C. For roughly two hundred years, 1400 to 1200 B.C., the Hittites ruled the eastern end of the Mediterranean, collected tribute from the Egyptians, and raided Babylon. For several centuries, at least, they were a power to be reckoned with in the Near East.

Like most less developed cultures, the Hittites borrowed heavily from the more complex civilizations with which they came in contact. From the Land of the Two Rivers they carried home such cultural booty as cuneiform writing, Mesopotamian myths, and the concept of a codified system of laws. The charioteers from the steppes retained much of their own culture too, legends and styles of art that looked back to their days as nomads of the great northern grasslands. Hittite religion particularly reminds us that they were a people whose culture had developed on the edge of the civilized world: There is, for instance, evidence of human sacrifice among them.

From the Hittites, however, came one great contribution to the civilization of the ancient Near East: the working of iron.

Bronze, alloyed usually of copper and tin, had been the hard metal since civilization first appeared in Sumeria. Now, in the smithies of Hittite towns and villages, in the double-walled mountain capital of Hattusas, brawny Hittite metalworkers discovered that iron ore, more plentiful than bronze, might also be used for hard-edged tools and weapons. The secret, which may have reached the Hittites from their old steppe homeland, involved much pounding of the heated but not melted ore to remove impurities, followed by a sudden quenching in cold water. The result was a sort of semi-steel more readily available and cheaper than the alloy of copper and tin on which older, more aristocratic Bronze Age cultures had been built.

Understandably, the Hittites did not distribute the secret of the new metal widely. But when new waves of invaders swept down across Asia Minor and tumbled Hattusas into ruin, skilled ironworkers were scattered across the Near Eastern world. The Hittites themselves vanished from the historical record until modern archaeologists unearthed their lost civilization. But their technological contribution left the Near East—indeed, all of western Eurasia—a new raw material to build with, one so important that some historians still date a new age of world history from the Hittites' twelfth-century prime—the Age of Iron.

THE FAR-TRADING PHOENICIANS

The Phoenicians were a Semitic-speaking people who settled the harbors and inshore islands along the coast of what is today Lebanon and Syria. They rose to prominence at the end of the second millennium, following the collapse of Hittite power, and flourished from 1100 to 800 B.C. They became the most famous traders on the sea before the Greeks and the chief bearers of developed Near Eastern culture to other peoples around the Mediterranean.

Politically, the Phoenicians were city-state dwellers, like the Mesopotamians. Failing to achieve political unity of their own, they were frequently absorbed into the larger polities of such powerful neighbors as the Egyptians, Hittites, and Assysrians. They borrowed Babylonian business methods and weights and measures and used Babylonian astronomy as a navigational aid. Their mythology was replete with Mesopotamian echoes, though their religion harked further back. Like the Hittites, the Phoenicians sometimes sacrificed human beings on the altars of their gods.

In one way, however, the Phoenicians made a major break with the practices of their Near Eastern neighbors. Unable to feed their numbers on the thin strip of mountain-girt coastline they inhabited, they turned gradually from agriculture to manufacturing and above all to trade.

The Phoenicians seem to have turned to profit everything their 120-mile stretch of coastline had to offer. The famous cedars of Lebanon provided them with a valuable early export item. After learning glassmaking from the Mesopotamians, they used a fine local sand to produce glass gewgaws that sold well to simpler folk around the Mediterranean. Even a tiny shellfish called the murex was used to make perhaps the most famous dye of all times, the Tyrean purple that would color the robes of emperors in centuries to come.

The location of the Phoenician cities—on the Mediterranean and astride the main trade route between Mesopotamia and Egypt—encouraged the Phoenicians to become traders as well as handicraft manufacturers. Byblos, Tyre, Sidon, and other cities were famous commercial centers in Old Testament times. The Phoenicians founded colonies on the islands of Cyprus and Sicily and on the coasts of Spain and North Africa. Among these Phoenician colonies was the North African metropolis of Carthage, Rome's great rival in later centuries. Other adventurous Phoenician sailors even passed out of the Mediterranean through the Strait of Gibraltar, the "Pillars of Hercules," beyond which few ancient seamen dared to venture. There is evidence that their little vessels braved the heavier swells and rougher winds of the Atlantic to trade for tin in western Britain and even to circumnavigate Africa, a feat not to be duplicated until early modern times.

The Phoenicians were carriers of culture rather than originators of it, but their impact, especially on European civilization, was not small. Their city of Byblos, which became famous for the export of Egyptian papyrus, gave its name to the Greek word for *book*—and our word *Bible*. And whether the Phoenicians developed their own written language or borrowed it from their neighbors, they passed that too on to the Greeks. The twenty-two consonants of the Phoenician alphabet, together with the vowels added by the Greeks, would evolve down the centuries into all the written languages of the Western world.

THE HEBREWS AND THE BIRTH OF MONOTHEISM

THE WANDERING YEARS

The Hebrew people of Palestine never produced an empire to rival that of the Hittites, nor did they wander as far as the Phoenicians, at least in ancient times. Yet they too left a great legacy to future ages, a heritage at least as valuable as either iron or the alphabet: monotheistic religion.

At the beginning of the second millennium before Christ, the Hebrews were part of the nomadic population of Semitic-speaking peoples that wandered and settled along the edges of the Arabian Desert, between the developed civilizations of Mesopotamia and Egypt. Abraham, the patriarch of the Hebrew tribes, trudges into history heading west from Ur with his wives and children, servants, shepherds, and flocks around him. The twelve tribes who claimed descent from Abraham apparently settled for a time in Palestine, between the Jordan River and the sea. Some of these, perhaps driven by drought, drifted on southward into Egypt, the great pillar of civilization at the other end of the fertile crescent from Mesopotamia. Oppressed—according to tradition actually enslaved in New Kingdom Egypt—they burst out once more in the thirteenth century B.C. to resume their wanderings.

The leader of the folk migration known in the Bible as the Exodus was a fiery preacher named Moses. Moses managed to hold his people together for forty years in the scorching deserts of Sinai. To accomplish this feat,

he seems to have rallied the Hebrew tribes around a single god, Yahweh. Perhaps as early as 1270 B.C., then, Hebrews became monotheists (believers in one god), sworn to obey the commandments of the divine Lord whose laws Moses had brought down from the mountain to Yahweh's chosen people.

THE KINGDOM OF DAVID

The wanderings of this pastoral nomadic people took them back to Palestine, which they now saw as the homeland promised to them by Yahweh. A hilly barren land along the Mediterranean Sea, Palestine nevertheless looked good after two generations in the wilderness. The region, however, was already settled by the Canaanites, a people who had built modest cities and established laws on the Mesopotamian model. Furthermore, in the second millennium B.C. this area was still subject to incursions by other nomadic peoples besides the Hebrews, including the powerful, iron-armed Philistines from the north. To conquer and hold their "promised land," then, the twelve tribes evolved once more, this time politically rather than religiously. In the fires of combat was the Hebrew kingdom forged.

Despite their monotheistic faith, the Hebrew tribes had frequently been disunited. A clan-based as well as an extremely religious society, they were guided by leaders called "judges" and sometimes by charismatic prophets who claimed divine inspiration for their warnings and injunctions. Shortly before 1000 B.C., however, all the tribes agreed to follow a single king, a war leader who might bring them final victory over their foes. The first of these rulers, Saul, proved unable to win either the victories the people demanded or the support of the influential prophet Samuel. With the latter's help, however, King David (c. 1010–960 B.C.) succeeded Saul, and under David and his son Solomon (c. 960–920 B.C.), the new state of Israel flourished as it would not do again until our own modern twentieth century.

A gifted military leader, David crushed the Philistines and completed the conquest of Palestine. He cemented the political unity of the twelve tribes, established a Hebrew state, and began to build a Hebrew capital at Jerusalem. Generally recognized as the mightiest of Hebrew rulers, David became the center of an admiring body of biblical legend and literature chronicling his rise from shepherd lad to war hero and finally to the founder of a centralized Near Eastern monarchy, the tenth-century B.C. kingdom of Israel.

THE SPLENDOR OF SOLOMON—AND AFTER

It was to be a brief flowering. David's successor, Solomon, would be the last to rule a united state encompassing all the twelve tribes. But the reign of Solomon would leave

The Realm of King David

The Kingdoms of Israel and Judah, c. 800 B.C.

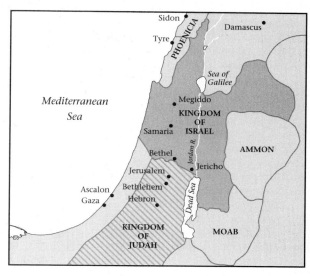

almost as deep a mark on the minds of future generations as the heroic achievements of the founder.

Celebrated in the Bible as the wisest of kings, Solomon was apparently a shrewd diplomat and a great builder. His harem, his huge stables, the palace he built for himself, and the temple he raised to the glory of Yahweh were all in the most opulent Near Eastern style. His army was strengthened and outfitted with chariots and new weapons. But these efforts to make Israel a small but powerful player on the Near Eastern chessboard of nations

Scale model of ancient Jerusalem as it looked after the return of the Hebrews from the Babylonian captivity. The modern state of Israel has encouraged archaeological excavation and welcomes tourists to Biblical sites. This concern to link up past and present, the ancient Jewish state with the modern one, is well illustrated by the stream of visitors here examining a model of the ancient city, very little of which remains even in Old Jerusalem today. (Israel Government Tourist Office)

cost huge amounts of labor and money. Oppressive taxation, forced labor, and other expedients made Solomon increasingly unpopular among his own people. Differences between the more sophisticated, urban, and commercial northern reaches of the kingdom and the pastoral, agricultural, more pious south further weakened the monarchy. Simmering rebellion split the kingdom after Solomon's death.

The result was the creation of two smaller nations: Judea in the south, inhabited by two of the Hebrew clans and still ruled from Jerusalem; and the new nation of Israel in the north, including ten of the original dozen tribes. Neither half of the old kingdom proved viable in the shark-infested waters of ancient Near Eastern politics. In the eighth century B.C., Israel fell to the powerful Assyrian Empire; in the sixth century B.C., Judea was overwhelmed by the New Babylonian Empire of Nebuchadnezzar. At the time of the latter cataclysm, in 586 B.C., Jerusalem and Solomon's great temple were leveled and many Hebrews were carried off into captivity in Babylon. Others scattered to Egypt and beyond, beginning the *diaspora*, or dispersal, of the people who became the Jews across the Western world.

Some returned from Babylon to rebuild the temple to their Lord, as they increasingly called Yahweh, before the end of the sixth century B.C. But though there were short-lived Jewish states at later periods, this small, intensely creative people would remain vassals of other peoples—Persians, Macedonians, Romans, Arabs, Turks— for most of the next twenty-five centuries. Only in 1948, in the middle of the twentieth century, did a new nation of Israel, approximating in size the nation ruled over by David, rise once again in Palestine.

THE FAITH OF THE HEBREWS

It was a history of wandering, warfare, and oppression that would have found a much less important place in global history if not for the contributions of the priests and prophets of this ancient people who, through all their misfortunes, thought of themselves always as uniquely chosen by God.

The Hebrews seem to have been particularly concerned with religion, even by Near Eastern standards. Prophets in goatskins wandered among them like loinclothed holy men in Hindu India. They carried the words of their god Yahweh carved on two stone tablets in a chest, and they believed that they were divinely ordained to rule a Promised Land somewhere in Palestine. Over the millennium and a half between Abraham and the return to Jerusalem from Babylon, the Hebrews evolved a unique conception of divinity and of humanity's relationship to it.

From the beginning, Yahweh had demanded an exclusive devotion from Hebrews that other Near Eastern gods did not. A Mesopotamian or an Egyptian could sacrifice to any number of divinities, but Yahweh was a jealous god and would tolerate no others. From this early Judaic view it was only a step further—albeit an immensely significant one—to the denial of the existence of other gods altogether.

Over the centuries the Hebrews added to this startling monotheism a powerful emphasis on the spiritual aspects of religion. Like Allah after him, Yahweh allowed no graven images of himself. He thus remained a purely spiritual presence, lacking the carven habitations where the gods of the two rivers dwelt. In addition, Yahweh's prophets of the first millennium B.C. stressed anew the ethical side of religious practice. For their god imposed particularly strict moral requirements upon his chosen people, requiring justice and mercy as well as the letter of the sacred law, ritual, and taboo.

Monotheistic, moralistic, highly spiritual, the religion of the Hebrews would maintain the cultural distinctness of this vital people through a long and often tragic history. The Hebrews may have borrowed their Flood story from Mesopotamia, proverbs from Egyptian wisdom literature, and psalms from both of these developed civilizations; but the faith of the children of Yahweh was distinctly their own, and a major contribution to the spiritual history of the world.

THE HEBREW HERITAGE

Some Hebrews at least were called *Yehudim*—whence, via a Greek intermediary, the English *Jew* is derived—even before the sixth-century B.C. Babylonian captivity. The *Judaic* religion as it has evolved since that time was clearly built on these ancient foundations of ethical monotheism, emphasis on the spirituality of God, and belief in the historicity of his manifest will in the world. In the first century A.D., Jesus Christ, born and raised in the Jewish community of northern Palestine, became the founder of the Christian faith, a creed that would spread around the world. And in the seventh century A.D., the Prophet Muhammad, an Arabian merchant conversant with both Judaism and Christianity, founded the third major world religion to emerge in this region—Islam. Down through the centuries, Hebrew leaders like Moses and Solomon would be honored, not only in later Judaism but also in the Christian Old Testament and the Muslim Koran.

The walls that enclose the narrow, winding lanes and crowded *souks* (markets) of Old Jerusalem today are mostly Ottoman Turkish battlements, built in the sixteenth century by Suleiman the Magnificent. Pass in through the Damascus Gate, however, and you can visit

 VOICES FROM THE PAST

"O Zion, that bringest good tidings, get thee up into the high mountain; O Jerusalem, that
bringest good tidings, lift up thy voice with strength; lift it up, be not afraid; say unto the cities
of Judah, Behold your God!

Behold, the Lord God will come with strong hand, and his arm shall rule for him, and his work
before him.

He shall feed his flock like a shepherd: he shall gather the lambs with his arm, and carry them in
his bosom, and shall gently lead those that are young.

Who hath measured the waters in the hollow of his hand, and meted out heaven with the span, and
comprehended the dust of the earth in a measure, and weighed the mountains in scales, and the
hills in a balance? . . .

Behold, the nations are as a drop of a bucket. . . . All nations before him are as nothing; and they
are counted to him less than nothing, vanity. . . .

It is he that sitteth upon the circle of the earth . . . that bringeth the princes to nothing; he maketh
the judges of the earth as vanity. . . .

But they that wait upon the Lord shall renew their strength; they shall mount up with wings as
eagles; they shall run, and not weary; and they shall walk and not faint."

This portion of the biblical book of Isaiah was probably composed by a Hebrew prophet
living at the time of the captivity in Babylon (550–538 B.C.). During this period, when the
Hebrew states of Judah and Israel had been absorbed by Assyrian and Babylonian conquerors and many Hebrews were living in exile in the New Babylonian Empire, the future
of this small band of people must have seemed very dim indeed. At such a time, the powerful preaching of Isaiah revived their confidence that their God would save them in the
end.

To what does Isaiah compare Yahweh when he wants to emphasize God's *care* for his
chosen people? Why was this comparison likely to move his hearers? How is the *greatness* of the Lord expressed here? Who are the "nations" and "princes" whom the Lord
"maketh as nothing"? Why would claims that worldly power is vain and that divine power
will strengthen true believers appeal to the Hebrews in Babylon? To Christians in Rome
centuries later?

Isaiah 40: 9–15, 17, 22–23, 31. The Holy Bible (Cambridge, England: Cambridge University Press).

in fifteen minutes three of the most sacred sites of the
great religions that emerged in the western portion of
Eurasia: the golden Dome of the Rock, built on the spot
from which Muhammad is believed by Muslims to have
ascended into heaven; the Church of the Holy Sepulcher,
allegedly encompassing the site of the Crucifixion of
Christ; and the Wailing Wall, all that is left of Solomon's
long-vanished temple, the holy of holies for Jews the
world over. Amid the tensions and explosive violence of
this long fought-over corner of the globe, it is chasten-
ing to remember that all three of these militant faiths
derive in large part from the spiritual intimations that first
took shape in the minds of a single people three thousand years ago.

THE PERSIANS: MASTERS OF THE MIDDLE EAST

THE MIDDLE EAST

To many Westerners, the Middle East is Arabs and oil—or Arabs, oil, and bloody little wars that never seem to settle anything. It is a tangle of states, middling or small in size but almost uniformly underpopulated, barren, and of interest only because of the oceans of petroleum beneath their sun-baked soil. Historically, the region is much more interesting than that. Geographically, it is certainly more complicated.

Even by a conservative definition, the Middle East is a huge slice of land.[1] It stretches from Egypt in the west to modern Afghanistan in the east, from the Black and Caspian seas in the north to the Red Sea, the Persian Gulf, and the Arabian Sea in the south. It is as far from Cairo to Kabul in Afghanistan, for example, as it is from New York to California.

The region is also much more heterogeneous topographically than the popular impression of a desert floating on oil might indicate. The northern tier of large Middle Eastern nations—Turkey, Iran, and Afghanistan—are high plateaus ringed by protecting mountains. The southerly tangle of states including Israel, Jordan, Lebanon, Syria, Arabia and the states of the Persian Gulf, Egypt, and Iraq have their share of rolling sands; but they also have the Nile and Tigris-Euphrates valleys, where civilization began.

North or south, however, most of the Middle East is low on both rainfall and population. The region has produced more than its share of nomads moving their flocks from one oasis or stubbly pasturage to the next. From the deserts of Arabia to the rugged Anatolian Plateau of Turkey and on to the mountains of Afghanistan, the area has bred hard people leading hard lives. Perhaps for this reason they have taken special pleasure in each historic Middle Eastern metropolis, from ancient Thebes and Babylon to Persian Persepolis and Islamic Damascus and Baghdad.

During the millennium centering roughly on the time of Christ, this diversified region enjoyed a period of intermittent unity presided over by a series of powerful dynasties. Of these, the first unifiers of the Middle East were the Persians of Cyrus the Great.

---

[1]The terms *Middle East* and *Near East* are frequently used almost interchangeably. In this book, *Near East* means primarily the states and regions of the eastern end of the Mediterranean, from Egypt and Mesopotamia up through Palestine and the Levant to Constantinople and the Straits connecting the Mediterranean and the Black Sea. The term *Middle East* will be used to denote the considerably larger area described in this section.

CYRUS THE GREAT

Cyrus the Persian (550–530 B.C.)—Cyrus the Shepherd, as they called him in his own time—was a self-made emperor if there ever was one. He seems to have been shrewdly merciful with defeated foes, judiciously tolerant of all religions, and automatically and totally courageous. He lived, fought, and died with the modest simplicity we would expect of a man who might have had trouble making his own mark on a Babylonian clay tablet. The fact that he devoted nearly all of his life, as far as we know it, to fighting with his fellow men is all the staunchest modern moralist could hold against him. And that, as they say, was a vice of the times rather than of the man.

The Persians and their overlords the Medes were Indo-Europeans, descendants of steppe nomads who had drifted south onto the Iranian Plateau hundreds of years before. In the sixth century B.C., they were still a warlike, semipastoral people living in the mountains of what is today western Iran. There they were within easy striking distance of the rich valley of the Tigris and Euphrates. The Medes had in fact participated prominently in the destruction of the penultimate Mesopotamian empire, that of the Assyrians.

By the middle of the sixth century B.C., however, the Medes had grown soft. This apparently put ideas into the head of Cyrus, hereditary chief of the tributary Persian tribes, in his mountain city of Pasagardae. In 550 B.C. Cyrus marched on the last Medean king, overthrew him, and made himself king of the Medes and the Persians. The twenty years of victories that followed constitute one of the most astonishing careers of blood and glory in the history of western Eurasia.

Cyrus's horse soldiers wore leather breeches and heavy felt boots, sat upon their rugged mountain ponies like centaurs, and were armed with the short, powerful compound bows of their steppe ancestors. They had a leader of genius in Cyrus. In his reign and that of his two successors, the Persians made themselves masters of the largest empire the sixth-century world had seen.

Three years after seizing control of the Median confederacy, Cyrus crossed the Taurus Mountains into what is today Turkey and there overthrew King Croesus of Lydia. The Lydians may have been the inventors of coinage, and Croesus was widely believed to be the richest king in the world. With the fabled wealth of Croesus at his command, Cyrus swung eastward, accepting submission from most of the tribes and peoples of modern-day Iran and Afghanistan. Only then, with a huge army and many victories behind him, did Cyrus turn south for the richest prize of all: Babylon.

The New Babylonian Empire was in decay and disarray. The unworthy heirs of Nebuchadnezzar, feuding with the powerful priesthoods of the city, had lost their authority over the people. With the help of a shrewd propaganda campaign, a Babylonian collaborator, and a well-placed victory or two, Cyrus was able to take possession of Babylon in 539 B.C. without even a token siege. It was the end of Mesopotamian independence and the beginning of Persian greatness in the Middle East.

Cyrus died in the saddle nine years later, fighting rebellious nomads in eastern Iran. His son Cambyses conquered the other earliest center of civilization, Egypt. Cambyses' successor, Darius I, extended the power of the Persians still further. His armies crossed both the Indus River into northwestern India and the straits of Bosporus and Dardanelles into southeastern Europe, where he accepted the submission of Macedonia, on the northern frontiers of Greece.

By 500 B.C. the Persian Empire was thus the master of the Middle East, the great power between Europe and farther Asia. For a thousand years, the Persians and their successors would maintain that position. Persia would be a powerful threat to its neighbors east and west and a crucial link in the chain of commerce and cultural influences that would connect the Roman and the Han Chinese empires in the days of the Caesars.

Cyrus the Shepherd was buried in a simple, house-shaped tomb on the grounds of his palace in mountain-girt Pasagardae. The Persian Empire itself was a far more splendid monument to the barbarian king.

DARIUS THE GREAT

But Cyrus was first and last a soldier. It was his successors Cambyses and particularly Darius I who transformed a patchwork of conquered tributary states into the most

impressive political structure—and the most physically impressive empire—in the western Eurasia of that time.

Darius I (522–486 B.C.), also sometimes called the Great, ruled a huge realm. He had to govern a considerable variety of peoples, from sophisticated Egyptians and Babylonians and businesslike Lydians and Greeks to his own vigorous Persians and Medes and the wilder steppe peoples, such as the Scythians and Parthians, with a handful of Indians from beyond the Hindu Kush thrown in. And he and those who followed him on the throne of Cyrus had to hold this vast empire together without the benefit of modern technology, modern bureaucracy, or the faintest shadow of modern national feeling. That they were able to do it at all is a tribute to the ingenuity and organizing ability of these barbarians turned empire builders.

Achaemenid Persia—so called after a revered ancestor of Cyrus—was divided into a couple of dozen provinces called satrapies. Each of these was headed by an appointed satrap, or governor, often a member of the imperial family or a prestigious local nobleman. The satraps were normally granted wide-ranging political, military, and financial autonomy. Indeed, as long as a satrapy paid its tribute on time and provided its share of recruits for the army, the province could pretty much go its own way in matters of local concern.

This loose-reined autonomy was balanced, however, by an ingenious array of imperial controls. There were garrisons of royal troops at strategic points across the empire, and there were also royal agents, known as "the

The Persian King of Kings on his throne. The emperor is Darius the Great; the bowing prince, his heir, Xerxes. Note the elaborately styled hair and beards of these Persian rulers and officials. (The Oriental Institute, The University of Chicago)

Persian archers march across a wall in Susa. Splendidly dressed and heavily armed, they are probably the "immortals" of the imperial bodyguard. What weapons did these conquering people favor? (The Bettman Archive)

king's eyes and ears," who kept tabs on both the satraps and their people, alert for signs of official conspiracy or popular rebellion.

Beyond these coercive measures, a more subtle web of common institutions brought a deeper unity to the empire. Darius formulated a single imperial code of laws, based on Mesopotamian models going back to Hammurabi, for all his peoples. He borrowed the idea of a minted coinage from the Lydia of Croesus, and soon royal gold and silver coins were in use all across Persia. A common set of weights and measures was also established, a system of royal couriers and mail, a common calendar (borrowed from Egypt), and a lingua franca, the Aramaic tongue already widely used for business purposes in the Near East.

Darius built extensively too. A network of hundreds of miles of roads linked the far places of the Persian Empire. The Royal Road from the capital at Susa in central Persia to the western city of Sardis, not far from the Aegean, was more than fifteen hundred miles long. Darius and his heirs took their ease in gardens they called "paradises" and in great palaces at Susa, Babylon, and, most splendid of all with its hundred-columned hall, Persepolis.

Gone were the rough leather breeches of Cyrus's rude cavalry; the marching soldiers sculptured on the walls of the palace at Persepolis wear the long robes called *kaftans,* heavy bracelets, and their hair and beards carefully curled in the Mesopotamian fashion. King Darius or Xerxes, his heir, robed in Tyrean purple, heavy with gold embroidery, golden jewelry, and a high tiara of gold, awed his prostrate nobles into the conviction that they were "in very truth . . . looking upon the lord of all the earth."[2]

---

[2]A. T. Olmstead, *History of the Persian Empire* (Chicago: University of Chicago Press, 1948), pp. 282–283.

SELEUCIDS AND PARTHIANS

The Achaemenid Persian Empire marks the climax of the strain of urban-imperial civilization that had first emerged in Mesopotamia and Egypt three thousand years before. But Persia also marks a transition from the relatively small polities of these earlier millennia to the much larger empires of later ages. And the Persian Empire itself remained at least an intermittent player on the great-power stage for centuries to come. Briefly, then, let us glance ahead at the future evolution of the impressive state that Darius the Great surveyed in 500 B.C.

At the beginning of the fifth century B.C. a handful of Ionian Greek city-states on the Aegean coast revolted against Darius and found support from the newly emergent Greek city of Athens. Darius suppressed the Ionian Greeks, but the punitive expeditions he and his successor Xerxes sent against Athens and the other Greek cities of the West were decisively defeated. And a century and a half later, as we shall see, the young Macedonian king, Alexander the Great, led the forces of the Greek West in a counter attack that overwhelmed the Achaemenid empire.

Later dynasties labored with varying success to rebuild the greatness of Persia. Two of these were dynasties of foreign kings, the Greek Seleucids and the Parthians, another wave of intruders from the northern steppes. The third was a new Persian dynasty, the Sassanids. Among them they carried the history of this ancient empire for a thousand years beyond this earliest age of human history.

Seleucus was one of Alexander's chief lieutenants. Within a decade or so after the Macedonian conqueror's death in Babylon in 323 B.C., his generals had parceled out his vast empire among themselves. Seleucus got the best of it—most of the Persian domain, minus Egypt. He and his successors were great builders of cities and great Hellenizers, spreading the Greek way of life at least to urban enclaves across the Middle East.

The Parthians replaced the Seleucids around 250 B.C. and ruled till A.D. 224, five long and tumultuous centuries. A warrior people from east of the Caspian Sea, the Parthians challenged the Romans for dominance of the ancient Near East. Their cavalry attacks and volleys of arrows combined with the blistering sun of the region to swallow up whole Roman legions.

These rugged fighters also played a more constructive role in the establishment of trade across the Eurasian continent. As we will see in a later chapter, this series of trade routes linked China in the east with the Roman Empire in the west. In so doing, the Great Silk Road curved down from the mountains of Central Asia into Persia. In Persia, Parthian and later Sassanid rulers guaranteed merchants safe passage—and took their share of the profits of this legendary road.

But the Parthians seem to have lacked the organizing ability of the Persians. They let much power go by default into the hands of local nobility, the Iranian barons who would play such an important part in Persian history from this time on.

THE SASSANIDS

The Sassanids, finally, expelled the Parthians in A.D. 224 and ruled the empire till 641, several centuries after the fall of Rome. The Sassanids—the word originally meant simply "Commanders"—were of Iranian stock, like the first Persians, and they claimed an Achaemenid connection. The four-hundred-year reign of the Sassanids is thus often seen as a restoration of the realm's legitimate rulers. Of the three dynasties, it certainly came the closest to equaling the splendor of the days of Cyrus and Darius.

During their four centuries on the Persian throne, the Sassanids constructed an elaborate system of power. It was a system based on a carefully structured bureaucracy and on two influential groups—the Iranian barons and the magi, or priests of Zoroaster.

A cluster of state officials directed the affairs of this most developed of Persian governments. In most periods, the chief of these was the grand vizier, the king's right hand and the operational head of the state. Other powerful officials were the chief priest, head scribe, and general of the armies. Below this exalted level, appointed officials spread out to the four main provinces, the lesser satrapies and other districts.

The Persian nobility, granted estates along the frontiers of the empire, provided a flexible border defense. In defending their own lands, these Iranian barons protected the Sassanid Empire as well. The ancient Zoroastrian priesthood, whose religious ideas will be discussed below, also served the state well. The magi collected the crucial peasant land tax on which government finances depended and provided religious sanction for Sassanid imperial power.

Under the Sassanids, that power was great enough to challenge the West once more, as Persia had done in the days of Darius and Xerxes. Under these rulers, Persia expanded until it briefly matched the vast extent of the original Persian Empire of the Achaemenids. At its greatest extent, the Sassanid Empire reached from Pakistan to Egypt, northward into Central Asia, and up to the suburbs of Constantinople.

The building of this vast empire, however, brought Persia once more into conflict with Western powers, first with ancient Rome, then with the medieval Byzantine Empire, whose capital was Constantinople. In later Sassanid times, when Rome and Byzantium were Christian states, the struggle acquired overtones of a religious clash between Zoroastrian and Christian. Exhausted by these wars, the Sassanid regime fell in its turn to the first wave of Muslim conquerors to come galloping out of Arabia.

Some of the pillars of the Persian emperor's royal audience hall in Persepolis, in modern Iran, still tower against an evening sky. If you had only the destruction of this palace by Alexander the Great to go by, whom would you judge more "civilized"—the Greeks or the Persians? (The Oriental Institute, the University of Chicago)

The Persian achievement was a monumental one indeed, with a geographical and historical dimension that reaches through classic and even into the medieval period of Western history. It is a powerful illustration of the scope of human political achievement across the western end of Asia.

THE FAITH OF ZOROASTER

The earliest religion of the Persians was probably the sort of polytheistic worship of natural forces that was common among ancient peoples. Indo-European Persians prayed to Anahita, goddess of the waters, and to Mithra, god of the sun. They sensed the presence of the numinous, the Wholly Other, the divine in the forces of light and darkness, earth and wind. Sacrificial fire played a central part in the religion of the early Persians, as it did among their Aryan relatives in India. There was a caste or tribe of priests among them—the magi—who like Indian brahmans performed all religious ceremonies.

Then, in the same sixth century that saw the emergence of the Persian Empire under Cyrus and Darius, a new and startlingly different religion appeared in Persia. Its founder was a prophet called Zoroaster, a mysterious figure about whom almost nothing is known with certainty. There are legends in plenty, of course, as there are surrounding most religious leaders. There are stories of his miraculous birth, his visions, his ten years' labor to find his first convert; of the Persian satrap who became his first patron, of his temporary happiness and later misfortunes, even of his murder by barbarous nomads while he prayed before the sacred flame. In actual fact, we scarcely know where or even when he lived, though best-informed guesses seem to be eastern Iran and sixth century. We do have his words, however, in *Avesta*, the Zoroastrian Bible, and we know what effect they had upon the Persians.

Six hundred years before Christ, Zoroaster preached a religion that had many of the elements of developed Christianity. There was, he said, not a multiplicity of gods but one god: Ahura Mazda, the Wise Lord, god of light, goodness, and truth. Ahura Mazda was the creator of all things, the judge of all people, the rewarder of virtue with an infinity of spiritual bliss.

It was a splendid vision. But, as in the later faith of the Christians, there was a dark side too. Zoroaster saw a principle of evil in the world also—the cosmic Liar, the prince of darkness, called Ahriman in developed Zoroastrianism. The universe itself was the battleground between Ahura Mazda and his chief lieutenant Mithra on the one side, and Ahriman on the other. All human beings, said Zoroaster, must take a stand in this eons-long struggle between light and darkness, good and evil. For in the end Ahura Mazda must win, and on that day his followers will enter rejoicing into paradise, while those who have served the Liar will be cast from the Bridge of Judgment into a pit of darkness and torment.

It was a creed suited to a militant people, and from the days of Darius the Great it was the faith of Persian royalty and nobility. The symbol of Ahura Mazda—a small human figure in profile, framed by vast horizontal wings—can still be seen carved in the ruined stone of Persepolis.

The Persians seldom sought converts to Zoroastrianism, and it remained largely the religion of an aristocratic elite. But even so carefully preserved a faith underwent change, as all faiths do. The fire sacrifice and the priestly role of the magi were annexed to Zoroastrianism from the beginning. Particularly under the Sassanids, every village had its sacred fire and two magi to tend it and perform all sacrifices. Other gods clustered around Ahura Mazda in popular folk belief. And Mithra, the Wise Lord's champion, became the protagonist of a growing cult of his own.

The Persians' Zoroastrian vision had its influence on neighboring peoples too. The faith spread eastward into India, where the Parsi sect comprises the largest body of Zoroastrians in the world today. The cult of Mithra the sun god, champion of light against darkness, spread westward to become a popular mystery religion in Rome and the favorite cult of Roman soldiers all over the empire. Even the Zoroastrian Liar found a place in foreign pantheons as the Satan of the Christians—the Father of Lies whose pit of fiery punishment carries more than an echo of the pit of Ahriman.

The Pillars of Persepolis

The pillars of Persepolis are the best-known relics of Persia's early glories. On a huge stone-faced platform projecting from a wall of cliffs, Darius the Great and his son Xerxes raised an intricate complex of palaces, monumental portals, harems, and audience halls in the fifth century B.C. Here was the celebrated hall of a hundred columns where Darius sat in state—the hall that Alexander and his drunken generals gave over to the flames a century and a half later.

This nude female figure from ancient Persia may represent a theatrical performance of some sort. Sculptured in stucco and worn away by the centuries, this elegant figure nevertheless preserves the memory of a vivid age long overlaid by a more puritanical Muslim society. (The Royal Ontario Museum)

One may climb the broad double stairway today, with its flanking bas-reliefs of marching soldiers and subjects bearing tribute, and pass through surviving doorways and porticoes carved with the royal figures of massive human-headed bulls. There is a huge fallen capital crowned with back-to-back bulls' heads that would be echoed centuries later on the pillars of Asoka in far-off India. And there are the soaring columns, sixty-five feet high, that once supported the lofty roofbeams of Achaemenid palaces.

Achaemenid glazed brick from Susa shows Persian soldiers in long embroidered *kaftans*, bows and quivers on their backs, long spears held vertically before them. Such figures give an idea at least of the blaze of color that once dazzled the eye of a Herodotus—or an Alexander—approaching a Persian royal residence for the first time. Persian treasure troves include gold and silver jewelry, cups of bronze and ivory, chased daggers, and plates of silver. From such exquisite work we may get an idea of life at the top among the most ancient Persians.

There is a monumental, formal, ceremonial quality to much of this art of ancient Persia that clearly derives from the Mesopotamian provinces of the empire. It is an art of audience halls and throne rooms, of silhouetted soldiers in embroidered robes parading solemnly around the walls. But there is a touch of life, a flowing freedom of movement to the bronze and gold and silver animals, the lions and griffins, a winged ibex leaping into space. There is a freshness and vitality here that breathes the cooler air of the Iranian Plateau—or the winds of the distant steppes.

And from time to time a living face looks out. From Susa the marble head of a Parthian queen, smooth-cheeked and calm, carved in polished stone in the Greco-Roman manner, gazes thoughtfully upon the world. From the distant Asiatic province of Tajikistan, a clay-sculpted head of a man, short-bearded and warmly capped, eyebrows raised, mustache tilted in a smile, radiates a sense of life. Such faces remind us that life did in fact once beat between the ribs of men and women who moved through the streets of even such exotic places as Persepolis and Susa.

SUMMARY

The dawn age of human history saw the emergence of other peoples besides the Mesopotamian states and ancient Egypt. Around the eastern end of the Mediterranean and on across western Asia, new cities, kingdoms, and empires bubbled up, many of them during the turbulent second millennium B.C. Between 1000 and 500 B.C., finally, the Hebrews and the Persians made very different contributions to the history of the world.

Among earlier peoples, the Ebla Tablets reveal a bustling society before 2000 B.C. Almost a thousand years later, the Hittites added iron to civilization's repertoire of workable metals. And during the centuries around 1000 B.C., the Phoenician city-states of what is today Lebanon traded by sea the length of the Mediterranean and beyond.

The Hebrews entered history as a pastoral nomadic people shortly after 2000 B.C. and established the short-lived kingdom of Israel under David and Solomon around 1000 B.C. The kingdom soon split into two halves, the northern half falling to Assyrian conquerors in the eighth century, the southern half to the Babylonians in the sixth century B.C. Through these trials and tribulations, however, the Hebrews developed a unique monotheistic religion, the direct ancestor of modern Judaism, Christianity, and Islam.

The Persian Empire, the largest in history up to that time, emerged with dramatic suddenness in the sixth century B.C., temporarily unifying the entire Middle East—western Asia—by 500 B.C. The founders and the most celebrated of Persia's four successive ruling houses were the Achaemenids (539–331 B.C.). Cyrus the Great and his rough, leather-clad Persian cavalry conquered most of the empire in the later sixth century B.C. Cyrus's heirs added to their inheritance, till by 500 the Persia of Darius the Great stretched from Egypt and Mesopotamia to the northwest frontier of India. Persian imperial administration of this sprawling system of satrapies, Persian roads, and palaces all set a new standard for western Eurasia. Persia's long struggle with the Greeks, however, proved its undoing. After two hundred years, the empire fell in its turn to Alexander the Great.

The inheritors of the Persian imperial tradition were a diverse line of dynasties—the Seleucids, the Parthians, and the Sassanids.

Persian high culture was significantly influenced by neighboring peoples, east and west, but produced lasting monuments that were distinctly Persian. The militant religion of Zoroaster—preaching life as a struggle between light and darkness, good and evil—influenced Persia's neighbors in their turn. And Persian palaces like those at Persepolis, despite traces of foreign influence, were magnificent embodiments of Persian imperial achievement.

SUGGESTED READING

BROOTEN, B. J. *Women Leaders in the Ancient Synagogue*. Chico, Calif.: Scholars Press, 1982. Inscriptions suggest a larger religious role for women among the ancient Hebrews. See also P. L. Day, ed., *Gender and Difference in Ancient Israel* (Minneapolis: Fortress Press, 1989), for essays on women's lives in Bible times.

Cambridge History of Iran (7 vols.). Cambridge: Cambridge University Press, 1983. Volumes 2 and 3 deal with the first four dynasties of Persia in scholarly detail.

COLLEDGE, M. A. R. *The Parthians*. New York: Praeger, 1967. See also N. Debovoise, *Political History of Parthia* (Chicago: University of Chicago Press,

1938), an older but scholarly outline of a tangled subject.

COOK, J. M. *The Persian Empire.* London: J M Dent, 1983. Achaemenid Persia in the light of recent archaeological discoveries.

CURTIS, J. *Ancient Persia.* Cambridge, Mass.: Harvard University Press, 1990. Brief but authoritative introduction to the subject.

DESCHESNE-GUILLEMIN, J. *Hymns of Zarathustra.* Boston: Beacon Press, 1963. Valuable introduction and commentaries accompany these translations of the Zoroastrian hymns, or *gathas.*

FERRIER, R. W., ed. *The Arts of Persia.* New Haven, Conn.: Yale University Press, 1989. Solid overview of the arts in ancient Persia.

GRAINGER, J. D. *The Cities of Seleukid Syria.* New York: Oxford University Press, 1990. Scholarly account of the cities of this part of the Persian Empire under Alexander's successors.

HEATON, E. W. *Solomon's New Men: The Emergence of Ancient Israel as a National State.* New York: Pica Press, 1975. Egyptian influences on the development of the Hebrew monarchy. For a popular account of the ancient Israeli kingdom, see E. H. Maly, *The World of David and Solomon* (Englewood Cliffs, N.J.: Prentice Hall, 1966).

MACQUEEN, J. O. *The Hittites and Their Contemporaries in Asia Minor.* Boulder, Colo.: Westview Press,

1975. Puts this innovative people in the context of their time and place.

MOSCATI, S. *The Phoenicians.* New York: Praeger, 1968. Recommended summary of the Phoenician cities and their overseas colonies. See also M. E. Aubet, *The Phoenicians and the West* (New York: Cambridge University Press, 1993), for a more detailed discussion of Phoenician commerce and colonial expansion.

NEWSOME, J. D. *By the Waters of Babylon.* Atlanta: John Knox Press, 1979. Compact treatment of the history and religious significance of the Babylonian captivity of the Jews.

SHERWIN-WHITE, S., and A. KUHRT. *From Samarkand to Sardis.* Berkeley: University of California Press, 1992. Survey of Hellenistic Persia. See also their edited collection, *Hellenism in the East* (Berkeley: University of California Press, 1987).

VAUX, R. DE. *The Early History of Israel,* trans. D. Smith. Philadelphia: Westminster Press, 1978. A standard history of the Hebrews. See also B. W. Anderson, *Understanding the Old Testament,* 4th ed. (Englewood Cliffs, N.J.: Prentice Hall, 1986), an authoritative survey linked to the familiar Bible account.

WERTIME, T. A. and J. D. MUHLY, eds. *The Coming of the Iron Age.* New Haven, Conn.: Yale University Press, 1980. Studies of the shift to iron-based technology in many cultures, based on archaeological remains as well as written sources.

CHAPTER 6

THE CITIES OF INDIA

LOST CIVILIZATION OF THE INDUS

The Indian Subcontinent

Harappan Culture

The Aryan Invasions

KINGDOMS OF THE GANGES

Cities in the Jungle

Social Structure: From Color Bar to Caste

The Rise of the Rajas

The Mauryas: Chandragupta

Asoka the Philosopher King

THE SOUL OF INDIA

The Lost Arts of Ancient India

Epic Poetry: The Song of God

Hinduism: From the Sacred Cow to Brahman

The Naked Philosophers

Buddhism: The Teachings of Prince Siddartha

Lost Civilization of the Indus

The Indian Subcontinent

The raw physical reality of India is mud in the monsoon, dust in the dry season. It is the high thin cold of the Khyber Pass and the glittering snowfields of the Himalayas, the lush green valley of the Ganges, the dry hills of the south. It is a mixture of peoples, a babble of many languages, a meeting place of some of the world's greatest religions. To Westerners today it is a richly physical world of hot curries and importunate bazaars from which, mysteriously, has emerged the profound spiritual tradition of the yogi and the guru, enlightenment and Nirvana.

India's history, like that of Mesopotamia, Egypt, and the Middle East, reaches back to a time before there was a Western world. Two thousand years before Athens or Rome, great cities flourished along the Indus. It is a history much less known than that of Egypt or Babylon, but one that deserves as large a place in any account of civilized beginnings around the world.

Indian civilization, like the civilizations of the Near East, was born in its river valleys, but it expanded inexorably thereafter, till it encompassed the entire subcontinent. On the map, this Indian subcontinent is one of the most readily recognizable of global features. It is a vast triangle, two thousand miles from north to south, about half the size of the United States. Like Arabia to the west and Indochina to the east, India is a gigantic peninsula jutting down from the underside of Asia.

Within this huge triangle, three main geographical subdivisions stand out. In the north the colossal ranges loom—the Hindu Kush in the northwest and the snow-shrouded Himalayas, including the world's highest peaks, Everest and K2, backed by the high, icy plateau of Tibet. Just south of the mountains run India's most celebrated rivers: the arid basin of the Indus in the northwest, the five rivers of the Punjab, the winding Brahmaputra, and the long green valley of the Ganges in the northeast, flowing from the Himalayas to the Bay of Bengal. South of the rivers, finally, lies the wedge-shaped Deccan, a dry, hilly plateau fringed by lesser ranges and narrow coastal plains as it runs down to Cape Comorin at the southern tip of the subcontinent.

To the west is the Arabian Sea and to the east the Bay of Bengal. Bathing the triangular land mass from the south are the heavier swells of the Indian Ocean. The monsoons, the great seasonal winds, blow in from the sea every June, bringing torrential rains through the summer and into the fall.

Each of the major regions of India has its distinctive and historic features. But the first center of Indian civilization was along the low, intensively cultivated banks of the great northern rivers, especially the sacred Ganges. It is along the shores of these rivers, then, that any history of India must begin.

Harappan Culture

The first of the Indian civilizations emerged not on the fertile banks of the Ganges but in the more arid valley of the Indus on the opposite side of the Indian landmass, in what is now Pakistan. Here, not long after the appearance of civilization in Mesopotamia and Egypt, the culture centered in the twin cities of Harappa and Mohenjodaro took shape.

The origins and development of Harappan culture, as the civilization of the Indus is usually called, remain a mystery. The very existence of this great center of early civilization was unknown until the 1920s, when archaeologists stumbled upon its remains. We have only recently learned to read the Harappan script, which survives only on small stone seals. The result is a great deal of intriguing speculation based on a dearth of hard information. Yet the impressive ruins are there, and archaeologists have come to at least some conclusions about their builders.

We know that Harappan culture flourished over an area larger than present-day Pakistan, leaving ruins scattered up and down the Indus basin and along the coast of the Arabian Sea. We know that it endured as long as a thousand years, from roughly 2500 to about 1500 B.C. We know nothing of Harappan kings and dynasties and wars, or even if they had kings or central government at all. But we can learn a good deal from the remains about the lives, the social organization, and even the attitudes of the people who produced them.

Harappan culture was built on agriculture, as most ancient civilizations were. Harappan villagers cultivated grain, especially wheat and barley, along the Indus and its

A straight street in ancient Mohenjadaro linked residential quarters, shops, state granaries, and public buildings. Houses typically opened onto narrow side streets rather than main avenues. The heavy clay and brick construction, shown here, kept citizens cool in the hot Indus River valley of what is today Pakistan. (Embassy of Pakistan)

tributaries. A considerable portion of this produce found its way down the rivers to the granaries of Harappa and Mohenjodaro, probably as taxes or tribute.

These early Indians worked copper and bronze, though stone tools continued to be used even after Neolithic times. They knew how to build bullock carts and small boats for transport. They exchanged goods, not only up and down the rivers of northern India but around the shores of the Arabian Sea and up the Persian Gulf to Mesopotamia. The distinctive rectangular Harappan seals have in fact been found as far away as Persia and Egypt.

We know little of the political organization of these Indian contemporaries of Sargon of Akkad and the Middle Kingdom pharaohs. Yet some degree of municipal authority was clearly required for the planning of their straight, right-angled streets and the maintenance of their remarkable system of underground drains and sewers. Centralized authority over an even larger area seems to be implied by the city granaries, the uniform brick construction, and the standardized system of weights and measures found all across the Indus basin. Whether

Harappa and Mohenjodaro were really twin capitals of a Harappan Empire, as is sometimes suggested, we do not know. It is certainly possible, however, that some degree of political unification was achieved in India even this early.

As the Harappan script reveals, the builders of this lost civilization were the ancestors of the Dravidians of southern India today. We have representation of them in small figurines and in seal carvings, and fragments of cotton cloth give some indication of how they dressed. A highly stylized bust of a bearded man with an embroidered robe fastened at one shoulder may be as close as we will get to an idea of what Harappan people looked like.

Religion was probably important among them, as among other early peoples. A mother goddess may well have been preeminent. There is evidence of cults devoted to the worship of animals. A famous seal shows a seated god surrounded by animals—perhaps a precursor of the great Hindu divinity Shiva in his capacity as Lord of the Beasts.

Above all, perhaps, an overwhelmingly conserva-

Head of a bearded man from Mohenjodaro. Some scholars believe this type of statue is intended to represent a Harappan priest. The robe leaving the right shoulder bare is typical of the costume of later Buddhist holy men, while the eyes, which seem to focus on the (broken) tip of the man's nose, may illustrate a meditative technique practiced by Hindu yogis in later periods. (Embassy of Pakistan)

THE ARYAN INVASIONS

The passing of Harappan culture is in some ways as obscure as its origins. Shifts in the course of the Indus or repeated flooding of the cities may have contributed to its decline. But the fall of the Harappan world was almost certainly due to the intrusion of a new people into north-western India: the Aryans.

The Aryan invaders who broke in upon the peaceful Indian world of 1500 B.C. were drifting tribes of pastoralists and intermittent agriculturalists. They were probably taller and paler than the Dravidian builders of the Indus culture, and considerably less civilized. Their original home, like that of other Indo-European peoples, was somewhere on the steppes of European Russia, perhaps north of the Caspian Sea. They traveled like many nomadic peoples, seeking water and pasturage for their herds of cattle, horses, and sheep. Their gradual filtering through the passes of the Hindu Kush and down into northwest India was a folk migration lasting several centuries, not an organized military campaign like those of Mongols and other later nomads. But the impact of the Aryans was every bit as devastating.

We have no detailed contemporary accounts of the Aryan conquest. The Hindu Vedas, a collection of Aryan hymns to their northern gods, give us our best information, but they tend to be couched in highly figurative language. We do know that the newcomers charged into battle in chariots against the Harappan infantry, and there is good evidence that at least some of the Aryan tribes wielded iron weapons against the native bronze. We know that Indra, the Aryan war god, proudly styled himself *Purandara*, "Breaker of Cities," and that his followers left the corpses of their foes to rot in the streets of Mohenjodaro.

Within a few generations of Aryan infiltration and intermittent warfare, only crumbling ruins remained of the great urban centers of the Indus. In Aryan India the cities of an older world were left uninhabited and unvisited, shunned as demon-haunted places by the descendants of those who had destroyed them.

 ## KINGDOMS OF THE GANGES

CITIES IN THE JUNGLE

The period of the Aryan predominance in India, roughly 1500 to 500 B.C., thus began with the destruction of a civilization. Cities were abandoned for hundreds of years. Writing was forgotten. Much of Vedic India—the Aryan-dominated northern India described in the Vedas—returned to the village life that had characterized pre-Harappan, Neolithic India.

The Aryans themselves continued to be herders of horses and cattle. During India's long summer monsoon rains, the intruders retreated to higher ground to grow a

tive cast of mind that makes the Egyptians look boldly innovative by contrast is indicated by what we know of Harappan civilization. For hundreds of years, the cities of the Indus were built and rebuilt on precisely the same rectilinear ground plan, and new houses were raised on the foundations of old. Foreign ideas seem to have been consciously rejected. Harappan merchants must have seen the elaborate irrigation works and the records on clay tablets developed in the Tigris-Euphrates valley, for instance, yet these valuable innovations were apparently never introduced along the Indus. The culture of Harappa and Mohenjodaro was one of the great breakthroughs into civilization, but it was dominated, like many early civilizations, by a profoundly conservative spirit.

HINDU KUSH

HIMALAYAS

(AFGHANISTAN)

Kabul R.

Chenab R.

Zhob R.

Indus R.

(Lahore)

BAHAWALPUR
DESERT

Ravi R.
Harappa

Sutlej R.

SMALL STATES

Bramaputra R.

(PAKISTAN)

Indus R.

Mohenjo-daro

Ghaggar R.

THAR
DESERT

(INDIA)

Ganges R.

MAGADHA

(Karachi)

Sabarmatir R.

Narbada R.

Tapti R.

20°

Gulf of
Cambay

(THE
DECCAN)

Arabian Sea

TRIBAL
AND
LOCAL
GROUPS

Bay
of
Bengal

15°

INDIAN OCEAN

10°

(SRI LANKA)

Aryan lines of penetration
1200–500 B.C.

Consolidation of New Monarchies
1000–500 B.C.

• Site where some sort of remains
from the Indus Civilization have
been found.

Modern place names in parentheses

| 0 | | 200 | | 400 Miles |
| 0 | 200 | | 400 Kilometers | |

65°   70°   75°   80°   85°   90°

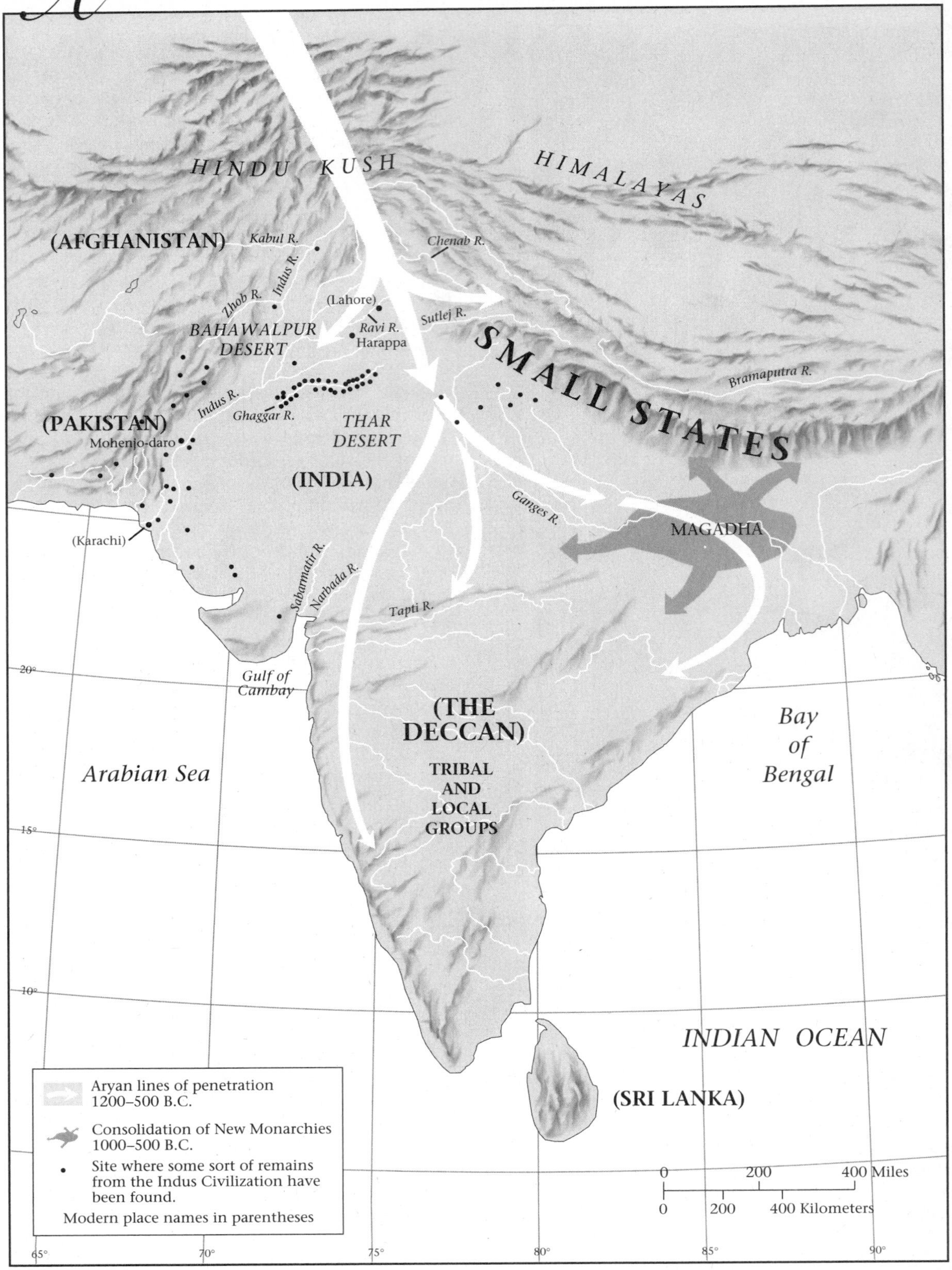

crop of grain, as Indian farmers had been doing for centuries. Year round they seem to have enjoyed chariot racing, gambling, drinking, and war, fighting as enthusiastically among themselves as with the original Dravidian inhabitants of the land.

Pastoralists and primitive agriculturalists, village dwellers and breakers of cities, these Indo-European intruders seemed an unlikely foundation upon which civilization might rise again in the Indian subcontinent. But during the first half of the first millennium B.C., urban culture did reemerge, slowly and painfully, in northern India. And its primary architects were the barbarian conquerors themselves.

This new birth of Indian culture involved a number of processes taking place concurrently.

There was, in the first place, an eastward migration by the restless Aryans from the Indus into the valley of the Ganges. The heavy rain forest there, which had resisted the bronze tools of Harappan times, yielded to the iron of the Aryans. The result was the opening up of rich soil for cultivation. The broad Ganges also contributed significantly to the economic development of the region, emerging as a busy avenue of trade.

Another aspect of the new India was the mingling of peoples and blending of cultures known as the Aryan-Dravidian synthesis. This subtle interpenetration of everything from religious beliefs to modes of production eventually turned the nomadic Aryans into settled farmers and their worship of anthropomorphic nature gods into the sophisticated concepts of Hinduism.

Accompanying the eastward migrations and the cultural synthesis of later Aryan centuries was the transformation of society. Some Aryans became sedentary landowners along the fertile Ganges valley, the more powerful of them using Dravidian farm laborers to work their land. Other Aryans became traders on the river itself. Crafts increased in complexity, providing heavy iron plows, trade goods, and the rough luxury items favored by the new, primarily Aryan aristocracy of landed and commercial wealth.

Here and there along the Ganges valley, finally, cities reappeared. Mere clearings in the jungle initially, these stockaded villages expanded into recognizable urban centers with substantial populations of artisans, traders, resident landowners, priests, warriors, and kings. Thus emerged such rude metropolises as Patna, the future capital of the Mauryan Empire, and Benares on the Ganges, still the holy city of the Hindus and perhaps the oldest continuously functioning city in the world.

SOCIAL STRUCTURE: FROM COLOR BAR TO CASTE

In this more complicated world, an institution developed that was to become one of the central features of Hindu Indian society. This was the immemorial Indian system of caste.

In a world of more elaborate social subgroupings, the old simple distinction between Aryan and non-Aryan was no longer adequate. In its place there emerged a division of society into four classes, or castes. The word for caste was *varna*, meaning "color" and clearly referring to the old racial differences between conquerors and conquered. But the actual basis of caste divisions was social and economic rather than racial. These divisions represented a clear shift from color bar to social classes in Indian society.

The four original castes were *kshatriyas*, the warrior nobility; *brahmans*, the priests; *vaisyas*, landowners and merchants, and *sudras*, cultivators of the land and other manual laborers. The system was not as rigid as it became later. Intermarriage between castes, for example, was possible in Vedic times. As warfare became less perpetual and religion more complex and important, the ranking of the top two castes was reversed; priests came to be regarded as the highest caste, followed by warriors.

The caste system grew more complicated and more rigid, however, with the passing of the centuries. In time the system would subdivide into hundreds of occupational categories. The religious sanctions would grow more strict, forbidding all forms of social interaction between castes, from eating together to intermarriage. Even the touch of the "untouchables" at the bottom of Indian society would come to be thought of as polluting to a high-caste Indian.

But there was also an open-ended quality to the caste system that made it remarkably easy for later immigrants—and there were many of them—to be absorbed into Indian society. Newcomers in later centuries would be assigned a place in the structure of castes based on their traditional skill, craft, or occupation. Paradoxically, this undemocratic system of traditional classes thus made India a very tolerant society into which newcomers could be accepted with minimal social tension.

The caste system as it developed in post-Vedic times was to remain a distinguishing feature of Indian civilization to the twentieth century, generating attitudes that survive today.

THE RISE OF THE RAJAS

The great transformation of later Vedic times was political as well as social. It introduced larger and more complex political units in northern India to accompany the more complicated social and economic institutions of the age.

Politically, the Aryan invaders had been loosely organized into tribes, clans, and families. Tribes were headed by chiefs or kings called *rajas*, most of them elected or chosen by rotation among the leading families. Councils of elders and assemblies of adult males normally shared political power with their kings. But the centuries of social evolution that carried India out of the dark ages following the Aryan conquest also transformed these simple tribal political institutions.

Most important, two new forms of state emerged

This bas relief from Bharhut near Calcutta, with its sculptured pillars, balconies, and gateways, hints at the vanished architectural splendors of the Mauryas, India's first unifiers. The central figures symbolize the veneration of the Buddha, embodied in the Wheel of Law. (New York Public Library Picture Collection)

in northern India: republics and kingdoms. The republican form retained many tribal institutions, including powerful councils and an oligarchy of leading families. In the developing kingdoms, however, the power of the *rajas* grew steadily at the expense of councils and assemblies. The new monarchies frequently became hereditary. They also developed administrative systems, headed by chief priests and military leaders, that exercised some degree of central control over the villages that composed the state.

Much of the new wealth generated by the rich soil, the renascent handicraft industry, the increased mining and utilization of iron, and the Ganges River trade funneled into the hands of these petty princes. It was crude splendor by later standards, a grandeur of rich robes and wooden palaces, but it was splendor nonetheless. As the caste system acquired religious support, so too did the institution of the monarchy. The brahmans conducted elaborate sacrifices, sometimes lasting as long as a year, to consecrate each new *raja*. The *rajas* in turn supported the evolving Hindu priesthood, establishing a close relationship between throne and altar. In India as elsewhere, the odor of sanctity thus hovered early over the kings of the Ganges, augmenting their growing authority over their people.

By the sixth century B.C. there were at least sixteen separate little states—many monarchies and some surviving republics—in the Ganges valley. These states retained some of their ties with the more traditional Aryan societies left behind in the Indus region to the west. They also continued the long-established Aryan tradition of

incessant warfare among themselves and against the Dravidian peoples of the Deccan to the south.

Increasingly, however, one principality loomed larger than any of the others in the little world of the Ganges—the kingdom of Magadha. Its rulers, the Nanda clan, had by the fifth century B.C. expanded its power at the expense of its neighbors, pushing their way down the delta of the Ganges to the head of the Bay of Bengal. From this jumping-off point the Nandas even opened up trade with Burma, which lay still farther east. It was the beginning of an eastward orientation that would be typical of India for the next two thousand years, replacing the westward orientation of Harappan times.

Domination of the Ganges valley thus came into the hands of a single state. From this power base the dynasty that followed the Nanda to the throne of Magadha would provide the foundation for the first genuine Indian empire—that of the Mauryas.

THE MAURYAS: CHANDRAGUPTA

The Mauryan dynasty (321–185 B.C.) was the first to bring almost the entire subcontinent under a single government. And the earlier Mauryas—Kings Chandragupta and Asoka in particular—seem to have presided over one of those rare occurrences in human history: a genuine golden age.

The Mauryan conquest of India, as it happens, began two years after the brief intrusion of one of the most famous of European conquerors, Alexander of Macedon. Many historians have theorized that Alexander the Great's long march from Greece across Persia to the frontiers of India may at least have stimulated the expansive imagination of the first of the great Mauryas, Chandragupta. In fact, there is very little historical likelihood that Alexander and Chandragupta ever met, and the Macedonian conqueror was certainly on his way home to Babylon to die when the first of the Mauryas set out on his own march to glory.

Legend—which must here make do for history—has it that Chandragupta Maurya (321–297 B.C.) was the son of a concubine at the Nanda court. He is supposed to have seized the throne of Magadha from the last of the Nandas with the help of his mentor and evil genius, a shrewd but unscrupulous brahman named Kautilya. With their authority thus firmly established along the Ganges, Chandragupta and Kautilya turned their eyes to a field of operations much larger than any of the princelings of the Ganges had ever dreamed of—the whole of India.

Chandragupta first led the large and powerful army of Magadha back to the old Aryan heartland on the Indus for a confrontation with the Greek forces of Alexander's heir in that part of the world, the shrewd general Seleucus. The founder of the Seleucid dynasty, however, chose not to fight for his distant Indian satrapies. He ceded to Chandragupta not only the Indus and the five rivers of the Punjab, but also much of what is today Afghanistan.

Thus strengthened, the Mauryan leader turned back eastward and pushed the frontiers of his growing domain all the way to the mouth of the Ganges in Bengal. He thus came to rule an empire that stretched some two thousand miles across northern India, from the head of the Bay of Bengal in the east to the high passes of the Hindu Kush in the west.

We know little of Chandragupta Maurya personally. He is said to have been a severely autocratic ruler, and indeed he would almost surely have had to be to hold such an expanse of recently conquered territory together. Thanks to the writings of his Machiavellian advisor Kautilya, Chandragupta has been associated with a foreign policy of ruthless self-aggrandizement. A Greek ambassador records that the self-made emperor, who had seized the throne by force, employed a notoriously efficient secret police and was heavily guarded in his palace at Patna.

Chandragupta's heir Bindusara expanded the Mauryan empire southward almost to the tip of the continent. Actual Mauryan rule ended in what is today Mysore, but Mauryan influence extended even to the island kingdom of Ceylon (Sri Lanka). Most of India already acknowledged the overlordship of the Mauryas when the third of that redoubtable line came to the throne—Asoka, the most famous of them all.

Before going on the most celebrated of the Mauryas, however, we should clearly note the scope of their achievement thus far. The empire of the Mauryas was no mere ten thousand square miles, like those of the Babylonians or the Egyptians. We are speaking of hundreds of thousands of miles, a feat of empire building comparable to those of the Persians before them and the Romans and Han China shortly thereafter.

The governing of such vast lands and peoples evidently required some doing in the third century before Christ. Some historians have suggested a rough system of more or less feudal allegiance on the part of local *rajas* to the Mauryan ruler at Patna. There is also some evidence of appointed Mauryan officials governing sizable chunks of the empire. However it was ruled, the Mauryan Empire was an amazing accomplishment, one of the most impressive feats of empire building in all of ancient history.

ASOKA, THE PHILOSOPHER KING

The reign of Asoka (c. 268–231 B.C.) was an even more astonishing achievement than that of Chandragupta. Like the Greek Age of Pericles or the Augustan Age in Rome, the Age of Asoka seems to have been one of the high points of human governance.

Specific facts about the life of the celebrated Asoka are very hard to come by. He is reputed to have had to fight for his throne, a struggle that may have involved an older brother. He almost certainly completed the conquest of the eastern coastal region of Kalinga, on the Bay of Bengal. And he was beyond doubt a very pious king. On

Asoka's royal lion capital once crowned a seventy-foot-tall column at Sarnath, on the site of Buddha's first sermon. The style shows Persian influence, but the symbolism and the inspiration are distinctly Indian. Can you think of other cultures in which the lion was the royal beast? (Indian Museum, Calcutta)

this thin scaffolding of fairly well attested fact, on awesome edifice of tradition, elaboration, and symbolic truth has been raised. For the life of Asoka as he himself presented it, and as it has been popularly recounted down the centuries, constituted a morality play of profound significance to the Indian people.

VOICES FROM THE PAST

"The circle of states is the source of the sixfold policy. The teacher says: "Peace, war, marking time, attack, seeking refuge, and duplicity are the six forms of interstate policy." "There are [really] only two forms of policy," says [the teacher], "for the sixfold policy is actually accomplished through peace and war. [Nevertheless], the forms of policy are, verily, six in number, for conditions are different in different cases."

Of these six forms: binding through pledges means peace; offensive operation means war; apparent indifference means marking time; strengthening one's position means attack; giving oneself to another [as a subordinate ally or vassal] means seeking refuge; keeping oneself engaged simultaneously in peace and war with the same state means duplicity. These are the six forms of policy.

When one king [the would-be conqueror] is weaker than the other [i.e., his immediate neighbor, the enemy], he should make peace with him. When he is stronger than the other, he should make war with him. When he thinks: "The other is not capable of putting me down nor am I capable of putting him down," he should mark time. When he possesses an excess of the necessary means, he should attack. When he is devoid of strength, he should seek refuge with another. When his end can be achieved only through the help of an ally, he should practice duplicity.

So is the sixfold policy laid down."

In this extract from Kautilya's <u>Arthasastra,</u> Chandragupta's shrewd advisor offers some calculated advice on foreign relations. And as this very worldly brahman had guided the founder of the Maurya dynasty to success in the interstate relations of northern India, his advice probably carried some weight.

Does this summary cover all the possible varieties of international relations, or can you think of others that have emerged since the fourth century B.C.? Do you feel the lack of a moral or ideological dimension here? Why or why not?

W. de Bary and others, eds., <u>Sources of Indian Tradition</u> (New York: Columbia University Press, 1958), p. 247.

It seems to have been the bloody Kalinga campaign that changed Asoka's life. Before he saw the heaped-up corpses and heard the wailing of women seeking their kindred among the dead, he was a Mauryan sovereign, wielding power and expanding the empire as his predecessors had. After the horrors of Kalinga, he was a man determined to live and rule in a different spirit.

That spirit was not that of Brahmanical Hinduism, but of Buddhism, a religion now two and a half centuries old in India. Asoka became a convert and apparently dedicated much of the rest of his life to the pursuit of *dharma*, the saving truth of the Buddha. He founded many shrines, sponsored a Buddhist council that dispatched missionaries to spread the faith as far as Tibet and Ceylon, and

devoted the rest of his reign to Buddhist virtues, public service, and the spiritual unification of his vast empire.

Asoka declared his new principles in an extraordinary series of public inscriptions carved on the walls of caves and on stone pillars erected along high roads from the Northwest Frontier to Mysore in the south, from the Arabian Sea to the Bay of Bengal. Some of these sermons in stone clearly reflected Asoka's conversion, urging upon his people such Buddhist virtues as reverence for parents and teachers, compassion, religious piety, and *dharma*. Others declared the emperor's larger public policies, a firm intent to see that his government would follow righteousness and serve the people.

Asoka particularly advocated the distinctly Indian

virtue of *ahimsa*—nonviolence—and promised to live by this principle as king. He would be mild toward his own subjects and would refrain from foreign conquests—as in fact he did. He renounced violence even toward animals, curtailed the mass animal sacrifices of Vedic days, and imposed a vegetarian regimen upon himself and his court.

A good deal of more practical public service accompanied Asoka's edicts. He dug public wells, built rest houses for weary travelers and clinics for the sick, and lined the roads of his empire with shade and fruit trees for the use of passersby. His masterpiece was the Grand Trunk Road, the commercial artery of north India, which ran many hundreds of miles from Patna to the Northwest Frontier and was still in use more than two thousand years later.

Unlike the pharaoh Akhenaton, the Indian ruler did his good works without attempting to force his new faith on his people. Religious toleration was unquestioned, and followers of other sects went their ways in peace while the emperor went his.

There may have been a practical side to the saintly Asoka's philosophy as well. He may have been trying to impose a broad spiritual unity upon his diverse peoples, many of them annexed to the Mauryan Empire by force during the last two generations. The emphasis on toleration may thus be seen as an attempt to undercut the inevitable social and religious tensions in the newly unified subcontinent. In the long run, this spiritual outreach may have been more successful than the military conquests of his predecessors. In fact, the far-flung Mauryan Empire fell to pieces less than half a century after Asoka's death. But India has ever since been one of the more spiritually open corners of the globe, a land where people worship many gods and follow many roads to truth.

THE SOUL OF INDIA

THE LOST ARTS OF ANCIENT INDIA

Nature and history have not been kind to the earliest achievements of Indian art. The cities of Harappan India were built of clay, those of Mauryan times of wood, and only the faintest traces of either have survived. History, in the form of Aryan and later barbarian invaders, has conspired to prevent the transmission of a substantial body of Indian art and craftwork. The Aryans in particular not only shattered the material culture of the first thousand years of Indian civilization, but they also produced little or no artwork themselves during most of their centuries of power. Yet enough fragments have survived to give us some idea at least of the high levels of artistic accomplishment reached by the earliest dwellers along the Indus and the Ganges. This is especially so of the Harappan and Mauryan high points of India's ancient history.

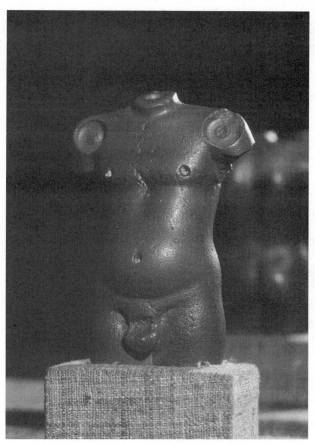

This flawless stone torso comes from Harappan Mohenjodaro. Many centuries before the ancient Greeks, the people of what is today Pakistan carved exquisitely shaped realistic statuettes like this. Art historians emphasize the distinctive South Asian qualities of the figure, including the slightly inflated feel of the body, probably intended to illustrate the breath-control techniques of Indian mystics. (Borromeo/Art Resource)

The geometrical beauty of what we know of the "planned cities" of Harappa and Mohenjodaro, with their rectilinear street patterns and public bathing places, has already been mentioned. The meticulously laid out blocks with water gurgling under the streets and residential structures rising two or more stories above them must have made an imposing spectacle in a world of Neolithic villages and tent-dwelling nomads.

The pieces of Harappan sculpture that remain—hundreds of carven seals and small figurines of terracotta, stone, or copper—reveal even more sophisticated traditions. The small rectangular seals usually depict animals, beautifully chiseled in low relief, as well as inscriptions in the unknown Harappan tongue. There are also examples of much more sophisticated sculpture, such as a lovely limestone torso only three and a half inches high, yet so exquisitely and naturalistically carved that it is often compared with the classic sculpture of Hellenic Greece. The lost civilization of the Indus would indeed have been a world worth seeing before the breakers of cities swept down from the north.

But the new civilization that eventually emerged in the Ganges valley to the east, the jungle-girt world of the first *rajas*, also nurtured builders of great skill. The climax of this second Indian artistic tradition dates from the Mauryan Empire, particularly from the reign of Asoka in the third century B.C.

The palace of Chandragupta at Patna was described by Greek envoys as more splendid than the Persian cities of Susa and Ecbatana. Its pillared audience hall echoed the columns of Persian Persepolis. Patna itself stretched for miles along the river and may have been the greatest city in the world in the third century B.C. Contemporary Buddhist bas-reliefs show high walls, many towers, and railed balconies over the streets. But all of it was made of wood cut from the great rain forests, and today only sections of the palisaded teak walls remain.

Among the Mauryan carvings that survive, most famous are the large animal figures—lions, bulls, and others—that top Asoka's famous inscribed pillars. In particular the conventionalized lion capitals of these smoothly polished forty- to fifty-foot freestanding columns show clear Persian influence. But they are nonetheless triumphs of Indian art.

There was a more completely Indian style in Mauryan sculpture, however, a style notably embodied in the massive statues of *yakshas*, or nature spirits. These big-bellied, larger-than-life figures are depicted naked to the waist, their powerful legs swathed in what looks like the *dhoti* that Indian men still wear in the villages. The *yakshis*, the female of this spiritual species, clearly reveal the supple, swaying stance, the narrow waist, and the swollen breasts that would be hallmarks of the female figure in Indian sculpture for centuries to come.

It is a scanty harvest for a culture whose later epochs would produce such numerous temples, such a multitude of softly smiling divinities in stone. But the art of Harappa and the Mauryas constitutes another of the great beginnings in the arts across Eurasia.

EPIC POETRY: THE SONG OF GOD

The literature that survives from these early Indian centuries is also sparse. There are, however, three literary peaks in that dawn age of Indian civilization. Two of these are epic poems: the *Mahabharata* and the *Ramayana*. The third is a hard-boiled treatise on statecraft called the *Arthasastra*.

The *Mahabharata* is, at 100,000 verses, the longest poem in the world. It is a Homeric saga of the struggle between two powerful Indian clans, the five Pandava brothers—particularly Prince Arjuna, the famous bowman—and their cousins the Kuravas. It clearly reflects the Aryan age of chariot fighters and kinship loyalties, of great archers, wild gamblers, and pious holy men wandering in the uncut Gangetic forest. Gods and other supernatural beings also play their part in a story that has a cosmic as well as a human dimension. The final victory of the Pandavas comes only after a colossal battle that, in the final version at least, seems to pit half the peoples of India against the other half.

The other great Indian epic, the *Ramayana,* is the more romantic story of how Prince Rama of one of the settled Ganges states rescues his lovely wife, Sita, from Ravana, the demon king of Ceylon. There is plenty of excitement in the adventures of Rama, Sita, and the friendly general of the apes, Hanuman, first exiled in the northern forests, then fighting epic battles in the south. But the original adventure story has been thoroughly reworked by brahman editors, so that Rama emerges as the ideal Hindu man, Sita as the perfect woman, and their relationship a model of the sort of conjugal loyalty and devotion expected in the settled agricultural states of the middle of the first millennium B.C.

The political commentary called the *Arthasastra*, attributed to Kautilya, Chandragupta's unscrupulous chief advisor, is a tract for a ruthless time of territorial state-building. For Kautilya, as apparently for his royal master, efficiency and success are the sole criteria of princely governance; morality is never taken into account. The people are to be kept in line by any means that work, including draconian laws vigorously enforced, hordes of bureaucrats, and battalions of what we would today call secret police.

A hard-nosed realist, Kautilya advises the shrewd *raja* to consider all his neighbors as enemies and all states beyond that inner ring as potential allies against the future victims between them. In the pursuit of ever-widening sovereignty, such practices as war, subversion, bribery, and assassination are clearly justified. The *Arthasastra* thus projects a grimly convincing image of political and diplomatic affairs among the raw new states along the Ganges.

Without these assorted literary efforts, our knowledge of war and politics, historical ideals, and intrigues in India's reemergent civilization would be vastly the poorer. Yet it is the religious content that is most striking in most of these works.

Before the brahmans had done with the *Mahabharata* and the *Ramayana*, central figures in both these epic adventures had turned out to be incarnations of the god Vishnu or of Brahman, the spiritual foundation of the universe. This is illustrated most vividly in the section of the *Mahabharata* called the *Bhagavadgita*, the famous Indian *Song of God*. This best-loved of all Hindu texts is a dialogue between Arjuna the archer, youngest of the Pandava brothers, and his divine charioteer Krishna. Its climax comes when Krishna reveals that he is actually the incarnation of Brahman, the divine ground of all things, in a vision that dazzles Arjuna like "a thousand suns":

O Lord of the universe [cries Arjuna] I see You without beginning, middle or end . . . endowed with numberless hands, having the moon and the sun for Your eyes and the blazing fire for Your mouth, and scorching the universe with Your radiance.[1]

The great victories of Prince Rama, the god-hero of the *Ramayana*, have become major festivals in the Hindu religious calendar. The feast of Diwali, a night of lights, candy, and toys for children rather like Christmas in the West, celebrates the victorious return of Rama and Sita to their kingdom in this ancient epic, which is still widely read. Even Hanuman the monkey prince has his share of temples and festivals over the length and breadth of India.

The Indians were a profoundly religious people, as concerned with the spiritual dimension of life as the ancient Egyptians or Hebrews. It would therefore be worthwhile to devote some space to this central aspect of the thought of ancient India.

HINDUISM: FROM THE SACRED COW TO BRAHMAN

Like a Hindu temple thick with statuary and other carved decoration, the Hindu religion is extremely ancient, very complicated, and more than a little exotic to Western eyes. At the popular level, it can look quite primitive—polytheistic, idolatrous, involving even the worship of animals. Yet at its heart stands a belief in a universal spirit—Brahman—who is often presented as three-personed, like the God of the Christians. And for the Hindu holy man, the meditating yogi or guru, religion is the mystical experience of a divine ground so ineffable that it cannot be described in words.

We know little or nothing about the religion of Harappan India. Worship of a mother goddess, mentioned earlier, seems a likely explanation for the many small female cult figures found in Harappa and Mohenjodaro. Harappan seals point to some veneration of animals, and one in particular may indicate a Harappan origin for the cult that was to grow up around the great god Shiva as Lord of the Beasts.

The Aryans brought to India the gods of the northern steppes, gods of thunder and sun—Indra, the god of war; Agni, the spirit of the sacrificial fire; and Varuna, lord of the big sky over the endless Eurasian plains. Aryans sacrificed to these divinities, slaughtering dozens or even hundreds of animals, and sometimes human beings too. The hymns, prayers, and rituals committed to memory syllable by syllable by the brahman priests were passed down to become the core of the oldest Hindu scriptures, the Vedas.

Hinduism as it developed in Vedic times involved a merging of the pantheons of the Aryan invaders and the conquered Dravidians, and perhaps even a certain gentling of the brawling gods of the breakers of cities. Most important, there was a striking evolution from naïve anthropomorphic divinities to a profound philosophic search for the deepest spiritual principle of the universe, the Brahman of later Hindu thought.

There were from the beginning many focuses for spiritual experience among the Indians, as among other older peoples. For ancient Hindus, there were many nature spirits like the *yakshas* and *yakshis* mentioned above, while hordes of demons lurked in the shadows, ready to tear and rend the souls of the unwary. Living among the teeming life of the Ganges rain forest, furthermore, early Hindus saw some of their gods in the shape of monkeys, snakes, or the sacred cow, which was the measure of wealth and source of life for their pastoral Aryan ancestors. To this day sacred cows browse more or less unopposed in the lanes and market squares of Indian villages. Grocers shoo them away from the vegetables and pedestrians step around the piles of dung they leave in their wake, but no one would deny them the streets.

The greatest Hindu divinities, however, were neither demons nor animals. Among the most popular gods were Indra's rambunctious successor Krishna, the divine charioteer of the *Bhagavadgita;* Rama, the incarnation of the great god Vishnu; and the divine wife of ancient Shiva, a goddess celebrated under the two contrasting personalities of Parvati, the universal mother, and Kali, the terrible goddess of destruction.

The most important of all the gods were—and are—Brahma, the rather hazy creator god; Vishnu, the preserver of the universe; and Shiva, the four-armed dancing divinity who is often presented simplistically as the destroyer of all things. These three were in time subsumed theologically under the persona of Brahman, the universal spiritual principle underlying all that exists. Brahman is not a personal god at all, but the unimaginable spiritual essence permeating the entire cosmos, "the One . . . hidden in all things."

The fabric of Hindu belief generated such peculiarly Indian concepts as the brotherhood of all living beings, reincarnation, karma, and *ahimsa*. For Hindus, all life is one and all living things have souls. This view was amplified by a later belief, first expressed around 500 B.C. in the philosophical dialogues called the Upanishads, in reincarnation, the transmigration of the soul. The Hindu doctrine of transmigration holds that each human soul is reincarnated, or reborn, in the body of some other creature—human, animal, or even supernatural—over and over again. In precisely what form one is reincarnated depends on *karma*, the "actions" one takes during one's present life. If you lead a good and pious life, you may be reborn as a brahman or other high-caste Indian; if you wallow in self-indulgence and sin, you may live your next life in the body of a rooting hog or a worm to be crushed by any passing sandal.

---

[1]*The Bhagavadgita or The Song Divine* (Gorakhpur, India: Gita Press, 1975), pp. 233–235.

From belief in reincarnation and the brotherhood of all life, finally, sprang the doctrine of *ahimsa*, or nonviolence. Arising first among Buddhists and Jains (see below), it eventually permeated all of Indian society.

The heart of developing Hinduism, however, lay not in its ceremonies and scriptures but in the central role of the mystical element in Indian religion. As early as the first millennium B.C., Hindus decided that they might escape the endless round of lives filled with human suffering through the mystical concentration of their psychic forces known as meditation.

The goal of the yogi's meditation is not "life everlasting" for the individual soul but rather the submergence of the ego in the supreme unity of Brahman. This mystic merging of the self with the spiritual oneness of the universe is sometimes compared to the dissolving of a drop of water in the ocean. It is to be achieved through spiritual enlightenment—the simple realization that all differences are illusions, or *maya*, that all that really exists is the totality of Brahman. "Those who know the High Brahman," the Upanishads declare, "they become immortal."

From the sacred cow to the unity of life and the oneness of all things, the spiritual quest of the Indians had by Upanishadic times—500 B.C.—already accomplished an awesome odyssey. By that time, however, Indian religion was spawning two other major faiths that were to follow their own historic paths, one of them to the spiritual conquest of the Far East. Let us then turn to the teachings of Mahavira the conqueror and of Siddartha, the compassionate Buddha.

THE NAKED PHILOSOPHERS

Hinduism as it emerged in the first millennium B.C. had already established itself as a basic social cement for evolving Hindu society. The ancient faith sanctified the caste system and sanctioned the rule of the *rajas*. The brahmans were the highest caste in society and could demand rich rewards for putting their ritualistic expertise at the service of rulers and people.

But the middle of the first millennium B.C. was a time of many changes and strains in Indian society. Out of these tensions a restless new impulse toward spiritual exploration emerged in northern India. In particular, this spirit produced the gurus (spiritual teachers) of the sixth century whom Western envoys would later describe as gymnosophists—the "naked philosophers."

Some of these wandering holy men were in fact naked, going unclothed in monsoon rains and under the Indian sun to discipline the flesh. Others starved themselves for long periods or engaged in exhausting exercises that would soon develop into the sacred discipline of yoga. A few sought to rediscover ancient sorceries in backwoods tribes, or even attempted spiritual growth through alcohol and orgiastic sexual practices. Of all the gurus of this age of intellectual ferment, however, two left by far the most important imprints on the Indian mind.

The first was Mahavira (c. 540–476 B.C.), founder of the sect of the Jains ("Conquerors"). Mahavira actually accepted a broad range of conventional Hinduism, from the caste system to reincarnation. But he did have some extreme notions—such as complete celibacy, total honesty, and the rejection of all earthly possessions. Like the most extravagant seekers of his generation, he practiced rigorous asceticism, meditated intensively, and went naked in rain and sun.

His major contribution to Indian thought, however, was the doctrine of *ahimsa*, which he defined as the nonviolent refusal to take a life. In pursuit of *ahimsa*, the Jains carried brooms to sweep insects from under their feet, fed ants, and filtered the water they drank and the air they breathed in order to avoid accidentally extinguishing some minute form of life. Their piety took extreme forms. But it sometimes takes extremists to get a hearing for a new doctrine, and the notion of nonviolence was clearly thrust into the mainstream of Indian thought by the extravagant commitment of the followers of Mahavira.

BUDDHISM: THE TEACHINGS OF PRINCE SIDDARTHA

The other great preacher of the sixth and fifth centuries B.C., the Buddha, or Enlightened One, made an even larger contribution to the religious thought of the East.

One approaches the historic Siddartha, or Gautama Buddha (563–483 B.C.), through a thick incrustation of image and legend. And the fairy-tale version of Siddartha's life has an undeniable charm. He grew up in splendor as a king's son, protected from any sight of human suffering until as a young man he beheld illness, age, and death for the first time. The stricken prince thereupon left his young wife and infant son and set out to find a way to escape the wheel of human misery. After many years of self-denial, he found enlightenment at last under the great bodhi (or bo) tree at Gaya, and devoted the rest of his life to spreading his new gospel.

He was not actually a *raja*'s son: his Sakya people were an undeveloped hill tribe among whom the headship rotated, his father being one of a number of sturdy *kshatriyas*—farmers who had a right to a turn as chief. But the rest of the legend—the years of rigorous asceticism, the meditation under the bo tree at Gaya, the famous first sermon in the deer park at Sarnath outside Benares, the monkish order he founded, and the long lifetime of wandering the roads of India with his disciples—all these are likely enough, given the spiritual ferment of the times.

Gautama Buddha found the fundamental cause of all suffering in one great human failing: desire, the almost universal human attachment to the good things of this world. Desire in turn fosters the central human illusion: that the things of this world are real. The Buddha agreed with orthodox Hinduism that worldly things are a grand illusion, a fantasy world of *maya*. Behind this illusory separateness of things, he further agreed, lies an ineffable spiritual unity—what the Hindus called Brahman. Buddha himself tended not to call it anything. His goal was to get there. Escape from desire, from the wheel of life and the *maya* world, was to be found along the eightfold path that Buddha preached for half a century in the growing cities and along the jungle trails of Gangetic India.

The eight steps to Nirvana—union with the ultimate spiritual reality of things—begin with the recognition and rejection of selfish worldly desires as the blind follies they are. Next comes the cultivation of unselfishness, compassion, and honesty; then rejection of such injury to others as murder, theft, and adultery; and finally the choice of a source of livelihood that does not bring harm to other living things. The path leads through a turning away from evil thoughts and all physical concerns to deep meditation and final escape from the wheel of unending lives through Buddhahood—that is, enlightenment—and Nirvana, the extinction of the suffering ego in the great ocean of eternal peace.

Buddha and his followers wore only the simplest of robes, owned nothing but their begging bowls and staves, traveled always on foot, and never slept under a roof—a striking contrast with the patrician, sometimes greedy and worldly brahmans. The Buddha presented his faith to live by in simple language that the layperson could understand, without the elaborate theology of developed Hinduism. Perhaps most radically, he accepted people of all castes as equals on the eightfold path.

Men joined him to escape the chains of caste, women to break with the exhausting load of family obligations. Men and women both shaved their heads and donned the saffron robes of the mendicant in search of the higher truth he preached. His orders of monks and nuns would carry his doctrines far across the eastern half of Asia over the next thousand years.

The results are still visible today. You can still see Buddhist temples in the People's Republic of China or at Kamakura in business-like modern Japan. In rapidly modernizing Indonesia, the hundred Buddhas of the hilltop temple of Borobudur still meditate over the lush jungles of Java. And in Tibetan monasteries beyond the Himalayas, the gold-painted Buddhas of the Past, the Present, and the Future gaze down at you over flickering candles of yak butter.

Paradoxically, after becoming royal orthodoxy under sovereigns such as Asoka, Buddhism would all but die out in India in later centuries. But there are temples in all the architectual styles of the East in the Buddhist shrine at Bodh Gaya on the Ganges today. There pilgrims from many lands remove their shoes and pass reverently under the shadow of the giant bo tree where Prince Siddartha found enlightenment and into the hall where a huge gold statue of the Buddha still meditates on human folly and desire.

SUMMARY

City-based civilization emerged twice in India between 2500 and 200 B.C., reaching a first climax under the Mauryan dynasty at the end of this period.

India's first civilization, that of Harappa, was born in the Indus River valley around 2500 B.C. and perished in the Aryan invasions of 1500 B.C. Harappan Indians built gridlike cities and had an integrated agricultural society. We do not know whether they developed a political empire or not, since they left no written records like those of Egypt or Mesopotamia. The Aryans, nomadic Indo-European cattle-herders from the northern steppes, destroyed the cities of the Indus and drove most of their Dravidian builders southward into the Deccan.

Civilization reemerged between 1000 and 500 B.C. in the Ganges River valley, east of the Indus. During this period the rude Aryans merged with the more settled Dravidians. Aryan iron tools succeeded in opening up the dense jungles of the Ganges valley and in rebuilding urban society once more. Although the institution of caste erected rigid barriers among races, classes, and occupations, it also made a place for future newcomers as new castes.

A number of small kingdoms ruled by divinely sanctioned *rajas* grew up along the Ganges around 500 B.C. One of these, Magadha, under the Mauryan dynasty (322–185 B.C.) unified much of the Indian subcontinent by force of arms during the fourth and third centuries. But the greatest of the Mauryas, the Buddhist Asoka, rejected the use of force and ruled as an Indian philosopher king.

Under the Mauryas, sculpture and palace architecture flourished, though most of these early monuments, made of wood, have vanished. But it was religion, a central feature of Indian history, that produced some of Asia's most influential insights during these early centuries.

Hinduism, the complex faith of most Indians, evolved during the Aryan-Dravidian synthesis shortly after 1000 B.C. It developed a range of religious sects and practices ranging from veneration of sacred cows to the mystical meditations of Indian gurus. Buddhism emerged as part of a new religious ferment around 500 B.C. Prince Gautama the Buddha and his monks preached escape from earthly suffering and desire through spiritual enlightenment. Even India's most famous epic poems, the *Mahabharata* and the *Ramayana,* reflect not only the warlike ways of the Aryans but the spiritual insights of the brahmans who edited them as well.

Suggested Reading

ALLCHIN, B. *The Rise of Civilization in India and Pakistan*. New York: Cambridge University Press, 1982. Archaeological insights into Indus and Ganges river civilizations.

BADER, C. *Women in Ancient India*. London: Kegan, Paul, Trubner and Co., 1925. Old but widely cited; perhaps paints too rosy a picture of the condition of women in early Indian civilization. See also I. B. Horner, *Women under Primitive Buddhism* (Delhi: Motilal Banarsidass, 1975) on the liberating influences of Buddhism.

BASHAM, A. L. *A Cultural History of India*. Oxford: Clarendon Press, 1975. Useful summary of India's cultural evolution.

BURTON, T. R. *Hindu Art*. Cambridge, Mass.: Harvard University Press, 1993. Brilliantly illustrated survey.

CHAKRAVARTI. *The Social Dimensions of Early Buddhism*. New York: Oxford University Press, 1987. Useful focus on social teachings and consequences. See also C.-S. Yu, *Early Buddhism and Christianity* (Delhi: Motilalsidass, 1981), comparing Christ and the Buddha in terms of authority, community, and the discipline they taught.

CORLESS, R. *The Vision of Buddhism: The Space under the Tree*. New York: Paragon, 1989. Good introduction to the life and teachings of the Buddha. Two recent and readable lives of the Buddha are R. A. Mitchell, *The Buddha: His Life Retold* (New York: Paragon, 1989), and D. J. Kalupahana, *The Way of Siddartha: A Life of the Buddha* (Lanham, Md.: University Press of America, 1987).

DUNDAS, P. *The Jains*. London: Routledge, 1992. Creeds and customs of this ancient Indian faith.

DUTT, R. C., ed. and trans. *Mahabharata and Ramayana*. New York: Dutton, 1961. Free translations of the two great Indian epics.

EDWARDS, M. *Everyday Life in Early India*. London: Batsford, 1969. Covers the period from Mauryas through Guptas; splendid illustrations. See also J. Auboyer, *Daily Life in Ancient India From Approximately 200 B.C. to A.D. 700* (London: Weidenfeld and Nicolson, 1961).

HUTTON, J. H. *Caste in India*. Cambridge: Cambridge University Press, 1946. Account of the history and nature of this distinctive feature of Indian civilization.

KAUTILYA. *Kautalya's Arthasastra*, trans. R. Shamsastry. Mysore, India: Mysore Publishing, 1967. The classic political tract by Chandragupta's right-hand man. For a modern political analysis, see N. P. Sil, *Kautalya's Arthasastra: A Comparative Study* (New York: Lang, 1989). For a picture of early Indian political culture, see B. A. Saletare, *Ancient Indian Political Thought and Institutions* (New York: Asia Publishing House, 1971).

KOSAMBI, D. *Ancient India: A History of Its Culture and Civilization*. New York: Pantheon, 1965. A study of India's beginnings, with a cultural emphasis.

KOSTERMEIER, K. K. *A Survey of Hinduism*. Albany, N.Y.: State University of New York Press, 1989. Expert overview of the world's oldest religion. See also D. M. Knipe, *Hinduism: Experiments in the Sacred* (San Francisco: Harper, 1991), and D. R. Kingsley's brief but penetrating *Hinduism, A Cultural Perspective* (Englewood Cliffs, N.J.: Prentice Hall, 1982).

KULKE, H., and D. ROTHERMUND. *A History of India*. Totowa, N.J.: Barnes & Noble, 1986. Solid survey of Indian political history, incorporating recent research.

MOOKERJI, R. K. *Chandragupta Maurya and His Times*, 4th ed. Delhi: Motilal Banarsidass, 1966. As much as we are likely to know, by an eminent scholar.

PARPOLA, A. *Deciphering the Indus Script*. New York: Cambridge University Press, 1993. Recent decoding of this writing system from ancient Pakistan.

QUIGLEY, D. *The Interpretation of Caste*. Oxford: Clarendon Press, 1993. Anthropological analysis of India's "peculiar institution." On the origins of caste, see B. K. Smith, *Classifying the Universe: The Ancient Indian Varna System and the Origins of Caste* (New York: Oxford University Press, 1994), and H. A. Gould, *The Hindu Caste System: The Sacralization of a Social Order* (Delhi: Chanakya, 1987).

STRONG, J. S. *The Legend of King Asoka*. Princeton, N.J.: Princeton University Press, 1983. Translation and analysis of the *Asokavadana*, an early account of the Buddhist philosopher king. See also R. Thapar, *Asoka and the Decline of the Mauryas* (London: Oxford University Press, 1960), for a less glowing treatment.

WHEELER, R. E. M. *The Indus Civilization*. Cambridge: Cambridge University Press, 1968. A good look at what the excavations tell us, by a leading excavator.

CHAPTER 7

THE CHINESE EMPIRE EMERGES

SHANG CULTURE

THE MIDDLE KINGDOM OF EAST ASIA

Sprawling across the far end of Eurasia, China is the world's third largest nation today. It has by far the largest population: well over a billion strong, the Chinese constitute a quarter of the population of the earth. A great power and a powerful influence on all its neighbors, China is to East Asia what India is to South Asia—and then some.

Nor is China's preeminence a new thing in the world: it has probably been the most populous of nations since its first unification in the third century B.C. Cut off from other centers of civilization by formidable barriers such as the Gobi Desert, the Pamir and Himalaya mountains, the jungles of Southeast Asia, and the Pacific, the world's largest ocean, China has been removed from much of the rest of world history. At the same time, the giant of East Asia has inevitably emerged as the predominant force in its own very substantial corner of the globe, from Tibet to Korea and Japan.

This combination of isolation and predominance has fostered distinctive patterns of behavior and attitude among the Chinese. This unique combination has, for instance, contributed substantially to the phenomenal cultural continuity that marks Chinese history. In fact, twentieth-century China is still governed to a striking degree by ideas that first emerged two or three thousand years ago.

Isolation and cultural supremacy have also bred a strong belief in China's uniqueness, a sense of being "the Middle Kingdom," the center of civilization, indeed the only civilized people in a barbarous world. This conviction—which China shares with many other peoples—would help to hold together a huge nation marked by great geographical diversity over many centuries. This self-confident sense of superiority would also make China one of the last of the old centers of civilization to succumb to the technological and ideological influence of the West in the twentieth century.

A glance at the geography of this vast and isolated land makes China's historical achievement all the more impressive. China today is slightly larger than the United States, stretching, like America, roughly three thousand miles from west to east and two thousand north to south. The land stairsteps down from the inhospitable Tibetan Plateau, the world's highest landmass, to the densely populated sea-level plains along the Pacific rim.

North to south, China is divided into three main regions, two of them defined by great rivers. The Huanghe (Yellow River) of north China, with its light yellow loess soil blown south from the Gobi, has been the political core of Chinese development. Beijing, the political capital, is the metropolis of north China today. The Yangzi River of central China is the main artery of a spreading web of tributaries and lakes that water some of the nation's most fertile farm land. Central China, with its wheat fields and rice paddies, bamboo groves and mulberry trees, has a major outlet at Shanghai today. The more mountainous south is monsoon-drenched and semitropical, rich in rice and tea production, the nation's historic commercial center and not infrequently the center of revolt. Guangzhou (Canton) and Hong Kong are its gateways to the world.

Such a topographical survey utterly fails, however, to convey a sense of the geographical diversity and picturesqueness of the ancient Middle Kingdom. The Great Wall and the Ming tombs are readily accessible from a Beijing hotel, and well-heeled visitors may even be flown across the length of China to see the colorful lamaseries of Tibet. But the desolate plains of Xinjiang, where nomadic herdsmen still raise their round felt yurts against the gigantic snow-draped background of the Pamirs, remain as unknown to outsiders today as in the days when it took two months by yak to reach the region from Beijing.

In the northeastern corner of this huge and ancient land, then, another center of civilization emerged sometime in the second millennium B.C.

FROM PREHISTORY TO HISTORY

The arts of civilized living, according to the oldest Chinese traditions, were taught by a series of wise men—at most *semi*divine—called sages. It was the most ancient sages who taught human beings to climb down out of trees, to domesticate animals and till the soil, to make silk and work bronze. It was the sages who instituted the family and created monarchical government, who invented the arts of music, writing, astrology, and other aspects of the higher culture. This is, of course, a drastic simplification—and dramatization—of a much slower historical evolution. But it comes closer to history than most such early accounts, which tend to attribute all good things to beneficent gods.

Some of the earliest relics of Paleolithic people have been found in China, including the bones of "Peking man," which disappeared in the chaos of World War II. More than one Neolithic Culture has also been detected, particularly centering in the valley of the Huanghe, where the first historic dynasties would presently appear. A late Neolithic village excavated at Banpo Xian reveals polished stone axes, handcoiled pots, and a collection of postholes and foundation pits from which a whole Stone Age village can be reconstructed. Square tent-like structures joined more permanent wattle-and-daub structures, some of them partially below ground, like the "pit houses" of the early dynasties.

Along the banks of the Huanghe and its tributaries, several hundred miles in from the sea, these Neolithic Chinese still hunted and fished, but they also farmed, cultivating millet and vegetables with the aid of hoes and other polished-stone tools. They domesticated dogs and pigs—both for meat—and oxen and horses for their labor. They made pottery. In many ways, in short, the early Chinese were much like other Neolithic people all across Eurasia.

In particular ways, however, the culture of these Stone Age people pointed toward the specifically Chinese high culture that would soon evolve on this simple foundation. Neolithic Chinese ceramic forms and techniques, for example, would influence the bronze ritual vessels that became one of the artistic glories of the first Chinese dynasty, the Shang. The prehistoric practice of scapulimancy—divination by "reading" the cracks that appear in heated animal bones—would in Shang times provide our first samples of Chinese writing. The care these early villagers took to bury their dead with a full array of food, tools, and weapons is usually seen as a precursor of the veneration of ancestors that would be a distinguishing feature of Chinese civilization.

These Stone Age farmers and hunters, squatting before their round mud houses along the Huanghe and its tributaries, did not of course see themselves as precursors of anyone. It is barely possible, however, that they did recognize the crucial change that they had pioneered: the invention of agriculture in the Far East. For it was on the backs of laboring Chinese farmers down the centuries, and with the leisure that labor made possible for a favored few, that one of the great world civilizations would be built.

Shang Society

Traditional Chinese historiography divides the history of the Middle Kingdom into two dozen dynasties, running from the third millennium B.C. to the present century. This scheme exaggerates the continuity even of Chinese history. There were, in fact, periods of hundreds of years when no single dynasty ruled the fragmented nation. Like most such schemes, furthermore, this one is especially

dubious in the earliest periods, where history merges into the mists of legend and myth.

Traditionally, Chinese history begins with the Three Dynasties—the Xia, the Shang, and the Zhou. Of these, the Xia was probably mythical; the Shang, once dismissed as legendary also, has in the present century been proved real enough; and the Zhou, China's longest historic dynasty, is as thoroughly documented as any age so far back is likely to be. It was in the wake of the Zhou, finally, that China for the first time found genuine unity under the short-lived dynasty of Qin—the climax of China's early history.

As far as we presently know, then, Chinese civilization began with the hazily documented Shang dynasty (roughly 1500 to 1000 B.C.). Shang society was considerably more complicated than the Neolithic agricultural villages that preceded it along the banks of the Huanghe. Granted, most subjects of the Shang kings still lived in pit houses or similarly simple dwellings and worked their fields with stone tools. But there were other classes of society too. There were skilled artisans, workers in bronze and silk as well as in stone and ceramics. There was an embryonic merchant class that traded at some distance in

A bronze brazier, decorated with dragons, shows the intricate patterning and skilled bronze work for which ancient Chinese art was famous. This one dates from later Zhou times. The mythic dragon, a symbol of the emperor and a common element in Chinese art of all periods, was probably derived from the real alligators who lived in some Chinese rivers. (New York Public Library Picture Collection)

salt and shells and the metals needed by the bronze workers, especially copper and tin. At the top of Shang society, finally, there was an aristocracy who hunted, fought, and enjoyed the finer things of Shang life—jade jewelry, bronze weapons and ritual vessels, silken robes, leather armor, and four-horse chariots from which to direct their frequent wars.

Presiding over this developing society were kings who, despite their titles, enjoyed only very limited powers. Shang kings were above all military leaders, defending northeastern China from border raids or embarking upon campaigns for loot or tribute. In peacetime, the monarch performed essential religious rituals and sacrifices on behalf of his people, entreating the gods for victory or good harvests. The throne was hereditary, though it frequently passed from brother to brother, or from uncle to nephew, rather than from father to son.

In performing these narrowly defined but important functions, rulers were aided by a still modest number of officials. These included expert scribes and diviners, the earliest specialists in the Chinese administration.

This Shang state sounds more like unified Egypt than the collections of independent states that composed early civilization in Mesopotamia and India. In actuality it was probably a loose confederation of clan states. The clans acknowledged the Shang king as leader in war and as a special intermediary with the gods. Beyond that, the power of the monarchy was almost certainly circumscribed by that of the more ambitious nobles. Royal authority probably seldom extended very far beyond the capital.

Shang cities were substantial if in some ways rudimentary accomplishments. The city walls, sometimes as high as thirty feet, were made of pounded earth and must have involved the regimented labor of thousands of workers. Within the walls were the large houses of nobles and kings and the temples of the gods, all constructed of wattle and daub hung on a framework of heavy timber. Aristocrats and commoners alike seem to have built exclusively of wood, reeds, and mud and to have depended on thatched roofs to keep the rain off floors of beaten earth.

Yet this newly civilized folk also produced the beginnings at least of one of the most sophisticated cultures the world has seen. Shang artisans, for instance, learned very early to alloy bronze out of copper, tin, and sometimes other metals. Writing, as mentioned above, also developed early, as a means of recording prophecies. Religion was polytheistic, embracing a welter of nature gods, goddesses, and other spiritual beings. These included the ancestral sky god Shangdi, later referred to as Tian (Heaven), and the Dragon Woman, as well as countless local spirits of earth and air and water. Among Shang aristocrats, however, one other element of Chinese religious belief began to take shape: the worship of ancestors.

The elite seem to have believed that Shangdi in particular was too awesome and elevated to be approached directly. Therefore they prayed to their own most celebrated ancestors, now transported to that spirit world where Shangdi reigned, to intercede with the god on behalf of living generations here below. This procedure had the practical advantage of giving the aristocracy, who alone had celebrated ancestors, exclusive access to the greatest of the gods. Ancestor worship thus effectively excluded all other classes from any concern with public affairs.

The veneration of ancestors was therefore a powerful conservative force from the beginning. It was not the least important legacy from the Shang period of Chinese history.

THE ZHOU DYNASTY AND CHINESE FEUDALISM

THE KINGS OF THE WESTERN ZHOU

The coming of the Zhou dynasty to northeastern China in the eleventh century B.C. is clearly explained in the dynastic histories—altogether too clearly, in fact, to be wholly convincing. According to the traditional version, the house of Shang reigned, and sometimes ruled, for more than five hundred years during the second half of the second millennium B.C. The last Shang king, however, was a royal monster, a man steeped in crimes against gods and humanity. Then, out of the west, came two brothers, King Wu and the famous Duke of Zhou, at the head of a great army. These two princes of the western tributary state of Zhou are the heroes of this version of the change of dynasties.

We do not know what really happened, of course. But the outcome of the decades-long struggle between the ruling houses of Zhou and Shang was the establishment of the longest-reigning dynasty in Chinese history.

The Zhou dynasty came to power in north China shortly before the year 1000 B.C. This house was to be recognized as at least the nominal overlord of China's political heartland until the year 221 B.C. Within this broad tract of time, two major periods are customarily distinguished: the comparatively successful Western Zhou, comprising the first two and a half centuries of the period, and the long debacle of the Eastern Zhou, five hundred years of anarchy under a house that reigned in name only. And yet, paradoxically, the turbulent later-Zhou centuries may have seen more progress than the more renowned reigns that began the dynasty.

The Western Zhou is so called from the fact that the early Zhou kings continued to rule from their hereditary lands in the west. Here in the mountain-girt Wei River valley, on the edge of civilization, they were able to retain the martial spirit of border lords while profiting from the more advanced institutions of the principalities they had conquered to the east. Their nominal rule reached as far north as the future site of Beijing, as far south as the

Yangzi valley of central China. To the peoples of a hundred city-states and other principalities, the Zhou kings thus became the true Sons of Heaven, the divinely ordained rulers of all civilized peoples.

ZHOU FEUDALISM

The rule of the Zhou kings, however, was at best indirect. Zhou monarchs in fact appointed others—princes of the Zhou clan, noble supporters, powerful allies—to rule the far-flung territories of the Zhou "kingdom." In short, Zhou China was essentially a feudal state, as Shang China had been. The Kings of the Western Zhou did, however, boast a more elaborate bureaucracy than that of Shang times. They also propounded a far more ingenious—and influential—set of justifications for the power they had seized with the sword.

At the top of the Zhou administration was a chief advisor who could sometimes be the actual formulator of royal policies. The prototype of this traditional chief minister was the Duke of Zhou, who labored by his brother King Wu's side through the long struggle that led to Zhou supremacy. The best of later-Zhou ministers strove to emulate this spirit of selfless dedication to the welfare of the monarchy. The worst of them, like grand viziers and mayors of the palace elsewhere, exploited their power for their own benefit.

Beneath the king and his chief minister, six administrative departments, charged with such matters as agriculture, war, public works, and religious observances, developed under the Zhou. These administrators collected tribute and issued communiqués, though the tributary princes were often too involved with their own affairs to pay much attention to royal officials.

Zhou kings, or their shrewder advisors, did, however, evolve what became the standard Chinese rationalization for their rule: the Mandate of Heaven. As Sons of Heaven, Zhou rulers claimed to govern by a special mandate or sanction of Heaven, a divine charge to govern the land. They further claimed that it was the heinous crimes of the last Shang king that had led Heaven to dispatch the princes of Zhou to replace the Shang. This ingenious doctrine had only a single drawback. Any failing of moral force in the Zhou themselves—or any striking series of public calamities, from earthquakes to invasions—could lead to the charge that the Zhou in their turn had lost the Mandate of Heaven. And without the clearly perceived divine right to rule, how long would the descendants of the Zhou continue to govern China?

The doctrine of the Mandate of Heaven thus introduced by apologists for the Zhou dynasty remained an essential feature of Chinese political theory. The chaotic rise and fall of later Chinese dynasties was explained by this cosmic pattern of interrupted harmony and reestablished order. It was a pattern that would be repeated over and over again throughout the long history of the Middle Kingdom.

THE EASTERN ZHOU: PROGRESS IN A WORLD AT WAR

The Zhou rode to feudal supremacy in the eleventh century B.C. In the eighth century a military disaster signaled a second fundamental turn in the fortunes of the dynasty—but this one a turn for the worse. Barbarians broke through into the Wei valley and sacked the Zhou capital. The monarchy thereupon prudently moved the capital eastward to Luoyang, in the civilized heart of northeast China. It was, apparently, a mistake.

From that time on, the authority of the Eastern Zhou—as the royal house is henceforth called—declined to the merest nominal allegiance. Feudal barons failed even to come to Luoyang for investiture, frequently failed in their tribute payments, sometimes refused even to respond when summoned to support the king in arms. Other princes took the title of king. During the latter part of the Eastern Zhou—the so-called Warring States period (fourth and third centuries B.C.)—this loose feudal empire dissolved entirely into a patchwork of separate states and clashing ambitions.

The Eastern Zhou has traditionally been considered a long decline after the more coherently ordered Western Zhou. More recently, however, historians have discovered some strikingly progressive elements in the politically anarchic later-Zhou centuries.

Perhaps most obvious—but no less important—the population grew substantially. By the third century the civilized areas of northeastern and central China had the largest population of any center of civilization in the world. The dynasty that succeeded in unifying the warring states would thus emerge as master of the world's most populous nation, a rank China would continue to hold down to the present.

Economic development seems to have accompanied demographic growth. For one thing, China moved from the Bronze Age to the Iron Age during the later Zhou, producing iron axes, scythes, plows, and swords from approximately 500 B.C. on. New crops such as soybeans were introduced, and large-scale irrigation works sponsored by later-Zhou princes are mentioned for the first time. The merchant class particularly seems to have prospered during the Warring States period, making use of new military roads, standard weights and measures introduced by some princelings, and the first real Chinese coins, copper "cash" with holes in the center. Strung on cords, copper cash was from that time on China's most common medium of exchange.

Some historians have also detected a decline in the nobility and the rise of a new, self-made social type in the more fluid society of the Eastern Zhou. Men of humble background could rise at the courts of competing princes on the basis of energy, intelligence, and expertise in war or politics. This was especially so if the ambitious new man also possessed the winning social grace and air of spiritual force called *shi*. Shi was a debonair mastery of gentlemanly forms, religious ritual, and traditional wisdom that seems to have gained the pushiest social climber an entrée at the courts of the warring states.

Finally, the later Zhou was one of China's cultural golden ages. The book was invented during these centuries, and learning came to be respected for the first time in China. Princes and barons supported schools at their capital cities that would teach an aristocratic elite reading and music as well as archery and chariot fighting. There were still altars to Shangdi or Tian at every court, but philosophic secularism also spread, and human sacrifice—an ancient custom in China, as elsewhere—declined considerably. From court to court, finally, there wandered not only unemployed officials and military commanders but sages as well. For the later Zhou was also, as we shall see, the Age of Confucius.

The Qin Dynasty Unifies China

The Rise of the House of Qin

These progressive changes were real enough, and modern historians have come to emphasize them. But the period of the Warring States was also, as the traditional chroniclers recorded, a time of political instability and violence. And out of this welter of rivalries and alliances, war and betrayal, a new power emerged that was to accomplish something neither the Shang nor the Zhou had achieved. The short-lived house of Qin, China's third historic dynasty, was to bring genuine unity to the nation at last.

The state of Qin was located in modern Shaanxi in the mountain-walled valley of the Wei River, where the old Zhou capital had been. But the kings of Qin, rising to prominence eight hundred years later in China's social evolution, developed along very different lines from the loose feudalism of Zhou.

The Qin began with much of the border-lord military spirit that had distinguished their predecessors. They too evolved as a society on the dangerous edge, between the barbarian intruders from the north and west and the heartland of Chinese civilization to the east. To this militant heritage they added a rigorous new approach to governance—a philosophy known as Legalism. The result was a potent mix of military toughness and authoritarian control that carried the Qin state to mastery of China in the third century B.C.

Defending the mountainous northwestern frontiers of Chinese civilization against raiders on horseback from the northern steppes, Qin warriors became expert cavalrymen themselves. During the fourth century B.C., the Qin kings used this cavalry arm to conquer a number of neighboring states in the northwest. They then pushed south into central China to overrun the fertile Red Basin of Sichuan. In the third century, finally, they turned their powerful cavalry and the large armies recruited from their new subject states upon the civilized Zhou states to the east.

By the time the Qin began marching against the Zhou dynasty and its nominal tributaries, this aggressive western state had also been strengthened in another way. Qin rulers had profitably applied the rigorous new authoritarianism of a school of sages called Legalists to their growing realm. It is a clear illustration of the proverbial power of an idea whose time has come.

Discussion of the theory of Legalism may be deferred to a later section on the philosophical schools. In practice, however, Qin Legalism meant emphasis on law and punishment, rationalization and strengthening of the bureaucracy, and autocratic control from the center. The best-known Qin Legalist, the fourth-century minister of state Lord Shang, constructed a strongly centralized administrative structure for military and civil government. He made appointments and promotions exclusively on the basis of merit and pushed policies that would keep the whole nation productively at work for the good of the state. Like his contemporary Kautilya in India, Shang also put heavy stress on the military, planted secret police across the land to spy on the populace, and inflicted savage—if rigorously impartial—punishments for infractions of his draconian laws.

In the middle of the third century B.C., then, this militarily powerful, rigorously authoritarian state marched east against the collection of separate little kingdoms that still formally acknowledged the primacy of the decaying house of Zhou. The King of Qin was a young and aggressive prince surrounded by cadres of ambitious advisers, most prominent among them Li Si, a latter-day Legalist. The Qin army was ready, the rival Zhou monarchy moribund. Luoyang fell, and with it the house of Zhou.

One by one thereafter the other major states were overwhelmed, gobbled up, as a famous Chinese historian later put it, "like a silkworm devouring a mulberry leaf." In 221 B.C., the last of them fell. The King of Qin assumed a new throne, and Chinese chroniclers later gave him a new name and title to go with it—Qin Shi Huangdi, the First Emperor.

Shi Huangdi: The First Emperor of China

Shi Huangdi is one of those larger-than-life figures who sometimes erupt into history, wrenching events out of their time-worn course, dazzling and often horrifying their contemporaries. "Cracking his long whip," even a hostile Chinese historian admitted, "he drove the universe before him,

MONGOLIA

GOBI DESERT

NAN SHAN

(Beijing)

SHENSI

Anyang

Yellow R.

• Xian

SHAN TUNG

Yellow Sea

KOREA

Sea of Japan

JAPAN

Luoyang

Birthplace of
Confucius, 551 B.C.

Site of Capital of Western
Zhou, 1127–770 B.C.

Wei R.

• Nancheng

Chengtu •

SZECHWAN

Yangtze R.

(Shanghai)

(Hangzhou)

*East
China
Sea*

Mekong R.

Yangzi R.

**TRIBAL AND
LOCAL GROUPS**

TAIWAN

BURMA

Pearl R.

(Canton)

(Hong Kong)
(Br.)

Hanoi •

VIETNAM

SIAM

*South
China
Sea*

	Shang States 1520–1027 B.C.
	Zhou Empire c. 300 B.C.
	Qin Empire c. 220 B.C.
∿∿	Great Wall
	Modern place names in parentheses

0   200   400 Miles

0   200   400 Kilometers

110°   120°

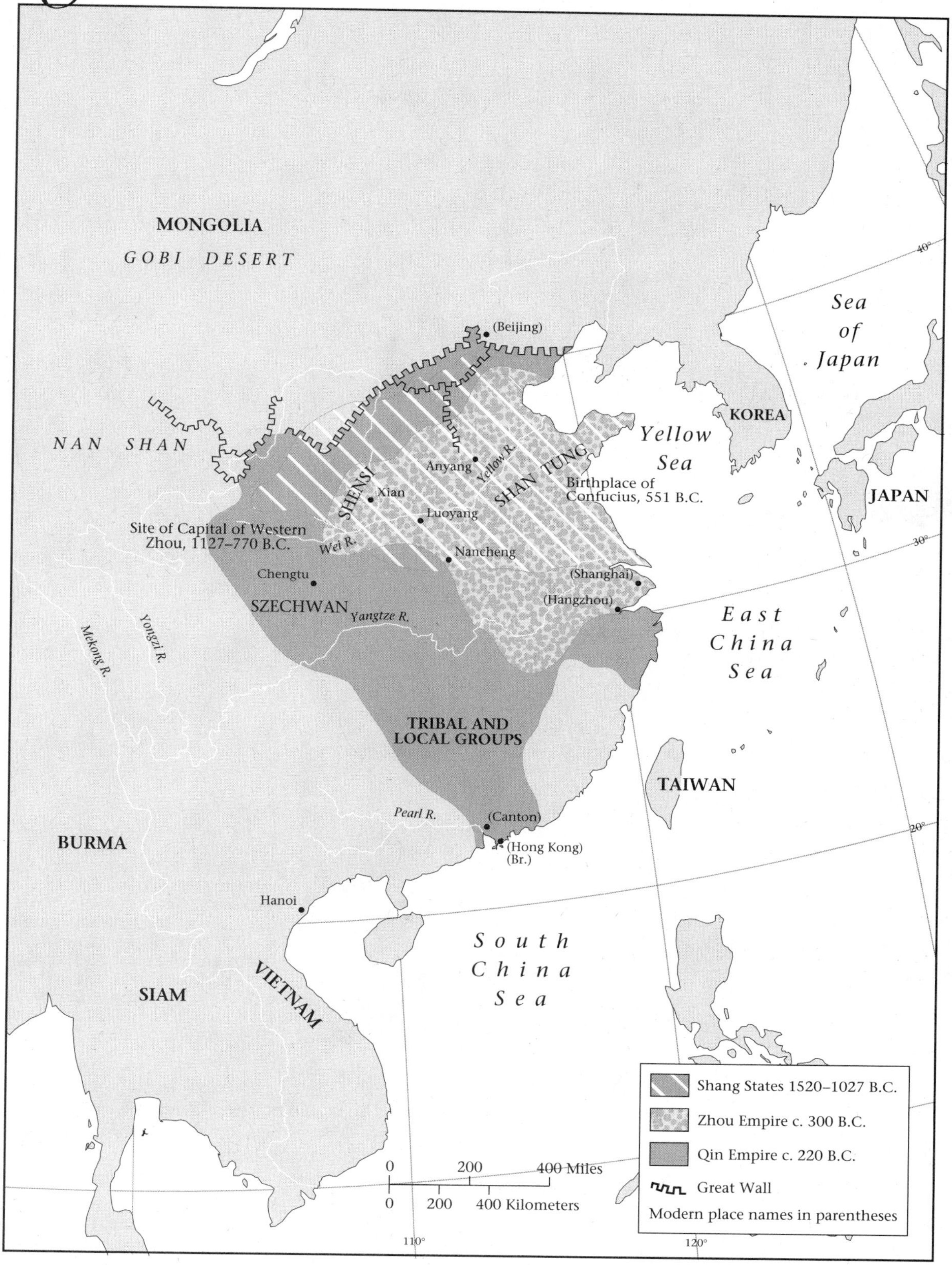

The Great Wall of China, with its crenellated battlements and frequent watchtowers, is often described as the only work of human hands visible from outer space. The road along the top of the wall made it possible to deploy troops and move supplies rapidly from one sector to another. How would you explain the similarity of the crenellations to those of Medieval European castles? (The Bettmann Archive)

swallowing up the eastern and the western Zhou and overthrowing the feudal lords. He ascended to the highest position and ruled the six directions, scourging the world with his rod, and his might shook the four seas."[1]

Certainly Shi Huangdi was a man of feverish energy. By 221 B.C. he ruled the largest part of modern China. But he did not stop there. His armies hurled back the nomadic barbarians of the northern steppes and pushed far south into what is today Vietnam. His archers and spearmen in their bronze and leather armor, his lumbering chariots and light cavalry clattered back and forth across the land, garrisoned the passes, held princes and people alike in awe. He was by far the greatest conqueror China had yet seen.

[1]Theodore de Bary, Wing-tsit Chan, and Burton Watson, eds., *Sources of Chinese Tradition*, Vol. 1 (New York: Columbia University Press, 1960), p. 151.

Yet it is the domestic achievements of Huangdi that most boggle the historical imagination. In the decade left him after unification, the First Emperor seems almost to have lifted the land out of one path and set it upon another.

Almost at a stroke he abolished both the warring states and the feudal system that had spawned them. The strongholds of the defeated princes were destroyed, and the nobles of the old order were decimated or compelled to live in the new Qin capital under the watchful eye of the emperor. The new China was divided into thirty-six districts, each with a military and a civil governor, and into many more county-sized subdistricts, each with its appointed administrator. A centralized bureaucracy thus for the first time genuinely governed a united nation in East Asia.

Within the nation Shi Huangdi labored to effect a degree of uniformity never attempted before. He standardized weights and measures for the whole of China, issued a uniform coinage, and commissioned scholars to produce a simplified standard set of Chinese characters for writing in all parts of the empire. Even the length of cart axles was made uniform by decree, so that cart wheels could all follow the same ruts in the soft loess soil of north China.

THE MAN WHO BUILT THE GREAT WALL OF CHINA

Like kings and conquerors in other lands, the First Emperor also embarked upon an astonishing number of large-scale building projects. Roads crisscrossed the empire as never before, facilitating troop movements but also encouraging merchants to ply their trade once more. Canals were dug or refurbished, both for inland transport and to irrigate cropland. The emperor constructed elaborate palaces in his capital, including one allegedly large enough to house ten thousand people. And he built himself a tomb at Chang'an—modern Xi'an—which traditional Chinese historians described as one of the miracles of the age—and in fact it awed a later age when parts of it were excavated in the 1970s.

All this, and still more. Somewhere between conquest and unification, among irrigation projects, royal palaces, and tombs, the First Emperor found time to build the Great Wall of China. In its final form, this amazing monument would stretch for fifteen hundred miles across China's northern frontier. It would average twenty-five feet in height over all those hundreds of miles, with watchtowers every two or three hundred yards. Huangdi did not build it all, of course. Sections had already been constructed by the lords of the northernmost Zhou states, and much of the emperor's work consisted of joining up these sections into a continuous barrier. Later rulers and dynasties revamped and added to the marvel, and most of the ramparts up which tourists toil and camera-toting Chinese

teenagers mill today were actually raised in the sixteenth century A.D. rather than the third century B.C. Yet the Great Wall remains a monument to the will and vision of Huangdi, and one of the undoubted wonders of the world.

To accomplish so much in so little time, the First Emperor had to drive his people mercilessly. Heavy taxes were laid on the peasant population. Forced labor was utilized for his enormous building projects. Whole populations were moved from one part of the country to another to carry out the emperor's orders. It was a triumph of the will unparalleled in China's ancient history—and one that many laboring Chinese probably could just as well have done without.

Legalists like Li Si particularly urged Huangdi to clamp down on intellectuals, the Confucian officials and other philosophers who objected to the rigors of the new regime. The books of philosophers who disagreed with the Legalists were collected and burned. Dissidents were imprisoned or executed, sometimes by the hundreds. They were harsh measures, but the men around the emperor justified them by the most powerful of Legalist arguments: success.

It took Shi Huangdi a quarter of a century to unify China. For another decade he labored to shape the empire to his will, perusing endless reports, traveling ceaselessly around the country on inspection tours. Tormented in his last years by fears of conspiracy, clinging to superstitious dreams of an elixir of eternal life, he died suddenly in 210 B.C., in the middle of one of his endless tours of inspection.

No longer infused with the emperor's fierce will, the vaunted Legalist order collapsed like a house of cards. Huangdi's chief ministers turned upon his heirs and then upon each other. Intrigue, executions, and royal suicide turned the dreamlike pleasure palaces of the First Emperor's capital into a nightmare world. Popular uprisings broke out among a people pushed to the breaking point and beyond. Within four years of Huangdi's death the dynasty of Qin followed its founder into extinction.

The unifier and his house perished; his capital was ravaged and looted, his tomb defiled. The Mandate of Heaven passed on to new hands. But the First Emperor's greatest achievement, the united China that he had created and to which the Qin dynasty had given its name, lived on. There would be later breakdowns of authority, later collapses of the empire into separate warring states. But the ideal of unity, order, and centralized authority, once achieved, was never forgotten. The history of the Chinese Empire from the third century B.C. to the twentieth century A.D. is itself the greatest monument to the driving will and extravagant dreams of China's First Emperor.

The Great Wall he built is today lost in a madhouse of souvenir stands, fluttering flags, clicking cameras, and well-dressed young Chinese on holiday. At the head of the stairs, as you step out on top of the crenellated wall

PROBING THE PAST

> *After Ch'in [Qin] had unified China, it replaced feudal domains with commanderies and prefec-tures and replaced dukes and counts with administrators and prefects. It held sway over all parts of China and located its capital at the most strategic point. How triumphant it must have felt! Yet in a few years its empire began to collapse. Why? It was so brutal as to put thousands of men into slave labor and so avaricious as to take away the material wealth of its subjects. The masses—ordinary farmers as well as convicted exiles—rose up in anger; together they formed alliances for the over-throw of the Ch'in regime. However, it should be recalled that the appointed officials remained loyal during this period of rebellion; it was the people who revolted. While the people were complaining below, these officials were afraid of punishments from above. Caught in the middle, they were either killed or kidnapped in numerous cases. The downfall of the Ch'in regime did not in any way result from defects on the part of a centralized administrative system; rather, it came about as a result of adopting harsh and inhuman policies, which caused grievances among the people.*

This treatment of the overthrow of the Qin dynasty after the death of the First Emperor is by Liu Tsung-yuan, a celebrated poet and commentator of the Tang dynasty. Writing during a period of weak government when China seemed menaced by revolt and invasion, Liu rejects the tendency of earlier historians to blame the fall of the short-lived Qin ruling house on the rigidly centralized government imposed by the First Emperor. Instead, Liu sees the cruelty of the regime as a prime cause of the upheaval.

Does Liu's analysis of the attitudes of the civil service sound realistic to you? Do you see any possible connection between Liu's own times and his view of the past? The inter-pretation offered here was popular with the Chinese Communist government in the later twentieth century. Can you see why the Communists would favor an explanation that did not blame strongly centralized government?

Liu Tsung-yuan, "Essay on Feudalism," in Li Yu-ning, ed., The First Emperor of China (White Plains, N.Y.: Interna-tional Arts and Sciences Press, 1975), p. xvii.

itself, you will do well to ignore the soldier who points to your right and go left instead. It is steeper that way, but there are fewer people. And near the end of the restored section, you can descend the stairs on your left, slip through an open doorway, and do a little exploring on your own.

Follow the path through dry rock and spiky plants to the end of the restoration—and the beginning of the real Great Wall. Following the crumbling crenellations down the slope, sit on a broken stone. Alone among the Chinese hills, you can meditate in peace on one of the wonders of the ancient world.

ART AND THOUGHT OF ANCIENT CHINA

ART: BRONZE DRAGONS AND CLAY SOLDIERS

There was much that was harsh and violent about the his-tory of the first three Chinese dynasties. But even a sketchy survey of the architecture and sculpture, the poetry and philosophy of the first millennium and a half of Chinese history will strikingly brighten the perhaps too grim political picture thus far presented.

A serious problem arises at the outset for the student of Shang, Zhou, and Qin architecture. Since it was built primarily of wood, like Indian architecture of that period, there is simply none of it left to study. Yet it is possible, on the basis of surviving postholes and poetic descriptions, to reconstruct at least the shape and color of those vanished cities.

In some ways they were quite crude, as we have seen: towns walled with pounded earth, wooden houses roofed with thatch in Shang times, with tile under the Zhou and Qin. Yet we also read of luxurious noble residences set in large courtyards and raised on high platforms reached in many cases by a double ceremonial staircase. Spacious halls and chambers are mentioned, as well as pergolas, terraces, galleries, and balconies. Gardens and lotus pools and banks of blooming flowers glimmer through the pages of Zhou poetry. Descriptions of scarlet-painted pillars, carved and polished rafters, and similar princely indulgences are convincing evidence that these kings and barons of the Chinese Bronze and Iron ages buily spendidly in their own way.

Where sculpture is concerned, we need no convincing. Considerable quantities of cast bronze in particular remain, collectors' items in China for hundreds of years. The archetypal Shang bronze is not a human figure but a vessel for holding meat, grain, or wine at a religious sacrifice. These ritual vessels stand on three or four legs and are typically covered with curvilinear or rectilinear designs in low or high relief, representing schematically the faces and bodies of animals. These animal-mask or monster-mask patterns became increasingly abstract and geometrical, until little remained but the eyes, polished bosses still peering out of the rhythmic interweaving of the sculptured bronze.

Fully figural sculpture still survives, some in marble or jade, but most elegantly cast in bronze. Animal motifs again are most common, including the water buffalo and rhinoceros as well as birds, horses, and dragons. The Chinese dragon shape in particular is fully developed by late Zhou times, with its undulating reptilian body, its wings and dorsal spines, and a scalelike patterning over its metal skin.

All this carved and cast sculpture from early China is small in size, and most of it is more decorative than realistic in style. But in 1974 the fabled tomb of the First Emperor of the Qin was discovered at Xi'an, and the

Elaborately decorated Shang ritual vessels like this one were used to make offerings to the gods of ancient China. Shang metalworkers had mastered the art of alloying copper and tin to make bronze tools, weapons, fittings for chariots, and drinking cups. This ritual vessel, only sixteen inches high, shows the abstract yet suggestively mask-like patterning typical of such Shang works. (Freer Gallery of Art, Smithsonian Institution)

Veterans of the last wars of the Warring States, this soldier and his horse helped bring the Qin dynasty to power and unify China for the first time. These figures were among the hundreds of life-sized clay statues excavated from the underground tomb of China's first emperor, Shi Huangdi. (Courtesy of the Cultural Relics Bureau, The People's Republic of China, and The Metropolitan Museum of Art)

emperor's fantastic army of life-size terracotta soldiers saw the light of day for the first time in twenty-two hundred years. There are reputed to be seven thousand of these clay statues—men, horses, even chariots—all life-size. Lined up in proper military formation, armed with real weapons, they were buried in underground tunnels to protect the emperor's subterranean tomb. Each figure is individualized and precisely detailed, from leather or bronze armor and intricate coiffeur to the furrowed brow of an officer or the smooth-faced good looks of an infantry recruit.

These clay figures in their silent hundreds, idealized though they may be, give some indication of how convincingly these ancient Chinese could model the human figure when they wished to. They bring us as close as we will probably ever get to the living faces of the human beings who built the Great Wall of China.

LITERATURE: CHINESE CHARACTERS AND THE BOOK OF SONGS

Writing was invented in China during the Shang period as a means of communicating with spirits. The first Shang examples we have, painted on charred and cracked oracle bones, are questions addressed to gods or noble ancestors; the answers received are written under them. During the Zhou dynasty, when writing began to be directed to human readers, books appeared—slips of bamboo or wood fastened along one edge. Under the First Emperor the characters were standardized. They have changed very little since—another instance of the remarkable continuity that is so central a feature of Chinese civilization.

The Chinese characters thus established are very different from any Western written language. Each character stands not for an alphabetical sound but for an entire word. The shapes themselves, executed with brush and ink, have a beauty of line that has made calligraphy a major art in China. Most striking, perhaps, there is a distinctly pictorial quality to many Chinese characters. Thus the symbol for *dragon* originally looked like a dragon; the character for *good* resembled a picture of a mother and child.

The sheer difficulty of learning these thousands of complex written signs—by contrast with the twenty-six letters required for written English, for example—severely limited the number of people who would become literate in China. The prestige of the scholar and the powerful place of the mandarin administrator in Chinese government are among the most important results of this elaborate Chinese system of writing.

Although China's complicated written language cut the elite off from the masses, it also helped unify the country regionally. A Chinese from Peking in the north cannot to this day easily understand the spoken language of Canton in the south. But speakers of both dialects can read the same newspapers, printed in characters that are their common heritage from ancient China.

There is no literature beyond oracle bones from the Shang, but the eight centuries of the Zhou dynasty were seen by subsequent generations of Chinese as a literary golden age. Perhaps the most immediately appealing products of this first great age of Chinese literature are poems, most notably the three-hundred-odd lyrics of the *Book of Songs*, first collected around 600 B.C.

The *Book of Songs* includes a variety of material, from elegant poems on the deeds of kings and courtiers to simple folk songs illustrating the lives of Chinese peasants. The latter, composed most commonly in short, rhymed lines comparable to those of European folk ballads, deal with many aspects of life in the fields and villages of ancient China. Farmers complain of the eternal tax collector. Soldiers lament the hardships of military service. Young people glow to the first tremor of love in an idyllic setting of pasturelands and country gardens:

> Mid the bind-grass on the plain
> that the dew makes wet as rain
> I met by chance my clear-eyed man,
> > then my
> > joy began.[2]

There are human misfortunes to complain of, and much talk of millet and rice, mulberry leaves, and the farmer's year. But after the hard work is over, there always seems to be a bountiful harvest, with country music and baskets full of food:

> . . . guests to feasting
> strike lute and blow
> pipes to show how
> feasts were in Chou [Zhou]
> > drum up that basket-lid now.[3]

Like Huangdi's soldiers in clay, these lines present an idealized version of ancient Chinese reality—but a salutary reminder too of the good times that, though perhaps rarer than the songs allow, were nonetheless a part of life in old China.

THE SAGES: THE TEACHINGS OF CONFUCIUS

There is a golden glow over this earliest epoch of Chinese history, especially as it was imagined by cultured Chinese of later ages. But that glow did not stem primarily from the deepening patina of Shang bronzes or the freshness of the folk songs of Zhou. The greatest glory of that antique age was the wisdom of its philosophers.

Nothing undercuts the stereotyped Western image of the mysterious East more sharply than Chinese philosophy. To plunge into the writings of these Chinese sages after an immersion in the religious teaching of ancient India, for example, is to move from one world of discourse into another. It is to move from mysticism to humanism, from metaphysical to social thought, even—dismayingly—from a longing for the infinite to a pious emphasis on good manners. It can be a disturbing experience; for a Westerner hungering for mystical insights, it can even be a bit of a letdown.

It should not be. The sages of China, like the philosophers of Greece, were concerned above all with *human* relations, with life in the world of living, breathing men and women. Considering how human affairs have commonly been managed down the centuries, this was surely no ignoble concern.

The sages and schools of the period between the sixth and the third centuries B.C. left a mark on the mind of China that no subsequent school of thought could match. They laid down the terms, defined their issues, fixed the categories for thought among their people for the next twenty-five hundred years. And the first and greatest of them, at least in the admiring eyes of later generations, was Kongfuzi—"Master Kong"—known to the West by the Latinized name of Confucius.

Confucius, the first of the Zhou sages, was born in what is now Shandong province in northeastern China, apparently in humble circumstances, though of aristocratic descent. He became one of the gentlemanly seekers after posts of authority at the courts of the kings of the later Zhou. Failing in this quest, he fell back upon teaching. Like Socrates and Jesus, he does not seem to have written anything himself, but his discussions with his students

---

[2]Cyril Birch and Donald Keene, *Anthology of Chinese Literature from Early Times to the Fourteenth Century* (New York: Grove Press, 1965), p. 8.

[3]Ibid., p. 12.

were preserved in the collection called the *Analects*. Respected in his own day, he was to be China's most honored sage in later centuries.

There is a deceptively conventional sound to many of Confucius's teachings. He earnestly urged such commonplaces of his day as respect for one's social superiors, reverence for one's elders and ancestors, pious observation of traditional religious rites, and formal courtesy. Unexciting ideas, perhaps too hierarchical for our democratic taste. Yet these principles would for many centuries help the Chinese people to live together in an increasingly crowded land where classes, generations, and ideas jostled one another for living space.

But Confucius had more startling things to say to his contemporaries. In a land where petty wars were more the rule than the exception, he was a pacifist. In a society still dominated by an arrogant hereditary aristocracy, he declared that the true gentleman was the man of wisdom and virtue, whatever his social origin. And in a Middle Kingdom ravaged by official exploitation, Confucius insisted that the care of the people should be the primary concern of their rulers.

It was an idealistic message, but ideals do sometimes have an impact on real life, at least in the long run. The finest of Chinese officials—the scholarly bureaucrats of later ages—would heed his message. And the people of China would have cause for gratitude for many centuries to come.

THE HUNDRED FLOWERS

In his own time, however, Master Kong was only one of several generations of sages who preached influential social philosophies to troubled times. There were sages on all the roads of China in Confucius's day. The later Zhou period, for all its social and political misfortunes, was hailed in later centuries as the age of the "hundred schools" of thought, the time when a "hundred flowers" of wisdom bloomed across the Middle Kingdom.

Mencius, a Confucianist who lived a couple of generations after Confucius, was a philosophic optimist. Mencius declared that human nature is fundamentally good, all appearances to the contrary. He urged self-perfection, the cultivation of virtue through study directed at bringing out our innate capacity for human decency. He was a political utopian as well, proposing the redivision of the land of China on a basis of eight parts for the people, one for the king. The voice of the people, he pointed out, is the real voice of the gods, since it is they who will finally decide by their actions whether a ruler possesses the Mandate of Heaven or not. There were enough rebellions in China's history to give this last point more of a realistic edge than some of Mencius's other ideas.

Han Faizi and the Legalists, or School of Law, declared by contrast that human nature is basically selfish and undisciplined. To govern such people required rigorous laws rigorously applied, as in the authoritarian state of Qin. "A 'tender mother,'" said Han Faizi, "has spoiled the children!" There is a grimly Machiavellian ring to maxims like "When a sage governs the state, he does not count on the people to do what is beneficial to him. Instead, he sees to it that [they] can do him no harm."[4] Ironically, this most celebrated of Legalist sages died in the dungeons of the Qin, according to tradition imprisoned and compelled to commit suicide by his most illustrious pupil—the First Emperor's legalist chief minister, Li Si.

Perhaps the most influential of all the hundred flowers to bloom after Confucius's day, however, was a school that was more a religion than a philosophy. It was a mystical view of the human condition whose founder may himself have been a myth.

The name Laozi, the legendary founder of Daoism (Taoism) means simply "Old Master." According to tradition, he was a sage of Confucius's own day, a keeper of the archives in the state of Zhou. Confucius once met him, so the story goes, and later told his pupils that he had seen that day a being that was neither fish nor fowl—but a dragon. At the end of his life Laozi, seeing Zhou China collapsing around him, left by the western gate and disappeared, leaving behind him only one short book, the *Daodejing (Tao Te Ching, The Classic of Virtue and the Way)*—the most commented upon and most widely translated of all the Chinese classics. That the book dates from the fourth century and not the Confucian sixth, and was almost certainly the work of several hands rather than the legendary Laozi, does not detract from its vast influence.

Dao means *the Way*—but what the Way means is a mystery wrapped in an enigma. The Way is the way of virtue; it is the way of nature. And it is something more. It is the ultimate ground of all being, the way things work, the way things are.

Virtue for many Daoists was to do nothing at all but relax and get in tune with the universe, with nature and the ultimate. Confucianists and Legalists argued incessantly, labored interminably to change things. Daoists tended to feel that the best society was a simple preliterate life synchronized with the rhythms of nature, and they would rather go fishing than argue about it.

Chinese hermits, nature poets, and landscape painters or later centuries would all practice in their various ways this philosophy of simplicity, acceptance, and harmony with the larger natural forces of the universe. Pressed to define the Way, the philosophical Daoist could only join the muted chorus of mystics down the ages in asserting that

> those who know do not talk
> and talkers do not know.[5]

---

[4]Han Fei Tzu [Faizi], *The Complete Works,* vol. 2, trans. W. K. Liao (London: A. Probsthain, 1959), pp. 306–307.

[5]Lao Tzu [Laozi], *The Way of Life,* trans. R. B. Blakney (New York: The New American Library, 1955), p. 109.

SUMMARY

Under its first three historic dynasties (1500–200 B.C.), China laid the foundations for what became, under the house of Qin, the largest unified nation in the world.

Shang China (1500–1000 B.C.) was really a collection of separate states in the valley of the Huanghe and neighboring regions. China's peasant masses and warlike aristocracy gave only nominal allegiance to the king of Shang. Their unity was that of a common culture—shared skills from bronze working to silk manufacture, ancestor worship, and reverence for the same pantheon of gods and goddesses.

The Zhou dynasty (1000–221 B.C.), a clan of border lords from the rugged northwest, conquered Shang China in the eleventh century. Their claim that they had the Mandate of Heaven helped them to govern in a loose feudal fashion longer than any other royal house.

It was the short-lived Qin dynasty (221–206 B.C.), however, that first imposed a centralized imperial order on all the Chinese states. Under the hard-driving First Emperor Huangdi, China was unified militarily, politically, and economically. Even the forms of Chinese written characters and the lengths of cart axles were officially prescribed. Among his many accomplishments, Huangdi linked the nation's northern defenses against nomadic invasion in the Great Wall of China.

Shang bronzes, the sculptured metal dragons of Zhou times, and the astonishing life-size clay soldiers from Huangdi's tomb are marvelous artistic achievements. The poetry of the *Book of Songs* has been beloved in China for more than two thousand years. But China's major contribution to world culture during these early centuries was the practical and humanistic philosophy of her sages.

The philosophers of the later Zhou period, around 500 B.C., played a central part in Chinese cultural tradition. Confucius's call for good government and human decency would echo down the Chinese centuries. So would Mencius's faith in human virtue and self-improvement, the Legalist's demand for rigor and justice, and the gentle urgings of Laozi to follow "the Way" of nature, goodness, and the cosmos.

SUGGESTED READING

ALLAN, S. *The Shape of the Turtle: Myth, Art, and Cosmos in Early China*. Albany: State University of New York Press, 1991. Intriguing analysis of Shang beliefs and art.

CHANG, K. *Shang Civilization*. New Haven, Conn.: Yale University Press, 1980. Archaeological approach; excellent on social structure and material culture. See also K. C. CHANG, ed., *Studies of Shang Archaeology: Selected Papers . . . on Shang Civilization* (New Haven, Conn.: Yale University Press, 1986), a collection of cutting-edge studies of the earliest known Chinese culture.

CHANG, K. C. *Early Chinese Civilization*. Cambridge, Mass.: Harvard University Press, 1976. Anthropological essays. See also his *The archaeology of Ancient China* (New Haven: Yale University Press, 1986), covering both prehistory and the early dynasties.

CONFUCIUS. *The Analects of Confucius*, trans. A. Waley. London G. Allen and Unwin, 1938. For a popular introduction to the man and his influence, see D. H. Smith, *Confucius* (New York: Scribner, 1973). Two valuable recent studies are R. L. Taylor, *The Religious Dimension of Confucianism* (Albany: State University of New York Press, 1990), and

W. M. Tu, *Way, Learning, and Politics: Essays on the Confucian Intellectual* (Albany: State University of New York Press, 1993).

COTTERELL, A. *The First Emperor of China*. Harmondsworth, U.K.: Penguin, 1989. Readable life of the Shi Huangdi.

FAIRBANK, J. K., E. D. Reischauer, and E. M. CRAIG. *East Asia: Tradition and Transformation*. Cambridge, Mass.: Harvard University Press, 1973. Especially good on political and economic developments. For culture and the arts, see C. Schirokauer, *A Brief History of Chinese and Japanese Civilizations* (New York: Harcourt Brace, 1978), and A. Cotterell, *China: A Cultural History* (New York: New American Library, 1988).

HSIAO, K. *A History of Chinese Political Thought from the Beginnings to the Sixth Century A.D.*, trans. F. W. Mote. Princeton, N.J.: Princeton University Press, 1978. An important contribution to our understanding. See also E. D. Thomas, *Chinese Political Thought: A Study Based on the Principal Thinkers of the Chou Period* (New York: Greenwood Press, 1968).

HSU, C., and K. M. LINDUFF. *Western Chou Civilization*. New Haven: Yale University Press, 1988. Solid overview of early Zhou times. See also Hsu's *Ancient China in Transition: An Analysis of Social Mobility, 722–222 B.C.* (Stanford, Calif.: Stanford University Press, 1965).

LAO-TZU. *Tao te ching*, trans. M. La Farge. Albany: State University of New York Press, 1992. Translation and commentary on the classic of Daoism. For the ongoing influence of Daoism, see J. Lagerway, *Taoist Ritual in Chinese Society and History* (New York: Macmillan, 1987).

LI, H. C. *Eastern Zhou and Qin Civilization*, trans. K. C. Chang. New Haven, Conn.: Yale University Press, 1985. Emphasizes the emergence of centralized imperial government in a feudal world. See also H. G. Creel, *The Origins of Statecraft in China* (Chicago: University of Chicago Press, 1970) on government under the Zhou dynasty.

LI, Y.-N. *Chinese Women Through Chinese Eyes*. Armonk, N.Y.: W. E. Sharpe, 1992. Chinese essays, including studies of ancient China.

MOTE, F. *Intellectual Foundations of China*. New York: Knopf, 1971. A brief but penetrating study of the early Chinese philosophers.

RAWSON, *Ancient China: Art and Archaeology*. New York: HarperCollins, 1980. Artistic achievements of the early dynasties.

SCHWARTZ, B. I. *The World of Thought in Ancient China*. Cambridge, Mass: Harvard University Press, 1986. A learned survey of Chinese thought through the second century B.C., making illuminating comparisons with other cultures.

WATSON, B. *Early Chinese Literature*. New York: Columbia University Press, 1962. Highly praised account covering the entire period dealt with here.

WILLIER, R. "Confucian Ideal of Womanhood," *Journal of the China Society*, 13 (1976). An apologia for the Confucian view of women.

WITTFOGEL, K. A. *Agriculture: A Key to the Understanding of Chinese Society Past and Present*. Canberra: Australian National University Press, 1970. Application of the hydraulic-society thesis to the origins of Chinese government and to its amazing longevity.

WALDRON, A. *The Great Wall of China: From History to Myth*. New York: Cambridge University Press, 1989. Carefully researched history of the wall, debunking many myths.

CHAPTER 8

THE OLMECS AND CHAVÍN CULTURE

THE FIRST NORTH AMERICANS

THE AMERICAS BEFORE COLUMBUS

From the beginning, most of the main centers of civilization scattered over the three continents of the Old World were linked by filaments of communication. Tiny ships and straggling caravans connected Mesopotamia with Egypt and even India, bound southern Europe to northern Africa. In its earliest centuries China may have stood largely outside this continental connection, but it too would soon be part of the modest network of trade and travel. Goods, crafts, religions and other ideas thus passed from one center of Old World culture to another, fertilizing and stimulating the growth of civilization.

In the two continents of the New World, things seem to have been different. In North and South America and the narrow isthmus of Central America between, civilization also emerged. But it did so essentially in isolation. The New World was severed from the Old by two of the world's most formidable ocean barriers. And the two primary American cultural centers seem to have taken shape with almost no contact between them. If China grew in splendid isolation on the far edge of Eurasia, the Native American civilizations of the New World developed completely alone beyond the Ocean Sea.

The geographical factor is thus particularly deserving of attention here. Pablo Neruda, the Chilean poet, evokes it vividly in his memoirs of his Latin American childhood:

> Under the volcanoes, beside the snow-capped mountains, among the huge lakes, the fragrant, the silent, the tangled Chilean forest . . . I pass through a forest of ferns much taller than I am . . . a butterfly goes past, bright as a lemon, dancing between the water and the sunlight. . . .
>
> Anyone who hasn't been in the Chilean forest doesn't know this planet.[1]

It is a world as exotic in its way as the Sahara or the high Pamirs, and as crucial in shaping the history of its people.

The geography of the Americas is of course familiar in broad outline to all Americans; we have seen the globe turned our way all our lives. We have some notion of the mountainous spine that runs down the western side of the new World, the Rockies and the Andes. We know about the great plains and icy tundras of Canada, the plains and deserts of the western United States, and the dark forests that once covered eastern North America. We should know more than we do of the mountains and jungles of Central America and the Caribbean, of the world's largest rain forest in Brazil, of the southward-flowing pampas of Argentina, and of the howling seas and bitter winds around Cape Horn.

As recently as five centuries ago, this vast and varied sweep of continents and islands was inhabited by a single people, known through Columbus's fundamental error of geographical judgment as Indians. Among these Native Americans, a series of civilizations had arisen long before Columbus came.

These highly developed cultures emerged in two parts of the New World especially, in what are today Mexico and Peru. They are usually represented in the modern imagination by their final formulations, those that the European conquerors encountered—the Aztecs and the Incas. But civilizations far older than these flourished and faded in the Americas hundreds and even thousands of years before the coming of the conquistadores. It is with these beginnings of civilization in the New World—with the long-vanished Olmec people of Mexico and the Chavín culture of Peru—that this chapter must finally concern itself.

We will begin, however, with a look at the earlier Amerindian cultures from which these early American civilizations emerged—the food-gatherers and farmers of Stone Age America.

HUNTERS AND FARMERS

In 3500 B.C. the great hunts on the western plains of North America were already thousands of years in the past. When the first Paleolithic hunters had passed through the gap in the Canadian ice sheet into what is today the western United States, they had found a hunter's paradise of big game. Endless herds of mammoths and mastodons,

---

[1]Pablo Neruda, *Memoirs*, trans. Hardie St. Martin (New York: Farrar, Straus, and Giroux, 1977), p. 5.

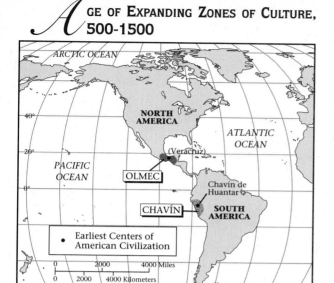

Age of Expanding Zones of Culture, 500-1500

ARCTIC OCEAN

NORTH AMERICA

ATLANTIC OCEAN

PACIFIC OCEAN

(Veracruz)

OLMEC

Chavín de Huantar

CHAVÍN

SOUTH AMERICA

• Earliest Centers of American Civilization

0   2000   4000 Miles
0   2000   4000 Kilometers
180° 160° 140° 120° 100° 80° 60° 40° 20° 0°

camels, prehistoric horses, giant bison, lion-sized cats, and many other creatures roamed the grasslands. The mongoloid hunting bands from Asia had grown fat in this Eden of raw meat on the hoof. They had also spread rapidly southward, as we have seen, occupying both continents of the New World in no more than a millennium or two.

Then things began to change.

The last ice age drew to a close. The retreat of the glacier and the resulting changes in temperature and vegetation transformed the New World environment. The warmer, drier climate substantially diminished the variety and numbers of the great herd animals of earlier times. In addition, the growing numbers and increasing skill of human hunting bands apparently led to vast overkill and the extinction of whole species. Most of the big game, the so-called megafauna of the Americas, was thus wiped out thousands of years ago.

A changing environment inevitably led to changes in the ways of life of the people who lived on the land. By the time civilization began to take shape on the faroff plains of Sumer, cultural change was also under way among the peoples of the Americas.

Diversification was the basic response of the Native Americans to their changing environment and the thinning game supply. In place of a single Paleolithic hunting culture, a variety of hunting, gathering, and Neolithic agricultural ways of life evolved up and down the linked continents of the New World.

In the farther north and south, the life of the hunting band still prevailed. The Inuit and other peoples still hunted in the arctic snows and the subarctic forests of northern Canada. In South America, hunters prowled the savannas of the Gran Chaco and on down the steppelike

pampas of Argentina. Shellfish collectors heaped up great middens (garbage dumps) of shells along the coasts of both continents, from the pacific Northwest to Patagonia. There probably already existed cultures based on desert gathering in the far western and southwestern portions of North America, exploiting small animals and vegetable food.

In the middle parts of the Americas, Neolithic agriculture developed. In the parklike forests of eastern North America, kept clear of undergrowth by regular burning, Native Americans preyed on surviving herds of deer. But they also practiced a modest woodland agriculture, perhaps including the cultivation of maize, or Indian corn. And in the forests of northeastern South America—particularly the rain forests of present-day Brazil—Neolithic peoples may have been growing manioc and other root crops this early.

In Mexico and Peru, finally, the full range of what was to be the basic American agricultural complex appeared. Maize cultivation mixed with that of squash and beans was widely in evidence by 1500 B.C. Here in the heart of the Americas, agricultural villagers ate as well as their hunting ancestors once had, and the population grew. In parts of Mexico and Peru, the villages of maize growers began to cluster around temple pyramids of earth and then stone as the Olmec and Chavín cultures slowly took shape.

REGIONAL ECONOMIES OF NORTH AMERICA

The native population of North America was once dismissed as a uniformly primitive collection of tribes. Archaeological and anthropological studies, however, have emphasized the range, diversity, and achievements of even the earliest peoples of North America.

The Native American population had come in several waves from Asia across the ice-age land bridge where the Bering Strait lies today. Ethnically, they were kin to the East Asian peoples we looked at in the last chapter. While the Chinese evolved toward greater unity, however, the mongoloid peoples of the New World diversified as they spread widely over two continents. By the time the first Europeans arrived, the Native Americans they encountered spoke hundreds of languages and had developed a wide variety of cultures.

On the great plains, the extinction of most of the American megafauna led the Indians to concentrate increasingly on one surviving species: the enormous herds of bison or buffalo that grazed from the Mississippi to the Rockies. Using spears tipped with deadly new "Fulsome points," the hunters of the plains brought down these large meat animals with growing efficiency. Once the kill was made, they also learned to dry the flesh into jerky or mix it with berries and fat to produce pemmican, both of which would keep much longer than untreated meat.

The woodland hunters of eastern North America prowled vast forests of hardwoods and pine. Like hunter-gatherers in many lands, they foraged for fruit, nuts, and roots and hunted deer and other grazing animals. They also fished the rivers and streams of eastern America, building fish traps or weirs composed of hundreds of stakes connected by tangles of brushwood.

In the North as well as on the Pacific and Atlantic coasts, early Native American peoples harvested the wealth of the sea as well as the land. In the Far North, Inuit peoples, lacking plant foods, lived entirely by hunting and fishing, killing bears, seals, and other mammals for food and clothing. In the Pacific Northwest, the Indians killed forest animals and depended heavily on the rich harvest of the salmon streams. On the Atlantic coast, Native Americans also hunted and fished. All these peoples lived in semipermanent dwellings, ranging from pit houses to tents. They also developed boats, including kayaks, birch-bark canoes, and log dugouts.

In the deserts west of the Rockies and north to the Rio Grande, finally, a surprisingly productive foraging economy took shape. Small bands of food-gatherers moved across these desert lands, killing lizards, birds, and other small game. They collected prickly pear in the lowlands, berries and nuts on the flat-topped mesas. These desert gatherers lived in caves and rock shelters, made early baskets, nets and traps, and, like most of their fellow Native Americans, chipped tools out of stone. It was to these foraging peoples of the American Southwest that agriculture would first spread up from Mexico around 2000 B.C.

HARMONY WITH NATURE

It is not easy to penetrate the minds of the hunters and gatherers who populated North America thousands of years ago. What we know or think we know must be deduced from archaeological remains or from our knowledge of their much more recent descendants.

Archaeological digs in various parts of the continent have uncovered some striking accomplishments. Most ancient Native American art was decorative, enlivening tools, weapons, or clothing. Much of it was geometrical in design, but there were also many representations of animals. Indian peoples from the northwest, for example, engraved or carved wood, bone, horn, and ivory to represent animals, birds, and whales. In the Great Lakes region, Indians cold-hammered copper into lovely ornaments as well as tools.

The religious views of these first Americans are almost entirely inferred from beliefs that survived into modern times and from parallels with preurban peoples elsewhere in the world. In North America, as in South America, Africa, and indeed, almost everywhere in early times, people had a strong sense of the oneness of nature and of the need to live in harmony with the natural world. Like animists elsewhere, early Native Americans attributed life to all things and sought only to take their fair share of nature's plenty.

Modern examples must suffice. Thus, for instance,

a twentieth-century Papago woman, digging in the Arizona earth for clay to make a pot, expressed her gratitude to the clay. "I take only what I need," she declares. "It is to cook for my children."[2] Far to the east, in the forests along the Mississippi, a Fox Indian explained his people's attitude toward the timber they used for many things:

> We do not like to harm the trees. Whenever we can, we always make an offering of tobacco to the trees before we cut them down. We never waste the wood, but use all that we cut down. If we did not think of their feelings . . . all the other trees in the forest would weep, and that would make our hearts sad too.[3]

And on the great plains, a Sioux priest expressed the total dependence of his people on the buffalo in a prayer to Wakan-Tanka, the Sacred Great One:

> Behold the buffalo, O Grandfather,
>   which you have given to us.
> He is the chief of all the four-leggeds
>   upon our sacred Mother [the Earth].
> From him the people live, and with him they
>   walked the sacred path.[4]

 # MEXICO: THE OLMECS

ORIGINS OF THE OLMECS

The geography of Mesoamerica ("Middle America"— Mexico plus Central America) is confusing at first glance. It appears to be a twisting line of mountains and lowland plains choked with tropical rain forest that winds between the continents. A cross-sectional view, however, reveals an underlying symmetry. There are frequently coastal plains on both Pacific and Caribbean shores, inland mountain walls, and, especially in Mexico, high plateaus among the mountains. Civilization developed toward the center of this three-thousand-mile isthmus, in the region that today comprises southern Mexico, Guatemala, and Honduras, in areas that included both highlands and the coastal plains.

Mexico's jungle-shrouded Yucatán Peninsula, home of the Maya, and the fertile Mexican plateau called the Mesa Central, the center of the Aztec Empire, are the sites of the most famous Mesoamerican civilizations. But they were not the oldest.

[2]Ruth M. Underhill, *Red Man's Religion: Beliefs and Practices of the Indians North of Mexico* (Chicago: University of Chicago Press, 1965), p. 116.
[3]Ibid.
[4]Ibid., p. 126.

America's first civilization emerged in southern Mexico between 1500 and 400 B.C. It did not develop in the highlands, as the more celebrated cultures of the Aztecs and the Peruvian Incas did, but on the coastal lowlands around present-day Veracruz. This oldest American civilization is called Olmec culture, after the Aztec name for the tribes who lived there at the time of the Spanish conquest. We have no idea what the people who created that ancient civilization called themselves.

We know that much of the Old World pattern of cultural evolution was duplicated in Mesoamerica. We have stone tools left by hunter-gatherers who drifted south twenty thousand years ago. We have archaeological remains of the villages of their Neolithic descendants in Mexico, settled village-dwellers who were making the delicate transition from foraging to agriculture. We know that the population grew, here as elsewhere, until it reached numbers sufficient to produce more complex forms of social organization.

OLMEC CULTURE

And then, out of the mists of the second millennium before Christ, the high culture of the Olmecs rises before the astonished gaze of the seeker after civilization's beginnings.

The head is nine feet high, carved from solid stone, and weighs perhaps fifteen tons. It stands on the grass,

An Olmec head. The realistic modeling was rare in pre-Columbian American art. Some have suggested that the features look more African than Native American, seeing in this resemblance evidence of an African presence in the New World 2400 years ago. Other experts believe that the flattened nose and ears may have been carved this way to avoid breakage when the sculptured heads were drawn overland from the deposits of basaltic rock where they were carved to the Olmec ceremonial center where they were displayed. (Museo Nacional de Anthropologica)

bodiless, neckless, wearing a round, close-fitting helmet, staring back at you. This is not some Easter Island primitive, but a startlingly realistic face. It is one of a number of similar monumental heads unearthed so far, carved by the Olmec Indians while Greece still languished in its dark age and before Rome existed.

The famous Olmec heads are only part of a growing archaeological treasure of sculpture and architecture, all clearly linked by the Olmec style, the best of it radio-carbon-dated between 800 and 400 B.C. Most of the finds are clustered in such tropical lowland sites on the Caribbean shore of Mexico as La Venta, in the Veracruz region. These sites include ruins that clearly point ahead to Maya and Aztec culture. And they have yielded up artifacts that would not be bettered by these later civilizations—that would not in fact be matched by them, for their realistic mode was developed by the Olmecs alone in Middle America.

La Venta and similar sites are usually described not as true cities but as ceremonial centers for the surrounding villages. Typical architectural finds include large pyramidal earthern mounds, precursors of the stone pyramids of the Mayans and Aztecs. There are also engraved stone altars, stelae, and sarcophagi. Such complexes are quite large and must have required the labor of all the surrounding peoples to build.

Besides the great carved heads there are smaller heads and figurines in clay, jade, serpentine, and other stone. Some of these are masks, as lifelike as the great heads, or perhaps even idealized portraits. Some are either infants or dwarfs, the latter freighted with supernatural significance for Mesoamerican Indians. There are life-size clay "tomb watchers," some of them sinister enough to suit their grim task admirably.

The most common motif of all, however, is that of the jaguar, which was probably a rain god, and the strangest of these are the half-human, half-cat werejaguars. So pervasive is this feline presence that one authority has called his study of the Olmecs simply *The Jaguar's Children*. Were-jaguars in the form of children are a particularly common—and startling—form of this sculptural type. We do not know what a smoothly sculptured, soft-fleshed infant with jaguar claws on its little hands and jaguar teeth just showing between softly parted baby lips may have meant to the ancient people of Mesoamerica. But we can be properly terrified ourselves.

OLMEC SOCIETY

What then can we say with any confidence about the builders of Olmec culture?

Much more can be deduced with some certainty about socioeconomic and even intellectual achievements than about the precise political organization or history of the Olmec people. Olmec culture seems to emerge full-blown on the Mesoamerican scene; there is little evidence of the slow development we would expect. It ends as suddenly, around 400 B.C., when the great complex at La Venta apparently expired in violence. Whether it was a rebellion against priestly overlords or an invasion by less developed peoples we do not know.

What political structure the Olmecs had, or whether any large political unit existed at all, also remains controversial. Some archaeologists have suggested than an Olmec empire, headed perhaps by priests or warlike traders, linked the Veracruz centers with more distant Olmec-influenced areas as far away as central Mexico and even Guatemala. Others have postulated the spread of a new religion centering in the worship of the jaguar god, or the simple exchange of Olmec goods in distant parts of Middle America.

More can be said about the economic aspects of Olmec life. Most Olmecs, to begin with, seem to have lived in pole-and-thatch houses in the tropical lowlands along the Caribbean, or in adobe-and-stone huts on the highland fringes. They grew maize and beans and other vegetables and wore clothing made of cotton and maguey. They made clay pots and small figurines by hand.

Social classes higher than peasant agriculturists are also indicated. Priests ran great ritual centers like La Venta. Richly furnished tombs indicate an aristocratic elite, as does the depiction at one site of a man kneeling before another, a much more gorgeously clad person. Farmers, artisans, priests, and perhaps nobility, then, existed in the Olmec world.

Something more, finally, can be said about the highest expressions of the culture. The religion of the Olmecs was evidently of primary importance to them; no palace ruins have been found, only the remains of temples. Their cults very probably included sky gods and earth gods, a female fertility goddess, the jaguar divinity, and the strange jaguar people who were perhaps that rain god's human representatives. Gods are also shown in bas relief hovering over clubwielding soldiers locked in combat, indicating that war too had its divine patrons in this oldest of Middle American civilizations.

 # PERU: CHAVÍN CULTURE

ORIGINS OF THE CHAVÍN CULTURE

The condor is the largest of all flying birds. Balancing on ten-foot wings, it cruises above the longest mountain range in the world, from Patagonia in the far south to the peaks that loom above the Amazon. It is an ugly bird close up, vulture-headed and ungainly on the ground. But riding on the icy winds that whistle among the crags, it is the sovereign of the Andes skies.

A condor's-eye view of the Peruvian Andes, where civilization first appeared in South America, would reveal a rather simpler topography than the tangled mountains and jungles of Mesoamerica. To the east of the north–south mountain chain, the jungles of the Amazon basin flow eastward beneath mist and rolling clouds two thousand miles to the Atlantic. To the west the Andean foothills descend to a narrow strip of desert between the mountains and the Pacific shore. Rain is rare, but river valleys carve their way through the arid land to the ocean. The mountainous highlands are much less fertile than the high plateaus of Mexico. Maize will not grow there naturally, though flocks may be grazed on the slopes.

Tropical jungles, forbidding heights, and a strip of rock and sand along the sea—it seems an unlikely area for civilization to emerge in. But that is precisely what happened on the western slopes of the Peruvian Andes and the arid Pacific coastlands early in the first millennium B.C.

In the end, civilized societies were to evolve over a large part of the central Andean region of South America, including portions of what are today Peru, Bolivia, Ecuador, and northern Chile and Argentina. But it began with the Chavín culture of Peru, named for the highlands site of Chavín de Huantar and usually dated between 800 and 400 B.C. Like Olmec culture in Mexico, Chavín culture was to spread widely and to be hailed by later archaeologists as a mother culture for the entire region.

The cruising condor probably paid no particular attention to the first people to appear in Peru, filtering southward through the Andean gorges perhaps twenty thousand years ago. These Paleolithic people hunted deer and llamas in the mountains and hauled in huge catches of fish along the shore. Within ten or twelve thousand years, they had settled into the universal Neolithic village. Soon they were raising potatoes and herding woolly llamas and alpacas in the highlands, growing cotton and making fishnets on the coast. They learned, probably as late as the second millennium B.C., to make ceramic pottery and to grow maize.

Maize cultivation required elaborate irrigation and terracing procedures, and these soon appeared in both the dry coastal valleys and the highlands. Regional exchange also developed, with potatoes, meat, and wool flowing down the mountains, and maize and cotton coming up from the lowlands.

Then, early in the first millennium B.C., Chavín culture happened.

RUINS IN THE ANDES

Chavín de Huantar is not the center of the culture that is named for it. Indeed, Chavín culture seems to have had no single center. But the Chavín site, almost 9000 feet up in the Cordillera Blanca of northern Peru, is a splendid example of the style that would impose itself on much of the central Andes over succeeding centuries.

This extremely old temple complex of truncated pyramids, plazas, and raised platforms impressed the con-

quistadores in the sixteenth century and continues to impress archaeologists in the twentieth. Perhaps the best brief description is still that of a Spanish chronicler who was closer to the living reality than we are. The temple at Chavín de Huantar, wrote Vasquez de Espinosa, was "a large building of huge stone blocks, very well wrought . . . one of the most famous heathen sanctuaries, like Rome or Jerusalem with us." The Indians, he said, "used to come and make their offerings and sacrifices, for the Devil pronounced many oracles from here, and so they repaired here from all over the kingdom."[5] That was written in the days of the Inca Empire; two millennia before, there was very probably no "kingdom." But the ceremonial center was there, and flourishing.

From the battered walls and chambers of dry stone-masonry that remain, here and elsewhere, a lost way of life may still be reconstructed today.

Agricultural terracing had become extremely elaborate by the first millennium B.C., and the multilevel stone terraces followed many winding rivers through the mountains and down to the sea. Large numbers of disciplined workers labored on the temple complexes. Cotton textiles and ceramics still flourished on the coast, where the temples tended to be built of sundried adobe brick instead of stone. In the uplands, the llama and the alpaca provided meat, wool, and the beast of burden that was so notably lacking elsewhere in the Americas. Trade was well established between regions in Peru, and pilgrims may have threaded the mountain trails to cult centers like Chavín de Huantar, where organized priesthoods served as intermediaries between native American people and their gods.

CHAVÍN RELIGION AND ART

Beyond such concrete details, however, early Peruvian society, even more than that of Mexico, is generally the object of speculation or dispute. Was there a Chavín polity, an empire coextensive with the reach of the culture? It seems extremely unlikely, given the broken country and the size and resources of the population. How then, was that culture disseminated over so wide an area of the central Andes? Opinion inclines to a spreading religious cult that perhaps included a feline god like the Olmec jaguar. It has recently been suggested that the new religion spread together with a new form of maize, which provided the caloric intake to support larger populations and a more diversified society of specialists.

As with Olmec culture, finally, art and religion are the heart of what we know or guess about Chavín.

Chavín religion, like that of the Olmecs, probably involved nature and animal divinities, gods of earth and air and water, and deities who manifested themselves pri-

[5]George Bankes, *Peru before Pizarro* (New York: Phaidon Press/E. P. Dutton, 1977), pp. 132–133.

More typical of ancient American art than the realistic Olmec heads is this heavily stylized puma from the Chavín culture of South America. Restlessly detailed, almost geometric designs animate this hard stone carving. Yet there is a cat-like feel, a recognizably feline curve of the tail and set of the ears. Many Peruvian villages revered the great cats as divinities, yet there remains a strong sense of observed reality behind this stylized representation. (The University Museum, University of Pennsylvania)

marily as great cats with snaky hair and monstrous fangs. Sacrifice was also important; one gallery at Chavín de Huantar is heaped with the bones of sacrificial beasts and with fragments of exquisite ceramic ritual vessels. Goods found buried with the dead indicate some hope for an afterlife. Beyond such basic guesses we can know little about the rites, myths, and theologies of the people in the long fringed shirts and simple loincloths who came down the mountain paths to the temple, or of the priests who met them at the gates.

The stone itself remains, as does the ceramic ware and, on the dry coast of Peru, some remarkably preserved textiles and rudely worked gold. All tell us something of the artistic sensibilities of the people who created the Chavín culture.

Unlike the La Venta and other Olmec temples, those of Chavín de Huantar are not solid but are honeycombed with rooms and passages. The largest of them, nicknamed the Castillo (Castle), was originally a three-story structure 250 feet square. Inside, it was a maze of chambers, narrow corridors and galleries, ramps, stairways, and an intricate system of air shafts that brought the bracing air down to the lowest level. It was decorated inside and out with carved heads of eagles, cats, and other creatures—many of them, puzzlingly, native to the Amazon jungles rather than to the mountains or the coast.

These examples of Chavín sculpture look much more like the highly stylized, symbolic carving we associate with pre-Columbian America than does the preco-

cious realism of the Olmec. It is mostly flat bas-relief on stone, though there are some decorative heads, human and animal, protruding from the exteriors of the more elaborate temples. It is as hard to see the falcons in the symmetrical lines and curves and scrolls of a low relief at Chavín de Huantar as it is to pick out the animal masks in a Shang bronze. But the space is as full of restless movement, and the sense of design is as strong in America as it is in the first Chinese culture five hundred or a thousand years before.

Distinctive "stirrup-spout" pottery, woven cloth with painted designs and representations of the cat god, gold beaten into sheets and worked by technique of *repoussage* into the familiar snarling feline face—all reveal the presence of the common culture we call Chavín.

Then as now, the mountains changed color in the sunset, the wind cried among the peaks, and the big bird floated on the wind. From the height of the drifting condor, the changes in the world below could not have looked like much. Stone terraces along the rivers, temples in isolated valleys or on far coastlines, perhaps larger clusters of dry-stone or wattle-and-daub huts here and there. But in the large cult centers, in the restless patterning of stone and clay and cloth, in the cat god and the unknown prayers of Chavín people, there was something new in the Andean world. There was a shared spirit, a common culture, a beginning of a pan-Andean civilization before any documentable political union had yet emerged on the wrinkled land below.

SUMMARY

The ancient history of the Americas is hard to recover because of the lack of written sources of information. With the help of archaeology and other disciplines, however, it is possible to reconstruct the early societies of the New World.

The earliest Native American peoples to cross the land bridge from East Asia settled in America north of the Rio Grande. There they passed through an evolution comparable to that of the Old World. After thousands of years as hunters and gatherers, they moved toward the settled life of predominantly agricultural villages. The shift toward villages and crops began in the desert Southwest and the eastern woodlands.

The larger Indian populations living south of the Rio Grande moved still further from their food-gathering beginnings. The mother cultures of Middle and South America were those of the Olmecs and the Chavín, both of which flourished during the first millennium B.C.

Olmec culture, which produced the famous giant stone Olmec heads, developed on the Caribbean coast of Mexico around modern Veracruz. Sites like La Venta were probably religious ceremonial centers rather than cities. But the structured society and uniquely naturalistic art of the Olmecs indicate a culture that had passed well beyond village agriculture.

The Peruvian culture named for the elaborate stone temples at Chavín de Huantar was also socially complex. Elaborately terraced fields and large stone structures reveal an impressive material culture. As with the Olmecs, however, there is no evidence of centralized political institutions.

SUGGESTED READING

BENSON, E. P., ed. *Proceedings, Dumbarton Oaks Conference on the Olmec*. Washington, D.C.: Dumbarton Oaks, 1968. Widely cited collection of papers.

BERNAL, I. *The Olmec World*, trans. D. Heyden and F. Forcasitas. Berkeley: University of California Press, 1969. A good summary of ancient Mexico's mother culture.

COE, M. *The Jaguar's Children*. New York: Museum of Primitive Art, 1965. Authoritative presentation of Olmec culture and the problems of interpreting it.

GILL, S. *Native American Religions: An Introduction*. Belmont, Calif.: Wadsworth Publications, 1982. Insightful study with good examples.

HURT, R. D. *Indian Agriculture in America: Prehistory to the Present*. Lawrence, KA: University of Kansas Press, 1987. Includes some emphasis on pre-Columbian agriculture.

JENNINGS, J. D. *Prehistory of North America*, 2nd ed. New York: McGraw-Hill, 1974. By a recognized authority.

KATZ, F. *The Ancient American Civilizations*. New York: Praeger, 1972. Perhaps the best general survey, including sections on both Olmec and Chavín cultures.

LANNING, E. P. *Peru before the Incas*. Englewood Cliffs, N.J.: Prentice Hall, 1967. A widely cited survey of archaeological studies of the ancient cultures of the Andean zone, including the Chavín mother culture of that region.

LEACOCK, E. B., and N. O. LURIE, eds. *North American Indians in Historical Perspective*. New York: Random House, 1971. Gives more attention to historical change among early Native American peoples than many do.

MASON, J. A. *The Ancient Civilizations of Peru*. Baltimore: Penguin Books, 1957. Includes material on Chavín culture.

MEGGERS, B. J. *Prehistoric America: An Ecological Perspective*, 2nd ed. New York: Aldine, 1979. Culture and environment in the New World; all levels of cultural development.

ROWE, J. H. *Chavín Art: An Inquiry into Its Form and Meaning*. New York: Museum of Primitive Art, 1962. A controversial explanation for traditional Chavín forms and motifs.

SNOW, D. *The Archaeology of North America*. New York: Viking, 1980. Overview.

WICKE, C. *Olmec*. Tucson: University of Arizona Press, 1971. Comparatively recent view, part of the continuing fascination with the oldest Mexican civilization.

CHAPTER 9

THE GREEK CITY-STATES

Minoans and Mycenaeans

Mountains and the Sea

> The mountain looks on Marathon—
>   And Marathon looks on the sea;
> And musing there an hour alone,
>   I dream'd that Greece might still be free.[1]

Lord Byron's famous lines tell us as much about Greek geography as they do about the continuing Greek dream of freedom. Greece *is* mountains and the sea. Greece is a jagged peninsula protruding some 350 miles southward from the Balkans into the Mediterranean, the central sea of European ancient history. The land of the Hellenes, as the Greeks called themselves, was all mountains and narrow valleys, capes, blue bays, strings and clusters of rocky islands—a place very different from the vast continental expanses of China and India, or the inward-looking Near Eastern river valleys of Mesopotamia and Egypt.

Greek civilization—the first of European civilizations—thus developed in a naturally fragmented little world. Each mainland city-state was walled off by mountains from its neighbors. Many Greeks, furthermore, lived on islands in the Aegean or in colonies along the nearby coasts of Asia Minor (Turkey today), isolated by the sea from their fellow Hellenes. Where the huge landmasses of India and China were cut off from other cultures by natural frontiers, the tiny world of Greece was, geographically speaking, divided against itself.

Much about Greek history is at least partially explainable in terms of this basic geography. Most obvious, perhaps, Greek culture was a seaborne one from the beginning. The first of European civilizations flourished on the Greek island of Crete, and the Greeks of later centuries were great traders, colonists, and sea fighters. The wanderings of the mythic hero Odysseus are the wanderings of his people, restless seafarers from Homer's day to our own.

The institutions of the Greek city-states, taking shape in isolated valleys, on islands, or in colonies along the coasts of other peoples' countries, were also influenced by this geographical fragmentation. The passionate sense of independence that was the glory and the downfall of the Greeks emerged quite naturally in this divided land. Fiercely independent toward other nationalities and even other Hellenes, the Greeks also developed a powerful sense of loyalty to their own isolated communities. The loyalty to the *polis*—the Greek city-state—was the loyalty of people who knew each other well and saw others only as outlanders, intruders in their own little world of mountains and the sea.

The great gods dwelt on Mount Olympus, but the "wine-dark sea" of Homer's poetry was the element where Greeks were most at home. The mountains divided them and made them love their homes. The sea made them rich and powerful. They were as much a part and product of their world as Arabs in their desert solitudes, or Polynesians on the far Pacific.

As much a part of it and much more.

The Minoan Sea Kings

We know very little about the first people to drift into this sunny, sea-washed world of gray rock and gray-green islands. We believe that they filtered in from Asia Minor as early as 3000 B.C., while pyramids were rising in Egypt and ziggurats in Mesopotamia. But it would be a dozen centuries before these seagoing people built anything comparable to the towering monuments of the Near East among the Greek islands.

By about 1800 B.C., however, a great palace had been built at the city of Knossos on Crete, the largest of the islands. Around this center, a glittering seaborne civilization briefly flourished. Minoan culture, named for the mythical King Minos, was not the work of Greek-speaking people. But there were Greeks living among them, and down the centuries some aspects of Minoan culture passed from them to the glorious fifth-century Greece of Pericles.

The civilization of Minoan Crete and its scattering of trading posts around the Aegean were clearly built on commercial exchange. Minoans traded in Egypt and the Levant, exporting pottery and bronze, olive oil and timber, and bringing back, among other things, the scripts that we call Linear A and Linear B. Minoan culture, in turn, dominated the islands and much of the mainland of Greece.

The kings who ruled at Knossos lived in considerable splendor in the vast, labyrinthine palace excavated by archaeologists thirty-five centuries later. There were

---

[1] George Gordon, Lord Byron, "The Isles of Greece," from *Don Juan,* ed. Leslie A. Marchand (Boston: Riverside Press, 1958), p. 127.

ANCIENT GREECE

Athenian Empire, 450 B.C.

Battle sites

THRACE

Black Sea

MACEDONIA

Byzantium

Propontis (Sea of Marmora)

CHALCIDICE

Aegospotami

Mt. Olympus

EPIRUS

Troy

• Dodona

Aegean Sea

PERSIA EMPIRE

THESSALY

LESBOS

LYDIA   **PHRYGIA**

ARGINUSAE IS.

Thermopylae

ITHACA

Delphi   **EUBOEA**

CHIOS

• Sardis

Thebes

Corinth

Gulf of

Athens

SAMOS

Mycenae   Corinth

Argos

Olympia

Miletus

PELOPONNESUS

See Inset Below

DELOS

Halicarnassus

COS

Sparta

LACONIA

Ionian Sea

MELOS

THERA (SANTORIN)

RHODES

CYTHERA

Cretan Sea

CRETE

Knossos

Mediterranean Sea

PHOCIS   Chaeronea   **EUBOEA**

BOEOTIA

Delphi   Thebes   Delium

Leuctra   Plataea

Gulf of Cornith

Marathon

ATTICA

Eleusis

Megara   Athens

Piraeus

Corinth

Saronic Gulf

Mycenae   Tiryns   *AEGINA*

Mantinea   Argos

Epidaurus

Areas of Greek settlements

ALPS   **ILLYRIA**

CRIMEA   Panticapaeum

Massilia (Marseilles)

PYRENEES

Rome

ITALY

Adriatic Sea

Black Sea

Byzantium

Trebizond

IBERIA

CORSICA

Neapolis (Naples)   Paestum

SARDINIA

Apollonia

ASIA

Cadiz

Croton   **GREECE**

Strait of Gibraltar

MAGNA

Segesta   *GRAECIA*

Corinth   Athens

MINOR

IONIA

Selinus   *SICILY*

Carthage   Syracuse

MELITA

CRETE

RHODES   *CYPRUS*

PHOENICIA   **SYRIA**

Mediterranean Sea

Cyrene

AFRICA

LIBYA   **EGYPT**

This Cretan fresco painting from Knossos evokes something of the spirit of Minoan culture, court life, and probably religion. The gracefully outlined bull is flanked by "toreadors" or "bull dancers" who vaulted over the horns of the powerful beasts. Painted on a Minoan wall a thousand years before the Greek golden age, this and other murals from ancient Crete reveal a sense of grace and drama in this island trading people. (Nimatallah/Art Resource)

scribes and bureaucrats in attendance and an elegant court life. But there were few soldiers, if we are to judge from archaeological evidence: Knossos and the other port cities of the Minoans were unfortified. Nor is the political authority of the kings of Knossos likely to have extended much beyond the island of Crete itself and a few entrepôts in other parts of the eastern Mediterranean. Theirs was a network of trade, not a military or political imperium.

The religion of the Minoans seems to have focused on gods, goddesses, and myths, some of which would reappear a thousand years later in Greek mythology. Early incarnations of gray-eyed Athena and of Astarte—here a snake goddess—first emerged in this ancient Cretan pantheon. The odd Minoan cult of the sacred bull seems to have been central to the island's religion. It was celebrated by scarifying performances of "bull dancing" or "bull leaping" by naked young men and women on the backs and over the horns of the beasts themselves. The bull would reappear in grotesquely distorted form as the Minotaur of Greek legend.

Life at the center of this small island world, the friv-

olous, fragile, lovely court life of the Minoan sea kings, comes vividly to us across the centuries in the brightly colored wall paintings of the royal palace at Knossos. In these murals, bare-breasted, bejeweled court ladies stroll in gardens full of flowers, and bronzed youths lift goblets of Cretan wine to a future that must have seemed as unlimited to them as our own does to us—and as pleasant as the life of any civilization we know.

The end seems to have come swiftly. They lived, traded, and danced on the horns of bulls for a few short centuries: the standard dating of Middle Minoan, the heyday of Cretan civilization, is from 2200 to 1500 B.C. Then they vanished, swept away in a series of catastrophes perhaps partially the work of nature—earthquakes and volcanic eruptions have been suggested—but almost surely in part the work of humans. The first Greeks lived among them and learned to read and write and worship their gods. But other Greeks came later, perhaps around 1500 B.C., from the mainland city of Mycenae, bringing fire and sword.

Minoan Crete glows like ancient amber for us today,

one of the happiest of the lost worlds of the early days of civilization. There seems to have been nothing before it in this part of the world, and very little for many slow centuries after it, to dim its aura. If the Greeks had a model in mind for their legendary golden age, it was surely Minoan Crete.

THE MYCENAEANS: LORDS OF THE LION GATE

To hurrying travellers or browsers in Greek art books, Mycenae is the Lion Gate and the death mask of Agamemnon. The gate is real enough, with its rough-hewn lions of pitted stone. The death mask is real too, carved of thin gold, its lowered eyelids, beard, and mustache clearly if conventionally incised in the ancient metal—though the attribution to the Homeric King Agamemnon is purely traditional. But the world these artifacts represent is sunk in myth and legend even more deeply than Minoan Crete.

The Mycenaeans were part of the great wave of migrating barbarian conquerors who intruded upon most of the main Eurasian enclaves of civilization during the second millennium B.C. These so-called Indo-Europeans—"tamers of horses" as Homer called them, chariot fighters, speakers of the lost tongue that would father all the major languages of Europe—constituted one of the most terrible of all barbarian onslaughts on civilization. In Minoan Crete as in Harappan India, the destructive force

The rude strength of the Lion Gate at Mycenae in the southern part of Greece reflects the temper of the warrior lords who built it. Notice the post-and-lintel structure of the gate, the lintel or cross beam supporting the sculpture above. (New York Public Library Picture Collection)

of their attack left little but wreckage for future archaeologists to pick over.

But the Mycenaeans were builders too. Their political structure was probably minimal, an earlier version of the world of separate city-states that rose again centuries later in classical Greece. Yet there was a structure of authority within the typical Mycenaean city-state—rule by an independent kinglet, rather than by council and assembly as in later centuries—and some records were kept in Minoan script. Their economic life is sometimes dismissed as little more than piracy and conquest, but they were traders too, exchanging goods around the Near East as the Minoans had done, pressing in where the declining Hittites and Egyptians gave way. Mycenae was a rich city, if we are to judge by the gold unearthed from the tombs of their nobles and kings.

Most noticeable from the distance of many centuries, the Mycenaeans left their share of substantial stoneworks on the land, both on mainland Greece and on the islands. They built walled cities and stone castles to garrison the lands they conquered. They raised the Lion Gate and the beehive-shaped *tholos* tombs of Mycenae. Sometimes they built on Minoan foundations; and Greek cities would rise in turn on the sites of Mycenaean ones.

But they were warriors above all, ruling the blue seas and rocky promontories by the strength of their arms and the power of their bronze-tipped spears. Their most celebrated exploit was the great armada of ships and soldiers that descended on Troy, a wealthy Near Eastern city on the shores of the Hellespont. That famous conquest, probably undertaken by a loose confederation of warlords bent on plunder and headed by the king of Mycenae, would provide the half-legendary basis for the first great monument of Greek literature, the *Iliad* of Homer.

THE GREEK DARK AGE

After the Mycenaeans, the mists close almost totally over the life of this southeastern corner of Europe where Western civilization began. Other tribes and clans of northern barbarians followed the Mycenaeans and crushed them in their turn. For at least three centuries—from around 1100 B.C., when the city of Mycenae itself fell to new invaders, to approximately 800—a genuine dark age settled over Greece.

Wave after wave of Indo-European peoples drifted down the valleys and on to the neighboring islands and the shores of Asia Minor beyond. There were rude Dorians, who settled in the Pelopponesus and became the ancestors of the militaristic Spartans of later centuries. There were Ionians, who moved on to the islands and the Asian coast of the Aegean, where, fertilized by contact with the older civilizations of the Near East, the Greek intellect would soon kindle into life with particular vigor.

But wherever these people came during the dark centuries, they blighted what remained of the wealth and

culture of Minoan-Mycenaean times. The kings of the Mycenaeans disappeared, monumental architecture ceased, pottery grew cruder, the use of the Minoan script was forgotten. As in Harappan India, Greece's first flowering was cut off from its later glories by a centuries-long resurgence of older, simpler lifeways on the land.

It was not all dark, of course. Toward the end of this period, in the eighth century, two of the most famous of Greek poets, Homer and Hesiod, composed their works—or, more likely, sang or chanted them before gatherings of Greeks in rude halls or village squares. The more basic arts of agriculture were not forgotten; settlers old and new went on scraping a meager living out of the dry, light Mediterranean soil. The petty Mycenaean kingdoms were destroyed, but this may have been an advantage in the long run, since imperial, divine-right monarchies like those of the ancient East were thus prevented from gaining a firm foothold in Greece, leaving the way open for wider participation in government during the next age.

It is unlikely, however, that such long-range advantages were imagined by contemporaries. For the Greeks of Homer's and Hesiod's time, greatness had passed from the land, and there was little future to look forward to.

CLASSICAL GREECE

WEALTH AND COLONIES

One thing that did continue to grow during the Greek dark ages was the population. And one consequence of population growth was the spread of Greek-speaking people still further around the Mediterranean world.

Indo-European nomads from the north continued to wander down the Greek valleys. Sometimes they dislodged their predecessors, forcing them to seek new homes, often over the narrow seas. Sometimes the invaders themselves continued on down to the sea and beyond. Greece itself simply could not support them. Its dry soil lay too thin over the rock to grow much grain or pasture many cattle. Many Greeks were thus driven to emigrate by pure Malthusian pressure; their numbers were pressing too hard upon the food supply. Others, especially after the revival of the city-state around 800 B.C., emigrated as traders or as mercenary soldiers.

This surge of expansion, which was especially intense from about 750 to 600 B.C., carried Greek-speaking people much further than their Mycenaean or Minoan predecessors had gone. Greek colonies were established not only on nearby islands and along the Ionian coasts of Asia Minor, but farther to the east around the Black Sea, and much farther to the west—in southern Italy and Sicily, in Libya and France, and on the coast of Spain at the far end of the Mediterranean.

The Acropolis of ancient Athens, with its white-columned temples, still rises above rocky, tree-fringed slopes. The Parthenon, dedicated to Athena, is right of center in this picture. Despite the carefully chosen angle from which this photograph was taken, the Acropolis actually sits in the center of the modern city of Athens, where the ancient stone is seriously threatened by pollution. (D. A. Harissiadis Photographic Agency, Athens)

The Greeks maintained a loose cultural unity wherever they traveled and settled. No matter how great a colony became in its own right, it tended to retain ties with the city-state that had fathered it. All Greeks spoke dialects of the same language. They worshiped the same gods and goddesses, some brought down from the north, some found among the older peoples of the eastern Mediterranean. Early on they gathered for athletic competitions in honor of their gods. Among these contests were the first Olympic games, traditionally believed to have been held as far back as 776 B.C.

Through this sea-linked network of settlements, the Greeks became the greatest traders in the classical Mediterranean. At home they produced elegant pottery, olive oil, and wine for sale overseas. From more lavishly endowed lands they brought back staples such as grain, essentials such as copper and tin and iron, and—from the Near East, for the second time—a written language. The characters were Phoenician in origin, but the language was Greek.

The earliest surviving written record of the language in which Homer had already sung and in which Plato was to write appears on a Greek pot dating from perhaps 750 B.C., the early days of the great Greek diaspora.

Well before 500 B.C., when the Greek golden age is usually said to have begun, Greeks thus swarmed over the peninsulas and islands and farther shores of the Mediterranean world. They had rediscovered trade, elegant handicrafts, and writing. And they had evolved a new form of political organization for themselves—the city-state, or *polis*. The city-state was as old as civilization, but the Greek *polis* developed in a different direction from any we have seen so far.

THE GREEK CITY-STATE

The Greek city-state of the classical period was one of the wonders of human social organization, a delicate balance that could not and did not long endure. But while it lasted, it gave some selected human beings more say in their own lives than some peoples know even today.

Physically speaking, the *polis* was two cities: a lower city, where the people lived, and an *acropolis* (high city) on a hill in the center of town, where the gods had their temples. In fact, however, the whole of the *polis* became in classical times the possession of the Greek citizenry. The all-too-human gods, glorified in white temples, were more objects of civic pride than sources of superstitious awe. The citizens owned the *polis*, and the city itself, with its unique political, social, economic, and military structure, governed and shaped the lives of its people.

The Greek-speaking invaders from the north brought with them the tribal and clan organization of the distant steppes. The typical *polis* thus took shape initially as an alliance of such tribes, governed by a council of leading families. This aristocracy, tribal in origin and now commonly including the leading landowners, sometimes tolerated a chief or petty king for a time, "a first among equals" like the kings of the ancient Mycenaeans. But real power lay with the landowners and the tribal leaders, and the last generation of Greek kings seems to have faded away without much struggle, transformed into elected magistrates or simply expiring as an institution.

In the seventh and sixth centuries, however, the aristocracy soon followed the monarchy into decline, opening the way to an astonishing degree of freedom among the Greek cities. A number of factors contributed to the decline of the aristocrats. One was the continuing growth of trade, which raised the social status of merchants as well as of farmers and potters, who produced wine, oil, and jars for overseas sale. Another cause was a radical change in military tactics, the replacement of the chariot-fighting aristocracy by a heavily armed phalanx of citizen infantry. The phalanx, composed of all who could afford the sword, spear, shield, helmet, and basic body armor of a *hoplite* (infantryman), rapidly replaced the Homeric charioteer as the backbone of Greek armies.

Land, money, and military service simply could not be excluded forever from political power. A military assembly of hoplites—the farmers, merchants, and craftsmen who could afford the weapons—was one road to political involvement for these solid citizens. Frequently also, men called "tyrants" (without the negative connotation of later times) became their spokesmen. These extralegal rulers, often former military leaders, proceeded to modify political institutions in order to strengthen their citizen-supporters. Tyrannies tended to last only a generation or two. But the citizen assemblies they fostered survived, establishing the predominance of the middle ranks in the Greek *polis*.

By the end of the sixth century B.C., these uniquely Greek versions of the city-state were scattered all over the eastern half of the Mediterranean Sea and north to the shores of the Black Sea. They were not as splendid to look at as Babylon or Patna. But they were filled with a thriving, bustling people, citizens whose simple diet, clothing, and private housing were balanced by impressive public gymnasiums, assemblies, and theaters. And when they strolled in the colonnades of the *agora* (marketplace), they were almost as likely to be talking about matters of public policy as the price of oil or wine. By 500 B.C., in fact, the *polis* was on the verge of producing the prosperous, comparatively democratic Athens of Pericles.

The famous "democracy" of the Greek city-state was of course far from democratic by any modern definition of the term. The total population of Athens and its surrounding villages in the fifth century B.C. was perhaps two hundred thousand—of whom thirty thousand were free citizens. Only native-born free adult males of a certain economic standing—hoplite material—could be citizens. The rest—women and children, slaves, resident foreigners, and the lower orders generally—had no voice in the state or any place in the philosophical conversations of thinkers like Socrates.

Nevertheless, this is still a long way from the autocratic rule of pharaohs, *rajas*, or Sons of Heaven. Greek citizens did meet in political assemblies to thrash out public policy. They did elect their own magistrates, war leaders, even a surviving electoral monarch here and there. They were citizens, not subjects. And it made a difference.

The life and culture of the Greeks were governed and shaped by the unique form the city-state took among them. Participation in politics bound the fate of the individual to that of the community. "Our constitution is named a democracy," said the celebrated Athenian leader Pericles, "because it is in the hands, not of the few, but of the many."[2] If the *demos* of ancient Greece was not as numerous or as broadly based as we would like, if slaves still toiled in the silver mines and women languished in virtual exclusion from public life, yet democracy was perhaps nearer to reality in the Greek *polis* than ever before.

THE PERSIAN WAR: MARATHON TO SALAMIS

Against this small, bustling people, the biggest empire in the western half of Eurasia came awesomely in arms at the beginning of the fifth century B.C. The Persian Empire, built by Cyrus the Great less than half a century before, stretched from the eastern Mediterranean to the banks of the Indus, from the mountains of the Caucasus to the shores of the Arabian Sea. Cyrus and his son had conquered rich Lydia, crushed ancient Babylon, overrun Mesopotamia and Egypt, and pushed their frontiers eastward to the nearest of the rivers of India. Darius I, who had inherited this vast realm in the late sixth century, was no leather-clad barbarian like Cyrus. He built roads and canals, divided his domain into twenty more or less efficiently governed satrapies, adopted the enlightened faith

---

[2]George Willis Botsford and Charles Alexander Robinson Jr., *Hellenic History,* 3rd ed. (New York: Macmillan, 1950), p. 201.

of Zoroaster, and reigned in civilized splendor from his great palaces at Persepolis and Susa.

Darius, of course, suppressed rebellion wherever it emerged among his many peoples. It was the suppression of one such insurrection, among the Greek city-states of Ionia, that triggered what the Greeks came to call the great Persian War.

The Ionian city-states of Asia Minor revolted in 499 B.C. under the leadership of the famous trading city of Miletus. Like others before them, the Milesians and their allies were crushed. But before they fell, the Ionians sent pleas for help to the Greeks of the mainland; and some small assistance was sent, most notably by the Athenians. For this act of defiance, Darius of Persia resolved to punish the mainland Greeks.

Of all the cities of the Hellenes, two were already prominent at the beginning of the fifth century: Athens, the largest and the most civilized, and Sparta, the most militaristic and most disciplined. These two were to dominate the history of that turbulent and splendid century. It was the Athenians, however, who bore the brunt of the Persian War and carried off the rewards of victory.

The first Persian punishment force drew their ships ashore at the edge of the small plain of Marathon, northeast of Athens, in 490 B.C. The mere sight of the iron-armed hosts of the Medes and the Persians, twenty thousand of them, with their royal guard of "Immortals" in the van, was enough to shake most enemies. The Athenian phalanx, outnumbered probably two to one, charged them at a dead run. The Athenian center broke, and the Persians poured through. But the Greek wings overwhelmed the Persian flanks, closed upon the Asian center, and drove the invaders in disarray back to their ships.

Retribution, however, was sure. Darius died before he could take further action, but his son Xerxes spent four years preparing a huge fleet and a massive army to avenge his father's humiliation and to add the lands of the Hellenes to his already swollen empire.

The new Persian host arrived in 480. They swarmed into northern Greece in unstoppable numbers, perhaps sixty thousand strong: Medes and Persians in leather breeches and fishtail iron jerkins, with their short, powerful bows; Assyrians with their bronze helmets and long lances; Arabs in long robes; Ethiopians in leopard and lion skins; and many more. The Spartans headed a coalition army that tried to halt them at a narrow northern pass called Thermopylae—the Hot Gates—and died almost to the last man when a Greek traitor showed the invaders a way to take the defenders in the rear. The Persians moved on southward, like locusts over the land, while a Persian fleet closed in on southern Attica by sea. Athens was taken and burned. All northern Greece lay open to Persian arms, and the defense of the south seemed no more than a forlorn hope.

But the Greeks bred brilliant leaders as well as soldiers who knew how to die for their homeland. Themistocles the Athenian had for years urged his countrymen to pin their faith on their fleet. Hundreds of new *triremes*—the long, oar-driven warships of the Mediterranean—had been built. These vessels, with their contingents of disciplined Greek hoplites, now turned the tide against the Persian host.

The turning point came at Salamis. Between this small island off the port of Athens and the shore, the Athenians tricked the larger Persian fleet into giving battle. Ramming and swarming aboard the demoralized Persian vessels, the Athenians once more routed their enemies. "No longer could we see the water," a Persian in a Greek play later lamented, "charged with ship's wrecks and men's blood."[3]

The Persian army was thus left without the support of its fleet. They wintered in Thessaly and marched south again the following year, 479. But this time a large Greek force led by a Spartan general met them at the village of Plataea, northwest of Athens, and shattered them on land as the Athenians had by sea. What was left of the Persian army stumbled home in defeat.

The war was not over. It dragged on nominally for some thirty years. But after Salamis in 480 and Plataea in 479, the struggle took the form of annual plundering raids by Greek fleets on the shores of the Persian Empire. The Persians never came again to Greece.

You can stand on the mounded cenotaph of the Athenian dead at Marathon today and observe, as Lord Byron did, how the mountains loom over the battlefield and how Marathon itself looks on the sea. Try it on a misty morning sometime, and the clash of ancient arms may seem to echo in your ears. The offshore island of Salamis you will pass on the highway outside Athens and probably never notice at all. Whether we indulge in romantic fantasies or not, however, the fact remains that few famous victories have been more consequential than the Greek triumph over the Persians in that war twenty-five centuries ago.

THE ATHENS OF PERICLES

The middle third of the fifth century B.C. is called the Age of Pericles, after the most famous of all Athenian statesmen. He, more than any other man, was the architect of Athens' greatness. Yet Pericles's predominance was itself the product of Athenian history—of a social and political evolution that had made fifth-century Athens the most democratic of all the Greek cities before Pericles was born.

The history of Athens was in some ways similar to that of other Greek city-states. Its kings were replaced by a government of aristocratic councils early in the seventh century B.C. At the beginning of the sixth century the *archon* (magistrate) Solon—a member of the city's chief elected council—became Athens' most famous lawgiver.

---

[3]Aeschylus, *The Persians,* trans. Seth G. Bernadete, in *The Complete Greek Tragedies,* vol. 1, eds. David Grene and Richmond Lattimore (Chicago: University of Chicago Press, 1959), pp. 234–235.

The laws of Solon freed poor farmers from debt slavery and opened up public office to citizens of less than aristocratic birth. Later in the sixth century the tyrant Pisistratus destroyed the residual power of the old clan-based aristocracy and transferred land from the aristocrats to the landless farmers who supported him. Pisistratus also encouraged handicraft manufacture and foreign trade and began the vast program of temple building that Pericles would carry to a triumphant climax.

Paradoxically, it was the aristocratic Cleisthenes who, during the last decade of the sixth century, brought participatory democracy to Athens. Winning popular support in 508, Cleisthenes instituted a Council of Five Hundred, chosen by lot, which was given sweeping authority to guide foreign and domestic affairs, to control government finances, and to prepare the crucial agenda for assembly meetings. The assembly of citizens still elected archons, passed all new laws, voted on questions of peace and war. A citizen-jury system began to edge out the aristocratic Areopagus court in judicial power. *Demokratia*, the rule of the citizens, was from this time on—a dozen years before the onset of the Persian War—the basic political reality of Athens.

Athens had thus become the freest of the Greek city-states by the beginning of the fifth century B.C. The mid-century Age of Pericles saw this city grow into the most powerful, prosperous, and admired center of civilized living among the Hellenes.

Pericles, who dominated Athenian politics between 450–429 B.C., was another of those descendants of the old aristocracy who seemed to flourish under Athenian democracy. The sculptured head that has come down to us, bearded and helmeted, the eyes gazing out calm and blank like those of all Greek gods and heroes, gives us only an idealized notion of what he was like. The Athenian historian Thucydides says he was famous for financial integrity and enormously popular among the people. Beyond these bare facts, Pericles seems to have been a man with a vision of Athenian greatness, a policy of grandeur that carried Athens to the climax of the Greek golden age.

Pericles put the finishing touches on the democratic constitution of Athens. He also presided over the conversion of Athens's victory over the Persian Empire into an Athenian empire among the Greeks.

The decades of naval warfare against Persia that followed Salamis added a new element to the turbulent mix of Athenian politics. The Athenian sailors, fundamentally oarsmen whose straining backs propelled Athenian triremes into battle, were typically landless city dwellers too poor to afford arms and armor. Thanks to their military contribution, this less affluent group now acquired a share of power in the assembly comparable to that of the hoplite class. Their growing participation in government represented a clear gain for *demokratia* in the Athens of Pericles.

Meanwhile, to keep up the pressure on the Persians and to bring home as much of the pillage of Asia as their

Pericles, the most celebrated statesman of ancient Greece, broods on the fate of nations in this idealized funerary sculpture. Is this a "realistic" representation? Look particularly at the hair, beard, and eyes. (New York Public Library Picture Collection)

arms could win, the Greeks organized the Delian League. This military alliance, originally voluntary, was gradually transformed into an Athenian empire. Under the leadership of Pericles, membership in the league became compulsory for some fifty Greek city-states. The headquarters—and the treasury—of the league were moved from the sacred island of Delos to Athens. Free contributions became required tribute. And the funds contributed by all the members began to be spent to build temples on the Athenian acropolis.

Under such leadership Athens flourished. Trade boomed, and the docks at the Athenian port of Piraeus were jammed with long ships and jars of wine and oil. There was plenty of work in the city—laboring on the public works on the acropolis or producing goods for export. And the city itself was a joy to live in. Philosophers such as Socrates disputed in the agora; the hands of Phidias sculptured stone among the columns of the Parthenon; Aeschylus and Sophocles produced moving tragedies for the annual festival of Dionysus.

Loyalty to the *polis* had never been greater. An aging Pericles appealed to it when he urged his hearers to "draw strength . . . from the busy spectacle of our great city's life as we have it before us day by day, falling in love with her as we see her."[4] These men of ancient Athens, with all their faults, had come as close to genuine self-government as any ancient people ever would. And they had found uses for their freedom that would seldom be matched, and perhaps never exceeded.

THE PELOPONNESIAN WAR

The Greeks were always a rivalrous, contentious people. The war between Athens and Sparta that brought the fifth century B.C. to its disastrous close was more than a typical Greek feud, however. It was a clash of principle, a conflict between two irreconcilable ways of life.

Sparta had retained the virtues of virile Homeric warrior heroes, the stress on personal courage, and the conservative institutions of an earlier day. As late as the fifth century the Spartans still had not one but two kings. Though they had an assembly, their politics was dominated by an old-fashioned council of elders. Military service was normal for full citizens of any *polis*, but in Sparta all males lived in barracks till the age of thirty. They were a people in arms, widely reputed to be the best soldiers in Greece.

There was more to all this than conservative sentiment, of course. The fields of Sparta were worked not by Spartan citizens but by subject peoples called *helots*. Since the helots vastly outnumbered the Spartans, every Spartan had to be a soldier simply to keep the helots in their place. This need to dominate by force had also led the Spartans to impose their will on their neighbors in the Peloponnesus, the sprawling peninsula of southern Greece, through a compulsory alliance called the Peloponnesian League. In the last decades of the fifth century, the Peloponnesian League and the Delian League—the land-based Spartan coalition and the seaborne empire of the Athenians—came to an all but inevitable conflict.

The rise of Athenian power was bound to cause concern in Sparta. When the Athenians began to interfere in the affairs of Spartan allies, the leaders of the southern alliance responded violently. The Peloponnesian War, which erupted in 431 B.C., dragged on for more than a quarter of a century. It was a civil war, pitting Greeks against Greeks, and it was the Hellenes as a whole who suffered.

From the beginning the Athenians had the worst of it. Sparta, located in the interior of the Peloponnesus, was

safe from the Athenian navy, which had been Athens' most powerful military arm ever since Themistocles. Athens, by contrast, lay open to repeated incursions by the redoubtable Spartan army. Other misfortunes fell upon the Athenians. In the second year of the war, a plague ravaged the city, costing many lives, including that of Pericles.

The Athenian government fell thereafter into the hands of lesser men, demagogues, and war hawks who kept the futile conflict going years after both sides might well have called it quits. The worst disaster of the war befell the Athenians in 415, when they allowed the brilliant but erratic Alcibiades to talk them into the catastrophic Sicilian Expedition, from which "few out of many returned home."

There were battles without number, bloody massacres and shocking betrayals, tangled alliances involving even the Persians, the old enemies of all Greeks. From this fratricidal carnage, the Spartans finally emerged victorious in 404 B.C. Athens was humiliated, stripped its navy, deprived of its empire. The city was forced to raze the "long walls" connecting it with the Piraeus and the sea, which had been the source of its wealth and power. The Spartans imposed upon the city the notorious Thirty Tyrants—a council of Athenian collaborators—and returned home in triumph.

Athens was the loser, but no one gained permanently. The Athenians regained their freedom almost at once, but other wars and intrigues followed, dragging on into the fourth century. Peace was at last imposed from without—by a half-barbaric northern power called Macedon. Long before the Macedonian conquest, however, the Greeks had sacrificed their freedom on the altar of their own eternal contentiousness.

ALEXANDER THE GREAT: LONG MARCH TO GLORY

Philip and Alexander of Macedon, father and son, composed a strange, brief dynasty. Philip's triumph brought a rough unity to Greece at least. Alexander's unrivaled string of victories spread at least an approximation of Greek ways and Greek culture from the Nile to the Indus. But it is unlikely that this violent duo aimed at either Hellenic unification or the Hellenization of the East. Conquest pure and simple was their most obvious goal. There is poetic truth in the story that when Alexander the Great could find no more worlds to conquer, he sat down and wept.

Philip II seized the throne of the northern kingdom of Macedon from his own ward in the middle of the fourth century. He built up a powerful army of hard-bitten Macedonians, conquered his more barbarous neighbors, and soon became involved in the tangled wars and alliances of the Greeks. In 338 B.C., Philip's soldiers smashed the combined armies of Athens and Thebes on the brutal field of Chaeronea. Two years later Philip was dead, murdered by his own officers.

---

[4]Bottsford and Robinson, *Hellenic History*, p. 202.

His son, Alexander, replaced him as king and warrior lord. He was apparently a youth of more subtlety than his father. Having been tutored by the Athenian philosopher Aristotle, he was perhaps capable of imagining a more sophisticated world order than conquest and pillage. But he was a warrior first and always. He began at once a twelve-year trek across western Eurasia seldom matched in the annals of warfare.

The tale of Alexander's victories reads like a gazeteer of the ancient Middle East. He crossed the Hellespont into Persia in 334, repeatedly defeated the Persians, brought the Phoenicians to heel, and besieged and captured Tyre. He swung south into ancient Egypt and founded Alexandria in the delta of the Nile, the first of many cities to bear his name. Plunging back into Asia Minor, he finally crushed the Persian emperor Darius II at the Battle of Gaugamela in 331 B.C., and then marched farther and farther east across the far-flung Persian satrapies. He passed south of the Caspian Sea, crossed what is today Afghanistan, and went beyond the reach even of the Persians, into northern India.

He won victories on the Indus, in the India of Chandragupta. But his battle-weary Macedonians refused to follow even the ever-victorious Alexander further. And so, after tracing the Indus south to the Indian Ocean, Alexander turned back across the great desert to bring his odyssey to an end in Babylon. Here, his destiny accomplished, he died suddenly of a fever in 323 B.C. He was thirty-three years old.

For good or ill, Alexander's long march accomplished more than can ever have been imagined in his narrow Macedonian skull. He himself had "gone native" on the long road east, adopting Persian garb, marrying a Persian princess, declaring himself a king and a god after the Oriental manner. But he had also founded twenty-five Greek city-states along his march, and married off thousands of his Macedonian officers and soldiers to native women. Henceforth Greek administrators, Greek traders, Greek ways of living, thinking, and carving stone would become part of the life of this half of Asia.

A new and wider world was opened up by Philip of Macedon and Alexander the Great. But an old world died too—the untidy little world of craggy mountains, blue water, and white cities where a small, combative,

Alexander the Great charges into battle in this fragment of a wall painting from Pompeii. The picture, done long after the event, nevertheless captures a hint at least of the hectic life and violent energy of the most successful warrior in Greek history. The horse is probably intended to be Bucephalus, the faithful steed that Alexander loved so much that when it finally died he gave it an elaborate military funeral. (Art Resource)

immensely energetic people had brought to a climax one of the great human efforts at civilized living.

THE FOUNTAINHEAD OF WESTERN CULTURE

THE GREEK ACHIEVEMENT

Greece is a smaller part of Europe than the river valleys of northern India and the northeastern corner of China are of their wide realms. But the part Greece played in defining key aspects of European culture is similar to the seminal role played by Gangetic India or the northeastern heart-land of Zhou China. Greece was in many ways the cultural fountainhead from which European civilization sprang.

Europe did not evolve into a single nation, as India and China did. For most of its history Europe has been many nations, frequently as violently antagonistic toward one another as the Greek city-states were among themselves. Yet there is a single European civilization that transcends all differences of region and nation, a common Western cultural heritage that sets off Europeans—and their cultural heirs in other lands—from other peoples of the world. And the first great source of that common culture was the astonishingly vital intellectual and artistic life of Athens and its sister cities in ancient Greece.

The art and thought of classical Greece are usually explored in at least two phases: the Hellenic and the Hel-

ALEXANDER'S EMPIRE AND THE HELLENISTIC WORLD

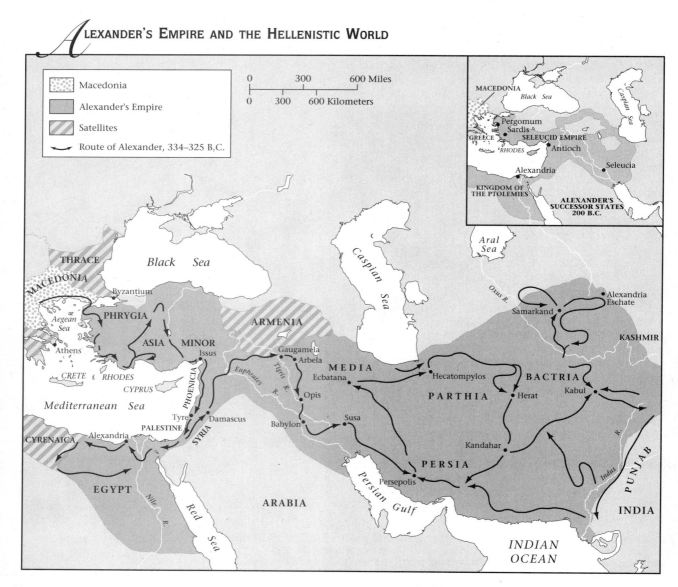

lenistic ages. The Hellenic Athens of the fifth century B.C. in particular glows like the China of Confucius and the *Book of Songs* in the cultural memory of the Western world. This golden age of Pericles, the century of Greek philosophy and drama, the art and architecture of the Parthenon, is for many the high point of Greek artistic accomplishment. But the Hellenistic age that followed Alexander the Great in the later fourth and third centuries B.C. has left us its share of art and an amazing first flowering of Western science as well.

There is space here for only a quick overview of our cultural legacy from ancient Greece, a pause here and there to sample an argument or touch the curve of a sculptured cheek. Yet even so brief and superficial a survey will be crowded with the cultural plenty of the Greeks.

THE ART OF THE ACROPOLIS

For many people, ancient Greece *is* white temples and statues carved in breathing stone. Even when we learn that the white marble was once painted and the streets of Athens much gaudier than our imaginations might allow, we cling—with some artistic justification—to the formal beauty of the stone beneath.

Greek sculpture apparently began, as the Greek dark age ended and the city-state emerged, with models borrowed from immemorial Egypt. The stiff frontality of Greek archaic statuary—the gowns like a fluted column, the fixed "archaic smile"—seem to look back to Memphis and Karnak. However, these stiff sixth-century Apollos and skirted female figures probably also reflect the limitations of the log from which earlier figures were fashioned by Greek woodcarvers.

Yet from these crude beginnings developed the perfect physical proportions and idealized shapes of fifth-century sculpture. The classic simplicity of the head of Pericles (see p. 133) or Phidias's *Athena Lemnia* became a model for later ages. The calm strength of the *Apollo* from the Temple of Zeus at Olympia and the incarnate majesty of the great bronze *Zeus* from the sea off Euboea have a power that challenges all efforts at emulation since.

But the restless mind of the ancient Greeks appears never to have been content, even with classic perfection. Greek sculptors of the fourth, third, and second centuries went on to more intricate, more violent, and perhaps more human things. Hellenistic sculpture included the tangled draperies of the *Winged Victory*, which stands in the Louvre today, and the writhing bodies of the muscular *Laocoön* and his sons in the serpent's coils. It also included the living flesh of perfect Hellenistic Aphrodites—the Greek goddess of beauty—and the wrinkled skin, taut tendons, and swollen veins of the *Old Market Woman*. Realism, melodrama, and sentiment thus replaced classic idealized forms as human concerns replaced ideal ones among the ever-changing Greeks.

Greek architecture evolved and changed much less,

The soft flesh of Aphrodite, the Greek goddess of love (known to the Romans as Venus), pulses with warmth and life in this Hellenistic rendering. Head and arms, often carved from separate pieces of stone, are easily broken off by vandals. (Art Resource)

yet it also left its legacy, as Greek-style facades on both sides of the Atlantic built within the present century will testify. Greek building, for all its subtlety of proportion, was very simple. Post-and-lintel structure—pillars and pediments and a gently sloping roof—made a Greek temple. The plain Doric order predominated, at least through the fifth century: a flat abacus at the head of the column and no base at all below. Yet the ruined beauty of the Parthenon, the Temple of Athena Parthenos (Athena the Virgin), on the Athenian acropolis testifies to what could be done with such economy of means.

A city crowned with such beauty—marble temples against the mountains and the sky—was a city that any people could, as Pericles said, fall in love with day by day.

HOMER'S EPICS AND ATHENIAN TRAGEDY

Greece is subtlety: the play of light across a sculptured cheek, the cling of diaphanous draperies of solid stone, the delicate patterning of pillars that only *seem* to be

Contrast the wrinkled humanity of this *Old Market Woman* with the triumphant youth of Aphrodite in the preceding illustration. Both reveal the Hellenistic passion for realism and sentiment, as well as the unsurpassed technical mastery of Greek sculptors. (The Metropolitan Museum of Art)

ticular stands alone in the classical canon as a powerful poem of men at war. The long hexameter lines boom with the rolling of the sea and the clash of battle on that distant Asian coast where Bronze Age Greeks and Trojans fought before Troy. The whole of that mythic struggle seems to be encompassed in this story of a single fatal incident in the ten-year war, when the angry Achilles, greatest of Greek warriors, defied his general and by so doing

> hurled in their multitudes to the house of Hades
>   strong souls
> of heroes, but gave their bodies to be the delicate
>   feasting
> of dogs. . . .[5]

The story of the wrath of Achilles—vain of honor, grieving terribly for the friend who dies in his place, and exploding at last, a blood-stained meteor across the battlefield—brings back with unparalleled power a savage age long gone.

Later Greek times produced lovely poetry as well. There are the fragile lyrics of Sappho, the Greek poet of the islands. Only fragments of her verse remain, yet they combine with unmatched beauty the poet's love of other women with a sensitive awareness of the legends of her people and the loveliness of the Greek isles. There are Pindar's famous odes, celebrating the transient glory of the heroes of his day and later imitated by many Western poets. But there would never again be the sheer poetic drive and power of Homer, the half-mythical blind bard of the Greek dark ages.

The ancient Greek theater apparently began with primitive hymn-singing and dancing in honor of Dionysus, god of the grape in particular and of fertility and generation in general. By the fifth century B.C., this simple celebration of divine beneficence had evolved into a complex dramatic form. In this classic Greek tragedy, characters in stylized masks acted out the story while a chorus danced, sang, and chanted a commentary between the "acts" of the play. The stories themselves normally derived from Greek mythology, but the old tales of gods and heroes often emerged with universal reference in the work of fifth-century Athenian playwrights such as Aeschylus, Sophocles, and Euripides.

The dramatic heroes of Sophocles perhaps best embody what Aristotle considered the perfect tragic type: the noble character marred by a single tragic flaw. Thus *Oedipus the King* attempts to discover the crime against the gods that has brought divine retribution in the form of a plague upon the city he rules. The dramatic tension of the play grows out of the inability of this great king to see what would be obvious to the audience even if they

straight and uniformly separated. But Greece is more. Greece is a literary power that the West has not been able to forget for twenty-five hundred years.

"Sing, goddess, the wrath of Achilles," begins Homer's *Iliad,* the oldest and for many still the greatest of Greek poems. It dates from the Greek dark ages—perhaps 800 B.C.—and harks back for its warlike theme to the wars of Mycenaean times. But it was as close to a Bible as the worldly Greeks ever got, even in the vastly more sophisticated centuries after 500 B.C.

The strength of Homer's twin epics, the *Iliad* on the Trojan War and the *Odyssey* on the wanderings of the hero Odysseus, would not be easily equaled. The *Iliad* in par-

---

[5] *The Iliad*, trans. Richmond Lattimore (Chicago: University of Chicago Press, 1951), p. 59.

did not know the story: that Oedipus himself is the criminal, the man who in defiance of all the laws of gods and humans has inadvertently murdered his father and married his own mother. The spiritual blindness that prevents him from seeing the truth for so long is symbolically expressed in the punishment Oedipus decrees for himself: self-inflicted blindness and expulsion from his city. He will wander the roads of Greece a sightless beggar for the rest of his days.

There was laughter in ancient Greece as well, evidently, and a comic theater to stimulate it. Most celebrated is the so-called Old Comedy of fifth-century Athens, embodied in the plays of Aristophanes. A comedy such as *The Clouds,* which lampoons the generation gap, the teachings of the philosopher Socrates, and much else, is typical. Aristophanes offers a rich mixture of social satire and personal innuendo, of bawdy farce and lyric flights of great beauty. We would expect nothing less complex and subtle of the Age of Pericles. Even Greek laughter was a many-splendored thing.

PHILOSOPHY: SOCRATES, PLATO, ARISTOTLE

From ancient Greece, as from Confucian China and ancient India, however, it is not shaped stone or patterns of words that have survived the longest, but the ideas of Greek teachers. The Greeks called their equivalents of the sages and gurus of the East *philosophers*, "lovers of wisdom." And in both their philosophy and their science, reason was the heart of the Greeks' achievement.

In the cosmopolitan city-states of the Ionian coasts in particular, a handful of choice spirits among the Hellenes went beyond mythology to ask themselves, "What is the universe *really* made of?" The answers Thales, Anaximander, Pythagoras, and others came up with— water, the four elements, fire, number, and so on—are of largely antiquarian interest. But from them descended both the philosophy of the fifth and fourth centuries and the Hellenistic science of the fourth century and after.

The most famous of Greek philosophers were Socrates in the fifth century B.C. and Plato and Aristotle in the fourth.

Socrates called himself the "gadfly" of Athens, an intellectual horsefly stinging Athenians into questioning traditional values, examining their own lives, thinking seriously about the real meaning of life itself. More of a crackerbarrel philosophizer than a systematic thinker, Socrates buttonholed his fellow citizens in the agora, asking judges what justice was, querying poets about the function of art, discussing with the young people who gathered around him how society ought to be organized, how the good life ought to be lived. "The unexamined life," he told his disciples, "is not worth living." In the terrible years after the Peloponnesian War, Socrates was tried and executed by his fellow countrymen, less for his words than for his insistence on his right to speak them.

One of the admirers who mourned Socrates was a broad-shouldered, poetic young man called Plato. For the rest of his life, this most influential of all Western philosophers would immortalize his teacher in a series of *Dialogues* expounding first the views of Socrates and later Plato's own mature notions of the nature of reality, of the good society, of the ideal life, and much more.

This most famous of Greek philosophers insisted that there is more to reality than meets the eye. There are two levels to the universe, said Plato, a lower world of matter, or "particulars," and a higher, nonmaterial realm of Ideas, Forms, or Absolutes. A triangle drawn in the dust by a Greek geometer is a particular triangle, and it ceases to exist with a sweep of a sandaled foot. The Form of the Triangle—the definition of a triangle, we might say—is an Idea, invisible, immaterial, and eternal. The courage you show in a tight spot, your sense of justice, whatever wisdom you may have—all these are temporary, finite, bounded by one imperfect human heart and mind. The Idea of Courage, of Justice, of Wisdom would survive even if there were not one wise or just or brave person left alive to think such thoughts, or to embody them. Ultimate reality, then, is not material at all but rather is pure, transcendental Idea. The Idea of Man, the Form of the Good, Absolute Beauty—these Platonic formulations would be powerful shapers of Western minds for centuries to come.

Plato's ethical teachings stressed one of these capitalized abstractions especially: Reason. The goal of life, Plato said, was happiness. But happiness comes from the practice of virtue, and the highest of virtues is wisdom. Since wisdom is achieved through reason, the best possible life is a life dedicated wholly to rational inquiry and the pursuit of truth. Philosophy ("love of wisdom") is thus itself the highest of human activities, and the philosophical life is the best life.

The good society, in turn, would be one in which philosophers were kings, or kings philosophers, and in which the rest of us performed the functions to which we are best suited by nature, class, or profession. Plato was no democrat: his family was an ancient aristocratic one, and it was the popular demagogues who had executed Socrates. Let the best minds guide the state, said Plato, as the brain rules the body. It was a beguiling notion, one that can tantalize us even today.

Other Greek sages proposed other theories of the ultimate nature of things, and of the good life for human beings. For Plato's disciple Aristotle—himself "the master of those who know" to later ages—the Forms are real enough but exist only *within* the particulars that derive their structure from them—not in some transcendental realm of nonmaterial being. For Aristotle as for Plato, the best life was the philosophical life, a life devoted to the

"*Croesus [reputed to be the richest king in the world] received Solon [the wise Athenian lawgiver] as his guest, and lodged him in the royal palace. On the third or fourth day after, he bade his servants conduct Solon over his treasures, and show him all their greatness and magnificence. When he had seen them all . . . Croesus addressed this question to him. 'Stranger of Athens, we have heard much of thy wisdom, and of thy travels through many lands, from love of knowledge and a wish to see the world. I am curious therefore to inquire of thee, whom, of all the men that thou hast seen, thou deemest the most blessed?' This he asked because he thought himself the happiest of mortals; but Solon answered him without flattery, according to his true sentiments, 'Tellus of Athens, sire.' Full of astonishment at what he heard, Croesus demanded sharply, 'and wherefore dost thou deem Tellus happiest?' To which the other replied, 'First, because his country was flourishing in his days, and he himself had sons that were noble gentlemen, and he lived to see children born to each of them, and these children all grew up; and further because after a life spent in what our people look upon as comfort, his end was surpassingly glorious. In a battle between the Athenians and their neighbors . . . he came to the assistance of his countrymen, routed the foe, and died upon the field most gallantly. The Athenians gave him a public funeral on the spot where he fell, and paid him the highest honors.'*"

◆◆◆

This anecdote from the early portion of Herodotus's *History of the Persian War* contrasts Western social values with the material wealth of Asia, at least as these qualities looked to the first of Western historians. The literal accuracy of this account may be dubious, but its intent was to illustrate what seemed to the author to be a larger truth.

What can you deduce from Solon's description of Tellus, the ideal Athenian, about the basic social loyalties of the Greeks? About their traditional attitudes toward the family and the sexes? Toward material wealth? Toward war? How would you compare or contrast these ancient values with those of Western peoples in our own time?

Herodotus, The History of Herodotus of Halicarnassus, trans. George Rawlinson (London: Nonesuch Press, 1935), p. 30.

---

search for truth. But since philosophy was not possible for ordinary minds, Aristotle declared that for most people virtue consists of a practical search for the golden mean—the avoidance of excess, moderation in all things.

Aristotle's wide-ranging intellect left Western people ideas on every subject, from politics to science to art. He developed basic definitions of major forms of government, from monarchy to aristocracy to democracy. He meticulously catalogued biological species and left theories that dominated physics until modern times. His writing on poetry and drama explained the "cathartic" effect, the sense of psychological purging and relief, that comes from great drama. Aristotle also laid out the means of con-

structing a "well-made play," methods still taught in many drama and film schools today.

HISTORY AND SCIENCE

The eager Greek intellect explored this world as well as the transcendent realm of the philosophers. Both Western science and Western history were founded by the ancient Greeks.

The two most honored of Greek historians were Herodotus and Thucydides, chroniclers of the two great fifth-century B.C. wars that bracketed the age of Pericles. Herodotus' *Persian War,* perhaps the first real history book ever written, recounted in colorful detail the epic struggle between the Greek city-states and the huge Persian Empire. Breaking with the ancient tradition of mythic and poetic accounts of the past in which gods and goddesses always played important parts, Herodotus sought to explain how human beings, Greeks and Persians, settled their differences by a resort to arms. Though he was not above inventing inspiring speeches for kings and generals and reading sententious morals into past events, Herodotus did travel widely, seeking evidence and talking to eyewitnesses, earning for himself the title "father of history."

Thucydides' history of the grim and disillusioning *Peloponnesian War* offers subtler analysis and more thoughtful syntheses than his predecessor. Like Herodotus, however, Thucydides was a literary artist of the first order. He also shared Herodotus' passion for getting at the truth. Thucydides' account of the cruelty, corruption, follies, and defeats of Athens at war is all the more moving when we remember that he was himself an Athenian commander. Exiled by his fellow citizens for an early failure in the struggle, he gave the rest of his life, not to justifying himself, but to compiling an unbiased yet deeply moving history of the great conflict.

There seemed to be no end to the intellectual curiosity of the Hellenes. By Hellenistic times much of the Greek thirst for ultimate understanding had shifted from philosophy to science. Here the Greeks made more substantial contributions than did any Western people before the Scientific Revolution of Copernicus and Newton.

The names of some of the early Greek scientists are well-known still. Pythagoras, the only sixth-century mind among them, is most familiar as a mathematician. His famous theorem about the squares of the sides of a right-angle triangle is part of the bric-a-brac of every schoolchild's mind today. Aristotle's researches in biology and physics were so impressive that later ages would revere even his occasional mistakes. Euclid's *Elements* of geometry remained the standard text into our own century, and doctors to this day begin their careers with the Oath of Hippocrates, most renowned of ancient Greek physicians. Archimedes' promise to move the world itself if you could give him a lever long enough and a place to stand has the ring of Greek speculative daring at its best.

Perhaps as far back as Pythagoras, Greek astronomers recognized that the earth is a ball. They calculated its size by mathematics and used trigonometry to estimate its distance from the sun and the moon. They made one fundamental error; in the end they agreed with Ptolemy's earth-centered theory of the structure of the universe rather than with Aristarchus's sun-centered view. But the ingenuity and influence of the Greeks were never manifested more impressively than when they were wrong. For Ptolemy's elaborate cosmological explication and mathematical calculation—it took some doing to present so erroneous a theory convincingly—carried the best scientific minds of Roman, Byzantine, Arab, and medieval Christian times along with him, till Copernicus in the sixteenth century set them right.

Reason was the heart of it, the core of Greek achievement in the linked fields of philosophy and science. Modern scholarship has taught us more about the Greeks, rational and irrational, from prophetic madness to mystery cults. But when they set their minds to work, this ancient Mediterranean people produced a body of rational speculation and calculation that is a major human effort to explain the meaning of it all, the nature of things.

SUMMARY

European history began in southern Europe, in the islands and mountainous mainland of Greece, where a series of cultures flourished between 2200 and 300 B.C., climaxing in the fifth century with the Age of Pericles.

The first two societies to develop in this area were those of the Minoans and the Mycenaeans. The Minoans (2200–1500 B.C.) migrated from the Near East to the large island of Crete, which they made the center of a city-based, seaborne, commercial hegemony over neighboring islands and coasts. The Mycenaeans (1500–1100 B.C.), Indo-European nomads from the north, overran this first European urban culture and became pirates, traders, and builders of rude cities. As subsequent waves of Dorians, Ionians, and other northern intruders continued to drift down into Greece, however, both trade and cities vanished entirely, and the area sank into a dark age of subsistence agriculture. Against this background, classical Greek civilization gradually took shape.

As early as the eighth century B.C., the Greek population began to outgrow the peninsula. Cities and city-states were built again, and Greek traders took to the sea. Soon thereafter, archaic kings and hereditary aristocracies faded away. The Greek city-state, or *polis*, ruled by a popular assembly with elected magistrates and other officials, became perhaps the most democratic of ancient urban institutions.

The history of the celebrated fifth century B.C. began with Greece's victorious war against the huge Persian Empire. The century centered on the rich and culturally brilliant age of Pericles in Athens, and it ended with the self-destructive civil war between Athens and Sparta, in which

Sparta won but all Greece was the loser. In the fourth century the Greek peninsula fell under the military domination of Philip and Alexander of Macedon. Alexander brought the long feud with Persia to a climax by overrunning the empire and scattering Greek cities across much of western Asia.

The culture of Greece provided a vital legacy to all later European peoples and to all Western culture. Greek literature—from Homer's epics the *Iliad* and the *Odyssey* to the delicate lyrics of Sappho or the dramas of Sophocles—provided models for later writers. Greek sculpture idealized the human form in lifelike figures of gods and famous citizens. The architecture of the Athenian acropolis was a model for later ages.

Above all, the philosophy of Greek thinkers like Socrates, Plato, and Aristotle left the West a legacy of daring ideas. From Socrate's challenge to "know thyself," through Plato's belief in absolute Ideas like Truth and Beauty, to Aristotle's conviction that ethics is a golden mean between extremes, their views have shaped Western thinking ever since.

SUGGESTED READING

BERNAL, M. *Black Athena.* London: Free Association Press, 1987. Scholarly, controversial study emphasizing Egyptian influence on Greece.

BOARDMAN, J., and others, eds. *The Oxford History of the Classical World.* New York: Oxford University Press, 1986. Leading contemporary authorities present the latest research findings on Greek and Roman political and cultural achievements.

CHADWICK, J. *The Mycenaean World.* Cambridge: Cambridge University Press, 1976. Overview by a scholar known for his exposition of the Minoan script, Linear B.

CONNOR, W. L. *New Politicians of Fifth Century Athens.* Princeton, N.J.: Princeton University Press, 1971. The political scene in the century of Pericles.

FARRINGTON, B. *Greek Science,* rev. ed. Harmondsworth, England: Penguin Books, 1961. Authoritative and readable, stressing the Greek contribution to the broader history of Western science.

FINE, J. V. A. *The Ancient Greeks: A Critical History.* Cambridge, Mass.: Harvard University Press, 1983. Solid scholarship, critical perspective.

FINLEY, M. I. *Economy and Society in Ancient Greece.* New York: Viking, 1982. Scholarly papers by an authority on Greek society. See also his *Politics in the Ancient World* (New York: Cambridge University Press, 1983), lectures on political institutions and practices in Greek and Roman cities.

FLACIERE, R. *Daily Life in the Athens of Pericles.* New York: Macmillan, 1965. Lively description.

GRENE, D., and R. LATTIMORE, eds. *The Complete Greek Tragedies* (4 vols.). Chicago: University of Chicago Press, 1959–1960. All the surviving plays by the three greatest Greek tragic dramatists—Aeschylus, Sophocles, and Euripides—translated by various hands.

GUTHRIE, W. K. C. *The Greek Philosophers from Thales to Aristotle.* New York: Philosophical Library, 1950. Good survey of the ideas of Socrates, Plato, Aristotle, and their precursors.

HERODOTUS. *The History of Herodotus,* trans. G. Rawlinson. Chicago: Encyclopaedia Britannica, 1955. The first Western historian's account of the Persian War and of the Near East in his own time.

HOMER. *The Iliad,* trans. R. Lattimore. Chicago: University of Chicago Press, 1951. Excellent rendering by an experienced translator and poet. See also *The Odyssey.*

HOOD, S. *The Minoans.* New York: Praeger, 1967. One of a number of surveys of this appealing culture.

JUST, R. *Women in Athenian Law and Life.* London: Routledge, 1991. Illuminating anthropological approach.

KITTO, H. D. F. *The Greeks.* Chicago: Aldine, 1964. Profile of this contradictory people by a leading student of Greek literature.

LACEY, W. K. *The Family in Classical Greece.* Ithaca, NY: Cornell University Press, 1984. Solid older treatment.

LEFKOWITZ, M. and M. B. FANT. *Women's Life in Greece and Rome.* Baltimore: Johns Hopkins University Press, 1982. Perhaps the best description, but see also the highly praised S. Pomeroy, *Goddesses, Whores, Wives and Slaves: Women in Classical Antiquity* (New York: Schocken Books, 1975).

MEIGGS, R. *The Athenian Empire.* New York: Oxford University Press, 1972. Standard account of the transformation of a voluntary alliance into an empire.

ROBERTSON, C. M. *A Shorter History of Greek Art.* New York: Cambridge University Press, 1981. Perhaps the best one-volume treatment available. See also J. Boardman, *Greek Art* (New York: Praeger, 1964).

SEALEY, R. *A History of the Greek City States ca. 700–338 B.C.* Berkeley: University of California Press, 1977. Revaluations of earlier views of Greek political history.

STARR, C. G. *The Economic and Social Growth of Early Greece, 800–500 B.C.* New York: Oxford University Press, 1977. Economic development of the Greek Mediterranean in preclassical times.

TARN, W. W. *Alexander the Great* (2 vols.). Cambridge: Cambridge University Press, 1948. A standard life. See, among others, the more recent and well written P. Greene, *Alexander the Great* (New York: Praeger, 1970) and N. C. L. Hammond's *Alexander the Great: King, Commander, and Statesman* (London: Chatto and Windus, 1980), combining deep classical learning with firsthand knowledge of Near Eastern lands.

THUCYDIDES. *The Peloponnesian War*, trans. R. Crawley. Chicago: Encyclopaedia Britannica, 1952. The greatest Greek historian's account of the Greek civil war.

WALBANK, F. W. *The Hellenistic World*. Cambridge, Mass.: Harvard University Press, 1982. Scholarly introduction to the fascinating later Greek centuries. But see also the equally scholarly, longer, and more detailed work of E. S. Gruen, *The Hellenistic World and the Coming of Rome* (Berkeley: University of California Press, 1984) as well as M. Grant's readable and sensitive *From Alexander to Cleopatra: The Hellenistic World* (New York: Scribner's, 1982), especially interesting on Hellenistic culture.

ZIMMERN, A. E. *The Greek Commonwealth*. London: Oxford University Press, 1961. A classic study, less critical of Greek society than more recent works.

CHAPTER 10

CULTURAL EVOLUTION

DIFFUSION VERSUS PARALLEL EVOLUTION

CULTURAL DIFFUSION

Ten thousand years ago the world's population of *Homo sapiens sapiens* embarked upon a cycle of unparalleled social and cultural change. As we have seen, the great transformation began as early as the eighth millennium B.C. with the development of agriculture. In the latter part of the fourth millennium, civilization was born. By approximately the time of Christ, as we shall see, empires spanned the entire Eurasian world island, and developed civilizations had sprung up elsewhere. Over the last two thousand years, finally, commercial ties, political empires, world religions, and modern technology have brought first neighboring peoples and then all the peoples of the globe into ever closer contact.

A central theme of any world history is thus the *interrelatedness* of the world's peoples, the *global* nature of the human venture. It is not surprising, then, that we should seek patterns of interaction as early as possible in humanity's recorded history. Are such patterns to be found in the record of the first three thousand years of the history of civilization?

Efforts have been made to tell the human story as the tale of one people from the beginning. In an extreme form of this approach, each major discovery—agriculture, the city, metalworking, monumental architecture—is made once only. Each ingenious new technique is then passed on to other peoples until all continents have come to share it. This spread of cultural innovations from one people to another is known as *cultural diffusion*.

There is no doubt about the diffusion of some aspects of culture over some parts of the world. The spread of Indo-European languages from somewhere in southern Russia to places as far apart as Aryan India, Greece, Rome, and Celtic Britain is a classic case in point. Virtually all we know about the history of Olmec culture is the story of its diffusion over substantial portions of Mesoamerica. Such powerful centers of civilization as China and India clearly had a strong influence on the development of culture in the nearby regions of East, South, and Southeast Asia.

But there are other cases of strikingly similar developments in which scholars can find little convincing evidence of outside influences. Such basic economic patterns as pastoral nomadism or commercial exchange of goods almost certainly developed independently in more than one place. The same is likely to be true of some forms of monumental architecture: Pyramidal structures in the Near East and in the Americas, megalithic standing stones in Western Europe and on the fringes of East Asia do not prove common origin in one place or the other. It is not necessary to assume that all the boats in the world go back to a single primal dugout.

In our own twentieth-century world, the lives of all people are closely bound up with the lives of peoples in other parts of the globe. The problem is how far back to push our search for the tangled patterns of international influences, the global interdependence of today.

PARALLEL EVOLUTION

Genuinely global connections are not as easy to come by during the first three millennia after civilization was born in ancient Sumer as they would be later. In these early centuries, in fact, the peoples of the world seem frequently to have followed separate roads to a common goal.

There is some trade and travel between adjacent areas, of course. Established caravan routes and port cities linked Mesopotamia, Egypt, and the rest of the Near East from very early times. Trading peoples such as the Greeks, the Phoenicians, and the Carthaginians bound the whole of the Mediterranean and neighboring regions in a web of commerce. Harappan Indian merchants left their seals in the Near East, and Olmec artifacts have been found over much of Mesoamerica. Peoples at varying levels of social evolution traded with each other, as the Greeks did with preurban people north of the Black Sea and as the Egyptians did up the Nile. Some degree of mutual influence was certainly likely in such cases.

During the dawn age of civilization, however, the influence of one culture on another does not seem to reach very far. We may legitimately speak of the spread of slash-and-burn agriculture from Western Europe into the forests of Russia, but there is no evidence that Europeans contributed to the development of that same technique across the Atlantic in the New World. The cultural influence of the first civilization in Mesopotamia was evidently felt among its nearer neighbors on the Nile and the Indus, but not along the much more distant Huanghe River of northeastern China.

Efforts to prove the existence of communication between more distant continents—particularly between the Old World and the New—have shown that such voyages were possible, not that they occurred. And even if a few storm-tossed mariners did reach the Americas from Europe, Africa, or Asia, there is little likelihood that they could have decisively shaped the course of cultural development in the New World.

During this earliest period, in short, we must accept coincidence, parallel evolution, or common causal factors such as ecological change as explanations for many similarities between widely separated cultures.

It is not so surprising, after all, that the gradual extinction of big game should lead hunters on both sides of the Atlantic to turn to smaller game, intensified gathering, and finally agriculture. The resulting increases in wealth, economic and technological complexity, and political hierarchy quite likely generated a more elaborate hierarchy of social classes as well. And so on, until parallel evolution explains many of the parallel results we see in many places during this early age of civilization scattered around the globe.

Some such parallels appear to deserve special attention. This chapter will deal briefly with three such parallel ventures. All three of these major thrusts in human history seem almost close enough to lead us to look for cultural diffusion behind them. In each case, however, we are probably dealing with common enterprises generated independently, with parallel evolution in similar societies.

PARALLEL DEVELOPMENTS AROUND THE GLOBE

AGRICULTURE IN THE AMERICAS

The basic discovery that made civilization possible was the development of agriculture. Since agriculture probably demanded more work than hunting and gathering did, it may have been initially taken up only when the game supply began to dwindle. In whatever way agriculture began, however, it proved a far more productive way of providing food energy for humankind. The simple fact was that a tract of land put to the plow could feed many more people than a similar expanse exploited through hunting and gathering. The rising population that resulted provided extra labor, not only for putting more land under cultivation but also for building cities, manning bureaucracies and armies, and staffing all the arts and crafts of civilization.

It is not surprising that some students of the past should feel that so basic a discovery should have been made only once, and diffused from that single center to a

grateful world. Historians and archaeologists today, however, are generally willing to allow that agriculture was probably discovered independently at least half a dozen times around the globe. It seems especially likely that farming evolved separately in the New World and in the Old World, rather than spreading by diffusion across either the stormy Atlantic or the contrary currents of the Pacific.

The development of agriculture in Mexico and Peru, the two major radiant centers of civilization in the New World, illustrates with particular clarity the complexity of the ideas of cultural diffusion and independent evolution. It also illustrates the many facets of the idea of agriculture itself.

Maize, or Indian corn, was the most widely grown grain in the Americas, the equivalent of wheat, barley, or rice in various parts of Eurasia. Studies of grains and even whole ears of corn preserved from early centuries indicate that this staple was indigenous to Mesoamerica. Corn as we know it apparently developed in Mexico from a miniature original to the large, easily harvested, and widely cultivated food crop that was found all over the Americas when Columbus arrived.

Peru, like the rest of the two continents, must therefore have acquired corn from Mexico. This could have happened through a system of overlapping trade patterns that made it possible for goods to pass from Mexico to the central Andes without Mexicans and Peruvians ever coming face to face—or even knowing of each other's existence. Such overlapping patterns of exchange account for much of the long-distance trade of early times, in the Old World as well as in the Americas.

This seems like a strong argument for a single origination of agriculture in Mexico, with diffusion to Peru. This argument depends, however, upon the confusion of a single crop, however important, with the idea of agriculture itself—a very different thing.

Archaeological evidence in fact indicates that the notion of planting and tending food plants, rather than merely gathering wild plants, arose independently in Peru. The equally important decision to abandon the wandering life of hunting and gathering for a settled existence dependent almost entirely on agriculture also seems to have been taken in Peru at an earlier date than could be accounted for by the arrival of maize from the north.

The same is true of other elements of the complex of institutions and traditional practices that made up agriculture in Peru. The farming village, the irrigation of plants, the impressive system of terraces up the slopes of Peruvian valleys all appear to have evolved independently there. In fact it was the potato, not maize, that eventually emerged as the staple food of Peru, though corn continued to be grown there.

The independent evolution of the idea of agriculture in the two prime centers of urban culture in the Americas thus seems established. It is an important example of the sort of similar, but not causally linked, parallel venture

Expert breeding by skilled Mexican Indian farmers turned the small food grain on the left into the familiar corn cob on the right. Indian corn, or maize, was grown all over the New World when Columbus came, and today it feeds millions around the world. (Courtesy of Paul Mangelsdorf and R. S. MacNeish)

that constitutes much of the fundamental unity of this age of civilization's beginnings.

Ironworking in Africa

Another fundamental step in human cultural evolution was the development of metalworking, the shift from stone to bronze and then to iron for hard-edged tools and weapons. We have noted the coming of the Bronze and Iron ages to one center of civilization after another across the Old World. One of the great unsolved problems in this story, however, is that of the coming of the Iron Age to the various parts of Africa.

Africa south of the Sahara seems to have moved directly from stone to iron tools, skipping the Bronze Age, which came between the ages of stone and iron elsewhere. As we have seen, the slag heaps of Meroe reveal the existence of a well-developed iron industry in ancient Kush in the fourth century B.C. Iron was smelted and worked in West Africa not long thereafter, while iron tools would help Bantu migrants cut their way through the rain forests of Central Africa in later centuries. Is there a connection between ironworking in East and West Africa? The problem is, once more, that of cultural diffusion versus separate development.

An older and at first glance very tempting theory

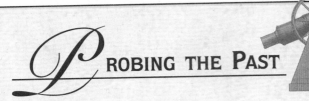

PROBING THE PAST

"*By the mid-1840s the existence of ruins of advanced civilizations in Mexico and Central America could no longer be seriously challenged. But when questions arose concerning the identity of their builders, most antiquarians steadfastly retreated to the only acceptable sources of possible inspiration: Europe, Asia, the Near East, Africa—in short, any area of influence which precluded the suggestion of an indigenous development.*

For years the debate over the origin of the Indians raged on . . . and endless analogies were drawn between various pre-Columbian cultures and the whole panoply of Indo-European civilizations. The existence in Mexico and Central America of terraced pyramids (similar to Sumerian ziggurats), calendrical systems, mathematics, and sculptured figures with beards or negroid features implied to many observers a connection with such peoples as the Assyrians, Phoenicians, Hittites, Babylonians, or Carthaginians. Other students viewed certain motifs in Mesoamerican art—lotus blossoms, tree-of-life designs, scrolls, dragonlike creatures, sun disks, and sea monsters—as conclusive evidence that massive migrations had reached America from India, Southeast Asia, China, or Japan. Inscriptions on a stone found near Paraíba, Brazil, in 1872 were pronounced to be a Canaanite text. Burial mounds in the Mississippi Valley yielded tablets inscribed with markings variously interpreted as Arabic, Chinese, Hebraic, Greek, Celtic, Sumerian, and Gaelic. . . . But regardless of how much these arguments differed in specific details, they all served the same basic purpose—to prove that America's aboriginal cultures were either founded or strongly influenced by immigrants from distant lands, a concept which is still being expounded today."

◆━◆━◆

The widely traveled American archaeologist and writer Charles Gallenkamp specializes in the pre-Columbian cultures of Mexico and the United States. In the excerpt above he sums up the efforts of generations of scholars to prove that the civilizations that flourished in the Americas before Columbus could not have been "an indigenous development." Instead, these scholars believed, such cultures must reflect the influence of more "advanced" Old World peoples from Europe, Asia, or Africa.

What parallels did these researchers see between the civilizations of the Old World and the New World? What other attitude besides objective recognition of these similarities may have inspired such efforts to prove that "America's aboriginal cultures" could not be independent developments?

Charles Gallenkamp, <u>Maya: The Riddle and Rediscovery of a Lost Civilization</u>, 2nd ed. (New York: Penguin Books, 1981), pp. 55, 59–60.

suggests that the technology of ironworking diffused from Meroe to the rest of sub-Saharan Africa. A dramatic narrative can be constructed in which the rulers of ancient Kush, fleeing from the invading Axumites, retreated westward from Meroe to reestablish Kushite civilization—including ironworking—at Darfur in the eastern region of the Sudanic grasslands. From there, iron technology could have spread on into the western Sudan and down to the rain forest belt of the Guinea coast. From West Africa, Bantu-speaking people could have taken the new metal on their great migration into the central and southern reaches of the continent.

There are, however, problems with this view. For one thing, the pattern of language distribution across the Sudanic belt does not indicate a direct diffusion of culture from east to west. Techniques of ironworking also differ from one region to the other, at least insofar as we can reconstruct them from the archaeological remains. As a result, some scholars have urged an independent origin for West African ironworking in particular. Traces of worked iron are often found in this region in conjunction with stone tools and other Neolithic survivals, suggesting direct technological development from stone to ironworking in West Africa.

The dispute, however, does not end here. Opponents of the theory of indigenous origins argue that there is no evidence of copper smelting in West Africa, a process that taught other peoples basic skills necessary for iron production. Proponents of the independent development thesis respond that West Africans might have learned smelting from firing ceramic pots, adding that the iron ore available in West Africa was easier to work than that found elsewhere, and hence required less intermediate technology.

The argument continues, and future archaeological finds may yet prove one side or the other. For the present, we can at least assert that the case for cultural diffusion remains unproven, the possibility very real that even so complex a process as the working of iron was developed independently in West Africa. Looking down the vertical shaft of a mine outside a West African ironworkers' village today, or watching the artisans at work over a smouldering fire under a thatched lean-to, iron artifacts laid out on the yellow grass, you can easily believe that these craft workers have been practicing this skill for many centuries.

Iron working in South Africa as it looked to Europeans in the nineteenth century. These Zulu artisans, like contemporary European or American village blacksmiths, produced tools and weapons much as ironworkers had been doing in Africa since the great furnaces of ancient Meroe. Such techniques would look increasingly old-fashioned as the Industrial Revolution spread across the West. But ironworking had been practiced in Africa since the first millennium B.C., when most of Europe and all of America was still chipping tools out of stone. (British Museum, Museum of Mankind)

Master Kong—Confucius—explains his principles to a Chinese ruler. Like Plato in ancient Greece, Confucius believed that heads of state should heed the advice of wise philosophers. What in this picture shows the power of the actual duke? What indicates that Confucious is doing the talking? (New York Public Library Picture Collection)

THE SEARCH FOR TRUTH ACROSS EURASIA

During the middle centuries of the first millennium before Christ, finally, a remarkable series of prophets and philosophers spread new insights and new gospels across Eurasia.[1] The religious and philosophical ideas developed during the sixth, fifth, and fourth centuries B.C. would provide the basis for thousands of years of intellectual exploration and spiritual faith in the developing civilizations of East and West. Yet there seem to be few if any links among the founders of these great traditions.

It was not that human beings had never concerned themselves with questions of ultimate truth before the sixth century. Evidence from the caves of later Paleolithic times indicates a belief in life after death and in the control of the forces of nature through ritual. Animism,

totemism, belief in nature spirits and in anthropomorphic divinities are revealed at Neolithic sites and in the ruins of the earliest civilizations. Elaborate mythologies and even more elaborate rites, rituals, and prescriptions for sacrifice come down to us from all the many dawns of civilization around the world.

Human beings thus believed from before the beginning of recorded history that they shared the world with many gods and demons. They believed that the will of these supernatural presences had brought the world into being, ruled it today, and had to be propitiated in the interests of a better tomorrow. Shamans, priests, diviners, witch doctors, and other intermediaries explained the will of these supernatural powers. For thousands of years, spirits of rain and fire, gods of the brick mold and the toothache, the will of Zeus, the judgment of Osiris, and the Mandate of Heaven seem to have been more than sufficient to explain all things in this world and above. Then, in the emerging civilization of Eurasia at least, an amazing wave of intellectual and spiritual restlessness seems to have rolled across the land.

[1]The most influential, though not the first, recognition of this "Axial Period" of parallel philosophical probes is in Karl Jaspers, *The Origin and Goal of History*, trans. M. Bullock (New Haven: Yale University Press, 1953), Part 1.

THE AXIAL AGE

We have touched on many of these pioneers of faith and reason previously. In China, the turmoil of the later Zhou produced the age of the sages, the "hundred flowers" of thought whose most honored names include such profoundly influential social thinkers as Confucius, Mencius, and Laozi. In India, the tangled rivalries and social tensions of the Gangetic states from which the Mauryan Empire would presently arise produced large numbers of wandering gurus—the religious mystics described by foreigners as the "naked philosophers"—most influential among them Mahavira, the founder of Jainism, and Siddartha the Buddha. Among the Persians, the lofty dualistic doctrines of Zoroastrianism pointed the minds of the ruling elite toward a life of crusading zeal in the service of good against evil.

In the Near East the Hebrews, long almost unique in their monotheism, gained from generations of prophets such as Jeremiah and Isaiah a deeper sense of God's ethical demands and a still more exalted feeling for his historic intent. And in the white cities and blue bays of the Greek Aegean, Socrates, Plato, and Aristotle were only the most celebrated of a long line of philosophers and scientists to abandon myth-making and to seek through human reason answers to the most fundamental questions about the good life and the ultimate nature of things.

These men all operated for the most part within existing systems of thought, yet they profoundly challenged the orthodox beliefs and practices of their time. Confucius sought social order in a disordered world. Buddha condemned the rigid, increasingly worldly religious establishment of his day. The Hebrew prophets lashed out at impiety and oppression. The Greek philosophers so shook the old mythologies of their time that a popular playwright lamented that the "Whirlwind has unseated Zeus."

But they were not mere intellectual destroyers, skeptics and sophists intent only on exposing the hypocrisies and follies of their contemporaries. Above all, these were seekers after new truths—and they frequently found them within the very intellectual and spiritual traditions they challenged.

Thus Confucius preached respect for ancient rites, elders, and emperors even while he demanded good government from the powerful and virtue in all people. Buddha accepted basic brahmanical doctrines about karma and reincarnation even as he preached his own road to escape from the wheel of life—and condemned the worldliness of the brahmans. Plato subtilized traditional Greek respect for reason and common sense into his vision of the philosophical life as the highest form of human existence, while Aristotle transformed the Greek virtue of temperance into the golden mean.

It is a dazzling array of new insights and beliefs. Confucius's vision of an ordered and harmonious soci-

Socrates, the "gadfly of Athens," stung his contemporaries into thinking seriously about some of the largest problems in life. This Roman copy of a Greek statue shows the philosopher as he was, physically unimpressive but intellectually magnetic. The Hellenistic original, now in the British Museum, follows the tradition that the great philosopher was actually overweight and ugly, unlike his handsome pupil Plato or the majestic Aristotle. (The Bettmann Archive)

ety, Buddha's dream of Nirvana, the prophetic Hebrew vision of a universal God, Socrates' gadfly insistence on free debate and fearless self-analysis—to mention only a few—reveal a range and depth of innovative thinking about the greatest human questions that would be hard to match in any other time. When we reflect that these defiant voices were first raised amid the reek of sacrificial altars, the chanting of ancient rituals, and the muttering of soothsayers poking about for truth in the entrails of dead animals, this surge of intellectual questioning and spiritual questing verges on the miraculous.

Inevitably, one wonders whether any of these contemporaneous intellectual challenges influenced any of the others. Yet there seem to be a few points of contact. The differences between these new doctrines and their clear roots in the traditions of their own societies indicate that we are dealing with independent adventures of the mind. They are one in intellectual daring, in conceptual scope, and in the passion of their seeking. But their origins are as diverse as the different human civilizations that produced them.

Here again, in short, we have parallel ventures produced by societies at roughly the same stage of social evolution. The parallel emergence of agriculture in the Amer-

icas produced food for the belly; the development of iron-working in West Africa forged tools that would open a continent to Bantu-speaking people; and the common search for truth across Eurasia generated as remarkable a range of spiritual and intellectual insights as the world has known. All three exemplify the common humanity that united all people long before trade and imperial conquest, technology and ideology had begun to shape the truly global civilization of our own times.

SUMMARY

Evolving human cultures in many parts of the world often came out looking remarkably alike. Sometimes this was because of cultural diffusion—the influence of one society on another. In these early centuries, however, similarities were also often the result of parallel evolution arising out of common circumstances.

In the New World, maize cultivation, originally developed in Mexico, spread far and wide, even as far as the other major cultural center in Peru. In Peru, however, the idea of agriculture itself, with its settled village life, terracing, and other agricultural techniques, evolved quite independently of any outside influence.

In Africa, the ironworking technology of Meroe may have spread across the grasslands south of the Sahara and down to the Guinea coast of West Africa. It is at least as likely,

however, that the breakthrough into the Iron Age was an independent West African achievement.

In Eurasia, finally, the centuries around 500 B.C. saw a remarkable series of spiritual explorations. These included the insights of the Greek philosophers, the Hebrew prophets, Buddha and other gurus in India, Confucius and other sages in China. There was, however, no apparent connection between these various quests for truth. Each grew out of its own cultural milieu and built on its own particular intellectual traditions.

Connections between cultures would intensify in later centuries. During these first three thousand years of history, however, each human culture, despite some contacts with its neighbors, for the most part followed its own independent line of historical development.

SUGGESTED READING

GROBMAN, A., W. SALHUANA, and R. SEVILLA. *Races of Maize in Peru and Their Origins, Evolution, and Classification.* Washington, D.C.: National Academy of Science, National Research Council, 1961. Corn and agriculture in the Andes.

JASPERS, K. *The Origin and Goal of History,* trans. M. Bullock. New Haven: Yale University Press, 1953. Part 1 structures the entire human past around the "Axial Period" in the history of philosophy and sees the origins of parallel intellectual movement in similar social, political, and historical circumstances.

KROEBER, A. L. "Diffusionism," in *Encyclopaedia of the Social Sciences,* vol. 5, E. R. A. Seligmen and A. Johnson, eds. New York: Macmillan, 1963. A brief if dated definition of the controversy over cultural diffusion.

MANGELSDORF, P. C., R. C. MACNEISH, and G. R. WILLEY. "Origins of Agriculture in Middle America," in *Handbook of Middle American Indians,* R. Wau-

chope, ed. Austin: University of Texas Press, 1964. Mexican beginnings. See also P. C. Mengelsdorf, R. C. MacNeish, and W. C. Galina, "Domestication of Corn," *Science,* 143 (1964), 538–545.

PHILLIPSON, D. W. "The Beginnings of the Iron Age in Southern Africa," in *Ancient Civilization of Africa,* G. Mokhtar, ed. Clear and detailed account of the impact of the Bantu migration. But see F. van Noten, "Central Africa," in the same volume, for a more cautious view of the evidence for the Bantu impact.

ROWE, J. H. "Diffusionism and Archaeology," *American Antiquity,* 31, no. 3 (January 1966), 334–337. Opposes the diffusionist thesis on the birth of American civilization.

SMITH, G. E., et al. *Culture: The Diffusion Controversy.* London: K. Paul, Trench, Trubner & Co., 1928. Smith was an extreme diffusionist, urging that all developed cultures could be traced back to the Near East.

THE CLASSIC AGE

Classic is a word with a ring to it. It conjures up the polished enamel and gleaming chrome of ancient automobiles, or orchestras tuning up. A classic age should be something splendid.

What makes the half-dozen centuries centering upon the time of Christ so distinctive as to earn them such a label?

In the first place, there is a certain scale and grandeur to them. Both the Roman Empire and Han China were about the size of the United States today. The Guptas ruled the subcontinent of India, and successive Persian empires filled most of the Middle East most of the time. The slightly later New World civilization of the Classic Maya did not fill so much space, but the Mayans did rule more of Central America than any of their predecessors. Important political units of this second age of human history were thus considerably larger than those of the dawn age.

A special feature of the so-called classic age of world history is an increased level of contact between neighboring societies, particularly between the formerly islanded civilizations of Eurasia. Goods could travel from China to Rome in the time of Christ. This degree of communication and exchange is particularly striking because it would decline drastically with the collapse of the classical civilizations, to reappear only briefly during the following thousand years. The great civilizations of the classic age thus accomplished a degree of continental interaction that would rarely be achieved again until modern times.

Still, there is more to the claim that these centuries constitute a classic age than the size of empires and the reach of trade. There is a breadth of accomplishment here too that is hard to match in even the most brilliant of the earlier cultures.

The cultural achievements of the fifth-century Greeks and the later Zhou dynasty were awesome—golden ages by any standards. But neither the Warring States period in China nor the Greek century that ended with the Peloponnesian War can be considered to have solved their basic political problems. Despite their temporary mid-course breakdowns, both the Roman and Han empires of the classic age project a sense of political power and stability as well as of cultural brilliance.

There is depth of accomplishment here as well. The civilizations of the classic age had the advantage of being able to draw upon the cultural, political, economic, and technological heritage of their predecessors—and go on from there. The Classical Maya, for instance, had hundreds of years of Mesoamerican experience in monumental architecture, stone carving, even mathematics and astronomy, to build upon. It is not surprising, then, that they went beyond any of their predecessors in most of these areas. The people of Axum brought with them into East Africa the skills at building and trading developed over centuries in their Yemeni homeland and soon outdistanced their Kushite neighbors and predecessors in that corner of the continent.

To some degree, it is perhaps a matter of tone—a tone of confident supremacy that few before or since can match. Like the rich, full tones of a symphony orchestra, the civilizations of the classic age radiated a powerful confidence that they knew what they were doing. It is an attitude that has a special power all its own.

In the culture of ancient Rome, "classical" means just such a tone of confident mastery, a conviction of having achieved what no other western people had done—the crafting of a "Roman world." Farther east, the bustling world of Gupta India projects a sense of supremacy in many fields, from political sovereignty to cultural flowering to religious rebirth. Han China is matched by few other civilizations in both achievement and calm certainty of its own centrality. Even where little beyond stone ruins survive of once-great civilizations, as in African Axum, the towering obelisks that remain seem to speak of vanished splendors.

Tone is hard to footnote, but it is real nonetheless. Some of us may be tone-deaf to the beauties of Bach or the Beatles in their prime, to the confident supremacy of Romans or Han Chinese, the complexities of Mayan culture, or the rich variety of India in its classic age. But few today could speak with the confidence of Roman poets or Han historians of our place in the world as one of absolute supremacy—as they spoke of Rome as "the city and the world" or of China as the "Middle Kingdom" ringed by hopelessly inferior barbarians. At the core of the civilizations of the classic age, there perhaps lies above all this a tone of sureness about their own place in world history.

A grand scale of political organization, sustained trade and communication between peoples, breadth and depth of cultural achievement, and a tone of confident certainty about it all are pehaps as close as we can come to defining the classic age. Yet there is an undeniable feel of cultural climax to these centuries immediately before and after Chirst—we can scarcely be more precise—that other ages of civilization cannot claim.

Let us now turn from definitions to realities and see how well our terms do characterize this second age of global history.

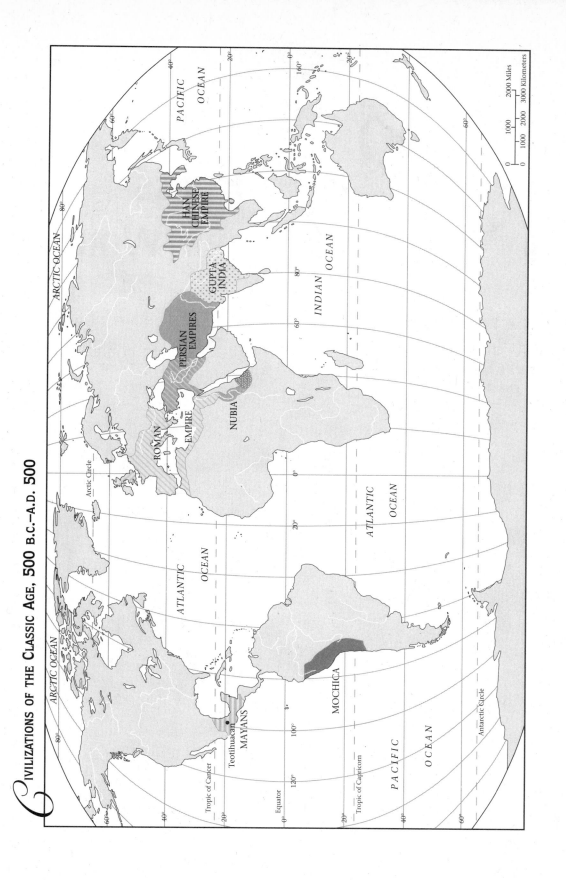

Civilizations of the Classic Age, 500 B.C.–A.D. 500

HAN CHINESE EMPIRE

GUPTA INDIA

PERSIAN EMPIRES

ROMAN EMPIRE

NUBIA

MOCHICA

MAYANS

Teotihuacan

PACIFIC OCEAN

INDIAN OCEAN

ATLANTIC OCEAN

ATLANTIC OCEAN

PACIFIC OCEAN

ARCTIC OCEAN

ARCTIC OCEAN

Arctic Circle

Tropic of Cancer

Equator

Tropic of Capricorn

Antarctic Circle

2000 Miles
3000 Kilometers
1000
2000
1000
0

CHAPTER 11

ROME RULES THE WESTERN WORLD

THE ROMAN REPUBLIC

THE ROMAN CITY-STATE

The Romans have an image in history very different from that of the creative, liberty-loving, self-destructive Greeks who preceded them as the dominant European people in the Mediterranean world. Champions of order, builders of empire, the Romans still cannot help but look a bit stodgy in the history books beside their brilliant kin across the Adriatic.

We shall have to look more closely at this problem later. It did, after all, take the two of them to forge the immensely potent alloy we call Greco-Roman culture, whose influence was to be so great upon later generations of Western people. At this point, however, it is sufficient to stress the simple fact of their kinship one with the other. For these two strikingly dissimilar peoples were in fact descended from common Indo-European origins somewhere on the long-forgotten Caucasian steppes. Speakers of various Italic dialects, including Latin, probably drifted into the Mediterranean basin at roughly the same time—early in the first millennium B.C.—as the Greek speakers to the east. Their histories were to be closely linked from then on.

Other peoples lived and flourished in the Italian peninsula before Rome rose, of course, most prominent among them the Etruscans. But, like the Minoans and Mycenaeans, whose civilizations preceded that of the Greeks in the Aegean, the ancient Etruscans are a people all but lost in the mists of history.

The Etruscans probably came, like the Minoans, from somewhere in Asia Minor. They imposed their rule upon the Iron Age natives living north of the Tiber River in central Italy sometime early in the first millennium B.C. They built a loose league of fortified cities, made lovely pottery, and furnished their tombs with grave goods of bronze. They learned to read and write from Greek colonies established in southern Italy and Sicily, and they passed this skill on to the Romans. By 500 B.C., however, Etruscan sovereignty over central Italy was drawing to a close. In the fourth century a decadent Etruria was absorbed by Rome; in the third the Greek colonies of the south followed the Etruscans into the Roman maw. It was a fate that awaited many other peoples then tilling their tiny fields and fighting their petty wars around the Mediterranean in blissful ignorance of the powerhouse that was building on the Tiber.

The core of Roman power lay for centuries in the hardfisted Roman peasantry and their grim patrician overlords. Between them they provided the backbone of the Roman army. They were a hardy people, practical, disciplined, and traditionally brave. "Roman courage," said Ennius, the first of Roman poets, "is an endless sky." Looking at portrait heads of men of the old Republic, realistically reproduced in bronze or stone, the warts decidedly left in, one sees strength, common sense, harsh justice perhaps, but little mercy. They were, above all, an intensely conservative lot. Not for these Romans the restless political experiments of the Athenians, or the Greek delight in the free play of the intellect. As their Roman forefathers had done, so would they do. "This thing, Rome," Ennius said also, "is simply men who know what their past means."[1]

They were, in their own judgment, a people made to rule. "Others, I know," wrote Vergil, the most famous of all Roman poets, "will mould the breathing brass with a finer touch; in marble trace the features of the life." But "these shall be your arts, [Romans:] to rule the subject nations with imperial sway . . . to impose the arts of peace, to spare the humbled, and to crush the proud."[2] In time, much of the Western world would come to accept that judgment—and that imperial sway.

There were many myths of Roman origins, among them Aeneas's flight from burning Troy, and Romulus and Remus suckled by a wolf. In fact the city of Rome seems to have been founded by descendants of a number of tribes—Latins, Sabines, Etruscans—living among the seven hills, meeting in the little valley that would become the Forum. Among these Latin tribes there were two important classes: *patricians*, who were the better-off farmers, and *plebeians*, the poorer. The real centers of authority among them remained for a long time the old

[1]Ennius, *Fragments*, in Garry Wills, ed., *Roman Culture* (New York: G. Braziller, 1966), p. 243.

[2]*The Aeneid*, in *The Works of Vergil*, trans. A. Hamilton Bryce (London: Bohn's Classical Library, 1907), pp. 320–321.

tribes and clans, whose heads were the chief men in the emerging Roman state.

Under the Etruscans Rome became a sizable city, important for trade and a power in that part of Italy. Probably sometime around 509 B.C., the traditional date of the founding of the Roman Republic, the Latin tribes overthrew their Etruscan kings. The constitution they established to replace the old Etruscan monarchy was dominated by the Senate, a patrician council composed of elder statesmen, former magistrates, and other leaders of the old clans. The magistrates, especially two executive officials called *consuls*, were chosen for short terms by assemblies of the free male fighting men.

Roman women did have more freedom than Greek women did. Upperclass women joined their husbands at the theater, the circus, and the banquet table. Working-class women labored as servants, artisans, shopkeepers, garment workers, nurses, midwives, doctors, entertainers, actresses, dancers, prostitutes, and servers in restaurants and taverns.

In general, early Roman society was very similar to that of their Greek kindred across the Adriatic, evolving from tribe and clan to monarchy and assemblies. In some important ways, however, things took a different course among the Romans.

For one thing, the Romans settled their domestic disputes, between patrician and plebeian in particular, with comparatively little violence. The "struggle of the orders" in Rome was settled by a striking conservative compromise. The championship of the interests of the lower social orders was vested in elected officials called *tribunes of the people*—who more often than not supported the will of the patrician Senate. The Roman Republic was to have its share of destructive domestic conflict, but that lay centuries in the future.

The other great difference between the rise of Rome and that of the Greek city-states was the rapidity with which the city on the Tiber River extended its sway over the entire Italian peninsula. Fear impelled some of the neighboring states to accept the protection and sovereignty of Rome—fear of a resurgence of Etruscan power, or of the barbarian Goths who had once stormed

A Roman triumphal arch—this one dedicated to Emperor Titus and located in the Roman Forum—symbolized the long series of victories that established the supremacy of the Empire around the Mediterranean and across Western Europe. Victorious legions with their loot and prisoners once paraded through such arches to the cheers of their fellow citizens. (Library of Congress)

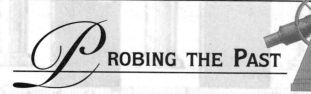

PROBING THE PAST

"*The momentum of social change in the Hellenistic world combined with Roman elements to produce the emancipated, but respected, upper-class woman. The Roman matron of the late Republic must be viewed against the background of shrewd and politically powerful Hellenistic princesses, expanding cultural opportunities for women, the search for sexual fulfillment in the context of a declining birthrate, and the individual assertiveness characteristic of the Hellenistic period. The rest of the picture is Roman: enormous wealth, aristocratic indulgence and display, pragmatism permitting women to exercise leadership during the absence of men on military and governmental missions of long duration; and, as a final element, a past preceding the influence of the Greeks—a heritage so idealized by the Romans that historical events were scarcely distinguishable from legends, and the legends of the founding of Rome and the early Republic were employed in the late Republic and early Empire for moral instruction and propaganda. The result was that wealthy aristocratic women who played high politics and presided over literary salons were nevertheless expected to be able to spin and weave as though they were living in the days when Rome was young. These social myths set up a tension between the ideal and the real Roman matron.*"

This passage from Sarah Pomeroy's widely admired <u>Goddesses, Whores, Wives, and Slaves</u> puts the condition of women in the Roman Republic in the double context of Roman society and the larger world of the Hellenistic Mediterranean. From this brief extract do you see any particular historiographical assumptions or methodologies that make this example of "women's history" different from other social and cultural history? Is Pomeroy attempting to generalize about all Roman women here, or does she focus on a particular class?

Sarah B. Pomeroy, <u>Goddesses, Whores, Wives, and Slaves</u> (New York: Schocken Books, 1975), p. 153.

down from the north. The primitive ethnic organization of the other Italian tribes favored the Romans too: the loosely structured tribal societies that surrounded Rome offered little resistance to the imposition of Roman authority.

The Roman Republic was founded as a city-state around the beginning of the fifth century B.C. By the end of the third, Rome was the undisputed master of the Italian peninsula. And the centuries of the Roman conquest were just beginning.

ROME RULES THE MEDITERRANEAN

During the last three centuries before Christ, Rome became the political center of the Mediterranean world. But Italy had been the geographical center of that world from the beginning. Roman Italy was protected by sea and by the Alps from frequent conquest. Thanks to Rome's central position in the Mediterranean, the city on seven hills was also ideally located to reach out east and west, south to Africa and north into Europe, imposing Roman rule.

But geography is not destiny, and many scholars have concluded that the Roman Empire, like the British Empire of many centuries later, was largely unintended by those who built it.

The empire that grew up around the Mediterranean Sea in the later centuries of the Republic was an oddly improvised, ramshackle, even reluctant affair. The Romans fought a good deal during those centuries, but most commonly in defense of their own interests or those of their allies and their expanding provinces. Cato the elder's thundering insistence that *Carthago delenda est*—"Carthage must be destroyed"—was the exception, not the rule. The rule was unenthusiastic involvement—followed by famous victories—and an expanding empire that led the Romans into more foreign involvements, more wars, more provinces to rule.

Reluctant imperialists though they might be, the Romans were extremely good at empire building. Italy was Roman by 285 B.C. Carthage, Rome's powerful North African rival, which had come to dominate the western Mediterranean, had been decisively defeated by 200 B.C. and was destroyed shortly after 150 B.C. Macedon and Greece also fell to Roman arms in the middle of the second century, western Persia and Ptolemaic Egypt in the first. It was an impressive record, and there were still many lands to conquer, even after the ancient powers of the Mediterranean and the Near East had been absorbed.

The Romans earned their place in history. Roman discipline and the Roman short sword, the eagle standards, and the tramping legions had a fierce implacability, tenacity of purpose that carried them inexorably, decade after decade, generation after generation, to the mastery of their world. The epic wars with Hannibal's Carthage illustrate this determination as well as any in the long litany of Roman victories.

There were three Punic Wars, stretching from the middle of the third to the middle of the second century B.C. The first was a struggle over Sicily (264–241), where the Carthaginians had replaced the Greeks as the predominant power. The Africans were driven from the island only at the cost of fearsome Roman casualties. The second was the Hannibalic war (212–202), begun when that brilliant general brought an African army down from the Alps on the backs of elephants to take the Romans in the rear. Hannibal was dislodged from Italy only when the Romans, after suffering repeated defeats on their home ground, turned the tables by invading North Africa to shatter the Carthaginians at Zama in 202. The Third Punic War (149–146) was a bitter piece of Roman chauvinism, in which the jingo slogans of the elder Cato prevailed at last. Carthage was taken, pillaged, and much of it burned. The stubborn Roman refusal to admit defeat despite Hannibal's victories, the pragmatic shrewdness of the Roman general Fabius "the Delayer" in wearing out the Carthaginians by refusing to give battle, the final harsh implacability of Cato's *Carthago delenda est*—all were typical of the builders of the Roman Empire.

It is recorded of Scipio Aemilianus, the general who presided over the destruction of Carthage, that he "wept and openly lamented the enemy's fate." He is said to have stood brooding for a long time over the fate of empires:

> Troy had fallen, once so prosperous a city; the empires of the Assyrians, and the Medes, and the Persians after them. . . . Consciously or unconsciously, Scipio recited Homer's lines:

> There will come a day when sacred Ilium shall perish,
> And Priam, and the people of Priam of the strong ash spear.[3]

The spears of the Romans had half a dozen centuries yet to hold the world in awe. But—if this passage is not pure literary flourish—there were men even among these grim old Romans of the Republic who saw their own future in the rubble of once-mighty Carthage.

THE ROMAN CIVIL WAR

The greatest danger to the Roman polity during the last centuries of the Republic, however, lay not in foreign wars but in the threat of civil war. The two were not unrelated.

The conquest of the eastern Mediterranean in particular made the Romans very rich. Opportunities multiplied for pillage in war and for corruption among the *proconsuls*, who governed conquered provinces. Land was cheap, tens of thousands of slaves were there for the taking, taxes and tribute flowed into the hands of the few. They spent their new wealth on broad estates and large houses, on Greek culture and Asiatic luxuries, and forgot the spartan virtues of earlier centuries.

The poor, by contrast, rapidly grew poorer as Roman power spread. Hannibal's campaigns in Italy ravaged the countryside, and long service in the East left farms untenanted. Rich men bought out small holdings, combined them into great estates called *latifundia*, and worked them with slave labor. Roman farmers, landless and unemployed, swarmed to Rome, where the Senate and the consuls now governed in splendor from the white-columned buildings that rose around the ancient Forum. Generals and proconsuls built themselves palaces in Rome; the poor sweltered in multistoried tenements and lived on the grain dole taken in tribute from Sicily and Egypt.

The resulting bitterness of the masses was exacerbated by the flagrant and increasingly violent political ambitions of the mighty. In the old days, so the patriotic legends ran, Roman generals like the fabled Cincinnatus had served from a sense of duty to the Republic, won their victories, laid down their arms, and returned to their bean fields. It was not so, however, with the generals whose victories turned the Roman Republic into an empire. These new-style heroes brought their armies home with them and became a menace to domestic tranquility, indeed to the very existence of the state.

The result of this unhappy mix of social pressures and political ambition was a turbulent century of tension and recurrent violence called the Roman Civil War (roughly 133–31 B.C.).

The history of those troubled decades is studded

---

[3]Appian, *Punica*, in Moses Hadas, *A History of Rome from Its Origins to 529 A.D. as Told by the Roman Historians* (Garden City, N.Y.: Doubleday, 1956), p. 44.

with the names of famous politicians such as the reforming Gracchus brothers, Tiberius and Gaius, and the eloquent orator Cicero, and of such celebrated generals as Marius and Sulla, Pompey and Julius Caesar. Their deeds will be briefly chronicled below. But it is well to remember that beneath the surface of high politics and military challenge there rumbled the bewilderment, bitterness, and sudden furies of a whole people caught in the grip of trends and currents that were as far beyond their understanding as the political tensions and economic pressures of our own times often are of ours.

The brothers Tiberius and Gaius Gracchus, tribunes of the people in 133 and 123, respectively, stirred up the popular assemblies, passed laws to provide land for the landless at the expense of the *latifundia*, and were hounded to death by the Senate. A series of victorious generals next took the center of the stage, mobilizing conservative sentiment and factional political support in the capital to slaughter their enemies. The army reformer Marius and the arch-conservative Sulla thus competed all their lives for leadership in the Roman Republic.

JULIUS CAESAR

The penultimate round of the Roman Civil War nearly tore the empire apart. It was a savage time, dominated by the powerful personalities of the generals Pompey the Great and Julius Caesar, the latter the only one of them all whose name is a watchword to this day.

As a general, Pompey won many victories for Rome. As a politician, he organized the so-called First Triumvirate, a loose political alliance including a rich nonentity and a much younger but equally ambitious man named Julius Caesar. Caesar spent most of a decade conquering Gaul—most of modern France. Then, feeling threatened by both allies and enemies at home, he turned back toward Rome to face more deadly enemies there than he had among the Gallic barbarians.

In 49 B.C. Caesar crossed the Rubicon River into Italy with the famous remark that "the die is cast"—and all his future hung on that cast. In Rome he smashed an alliance of convenience between Pompey and the Senate. He thereafter drove Pompey from the Italian peninsula and crushed him for good in Greece. He pursued his foes around the Mediterranean, enjoyed a brief liaison with Cleopatra in Egypt, and returned triumphantly to Rome in 46 B.C.

He was the undisputed master of the Roman world. He had a little more than two years to live.

Julius Caesar seems to have been a somewhat more complex person than such pithy communiqués as the celebrated *Veni, vidi, vici*—"I came, I saw, I conquered"— might lead us to expect. A famous portrait head of him shows what appears to be a rather thoughtful man, half smiling, shadowed at the temples. He was as ambitious as other victorious Roman generals had been. He may also have had a touch of the reforming Gracchus brothers in his makeup. He claimed at least to be the people's champion, and the aristocratic Senate was terrified of him. The Republic, he said, was a hollow sham.

What exactly he might have done about it if he had lived we cannot know. What he did do was make himself dictator for life, pack the Senate with his officers, and give land to his soldiers. He also inaugurated a program of public works, reorganized the administration of Italy, reformed taxation in the provinces, extended Roman citizenship to at least some conquered peoples, lowered the debt burden, and reformed the calendar. His enemies said he planned to make himself king of Rome.

On the Ides of March, 44 B.C., he was stabbed to death in the Senate house by a group of senatorial conspirators led by two of his own lieutenants. Caesar thus died as he had lived—dramatically. The battered shell of the Republic survived him by a dozen years. The wars and intrigues that followed were complicated and brutal, the last bloody gasp of the Roman Civil War. Caesar's assassins and his old commanders fought while champions of the old order such as the eloquent orator Cicero labored to save the Republic. In the end, they were all out-fought and out-intrigued by a young man who was only nineteen when Julius Caesar died: his grandnephew and adopted son Octavian, known to history as Augustus Caesar.

BUST OF JULIUS CÆSAR (NAPLES).

The enigmatic face of Julius Caesar—solider, statesman, and the man many thought would be king in Rome. Murdered in the Senate house, Caesar left his name and legend to a line of emperors. Yet the thinning hair and thoughtful eyes are those of a very human individual. (New York Public Library)

Augustus, Rome's "second founder." The armor, the pose, the upraised arm all embody the force of character and confident authority that made Augustus not merely another successful general and shrewd politician, but the first emperor of Rome's golden age. This idealized portrait, however, probably bears little physical resemblance to the real Octavian. (Library of Congress)

The year after his uncle's assassination, Octavian and his allies of the Caesarian faction formed the Second Triumvirate and forced the Senate to grant them—and their legions—the power to restore order to the state. In the year 42 B.C. at Philippi in northern Greece, they defeated the men who had murdered Caesar. Octavian then fell out with his own allies, most importantly with Caesar's old friend (and Cleopatra's new lover) Antony. In 31 B.C. Octavian's forces destroyed Antony's in a naval battle off Actium, and the Roman Civil War was over.

"Who could venture," a Roman historian of the next generation asked rhetorically, "to express the benefits that day conferred upon the world or the improvement in the fortunes of the state?"[4] To an unbiased observer, all that could be said with any certainty was that another ambitious general had crushed his foes. In fact, however, the ancient historian was right. From the reign of Augustus Caesar, we date the most successful and prosperous period of Roman rule: the Principate at home and the Roman Peace over the length and breadth of their wide empire.

THE ROMAN EMPIRE

AUGUSTUS CAESAR

Gaius Julius Caesar Octavianus, holder of the *imperium* (military command) and of the tribunician power (and hence spokesman for the people), *pontifex maximus* (chief priest), *princeps* (which then meant not "prince" but

---

[4]Velleius Paterculs, in Hadas, *History of Rome*, p. 87.

simply "first citizen"), voted the title of *Augustus* (the Fortunate and Blessed) during his lifetime and "the Divine" after his death, was never officially emperor of Rome at all. Nor were his successors during the most successful centuries of what we call the Empire, as contrasted with the Republic. The purple robe and the diadem, the bowing and scraping as before a Near Eastern potentate, were adopted at Rome only in the fourth century A.D. by rulers desperate to hold the empire together. Augustus had no need for such trappings.

Historians call the order he established the Principate—rule by the princeps. It was a typical conservative Roman compromise, yet it amounted to little less than a second founding of Rome after a century of civil strife.

During the forty-five years of Augustus's rule (31 B.C.–A.D. 14), the Senate and the popular assemblies still met. But the former was filled with friends of the first citizen's, and the assemblies seem to have lost all political function. Consuls, proconsuls, tribunes, and other officials were still elected, but only after securing Augustus's political blessing. He ruled the vast empire, whose frontiers now reached to the Rhine and the Danube, as commander of the Roman armies. He dominated Rome on the strength of his great-uncle Julius Caesar's name, his own military triumphs, and the simple fact that he had brought peace and order after decades of civil war. He earned a reputation for piety as the rebuilder of the temples and refurbisher of the cults of the Olympian gods, but he also built temples to the "divine" Julius Caesar and to "Rome and Augustus," thus surrounding the name of the emperor with the faint aura of divine right. He did not go beyond that. But then he did not need to.

Augustus claimed to have "found Rome brick and left it marble"—a bit of an exaggeration. But he did build or rebuild many temples and public buildings, as well as roads, bridges, and aqueducts. He established a sound currency, fostered honest government, paid the troops, and kept the land, internally at least, at peace. He encouraged literature and the arts in the age of Vergil and Horace and Ovid, three men whose poetry is still being read in schools two thousand years later. It is perhaps no wonder that Romans called him "blessed," "fortunate," and "the divine," or that the Age of Augustus has become known as Rome's golden age.

The idealized contemporary statue of him that we possess—he is clad in armor, the rod of authority resting easily across his left arm, the right hand raised in a gesture of command—does not tell us much. A shrewdly calculating man, dismissed by some as a military adventurer, he was no philosopher king, yet he was not a tyrant either. Sickly in youth, never robust, he nevertheless possessed a quality the Romans called *auctoritas*, an air of confident authority that made it unnecessary for him to resort to force. Conservative by nature, he became the most effective political innovator in Roman history— something perhaps only such a man could have managed,

given the profoundly conservative character of the Roman people.

The peace and prosperity fashioned by Augustus Caesar lasted for the better part of two hundred years.

THE ROMAN PEACE

The Roman Empire, which now brought the Mediterranean world, western Europe, and a sizable chunk of the Near East under a single government, was above all a supreme exercise of power. In the great days of the empire, at least, Roman subjects had little cause to regret it.

The "good emperors"—Claudius and Trajan, Hadrian, Marcus Aurelius, and others—who reigned during the first and second centuries A.D. perpetuated and expanded the Augustan heritage. They completed the building of the splendid city on the seven hills that future generations would revere as the Rome of the Caesars. They brought the protection of Roman power to more and more of their subjects. And they expanded the empire beyond anything the West had seen before—or was ever to see again, at least down to the present day.

Among the material benefits of the empire, three deserve special attention: Roman administration, Roman citizenship, and Roman law.

Roman administration under the Republic had been relatively simple, a matter of the short-term proconsuls, who not infrequently milked their provinces mercilessly. Under the emperors of the first two centuries A.D., however, a much more elaborate system of imperial administration was carried out by paid permanent officials closely supervised by their superiors. It was a system that provided lower taxes and more effective government than most parts of the Roman world had ever known before.

Roman citizenship was also extended far more widely by Augustus and his successors; by approximately A.D. 200, all free provinces had been granted citizenship, making them equal in every way to their conquerors. The army, the bureaucracy, and even the higher reaches of the government were thoroughly opened up to Gauls and Spaniards, Near Easterners and North Africans.

Roman law, finally, embodied the benefits of Roman government more concretely and longlastingly than almost any other aspect of the Roman predominance. The first laws of the Romans had been inscribed on the famous Twelve Tablets as early as the fifth century B.C. Over the following centuries, Roman civil and criminal law grew through legislation by the assemblies and decrees promulgated by the emperors, but above all through precedents established by Roman magistrates down the years. The resulting system of justice was among the most impressive bodies of law ever produced.

"Let justice be done," the Roman maxim ran, "though the heavens fall." Mercy was not a Roman strong point; stern justice seems to have been.

The sheer size of the empire, as well as the com-

GROWTH OF ROMAN DOMINIONS UNDER THE EMPIRE, 44 B.C.–A.D. 180

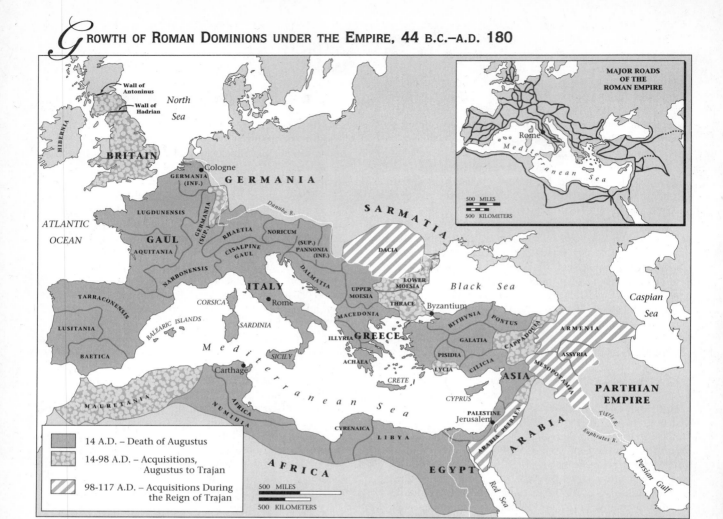

MAJOR ROADS OF THE ROMAN EMPIRE

Legend:
- 14 A.D. – Death of Augustus
- 14-98 A.D. – Acquisitions, Augustus to Trajan
- 98-117 A.D. – Acquisitions During the Reign of Trajan

plexity of its government, grew significantly under the *imperators* who followed Augustus. Roman legions pushed farther east into former Persian lands, north across the Danube into central and eastern Europe, north across the Channel to overrun most of Britain. There were setbacks and withdrawals, especially in what was to become Germany, but the legions were generally victorious. At its height, the Roman Empire covered more than three million square miles, only slightly less than the size of the United States today. Recent estimates of the population of the empire run to eighty million, about a third that of modern America.

"By allowing the vanquished to be sharers in thine own law," a late Roman poet boasted, "thou hast made a city out of what was once a world."[5] Rome: *urbi et orbi*—the city and the world. Egyptian *fellahin* laboring in the

fertile fields along the Nile, tenders of olive trees in Greece and orchards in Britain, merchants at Byzantium, and philosophers in Athens all lived under the protecting shadow of the *Pax Romana*—the Roman Peace.

Roman roads snaked out from their central hub at Rome, girdling the entire Mediterranean, spanning the Alps, the Pyrenees, and the English Channel. Trade followed the flag, and Roman styles of life and culture followed the soldiers, the traders, and the governors. The ruins are still there to testify to that vanished supremacy. Roman amphitheaters and triumphal arches, country villas and towns once dotted the map of Europe as outposts of the civilized south. You can see them today, from fortifications along the Scottish frontier in the mists of northern Britain to cities in the sundrenched sands of Jordan in the Middle East. And wherever you find the old foundations, there are the remains of temples as well as forts, the streets run at crisp right angles, and under the mosaic of a Roman floor lie the telltale ducts of Roman central heating.

---

[5]Rutilius Namatianus, in Frederick Brittain, *The Penguin Book of Latin Verse* (Baltimore: Penguin Books, 1982), p. 104.

THE CRISIS OF THE THIRD CENTURY

There were breakdowns, of course, as there are in any human institution, even during the early centuries of the empire. There was the increasing interference of the Praetorian Guard—the elite troops who served as the emperor's bodyguard and policed the city of Rome—in selection of each new emperor. There were tyrants even among the good emperors, men such as the insane Caligula and Nero, who crucified the Christians and drove all Gaul to revolt. And there was plain brutality: the severed hands of those who took up arms against Rome, the enslavement of whole armies of her foes, the popular savagery of gladiatorial contests, and public executions.

Neither anarchy nor tyranny, however, was new to either Europe or the Mediterranean. What was unprecedented was the level of general prosperity, the long years of peace. It was when these began to fail seriously that the decline and fall of the Roman Empire began.

It came in two stages. There was a first major breakdown in the third century A.D. This was followed by recovery under an increasingly autocratic regime in the fourth century. But the recovery was only temporary. In the fifth century came the collapse.

The good times seem to have ended with the reign of Marcus Aurelius (161–180), the celebrated Stoic emperor, last of the benevolent successors of Augustus. The next hundred years, the disastrous third century A.D., saw a bewildering series of short-term rulers, many of them provincial generals who were elevated by their troops and then killed by their own or rival legions. Standards of living declined sharply. The countryside was depopulated, the cities swollen with poor people living on the government grain dole, the solid middle classes of society shrinking under the pressures of government exactions. There were rebellious rumblings in the provinces—Gaul, Spain, North Africa—and new pressure on the frontiers from Germanic peoples in Europe and a revived Persian Empire in the East.

This century of disasters was ended by the reforms of the emperors Diocletian and Constantine, who between them at least temporarily restored the Roman order on a more autocratic basis than ever before.

Diocletian (284–305), a strong-willed Balkan peasant from Illyria who had risen through the army, attempted to quell anarchy by the installation of the so-called Tetrarchy. Imperial power was shared among four rulers, two senior *Augusti* and two junior men called *Caesars*. Diocletian strengthened the bureaucracy, reformed taxation in the direction of greater equality—and rigor—and even attempted to fix prices. In his last years he embarked upon the last major persecution of the Christian church, in whose growing power he apparently detected a threat to the restored authority of the state.

The Tetrarchy collapsed after Diocletian, and Constantine (306–337), son of one of the tetrarchs, fought his way to sole mastery of Rome. Constantine carried Diocletian's bureaucratic reforms to even greater lengths. He established two capitals, one at Rome and one at Byzantium (renamed Constantinople in his honor) in the east, where a Byzantine (or East Roman) Empire would survive for another thousand years. He set up an elaborate centralized system of administration involving four huge imperial prefectures, a dozen dioceses, and 120 separate provinces from Britain to Egypt. He also shrewdly separated civil government from the military and encouraged a series of army reforms in order to strengthen the frontiers.

At home the autocratic Constantine prescribed fixed hereditary membership in the crafts and professions. He levied taxes for defense that were so oppressive that free farmers had to be reduced to near slavery if they were to be kept on the land. Only the Christians had obvious cause to love him, for he finally legalized the Christian church in Rome in 313.

This rigidification of the system worked, however. For a century after Diocletian and Constantine, Rome at least survived. But the benefits of Roman rule were so reduced that many Romans may have tolerated, even welcomed, the barbarian incursions that came at last in the fifth century A.D.

DECLINE AND FALL

Rome's preurban or "barbarian" neighbors were often great admirers of all things Roman. As one dazzled chief declared, gazing at Constantinople with its towering walls, crowded streets, marching troops, and harbor full of ships: "Surely the emperor is a god upon earth, and whoever lifts up his hand against him is committing suicide."[6] Less than a century later, however, the Roman Empire of history was no more, and this barbarian's descendents were struggling to hold together the empire they had occupied.

Of all Rome's preurban neighbors to the north—Germans, Celts, Slavs, and others—the Germanic tribes along the Rhine-Danube frontiers had generally been the most important. Half-Romanized Germans had infiltrated the empire for centuries, as settlers on deserted lands and as mercenary soldiers. Late in the fourth century, however, these Germanic peoples were thrust more violently against Roman frontiers by the onslaught of warlike East Asian nomads following the steppe gradient westward. Thus pressured from the rear, armies of Visigoths, Ostrogoths, Vandals, Franks, and others crashed through the Roman boundaries in force in the fifth century. Barbarian cavalry broke the Roman phalanxes, ravaged whole provinces, and twice sacked Rome itself, the Visigoths in 410, the Vandals in 455. The invaders ended by estab-

---

[6]Quoted in E. A. Thompson, *Romans and Barbarians: The Decline of the Western Empire* (Madison: University of Wisconsin Press, 1982), p. 5.

lishing kingdoms of their own all across the western half of the Roman Empire.

There is little argument about the unhappy sequence of events that Edward Gibbon, in perhaps the most famous of all history books, christened *The Decline and Fall of the Roman Empire*. What fills the pages of more recent historical studies are attempts to explain the underlying causes of this mighty fall.

Before the barbarians came, so most modern historians believe, the empire had been fatally weakened from within. It is these internal weaknesses that have preoccupied students of Roman history since Gibbon.

There were obviously political factors at work. The lack of orderly procedures for the transfer of power, thanks to Augustus's shying away from hereditary monarchy, clearly opened the door to political turmoil. After Diocletian and Constantine, there was also the increasing remoteness of government—of emperors in purple and gold glittering with jewels, of elaborate court ceremonies, of corrupt and arrogant bureaucrats.

A wide range of social and economic problems also existed. There was the widening gap between rich and poor, the heavy cost of bread and circuses to keep the poor properly docile, the squeezing of the middle classes of society by government regulation and economic pressure. And there were more technical problems: the diminishing quantities of silver available for coinage, the exhaustion of soil, the abandonment of farmlands. They all added up to a substantial decline in the prosperity that had been one of the empire's chief claims on the loyalty of its subjects.

Demographic factors have been stressed in some analyses. The "barbarization" of the army and much of the bureaucracy that took place when Romans refused to serve seems a major weakness to some. Population decline, especially among the millions of slaves who did much of the work of the empire, may also have weakened the empire seriously. Even a gradual self-poisoning by the Roman ruling class, due to the lead pipes and drinking vessels they used, has been suggested as a source of social decay.

Cultural and ideological causes may also have played a part. A general malaise, or failure of nerve, as the center failed to hold and things fell apart may have further undermined Rome's will to fight. Gibbon himself put some of the blame on the subversive influence of early Christianity, which siphoned off the best minds for the church and encouraged pacifist and antistate attitudes among its otherworldly followers.

There are historians who throw up their hands at this complex array of causes and simply blame the colossal difficulty of governing so vast an assemblage of lands and peoples with the limited personnel and resources available in Roman times. The wonder was not that Rome fell, this school declares, but that it lasted as long as it did.

Other historians urge that what took place was less the "decline and fall" of a great civilization than the transformation of one society into another one. They empha-size the fact that the Germanic invaders of the Roman Empire had been living on its borders and infiltrating the empire itself for centuries. German chiefs had become landowners, married Roman ladies, taken Roman names, and tried to take part in Roman public life. Even the Germanic invaders of the fifth century sought less to destroy the sophisticated society they had long admired than to take it over and live as the Romans did. Their alien ideas and customs led to the failure of this effort; but the result was less a savage destruction than a slow change from ancient to medieval civilization in the West.

Nevertheless, by the end of the fifth century, there were barbarian kingdoms where once Roman eagles stood, from North Africa to Britain. And in centuries to come, though Rome later became the city of the popes and the center of western Christianity, the teeming metropolis of half a million souls shrank to tens of thousands. The villas of a ruder nobility were built within the gigantic shells of public baths, and goats grazed on the palatine hill where palaces had once stood. Difficult as it is to define or explain the end of an era, one surely ended here.

For Gibbon, the decline and fall of the Roman Empire constituted "the greatest, perhaps, the most awful scene in the history of mankind." We need not go so far to see in the passing of the Roman world the ending of one of the great ages of the human race.

THE ROMAN ACHIEVEMENT

GREEKS AND ROMANS

Of all the conquests of that great Empire of the West, the absorption of the Greek city-states had the greatest long-range consequences. Here, in a cultural sense at least, "the vanquished led the victors captive."

The Roman aristocracy, like many people since, were dazzled by the Greek cultural achievement. They read Greek writers, imported Greek statues and Greek slaves to tutor their children, and sent their older sons to the Athenian "schools" to study at the feet of Greek philosophers. They also did their best to model Roman culture after Greek.

Thus, Roman official religion, literature, art, and philosophy were all based to a considerable degree on Greek mythology, writing, carving, and thought. Over centuries of emulation, the Romans did succeed in absorbing much of Greek culture, in making its conventions theirs, even in going beyond their brilliant neighbors in some areas. But the overall consequence was as clearly derivative as, say, modern American culture is derived from that of Europe. Roman culture, therefore, cannot be discussed without repeated backward glances at the cultural achievements of the first of Western civilizations, that of the ancient Greeks.

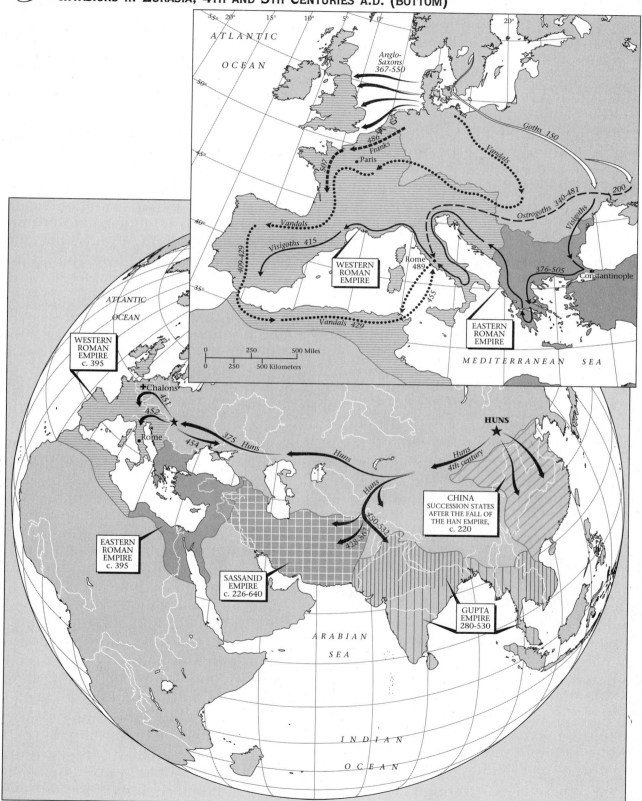

ATLANTIC OCEAN

Anglo-Saxons 367-550

Goths 150

Franks

Paris

486

507

Vandals

Ostrogoths 340-481

Visigoths

200

Vandals

Visigoths 415

409-429

WESTERN ROMAN EMPIRE

Rome 489

455

376-505

Constantinople

EASTERN ROMAN EMPIRE

Vandals 429

0   250   500 Miles

0   250   500 Kilometers

MEDITERRANEAN SEA

ATLANTIC OCEAN

WESTERN ROMAN EMPIRE c. 395

Chalons

451

452

Rome

454

375 Huns

Huns

HUNS

Huns 4th century

Huns

EASTERN ROMAN EMPIRE c. 395

Huns

450-532

428-567

CHINA SUCCESSION STATES AFTER THE FALL OF THE HAN EMPIRE, c. 220

SASSANID EMPIRE c. 226-640

GUPTA EMPIRE 280-530

ARABIAN SEA

INDIAN OCEAN

Such comparisons, however, are not necessarily to the detriment of the Romans. After all, Rome left its own distinctive cultural image to future ages. Greece is calm white temples and exquisitely modeled statues; Rome is triumphal arches, aqueducts, the crumbling grandeur of the Colosseum repeated on a thousand travel posters. Greece symbolizes the speculative mind, at least in its Western form. Rome is practicality, the pragmatic temper that made a science out of engineering and a fine art out of government.

We refer to the Western classical heritage as a Greco-Roman one. The Roman share in that joint legacy, all things considered, was not less significant.

ART AND ENGINEERING

Greece had left the Romans awesome models of sculpture and architecture. The Romans matched their models in their own styles of carving human likenesses in stone. And in building, the Romans in some ways outdid their neighbors.

The Greeks had produced highly idealized representations of gods and great leaders in the Hellenic fifth century B.C. and extremely realistic statues in the later, Hellenistic period. Both the ideal and the realistic legacy in sculpture were taken over wholesale by the Romans.

Many Greek statues, for instance, exist today only as stone copies preserved in Rome. But the Romans used Greek styles for their own purposes too. Portrait heads of Roman citizens from the late Republic were as hyperrealistic as any Hellenistic achievement. Yet Roman statuary projects a special force of its own. The strength of a Roman *paterfamilias*—the strength of character that befits the head of an old Republican clan—shows through the craggy features. The whole figure of *Augustus* in armor, one arm upraised, radiates idealized authority as effectively as any fifth-century Greek god—as the image of the refounder of the Roman Empire should. Roman sculpture was thus not merely a matter of copying Greek originals but a genuine expression of the Roman spirit.

Nowhere was that spirit expressed more powerfully than in Roman building. With Rome came monumental architecture of a size and elaborateness seldom seen before in the Mediterranean world. The Romans had vast spaces to cover, public baths and basilicas (law courts), palaces and temples built on an imperial scale. To roof such buildings they introduced the arch, the vault, and the dome. They embellished these great buildings with scrolled Ionic and complicated Corinthian columns, with carving and tile and gold leaf. Most of that ornate splendor is gone today. But even the ruins of the Baths of Caracalla and the Basilica of Constantine have a spaciousness and a grandeur not to be found in the Greek world.

In engineering, finally, the pragmatic Roman spirit found one of its truest expressions. The Romans crisscrossed Europe with more than fifty thousand miles of stone-paved roadway, a system not equaled until modern times. The soaring arches of Roman aqueducts awed and baffled the peoples who came after them; the one built to supply Segovia with water was known as the Devil's Bridge to medieval Spaniards. Into the city of Rome itself a total of fourteen aqueducts brought 100 million gallons of water every day.

POEMS AND PLAYS: VERGIL

The Roman cultural debt to Greece is nowhere clearer than in Roman literature. Again, though, there are distinctive Roman accomplishments to admire.

The arches of a Roman aqueduct still tower over the city of Segovia in Spain, once a province of the Roman Empire. Like Roman roads and Roman law, Roman cities—with their aqueducts, theaters, and other amenities—were major benefits of the only period of political unity in European history. Can you think of any structures in modern America that will probably still be standing two thousand years from now? (Photo Researchers, Inc.)

Most of the common elements in the literature of the two peoples—style, themes, mythological foundations, literary conventions—were the result of conscious modeling of Roman work upon Greek. Thus, if Homer opens his epic *Iliad* by calling upon the gods for divine inspiration, Roman Vergil will not go many lines before he calls upon his Muse for inspiration too. If there is a catalogue of the ships that brought the Greeks to Troy with all their colorful crews in Homer's epic, there will be a catalogue of the peoples that followed Aeneas to Italy in the later poem. And so on, through much of Latin literature. The literary genres are the same for the two peoples; epic and lyric poems, tragedy and comedy, pastoral and satirical modes flourish among them both. There is similarly bawdy humor on both their stages, a common nostalgia for a simpler, pastoral past in much of their verse.

In some cases, the Greeks clearly carry off the prize. Roman tragedy and comedy, for example, never achieved the dramatic fullness of their Greek predecessors. The only surviving Roman tragedies, the seldom performed post-Augustan works of Seneca, read more like melodrama than tragedy. The comedies of Plautus and Terence, produced under the Republic, were based on the Greek New Comedy and are full of confusions of identity, prodigal sons, clever slaves, and other stereotypes. Unpromising material, certainly—though no less a playwright than Shakespeare borrowed from both Seneca and the Roman comedy.

Roman poetry, however, needs no excuses: it clearly matched the best of its Greek precursors and left an influential legacy. There is a barbaric strength to Homer not to be found in later epics, but Vergil's *Aeneid*, the Augustan epic of the founding of Rome, has a perhaps subtler power of its own. Vergil's Aeneas is a much more complicated character than the half-savage Achilles. He is a man with a mission, driven by a Roman sense of duty, yet he is tempted by very human feelings along the way. The mythic core of the story was simple enough: the ancient tale that Rome had been founded by the last Trojan, the hero Aeneas, escaped from flaming Troy and charged by the gods to found a new city in a new land. But it took the genius of Vergil to ask: How would the future founder of Rome feel when his wanderings took him to North Africa and he was welcomed by Queen Dido, busy raising the walls of her own city—Carthage? How would he react, and how would she, when the founders of the two great imperial rivals of Roman times fell passionately in love?

There is much more to the *Aeneid*. But the love of Aeneas and Dido has enthralled readers over the almost two thousand years since Vergil wrote it, in the days of Caesar Augustus.

Many other forms of poetry flourished among the Romans, as they had among their Greek precursors. The sophisticated sexuality and wit of the Romans Ovid and Catullus have found as many readers down the centuries as the lyrics of the Greek Sappho. The odes of Horace have been imitated by poets of later ages as often as those of his Greek predecessor Pindar. The poets of the two peninsulas wrote in their own ways, with skill and passion, and when those ways merged, neither the Greek original nor the Roman poem modeled on it was the worse for that mingling of genius.

THE MESSAGE OF JESUS

"And it came to pass in those days," the second chapter of the third Gospel informs us, "that there went out a decree from Caesar Augustus, that all the world should be taxed." So Jesus of Nazareth was born in Bethlehem, where his parents had gone to render unto Caesar, around the year 4 B.C.

He was thus born at a time when the Roman Republic was turning into the Empire, and a time when Greek ideas had been thoroughly assimilated by the Romans. His story sits oddly in the middle of Roman history, so largely secular and practical in spirit. Yet the religion that grew up around the name and teachings of Jesus Christ constitutes a crucial part of the legacy of those times. Modified by Greek ideas, adopted as the Roman state religion, Christianity would survive the Greco-Roman world to become the basic religion of the West.

We do not know what Jesus looked like—there are no dependable contemporary likenesses—but the traditional medieval image of a gaunt man with long hair and a beard is likely enough, given the styles of his time and province. The Bible does offer a vivid picture of his wandering ministry, of his style of preaching in vigorous parables, of his ability to move the hearts of his hearers. He was clearly a charismatic figure, whatever he looked like.

According to the Testament of his followers in the first and second centuries A.D., his birth was heralded by angels, his life replete with miracles, his passing accompanied by storms and earthquakes and climaxed by the greatest miracle of all, his rising from the dead and ascending to heaven. Jesus began his active ministry—which apparently was limited to the last three years of his life—at the age of thirty, when he became a wandering holy man in the far Roman province where he was born and put to death. Here his messianic claims—that he was the Messiah prophesied of old, come to save the world—led to his arrest at the instigation of the Hebrew priestly hierarchy in Jerusalem and his execution by the Roman authorities. And here in the eastern provinces of the empire, the Christian church began to grow.

The moral passion of Jesus had gone straight to the heart, and it would reach many others in the Roman Empire whose needs were like those of his first hearers: "Blessed are the poor in spirit, for theirs is the kingdom of heaven" (*Matthew* 5:3). His commandments had a scope that would stir even the skeptics of a later age:

Thou shalt love the Lord thy God with all thy heart, and with all thy soul, and with all thy mind. This is the first and great commandment. And the second is like unto it. Thou shalt love thy neighbor as thyself. On these two commandments hang all the laws and the prophets. (*Matthew* 23:37–40)

The new religion thus began with the law and the prophets of the ancient Hebrews and looked at first like a schismatic form of Judaism. From his Hebrew heritage Jesus derived the monotheism that had long distinguished the Jews and the ethical emphasis brought to their faith by the prophets of earlier centuries. But Jesus added his own unique beliefs to the faith of his fathers, and it was these additions that were to carry Christianity from obscurity and persecution to the top of the Roman world.

The two distinguishing features of Jesus's message were, first, the assertion that he was not a mere prophet, like his predecessors, but the Son of God himself, and, second, that he came to bring to his followers the supreme gift of eternal life. "Dost thou believe in the Son of God?" he asked the man that was born blind. "Thou hast seen him, and it is he that talketh with thee" (*John* 9:35,37). And to Martha: "I am the resurrection and the life: he that believeth in me, though he were dead, yet he shall live: and whosoever liveth and believeth in me shall never die" (*John* 11:25–26).

THE TRIUMPH OF THE CHURCH

This message was spread by the twelve disciples who had followed Jesus during his lifetime. But the new faith was carried outside the Hebrew community most effectively by a man who had never seen Jesus of Nazareth in life—Saint Paul. This Greek-trained Hebrew was able to preach the message of Christ to the Greek-speaking Eastern Roman Empire particularly. More than anyone else, he saw Christianity not merely as a Hebrew sect but as a religion open to all believers. Through his endless travels, his letters to Christian communities around the eastern end of the Mediterranean, and his total conviction of the truth of the Christian message, Paul became almost a second founder of the new religion.

There is no doubt that Jesus believed in his own divinity and in his mission to bring salvation to suffering humankind. Nor is there any doubt of the spark these messianic claims of divinity and salvation kindled in the souls of the faithful. The sign of the fish, under which Christians met in secret in the early years, was used because the letters that spelled *fish* in Greek—the lingua franca of the Roman East—were also the initials of the key words in the Christian message: "Jesus Christ—Son of God—Savior."

Various eastern "mystery cults" had made a similar offer of eternal life, and indeed had practiced some of the same rites and rituals that emerged in the early church. The cults of Dionysus, Demeter, the Egyptian Isis and Osiris, and others had promised life after death. Osiris and Dionysus had returned from the dead themselves. Magna Mater—the Great Mother—and Mithras, the Zoroastrian god of light, required baptism of initiates. Dionysus, the Great Mother, and Isis and Osiris all offered a communion feast. But the Christian forms of these practices and promises, rooted in a claim of recent historicity rather than ancient myth, had a special appeal. Christianity gradually outdistanced all the rest.

The spread of the new cult was also fostered by men of learning who took up the new ideas, interpreted them in the familiar light of Greek philosophy, and thus made them acceptable to respectable Romans. In this way the Greek doctrine of the *Logos* (the Word, or the spiritual manifestation of the World Soul) was used to explain Christ's coming into this world: "And the Word [*Logos* in the original Greek of the New Testament] was made flesh, and dwelt among us . . . " (*John* 1:14). Thus also Saint Augustine, writing in the last days of the Roman Empire, explained the problem of evil in a world made by a beneficent and all-powerful God by referring to well-known Neoplatonic doctrines of the distance between spirit and matter. From Paul in the first century to Augustine around 500, the simple story and dramatic claims of Jesus were supported and elaborated by men imbued with the rational spirit of Greco-Roman culture, till Christ's message emerged as the core of a formidable system of theology.

The rise of Christianity was not as rapid as that of Islam seven hundred years later. The early Christians were accused of atheism as the Jews had been—they did reject all but *one* of the gods, after all—and were rumored to practice abominable rites in secret. There were brutal persecutions in the first three centuries, mob violence in provincial cities, and mass executions in Rome. Saint Paul and other spreaders of the new faith were martyred for their beliefs.

Slowly but surely, however, the church found social and political recognition. Its own institutions were strengthened and systematized as its doctrine was. The isolated, persecuted Christian communities of the early centuries grew into a structure of episcopal sees, each headed by a big-city bishop. Even this early, furthermore, there was a tendency to defer on doctrinal matters to the bishop of Rome, the head of the Christian community at the imperial capital.

After one final round of savage persecutions under Diocletian at the beginning of the fourth century, then, the Christian church was finally recognized by the emperor Constantine in the Edict of Milan (A.D. 313). At the end of the fourth century, under Theodosius, the pagan temples were closed at last and Christianity became the state church of the Roman Empire.

The Greco-Roman world was a shell of its former self by then, deeply split and ready to crumble. But when the superstructures of the state fell away under the hammerblows of the barbarians, the Christian church would stand. It would go on alone into the darkness that lay ahead.

Roman women celebrate the secret rites of the mystery cult of Dionysus in this wall painting from Pompeii. On the left, a young initiate kneels, clinging to an older woman for moral support. On the right, a celebrant clashes cymbals overhead to the rhythm of the orgiastic dance. What elements in the picture give it a feeling of graceful movement? (PH Archives)

SUMMARY

The ancient Romans, a practical, conservative people, were among the world's most successful empire builders—and the only ones ever to bring most of Europe under a single government.

Beginning around 500 B.C., the city of Rome in central Italy grew into the largest empire western Eurasia had yet seen during the last five centuries before Christ. Roman toughness, tenacity, and discipline accounted for much of this success. But Rome's endless wars and vast imperial holdings corrupted its aristocracy, impoverished many of its people, and tempted its generals to use their armies to advance their own political ambitions. The resulting civil war was ended by two remarkable men, Julius and Augustus Caesar. Augustus found Rome divided in the first century B.C. and left it united, powerful, and prosperous in the first century A.D.

The period of the Roman Peace—the first two centuries A.D.—saw Roman power established from London to Constantinople, all around the Mediterranean Sea and over most of Western Europe. The third century, however, saw political chaos in the capital once more. Diocletian and Constantine reestablished order during the fourth century. But Rome was decaying economically, socially, culturally, and in other ways; and in the fifth century, the Western Roman Empire collapsed under waves of invasion by preurban peoples who lived on its frontiers.

During their centuries of power, the Romans benefited from the culture of their most brilliant conquest, the Greeks. But they also developed practical arts like engineering and architecture themselves, building roads, aqueducts, theaters, and temples across Europe. Roman administration was efficient, Roman law a major cultural accomplishment. Rome's great writers left an unexcelled literary heritage to the West, including Vergil's epic of Rome's founding, the *Aeneid*. And it was in the days of the Roman Peace that Jesus Christ lived in Palestine, and Christianity grew and spread till it became the state church of the empire—an even more important legacy to future generations.

SUGGESTED READING

BALSDON, J. P. V. D. *Roman Women*. Westport, Conn.: Greenwood Press, 1975. The best place to start. Equally scholarly are M. Lefkowitz and M. B. Fant, *Women's Life in Greece and Rome* (Baltimore: Johns Hopkins University Press, 1982) and Sarah Pomeroy, *Goddesses, Whores, Wives, and Slaves: Women in Classical Antiquity* (New York: Schocken Books, 1975) See also J. P. Hallett, *Fathers and Daughters in Roman Society: Women and the Elite Family* (Princeton: Princeton University Press, 1984). Impressionistic discussion of women's influence on society, exercised through family connections.

BARNES, T. D. *The New Empire of Diocletian and Constantine*. Cambridge, Mass.: Harvard University Press, 1982. Scholarly treatment.

BRILLIANT, R. *Roman Art*. New York: Praeger, 1974. Good survey.

BROWN, P. *The World of Late Antiquity*. New York: Harcourt Brace, 1971. Stimulating interpretive discussion of the Western world in later Roman times.

BRUNT, P. A. *Social Conflict in the Roman Republic*. New York: W. W. Norton, 1972. The Roman Revolution and its social roots. See also the classic—and highly readable—work by Ronald Syme, *The Roman Revolution* (London: Oxford University Press, 1960).

COCHRANE, C. M. *Christianity and Classical Culture*. New York: Oxford University Press, 1957. Stimulating analysis of the roots and place of early Christianity in Roman society and culture.

EVANS, K. K. *War, Women and Children in Ancient Rome*. London: Routledge, 1991. Studies of the legal, familial, and workday problems of Roman women.

GARNSET, P. and R. SALLER. *The Roman Empire: Economy, Society, and Culture*. Berkeley and Los Angeles: University of California Press, 1987. Particularly useful on government administration and social relations.

GIARDINA, A. *The Romans*, trans. L. G. Cochrane. Chicago: University of Chicago Press, 1993. Intriguing collection of essays on Roman social types, from citizens and priests to bandits and slaves.

GRUEN, E. S. *Cultural and National Identity in Republican Rome*. Ithaca, N.Y.: Cornell University Press, 1992. Analysis of the republican ideology before the rise of the Caesars.

HARRIS, W. V. *War and Imperialism in Republican Rome 327–70 B.C.* New York: Oxford University Press, 1985. Scholarly account of Roman expansion around the Mediterranean Sea.

JENKYNS, R., ed. *The Legacy of Rome: A New Appraisal*. New York: Oxford University Press, 1992. New collection based on a classic anthology of scholarly essays on Rome's cultural legacy to later ages.

JOLOWICZ, A. *Historical Introduction to the Study of Roman Law*. Cambridge: Cambridge University

Press, 1952. The evolution of the Roman legal system.

JONES, A. H. M. *Augustus*. New York: Norton, 1970. Life and role of the founder of Rome's golden age.

————. *The Decline of the Ancient World*. New York: Longman's, 1966. Shortened version of his widely cited three-volume work, *The Later Roman Empire*.

LAZENBY, J. F. *Hannibal's War: A Military History of the Second Punic War*. Warminster, England: Aris and Phillips, 1978. Detailed narrative account of the great African general's long struggle against Rome.

MACDONALD, W. L. *The Architecture of the Roman Empire*. New Haven: Yale University Press, 1965. Excellent study of this quintessential Roman art form.

MACMULLEN, R. *Roman Social Relations*. New Haven: Yale University Press, 1974. Society under the Caesars. See Brunt, above, for society under the Republic.

MEEKS, W. A. *The First Urban Christians: The Social World of the Apostle Paul*. New Haven: Yale University Press, 1983. Sees leading converts to Christianity as socially isolated people—wealthy women, Jews, freedmen—in need of a sense of spiritual community.

SAINTE CROIX, G. E. M. DE. *The Class Struggle in the Ancient World: From the Archaic Age to the Arab Conquests*. Ithaca, N.Y.: Cornell University Press, 1981. Impressive presentation of a class-based interpretation. Compares with the equally celebrated M. I. Finley's *Ancient Slavery and Modern Ideology* (New York: Viking, 1980). And see the less the-oretical work by K. R. Bradley, *Slaves and Masters in the Roman Empire: A Study in Social Control* (Brussels: Latomus, 1984), a grim picture of Roman slavery, with intriguing guesses at attitudes of the enslaved.

SNOWDEN, F. M., Jr. *Before Color Prejudice: The Ancient View of Blacks*. Cambridge, Mass.: Harvard University Press, 1983. Artistic representations and high positions in state and society achieved by black Africans indicate little racial prejudice in ancient societies from Egypt to Rome.

STAMBAUGH, J. E. *The Ancient Roman City*. Baltimore: Johns Hopkins University Press, 1988. Physical and social parameters of Roman urban life, based on literary sources as well as historical and archaeological materials.

STARR, C. G. *The Beginnings of Imperial Rome: Rome in the Mid-Republic*. Ann Arbor: University of Michigan Press, 1980. Roman expansion in the fourth and third centuries B.C. See also C. Wells, *The Roman Empire* (London: Fontana, 1984) combining narrative with analysis of Roman institutions and society during the first two centuries A.D.

WEBSTER, G. *The Roman Imperial Army*. London: Black, 1969. Recommended account of this central Roman institution. See also G. R. Watson, *The Roman Soldier* (Ithaca, N.Y.: Cornell University Press, 1970).

WILLIAMS, S. *Diocletian and the Roman Recovery*. New York: Methuen 1985. Sound evaluation by a nonacademic deeply versed in the Latin sources.

VERGIL. *The Aeneid*, trans. R. Fitzgerald. New York: Random House, 1983.

CHAPTER 12 ——————

Golden Age on the Ganges

India between the Mauryas and the Guptas

A Geographical Expression

Of the half-dozen major centers of civilization of the classical age, India is surely the easiest to draw with a pencil. The familiar triangle with the short side on top may not make due allowance for the northwestern bulge of the Punjab and Kashmir. But the V-shaped sketch would at least make one point strongly: Of all the Eurasian civilizations, India, bounded on two sides by the sea and to the north by the world's most colossal mountains, should surely have been the easiest to unify.

In fact, of all the centers of Eurasian high culture, India had the least political unity for most of the age of the classical civilizations.

From the fall of the Maurya dynasty in 185 B.C. to the rise of the Guptas in A.D. 320, India was without even a shadow of a central government. During this period of five centuries, while Rome and Han China constructed vast systems of public administration, India wallowed in what must look to the seeker after empires very much like anarchy.

During these centuries the kingdom of Magadha, from which the Mauryas had sprung, was a middle-sized state on the Ganges again. Foreign invaders shouldered their way down through the Northwest Frontier once more, as in the days of the Aryans and of Alexander the Great. Separate Dravidian kingdoms rose and fell in the Deccan. It would be easy to wonder whether the Indian subcontinent was not, as a nineteenth-century statesman once said of Italy, a geographical expression rather than a nation.

Actually, a tough nucleus of cultural elements, from religion to caste, was already binding India together. And even the foreign invaders of this period would enrich rather than undermine the traditional culture that was the heart of India.

Invaders of the Punjab: The Kushans

During these centuries foreign invaders thrust far beyond the Punjab, the region of the five rivers that branch out of the Indus. It was one of those times in India's history when the Northwest Frontier, the subcontinent's traditional invasion corridor, seemed clogged with invading armies and migrating peoples moving through the mountain passes into the plain below.

There were Greeks after Alexander, adventurers from the eastern provinces of Seleucid Persia. There were Parthian Persians in Roman times. There were nomadic peoples from the northern steppes, first Scythians and later an aggressive and extremely successful Turko-Mongol people called Kushans. One by one they came down through the mountain-rimmed passes into the warm country of the five rivers: nomads on horseback with their flocks and wagons or sharp-eyed soldiers with long lances or exotic bows. Some were Indo-Europeans, some mongoloid peoples shifted westward by Shi Huangdi's Great Wall. The Indians of the Punjab and the Indus valley watched them pass.

Over several hundred years, these foreign intruders set up kingdoms of their own over various parts of northwestern India. The mongoloid Kushan Empire, for example, stretched for a time all the way from the frontiers of Parthian Persia into the heart of the Ganges valley. But all the newcomers followed one of two patterns. Some adopted Indian names, religions, and culture, and were absorbed into a population that was already becoming adept at absorbing foreigners. Some were eventually dislodged and went their way. In either case, India survived the onslaught of each new intruder in turn.

Most of the invaders of these five centuries, however, left something of their own to add its tang to the rich mix of Indian tradition.

The Greeks brought coinage to India, and helped develop trade between India and the Mediterranean. The Kushans patronized Buddhism and presided over the emergence of a new form, the Mahayana Buddhism that would spread far across Asia. Even the wild Scythians brought something; as the Saka people, they added their blood and energies to the population of the Indian subcontinent.

Kingdoms of the Deccan: The Tamils

Indian history thus far had centered in the north, in the valleys of the Indus and the Ganges, in the shadow of the Himalayas. What was probably a Dravidian Harappan culture had flourished and faded here during the dawn age

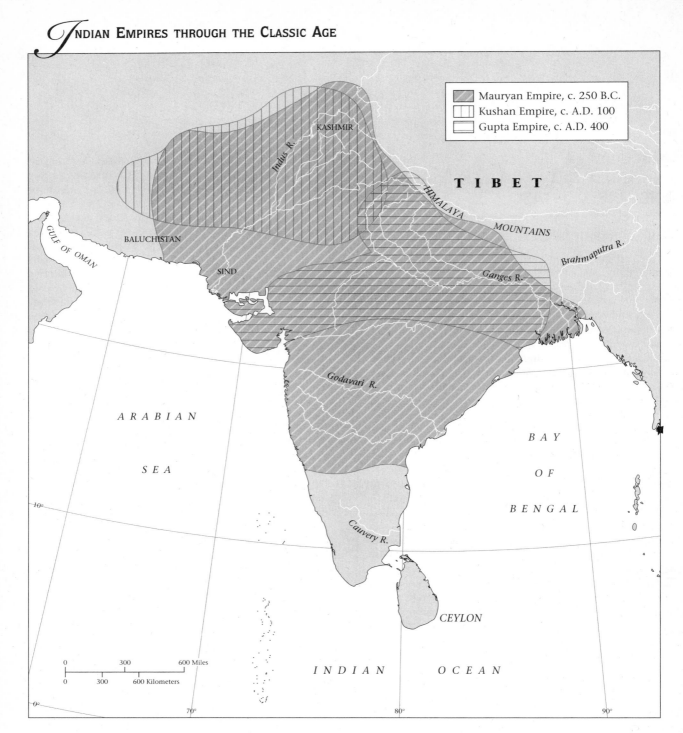

Maimuryan Empire, c. 250 B.C.
Kushan Empire, c. A.D. 100
Gupta Empire, c. A.D. 400

of human civilization. Here Aryan and Dravidian had merged to produce a new civilization on the Ganges and its first flowering in the Mauryan Empire of Asoka. Here the Gupta golden age would presently take shape.

But there were also cities and kingdoms in the south during these centuries around the time of Christ—highly developed Dravidian cultures in the great southward-reaching triangle of peninsular India. Their people too are part of the confused but fertile history of the centuries between the empires.

The south was cut off from the north by the Narmada River and by ranges of thickly forested hills. Geographically, the center of the south is an arid plateau called the Deccan. This ill-watered region, then still heavily wooded, could not support either a large population or centers of developed culture. But the hills of the Deccan stairstep down to fertile coastal plains on both sides of the peninsula, and these plains became increasingly prosperous centers of both agriculture and trade in the first centuries A.D.

The peoples of the south were still almost purely Dravidian stock, as yet little affected by the long-established Aryan predominance in the north. The Southerners spoke their own languages and had their own culture and social patterns. Trade, both overseas and with north India, appeared and grew during this period. Commercial contacts with the cities of the Indus and Ganges began to bring such northern cultural characteristics as Hinduism and the caste system into the south. In the first centuries after Christ, there were southern kingdoms that could challenge the most powerful northern principalities.

One of the most successful of these southern states was the Andhra monarchy of the northern Deccan. Powerful in the first and second centuries A.D., the Andhras for a time controlled a slice of India from coast to coast. The Andhra *rajas* never enjoyed more than a loose sovereignty over the chiefs and village headmen among their subject peoples. They did, however, manage to exercise a profitable control over the increasing trade between north and south India, all of which had to flow through their territories or along their coasts.

The most important peoples of the further south were the Tamils. Their language was the most widely spoken southern tongue, and they dominated the whole region from what is today Madras down to Cape Comorin, at the tip of the subcontinent.

During the first centuries A.D. the Tamil peoples were just moving from village culture into larger political units—chiefdoms and monarchies. Village councils were still central decision-making bodies, even after hereditary monarchy was introduced. The people still prayed to commemorative "hero stones" or made sacrifices of blood and rice to ancient gods of fertility, regarding the elaborate Vedic rituals—so ancient in the north— as modern novelties.

But change came rapidly to the shrewd Tamils. The source was growing prosperity as they developed the agricultural potential of their converging coastal plains and above all the mushrooming trade that flourished on both coasts. Southern India thus became a booming center of commerce and handicraft industries, and the land along the southern rivers bloomed.

Political and cultural evolution came with economic growth. Matrilineal succession prevailed in many parts of the south. The queen of the Pandyas, a powerful Tamil people, could field an army of thirteen thousand infantrymen, four thousand cavalry, and five hundred elephants.

Tamils for a time conquered and occupied northern Ceylon (Sri Lanka) where they are still a revolutionary force today—and they fought epic battles among themselves. Poetry also flowered among them very early, and the songs of the Tamil bards are among the treasures of India's literary heritage.

NATIONS OF SHOPKEEPERS

The lack of a strong central government during the five hundred years between the Maurya and Gupta empires seems in no way to have handicapped the rapid growth of hand manufacturing, trade, and cities in both northern and southern India. Indeed, the half-envious label applied to industrial Britain many centuries later—"a nation of shopkeepers!"—would seem almost equally appropriate to India in the last centuries before Christ and the first centuries A.D.

Over a region approximately half the size of the continental United States. Indians found raw materials in considerable quantity. Iron and copper, gold and silver and precious stones were mined. The subcontinent's still abundant forests provided woods of all sorts, from teak to aromatic sandalwood. Cotton was widely grown and silk introduced. Even the sea contributed, providing pearls for Indian jewelry and for export.

These materials were processed by a complicated array of guilds, most of them organized by castes or subcastes who traditionally practiced particular hereditary crafts. Guilds of carpenters, metalworkers, and ceramicists were especially powerful in many urban areas. Women worked extensively in the widespread cotton-textile industry, weaving fabrics so fine that it was impossible to detect the separate threads. Like guilds in medieval Europe centuries later, Indian guilds regulated quality, prices, and competition, contributed substantially to religious foundations—especially Buddhist and Jain—and made the streets of Indian cities colorful with banners and processions on their feast days.

Trade also boomed during these centuries, especially in the port cities of the south. North and south were linked by sea trade along the coasts and by a more modest system of roads begun in Asoka's day. Flotillas of coastal trading vessels, caravans of mules, oxen, and camels in the arid north bound all the regions from the Himalayas to Cape Comorin as no political organization had ever done. Foreign trade also prospered. The Greek and Kushan states in the northwest encouraged Indian trade with the Mediterranean and China. The location of the south made it a crucial link in the east-west trade that drained the Roman Empire's wealth—so its social commentators lamented— for spices from the East Indies and muslins and precious stones from India. Indian merchants searching for the spices that brought such good prices in the West increasingly traded and even settled in Southeast Asia, where Indian religious influence was also growing.

It was, in sum, a bustling, prosperous time in the cities of India. Coinage replaced barter in the urban centers; gold, silver, and copper coins of many kinds were minted, and even Roman *sesterces* circulated freely. The literature of the age describes a colorful urban population of guild craftsmen, wealthy caravan masters, and shipowners mingling with Hindu brahmans and Buddhist monks, prostitutes and poets, in narrow city streets. The courts of the *rajas* and of kings with even more exalted titles borrowed from Persia or China were centers of luxurious living and cultivated taste.

Most Indians, of course, still lived like most people everywhere—by plowing and harvesting, herding and shearing, according to the ancient rhythms of village life. But the groundwork had at least been laid in the caravan tracks and sea lanes and in India's busy bazaars for the subcontinent's next great experiment in empire building—the age of the Guptas.

 # THE GUPTA GOLDEN AGE

CHANDRA GUPTA I: THE RAJA OF THE RAJAS

India was a highly literate society by this time, one with several written languages. But her continuing lack of interest in mere history—plus the destruction in later centuries of what records might have survived—leaves us with almost as little detailed knowledge of the reigns of the Guptas as we have of their Maurya predecessors half a millennium earlier. Enough is known, however, to piece together some striking parallels between these two Indian empires.

To begin with, both centered in northern India, specifically in the Ganges valley, which had been the center of Indian development since the Aryan conquest. Both the Maurya and Gupta dynasties, in fact, rose to power first in the same Ganges state of Magadha. Both expanded westward from there to incorporate the old pre-Aryan heartland on the Indus and the five rivers of the Punjab. Both pushed much more tentatively southward. The greatest of the Guptas actually controlled less of the Deccan than Asoka had. The Mauryas ruled for only about a century and a half (321–185 B.C.), the Guptas nominally for two centuries (A.D. 320–540). But in both cases the first three reigns were the glory days, and then the empire began to fragment and decline.

The first of the Guptas, Chandra Gupta I, even had the same name as the founder of the earlier dynasty, Chandragupta Maurya, though they were not related. The second of the Gupta clan, Samudra Gupta, was the great conqueror. The third, Chandra Gupta II, presided, like Asoka, over the dynasty's golden age.

A word or two about each of these rulers, drawn from what meager sources remain, will have to suffice for the political history of the age of the Guptas.

Chandra Gupta I (320–330) seems to have been either a minor princeling or a wealthy landowner in the Ganges valley who married well. His bride, Princess Kumara Devi of the powerful Lichchhavi tribe, brought him an alliance powerful enough to make him ruler of the state of Magadha. From its now ancient capital of Patna, Chandra Gupta expanded his suzerainty over enough of the surrounding territories to kindle dreams of empire. In A.D. 320 he took the grandiloquent title—derived perhaps from the Persians via the Kushans—of *maharajadhiraja*, "great king of kings." Ten years later he left this title, with all its implied aspirations, to his son Samudra Gupta, who made good on them with a vengeance.

SAMUDRA AND CHANDRA GUPTA II

Samudra Gupta (330–375) is shown on some of the gold coins he minted with the profits of his wars reflectively strumming a lute, and he is supposed to have loved poetry. The most important single record of his reign, however, is a record of his conquests. According to this eulogy, Samudra broke many kings in the field, forcing some to accept his overlordship and pay tribute and others to do homage. He brought most of civilized northern India under Gupta rule and raided hundreds of miles into the southern jungles, returning laden with glory and plunder. He imposed direct Gupta government, collected tribute, or exercised a paramount influence from the mountains to a point well south of the Narmada. He became what his father had dreamed of being: *raja* of the *rajas*, great king of kings.

Chandra Gupta II (375–415), a grandson of the founder, fought his share of campaigns too. He completed the conquest of the northwest, so that Gupta power stretched all across northern India, from the Indus valley to the head of the Bay of Bengal. He also negotiated a shrewd series of marriage alliances with the preeminent princes of the south that cemented Gupta influence in the Deccan. An additional advantage of his wars and marriage diplomacy was that it gave the Guptas control of valuable west-coast seaports and their trade with the West.

Chandra Gupta II is most famous, however, for the cultural life of his reign and for his own patronage of the arts. Kalidasa the poet lived at his court, and literature and art flourished while he ruled. When we reflect that his forty years on the throne generally constituted a time of peace and prosperity, despite his celebrated conquest of the northwest, the "golden age" label so often affixed to the reign is easy to understand.

The first century of Gupta rule (the fourth century A.D.) was thus a time of expanding power, growing prosperity, and cultural splendor. The second Gupta century, however, was increasingly darkened by new invaders moving down from central Asia across the Northwest Frontier: the White Huns.

The White Huns were probably kin to those Huns who, under the notorious Attila, had reached the wall of

Rome a hundred years before. Now, in the fifth century, while Rome foundered and fell to half-civilized Germanic invaders, the White Huns battered at the gates of Gupta India.

Gupta leaders succeeded in turning them back until late in the century. By 500, however, the Huns ruled the northwest and the Guptas were drawing back once more upon their Ganges base. They were a local power thereafter, and one that would disappear from the skimpy records in a few decades more.

THE HINDU GOLDEN AGE

The profile of a golden age is not as easy to outline as one might think. What, after all, makes an age *golden*—or, as this one is also often called, *classic*? Most accounts of such periods tend to highlight intellectual and artistic achievements, and these will receive due emphasis in the following section. Some attention, however, must be given to more mundane matters—to the everyday lives of most people, who did not write or sculpt or even pay much attention to those who did. A look at the life provided for such people under the Guptas therefore follows—a look at government, the economy, and society in the Gupta age.

Government was probably less centralized and less intrusive in Gupta India than in Maurya times. Even in those parts of north India ruled directly by the great kings of kings, most of the day-to-day authority was in the hands of the provincial viceroys, district officers, and even the headmen and elders of the individual villages. The councils of major cities were chosen by local people—espe-

The interior of the sanctuary at Karli. The dimness, the heavy polygonal columns, and capitals thronged with spiritual presences generate the profoundly religious atmosphere for which India has been known for three thousand years. Note the balance of horizontals and verticals, circles and rectangles, in each column. (New York Public Library Picture Collection)

cially merchants and craft guildsmen—rather than appointed from the center, as was apparently done in Maurya times. Nor was there anything in the India of Chandra Gupta II to correspond to the secret police of Chandragupta Maurya's day.

Economically, the trends of more recent centuries continued. Indian farmers labored in fields of wheat and sugar cane in the west, rice in the east, and in orchards and vegetable gardens everywhere. Craftspeople in bustling Indian cities continued to produce large quantities of pottery, metal goods, and textiles for home and foreign consumption. Trade with the west, by caravan and ship, dwindled in Gupta times as Rome declined. But Indian merchants were still frequently seen in East African ports, and they increased their activities in Southeast Asia. Spices, gems, perfumes, and sandalwood were exported; silk from China, ivory from Africa, and horses from Arabia and Persia flowed in.

The home of a reasonably affluent city dweller of Gupta India was thus likely to contain plenty of clothing and even some jewelry, well-made tools of copper and iron, numerous servants, and perhaps some slaves. The cultivated urbanite enjoyed plays, musical performances and poetry readings, gambling and courtesans. Some of the latter, incidentally, were as sophisticated as any earlier Greek *hetaera* or later Japanese *geisha*.

Women's lives in general were varied. Upper-class girls were given some education, and girls of all classes were married young. Outside of marriage and motherhood, the only ways of life commonly open to women were withdrawal to a Buddhist nunnery, acting in a theatrical company, or prostitution. There were women who were teachers and even philosophers. On the other hand, the sixth century saw the first recorded case of widow burning: pious self-immolation by a high-caste Hindu widow who believed she would thereby become a *sati*, or woman of great virtue. This supreme act of loyalty was considered to prove the widow's faithfulness to her husband and to guarantee their reunion after death. Widows also occupied a very low social status, which may have encouraged some to commit suicide in this way.

A Chinese Buddhist pilgrim who visited northern

This famous Gupta statue of the Buddha from Sarnath in northern India shows the Enlightened One preaching his first sermon. By Gupta times, every detail of such representations of the Buddha was thick with symbolism. Note here the ishnisha or bump of enlightenment on the Buddha's head, the eyes lowered in spiritual contemplation of the infinite. The hand gesture, or mudra, one of many symbolic gestures given to such statues, is the "wheel-turning" mudra, reminding pious viewers of the wheel of life from which Buddhism offered ultimate escape. (PH Archives)

India in the reign of Chandra Gupta II described the Indians as on the whole a fortunate people. The land was prosperous, yet the people, he said, religiously refrained from both meat and wine. Charity hospitals were provided for the poor by pious citizens. Even the untouchables, the caste at the bottom of society, knew their place. These pariahs never entered a city without beating on a piece of wood so that their betters might avoid being polluted by contact with them.

Even allowing for the exaggerations of an enthusiastic visitor, it was a model society by the standards of its time.

ART AND INDIAN PIETY

EVOLVING FAITHS: MAHAYANA BUDDHISM

The Buddhist visitor from China cited above noticed particularly the intense religious feeling of Gupta India. From the first century A.D., in fact, both Buddhism and Hinduism had been undergoing vital changes in the land of their birth.

The crucial changes in Buddhism took place in the centuries between the empires, particularly during the first two centuries A.D. It was in this period that Buddhist belief divided into the two great traditions that have characterized it ever since. This division, comparable to the Catholic-Protestant split in Christianity or the division between Shiite and Sunni Islam, produced two separate communities in international Buddhism. The older form, *Hinayana* ("Little Vehicle") Buddhism remained perhaps closer to the precise words and ideas of the founder. But the newer form, *Mahayana* ("Big Vehicle") Buddhism, was to reach much further, spreading in the end over most of East Asia.

Hinayana Buddhists saw Prince Siddartha the Buddha as the greatest teacher who had ever lived. He was the man who showed how an individual might, through right living, right thought, and assiduous meditation, escape from the endless wretched wheel of life into that blissful extinction of the self called Nirvana. It was a practical if profound message, from one enlightened human to those others, most commonly monks and nuns, who were capable of following him on the rigorous path of spiritual enlightenment.

Mahayana Buddhism expanded this conception drastically, and by so doing reached much larger numbers of people. Mahayana Buddhists saw the Buddha not merely as a wise teacher but as an incarnation of God. His goal, they asserted, was also larger: not only individual escape from the wheel, but the salvation of all humanity through the self-sacrificing labor of the spiritually enlightened few. In the Mahayana theology there was in fact not one Buddha but a whole series of such incarnations of

divinity, "blessed Buddhas . . . equal in number to the sands of the river" come to save humankind.[1] Before and after the historic Buddha there had lived, or would live, many other *bodhisattvas*, people who attained enlightenment but deliberately rejected escape into Nirvana in order to continue their pious work in this world, showing others the way to salvation. In addition, hosts of lesser gods clustered around the central figure of the Buddha in the art and thought of Mahayana Buddhism. Even Nirvana looked different to followers of the newer path, who envisioned a hierarchy of heavens and hells awaiting the faithful or the unbeliever after death.

Like Confucius, the historic Buddha had apparently refused even to speculate about gods; unlike Christ, he had never claimed to be divine himself. Seven centuries after Siddartha's death, many of his followers went further than the founder ever had, transforming Buddha into the central god of an immensely popular religion. His worship became a spectacle of impressive proportions, replete with huge temples, elaborate rituals, bells, and incense. The larger conception of salvation for the multitude was splendid, but one wonders what the simply dressed man who walked the dusty roads of the Gangetic states in the sixth century B.C. would have thought of the temples and the ritual, the incense and the bells.

THE HINDU RENAISSANCE

Hinduism, meanwhile, underwent even more impressive transformations, both before and during the Gupta era. Some of these changes paralleled those in Buddhism. Hinduism too saw a turning away from older texts toward more popular religion, and a widespread belief in a divine incarnation as savior. But the Hindu Renaissance, as it is often called, was a unique series of developments within India's oldest and always majority religion. These developments involved the priesthood, the scriptures, and the basic beliefs of Hinduism.

The brahmans, the hereditary priestly caste, remained widely respected and essential for ceremonial occasions. But the public turned more and more to a new collection of religious literature. These were the *Puranas*, popular myths and chronicles of Indian dynasties infused with religious significance and a prophetic framework by brahman authors.

The many gods, or *devas*, of the Vedic tradition remained, but there was a trend toward monotheism, the ancient sun god Vishnu or the fertility god Shiva emerging as the one true God in the thinking of his followers. Thus Shiva *nataraj*, "lord of the dance," embodied the cosmic rhythms of the universe. Depicted as a four-armed deity dancing in a ring of fire, crushing the demon of igno-

---

[1] *The Smaller Sukhavati-Vyuha* in *Buddhist Mahayana Texts*, trans. E. B. Cowell (New York: Dover, 1969), p. 99.

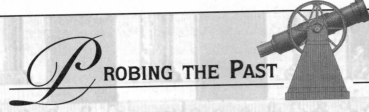

PROBING THE PAST

"In the Kūrma Purāna, Śiva [Shiva] says of himself, "I am the originator, the god abiding in supreme bliss. I, the yogi, dance eternally". . . . the whole cosmos was the scene of Śiva's dance. At the end of time, he dances the awesome Tāndava. The stamping of his foot, the gyrations of his body, his flailing arms toss the mountains into the air; the ocean rises, the stars are lashed and scattered by Śiva's matted hair. In order to save the world, Śiva in his perverse power dances the world out of existence . . . wildly laughing . . . scattering ashes from his body . . . so that the world may be renewed. This is the Tāndava dance of Śiva, as Kāla-Māhākala, the Destroyer, Destroyer of destruction. But, from his flowing hair the rivers will flow again into existence . . . and the rays of sun and moon will be seen again for what they are, the hair of Śiva. . . ."

A leading authority on Indian art and Hindu religion, Professor Stella Kamrisch of New York University, is also curator of Indian art at the Philadelphia Museum of Art. Here she weaves fragments of Hindu scripture and legend into a vivid evocation of Shiva as destroyer and creator of the cosmos.

In a culture that has not traditionally put great emphasis on the linear succession of events we call history, cyclical patterns of development have acquired great significance. What does Shiva destroy "at the end of time"? He is described as "wildly laughing." Can you imagine the God of the medieval Christians laughing and dancing the world into extinction at the Last Judgment? Does this passage describe the end of history? How can you tell that a new cycle of human life is beginning?

Stella Kamrisch, The Presence of Siva (Princeton, N.J.: Princeton University Press, 1981), p. 439.

rance underfoot, he was seen as the cyclic force that both created and destroyed worlds.

There was also a tendency to group three of the most prominent old divinities as a sort of Trinity, embodying the three main forces in the universe. In this Hindu tradition, Brahma was the Creator of the universe; Vishnu was the Preserver, frequently appearing in human incarnation to save the virtuous; and Shiva was the Destroyer who brings a deserved end to all things when evil has corrupted the cosmos beyond hope of salvation. The process is cyclical, however, and Brahma soon creates heaven and earth anew.

The richness of this evolved Hinduism made a wide variety of religious experience available to Indians. An individual might worship the *lingam* (phallus) in the temples of Shiva or practice one of the many forms of *bakhti* (personal piety) encouraged by the cult of Vishnu. Buddhists too enjoyed many forms of religious celebration. The Chinese visitor quoted earlier described a religious festival in which towering floats were dragged through the streets, decorated with devas and spirits, Buddhas and bodhisattvas, canopies and streamers, and accompanied by singers, musicians, monks, and throngs of worshipers expressing their devotion with "flowers and incense."[2]

The Gupta rulers were Hindus: Chandra Gupta II was even a theologian of sorts. Yet religious toleration prevailed, as it had under the Buddhist Asoka. Comparative tolerance of other people's beliefs would continue to characterize Indian religion until the coming of more militant faiths from the western end of Eurasia in later centuries.

THE ART OF CAVES AND STUPAS

The classic art of the half-dozen centuries climaxing in the Gupta age is the architecture and, above all, the sculpture of Buddhism. It is the art of the cave temple and the

[2]Fa Hsien, *A Record of Buddhist Kingdoms Being an Account by the Chinese Monk Fa-Hsien of His Travels in India and Ceylon* A.D. *399–414*, trans. James Legge (Oxford: Clarendon Press, 1886), p. 79.

stupa, and it shows what beauty Buddhism could inspire even in this dawning of the Hindu Renaissance.

The *stupa*, a center of worship that goes back before the time of Christ, was a large domed mound with a relic of the Buddha buried at the center of it. Around this masonry-covered mound ran a circular paved path where monks walked, murmuring their devotions. Enclosing the entire precinct was a circular railing with four ornamental gateways set at the four cardinal points of the compass.

It is on these high, elaborately carved stone gateways that we see for the first time the interwoven tangle of figures that will be so typical of later Indian temples of many faiths. Thus, the three transverse panels that top the gateways of the Great Stupa at Sanchi, in the north-ern Deccan, are already bursting with sculptured life—elephants and lions, peacocks and lotuses, kings and surging crowds. The gods are there too: benevolent bodhisattvas and full-breasted, narrow-waisted *yakshis* (nature spirits) swaying under mango trees. Buddha himself is never shown, but the stone is thick with Buddhist symbols, from the glowing footprints left by Prince Gautama's departure from his father's palace to the bo tree—the throne of his enlightenment—and the great spoked wheel of life.

Perhaps even more striking to Western eyes are the "cave temples," rock-cut sanctuaries where the western hills stairstep down to the coastal plains above Bombay. These temples, complete with facade, long interior nave,

Dome-shaped stupa shrines like this, with their sculptured gates and railings, served as centers of religious devotion for Buddhist monks before the time of Christ. Buddhist veneration of the relics—portions of the physical body of the Enlightened One, whose soul had vanished into Nirvana—resembled Christian devotion to similar relics of saints in pilgrimage churches all across medieval Europe. (The Bettmann Archive)

flanking pillars, side aisles, and a mounded stupa at the far end, are carved entirely out of the living rock of the cliffs. They were sculpted, even to the obviously nonfunctional ribbed vaults overhead, in perfect imitation of the wooden, thatch-roofed temples then in use in the world outside.

In the dim light of the most imposing of these sanctuaries, the one at Karli, the rows of close-set polygonal pillars with their lotus and elephant capitals give one a dizzy sense of moving in a world where nothing is what it ought to be. All that would be needed to catapult the viewer back a score of centuries would be the murmur of shaved, saffron-robed monks moving down the shadowy aisle beyond the sixteen-sided pillars.

Nowhere does Buddha himself appear in these earlier monuments to Hinayana purity. Soon, however, the traditional figure of the more popular religion of later centuries begins to show. The Indo-Greek sculptors of the Gandhara school in the Northwest offer an almost Hellenic Buddha, replete with acanthus leaves and even cupids. Farther south, however, the Mathura school presents a more convincingly Indian figure—the round face, the shaved crown, the bump of enlightenment, the right

A bodhisattva—a Buddha who has renounced Nirvana to help bring enlightenment to humankind—meditates on a lotus (held in his right hand) in this famous painting from the Ajanta caves. The graceful pose, the tilted head and air of brooding spirituality are typical of the best of the great Ajanta murals. Compare this religious painting with the cult painting from Pompeii in Chapter 11. Can you see how these modes of worship—rhythmic motion or focused meditation—could produce spiritual feelings comparable to those produced by hymn singing in Christian churches? (New York Public Library Picture Collection)

hand raised in a gesture not of blessing but of fearlessness. Here if anywhere the classic simplicity and calm strength of Gupta art look out at us.

To see the best of what remains of Gupta painting, finally, one would have to go to the famous Ajanta caves in the mountains of the Deccan. Here, on the walls of some thirty cave temples and monks' cells hollowed out over several hundred years, the lives of the aristocracy of that long-vanished age live on in faintly glowing colors. Here lovers lounge eternally on the veranda of an elegantly pillared palace. A prince and princess stroll among the palms and flowers. And a bodhisattva, his handsome head bowing under the weight of a high jeweled crown, gazes beneath half-lowered lids into his divine destiny. The smoky modeling of cheeks and lips, the glimmering colors on the cave walls, illuminate that forgotten world of sensuality and mystic faith with a somber beauty.

BEAST FABLES AND COURTLY LOVE

The age of the Guptas was the great age of Indian literature as well. It was the age of Kalidasa, frequently described as the Indian Shakespeare, of the final versions of the great Indian epics, and of the triumph of literary Sanskrit in plays, poetry, and prose.

The great technical breakthrough was the adoption of a version of Sanskrit, the language of the ancient Vedas and other Hindu religious texts, as the language of a brilliant living literature. Kalidasa and other playwrights and poets of this Indian "nest of singing birds" used this two-thousand-year-old tongue with refined and courtly elegance. They also used the vernacular Prakrit language in plays for the speeches of the lower-class characters.

If Buddhism shaped the painting and sculpture of the Gupta age, the Hindu Renaissance inspired much of its literature. It was at this time that the ancient epics— the *Ramayana* and the *Mahabharata*—were put into the versions we have today under the judicious guidance of brahmanical scholars. Thus interpreted, these old poems of war and adventure acquired heavy religious overtones; the *Song of God* episode, with its revelations of princely duty and the nature of the godhead, was added to the *Mahabharata* at this time. The *Panchatantra*, the widely popular collection of Indian beast fables and fairy tales, was also assembled during this period. The wisdom here is more worldly, but this world of talking animals, of beast and human life commingled, seems distinctly Hindu in spirit.

There is even a substantial mythological framework to the romantic plays and poems of Kalidasa, the most celebrated secular writer of the Gupta age. Shiva and Vishnu, the two ancient epics, and the even older Indian myths of gods and nature spirits hover over his works as Greek mythology informs Greek tragic drama. Kalidasa's most famous play, *Shakuntala*, is based on an incident from the *Mahabharata*, and gods move freely in and out of the story.

As writers have learned in many lands, however, much can be done with sacred material. *Shakuntala*, the story of a king's love for the lovely daughter of a pious hermit, is as romantic a piece as a Gupta court audience could have wished. The lyric passages, which were apparently sung, give the performance something of the air of a modern musical comedy. But the depth and endless variety of emotional tones, the joy in nature, the humanity of the middle-aged king, and the shy eagerness of Shakuntala herself carry Kalidasa's masterwork far beyond any such simplistic modern parallel.

MATHEMATICS, MEDICINE, AND SCIENCE

Religion seems to infuse so much of the Indian consciousness that it is perhaps surprising that some of the most impressive achievements of the Gupta age came not in mystic insight or theology but in science. As it happens, no great conflict was felt between science and religion in Gupta India. Buddhist monasteries and Hindu schools taught mathematics and medicine as well as philosophy and their respective sacred texts. The Buddhist institution of learning at Nalanda, the largest "university" in India, taught medicine and physics along with languages, literature, and metaphysics.

Gupta medicine was based too little on empirical observation to make much progress. Gupta astrology was very popular, but it is hard to establish progress in a pseudoscience. In astronomy and mathematics, however, Indian scientists clearly rivaled the Greeks and the Chinese.

The great leap forward made by Indian mathematicians was the development of what Westerners came to call Arabic numerals—a vast improvement over the Roman numerals that remained standard in the West for another thousand years. With nine numerical symbols and that wonderful little invention, the zero, India immensely simplified the process of mathematical calculation. With the decimal system and the concept of place value, new spheres of mathematical operation were opened up. The value of pi and the beginnings of algebra were also developed here.

Greek astronomy was in circulation among Indian scientists, and Greek scientific terminology was absorbed into Indian texts. But the astronomers of the subcontinent discovered for themselves that the earth was a rotating sphere and learned the causes of lunar eclipses. They also calculated the length of the solar year to the seventh decimal place.

The life of the scientific mind, at any rate, has never been limited to any one corner of this spinning globe.

SUMMARY

India's second golden age, the reign of the Guptas, came as the climax of a long period of turbulence and growth in the subcontinent.

After the disintegration of the unified Maurya Empire in the second century B.C., India did not know unity again for more than five tumultuous but prosperous centuries. During this period repeated waves of invaders swept down through the passes of the Northwest Frontier, including Greeks, Scythians, and Kushans, whose empire included part of northwestern India. Prosperous cities and kingdoms also grew in southern India, which now rivaled the north in wealth and power for the first time. The growing number of cities, the increasing sophistication of handicraft industries, and above all the expansion of trade both within and beyond the subcontinent made this a prosperous period for the many peoples of India.

A true golden age came with unification under the Gupta dynasty (A.D. 320–540). The two earliest of these maharajas, Chandra Gupta I and Samudra Gupta, repeated the Maurya feat of conquering much of the land between the Himalayas and the southern cape. As Asoka had earlier presided over India's Buddhist golden age, Chandra Gupta II gave India a Hindu Renaissance. For a brief time order and prosperity pervaded the land, and the arts flourished under the patronage of this great Hindu dynasty. Then new invaders, a Turko-Mongol people called the White Huns, swept down across the Northwest Frontier, and the Gupta supremacy too passed into history.

Religious piety continued to be central to the high culture of India. Buddhism divided into two historic traditions, the Hinayana and Mahayana schools, and completed its evolution into an elaborate popular religion. Hinduism grew even more dramatically, tending toward monotheism and popular diversity and undergoing a genuine spiritual revival all across India.

Artistic developments reflected the continuing importance of religion and the power of the *rajas*. Architectural remains reveal Indian piety in the unique cave temples and *stupas* of these centuries, and their sculpture projects a sense of the many forms of life. Ordinary Indians enjoyed the beast fables of the *Panchatantra*, while the plays of Kalidasa flourished in the sophisticated atmosphere of India's princely courts. Indian scholars invented the zero and compiled a calendar very similar to our own.

SUGGESTED READING

ALTEKAR, A. S. *The Position of Women in Hindu Civilization.* Banaras: Motilal Banarsidass, 1956. Recommended survey of the subject; especially useful for earlier periods.

BASHAM, A. L. *The Wonder that Was India.* New York: Taplinger, 1968. History and culture of the subcontinent to the Muslim conquest; illustrated.

DE BARY, W. T., ed. *Sources of Indian Tradition.* New York: Columbia University Press, 1958. Valuable collection of source materials.

KALIDASA. *Shakuntala and Other Writings,* trans. W. Ryder. New York: Dutton, 1959. Highly praised translation of the Gupta dramatist.

KAR, C. *Classical Indian Sculpture: 30 B.C. to A.D. 500.* London: Alec Tiranti Ltd., 1956. A little book providing a clear overview and many good photographs. See also the large format with examples from earlier centuries in M. M. Deneck and W. and B. Forman, *Indian Sculpture* (London: Spring Books, 1962).

KEITH, A. B. *History of Sanskrit Literature.* London: Oxford University Press, 1928. Old but still recommended on the Sanskrit literary renaissance.

MAZUMDAR, R. C., *History and Culture of the Indian People* (10 vols.) Parts of Volumes 2 and 3 are relevant, particularly on cultural and social aspects.

MOOKERJI, R. K. *Gupta Empire,* 3rd ed. Bombay: Hind Kitabs, 1959. One of the standard surveys of the period.

NEHRU, J. *The Discovery of India.* New York: John Day, 1946. Insights into his country's past by the first prime minister of independent India.

RAWLINSON, H. G. *Intercourse between India and the Western World: From the Earliest Times to the Fall of Rome,* 2nd ed. New York: Octagon Books, 1971. Old standby on the subject.

SALETORE, B. A. *Ancient Indian Political Thought and Institutions.* New York: Asia Publishing House, 1972. Origins of long-lived Indian political ideas and structures.

SMITH, B. L., ed. *Essays on Gupta Culture.* Delhi: Motilal Benarsidass, 1983. Well-illustrated collection of studies.

ZIMMER, H. *The Art of Indian Asia.* New York: Pantheon, 1955. Good on this and earlier periods.

CHAPTER 13

THE HAN CHINESE EMPIRE

THE HAN DYNASTY

THE FOUNDER OF THE FORMER HAN: HAN GAOZU

On the great eastward bulge of Asia, the first attempt at a unified China had collapsed in ruins in 207 B.C. The awesome First Emperor, Shi Huangdi, had scarcely been placed in his fantastic tomb when court intrigue, peasant rebellion, and rival warlord armies tore his empire apart. From the Great Wall in the north to the warm, typhoon-swept south, the river valleys and tile-roofed cities were tumbled into chaos once more. With the collapse of the Qin dynasty after a single reign, China seemed to be sliding back into Zhou feudalism and the anarchy of the Warring States.

But this was not what happened. When the Mauryas succumbed in India, no new unifying power emerged for five centuries. In China the violence burned itself out, and a new dynasty took up the task of unification in less than twenty years.

Two strikingly different rivals for supreme power emerged in the chaos of feuding warlords that followed the death of Huangdi. One was a dashing southern aristocrat named Xiang Yu. Xiang Yu was willing to leave other princes and warlords in possession of their own lands in return for the sort of semifeudal suzerainty that had been wielded by the Zhou kings. The other contender was a rare type in Chinese imperial annals: a one-time village official and former bandit turned rebel general named Liu Bang. Liu Bang was not an aristocrat or even a gentleman, and his ambitions went considerably beyond feudal suzerainty.

According to later Han historians, dragons and omens presided over Liu Bang's humble birth, and the Mandate of Heaven passed into his hands by divine decree. He seems to have had a good deal of peasant cunning and more than his share of dogged determination. He possessed a politician's understanding of human needs and an ability to shape them to his ends through generosity and praise. Like Augustus Caesar, the first Roman emperor, Liu Bang was no great military leader; at one point he was even captured and held for ransom by the Xiongnu barbarians from beyond the Great Wall. In his protracted struggle with Xiang Yu, he won only one battle—the last one.

Surrounded, outmaneuvered, and outlasted, the aristocratic Xiang Yu committed suicide—and has lived on ever since as a tragic figure in Chinese opera. Liu Bang got on with the business of organizing power in China.

The Han dynasty he founded was to rule, with a single brief interregnum, for more than four hundred years, from 202 B.C. to A.D. 220. The Liu family took their dynastic name from the river Han, which flowed through the territory that had been Liu Bang's home base. The peasant emperor himself was posthumously awarded a new name by the historians of his reign. He is officially known to history as Han Gaozu, "Exalted Founder" of the Han dynasty. It was a dynasty that would be so honored in Chinese history that to this day the Chinese call themselves "people of Han."

In the few years left to him after his long struggle for power (he died in 195 B.C.), Gaozu set the dynasty on the basic political course it would follow thereafter. He chose to reject Zhou feudalism and to continue instead the centralizing policies of the Qin. But he also had the common sense to proceed with less rigor and more moderation than the hard-driving First Emperor had used. Taxes were easier to bear under Gaozu, punishments less savage than they had been under Huangdi's Legalist advisers. Some elements of the feudal order were preserved temporarily by the pragmatic Exalted Founder—notably, feudal domains for some of his own supporters and relatives.

The Chinese people, exhausted by Huangdi's grand schemes and by the years of civil war thereafter, responded to this more temperate course by conferring their support on the new dynasty. Ill defined and largely passive as such popular decisions generally are, this collective acceptance of the new order proved to be a wise one. It brought the Chinese a period of relative peace and prosperity comparable to that enjoyed by Romans after Augustus or Indians in the age of Asoka. It established traditions that would shape the lives of generations far into China's future.

THE SUSTAINER: EMPRESS LÜ

Life was easier along the Yellow River, the Yangzi, and their webs of tributaries wandering among the misty mountains of China. Labor in the millet fields of the north and

"*The king of Han, now emperor, considered that Hsiao Ho had achieved the highest merit, and hence enfeoffed him as marquis of Tsuan with the revenue from a large number of towns. But the other distinguished officials objected, saying, "We have all buckled on armor and taken up our weapons, some of us fighting as many as a hundred or more engagements, the least of us fighting twenty or thirty. Each, to a greater or lesser degree, has engaged in attacks upon cities or seizures of territory. And yet Hsiao Ho, who has never campaigned on the sweaty steeds of battle, but only sat here with brush and ink deliberating on questions of state instead of fighting, is awarded a position above us. How can this be?"*

"Gentlemen," the emperor asked, "do you know anything about hunting?"

"We do," they replied.

"And do you know anything about hunting dogs?"

"We do."

"Now in a hunt," the emperor said, "it is the dog who is sent to pursue and kill the beast. But the one who unleashes the dog and points out the place where the beast is hiding is the huntsman. You, gentlemen, have only succeeded in capturing the beast, and so your achievement is that of hunting dogs. But it is Hsiao Ho who unleashed you and pointed out the place, and his achievement is that of the huntsman. Also in your case only you yourselves, or at most two or three of your family, joined in following me. But Hsiao Ho dispatched his whole family numbering twenty or thirty members to accompany me. This is a service I can hardly forget."

Sima Qian (Ssu-ma Ch'ien) (145–90 B.C.), the "Grand Historian" of Han China, was famous for his dramatic style and for his ability to bring historical figures to life. Here Gaozu, the founder of the Han dynasty, faces the difficult problem of rewarding his chief supporters after their victory and accession to power. Which does the new emperor seem to value more, military or administrative skills? From what you know thus far, does this seem typical of China's attitude toward the military and civil government? From what you know about Gaozu, does this homely parable sound like something he might actually have said? Do you get a sense of his character from this anecdote?

Ssu-ma Ch'ien, Records of the Grand Historian of China: The Shih Chi, trans. Burton Watson (New York: Columbia University Press, 1961), pp. 127–128.

the rice paddies of the south brought the peasant farmer a larger share at least of his just reward, thanks to the dynasty established by the peasant emperor. But at the imperial capital at Chang'an (modern Xi'an), politics went on as usual. And politics in China, even under the Han, could be as full of intrigue and violence as it has ever been anywhere, particularly at the beginning of a new dynasty. Factional feuding at the imperial court was a potential danger to the newfound domestic tranquility of the nation.

Augustus Caesar reigned for forty-five years after

the defeat of his rivals for power. Gaozu had his hands on the levers of power for only seven years after Xiang Yu's defeat in 202. Someone was desperately needed to carry on the work, to sustain the drive for unification and conciliation he had begun. Fortunately for China—if not for her court rivals—there was such a person: the empress dowager Lü.

Empress Lü was not Gaozu's only wife, nor was her son the late emperor's oldest or even his favorite. But Lü was well known to Gaozu's old comrades in the long

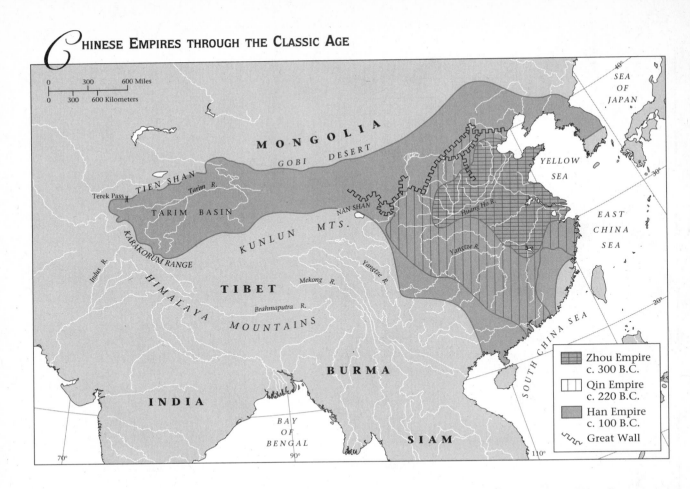

Zhou Empire
c. 300 B.C.

Qin Empire
c. 220 B.C.

Han Empire
c. 100 B.C.

Great Wall

struggle for power, now the chief ministers of the Han Empire. Two of her brothers had been generals in the wars, and she herself had contributed substantially to the successful struggle and suffered in the cause. When her undeniable intelligence, firmness of purpose, and driving ambition are added to this record, the rise of the empress to power has almost a ring of inevitability about it.

In fact, she rose through a court struggle as devious and cruel as anything the Hans had faced in the field. Lü ruled first through her son, a well-meaning but unaggressive sixteen-year-old. When the boy emperor suffered a nervous collapse, allegedly out of horror at his mother's brutal treatment of her defeated rivals, the dowager empress governed directly. There was no doubt of her vindictiveness toward rivals. There was no doubt either that hordes of ambitious members of the Lü clan descended on Chang'an during the years of her supremacy, challenging even the old fighters for the empress's favor.

Precisely because of her need for supporters, however, Dowager Empress Lü endeavored to earn the support of the people through moderate and humane policies. Like Gaozu, she eased the tax burden. She allowed the substitution of fines for physical punishments, and she rescinded the Qin book-burning laws. Her rule was strong and beneficent enough to earn the grudging admiration even of those of the old guard who objected to the growing power of the Lü clan.

Despite all the feuding of the factions, then, the great Han historian Ban Gu wrote approvingly of her reign:

> During the times of [Empress Lü] the world had succeeded in putting behind it the sufferings [during the period of] Contending States.... the world was quiet, [mutilating] punishments and other penalties were seldom used, the people were busy in sowing and harvesting, and clothing and food multiplied and were abundant.[1]

But the years rapidly grew heavy on the empress, who was not young when she acceded to power, and her strength waned as her years advanced. She appointed favorite nephews to supreme civil and military authority, advanced her family in the crucial tables of precedence—

---

[1]Ban Gu, *The History of the Former Han Dynasty,* trans. Homer H. Dubs (Baltimore: Waverly Press, 1938), p. 210.

and then quite suddenly died. The cause of death was the bite of a black dog, which Lü swore on her deathbed was the spirit of a long defeated rival come back to take its revenge.

Like the First Emperor of the Qin, the great sustainer of the Han could do nothing to impose her will from beyond the grave. Within weeks of her death, old fighters and members of Gaozu's clan had joined with leading officials and military men to massacre the entire Lü family and to put another of the Exalted Founder's line on the dragon throne of China.

THE MARTIAL EMPEROR: HAN WUDI

The greatest of the Han emperors came to the throne half a century after the founder's death. Han Wudi, "the Martial Emperor" (141–87 B.C.), was a man of extravagant ambitions and sometimes fantastic beliefs. But he did more in his fifty-four-year reign to strengthen the empire—and the autocratic power of the emperor—than any ruler since Shi Huangdi.

Wudi believed totally in the Mandate of Heaven and the mystique of the emperor. To fortify his claim to absolute sovereignty, he revived or instituted what became traditional imperial prayers and sacrifices to Heaven, to Earth, and to many other supernatural powers. To strengthen the developing system of imperial administration, he recruited, trained, and appointed a pyramidal bureaucracy of tens of thousands of officials. Both his invocation of supernatural forces and his expansion of the machinery of government measurably strengthened the authority of the central government over the Chinese people.

Wudi's economic policies built consciously on the prosperity of the earlier Han. To encourage continued economic growth, he expanded the transportation system through an extensive program of canal building. He established a system of imperial granaries to store grain for resale in time of bad harvest—a system that both stabilized agricultural prices and provided a tidy profit for the imperial treasury. To pay for his large-scale foreign and domestic projects, however, Wudi tapped the growing wealth of the empire through expanded taxation on trade, handicraft industry, and agriculture and through state monopolies on the sale of such essentials as iron, salt, and liquor. In his need for funds he even went to such ultimately disastrous lengths as the sale of government offices and the inflationary measure of licensing the right to mint coins.

The Martial Emperor's most obsessive concern, however, was with foreign wars, both defensive and expansionist. Perhaps his greatest military efforts were lavished on a series of campaigns against the nomadic Xiongnu north of the Great Wall. Wudi sent huge armies north to push the intrusive nomads back across the Gobi. He extended the Great Wall itself and set up military colonies to keep watch over the northern frontiers. He also developed what became a traditional Chinese policy of

A multistoried house in Han China, with wide tile roofs, decorated walls and balconies, and heavy doors at the street level, is depicted in this pottery model. Notice the elaborate decoration of the building from top to bottom. (New York Public Library Picture Collection)

"using barbarians to control barbarians." This involved an intricate combination of marriage alliances, tributary relationships, and hostage taking in the guise of providing court education for the children of Xiongnu chieftains.

The result of these costly efforts was to repulse the restless peoples of the northern steppes. But pressure from northern nomads remained a prominent feature of most of Chinese history thereafter.

Wudi also embarked on a grandiose program of Chinese imperial expansion. Following in the footsteps of the First Emperor, the Martial Emperor pushed into both Korea and north Vietnam. His reaffirmation of Chinese authority made Vietnam a Chinese colony for most of the next millennium. His aggressiveness also helped transform Korea into the cultural base from which the offshore islands of Japan would later be reshaped in China's image.

But the ambitions of Wudi did not stop with domination of East Asia. He sent expeditions far across the northwestern frontiers as well, into the heart of Eurasia. His expeditions had several goals: alliances with western barbarians against the Xiongnu, acquisition of the famed war-horses of Ferghana in central Asia; and quite possibly control of the east-west trade routes across Eurasia as well. These military campaigns established Chinese provinces from Mongolia to Tibet, pushed on over the towering Pamirs into central Asia, and established Chinese control over crucial oases on the caravan roads around the Tarim Basin.

China's interest in westward expansion was to continue, and Chinese armies were to push westward still farther. But the Martial Emperor had done his share for Chinese territorial expansion north, south, and west. By the time of his death in 87 B.C., the borders of the Middle Kingdom were beginning to look a good deal like those of modern China.

WANG MANG AND THE INTERREGNUM

In traditional Chinese historiography, the four centuries of Han rule are divided into two halves: the Former or Western Han, from 202 B.C. to A.D. 9, and the Later or Eastern Han, from A.D. 25 to 220. The years in between constitute the brief, colorful period of the usurping emperor Wang Mang.

The emperors of the Former Han fell victim to what was to become a familiar combination of peasant unrest and weakness at the center. Peasant revolts broke out during the last two decades of the first century B.C., partly because of excess taxation, partly because of population growth that outstripped the land available to feed the people. At the same time, the government faced dwindling tax revenues as once-taxable peasant farmers became farm laborers on the traditionally untaxed estates of large noble landowners.

Amid this crisis, Wang Mang, nephew of a reigning empress, assumed power, proposing radical surgery to cure the ailing state. In the process he temporarily replaced the Han dynasty with his own imperial house.

The usurper claimed that he was reviving traditional policies of pre-Han rulers. In fact, some of his reforms look rather like revivals of some of the most extravagant policies of his great Han predecessor Wudi. Thus Wang also expanded government monopolies, strengthened the system of imperial granaries, and even indulged in inflationary coinage to put more money into circulation. His most drastic innovation, however, was a scheme to boost government revenues—and benefit the peasantry—by nationalizing the great estates of the aristocracy and parceling them out among taxable peasant proprietors.

Needless to say, this plan quickly alienated the great landowners from the new government. Bad harvests and terrible flooding by the Yellow River then triggered a new wave of peasant rebellions—the bloody revolt of the Red Eyebrows. Crusading for vaguely Daoist ideals, this group adopted red as its symbolic color because this was the color of the Hans, whose restoration they championed. They rose first in Shandong, China's great northeastern peninsula and the site of its most sacred mountain, and

were soon ravaging the central plains. When nomads from beyond the Wall broke through the depleted border garrisons, it was clear to all that the Mandate of Heaven had not passed to Wang Mang after all.

Wang was slaughtered by rampaging rebels in his own capital in A.D. 23. Two years later the head of a branch of the ruling house of the Han Empire seized power, and the Han began two more centuries of rule over China.

THE LATER HAN: NEW FRONTIERS

The first century of the Later Han dynasty—the first century A.D.—was a period of internal recovery and renewed external expansion. The restored Han moved the capital from Chang'an eastward, down to the city of Luoyang. They suppressed remaining pockets of rebellion and reestablished the strong centralized administration of earlier Han times. Prosperity was revived across the country and relative peace reigned. After four decades of natural disasters, rebellions, and invasions, which had substantially diminished the population of North China, the Chinese people were grateful to have the Mandate of Heaven back in good hands.

The Later Han also saw a revival of Han imperial expansion. Armies from Luoyang reestablished Han authority over South China and north Vietnam, and Chinese influence grew in Korea. The first respectful embassy from one of the "hundred tribes" of Japan was received during Later Han times. The Xiongnu were dealt so crushing a defeat toward the end of the first century A.D. that they began the long westward drift across the steppes that would eventually bring them up against the walls of Rome—under the name of Huns.

Most striking, however, was the renewed westward drive under the Later Han emperors. The leading spirit in this expansion was Ban Chao, one of China's most celebrated proconsuls of empire. In two major expeditions he reestablished Chinese authority over the Tarim Basin and pushed on over the Pamirs and across central Asia as far as the region of the Caspian Sea. At the moment of Han China's farthest westward penetration, only the Parthian Empire of Persia lay between the great Empire of the East and the Roman Empire of the West. Direct contact eluded the two greatest Eurasian empires of the classical age during the second period of Han imperialism, as it had during the first. But the Later Han emperors actively encouraged trade with the West over the Silk Road—a connection that would continue for some time even after the fall of the dynasty.

THE MANDATE PASSES

The second century of Later Han rule—the fourth of the dynasty's total tenure of power—was far less successful. As usual, the troubles were both political and economic, focusing in the court and in the country as a whole.

A special political difficulty was one that surfaced as early as the reign of the Empress Lü in Former Han times: the ambitious families of Empresses. In the feudal times of the Shang and the Zhou, before unification was achieved, the kings of the various affiliated Chinese states could marry each other's daughters—their equals in rank. But under the unified empire of the Han, there were no other monarchs in China, and the neighboring peoples were dismissed as barbarians, unsuitable sources of Han empresses. Han emperors therefore had to marry the daughters of aristocratic subjects. The multitudinous kin of the empress invariably flocked to court to take advantage of the family's good fortune by establishing themselves in as many positions of power as possible. When an empress outlived her imperial husband and governed as regent for a minor emperor, the power drive of her clan could tear the Luoyang court apart. This in fact happened more than once under the Later Han.

Other centers of factional rivalry existed at the imperial court as well. These included the large numbers of eunuchs, whose power extended far beyond the imperial harem; the most successful generals; and the chief ministers of state. All these groups contributed to the downfall of this and more than one later dynasty.

Finally, economic factors and peasant upheavals once more played crucial parts in the coming catastrophe. Rich landowners, recovered from the disasters of Wang Mang's regime, once more acquired tax exemptions for their large estates. Buckling under the increased tax burden thus shifted to their shoulders, peasants sought to escape the tax collectors by fleeing into South China, as far as they could get from Luoyang. And some of these embittered farmers inevitably rebelled.

Like the Red Eyebrows, the Yellow Turbans of the later second century A.D. had Daoist sympathies and social grievances. They also had the usual share of peasant superstitions; the yellow cloth they wore wrapped around their heads symbolized the color of Chinese earth, which would quench the red fire of Han. Like the Eyebrows, the Turbans rose first in the great northern peninsula of Shandong and were soon terrorizing much of North China.

The collapse of the Later Han thus came in a typical turmoil of court conspiracy, peasant revolt—and finally warlord generals carving up the crumbling empire into their own separate fiefdoms. By A.D. 220 China was once more divided, this time into the Three Kingdoms. The generals who headed these successor states began four centuries of political fragmentation and disarray in China. The first and one of the greatest of Chinese experiments in empire, that of the Qin and the Han, was over.

In a sense, the Han Empire was the victim of its own success. The centralized administration that was one of its greatest achievements could not work without close ties with the landed aristocracy. But the landed magnates milked this special relationship so successfully that they became too rich and powerful to control and created autonomous power centers all over the empire. Again, the very peace and prosperity of Han times seem to have led to an unprecedented growth in the peasant population—until there were simply more people than the government could support or control. Even imperial expansion created a Frankenstein's monster, in the form of the half-settled Xiongnu principalities established along the northern frontiers. These half-civilized kingdoms, like their Germanic counterparts along the frontiers of Rome, finally poured through the defensive line they were supposed to guard. But by the time this catastrophe occurred, in the fourth century A.D., Han China had been a hundred years in its grave.

THE STRUCTURE OF HAN CHINA

THE IMPERIAL MYSTIQUE

China under the Han was the great empire of the East, as Rome—at almost exactly the same time—was the empire of the western end of Eurasia. The two had much in common: vast size and population; increasing power in the hands of the emperors; increasingly centralized bureaucratic administration; a sense of being the only truly civilized people, surrounded by barbarians; even an important breakdown of authority midway in their history, in both cases about the time of Christ. The two were aware of each other's existence and traded through intermediaries from one end of the world island to the other.

The similarities were real, but so were the differences—and most of them favored China over Rome. The Roman Empire, for instance, was comparatively scattered geographically, consisting in large part of an irregular ring of provinces around a central sea, whereas China was a single block of contiguous mainland territory. The Romans ruled a polyglot diversity of peoples, ranging from Britons to Berbers, from Spaniards to Macedonians; China, by contrast, was populated primarily by people of common language and culture. Hence the Chinese were far more likely to accept an image of their emperor as a paternal autocrat, the head of the state in the same sense that the father was head of his extended family. Romans might vote their emperor a title such as *pater patriae*, but Gauls and Arabs were less likely to actually see him as a father figure than the Chinese were to see their emperor as the "father of his country."

The Han emperors built a significant bastion of imperial authority on the Zhou doctrine of the Mandate of Heaven. It was under the Han that this doctrine of divine right to rule became associated not with a weak feudal regime like the Zhou but with a powerful centralized monarchy. From Han times the Chinese tended to believe that legitimate government meant strong rule by a single benevolent despot—a fatherly, authoritarian emperor whose governance was both virtuous and divinely sanctioned.

That the facts of political life at the Chinese court seldom corresponded to this pious theory was much less important for China's subsequent history than was the impact of the theory itself. The belief in paternal, virtuous, and divinely mandated governmental authority was a powerful unifying and centralizing force in Chinese life. Reinforced by a common written language, shared traditions, and—as will be emphasized presently—Confucian beliefs and a classically educated centralized bureaucracy, this image of the emperor helped to weld China's tens of millions of people into something that Rome and India could never be: not a polyglot empire but a gigantic unified nation.

There were major breakdowns of Chinese unity still to come. But the centralizing rule of the Han set China on the road to national unity and strong central government infused with a sense of its own righteousness and right to rule. China has followed this road ever since, despite all that her huge size, vast population, and strong regional loyalties did to pull it apart.

THE SCHOLAR-BUREAUCRATS

The Han period also saw a crucial institutional development that made the authority of the imperial government much more than a theory. For in Han times, China's famous system of scholarly bureaucrats began to evolve.

The great shift from government by an autonomous feudal aristocracy to government by appointed officials of the central government had had a brief, violent trial run under the Qin. But the Legalist rigor of Qin administrators had made the system too brutal for widespread acceptance. Infused with the more moderate spirit of Confucianism—and with due concessions to the existing social elite of the countryside—China's administration under the Han dynasty became the most impressive in the world.

At the center of the Han administrative system were a small number of powerful court officials. These included a chancellor who chaired meetings and wielded substantial authority under the emperor; a director of the secretariat, whose power came from his control over what documents actually reached the emperor for signature; and a commandant of the Chinese armed forces. There were also nine ministers of state charged with the daily business of government, with running the huge imperial palace, and with the crucial religious rituals required of the Son of Heaven.

Outside the capital at Chang'an or Luoyang, the nation was divided and subdivided into administrative districts. There were a dozen main regions, 20 princedoms (holdovers from the feudal system), more than 100 commanderies, 240 marquisates, and 1300 counties in Han China—all governed by officials appointed by the emperor. In the Han period, as noted above, most of these officials were still members of wealthy landowning families who thus obtained official sanction for their supremacy in the countryside. The structure of officialdom also tended to be self-perpetuating, since openings were frequently filled by people nominated by current officeholders.

Under the Han, however, the system of civil-service examinations that would eventually undermine the remaining power of the landed magnates slowly took shape. Exams on Confucian principles and classics were given annually at Chang'an to young gentlemen nominated for office. To prepare them, an imperial university was established at the capital. Again, the children of the wealthy, who had money for books and tutors, were evidently the ones most likely to succeed. Nevertheless, the result was to produce a ruling elite of government administrators who had a common family background and whose heads were filled with common Confucian theories, shared historical understanding, and the same basic values—a powerful force for stability in the ancient Middle Kingdom.

Around 100 B.C. China's governmental bureaucracy, divided into eighteen civil-service ranks, included upwards of 130,000 people—not many to govern tens of millions of Chinese, but an astonishing number of educated, centrally appointed officials for those days, when most of the world was still ruled by village elders, hereditary clan chieftains, and local princes.

SIXTY MILLION CHINESE—AND COUNTING

The land they administered was large, populous, and generally prosperous in spite of some startling social and economic changes over the four centuries of Han rule. The size of the Han Empire, with the cementing of Chinese authority over northern Vietnam and the addition of Xinjiang—China's far west—was close to the size of twentieth-century China. The population, according to tax censuses taken around the middle of the dynasty, ran higher than sixty million people. We are thus dealing with a nation approaching the geographical size of the United States today, though with a population approximately one quarter that of the present United States.

Most of the Chinese emperor's subjects, as indicated above, were Chinese-speaking and raised according to a common set of ancient beliefs and traditional mores. This is not to say that unification or centralized authority was inevitable in China. Ancient Sumeria and ancient Greece, for two examples, shared similar advantages yet seldom managed even temporary unity. But given the organizing ability and determination of the most energetic Han emperors and administrators, unity was at least possible. And a roughly homogeneous culture was very likely indeed.

Even within this framework of ethnic and cultural homogeneity, however, Han society underwent significant changes. Han China was particularly affected by the destruction of the ancient pattern of provincial feudalism by Gaozu and his successors. Their methods were less ruthless than those of Huangdi, but they had the same effect. Gaozu had abolished most of the autonomous states upon his seizure of power, leaving only a few such feudal enclaves to reward his own followers. Later Han emperors undermined even those few by edicts requiring feudal landholders to divide their estates equally among their male offspring. Within a few generations, this procedure had so thoroughly fragmented the great feudal holdings that they easily came under imperial control.

From this change emerged the basic social structure of China from Han times to the present century. When feudal landholding was replaced by freehold property, three main classes quickly developed across the vast expanse of China's countryside. There was a class of locally powerful, often very wealthy large landowners. There was a larger class of peasant freeholders who often had to struggle to keep enough land to feed themselves. And there was an even larger class of tenant farmers and farm laborers. The interaction among these social classes, who composed the bulk of China's population, would determine much of its subsequent history.

The relative peace and prosperity of the Former Han transformed the nation economically as well. A true money economy, for example, was established for the first time. The widespread use of coins instead of barter brought with it such exotic problems as inflation and the need for a firm governmental monetary policy. But the growing wealth of China also filled the government's treasury with strings of copper cash, revenues that accumulated through so many reigns that the strings actually rotted away—an enviable situation for any government.

Under the expansionist Han emperors, furthermore, foreign trade expanded significantly. China traded, in the first instance, with the less developed tributary peoples around it. More important, Chinese goods moved westwards across Eurasia along the great Silk Road to India or to Rome, where Chinese silk became a major luxury import. Chinese merchants themselves did not travel that far. But the trade overland through central Asia or by sea through the archipelagoes of Southeast Asia became one of the basic ties that bound the world island into a single, if loosely linked, unit during the classical period.

It should be stressed, finally, that even in this cosmopolitan, centrally ruled nation, the lives of most of China's peasant millions were still bounded by the village and the province. Government officials intruded into the countryside mainly to collect taxes, schedule the annual labor service required of all peasants, or perhaps to recruit soldiers for the army. The resident magistrate of a district town dealt mainly with landed magnates and village headmen, not with ordinary citizens. The real rulers of the countryside on a day-to-day basis remained the larger landowners, who controlled the peasantry through favors and patronage, through economic clout, and sometimes through the bullying of their retainers or henchmen. Since the wealthy landowners also staffed the imperial administrative system, their overall power was very great.

On this foundation of rural stability and landowner control, the small, far-off Han court stood. Forbidden even to pronounce the emperor's name with their profane lips, the peasants could only pay their taxes, do their road work or garrison duty, and hope for the best from on high. Under the Han, fortunately, they very frequently got just that.

THE WOMEN OF THE HAN

The Han dynasty is commonly characterized as one of China's most splendid periods. In the lives of the female half of the huge Chinese population, it was also a time of considerable variety and significant achievement.

During this age in which much of the traditional Chinese way was first established, the position of women was also apparently set. Widely accepted maxims and popular anecdotes illustrating admired feminine qualities came into circulation. Like so much else, these precepts were sanctified in Han times by attribution to Confucian sages. They added up to a prescription for ideal womanhood that would prevail in China through most of its history.

According to this Confucian view—as in Christian, Muslim, and other groups in later centuries—women's virtues were family virtues. Chinese women were expected to be devoted to their parents in childhood and youth, to their husbands thereafter. Care of their family and children was to be their central preoccupation as adults. Fidelity, chastity, and modesty were the ideal female qualities.

In actuality, however, Han China produced a number of women who transcended this image. Women of several important classes became highly educated and much respected for their learning during the Han dynasty. At the top of the social pyramid, Han empresses and imperial concubines were sometimes celebrated for their culture, as were the wives and daughters of some of the landowning aristocracy. Daoist and later Buddhist nuns might be both educated and relatively independent in traditional China. A few at least of the courtesan class were also highly cultured, as *geishas* would be in Japan at a later date.

Pan Chao, perhaps the most honored of all Chinese women writers, composed her widely admired verses, essays, and treatises—sixteen volumes in all—during the Han period. Pan Chao's classic *Precepts for Women* became the basis of Chinese women's education for most of the next two thousand years. Her *Precepts* included an idealistic view of marriage as "the fusion of Yin and Yang"—the male and female principles of the universe. "If the wife carry not to completion [the] management of her husband's affairs," she wrote, "the rule of rightness, polished jewel of correct action, crumbles, is lost."[2]

---

[2]Pan Chao, *Nu Chieh: Precepts for Women*, in Florence Ayscough, *Chinese Women Today and Yesterday* (New York: Da Capo, 1975), pp. 240–241.

Chinese court ladies, hair elaborately dressed, hands concealed in long sleeves. The well-fed self-assurance of the Middle Kingdom in one of its greatest ages is eloquently captured in these clay figurines, which have survived remarkably undamaged over twenty centuries. (New York Public Library Picture Collection)

We shall meet all these groups of learned ladies in later periods of Chinese history. But the Han period—the very time when the constricting Confucian ideal of womanhood was taking shape—was also a time of relative success, for the elite at least, of China's female population.

THE MIND AND ART OF THE HAN

THE TRIUMPH OF CONFUCIANISM

If Shang bronzes were the glory of that dynasty, and if the supreme cultural achievement of the Zhou lay in philosophy and poetry, then Han China's major cultural monuments are to be found in the somewhat less exalted fields of scholarship and history. But Confucian scholarship and the study of the great dynastic cycle of Chinese history also had their contributions to make to the many-splendored culture and the amazing longevity of Chinese civilization.

The triumph of Confucianism in Chinese thought during the Han period was a complicated and in some ways rather unedifying spectacle. But that triumph would make a great difference to China's future.

All the schools of philosophy that had survived the "burning of the books" under the Qin had their place under the Han. The Qin Legalist tradition itself, with its justification of ruthless efficiency and rigorous punishment, was often the actual policy of Han emperors, even those who paid reverent lip service to Confucius. The romantic mysticism of Daoism became in Han times the basis of a widely popular farrago of nature worship, dietary regimen, research into methods of preserving life indefinitely and transmuting base metals into gold, and plain magic.

Nevertheless, the Confucian tradition did become the predominant philosophy of China during the Han period. Han emperors, from the classically uneducated Exalted Founder to the ruthlessly Legalistic Martial Emperor, filled their edicts with Confucian invocations of government for the good of the people, respect for the sages, and other pieties. The official examinations were based on the Confucian classics, so that all government administrators had at least studied the master's writings. Official sacrifices were made to his immortal spirit, and the classics themselves were engraved in stone and set up for all to see. From Han times on, Confucian philosophy was the national philosophy of the Chinese people.

In many ways the Confucianism thus established bore little resemblance to the social and ethical doctrine preached by Master Kong five hundred years before. Confucian scholars of the Han period attributed to their founder many views he never held. He was presented as a supporter of harsh punishments, as the author of a book on fortune-telling, and as an ardent champion of the doctrine that the emperor was the Son of Heaven. Many Confucianists ceased to be social and ethical philosophers at all and became scholars dedicated to editing and commenting on every surviving character of the master's alleged works.

Like Buddha in India, Confucius was thus oddly transformed at the moment of his triumph. Confucianism became "a great synthetic religion, into which were fused all the elements of popular superstition and state worship."[3] Yet there was an important sense in which Confucius's canonization as the nation's official philosopher was a very good thing for China.

---

[3]Hu Shih, "The Establishment of Confucianism as a State Religion during the Han Dynasty," *Journal of the North China Branch of the Royal Asiatic Society*, vol. 60 (1929), pp. 34–35.

Many Confucian sages did not take official jobs or become pedantic scholars but remained poor men—and social critics—all their lives. Such men could still speak for the people whose ragged robes and torn sandals they shared. Official doctrines attributed to Confucius still included much of the master's spirit, including his insistence that virtue should rule, and even his radical notion that government should serve the people rather than exploit them. The endless repetition of these views over many centuries, by everyone from the emperor to the raggediest Confucian student, gave these principles of duty and decency, harmony and order, some weight at least in shaping the policies that ruled China.

THE GRAND HISTORIAN

The study of history was another area in which the Han dynasty made significant contributions to Chinese culture and political understanding. Han China actually nurtured not one but two of the greatest historians her civilization has ever produced. In addition, Han historical scholarship developed a central concept of Chinese social thought: the idea of the dynastic cycle.

Sima Qian lived during the Former, Ban Gu during the Later Han. Both men were close to great events and the great men of the age—Sima Qian as court historian to Wudi the Martial Emperor, and Ban Gu as the twin brother of Ban Chao, the most famous of Han empire builders. Their books followed what became a Chinese historiographical tradition by incorporating large amounts of source material, from government documents to snatches of poetry, into their texts. Otherwise, however, the two historians and their histories were very different.

Sima Qian's *Records of the Grand Historian* was a monumental attempt at a universal history of China, from the age of the mythical sages through the Shang, Zhou, and Qin to his own time. He passed judgments, told colorful stories, invented speeches for his historical figures, and generally filled his ten thousand or so pages with fascinating and thoroughly humanized history.

Ban Gu's *History of the Former Han* was more restrained in tone and more restricted in scope. But it became a model for a standard form of Chinese history thereafter: the history of a single dynasty, from vigorous beginnings to final collapse.

The interpretation of China's past as a series of such more or less uniform dynastic cycles became the core of traditional Chinese historiography—and the Former Han the great exemplar of this pattern. Each of the great dynasties thereafter was seen as beginning vigorously, rising to great achievement, then settling into a long decline and fall as the Mandate of Heaven passed on to strong new hands.

The traditional approach embodied this pattern in vivid personalities, often modeled on the rude but robust Gaozu, the greatness of Wudi, and the degeneracy and debauchery of the last emperors of the line. A more modern approach sees the dynastic cycle as a pattern of institutional, social, and economic development and decline. Thus, the success of a new dynasty is seen in its centralizing policies as much as in its personalities, and factional feuds built into the structure of the court contribute to its downfall. All dynasties build grandly, send out great armies, and in so doing overspend, leading to pressure on the tax-paying peasantry that will finally drive them to rebel. As revenues dry up, inadequately maintained dikes and border garrisons are likely to give way, leading to natural disasters and barbarian invasions. These catastrophes indicate that the Mandate of Heaven has been withdrawn—and yet another dynasty is swept away.

There is probably truth in both the approach that concentrates on personalities and the approach that concentrates on institutional analysis and impersonal forces. There certainly seems to be truth in the concept of the dynastic cycle itself—one form of the eternal recurrence of rise and fall that plays over the history of all civilization. In China's case, however, we can chart the cycle in remarkable detail, thanks to the scrupulous efforts of Chinese historians to record the histories of their dynasties over the two thousand years since the Former Han.

ART IN THE PALACE OF HAN

Surprisingly little remains of the art and architecture of Han China. The Han Chinese left us no crumbling Forum like that of ancient Rome, no Ajanta caves full of wonders. Their magnificent palaces were built of wood, and the paintings that literary sources describe have vanished with the plastered walls that held them. From such literary accounts, however, and from surviving fragments of metalwork and lacquerware, pottery, pressed tile, and the walls of tombs, we may get some idea at least of the subjects and styles of Han art.

The subjects are human, social, and historical: laborers in the fields, banqueters at the table, dignitaries parading in their parasol-shaded chariots, ancient sages, famous kings. There are few gods and no heavens, hells, or judgment halls of the dead, even in Chinese tombs. The style is simple, vigorous, and full of energy. Human figures are clearly outlined, rather flat, almost cartoonlike at first glance. But they move, gesture, reach out—their horses prance or charge at a flying gallop—with the dash and vigor that made the Han age great.

For the architecture of Han, we have some small pottery models, a few sketchy pictures, and the usual extravagant literary descriptions. From the models we get a sense of multistory tile- or thatch-roofed houses, walled courtyards, pig-pens and kitchens, balconies, people sitting in open doorways. From the written descriptions of Han palaces, we get a picture of something much more splendid.

The vigor and dynamism of the Han Empire are powerfully conveyed by this beautiful bronze horse, dating from the second century A.D. Note the "flying gallop" pose. What conveys the sense of rapid motion in this statue? (New York Public Library Picture Collection)

The scale of Han public building clearly matched and even exceeded that of Huangdi. Gaozu's palace complex at Chang'an was more than a mile square and filled one ninth of the capital city. One of Wudi's even larger palaces, located outside the city walls, was connected to a royal residence inside the ramparts by an overpass that soared across the city moat as well as the walls. Inside a royal compound were many sumptuous buildings with ornamental gates and towers, mazes of courtyards, and vast audience halls, the whole surrounded by extensive parklands dotted with artificial lakes and stocked with exotic plants, beasts, and birds. Interiors of palaces or mansions were bright with plaster, paint, and gilt, bronze, and lacquer.

Gaozu, a peasant's son long used to field and camp, may have felt faintly ill at ease moving through such newly painted splendor in his elaborate silk robes. But the great Wudi surely strode with perfect confidence across an audience hall apparently larger than the one that graced the royal palace in twentieth-century Beijing. For the Han emperors built to their own measure, and that scale was often significantly larger than life.

SUMMARY

China under the Han dynasty was the great empire of the East, as Rome was of the West. But while Europe has not known unity since the fall of Rome, the Han emperors were laying the foundations for an imperial unity that would be reestablished again and again over the next two thousand years.

The political history of the Han (206 B.C. to A.D. 220) produced its most famous rulers during its earlier centuries. Gaozu, "Exalted Founder" of the dynasty, was a tough, hard-driving peasant who imposed order by force on the anarchy that had followed the death of Huangdi, the first unifier of China. Gaozu, however, did not live to enjoy his victory long. It was his successor, the Empress Lü, who established the new order firmly across the Middle Kingdom. The empress's grandson and the most famous of all the Hans, Wudi, the "Martial Emperor," was a true ruler for all seasons. He expanded China's frontiers by conquest, pushed back the Xiongnu nomads, built immense public works, and encouraged the establishment of a Confucian administrative system that would long outlast his dynasty.

Lesser Han rulers were briefly displaced around the time of Christ by the short-lived reforming regime of the usurper Wang Mang; but the Hans of the first century A.D. were again vigorous and successful. Under them China's wealth and empire grew once more, until Chinese armies almost confronted Roman armies on the distant steppes of central Asia. Internal decay, rebellious generals, and invasions by northern peoples finally brought the Han dynasty down in the third century A.D. But by that time four centuries of Han rule had left such a mark on China that Chinese today still call themselves the People of Han.

Under this vigorous ruling house, the imperial mystique was honored, and the astonishing system of highly trained Confucian scholar-bureaucrats, which would make China perhaps the best-governed of all nations for many cen-

turies, took shape. The population of China passed sixty million, and the wealth of the land supported such growth.

Han culture was solid rather than creative. Confucius became the empire's official philosopher and the core of China's educational system. Two of the greatest of Chinese historians, Sima Qian and Ban Gu, established history writing as one of China's major cultural achievements. And the Han emperors patronized art and literature on a scale suited to the wealth and splendor of the Middle Kingdom during one of its greatest ages.

SUGGESTED READING

BIELENSTEIN, H. *The Bureaucracy of Han Times*. Cambridge: Cambridge University Press, 1980. Origins of the remarkable system of scholarly bureaucrats.

CHÜ, T. *Han Social Structure*. Tokyo: University of Tokyo Press, 1972. Useful overview.

CREEL, H. G. *Chinese Thought from Confucius to Mao Tse-tung*. Chicago: University of Chicago Press, 1953. See chapter on "The Ecclectics of Han."

FAIRBANK, J. F., E. O. REISCHAUER, and A. M. CRAIG. *East Asia: The Great Tradition*. Boston: Houghton Mifflin, 1960. Valuable source, especially on institutions and society.

HIRTH, F. *China and the Roman Orient*. Chicago: Ares Publishers, 1985. Contacts between the two empires.

HSU, C. *Han Agriculture: The Formation of Early Chinese Agrarian Economy*, ed. J. L. Dull. Seattle: University of Washington Press, 1980. Social, technological, and economic bases of Chinese society.

LOEWE, M. *Crisis and Conflict in Han China*. London: Allen and Unwin, 1974. Breakdown of the Former Han.

———. *Everyday Life in Early Imperial China*. London: B. T. Batsford, 1968. Brings ancient China to life.

NEEDHAM, J. *Science and Civilization in China*, 6 vols. New York: Cambridge University Press, 1986. Massive ongoing study directed by a scholar who has given his life to examining China's scientific and technological achievements.

PAN, K. *Courtier and Commoner in Ancient China: Selections from the History of the Former Han*, trans. B. Watson. New York: Columbia Press, 1974. More courtiers than commoners, but provides a range of

short biographies from princes and generals to concubines and even a court fool.

SCHIROKAUER, C. *A Brief History of Chinese and Japanese Civilizations*. New York: Harcourt Brace Jovanovich, 1978. More political and social history than usual in the Han chapter of this recent and readable overview.

TWITCHETT, D., AND M. LOEWE, eds. *The Ch'in and Han Empires, 221 B.C.–A.D. 220*. New York: Cambridge University Press, 1986. Scholarly.

WANG, Z. *Han Civilization*, trans. K. C. Chang. New Haven: Yale University Press, 1982. Lectures on aspects of Han culture as revealed by archaeological research.

WATSON, B. *Ssu-ma Ch'ien: Grand Historian of China*. New York: Columbia University Press, 1968. See also Watson's translations of Sima's *Records of the Historian* and *Records of the Grand Historian of China* (New York: Columbia University Press, 1961).

———. *Early Chinese Literature*. New York: Columbia University Press, 1962. Excellent survey that goes through the Han period.

YANG, L. "Female Rulers in Imperial China," *Harvard Journal of Asiatic Studies*, 23 (1960–1961), 47–61. Includes empresses during the Han, when women rulers were particularly prominent. For a contemporary life of Empress Lü, see Ban Gu's *History of the Former Han Dynasty*. vol. 1, trans. H. H. Dubs (Baltimore: Waverly Press, 1938), chaps. 2 and 3.

YÜ, Y. *Trade and Expansion in Han China: A Study in the Structure of Sino-Barbarian Economic Relations*. Berkeley: University of California Press, 1967. A major contribution.

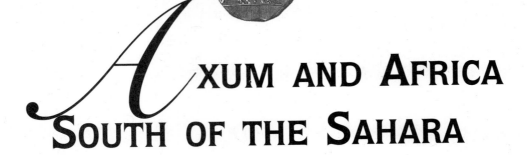

CHAPTER 14

AXUM AND AFRICA SOUTH OF THE SAHARA

AFRICA AND THE MEDITERRANEAN
Greek and Roman Africa
Alexandria

AXUM
Axum and the Red Sea
Axumite Society
The Culture of Axum

AFRICA SOUTH OF THE SAHARA
Saharan and Sub-Saharan Cultures
Technology—Metals and Salt
Trade—the Camel Revolution
Political Organization—Hints of Things to Come

AFRICA AND THE MEDITERRANEAN

GREEK AND ROMAN AFRICA

The centers of most of the world's more developed cultures during the classic age remained on the linked continents of Asia and Europe. On this huge landmass complex cultures interacted in ways that fostered comparatively rapid growth and development. But civilization had already begun outside the world island, and there were further developments on other continents during this period too.

Africa, closest to Eurasia and the home of one of the earliest civilizations, that of Egypt, continued to be integrated into the large patterns of Old World civilization. But sophisticated societies continued to emerge outside the older cultural areas as well.

North Africa's ties to the Near East and the Mediterranean world remained strong in the classic age. Thus, Egypt was ruled first by the Ptolemies, heirs of one of Alexander the Great's generals, then by the Romans. The Romans especially squeezed the Egyptian peasantry unmercifully to ring all the grain possible out of the fertile Nile valley to feed the populous cities across the Mediterranean. Egypt's monuments and reputation for deep wisdom survived, however. Alexandria, in the Nile delta, became, as we will see, one of the great Mediterranean centers of learning.

By the time of Christ, all the rest of North Africa had also been incorporated into the Roman Empire. From the mouths of the Nile to the site of ancient Carthage and on west to the Strait of Gibralter, Roman soldiers maintained domestic order and turned desert raiders back into the Sahara. The Romans also sowed the fertile strip along the Mediterranean coast with ordered farms and public wells, aqueducts and cities. The ruins are still there today, fluted columns and fallen capitals that might as easily have been quarried in Italy or Greece as here on the northern edge of Africa.

North Africa was thus an important part of one of the great civilizations of the classic age. It contributed significantly to the rich mix of cultures that would increasingly characterize human life everywhere on earth.

ALEXANDRIA

The Egyptian city of Alexandria was famed for its harbor in Greek and Roman times. Its towering Pharos, a 400-foot lighthouse, was hailed as one of the wonders of the ancient world. Visitors from Africa, Asia, and Europe gazed in awe at the great Delta city's commercial wealth, palaces, and temples.

Alexandria's cultural institutions in particular were unrivaled. Its zoological and botanical gardens drew throngs of citizens. Its museum was true to its name, a temple of learning dedicated to the Muses. Most celebrated of all was the great library of Alexandria, which may have contained as many as 400,000 books. Here Egypt's Ptolemaic dynasty supported scholars, scientists, and other learned people, freeing them for study and writing in an atmosphere like that of a modern research institution.

Many writers and thinkers flocked to this new Athens on the southern shores of the Mediterranean. The geographer and astronomer Ptolemy worked here, assembling the theory of the structure of the universe that would dominate Western thought down to the time of Copernicus. The philosopher Plotinus, founder of the Neo- or New Platonism, probed the metaphysical limits of human understanding in the shadow of these brightly painted, multistoried buildings. The Greek-speaking Ptolemaic dynasty gave way to Roman emperors, but Egypt's reputation for wisdom continued to draw the best minds from Hellenistic into early Christian times.

The intellectual brilliance of Alexandria owed much to the city's Egyptian setting. Egypt's ancient skill at surgery and medicine, for instance, helped make Alexandria a leading medical center. There, thanks to the prevailing intellectual freedom, doctors conducted valuable anatomical studies by dissecting corpses. Greek and Egyptian styles of art and architecture began to blend and mingle here.

Greek and Egyptian taste for artistic representations of black Africans has left us a particularly valuable legacy of statuettes in marble, bronze, and terra cotta clay. Here these people of the Upper Nile are shown riding elephants, battling crocodiles, wrestling, dancing, juggling, making speeches, or playing musical instruments. These small figures are a vivid reminder that Hellenistic and Roman Alexandria was still an African city.

This conjectural rendering of Alexandria's great lighthouse, the Pharos, gives at least some sense of the scale of and grandeur of the building. It also reflects an Egyptian tradition of building on the grand scale that goes back to the pyramids. (The Bettmann Archive)

Meanwhile, an impressive African civilization flourished far from the intersecting cultures of the Mediterranean during this period. This was the East African empire of Axum, south and east of Egypt on the shores of the Red Sea.

AXUM

AXUM AND THE RED SEA

Axum rose to supremacy in northeastern Africa on the ruins of ancient Kush and its capital, Meroe. The Axumite troops of King Ezana ravaged this ancient African king-

dom on the upper Nile around A.D. 350. But Kush may already have been tributary to the kings of Axum when Ezana's armies desecrated its temples, for Axum was nearing the apogee of its power in the fourth century A.D. Axumite civilization, in fact, had its complex origins the better part of a thousand years before.

Axum was located southeast of the Sudan, in an area that straddles both the high Ethiopian plateau and the sun-bleached coast of the Red Sea. Perhaps as early as the seventh century B.C., Semitic-speaking Arab people had crossed the southern end of the Red Sea from Yemen to Africa. The newcomers, known as the Habashat people, settled both on the African shore and in the high country back from the coast. Here they met,

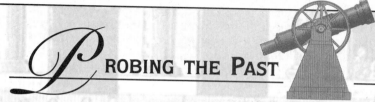

PROBING THE PAST

"*By the first century A.D. the development of the town of Aksum begins the third period, known as "Aksumite," which continued until the tenth century. The evidence suggests that many of the earlier sites were abandoned and new towns founded. Of these, Aksum, perhaps by reason of its sheltered situation, plentiful water supply and adequacy of agricultural land, became the most important, and the seat of a long line of rulers. This Aksumite period is marked by a number of important changes in the styles of architecture, as well as of pottery and other manufactured articles. A coinage was developed by the third century A.D., and from the representations of royalty, often with their names, on the coins, a list of kings can be established. There was certainly an increase in prosperity, largely as a result of trading activities. Many more sites are known than from pre-Aksumite times, and there is a greater richness in the material culture, together with a considerable import of objects from the eastern Mediterranean.*

During this period Aksum became a town of some size and contained numerous temples and palaces, as well as the large monolithic stelae for which it is best known. . . . some idea of the nature of the richer, perhaps royal, buildings can be got from the large "chateau" (as the excavator has described it) of Dongour on the western outskirts of the town. This complex building is an irregular rectangle with each side about 57 meters long. Some walls still stand to a height of 5 meters, and it contains over forty rooms ranged round a central pavillion reached by a monumental stone staircase. It is a massive and splendid construction bearing witness to the wealth and technical competence of the Aksumite kingdom."

◆◆◆

The above description of the golden age of Axum is by Professor P. L. Shinnie, an archaeologist from the University of Calgary who has specialized in the region of Axum, Kush, and Nubia. Though there are references to Axum in ancient accounts by merchants who traded there, the evidence drawn upon here is mostly archaeological in nature.

What natural advantages does Professor Shinnie believe classical Axum had? What do the surviving Axumite coins tell us about the economic life of Axum? What can we learn from coins about its political history? What can be deduced from archaeological investigation about the quality of life and technical skills of the Axumites?

P. L. Shinnie, "The Nilotic Sudan and Ethiopia, c. 660 B.C. to c. A.D. 600," in J. D. Fage, ed., The Cambridge History of Africa, 8 vols. (Cambridge, England: Cambridge University Press, 1978), vol. 2, p. 263.

dominated, and merged with a farming, herding Kushite-speaking people to produce the Axumites of the first millennium A.D.

The intruders came with experience in agriculture, trade, and other skills. The Habashat had already made southern Arabia bloom through the judicious deployment of dams and aqueducts. They had for generations been trading along the Red Sea and around the Indian Ocean. They were literate in their own Ge'ez tongue, and they knew how to build with stone.

AXUMITE SOCIETY

The new land the Habashat came to combined one of the hottest strips of territory on earth—the African Red Sea shore—with the mile-high mountains, deep gorges, and rushing rivers of the Ethiopian highlands inland. The Kushite people they found there lived in farming villages or followed their herds through the hills down to Lake Tana or the wide bend of the Blue Nile. The Habashat first overwhelmed and then blended with this older people on the land, as Aryans had with Dravidians in India, to produce a new African people—the people of Axum.

Such inland African products as ivory, hides, rhinoceros horn, and gold passed to the outside world through their highland capital, the city of Axum itself. Adulis, their port city in the lowlands, became a collecting point for goods from further down the coast of East Africa, or from as far away as India and Ceylon, across the Indian Ocean. From Axum and Adulis these African and Asian goods would flow north up the Red Sea to the eastern Mediterranean, to the Near East, Greece, Rome, and beyond.

During its most prosperous time, from the third century B.C. to the fourth century A.D.—the heart of the classical age—these Axumite cities were thriving centers of trade. Greek, Arab, and Jewish merchants mingled in its port cities, and caravans from the Sudan and beyond jostled each other in the streets of its capital. This bustling nation of traders became a key juncture in the flow of goods and ideas between the three continents of the Old World.

With wealth from overseas, furthermore, there came power in Africa.

The Habashat invaders did not originally have a centralized political structure. Priests were important among

A carved megalith from Axum, in today's Ethiopia, dwarfs the tiny human figure standing at its base. Notice the false door inscribed in the solid stone at the base of the structure. Where else have we seen inscribed vertical shafts set up as commemorative and decorative structures? (The Smithsonian Collections)

them in the early days, and there were governors who collected tribute from local areas. Like so many others around the world, they were one people culturally but not yet a political nation. More centralized political institutions, however, evolved with time. By the first century A.D. the written guide to the Red Sea used by Greek traders reported that there was a king at Axum—and that he had some Greek education. A traveler of a later century described the Axumite ruler progressing in splendor, clad in gold-embroidered linen and standing in a four-wheeled chariot drawn by four elephants. Both the king and his counselors were armed with gilded spears and shields, and flutes made music for them as they passed.

THE CULTURE OF AXUM

The soldiers of the kings of Axum carried the power of the coastal kingdom inland. Axumite armies pushed north through the Ethiopian mountains as far as the frontiers of Egypt. They thrust west across the grasslands of the Sudan to ravage Kush and Meroe. For a time they controlled all the land from the Ethiopian uplands to the Horn of Africa, dominated a long stretch of the Red Sea coast, policed the interior caravan trails, and kept all the neighboring pastoral peoples in awe.

The city of Axum itself, settled in the well-watered highlands some days' journey back from the coast, developed a unique material culture under the Axumite kings. The ruins that remain remind the traveler of no place else on earth. There are crenelated castles and thrones of carven stone. There are "stepped walls" and the giant obelisks of Axum, sixty-five feet high and carefully sculptured to look like towers with false doors and windows and strange round arches at the top.[1]

In pagan Axum there were temples to the old gods of Arabia—gods of earth and war and the blazing sun—and blood sacrifices to these deities, even of humans. But in the fourth century A.D. the celebrated King Ezana accepted conversion to Christianity at the hands of his old tutor, an Eastern Orthodox priest. Thereafter churches began to rise in Axum. Thereafter also the fortunes of the Axumites began to change.

The coming of Christianity ended the blood sacrifices—if they had not ended before—and strengthened commercial ties with the Christian Near East. But conversion also had a powerful isolating effect on Axum, which became the only Christian country in this part of the world. This effect was intensified in the seventh century A.D., when Islam swept like a prairie fire across North Africa and down through Arabia. The Christian Axumites then found themselves alone indeed, between the pagan peoples south and west of them and the Muslims to the north and east.

[1]G. W. B. Huntingford, "The Kingdom of Axum," in *The Dawn of African History*, Roland Oliver, ed. (London: Oxford University Press, 1961), p. 23.

These enemies encroached slowly upon the greatness of Axum. Adulis was taken by the Arabs, and other Axumite harbors by neighboring African peoples. The herdsmen that king Ezana had held in check now raided at will across the croplands of the Axumites. There were kings in the city of Axum for another century or two; then they too disappeared from history.

The survivors of once proud and prosperous Axum clung to the faith of Ezana, if they could not keep his wealth and power. Christianity persisted and strengthened them in their long isolation. They survived to become the ancestors of Africa's oldest continuously independent people, the Ethiopians of today.

AFRICA SOUTH OF THE SAHARA

SAHARAN AND SUB-SAHARAN CULTURES

During the thousand years before and after Christ, Africa south of the Sahara desert developed at its own pace. There were as yet no Alexandrias or Axums in these regions, any more than there were in Europe north of the Alps or Asia north of the Great Wall of China. Nevertheless, archaeological research reveals technological and economic progress and suggests the emergence of more complex political forms in the western and southern parts of Africa during the classic age.

TECHNOLOGY—METALS AND SALT

Many African peoples of this period continued to shape stone into hard-edged tools for everyday use. Some of them also learned to work copper, iron, and gold and to mine salt during these centuries.

Of the chief metals, copper was mined in Mauretania in northwestern Africa in pre-Christian times. Copper ornaments and use objects have been found in tombs in this area. The West Africans of Senegal and the central and southern Africans of today's Zaire, Zimbabwe, and Zambia also worked copper, though we know less about these regions.

Ironworking, as we have seen, may have radiated from ancient Meroe or may have emerged spontaneously in several parts of Africa. Some authorities believe Africans outside of the Nile valley both mined and worked iron during the first millennium after Christ. Khoi-San peoples may have mined iron in southern Africa as Bantu-speaking Africans did in West Africa. Certainly, the great Bantu migrations, to be discussed below, spread iron far across central and southern Africa.

Gold, which would emerge as a key African export in the next stage of African history, also came into use south of the Sahara this early. Far up the Senegal and Niger rivers of West Africa, people probably panned and mined for gold as early as the first millennium A.D.

The lowly mineral called salt became increasingly valuable as more and more Africans settled down in agricultural villages. Hunting peoples got plenty of salt from the animals they killed, but people dependent on crops had little salt in their diets. Living as they did in an increasingly hot climate, Saharan and equatorial Africans also lost much salt each day through perspiration. While archaeologists still have much digging to do, salt works from the first millennium A.D. have been found in the Sahara itself as well as in East Africa.

TRADE—THE CAMEL REVOLUTION

Commercial exchange, as we have seen, goes back a long way in Africa. Both food-gathering and agricultural peoples traded stone and metal for tools, decorative beads, meat, grain, dried fish, and many other things. Most of this exchange, however, was local and small in scale. Only with the spreading use of metals and the introduction of the camel into Africa did long-distance trade emerge.

Metal deposits were found only in widely scattered sites. As peoples began to work them, however, metals became the most widely valued of trade goods. Evidence of exchange includes the discovery of copper ingots in South Africa and of ornaments made of metals not locally available in West African graves. Other things were widely traded too, including salt from the Sahara and glass beads, which may have been made as far away as India.

A key development that made wider trade possible was the "Camel Revolution." This major improvement in transportation spread westward from Asia during the centuries around the time of Christ. Capable of carrying heavy loads for many days with little water and only the scantiest grass, camels were ideally suited for desert travel across northern Africa.

The hardy beasts were probably introduced from the Near East into Egypt by the Greek Ptolemies and to the rest of North Africa under the Romans. The African Berbers quickly adopted camels, using them for travel across the Sahara to the Western Sudan and the forests of the Guinea coast.

POLITICAL ORGANIZATION—HINTS OF THINGS TO COME

While African city-states, kingdoms, and empires had risen and fallen for many centuries along the Mediterranean and down the Nile, most of the rest of the continent still favored social organization based on family and clan. But the day of the major East African city-states, the South African kingdoms, and the great West African empires lay just ahead. And here and there during the classic age, first steps were probably being taken toward these more complex political forms.

The evidence, once more, is scattered and much disputed. There are tombs in Mali 180 feet long and 35 feet high, monuments requiring the work of so many people that some scholars believe they must have been built to house the bones of kings. The art and artifacts of the lower Niger region include evidence of ironworking, copper casting by the sophisticated "lost-wax" process, and remarkably realistic terra cotta figurines. This dazzling array seems to many experts to demonstrate the existence of a socially stratified society that may well have been headed by a hereditary ruler.

In the grasslands of the Western Sudan, finally, the first of the West African empires, Ghana, was probably taking shape in the middle of the first millennium B.C. No Ghanian ruins have survived from these ancient days. But later Muslim visitors heard of a dynasty of twenty kings who ruled there before A.D. 718. This would push Ghana's political beginnings back to the sixth or seventh century, into the classic age.

SUMMARY

North Africa continued to flourish as part of the Mediterranean culture that surrounded the world's largest inland sea. Alexandria, in Egypt, became a great intellectual center of the Mediterranean world during Hellenistic and Roman times. The fertile North African shores played an important role in the larger Roman imperium of these centuries.

Eastwards in Africa, on the blistering Red Sea shore and in the cool Ethiopian highlands, the Kingdom of Axum (third century B.C. to fourth century A.D.) built its independent place in the commercial life of the Old World. Serving as a meeting place for goods from inner Africa, the Mediterranean, the Indian Ocean, and the lands beyond, Axum enjoyed many prosperous centuries before succumbing to isolation and conquest early in the Christian era. Trade grew across northern Africa as Africans turned to new technologies and forms of political organization.

SUGGESTED READING

ANFRAY, F. "The Civilization of Aksum from the First to the Seventh Century," in *Ancient Civilizations of Africa*, vol. 2 of the *UNESCO General History of Africa*, G. Mokhtar, ed. London: Heinemann, 1981. By a leading excavator of Ethiopian ruins. See also Kobishanov and Mekouria, below.

BROOKS, L. *Great Civilizations of Ancient Africa*. New York: Four Winds Press, 1971. Covers Nile states and Ethiopia as well as empires of West Africa.

BULLIET, R. W. *The Camel and the Wheel*. Cambridge, Mass.: Harvard University Press, 1975. Spread of the camel revolution from the Middle East to North Africa.

CANFORA, L. *The Vanished Library*. Berkeley: University of California Press, 1989. Alexandria's vanished treasure trove of ancient learning.

DAVIDSON, B. *The Lost Cities of Africa*. Boston: Little, Brown, 1970. Includes Nubian cities but not Egypt.

JULY, R. W. *Precolonial Africa: An Economic and Social History*. New York: Scribner's, 1975. Especially useful on earlier periods, where little political detail is known.

KOBISHANOV, Y. *Axum*. Pennsylvania State University Press, 1979. Good treatment by a scholar with both historical and anthropological expertise.

LINDSAY, J. *Daily Life in Roman Egypt*. London: F. Muller, 1963. Social history of the most valuable part of Roman North Africa.

MEKOURIA, T. T. "Christian Aksum," in *Ancient Civilizations of Africa*, G. Mokhtar, ed. The last centuries of Axum. With Anfray and Kobishanov (see above), provides solid coverage of what is known of Axumite culture.

PANKHURST, R. ed. *Travellers in Ethiopia*. London: Oxford University Press, 1965. Includes the two basic accounts of travelers to ancient Axum.

RAVEN, S. *Rome in Africa*. London: Evans Brothers, 1969. Roman rule in North Africa, with many photographs.

SNOWDEN, F. M. *Before Color Prejudice: The Ancient View of Blacks*. Cambridge, Mass.: Harvard University Press, 1983. Classic study of Greco-Roman views of Africa. See also W. L. Hansberry, *Africa and Africans as Seen by Classical Writers*, J. E. Harris, ed. (Washington, D.C., 1981).

VLAHOS, O. *African Beginnings*. New York: Viking, 1967. Popular survey, from Egypt to the Arabs.

CHAPTER 15

FROM THE MOCHICA TO THE MAYANS

NORTH AMERICAN CULTURES

SPREAD OF AGRICULTURE

Agriculture replaced hunting and gathering in Mexico thousands of years before Christ. Slowly, this pattern of life, with its settled villages and increasingly structured society, spread north of the Rio Grande.

Not all North American peoples saw obvious advantages in the new way of life. Where plenty of animal and vegetable foods were available for the taking, as in bountiful California or the salmon-rich Northwest, the difficult shift to agriculture seemed unnecessary. Some Native Americans probably agreed with more recent food-gathering peoples that farming was much harder than foraging. The sheer dullness of sedentary village life may also have caused some Indian peoples to stick to their old migratory hunting-and-gathering ways.

Others, however, particularly under pressures created by climatic changes or declining game supplies, did begin to see the advantages of agriculture. Foremost among these advantages was the far greater carrying capacity of land that was devoted to farming over terrain used for hunting and gathering. In the Americas, an area that could support one forager could feed a hundred farmers. In the old world as in the new, furthermore, larger populations also led to more complex societies.

THE DESERT SOUTHWEST: MOGOLLON AND HOHOKAM

An early such shift north of Mexico occurred in what became the American Southwest before 1000 A.D. In Arizona and New Mexico, a hotter, drier climate menaced the stable foraging society that had taken root there. Threatened with extinction, the Mogollon and Hohokam peoples moved toward settled farming.

The Mogollon people used digging sticks to cultivate the basic trio of crops that had first developed in Mexico: corn or maize, beans, and squash. They built permanent pit houses that were cool in summer and warm in winter. They also constructed underground storage rooms for harvested food.

The Hohokam were themselves immigrants from Mexico. One thoroughly excavated Hohokam site reveals a hundred pit houses. The site also includes perhaps the first irrigation system constructed in America, here used to bring river water to arid fields several miles away. The Hohokam grew not only the basic food crops mentioned above but cotton and tobacco as well.

THE EASTERN WOODLANDS: ADENA AND HOPEWELL

Farming began to spread to eastern North America about this time also, though it complemented rather than replaced hunting and gathering. On the Ohio River, the Adena culture emerged earlier than the Mogollon tradition—before 500 A.D. The existence of settled villages shows that the Adena people spent a large part of the year in one place, probably tending crops. They combined pumpkins and other food plants with nuts, fish, and game gathered or hunted in the forest.

Around the first century A.D., the much more widespread Hopewell culture emerged in the Mississippi and the Ohio River valleys. Like their Adena predecessors, the Hopewell people combined foraging with limited farming. But maize was not yet effectively adapted to the colder northern environment. Further development would await both new strains of corn and some crucial technological advances.

SOCIETY AND CULTURE

During the thousand years around the birth of Christ, however, these Native American peoples of the classic age did make some remarkable social and cultural breakthroughs. The people of the Southwest, for instance, learned to weave cotton into cloth and to make pottery. Besides their impressive irrigation works, the Hohokam people mined for turquoise. This they traded with the city-dwellers of Mexico for copper bells and earrings, rubber balls, and other handcrafted products. They also imported from Mexico such cultural practices as mounds for religious ceremonies and large outdoor ball courts.

The Eastern forest peoples traded even further and built even more impressively. The Hopewell culture constructed large and elaborate burial mounds for their most honored dead. These graves have yielded trade goods accumulated by Hopewell people, sometimes from half-

Carved figure found in a North American Indian mound in Tennessee. Such artifacts of stone or clay reveal the artistic skills of the Native Americans whose towns once dotted this part of the continent.

way across the continent. Among these were shells from the Gulf Coast, copper from the Great Lakes, and obsidian from the Rocky Mountains. Their Adena predecessors were even greater builders. The Great Serpent Mound in southern Ohio, winding for some 1300 feet, is the largest representational earthwork in the world.

The artistic achievements of these peoples could be striking. Human figures dance around an elaborately decorated Hohokam pot dating from the first millennium A.D. Hopewell artisans shaped a flat sheet of mica into a startlingly lifelike silhouette of a human hand around A.D. 500. The great traditions of Native American art thus began to take shape even before many of these people had settled into fully agricultural societies.

SOUTH AMERICAN SOCIETIES

GROWING POPULATIONS

The rise of the United States to prominence over the past two centuries has fostered a completely unhistorical sense of "natural" North American predominance in the Western Hemisphere. For most of the history of civilization in the New World, Middle and South America have in fact been the leaders, and North America the less-developed continent of our hemisphere.

At the time of the Spanish conquest, the Amerindian population of Mexico was, by conservative estimate, around twenty million people, while the entire area currently occupied by the United States held perhaps two million. These figures would not, of course, hold for the period fifteen or more centuries before Columbus, but the ratios would be comparable. Population growth had taken place in northwestern South America as well. Both here and in Mexico intensive advanced agriculture centering in corn, beans, squash, and, in South America, potatoes had produced a population base adequate to support societies more elaborate than any to be found north of the Rio Grande.

The Olmec culture of Mexico and the Chavín culture of Peru had begun the social evolution of Mesoamerica and South America during the first millennium before Christ. During the first thousand years A.D., that process of cultural evolution continued in Mexico and Central America on the one hand, and in northwestern South America on the other.

In both these areas the process of state formation was a key element in this development. From agricultural villages linked by religion and culture, there evolved states with populations of tens and hundreds of thousands, specialization of labor, structured systems of social classes, and sometimes true cities and central governments as well. Unification into larger empires like those of the Aztecs and Incas of later centuries was rare. Nevertheless, during the classical period areas of advanced culture were scattered all over the highlands and lowlands of Mexico, Honduras, Guatemala, and through the central Andes and neighboring coastal lowlands of Peru.

While North America remained the preserve of hunting-and-gathering tribes and agricultural villages dominated by hereditary chiefs, impressive civilizations had thus emerged in Middle and South America. Three of the better known of these societies will be dealt with here, including perhaps the most sophisticated of all Amerindian cultures, that of the Classical Maya.

THE MOCHICA POTTERY MAKERS

We will begin with South America and the continuing evolution of civilization in the shadow of the Andes.

The first highly developed culture in Peru, the Chavín culture of the first millennium B.C., had faded several centuries before Christ. But its influence lingered on, giving rise to several successor cultures during the first millennium A.D. One among these has particularly impressed the archaeologists, who are once more our primary sources of understanding: the Mochica culture of the Moche River region of northern Peru.

The cult centers of the old Chavín culture had been in the Andes. Mochica culture, like most of the successor

The faces of the Mochica look out at us from a collection of portrait jugs. The work of these most admired of South American ceramicists is much sought by collectors today. What features of these clay faces look much the same to you? Which seem to show the individuality of a portrait? (The Bettmann Archive)

cultures to Chavín, developed on the coastal strip along the Pacific and in the river valleys that spread through the foothills of the Andes down to the sea. Like most of the classical American cultures, they flourished rather later than the classic civilizations of the Old World: Mochica culture was probably at its height between A.D. 300 and 700.

Although they were preliterate, the Mochica people have left us a great deal of concrete information about themselves in their unique pottery. In the naturalistically sculptured forms of many of their ceramic works and in the pictures with which they decorated them, a whole vanished culture comes to life. These, coupled with huge clay-brick ruins, reveal one of the most sophisticated South American societies before the Inca.

The Mochica civilization was almost surely that of an organized state, and one that dominated the coastal valleys of much of Peru. The ruling elite must have included a priestly class that supervised the large temple complexes. It must also have involved a warrior class, since the Mochica were a warlike people who built their empire, as empires have generally been built, by force.

The bulk of the population were farmers, though they supplemented their diet with game and fish. The Mochica were, in fact, very advanced agriculturists, cultivating maize, beans, potatoes, and other crops on the narrow green patches along the rivers. These they irrigated by elaborate systems of ditches and fertilized with bird dung fetched on large seagoing rafts from offshore guano islands.

The were also large-scale builders, mostly in adobe brick. They constructed genuine cities and raised massive step-pyramids in their religious ceremonial centers. One of these pyramids, the Huaca del Sol in the Moche Valley, was perhaps 150 feet high and required as many as fifty million clay bricks for its construction.

Beyond all this, the Mochica became some of the most skilled artists and artisans in the Americas. Their metalworkers made masks of copper, headdresses of gold, and jewelry of various metals. Mochica women specialized in textiles, doing both the spinning and the waving of cloth. They produced the elaborate tunics, shirts, and mantels worn by the men and the simpler garments they themselves wore. Mochica potters manufactured the sculptured ceramic ware that has provided information about their culture and the gems of many ceramics collections since.

Many Mochica pots and jars are fully sculptured and as realistically representational as the Olmec heads of Mexico. There are actual portrait heads on these Peruvian jars. A Mochica woman with a child on her back pro-

NORTH
AMERICA

ROCKY MOUNTAINS

Missouri R.

40°

BERMUDA

*ATLANTIC
OCEAN*

Rio Grande
SIERRA MADRE
ORIENTAL

*Gulf of
Mexico*

Teotihuacan

20°

Mississippi R.

SIERRA MADRE OCCIDENTAL

(Veracruz)

GREATER

BAHAMA IS.

*WEST
INDIES*

OLMEC

ANTILLES

*LESSER
ANTILLES*

MAYA

Caribbean Sea

Magdalena R.

Orinoco R.

*GUIANA
HIGHLANDS*

0°   Equator

GALAPAGOS IS.

Negro R.

Amazon R.

MT. CHIMBORAZO
20,577 FT.

ANDES

Madeira R.

SOUTH
AMERICA

São Francisco R.

*PACIFIC
OCEAN*

MOCHE AND
CHIMU

Chavín de Huantar

HUARI EMPIRE

*Lake
Titicaca*

20°

Paraguay R.

BRAZILIAN
HIGHLANDS

TIAHUANACO
EMPIRE

● Early Centers of
Amerindian Civilization

ANDES

Paraná R.

Uruguay R.

MT. ACONCAGUA
22,834 FT.

ANDES

Rio de la Plata

40°

0   1000   2000 Miles

0   1000   2000 Kilometers

FALKLAND IS.

Strait of Magellan

140°   120°   100°   80°   60°   40°

jects a powerful sense of individuality. A full-faced, strong-featured Mochica chieftain with a lily in his woven cap radiates the vitality of the living man.

Other ceramic works and the painted images on them show Moche warriors swinging their clubs in battle or leading home long lines of prisoners with ropes around their necks, probably for sacrifice. They depict reed boats on voyages to guano islands or peasant farmers laboring in shorts or even naked in the fields. And they show the gods. The sky god sits on his throne in the high mountains, monumental and unmoved, the sun rising behind his head. The jaguar-fanged god of the coast—the active force in Mochica religion—slays sea monsters with the help of a lizardlike lesser divinity.

This Mochica people of the north coast of Peru are only one of several Peruvian societies that developed on the Pacific coast and in the Andes between the ancient Chavín and the awesome achievement of the Incas. But thanks to their artistic and architectural accomplishments, they illustrate Peruvian civilization during the classical age more vividly and more impressively than most of the other societies of northwestern South America.

PERUVIAN CULTURE

Other cultures flourished in Peru, both on the coast and in the mountains, during this period. Archaeologists have a plentiful supply of ruins to explore, tombs to excavate, and surviving artifacts to evaluate. Partly because of the lack of a written script, however, firm conclusions are hard to come by. A brief survey of some of the remarkable remains of these vanished peoples will perhaps be more useful than a summary of debatable conclusions.

In the Peruvian highlands, multistoried stone buildings gaze out over the mountains, their purpose unknown. Statues of warriors or women and pottery decorated with hunting scenes give haunting glimpses of vanished civilizations. More striking are the gorgeous textiles discovered wrapped around mummies found on the arid south coast of Peru. Thanks to the dry climate, fabric thousands of years old has been perfectly preserved. Woven of a variety of threads—wool, cotton, even human hair—and dyed with more than a hundred different colors, the textiles of Paraca Necropolis have been described as among the most beautiful in the world. Yet we know almost nothing of the society that produced them.

Perhaps most tantalizing of all are the famous Nazca lines. These marks inscribed in the dry earth of southern Peru were discovered by accident when a plane flew over them in the first half of the twentieth century. Seen from that height, it was clear that many of the lines sketched out animals and birds, while others defined geometrical shapes or ran straight across the desert pointing at the horizon.

Those who have studied the enigmatic lines have seen astronomical significance in some, which point toward solstice or equinox points. The pictures, undetectable on the ground, must have been intended for the gods to contemplate.[1]

MIDDLE AMERICAN CIVILIZATION

THE PYRAMIDS OF TEOTIHUACÁN

There are more huge stone pyramids in Mesoamerica than there are in Egypt—striking testimony to the centuries of organized society and the sophisticated cultural heritage of Mexico and Central America before the conquistadores came. Some of the most impressive of these monuments are to be found not in the coastal Caribbean lowlands where Olmec and later Mayan culture flourished, but in the upland valleys of central Mexico. Of these peoples of the high plateau, the earliest and one of the most revered were the builders of the great city of Teotihuacán, the "sacred center . . . of the Mesoamerican world" around the time of Christ.[2]

The civilization of Teotihuacán emerged perhaps as early as 200 B.C. and expired in violence around A.D. 700. As usual, lacking significant documentary evidence, we know virtually nothing of the political history of this early Mesoamerican people and can do no more than speculate on their political institutions. But there is plenty of information—including, once more, pictorial evidence—concerning the economic life, social structure, and artistic capabilities of the people of Teotihuacán.

Settled and extremely productive agriculture, yielding several crops a year in the fertile mountain-walled upland plateau of central Mexico, provided the economic foundation upon which Teotihuacán culture was built. Huge markets in the city redistributed the crops to a thoroughly structured society, including large numbers of artisans and construction workers, priests, warriors, and some sort of political elite.

There is an aggressive tone to surviving Teotihuacán mural paintings—warriors with human hearts skewered on their blades—suggesting a predatory foreign policy similar to that of the Aztecs of later centuries. Evidence of Teotihuacán's cultural predominance is found as far afield as Guatemala. Whether this evidence proves trade and cultural contacts or actual conquest and rule must remain uncertain. We know only that we are dealing with a powerful people whose influence was widespread.

The best evidence of their greatness is, of course, the city of Teotihuacán itself. Several square miles in area with a population of well over one hundred thousand, this

---

[1]Alternative explanations relating the Nazca lines to flying saucers have not found favor with archaeologists.

[2]Jill Leslie Furst and Peter T. Furst, *Pre-Columbian Art of Mexico*. (New York: Ableville Press, 1980), p. 43.

Teotihuacán's immense Temple of the Sun, larger than the largest pyramid at Egyptian Giza, dominates this revered Mesoamerican "city of the gods." A four-chambered cave recently discovered under the huge pyramid may have been dedicated to a primordial Mother Goddess believed to dwell underground. (Jim Fox/Photo Researchers)

was one of the true cities—as opposed to ceremonial religious centers—in pre-Columbian America. It was a planned city, designed probably by priestly administrators. Its grid of streets and avenues provided space for the temples, palaces, and market plazas, the courtyards and arcades of the rich, and the single-story, flat-roofed "apartment houses" of the less affluent.

The arts of Teotihuacán included elegant ceramics, beautiful stone masks, and the carefully carved stone faces of the gods. There are also paintings, here in the form of thousands of murals found in houses and palaces throughout the city. The chief divinities of Teotihuacán were Tlaloc the rain god and Quetzalcoatl, the feathered serpent of later Aztec times. But the greatest monuments in the city are the gigantic pyramids of the Moon and the Sun. The Pyramid of the Sun, seven hundred feet long and more than two hundred feet high, built of stone over an earthen core, is one of the largest structures to be found anywhere in Amerindian Mexico.

Teotihuacán was a thriving place for nine hundred years before it perished by fire, perhaps in war or revolution, between A.D. 650 and 750. Eight centuries later the vast ruins of this dead city drew the Aztec emperor Moctezuma to pray and consult with the gods among its empty avenues and tumbled stones. But the gods of Teotihuacán, who could not save their own people from the common fate of empires, could not save the Aztecs either.

THE MAYAN CITY-STATES

The Classic Maya of Mesoamerica, who flourished between A.D. 300 and 900, produced what many scholars consider the most brilliant of all pre-Columbian Amerindian civilizations. Every enthusiast for "lost civilizations" knows their huge step-pyramids, bursting vertically out of the jungle, vines and bushes sprouting picturesquely from the ancient stone. Fewer know their faces, the convincingly modeled middle-aged cheeks and heavy lids of men in ceremonial headdresses reproduced in ceramic figurines, or the painted figures of priests, nobles, and warriors in fantastic regalia marching across the walls of temples. But it is only when we begin to penetrate the minds of the Maya that we glimpse the true dimensions of their accomplishment.

"And they called it Teotihuacán
because it was the place
where the lords were buried.
Thus they said:
'When we die,
truly we die not,
because we will live, we will rise,
we will continue living, we will awaken.
This will make us happy.'

Thus the dead one was directed,
when he died:
'Awaken, already the sky is rosy,
already dawn has come . . .
Thus the old ones said
that who has died has become a god,
they said: 'He has been made
a god there,'
meaning, 'He has died.'"

Long deserted Teotihuacán was still the city of the gods to the Aztecs of many centuries later. This Nahuatl song from Aztec times suggests that belief in an afterlife was associated with these massive remains.

Do the religious beliefs expressed here suggest the beliefs of any ancient Old World peoples? Do you detect parallels with the religious views of the Egyptians in particular?

Michael D. Coe, Mexico (New York: Praeger, 1962), p. 111.

There are many mysteries about Mayan civilization. We know that the Mayans lived in the lowlands of the Mexican Gulf Coast and in parts of Guatemala, Honduras, and El Salvador in the first millennium after Christ. We know that in some ways their culture derived from that of the ancient Olmecs—but even Olmec antecedents cannot explain mathematical insights that had not yet occurred to Europeans at that time. We know that after centuries of dynamic cultural development Mayan civilization withered and died. But we have only informed guesses as to why.

Even basic facts about the Mayan economy are debated. They were certainly a fully agricultural people, cultivating maize, beans, squash, and other foods and feeding a population of upwards of two million people. One of the long-standing puzzles of Mayan history has been how the Mayans managed to feed so many people using old-fashioned slash-and-burn agricultural methods. Recent research employing aerial photographs, however, seems to have detected intricate patterns of irrigation canals beneath the rain forest that blankets the region today. So one Mayan mystery at least may be on its way to a solution.

The political and social organization of the Mayans is clearer than that of any Amerindian culture we have glanced at so far. The Maya region was divided into a number of small states, all speaking related but not always mutually intelligible languages. Warfare was common among these states, and prisoners were brought home and ritually sacrificed to the gods of the victors.

Like Mesopotamian or Greek city-states, the lands of the Mayans shared a similar hierarchic social and political structure. They were normally ruled by a hereditary elite of priests and nobles. There was an intermediate social class of artisans and artists, traders and civil servants. And there was a majority population of peasant farmers and a smaller number of serfs and slaves.

THE MINDS OF THE MAYANS

Like other lowland Mesoamerican peoples, the Mayans were not yet a truly urban culture. But they did build huge ceremonial centers with the famous stone step-pyramids, multistory palaces, wide plazas, ceremonial ball courts, intricately carved stone stelae, and other impressive structures and carvings. Thousands of people could live at centers like those of Tikal in northern Guatamala, with its 230-foot pyramid, or at Palenque in eastern Mexico, with its great palace. Tens of thousands of others would live in wattle-and-daub thatched huts around the periphery of such a place. And countless more would come for the great celebrations before the temples of the gods.

In stone and plaster sculpture as well as in multicolored wall paintings, the Mayans have left even more detailed information about their daily lives than did the Mochica or the people of Teotihuacán. In these images from the past, a colorful aristocracy of warriors in jaguar skins and plumed headdresses and ladies in long white robes watch costumed dancers spin to the music of drums, rattles, and trumpets. Crowds cheer the young players of ceremonial ball games or watch the bloody sacrifices of prisoners from the last war. The excitement of these vanished spectacles lives still in moving limbs, an upraised hand.

But there were minds at work here whose concerns went far beyond such common pastimes as sports, music, and war. There was, for instance, as bewildering a pantheon of gods as we have encountered anywhere in the world. The chief of these was Itzamná, creator of humankind, inventor of the arts and sciences—a toothless old man often represented as a lizard, a crocodile, or a serpent. There was

Ah Kinchil, god of the sun, and Ah Puch, lord of death, with his spotted body and protruding spine. There were gods who protected the interests of all sorts and conditions of people in this complex Mayan world. There were patrons of traders, travelers, farmers, hunters, fishermen, and bee-keepers; gods of poetry and music, of war, sacrifice, and suicide; gods of the rain and the life-giving corn.

All of these divinities mingled traits of humans and animals, reptiles, or birds in monstrous, sometimes changing shapes. In the complicated Mayan theology, they presided over thirteen heavens above the earth and nine hells below it. Like gods in many other lands, they made the corn grow, the women fertile, and the warriors victorious.

Once again, however, we make them seem too simple. For the Mayans are most famous not for theology but for science. Mayan mathematics was in some respects distinctly superior to the mathematical thinking

The costumes of Mayans of the classic age are indicated in these deftly carved sculptures from Yucatan. Sandals, mantles, and headdresses seem to have been as varied in style then as in more recent times. Have you ever seen a poncho like that worn by the figure at lower right? (Bureau of American Ethnology)

of Greeks and Romans. Like the Indians of the Gupta era, for instance, the Mayans understood the concept of zero. Some Mayan astronomical observations were among the world's most advanced, and the Mayans had an elaborate calendar built on a 365-day year.

They were, finally one of the few truly literate peoples in the New World. Most surviving Maya books, unhappily, were destroyed by the Spanish conquistadores centuries later. But what remain indicate that Mayan glyphs (written symbols) were used mostly for religious texts, sacred songs and spells, horoscopes and prophecies—in short, for things that mattered to them, things not to be forgotten.

Even Mayan prophecies seem worthy of respect. After all, some of them predicted the coming of bearded men across the sea bearing the sign of a god—and utter ruin to the children of the gods of Mexico. And that, certainly, came to pass.

SUMMARY

Agriculture spread widely across North America during the last centuries before the beginning of the modern era. In the Southwest, the Hohokam and Mogollon cultures drew from neighboring Mexico to build their own village societies. In the Eastern woodlands, the Mississippi Valley produced the Adena and Hopewell cultures with trade links to distant parts of the continent.

Among a number of local cultures that rose in the Peruvian Andes on the foundations laid by the ancient Chavín "mother culture," the society of the Mochica people has perhaps most intrigued historians, archaeologists, and art collectors. These makers of some of the New World's most famous pottery also built a powerful state with a structured society and a brutally successful military class.

The metropolis of Teotihuacán in upland Mexico represented an urban achievement of the first order. Its predominant position in Middle America lasted for centuries and extended as far as Guatemala, where evidence of economic and cultural, if not of political, influence has been found.

The most impressive of American cultures during the classical age, however, was that of the Mayans (A.D. 300–900) of the Caribbean lowlands. Mayan society, like that of ancient Greece, never evolved politically beyond the city-state. But Mayan art, religion, and intellectual achievement, from early writing to mathematics and astronomy, were dazzling. Mayan culture went beyond anything achieved in the New World up to that time and provided a cultural reservoir for later civilizations in Middle America.

SUGGESTED READING

BENSON, E. P. *The Mochica*. New York: Praeger, 1972. Illustrated and clear exposition of the culture of the most intriguing of South American pottery makers.

BROSE, D. S., and N. GREBER, eds. *Hopewell Archaeology: The Chillicothe Conference*. Ohio: Kent State University Press, 1979. Unearthing the culture that built the Hopewell mounds.

COE, M. D. *The Maya*. New York: Praeger, 1966. One of the best surveys of this much discussed ancient Mesoamerican people.

CULBERT, T. P. *The Classic Maya Collapse*. Albuquerque: University of New Mexico Press, 1973. Probes one of the enduring Maya mysteries: What happened to the brilliant pre-Columbian culture? See also R. L. Hamblin and B. L. Pitcher, "The Classic Maya Collapse: Testing the Class Conflict Hypothesis," *American Antiquity*, vol. 45 (1980), pp. 246–267.

DRIVER, H. E. *Indians of North America*, 2nd ed. Chicago: University of Chicago Press, 1969. Topical study of Amerindians of all regions and cultural levels; includes Mesoamerica.

HAGEN, V. W. VON. *The Desert Kingdoms of Peru*. New York: New York Graphic Society, 1964. On the Mochica and the later Chimu states.

HAMMOND, N. *Ancient Maya Civilization*. New Brunswick, N.J.: Rutgers University Press, 1982. See also T. P. Culbert, *The Lost Civilization: The Story of the Classic Maya* (New York: Harper & Row, 1974).

HAURY, E. W. *The Hohokam: Desert Farmers and Craftsmen*. Tucson: University of Arizona Press, 1976. Archaeological excavations. See also D. E. Doyel, "The Prehistoric Hohokam of the Arizona Desert," *American Scientist*, vol. 67, No. 5 (1979), pp. 544–554.

HENDERSON, J. S. *The World of the Ancient Maya*. Ithaca, N.Y.: Cornell University Press, 1981. On the Mayan economy, see also P. D. Harrison and B. L. Turner, eds., *Pre-Hispanic Maya Agriculture* (Albuquerque: University of New Mexico Press, 1978).

LANDA, D. DE. *The Maya: Account of the Affairs of Yucatan*, trans. A. R. Pagden. Chicago: O'Hara, 1975. A fundamental source of the Mayans.

MILLON, R. *Urbanization of Teotihuacán, Mexico*. Austin: University of Texas Press, 1973. Introduction summarizes research on this ancient metropolis.

SCHELE, L., and M. E. MILLER. *The Blood of Kings: Dynasty and Ritual in Maya Art*. Fort Worth, Tex.: Kimbell Art Museum, 1986. Mayan art in its social context.

TEDLOCK, D. *Popol Vuh: The Mayan Book of the Dawn of Life and the Glories of Gods and Kings*. New York: Random House, 1985. Translation of a Mayan religious classic.

THOMPSON, T. E. *Maya History and Religion*. Norman: University of Oklahoma Press, 1970. A standard survey. See also the older but substantial work of C. W. Brainard and A. Morley, *The Ancient Maya* (Stanford: Stanford University Press, 1956).

WOLF, E. R. *Sons of the Shaking Earth*. Chicago: University of Chicago Press, 1959. Ecologically based poetic evocation of Mesoamerican cultures.

CHAPTER 16

CULTURAL DIFFUSION

CULTURAL CONTACT

FORMS OF CULTURAL INTERACTION

Part I of this book closed with some indication of the similarities that already characterized the scattered cultures of humankind by the end of the dawn age of human history. Many of these early similarities in styles of life and thought, however, proved to be the results of parallel but independent cultural evolution in various parts of the globe. The very fact that these separate ventures into history led so often to similar consequences may, of course, be seen as evidence for the unity of the human family at a very deep level. We are apparently very much alike, after all, and our historic group life has tended toward the same broad ends in even the most varied circumstances.

But the fact that so much of this earlier similarity was the result of independent ventures should also remind us how isolated the far-flung peoples of the world really were. It is, in fact, only in the classic age that we begin to see substantial ties binding the major civilizations one to another and increasingly linking preurban peoples as well. These developing links between regions and cultures are the subject of the present chapter.

The ties that bound the classic civilizations and peoples included three kinds of contact and connection between populations. The oldest of these was migration, movements of whole peoples that often brought them into direct physical contact with other populations. The second and probably the most thoroughly documented type of connection during the classic age, however, was long-distance trade, the exchange of goods between regions and civilizations. Finally, perhaps the most important developing bond between peoples was the diffusion of high culture from one civilization to another—most notably at this time the spread of great religions across regional and even continental boundaries.

Each of these three—migration, trade, culture—will be explored below.

FIRST STEPS ON A LONG ROAD

One warning before we start, however: the degree of unity among the peoples of the classic age should not be exaggerated. The primary unit during this period remained—as it probably remains today—the separate culture, the individual civilization, the particular society to which one belonged. These primary units of human group life were the centers of loyalty and the shapers of consciousness for all the world's peoples.

In this context, migrations, however important their long-range impact, would initially be felt as intrusions, perhaps as invasions pure and simple. A trickle of trade in luxury goods would affect the life styles of elites, but it would not significantly alter the tenor of life of a whole people. Cultural transplants could bring about important changes in the lives of peoples, but the acceptance of cultural influences tended to be on terms acceptable to the receiving culture. Thus, the incoming ideas would be modified to fit the traditional ideas of the people who took up the new notions—again, a measure of the power of a particular society over its children.

It is a long way from these first beginnings of ties among the world's peoples to the intricately interrelated global culture that may be emerging today. The massive population shifts, the economic interdependence, the worldwide reach of ideas and ideologies of our time lay far in the future during the classic age. And as the conflicts of the twentieth century make clear, true global integration has not been achieved even today.

Nevertheless, a beginning was made in these earlier centuries. And it is precisely as a beginning, the first steps on a long and immensely significant road, that the ties that so tentatively bound this earlier world will be examined here.

MIGRATION: AN URGE TO MOVE ON

WHOLE PEOPLES ON THE MARCH

Perhaps the oldest of all forms of linkage among the widely dispersed peoples of the globe has been the continuing human urge to pack up and move on, to see if the grass is really greener on the other side of the fence, the pasture better on the other side of the hill. Such migration from one part of the world to another brings whole peoples together. It may result in war, as so frequently

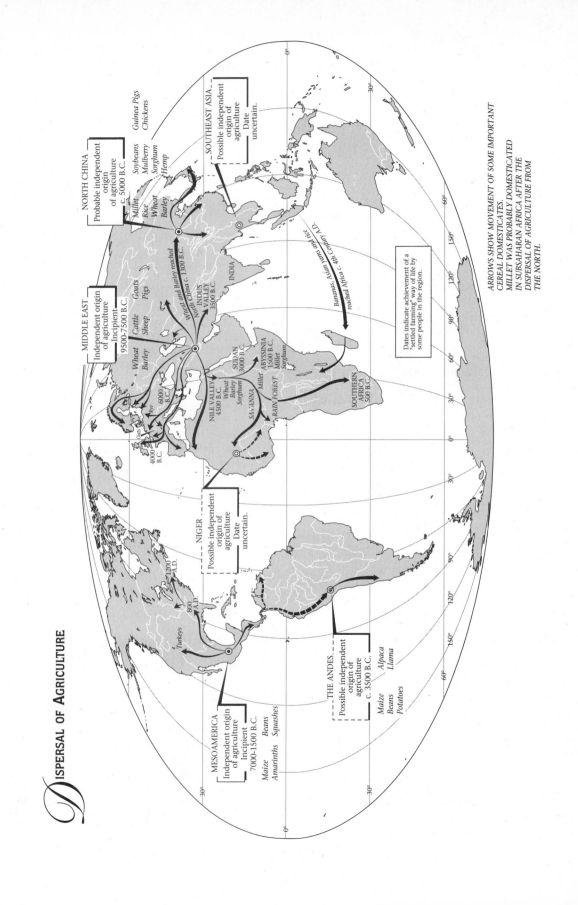

Dispersal of Agriculture

NORTH CHINA
Probable independent origin of agriculture c. 5000 B.C.

Millet
Rice
Wheat
Barley

Soybeans
Mulberry
Sorghum
Hemp

Guinea Pigs
Chickens

MIDDLE EAST
Independent origin of agriculture
Incipient 9500–7500 B.C.

Wheat
Barley

Cattle
Sheep

Goats
Pigs

SOUTHEAST ASIA
Possible independent origin of agriculture
Date uncertain.

Wheat and Barley reached North China c. 1300 B.C.

INDIA
INDUS VALLEY
3500 B.C.

6000 B.C.

Rye

Oats

4000 B.C.

Bananas, Asian yams and rice reached Africa c. 4th Century A.D.

Dates indicate achievement of a "settled farming" way of life by some people in the region.

SUDAN
3000 B.C.

ABYSSINIA
1500 B.C.
Millet
Sorghum

NILE VALLEY
4500 B.C.
Wheat
Barley
Sorghum

SAVANNA

Millet

RAIN FOREST

SOUTHERN AFRICA
500 B.C.

NIGER
Possible independent origin of agriculture
Date uncertain.

1200 A.D.

800 A.D.

Turkeys

MESOAMERICA
Independent origin of agriculture
Incipient 7000–1500 B.C.

Maize
Amarinths

Beans

Squashes

THE ANDES
Possible independent origin of agriculture
c. 3500 B.C.

Maize
Beans
Potatoes

Alpaca
Llama

ARROWS SHOW MOVEMENT OF SOME IMPORTANT CEREAL DOMESTICATES.
MILLET WAS PROBABLY DOMESTICATED IN SUBSAHARAN AFRICA AFTER THE DISPERSAL OF AGRICULTURE FROM THE NORTH.

happened with the Eurasian steppe peoples. It may also lead to trade or even a fruitful exchange of ideas. Or it may even result in a merging of peoples and cultures into a new people, a new culture altogether.

The great migrations of our prehistoric ancestors had peopled almost the entire globe with *Homo sapiens sapiens*, the most adaptable of all animals. Up from Africa, east and west over Eurasia, and across temporary land bridges to colonize Australia and the Americas we had gone. But we had not stopped then. Unable to sit still, or impelled by more practical urges to escape changing climatic conditions or to seize upon fat lands or fatter cities—we had kept on moving.

In the earliest age of urban culture, nomadic migrations had sometimes destroyed entire civilizations, as we have seen. Migration had also, however, forged new peoples and new cultures. The builders of some of the first civilizations in Mesopotamia, after all, were a mix of Akkadian and Sumerian peoples. The melding of Aryan and Dravidian was only the beginning of the fertile mixture of peoples in historic India. Several waves of Indo-European invaders, from Mycenaean to Dorian, overlying an earlier Minoan population went into the making of the classical Greeks. From the beginning of history, then, migration produced a yeasty mixing and melding of populations and ways of life.

A Nok figurine from the village interior of Nigeria, West Africa. The use of sharply decorative conventions and artistic emphasis on basic shapes and contours has here produced a startling vivid piece of sculpture. (New York Public Library Picture Collection)

This process continued in the classic age. Migrations and resulting mixtures of bloodlines and basic skills, folkways and mythologies, produced most of the great civilizations of this period in Europe, Asia, and Africa. An original mixing of Latin and Etruscan peoples produced the Romans, whose empire was as polyglot a mix as the world has seen. Indian culture was enriched during the classic age by the influx of new peoples—Greeks, Arabs, Kushans, and others—across the Northwest Frontier. Even China, in the most homogeneous end of Eurasia, felt the eternal pressure of nomadic steppe peoples such as the Xiongnu, and would be overrun by such peoples in the next stage of its history.

In Africa, the civilization of Axum was the result of a productive merging of the Habashat people from Arabia with indigenous African populations. Egypt in the classic age accepted a seemingly endless succession of foreign rulers and cultures—producing such wonders as the rich and brilliant Alexandria of Roman times.

We do not know as much as we would like about major migrations in the New World this early. But in a later period, the last and most powerful of Mesoamerican civilizations would be the fruit of the southward drift and acculturation of the immigrant Aztecs.

We will look in more detail now at two such instances of productive mass migrations: the great Bantu trek across Africa and the seaborne migrations of the island peoples of the Pacific.

THE BANTU MIGRATIONS

We are used to thinking of Africa, or at least of Africa south of the Sahara, as black Africa. In fact, as recently as the middle of the first millennium B.C., negroid peoples inhabited only a small slice of their future homeland—the tree-scattered Sudanic savanna just south of the Sahara. North of the desert predominantly caucasoid peoples were herding and trading. Over all the vast central and southern portions of Africa, Khoi-San and Pygmy hunters and gatherers were thinly distributed through the great rain forests and over the southern savannas and the wastelands of the southwest.

During the ten or fifteen centuries after 500 B.C., negroid peoples from the Sudan made themselves masters of most of this immense area—Africa south of the Sahara. The secret of their success seems to have been iron.

All that we know of this great southward expansion must come from archaeology or from anthropological or linguistic study of the present-day populations of Africa. But the picture that emerges from this study of archaeological digs and Bantu root words is as dramatic as any written history.

The African peoples who had moved south from the dessicating Sahara to the grasslands and the fringes of the rain forests farther south were typical Neolithic agriculturalists. They lived in small villages of wattle-and-daub huts, grew grains such as millet and dry rice, herded goats, sheep, and cattle. They made tools of carefully ground and polished stone. Apparently much of the labor was divided up by sex, women having traditional chores that were only slightly less heavy than those done by men. Social and political organization was based on family and clan, as it was in most of the world outside the walls of cities. Some of these peoples, especially in the West African end of the sudanic belt, spoke a language ancestral to the family of Bantu languages that are to be found in many parts of Africa today.

As indicated in an earlier chapter, we do not know for certain how these people learned to smelt and forge hard iron. But whether the new skill was developed independently in West Africa or acquired across the savanna from ancient Meroe, it proved an invaluable aid to the Bantu migrations. Equipped with iron tools and iron weapons, the peoples of the sub-Saharan grasslands pushed through or around the equatorial rain forests into central and southern Africa in a few centuries.

One stream of people, probably a thinner one, flowed down the Great Rift Valley of East Africa, a region of great lakes, green uplands, and vast plains. These were cattle herders primarily, like the Masai whose cattle still crop the dusty ranges today. The other and far broader flow of northern migrants into the south was that of the Bantu-speaking West African agriculturalists. These far trekkers penetrated the dense rain forests of the Guinea coast, then pushed eastward into the jungles of central Africa and south into the heart of the Congo. From the Congo basin they eventually emerged below the equatorial rain forests to spread still farther east to the Indian Ocean and still farther south to within striking distance of the southern tip of the continent.

It was one of the great migrations of history, comparable to the prehistoric Amerindian colonization of the Americas, or to the more recent American westward expansion of the last century. And everywhere they went, the Bantus—like nineteenth-century Americans—brought not only a new technology but a complex of cultural traits that added up to a new way of life for Africa south of the Sahara.

With iron tools came agriculture and a slow but certain withering away of the old hunting-and-gathering life. Cereals from the northern savannas came south with the Bantu cultivators. Another whole range of tropical crops—bananas, coconuts, and yams—were acquired by black settlers in East Africa from Indonesian immigrants. From northeastern Africa cattle and other domesticated animals spread into the south. With all these new peoples from the north came distinctive styles of pottery, distinctive patterns of village life. And with these new things came the

Bantu words for them—words that, like Indo-European roots in modern Eurasian languages, tell us much of what we know today about the spread of the culture that produced them.

By A.D. 500 or 1000 at the latest, Bantu-speaking ironworking agriculturalists were almost everywhere south of the Sahara. The Pygmy people and the bushmanoid folk with their Khoi-San click-languages were already in full retreat into the deepest jungles or the fiery wastes of the Kalahari, where they would preserve the life of the Paleolithic food-gatherer down to the present day.

The Bantu migrants who had occupied the better part of the world's second largest continent in a few hundred years still lived in small villages and organized themselves by family and clan. They were probably animists, believers in a multiplicity of nature spirits and in their own close relationship to gods, ghosts, and the rest of the natural world. Little remains of their art, but the famous Nok figurines show what they could do. These terra-cotta figures of animals and human beings, produced by the Nok people of northern Nigeria around the time of Christ, are relatively naturalistic by contrast with the normally nonrealistic traditions of most African art. The human figures are sometimes depicted wearing bracelets, beads, and other indications of a gracious style of life.

Agricultural villagers, like pastoral nomads, could thus make some remarkable contributions to history during the classic age. But even a people who still depended to a considerable extent on hunting and gathering for sustenance could leave some impressive memorials of their passing, as the next section of this chapter will attempt to show.

SEABORNE MIGRATIONS ACROSS THE PACIFIC

We have dealt thus far with the precivilized peoples of the great continental landmasses—Eurasia, Africa, and the Americas. With Oceania we enter a very different world. For Oceania, though it includes the continent of Australia, is largely a world of water.

Oceania straddles both the equator and the international date line. It stretches a quarter of the way around the world, from Southeast Asia to Easter Island, the westernmost possession of Chile. It consists of one continent, thousands of islands, and millions of square miles of South Pacific.

A remarkably wide variety of environments is encompassed in this fragmented collection of empty land mass, scattered archipelagoes, and open sea. The desiccated Australian Outback contrasts sharply with the steamy rain forests of interior New Guinea; countless barren atolls broiling in the sun differ from such tropical paradises as Tahiti and Hawaii. But the wide Pacific washes all their shores.

The ocean did not completely isolate Oceania from the rest of the world; there was probably considerable communication at least with the islands of Southeast Asia. But the surrounding waters did help shape the distinctive cultures of the region, affecting everything from their

The mysterious heads of Easter Island reveal the technical level of the Polynesians who penetrated farthest into the vastness of the Pacific. Like the megaliths of Stonehenge in ancient Britain, these monumental figures weigh many tons: simply erecting them must have been a formidable challenge for preurban peoples. (Photo Researchers, Inc.)

economies to their relations with one another. Above all, the Pacific became the pathway for the great Oceanian adventure—the long seaborne migration that is the heart of Oceania's history.

Laid out on the map today, Oceania consists of Australia and three far-flung island groups: Melanesia ("Black Islands"), which lies northeast of Australia and includes the huge island of New Guinea; Micronesia ("Little Islands"), still farther to the north; and, stretching thousands of miles to the east, the vast ocean triangle of Polynesia ("Many Islands"), anchored at Hawaii, New Zealand, and Easter Island. Each of these great groups is subdivided into lesser island groups, archipelagoes with indigenous names such as Samoa and the Fijis or more recent labels such as the Solomon Islands and the Bismarck Archipelago.

Of these areas, Australia and New Guinea had been reached by human beings during the great prehistoric migrations. The inhabiting of the rest of the jungle-clad volcanoes and coral reefs of the South Pacific would occupy the peoples of Oceania throughout most of their history.

The chronology of these immense seaborne migrations is much disputed by scholars. There seems to be a rough consensus among archaeologists and anthropologists, however, that Melanesia and Micronesia, closer to Southeast Asia, were settled first, during the period of civilization's beginnings. Most of Polynesia would not be explored and occupied by South Sea islanders till much later, during the first dozen centuries A.D.

The first inhabitants of these tropic islands came from southern Asia. Their canoes or rafts must have been capable of crossing considerable patches of open sea, since the partial land bridge to Australia was long gone. They came perhaps in successive waves, perhaps filtering in almost continuously from Southeast Asia over the third and second millennia B.C., slowly filling up the inhabitable islands of Melanesia.

From these Black Islands, and perhaps from mainland Asia as well, settlers were soon striking out northward over even larger expanses of ocean, into the Marshalls, the Marianas, the Carolines, and the other island groups of Micronesia. To undertake these longer voyages, they must have developed outrigger canoes and perhaps sails of matting.

Sometime before 1000 B.C., various of these drifting peoples reached Tonga and Samoa, on the near edge of the Polynesian triangle. But there they seem to have halted, not to move on again for more than a thousand years.

Then, around A.D. 300, intrepid Polynesian voyagers drove through to the far side of the Polynesian triangle, to the Marquesas Islands. The Marquesas and the neighboring Society Islands then became the bases from which the rest of Polynesia was colonized.

The three corners of the triangle were reached over the next five centuries. Easter Island far to the southeast had been colonized by 400, the Hawaiian Islands to the northeast by 500, and New Zealand to the southwest last of all, by 800 or 850. All the other scattered archipelagoes of Polynesia were settled, either from Samoa and Tonga or from the Marquesas and the Societies, between 1000 and 1300.

The aborigines who had settled Australia thousands of years before had come as Paleolithic hunters and gatherers. The new migrants to the islands of Melanesia and Micronesia were Neolithic agriculturalists, though they hunted and fished as well. Like most of North and South America, then, western Oceania filled up with very successful Stone Age peoples.

The first South Sea islanders hunted animals and birds or speared fish in the rivers of Australia or the lagoons of the islands. They cultivated root crops such as taro and yams and tree fruit such as the coconut. They made tools and weapons tipped with smoothly ground stone or shell, and the remains of their famous Lapita ceramic ware are found today on many widely separated islands.

In the farthest island societies of the Polynesians, social evolution continued between the eighth century and the eighteenth, when the Europeans "discovered" them. Some things were lost to these scattered island peoples— pottery making is the outstanding example. But some remarkable things were accomplished too. The Hawaiian Islands, the Society Islands (especially Tahiti), and the original Polynesians of Tonga developed strong chiefdoms, elaborate structures of class and rank, and a material culture that stands out today in museums of primitive art. The large island of New Zealand fostered the inward-looking society of the Maori, whose carved war canoes were things of beauty. Far-off Easter Island— much closer to South America than to Australia—produced the unique Easter Island statues. These huge heads, probably of former chiefs, make the hearts of true believers in the mythical lands of Atlantis and Mu beat faster to this day.

But the most amazing accomplishment of these long voyagers, these Vikings of the Pacific, as Europeans would call them, was surely the long voyages themselves.

They sailed in outriggers or—for long inter-island voyages—double canoes, lashed together with braces and a platform. Some of these vessels were reportedly a hundred feet long and could carry food, plants, and livestock for colonizing new islands, as well as a hundred or more Polynesians. They navigated by the stars, by the sun and moon, by the direction of the sea swells and the trade winds, by the ripples on the water, and by the formations of the clouds. Their long double canoes were liable to break apart in heavy seas and were almost impossible to bail when they took in water. But they were "sea-kindly craft," normally stable, and their single triangular sail could carry them a hundred miles in a day of good wind.[1]

They set out in search of new homelands for many reasons. Famine in the home islands, defeat in war, frustrated ambition for political leadership could all impel Polynesians to take to the sea and head east, where experience taught them there were always more islands.

Cross-fertilizing each other's cultures as they voyaged routinely among the islands, hundreds and even thousands of miles between landfalls, theirs is certainly one of the most remarkable achievements of peoples on the move.

TRADE: VOYAGING BY LAND AND SEA

THE HORSE-TRADING IMPULSE

Another potent source of cultural diffusion has been commercial exchange. This horse-trading impulse, originating often in ritual gift-giving and evolving into the classic exchange-for-profit of historic times, seems to be widespread among peoples at all stages of social evolution. But the great urban imperial cultures of the classic age developed long-distance interregional trade beyond anything seen before.

Exchange of goods between the original islands of urban society and less developed neighboring peoples went back as far as the city itself. There had been some culturally stimulating exchange between the major early civilizations of western Asia and Africa—the cultures of Mesopotamia, Egypt, and Harappan India. Still, most of the trade in early times was *within* the major civilized areas—back and forth across the Mediterranean, for example, or up and down the Maurya Indian empire.

It was not till the first two centuries A.D.—the heart of the classic age—that the three continents of Asia, Europe, and Africa were linked by highly developed regular trade routes. And even that late, trade between North and South America is hard to prove, and any trade at all between either the Americas or Australia and the Old World very unlikely indeed. Given the commercial underdevelopment of the rest of the world, the intricate web of commercial ties that bound Eurasia and Africa is all the more impressive.

CARAVANS ACROSS EURASIA

The Old World was linked by two great lines of trade during the first and second centuries.[2] The northern road was the clopping hooves of horses and mules, the tinkle of camel bells, the dust and heat and babble of caravansaries—the land route across Asia. The southern route was the ruffle of lateen sails, the strumming of the monsoon wind in the cordage, gulls calling, and the smell of tar and spices in a foreign port—the sea route from Asia to Africa and the Near East.

The two great empires of the eastern and western ends of Eurasia—Han China and Rome under the heirs of Augustus—were the anchors of the land route. The middlemen were the peoples of the Persian Empire and the Kushans, whose empire included part of northern India but also stretched far up into central Asia. Particularly when the Romans were not at war with the Persians and when the Chinese controlled the Tarim Basin north of Tibet, goods could flow in an uninterrupted stream from the banks of the Tiber to the Yellow River of North China.

Trade goods were normally carried across China's half-civilized far-west region of Xinjiang to the eastern end of the Takla Maklan Desert in the Tarim Basin, the beginning of the fabled Silk Road. There the route divided, following strings of oases either north or south of the Takla Maklan, north of the Himalayas into the Pamirs. From the western end of the desert, the road wound up through the passes north of the Pamir Knot, where all the great ranges of Eurasia seem to come together, and down into the rich horse country of Ferghana.

Here the road divided once again, northwest to Tashkent and southwest to Samarkand. From either of these central Asian trading centers, the route ran southwest across the Kushan Empire, across the Oxus and into Persia, and then west the length of the Persian Empire. South of the Caspian, south of the Black Sea through Asia Minor (Turkey today), the road wound on across the Anatolian Plateau and down at last to the warm shores of the Aegean, at the eastern end of the Mediterranean Sea.

No single set of intrepid merchants undertook so long a journey during the classic age. For example, goods flowing the other way, east from the Mediterranean, would be carried across the Near East by Greek, Syrian, or Arab merchants. They would then be turned over to trustworthy steppe nomads for the journey across central Asia, and then passed on to Chinese traders. Between the Roman and the Chinese zones, Persian and Kushan rulers maintained the roads, provided stopping places along the way, protected travelers from bandits, and collected substantial tolls for their services.

---

[1]Ben R. Finney, "Voyaging," in Jesse D. Jennings, ed., *The Prehistory of Polynesia* (Cambridge, Mass.: Harvard University Press, 1979), p. 331.

[2]These routes can best be followed on the colorful maps in Geoffrey Barraclough, ed., *The Times Atlas of World History* (London: Times Books, 1978), or see the map on p. 229.

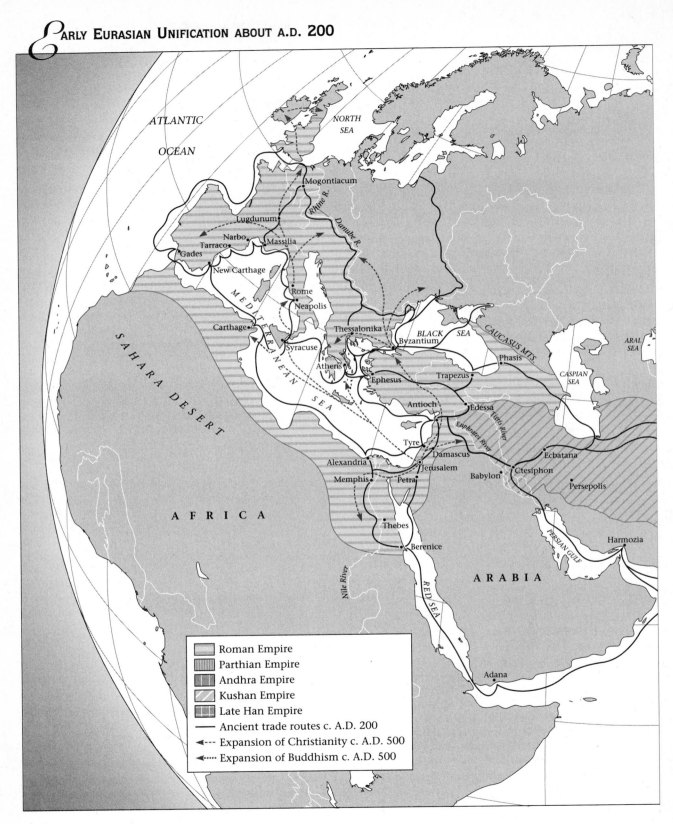

ATLANTIC OCEAN

NORTH SEA

Mogontiacum

Rhine R.

Danube R.

Lugdunum

Narbo

Tarraco

Gades

Massilia

New Carthage

Rome

Neapolis

MEDITERRANEAN SEA

Carthage

Syracuse

Thessalonika

Athens

Byzantium

BLACK SEA

CAUCASUS MTS.

Ephesus

Trapezus

Phasis

ARAL SEA

CASPIAN SEA

Antioch

Edessa

Tigris River

Euphrates River

SAHARA DESERT

Tyre

Damascus

Ecbatana

AFRICA

Alexandria

Memphis

Jerusalem

Petra

Babylon

Ctesiphon

Persepolis

Thebes

Berenice

ARABIA

PERSIAN GULF

Harmozia

Nile River

RED SEA

Adana

▦	Roman Empire
▦	Parthian Empire
▦	Andhra Empire
▨	Kushan Empire
▦	Late Han Empire
——	Ancient trade routes c. A.D. 200
◄---	Expansion of Christianity c. A.D. 500
◄····	Expansion of Buddhism c. A.D. 500

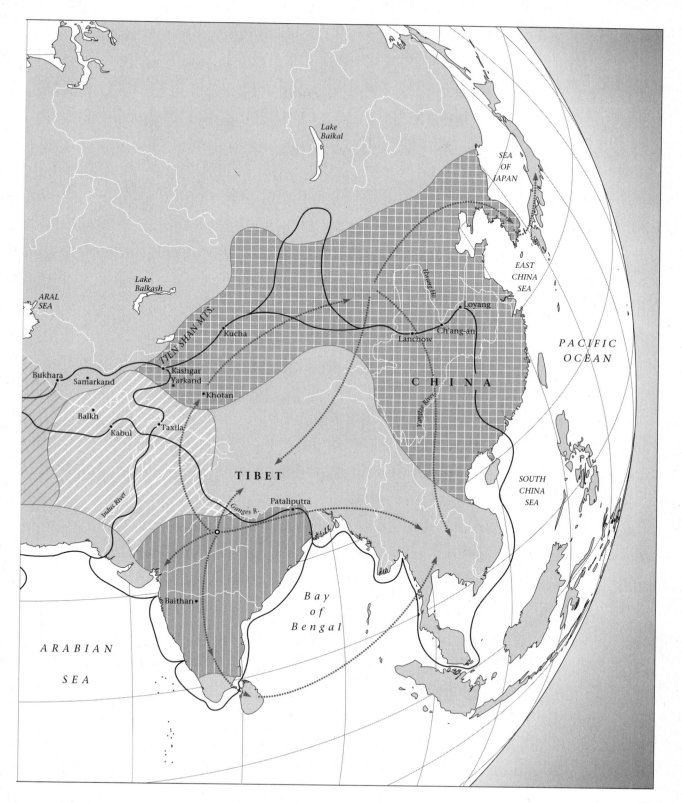

RIDING THE MONSOON WINDS TO INDIA

The sea route in the south hinged on India and Southeast Asia and included Africa in the complex equation. Chinese goods entered the flow of international sea trade in the far southeast of the Middle Kingdom, perhaps from Canton, perhaps from Haiphong, in what is today northern Vietnam. Merchandise flowed from there around the southern end of Indochina and through the Indonesian archipelago to Malaya. Goods were either transported by land through the jungles of the Malay Peninsula or carried by ship around the southern tip and northwest again between Malaya and Sumatra. Thence the sea lanes lay west to the southern end of India, or perhaps northwest across the Bay of Bengal to the muddy delta of the Ganges.

From the other side of India—the Malabar Coast of later times—one could follow the shore northwest around to the mouth of the Persian Gulf and up the gulf for final transport by land across western Persia to the Mediterranean. Or one could sail due west, riding the seasonal monsoon winds to the mouth of the Red Sea, and thence to the Axumite port of Adulis or to one of several Egyptian ports for transshipment to Alexandria, once more on the blue Mediterranean.

Still another flow of goods by sea began in Southeast Asia or in India and crossed directly on the steady monsoon winds to East Africa, perhaps with an intermediate break in the nation-sized island of Madagascar, early settled by Southeast Asian migrants. From East Africa, cargoes were carried by sea up to Axumite or Egyptian Red Sea ports, and from there overland to the Mediterranean.

Again, no single fleet undertook such long voyages. Greeks, Arabs, perhaps Phoenicians or Syrians dominated the western end of the sea route. Indian or Southeast Asian sailors undertook the middle ranges of the voyage, and the goods were probably turned over to Chinese merchants in what is today Kampuchea, at the southern end of the Indochinese peninsula.

The most popular of all the goods that circulated on this interregional trade system was silk from China. Indian muslin and precious stones, spices from Southeast Asia, incense and drugs from Arabia, metals, glass, and pottery from Rome, and many other luxury items, light

A reconstruction of one of the ancient lateen-rigged trading vessels that once plied the Indian Ocean, carrying goods from South Asia to East Africa or the Near East. These triangular sails, borrowed by European shipbuilders, would add greatly to the maneuverability of Western ships during Europe's "age of discovery" around the time of Columbus. Arab dhows similarly rigged still make the shorter runs up to the Red Sea or the Persian Gulf today. (G. A. Ballard)

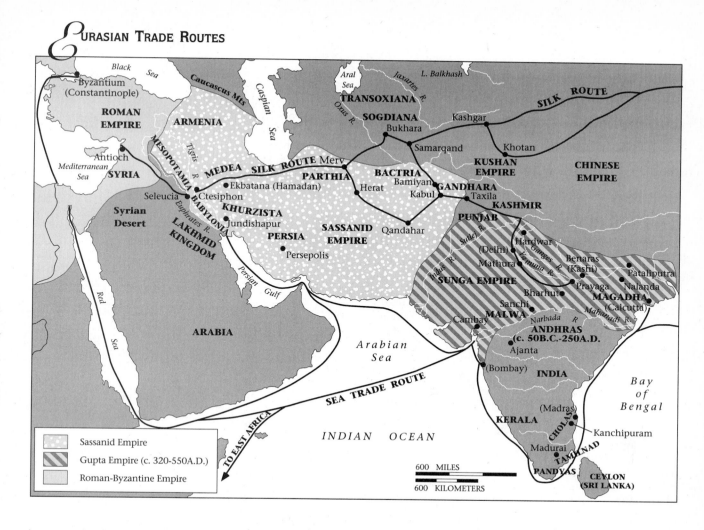

EURASIAN TRADE ROUTES

Legend:
- Sassanid Empire
- Gupta Empire (c. 320–550A.D.)
- Roman-Byzantine Empire

in proportion to their market value, were exchanged over the caravan trails and sea lanes of the classic age.

A great deal of coin of the realm also traveled from the West to Asia at this time. Asian goods were much more highly prized in Europe than anything the West could produce was in China or India. The Romans, therefore, had to pay cash—a substantial drain on the wealth of the empire.

The inroads of nomadic peoples had choked off most of this trade by the middle of the first millennium A.D. The fall of Han China and then of Rome further reduced the flow of interregional trade for centuries. But while it lasted, this long-range commerce at least began the process of drawing the peoples of Eurasia together economically.

CANOES ON THE CARIBBEAN

There was nothing like this elaborate system of long-distance, interregional trade anywhere else in the world this early in history.

Commercial exchange *within* the Mesoamerican and Peruvian cultural zones was highly developed. As noted in an earlier chapter, there must have been some diffusion of such products as maize southward from Mexico to Peru—that is, some interregional exchange. But this probably resulted from a succession of short-range exchanges between neighboring villages or peoples, a process that could have taken generations to move corn from Mexico to Peru.

The Mayans had large seagoing canoes, and Columbus encountered one laden with cotton clothing, copper axes and bells, swords edged with obsidian, and other trade goods. But these were on the Caribbean side of the Isthmus of Panama rather than on the Pacific side, and they could not have gotten anywhere near Peru.

There is, finally, no evidence of trade between the centers of civilization in the Old and New Worlds this early. It is possible that an occasional storm-swept mariner from elsewhere did end up in the Americas. But no trade goods made in Asia or Europe have been found in the New World. Commercial exchange across the Atlantic and Pacific would have to wait for the Europeans who arrived around 1500.

We have, then, a significant beginning at long-range trade across and around the three continents of the Old World during the classic age. But a genuine world market, a web of commerce linking all continents, would have to wait a thousand years more, until modern times.

CULTURAL DIFFUSION: THE OUTREACH OF IDEAS

DEFINITIONS OF CULTURE

Cultural influences of one region on another also increased significantly during the classic age. Again, the phenomenon is limited essentially to the three continents of the Old World. Nevertheless, the cultural diffusion of this period, particularly during the early centuries of the Christian era, constitutes an important increase in the interaction of regions and peoples. Like the expansion of trade and the movements of peoples, the spread of cultural elements is a notable step toward a genuinely global community.

Cultural diffusion is especially evident if we define culture as the anthropologist does—broadly, including not only "high culture" but *all* aspects of human lifeways. Thus defined, historic examples of cultural diffusion between regions would include the spread of ironworking from the Near East to Meroe or the spread of Greek cities from Europe across the Middle East. It would, of course, include such artistic diffusion as Roman culture transplanted to North Africa, Hellenistic Buddhas in northwestern India, and Han Chinese art in Korean tombs.

Such cultural diffusion may follow trade routes or travel with migrating peoples; it may come with victorious armies or political authority. In any case, it can make a profound impression on the alien peoples it reaches.

Probably the most important forms of cultural influence during the classic age, however, were the great world religions, some of which spread far and wide over the Old World during those centuries.

THE MISSIONARY IMPULSE

Not all of the world's more important religions have displayed the missionary impulse or the capacity to appeal to others outside the societies that originated them. Thus, the Greco-Roman pantheon does not seem to have traveled well, and Hinduism made few converts outside of India this early.

But Judaism spread with the Jewish diaspora from its Near Eastern homeland all around the Mediterranean, as well as south to Ethiopia and down to central Arabia. Mithraism, a Zoroastrian cult, followed the Roman legions into Europe, particularly to frontier areas such as the Balkans, Germany, and Britain. In the Far East, Confucianism spread with Chinese political power and cultural influence to regions as widely separated as north Vietnam and Korea.

Stone carvings of the sacrifice of the Mithraic bull can be found in the ruins of underground temples along Hadrian's Wall in northern Britain, and the story of Solomon and the Queen of Sheba is still told in Ethiopia. But the most important world religions that spread from one region to another during the later centuries of the classic age were Buddhism and Christianity.

The founding and early spread of these two faiths has already been outlined, and more will be said of their development in later chapters. Here, however, a rough review of the simple geographical dispersion of these religions during the early centuries of the Christian era will be given. Both religions are striking examples of the distance that ideas can travel, and of the transforming influence they can have far from their spiritual homes.

The Buddhist faith spread very far indeed from its birthplace on the Ganges. Carried by pious monks and Indian traders, Buddhism spread north into the Himalayan lands of Nepal and Tibet and south to the island kingdom of Ceylon. It also followed the trade routes southeast to Burma, Thailand, and the island of Sumatra. Most important, the Buddhist vision of salvation through enlightenment was carried north and east along the Silk Road into China, and later through Korea to Japan. Buddhism thus became the most widespread of East Asian religions even while, as noted above, it was rapidly losing ground in India to a resurgent Hinduism.

Christianity spread from its Near Eastern origins all around the Mediterranean and up into western Europe, becoming in the fourth century the state religion of the entire Roman Empire. Isolated Christian communities also emerged in places as widely dispersed as the Balkans, Kush, and subsequently Ethiopia, eastern Persia, and southern India. But the main body of Christians were grouped for the time being on the margins of the Mediterranean, where the three Old World continents met. Thus, three of the most influential fathers of the early Church were Ambrose, bishop of Milan in southern Europe; Augustine, bishop of Hippo in North Africa; and Jerome, the translator of the Latin Bible, who lived much of his life as a recluse near Bethlehem, in western Asia.

Both Christianity and Buddhism were spread by simple preachers of their gospels and initially offered salvation without elaborate ceremonial, powerful priestly establishments, or complicated theology. Both religions subsequently developed all of these, however, and became

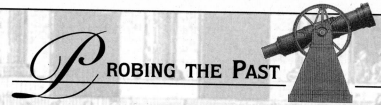

PROBING THE PAST

"People of a trade diaspora [scattering or dispersion of a people] were not only members of an urban society; they were also members of a plural society, where two . . . cultures existed side by side. . . . With the passage of time, cultural differences . . . would be expected to disappear . . . but the actual course of cultural integration was extremely variable. Some trade diasporas tried very hard to protect the integrity of their original culture. In spite of their roles as cross-cultural brokers, they developed intricate systems of social control to prevent their traveling merchants "going native." . . . In other circumstances, men who went abroad to trade without wives from home ended by marrying abroad, which could speed the process of culture change. On eighteenth-century Java, for example, the intermarriage of Chinese merchants with local women led to the creation of a new mixed culture called peranakan. . . .

Although some diaspora merchants sought only to protect their cultural integrity, others tried to convert their hosts. Their success was sometimes spectacular. Hindu merchants from India carried not only their religion but also a lot of Indian secular culture to Southeast Asia. Later on, Muslim Indians carried Islam throughout island Southeast Asia."

Here Philip Curtin, a widely respected specialist in the history of Africa and of the transatlantic slave trade, discusses three reactions to the cultural encounters that resulted from long-distance trade. What impact does Professor Curtin suggest a foreign environment might have on resident merchant communities from abroad? How might an entirely new culture sometimes be created? What forms of cultural transformation might foreign traders bring to the lands where they settled? Do you know of any more recent examples of the spread of religious or other ideals or of material culture through the commercial penetration of one cultural community by another?

Philip D. Curtin, <u>Cross-Cultural Trade in World History</u> (London: Cambridge University Press, 1984), pp. 11–12.

powerful institutions shaping the lives of millions in the lands where they took root. From agricultural reform to brilliant artistic traditions, these two world religions made immense contributions to the societies of eastern and western Eurasia. They also helped to bind region to region—East, Southeast, and some of southern Asia in the Buddhist community; Western Europe and for a time North Africa and the Near East in the Christian community.

We have, once more, much less evidence and little reason to believe in similar cultural diffusion between the two major areas of urban culture in the New World. Such common artistic motifs as the jaguar in Mesoamerican and Peruvian art and religion may reveal a spreading cult, like Buddhism or Christianity in the Old World. Or it may simply reveal parallel ventures, an animistic attribution of divinity to a fierce animal that was found in the rain forests of both regions.

Again, there is no convincing evidence of major cultural influence from the Old World on the New. Even if the odd European or Asian mariner did reach the Americas, it is generally deemed unlikely that such an isolated case could materially influence cultural evolution over the two American continents.

For further evolution toward a genuinely global culture, the world would have to wait another ten centuries at least. But where such cultural diffusion did already operate, across Eurasia and Africa, major religions, like trade routes or migrating peoples, were among the crucial ties that began to draw peoples together on the planet they shared.

SUMMARY

Cultural diffusion and links between peoples, particularly between major centers of civilization, became especially important during the classic age.

Such contacts were of three kinds: migrations and conquests involving whole peoples; trade by merchants; and purely cultural contacts, particularly the missionary efforts of great religions. The chief centers of urban imperial culture continued to grow independently, sometimes in total isolation from each other. Preurban peoples also cherished their individual traditions. But migration, trade, and cultural diffusion would bind them all increasingly in later centuries.

Migration, going back to prehistoric times, was the oldest form of contact between peoples. Mass migrations continued during the classic age, and thus continued to contribute to the yeasty mixing of peoples and the spread of whole ways of life from one region to another. Epic examples include the Bantu trek across southern and central Africa and the voyages of Melanesian, Micronesian, and Polynesian islanders across the western Pacific.

Commercial exchange reached unprecedented levels during the early centuries of the Christian era. Caravans linked Han China and the Roman Empire across Eurasia. Established shipping lanes carried goods from the China seas across southeastern Asia and the Indian Ocean to Africa and Europe. In the New World, there was apparently little or no commercial or other forms of contact between the developed cultures of Mexico and Peru. But goods from Middle America did circulate in the Caribbean, and systems of exchange linked the cultures of the Andes.

Cultural diffusion often accompanied trade and migration, and it exerted its own independent influence on the peoples of the world. Styles in art and ideas, as well as forms of material culture, thus passed from people to people, civilization to civilization. One powerful form of cultural diffusion was the missionary impulse. This urge to spread religious truth carried world religions like Christianity and Buddhism far across western and eastern Eurasia respectively.

This surge of contacts between peoples around the time of Christ would dwindle almost to nothing during the next thousand years. But it pointed toward the wave of genuine global integration that would begin between 1200 and 1500 and continue to the present day.

SUGGESTED READING

BARRACLOUGH, G., ed. *The Times Atlas of World History*. London: Times Books, 1978. Has excellent maps to illustrate the major Eurasian trade routes, as well as the spread of the main world religions.

BENTLY, J. *Old World Encounters: Cross-Cultural Contacts and Exchanges in Pre-Modern Times*. New York: Oxford University Press, 1993. Excellent brief summary.

CURTIN, P. D. *Cross-Cultural Trade in World History*. Cambridge: Cambridge University Press, 1984. Insightful overview of the part played by trade in binding distant cultures together.

GUHA, A. *Central Asia: Movements of Peoples and Ideas from Times Prehistoric to Modern*. New York: Harper & Row, 1972. Migration across Eurasia and its impact on history.

HUDSON, G. T. *Europe and China: A Survey of Their Relations from the Earliest Times to 1800*. London: Edward Arnold, 1931. An old survey of the subject. See also Needham below.

JENNINGS, J. D. *The Prehistory of Polynesia*. Cambridge, Mass.: Harvard University Press, 1979. Up-to-date, scholarly studies of major island groups and of significant aspects of Polynesian culture, from ecology to physical anthropology. See also B. R. Finney, *Pacific Migrations and Voyaging*. (Wellington, New Zealand: The Polynesian Society, 1976) on experimental research, from computer simulations to actual voyages, on the navigational techniques of the Polynesians.

MILLER, J. I. *Spice Trade of the Roman Empire, 29 B.C.–A.D. 641*. London: Oxford University Press, 1969. Trade between East and West from the Caesars to the Arab conquest.

NEEDHAM, J. *Science and Civilization in China*. Cambridge: Cambridge University Press, 1954–. Volume 1 of this monumental work in progress outlines cultural and other contacts between China and the rest of Eurasia.

PHILLIPSON, D. W. "The Beginnings of the Iron Age in Southern Africa," in *Ancient Civilizations of Africa*, G. Mokhtar, ed. London: Heinemann, 1981. Analyses of the cultural impact of the Bantu migrations.

RAWLINSON, H. G. *Intercourse between India and the Western World from the Earliest Times to the Fall of Rome*. New York: Octagon Books, 1971. Reprint of 1926 edition of this standard account of economic and other relations.

SIMKIN, C. G. F. *Traditional Trade of Asia*. New York: Oxford University Press, 1969. Good coverage.

TOUSSAINT, A. *History of the Indian Ocean*. Chicago: University of Chicago Press, 1966. Focus on the main sea–trade route of Eurasia.

VALERI, V. *Kingship and Sacrifice: Ritual and Society in Ancient Hawaii*, trans. P. Wissing. Chicago: University of Chicago Press, 1985. Anthropological investigation of the society and culture of the islands before Westernization.

WOODCOCK, G. *The Greeks in India*. London: Faber and Faber, 1966. The most important Western penetration of the East in ancient times.

ZURCHER, E. *The Buddhist Conquest of China* (2 vols.). New York: Brill, 1959. The most successful missionary faith before the coming of Islam and Christianity. See also his *Buddhism: Its Origin and Spread* (New York: St. Martin's Press, 1962) for the broader picture of Buddhism's Asian reach.

ZONES OF CULTURE AROUND THE WORLD

Civilization survived, despite the widespread destruction that brought the classic age to an end. Out of the ruins, as so often before, areas of order, prosperity, and high culture emerged once more.

If anything, the new cultures—or the reconstituted older ones—were larger and more impressive than those that had collapsed during the middle centuries of the first millennium A.D. For the emerging civilizations included not only those adjacent areas of the earth that could be brought under a single government. Civilization had grown till it transcended the reach of political authority, creating a series of *zones* of culture, harder to define historically than nations and empires, but real nonetheless.

Several types of cultural zones are detectable during the thousand years between A.D. 500 and 1500. The most obvious, perhaps, are the satellite civilizations appearing at the fringes of the great empires. In China's East Asian sphere, for example, related civilizations developed during these years in Korea, Vietnam, and, most important, Japan. Indian culture reached almost all of Southeast Asia, producing perhaps most strikingly the brilliant derivative civilization of the Khmer people of Cambodia.

A second sort of cultural zone was that created not by the cultural influence of a single great state, but by the rise and spread of a new international religion. The conversion of much of South and Southeast Asia to Buddhism—mentioned in the preceding chapter—had much to do with the spreading influence of Indian civilization. More striking examples of the shaping power of religion sprang up in western Eurasia during the next thousand years in the remarkable continuing growth of Christianity and the amazing upsurge of Islam.

Medieval Christianity, in both its Roman Catholic and Greek Orthodox forms, completed the process of civilizing Europe that the Roman Empire had begun. Islam, born in the seventh century, spread so rapidly that by the fifteenth century a series of Islamic states stretched from West Africa to Southeast Asia. Both the Christian and the Islamic zones of related cultures were thoroughly international, composed of many nations and even great empires. Yet the particular forms of urban, literate culture that developed in Christendom and in the Islamic sphere clearly reflected the shaping power of the religious faiths that dominated these two wide swathes of the Old World.

A third type of cultural zone was that created by the far-reaching conquests of a single people—the Mongols. The powerful armies of these nomads created for a couple of centuries the largest land empire ever assembled across northern Eurasia. And even when the Mongol Empire crumbled, a zone of Mongol culture still reached from the steppes of western Russia to the Pacific.

Impressive cultural zones, finally, had by this time also emerged in the New World and in Africa south of the Sahara. The kingdoms of the West African savanna constituted a zone of related cultures even before the shaping influence of Islam began to be felt. The peoples of Mesoamerica and Peru manifested common cultural traits well before the unifying power of the Aztecs and the Incas welded them into empires in the fifteenth century. A similar geographical environment—the West African grasslands or the Andes, for instance—might help to explain the phenomenon. A powerful common cultural heritage might thus bring together a number of peoples and states without either a religion or an empire at its center.

Of course, cultural zones were not new in the world of fifteen hundred years ago. A common civilization had infused the states of ancient Greece, of Shang China, even of ancient Mesopotamia. But the new zones of culture that flourished between 500 and 1500 had a size and a dynamism that pointed toward something still more impressive: the beginning of a truly global culture in centuries to come.

The major cultural zones remained separate for the most part during the period under consideration here. Except for the brief Mongol interlude, even Eurasia was without the unifying exchange of goods and ideas that had tentatively linked east and west during the classic age. But the new zones of culture were growing, catching up an ever larger percentage of the world's peoples in the great enterprise of civilization building. And the time would come when one among them, around 1500, would launch a drive for dominion that would dwarf even those of the Muslims and the Mongols.

As an unconscious step toward the global integration of modern times, then, the disparate cultural zones of the centuries between the end of the classic age and the beginning of our own era—roughly 500–1500—are of special interest.

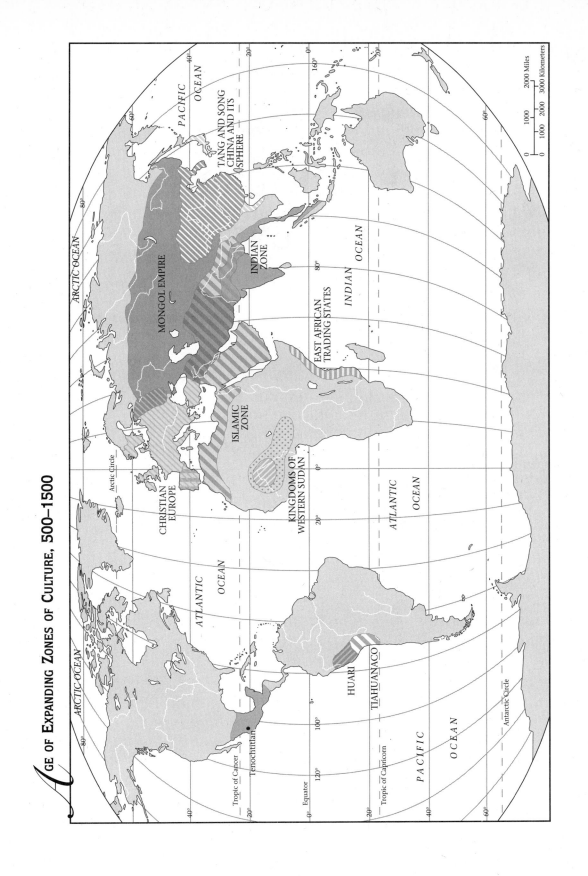

Age of Expanding Zones of Culture, 500–1500

Arctic Circle

ARCTIC OCEAN

PACIFIC OCEAN

CHRISTIAN EUROPE

MONGOL EMPIRE

TANG AND SONG CHINA AND ITS SPHERE

INDIAN ZONE

ISLAMIC ZONE

KINGDOMS OF WESTERN SUDAN

EAST AFRICAN TRADING STATES

INDIAN OCEAN

ATLANTIC OCEAN

ATLANTIC OCEAN

Tropic of Cancer

Tenochtitlan

Equator

HUARI

TIAHUANACO

Tropic of Capricorn

PACIFIC OCEAN

Antarctic Circle

2000 Miles

1000 | 2000 | 3000 Kilometers

CHAPTER 17

THE CENTURIES OF CHRISTENDOM

THE EARLY MIDDLE AGES

THE WESTERN END OF EURASIA

The geography of Europe, familiar as it is to most Western people, is extremely difficult to describe. In the broadest perspective, it is simply the western end of Eurasia—about a fifth of the double continent. But it has more than enough peninsulas and islands, mountains and inland seas, to confuse any more detailed description.

In political and cultural terms, Europe today is divided into a number of readily recognizable regions. There are the Scandinavian peninsulas to the north, the British Isles off the west coast, and the Iberian, Italian, and Greek peninsulas to the south. France, Switzerland, and the Low Countries complete the roster of Western Europe. Germany and Austria comprise the core of central Europe. And Eastern Europe runs from the Baltic Sea and the plains of Poland and Hungary down through the mountainous Balkans and east across the immensity of Russia.

Europe's traditional frontiers are the Atlantic in the west; the Mediterranean, Black, and Caspian seas to the south; Russia's Ural Mountains on the east (though Russia itself flows on across Eurasia to the Pacific); and the frozen arctic to the north. Europe's great rivers—the Rhone, the Rhine, the Danube, the Volga, and many others—have served it as roads of commerce throughout its history. The continent's largest mountain ranges, from the Alps and Pyrenees to the Carpathians and the Caucasus, have become important boundaries of European nations. Europe's rich croplands and pastures, from France to Russia's Ukraine, have fed one of the densest concentrations of human population on the globe.

Burgeoning commercial exchange, competitive nations, and a swelling population have all contributed significantly to the shaping of Europe's history. Particularly in modern times, its frontiers of ocean and steppe seem to have existed only as challenges, readily and even explosively transcended.

In the present chapter, however, we will be dealing with a medieval Europe whose dynamic qualities were less spectacularly on display. For much of the Middle Ages, in fact, Europe may quite legitimately be described as an underdeveloped area. Bordered by the glittering cultures of Byzantium and Islam, sharing the Eurasian land mass with the great civilizations of India and China, Dark Age Europe looks like a very backward cultural zone indeed. But medieval Europe did flower, briefly and brilliantly, in the High Middle Ages—the eleventh, twelfth, and thirteenth centuries. And its future greatness may be traced back this far at least, to the crusading religion, the increasingly productive agriculture, the enterprising merchants, the militaristic aristocracy, and the increasingly powerful kingdoms of the medieval centuries.

We must begin, however, where the story does, with a very different Europe from that of the High Middle Ages—with a Europe lying broken and helpless in the ruins of its greatest historic catastrophe.

THE REIGN OF THE BARBARIAN

> For the end of the world was long ago—
> And we all dwell today
> As children of some second birth,
> Like a strange people left on earth
> After a judgment day.[1]

G. K. Chesterton's "medieval" epic puts words into the mouths of Dark Age Britons. But those words may in fact sum up a genuine, if hazily felt, medieval sense of a better world long gone. The world that had ended, of course, was the Roman world—an authoritarian, sometimes brutal empire that had nevertheless brought a considerable degree of order and prosperity to Europe. In place of Roman soldiers, Roman roads, Roman merchants, Roman cities, and Roman law there came now the rule of the barbarian.

Chesterton's barbarians are typical of a popular—and considerably oversimplified—image of the type. His enemies of light are pagan Vikings, wading in from their long black ships with horns on their heads and battle-axes swinging. In fact, the earlier Germanic invaders had lived on the fringes of the Roman Empire for a long time and probably shared a basic pattern of village life with most Roman subjects. Others, however, like the seagoing Vikings, had less understanding of, and less respect for, the stable institutions of cities and empires. And both

---

[1]G. K. Chesterton, *The Ballad of the White Horse* (London: Methuen, 1911), p. 2.

groups, intentionally or not, contributed to the destruction of the only unified empire Europe has ever known.

From the fifth century to the tenth, then, barbarian kingdoms divided Europe among themselves, fought one another and each new wave of barbarian invaders, and gradually transformed life on the western end of Eurasia.

They came in two great surges. The first, composed mostly of semicivilized Germanic peoples, shouldered their way into the empire they had long admired, and established themselves as early as the fifth century. They set up an Ostrogothic kingdom in Italy, a Visigothic one in Spain, Franks in what would become France, Angles and Saxons in Britain, and Alemanni in Germany. A second, more varied wave of invasions began in the eighth century. Vikings pressed down from the north by sea, Magyars from the eastern steppes, and Muslim Arabs up from the south across Spain and the Mediterranean.

They came for a variety of reasons. In the early days, some came from envy of what remained of Roman prosperity, or in search of land, or simply as a result of being jostled down the steppe gradient by more powerful nomadic neighbors to the east. The Vikings came for loot, the Arabs in the grip of a new religion that sanctioned warfare in Allah's name. Some of the intruders took what they could carry and headed home. Others settled among the peoples of the broken empire or the unstable barbarian kingdoms that replaced it. Some of those who stayed became Europe's new masters, a military aristocracy distinguished by cavalry skills and increasingly heavy arms and armor—the mounted knights of the new age.

The process of transition from the civilization of the ancient Romans to the culture of the early Middle Ages was more gradual than was once imagined, more evolutionary than revolutionary in nature.

The new peoples brought some new ways of life with them, of course. The German royal entourage, a war band called the *comitatus*, would provide the germ of the new feudal political order, based on personal allegiance to an overlord. The proclivity of the Germans for country rather than urban living would contribute to the disintegration of the network of cities that had dominated ancient Greco-Roman civilization. Yet when towns reappeared in the later Middle Ages, German social brotherhoods called *guilds* would evolve into the merchant and craft guilds that played a central role in the medieval urban economy.

But there were Roman roots for medieval civilization too. Roman estates called *villas* worked by slave labor probably evolved in some places into medieval manors with their labor force of serfs. Roman roads and aqueducts continued to be used for a time; coins were only gradually replaced by barter as trade diminished; the cities the Romans had built were abandoned slowly, over generations. And the Roman Catholic Church, with its structure of episcopal administration and its communities of monks and nuns who preserved some vestiges of Latin culture, would reach new heights in the Middle Ages.

A mingling of folkways accompanied by a slow merging of peoples thus lay at the root of the new society of medieval Europe. Germanic chiefs intermarried with Roman aristocrats, while German freemen settled beside Celtic or other indigenous peasant cultivators. The Vikings who descended from Scandinavia established themselves in parts of northern Europe, including Normandy (in modern France) and northern England. Muslims from the other side of the Mediterranean colonized Spain, Sicily, and other places along the southern fringes of the Continent. If the Germans brought the *comitatus* and the early guild, the Northmen would develop the strongest feudal government in Europe, and the Arabs and Berbers, maintaining contact with the more cultivated cultures of North Africa and the Near East, would produce enclaves of civilized living along the southern margins of Europe.

Yet the disintegration of the Roman order must have seemed very much like a judgment passed on the world. There had been intermittent exploitation under the Roman eagles; under the barbarians, local tyranny and endless fighting became the rule. The new kings, operating without benefit of Roman administration, Roman legions, or a Roman sense of order, could do nothing. From the glory of Augustus in his far-off city of marble, it was a long comedown to the "do-nothing" kings of the Merovingian Franks, who, according to a contemporary chronicler, were sometimes trundled along the rutty lanes of the kingdom in a farm wagon while a servant trotted ahead blowing a ram's horn.

CHARLEMAGNE'S EMPIRE

Here and there, however, strength and capacity existed even in Dark Age Europe. The most impressive attempt to restore order and unity to the Continent was led by perhaps the most famous of medieval monarchs, the Frankish king Charles the Great, known to history as Charlemagne.

Charlemagne (768–814) was a half-literate giant, six feet and several inches in height, a tremendous toper, trencherman, and womanizer, and a mighty warrior in a war-battered age. The greatest of the ambitious Carolingian kings of the Franks who succeeded the do-nothing Merovingians in the eighth century, Charlemagne spent most of his long reign fighting. He hammered together a rude but sizable empire, with modern France at its core and chunks of Spain, northern Italy, western Germany, and neighboring regions as outlying provinces. On Christmas day, 800, a pope, grateful for his help against barbarian intruders and the pope's political enemies in Rome, placed a crown on Charlemagne's head, hailing him "Pious Augustus, crowned by God," and heir of all the Caesars.[2]

He was scarcely that, this huge, thick-bearded man who spoke vulgar Latin as well as the Frankish tongue and kept a slate beside his bed so that he could practice

[2]Robert S. Hoyt and Stanley Chodorow, *Europe in the Middle Ages* (New York: Harcourt Brace Jovanovich, 1976), p. 160.

tracing the letters of the alphabet in rare quiet moments. His endless campaigns spread Roman Christianity and Frankish rule far across western Europe. He organized his empire into a loose provincial structure of *counties*—each headed by a count—and tried to keep tabs on them, both in person and through royal inspectors sent out from his court at Aachen near the Rhine. He even presided over a temporary revival of learning, the Carolingian Renaissance, which at least made a virtue of Latin literacy and theological scholarship at Aachen. Charlemagne's scholars both preserved much of Rome's literary heritage for the future and developed a new form of writing—*Carolingian minuscule*, the small or lowercase letters we still use, along with Roman capitals, today.

But Charlemagne's heir had none of his strength of will, and his three grandsons divided the Carolingian Empire among them less than thirty years after his death. The Carolingian Renaissance too proved to be a false dawn in the Dark Ages. But it did at least halt the long decline and point out one way in which peace and prosperity might be restored to Europe. To the extent that they accepted this obligation, the strong kings of centuries to come were all Charlemagne's heirs.

THE FEUDAL LORDS

The forces that pulled Charlemagne's empire apart were rooted more deeply in medieval society than in the rivalries of feuding heirs. For the real rulers of Europe in the Dark Ages were not the kings of the barbarian states but the powerful dukes, counts, knights, and other warrior lords of medieval Europe linked in a loose structure of power called *feudalism*.

Feudalism did not emerge in its full complexity until after the collapse of the Carolingian Empire in the ninth century, but its roots went back to the customs of the Germanic tribes who had overrun the Roman Empire in the fifth. Among the ancient Germans it was common for young freemen to join the personal retinue, the *comitatus*, of a famous warrior, pledged to fight and die with their chief. In the violent centuries after the barbarian conquest, when government was weak and local warfare endemic,

Charlemagne, looking almost larger than his horse in this bronze representation, wears the crown and holds the orb of imperial authority. Note the heavy sword under his cloak, a symbol of his many victories and conquests. Notice also the monumental feel of this representation, which is in fact only a small figurine. (New York Public Library Picture Collection)

Dark Age Invasions of the West, 9th to 10th Centuries

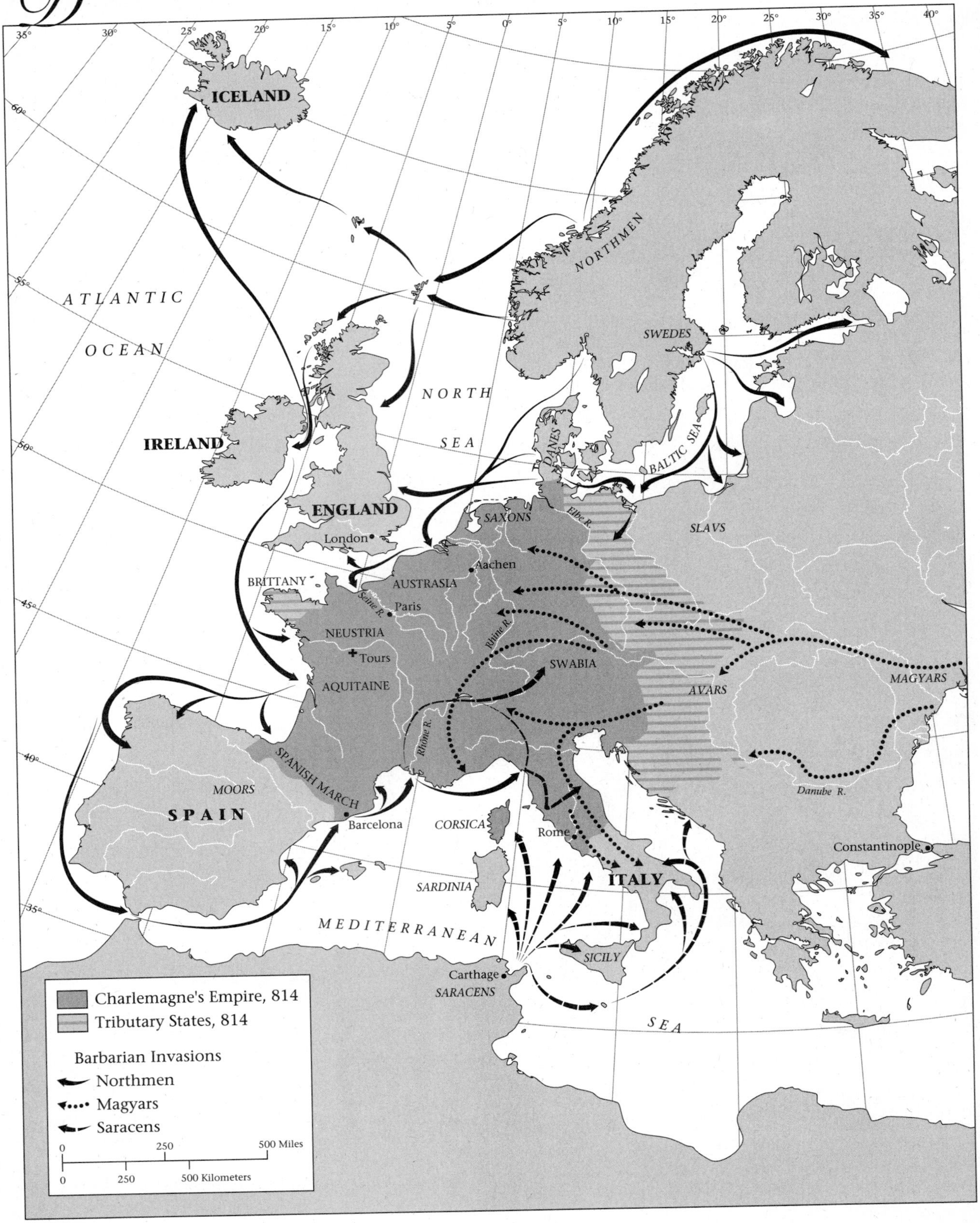

ICELAND

ATLANTIC

OCEAN

NORTHMEN

SWEDES

NORTH

SEA

BALTIC SEA

DANES

SLAVS

IRELAND

ENGLAND

London

SAXONS

Aachen

Elbe R.

BRITTANY

AUSTRASIA

Seine R.

Paris

Rhine R.

AVARS

MAGYARS

NEUSTRIA

+ Tours

SWABIA

AQUITAINE

Rhône R.

Danube R.

SPANISH MARCH

Barcelona

CORSICA

Rome

MOORS

SPAIN

SARDINIA

ITALY

Constantinople

MEDITERRANEAN

SICILY

Carthage

SARACENS

SEA

| | Charlemagne's Empire, 814 |
| | Tributary States, 814 |

Barbarian Invasions

➤ Northmen

▶•••• Magyars

◀--- Saracens

0   250   500 Miles

0   250   500 Kilometers

many freemen turned for sheer survival to the similar relationship of feudal vassalage.

Feudalism was a system of military service and land tenure that bound Europe's ruling classes into an elaborate pyramid of political and military power. Under this system the less powerful knights—called *vassals*—sought political protection and economic support, commonly in the form of a grant of land, from the more powerful, who became their feudal lords, or *seigneurs*. In return, feudal overlords required military service, money payments, and general support from their vassals.

The ceremony of feudal vassalage was solemn and symbolic. The vassal knelt, placed his hands between those of his lord, and took an oath of *fealty*, or allegiance. He pledged perhaps forty days of military service each year, plus money payments when the lord's son was knighted, his daughter married, or the lord himself captured and in need of ransom. In return the seigneur handed the vassal a clod of earth or a sprig from a tree, and with it conferred on him a *fief*, a parcel of land replete with villages of serfs to cultivate it.

This structure of interlocking obligations was quite suitable to a violent age in which only local authority was strong enough to offer any real protection. In time, however, the system became immensely complex and sometimes self-defeating. Loyal vassals might find themselves with a number of overlords, some of whom might feud with each other, creating embarrassing conflicts of interest. The strong kings of later centuries sometimes came into conflict with the most powerful of feudal overlords, "overmighty subjects" who could rival even kings for power. The royal rulers of the High Middle Ages would thus often prefer to depend on hired mercenary companies, whose services could be depended on as long as the monarch's money lasted.

Throughout the Middle Ages in Europe, the feudal lords would hold much of the Continent's political power. In the early Middle Ages—the first half of the thousand years of medieval history—the military leaders were the real rulers of the land.

SERFS OF THE MANOR

The feudal nobility lived with their families, military henchmen, and servants in manor houses or later in large stone castles, many of them located on hilltops for defensive purposes. But the true support of society was to be found not in the high, walled keep or castle, but in the small village at the foot of the hill.

If feudalism constituted the political power structure of Europe in the early Middle Ages, the manor system was the heart of the earlier medieval economy. In a world reduced to isolated, county-sized political units, subsistence agriculture was essential. The manor system fed the farm laborers themselves, the feudal aristocracy, the priests, the kings. And it provided at least a modicum of protection for masses of people who could no longer look to garrisoned legions or civil authorities for defense against violence or help in hard times.

The typical medieval manor consisted of a village surrounded by arable land, usually with the manor house or castle overlooking it. A dozen, perhaps several dozen, stone or mud huts clustered along a single unpaved village street. A small, rude church might occupy one end of the street, and perhaps a mill, bakehouse, smithy, and other adjuncts were mixed in among the houses of the peasants. The surrounding land would include, besides the arable for spring and autumn planting, a third field left fallow in rotation each year so that it could recover its strength. These three fields were typically divided into strips so that all might have a share of the best as well as the worst land. Beyond the three-field system of strips were blocks of common pastureland for farm animals and portions of uncut forest for firewood and foraging pigs.

Medieval peasants were totally subservient to the lord of the manor. They paid portions of their produce to support the lord. They also worked the lord's land for him and did other manual labor around the estate—the corvée work on roads, bridges, and so on. The blacksmith's shop, the bakehouse, and similar amenities were the lord's, and the peasants paid to use them. Peasants were tried for all but the most serious crimes in the baron's court, and married outside the manor only with his consent. They were not chattel slaves, as in the ancient world. But they were serfs, bound to the land and the village for life—and thus to the lord, for as long as he held that land.

In return for their many services, medieval serfs received the military protection of the lord and his strong-arm henchmen. They had their traditional manorial rights and would be cared for in old age, if they lived that long.

Life in the village under the hill during the early Middle Ages was a hard and narrow round. The typical peasant family—that is, the large majority of Europeans—lived in a meagerly furnished, earth-floored, one-room hut. They moved by day in a clutter of chickens and animals who shared the hut with them, slept whole families curled together for warmth on a straw-covered sleeping floor at night. They plowed with horses or oxen and a heavy wheeled plow, harvested and threshed their grain with rough homemade tools.

Starving time came in the spring, when the fall harvest was consumed and the winter wheat not yet in. Wolves howled in winter in the dark forests that still covered large parts of Europe. And there was always danger of disease in a world without doctors, of barbarian raids or local barons' wars that could bring fire to the thatch of manor house and peasant hut alike.

There had been such breakdowns of the great enterprise many times in many parts of the world. But this was probably the worst that Europe ever had to endure.

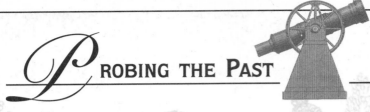

PROBING THE PAST

"*Changes in mortality rates are the final and the most telling witnesses in the indictment of the excessive population which oppressed certain western countries at the end of the thirteenth century. In effect, the only important study of this kind concerns England between the years 1240 and 1350, and rests on the extraordinary series of accounts preserved in the records of the bishopric of Winchester.*

It emphasizes how precarious was the existence of the peasant population, which in some districts appears by 1300 to have exceeded that of the eighteenth century by 20 percent. In 1245 the expectation of life for a man over 20 years of age was 24. For the entire period the death rate can be estimated at 40 per 1,000. . . . It became 52 per 1,000 for adults between 1297 and 1347 and the expectation of life therefore fell to 20 years. Fluctuations in the curve of mortalities were very frequent and expressed the sensitivity to epidemics of such a physically debilitated population; the fluctuations appeared also to be closely correlated with the curve of harvests, and an approximate analysis by social class shows that the richer peasants were less likely to die than their poorer neighbors. These statistics, imprecise as they are, provide the most striking proof of how utterly insufficient agricultural improvements were. In spite of the various changes in agriculture in the last years of the century, technical progress never succeeded in meeting the needs of a teeming population which lay at the mercy of a shortage of food as cruel perhaps as it had ever been in Carolingian times."

◆◆◆

Modern French medievalist Georges Duby is a leading practitioner of one form of the "new social history." Here he uses medieval records, particularly statistical evidence, to illuminate the lives of ordinary medieval people. How does Duby's approach to history differ from those of the ancient Greek historian Herodotus on p. 140 and China's Grand Historian on p. 189? How important is statistical evidence to Duby? In the present instance, do you think he has sufficient statistical data to justify his assertions about medieval demography?

Georges Duby, <u>Rural Economy and Country Life in the Medieval West</u>, trans. Cynthia Arnold (London: Edward Arnold, 1968), pp. 124–125.

THE LIFE OF THE CHURCH

In this harsh, subsistence-level world, one institution worked still for higher ends and provided islands of culture in a backward Europe. The Christian Church survived the Fall of Rome and actually expanded and grew more powerful through the medieval centuries.

As we shall see, Christianity spread north from two radiant centers in the Mediterranean world during the Middle Ages. The popes of Rome sponsored the vast expansion of Roman Catholicism over Western Europe, while the patriarchs of Constantinople, capital of the Byzantine or Eastern Roman Empire, spread Greek Orthodox Christianity across much of Eastern Europe. Even in the early Middle Ages, daring missionaries converted pagan kings and queens, and through them their peoples.

Churchmen like Charlemagne's advisor Alcuin preserved some Latin learning, produced beautifully decorated handwritten books, and presided over such heroic attempts at cultural revival as the Carolingian Renaissance.

Humbler monks and nuns, seeking refuge from worldly temptation behind the walls of monasteries and convents, created outposts of order, charity, and often relatively efficient agriculture. Monastic establishments planted among non-Christian populations also provided centers from which pagans might be converted to Christianity. The pious men and women who lived within monastic walls alternated hard work in the fields or cloisters with religious meditation and prayer. Most importantly, from their own point of view, they provided a desperately needed link between the peoples of the western end of Eurasia and their God.

How many medieval villages had their own priests and little churches, or even a cross on a hill around which to pray, we do not know. Many probably did not, especially during the earlier medieval centuries. In many parts of Europe, old religions worshiping the forces of nature, pre-Christian cults, folk beliefs, and superstitions undoubtedly survived. But the Christian Church remained the most determined and dynamic of Western institutions even during this grim time.

WOMEN IN EARLY MEDIEVAL SOCIETY

The role of women at all levels of medieval life, finally, was extremely important. In a time when Western civilization struggled simply to maintain itself, women may in fact have played a particularly important part in society.

In a world reduced to fundamentals, the family was a central institution. The peasant household, which included the large majority of medieval people, was the basic unit of production, one in which women carried at least their half of the common burden. Caring for farm animals and children, tending vegetables near the house, preparing food, making all clothing by hand, and often doing a share of sowing or harvesting crops in distant fields as well, medieval peasant women needed nimble fingers and strong backs.

Higher up the social ladder, women of noble families often shared in the ruling functions and responsibilities of the upper classes. The structure of power and prestige, like the system of economic production, was based on the family, on inheritance and marriage. Women born of great families could inherit vast estates. As wives of fighting barons, they were often called on to administer and sometimes defend their lands and manor houses while their husbands were away at the frequent wars.

Women, finally, could also make an independent place for themselves, and even exercise considerable authority, within the Church. Women who found the burdens of family life oppressive could dedicate their lives to God by "taking the veil" and entering a convent. Women with large estates could even establish and run their own convents. Within these holy institutions, they could wield the absolute authority of a mother superior or an abbess. Women as well as men, finally, might lead lives so pious that they achieved the ultimate medieval accolade of sainthood. Hildegarde of Bingen, whose convents carried Christianity to the Germanic peoples, was famed for her learning and visionary insights. The pope himself wrote to her that "We are filled with admiration, my daughter . . . for the new miracles that God has shown you in our time, filling you with his spirit so that you see, understand, and communicate many secret things."[3]

---

[3]*Patrologia Latina*, vol. 197, col. 145, quoted in F. and J. Gies, *Women in the Middle Ages* (New York: Crowell, 1978), p. 81.

THE HIGH MIDDLE AGES

THE REBIRTH OF CITIES

In the year A.D. 1000, Europe was a cramped and drafty fortress on a hill, a dozen families huddled in huts along a muddy street below, and all around, a world of fen and forest stretching to an empty horizon. It was as though the Greek city-states and the metropolis on the seven hills of Rome had never existed.

A century later, two centuries, and it was a world transformed.

Once again the gates of cities swung wide, and to the braying of donkeys and the baaing of sheep, country folk could pass through an arched gateway into crowded cobblestoned streets. Steep-roofed multistory houses pressed close above. There were market squares and gingerbready guildhalls, street after street of artisans and merchants, and rising against a misty gray sky, the half-finished towers of a cathedral. This was the twelfth century, or the thirteenth—the greatest of centuries, medieval enthusiasts have insisted since. Paris was the cultural capital of one of Europe's great ages—the Athens of the age of faith.

But where did it come from, this new urban sprawl, this urban splendor reborn? The reappearance of cities in medieval Europe after centuries of largely rural life has been explained in a number of ways by modern scholars. Among the factors most commonly selected, three stand out: agricultural improvements, population growth, and perhaps most important, the revival of trade.

The medieval European manor, primitive as it was in many ways, produced several crucial agricultural innovations. These included the three-field system, the heavy wheeled plow (both mentioned above), the horseshoe and the horse collar, and the windmill for grinding grain where no river was available for a water mill. After the year 1000 there was also a significant expansion in the amount of land under cultivation, due to the clearing of woodlands, the draining of swamps, and the movement of productive western European lords and peasants into less developed eastern Europe. Because of this increase in food production, the population began to grow, after centuries of stagnation. And some of these additional people concentrated in islands of dense population in which cities rapidly took shape.

The heart of the new towns, however, was commercial exchange and skilled handicraft manufacturing. The revival of trade in Europe in the eleventh, twelfth, and thirteenth centuries is thus a central cause of the rebirth of cities.

Trade grew up in Europe once more, partly because of the increased demand for goods created by the expanding population. Another cause was the taste for Eastern luxury goods encouraged by the Crusades, which began at the end of the eleventh century. And a prime stimulus was the expanded commercial exchange between the Near East and Italian trading cities such as Venice, which had survived the Dark Ages because of their connection with the powerful Byzantine Empire, Rome's heir to the east. The merchants who participated in this commercial revival became the builders and rulers of the medieval cities.

The trading cities were dominated first by merchant and craft guilds—trade associations of dealers in or makers of particular products, from cloth to goldsmith work. In time cities acquired independent political authorities—magistrates and city councils elected by this oligarchy of business people. Around the leading merchants and the master craftsmen, a colorful urban population soon gathered. The craft guilds included journeymen assistants and apprentices to the trade as well as masters. Merchants required stevedores, porters, muleteers, and other adjuncts. Priests, students, lawyers, runaway serfs, and other masterless men sought the protection of the city's walls.

In this stimulating environment—a world within the walls once more—what is sometimes called the commercial revolution of the High Middle Ages took place. The robed and ermined merchants of the twelfth and thirteenth centuries revived the use of coins after long centuries of barter and payment in kind. They began once more to lend money at interest and to develop such important modern business practices as double-entry bookkeeping and letters of credit. They began the pooling of capital for large-scale economic investments through the joint-stock company—an institution pointing ahead to all the stock markets of the modern world. Modern Western capitalism was thus born well before modern history began, in the cathedral-dominated cities of the age of faith.

THE FEUDAL MONARCHS

This burgeoning economic revival was accompanied and encouraged by the equally striking resurgence of centralized political power in the hands of medieval kings.

Their faces sleep in stone effigies on the lids of their sarcophagi or store blankly at us out of the simple illustrations of illuminated manuscripts. But their names still echo to a distant sound of trumpets: England's William I the Conqueror and Henry I the Lion of Justice; the Germans Frederick I Barbarossa ("Red Beard") and Frederick II *Stupor Mundi* ("The Wonder of the World"); France's Philip II Augustus and Louis IX, Saint Louis. There are less noble-sounding titles too, like Louis the Fat and Charles the Bald and Ethelred the Unready. But the famous rulers of the eleventh, twelfth, and thirteenth centuries—the William the Conquerors and the Philip Augustuses—deserve their places in the history books. They were the architects of the nation-states that would dominate the history of Europe for hundreds of years to come.

They were a varied lot. William the Conqueror still signed his name with an X; Frederick II spoke half a dozen languages fluently. Frederick Barbarossa was tall and powerfully built, a chivalric legend in his own time; Philip Augustus was bald, one-eyed, and crafty. Nor were their lives textbook models of selfless statesmanship. They hunted, wenched, squeezed their subjects for funds, and fought endless wars. They feuded with each other, with the popes, with their own barons, and embarked on the futile crusades and extremely successful programs of state building with indiscriminate enthusiasm. In the end it was this last-mentioned effort that has earned most of them their places in history.

Not all even of these famous names succeeded. None of the Holy Roman Emperors of the Germans—not even the redoubtable Fredericks—were able to impose genuine unity on the many German-speaking states of central Europe over which they held feudal suzerainty. Throughout most of its history the Holy Roman Empire would remain a ramshackle collection of separate principalities giving only minimal allegiance to its emperor. England and France, by contrast, were among the best examples of the centralized monarchy in medieval Europe.

Duke William the Bastard of Normandy overwhelmed Anglo-Saxon England in 1066, thus earning the more dignified sobriquet of William the Conqueror (1066–1087). He brought developed Norman-French feudalism with him to backward Britain. By asserting his position as king of England at the top of the feudal pyramid of power, he gave the country stronger centralized rule than it had ever had. His successors, including Henry I and Henry II, developed such governmental institutions as the royal council, the exchequer (treasury), and a system of royal justice based on English common law. By the end of the twelfth century—less than a century and a half after the conquest—England had the strongest monarchical government in Europe.

Close behind was the thirteenth-century French monarchy of Philip Augustus (1180–1223) and Saint Louis (1226–1270). Personally unprepossessing, Philip emerged as France's most successful medieval monarch. Like the English kings, he used his place at the apex of the feudal system to increase his power over the nobility. Like English rulers also, he developed an independent royal administrative system, including a more effective chamber of accounts, or treasury, and a stronger legal system. He did not conquer a new country for himself, like William of Normandy, but he did launch a calculated crusade against the heretical barons of southern France that tripled the size of the royal domain, and he took from the heirs of Henry II some important English holdings in France.

Under Philip Augustus thirteenth-century France replaced the Holy Roman Empire as the most powerful nation on the European continent. Under Louis IX the French monarchy acquired the prestige of having a duly canonized saint in its roster of kings. Louis was no weakling: he increased royal power over French towns, dared to issue royal edicts without consulting his baronial vassals, and strengthened the French system of law courts, or *parlements*. But he was also a paragon of medieval Christian and chivalric virtues, washing the feet of lepers, meting out justice under an oak tree, and earning such a reputation for fairness and piety that he was known as Louis the Just in his own time and was canonized only thirty years after his death. In the age of faith, a saintly life was no small contribution to the power of the French monarchy over its people.

It was a long step up from the "do-nothing" Merovingian kings of the Dark Ages to the power and vitality of William the Conqueror or Philip Augustus. And even the conflicts and competitiveness of Europe's kings and the taut power of the kingdoms they built generated a dynamism that would prove in later centuries more than a match for the great empires of other parts of the globe.

THE FEUDAL MONARCHIES

Undergirding the achievements of individual feudal monarchs, medieval government itself was evolving. The *feudal monarchy* as a set of political institutions and relationships would survive the Middle Ages and continue to develop through early modern times. In the end, modern bureaucratic government is a distant descendant of the monarchical institutions of the Middle Ages.

Basic problems for medieval rulers who truly wished to rule their lands included the need to impose the royal will on powerful vassals, the necessity of replacing a ragbag of feudal law with some sort of royal law, and perhaps most important, the need to get the right to tax the nation. Where these goals were met, as they were to a considerable degree in England and France, monarchs had to pay for their growing power by the rights of representative bodies speaking for the chief estates or classes of medieval society—the nobility, the Church, and the wealthy new towns.

The Norman feudalism that William the Conqueror imposed on England was the most developed in Europe. William claimed all the land in England for his own after the conquest: what he distributed as fiefs to his followers came with stringent feudal obligations. All the new vassals were actually required to gather on Salisbury Plain and take a mass oath of allegiance to their king. The legal reforms of William's successors began the process of replacing feudal law with the traditional English Common Law, which had been evolving for centuries before the Norman Conquest.

The right of English kings to tax their people, finally, was acquired with much more difficulty and in return for significant concessions. During the later Middle Ages, the English Parliament claimed the right to have the nation's grievances redressed before voting the monarch customs duties, taxes, or other sources of government revenue. Granted, Parliament met only when the monarch summoned it and represented only the elites of medieval society—ecclesiastical institutions, the nobility and country gentry, and the urban middle classes—not the masses of the people. But Parliament would in later centuries challenge royal authority and finally bring modern democracy to Britain.

The royal rulers of France had to deal with nobles whose claims went back many centuries and who saw the monarch as merely "first among equals" in the feudal structure. Great landed magnates whose holdings were sometimes larger than the king's would prove very hard to bring under royal control. The royal law the French kings strove to impose was Roman law, which had reached the West from the Byzantine Empire in the eleventh century. This strongly centralized code of laws, with its origins outside feudalism altogether, did significantly strengthen royal claims to overarching authority.

In France as in England, finally, the royal right to collect revenues outside the ruler's own domains was challenged. Again, a body representing the three estates emerged and demanded to be consulted. The French *Estates General* would not prove as successful as the English Parliament in limiting royal power; indeed, in early modern times it would become moribund for the better part of two centuries. But it would be revived in time to trigger the great French Revolution, which would turn that nation toward democracy.

In the vast central European area of Germany, the German or Holy Roman Emperors, as we have seen, failed to establish either central authority or the foundations of later representative government. The emperors could not tax the increasingly independent dukes, bishops, free cities, individual knights, or other autonomous powers who acknowledged a vague imperial suzerainty. Nor could they impose a single legal system on such a heterogeneous array of nominally subordinate powers, seven of whom—the "electors"—in fact had the power to choose each new emperor. In addition, debilitating struggles with the popes of Rome and unsuccessful efforts to impose imperial authority on the rich north Italian cities both distracted and weakened the emperors at home. In the end, the German emperors really *were* little more than "first among equals," exercising real authority only in their own dynastic lands.

Shadow rulers of hundreds of virtually independent princes, the German emperors entered the modern world with little but the prestige of an ancient title and a crown officially characterized as holy and allegedly descended from that of the Caesars. There would be no unified German nation until the later nineteenth century; and then it would be forged, not by the heirs of the medieval emperors, but by the descendants of one of the subordinate German princes of 1500, the electors of Brandenburg-Prussia.

THE POPES AND THE POWER OF THE KEYS

The power of barons in the countryside, business oligarchies in the cities, and the stronger kings in the nation as a whole could be great. But in some ways the power

Christ in glory, flanked by the Virgin Mary and the saints, judges both the quick and the dead. This relief from the facade of Autun Cathedral in France embodies the central conceptions of medieval Christian thought: Christ as Lord and Judge, and the concrete reality of heaven and hell. (Photograpahic Bulloz)

of the Catholic church—the power of the keys of heaven—was greater still. And the wielders of that vast power were the popes of Rome, the heads of the Roman Catholic church.

Because Saint Peter, the "rock" on whom Christ had said he would build his church, had been martyred in Rome, the popes, as bishops of Rome, claimed to be Peter's heirs. As successors to Peter, to whom the keys to heaven's gate had traditionally been confided, the popes wielded the vast power of spiritual life and death over Western Christians.

Some Roman popes even asserted a double legacy of authority, declaring themselves to be the custodians of the "two swords" of spiritual and secular sovereignty. They thus claimed supremacy not only in the Church but also over any earthly sovereign—a claim hotly contested, of course, by earthly sovereigns. On the basis of this religious supremacy, the papacy over the centuries built the most impressive of all medieval European institutions: the Roman Catholic church.

The papal administration of the High and later Middle Ages was larger and more sophisticated than that of any king or emperor. The wealth of the Church, which had been collecting tithes, fees, and contributions and receiving gifts and bequests from the faithful for centuries, was greater than that of any landed magnate, merchant prince, or monarch. The Church owned a good percentage of the land of western Europe, and cathedral spires dominated the skylines of medieval cities. Indeed, a significant proportion of the population of medieval Europe held holy orders or otherwise worked for the Church.

Popes contended on roughly equal terms with kings and emperors. Their weapons were the spiritual powers of excommunication and interdict—exclusion from membership in the Church and prohibition of the performance of essential religious ceremonies. Powerful popes such as Gregory VII in the eleventh century and Innocent III in the thirteenth could bring sovereigns as powerful as Philip Augustus to their knees by threatening to excommunicate them or by absolving their vassals of their feudal oaths of loyalty.

But Gregory was a great reformer of the Church as well, and Innocent labored as hard for Christian unity as he did to establish papal sovereignty over European rulers. In the end, the power of the medieval Church lay precisely in its grip on the hearts and minds of millions of ordinary Christians and its power to console and guide their spirits.

Not every hamlet and manor village had its priest, but most probably did. There were also thousands of monasteries and convents scattered over Europe, to which brotherhoods of monks and groups of nuns had withdrawn from worldly temptation to give their lives wholly to prayer and good works. Beginning in the High Middle Ages, Franciscan and Dominican friars wandered the roads begging their bread and helping with the Church's mission of saving souls.

The priests were frequently illiterate, the monasteries sometimes wealthy, and the Church's rule of celibacy not always obeyed. Yet despite endless satire and sermons aimed at Church abuses, the people of the Middle Ages valued their religion as no other Western society has. The most prominent architectural feature of any medieval city, after all, was neither the battlements of its baronial citadel nor its Gothic guildhall, but the towers and soaring spires of its cathedral.

WOMEN IN THE LATER MIDDLE AGES

In later medieval society as a whole, some scholars believe, women lost many of the independent opportunities and positions of authority that had earlier been theirs. This seems to have been so despite the presence of some immensely celebrated individual women in the annals of the Middle Ages.

Some noblewomen still administered and defended large feudal holdings in later medieval times. Such queens as Eleanor of Aquitaine might accompany their royal husbands on crusades or govern their own realms. And aristocratic and royal ladies played a central role in the emergence of the elaborate code of chivalry that was supposed to govern the conduct of the knightly classes.

In its earliest formulation, chivalry meant mostly such warrior virtues as courage, skill with weapons, fairness to one's foes, and loyalty to one's feudal superior. Church leaders urged protection of noncombatants, including women and of course the Church. Medieval ladies, however, guided the development of the most striking element of the chivalric code—the cult of courtly love. The truly chivalrous knight was thus encouraged, not only to protect women, but to love, serve, and revere a particular lady, usually from a distance. Troubadours and minstrels, medieval entertainers whose reward came from the lady who ran the noble household, were responsive to the tastes of their patronesses, singing songs of love and praising knights who served their ladies well. In southern France especially, ladies ran informal "courts of love" where young knights and ladies discussed this chivalric devotion in great detail.

At a less elevated level, middle-class women shared in the works and profits of the evolving urban guilds. Indeed, some guilds, including some devoted to the cloth and clothing industries, were actually run by women. In other guilds, women sometimes inherited and continued to operate their husbands' handicraft workshops. At the same time, in the agricultural villages where most people lived, women continued to bear their share of the burden of feeding the medieval world.

Modern historians, however, have detected some decline in the independent power of women in medieval times. As the Church strove to assert its authority over religious appointments and institutions, for instance, wealthy noblewomen lost their right to run the monastic institutions they founded or supported. In the realm of high politics, modifications in feudal practice required even queens and noblewomen to surrender control of their landed property to husbands or male guardians. Among the middle classes, dowries, which had once given women of the burgher class some leverage in a marriage, were increasingly turned over

The grandeur of Hagia Sophia, the sixth-century Church of the Holy Wisdom at Constantinople, excelled that of any other cathedral in Christendom when it was built by Emperor Justinian. Converted into a mosque and then a museum, the church is still one of the sights of modern Istanbul. (Art Resource)

entirely to their husbands. Finally, during the late medieval economic decline (which we shall discuss shortly), guilds frequently refused to allow women to operate shops or to work in places run by their fathers or husbands.

The later Middle Ages was a hard time for all, but perhaps hardest for medieval women.

 EASTERN EUROPE AND BEYOND

THE BYZANTINE EMPIRE

All this time, of course, there was another side of Christendom. In western Europe Christianity spoke Latin, and Christians looked for spiritual guidance to the pope of Rome. But in eastern Europe during the Middle Ages, the language of the Church was Greek, and the fount of

Christian consolation was the patriarch of Constantinople. To the eastern half of Christendom and the Byzantine Empire that was its heart we must now turn.

In many ways, medieval Byzantium and Western Christendom were historically opposite and complementary. Western Europe in the Middle Ages was comparatively practical, noisily disunited, and increasingly dynamic. The Byzantine Empire—or Eastern Roman Empire, as it was officially called—was more mystical, united by a rigid autocracy, and intensely conservative. Western Europe began the medieval period in the depths of a dark age and slowly evolved to a twelfth-century apogee. Byzantium's greatest age came at the beginning of the medieval period, during the sixth-century reign of the Emperor Justinian, and the later medieval centuries saw its greatest misfortunes.

Militarily there is also a striking contrast. In the early Middle Ages, Byzantium provided Western Europe with essential protection against pagan or Muslim inva-

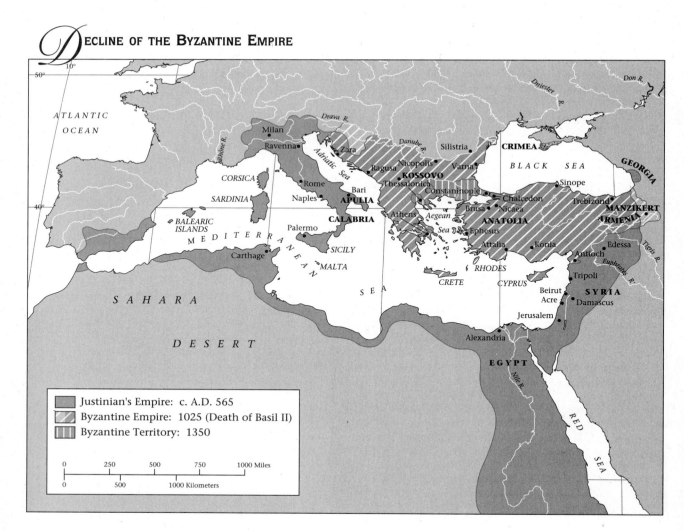

DECLINE OF THE BYZANTINE EMPIRE

Justinian's Empire: c. A.D. 565
Byzantine Empire: 1025 (Death of Basil II)
Byzantine Territory: 1350

sion from south and east; in later medieval times, Western Christian Crusaders first seized and looted Constantinople and later ignored Byzantine pleas for help until the Muslim Turks overwhelmed the empire.

The high point of Byzantine power and cultural creativity came under Emperor Justinian (527–565) and his formidable empress, Theodora, a former courtesan who put steel into the emperor's backbone when he needed it. Justinian's greatest effort went into a massive drive to reclaim the West from the barbarian. After decades of campaigning, his generals succeeded in overthrowing the Ostrogothic kingdom in Italy, the Visigoths in southern Spain, and the Vandals in North Africa. For a short time a "Roman" empire—this one ruled from Constantinople—almost girdled the Mediterranean once more.

Justinian is probably best known, however, for his sponsorship of an immense collection, abridgment, and codification of Roman law. Justinian's Code, as it is commonly called, passed Roman law on to medieval and modern Europe, where it proved extremely influential in shaping the law codes of many modern nations.

The greatest crisis of the reign, paradoxically, was a breakdown of law and order—the terrible Nika riots. This week-long outburst of popular violence saw leading political factions rise in protest against government corruption, burning and looting the heart of Constantinople. At one point Justinian was urged to flee the city for safety, but Theodora stiffened his courage by reminding him that the imperial purple would make a splendid winding sheet. Having resolved to live or die an emperor, he stayed and triumphed.

Justinian's greatest passion after the reconquest of the empire in the West was the Eastern Orthodox church. He built the largest church in Christendom in its honor—Hagia Sophia, the Church of the Holy Wisdom. With its marble and mosaics and its great dome, Hagia Sophia has been an awesome symbol for fourteen centuries of the splendor of Byzantium in the days of Justinian and Theodora.

For the next five hundred years, the Byzantine Empire remained proverbial for wealth, power, and military strength. Its emperor, served by a large and efficient bureaucracy, dominated his church, his nobility, and his people. So great was the power of the Byzantine emperors that one of their titles, *autokrator*, has come into modern languages as a synonym for absolute power—*autocrat*. The Byzantine army and navy, well trained and organized and equipped with such technological innovations as "Greek fire" (a flammable chemical substance sprayed on enemy ships) threw back wave after wave of would-be conquerors—Persians, Arabs, Turks, and many others. In so doing, Byzantium incidentally protected western Europe from foreign invasion during its weakest centuries.

Constantinople, controlling the bottleneck of east-west trade across Eurasia, became perhaps the richest city in the world during those centuries. From its famous harbor, the Golden Horn, Byzantine goldsmith work, Chinese silks, and Persian carpets reached Europe through the Italian trading cities. The Byzantine capital teemed with shrewd Greek and Levantine merchants and skilled artisans—a profit-hungry business community whose most popular leaders were monks!

With its palaces and churches rich with mosaic and gold leaf, Constantinople flourished down the medieval centuries, while Western Europe was slowly pulling itself out of mud huts and manor villages. Byzantines called their capital, located on a narrow peninsula protected by water and heavy walls, "the city protected by God." For many centuries it seemed that it was so.

Then in the early 1200s, an army of Norman Crusaders, encouraged by Venetians envious of the city's wealth, captured and looted Constantinople. And in 1453 the Ottoman Turkish sultan, Muhammad II, breached the ancient walls, killed the last emperor, and turned the Church of the Holy Wisdom into a mosque. The Eastern Roman Empire had finally fallen—a thousand years after the fall of the Empire of the West.

FROM KIEV TO MOSCOVY

The history of Eastern Europe is commonly neglected by European historians—a serious mistake, especially in a world that was divided for much of the twentieth century along a line that split Europe precisely into eastern and western halves. A few words, then, about Eastern Europe in these earliest centuries will be in order here.

Even in medieval times, Eastern Europe was never the land of cossacks, gypsies, and Transylvanian vampires of the popular Western imagination. Yet there were distinctive differences between the two halves of Europe long before our own century divided the continent. A prime source of these differences was the influence of Byzantine and later of Mongol culture on the Slavic population of Russia in particular. Slavic origins and Byzantine influences will be glanced at here, and Mongol influences deferred to Chapter 22.

The Slavs settled much of the eastern half of the continent from the Balkans to the Baltic, from predominantly German-speaking central Europe to what became European Russia. These Slavic herders and farmers soon came to be ruled by more warlike minorities—Bulgars and Avars from Asia and Vikings coming down the Russian rivers from the fjords of Scandinavia. The East Slavs, who had settled in what became Russia, were governed by a loose confederation of Viking princes known as Varangians. From their metropolis at Kiev, Varangians and Slavs voyaged down the Dnieper to the Black Sea and on to Byzantium to trade their wheat and honey, furs and amber for the luxury goods to be had in the bazaars of Constantinople.

From Constantinople, then, Eastern Europe in general and Russia in particular received the first impress of a more complex civilization toward the end of the early Middle Ages. But it was a set of cultural influences very different from those Rome had imprinted on Western Europe.

Byzantine missionaries carried Christianity to pagan Slavs, Varangians, and other East European peoples. Thus, the faith to which Russia was converted was the mystical, liturgical Greek Orthodox form of Christianity, with its particular reverence for monks and the lovely little sacred images called *ikons*, and its Byzantine sense of the emperor as head of the church as well as the state. Russia learned to write in the Greek-based Cyrillic alphabet devised by Byzantine missionaries rather than the Roman alphabet used in Western Europe, and Russian art echoed that of the Byzantines. And when the czarist Russian state began to take shape centuries later around Moscow, far to the north, the czars took upon themselves all the autocratic claims of Byzantine emperors in their prime.

The shift in the center of Russian power from Kiev in the southern grasslands to Moscow in the darkly forested north was precipitated by one of Russia's greatest historic catastrophes—the Mongol conquest of the thirteenth and fourteenth centuries. The impact of the Golden Horde on Russian development will be dealt with presently. One key consequence, however, should be stressed here. The primacy of Kiev, already weakened by feuds among the princes, was ended with its destruction by the Mongols. Leadership passed from the open steppes to the more defensible northern woodlands, and finally to the palisaded river city of Moscow. And Moscow, far from a now rapidly declining Constantinople, oriented its policy toward the Baltic and Western Europe, rather than the Black Sea and Byzantium, in centuries to come.

Yet the Byzantine influence lingered on. The Russian Orthodox church continued in the Byzantine pattern: monasteries owned huge tracts of land; the church supported the evolving monarchy (instead of feuding with it, as the popes did in Western Europe); and the people prayed devoutly before their ikons. The grand dukes—later czars—of Muscovy shaped their new nation on a hazily conceived model of Byzantine autocracy—with a dash of Mongol rigor. And when Constantinople fell to the Turks in 1453, the Moscow rulers took for their own state the title of "third Rome," the heir to both Byzantine civilization and to the imperial tradition of the ancient Caesars.

THE CRUSADES: REHEARSAL FOR EMPIRE

Medieval Christian civilization was in general a more dynamic, expansive culture than is often realized. Its growth was by no means as spectacular as that of Islam—whose story will begin in the next chapter—yet Christendom also spread outward from its Mediterranean and Western European base during the Middle Ages. It constituted not a single state or a static region of cultural predominance but an expanding zone of culture.

Christianity had spread to the limits of the Roman Empire during its last centuries. When Rome fell, the Roman and the Byzantine churches continued to reach out for new souls to save, converting new waves of barbar-

ians and reaching well beyond the Rhine-Danube line into areas the Romans had never penetrated. The new kingdoms that emerged in Europe also expanded, carrying developing medieval civilization with them. During the High Middle Ages, finally, international Christian armies of Crusaders marched on the Muslim lands of the eastern Mediterranean. Pious Christian missionaries and aggressive monarchs, land-hungry barons and peasants, Crusaders driven by piety or greed, and merchants seeking commercial footholds in the Levant—all contributed to the beginnings of a European expansion that would one day astonish the world.

Some of these expansive forces have already been illustrated. We have seen how the far-reaching conquests of Charlemagne carried Frankish rule beyond the eastern frontiers of the former Roman Empire. Missionaries such as Cyril drove a wedge for Byzantine civilization into Russia. The economic expansion of the High Middle Ages stimulated the spread of manorial agriculture over the Pyrenees into Muslim Spain and especially to Slavic Eastern Europe. The latter movement was the beginning of the *Drang nach Osten*, or "drive toward the East," of German-speaking central Europeans.

The medieval European Crusades, finally, accomplished little in the way of territorial expansion. But they did set in motion a Western outreach that would in later centuries swell into the greatest wave of imperial conquest in history.

The beginnings were small enough. The First Crusade began in 1095, sending tens of thousands of Christian holy warriors swarming into the Near East to liberate from Islam the lands where Christ had lived. The movement was triggered by a plea from the Byzantine emperor for help against the Muslim Turks, and was encouraged by Pope Urban II's assurances that the liberation of the Holy Land from the infidels was a good work in God's eyes. Other important causes included such nonreligious factors as population pressures in Europe, land hunger, and the restless ambitions of European nobles.

The First Crusaders did "liberate" Jerusalem, massacring most of its Jewish and Muslim population in the process. They then set up a series of Crusader States stretching along the eastern end of the Mediterranean from Gaza through Lebanon. European pilgrim traffic, Italian trading colonies, and a steady flow of men and money maintained this Western toehold in the Near East for two hundred years (though Jerusalem fell to the famous Muslim leader Saladin in less than a century). European taste for Asian spices and other luxury goods and Christian zeal for spreading the faith by force of arms were both whetted by the Crusades. The Western money economy of the High Middle Ages was stimulated by the expanded trade with the East, and Europeans learned to tax themselves and to organize large-scale overseas ventures while mounting these international military campaigns.

All the later Crusades were costly failures, however,

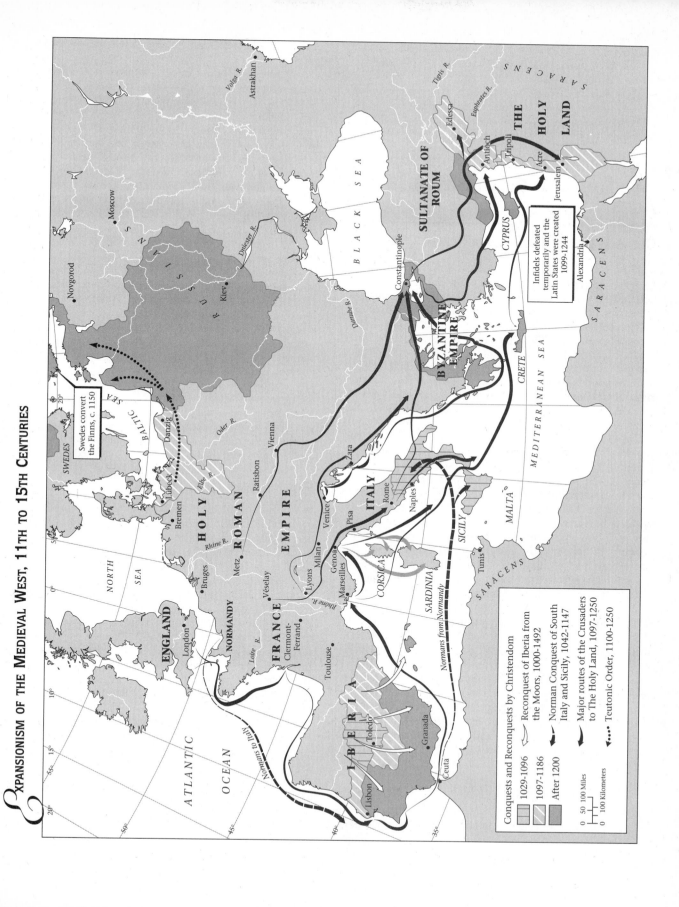

EXPANSIONISM OF THE MEDIEVAL WEST, 11TH TO 15TH CENTURIES

ATLANTIC OCEAN

NORTH SEA

BALTIC SEA

SWEDES

Swedes convert the Finns, c. 1150

Novgorod

Moscow

Astrakhan

Volga R.

R U S S I A N S

Kiev

Dnieper R.

Dniester R.

BLACK SEA

SULTANATE OF ROUM

THE HOLY LAND

Tigris R.

Euphrates R.

S A R A C E N S

Edessa

Antioch

Tripoli

Acre

Jerusalem

Alexandria

CYPRUS

Infidels defeated temporarily and the Latin States were created 1099-1244

BYZANTINE EMPIRE

Constantinople

Danube R.

CRETE

MEDITERRANEAN SEA

MALTA

S A R A C E N S

SICILY

Tunis

Ceuta

SARDINIA

CORSICA

Rome

Naples

ITALY

Genoa

Pisa

Venice

Milan

Zara

Marseilles

Lyons

Rhône R.

FRANCE

Clermont-Ferrand

Toulouse

Vézelay

Metz

NORMANDY

ENGLAND

London

Loire R.

Rhine R.

Bruges

Bremen

Lübeck

Danzig

Elbe R.

Oder R.

Ratisbon

Vienna

HOLY ROMAN EMPIRE

IBERIA

Lisbon

Toledo

Granada

Normans to Italy

Normans from Normandy

Conquests and Reconquests by Christendom

| 1029-1096 |
| 1097-1186 |
| After 1200 |

Reconquest of Iberia from the Moors, 1000-1492

Norman Conquest of South Italy and Sicily, 1042-1147

Major routes of the Crusaders to The Holy Land, 1097-1250

Teutonic Order, 1100-1250

0   50   100 Miles
0   100 Kilometers

and the movement dwindled to talk and minor skirmishes after 1250. It would be another two and a half centuries before Europeans would again reach out for spices and converts, land and booty, beyond the confines of their own end of Eurasia. But the dynamism, the organizing ability, the ruthlessness, courage, and greed of the West had been demonstrated in this first rehearsal for empire.

 # The End of the Middle Ages

God's Heavy Flail—or a Time of Change?

Like their spiritual ancestors, the ancient Hebrews, medieval people believed that their misfortunes were divine punishments for their sins. Even nomadic invaders such as the Huns and the Mongols were "the scourge of God" laid across Christian shoulders. From this medieval perspective, God's heavy flail fell more fiercely and with more devastating effect than ever before during the fourteenth and fifteenth centuries—the period described by the Dutch historian Johan Huizinga as the autumn of the Middle Ages.

After the splendid achievements of the High Middle Ages in the twelfth and thirteenth centuries, the next century and a half was a trough indeed. Disaster struck all major segments of society, decimated the population, plunged the economy into a long depression. It was, in many important ways the end of an era, and the modern age that emerged from its ashes would be a different world.

Yet in dealing with the end of the Middle Ages, as with its beginnings, recent scholarship has come to see this period as a time of transition rather than one of cataclysm. Between 1300 and 1500, important medieval institutions suffered massive setbacks, often accompanied by traumatic experiences for large segments of the population. Plagues, wars, popular rebellions, economic turmoil, and struggles between rival claimants to the papacy itself scarred the lives of generations of Europeans. But there was a revival too, a recovery from these disasters that was well under way by 1500, when the modern world was clearly emerging. What must have felt like divine punishment to many also stimulated a surge of creative restructuring that produced the modern age.

We will look here for the most part at the negative side of this period of transition from medieval to modern. The story of Europe's revival and embarkation upon more expansive ventures will be reserved for later chapters focusing on modern times.

Schism and War

The papacy fell into the deepest decline of its history during this period. The linked crises of the Babylonian Captivity and the Great Schism filled the century from 1305 to 1415.

The Babylonian Captivity—the name deriving from a fancied parallel with the Hebrews' ancient captivity in Babylon—was the Avignon papacy of the fourteenth century. During this period the popes, once so powerfully independent, fell under the influence of French kings, lived at Avignon in southern France, and became a byword in Christendom for extortionate greed. The Schism followed soon after. For several decades around 1400, there were two and even three claimants at a time to the throne of St. Peter, each excommunicating his rivals, and further degrading the Church in the eyes of bewildered and increasingly cynical Christians.

There were other disasters during this long season of Europe's discontent.

For more than a century England and France, the most successful of the medieval monarchies, mired themselves in the long agony of the Hundred Years War (1337–1453). The great early victories won by the English longbow—Crécy, Poitiers, Agincourt—go into every English schoolchild's notebook, as Joan of Arc's later heroism does on the French side of the Channel. In fact, the protracted conflict devastated France in the fourteenth century and drained England in the fifteenth. The success of the longbow—which could pierce a knight's chain mail at a hundred yards—marked the beginning of the end of the baronial cavalry as masters of European battlefields. The marauding of mercenary companies and of rebellious peasants added to the havoc of this worst of medieval wars.

Plague and Depression

In the middle of the fourteenth century, meanwhile, an even more terrible calamity befell Europe as a whole. It came with the shiny little fleas that infested a species of black ship rat brought up the Mediterranean from Byzantium or the Black Sea. It was the Black Death.

The Black Death was an excruciatingly painful, almost inevitably fatal, and extremely contagious disease, technically known as bubonic plague. After ravaging the cities of China and traveling west along the caravan routes, the plague struck Europe first in 1348 and ravaged its populations repeatedly for three centuries thereafter. During this first horrifying visitation at the end of the Middle Ages, the plague may have killed a quarter of Europe's people. The population growth of the preceding centuries ended with a crash.

Add to all these catastrophes the deep Europe-wide depression that began in the middle of the fourteenth century, in part as a result of the wars and the plague. The economic hard times shattered the boom of the high-medieval commercial revolution and plunged the European economy into turmoil for a hundred years.

Drastic reduction in the size of the population raised the cost of labor, cut production, and thus inflated the prices of the goods that were produced. Landowners suffered from the high cost of labor, consumers from rising prices. In response, landholders often turned from farming to less labor-intensive sheep raising, while governments at all levels tried to fix both wages and prices. Another expression of this conservative reaction was the organization of protective associations of cities like the German Hanseatic League, dedicated to defending their own economic interests in a shrunken economic arena.

There was a more positive response to the economic upheaval as well, however. The workers who survived the plagues and famines, for example, earned much higher wages than before; merchants profited from rising prices; and sheep raising proved quite lucrative for many landowners. Some alert entrepreneurs, furthermore, adapted to changing times with more flexible business organization and with real technological innovations. In mining, metallurgy, printing, and ship building, lost labor was replaced with labor-saving devices that made these industries considerably more efficient. A new economic order would thus take shape in early modern times. But the upheaval itself must have been enormously painful for most who experienced it.

Thus, the Middle Ages ground to an end in western Europe, to the wail of penitent flagellants lashing each other along the roads, in waves of heresy and a din of prophecies of the coming end of the world. By this time medieval memory reached back only hazily to the Fall of Rome. But the fifteenth-century Europeans who did see that far into their past must have felt a disturbing sense of déjà vu. Confronted with images of the Apocalypse glowing darkly on the walls of churches and the Dance of Death—skeletal figures leading knight, burgher, and peasant to the grave—a staple of the newborn printing press, late-medieval people must have felt that they were living through another Judgment Day.

MEDIEVAL CHRISTIAN CULTURE

THE DAUGHTER OF GOD

The Christian religion was the pulsing heart of medieval European culture. And there is no better illustration of the power of religious belief in medieval life than the briefly glorious but tragic career of Jeanne d'Arc—Joan of Arc— one of the most amazing of medieval saints.

The familiar story can be retold in a couple of paragraphs. Born in a small village in northeastern France early in the fifteenth century, Saint Joan grew up illiterate and pious in the middle of the Hundred Years War. In 1429, at the age of seventeen, she began to hear the voices of angels telling her to go forth and save her country from

Joan of Arc's brief, meteroic career did not include time out to sit for portraits. This modern rendering, however, tries to give a sense of the youth, vigor, and naïve piety of this most beloved of medieval French saints. Can you imagine this Joan as an athlete today, or an officer in a modern army? (Library of Congress)

the unending ravages of the wars. With the simplicity of total belief, she thereupon set off for the court of Charles VII, where she miraculously picked that unimpressive— and as yet uncrowned—monarch out of a crowd of his own courtiers. Even more astonishing, she then convinced the unhappy French king that she should be allowed to ride off with the troops currently gathering for a major confrontation with the English.

Inspired by the Maid, as she was universally called, the disheartened French rallied. Joan's soldiers lifted the siege of Orleans—a key French bastion— defeated the English repeatedly, and swept triumphantly through to Reims. There, in the heart of English-held territory, in July of 1429, Charles VII was at last formally crowned King of France in a traditional ceremony in Reims cathedral.

Thus anointed with holy oil by the Church, Charles could look forward to a new loyalty from his people, who everywhere began to flock to the king's support against the English. Joan, hearing no more from her angelic voices, deemed her mission accomplished and wanted to return home. But she was too potent a symbol to be let go. She was kept in service and sent off to hearten the French troops then marching on Paris, which the English still held.

Here, however, fortune turned against the Maid. The attack on Paris failed. Joan was captured by England's Burgundian allies, sold by them to the English, tried for witchcraft by a subservient ecclesiastical court, and burned at the stake in Rouen in 1431.

Joan of Arc's entire public career lasted only two years, and half that time was spent in prison after her capture. Yet she remains one of the most fascinating and enigmatic of medieval people. She was an astonishing anomaly: a peasant knight, a woman leading soldiers into battle. Though she did not actually command the armies, she was fearless, had a charismatic capacity to stir her troops to new efforts, and displayed a wonderful knack for showing up in the thick of the fray at precisely the right time to turn the tide. Above all, she believed completely in her voices—Saint Catherine and the archangel Michael—and in the unheard-of task they called her to perform.

In this, at least, she was completely typical of her time. The English called her "a disciple and limb of the Fiend"; she insisted that her voices called her a "daughter of God."[4] But no one in that far distant century questioned the reality of the supernatural presences that urged her on.

FAITH AND FANATICISM

The mind of the Middle Ages was as thoroughly dominated by religion as were the minds of ancient Egyptians, Hindu Indians, or Europe's own Muslim neighbors. During the medieval centuries, the simple faith of a Saint Joan mingled with the savage fanaticism of the Inquisition and the burners of witches and heretics. From this mixture came the profound religious thought, the great art, and the moving literature of the Western World's great age of faith.

The doctrines of the developed medieval church went far beyond the simple teachings of Jesus of Nazareth. Jesus's basic message remained central: Christ the Son of God still offered eternal life to those who believed. The Pauline virtues of faith in Christ, hope of salvation, and charity toward one's neighbor were still preached. But there was much more now.

Medieval priests catechized Christians on more elaborate creeds established by Church councils over the centuries. God was the Three-in-One—Father, Son, and Holy Ghost. There were seven deadly sins—pride, greed, envy, sexual self-indulgence, violence, laziness, and gluttony. Heaven, hell, and purgatory (a halfway house for purging away modest quantities of sin) were minutely anatomized, with all their angelic and demonic caretakers.

Religious duties were central to every human life. The seven sacraments brought religion into the lives of Christians at crucial points in the life cycle, sanctifying birth with baptism, coming-of-age with confirmation, marriage with matrimony, and death with extreme unction.

The sacraments also provided penance and absolution for sins freely confessed, conferred spiritual powers on priests through ordination, and celebrated the communion of believers with their Savior in the central Christian mystery of the Mass.

But there was always that other side to the age of faith. There was the fanaticism that produced popular pogroms against Jews and official persecution of heretics, witches, and others believed to be in league with Satan. The Holy Office of the Inquisition, which was charged with maintaining the purity of Christian thought, used the most unscrupulous methods, including torture, to get confessions from those accused of heresy. Incorrigible enemies of Christ were turned over to the secular authorities to be burned alive in public marketplaces.

A faith founded on the love of God thus sponsored the cruel persecution of all who rejected its tennets. It was a feature of many creeds, past and yet to come, which claimed to offer universal truths to humankind.

THE TWELFTH-CENTURY RENAISSANCE

It is evident that medieval religion was far from a simple matter. The Christian leaders of the High Middle Ages, in fact, devoted their most intense intellectual efforts to making sense out of their immense and complex religious heritage. And they produced one of the major intellectual triumphs of Western history: the scholastic synthesis of the Twelfth-Century Renaissance.

Dubbed a *renaissance*, or "rebirth," by historians after the more famous cultural revival of the fifteenth century, this medieval cultural flowering was actually a remarkably original synthesis. It took ancient materials—Greek philosophy and science, Roman law, and above all the revealed truths of the Judeo-Christian religious tradition—and wove them into something original and profound.

Paradoxically, this first recovery of Greco-Roman ideas came to Christian Europeans mostly by way of their archenemies, the Muslims. The culture of Islam had flowered several centuries before that of Christendom and had absorbed the wisdom of the restless Greek mind during the Muslim conquest of Byzantine territories in the Near East. Greek books had then traveled across North Africa to Muslim Spain at the other end of the Mediterranean. Here, in the flourishing cultural centers of Córdoba and Toledo, Christian scholars from western Europe had come to study the pre-Christian philosophy of Aristotle at the feet of learned followers of the non-Christian Prophet Muhammad!

European scholars thus recovered the mathematics, astronomy, and medical ideas of the ancient Greeks and—from Byzantium directly—Justinian's Code of Roman law. Most important, they immersed themselves in the encyclopedic writings of Aristotle, "the master of those who know" in medieval times. From these varied sources St. Anselm drew arguments for the primacy of Christian faith, while Abelard raised probing questions that strengthened

---

[4]Joseph R. Strayer and Dana C. Munro, *The Middle Ages: 395–1500* (New York: Appleton-Century-Crofts, 1959), p. 486.

the structure of belief it subjected to challenge. The beloved St. Bernard condemned the immoralities of his age, and St. Thomas Aquinas summed up the knowledge of his age in a vast structure of Christian thought.

To study and spread this newly acquired knowledge, medieval scholars invented the university. In the twelfth and thirteenth centuries, these associations of teachers and students, operating in rented halls or in churches, sprang up in many cities in western Europe. They taught undergraduates rhetoric, law, and above all Aristotle's logic, while graduate faculties gave professional training in law, medicine, and the queen of the sciences, theology. For it was in theological speculation, explored with the help of Aristotelian logic, that medieval thinkers made their greatest contributions to the history of Western thought.

Anselm and Abelard, the eloquent preacher Saint Bernard, and even the most honored of medieval thinkers, Thomas Aquinas, are not household words today. Yet in their learned lectures and their volumes of abstruse theology, they accomplished something that our finest minds

have yet to manage. By applying Aristotelian rigor to their inherited Christian insights, they achieved a remarkable synthesis of faith and reason. Even more impressive, they produced a coherent view of the world that was rationally and emotionally acceptable—indeed inspiring—to the simplest peasant and the deepest doctor of theology. They anatomized in convincing detail a world made by God's fiat, guided by God's providence, yet comprehensible by human minds and deeply moving to the human heart.

THE ART OF THE CATHEDRALS

Between 1050 and 1350 no less than eighty cathedrals and hundreds of churches of comparable size and grandeur were built in France alone. They were not built by the people themselves, exalted mobs of true believers with kings and commoners pulling together on the ropes, as romantic historiography once believed. The cathedrals were raised over long, slow decades by master builders, skilled architects who called themselves masons and who

Chartres Cathedral was one of the most beautiful of the hundreds of great churches built to the glory of Mary the Mother of God during the later medieval centuries. It is seen here as it must have looked then, towering above the cobbled streets and peaked roofs of a medieval town. The two towers flanking the portals in front, built at different times are very different in design. (Photo Researchers, Inc.)

hired the best medieval artisans to make God's house a thing of beauty. These towering Christian temples, dedicated to the Virgin Mary, still constitute the finest expression we have of the religious spirit of the age of faith.

The image of Paris's Notre Dame leaps quickly to mind, of course. But it is well to remember that not all the great churches of the Middle Ages were gothic, like Notre Dame de Paris. There were many lovely romanesque cathedrals in the earlier medieval centuries, built with round instead of pointed arches, mural paintings instead of stained-glass windows. There were also Eastern Orthodox churches, from Constantinople to Kiev and Moscow, built with wide domes instead of spires, gold leaf and mosaic decorating their labyrinthine interiors. And there is as much beauty and spirituality in Constantinople's Church of the Holy Wisdom as there is in Paris's more familiar Church of Our Lady.

Nevertheless, the great gothic churches built in western Europe in the High Middle Ages remain the most celebrated artistic achievements of the age. Rising hundreds of feet above the rooftops and the cobblestoned streets of the medieval city below, gothic cathedrals such as those of Paris or Chartres, Salisbury or Cologne (not completed until the nineteenth century) were marvels of architectural skill and daring. The basic ground plan was a cross, with the altar at the crossing and a single soaring spire rising above it. The longest arm of the cross was the nave, where the faithful gathered for worship. At the foot of the nave stood the two main portals, flanked on either side by two huge towers with a belfry for summoning the worshipers.

Lofty verticality was the keynote of the gothic style. Pointed gothic arches, clustered pillars, and ribbed vaulting support a thin fabric of stone and glass many stories high. This immense height and the weight of the roof was supported by graceful external braces called flying buttresses. All of it, finally—towers and buttresses, inside and out—was thick with restless gothic decoration: statuary, carved wood, stained glass, finials and spires, kings, saints, and gargoyles. This too was a hallmark of the gothic—abhorence of empty space, so that every inch is filled with intricately interwoven shapes.

The other arts of the medieval period clustered about the churches. Stone figures flanking the deepset portals combine convincingly real faces with robes whose folds blend into the verticality of the surrounding pillars. Along the walls, high arched windows ablaze with stained glass trace scenes from the Bible or the lives of the saints. Under the seats in the choir, animals and humans, bunches of grapes, and leering demons show what the art of the wood-carver could do. Even the great handmade Bible in the lectern was bright with illuminated capitals and glowing illustrations of events that happened long ago and far away in fairy-tale places with names such as Jerusalem and Bethlehem, Golgotha and Galilee.

The walls and columns and gothic arches of medieval cathedrals, dark now with the soot and grime of two industrial centuries, were once white with the rawness of fresh-cut stone. There is a certain slant of afternoon light that can bring back that earlier time—and with it some of the spiritual refreshment of an age that had much need of such consolation.

MEDIEVAL LITERATURE: ROLAND'S HORN, DANTE'S HELL, AND THE CANTERBURY PILGRIMS

Most of the serious religious literature of the Middle Ages, in Western Europe at least, was written in Latin and thus inaccessible to most medieval people. But in the High and later Middle Ages, some impressive popular literature began to appear in the vernaculars—the living languages of modern Europe. Most of this writing was in verse, and the religious element was often powerfully present (two strikes against it for many modern readers). Nevertheless, there is a life to the work of Chaucer or Dante or the unknown author(s) of *The Song of Roland* that is hard to find in the staider, more respectable writing of the time.

The Song of Roland is one of many French "songs of deeds," long epic war poems sung in the halls of medieval barons, much as Homeric bards sang of the deeds of Greek and Trojan heroes to the warlords of an earlier age. It is the story of the heroic death of Roland, one of Charlemagne's mythic paladins, the French equivalent of King Arthur's knights of the round table. Ambushed in the pass of Roncesvalles in the high Pyrenees while returning from a raid into Muslim Spain, Roland and his knights—the rear guard of Charlemagne's army—are massacred to the last man. Almost to the last moment the chivalrous Roland refuses to blow his great horn Olifant, whose high clear note echoing among the crags would bring Charlemagne and the main body of the French host galloping to the rescue. When Roland's horn is blown at last, it summons the Christian cavalry only to bury their dead—and guarantees chivalric immortality for Roland and his horn.

With the Italian poet Dante Alighieri, we follow the medieval spirit to the other side of death, into the Christian otherworlds beyond the grave. Dante's *Divine Comedy*, an epic poem on the afterlife, traces the poet's imaginary descent into hell, the inferno at the center of the earth, up the steep slopes of purgatory on the other side of the world, and on beyond the stars into the radiance of paradise. It is a journey thick with history and symbol, told in musical Italian verse. Yet it is Dante's inferno, that "nation of the lost," that has always fascinated modern readers.[5] It is a lurid vision of living souls wrapped in agony, punctuated with vivid flashbacks to the

---

[5]Dante Alighieri, *The Divine Comedy*, trans. Thomas G. Bergin (New York: Appleton-Century-Crofts, 1955), p. 8.

world above and the sins that have doomed these men and women to their eternal torment. Even in our calloused age, this plunge into the nightmare geography of the pit, the deepest netherworld of the medieval imagination, is not to be undertaken lightly.

But there was a world above, birdsong and spring flowers glittering with dew along the road to Canterbury—the world of the English poet Geoffrey Chaucer's *Canterbury Tales*. Among the company that assemble at the Tabard Inn in the London suburb of Southwark for the short spring pilgrimage to the cathedral at Canterbury are representatives of all walks of medieval life. The merchant, the friar, and the Oxford university student, the nun and the much-married wife of Bath, the earthy miller and the "gentle, perfect knight" all have their characteristic tales to tell to help pass the journey. The wit, variety, and high good humor of the whole remind us finally that there was more in the medieval mind than crusades and hellfire. There were bawdy tales, high ideals, and busy worldly lives to be led, even in the shadow of cathedral spires.

SUMMARY

The period of European medieval history, once dismissed as a barbaric "middle age" between the cultural peaks of ancient and modern history, is no longer seen in that way. The European Middle Ages actually represent the rise and fall of a great independent civilization: the culture of medieval Christendom.

The European Dark Age that followed immediately upon the Fall of Rome was admittedly a hard time of political and social disintegration, poverty, and violence. To deal with waves of invasion, Europeans developed the feudal system, a loose structure of political power based on military service in return for land. To survive after the collapse of Western trade, Europeans evolved the manor system of subsistence agriculture. Rude empires even emerged from time to time, the most famous being the Carolingian Empire of Charlemagne, who was crowned on Christmas Day, 800.

During the High Middle Ages—the eleventh, twelfth, and thirteenth centuries—European society and culture experienced a brilliant revival. Thanks in large part to the reemergence of trade by land and sea, great cities appeared in Europe once more. Kings, by imposing their will on the feudal barons, began the building of modern nation-states in France, England, Spain, and elsewhere. And the Roman Catholic church, led by powerful popes and fueled by the passionate belief of many medieval people, became the most impressive single institution in Western Christendom.

In East Europe and on the fringes of the Middle East, both autocratic imperial government and Greek Orthodox Christianity were centered in Constantinople. This strongly centralized Byzantine Empire spread Christianity and civilization in East Europe, provided economic stimulation, and survived for a thousand years, from the fifth to the fifteenth century. Muscovy, the core of the future Russian state, emerged at the end of the Middle Ages, modeling its political and religious institutions on those of fallen Byzantium.

The Crusades of the High Middle Ages represented Europe's first rehearsal for the great overseas imperial expansion of modern times. But in the fourteenth and fifteenth centuries, medieval society collapsed in a welter of economic disaster, plague, wars, and religious schism.

At its peak, however, medieval Christendom was an impressive cultural achievement in its own right. Built on a mixture of ardent faith and sometimes savage fanaticism, the culture of the Middle Ages was as intensely religious as any the world has seen. The Twelfth-Century Renaissance provided rigorous intellectual underpinnings for medieval Christianity in the scholastic philosophy of Thomas Aquinas. The great church builders of the age raised cathedral spires over hundreds of European cities. The poetry of Dante, Chaucer, and other medieval writers reflected a culture in which this world and the Christian "other world" met and mingled in the minds of Western people.

SUGGESTED READING

ALIGHIERI, Dante. *The Divine Comedy*, ed. and trans. T. G. Bergin. New York: Appleton-Century-Crofts, 1955. Many other translations of the greatest medieval epic are available.

ALLMAND, C. *The Hundred Years War: England and France at War, c.1300–c.1450.* New York: Cambridge University Press, 1988. Concise topical treatment, including a clear and brief summary of the military campaigns.

ATIYA, A. S. *Crusade, Commerce, and Culture.* Bloomington: Indiana University Press, 1962. Impact of Christendom's holy wars on European society.

BARTLETT, R. *The Making of Europe: Conquest, Colonization, and Cultural Change 950–1350.* Princeton: Princeton University Press, 1993. Impressive social and cultural overview of the High Middle Ages.

BROWNING, R. *Justinian and Theodora.* New York: Praeger, 1971. Does not assign Theodora as much weight in the partnership as some do. On the empress, see C. Diehl, *Theodora: Empress of Byzantium* (New York: Friederich Unger, 1972).

CANTOR, N. F. *Inventing the Middle Ages.* New York: Morrow, 1991. Provocative account of the "lives, works, and ideas" of recent medieval historians.

DUBY, G. *The Early Growth of the European Economy: Warriors and Peasants from the Seventh to the Twelfth Century*, trans. H. B. Clarke. Ithaca, N.Y.: Cornell University Press, 1974. Economic life from the feudal age to the revival of trade and towns.

———, ed. *A History of Private Life,* Vol. 2: *Revelation of the Medieval World*, trans. A. Goldhammer. Cambridge, Mass.: Belknap Press, 1988. Social and cultural aspects of the private lives of French and Italian people, lavishly illustrated.

FOSSIER, R. ed. *The Cambridge Illustrated History of the Middle Ages*, trans. S. H. Tenison. 3 vols. New York: Cambridge University Press, 1987. Includes a more extensive treatment of eastern Europe and of the southern margins of medieval Christendom than is usual, and some rare pictures. See also N. Cantor, *Medieval History: The Life and Death of a Civilization.* New York: Macmillan, 1963. Sees medieval Christendom as a self-contained culture, rather than as an interlude.

GANSHOF, F. L. *Feudalism*, trans. P. Grierson. London: Longman's, 1964. A standard source. For a brief introduction by an eminent scholar, see J. Strayer, *Feudalism* (New York: Van Nostrand, 1965).

GEIS, F., and J. GEIS. *Women in the Middle Ages.* New York: Crowell, 1978. Combines a general outline of the condition of women with profiles of exemplary medieval women, from Queen Blanche to "Piers Plowman's Wife." See also M. W. Lebarge, *A Small Sound of the Trumpet: Women in Medieval Life* (Boston: Beacon Press, 1988).

GOTTFRIED, R. S. *The Black Death: Natural and Human Disaster in Medieval Europe.* New York: Free Press, 1983. Ecological analysis of the plague and its impact on society.

HUIZINGA, J. *The Waning of the Middle Ages.* Garden City, N.Y.: Doubleday, 1956. Vivid evocation of late medieval culture dating from the 1920s.

LABARGE, M. W. *A Small Sound of the Trumpet: Women in Medieval Life.* Boston: Beacon Press, 1986. Vigorous evocation of women's lives in western Europe in the High and later Middle Ages. M. C. Howell, *Women, Production, and Patriarchy in Late Medieval Cities* (Chicago: University of Chicago

Press, 1986) sees a decline in women's economic position in the later Middle Ages.

LE GOFF, J. *The Medieval Imagination*, trans. A. Goldhammer. Chicago: University of Chicago Press, 1988. Challenging probe of the medieval mind through analysis of changing words and conflicting intellectual structures.

MAYER, H. E. *The Crusades.* New York: Oxford University Press, 1988. Thorough updating of an excellent one-volume survey. See also N. Housley, *The Later Crusades 1274–1380* (New York: Oxford University Press, 1992), on the crusades of the thirteenth and fourteenth centuries.

MUNDY, J. H. *Europe in the High Middle Ages.* New York: Basic Books, 1973. A good overview.

MUSSET, L. *The Germanic Invasions: The Making of Europe, A.D. 400–600,* trans. E. and C. James. University Park: Pennsylvania State University Press, 1975. Fine recent survey of the earlier Germanic incursions.

PANOFSKY, E. *Gothic Architecture and Scholasticism.* Latrobe, Pa.: Archabbey Press, 1951. A classic essay comparing the underlying principles of these two expressions of the medieval world view.

PHILIPS, J. R. S. *The Medieval Expansion of Europe.* Oxford, England: Oxford University Press, 1988. Valuable summary of European contact with and information about Asia, Africa, and America during the later Middle Ages.

RUSSELL, J. B. *A History of Medieval Christianity: Prophecy and Order.* New York: Crowell, 1968. Older but readable and authoritative history of the medieval church.

SAWYER, P. H. *Kings and Vikings: Scandinavia and Europe, A.D. 700–1100.* New York: Metheun, 1982. The Viking age in European history.

STUARD, S. M. *Women in Medieval History and Historiography.* Philadelphia: University of Pennsylvania Press, 1987. Useful overview of recent trends in medieval women's history.

TURBERVILLE, A. S. *Medieval Heresy and the Inquisition.* Hamden, Conn.: Archon Books, 1964. Fair evaluation. R. I. Moore, *The Formation of a Persecuting Society: Power and Deviance in Western Europe, 950–1250* (New York: Basil Blackwell, 1987), views religious and other persecution as intrinsic to the society of the high Middle Ages.

WARNER, M. *Joan of Arc: The Image of Female Heroism.* New York: Knopf, 1981. Feminist interpretation of the enigmatic Maid.

CHAPTER 18

THE MUSLIM CENTER

THE PROPHET AND THE HOLY WAR

Muhammad, the Messenger of God
The Teachings of the Prophet
Jihad: The First Muslim Holy War

THE ARAB EMPIRE

The Caliphs: Successors to the Prophet
The Omayyads
The Abbasids
The Splendors of Baghdad

THE FAITH AND ART OF ISLAM

The Koran, the Law, and the Five Pillars of Islam
The Sufi Tradition: Ecstasies and Trances
Islamic Art: Mosques and Minarets
Arab Literature: Poems and Tales
Philosophy and Science: Knowledge Lights
the Way to Heaven

THE PROPHET AND THE HOLY WAR

MUHAMMAD, THE MESSENGER OF GOD

Muhammad the Messenger of God (570–632) lived six centuries after Jesus Christ, twelve centuries after Gautama Buddha. He became the prophet of Islam, the last of the great world religions to emerge in history thus far.

Muhammad was born in Mecca, an oasis city on the caravan routes of western Arabia about forty miles from the Red Sea. It was a busy town, full of merchants, handicraft artisans, and pilgrims. The caravans came and went, carrying silks and spices, frankincense, and other luxury products to and from Damascus, Byzantium, Basra. But Mecca was also a religious center. Its central temple, the odd cubical structure called the Kaaba, contained a mysterious black stone that God—Allah in Arabic—was believed to have cast down from heaven, as well as idols dedicated to a number of other gods, to *jinn* and desert demons.

Beyond Mecca, with its gardens and bustling markets, the sea of sand began: shifting sand hills, dry *wadis*, and the desolate crags of the Najd, the Exhausted Land. Here roamed restless tribes of bedouin—the desert Arabs, herding their flocks, conducting their blood feuds, swooping down on hapless caravans.

It was a world not much changed from Jesus's time, or the time of the Hebrew prophets. It was about to produce a third great religion, and one integrally related to Judaism and Christianity. Muhammad never claimed to be the first Prophet—only the last.

Muhammad, the son of Abdullah, son of Abdul Muttalib, of the tribe of Qureysh, was orphaned early in life and had to make his own way in the marketplaces of Mecca. He probably traveled with the caravans, perhaps as far as Palestine, and picked up the rudiments of the religions of Moses and Jesus there. At twenty-five he married a wealthy and intelligent woman fifteen years older than himself, who gave him a modest place among the Meccan merchants, to whom he was known as *Al Amin*, the Trustworthy. According to Islamic tradition, he was a husky man with a black beard and fair skin, a hooked nose and black, luminous eyes. An upright, sometimes melancholy man, he was given to long silences.

At the age of forty, meditating in a cave outside the town, he had his first vision. "Read!" a voice thundered. "I cannot read," replied Muhammad, who was apparently illiterate. "Read!" the voice intoned twice more. And then, beyond the cave mouth, the Arab saw standing in the sky an angelic figure who spoke once more: "O Muhammad! Thou art Allah's Messenger, and I am Gabriel."[1] The "reading" of the divine message to the world ("recitation" or even "speaking forth" are perhaps better renderings of the original Arabic) occupied Muhammad for the rest of his life and was preserved for the Islamic world in the verses of the Koran. For countless millions of Muslims, the visions of Muhammad would constitute God's final Message to humankind.

He was at first a prophet without honor in his own country, ridiculed and dismissed as mad or possessed. Some of the poor listened to his revelations, and his wife, Khadijah, stood staunchly behind her husband. He also won the support of a wealthy merchant named Abu Bakr, and Omar, a leading citizen of Mecca. A persecutor of Muhammad in the early days, Omar was to become his most effective successor as leader of Arabic Islam.

For the time being, however, his enemies prevailed. In 622 Muhammad fled from Mecca, taking his prophecies north to the oasis city known today as Medina. He was then a man in his fifties, and the black beard must have been at least flecked with gray.

The *Hegira*, or flight from Mecca, was a great success. At Medina Muhammad won many converts to his doctrines of *Islam*, "Submission" to the will of Allah. He preached an end to idolatry, monotheistic worship of Allah, prayer five times a day, fasting from dawn to dusk through the month of Ramadan, paradise for the faithful, and hellfire for the wicked. He also urged social reformation on the Arabs: limits on slavery, polygamy, and divorce; compassion for the poor; an end to blood feuds. He recognized Moses and Jesus as earlier prophets and seems to have expected Jews and Christians to accept him as God's Messenger too. When the Jews of Medina refused to do so, he exercised his newfound ascendancy by expelling them from the city.

There were external enemies of the new faith to deal with as well. Whereas Jesus's three-year ministry was

---

[1]Mohammed Marmaduke Pickthall, *The Meaning of the Glorious Koran* (New York: New American Library, 1953), p. x.

strewn with miracles, Muhammad's career was punctuated with battles. The aging merchant turned holy man personally led some two dozen campaigns during his last ten years. His struggles with his most obdurate foes, the Meccans, climaxed in 630 with his victorious return to his birthplace. There the Prophet cleansed the Kaaba of its idols, prayed before the Black Stone, and forgave his enemies.

He died two years later, the founder of a new religion whose phenomenal spread over the coming centuries would perhaps have awed even Muhammad, the Trustworthy, the Prophet, the Messenger of God.

THE TEACHINGS OF THE PROPHET

The force unleashed by the Arab prophet dreaming in the marketplace in Mecca was to have a genuinely seismic impact on history. Yet this militant faith, spreading over substantial portions of all three continents of the Old World, was less focused and considerably more complex than some of those we have examined thus far.

We are not dealing here with a single empire, a territorial polity like ancient Egypt or the Roman Empire. Islam was a living, growing organism, dividing into separate and sometimes antagonistic states, spreading ever farther across Eurasia and beyond. Its extent became in time so vast that it is quite unlikely that the Muslim kings of Sokoto in North Africa, for instance, were even aware of the existence of the Islamic coastal states of Borneo. Yet there are fundamental historical patterns to be detected in this vast intercontinental sprawl that we call Islam.

Islam was above all a religious community, bound together in the first instance by the Holy Koran, the "reading" that Gabriel had enjoined upon Muhammad and that Allah had inspired in his Messenger. This volume of sacred verses, read and memorized in Arabic all across the Muslim world, served as a powerful cultural cement. So did the Muslim Law, a detailed body of religious strictures and traditions professed by holy men sitting in dusty market squares from Spain to Samarkand. Paradoxically, finally, the religious unity of Islam was actually strengthened by the sectarian upheavals that swept through it from time to time. Initially divisive, such challenges to orthodoxy as the mystic Sufi movement or the Sunni–Shiite split—to be examined in a later section—stirred new fervor in the faithful and sometimes, as in the case of the Sufis, contributed significantly to the further expansion of Islam.

Submission to Allah was thus a religious submission first of all. But Islam was also a human dominion, and its bearers, while a diverse lot, fitted a pattern nonetheless. Typically, the ruling peoples of the Muslim world began their rise to predominance as rude converts—hard-fighting, comparatively barbarous warriors of Allah. They ended as cultivated Oriental princes, more worldly and more sophisticated than the founder of their faith had ever been. The Arabs first, then Turks, Mongols, Africans, and others still farther east followed this historic cycle,

rejuvenating Islam and reaching out for new converts and new dominions each in turn.

Islam is, finally, a variegated and brilliant civilization, a pattern of culture as distinctive in its way as those of China or the Greco-Roman Mediterranean. Mosque and minaret and the Arabic script of the Koran flourished all across this broad swath of northern Africa, southern Europe, and western Asia. Men of Muslim beliefs and ways of life traded on all the caravan routes across Eurasia and rode the monsoon winds across the Indian Ocean. Their rulers lived cultivated court lives in Damascus or Baghdad, Córdoba or Constantinople, Samarkand or Timbuktu.

A complex entity, Islam was thus not only a religion but also a succession of political hegemonies and a variety of linked cultures. For a thousand years, from the seventh century to the seventeenth, Muslim power reached out, winning converts from the Russian steppes to the African savannas, thrusting into Christian Europe, conquering most of Hindu India, and reshaping the lives of millions of human beings. But there was order beneath the tumult. Islam bound all its millions to a religion, a civilization, and a pattern of history.

JIHAD: THE FIRST MUSLIM HOLY WAR

When Muhammad died, he had left his mark upon most of the oasis towns and primitive bedouin of northern Arabia. In the centuries that followed the Prophet's death in 632, his followers were to seize with the sword an area larger than the Roman Empire, all in the name of Allah and his Messenger. A survey of Arab Islamic expansion during the first few centuries after Muhammad will give us some idea of the realm with which we will be dealing in subsequent pages and chapters, and of the general pattern of Islamic expansion across the Old World.

The ragged bedouin from the Exhausted Land of Arabia were a proud, tough people. They wore clothing and lived in tents made of the hides of their beasts, milked and slaughtered them for food, warmed themselves around small fires of dried camel dung under the brilliant stars. Beyond that they had their *jinn* and demons, their clan feuds and intermittent banditry, and the endless quest for the next hillside of dry salt grass. The simple pressure of overpopulation in their arid land has often been seen as a spur that drove the Arabs on to conquest elsewhere.

But the Message of the Prophet was clearly the precipitating factor. Muhammad had preached the duty of expanding the Islamic zone of true believers. The holy war—*jihad*—was in a sense a deal the Arabs couldn't refuse. If they won, they came home laden with more booty than any caravan raid provided. If they died in the attempt, they would come home to Paradise: "What though ye be slain or die," the glorious Koran declared, "when unto Allah ye are gathered?" (*The Koran*, III, 158).

When the Prophet died in 632, his old companion Abu Bakr was hailed as caliph ("successor") in the cities

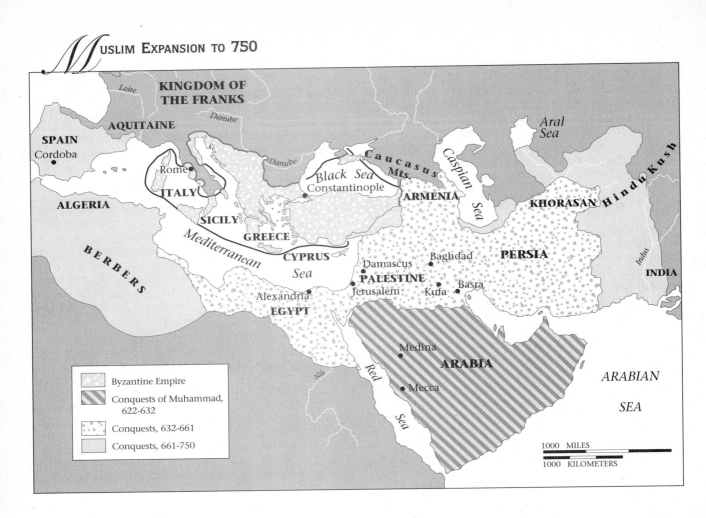

of Arabia. Some of the desert sheiks resisted, but Abu Bakr brought them around, sometimes by force, before he died, two years after Muhammad.

Omar, the Prophet's earlier persecutor and first official patron, became the second caliph. A man of vision and organizing skill and the best general among the Muslims, Omar fused the desert tribes into an army and turned their first tentative probes into the great *jihad*.

The Arabs were not vastly numerous or well equipped. But by sticking to the barren wilderness they knew, and to their camel cavalry and hit-and-run tactics, they proved quite effective. Their fierce traditional pride and their new faith gave a sharp edge to their swords. As with true believers in other times and lands, their strength would sometimes seem the strength of ten because their hearts were, if not purer than other men's, at least more passionate.

The neighboring lands turned out to be plums ripe for the plucking. The Persian and Byzantine empires northeast and northwest of Arabia were old and worn out with fighting each other. The Berbers of North Africa, oth-

erwise much like their Arab assailants, had no *jihad* to unify them. And once the holy war was well begun, the warriors of Allah developed a momentum that would take some stopping, even by more formidable rivals.

Under Omar (634–644), the ragtag army took the provinces of Syria and Palestine from the Byzantine Empire, occupied most of Sassanid Persia, and conquered Egypt. Under the Omayyad dynasty that followed, despite internal divisions and civil strife, the Arabs swept on westward across North Africa, crossed the Strait of Gibraltar, overwhelmed the Visigothic kingdom in Spain, and swarmed over the Pyrenees into western France. There they were finally stopped by a Frankish army under Charles Martel at the Battle of Poitiers (Tours) in 732. In the eastern Mediterranean, meanwhile, Arab warriors had built themselves ships, destroyed the fleet of the Byzantines, and mounted a massive siege of Constantinople. Here again they met with a substantial check, and in 718 they abandoned the assault on the impregnable walls of the Byzantine capital.

But these reverses at Constantinople and Poitiers did

The splendor of the far-reaching Muslim imperium was dazzlingly displayed in the Alhambra, palace of the Moorish rulers of Granada in fourteenth-century Spain. The famous Lion court is tile roofed and decorated with fillagree work over the slender arches. The palace is cool in the noon-day heat, bright with flowers, garnished with reflecting pools. (PH Archives)

not stop the far-ranging soldiers of the Prophet. In the early eighth century, roving bands were already pushing northeast into the Caucasus and central Asia and east beyond Persia into the valley of the Indus.

The victorious Arabs tended to be less fanatical than Christian legend long believed. Christians and Jews in particular, as followers of earlier prophets in Muhammad's line, were usually allowed the freedom of their religion, though they paid a special tax for the privilege. Persians and Byzantines, with their long experience of government, were soon managing conquered territories for the victorious but administratively unsophisticated Arabs.

Yet the legend of that first eruption out of Arabia lived on—above all, perhaps, for their most persistent enemies, the Christian peoples still sunk in the depths of the early Middle Ages on the other side of the Mediterranean. Muhammad became Mahound, the Devil himself, to medieval Christians, and "Lord, save us from the Saracens" their most fervent prayer.

Only the first stage of Muslim expansion was ended. Indeed, the Arab conquest had laid the foundation for a predominance that would fill the center of Eurasia with Islamic power by the beginning of the modern period.

 # THE ARAB EMPIRE

THE CALIPHS: SUCCESSORS TO THE PROPHET

The Arab Empire founded by Omar would flourish for some three centuries. Thereafter Islam would march on under other banners than those of its Arab founders. But the development of the two Arab caliphates, the Omayyads (661–750) and the Abbasids (750–1258; flourished 750–946), was typical of much that was to come.

Under Muhammad's early successors—the "rightly guided" caliphs who immediately followed him and the Omayyad dynasty thereafter—Arabs came to rule vast tracts of the Near East, North Africa, and parts of southern Europe. In attempting to govern their new conquests, they found that their ancient desert heritage of tribal life and their new power in the world interacted to produce unforeseen social and economic problems and some sanguinary political history. However, the Arab Empire also fashioned an integrated society and a brilliant flowering of Islamic culture. These aspects of their history deserve as much attention as the dazzling conquests that carried the Arabs with such rapidity to the mastery of their substantial corner of the globe.

The problems began at the heart of Islam, with the religious leadership of the faithful, which was vested from the beginning in the caliphs.

The institution of the caliphate was intended to be a theocracy. The caliph was initially the religious as well as the political head of Islam, as Muhammad had been. In Islamic thinking there was no difference between these two spheres of activity, secular and ecclesiastical, sacred and profane. As the caliphs became more worldly and luxury-loving, however, their spiritual leadership was harder and harder to reconcile with the style of life their political ascendancy brought them. Under these circumstances they allowed their spiritual authority to pass largely into the hands of the *ulama*—the experts on the life and teachings of the Prophet, the shapers and masters of the Muslim Law. While retaining their nominal

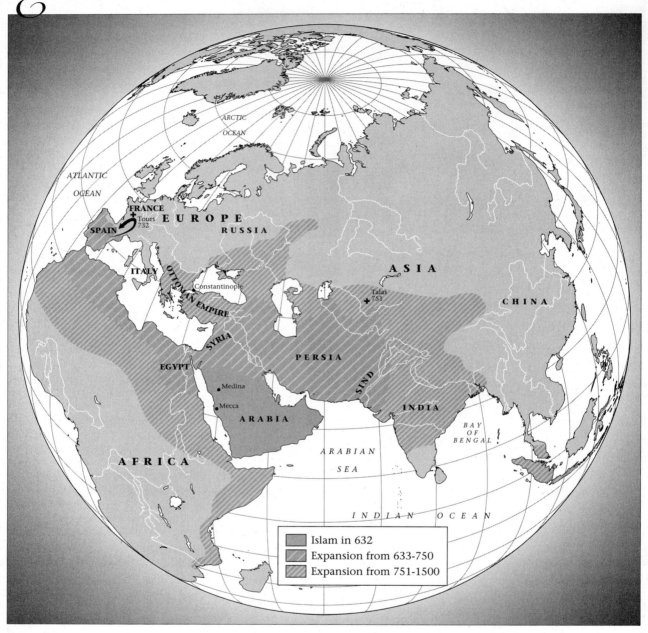

ARCTIC
OCEAN

ATLANTIC
OCEAN

FRANCE
Tours
732
SPAIN
EUROPE
RUSSIA

ITALY
OTTOMAN EMPIRE
Constantinople

ASIA

CHINA

Talas
751

SYRIA
PERSIA
SIND

EGYPT
Medina
Mecca
INDIA
BAY
OF
BENGAL

ARABIA

AFRICA
ARABIAN
SEA

INDIAN OCEAN

Islam in 632
Expansion from 633-750
Expansion from 751-1500

headship of the faithful in religious matters, the caliphs thus became concerned more and more exclusively with politics.

Abu Bakr, the first caliph, was chosen by the acclaim of the believers, at least in the Arabian cities. After the first four caliphs, however, the dynastic principle came into play. During both of the two main Arab caliphates, family succession determined the leadership of Islam. The dynastic succession was punctuated, however, by some of the bloodiest high politics since third-century Rome.

THE OMAYYADS

Of the four "rightly guided" caliphs, only Abu Bakr died peacefully in bed. Omar was assassinated in 644; so was his successor, in 656; and so was the next in line, Muhammad's son-in-law Ali, in 661. Nor did the establishment of the Omayyad clan that year put an end to fratricide among the Arab rulers. There was civil strife again in the last decades of the seventh century, and the Omayyad dynasty expired finally in a massacre that all but wiped out their house.

The sources of this sanguinary political history lay in a number of unresolved problems that plagued the Omayyads throughout that first century of Islam. There was the traditional bedouin penchant for clan vendettas that a century of common victories did not abolish. There was the inevitable tendency of recently conquered peoples to revolt, producing recurring civil wars in the Arab Empire. And there was the appearance of the sectarian spirit within the body of the Muslim faithful as early as the death of Ali, whose Shiite followers constitute to this day a sometimes violent minority in the Islamic world.

Other transformations, less violent but more far-reaching, were also going on beneath the surface of victorious conquest and self-destructive civil conflict that characterized the rule of the Omayyads.

In the first place, there were transformations in the conquered peoples. The Arabs did not give much attention to conversion of unbelievers during the early years. They collected taxes and tribute regularly, making effective use of the existing Persian or Byzantine bureaucratic structures for these purposes, and otherwise asking—and offering—little more. Before the end of the Omayyad century, however, this policy began to change. The defeated peoples, impressed with the theology and military success of Islam, slowly began to seek conversion to the religion of the victors. This process was no doubt encouraged by the fact that by converting to Islam non-Muslims escaped the taxes levied on infidels. At the same time, the Arabs began to fraternize more with the natives, so that the Arabic language came into increasingly common use all across the Muslim world. The spread of Arabic was also hastened by the spread of the faith, since the Koran could be read and prayers addressed properly to Allah only in the language in which he had spoken to the Prophet.

The spread of the Islamic religion and the Arabic language provided the basis for a slow but extensive change in the peoples the Arabs had overwhelmed during the century after the Prophet's death. It was a process that would continue under later dynasties and other regimes, imposing a far-reaching cultural unity on the Islamic world.

Changes also came about in the Arab conquerors themselves during this early period. Once they had abandoned their isolated garrisons and mingled with the peoples they ruled, Arabs everywhere gradually became part of the indigenous ruling classes. Some of them turned into wealthy landowners, adopted the luxurious lifestyles of their former enemies, and increasingly left the fighting to new, non-Arab converts to Islam. Arab viceroys and governors built themselves palaces and even whole new cities, where they lived in opulence, cut off from the people they ruled. The Omayyad caliphs transferred the capital of Islam from its old center of Mecca to the rich city of Damascus, where a more imperial style of life might be lived more easily. In their new capital, they created a court to rival the most luxurious of earlier Near Eastern emperors.

By the end of its first century, then, the Arab Empire had produced a style of life very different from the desert wandering of Muhammad's day. Under the Abbasid dynasty, which seized the caliphate in 750, Arab rule was to reach its apogee of grandeur. It was also to undergo one final metamorphosis before slipping slowly and lingeringly out of the pages of history.

THE ABBASIDS

The founder of the new dynasty was a powerful and ruthless man named Abu al-Abbas. He had himself proclaimed the true caliph in Persia in 749 and marched at once on Damascus. With him marched the disaffected of the Arab Empire. There were, as always, poor men hoping to better their lot under the new regime. There were Shiites who, believing that only blood ties with Muhammad could confer legitimacy on a caliph, were duly impressed by Abu's assertion of kinship with the Prophet. There was, finally, a group with a powerful future in Islam: the new, non-Arab converts to the faith who had been relegated to second-class status among the faithful.

The new dynasty would not make poor men rich, nor would it turn the Shiite heresy into orthodoxy. But over the two centuries of their actual supremacy—and the five centuries of their nominal rule—the Abbasids would preside over a complete transformation of the ruling class of Islam. The Arab conquerors would merge with the ancient aristocracy of Persia, and with Turks and even Mongols, vigorous new converts from the nomadic northern steppes.

With this support from the disaffected, Abu al-Abbas seized Damascus in 750. He invited all the princes of the defeated Omayyad clan to a conciliatory banquet—and sent the executioners in. Afterwards, according to legend, the victorious Abbasids enjoyed the meal themselves.

Among the Abbasids there were names more famous than that of the founder. The most celebrated was the legendary Harun al-Rashid, the wealthy, sophisticated caliph immortalized in *The Arabian Nights*, who ruled in the decades around 800. The most beneficent was perhaps his cultivated son, Mamun the Great. There were still fighters among them too—the pleasure-loving Harun fought many military campaigns. But the political history of the dynasty during its first two centuries—the period of its real power—was dominated by three new trends: centralization, secession, and the gradual decline of Arab supremacy at the center of the web.

Some sort of centralization of government power was clearly necessary if the Abbasids were to rule so vast

The ninth-century mosque of Ibn Tulun in Cairo shows the open Abbasid form, with minarets and an arcade around the central court. Like the cathedral shown in the preceding chapter and the temples in the next chapter, this thousand-year-old mosque is still in use today. Contrast the calm simplicity of basic forms and the regularity of the decoration here with the variety and elaboration of Chartres cathedral in the last chapter. (Photo Researchers, Inc.)

a realm at all. By the time of Abu al-Abbas, the Arabs nominally governed territories that stretched from Spain to Afghanistan. Building on Omayyad beginnings and drawing as their predecessors had on the long experience of the Persians in particular, the Abbasid dynasty constructed an elaborate system of administration.

Persian influence became crucially important to the emerging Arab Empire. Persian aristocrats converted to Islam and continued to form an important part of Baghdad's Islamic elite. Besides staffing the emerging administration of the Arab Empire, Persians also helped reorganize a guerrilla Arab army into a more tightly structured military machine.

Baghdad, the new Abbasid capital, thus became the center of an impressive bureaucratic structure. At its head, just beneath the caliph himself, stood the grand vizier (chief counselor), a position that might also have become hereditary if Harun al-Rashid had not shrewdly decided to root out the family that had come to dominate the office

in his reign. Beneath the vizier, the will of the caliph was to be carried out by provincial governors all across the empire. Governorships did become hereditary, and the central authority did not always reach effectively into distant provinces dominated by local dynasties. Yet there was a structure of authority, which in the person of the *qadi*, the judge and authority on Muslim law in almost every town and city, reached even to the local level. It was a governmental system far superior to that of contemporary Europe, then struggling out of the earliest Middle Ages into the uncertain light of the Carolingian renaissance.

A structure of power thus grew up under the Abbasids. But not all the caliph's far-flung realms accepted his authority. Secession also spread, fragmenting the western portions of the empire in particular. Only one of the Omayyad princes escaped Abu's executioners in 750; five years later he founded an independent Omayyad caliphate in Spain. Other secessionist regimes established themselves across North Africa: in Morocco in 788, in Tunis in 800, and the Fatimid dynasty, which traced its lineage back to Muhammad's daughter Fatima, in Egypt in 868. A separatist movement even succeeded in eastern Persia in 820. All these remained part of the great body of Islamic religion, civilization, and commerce, but politically they were lost to the Arab government in Baghdad.

An even more dangerous threat to the Arab predominance, finally, was nourished within the empire itself. As the descendants of the Arab conquerors settled into splendor in Baghdad, other peoples came to the fore. Persian power predominated increasingly in council and among the cadres of lesser officials. At the same time, as noted above, a new wave of hardy nomads infiltrated the empire from the Eurasian steppes. Among them the Seljuk and Ottoman Turks and the Mongols were to be the most important for the future of Islam.

The Turks infiltrated the frontier cities first, often coming as mercenary soldiers. Sometimes whole tribes of them accepted conversion. By the middle of the ninth century, less than a hundred years after the Abbasids had seized power, Turkish guards were providing the caliph with the heart of his standing army. They proved their value as willing repressers of disorders among the native peoples of the caliphate. In time they became as powerful in Arab affairs as the Praetorian Guard had been in Rome.

The Persians, however, were the first to profit from the decline of Arab vitality and power. In 946 a Persian general unmade one caliph and made another a puppet, content to live in Persia and rule as his masters willed. The Abbasids would reign in name only for three more centuries, till 1258. But Persians and Turks dominated the empire in the east, and secessionist regimes still flourished in the west. Abbasid splendor was not diminished, but Abbasid power was a shadow of what the Arabs had once wielded. The peoples of the northern steppe soon replaced the people of the southern desert as the masters and builders of Islam.

THE SPLENDORS OF BAGHDAD

In "The Tale of the Porter and the Three Ladies of Baghdad" (told on the ninth night of the Thousand and One), a beautiful Muslim lady leads a ragged porter about the bazaars of the great city, heaping the basket he carries on his back with good things to eat and drink and see and smell. The list includes, among many, many others, Syrian apples, Arabian peaches, and cucumbers and limes from Egypt. She purchases ten kinds of perfume, along with incense, aloewood, ambergris, musk, and "candles of Alexandria wax." The house to which she leads the eager porter is a "fair mansion" with a broad courtyard, gates of ebony, and a great hall replete with "balconies and groined arches and galleries," a pool and a fountain in the center and a raised dais at one end with "a couch of juniper wood set with gems and pearls" and

"a canopy . . . of red satin-silk looped up with pearls as big as filberts."[2]

Due allowance must, of course, be made for the fact that *The Arabian Nights' Entertainment* is a collection of fairy tales, and for the need of Scheherazade to drag out her story through the night with lengthy catalogues of good things. Nevertheless, they were things familiar enough in the Baghdad of the Abbasids. And Harun al-Rashid, the caliph most reflected in *The Arabian Nights*, was the most celebrated of all the Abbasids.

Through all the conflicts and transformations outlined above, the Arab Empire in general and the Abbasid caliphate in particular did much to advance the welfare of their subjects. The Arab peace fostered agriculture in Egypt and Persia, in Muslim Sicily and Spain. Most important, the spread of a common culture across a wide swath of western Eurasia encouraged trade, by caravan and swift Arab dhow, from Spain to India.

A common language and religion, a Muslim law code based on the life of the merchant and the caravan town all encouraged commercial development. And commerce in turn contributed to the development of handicraft industry; Damascus steel, Córdoba leather, and silks and cottons from the East were all internationally known. The Syrian apples and Arabian peaches in the Baghdad bazaar of "The Porter's Tale" are perhaps as realistic as the red silk canopy from the Far East or the candles of Alexandria wax.

Baghdad itself—"City of Peace, Gift of God, Paradise on Earth"—was one of the wonders of the age. Built up by the Abbasids from a small market town on the Tigris, the third capital of Islam (after Mecca and Damascus) grew into a city that rivaled even Constantinople in size, wealth, and beauty. Palaces and gardens, the domes and minarets of mosques, and the endless bustle and color of the bazaars dazzled the eye and bewildered the ear. Arabs, Persians, Turks, and all the rest of the empire's kaleidoscope of peoples mingled in the streets of the city. There were many libraries, a House of Wisdom for the study of theology, and an observatory for the study of the stars.

At the courts of the caliphs, poetry, music, and the other arts all flourished, along with the self-indulgence indigenous to the courts of princes. There were fragrant gardens and fountains, alabaster halls and Kabul carpets, robes of silk and jeweled turbans enough to outfit any Arabian night's entertainment in fitting splendor. At first glance there would seem to be little connection between that paradise and the lives of the majority of the faithful the caliphs claimed to rule. But there were crucial connections nonetheless.

Across the empire, in a thousand dusty villages set among the slender trunks of date palms, farmers drove plodding beasts that turned their water wheels, or squat-

[2]Richard F. Burton, *The Book of a Thousand Nights and a Night*, vol. 1 (London: Burton Club private edition, n.d.), pp. 82–85.

ted around the food pots as their ancestors had done and their descendants would continue to do. But now there was a *Qadi* in the town to enforce the Law of the Prophet. From time to time a caravan came tinkling past and stopped to display unlikely wares from far away. At times, a black-robed, black-turbaned Abbasid prince might ride by with a troop of Turkish mercenaries, on his way east to defend the frontier. Whether they knew it or not, the life of those silent farmers tending their immemorial water wheels was the better for the men who ruled in Baghdad, for the commerce, the protection, and the Law of the Prophet—the good things that Baghdad symbolized and in varying degrees provided over the centuries.

THE FAITH AND ART OF ISLAM

THE KORAN, THE LAW, AND THE FIVE PILLARS OF ISLAM

In the early days of Islam, the simplicity of the religion of Allah appealed to Christians, Zoroastrians, pagans, and other potential converts. Muhammad had fixed upon the Black Stone of the Kaaba, allegedly cast down from heaven, as the earthly focus of his faith. In the beginning any enclosed area with a clearly designated side facing Mecca seems to have done for a mosque. Beyond that there was only the Book, the Law, and the worship they enjoined.

The Koran, the sacred book of Islam, was spoken aloud by Muhammad in oracular, poetic verse in a series of revelations over a period of more than twenty years. These prophecies and injunctions, taken down by disciples, were assembled within a few years of the Prophet's death into a book about the size of the Christian New Testament. Its 114 *suras*, or chapters, are composed in Arabic poetry so moving that Muslims regard this alone as evidence of its divine origin. Small boys memorize its thousands of verses entire, and grown men weep when it is chanted in the mosque.

The faith whose essence is Submission (*Islam*) to the will of God (Allah) begins with a *sura* often described as the Lord's Prayer of Islam:

> In the name of Allah, the Beneficent, the Merciful.
>   Praise be to Allah, Lord of the Worlds,
>   The Beneficent, the Merciful.
>   Owner of the Day of Judgment,
> Thee (alone) we worship; Thee (alone) we ask
>   for help. (*The Koran*, I, 1–5)

The briefest summary of the faith, offered daily in the mosque, goes simply: "There is no God but Allah, and Muhammad is his prophet."

The most obvious differences between Islam and the Christian tradition lies in the part played by Muhammad himself in the Islamic revelation. The Muslim Prophet claimed no divinity, performed no miracles save the one great miracle of bringing God's will to humanity. The Koran was thus believed to embody God's final revelation, and to be superior to any other holy book.

But the Koran was the beginning, not the end, of the development of the Islamic faith.

Theology came to Islam a century after Muhammad's death. Muslims argued like theologians of other religions over such abstruse points as predestination, major and minor sins, the role of reason in expounding the faith. But it was in the Muslim Law that the theological genius of Islam was expressed most strikingly.

The Muslim Law is an attempt to bring the Islamic faith to bear on every aspect of the life of the believer. The Arab compilers of the Law sought to explicate God's will toward people in such detail that the faithful need never be in doubt about how a good Muslim ought to act in any situation. Experts in the Law—the *qadis*—sat in the market squares of all Muslim towns, adjudicating civil disputes and ruling in criminal cases on the basis of their detailed knowledge of the words of the Prophet and the traditions of his faith.

The compilation of Islamic Law was a monumental effort undertaken in the earlier Muslim centuries by the *ulama*, the body of Muslim priests, judges, and scholars. These learned men drew upon four sources of divine truth: the Koran, the traditions, consensus, and analogy. The Koran itself stood first in authority, of course. When the Koran provided no clear direction, the *ulama* turned to the traditional accounts of the Prophet's deeds and opinions expressed outside the Koran. The scholarly study of these traditions, or *Sunna*, occupied generations of Islamic scholarship.

Where neither the *Sunna* nor the Koran offered sufficient insight, the Law was based on the consensus of the Islamic community, on the theory that God would not allow the faithful to be in error about any important matter down the centuries. Finally, where all else failed, the makers of the Muslim Law undertook to reason by analogy; if the Prophet forbade wine, for instance, this prohibition might be extended to other intoxicants as well.

The result was an immense body of requirements and prohibitions concerning religion, personal morality, social conduct, and political behavior. Business and marital relations, criminal law, ritual practices, and much more were covered in this vast system. Even where central government broke down, Muslim Law provided an effective framework for living for peoples all across the Islamic world.

Besides the Koran and the Law, lifelong routines of worship welded Islam into a cultural unity. From the earliest centuries the Islamic faith had five essential practices, the Five Pillars of Islam: witnessing to one's belief, prayer five times daily, fasting, almsgiving, and pilgrim-

The golden-roofed Muslim shrine of the Dome of the Rock in Jerusalem marks the spot from which Muhammad is believed to have ascended into heaven. Located in modern Israel, this seventh-century building is still a sacred place to the world's Muslims. Again, notice the combination of monumental forms and patterned decoration in this Muslim structure. (Israel Government Tourist Office)

age, particularly the great pilgrimage to Mecca that every Muslim dreams of making at least once in a lifetime.

The Book, the Law, and the life of Islam thus blended to produce one of the most successful of all the major religions of humankind. But like all religions, the Muslim faith had its divisions and revisions. And these too are part of the story of the intercontinental reach of Islam.

THE SUFI TRADITION: ECSTASIES AND TRANCES

Sectarian divisions broke out early in Islamic history. Theology, history, and the mystical impulses to which all religions are liable all helped to divide the faith of the Prophet.

Near Eastern Christianity, Persian Zoroastrianism, and even Buddhism—all highly sophisticated systems of religious thought when the Arabs first came in contact with them—challenged Muslims to think through their own beliefs more carefully. Perhaps most disturbing, Greek philosophy, encountered in the Hellenized East, raised the same questions of faith versus reason that it kindled among Christians.

The most historically important sectarian outbreaks, however, were rooted in the political realities of the early Muslim centuries. The most long-lived and devastating of these Muslim religious schisms was the Shiite revolt, which began in the first century after Muhammad's death and has persisted to the present. It began with the murder of the fourth caliph, Ali, son-in-law to the Prophet, and the accession of the Omayyad dynasty. The Shiites were those Muslims who objected to the Omayyad succession on the grounds that only descendants of Ali and Muhammad's daughter Fatima—Ali's wife—could be legitimate

successors to the Prophet. In time the Shiites became opponents of the whole orthodox, traditional approach taken by the Sunnite majority. Habituated to martyrdom at the hands of the orthodox, Shiite Muslims remain today a powerful movement, particularly in that part of ancient Persia that is now Iran.

The most successful new direction in the Islamic religion, however, was the Sufi movement. The Sufis were Muslim mystics, seekers after Islamic truth through direct spiritual experience. Like Buddhist or Christian monks, Sufis reacted to the increasing worldliness of the caliphate by stressing self-denial. They saw asceticism as the beginning of the arduous road to mystical union with Allah himself.

They began their preaching in the seventh century, the first century of Islam. For some time the oddness and immediacy of Sufi religious experience brought them into conflict with the keepers of the Book and the Law. One of the most famous of all Sufi seekers, al-Hallaj, was crucified in the tenth century for asserting, "I am the Absolute Truth."[3] In time, however, Sufism found its place and became an immense influence in Islam. By the twelfth century there were orders of Sufis all across the Muslim world, each with its revered masters and saints, its diverse practices and doctrines, its own version of the mystic way to union with Allah.

These ceremonies included chanting, rhythmic motion, and sometimes the singing of Sufi poems to musical accompaniment. In a murky atmosphere of incense and ritual, prayers, incantations, and invocations of angelic

[3]Annemarie Schimmel, *Mystical Dimensions of Islam* (Chapel Hill: University of North Carolina Press, 1975), p. 72.

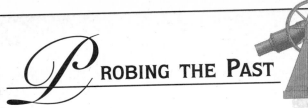

PROBING THE PAST

"*Muslims are assured in the Qur'ân [Koran], "You have become the best community ever raised up for mankind, enjoining the right and forbidding the wrong, and having faith in God" (111,110). Earnest men have taken this prophecy seriously to the point of trying to mould the history of the whole world in accordance with it. Soon after the founding of the faith, Muslims succeeded in building a new form of society, which in time carried with it its own distinctive institutions, its art and literature, its science and scholarship, its political and social forms, as well as its cult and creed, all bearing an unmistakable Islamic impress. In the course of centuries, this new society spread over widely diverse climes, throughout most of the Old World. It came closer than any had ever come to uniting all mankind under its ideals.*

Yet the "civilization of Islam" as it has existed is far from being a clear expression of the Islamic faith. From the first, pious Muslims themselves differed as to what the "best community" should be like. The Islamic vision of what mankind might be has been seen and interpreted variously: no one ideal has ever fully prevailed among the Muslims. Moreover their efforts, such as they were, to build a good society often produced actual results strikingly different from what anyone had anticipated. Some of the greatest triumphs of culture under an Islamic aegis have been such as many devoted Muslims could not look on with favour; and while Islam has seen some outstanding successes which all could acclaim, it has seen failures at least as outstanding. Those who have undertaken to rebuild life in Islamic terms have ventured on an enterprise with a high potential reward—that of winning through to the best that is open to mankind; but with correspondingly great risks of error and failure."

The legendary twentieth-century Islamicist Marshall Hodgson had a powerful concern—rare among scholars—for breadth of coverage, for the "big picture" of an entire civilization. When he died prematurely at forty-seven, he had his six-part masterwork on <u>The Venture of Islam</u> nearly complete (a colleague finished it for him) and had begun what would have been a remarkable world history as well.

In this extract from his "General Prologue" on "The Islamic Vision in Religion and Civilization," Hodgson discusses the extent to which this world civilization is and is not truly "Islamic." What elements of this society does he feel bear an "Islamic impress"? In what ways does he feel Muslim history is *not* entirely a product of the Muslim religion? How important do you feel an underlying system of beliefs is to any civilization?

Marshall G. S. Hodgson, <u>The Venture of Islam: Conscience and History in a World Civilization</u>, 3 vols. (Chicago: University of Chicago Press, 1974), vol. I, p. 71.

beings, these Sufi performances could bring the adept into a state of religious exaltation.

The Sufis were among the most effective propagators of the faith to unbelievers. Their direct, emotional approach could touch the hearts of potential converts. Later would come Arabic and the Koran, the *qadi* and the Law. But simple faith, a call to the heart, ecstasies and trances were a quicker way to win new converts to the

teachings of a prophet who had himself been summoned to his task by angelic voices.

ISLAMIC ART: MOSQUES AND MINARETS

In the Arab Empire, as wherever the faith of the Prophet spread, religious experience and theological prescriptions profoundly influenced the practice of the arts. The most obvious example of this influence is the Muslim ban on the depiction of the human figure in art. This prohibition, honored particularly in the broad spectrum of religious art, all but abolished sculpture and severely limited the figurative element in painting. This rejection of the representational also contributed to the highly abstract nature of Islamic design. Muslim art thus stressed geometric shapes, arabesque curvilinear patterns abstracted from floral designs, and religious maxims in angular or flowing Arabic scripts used as decorative motifs.

The overwhelming influence of religion also made itself felt in more positive ways. Like the cathedral in medieval Christendom, the mosque became the most characteristic artistic achievement of the Muslim peoples, and architecture generally their central art.

The mosque was the center of any Arab town. Its essential features as a place of worship include a large court with a fountain for ceremonial ablutions; a prayer hall with a wall facing Mecca; a decorated niche in that wall providing a focus for the devotions of the faithful; and a pulpit near this niche for readings from the Koran and for sermons. The most readily recognizable element, however, is the tall, often slender tower called a minaret, from which the faithful are called to prayer five times daily.

This simple pattern of court and hall, with inner and outer adjuncts, proved capable of immense elaboration. Typical Arab extrapolations included the addition of an impressive facade flanked by towering minarets, roofed galleries around the courtyard, and forests of pillars in the prayer hall itself. The Great Mosque of Córdoba, built by the Omayyad caliphs of Spain, and the Fatimid Mosque of El-Hakim in Cairo follow this elaborated model.

Other characteristic types of Muslim architecture include the *madrasah*, or Muslim seminary, the mausoleums of sultans and saints, bazaars, and royal palaces. Of the few palaces that survive, the late medieval Alhambra with its famous Lion Court, located in the Spanish city of Granada, is by far the best known. The immense "desert castles," such as that of Ukhaydir in the sea of sand south of Baghdad, give us only the roughest idea of what Abbasid Baghdad itself must have been like in its glory.

Muslims were masters of all the decorative arts—ceramics and tiles, metalwork and textiles, calligraphy, the art of miniature, and many more. A gilded and illuminated copy of the Koran is a thing of beauty to set beside any medieval Christian Bible. But nowhere did the decorative artistry of the Muslim peoples stand out more clearly than in their efforts to express "the experience of the infinite" in the Muslim house of prayer, the mosques that are the glory of Islam.

ARAB LITERATURE: POEMS AND TALES

The mosque is a luminous artistic achievement accessible in some degree, at least, even to the non-Muslim. The same cannot be said for the literature and thought of Islam. Poetry, fiction, history and biography, philosophy, and the sciences all seem to date more rapidly than the direct formal statements of architectural design and decorative motif. Between the modern Western reader and the words and ideas of the medieval Arab Empire lies a gap as great in time as that which separates us from our own Middle Ages—and an even greater cultural divide. Nevertheless, a glimpse must be attempted, particularly into Arab literature, which is one of the great literatures of the world.

Arabic literature began as verse, the oral poetry of the desert Arabs. Poetry was as highly developed an art among these otherwise unsophisticated people as it was among Homeric Greeks, or among the medieval minstrels who sang the *Song of Roland* along the pilgrim routes of Europe. Like these other singers of a simpler world, Arab bards celebrated the greatness of their clans and the perfidy of their enemies; they described the harsh beauty of their desert world and the joys of fighting and fast riding. By the time Muhammad came, Arabic poetry was a highly developed art, and it was the poetic language of the desert Arabs that the Prophet used in speaking the revelations of the Koran.

Arab experience of the world changed drastically after Muhammad, however, and in the centuries that followed, both the subjects and the forms of Arabic literature expanded dramatically. Wine songs, love songs, and poems of a markedly mystical tone replaced the older verses devoted to horses and camels and the pride of the clan. Verse forms became more complex still, and poets reached for more ingenious metaphors, more complicated tropes and figures than before. From the celebration of a hard ride over the desert, they moved to al Masudi's famous ode to the banquet table or Ibn Hazm's frequently erotic *Ring of the Dove*:

> Her body was a jasmine rare,
> Her perfume sweet as amber scent,
> Her face a pearl beyond compare,
> Her all, pure light's embodiment. . . .[4]

Arabic prose was as varied and ingenious as Arabic poetry. This was the golden age of the professional Arab storyteller, whose repertoire of popular romantic tales was often arranged in cycles like that of *The Arabian Nights*. Collections of brief anecdotes were also popular, ranging in content from the most pious to downright bawdy tales. Styles varied from the easy flow of the teller of tales to the most elaborate rhetorical devices. The Arabs appreciated a flow of literary eloquence, whether it was the simple tale of the desert bard or the ornate literary construct of a court poet.

---

[4]Ibn Hazm, *The Ring and the Dove*, in A. J. Arberry, *Aspects of Islamic Civilization* (Ann Arbor: University of Michigan Press, 1967), p. 186.

PHILOSOPHY AND SCIENCE: KNOWLEDGE LIGHTS THE WAY TO HEAVEN

More substantial genres flourished during the centuries of Arab greatness. Biographies of Muhammad and of Muslim saints and scholars, histories of the caliphs and their wars, of the great cities of the Islamic world—Mecca, Damascus, Baghdad—and general accounts of the history of the Arabs and the civilization of Islam all appeared from the eighth century on. Travel books and geographies surveyed the Mediterranean world and took readers as far afield as central Europe and East Asia. Collections and encyclopedias multiplied on the bookshelves of Arabic scholars.

In all this array of learning, Arabic philosophy and science were perhaps the fields known and admired the most widely.

Arab philosophy, like medieval European theology, drew upon translations of the works of ancient Greek thinkers. Aristotle, Plato, and the Neoplatonists were all still readily available in the Greek-speaking Byzantine region when the Arabs swept in. Much of the Arabs' own philosophizing, therefore, took the form of commentaries on the ancients. Avicenna's vast encyclopedias of philosophic knowledge and Averroes' commentaries on Aristotle, both monuments to Arab scholarship, were clearly rooted in the thinking of the ancient Greeks.

Arab philosophers of the ninth and tenth centuries, however, embarked upon some daring speculative paths of their own. Muslim philosophers meditated more boldly than medieval Christian thinkers on such matters as the creation and nature of the universe, divine providence, and even the relative value of rational philosophy and revealed religion as roads to an understanding of the world. From the end of the eleventh century on, however, such speculations came under fire from religious fundamentalists, and philosophical originality and daring declined in the Arab world thereafter.

The sciences bloomed among the Arabs as they had nowhere else in the western half of Eurasia since Hellenistic times. Again, the Arabs began by drawing upon their neighbors, translating Aristotle's biology, Ptolemy's astronomy, and Galen's medical writings, and acquiring the decimal system from the mathematicians of Hindu India. On these foundations, Muslim scientists built an impressive structure of ideas about the natural world.

Arab scientists excelled particularly in astronomy and mathematics, where they made important contributions to algebra and trigonometry. They added significantly to the world's store of knowledge in optics, pharmacology, and other branches of natural science. Arab alchemy and astrology—recognized sciences everywhere in those days—were considered authoritative in Europe. The reputation of Arab medical expertise was so high in the West that Christian kings preferred Saracen physicians to Christian doctors.

"Knowledge," the Prophet had said, "enables its possessor to distinguish what is forbidden from what is not; it lights the way to Heaven."[5] It led at least some of its devotees far beyond the revelations of the Arab merchant of Mecca. The Muslim religion might harden into a more rigid orthodoxy in later centuries. During the Arab golden age, however, the faith of Muhammad and the ideas of ancient Greeks and Hindu Indians were able to coexist within Islam, a striking testimony to the flexibility of this world religion.

The whole of the Muslim cultural experience had, in fact, carried these true believers quite a distance from the marketplaces of Mecca and the camps of desert bedouin. Muhammad the Trustworthy, who told the angel Gabriel "I cannot read!" would surely have been astonished at, and perhaps not always approving of, some of the paths the agile minds of his followers took in later centuries. Yet it is likely that the most erotic of later Arab poets, the most daring of Muslim philosophers, began and ended most of his days as his simpler neighbors did, prostrate with his face toward Mecca, murmuring the immemorial *Bismillah, al-Rahman, al-Rahim*—"In the name of Allah, the Beneficent, the Merciful. . . ."

---

[5]Syed Ameer Ali, *The Spirit of Islam* (London: Chatto & Windus, 1964), p. 360.

SUMMARY

The first half-dozen centuries after the coming of the Prophet Muhammad—the period of the Arab predominance in the Muslim world—was one of the great ages of Islamic history.

Muhammad preached his gospel in Arabia in the seventh century of the Christian calendar—the first century of the Muslim one. Muhammad's inspiration turned a rabble of desert bedouin and a scattering of oasis traders into an Arab army embarked upon a holy war. This first great jihad carried Muslim power across North Africa, up into Europe, and back across the Middle East in less than a century.

The Arab Empire that resulted was ruled by two successive dynasties of caliphs ("successors to the Prophet"), the Omayyads (661–750) and the Abbasids (750–1258). From the seventh through the tenth century, this first Muslim empire brought a degree of political order, real commercial prosperity, and unparalleled spiritual unity to this broad central swathe of the Old World. Baghdad was one of the world's great metropolises, and even humble villagers benefited from Muslim Law and Arab protection.

The history of the Arab Empire after 1000 saw a decline in its material strength. Western provinces from Egypt to

Spain seceded. In the east, Persians and Turks became the real political powers under the later Abbasids. The rise of medieval Christian power raised the possibility of a serious challenge to Islam in western Eurasia. The faith of the Prophet, however, continued to generate one of the greatest of world cultures.

Islam, built on the Koran, Islamic tradition, and the Muslim Law, provided a framework for living throughout the Arab domains. Sects of Sufi mystics offered a more emotional expression of Islam and were particularly effective as missionaries for the faith.

Muslim art produced beautiful mosques, while Arab scholarship explored and expanded Islamic theology as well as Greek philosophy and Indian science. Arab literature, building on a poetry that predated the Prophet and was incarnated in the verse of the Koran itself, found expression in a glittering spectrum of sophisticated poetry and prose.

The cultivated and worldly court of Harun al-Rashid in ninth-century Baghdad was a far cry from the marketplace at Mecca where Muhammad had preached. But Islam, like medieval Christendom, remained a profoundly religious hegemony.

SUGGESTED READING

ABBOTT, N. *Aishah: The Beloved of Mohammed*. Chicago: University of Chicago Press, 1942. The Prophet's favorite wife and a powerful figure in the clan politics of early Arab times. For accounts of women of wealth and power in the more sophisticated society of the Abbasid caliphate, see Abbott's *Two Queens of Baghdad* (Chicago: University of Chicago Press, 1946).

ARNOLD, T. W., ed. *The Legacy of Islam*, 2nd ed. Oxford: Clarendon Press, 1974. Focusing on Islamic impact on Europe, this is also an excellent introduction to Islamic culture.

CRONE, P., and M. HINDS. *God's Caliph: Religious Authority in the First Centuries of Islam*. New York: Cambridge University Press, 1986. Challenges the view that the caliphs early abandoned their religious role in Islam for purely political functions.

DUNN, R. E. *The Adventures of Ibn Battuta: A Muslim Traveler of the Fourteenth Century*. Berkeley and Los Angeles: University of California Press, 1986. Scholarly, thoroughly readable account of the life and voyages of the great Muslim voyager.

FYZEE, A. A. A. *Outlines of Muhammadan Law*. London: Oxford University Press, 1949. Good introduction to this crucial element in Islamic culture.

GHAZZALI, A. H. M. *The Alchemy of Happiness*, trans. C. Field. New York: Sharpe, 1991. Eleventh century Arab summary of Islamic values, with emphasis on the Sufi way.

GLUBB, J. *The Life and Times of Muhammad*. New York: Stein & Day, 1970. The founder of Islam interpreted for Western readers.

GRUBE, Ernest J. *The World of Islam*. New York: McGraw-Hill, n.d. Clearly written, very well illustrated coverage of Islamic arts and architecture by region and period.

GRUNEBAUM, G. E. VON. *Classical Islam: A History 600–1258*, trans. Katherine Watson. Chicago: Aldine, 1970. By a celebrated Islamicist.

HITTI, P. K. *The Arabs*, 5th ed. New York: St. Martin's Press, 1951. Much reprinted standard history of the rise of the Arab Empire.

HODGSON, M. G. S. *The Venture of Islam: Conscience and History in a World Civilization* (3 vols.). Chicago: University of Chicago Press, 1974. An impressive interpretive study of Islamic history, beliefs, and values.

KEDDIE, N. R., and B. BARON, eds. *Women in Middle Eastern History*. New Haven: Yale University Press, 1991. Scholarly papers on Muslim women in various times and places, including the Arab Empire.

LASSNER, J. *The Shaping of Abbasid Rule*. Princeton, N.J.: Princeton University Press, 1980. Scholarly recent account of the Baghdad caliphate.

NICHOLSON, R. A. *A Literary History of the Arabs*, 2nd ed. Cambridge: Cambridge University Press, 1930. Old, but the best introduction to the remarkable flowering of Arab literature under Islam.

PETERS, F. E. *Allah's Commonwealth: A History of Islam in the Near East A.D. 600–1100*. A good overview of the subject.

PICKTHALL, M. M. *The Meaning of the Glorious Koran*. New York: New American Library, 1953. Readily accessible translation of the Muslim holy book.

RAHMAN, F. *Islam*, 2nd ed. Chicago: University of Chicago Press, 1979. Excellent concise summary of Islamic ideas and institutions: a good place to begin.

SCHIMMEL, A. *Mystical Dimensions of Islam*. Chapel Hill: University of North Carolina Press, 1975. The emotionally accessible Sufi movement. See also J. S. Trimingham, *The Sufi Orders in Islam* (Oxford: Clarendon Press, 1971).

WATT, W. M. *Muhammad at Mecca*. Oxford: Clarendon Press, 1953. Also *Muhammad at Medina* (Oxford: Clarendon Press, 1953). Life of the Prophet by a noted authority. See also the abridged edition, *Muhammad: Prophet and Statesman* (London: Oxford University Press, 1961).

GHANA AND MALI, ETHIOPIA AND ZANJ

West African Empires

The Bilad al Sudan

It is sometimes suggested that Africa "enters history" during the period, contemporary with Europe's Middle Ages, when substantial quantities of written evidence about Africa (in Arabic) first became available. Africa had, of course, already contributed significantly to human history, from the "African genesis" of the human race through the early civilizations of Egypt, Kush, Carthage, and Axum. But the period between the tenth and fifteenth centuries did see the emergence of a number of new African kingdoms and empires, mostly in the Western Sudan, the West African savanna south of the Sahara.

This West African zone of culture should therefore be added to the great cultural areas of European Christendom and the sprawling Muslim hegemony as a center of world civilization during this age of expanding cultural zones.

A number of interrelated factors contributed to the emergence of a distinctively West African civilization on the great westward bulge of Africa shortly before the year 1000. These linked causal factors included geography, trade, and religion.

While North and East Africa were geographically oriented outward toward the developing civilizations of the Mediterranean and the Indian Ocean, West Africa faced inward. Owing to a lack of natural harbors on the coast of West Africa, transport and trade were largely internal. And since commercial exchange was an essential ingredient in the development of kingdoms in West Africa, these new states emerged primarily in the interior, rather than along the coasts.

The interior of Africa, it will be remembered, is divided into a series of horizontal belts of land and climate. These belts are nowhere more clearly marked than in West Africa, and they are crucial to the emergence of trade in that region. In the north there is the thin strip of fertile land along the Mediterranean—the Maghreb, site of ancient Carthage, home in the year 1000 of Muslim Berber and Arab kingdoms, from Tunis to Morocco. South of this coastal strip the Sahara Desert stretches the width of Africa, with its scattering of oases and caravan trails. Farther to the

south lies the Western Sudan, the western end of the belt of lightly wooded savanna that also runs the width of the continent. Still farther south, finally, the dense rain forest of the Guinea coast extends eastward around the internal angle of Africa into the jungles of the Congo basin.

Trade in West Africa flowed predominantly north and south across these belts of climate and terrain. From the Maghreb in the north, camel caravans crossed the desert southward to the savannas to trade in the cities of the *Bilad al Sudan*, the "Land of the Black People," as the Western Sudan was then called. The goods and products these traders took back with them, including the famous gold of Africa, came mostly not from the Sudan itself but from the forests beyond. It was by building their power in this strategic location between the Sahara and the forest peoples of the Guinea coast that the Sudanic kingdoms waxed rich and famous as centers of trade.

With the traders from the north there also came the new religion of Islam. Muslim merchants and teachers, Arab or Berber, settled in the growing cities south of the Sahara and contributed their faith and their skills to the new West African states. They brought with them literacy and administrative experience, and they often held high offices under African kings. They also brought one of the great world religions, a faith which, while always that of a minority, helped to integrate the African kingdoms into the larger world of Muslim trade, Islamic pilgrimage, and the hospitality of their coreligionists wherever they traveled. Under these stimuli, the ironworking agricultural villages of the Western Sudan evolved into impressive African empires over the half-dozen centuries after 1000.

The typical Sudanese state could be as large as, or larger than, the European nations that were developing about the same time. They were ruled by divine-right kings who served as essential intermediaries between their people and their gods. Women often played an important part in governance, queen mothers and senior wives having especially important roles in African kingdoms.

These rulers governed through a combination of appointed bureaucrats and alliances with lesser kings and maintained substantial armies for the constant warfare of the region. For long stretches of time the peoples of West Africa seem to have been well governed and prosperous. European as well as North African goods were on sale in the cities of the Sudan, and West African gold contributed significantly to the European economic revival of the High Middle Ages.

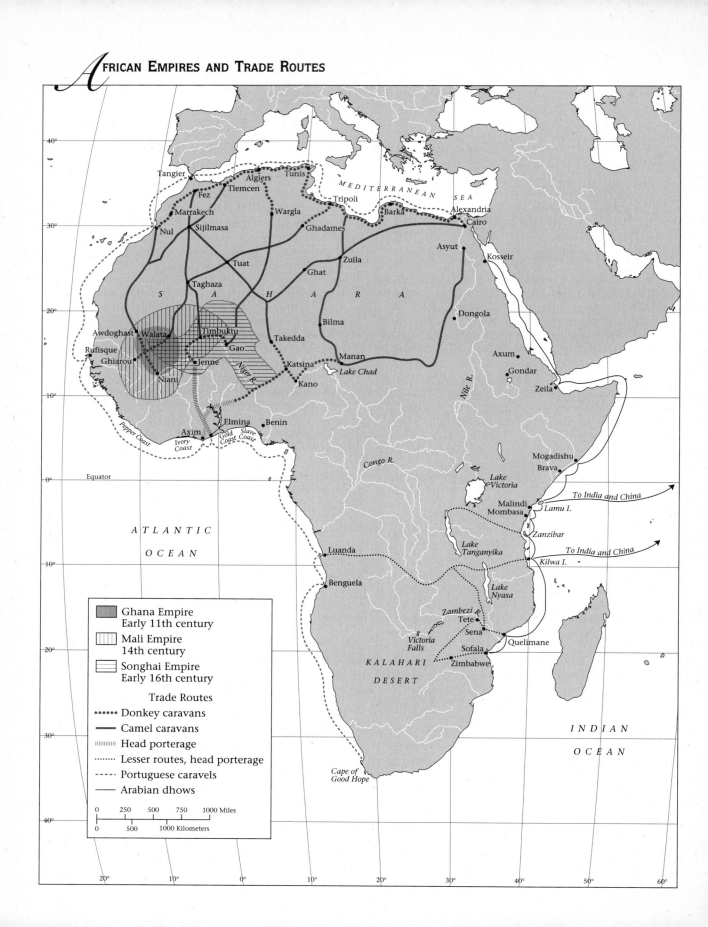

African Empires and Trade Routes

MEDITERRANEAN SEA

Tangier
Algiers
Tunis
Fez
Tlemcen
Marrakech
Wargla
Tripoli
Alexandria
Nul
Sijilmasa
Ghadames
Barka
Cairo
Tuat
Zuila
Asyut
Kosseir
Taghaza
Ghat
S A H A R A
Bilma
Dongola
Awdoghast
Walata
Timbuktu
Takedda
Axum
Rufisque
Gao
Manan
Gondar
Ghiarou
Jenne
Katsina
Lake Chad
Zeila
Niani
Kano
Niger R.

Elmina
Benin
Axim
Ivory Coast
Gold Coast
Slave Coast
Pepper Coast

Congo R.
Mogadishu
Brava

Equator

Lake Victoria
To India and China
Malindi
Mombasa
Lamu I.
Zanzibar

ATLANTIC OCEAN

Lake Tanganyika
To India and China
Luanda
Kilwa I.

Benguela
Lake Nyasa

Zambezi R.
Tete
Sena
Victoria Falls
Quelimane
Sofala
KALAHARI DESERT
Zimbabwe

INDIAN OCEAN

Cape of Good Hope

Nile R.

Legend

	Ghana Empire Early 11th century
	Mali Empire 14th century
	Songhai Empire Early 16th century

Trade Routes
- Donkey caravans
- Camel caravans
- Head porterage
- Lesser routes, head porterage
- Portuguese caravels
- Arabian dhows

0 250 500 750 1000 Miles
0 500 1000 Kilometers

There were problems in the Sudanese kingdoms, as in all the efforts at civilization building we have chronicled so far. These African empires seldom had clearly defined boundaries; they are often represented by circles on maps. And as in their medieval European counterparts, royal power faded rapidly the further one moved from the capital. There were serious problems with succession as well, since succession in West Africa was based not on direct patrilineal hereditary descent, but on a more generalized lineage concept that often produced more than one possible heir to a throne. As in most early civilizations, finally, rebellious generals and revolts by recently conquered peoples were common problems.

All such difficulties notwithstanding, the empires of the Western Sudan did represent a major expansion of urban imperial culture, and as such will be examined here. We shall focus on two of the most famous: Old Ghana and Mali.

GHANA: THE LAND OF GOLD

The Western Sudan in the tenth century was open grassland dotted with scattered trees and groves. The people lived in villages of round, thatch-roofed earthen huts and granaries, cultivated millet and sorghum, and worked iron. The oldest male in a particular village normally ruled the village or sometimes a collection of villages, often with the strong advice and consent of a queen mother or a council of elders. Spirits dwelt nearby in sacred pools and groves of giant baobab trees, and carefully carved fetishes were kept in a special hut and consulted on all serious problems. It was a life, in short, much like that of other peoples outside the walls of urban culture.

Then, sometime before 1000, the walls of cities began to go up in West Africa too.

Ghana, the oldest of the two medieval West African kingdoms to be discussed here, flourished from the eighth through the eleventh centuries, and Mali, its successor, from the twelfth through the fourteenth. Both Ghana and Mali were dominated and most frequently ruled by Mande-speaking peoples: the Soninke, or northern Mande, and the Mandinke, or southern Mande, the latter the famous Mandingo of later history.

Ghana set the pattern of wealth and power built on trade that its successors would follow. As early as 800, while Charlemagne was being crowned in Rome and most of Europe was sunk in feudal chaos and subsistence agriculture, Ghana was already being described by Arab chroniclers as "the land of gold."

The origins of Old Ghana are lost in the mists of time and scholarly dispute.[1] By the eighth and ninth centuries, however, the Soninke kings of Ghana ruled all the lands bounded by the shallow V formed by the upper Niger and Senegal rivers. They governed many villages and clans through a centralized administrative structure and a powerful army. They claimed divine sanction for their governance; like rulers everywhere, they were the chief link between their subjects and the gods. In fact, however, it was commercial exchange that made them great.

From the north came Tuareg camel caravans down across the desert, navigating from oasis to oasis by sun, stars, and wind patterns on the dunes. The Arab and Berber merchants in these caravans brought cloth, brass, glass, and above all, blocks of salt—essential to life in the tropics—to the metropolises of Ghana. From the south, Ghanaian traders brought back agricultural products, slaves, and most important, gold from the mines of Wangara, just south of the Ghanaian frontier. Both African and Arab profited from the exchange. And the kings of Ghana collected heavy customs duties on all the gold and all the salt that crossed their borders. So great was the northward flow of gold that medieval Arab travelers and historians thought the king of Ghana must be the richest ruler in the world.

In the end, it was apparently excessive ambition and the slow southward advance of the Sahara that brought Ghana down.

The ambition of the Soninke kings led them to try to extend their authority northward along the trade routes into the Berber lands on the southern edge of the Sahara. The disunited Berbers fell easy victims at first. But in the eleventh century, unified and filled with crusading zeal by the puritanical Almoravid sect of Islam, they struck back. Within a few decades the Almoravids had swept north as far as Morocco and on into Spain—and south to overwhelm Old Ghana.

The southward creep of the Sahara completed what the Almoravids had begun. The continuing drying-out of northern Africa parched the former heartland of Ghana. Before the slowly advancing sands, black power retreated farther to the south.

MALI: WHERE THE KING DWELLS

The Almoravids broke the back of Ghanaian power, but they were not strong enough to rule for long. The result was to create a power vacuum in the Western Sudan where a number of African kingdoms fought for mastery. Another branch of the Mande-speaking people, the Mandinke, emerged victorious by the early thirteenth century from this anarchic period. They became the builders and rulers of an even larger realm than Old Ghana had been: The Empire of the Mali.

Mali is an Arab corruption of a southern Mande word meaning simply "Where the King Dwells"—and the Mandinke rulers of Mali were kings indeed. They governed in conscious emulation of their Ghanaian prede-

---

[1]"Old Ghana" is sometimes so called to distinguish it from the modern nation of Ghana, which is located some hundreds of miles southeast of the empire discussed here.

Voices from the Past

"*The city of Ghana consists of two towns situated on a plain. One of these towns, which is inhabited by Muslims, is large and possesses twelve mosques, in one of which they assemble for the Friday prayer. There are salaried imāms and muezzins, as well as jurists and scholars. In the environs are wells with sweet water, from which they drink and with which they grow vegetables.*

The king's town is six miles [about 10 km] distant from this one and bears the name of al-Ghāba. Between these two towns there are continuous habitations. The houses of the inhabitants are of stone and acacia wood. The king has a palace and a number of domed dwellings all surrounded with an enclosure like a city wall.

In the king's town, and not far from his court of justice, is a mosque where pray such Muslims as pay him formal visits.

Around the king's town are domed buildings and groves and thickets where the sorcerers of these people, men in charge of the religious cult, live. In them are their idols and the tombs of their kings. These woods are guarded and none may enter them and know what is there."

This famous eleventh-century description of the capital of Ghana clearly reflects both the impact of Islam and the persistence of older African traditions. The Arab chronicler Al-Bakri records that the capital was really two "cities"—or city centers, since houses filled all the space between them. The Arab quarter is dominated by its mosques, while the "king's town," or political center, has its sacred grove consecrated to older gods.

According to this Arab account, the king received visitors in state in his royal pavilion, surrounded by the sons of subordinate chiefs, leading advisors, and governors. Guards with swords and shields stood behind him. The royal turban and robes, the shields of the sentries, and even the collars of guard dogs stationed at the door were all of gold.

What does this description tell you about the economy and political structure of Ghana? What do you deduce about the importance of the Arab traders from the fact that, while his majesty's African subjects were required to prostrate themselves on the ground before him and throw dust on their heads, Muslims were allowed to greet him simply by clapping their hands?

Al-Bakri, Kitab al-masalik wa'l mamalik in Nehemia Levtzion, "The Sahara and the Sudan from the Arab Conquest . . . to the Rise of the Almoravids," in J. D. Fage, ed., The Cambridge History of Africa (Cambridge: Cambridge University Press, 1986), Vol. 2, p. 668.

---

cessors, with appointed officials—including departments of defense, foreign relations, and finance—and with an effective army to enforce the royal will. They revitalized the trans-Saharan trade in gold and salt and grew richer than the Soninke Mande of Ghana. They turned caravan-route cities like Timbuktu into famous emporiums of trade and centers of culture.

Mali reached its highest point in the fourteenth century under its most famous ruler, Mansa (King) Musa (c. 1307–1332). Musa expanded the empire to its greatest territorial extent, to the big bend of the Niger. He was celebrated not only in Arab lands to the north but as far away as Europe.

The famous Arab traveler and historian Ibn Batuta, who visited Mali around the middle of the fourteenth century, was impressed with what he saw. He received good medical attention there when he fell ill, and he had respectful words for the scholars he met. Above all, he was struck by the strong sense of justice and the rigorous enforcement of it that he found in Mali. The roads of Mali were safe for travelers, he wrote, as they were in few other parts of the world.

This picture of a well-governed, wealthy, and powerful state has its darker side. There were frequent disputes over the succession to the throne, and factions feuded at the courts of the kings of Mali, as they did in royal courts from China to Britain. Conquered peoples were often restless and ready to rebel. Religion became an important divisive factor too, with Mandinke rulers turning to Islam while their peasant subjects and the neighboring peoples with whom Mali traded remained faithful to the old gods and the spirits of the land.

Like all great nations, the kingdom of Mali had its enemies, rivals awaiting only the opportunity to pull the greatest of West African powers down. In the fifteenth century, as we will see, one of them took advantage of internal weakness to do just that.

MANSA MUSA'S PILGRIMAGE

Like all the kings and increasing numbers of the ruling classes of Mali, Mansa Musa was a Muslim, and his most renowned exploit was a pilgrimage to Mecca. His royal progress across Africa astonished the peoples through whose lands he passed. On this long journey to the north and east across Africa, Musa was accompanied by his wife, his chief officials, thousands of servants, and a hundred camels laden with gold. He was given a palace in Cairo by the Egyptian sultan and spent three months there before continuing on to the holy city. He and his retinue had spent so much gold in Cairo that the price of that precious metal declined because there was so much of it in circulation. As an Egyptian official reported:

> This man spread upon Cairo the flood of his generosity: there was no person, officer of the court, or holder of any office of the Sultanate who did not receive a sum of gold from him. The people of Cairo earned incalculable sums from him, whether by buying and selling or by gifts. So much gold was current in Cairo that it ruined the value of money.[2]

On his return, Mansa Musa glorified his capital city. From his pilgrimage, he brought back artists, scholars, and a famous architect to build him palaces and mosques. He established diplomatic ties with African states as far away as Egypt and Morocco. It was from this time on that European map-makers began to put Musa's picture on their maps of West Africa with a lump of gold in his hand.

[2]ál-Omari, in E. Jefferson Murphy, *History of African Civilization* (New York: Crowell, 1972), p. 120.

2 CHRISTIAN KINGDOMS OF EAST AFRICA

THE CHRISTIAN STATES OF NUBIA

The influence of Islam was profound across North Africa, West Africa, and—as we will see—down the eastern coast of the continent as well. In one area, however, another great world religion exercised a determining influence. In the northeastern corner of Africa, several Christian kingdoms flourished, including the states of Christian Nubia and the Christian kingdom of Ethiopia.

Nubian civilization already had a long history when Christianity reached the Upper Nile in the sixth century. Nubia had been the home of a flourishing culture in the days of ancient Egypt. Kush and Meroe had flowered there, and Axum had overrun the southern core of the region. But great changes came over Nubia when Greek Orthodox preachers from the north converted first the kings and then the upper classes of the Nubian zone.

The political history of Christian Nubia covered eight hundred years, from the sixth to the fourteenth centuries. The most powerful of the Christian kingdoms of Nubia was Makouria, whose chief cities were the royal capital at Old Dongola and the chief religious center at Faras.

At the height of its power, Makouria's King Kyriakos could march up the Nile into Muslim Egypt to force the sultan to release the imprisoned head of Egypt's Christian minority. In its heyday around 800, Makouria was ruled by a hereditary monarch who dictated to a dozen subsidiary kings and commanded a large number of officials.

Converted to Christianity by missionaries from the Greek-speaking Byzantine Empire, the Christian Nubian elite also spoke Greek, used Greek titles for officials, and used Greek as the official language of the church. Pictures of Nubian kings show them wearing golden crowns encrusted with jewels and clad in sumptuously embroidered robes like those worn by Byzantine rulers in Constantinople.

In its best days, Christian Nubia was a lovely land of cities and villages, churches and monasteries. A tenth-century Arab visitor recalled "villages with beautiful buildings, churches, monasteries and many palm trees, vines, gardens, fields and large pastures in which graze handsome and well-bred camels."[3]

By the 1300s, however, royal power had declined, and bloody coups were frequent. A feudal aristocracy with castles scattered across the land divided real power between them. Then Arab tribesmen broke through the frontiers, and Egypt's new rulers, the military aristocracy

[3]Ibn Selim, quoted in William Y. Adams, *Nubia: Corridor to Africa* (Princeton, NJ: Princeton University Press, 1984), p. 461.

known as the Mamelukes, interfered repeatedly in Nubian royal politics. Cut off from the main body of medieval Christendom in Europe, Christian Nubia held out as long as it could against the growing power of Islam in Africa. By 1400, however, a Muslim dynasty ruled Makouria, and almost all of Nubia was in Islamic hands.

THE CHRISTIAN KINGDOM OF ETHIOPIA

Southeast of Nubia, the Christian survivors of ancient Axum had withdrawn ever deeper into the mountainous regions of their corner of Africa in the latter part of the first millennium A.D. A one-time trading people, they were now cut off from their former trading partners in the eastern Mediterranean and the Red Sea. Christian converts from the fourth century, they were surrounded by pagans and, from the seventh century on, by Muslim Arabs. Forgotten by their fellow Christians and by those whose ancient civilization they had shared, the people who would come to be known as Ethiopians struggled to survive in their isolated upland home.

Only in the twelfth century did a fusion of Ethiopian peoples under the Christian Zagwe dynasty bring a new flowering of this African kingdom. Under the Zagwe kings, a uniquely Ethiopian form of Christianity took shape. Heavily imbued with both local pagan and ancient Judaic elements, the Ethiopian church also forged a close alliance with the monarchy, a cooperation that strengthened both. The most striking relics of this era still remaining are the dozen rock-carved churches hacked out of the volcanic stone of the Ethiopian mountains at Roha during the reign of King Lalibela (c. 1181–1221). According to a later medieval account, the king's stone carvers labored on the churches by day, while angels carried on the work at night.

The Solomonid dynasty succeeded the Zagwe kings in 1270 and at least nominally ruled the land for the next seven centuries. Claiming direct descent from Israel's King Solomon and the Queen of Sheba, the Solomonids reached their apogee under King Zara Jacob (1434–1468). Still depending heavily on religion as a social cement, these Ethiopian rulers suppressed heresy at home and crusaded vigorously against neighboring Muslim peoples. From the fourteenth century, priests and monks generated a literary renaissance that produced hymns, royal chronicles, and biographies of kings and saints. By the beginning of modern times, sixteenth-century Ethiopia was an extensive if still isolated kingdom.

Medieval Europeans told legends of the golden realm of Prester John, a fabulously rich Christian king lost somewhere in the unknown southern lands of Africa. A hardy Portuguese traveler even reached Ethiopia in 1494, two years after Columbus reached the New World. But this and other early contacts came to nothing. Muslim mil-

itary pressure was renewed in the later sixteenth century, and Ethiopian Christians themselves fell into a bloody schism. By 1600, the Solomonid monarchs were little more than figureheads, the kingdom itself a loose confederation of princes.

A CAPITAL ON THE MOVE, A MOUNTAIN OF KINGS

Medieval Ethiopia's political system, at its apogee under the Solomonids, evolved some unique features all its own. Ruling over a large, geographically fragmented realm, over Christians, Muslims, Jews, and traditional animists, over Africans, Arabs, and other peoples, Ethiopia's kings devised a governmental system combining flexibility with strength. A loose feudal regime of vassal kings and nobles meant that the king of Ethiopia delegated a good deal of authority to regional powers. A large military force, ready to move at the first threat of serious disorder, gave the ruler the final say.

Two other institutions emphasized the flexibility of the Ethiopian system. One was the traveling royal court, the other Ethiopia's unique Mountain of Kings.

The court of the Ethiopian king was not settled in a single capital city but was always on the move. In some ways it resembled the restless monarchies of medieval Europe, moving from one castle or province to the next to keep an eye on feudal vassals whose loyalty was often fickle. In Ethiopia, however, the kings seem to have had no favorite seat. The royal court was a movable camp, ever ready to pull up stakes and move on to the next valley, to march against a rebellious prince or an aggressive neighboring people.

It was a colorful array of royalty and powerful officials, courtiers and soldiers, many priests, and thousands of royal retainers. Merchants, Christian and Muslim alike, gathered around this caravan to display their wares. Subordinate princes and provincial governors came and went, offering submission, tribute, or taxes, asking for decisions on matters of state from powerful royal ministers or from the king himself.

The royal caravan brought all the upper classes, ethnic groups, and religious sects together, while moving majestically from one part of the kingdom to another. Thus, the traveling court of Ethiopia performed a vital integrative function for this extremely heterogeneous society.

Ethiopia's legendary Mountain of the Kings combined stability with flexibility in a very different way. King Yikunno-Amlak, who established the Solomonid dynasty in 1270, was determined to avoid future palace coups or revolutions. He therefore sent all his relatives except his designated heirs up to the heights of Mount Geshen, an inaccessible retreat guarded by picked troops garrisoning all the passes below. On Mount Geshen, all

Mansa Musa of Mali, shown on a European map with crown, scepter, and a royal orb of authority which is a lump of solid gold. West Africa's reputation as a golden land went back as far as ancient times and earned one stretch of coastline the European colonial label of "Gold Coast" (today's Ghana) as recently as the present century. (New York Public Library)

the princes of the realm who could be rivals for the throne lived in luxurious isolation. They were free to enjoy all the pleasures that went with their high birth—but cut off from political ties to the world below.

As the years passed, many of these royal exiles turned to religious study, took up poetry or music, became wise or creative spirits. And if ever the direct royal line failed in the kingdom, the wisest of all the denizens of the Mountain of the Kings could be summoned down to take his place on the throne of Ethiopia.

CHRISTIAN ART OF AFRICA

The cultural life of Nubia and Ethiopia, like the contemporary culture of medieval Europe, was powerfully shaped by religious belief. The manuscripts and inscriptions that have survived from this period in both areas are heavily Christian, including Scripture, prayers, and the lives of saints. Surviving pictures include manuscript illustrations and frescos on church walls depicting scenes from the Bible and leaders of African churches. In Ethiopia especially, education and culture were in the hands of monks. In both areas, churches and monasteries dotted the land.

Many impressive artistic achievements remain to us from these Christian centuries in northeastern Africa. Among them are the beautiful frescos rescued from the Nubian cathedral at Faras and the rock-cut churches built by Lalibela, mentioned above.

The mural paintings of Faras had to be removed in the mid-twentieth century when much of Nubia was flooded by Egypt's Aswan High Dam. Carefully separated from the walls by Polish experts, these dazzling religious paintings may now be seen in museums in Khartoum and Warsaw. In the most famous of them, the three Hebrew youths cast into the fiery furnace are shielded from harm by the towering Archangel Michael. The figures, garbed in blue and gold, stand out vividly against a wall of leaping scarlet flames.

Ethiopia's churches of Lalibela were for a long time believed to be the work of foreign artists and masons. More recent study of the many other surviving buildings in the region, however, make it clear that the churches were done by local builders and artists trained in traditions of stone carving that go back to ancient Axum.

The eleven churches of the Lalibela complex were and named after structures in Jerusalem. A stream flow-

Ethiopia's remarkable rock-cut churches at Lalibela, carved entirely from the living stone, are among the most striking monuments of African Christianity. This interior is still crowded with Ethiopian worshipers on church holy days. (Comstock)

ing through the center was called after the river Jordan, and a high spot overlooking the churches was labeled "Calvary" after the site of Christ's execution. According to legend, King Lalibela had been mystically transported to Jerusalem, where Christ himself showed him the holy places as they were later duplicated in the king's rock-cut church center. There each year Christ's baptism, crucifixion, and resurrection were re-enacted in a passion play at this sacred site high in the mountains of Ethiopia.

EAST AFRICAN TRADING CITIES

THE CITY-STATES OF ZANJ

Down the east coast of Africa, along the shores of the Indian Ocean, a similar process of commercial growth, Islamicization, and cultural synthesis was taking place. The result was the flourishing string of East African ports and city-states the Arabs called the Land of Zanj—mostly Kenya and Tanzania today.

Towards the end of the first century A.D., a Greek vessel sailing out of the Red Sea and down the East African coast would find little but crocodiles and a few people fishing with wicker traps along the shore. A millennium later cities were to be found all along these coasts, their ports humming with the trade of the Middle and the Far East.

In the interim wave after wave of migrants had settled along this edge of the continent. The Bantu-speaking Africans were migrants across central Africa to these coasts, bringing iron and agriculture. Other peoples had come by sea. Southeast Asians had been coming for centuries, populating the huge southern island of Madagascar and introducing the ubiquitous banana to Africa. Shirazi Persians, probably moving south from earlier settlements on the Horn of Africa, came as traders. But the most successful immigrants, merchants, builders, and sometimes rulers were the Muslim Arabs we have already met in so many places.

The history of evolving relationship between African animists and agriculturists on the one hand and Arab Muslim traders on the other must be worked out largely from archaeological remains and oral tradition. Arabs, by that time masters of the most of the Indian Ocean trade, seem to have settled in East Africa in growing numbers from the twelfth century on. They may have established trading posts alongside African towns, as they did in the Western Sudan, accepting the protection of African kings. Or they may have imposed Arab overlordship, as they would do along these coasts in later centuries.

SWAHILI CULTURE

In either case, the Muslim faith spread here as well as in West Africa. A mixed Afro-Islamic culture developed. A Bantu language, Swahili, continued as the lingua franca of the coast, and African customs persisted even among the rulers of the new city-states that emerged. But there were Arabic influences in Swahili too, and the architecture of the new towns was more likely to be Arabic or Persian than African in design.

The wealth of East Africa, like that of the Western Sudan, was based on commerce. Here the trade routes of inner Africa met the sea lanes of the Indian Ocean, linking Africa with the Mediterranean, Arabia, India, Southeast Asia, and China. Ivory, gold, iron, copper, pearl, coral, and slaves left African shores; Indian beads, Chinese porcelain, and silks flowed into Africa from overseas.

The East African cities of Kilwa, south of Zanzibar, and Sofala, still farther to the south beyond the Zambesi, dominated the region. The first Portuguese intruders around 1500 reported a number of such cities, with fine stone buildings, women wearing imported silks and beads, and rich agriculture produce. The houses of Mogadishu in the north were multistory structures, and the palace at Kilwa covered two acres, with courtyards and vaulted chambers on a cliff overlooking the sea.

The quality of life in these coastal cities would later be testified to by the Portuguese. The narrow stone-walled city streets were similar to their own. Doors were elegantly carved, beds sometimes inlaid with ivory, walls inset with Chinese porcelain or Persian ceramics, like the dishes on which the wealthy ate. Early European visitors also noticed the luxurious silk and cotton garments of wealthy Swahili women, their gold and silver bangles and earrings set with precious stones.

Foreignors seldom penetrated the inner courtyards of the homes of the well-to-do. But baked clay lamps lit interior rooms, and one Arab author reported that the elites of these East African towns "take spiritual delight in the study of philosophy."[4]

A stroll down the streets of the island town of Lamu off the coast of Kenya today may give a general impression of that lost world. Close-pressing walls of white-washed stone, intricately carved doorways, cool courtyards and tangled gardens frame the life of what is now a quiet backwater. The muezzin still wakes you before dawn each morning with his call to prayer. And the old stone pier where you land and leave still shelters Arab dhows in from the Red Sea or the Persian Gulf.

---

[4]Abu 'l-Kasim al-Andalusi, quoted in V. V. Matviev, "The Development of Swahili Civilization," in D. T. Niane, ed., *General History of Africa* (London: Heinemann, 1984), Vol. 4, p. 457.

SUMMARY

Commerce and religion were at the heart of the new zones of urban imperial culture that took shape in Africa between A.D. 600 and 1500. These two factors shaped West African empires and East African kingdoms and city-states

The lightly forested plains of the Western Sudan saw the emergence of a distinctive type of African kingdom during this period. The kings of the Western Sudan, located between the Sahara and the deep forests, became middlemen in the lucrative trade between the Arab states of the Maghreb and the forest peoples of the Guinea coast. These African kings built powerful states on the grasslands, and Arab merchants brought Islam, literacy, and other innovations to their urban elites.

The most famous early Sudanic kingdom was Ghana (eighth to eleventh centuries), known to Arab travelers as "the land of gold." Mali (twelfth to fourteenth centuries) emulated earlier Ghanaian practices with even greater success, building such commercial metropolises as Timbuktu and producing one of the most famous of West African rulers in Mansa Musa.

The spread of early Christianity up the Nile strongly influenced the new civilizations that emerged in Nubia and Ethiopia (ancient Axum) between 500 and 1500. Powerful monarchs ruled these countries while churches and monasteries generated new schools of art, architecture, and religious literature. The Nubian states were absorbed into the growing body of Islam, but Christian Ethiopia, though declining politically, survived as an independent state on into modern times.

On the East African coasts a number of African city-states played an important part in trade on the Indian Ocean between the seventh and the fifteenth centuries. Cities like Kilwa or Sofala also had Muslim Arab commercial communities (and perhaps rulers). They traded with Arabia, India, and countries even farther east.

SUGGESTED READING

BROOKS, G. E. *Landlords and Strangers: Ecology, Society, and Trade in Western Africa, 1000–1630.* Boulder, Colo.: Westview Press, 1993. Ecologically rooted study of social and commercial patterns among West African peoples during the period of the great West African empires.

CONNAH, G. *African Civilizations: Precolonial Cities and States in Tropical Africa: An Archaeological Perspective.* Cambridge, England: Cambridge University Press, 1987. Geographical and archaeological analysis of centers of civilization from the Nile to the West African Sudan.

DAVIDSON, B. *The African Past: Chronicles from Antiquity to Modern Times.* Boston: Little, Brown, 1964. Material on Sudanic and east-coast African states.

FAGE, J. D. *A History of West Africa,* 4th ed. Cambridge, England: Cambridge University Press, 1969. An old standard, but still a good place to begin.

IBN BATTUTA, M. *Travels in Asia and Africa, 1324–1354,* trans. H. A. R. Gibb. New York: McBride, 1929. Vivid descriptions of the kingdom of Mali are among the selections translated here.

JONES, A. H. M., and E. MONROE. *A History of Ethiopia.* Oxford: Clarendon Press, 1955. Brief survey of the political history, with emphasis on medieval and early modern periods.

JULY, R. W. *Precolonial Africa: An Economic and Social History.* New York: Scribner's, 1975. Useful for both sides of Africa in this period, when trade was central to development.

LEUTZION, N. *Ancient Ghana and Mali.* New York: African Pub. Co., 1980. Scholarly study, originally published as a volume in the Methuen Studies in African History; based on oral as well as Arabic sources.

NIANE, D. T., ed. *UNESCO General History of Africa,* Vol. 2: *Africa from the Twelfth to the Sixteenth Century.* Berkeley and Los Angeles: University of California Press, 1984. African perspectives on the history of the continent during the centuries before major Western penetration.

NURSE, D., and T. SPEAR. *The Swahili: Reconstructing the History and Language of an African Society, 800–1500.* Philadelphia: University of Pennsylvania Press, 1985. Swahili interaction with Arabs and Persians in the shaping of East African society.

OLIVER, R., and A. ATMORE. *African Middle Ages, 1400–1800.* New York: Cambridge University Press, 1981. Authoritative account of the period.

OSAE, T. A., S. N. NWABARA, and A. T. O. ODUNSI. *A Short History of West Africa A.D. 100 to the Present.* New York: Hill and Wang, 1973. Stimulating and balanced, with brief discussions of Ghana, Mali, and other early West African states.

SMITH, R. S. *Warfare and Diplomacy in Pre-Colonial West Africa,* 2nd ed. Madison: University of Wisconsin Press, 1989. The art of war as practiced among the West African kingdoms.

STRIDE, G. T., et al. *Peoples and Empires of West Africa.* New York: Africana Publishing Corp., 1975. First half covers the story through the West African empires.

CHAPTER 20

INDIA AND SOUTHEAST ASIA

INDIA BETWEEN THE GUPTAS AND THE MOGULS

THE TIMELESS LAND

The Himalayan mountain chain that shuts northern India off from the rest of Asia loomed over the Gangetic plain as it had always done. The sacred Ganges, brown and rich between green banks flowed southeastward across northern India. South of the Ganges, forested hills blended into the wedge-shaped Deccan, the plateau of peninsular India, narrowing between the Arabian Sea and the Bay of Bengal toward the equator.

The Northwest Frontier remained uneasy as always, inviting foreign armies through the passes into the Indus valley and the Punjab. At the other end of India, the large island of Ceylon (Sri Lanka) floated lush and tempting on the southern seas; even more tempting lands lay in Southeast Asia beyond.

By A.D. 500 three thousand years of history had happened in this ancient land. Perhaps half that time was lost in a haze of legend and obscurity—the vanished Harappan hegemony of the Indus and the barbarous, epic centuries of the Aryan conquests. But the thousand years between the rise of the Gangetic city-states and the living India of 500 had left a continuous trace upon the land.

The Mauryas and the Guptas had shown that much of India could be governed from a single center, at least for a time. But other cities, states, and dynasties had emerged all over the subcontinent in those ten centuries, and their conflicting ambitions and determined independence would make the imposition of a single political order no easy thing in the future.

Cities full of bustling merchants and skilled artisans were scattered liberally along the coasts and rivers of India in the middle of the first millennium A.D. Countless tiny villages dotted the land, their populations plowing, planting, and harvesting to the seasonal rhythm of the monsoon. The complex system of castes structured Indian society, determining from birth to death what every Indian would do for a living, whom he might marry, what foods he would eat, what gods he would pray to. The long, slow evolution of Hindu, Buddhist, and other faiths had marked India with an ancient passion for religion as powerful as the newer faiths of Christianity and Islam in the west.

India's history in this age of growing zones of culture was thus rather different from that of the newer Christian and Muslim cultures of western Eurasia. Indian history between 500 and 1500 was given its shape and texture by a matrix of already ancient geographical adaptations, institutional and social patterns, and traditional ideas. This matrix of faith and caste, palace and village, the rolling river and the looming mountain range would impose cultural continuities on these unsettled centuries. The trends of the new millennium would evolve naturally out of what had gone before, till past and present blurred into one. Already India was assuming that air of timelessness that would distinguish it among the nations.

ATTEMPTS AT UNITY: HARSHA AND THE DELHI SULTANATE

The political history of India for much of the thousand years between the decline of Gupta rule in the fifth century and the coming of the Mogul dynasty not long after 1500 is a tangle of short-lived states, foreign invasions, and power struggles leading nowhere. Some of the peoples of this millennium, such as the chivalric Rajput princes in the north and the ambitious Cholas in the south, left a mark on India's history. There were also two significant attempts at national conquest: the empire of King Harsha and the Turkish regime called the Delhi Sultanate. But none of these matched the political achievements of the Mauryas and Guptas before them or the Mogul Empire to come.

The seventh-century reign of King Harsha (607–647) saw a brief futile attempt to impose order on the peoples and kingdoms of the subcontinent. The cultured warrior King Harsha conquered all of northern India from the Himalayas to the river Narmada, the traditional divide between northern India and the Deccan. Between campaigns, he—like Charlemagne two centuries later—patronized religion and the arts and gave lavishly to the poor. Considerably more literate than the great Frankish king, Harsha may actually have written the plays and poems that are attributed to him.

He moved his capital from Patna, the traditional center of political unification since the Mauryas, to the city of Kanauj farther up the Ganges valley. But—again like Charlemagne—he controlled his north Indian empire

The <u>Descent of the Ganges</u>, India's sacred river, from heaven to earth is depicted in this celebrated sculpture at Mamallapuram. All earth's teeming life—animal, human, and divine—gathers to give thanks for the divine gift in this awesome life-size granite carving, only a detail of which is shown here. A lush plenitude of figures and detail is as typical of Indian as of European gothic religious art. (New York Public Library Picture Collection)

primarily by moving about it at the head of his army. The empire itself was probably no more than a loose collection of kingdoms and principalities, and most Indians can have been little affected by the transitory power at Kanauj. With Harsha's death, his empire crumbled and political division reasserted itself.

The second significant effort to impose order on the subcontinent was the work of foreigners—the Turkish Afghan regime known as the Delhi Sultanate, which dominated much of northern India from the thirteenth into the sixteenth century. It was an impressive span of years, but the size of the realm the newcomers ruled varied drastically from reign to reign. For a few brief years in the mid fourteenth century, one sultan of Delhi held at least feudal suzerainty over most of the kingdoms of the south as well as northern India. But this was exceptional, and during the fifteenth and early sixteenth centuries the Turkish sultans really governed little beyond the immediate environs of the city of Delhi itself.

They did make this city, still farther up the Ganges, into the third political center of northern India—and New Delhi is, of course, the nation's capital today. But the Delhi sultans had only a rudimentary system of adminis-

tration, and their rule was essentially feudal. Provincial governors were really soldiers granted control of villages or larger territories in return for military service. These local rulers governed only as far as their troops could reach. Again, most Indians had little significant contact with those who claimed to govern them.

There were more impressive examples of governance on a regional basis. The Cholas in the south, a Tamil-speaking Dravidian dynasty whose ambitions once carried them almost to the Ganges, apparently had a more centralized administrative system, based on unions of villages. But even in the Chola Empire, village autonomy was great. And most of the other "kingdoms" of those centuries were little more than military hegemonies or clan supremacies headed by self-styled *rajas*. There were no Asokas, no Chandra Guptas to do more.

INVASIONS AND DIVISIONS

Besides political disunity, another disturbing feature of the history of those centuries of disarray was the unending series of invasions from without and power struggles within the subcontinent.

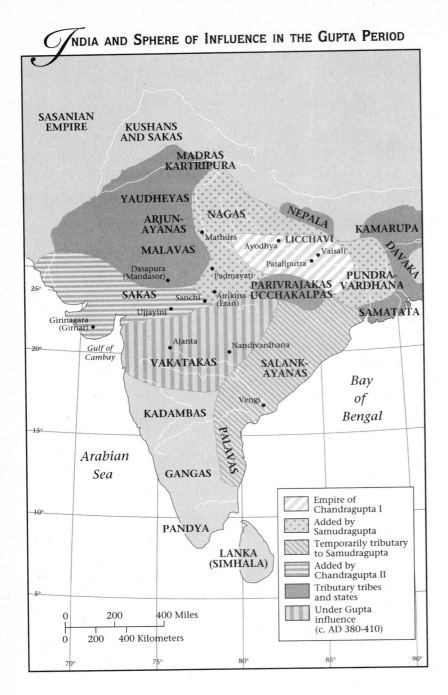

SASANIAN EMPIRE

KUSHANS AND SAKAS

MADRAS KARTRIPURA

YAUDHEYAS

ARJUN-AYANAS

NAGAS

NEPALA

KAMARUPA

DAVAKA

• Mathura

Ayodhya

• LICCHAVI

• Vaisali

MALAVAS

Pataliputra

Dasapura (Mandasor) •

• Padmayati

PUNDRA-VARDHANA

PARIVRAJAKAS

SAKAS

Sanchi •

• Airikina (Eran)

UCCHAKALPAS

25°

Ujjayini •

SAMATATA

Girinagara (Girnar) •

Gulf of Cambay

• Ajanta

• Nandivardhana

20°

VAKATAKAS

SALANK-AYANAS

Bay of Bengal

Vengi •

KADAMBAS

15°

Arabian Sea

PALAVAS

GANGAS

Empire of Chandragupta I

Added by Samudragupta

Temporarily tributary to Samudragupta

Added by Chandragupta II

Tributary tribes and states

Under Gupta influence (c. AD 380-410)

10°

PANDYA

LANKA (SIMHALA)

5°

0   200   400 Miles

0   200   400 Kilometers

70°   75°   80°   85°   90°

Among the foreign invaders who took advantage of India's weakness to push down through the passes of the Northwest Frontier were the White Huns who undermined the Guptas, the Arabs, the Rajputs who became India's military aristocracy, the Muslim Turks who established the Delhi Sultanate, Tamerlane and his Tatars, and finally the Muslim Moguls who reunified India at last in the sixteenth century. This succession of nomadic invasions made things lively along the frontier. Most of them, however, made scarcely a ripple on the steady flow of Indian life that went on as it always had beneath the marching of armies and the feuding of princes.

When there were no new hordes swarming down the Afghan passes, there was still princely feuding to contend with. Two major power struggles within the subcontinent should at least be mentioned here.

In the north, during the centuries following the brief meteoric passage of Harsha, three separate kingdoms struggled to dominate his short-lived empire. There was no decisive outcome but only the gradual decline and fragmentation of the contenders. In southern India, the Tamil-speaking Cholas, mentioned above for their administrative sophistication, also embarked on a campaign of conquest. For a time it seemed possible that the Cholas would reverse the historic pattern by conquering the north from a southern base. But they were unable to prevail, and their administrative skills and lavish patronage of the arts never spread beyond the southern end of India.

It is a frustrating political picture. *Rajas* and *maharajas* appointed officials with high-sounding titles and sent their armies off to war, and nothing much came of it at all. Compared with the dynamic expansion of Islam or the rhythmic dynastic cycles of China, the Indian political scene seemed shapeless and chaotic, going nowhere.

RAJPUTS AND DRAVIDIANS, CASTE AND SEX

But there was order to the Indian experience, even during these disordered centuries. Beneath the aimlessness of politics, profound social and cultural changes were taking place. Many of these changes represent continuations of earlier trends. But they reached a climax of sorts during the millennium of political disarray between the Guptas and the Moguls.

The greatest social transformation, a continuation of a much older tradition, was the absorption of new peoples into the already complex fabric of Indian society. This was basically the result of creative compromise by Hindu India's brahman elite, who found room in the ancient caste system for the newcomers. Thus, when nomadic invaders such as the Rajputs actually settled in India, their leaders would be accepted as *kshatriyas* (the ancient Aryan warrior caste), less prominent tribesmen as *sudras* (farmers), and even their priests as brahmans of a sort. Like Mongols in China or Germans in the Roman world, these steppe peoples were typically seduced by life in the host culture's rich cities and princely courts and were glad to be part of it. As caste allegiances grew among the new peoples, old loyalties to tribe and clan decreased, until the newcomers were thoroughly assimilated into the polyglot Indian population.

The fiercely proud Rajputs—"Sons of Kings"—in particular provided ruling houses for many north and central Indian kingdoms. They fought chivalric wars with one another, provided the strongest military force India could muster against subsequent invaders, and still compose an important part of the Indian army's officer corps today. As *kshatriyas*, their warlike proclivities were thus channeled into the service of the ancient Indian society that had absorbed them.

A similar process of assimilation went on in south India. The great triangle of peninsular India had been the

The patterned movement of Shiva Nataraja, Lord of the Dance, symbolizes the pulsing cosmic energy of the universe. This famous figure of the multiarmed god, grinding the demon of ignorance underfoot as he dances the universe into being, is a product of the Dravidian Hindu imagination of southern India. The god holds an hourglass-shaped drum in one of his four hands, fire in another, symbols of his power to awaken the natural world to life and to destroy it at the end of a cosmic cycle. ("Shiva Nataraja" 13th Century Sculpture-Bronze-Indian, 34.25 × 27.5 × 13 inches [87 × 69.9 × 33 cm], The Nelson-Atkins Museum of Art)

haven of the Dravidian peoples driven south by the conquering Aryans many centuries before. Dravidians, particularly the Tamil-speaking people of the far south, had built a flourishing city-based society on foreign trade and agriculture during the preceding half-dozen centuries. The absorption of the Dravidian south into a single cultural zone with northern India, however, dates from approximately the year 500.

Again, the vehicle was the spread of Hinduism and the caste system. The worship of the great Hindu divinities Vishnu and Shiva grew in the south, and Sanskrit began to challenge Tamil as the literary language. Above all, a modified caste system—almost excluding the warrior *kshatriyas* but containing many "untouchable" groups—was gradually imposed upon Dravidian society.

Henceforth, the Indian subcontinent would constitute a single zone of culture, though there would continue to be significant regional differences. The north would remain politically dominant; the south would be a center of artistic and intellectual development.

Another important change during this period—again, a continuation of an older trend—was the rigidification of the caste system. The number of castes continued to grow far beyond the four original divisions generated at the time of the Aryan-Dravidian synthesis. Categories and subcategories multiplied, and the obligations imposed by membership in a given caste grew more elaborate—and more rigorous. Respect for caste grew especially as Buddhism—which had ignored caste distinctions—declined in India. And new recruits, among northern tribesmen or in the Dravidian south, took up the system with the fervor of converts.

There was still some freedom of choice in occupation, and marriages across caste lines could occur, if perhaps uncommonly. But the direction of development toward a caste-bound society was clearly established during these centuries before 1500.

The freedom of women in society, which would come to be curtailed more rigorously in India than in many other places, was considerably less constrained during this millennium. The strict seclusion of respectable women was not common yet. And the brutal practice of self-immolation by widows was still rare; some widows even remarried without losing popular respect. Ladies of the upper classes seem generally to have been educated and cultured during this period. They enjoyed music and dancing and shared freely in the pleasures of life at the courts of the *rajas*.

For the peasants in their millions, clustered in dusty villages or creaking in a bullock cart past the gardens of the palaces, the culture and pastimes of the great were matter for fairy tales, not part of real life. But there was one central part of Indian culture that was open to all. This was the life of the spirit, the rich religious culture of many faiths and increasingly magnificent temples that flourished in this as in earlier periods of Indian History.

 # RELIGION AND ART IN INDIA

A FERMENT OF RELIGIONS: HINDUISM AND BUDDHISM

The rich variety of India's religious heritage is unparalleled. A thousand years ago, while Christians and Muslims burned and crucified famous heretics across their zones of the Old World, there were in the sprawling subcontinent of India separate but generally tolerant communities of Hindus, Buddhists, Jains, animists, Parsis, Muslims, and even some Christians and Jews. But the religious history of the centuries between 500 and 1500 is really concerned with only three of these religions. It is the story of a continued Hindu flowering, of the virtual disappearance of Buddhism in the land of its birth, and of the coming of Islam to India in force.

Hinduism, as we have seen, played a large part in the assimilation of new peoples into the mainstream of Indian life. In so doing, the Vedic tradition and the dominance of the brahmans were increasingly identified with that Indian mainstream. The brahmans also consecrated new generations of monarchs, conferring the status of *devaraja*, "god-king," and suitably divine ancestors on princes all over India. In the process, the status of the brahmans rose still further, till they were commonly accorded the same sort of spiritual standing and powers that Christian priests enjoyed in Europe. Waves of new converts, royal patrons, and the increasingly exalted spiritual status of the brahmans all helped to advance the cause of India's oldest religion.

Main trends in Hinduism during this period included a variety of mystical paths to salvation. The most important of these mystical schools of religious thought, called Vedanta, was the work of a brahman named Sankaracharya. Seeking to purge traditional Vedic thought of its tangled and sometimes obscure theology, the prophet of Vedanta Hinduism declared the true goal of religion to be quite simple: it was the mystic union of the individual soul of the worshiper with the Absolute Soul of the universe. It was vigorous assertion of an ancient emphasis in Hinduism, and it would be an even more central theme thereafter.

The decline of Buddhism in the Buddha's own country is perhaps harder to understand. It is sometimes explained by the scarcity of powerful royal patrons to advance the Buddhist cause. Kings in search of sacred support for their right to govern turned increasingly to Hinduism. There were more divine ancestors available in the elaborate pantheon of the brahmans, who had been providing religious sanctions for society and its rulers since Vedic times.

Persecution also undoubtedly played a part, particularly in the Muslim-dominated north. The massacres of Buddhist monks and the burning of monasteries at the time of the establishment of the Delhi Sultanate dealt a fatal blow to Buddhism in the northeast, as well as depriving India as a whole of one of its most vital centers of religious culture.

A more subtle but nonetheless important development was the slow convergence of the Buddhist and Hindu traditions in India. Hinduism became more and more monotheistic in all but name, though the one true god might be Vishnu or Shiva, depending on the cult one belonged to. Since Buddhism was already monotheistic, transferral of allegiance from one faith to the other was made that much easier. Buddha himself was absorbed into some versions of Hinduism as an incarnation of Brahma, like Krishna or Rama in earlier Hindu mythology.

Given the growing prestige of the brahmans, the lack of powerful patrons for Buddhist monks, and the acceptance of Buddhist insights by the older faith, it is not surprising that the number of Buddhist believers dwin-

"*What could, then, be the cause of our country having been over-run so easily from the Indus to Banaras within a short space of thirty years by the Ghaznavid hordes? The first and foremost cause seems to be the fact that the country having been parcelled out into numerous independent States, it was nobody's concern to make effective arrangements for the protection of the north-western frontier and to check the progress of the invader. While the Hindustani king of the Panjab fought to resist Mahmud within his own territory, he did not think it to be his business to prevent his march into the dominions of his neighbours.*

Secondly, the masses had developed an attitude of unconcern towards politics, the rise and fall of empires and coming and going of rulers. They did not care as to who their rulers were. They went on tilling their fields without minding the great conflicts between our rulers and the invader. Political apathy, combined with lack of patriotism, territorial or emotional, created a frame of mind in the generality of the Indians of that age which made little difference between foreigners and their countrymen. But the greatest cause of our country having been over-run so easily and quickly was the employment of shock tactics by Mahmud. He pursued the policy of falling upon our prosperous towns with lightning rapidity and withdrawing himself suddenly and returning to Ghazni with equal speed. His mobile and rapid marches created great confusion and demoralisation in our ranks. Our people looked helpless like the peaceful, though brave, members of a household before a daring and callous robber. Before they could gather themselves and make improvised arrangements for protection, the invader, like a robber, was off. They felt that they were now safe; but the invader returned again with his former suddenness."

Ashirbadilal Srivastava, professor emeritus at Agra College, India, wrote the volume from which this passage is taken as a textbook for use in Indian schools. In this account of the rise of the Muslim-ruled Delhi Sultanate, the author seeks to explain the rapid conquest of one of the richest, most sophisticated, and most populous regions of Eurasia by Turkish raiders led by Mahmud of Ghazni.

What effect does the historian believe India's political divisions had on India's ability to resist invaders? Why does he think the masses of the Indian people did not resist? How did the hit-and-run tactics of the Turks prove especially effective in India?

Ashirbadilal Srivastava, The History of India (1000 A.D.–1707 A.D.) (Jaipur, Agra, India: Shiva Lal Agarwala, 1964), pp. 301–302.

dled. By 1500 Buddhism was essentially dead in India, while—as we shall see below—it flourished all across Southeast and East Asia.

THE SPREAD OF ISLAM

Islam descended upon northern India in waves during the later centuries of this period. There were Muslim Arabs in the far northwest before 1000, and Muslim Turkish raiders pushed still further into the north in the eleventh century. But it was the Turko-Afghan regime of the Delhi Sultanate in the thirteenth century that made Islam a vital force from the Punjab in the west to the frontiers of Bengal in the east.

In subsequent centuries Islam was to replace Buddhism as India's second religion, until in the first half of the twentieth century a quarter of India's huge population was Muslim. The process began, however, under the Delhi sultans. Some Indians were converted by the sword during the Turkish invasions. More probably accepted Islam as the high road to political advancement, once the sultanate was established. Many, finally, were drawn to the faith of the Prophet by the Sufis, whose mystical approach to religion appealed to the hearts of Indians even when their heads rejected the rigor of Muslim theology and law.

At the upper levels of Indian society, Hindus and Muslims found it quite possible to live in intellectual and religious harmony in these early days. Fifteenth-century Indian religious leaders argued that there were no spiritual differences between Allah and Vishnu. Intellectuals of both faiths sought to understand the Supreme without theological hairsplitting and undue attention to labels. But at the level of worship and ritual, the masses of north Indians had already drawn the line. Music in front of a mosque (where music was forbidden) or a Muslim beef feast (the cow still being sacred to Hindus) could trigger a riot in an Indian town at any time over the past eight centuries.

Tolerance thus had its limits, even in India. To this most religious of peoples, religion has never been a matter of lip service and formal ceremonies. Religious beliefs are woven into their lives. To this day they have remained a source of potentially explosive interaction with other aspects of Indian history.

THE AGE OF THE TEMPLE BUILDERS

The high culture of India during the millennium 500–1500 was thus, as usual, profoundly shaped by religion, and particularly by the renascent Hindu faith. This highly developed civilization did produce a complex secular culture over these centuries, ranging from royal biographies and histories of the various Indian kingdoms to popular tales and erotic poetry. But the most striking art forms of the age were religious architecture and sculpture, as combined in the stone temples then beginning to rise all over India. Just as cathedrals and mosques were being built during this period across western Eurasia, this was the age of the temple builders in India.

A Westerner's first impression of an Indian temple is likely to be one of confusion. Here is none of the simplicity of a Greek temple, or even the underlying structure of a Gothic cathedral. Buddhist, Jain, and especially Hindu temples of this and later periods, with their beehive-shaped or pyramidal towers and courtyards alive with sculpture, look at first glance rather more like organic growths than human constructs.

In fact, these Indian temples are designed very carefully according to intricate architectural—and metaphysical—principles. The ground plan is a complex of *mandalas*, or squares enclosed in circles, intended to reflect the shape of the world as it was theologically understood at the time. The tower (or *shikara*, meaning "mountain") is the image of the "world mountain," the pillar between heaven and earth, pointing to God. In the north the typical Indo-Aryan *shikara* is shaped rather like a cucumber, or one of the finger-length bananas vendors sell in the streets. In the south, the Dravidian *shikara* is a pyramidal series of terraces of decreasing size, each dedicated to a different god. Over all available surfaces, intricate decorative motifs and the swaying, dancing figures of gods and mortals, animals and plants move round and round the terraces, friezes, bases, and towers.

Whole cities of these great temples—some of them all but deserted now—were built during the centuries between the Guptas and the Moguls across the vast land of India. Perhaps the finest in the Indo-Aryan style is Khajuraho in central India, a score of huge towers (where more than eighty once stood) looming above the plain. Built by Rajput sovereigns a thousand years ago, each mountain of stone, seen closer up, is a mass of detailed, if time-worn, carving.

In the south, the Dravidian style reached its culmination in the Chola temples at Tanjore. Here Rajaraja the Great, also around 1000, erected a gigantic temple to Shiva the Destroyer. The main building is almost two hundred feet long; the *shikara* soars in thirteen receding terraces almost the same distance into the sky. The whole is topped by a single dome-shaped stone weighing more than eighty tons. Looming behind the palms and ornamental gateways of its courtyards, Rajaraja's masterpiece is one of the great achievements of Indian building.

The statues that fill the niches and walls and pillars of these buildings and the carven gods in their inner sanctums all have the usual burgeoning life of Indian sculpture. The famous *Descent of the Ganges*, a gigantic bas-relief cut from living rock at a temple complex near Madras, shows the sacred river, which once flowed only through heaven, descending at last to earth, to the admiration of all its creatures. Gods and spirits, men and women, and gentle deer and lumbering elephants converge upon the holy spot in the great stone panorama.

Even more famous are the widely imitated and worshiped south Indian bronze sculptures of the *Dance of Shiva*. In this vivid pose, the Destroyer is shown dancing the universe back into being. Wreathed with a ring of fire, trampling the demon of ignorance, Shiva deploys his four arms gracefully as he moves to the cosmic measure that makes worlds—and destroys them.

THE INDIAN ZONE: SOUTHEAST ASIA

A PATTERN OF VILLAGE LIFE

We have touched down in Southeast Asia before, usually on our way somewhere else. This collection of islands and peninsulas at the southeastern corner of Asia was the way station for prehistoric immigrants passing on out through the islands towards Australia and Oceania. We have mentioned the beginnings of Chinese imperial penetration into Vietnam and will have more to say about that directly. In the present chapter, we focus on the profound influence of Indian culture on the region as a whole.

But Southeast Asia is not a mere way station to somewhere else, nor is it a passive recipient of other people's culture. Since the region received its modern name—as recently as World War II, when it was the locale of the Anglo-American Southeast Asian Command against the Japanese—scholars have increasingly recognized not only the geographical but the cultural uniqueness of this Europe-sized sprawl of peninsulas, islands, and seas across the equator.

Geographically, Southeast Asia juts south between India and China, pointing roughly toward Australia. Mainland Southeast Asia is Myanmar (Burma) Thailand, Kampuchea, (Cambodia) Laos, Vietnam, and the long curving peninsula of Malasia, with Singapore today at its southern tip. Island Southeast Asia is mostly Indonesia now, including Java where most of the population live, Sumatra, the large central island of Borneo, the heavily touristed island paradise of Bali, and part of New Guinea, just off the Australian coast. Add the Philippines for the eastern flank—and some 13,000 smaller islands scattered between the Indian Ocean and the China seas, and you have a substantial zone of culture indeed.

But the region had its own culture before the foreigner came. The mountains and rain forests, the rich, fertile river valleys, and the waters full of fish have sheltered human life for many centuries. Bamboo villages on stilts, water buffalo, and rice paddies were all in place before the first Chinese soldier or Indian merchant came marching through the jungle or poking up the muddy rivers. Dong-Son culture developed its special combination of agriculture, trading, and piracy with minimal foreign input. If bronze working filtered down from China, the unique bronze drums that symbolize the Dong-Son achievement are a Southeast Asian artifact.

Perhaps most important, the pattern of Southeast Asian village life—the life of most Southeast Asians to this day—was firmly established long before civilized Indians and Chinese, Muslims and Christians came to bring the splendors and miseries of urban-imperial culture to this substantial corner of the world.

It is too easy to slip into the dismissive frame of mind that sees one peasant as much like another, an agricultural village in Java as really no different from one in Nigeria or Peru. But there are differences, some of them extremely important still.

Southeast Asian villagers were still animists, worshiping natural objects and the forces of nature, while Indian peasants were adopting the larger and more complex creeds of Hinduism, Buddhism, and later Islam. Many parts of Southeast Asia built societies around the small nuclear family of parents and children—as most modern societies do—rather than the extended family prevalent in India and China. Perhaps most striking, Southeast Asians from early times accorded a higher degree of equality to women than their neighbors did.

Women in Southeast Asian villages shared more than labor with their men. In ancient times they were often priestesses and even chiefs. Women sometimes chose their husbands (instead of the other way around), and matrilineal descent—inheritance through the wife's rather than the husband's side—was common. Against this ingrained tradition of relative female equality, such later influences as the Indian drift toward seclusion for married women or such Muslim institutions as harem isolation and the veil could make little progress. Today you are considerably more likely to see young women jogging in the streets of Indonesia's capital Jakarta, for instance, than in New Delhi or any Arab city.

Most of what follows concerns the absorption of Southeast Asia into a larger zone of culture whose radiant center was India. But it should be remembered that the glories of Angkor Wat or Borobudur were built by the labor of village people whose hearts and lives were still shaped to a large extent by an older world where such incongruous beliefs as nature worship and female equality lived on in perfect harmony.

MISSIONARIES AND MERCHANTS OF THE INDIES

Indian influence in Southeast Asia goes back to the classic period, the age of the Guptas and before, but it reached its peak during the thousand years between 500 and 1500. As a source of cultural influence, India substantially outweighed China, whose impact during these centuries seldom reached much further than northern Vietnam. Indian influence, by contrast, spread to most of the mainland peoples, from Burma into southern Vietnam, and to a number of the larger islands, including Sumatra, Java, and Borneo.

This Indian influence differed strikingly from the looming Chinese presence. When the Chinese did come south, it was as conquerors, the organized political and military agents of the world's most populous and powerful nation. Indians, by contrast, filtered into the region primarily as merchants and missionaries. In the end, the cultural impact of Indian civilization, built on mutually beneficial trade and on the emotional and spiritual appeal of India's religions, penetrated Southeast Asian culture as Chinese political influence seldom did.

Indian traders settled into the port towns of Malaya, Java, and Sumatra, even Thailand and south Vietnam, as easily as they did along the coasts of East Africa, far to the west. They gave village chiefs impressive gifts, the products of an Indian handicraft industry that local arti-

The Cambodian "lost city" of Angkor Thom built in the twelfth century while the gothic cathedrals were rising in Europe, has awed generations of Western visitors. Closely shaped by Indian artistic and religious influences, the towers and walls and endless sculptured galleries of Angkor remain one of the greatest monuments of ancient Southeast Asian civilization. (Library of Congress)

sans could only envy. They exchanged textiles, jewels, jars of oil, and perfume for spices and timber, gold and tin. In time they married the daughters of local dignitaries and became influential citizens of communities that grew increasingly prosperous thanks to Indian trade.

Indian missionaries came to spread all three of the greatest Indian religions. Buddhist monks brought a simple, caste-free, faith that had a great appeal to ordinary villagers. Brahmans brought a Hinduism that sanctioned *rajas* in Southeast Asia as easily as it did in India and that soon became a common cult among rulers and aristocrats. Islam, when it came, came often in the simple, straight-from-the-heart Sufi form. But Indian Muslims came frequently as conquerors too, and some prudent Southeast Asians accepted Islam as a rapid road to success in Muslim controlled areas.

Sometimes Indians taught techniques of land irrigation and terraced hillside agriculture, though these skills had been developed in many areas before they came. In many places Indians helped Southeast Asian rulers to develop bustling port cities for further trade with India and elsewhere. And Indian monks, brahmans, and Islamic mullahs raised temples to Vishnu and Shiva, to Buddha or to Allah, among the palms and paddies of these lands of the eastern seas.

Climbing over the mountain of terraces, statues, carved gateways, and broken stairs of Borobudur, in Java, one has the odd feeling of exploring a Gothic cathedral turned inside out. All the stairs and gates and statues are on the outside; there is no inside. But there is the same careful stonework in a carved Buddha meditating on the Javanese jungle as in any sculptured Christ looking down on a Gothic nave. The religious symbols and the religious stories are different, but the Buddhist temple at Borobudur is as much a holy mountain reaching up to God as any Notre Dame.

LANDS OF A MILLION ELEPHANTS: FROM MALACCA TO ANGKOR WAT

The fusion of traditional ways with Indian influence produced a whole series of kingdoms and empires across Southeast Asia, a number of them comparable in splendor to those of India itself.

Almost every modern Southeast Asian nation can point to some such glorious center of civilization in the past. The islands of today's Indonesia, especially Java and Sumatra, were the sites of briskly feuding Indianized nations between 500 and 1000, a period when Europe was languishing in its Dark Ages. As early as the ninth century, the huge Buddhist temple at Borobudur and the Hindu temple complex at Palambanan had risen over the jungles of central Java. The great Anirudda filled the far-famed Burmese capital of Pagan with temples and shrines dedicated to Buddha in the eleventh century, at about the same time that the gothic cathedrals were beginning to rise in Europe. Laos looks back to the great days of Lan Xang—Land of a Million Elephants.

Malaya remembers the meteoric career of the great port city of Malacca, which under the leadership of Muslim Indian merchants dominated East Indian trade and spread the faith of Muhammad to many parts of Southeast Asia. Dazzled by bazaars heaped with Indian fabrics and Chinese porcelain, spices, aromatic woods, and precious metals, pearls, and perfumes and silks, a Portuguese visitor in the 1400s declared that "Men cannot estimate the wealth of Malacca."

In 1511 the Portuguese captured Malacca, and a new era began for Southeast Asia. But the long millennium between the end of the classic age around 500 and the beginning of the modern era around 1500 had produced achievements in civilization second to none. Perhaps the most famous of all was the kingdom of the Khmer in what became Cambodia—the civilization whose most awesome monument is the great lost city of Angkor Wat.

The Indianized, Hindu-Buddhist state of Kambuja (Cambodia—today Kampuchea) flourished from the ninth to the fifteenth centuries. The Khmer peoples who ruled it extended their sovereignty into parts of southern Vietnam and Thailand. Over its half-dozen centuries of splendor, the Khmer Empire learned Sanskrit, mathematics, architecture, and art from the Indians. Khmer rulers became *devarajas* and pious Hindus, while many of their people accepted the less hierarchical Buddhist faith, the

religion of most Cambodians today. The ancient Indian epic poems, the *Mahabharata* and the *Ramayana*, were widely known in southern Indochina. And the great temple city of Angkor Wat was built to reproduce on earth the Hindu vision of the shape and structure of the cosmos.

The Khmer Empire was never large in size or population. But the Angkor dynasty channeled the wealth of the land and the labor of their million subjects into huge building projects dedicated to the greater glory of their gods and their god-kings. The temple complex of Angkor Wat is the most splendid evocation of the wealth and dedication of this vanished civilization.

Here the moated city of Angkor once stood, several miles around, surrounded by a green plain criss-crossed by irrigation channels and lush with rice paddies and orchards. Within the city swarmed a mongoloid population many times as large as that of medieval London. The booming business of the city was dominated—like so much else in Southeast Asia—by women. But the city's great centers, clearly visible over the rooftops of the earth or wooden houses of the people, were the bristling stone towers of the royal city of Angkor Thom and the temple complex of Angkor Wat.

Even the ruins that survive today—overgrown with jungle, discolored by monsoon rains, pocked by the bullets of more recent Southeast Asian wars—are among the most impressive to be found anywhere. Angkor Wat itself, six hundred feet on a side, has been described as the largest temple in the world. Around its courtyards and galleries and up the sides of its *shikara*, hundreds of carven figures retell Hindu myths and glorify the Khmer King—Suryavarman II—who built it in the twelfth century. The style is distinctly that of this great Southeast Asian people, but the images of Vishnu and Shiva and Buddha, the creation myths, and the cosmological design all reflect the cultural influence of India.

The Khmer Empire spent its substance on these mighty monuments. Weakened by plague and the eternal factional feuding of courts, the kingdom fell to the neighboring Thais in the fifteenth century. Angkor Thom was pillaged, Angkor Wat surrendered to the jungle. Roofs fall in today, and vines trail across smiling Asian faces in crumbling stone. But the Southeast Asian achievement—and the long reach of Indian culture—are revealed as clearly here as anywhere else in this far-spreading zone of culture south of the Himalayas.

SUMMARY

The thousand years of Indian history between the Guptas and the Moguls were tangled and confused politically, like so much of India's history. But they were also centuries of cultural flowering and of the spread of Indian influence, above all into Southeast Asia.

During this period, from roughly A.D. 500 to 1500, the Northwest Frontier admitted Rajputs, Turks, Tatars, and others to find their place in the polyglot population of India. The Dravidian south merged with the north in a single arena of competitive states. The caste system grew more complex and more rigid, and women's place in society became fixed. Attempts at imposing political unity included the short-lived empire of King Harsha and the longer but no more substantial regime called the Delhi Sultanate.

India's culture, with its roots still deeply planted in the subcontinent's many religions, continued to probe spiritual profundities and to generate artistic splendors.

Hinduism, which had experienced a spiritual revival under the Guptas, still flowered during the following millennium. But Buddhism lost favor in the Buddha's own homeland, expiring finally in the turmoil following the Muslim invasions. The rise of Islam itself, particularly in the north, made the Muslim faith the third main current of Indian religious history during this period, India's second largest religion in later centuries.

As Western Christian art centered on the cathedral and that of Islam on the mosque, so Indian art focused on the countless huge stone temples that were built in all parts of India in this age. Dense with life, myth, and symbol, the temples of Hindu, Buddhist, Jain, and other faiths glorified Indian cities, as churches of Our Lady did the cities of Christendom.

This ancient and complex culture, finally, has an important impact on a large cultural zone comprising almost all of Southeast Asia in this period.

Indian merchants and Buddhist, Hindu, and Muslim missionaries guided the developing cities and empires of these lush islands and peninsulas. Southeast Asian village culture was significantly affected by the new faiths. Kingdoms in Burma, Java, Sumatra, and the famous Angkor Wat of Cambodia all reflected the influence of the timeless culture of India.

SUGGESTED READING

CHAUDHURI, K. N. *Asia before Europe: Economy and Civilization of the Indian Ocean from the Rise of Islam to 1750.* Cambridge, England: Cambridge University Press, 1991. Regional study of the ocean and its neighboring peoples. See also K. R. Hall, *Maritime Trade and State Development in Early Southeast Asia* (Honolulu: University of Hawaii Press, 1985).

DEVAHUT, D. *Harsha.* London: Oxford University Press, 1970. The brief empire of Kanauj. See also R. C. Majumdar, *The Age of Imperial Kanauj* (Bombay: B.V. Bhavan, 1955) for the subcontinent as a whole during Harsha's ascendency and S. R. Goyal, *Harsha and Buddhism* (Meerut, India: Kusumanjali Prahashan, 1986) on institutional, economic, and other aspects of King Harsha's religious policy.

HALL, D. G. E. *History of Southeast Asia.* London: Macmillan, 1955. The best overall account.

KAMRISCH, S. *Indian Sculpture.* London: Oxford University Press, 1937. A commonly recommended source on the subject.

MAJUMDAR, R. C. *Ancient India*, 5th ed. Delhi: Motilal Banarsidass, 1968. Political history to 1200 by the dean of Indian historians.

————, *The Arab Invasion of India.* Banaras: Motilal Banarsidass, 1952. Old, but probably still the best one-volume treatment.

————, ed. *The Delhi Sultanate.* Bombay: Bharatiya Vidya Bhavan, 1960. A standard source.

————, ed. *The Struggle for Empire.* Bombay: Bharatiya Vidya Bhavan, 1957. Articles on the impact of the Muslim conquest on India.

MUJEEB, M. *Indian Muslims.* Montreal: McGill University Press, 1967. Recommended. See also A. Ahmad, *Studies in Islamic Culture in the Indian Environment.* (Oxford: Clarendon Press, 1964).

MUKERJEE, R. *The Culture and Art of India.* London: Allen and Unwin, 1959. Pictures and extracts, both well chosen by a wide-ranging scholar.

NILKANTASASTRI, K. A. A. *History of South India.* London: Oxford University Press, 1965. Covers the period to the sixteenth-century rise of the Moguls for this culturally distinct part of India.

PRASAD, I. *History of Medieval India*, 3rd ed. Allahabad: The Indian Press, 1950. Good on the political structures of Indian society between Guptas and Moguls.

RAWLINSON, H. G. *India: A Short Cultural History.* New York: Praeger, 1952. Still a good introductory survey.

SPEAR, P. *India: A Modern History*, rev. ed. Ann Arbor: University of Michigan Press, 1972. An excellent overview of a tangled age, seeing order where others see only complexities.

ZIMMER, H. *The Art of Indian Asia* (2 vols). New York: Pantheon Books, 1960. Outstanding study, beautifully illustrated, of the art of the Indian zone of culture.

CHINA AND EAST ASIA

3 THE TANG DYNASTY

THE CENTER OF THE WORLD

There are sober businessmen in Singapore or Hong Kong or Tokyo—and even soberer scholars in America—who will tell you that the twenty-first century will be the century of the Pacific rim. The Atlantic powers have had their day, they will say. The nations that border the Pacific will be the arbiters of the planet's destiny in the century that will soon be beginning—and Asian nations will lead all the rest.

A traditional Chinese scholar would tell you that the Asian rim of the Pacific has actually been the center of world history for a couple of thousand years already. Since the Qin and the Han dynasties united China in the third century B.C., creating at a stroke the largest and most populous nation on earth, Chinese primacy has been an article of faith in the land they call the Middle Kingdom.

Basic geography—and basic history—certainly seemed to support the Chinese sense of being the center of human civilization during most of the millennium between the end of the classic age and the beginning of the modern era.

China sprawls massively across the eastward bulge of Asia. For most of its history it has been a large, powerful, centralized state with a proud and ancient culture. During much of the period under consideration here, China basked in the renewed glories of two of its greatest ages, the Tang and Song dynasties. Most of the other centers of developed urban-imperial civilization were far away, at the other end of the Old World or across the Pacific in the New—hazy or unknown to the Chinese.

Particularly during the centuries of the Tang and Song—from the seventh to the thirteenth A.D.—Chinese influence decisively shaped the history of most of its neighbors. China's sense of centrality can seldom have been greater than it was as the Chinese Empire guided—by domination, influence, and example—the development of an entire zone of culture along Chinese lines.

Over these centuries, which saw the rise of Islam and the climax of the Christian age of faith at the other end of Eurasia, another major zone of civilization thus emerged and produced great things along the far Pacific rim.

THE SIX DYNASTIES

The four hundred years that elapsed between the collapse of the Han dynasty in 220 and the accession of the Tang in 618 are a hopeless tangle politically. The epoch may be subdivided into the sometimes overlapping periods of the Three Kingdoms, the Six Dynasties, and the brief pre-Tang unification under the Sui dynasty. But the essential elements of this age—which we may refer to for convenience simply as the Six Dynasties—lay not in its political confusion but in other areas of Chinese history and culture.

Perhaps the decisive event was not political but military. It was not so much the third-century collapse of the Han monarchy that shattered Chinese unity but the fourth-century overrunning of northeastern China by a chaotic flood of preurban nomadic peoples from beyond the Great Wall. The result of this barbarian conquest of the old Chinese heartland was to leave China culturally as well as politically divided between north and south for most of the next three hundred years.

These centuries of division, it should be stressed, were not centuries of demoralization or decay in other ways. China under the Six Dynasties did not resemble Europe in the grim centuries after the Fall of Rome. China's case was much closer to that of India during the long stretches of political fragmentation between empires, periods when the subcontinent often flourished economically and culturally in spite of its lack of political unity.

In the south, floods of Chinese fleeing from the barbarians in the north carried the center of Chinese culture south of the Yangzi for the first time. Under the politically ineffectual Six Dynasties, wet-rice agriculture was developed and urban culture flowered impressively. There was progress in everything from bridge building to the beginning of China's great schools of painting.

But the impulse toward complete political unification was always there. Toward the end of the sixth century, finally, the brief Sui dynasty (589–618) reunited most of China and began the great unifying works that the Tang emperors were to bring to a triumphant climax.

The two Sui emperors, Yang Jian and his brilliant, unscrupulous son Yang Guang, were northerners with the blood of the Xiongnu in their veins. The armies of the militant Sui broke through the Yangzi demarcation line to conquer the south. Then this vigorous father and son labored successively to rebuild an administrative system for all China. They worked also to extend the Grand Canal system begun by the Han and the Great Wall built by the Qin emperor Huangdi. They strove with considerable success to keep out the barbarians and to impose Chinese rule once more upon the Vietnamese and Chinese influence on the Koreans.

The Sui emperors, like Huangdi, exhausted the country with extravagant building projects at home and costly military campaigns abroad. A nation strained beyond the breaking point rebelled, and the dynasty fell after less than thirty tumultuous years. But like the Qin, the Sui had paved the way for something more long lasting.

THE GREATEST OF EMPERORS: TANG TAIZONG

For some Chinese historians, the Tang dynasty (618–907) was the greatest of dynasties and the three hundred years of Tang rule the most lustrous of China's several golden ages. For others, the Han and Tang stand roughly on a par, twin peaks in China's history.

Like the Han, the Tang combined political and economic strength, imperial expansion, and cultural brilliance in a uniquely successful way. The earlier Tang, like the former Han, was an era of powerful personalities and glittering accomplishment, a period when China's preeminence and influence were unquestioned throughout East Asia. The latter half of the Tang period, like the Later Han, was a time of retrenchment and decline. In both cases,

Li Shimin, known to history as Tang Taizong, the reunifier of China and founder of the great Tang dynasty, looks pardonably self-satisfied in this drawing based on a rubbing from Shensi. Notice the elaborately embroidered robe, the carefully trimmed and curled beard, and the traditional full sleeves. (New York Public Library Picture Collection)

however, a long-reigning dynasty and frequently competent leadership gave China a considerable spell of domestic tranquility and foreign splendor.

The first two Tang emperors, like the two Sui, were father and son. But in the case of the Tang founders, the son was so clearly the dominant personality that it is common to see him as the true establisher of the dynasty, though he was its second emperor. This hard-driving second son is in fact often considered the greatest of all China's many emperors.

The father, Li Yuan, was the scion of an ancient northwestern Chinese family who married a daughter of the northern steppes, sired three sons, and became a leading general under the Sui. He seems, however, to have fallen strongly under the influence of his second son, an ambitious young war hero named Li Shimin. When the brief Sui restoration of imperial unity began to crumble, Li Shimin urged his father step by step along the road to power.

The older man was still at the fore when a key alliance was forged with the northern Turks against the crumbling Chinese regime. Father and son took the Sui capital of Chang'an (modern Xi'an) together, and soon thereafter Li Yuan was installed with all due solemnity as the new Son of Heaven, emperor of China. In the eight years of his reign, the new emperor firmly established the Tang regime at Chang'an, crushed several drawn-out rebellions in South China, and repelled an invasion by the new dynasty's former allies, the Turks.

In the end, however, the stronger personality of Li Shimin thrust its way forward. Returning from the wars, where he had spent his youth fighting for his country and his clan, the second son confronted a conspiracy hatched against him by the crown prince and by the third Li brother, both envious of Shimin's fame. The border warrior reacted with the directness of the military commander he was. He took a squad, ambushed his brothers and their retainers outside the palace gates, and shot both the plotters down with bows and arrows. He then compelled his aging father to step down and mounted the throne himself—emperor at the age of twenty-six.

Li Shimin would be listed in the history books as Tang Taizong (629–649), Grand Ancestor of the Tang. Brilliant general, governmental reformer, famous historian, and master of the calligraphy brush, he would be one of the most admired of all Chinese emperors.

Taizong's governmental reforms were in part a restoration of the Han system already partially revived by the Sui, in part a long step beyond these traditional ways. This real founder of the Tang put government in the hands of an administrative system of six central ministries (for state revenues and public works, defense and justice, personnel and religious rites), ten provinces, and hundreds of prefectures and lesser administrative units. He expanded the Confucian examination system for civil servants and established a structure of schools, including a central university at Chang'an that would prepare students for the exams. He promulgated a flexible new law code and a new state-supported court aristocracy in nine graduated ranks. He laid the groundwork, in short, for the whole Tang system of imperial government.

Taizong also launched the reunited Chinese nation on the road to renewed imperial preeminence in East Asia. He led his armies himself, following the trail of westward expansion already blazed by the Han. Taizong's armies pushed the Turks back out of the Tarim Basin and carried Chinese power all the way to the Pamirs and into the valley of the Oxus River beyond. South of the Tarim Basin he imposed Chinese authority on the newly unified mountain kingdom of Tibet. He thus opened the doors to trade with western Eurasia once more—though in the seventh century there was no developed civilization in Europe with which to trade.

Tang Taizong ruled for more than twenty years, building palaces for himself and public granaries for his people, exalting Buddha at his court and establishing temples to the honor of Confucius across the land. He died at the comparatively young age of forty-nine, his health destroyed by a hard military campaign in Korea.

In the end, Taizong's one great failure was that he produced no heir strong enough to hold and build upon this heritage. But even this turned out to be for the best, for weakness at the top allowed his true successor to fight her way up through the cauldron of court politics—his former concubine who became the formidable Empress Wu.

THE GREATEST EMPRESS: WU ZETIAN

Like the Han empress Lü, Empress Wu Zetian (649–705) of the Tang period owed her initial power to male connections. Concubine of the second Tang emperor, wife of the third, and mother of the next two, Wu finally dispensed with surrogates and ruled in her own right and name. Beautiful and cruel in her early years, she displayed in later life the intelligence, good judgment, and foresight that make a great ruler.

In her climb to the throne of China, Wu Zetian struck down her rivals ruthlessly, exalted her own family, and even tried to establish a new dynasty of her own. She fostered the Buddhist faith as her predecessors had, fell temporarily in love with a Buddhist monk, and even had herself proclaimed a new incarnation of the Enlightened One. In her later years she declared herself emperor, performed the rites, and received the homage due the Son of Heaven. Though other women governed China—from the Han empress Lü to imperial China's last great ruler, Ci Xi in the nineteenth century—Empress Wu was the only woman to hold the titles as well as the power in her strong hands.

Beneath the gaudy surface of her long tenure of power, however, Wu Zetian governed capably and well. Her chief ministers tended to be men of talent, the provincial officials stayed loyal, and the state prospered. In foreign affairs, she shrewdly supported the unification of Korea—

This later representation of the Empress Wu Zetian probably does not do justice to the powerful preserver of the Tang order even in her later years. Can you detect winged dragon motifs—symbolic of imperial power—in the empress's headdress? (New York Public Library Picture Collection)

which the Chinese had been trying and failing to conquer for generations—and thus enjoyed cordial relations with the new state throughout her life. In the west, she sent Chinese armies out as her predecessors had to chastise Turks and Tibetans and keep open China's trade routes across the Tarim Basin into western Asia and beyond. She was "perspicacious, and rapid and sure in decision" and enjoyed an international reputation for astuteness and success.[1]

Empress Wu's efforts to establish a new dynasty—her own—finally brought her down. She was deposed at last in her eighties, after more than half a century of ruling China. She left the nation more firmly united, wealthier, and more powerful than it had ever been before. What Tang Taizong had begun, Wu Zetian finished, and she was as much the architect of Tang greatness as he.

THE BRILLIANT EMPEROR: TANG XUANZONG

The last in this colorful line of great early Tang rulers was Empress Wu's grandson Tang Xuanzong (713–756). The long reign of Xuanzong, known to history as the Brilliant Emperor, covered most of the first half of the eighth century and is often seen as the cultural apogee of the Tang period.

[1]C .P. Fitzgerald, *The Empress Wu* (Vancouver: University of British Columbia Press, 1968), p. 146.

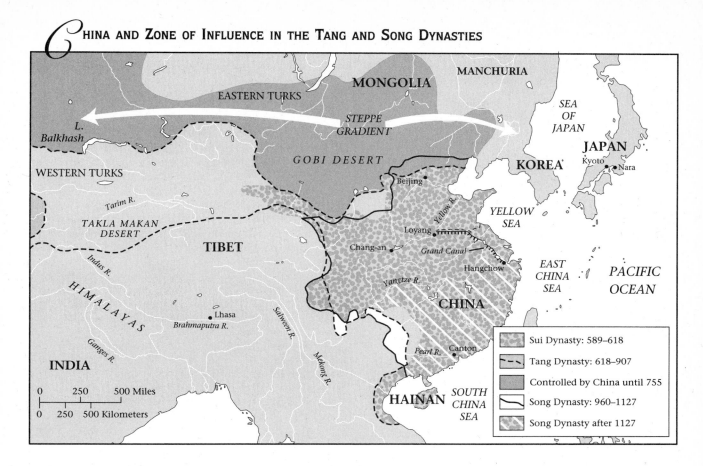

CHINA AND ZONE OF INFLUENCE IN THE TANG AND SONG DYNASTIES

Xuanzong's huge palaces and gardens at Chang'an and elsewhere glittered with the work of some of the most famous of Tang poets and painters. Some of the most exquisitely beautiful of Chinese porcelain was produced for him, and he and his courtiers ate off silver dishes that were works of art. The magnificence of his court is often illustrated by his enthusiasm for fine horses, which he reportedly gratified by keeping forty thousand of them in the royal stables.

The Brilliant Emperor made more concrete contributions to the history of China than just living magnificently, however. It was during his reign that the fertile Yangzi River valley of central China was made to produce agriculturally on a scale that substantially increased the wealth of the nation. The imperial armies pushed still farther to the west under Tang Xuanzong, down into Kashmir and on toward the Caspian once more.

But it was here in central Asia that a disastrous encounter with the Arabs, driving eastward as the Chinese pushed west, ended Chinese expansion in that direction forever. China's defeat by Muslim armies at the Talas River near Samarkand in 751 was, in fact, a turning point in Chinese imperial history. It began a centuries-long decline of Chinese power in central Asia.

At home there was a similar turn in the emperor's—and the dynasty's—fortunes. It came in the guise of a September-and-May love affair between the aging Xuanzong and an attractive concubine named Yang Guifei. Yang's influence, that of her family, and finally that of her ambitious young protégé, An Lushan, predominated at court thereafter. When An Lushan openly revolted, the imperial troops demanded the death of the concubine whose influence had raised him so high. Yang Guifei was executed, and the Brilliant Emperor abdicated, a broken king.

The revolt of An Lushan was ultimately suppressed. But there were other revolts and other palace intrigues to come over the next century and a half. And there were no more Taizongs, no more Empress Wus, in the second half of the Tang era. The road, if not downhill all the way, was distinctly bumpier.

THE WORLD'S LARGEST COUNTRY

The Tang capital at Chang'an was a fitting symbol for the majesty of the Tang imperial achievement. A planned city thirty square miles in extent, its rectangular wards and blocks held a population of perhaps a million people. Another million lived in the outlying suburbs, making Chang'an the largest city in the world at that time. The administrative offices and the emperor's palace and grounds filled an area of several square miles on the northern side of the city. This governmental center of the empire was reached by an avenue five hundred feet wide that started from the main city gates in the south and ran the length of the metropolis. In the eastern and western parts of the city, two huge government-run marketplaces bustled with life and business. The high pagoda roofs of Buddhist and Daoist temples beautified the skyline, and there were scenic parks such as the celebrated Hibiscus Gardens for rest and recreation.

There were many foreigners in Chang'an including merchants from India, Persia, and the Levant and students from Korea and Japan. Women enjoyed much more independence in aristocratic society than they would in later centuries. We have figurines of them riding horses and even playing polo, an athletic sport imported from Persia.

From the administrative capital at Chang'an, a nation as large as all Europe was governed by a handful of courtier-politicians and an army of scholarly civil servants. There were too many bureaucrats, as is frequently the case—secretariats and chancelleries to check every piece of paper the emperor saw. But the six ministries for revenue and pubic works, justice and defense, personnel and rites and ceremonies did their jobs with relative efficiency. There was a board of censors, who kept tabs on the whole elaborate system and reported inefficiency, malfeasance, and treason directly to the palace. The nation beyond the walls of the capital was administered at three levels, including ten provinces, 360 prefectures, and hundreds of subprefectures or districts.

Office seekers were trained in the unique Chinese educational system of local schools, provincial colleges, and a national university at Chang'an where one could study not only the Confucian classics but science, mathematics, and law. This system of education, keyed to examinations for civil-service jobs, in time perfected the ancient Han system of scholar-bureaucrats. Most officeholders henceforth came not from the ranks of the aristocratic large landowners but from the literate gentry class of lesser landholders whose sons qualified for office by study and high marks. It was a system based substantially on merit, awarding the highest posts in government to those most qualified.

The power of this centralized administration was, for the seventh or eighth century A.D., very great indeed. Every ward in the great planned city of Chang'an was locked at midnight, and no one moved around thereafter. Every peasant belonged to a "collective-guarantee" group of neighbors, all of whom were responsible for one another's taxes and general good behavior—and all of whom thus kept an eye on one another for the government. Military service and corvée labor were rigorously imposed and could fall heavily on whole villages.

Responsibility, not freedom, was the keynote of a system of government that became traditional in China—and may sound oppressive to a Western ear. On the other hand, at a time when emperors like Charlemagne in Europe and Harsha in India had to mount many military campaigns to maintain their empires intact, China was ruled in a rather more modern way—by a steady flow of paper from the capital out across the provinces of the world's largest nation.

EQUAL FIELDS AND WIDE EMPIRE

Tang officialdom developed further the "equal-field" system originated by earlier dynasties, a form of land nationalization that assigned most of China's agricultural land on an equal basis to free peasants. The practice was intended to regularize—and maximize—the land tax. It also had the effect of limiting the amount of land held by wealthy landowners and hence of further undermining their power.

The government, like the governments of many developed nations, involved itself vigorously in the economy. A hundred mints produced strings of copper cash, and government-issued paper money was widely used. Royal roads radiating from Chang'an were equipped with hostels every ten miles and an impressive system of royal posts. Both the roads and the canal system were thronged with domestic traders.

Government incentives also helped turn the huge Yangzi valley into China's rice bowl. The emperor built ten shipyards in central China alone to give China a merchant marine, and entertained foreign merchants in growing numbers at Canton and other southern ports. Tang China was a great deal richer than Han China, and the imperial government played a significant part in this development.

Empire building and foreign trade, finally, were carried to new highs under the Tang.

At the height of their power, the Tang emperors dominated Asia. Their writ ran more or less effectively from the southern margins of Siberia down to Southeast Asia and west from the Pacific to somewhere beyond Ferghana—sometimes even to the neighborhood of the Caspian Sea. Chinese armies intervened in the affairs of northern India and Afghanistan, and China established a temporary protectorate over eastern Persia.

China's network of foreign trade reached out to the whole of Asia, from Japan to Syria. Foreign influences played more freely on Chinese culture than ever before—or since. And China's manifest superiority was admired and imitated by a larger proportion of the human race than ever previously. If it was not China's greatest age, it was certainly a strong candidate for this highly competitive honor.

 # THE SONG DYNASTY

THE FIVE DYNASTIES

The last years of the Tang seem to have been typical of that cyclic dynastic end game that recurs so frequently in Chinese history. There were fractious governors in the provinces, feuding bureaucrats and eunuchs at court, and underage or ailing emperors trying to hold it all together. Unpaid armies revolted, provinces seceded, short-lived emperors became tools in the hands of scheming subjects. In the 880s the nation slid helplessly into anarchy. In the early 900s the last Tang emperor and all his family were slaughtered, the magnificent capital at Chang'an pillaged and burned.

The period of the Five Dynasties that separates the Tang from the Song lasted only a little more than fifty years (907–960)—a striking contrast with the several hundred years of the Six Dynasties between the Han and the Tang. The five dynasties in question—all in the north—were necessarily brief, usually no longer than the life of the founder. There were at least ten other secession states in the south, all feuding, conniving, dreaming of unity, and destroying any of their number who strove to impose it. Rebellion was endemic, and invaders from beyond the Great Wall once more overran the north. A famous poem of the time, "The Lament of Lady Qi," describes fountains running with blood, palaces in ashes, feet crunching through the calcined bones of court officials.

Yet it ended. In 960 a group of loyal and no doubt ambitious officers threw an embroidered dragon robe around the shoulders of a general named Zhao Kuangyin and told him he should be their emperor or die on the spot. General Zhao, who commanded the armies of one of the northern dynasties, chose to live and reign. He became the founder of the Song.

The Song dynasty would not achieve the universality, the range of achievement of the Han or the Tang; in some areas, however, it would exceed these predecessors. When it came to governing, to getting and spending, and to art and poetry, the Song have seldom been excelled.

NORTHERN SONG, SOUTHERN SONG

General Zhao Kuangyin (960–976) seems to have been the only one of the twenty Song emperors whose personality stands out in the traditional historiography. He was a scholar as well as a general, an autocrat—and a man who saw that unity had become China's destiny.

As a general, Zhao Kuangyin first unified as much as he could of the north, leaving a wedge of territory still in barbarian hands, and then reconquered the fragmentary kingdoms of central and southern China. As a scholar, he revived the traditional Confucian education and examination system, which had fallen into abeyance during the Five Dynasties period, and fostered culture at his court. As an autocrat by nature, he revived and strengthened the Tang system of provinces and prefectures and strove to concentrate as many functions of government as possible in his own hands. And as a man with a sense of Chinese unity, Zhao Kuangyin benefited from the fact that many educated Chinese had come to believe that the secret of peace, prosperity, and order lay in unity and centralized

authority. Many cities opened their gates to Zhao simply on the assurance that unity, not loot, was his object. The Song thus became in a sense the first dynasty established as much by consensus as by conquest.

The Song dynasty (960–1279) lasted about the same length of time as the Tang—three centuries. Like the Han and the Zhou before it, the Song was a clearly divided dynasty. The Northern Song (960–1127) governed from Kaifeng in the northern Yellow River valley; the Southern Song (1127–1279) fell back to the great city of Hangzhou in the valley of the Yangzi, central China's great waterway. The whole era, contemporary with the High Middle Ages at the other end of Eurasia, was another high point in Chinese history.

In domestic affairs, the Song period was one of China's golden ages. Song emperors further improved on the Tang administrative structure. They controlled the military more effectively than their predecessors had, and they tried to tax large and small landowners alike. Song China was freer from popular discontent and rebellion than China had ever been before.

The dynasty even produced a great reforming minister of state in Wang Anshi, who in the eleventh century, a hundred years after Zhao Kuangyin, tried to revitalize the Northern Song with innovations in agriculture, trade, education, and the army and navy. Wang's Legalist rigor and his attack on wealth alienated Confucian bureaucrats and wealthy landowners and led to the frustration of many of his reforms. Nevertheless, Wang Anshi was one of a long line of reforming spirits who periodically shook up and infused new vigor into the Confucian system, which otherwise tended to become set in its ways.

China's problems under the Song dynasty—and the nation had serious ones—were rather foreign than domestic in origin. Most of these difficulties were with China's northern neighbors, the eternal peoples of the steppe. These conflicts climaxed with the loss of North China to the barbarians in the twelfth century.

Throughout the Song period parts of northwestern China were occupied by the Tibetans, and a slice of territory south of the Great Wall in the northeast was controlled by semiagricultural peoples from Mongolia. The Northern Song emperors were never able to dislodge these northern barbarians, who had established themselves during the anarchy of the Five Dynasties. In the first half of the twelfth century, finally, the Ruzhen (Jürched) people descended from the Manchurian steppes in the far northeast, helped the Song overpower the rulers of the northeast, and then rampaged on south, conquering all of North China and carrying off the last emperor of the Northern Song to live out his life as a prisoner beyond the Great Wall.

The Southern Song, established by a son of that unhappy exile, set up a new capital at Hangzhou and ruled a truncated empire for the next century and a half. China under the Southern Song was vastly wealthy, immensely cultured, peaceful, and well governed. But the Chinese failed in all efforts to expel the Ruzhen and were actually forced to pay them tribute and to recognize China's status as vassal to the northern barbarians.

The Song emperors' de-emphasis of the military, while it minimized the risk of warlordism and civil war, thus cost them dearly in the international arena. It was the middle passage of a long decline in China's power in East Asia. That decline, which began with the Brilliant Emperor's defeat on the Talas River in central Asia in 751, would climax in the thirteenth century with the overthrow of the Song and the conquest of the entire nation by the Mongols of Genghis Khan—to be dealt with in the following chapter. Through it all, however, China's wealth, its remarkable administrative institutions, and its cultural brilliance would continue to dominate the life of East Asia—even when Chinese armies could not.

THE FIRST MERITOCRACY

Despite foreign-policy setbacks and the catastrophic loss of North China, the Song period saw material achievements that deserve further notice. These include the perfection of the scholar bureaucracy and its examination system and the immense wealth of the nation.

China's civil-service examinations and the resulting governmental meritocracy are as uniquely Chinese as the caste system is Indian or the Muslim law and its powerful local judges is Islamic. The examination system, originated by the Han dynasty and developed under the Tang, reached what was essentially its final form under the Song. For the next ten centuries it was to give China a stable administration that for most of that time was the envy of all who observed it.

The people who took the exams were for the most part children of China's gentry class—not aristocrats or holders of large estates, but men whose families were well enough off to spare them from agricultural labor while they devoted their lives to study. They typically spent many years reading the Chinese classics—Confucius above all—memorizing and analyzing every line. The tests required them to write passages from memory, to discuss and explain them, to compose a poem or other literary work in the style of particular masters, and to discuss theoretical problems of government having contemporary relevance.

Examinations were prepared with scrupulous attention to fairness. Papers were identified by number rather than name, and were even recopied before being graded so that the calligraphy might not be recognized by a grader. Exams were taken at several levels, beginning locally, where between 1 and 10 percent passed, and climaxing with the palace examinations, which passed perhaps a couple of hundred men a year into high governmental posts. The average "presented scholar" at this top level was in his middle thirties, well off but not wealthy, immensely learned, and one of a handful chosen out of China's millions to govern.

ECONOMICS AND SOCIAL CLASSES

The Chinese were also more numerous and wealthier than they had ever been. And two thirds of the population and wealth were for the first time concentrated in central and south China, rather than in the old northeastern heartland.

In Song times, China's population passed the hundred-million mark, twice the number counted in the Han period. This growing population created a huge economic demand, which in turn generated what is sometimes called an economic revolution in the Middle Kingdom.

Agriculture grew rapidly, and its center shifted with the center of population from the millet- and wheat-growing north to the rice paddies of the Yangzi and the southeast, where two crops a year of special strains of rice could be grown. Agricultural reforms included increasing use of fertilizer, improved irrigation, and better iron farming tools.

The iron and related coal industries developed rapidly under the Song, and there was widespread production of fine steel for tools, weapons, stoves, nails, and much more. Other growth industries included shipbuilding, the manufacture of ceramics, silk, and paper, and tea and salt processing. Many of these manufacturing enterprises were small craft-shop operations, but some were much larger in scale, employing hundreds of workers.

Trade flourished in Song China. Domestic traders frequently organized themselves in guilds and set up shops dealing in the same articles in the same streets, as in medieval Europe. Inland trade was carried out more commonly on the nation's elaborate network of waterways, both rivers and canals, than by road. It was a large country, and water was the cheapest form of transport.

Southern Song cities such as Guangzhou (Canton) carried on long-distance foreign trade, both through foreign merchants—whom the Chinese government, for once in its history, eagerly encouraged to come to China—and in Chinese vessels plying foreign waters. Chinese ships were among the most impressive in the world, large enough to carry hundreds of men and large cargoes. They were equipped with such up-to-the-minute technology as watertight bulkheads, sea anchors, rudders (instead of steering oars), depth-sounding lines, compasses, and gunpowder-powered rockets for use in war or against pirates.

China imported drugs, textiles, and some luxury goods. The nation also exported silk in large quantities, metals, and especially ceramics, an export encouraged by the government. Song Chinese porcelain has been found not only in Southeast Asia and India but in the Middle East and East Africa.

Urbanization continued in Song times, as the educated gentry joined merchants and officials in the pleasures of sophisticated city life. The cities were prosperous, colorful, and perhaps more relaxed than the planned city of Chang'an with its rectangular blocks and locked wards. The two Song capitals, Kaifeng and Hangzhou, as well as the booming port towns, were haphazard growths that repeatedly swelled beyond their walls. Their markets were full of food from the countryside, their streets lined with dealers in every known handicraft item. Avenues and alleyways were thronged also by the patrons of the shops, the outdoor restaurants, and the puppet theaters, by crowds gathering around storytellers, fortunetellers, acrobats, jugglers, and prostitutes. Marco Polo, who visited Hangzhou in the next dynasty, regarded it as the most splendid city in the world—and he had seen his share of the world's cities.

There are, however, no paradises on this earth, and Song China was no exception to this melancholy rule.

There were economic problems even under the Song. Growing population, increasing taxation, and played-out land drove peasants into pauperism even in so wealthy a time. The government's paper money encouraged trade—until too much paper currency was put in circulation, leading to inflation. Government spending grew beyond the capacity of even so wealthy a land to support—especially military expenses, which devoured 80 percent of the budget, supported an unheard-of army of a million men, and still could not defeat the northern barbarians.

The condition of women also began to worsen. The relative freedom and equality of women under the Tang gave way slowly to the subjugation of the female that was to be increasingly typical of Chinese society. Early signs were the spread of concubinage—the keeping of concubines by married men in addition to their legal wives—and the social stigma that began to attach to remarriage by widows. The most distinctly Chinese form of discrimination against women, however, was the practice of foot-binding, which began among aristocratic women of the Song era. This binding of the feet of young girls with long strips of cloth produced a "lily foot" about half normal size. This made women useless for work—hence advertised their husband's wealth—and gave them an odd, stilted walk that men found intensely attractive. The foot-binding itself was also an extremely painful process for the adolescent daughters of the aristocracy.

 # THE CULTURE OF THE TANG AND SONG

MISSIONARY BUDDHISM AND THE NEW CONFUCIANISM

The great intellectual currents of Tang and Song times were the spread of Buddhism in the earlier period and the resurgence of Confucianism in the latter.

Buddhism was brought by missionary monks from northern India to western China over the caravan routes of the great Silk Road. As early as the first century A.D., it was the faith of many foreign merchants resident in China. It appealed to Chinese and other East Asians through its direct dealing with human suffering, from which Buddhist enlightenment promised escape. In addition, evolving Mahayana Buddhism soon offered ritual and music, magic, art, and a variety of heavens and hells for people who couldn't grasp the nonbeing of Nirvana. During the Six Dynasties, Chinese Buddhist monks spread their faith all over China.

There were problems with translating abstract Indian concepts—like Nirvana—into Chinese. And the celibacy of Buddhist monks and nuns clashed jarringly with the Chinese emphasis on continuing the family line. But adaptable Buddhist missionaries in North China outdid the barbarian shamans at magic tricks, while Buddhists in the sophisticated south adroitly mixed religious propaganda with witty worldly conversation. Monasteries blossomed all over China, royal patrons were won, and the poor and unfortunate of the divided land found solace in the new faith.

But the real flowering of Chinese Buddhism came after the nation was reunited in Tang times. Despite the status of Confucianism as China's official philosophy and the penchant of a number of emperors for Daoism, Buddhism enjoyed its golden noon in Tang China. There was a proliferation of sects, providing a form of Buddhist belief for any Chinese. The *Tiantai* (Heavenly Terrace) sect tried to synthesize the conflicting doctrines of northern and southern Chinese Buddhism on various levels of truth, while claiming that all truth could actually be found in a single sermon—Buddha's famous Lotus Sutra. *Qingtu* (Pure Land) Buddhism, widely followed by ordinary Chinese with no head for theology, worshiped Buddha as ruler of a paradise in the west called the Pure Land and offered salvation simply through calling upon his name with a pure and sincere heart. *Chan* Buddhism, better known by its Japanese name of *Zen*, rejected all theology, scripture, and ceremony in favor of pure meditation, which alone would provide a true mystical understanding of the path to enlightenment.

In Tang times Buddhism thus channeled China's spiritual and intellectual impulses in an untypically religious direction. Under the Song, however, the Neo-Confucian revival—like the Hindu renaissance in Gupta India—drew China's educated classes back to an older faith. In China's case, it was a turn from an otherworldly religion back to a more typically Chinese secular philosophy.

Neo-Confucian scholarship produced many commentaries on the Confucian classics. It established the Four Books of Confucian wisdom that were to be China's core curriculum for the next millennium. Confucian scholars and philosophers reinvigorated historical study and revived public and private education. Perhaps most striking, however, they tried to answer the sort of question about the ultimate nature of things that Master

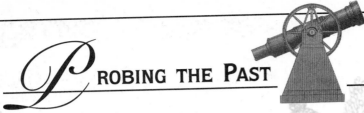

$\mathcal{P}$ROBING THE PAST

"*We may return for a moment to the general question raised in these paragraphs. Although this is not yet the place for final conclusions, there can be no doubt that China was, among the ancient civilisations of the Old World, the one which was most isolated from the others. The originality of its characteristic cultural patterns was therefore greater. But this does not mean that it did not participate in the spread of that civilising technological influence which radiated from the Fertile Crescent; furthermore, through all the successive centuries for three millennia, China was giving forth, and receiving, with ever-varying intensity, cultural and technical elements.*

Chinese civilisation . . . has always been "in the circuit" of the diffusion process. . . . It is, of course, equally necessary to make allowance for parallel development of ideas and techniques, independence of invention, and the like. In all these matters the repetition of generalisations is useless; what we need to know are more facts such as those to the elucidation of which the present work is devoted. It is probable that our final conclusion will be that there was far more intercourse and reaction between the Chinese and their western and southern neighbours than has often been supposed, but nevertheless that the essential style of Chinese thought and culture patterns maintained a remarkable and perennial autonomy. This is the real meaning of the "isolation" of China; contacts there were, but never abundant enough to affect the characteristic style of the civilisation, and hence of its science."

Joseph Needham's detailed, many-volumed history of science and technology in China is widely recognized as a monumental achievement of twentieth-century historiography. Here Needham confronts one of the key questions about Chinese history: the isolation of this great East Asian power and the resulting originality of its culture.

Does Needham see China as totally cut off from other centers of Old World civilization? Does he offer a final, dogmatic conclusion as to how original Chinese culture really was? How does he think historians may arrive at a surer conclusion on the matter? What is the cultural "diffusion" he refers to here? What does he mean by "parallel development"?

Joseph Needham and Wang Ling, <u>Science and Civilization in China</u>, Vol. I (Cambridge, England: Cambridge University Press, 1954), pp. 156–157.

Kong himself had always avoided—to provide a metaphysical foundation for Confucian social and ethical thought.

The most famous instance of Neo-Confucian metaphysical theorizing was the work of the philosopher Zhu Xi, a twelfth-century thinker who was to the Confucian revival what his contemporary Thomas Aquinas was to the Scholastic theology of the Christian Middle Ages. The best-known philosophical explorations of Zhu Xi involved a Platonic-sounding effort to explain the world in terms of *li* and *qi*. The *li* of anything was its basic form or fundamental principles, its *qi* the substance or stuff of which it is made. The most celebrated application of this doctrine had to do with the ancient dispute as to whether human nature was basically good, as Mencius had asserted, or evil, as the Legalists had always insisted. For the Neo-Confucianists, we are in a sense both. Our *li*, or basic principles, are good, but the substance of which we are made, our *qi*, is gross, corruptible, and bound to lead us into evildoing. Self-improvement, the cultivation of our human essence or *li*, is, of course, best accomplished through study of the Confucian classics.

SCIENCE AND TECHNOLOGY: FROM GUNPOWDER TO THE PRINTING PRESS

The physical sciences were an area in which there was striking progress from the third to the thirteenth centuries. In this as in so many things, the Chinese tended to be practical, to make contributions to technology rather than to pure science. It took the abstract mind of India to invent the zero; China developed the abacus.

Chinese science and technology during these centuries should, of course, be understood in the context of the mysticism and pseudoscience, often Daoist in origin, that framed its hardheaded practicality. Alchemical experimentation, the eternal quest for an elixir or regimen that would guarantee eternal life, and plain magic were as common in this as in earlier ages. Nevertheless, a striking array of useful discoveries in technology and applied science appeared in China before they did elsewhere.

Thus, the famous trio of inventions of which Europeans would boast during their own Renaissance—the compass, the printing press, and gunpowder—were all discovered many centuries earlier in China. Gunpowder was used more commonly for fireworks than for military purposes by the Chinese, but they did have forms of military rockets, hand grenades, and even explosive shells by Song times. The printing press was used most commonly for wood-block printing—whole sheets reprinted from single blocks—rather than printing with movable type, Gutenberg's great contribution. But this was simply because movable type was impractical where thousands of characters, instead of twenty-six letters, were involved. The compass was a clear advantage; it opened all the eastern seas to Chinese junks.

The Chinese of these centuries studied acoustics, optics, astronomy, and mathematics. Chinese cartographers made elaborate maps of Asia, some with a superimposed grid indicating elevations and trade routes across the Far East. They compiled botanical studies classifying many sorts of plants, from garden herbs to trees. Even such apparently superstitious exercises as alchemical experimentation taught the Chinese a good deal about genuine chemical reactions.

Chinese medical studies included treatises on drugs, diagnosis, and other aspects of disease and its treatment. Tea and hot baths were recommended for many ailments, but quite convincing drug treatments were urged in other cases. Chinese doctors took the pulse as an aid to diagnosis and inoculated people against smallpox. Acupuncture, the famous Chinese practice of sticking needles into patients to anesthetize them for surgery, still puzzles Western doctors, who are unsure whether it impedes the flow of pain signals through the nerves or stimulates the body

to secrete its own anesthetic substances. Whatever it does, it apparently often works.

The list of practical Chinese inventions goes on and on, well beyond the celebrated trio of compass, gunpowder, and printing press. Sedan chairs for the wealthy and wheelbarrows for the peasants, water mills and suspension bridges, paper and porcelain, ships' rudders and sea anchors, and many other handy devices were produced by the pragmatic Chinese intellect.

POETRY: MOON IN THE WATER

Besides Buddhist religious writing, Neo-Confucianist scholarship and philosophy, and China's pace-setting performance in science, the Tang and Song periods produced a flood of literary prose and poetry of all kinds. The literary legacy of these centuries is as rich as any in the history of this immensely literate civilization.

The prose production of the millennium between the fall of the Han in the third century and the fall of the Song in the thirteenth was impressive, even during the disunited centuries of the Six Dynasties. Commentaries on the classics, historical writing, and—something new—literary criticism and books on art passed through many schools and periods. There was a continuing dispute between a majority who favored the stately, formal prose styles of ancient times and a minority who urged a freer, more colloquial and colorful style of Chinese.

Poetry appeared in massive quantities. We have the names of more than two thousand Tang poets and almost four thousand from the Song period, as well as tens of thousands of surviving poems. Poetry, calligraphy, and painting were the gentlemanly arts, and every gentleman, scholar, or official seemed to feel a social if not an aesthetic compulsion to grind out a few verses at least.

Some of the best-known of these poets are still read today. China's most famous poets, in fact, are the Tang masters Du Fu and Li Bo.

Du Fu, perhaps the most admired of all Chinese poets, was an eighth-century writer who wrote in elaborate verse forms. Yet he expressed a deep involvement with ordinary Chinese people, particularly with the oppressed and exploited. His "Song of War Chariots," for instance, opens with a stirring call to battle:

The war-chariots rattle,
The war-horses whinny.
Each man of you has a bow and a quiver at his
    belt.

But it soon moves on to a grimmer assessment of the famous wars of the Tang:

We remember others at fifteen
    sent forth to guard the river. . . .
The mayor wound their turbans for them
    when they started out.

With their turbaned hair white now,
   they are still at the border,
At the border where the blood of men
   spills like the sea—
And still the heart of Emperor Wu
   is beating for war.[2]

Du Fu thus wrote with grave Confucian concern of the misfortunes that have afflicted humankind from that day to this.

Du Fu's friend and contemporary Li Bo was as bohemian a poet as ever drank himself under a table or declaimed his verses at the moon. Like Du Fu a minor official, Li was a footloose wanderer, a lover of wine, good company, and nature—all of which he celebrated in his poetry. Actually, he seemed quite capable of conjuring up his own company, given the wine and a suitably romantic slice of nature. According to a famous legend, Li Bo drowned during a drunken boating party when he reached over the side to scoop up the moon from the water.

The poets of the Song period wrote masses of verse on such traditional topics as country life, oppressive officials, friendship, and unhappiness. The most famous of them was probably the eleventh-century writer Su Shi. He and his artistic coterie often combined all three of the gentlemanly arts by writing their poems in elegant calligraphy as part of a painting. Su Shi was also a thoughtful critic of both literature and art. Poems, he once said, are "pictures without form," and paintings "unspoken poems."[3]

ART: MOUNTAINS IN THE MIST

The arts of the thousand years encompassing the Six Dynasties, the Tang, the Five Dynasties, and the Song created beautiful things in many forms. Of them all, Tang architecture was perhaps the most admired in its day, Song painting today.

Of the other arts, the two most distinctively Chinese were probably calligraphy and ceramics. Song pottery is particularly sought after. The simple, graceful vases and jars, sometimes porcelain and sometimes stoneware, manage to blend the strength of earlier pottery with the elegance and delicacy of later ceramics. One style of decoration popular even in the imperial palace was the crackle design, an array of thin cracks produced by a glaze that cooled and broke over the surface of the vessel as it did so.

Calligraphy is one of the hardest of Chinese arts for a foreigner to understand. Chinese characters, executed with brush and ink on paper or silk have, however, a striking beauty to the cultured Chinese eye. The abstract pattern of the character itself, the strength, dash, fluidity, or grace of the brush stroke, the revelation of the personality behind any particular calligraphic style—all have an endless fascination.

Most of the surviving sculpture of the period is Buddhist in origin and includes Buddhas and bodhisattvas, especially Guanyin, the bodhisattva of mercy. The fullness and swaying poses of Indian sculpture frequently merge here with the linear quality of much Chinese art, usually in the folds of clothing. There is some awesome stone statuary, notably the huge figures in the seventh-century Longmen cave temples centering on an immense fifty-foot Buddha. There are many smaller, extremely realistic figures in wood, bronze, or china, including graceful Guanyins seated at ease, one hand extended in gentle blessing. In Song times vivid portrait figures of *lohans*, mountain hermits adept in both Buddhist and Daoist mysticism, give us a close look at the faces of these saints of other faiths.

The most massive and sometimes extravagant architecture of these centuries was that produced during the Sui and the earlier Tang. This age of empire builders built on an imperial scale that was still admired in Song days. Huge palaces, pavilions, pagodas, and other structures are described in surviving literature, and some surviving pagodas give at least a flavor of the age. Pagoda towers, with their multiple, gracefully sloping eaves curving up at the corners, were built in connection with Buddhist temples or tombs.

Palaces also called for monumental building. Empress Wu Zetian, a great builder, once erected a royal hall three hundred feet on a side and almost three hundred feet high. An earlier ruler caused a pavilion to be constructed in which hundreds of guests could dine, and which could be rotated by machinery while they did so.

Not much remains of these great works except a few pagoda towers. But Song painting survives to delight us still. Painting on wall hangings or hand scrolls (to be unrolled horizontally, giving a gradual exposure to the work) was common from the Six Dynasties on. The most common Chinese word for painting is *hua*, meaning "to define by line," and Chinese painting has always been strongly linear.[4] Done with brush and ink, like calligraphy, it frequently looks more like drawing than painting to Western eyes. By whatever name, it is a major achievement.

Tang painting tended to use more color than was usual later. It also concentrated on the human figure, including some thoroughly convincing portraits and many figures of monks and other religious personages, elegant ladies, and other stock subjects. Other painters specialized in particular genre subjects, such as horses, birds, or flowers.

There was some Tang landscape painting, but this form really came into its own under the Song. Here, land-

[2]"A Song of War Chariots," in Cyril Birch, ed., *Anthology of Chinese Literature from Early Times to the Fourteenth Century* (New York: Grove Press, 1965), pp. 240–241.

[3]Susan Bush, *The Chinese Literati on Painting: Su Shih (1037–1101) to Tung Ch'i-ch'ang (1156–1636)* (Cambridge, Mass.: Harvard University Press, 1971), p. 25.

[4]Wan go Weng, *Chinese Painting and Calligraphy: A Pictorial Survey* (New York: Dover Publications, 1979), p. xvi.

scape painters largely abandoned color to concentrate on poetic line and on the famous Chinese composition that makes empty space an important part of the picture. The subjects define the face of the Chinese land as it looked a thousand years ago: bamboo and water, naked tree branches against snow, and again and again mountains in the mist.

Unrolling a hand scroll such as Gao Keming's eleventh-century *Streams and Hills under Fresh Snow* is like taking a walk along the wintry river, with here a laden coolie, there a barge, gnarled trees close up, and further off a cozy house along the snowy bank, the master and mistress just glimpsed through an open door as they are served their dinner. Fan Guan's magnificently vertical *Travelers among Streams and Mountains* shows the travelers in their carriages dwarfed by the pine-crowned hills just behind them, rendered utterly insignificant by the gigantic mountains that rise out of a veil of mist to dominate the picture.

Tang building is gone, Song painting survives. Both make it only too clear why Chinese civilization dominated the East a thousand years ago.

CHINA'S SPHERE OF INFLUENCE

THE BORDERLANDS

The Chinese sphere of influence consisted of a ring of states and peoples around the Middle Kingdom. All these cultures were less developed than China's during the ten centuries from the fall of the Han to the fall of the Song. Two distinct regions—and relationships—may, however, be distinguished among these peoples of China's borderlands.

Most of China's inner frontier, facing north and west upon Eurasia, opened onto relatively barren and thinly peopled terrain. The dusty deserts, the thin grass of the steppes, the high cold plateaus of Manchuria, Mongolia, Tibet, and the Tarim Basin encouraged a pastoral nomadic style of life very different from China's intensive agriculture and developed urban society. The languages of the Turko-Mongol peoples beyond the Great Wall were so different that they couldn't even be written in Chinese characters.

The normal relationships between China and its nomadic neighbors to the north and west was one of conflict. Every dynasty had to deal with "the barbarians," either defensively like the Song or by taking the offensive against them as the Tang emperors did. But large-scale assimilation to the Chinese way would prove very difficult in most of these inner Asian borderlands.

South and east, however, the case was very different. Here settled agricultural peoples had already made a beginning at a more developed culture. And here the impressive Chinese achievement in civilization decisively influenced what became the three most important East Asian nations outside of China itself—Vietnam, Korea, and Japan.

VIETNAM: THE LESSER DRAGON

Vietnam is a narrow S-shaped country running down the eastern edge of the Indochinese peninsula from South China into Southeast Asia. The country has two "rice bowls," the broad, fertile deltas of the Red River in the north and the Mekong in the south, connected by a long, curving mountain spine. Intruders from China began to push into north Vietnam toward the end of the first millennium B.C., just about the time of China's unification under the Qin.

They found a Bronze Age people, recently evolved from hunting and fishing yet already shaping an urban, seafaring society on a narrow agricultural base—the Dong-Son culture whose remains were to be found in many parts of Southeast Asia. Vietnam was no match for its huge neighbor. Shortly before 100 B.C., the Han emperors formally annexed the country, which would remain part of South China for the next thousand years.

Particularly under the aggressive Tang dynasty, Chinese rule brought Chinese administration and language, Confucian classics, and Mahayana Buddhism. Chinese influence also brought intensified wet-rice agriculture and a more elaborate urban culture. The Chinese presence, however, also generated a growing sense of national identity and resentment of foreign rule on the part of north Vietnamese officials and aristocrats in particular.

North Vietnam was never simply another Chinese province. The Vietnamese felt the cultural pull of their Indianized Southeast Asian neighbors. They were frequently preoccupied with the beginnings of their own long, slow conquest of southern Vietnam, which was then dominated by the Indianized kingdom of Champa. And resentment of their powerful neighbor to the north grew with every passing generation.

When the Tang dynasty collapsed into anarchy in the tenth century, the Vietnamese seized the chance to secede. After a long millennium as part of China, Vietnam was an independent—and growing—nation.

And yet before that century of independence was out, Vietnam's leaders had prudently accepted a tributary relationship with Song China. The cultural ties—and political enmities—that existed between the two nations would continue down the centuries, even to the present one. The troubled relationship between China and Vietnam, sometimes called the Greater and Lesser Dragons, remains a fact of East Asian life today.

KOREA AND CHINESE CULTURAL HEGEMONY

Korea is a broad, slightly hooked peninsula thrusting down between North China's Yellow Sea and the Sea of Japan. The country is broken up by mountain ranges extending throughout much of its length. The western and southern coasts, however, smooth down into level plains and finally break up into many harbors and islands. The population at the time of the first Chinese intrusion was sparse and not long removed from dependence on hunting and fishing, though the western coastal plains particularly were already under cultivation. The Koreans still lived in tribal societies dominated by hereditary chiefs and female shamans called *mudang*. Their major monuments were stone-walled tombs, or dolmens, of the sort found in many parts of Eurasia, from western Europe to Japan, in earlier centuries.

The expansionist Han Chinese pushed into northern Korea in the last centuries before Christ. Empress Lü temporarily annexed part of the northern peninsula around 100 B.C. But Korea itself was moving rapidly ahead with state formation by then, and Chinese political control soon evaporated. Nevertheless, an influential colony of Chinese remained in the northern part of the peninsula for several hundred years.

From about the fourth century A.D. on, the Three Kingdoms divided Korea among them. These three rival Korean powers competed for Chinese skills and cultural innovations to strengthen them in their endless feuds. When the Sui and Tang dynasties reunited China in the seventh century, massive Chinese expeditions were launched against Korea. Once more, the attempt at conquest failed. But Empress Wu's shrewd alliance with the Korean kingdom of Silla, which soon established control over most of the peninsula, enhanced the continuing Chinese influence.

Under Silla in Tang times and under the kingdom of Koryŏ in the days of the Song, Korea's own rulers set out to turn their recently unified nation into a carbon copy of their huge neighbor. What remained of the old tribal culture was replaced as far as possible by a structure of central bureaus and provincial officials. The Korean economy—particularly the commercial sector—remained comparatively backward by Chinese standards. But the Chinese written language and culture, and most especially Chinese Mahayana Buddhism, were widespread.

Like the Vietnamese, the Koreans traditionally paid tribute to China. But the Korean debt to the Middle Kingdom went far deeper than annual payments. The development of Korean civilization illustrates perfectly the pattern of cultural hegemony that underlay the phenomenon of growing zones of culture around the world.

JAPAN AND THE CHINESE MODEL

The offshore-island kingdom of Japan provides a variant and even more important example of the impact of Chinese culture. Japan was dramatically affected by its encounters with Chinese civilization, yet a distinctive Japanese form of East Asian culture, contrasting sharply with China's in some ways, evolved in the end.

The reason for China's limited impact on Japan was probably primarily geographic. Japan lies more than a hundred miles east of the Asian mainland—five times as far from Asia as Britain is from Europe. At such a distance China's armed forces, which were spearheads of Chinese influence in Vietnam and even Korea, had no impact on Japan. The Japanese were thus much freer to accept or reject Chinese influences, to seek contact with the giant power to the east or to cut themselves off from it for generations at a time. From this unique circumstance evolved the strikingly selective pattern of China's influence on Japan.

The four main Japanese islands run some 1300 miles, from jagged Hokkaido in the northeast through the long, indented curve of Honshu to the smaller islands of Kyushu and Shikoku in the southwest.

Four fifths of the island country is too mountainous for agriculture, but intensive rice cultivation in the narrow river valleys and coastal plains has made it possible for today's Japan to support the sixth largest population in the world. The mountains contribute to the nation's picture-postcard beauty and have given it a national symbol, the sacred snowcapped cone of Mount Fuji. As in ancient Greece, however, those same mountains inhibited national unity in Japan's early centuries.

The center of Japan's early history was not in the heart of the large central island of Honshu, where Tokyo sprawls today, but in western Japan, around the narrow Inland Sea framed by Kyushu and Shikoku and the southwesternmost tip of Honshu. Here prehistoric hunting, fishing, and farming bands, and settlements developed, matriarchal in social organization, worshiping nature spirits, working bronze and then iron.

During the early centuries of the Christian era, a simple clan-based society evolved around the Inland Sea, each small clan, or *uji*, having its hereditary chief and its ancestral god, often a totemic animal or other nature spirit. By the fifth century a loosely feudal state had appeared, dominated by the powerful Yamato clan; other *uji* were ranked in a rough hierarchy. By this time too the collection of cults and religious practices called *Shinto* had emerged, along with its simple rites and local shrines dedicated to mountains, waterfalls, ancient trees, and a few sanctified individuals.

Chinese influences reached this little world of clans and nature spirits, first from sinicized Korea and then from China itself, during the imperial age of the Tang.

In the sixth century Chinese Buddhism reached Japan through Korea, bringing Chinese culture with it. In the seventh and eighth centuries, reforming Japanese regimes sent repeated embassies, including many students and monks, to Tang China to acquire the skills and learn the ways of the East Asian colossus. Powerful Japanese statesmen encouraged this procedure. The famous Prince Shotoku, in particular, preached centralized government and court hierarchy and even imported the Chinese calendar.

Contrast this Japanese <u>bodhisattva</u>—a Buddhist "enlightened one" who has deferred entry into Nirvana in order to confer spiritual benefits on the human race—with the Indian version shown in Chapter 12. The spread of Buddhism from India to East Asia required many modifications in both religious ideas and artistic forms. Other world religions, including Christianity, have undergone similar modifications as they spread to different cultures. (Freer Gallery of Art)

The resulting changes seemed likely to turn Japan into another small version of the Tang state. Japanese rulers and *uji* chiefs, some of whom were more powerful than their sovereign, nevertheless preached centralized rule by an absolute emperor and urged a Confucian sense of duty and Buddhist reverence. Centralized bureaus were established, a Chinese-style law code was promulgated, and attempts were made to establish the equal-field system and centralized taxation of Tang China. A capital city called Nara was built at the eastern end of the Inland Sea, modeled on Xi'an, with proper royal palaces and massive monasteries. The Japanese elite learned Chinese and used Chinese script, borrowed Chinese court ceremonials, Chinese styles and entertainments.

Beneath these transformations at the top of Nara society, however, Japan remained in many ways the Japan of old. The *uji* aristocracy preserved much of its former feudal independence despite the emperor's exalted claims. The economy remained comparatively simple; money, for example, was still rare, barter far more common. And the great Chinese invention of an educated civil service based

on merit was never adopted at all beyond the Sea of Japan.

Then, as Tang China declined and crumbled into chaos in the ninth century, Japan turned away from its great model and began to develop its own distinctive style of civilization. The Heian period (roughly 800–1200), when the Japanese capital was at Heian (present-day Kyoto) was the period when this return to older ways was strongest. In three dynamic centuries Japan's ruling elite had absorbed all they could learn from China. The following four hundred years were given over to digesting and modifying these cultural acquisitions in terms of Japan's older native heritage.

The core of that heritage was *uji* feudalism, and the Heian period saw a significant resurgence of the power of the landed magnates in the *shoen* (estates) system. The *shoen* typically consisted not of a single estate but a dispersed collection of tracts owned by a single aristocratic proprietor. This proprietor looked up to a patron, usually a powerful figure at the royal court or in the Buddhist establishment. Below the proprietor were his estate managers, the farmers they managed, and the farm laborers the farmers hired. The result was a structure much like the feudal and manorial systems of Europe at that time—and very different from the centralized economy of China.

The chief patrons of the *shoen* system were wealthy court families, such as the Fujiwara, or religious institutions, commonly rich Buddhist monasteries. The great families in particular became the real rulers of Japan, using the royal court as an arena for their endless intrigues. The Fujiwara soon became the most powerful of these great clans, supplying the royal house with most of its empresses, monopolizing high government posts, and holding more *shoen* estates than any other family.

Occasionally feisty emperors challenged Fujiwara dominance, and there were damaging splits in the Fujiwara clan itself. But the real problem was that the authority of the government declined so drastically as to be a prize hardly worth controlling. As the power behind a powerless throne, the Fujiwara slowly went down with the monarchy they had themselves undermined.

THE CULTURE OF COURT AND MONASTERY

The Japanese cultural accomplishment during the seven centuries from the Yamoto state to the Heian period reflected even more strikingly the unique Japanese amalgamation of indigenous elements and foreign influences. This mixture is clear whichever of the twin centers of Japan's emergent culture we look at—the Buddhist monasteries or the imperial court.

The imported Buddhist faith comprised a variety of Chinese sects, from the ecclectic *Tendai* (Chinese: *Tiantai*) with its emphasis on the Lotus Sutra, through the popular Pure Land school, to the mystic withdrawal of medi-

A Kyoto temple today, with its curving pagoda roof line, reflecting pool, and setting of trees and flowers beautifully embodies both the Chinese Buddhist influence and the grace and elegance of Heian Japan. Lightness, graceful lines, and the integration of buildings with the natural world around were features of Japanese architecture. (Japan National Tourist Organization)

tative Zen (Chan). Pure Land Buddhism, offering hope of rebirth in the Buddhist paradise, had a particular appeal during the later Heian period, when the decay of central government and accompanying domestic violence made many fear that a Buddhist version of the end of the world was nigh.

Buddhist temples and Buddhist sculpture survive in considerable quantities, and Chinese influences are clear. The graceful lines of multiple pagoda roofs rose above the worldly capitals of Nara and Heian and among the forested mountains where some monks sought refuge from the world. Statues of Buddha, of various bodhisattvas, and of famous monks in meditation were crafted in stone, bronze, wood, and other materials. One of the most famous is the *Portrait of Ganjin*, a Chinese monk who tried six times to reach Japan, survived pirates,

storms, and shipwreck to do so, and finally arrived—blind, having lost his vision in the course of his tribulations. There is more than realism in this simple figure seated in the Buddhist posture of meditation; the gentle face, shaved head, and closed eyes blend with the curving folds of the robe to project a feeling of benevolence and great peace.

The secular culture of the Heian period especially was immensely sophisticated for a people only a few centuries removed from the rude life of feudal clans. The court life of that period of intrigue and conspiracy was elegant in the extreme. Fashion, aesthetics, and the most delicate sensibilities governed the dress and decorum, the love life and artistic creativity of these courtiers of old Japan.

Poetry and exquisite prose were produced in substantial quantities, much of it by highly cultured court ladies. The greatest subject was love, the medium a mix of prose and poetry. An unusual literary form was the poetic diary, a first-person account of a journey, a love affair, or simply the daily life of the court, much of it written in verse. Though a core of autobiographical fact was necessary, artistic requirements seem to have determined the shapely contours of the finished work.

The novel also appeared this early in Japanese literary history. The most famous Heian novel—indeed, the most famous and influential of all Japanese novels—was Lady Murasaki's eleventh-century *Tale of Genji*. Often described as the first psychological novel, this lengthy account of the life and love affairs of Prince Genji gives as much attention to nuances of feeling as to complex plotting and court life. Overlying it all, there is a romantic melancholy, a sense of the fragility of all things human, and of the heightened intensity this sense of transitory humanity gives to life, love, and beauty.

Among the rude barons of the back country, however, devotees of the warrior code of *bushido*, the builders of the next age, were already gathering their forces. The reign of the samurai was fast approaching.

SUMMARY

Between the third and the thirteenth centuries, many dynasties ruled China, but two loom gigantic in the history books: the empire-building Tang and the brilliant Song.

The Tang dynasty (618–907) was founded by Emperor Tang Taizong—"Grand Ancestor," victorious general, political reformer, scholar, artist, and perhaps the greatest of all Chinese rulers. The greatest of Chinese empresses, the Dowager Empress Wu, left the land richer and more powerful than it had ever been. Overall, China's political centralization, foreign trade, domestic wealth, and conquests beyond its own borders had never been greater than they were during the Tang.

The Song dynasty (960–1279) produced fewer great emperors, no foreign conquest, and diminished commerical exchange with the outside world. Yet the Middle Kingdom was never more brilliant. A population of one hundred million Chinese fed itself and was governed by the world's first meritocracy, the Confucian scholar-bureaucrats.

Chinese culture during this millennium from the fall of the Han to that of the Song was varied and colorful. Chinese learning probed the nation's lengthening past and analyzed the classics of Confucius. Buddhist monks carried that Indian religion far across China and beyond. The printing press, the compass, gunpowder, and acupuncture all enriched Chinese culture.

Poetry blossomed in unparalleled quantities, including the lyrics of China's most admired poet, Du Fu, who wrote with Confucian concern for the Chinese underdog. Song ceramics and landscape painting established Chinese traditions that have been admired around the world since.

Under the Tang furthermore, China's zone of influence among neighboring peoples exceeded even that of the Han. China ruled Vietnam as a loosely held province and exercised a decisive cultural influence on Korea. But Tang China's most important impact was felt by the still undeveloped islands of Japan.

Under Chinese influence, the island nation of Japan evolved from a culture of feuding clans into a Tang style monarchy. China's impact declined during the inward-looking Song era, when Japan's emperors lost most of their power to its great noble families. Yet Japan remained a sophisticated new nation, where Buddhist monks, court poets, and novels like the famous *Tale of Genji* reflected the seminal influences of the ancient empire more than a hundred miles away across the Sea of Japan.

SUGGESTED READING

BINGHAM, W. *The Founding of the Tang Dynasty*. New York: Octagon Books, 1970. Originally published in 1941 and perhaps still the best available account.

CARMODY, D. L. *Women and World Religions*. Nashville, Tenn.: Parthenon Press, 1979. Brief studies, including good summary of women's place in Buddhist and Daoist theory.

CHAFFEE, J. W. *The Thorny Gate of Learning in Sung China: A Social History of Examinations*. New York: Cambridge University Press, 1985. Widely admired study of the development of China's scholarly elite during a period of rapid growth..

CH'EN, K. *Buddhism in China: A Historical Survey*. Princeton, N.J: Princeton University Press, 1964. Outline of the spread of the Indian religion in China. For a more focused study on the period under consideration, see S. Weinstein, *Buddhism under the T'ang* (New York: Cambridge University Press, 1987) an examination of shifting government policies toward the spread of Buddhism in China.

FITZGERALD, C. P. *The Empress Wu*. Vancouver: University of British Columbia Press, 1968. Readable and scholarly life of one of the greatest of Chinese empresses.

————. *Son of Heaven: A Biography of Li Shih-min, Founder of the Tang Dynasty*. Cambridge: Cambridge University Press, 1933. Political history of the rise and reign of this famed ruler.

GERNET, J. *Daily Life in China on the Eve of the Mongol Invasions, 1250–1276*, trans. H. M. Wright. London: Allen & Unwin, 1962. Late Song Social life.

HUNG, W., ed. *Tu Fu, China's Greatest Poet* (2 vols). Cambridge: Cambridge University Press, 1952. The range of the poet's concerns comes through clearly.

KIDDER, J. E. *Japan before Buddhism*, rev. ed. New York: Praeger, 1966. A widely recommended book on Japan before the shaping influence of China.

KRACKE, E. A. *The Civil Service in Early Sung China, 960–1067*. Cambridge, Mass.: Harvard University Press, 1953. Standard work on the central feature of Chinese government at a crucial stage in its development. See also B. E. McKnight, *Village and Bureaucracy in Southern Sung China* (Chicago: University of Chicago Press, 1971), for government on the local level.

MURASAKI, S. *The Tale of Genji*, trans. E. G. Seidensticker. New York: Knopf, 1976. Accurate translation of this most famous of Japanese novels; Arthur Waley's older translation (London: Allen & Unwin, 1935) still has great literary appeal.

POLLACK, D. *The Fracture of Meaning: Japan's Synthesis of China from the Eighth through the Eighteenth Century*. Princeton: Princeton University Press, 1986. Complex interaction of borrowed ideas from China and indigenous Japanese concepts to produce Japan's own unique traditional culture.

REISCHAUER, E. O., ed. *Ennin's Travels in Tang China*. New York: Ronald Press, 1955. First-hand tale of society in Tang times by a traveling monk.

ROSSABI, M., ed. *China Among Equals: The Middle Kingdom and Its Neighbors, 10th to 14th Centuries*. Berkeley: University of California Press, 1983. Song times and after, in up-to-date and authoritative papers.

TWITCHETT, D. *Financial Administration under the T'ang Dynasty*, 2nd ed. Cambridge: Cambridge University Press, 1971. Good example of the sort of institutional study the remarkable Chinese records make possible.

WECHSLER, H. J. *Mirror to the Son of Heaven: Wei Cheng at the Court of T'ang T'ai-tsung*. New Haven, Conn.: Yale University Press, 1974. The founder of the Tang and his China.

WENG, W. *Chinese Painting and Calligraphy: A Pictorial Survey*. New York: Dover, 1978. Beautifully reproduced examples from a famous American collection, including many samples from the Northern and Southern Song.

CHAPTER 22

THE MONGOL EMPIRE

THE NOMADS OF EURASIA

The Double Continent
Nomads of the Steppes
Steppe Nomads and Civilization

THE RISE AND FALL OF THE MONGOLS

Genghis Khan, Lord of All Men
The Mongol Conquests
The Mongol Empire
The End of the Mongol Adventure

THE IMPACT OF THE MONGOL IMPERIUM

Mongol Culture
Russia and the Golden Horde
China and the Mongol Khans
China in the Days of Marco Polo
The Fall of the Mongols

THE NOMADS OF EURASIA

THE DOUBLE CONTINENT

Europe and Asia are normally considered as two continents divided by the Ural Mountains and by the straits between the Mediterranean and Black seas. In dealing with the wide-ranging Eurasian nomadic peoples who are the subject of this chapter, however, it will be useful to look at the world's largest land mass as a whole. Northern Eurasia in particular was in earlier times a vast empty stage across which peoples wandered and settled pretty much at will.

The "world island," as it is sometimes called, covers some twenty-one million square miles, four fifths of it Asia and one fifth Europe. It reaches from the equator in the south to the arctic in the north. West to east, it stretches halfway around the globe, from the prime meridian that runs through Greenwich, England, to a point beyond the 180-degree line in the Russian Far East.

Eurasia includes the largest country in the world today, Russia, and the two most populous, China and India. Some of its peninsulas, from Scandinavia to Korea, are nation-sized. Two of its major groups of offshore islands—Great Britain and Japan—are among the world's great powers.

The geographical diversity of Eurasia is immense. Its great ranges include the Alps and the Himalayas—the latter, the world's highest mountains. Its deserts run from Arabia to the Gobi. Its northern reaches are eternally frozen, and its bare tundra and dark taiga (subarctic coniferous forests) are almost as cold, while its southern extremities dissolve into the warm Mediterranean or melt into the jungles and tropic seas of Southeast Asia.

Deserts, mountains, jungles may divide; other aspects of Eurasian geography provided broad highways for people who had the skills and the courage to attempt them. The grassy steppes that flow from western Europe far across Russia and the passes around the Pamir Knot leading still further east to China were open roads from early centuries. The bodies of water that wash from the Atlantic and the Mediterranean to the Indian Ocean, the China seas, and the Pacific provided the broadest thoroughfare of all in later times. But these avenues were only for nomadic tribes and merchant caravans, ships and sailors who knew the ways of the world's oceans and the sea of grass.

Some of these nomadic peoples became great conquerors of more settled peoples. The most successful of them all were the Mongols, who in the thirteenth and fourteenth centuries, as we shall see, turned a large part of Eurasia into a Mongol-dominated zone stretching from one end of the world-island to the other.

NOMADS OF THE STEPPES

Because of their unique style of life, the nomads of Eurasia had created a cultural zone of their own that went back to the dawn age of human history. Their way of life was determined from the beginning by their dependence on moving herds of animals.

The animals they tended included goats, sheep, cattle, and even reindeer. The essential animals for riding and for transport were the horse, the ass, and the camel. Life built around these herds and flocks produced an evolving technology as different from that of the farming village as both were from life within the walls of the cities.

Pastoralists were the first to domesticate the horse and the camel, and thus to gain the mobility offered by these large, fast-moving animals. They adapted the wheel—discovered by the ancient Mesopotamians—to their own uses, producing sizable wheeled carts in which all their belongings might be moved from one decently watered pasturage to the next. They developed the oldest and most adaptable form of mobile housing ever devised—the tent. And they learned to live almost entirely off the milk, blood, and meat, the hides and the wool, of the animals they herded.

Certain social forms emerged naturally among the peoples living this wandering style of life, forms rather different from those that predominated among settled farmers. Nomads continued to organize by family and clan, as did more sedentary populations. But the need for guidance and decision making among a people who were constantly on the move encouraged strong leadership and powerful chiefs. The need to deal firmly with other peoples among whom they had no established traditional rights put a premium on fighting skills and gave many nomads a more militaristic tradition than farming areas had.

Three clear patterns of migration guided the ponderous but purposeful progress of the nomads of northern Eurasia in particular.

As a pastoral people, first of all, they followed an established annual round, back and forth across a predefined territory where they knew they would find water and pasturage at each season of the year. This was the primary nomadic pilgrimage, tracking the seasons across familiar ground, perhaps even using the same campsites year after year.

As warrior peoples defending—or deliberately invading—unmarked grazing grounds, nomads also frequently clashed with other peoples. If they were defeated in these conflicts, they necessarily retreated from their familiar pasturage and set out in search of new territories. These movements in turn often meant clashing with still other pastoral folk, perhaps jarring them out of their lands in their turn. This jostling could spread from one end of the steppe to the other over a period of decades or generations. Such dislocations tended to flow from east to west, as uprooted nomads turned their horses' heads toward the warmer and moister grasslands of the western steppes.

Besides the annual migratory round and the less common east-to-west movements of peoples, there were, finally, the predatory southward drives of nomadic peoples into the fat lands of the city-based civilizations. Tempted by the wealth or weakness of the developed societies that stretched from one end of Eurasia to the other, these mobile armies, whole peoples on the move, could have a devastating impact.

A nomad horde on the march must have been a striking sight, as it is today in those few corners of the world where this ancient style of life persists. There would be milling sheep or shambling cattle, high-wheeled wagons, laden beasts, and the herders themselves moving the flocks. There would be stinging flies thick around the animals, smells of sweat and leather, a haze of dust over the faces of men, women, and children. Most of the time, especially on the steppes, there would be the rudely garbed riders, so easy in their saddles as to remind an uneasy observer of old legends of the centaur, half human and half beast. And there would be weapons, certainly—glinting blades, unstrung bows, and deadly feathered shafts.

STEPPE NOMADS AND CIVILIZATION

Because they were constantly on the move, nomads were much more likely than settled farmers to brush up against lifeways other than their own. Such cultural encounters inevitably led to friction. Greed was also quickly kindled among these lean and quick-eyed herders: Much as they might despise farming, they knew well-watered land when they saw it. Nor were their own spartan ways proof against the temptations of the luxuries that accumulated within the walls of cities.

Powerful leadership, military skills, and elan, combined with unparalleled mobility and the toughness that went with their rigorous style of life, made nomads formidable opponents for the cities and empires of the civilized zones. Pastoral nomads—as we have seen—left more than one island of urban culture in ruins.

The most dangerous and successful of the nomads

Nomads of ancient and modern times have carried their homes with them folded up on the backs of camels, yaks, or other beasts of burden. Like these Tibetans of more recent times, the nomadic Mongols among whom Genghis Khan grew up ate and slept, talked and did chores inside their tents. (North Wind Picture Archives)

were those of the steppes, and over the centuries their impact was heaviest on the sedentary populations of western Eurasia. The reason for this nomadic pressure on the West was what is sometimes called the *steppe gradient*—the warmer weather and superior pasturelands of the more southerly western steppes. By 2000 B.C., the steppe gradient had already drawn Indo-European nomads into Europe, where they became the ancestors of the Greeks and Romans, the Slavs, Celts, and Germans of later centuries. Other Indo-Europeans in the second and first millennia B.C., and Turko-Mongols in the first and early second millennia A.D., followed this historic drift from eastern Asia toward Europe.

The inventiveness of the steppe nomads made them a particularly potent military threat. Shortly after 2000 B.C., they armed themselves with bronze and mounted themselves in light, fast war chariots that made them the masters of the battlefield. Thus equipped, they were to shatter most of the great civilizations of the turbulent second millennium, from the Mediterranean to India.

Beginning around 1000 B.C., the nomadic warriors of the Eurasian grasslands shifted from chariots to horseback and armed themselves with weapons made of iron, which was harder and more plentiful than bronze. The Persians and the Xiongnu were cavalry soldiers. So were the Mongols of Genghis Khan, with whom the present chapter is primarily concerned.

THE RISE AND FALL OF THE MONGOLS

GENGHIS KHAN, LORD OF ALL MEN

Genghis Khan (1167?–1227) was born plain Temujin (Ironsmith), son of a minor Mongol chieftain on the chilly steppes northwest of China. While he was still a boy, his father was poisoned by enemies. The heir apparent had to flee from the tents of his own people to wander with a few followers, an outcast among the drifting clans.

He had tremendous physical strength and the physical courage expected of his people. He was also a natural political intriguer and a born military strategist—in both areas patient, cunning, and ruthless when the time to strike finally came. He was a religious man, a believer in the nature gods of the steppe, yet tolerant and eager to have priests of all faiths around him, lest he give offense to any powerful divinity. Perhaps strangest of all in a wandering child of the steppes, he had a remarkable head for organization. He organized his armies and his empire with a rigor that would have done a Chinese or Byzantine bureaucrat proud.

The motives that drove Genghis Khan have been variously represented. To some degree, certainly, it was the simple imperative of many nomadic conquerors before him. He led his soldiers into battle, he once said, for the sheer exaltation of winning, the joy of seeing other men break and run before him, of taking their horses, looting their tents and cities. But there was a deeper motive at work as well behind that wind-darkened forehead, those enigmatic eyes—a religious motive. The Eternal Sky—chief of the Mongol gods—had ordered him to take the field against the world.

Drying pasturage and greed for the material luxuries of the cities, common motives for movements of steppe nomads, may also account in part for this greatest onslaught of the steppes against the softer, richer southern lands. But without the uniquely inspired leadership and genius for organization of this most remarkable of nomads, the long ride of the Mongols could never have happened.

Mongol warriors lived in the saddles of their stocky, shaggy ponies. They could travel for days without rest or food beyond the blood and mare's milk of their own horses. Their particularly fearsome version of the compound bow, more powerful than the English longbow or the Muslim crossbow, could kill at an eighth of a mile.

In combat the Mongols would circle their enemies, discharging flight after flight of arrows. They might also pretend to flee, drawing their antagonists into yet more devastating barrages. But when enough enemy mounts and men had fallen, they would turn and charge, screaming columns of leather and fur and flashing swords, with always that relentless cloud of armor-piercing arrows driving on before them. That was the last sight many a more civilized soldier ever saw—the charge of the Mongol cavalry—before the dust and blood engulfed him.

In 1206, at a tribal conclave on the Kerulen River in the wastes of Mongolia, the clan chiefs of these Mongol warriors chose Temujin to be their paramount leader. He was neither a boy nor an outcast by then, but a seasoned warrior and a skilled political tactician who had outmaneuvered and destroyed all his rivals among the Mongol tribes. They made him their great khan—Genghis Khan, Lord of All Men. He had twenty years left to lead the people of the tents, to shatter their foes, to earn the title of the most successful conqueror the world has ever known.

THE MONGOL CONQUESTS

The Mongol conquests, which began in Genghis Khan's time and lasted through most of the thirteenth century, astonished and horrified all the zones of civilization across Eurasia. Three major centers of urban culture were primary targets of Mongol raids, conquest, and eventual subjugation: Confucian China, the Muslim Middle East, and the eastern part of Christian Europe. Most of the world's largest land mass was thus shaken for a century by the pounding hoofbeats of the Mongol hordes.

Genghis Khan drove first down into North China, where he crushed the Tibetan and Jürched states that

"On the following day when from the reflection of the sun the plain seemed to be a tray filled with blood, the people of Bokhara opened their gates and closed the door of strife and battle. . . . Chingiz-Khan rode into the Friday mosque and pulled up before the maqsura, *[where he] asked those present whether this was the palace of the Sultan; they replied that it was the house of God. Then he too got down from his horse, and mounting two or three steps of the pulpit he exclaimed: "The countryside is empty of fodder; fill our horses' bellies." Whereupon [Chingiz-Khan's men] opened all the magazines in the town and began carrying off the grain. And they brought the cases in which the Korans were kept out into the courtyard of the mosque, where they cast the Korans right and left and turned the cases into mangers for their horses. After which they circulated cups of wine and sent for the singing-girls of the town to sing and dance for them; while the Mongols raised their voices to the tunes of their own songs. . . . After an hour or two Chingiz-Khan arose to return to his camp, and as the multitude that had been gathered there moved away the leaves of the Koran were trampled in the dirt beneath their own feet and their horses' hoofs. In that moment, the Emir. . . . famous for his piety and asceticism, turned to the learned* imam *Rukn-ad-Din Imamzada. . . . and said: "Maulana, what . . . is this? That which I see do I see it in wakefulness or in sleep, O Lord?" Maulana* Imamzada *answered: "Be silent: it is the wind of God's omnipotence that bloweth, and we have no power to speak."*

Joveyni (1226–1283) was a cultivated Muslim man of letters; he was also a Persian official in the employ of the Mongol conquerors of Persia. The desecration of the mosque at Bokhara by Genghis Khan and his pagan Mongols described here should be read with an awareness of the author's difficult position as a pious Muslim who served in the government of one of Genghis Khan's descendants.

Does Joveyni try to disguise the blasphemous behavior of the Mongols? How does the remark of the wise <u>imam</u> quoted here try to explain the desecration of Allah's house in terms of Allah's power? Does this explanation seem to mitigate the shocking behavior of the "World Conqueror" Genghis Khan?

'Ala al-Din 'Ata Malek Joveyni, <u>The History of the World Conqueror</u>, trans. John Andrew Boyle (Manchester, England: Manchester University Press, 1958), pp. 103–104.

shared a divided China with the Song emperors in the south. The Great Wall had been breached and Beijing left a smoldering ruin by 1215, opening the way to the subsequent conquest of all North China and Korea.

After this first assault on China, Temujin turned his horses westward and advanced against the Muslim Middle East. Ancient trading cities like Samarkand and Bokhara were pillaged, their inhabitants slaughtered. By 1220 Afghanistan and Persia lay helpless before the Mongols.

The armies of Genghis Khan pushed on into European Russia, riding through the rich pasturelands of the Ukraine. There a flying column of Mongol horsemen met and overthrew a coalition of Russian princes in 1223. It was only foreshadowing of what was to come.

Genghis Khan died in 1227, a greater conqueror than Cyrus the Persian or Alexander the Great had ever been. He left behind a huge empire, a carefully planned succession, and above all an army that was one of the most awesome fighting machines the world has seen.

Genghis Khan had disciplined his troops as no Mongol horde had been before. He had added military experts from conquered peoples, such as the Turks and Chinese, and more elaborate military technology, such as the catapults and battering rams that now rumbled along in the baggage train. He had developed the process of preliminary intelligence-gathering into a fine art. He had turned the casual terrorism of any nomad campaign into calculated psychological warfare. And his unbeaten cavalrymen were still there, tough, ever-victorious, eager to conquer and loot the rest of the world for his successors.

Mongol armies rode west once more in the 1230s and 1240s. They captured and devastated Kiev, the old southern capital of Russia, and overran a number of northern Russian cities as well, including the still modest town of Moscow. From a base on the Volga, they sent massive raids into eastern Europe. They ravaged Hungary and Poland and probed Austria before swinging back toward the northern grasslands.

In the 1250s powerful Mongol formations poured into Muslim Persia once more in a campaign that climaxed with the capture of Baghdad. The Abbasid capital was sacked and much of the population put to the sword. The last Abbasid caliph was trampled to death by Mongol ponies.

The conquest of the rest of Song China took the better part of half a century, but that too was accomplished—the first time all of China had ever been overrun by the nomads from beyond the Great Wall. In 1279 Genghis Khan's renowned grandson Kublai Khan overwhelmed the last Song emperor.

To their victims they were the scourge of God, the horsemen from hell. They came like a recurring nightmare out of the steppes, darkening the plain, descending on the sedentary populations of Eurasia, putting whole cities to the sword. They marked their passing with pyramids of skulls.

But they also did something that nomadic raiders had not done before. Following in the footsteps of their remarkable founder, they organized an empire.

THE MONGOL EMPIRE

The empire the Mongols put together was the largest the world had yet seen. It included both the largest and the most populous of modern nations, Russia and China, as well as much of the Middle East and portions of Southeast Asia. It stretched all across Eurasia, from European Russia to the Far East.

This vast expanse was divided into four khanates, with a splendid capital at Karakorum in the ancestral grasslands of Mongolia. The premier khanate, the realm of the Great Khan, was East Asia, centering in China but including Korea, Tibet, and Mongolia itself. The Jagatai Khanate dominated a vast slice of central Asia. The Ilkhanate ruled the Muslim Middle East. And the Khanate of the Golden Horde governed the rolling expanse of Russia.

The imperial order imposed upon this heartland of the world island was a free-form combination of ancestral ways, military discipline, and borrowed bureaucratic techniques.

The government at Karakorum included administrators from a number of conquered peoples, organized in rough imitation of the developed bureaucracy of China. There were ministries of justice, of the treasury, and of war, and officials were trained by a government academy. Records were kept in a system of Mongolian writing that used Arabic script. A famous system of couriers and post houses carried the word of the Great Khan out across his far-flung realms.

Out in the khanates, however, native officials were generally allowed to continue governing as they had before the Mongols came. They had to pay their tribute regularly and obey all decrees from the khans. Beyond that, the rough feudalism of the nomadic tribes and clans seems to have prevailed.

The final source of Mongol strength, however, remained neither borrowed bureaucracy nor traditional clan structure, but the army. Efficiently organized in groups of tens, hundreds, and thousands, and led by officers promoted on merit, Mongol troops remained ready to ride on the shortest notice. And it was terror of the return of that host that kept the tribute coming and secured obedience to all decrees.

For a time, in the thirteenth and fourteenth centuries, Mongol predominance guaranteed order across northern Eurasia. It may have prevented other, more developed Asian peoples from invading the West. It certainly opened the road to trade from one end of the world island to the other. Once more, as in the classic age, goods, ideas, and travelers could pass back and forth from Europe to China.

Marco Polo was the most famous merchant traveler to take that long road east and back again. The mere outlining of his route gives some sense of the magnitude of the Mongol achievement.

From Venice the Polos—Marco, his father, and his uncle—sailed to Acre (still a Muslim sultanate) and then plunged into the Ilkhanate, crossing today's Turkey, Iraq, and Iran to the Persian Gulf. They then turned up through Afghanistan and on across the Hindu Kush into the Jagatai Khanate of central Asia. They continued east across the Tarim Basin north of Tibet and on into the Great Khanate, crossed the Great Wall of China, and swung south at last to Beijing.

Later travels took Marco to Burma, to South China, and home by sea via India, the Middle East again, the Black Sea, Constantinople, and the Adriatic to Venice. The journey, which included much time spent in the service of the Great Khan, took him seventeen years. It was a journey that could not even have been undertaken a hundred years before.

Or a hundred years later. For the precarious Mongol imperium came soon to its end.

THE END OF THE MONGOL ADVENTURE

It was an amazing achievement—and one that because of its very nature could not last long.

The Mongol Empire, as indicated above, depended in the last analysis on the unbeatable Mongol army. When Mongol armies began to fail of their objectives—as inevitably they did—the Mongol predominance was instantly in jeopardy.

Before the thirteenth century was out, a diminished Mongol horde was beaten by the Egyptian Mamelukes in Palestine. Mongol expeditions dispatched to conquer Japan discovered that a lifetime of cavalry warfare on the steppes was no advantage in facing the perils of a seaborne invasion. And thrusts into the dank heat of Southeast Asia, toward Burma, Vietnam, and Sumatra fell afoul of climate and terrain as well as the tropic seas. There were limits, in short, to what even the Mongol military could do.

The political unity of the Mongol Empire also began to disintegrate within two generations of the death of Genghis Khan. There were too few Mongols to manage so vast a domain, even if they had developed the admin-

Western European merchants return from the far end of Eurasia along the Great Silk Road, reopened by the Mongols during the later Middle Ages. What sort of animals are being ridden and used as beasts of burden here? What features seem to be typical of the stylized cities shown on the map below the travelers? (The Bettmann Archive)

istrative skills to do so. There were inevitable quarrels among the khans themselves, and they tended to forget their redoubtable founder's warning that due recognition of the primacy of the Great Khan was essential for continued unity. When the Great Khan Kublai moved his capital from Karakorum to Beijing, he turned his attention more and more to Chinese affairs, and the lesser khans went their own ways in their own domains.

Most destructive of unity, finally, was the tendency of the victorious Mongols, like victorious barbarians in many other times, to adopt the culture of the more developed societies they had conquered. But since the Mongols had conquered peoples of so many different cultures, this process of acculturation soon divided the Mongols among themselves.

It will be necessary, then, to follow the Mongols into some of the separate khanates to see how the Mongol predominance fared at the local level—and how it came to an end.

THE IMPACT OF THE MONGOL IMPERIUM

MONGOL CULTURE

Mongol ideas of government, as noted above, were much less complex than those of many of the people they conquered. The empire they built thus tended to depend on other people's administrative techniques and frequently on non-Mongol administrators as well. At the crucial local level, finally, the indigenous ruling classes were soon in charge of affairs once more. The Mongol rulers took tribute, taxes, conscripts, land, and loot from conquered peoples, but they did not confer anything resembling Roman law or Chinese administration in return.

Mongol religion—to touch on one more element of Mongol culture—seems to have made little or no contribution to the spiritual lives of those they ruled. Their ancient faith in the old spirits of the hearth and the wide blue sky seems to have offered little to peoples raised in the faiths of Buddha, Muhammad, or Christ. Within a few generations, the Great Khan in China was a Buddhist of sorts and a patron of Confucian principles, the Ilkhan in Persia a Muslim, and the khan of the Golden Horde in Russia a strong protector of Greek Orthodox Christianity.

Were there, then, no long-range consequences of the great Mongol storm that roared across Eurasia, or of their admittedly brief mastery of so many lands and peoples? A look at the Mongol period in two contrasting portions of Eurasia will indicate that the heirs of Genghis Khan did leave their mark, in subtle or less subtle ways, on the peoples they ruled.

RUSSIA AND THE GOLDEN HORDE

The Mongols who burst into Russia for the second time in 1236 were not a cavalry detachment looking for loot, as on their first incursion twelve years before. They were a whole horde on the move, with wagons, families, and herds, come to stay on the steppes of southern Russia. The Russian princes and city-states, still organized in only the loosest of federations, were no match for the Mongols. City after city was sacked and burned, including the old southern capital of Kiev and the new one at Vladimir in the north. By 1240 the Mongols were effectively the masters of European Russia. They would remain so for the next two and a half centuries (1240–1480).

The khan of the Golden Horde—so called from the color of their tents—settled at a new city called Sarai on the lower Volga. Once the initial carnage was ended, the Tatar Yoke, as the Russians call the period of Mongol rule, was less onerous than it might have been. The khans retained control over princely successions and exercised a veto over all major policy decisions. Taxes had to be paid on time and recruits for the Mongol armies sent as ordered. Beyond this, the Russian cities, once they had dug out of their ruins, ordered their affairs pretty much as they wished. A senior Russian prince was even put in charge of tax collection for the Golden Horde, and Mongol officials rigorously punished any profanation of the Orthodox church.

The eventual fall of the khans came about as a result of a proclivity for self-destructive feuding as great as that of the Russian princes in earlier times. The earlier fifteenth century saw major Mongol secessions from the Golden Horde. Then in 1480 a weakened khan backed off from a confrontation with a Russian alliance now headed by the grand duke of Moscow. Twenty years later, the shrunken remnant of the Golden Horde was extinguished on the southern steppes by some of their own rivalrous Tatar kin.

But two and a half centuries of Mongol rule had left their mark on Russia.

On the negative side, Russian cultural development seems to have been impeded by the severing of contact with Western Europe during this period. Russian economic growth also suffered—from heavy tributes and from repeated punitive expeditions, the Mongol method of maintaining order in Russia. Politically, budding city assemblies that had had some power in the Kieven period withered under the Mongols. Thus, Russia lost the urban merchant oligarchies, the "rising middle classes" that appeared in western Europe about this time.

A Mongol element may be detected in the Russian population, and some Mongol influence on Russian coinage, military organization, and early administrative practices. But the most significant consequence of the centuries of Russian subservience to the Golden Horde was surely the impetus it gave to authoritarian rule in czarist Russia.

The Russian people, as one Russian historian pointed out, "were trained by the Mongols to take orders, to pay taxes, and to supply soldiers without delay."[1] They carried over these habits into later centuries, making them excellent subjects for future czars.

The ruthless methods used by the Moscow grand dukes to unify their country in the fifteenth and sixteenth centuries are also sometimes traced to the Mongol example. In matters of government, the subtler model of Byzantine autocracy was now reinforced by direct experience of the bludgeoning authoritarianism of the khans. It may not be too imaginative to see in these early models the seeds of a Russian style of autocracy that would be echoed in the hardfisted regimes of such later Russian rulers as Ivan the Terrible, Peter the Great, and Joseph Stalin.

CHINA AND THE MONGOL KHANS

In China the Mongols encountered not a loose federation of princes but a nation that had been unified under centralized government off and on for the better part of the preceding fourteen hundred years. The Mongol Yuan dynasty that reigned in China for a century (1260–1368) was in many ways an interlude rather than a major period in Chinese history. Yet this was the China of the Great Khan Kublai, the "Cathay" that roused the awe and wonder of Western visitors such as Marco Polo, and it should be noticed here.

The conquest itself was a long and bloody business. The population of the Tibetan empire in the northwest was decimated. Large sections of the Jürched-ruled northeast were so devastated that a Mongol horseman could ride for many miles without encountering any impediment sizable enough for his pony to stumble over. The Song emperors of South China resisted for decades, depending on rivers and broken country to slow the Mongols and falling back at last on the port cities and their navy. The last Song emperor was killed in a naval battle off Hong Kong in 1279, ending a struggle that had lasted for forty-five years.

Kublai Khan, the victor in the long war with the Southern Song, was the most remarkable Mongol after Genghis Khan. Grandson of the founder, he was also Great Khan, or Khan of Khans, nominal head of the whole sprawling Mongol Empire—though after he moved his capital south of the Great Wall to Beijing, his concerns were largely with his vast Chinese realm.

A Chinese portrait shows a well-padded face with a small, pointed beard and a moustache narrowing to carefully cared-for points. The eyes, under heavy lids, look small, clear, and thoughtful. Marco Polo eulogized him as a giver of alms, builder of public granaries, maintainer of roads, and so on, while allowing him the usual royal vices—overindulgence in food, concubines, and hunting.

Polo found the royal city of Cambaluc, as Beijing was then called, a vast twelve-gated metropolis several miles on each side, laid out foursquare with wide, straight avenues, splendid palaces, gardens, and courts. The royal

[1]George Vernadsky, *A History of Russia* (New Haven: Yale University Press, 1961), p. 80.

large numbers of Chinese clerks and bureaucrats. The new government also paid lip service to Confucian principles of government. But in practice the Mongol Yuan dynasty suspended the civil-service examinations, promoted few Confucian scholars to high positions, and turned most of the top spots in government over to a new, non-Chinese elite of Mongols and hired foreign officials, including Muslims from the Middle East and Christians such as the Polos.

CHINA IN THE DAYS OF MARCO POLO

Economically, China seems to have flourished under the Mongols—once it had recovered from the initial devastation. Kublai Khan facilitated internal trade by refurbishing the Grand Canal, sprucing up the roads, and issuing paper money as the sole legal tender. South China remained the nation's economic heart, as under the Song. The manufacture of silk and porcelain continued to prosper, and cotton textiles began to be produced in large quantities for the first time.

International trade grew as it had not since the heyday of the Tang. The reopened trade routes between eastern and western Eurasia brought merchants and their goods from as far away as Western Europe and North Africa. Mercenary officials, missionaries, and other travelers came too, and some, like Marco Polo and the Arab Ibn Batuta, left detailed accounts of life in Mongol China.

Cultural life in China under the Mongols relates only negatively to the alien culture of the conquerors. Because positions of power were now held by people without classical educations, for instance, a simpler form of written Chinese came into use in government—and soon became the vehicle of a new literature. Because educated Chinese could no longer depend on careers in government, some of them turned their hands to literature and helped to produce what amounts to a literary flowering of sorts under the Yuan.

Two new genres in particular developed in Mongol China: the drama and the novel. The theater combined music and dancing, mime, gorgeous costumes, bawdy humor, and violent action in an operatic drama that was widely popular. Yuan plays built on a popular dramatic tradition of puppet theater and shadow plays, and derived their romantic plots from Chinese history and legend. Love triumphed, official corruption was punished, and ancestors were duly honored—at least on the Yuan stage.

The popular novel also developed during Yuan times, mostly in the long, unstructured, but exciting tales of professional storytellers. Lower-class or soldier heroes, vernacular style, and sheer length that would have made Scheherazade pale earned huge audiences for these tales. The developed Chinese novel had to wait for the next dynasty, the Ming, but its precursors are to be found in the "prompt-books" of popular Chinese storytellers under the Mongols.

Marco Polo's arrival in the palace of the Mongol Khan Kublai is here imaginatively portrayed by a later illustrator. Marco and his older kin do not seem to be kowtowing as they may be presumed to have done before the most powerful ruler in the world, and the architecture and some of the accoutrements make little claim to authenticity. Nevertheless, some sense of pomp and opulence, and of alien cultures encountering each other, does seem to come across.

palace stood in walled parklands a mile square. The central complex was a lofty building on a high platform decorated with gold, silver, and dragons. According to Marco Polo, as many as six thousand people could sit down to dine in the great hall—off gold plate.

The Mongols retained much of the Chinese political system, especially the six central bureaus established by the Tang dynasty and the general division of government into the civil service, the military, and the censors. They even strengthened the system—one of their few lasting innovations—by tightening the links between the central government and the provincial authorities. The result was probably a harsher autocracy than China had seen before.

As elsewhere, the Mongols retained as many natives in power on the local level as possible—here, the

Kublai Khan, the most worthy of Genghis Khan's heirs, is shown here as Emperor of China. Kublai completed the conquest of southern China and ruled the Middle Kingdom capably and intelligently, earning the respect of foreign officials in his employ like the Polos. He was also the first Mongol emperor to abandon the tents of his Mongol ancestors for full-time residence in the Chinese capital, accepting Chinese ways and the Chinese dynasty name of Yuan. (New York Public Library Picture Collection)

Traditional arts of painting and calligraphy still flourished in China, but many artists looked to past styles for models rather than seeking inspiration in the Mongol present. Some painted horses in the Tang style, while others followed the Song landscape tradition. A leading painter of this period was Kuan Fu-yen, celebrated for her Song-style images of flowers and birds, bamboo and plum blossoms. Her painting *Plum Blossoms Across the Moon* perhaps embodies the longing of all educated Chinese for happier days gone by.

THE FALL OF THE MONGOLS

Mongol rule was never popular in China, and Mongols were never socially acceptable to cultivated Chinese. The conquerors dressed in leather and fur instead of silk, ate mutton and mare's milk instead of Chinese cuisine, could not read and write, gave their women too much freedom, had no last names, did not wash, and smelled bad. Only shrewd leadership and brute force could keep them in power, and though Mongol ferocity remained intact, after Kublai Khan there were no more great leaders in the Yuan line.

In the first half of the fourteenth century, eight lesser Mongol rulers tried to maintain the regime intact. Unbacked paper money led to inflation. The gods indicated their displeasure through repeated destructive flooding of the Yellow River and famine across North China. Secret societies such as the White Lotus proliferated, as in the last days of many dynasties, and rebellion flared in many provinces. During this prolonged crisis the Mongol leaders once more fell to fighting among themselves.

In 1368 a Chinese rebel leader expelled the Mongols from Beijing and declared a new dynasty—the Ming. The Yuan and their followers retreated northward to Mongolia, whence their famous founder had led their ancestors one hundred fifty years before.

The Mongols left only a scattered legacy. They had strengthened the government, as they did elsewhere. They had encouraged further economic growth. They had developed craftwork by fostering the establishment of hereditary crafts within families. They had unintentionally encouraged the arts by driving classically educated people out of government to seek their fortunes where they could find them—even in the arts.

The isolationist, inward focus of the Ming dynasty is often seen as a reaction to the trauma of foreign rule under the Mongols—a further negative legacy of the age. But China survived the whirlwind from the steppes, as developed civilizations have the capacity to do, and went on, at least modestly enriched.

SUMMARY

Nomads of the Eurasian steppes had been terrorizing the urban imperial cultures of the south for more than three thousand years. In the thirteenth and fourteenth centuries, however, the Mongols themselves established the largest of all the historic Eurasian empires.

Genghis Khan, the founder of the Mongol Empire, welded the nomadic tribes of the eastern steppes into an unstoppable cavalry army. Adding catapults and military exper-

tise from conquered peoples and imposing centralized authority for the first time on the discordant whole, Genghis and successive khans made themselves masters of much of the world-island.

In the end, like other conquerors before them, the Mongols reached their limits too. They penetrated only a short distance into Europe and failed to conquer Japan, India, or Southeast Asia. But Russia, China, Persia, and other substantial chunks of the heartland of human civilization fell under the rule of the Mongol hordes for the better part of two centuries.

Mongol cultural influence was in some ways no more than skin deep across most of Eurasia. They governed as much as possible through local agents and already established institutions. Yet Russia never forgot the Tatar period in its history, which even more than the Byzantine influence shaped the autocratic regime that emerged in Muscovy. And the Chinese Empire, despite much initial devastation, in the end achieved new levels of centralization under Marco Polo's much admired master Kublai Khan.

SUGGESTED READING

BOYLE, J. A. *The Successors of Genghis Khan*. New York: Columbia University Press, 1971. The later khans and their conquests.

CHAMBERS, J. *The Devil's Horsemen*. New York: Atheneum, 1979. Readable overview of the Mongol impact on Europe.

GROUSSET, R. *Conqueror of the World: The Life of Chingis Khan*, trans. D. Sinor and M. Mackellar. New York: Viking, 1972. Semipopular life of the founder of the Mongol hegemony. H. D. Martin, *The Rise of Chingis Khan and His Conquest of North China* (Baltimore: Johns Hopkins University Press, 1950), is more scholarly.

HALPERIN, C. J. *Russia and the Golden Horde*. Bloomington: Indiana University Press, 1985. The impact of the Mongol conquest on Russian history.

KWANTEN, L. *Imperial Nomads: A History of Central Asia, 500–1500*. Philadelphia: University of Pennsylvania Press, 1979. History of the Mongol peoples during the millennium when they dominated the Eurasian heartland.

LANGLOIS, J. D., ed. *China under Mongol Rule*. Princeton, N.J.: Princeton University Press, 1981. Scholarly essays.

MORGAN, D. *The Mongols*. New York: Blackwell, 1986. Readable illustrated overview of Mongol history and society.

PHILLIPS, E. D. *The Royal Hordes: Nomad Peoples of the Steppes*. London: Thames & Hudson, 1965. Useful survey of these restless peoples in history.

POLO, M. *Travels of Marco Polo*, trans. R. Latham. New York: Abaris, 1982. Report of the celebrated merchant traveler to Kublai Khan's China.

ROSSABI, M. *Khubilai Khan: His Life and Times*. Berkeley: University of California Press, 1988. Authoritative biography of the greatest of the Mongol emperors of China.

RUYSBROECK. *The Mission of Friar William of Rubruck . . . to the Court of the Great Khan Mongke, 1253–1255*, trans. P. Jackson. London: Hakluyt Society, 1990. Classic account of a visit to the Mongol Empire by a Western contemporary.

SAUNDERS, J. J. *The History of the Mongol Conquests*. New York: Harper, 1972. Chronicle of the establishment of the Mongol predominance.

SCHURMANN, H. F. *Economic Structure of the Yuan Dynasty*. Cambridge: Cambridge University Press, 1956. The Mongol rulers and the Chinese economy.

SEVERIN, T. *In Search of Genghis Khan*. New York: Atheneum, 1992. Illustrated by good photographs.

SPULER, B. *The Mongols in History*, trans. G. Wheeler. London: Pall Mall Press, 1971. Survey and evaluation of their place in the history of the double continent.

VERNADSKY, G. *The Mongols and Russia*. New Haven: Yale University Press, 1953. Part of Vernadsky's multivolume history of Russia; scholarly, but rooted in older historiographical perspectives.

CHAPTER 23

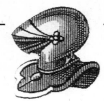

FROM THE TOLTECS TO CHIMU

NORTH AMERICA: THE PUEBLOS
AND THE GREAT MOUNDS

Pueblo Culture

The Mississippi Culture

Cahokia

MIDDLE AMERICA: THE TOLTECS

Mexico and Peru:
Continuing Centers of American Civilization

Changes in New World Civilizations

The Toltecs:
A Race of Legendary Heroes

SOUTH AMERICA: PEOPLES OF THE MOUNTAINS
AND THE SHORE

Tiahuanaco and Huari: Cities of the Andes

Chimu: People of the Coast

The Power of the Chimu State

NORTH AMERICA: THE PUEBLOS AND THE GREAT MOUNDS

PUEBLO CULTURE

Pueblo means "town" in Spanish, and we still apply this label to the unique collections of adobe or masonry houses under the red cliffs of the American Southwest that the conquistadores recognized with astonishment as "real towns" in that otherwise barren land. In fact, the Pueblo culture is only one phase of a general regional flowering that made Arizona, New Mexico, and the northern provinces of today's Mexico one of the two most impressive zones of preurban development in North America.

This transition was brought about by the arrival from Mexico of the three basic Amerindian crops—corn, beans, and forms of squash—and by their gradual adaptation to the arid Southwest. This was accomplished about the time of the Fall of Rome. As we saw, Indians of several cultures were thus transformed into village agriculturalists, living in settled communities of pit houses, making pottery, and cultivating a form of maize that would actually grow there.

Not much happened beyond this fundamental transition from gathering to village agriculture for several centuries. But there was further influence from Mexico, stimulating contact among the various regional cultures of the Southwest themselves, and a steadily increasing population. Finally, between 900 and 1300—a period roughly contemporary with the High Middle Ages in Europe—the later "pueblo" phases of what archaeologists call the Anasazi culture produced the most remarkable flowering of this impressive preurban society.

Pueblo culture, which has left such impressive remains, has been studied thoroughly, perhaps more intensively than any other Native American society. Archaeologists note their dikes and dams for collecting precious water, their woven cotton blankets, their feather robes, their bows and many specialized arrows, and their tiny cult figurines, perhaps related to fertility. Collectors treasure their black-and-white Mesa Verde pottery. But it is the pueblos themselves that impress the more casual visitor.

Constructed originally of mud and sticks, these clustered apartment buildings of the Southwest were soon being built of stone instead. They were sometimes erected against cliffs or even under rocky overhangs. Others were laid out in rectangular, L-shaped, or semicircular blocks that were several stories high and contained an enclosed court. There were sometimes towers and almost always a *kiva,* or underground ceremonial chamber. With the passing centuries these residential complexes grew larger, till some had more than a hundred units and scores of families living together.

It is possible to reconstruct from their middens and burial mounds the lives of these only slightly preurban people. Women did a great deal of the work, making pottery and clothing, gathering food and preparing it, gathering wood and preparing it, gathering wood, and even building and repairing the houses. Male duties included farming, weaving cloth for the women to make into apparel, some hunting still, and probably spending a great deal of time conducting ritual ceremonies in the *kiva.*

THE MISSISSIPPI CULTURE

The most impressive Native American culture in North America, however, flourished not in the Southwest but in the Southeast. Its major remains are to be found along the rivers of the Mississippi valley, and its cultural roots lie less in Mexico than in the classic Hopewell culture of the eastern woodlands of the future United States.

Mississippian sites, located usually on river banks, feature flat-topped pyramidal mounds, a particular sort of pottery made with eggshell, and a collection of exquisite artifacts—jewelry and even metalwork—found in graves and associated with what used to be called a death cult. These remains are found across a wide tract of well-watered, temperate, originally thickly forested land that includes the east coast of the United States, the southern Appalachians, and the whole length of the Mississippi River valley.

During the period between 750 or so and the appearance of the first Europeans in 1540, Native Americans in the Southeast shifted slowly from hunting and gathering toward dependence on agriculture. Most Mississippians lived in tiny hamlets of pole houses along streams and rivers, gathering nuts, hunting game with bow and arrow, but devoting increasing attention to straggling rows of corn and beans planted in the river mud. They must also have channeled significant energy into building their large ceremonial mounds, walls, and other earthworks at selected sites—the major evidence that we are dealing here not with a collection of Neolithic farming villages but with an integrated society capable of large-scale coordinated efforts.

Ceremonial religious centers point to a powerful priestly cult. But fortifying walls become more common at later Mississippian sites too, indicating warfare and war leaders. These leaders may even have been hereditary, which would have made the societies that built the great mounds true chiefdoms, only half a step from the bureaucratic political state.

Mississippian societies traded widely on the rivers of North America. They practiced some specialized crafts, whole villages manufacturing stone hoes or mining salt. Their ceremonial pottery included exotic human and animal shapes, and their graves have yielded copper and shell ornaments and flat copper representations of winged human beings.

CAHOKIA

The largest such center so far excavated was at Cahokia, a site near the modern city of St. Louis. Here a string of

North American pueblos built in the lee of a towering cliff face in the deserts of the Southwest. Limitations imposed by the barrenness of their environment prevented this gifted Native American people from moving from these agricultural villages to still more complex political units. The exquisite texture of the stone cliff is strikingly revealed in this nineteenth-century picture made by a photographer who lugged camera and plates into the wilderness by mule back. (Library of Congress)

some 85 mounds stretches for six miles along a river bank. In the 1200s, most of the people of Cahokia worked the hundreds of acres of corn that surrounded the complex, feeding a population of perhaps 30,000 people. Others, however, were already specializing in tool making, pottery manufacture, metalworking, or handcrafted jewelry. An extensive trade network also brought Cahokia copper from the Great Lakes, sea shells from the East Coast, and other goods from far across the continent.

The largest of Cahokia's impressive earthworks was the huge Monks Mound, a hundred feet high and built on a base seventeen acres in area. Constructed entirely by Indian labor equipped with baskets to carry the earth, this mound must have dominated Cahokia as an acropolis did an ancient Greek city-state. Like the mounded temple bases of Mexico, this man-made hill was almost certainly the location of temples and the rude palaces of chiefs. Religious ceremonies on the high mound would feature chiefs and priests in elaborate costumes and dazzling headdresses made of brightly colored feathers.

Scholars differ as to whether Cahokia is best described as a collection of linked agricultural villages, a religious ceremonial center like those of early Mexico, or a city and political center. The overall impression remains of a striking step toward a larger and more complex society.

MIDDLE AMERICA: THE TOLTECS

MEXICO AND PERU: CONTINUING CENTERS OF AMERICAN CIVILIZATION

The real centers of high culture in the pre-Columbian Americas, however, continued to lie south of the Rio Grande, in Mexico and Peru. By A.D. 1000 both these zones of developed and intermittently urban imperial culture were well established in the Americas.

The complex societies of both regions were built primarily on agriculture.

Mesoamerican culture was built on the traditional agricultural base of maize, beans, chilies, and squash, which supported a comparatively dense population of several million people. Mesoamerican societies were as hierarchical as any in the Old World. Amerindians in this part of the New World were learning the art of effectively governing large empires. They also suffered periodic influxes of skin-clad Indians from the north, attracted as Goths were to Roman Europe or Mongols to China by the seductive charms of civilization.

Agriculture was widely practiced in South America also, but the range of products was greater. Corn, beans, and various kinds of squashes were common in Peru as in Mexico. In addition, potatoes were the upland staple of the Andes, and coca and other tropical products came from the Amazonian interior. Huge flocks of llamas and alpacas were herded in the high country. Hillsides were terraced for agriculture, and irrigation canals and ditches spread water over lowland valleys.

In various parts of Peru, large ceremonial centers and even some true cities featured huge stone buildings, especially temples and palaces. Many crafts were practiced, including the ancient ceramics and textile industries and more working in metal than in Middle America. Society was acquiring the habits of specialization and hierarchical class divisions characteristic of urban civilization everywhere. These growing and increasingly complex civilizations fostered more elaborate political organization as well. In both areas, difficulties may have led to the rise of a strong military elite, perhaps displacing a priestly elite of earlier times.

In both these zones of culture, the daily agricultural round filled the lives of most Amerindians with a reassuring sense of permanence. In Mexico it was "my Lord the Corn" that stirred the most heartfelt reverence in village populations. In the high valleys of Peru the lowly potato was the staff of life. More elaborate social and political structures would grow on this agricultural base, like those of the Toltecs and Chimu, to be discussed later. But the agricultural basis of life would be there always, as it is today.

CHANGES IN NEW WORLD CIVILIZATIONS

The more complex cultures of Middle and South America, however, did more than continue along lines laid down by the dawn age and the classic age that preceded them. The period that began in some places as late as 1000 and ended with the coming of European conquerors in the 1500s also saw some major changes.

Some of these developments were material. Metalworking became more common in both Mexico and Peru, though carefully worked stone tools were still the rule. Large public buildings became even more widespread in both places. Both areas also saw the building of the largest irrigation systems constructed in the Americas before the coming of the Europeans.

Other changes were of a cultural nature. Some earlier intellectual trends seem to slow or even reverse themselves. Middle America made no more gains in mathematics, writing, or calendar development after the end of the period of Maya flowering. In South America, on the other hand, the *quipu* record system of knots as a substitute for writing came into existence during these postclassical centuries.

The biggest changes, however, were probably social or political in nature. After 1000, cities grew rapidly in Mexico, while the integration of larger political states

A Toltec pyramid at the Mayan sacred city of Chichén Itzá, in modern Mexico, shows how much the conquerors had absorbed from the subtle minds of the Mayans. The pyramid, for example, has 365 steps, one for each day in the Mayan—and the modern—solar calendar. Its nine levels correspond to the nine levels of the Mayan underworld, while the temple on top is dedicated to the god Kakulkan, the Mayan version of Quetzalcoatl, the Feathered Serpent whose cult went back to ancient Tenochtitlán. (The Monkmeyer Press)

advanced in Peru. In both areas, large empires emerged, bringing many peoples, cities, and states under central authority. In both regions, empire-building was accomplished by force, leading to extensive wars and the increasing prominence of a warrior elite.

In this section, we will take the story of the consolidation of the American Indian civilizations only to the eve of their finest flower, the Aztec and Inca empires confronted by the conquistadors after 1492. But we will leave our story in a world that will be familiar to anyone who has ever admired the Aztecs and Incas—the world of the legendary Toltecs, of Atlantean Tiahuanaco, and the awesome empire of Chimu.

THE TOLTECS:
A RACE OF LEGENDARY HEROES

The decline of the Mesoamerican civilizations of the classic age—of Teotihuacán and the cities of the Mayans—was apparently accompanied by widespread violence. Preurban, sometimes even preagricultural peoples, particularly from the north, overran central Mexico and the southeastern lowlands. Many of these invaders, like the ancient Aryans in India, did not occupy the cities they conquered but shied away, regarding them as supernatural places. Some used deserted cities as burial places for their dead.

One famous race of conquerors, however, surged down from the north not to destroy but to reinvigorate the crumbling urban culture of Mesoamerica. These were the legendary Toltecs, the most celebrated of all the precursors of the Aztecs in Middle America.

For a long time the people about whom so many tales were told at the time of the Spanish conquest were believed to be legendary—a mythical race of heroes like Homer's Trojans or the legendary Amazons. Archaeological research, however, has proven the Toltecs to be as real as buried Troy turned out to be.

Like the Aztecs who came after them, the Toltecs were apparently a Nahuatl-speaking, warlike, less developed people from the north. They descended into central Mexico around 900. They may have participated in the destruction of Teotihuacán; they certainly imposed their will on the surviving Mayans of Yucatan—and learned from them. Toltec power extended even into Guatemala.

Everywhere the central feature of their culture was the predominance of a warrior ruling class. Grim-faced soldiers of the orders of the eagle and the jaguar march across the walls of temples in their metropolis of Tula. Priests, who were the highest caste in most Mesoamerican cultures, yielded pride of place to soldiers under the Toltec hegemony.

These invaders were not barbarians, however. They had lived on the northern fringes of Middle American urban culture long enough to be at least partially civilized themselves. And some of their vigor went into other than warlike pursuits.

Far from destroying or abandoning cities, the Toltecs built new ones, like their capital at Tula, or expanded old ones, like Chichén Itzá in Yucatan. Tula included a number of typical Mesoamerican features, such as a central plaza with temples, palaces, and other large buildings around it, as well as such innovations as long roofed colonnades around the square.

Metalworking also developed among the Toltecs, though more commonly for jewelry than for useful objects. Most important, the Toltecs substantially expanded commercial relations within and perhaps beyond Middle Amer-

"The Toltecs were a skillful people;
all of their works were good, all were exact,
all well made and admirable.

Their houses were beautiful, with turquoise
    mosaics,
the walls finished with plaster,
clean and marvelous houses, which is to say
Toltec houses, beautifully made,
beautiful in everything. . . .

Painters, sculptors, carvers of precious
    stones,
feather artists, potters, spinners, weavers,
skillful in all they made, they discovered

the precious green stones, the turquoise;
they knew the turquoise and its mines, they
    found
its mines and they found the mountains
    hiding
silver and gold, copper and tin,
and the metal of the moon.

The Toltecs were truly wise;
they conversed with their own hearts. . . .
They played their drums and rattles;
they were singers, they composed songs
and sang them among the people;
they guarded the songs in their memories,
they deified them in their hearts."

During the first century of Spanish rule in Mexico, Christian missionaries and Indian converts together collected a substantial array of traditional Indian literature. This work, including myths and poems of many peoples, was rediscovered and translated out of the original Nahuatl and other Amerindian tongues only in the present century.

This poem on the ancient Toltecs—translated by the learned Miguel Léon-Portilla—reflects the reverence in which this legendary people were held by later Middle American peoples. What qualities are particularly praised here? What Toltec crafts are discussed? What else could you learn about the Toltecs from this poem? Does the fact that the poem was not composed by people who lived at the same time as the Toltecs raise any questions about the value of the verses as historical evidence?

Miguel Léon-Portilla, ed., Native Mesoamerican Spirituality (New York: Paulist Press, 1980), p. 207.

ica, linking the Mexican highlands with the tropical lowlands and conceivably even with South America.

Especially important trade goods were tropical products with a great appeal to the people of Mexico's central plateau: cocoa, feathers, and cotton. Cocoa was both a favorite drink in Middle America and a common medium of exchange, used as money for buying, selling, and paying debts. Feathers from tropical birds, used as a chief form of personal adornment, became a major medium of artistic expression. Cotton cloth grew in importance during this period and could even be worked into the armor of the warrior elite who dominated the era.

The famous semimythical Toltec ruler Topiltzin, identified with Quetzalcoatl as sage, founder of civilized arts, and spiritual leader, embodied the virtues the Toltecs most admired. Topiltzin was even alleged to have tried to keep his people from practicing the bloody religious rituals of human sacrifice. In the end, the living embodiment of Quetzalcoatl "went away," promising to return at some distant future time. With his passing, prosperity departed from the Toltecs. After a century of achievement, drought and famine spread over the land, and new waves of more barbarous invaders came down from the north.

This enigmatic statue from Tiahuanaco has some of the "Atlantean" feel of being totally unlike the work of any other culture. The roughly rectilinear decoration generally resembles other pre-Columbian carving, and the figure is no more naturalistic than most early American art. Nevertheless, an overall feeling of strangeness seems to hover over this robot-like survivor of a ruined city on the shores of Lake Titicaca in the stark Andean uplands. (D. Donne Bryant Stock Photography)

SOUTH AMERICA: PEOPLES OF THE MOUNTAINS AND THE SHORE

TIAHUANACO AND HUARI: CITIES OF THE ANDES

The postclassical period in the Andean region saw several substantial regional hegemonies emerge. One among them, the Chimu state, was the most impressive political structure erected anywhere in South America before the coming of the Incas. Two other names, however, also help to fill the centuries between the decline of the Mochica and other classical cultures and the rise of the Inca Empire: the linked names of Tiahuanaco and Huari.

Tiahuanaco, on the high Bolivian plateau south of Lake Titicaca, has left behind some huge stone temple ruins and some rare statues of human beings. Huari, in Peru, had dwelling places as well as public buildings and was evidently a true city, rather than a ceremonial center only. The surviving ceramics, textiles, and carvings of these two peoples bear enough resemblance to indicate some relationship between them. But as is usual where written records are lacking, the political history of Tiahuanaco and Huari—and any political ties between them—can only be conjectured.

The two may have been separate conquest empires, one ruling northern Peru, the other southern Peru and parts of Chile and Bolivia, between A.D. 600 and 1000. Or people from Tiahuanaco may have spread north to the Huari area, mixed with coastal peoples to build Huari itself, and then spread a modified Tiahuanaco-Huari culture by conquest over much of pre-Incan Peru.

Under such joint or divided Tiahuanaco-Huari hegemony, in any case, the Andean area saw some changes. The breeding of llamas, for instance, spread down into the valleys, bringing meat, wool, and other advantages. Bronze began to be worked on a modest scale. Most important, a number of small cities sprang up. Many of these were walled and included no temples at all, leading some archaeologists to suggest that here, as in Mexico, a military aristocracy was shouldering the priesthood aside.

It was in the coastal state of Chimu, however, that these tendencies reached their climax.

CHIMU: PEOPLE OF THE COAST

According to local legend, the founder of the royal house of Chimu and his entourage came on balsa rafts across the ocean—a story that has led some scholars to postulate an Asiatic origin for this remarkable society with its highly autocratic government. Others point to the elaborate irrigation system that was central to Chimu culture and see in it a typical example of a hydraulic empire requiring strong central authority to regulate the crucial water supply. Whatever its origins, this was a rigorously centralized and militaristic state, and one of the most culturally advanced of pre-Columbian times.

Located in northern coastal Peru, Chimu in the fourteenth century controlled some five hundred miles of coastal valleys along the Pacific. Its geographical and cultural core was the old Mochica region, its economic basis the much expanded irrigation systems of those valleys. The scope of these works, sometimes uniting several valleys in a single hydraulic network, was unprecedented.

A Chimu mask, made of thin beaten gold. Chimu metalworkers shaped copper and bronze as well as silver and gold, sometimes into useful objects such as knives and awls, but mostly into ornaments and other decorative objects. Note the exquisite detail of the earrings and the tiny pendants. To the eyes of a later age, at least, there is also a grimness to this mask that reminds us that the Peruvian Chimu, like the Incas who succeeded them, built their large empire by force of arms. (PH Archives)

The cities of Chimu, particularly the capital, Chanchan, were large and rich, with houses and gardens for the warrior nobles, pyramid temples, and administrative centers. Chanchan's walls were thirty feet high and several miles around. The population may have run as high as 100,000. Unlike Mesoamerican cities with their central plazas, however, the Chimu capital was built in ten separate walled wards or precincts, perhaps to house different clans or social classes. Chimu cities were built of adobe brick rather than of stone, but brick so good that surviving examples sell for ten times what a modern brick will bring in Peru today.

THE POWER OF THE CHIMU STATE

It is the government of the Chimu state, however, that arouses the most interest. The scale of irrigation projects and urban construction would have required a central authority with power over large numbers of laborers. The increasing proportion of palaces, fortresses, and other secular structures, as against temple architecture, indicates that here too a warrior elite was replacing a priestly one.

According to Inca evidence, the Chimu state was a kingdom, founded early in the fourteenth century by conquest. The king of Chimu—wherever he came from—was believed to be divine and had immense authority. Each separate valley had its own appointed governor, and a regular structure of government existed in which village headmen, or *curacas*, reported to *curacas* at higher levels up through the governors to the king.

The presence of large buildings, which apparently served as both administrative and religious centers of cities and wards, strengthens our sense of centralized authority. State power also extended to the frontiers, where large fortresses anchored a system of defense against the smaller states of the Peruvian coasts.

Trade was routinely controlled by the government. Craft workers were supplied with raw materials by the government and worked largely for the noble elite. Peasants probably labored as serfs on noble estates.

Chimu was the most powerful centralized state in South American history before the coming of the Incas, who, like the Aztecs in the north, would put empire building on a whole new level in the Americas.

SUMMARY

In the New World, different societies continued to emerge north and south of the Rio Grande. In North America, the Pueblo and Mississippi cultures evolved steadily toward the more complex urban economies and more centralized forms of government already developed by their southern neighbors. The Cahokia Mound Builders were closing rapidly on the developed civilizations of Middle and South America when the first Europeans reached the western hemisphere.

To the south, developed civilizations continued to flourish in Mexico and Peru and their neighbors. In both areas warrior elites seem to have been more prominent, priestly predominance less central, than in earlier times.

The Toltecs in Mexico were the most important conquerors before the coming of the Aztecs. Arriving in the ninth century, at the time of the passing of the Classic Maya and Teotihuacán cultures, the Toltecs created not one but several regional states. They encouraged trade and city building in many parts of Middle America.

Among the regional hegemonies of South America, the probably related Tiahuanaco and Huari cultures began as early as the seventh century. The most politically integrated was the fourteenth-century Chimu culture of the northwestern coast of Peru. With their elaborate cities and huge irrigation works, the Chimu dotted the land with fortresses and created the most impressive centralized government in South America before the coming of the Incas.

SUGGESTED READING

BENNET, W. C., and J. B. BIRD. *Andean Cultural History.* New York: American Museum of Natural History, 1964. Best on Tiahuanaco. See also Lanning, below.

BROSE, D. S., J. A. BROWN, and D. W. PENNEY. *Ancient Art of the American Woodland Indians.* New York: Abrams, 1985. Good account of the artistic achievements of these North American peoples. See also Brose and N. Greber, eds., *Hopewell Archaeology* (Kent State University Press, 1979).

DAVIES, N. *The Toltecs: Until the Fall of Tula.* Norman: University of Oklahoma Press, 1977. Tries to find the facts in the maze of ancient legend.

DRIVER, H. E. *Indians of North America,* rev. ed. Chicago: University of Chicago Press, 1975. Topical coverage; a standard work.

DENEVAN, W. M. *The Native Population of the Americas in 1492.* Madison: University of Wisconsin Press, 1976. Analysis of the Native American population before the shattering impact of the Western intrusion.

FEIDEL, S. J. *Prehistory of the Americas,* 2nd ed. New York: Cambridge University Press, 1992. Chronological survey, from the first comers to the emergence of complex societies.

HAGEN, V. W. VON. *The Desert Kingdoms of Peru.* New York: New York Graphic Society, 1964. On the Chimu state and its Mochica predecessor.

ISBELL, W. H., and K. J. SCHREIBER, "Was Huari a State?" *American Antiquity,* Vol. 43, No. 3 (1978), pp. 372–390. Examines the evidence for centralized government.

JOSEPHY, A. M., ed. *America in 1492: The World of the Indian Peoples Before the Arrival of Columbus.* New York: Knopf, 1992. Regional and topical studies of Native American cultures.

KOSOK, P. *Life, Land, and Water in Ancient Peru.* New York: Long Island University Press, 1965. Widely praised archaeological and ecological study of irrigation, with emphasis on the Chimu state.

LANNING, E. P. *Peru before the Incas.* Englewood Cliffs, N.J.: Prentice Hall, 1967. Sections on the South American cultures discussed here, on the archaeology and its interpretation.

LUMBRERAS, L. G. and D. B. SMITH. "Cultural Development in the Central Andes—Peru and Bolivia," in *Aboriginal Cultural Development in Latin America: An Interpretive Review,* eds. B. J. Meggers and C. Evans. Washington, D. C.: The Smithsonian Institution, 1963. Useful on Tiahuanaco, a much exaggerated and still little understood society. See for instance A. Poznansky, *Tiahuanaco—The Cradle of American Man* (4 vols.) (New York: J. J. Augustin, 1945–1957).

CHAPTER 24

DIVERSITY AND COMMUNITY

CULTURAL DIVERSITY

1500: AN END AND A BEGINNING

The earth turned slowly into the sunlight on the day the Christians of western Europe called January 1 in the year they called 1500 *anno Domini*, the Year of Our Lord. As the sun's disk lifted grandly into view over a succession of horizons around the world, the day's work was already under way in many places. Farmers had fed their animals, bakers were at their ovens, herders were already on their way to distant pastures. Hunters in America or Australia rose from the water holes where they had crouched for hours, picked up whatever unwary game they had brought down, and started for home. Astronomers in China or the Middle East or western Europe recorded their final observations in their widely varying scripts and called it a night—and a day's work well done.

The streets grew noisier and busier in London and Paris, in Constantinople and Madras and Beijing, in Timbuktu and Cusco and Tenochtitlán. Wares were laid out in market squares and crowded shops. The narrow lanes of all the world's cities slowly filled with mules or camels, human porters, impatient horsemen, or the sedan chairs of the rich.

There was snow in the streets of old Paris; the mist rose slowly off the mountains above Cusco; the heat was oppressive in Timbuktu and Madras. But everywhere the day advanced according to immemorial patterns of behavior, traditions older than the walls of cities, as old almost as the water holes and hills and fields where most of the world was at its day's work.

During the twelve months that followed that January morning, Pedro Cabral discovered Brazil, Shah Ismail founded a new dynasty in Persia, Lucrezia Borgia's second husband was murdered, and black lead pencils were used for the first time in human history. It would be pleasant to record that all this added up to the beginning of a new era. But of course it is not so.

New ages in the long and complicated history of the race do not emerge in a day or a year. Yet there are great sea changes in the history of humanity, fundamental shifts in the human condition, that deserve attention. And these must be dated somehow, rough though that dating must be.

Let us say, then, that somewhere in the years, in the lifetimes around the year 1500 of the Christian calendar, one era of the world's history ended and another one began. And let us at least attempt to define the nature and significance of this great change.

CULTURAL DIFFERENCES

As far as we know, most of the prehistoric hominid species that evolved on this earth lived much like their neighbors around the world. They hunted and gathered, wandered and reproduced and died in tiny, inbred hunting bands, differing in no striking ways from the hunting band in the next valley.

Approximately ten thousand years ago, the Agricultural Revolution began in the Middle East. Thereafter, increasing numbers of the last surviving human species, *Homo sapiens sapiens*, lived the settled life of the agricultural village rather than the nomadic hunting life of caves and temporary camps. Centuries later, a new nomadism appeared: the pastoral search for grass and water for herds, which made nomads out of dwellers on marginal lands that were too poor for easy cultivation and suitable only for meager pasturage for herds and flocks of animals.

Five and a half thousand years ago, finally, the great enterprise of civilization began. In the valley of the Tigris and Euphrates rivers, walled cities rose. People learned to erect monumental structures, to work metals, to read and write and make mathematical calculations. Society grew more complicated, producing social classes, centralized bureaucratic government, more elaborate religions and philosophies. And the people who lived within the walls began to impose their will on all around them—on agricultural villages most easily, on nomadic pastoralists and surviving hunters as they could.

These city-based cultures, as we have seen, differed strikingly from the varied cultures of village people, pastoralists, and hunter-gatherers. But differences also began to be noticeable among the major urban-imperial societies themselves. Developing in isolation from each other, brawling as often as trading when they did come in contact, the peoples of the world became passionately attached to their own myths and mores, their own systems of social relations and styles of life and thought. The result by A.D. 1500—five thousand years after the birth of civilization—was a motley array of human cultures scattered around the world.

A visitor from another planet might not have been particularly impressed by the differences. Such a trained anthropological observer from outer space might have seen the same basic processes of biological survival, social organization, mythmaking, and other fundamental patterns of human behavior at work everywhere, in villages and cities, in India and Europe, in Africa and Mexico. And in a sense, he or she would have been right.

But not in a historical sense. If our otherworldly visitor in 1500 had sought to understand the historical rather than the anthropological or sociological picture, he or she would have found a world of difference. For the sense of differentness, of *our* ways and foreign ways, of *our* lands, *our* rights, *our* gods—and theirs—had become immensely important in human life down the millennia.

Cain was a farmer and Abel a shepherd, and Cain struck Abel dead upon the ground. Some of us, said the ancient Greek historian Herodotus, burn their dead, and others of us eat them, and our mutual incomprehension and loathing are very great. In the sixteenth century, a whitewashed port city on one side of the Mediterranean might have looked very much like a white city on the other side. But if one were Muslim and the other Christian, they might confront each other—at the Battle of Lepanto, say—across a cultural and historic gulf far wider than the narrow Mediterranean Sea.

Anthropologists catalogue differences as well as similarities. And the specific felt differences among the many peoples of the world five hundred years ago were very great indeed.

CENTERS OF CIVILIZATION

The briefest of surveys of the world in 1500 will confirm this cultural diversity and give us a sense of the immensity of what is to come.

European Christendom at the beginning of the modern era comprised two major varieties of Christianity and a number of separate political states, all still bottled up at the western end of Eurasia. At the eastern end of the double continent, the Ming emperors had firmly reestablished a complex Confucian culture in a unified Chinese Empire, the oldest and largest nation in the world. Between the Christian and Confucian realms a sprawling "Muslim center" of the Old World dominated the nations and peoples of North Africa, the Middle East, northern India, and parts of Southeast Asia. But a sophisticated Hinduism still molded the lives of most Indians, and dynamic new societies had appeared over the preceding millennium down the Pacific edge of East Asia, from Japan to Cambodia.

There were fewer developed urban cultures outside the world island. Nevertheless, in Africa south of the Sahara, imperial nations dominated the savannas of the Western Sudan. Prosperous city-states were also distributed down the east coast of Africa, oriented toward the trade of the Indian Ocean.

In the New World, which had just begun to experience significant historical contact with the Old in 1500, there were also some areas of urban-imperial civilization. Yet the Aztecs in Mexico and the Incas of Peru had recently developed the most impressive reformulations thus far of the traditional Mesoamerican and Peruvian cultures.

Beyond these zones of city-based civilization, an immense variety of village-agricultural, nomadic-pastoral, and hunter-gatherer peoples jostled and squabbled across the world. And while an outsider might see little difference between the life of one South Sea island people and the next, between one tribe of North American Plains Indians and its neighbor, the Polynesians and the Indians knew.

Language and history, means of subsistence and forms of social organization, traditional religion and art, ethics and manners all set one people off from another around the globe. Everywhere, the cultural pluralism that had taken thousands of years to build was the most fiercely defended of all the unintended consequences of human cultural evolution.

A WORLD IN BALANCE

A number of factors made it possible for cultural pluralism to emerge and to survive for so long.

In the first place, there was world enough to go around. The older cultures, based on inefficient slash-and-burn agriculture, on pasturing flocks on marginal land, or on hunting and gathering, could feed only small populations. Such peoples were thus scattered thinly over the world from the beginning. They fought and feuded, of course. But if an aggressive neighbor proved too strong, they could always move on, down the steppe gradient, deeper into the forest, the hills, the desert. There was room for Pygmies even in the Africa of Bantu predominance, for tribes other than the mighty Sioux on the Great Plains of the American West.

There was space too between many of the centers of expanding urban-imperial cultures. The spaces between, normally difficult lands to survive on, also served as buffer zones between centers of civilization.

Thus, China was cut off from the rest of Asia by deserts from the Gobi to the Tarim Basin, by the high plateaus of Tibet, by the jungles and seas of Southeast Asia. India was walled in by the Himalayas and the Indian Ocean; only its Northwest Frontier lay open to large-scale incursions. Europe, bounded by water on three sides, had the great East European plain between it and most of the rest of Eurasia. Africa south of the Sahara was generally protected from large assaults by the sea of sand.

The New and Old Worlds were separated from each other by thousands of miles of ocean and developed in splendid isolation from each other. The great civilizations of Mexico and Peru, separated by more than two thousand miles of jungle and mountain, seem to have had little if any contact. Each was able to go its own way, developing its own style of civilized life without intrusion or challenge.

A second reason for the long-established pluralism of the world's cultures is the rough strategic balance of power that prevailed among peoples and empires.

We have looked already at the long seesaw struggle between urban-imperialism and preurban peoples. Nomads in particular had mobility and militarized societies to give them strength. City-based agricultural societies had numbers, depth of social organization, and long-run technological superiority. The city dwellers could outlast or absorb the nomads; the raiders could flee back into the steppe or the desert. For thousands of years, at least, neither had been able to destroy the other.

Between the various centers of urban-imperial society, there was also a rough parity of power. There were simply no gaping disparities between levels of political organization, economic and technological development, or the effectiveness of the cultural cement that held the great civilizations together.

Thus, when there were conflicts between the great powers of the first five thousand years of human history, the results tended to be indecisive at best. Sometimes they resulted in long standoffs or alternating success and failure, as in the centuries-long conflicts between ancient Rome and Parthian Persia, or between medieval Christian Europe and Islam. When victory did seem to come to one great developed culture over another, the results were often disappointing. The Hellenization of the Middle East was never more than skin deep, even after the famous victories of Alexander the Great.

There were important contacts among the major civilizations of the Old World, and sometimes important cultural influences of one on another. Commercial exchange could have a significant effect on the lifeways of the upper classes at least, as the long-standing European taste for Asian luxuries illustrates. Religions could travel from one great civilization to another, as Buddhism did from South Asia to East Asia, from India to China. Migration and military conquest could leave their mark, as with the Islamic expansion, though trade and of course religion also played their parts here.

But religion, trade, migration, and other forms of intercultural contact seldom uprooted old ways entirely. The great centers of civilization and even the traditional cultures of nonurban peoples were usually very stubborn nuts to crack. They resisted penetration, absorbed intruders, and maintained the tight, hard kernel of cultural identity that set one people off from another.

The traditional balance among cultural centers was thus maintained for thousands of years. By 1500 the world

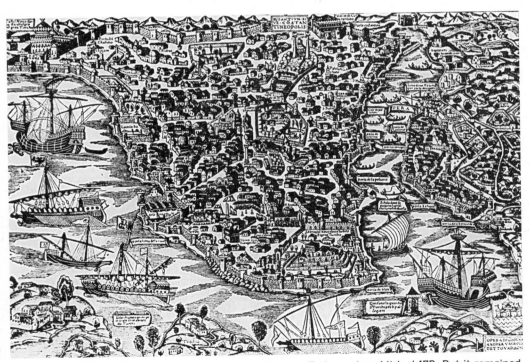

Christian Constantinople became Muslim Istanbul after the Turks captured it in 1453. But it remained the great emporium of Mideast trade. Note the famous "impregnable" walls and the busy shipping in the harbor in this view of the city in 1520. (The Bettmann Archive)

CULTURE AREAS OF THE WORLD ABOUT 1500

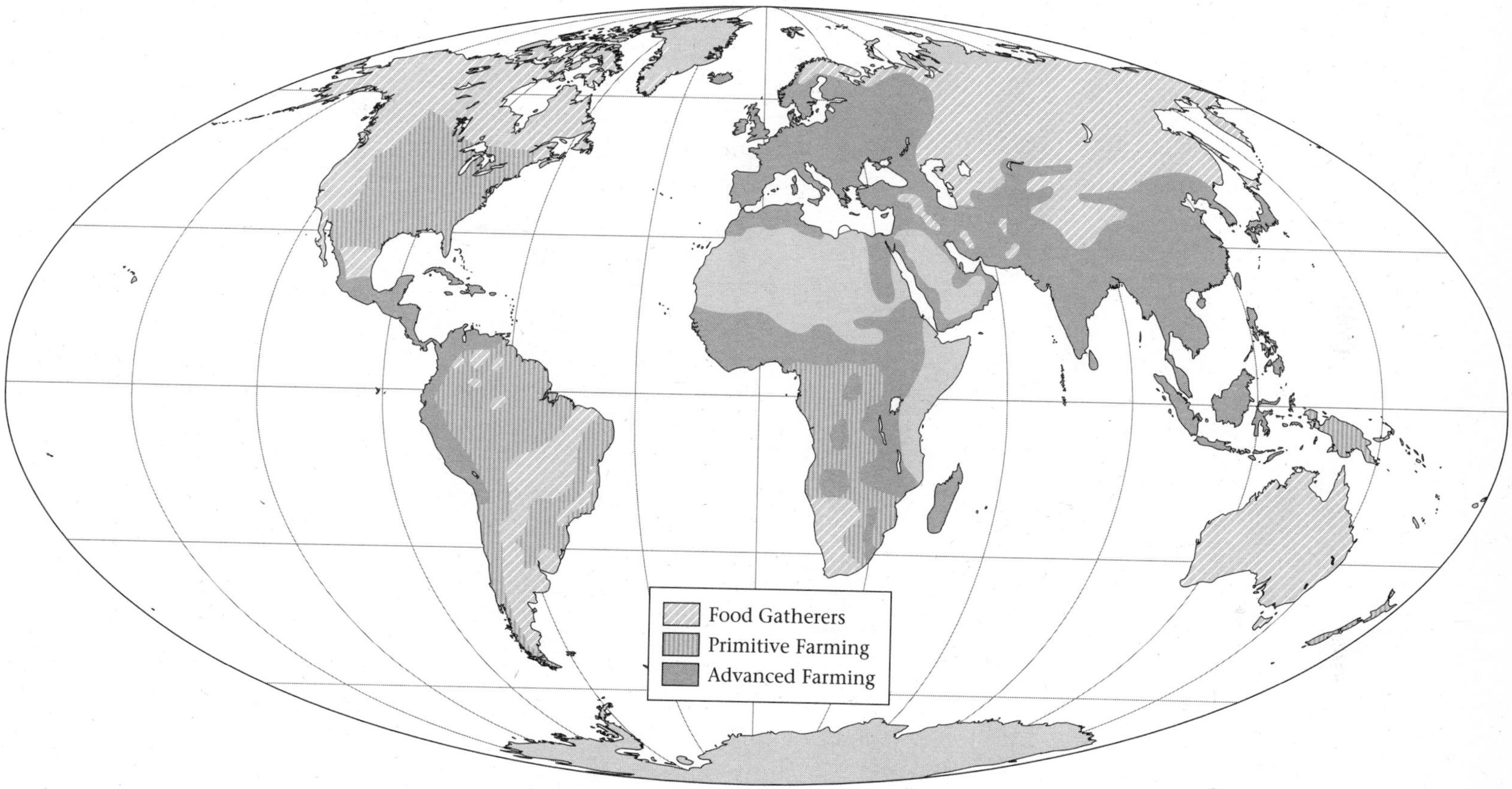

Food Gatherers
Primitive Farming
Advanced Farming

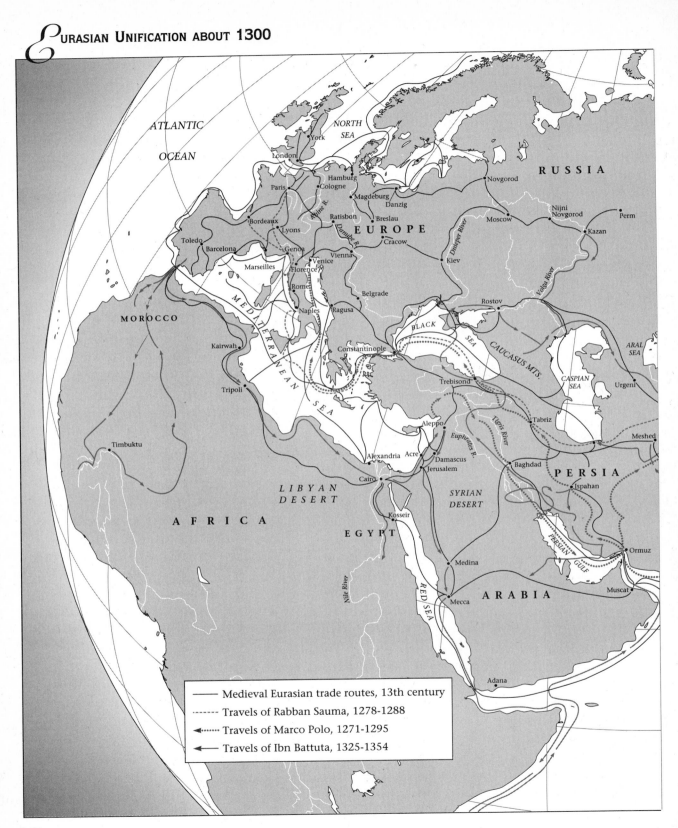

ᴇURASIAN UNIFICATION ABOUT **1300**

ATLANTIC

OCEAN

NORTH
SEA

RUSSIA

York

London

Hamburg
Cologne

Paris

Novgorod

Magdeburg

Danzig

Bordeaux

Ratisbon

Breslau

Moscow

Nijni
Novgorod

Perm

Lyons

Rhine R.

EUROPE

Danube R.

Cracow

Kazan

Toledo

Barcelona

Genoa

Vienna

Dnieper River

Marseilles

Florence

Venice

Kiev

Volga River

Rome

Belgrade

Rostov

**ARAL
SEA**

Naples

Ragusa

Urgent

MOROCCO

Constantinople

BLACK

SEA

CAUCASUS MTS.

**CASPIAN
SEA**

Kairwah

MEDITERRANEAN

Trebisond

Tabriz

Meshed

Tripoli

SEA

Aleppo

Tigris River

Euphrates R.

Baghdad

PERSIA

Timbuktu

Alexandria

Acre

Damascus

Ispahan

Cairo

Jerusalem

Ormuz

*LIBYAN
DESERT*

Kosseir

*SYRIAN
DESERT*

*PERSIAN
GULF*

Muscat

AFRICA

EGYPT

Nile River

Medina

RED SEA

ARABIA

Mecca

Adana

——————	Medieval Eurasian trade routes, 13th century
- - - - - -	Travels of Rabban Sauma, 1278-1288
·◄·····	Travels of Marco Polo, 1271-1295
◄———	Travels of Ibn Battuta, 1325-1354

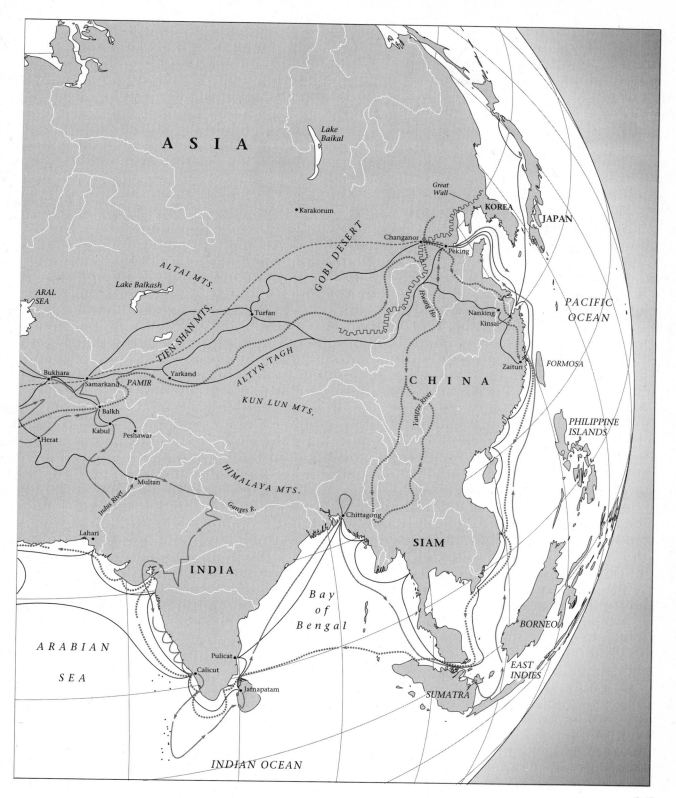

ASIA

Lake Baikal

• Karakorum

ALTAI MTS.

Lake Balkash

ARAL SEA

TIEN SHAN MTS.

Turfan

GOBI DESERT

Great Wall

KOREA

JAPAN

Changanor

Peking

Hwang Ho

Bukhara

Samarkand

PAMIR

Yarkand

ALTYN TAGH

Nanking

Kinsai

Balkh

KUN LUN MTS.

CHINA

Zaitun

FORMOSA

Kabul

Herat

Peshawar

Yangtze River

PACIFIC OCEAN

PHILIPPINE ISLANDS

Multan

HIMALAYA MTS.

Indus River

Ganges R.

Lahari

INDIA

Chittagong

SIAM

Bay of Bengal

BORNEO

ARABIAN SEA

Pulicat

Calicut

Jafnapatam

EAST INDIES

SUMATRA

INDIAN OCEAN

343

Timbuktu, sketched here by one of the first Europeans to visit the West African metropolis in the nineteenth century, must have looked much the same hundreds of years earlier, in its prime. Several mosques are shown, with steeply pyramidal minarets. A number of horsemen and a lone camel and camel driver represent the caravan trade that made Timbuktu one of the commercial centers of inner Africa. (Library of Congress)

was a genuinely pluralistic, diversified place, having a dozen major civilizations and many less extensive and complex cultures. Then, about five hundred years ago, something unprecedented began to happen.

 ## GLOBAL HEGEMONY

COLUMBUS: UPSETTING THE BALANCE

On August 3, 1492, Christopher Columbus sailed from Palos, in Spain, on what he called the "Enterprise of the Indies." His goal was to reach the Far East—Cathay (China), Cipangu (Japan), and the Spice Islands of Southeast Asia by sailing west across the Atlantic. On October 12, his little fleet made its historic landfall—at the island of San Salvador in the Caribbean Sea.

Columbus did not "discover" America: the native American peoples had done that thousands of years before. Nor, though he coasted parts of Central and South America, did he ever set foot in what would become the United States. Yet his achievement was immense. He opened the hitherto isolated Americas to penetration, conquest, and eventual transformation by the peoples of Europe, and subsequently by Africans and Asians as well.

It was not easy. During his four voyages to the New World, as Europeans soon took to calling it, Columbus confronted hunger and thirst, unfamiliar diseases, rotting ships, tropical hurricanes, increasingly hostile Amerindian populations, and the loss of whole settlements. He faced intrigue and mutiny among his own crews and imprisonment by the Spanish sovereigns who had financed his expedition. Obsessed by dreams of wealth and titles, convinced that he sailed under divine protection, a brilliant navigator, efficient seaman, wretched colonial administrator, and brutal enslaver of the Indians, Columbus combined all the qualities of the generations of Western explorers and conquerors who would follow him.

What Columbus and his successors accomplished was to upset the delicate balance of separate centers of power, separate cultures and communities around the world. In the perspective of history, it is possible to see a drift toward "one world," interdependent and increasingly homogeneous, beginning around 1500.

WESTERN IMPERIALISM

It began in what was really quite a conventional way, with a new wave of conquest: the great European imperial expansion that has been one of the defining features of modern history. But there were two aspects of this surge of European conquest that set it off from the many similar imperial ventures of the past. One was the element upon which this great conquest was launched; the other was the sheer scale of the enterprise.

The European empire building that began with the epic voyages of Columbus to the Americas in 1492 and of Vasco da Gama to India in 1498 was unique in that it began and continued not over land but on the sea. New ships, new maps, new techniques of navigation, and new levels of firepower made the European conquerors masters of all the world's oceans. And as such they became, for the first time, potentially the masters of all the world's continents as well.

The maritime medium thus made possible the second unprecedented feature of Western imperialism after 1500: its global scale. For the first time, genuinely intercontinental empires encompassing all the world's divided landmasses were possible. And over the next four centuries, just such global empires were achieved. By 1900 Europeans owned the world—or all they wanted of it and were willing to pay for in blood and treasure. The peoples of the West, whether they lived in Europe still or had migrated to the Americas, Africa, Asia, or Australia were the world's first global conquerors.

The great conquest did not last, of course. The political empires collapsed in the middle of the twentieth century, in the wake of World War II. The economic preeminence of the West is only now beginning to deteriorate, as such intrusive factors as Third World oil production and East Asian industry weigh more and more heavily in the world.

But the Western conquest of so much of the globe began something even more important. It began the unprecedented interaction and gradual integration of peoples around the world.

Most obviously, it was a matter of the spread of Western influences that accompanied Western hegemony in the world. The West established one more zone of culture in the centuries after 1500—this one global in its extent.

For much of the period of European colonial hegemony, admittedly, Western influence remained rather shallow over most of the world. The majority of the peoples whose rulers submitted to European overlordship lived pretty much as they always had. But Western power did bring about some critical structural changes in the non-Western world from the beginning. European invaders toppled empires in the Americas, transported millions of Africans to the New World to serve them as slave labor, and drove the Arabs from the sea lanes of the Indian Ocean—all as early as the sixteenth century. In later centuries, European domination continued to transform the political, economic, social, and intellectual lives of non-European peoples in all parts of the earth.

Empires and zones of cultural influence were nothing new in history, of course. But the sheer scale of the Western predominance was totally unprecedented. And it led to something even more startling. It brought about a complex mixing and mingling of cultures, the end of which is not yet in sight.

THE GLOBALIZATION OF HISTORY

Over the past two centuries in particular, other forces combined with the great conquest to bind the peoples of the world in more and more elaborate nets of interdependence. The result was something much more important than another conquest empire, however large. It amounted to the globalization of history.

Among the forces that combined to produce this

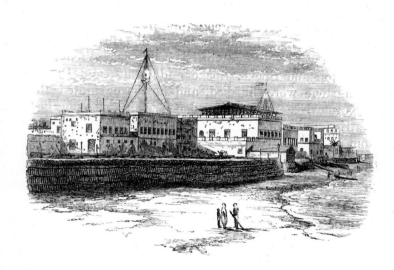

The waterfront at Zanzibar. This palm-fringed island with its ancient port was notorious as a center of the slave trade and remains famous for the export of much of the world's supply of the spice called cloves. Now part of the East African republic of Tanzania, Zanzibar was remembered by a traveler in the 1800s for its "gentle slopes clad with palms and mango trees" and the "pale blue sky and sleeping sea" that encompassed it—much the same impression that the island makes today. (From a photograph by Mr. Buchanan of Natal)

Voices from the Past

"In order to prove that the land he sees before him is indeed the continent, and not another island, Columbus engages in the following reasoning (in his journal of the third voyage, transcribed by Las Casas): "I have come to believe that this is a mighty continent which was hitherto unknown. I am greatly supported in this view by reason of this great river, and by this sea which is fresh, and I am also supported by the statements of Esdras in his fourth book, the sixth chapter, which says that six parts of the world consist of dry land and one part of water. This work was approved by Saint Ambrose in his Hexameron and by Saint Augustine. . . . Moreover I am supported by the statements of several cannibal Indians whom I captured on other occasions, who declared that there was mainland to the west of them."

Groping their way into the unknown, explorers like Columbus sought to understand the larger world that was unfolding before them. They depended on an often unreliable mix of empirical observation, information provided by the alien peoples they encountered, and interpretations authorized by their own Western culture. Here Christopher Columbus, as reported by the missionary priest Bartolomé de Las Casas in his sixteenth-century <u>Historia de las Indias</u> (I, 138), tries to decide whether a strip of coastline discovered in his exploration of the Caribbean basin is a large island like Cuba or an unknown continent. Since he seldom understood the languages of the Amerindian peoples and since the prophet Esdras—author of the first two books of the Apocrypha of the Bible—had no knowledge of the New World, the explorer's best guide proved to be shrewd observation.

What does a phrase like "cannibal Indians whom I captured" suggest about Columbus's views of and relations with the Indians? What does the citation of a Biblical prophet supported by two Fathers of the Church indicate about the admiral's commitment to Christian doctrine? How does the presence of a large river pouring out a volume of water sufficient to replace salt water by fresh water far out to sea support the theory that this is a large land mass? The coastline in question, encountered in Columbus's third voyage, was in fact the north shore of South America, the river the Orinoco in what is today Venezuela.

C. Tzvetan Todorov, <u>The Conquest of America: The Question of the Other</u>, trans. Richard Howard (New York: Harper and Row, 1987), p. 14.

unprecedented event, some, of course, were Western influences generated by Western imperial predominance. The world market established as early as the sixteenth century, for instance, was transformed by the Industrial Revolution into the vastly more potent and penetrating economic imperialism of the nineteenth century. Western ideologies also spread to the far places, until slogans coined in the English Revolution of 1688 or the French Revolution of 1789, or in the revolutionary tracts of the socialist Marx

or the nationalist Mazzini, returned to haunt Europeans on the lips of rebellious colonial peoples.

In the twentieth century particularly, however, intercontinental influences began to flow the other way in an increasingly interrelated world. Japanese militarism in the 1930s and Japanese industrial growth in the 1980s, price manipulation by a cartel of Third World oil-producing nations in the 1970s, revolutionary doctrines produced by Mahatma Gandhi or Fidel Castro—all these could send tremors through the West as great as those that Western deeds and thoughts once stirred across the non-Western world.

Institutional ties also emerged in a world already linked economically and ideologically. International organizations, many of them global in scope, have proliferated over the past hundred years. Some of these have failed ignominiously, as did the League of Nations between the two world wars. Others, such as the United Nations, have proved less effective than many had hoped. But some multinational organizations have made quite a difference in the lives of the world's peoples. Without the Common Market, Europe's history since World War II would surely have been vastly different. Without the World Bank and the International Monetary Fund, for all their faults, development in the Third World would have been much more difficult.

Common perils, finally, unite all of us in the great global venture of modern times. Pollution, overpopulation, and the possibility of a nuclear holocaust are problems for all the world's peoples. History remains today, as it was for the first builders of civilization five thousand and more years ago, as it has been for all peoples down all the centuries since, a most dangerous game.

Nevertheless, it is a game that we all must play. The lives of all the peoples of the earth are now linked as never before in modern times. A war in the Middle East, a revolution in Latin America, a fall on the New York stock exchange, a dispute between politicians in Washington and Beijing—each can change the futures of all of us. The history we are living today is one more risky stage in the great human venture—though the stakes are perhaps a little higher in our times.

Volume II of this book will attempt to trace the journey from Columbus's day to our own. It will try to explain how we got where we are today. And it will hazard a guess or two about where we may be this time next year, next century, in the next step on the long road from the Paleolithic caves.

MANY HISTORIES—OR ONE?

The second volume of this book will therefore attempt to tell two stories at once. The first will resemble the story told in the first volume. It will consist of the separate histories of the world's various peoples over the past five centuries. The second, however, will offer something new: It will try to tell the complex story of the merging of all these histories into a single global history.

The chapters concerned with the separate stories of the many peoples who live on planet Earth will build on what has gone before. Treatments of the histories of Europe, the Muslim world, India, China, Africa, the Americas, and other nations and regions will glance back repeatedly at the earlier histories of these areas. To understand modern peoples, we must remember the historic development of the institutions and ideas that govern their behavior today. We will therefore survey the rebirth and rapid development of Europe from the Renaissance to modern industrial society, the last great surge of Islamic expansion, the final formulation of China's traditional culture, the emergence of new states in Africa, the destruc-

A mapmaker of the 1500s works at his scholarly craft, symbolically flanked by a model ship and several globes. The shape and size of the earth and most of the continents were known by this time. Contrast this world view with the vision of a flat earth ringed by mythic seas revealed by the Babylonian world map in Chapter 1. What new functions had maps acquired by early modern times that the ancient Mesopotamian map was not expected to perform? (National Maritime Museum, Greenwich)

tion of the last great Native American empires, and the rise of powerful new nations in the Americas over the last two centuries.

Other chapters dealing with events since 1500, by contrast, will concentrate on genuinely global elements in modern history. These chapters will chronicle the rise, climax, and collapse of the Western intercontinental empires. They will outline such clearly global events and trends as the First and Second World Wars of the twentieth century, the Cold War, and the emergence of a host of international agreements and organizations. In the last chapters of this book, this global history will emphasize the emergence of such powerful forces for global integration as the reach of modern economic relations, technology, and culture, as well as the common global problems mentioned earlier.

A key concept that will help us to understand this increasing interdependence of the globe—and perhaps to make a start at solving its many problems—is the idea of human community.

🐚 TOWARD A GLOBAL COMMUNITY

HUMAN COMMUNITIES

Community is a term with many meanings.

Communities come in all sizes, from a tiny medieval farming village to the European Economic Community of today, encompassing a dozen nations. A "community of interests" may link peoples who have developed very different social structures or cultural values. Commercial exchange or diplomatic alliance, for instance, may make partners out of sometimes extremely diverse nations. A felt "sense of community," a feeling of being part of a larger group, can itself play a vital role in history. Thus, religious affiliation may create a strong sense of being part of a Christian or Jewish, Muslim or Buddhist community, while nationalism may make people feel that the most important thing about them is that they are Russians or Chinese or Americans.

Human communities in these varied senses have been key factors in history from the beginning. Since prehistoric times, the family and the clan, the food-gathering band and the agricultural village have provided a communal core to human life. From the beginning of history, the more complex community life of the city, the nation-state, and the empire have been crucial elements in the human story. Diffuse but essential links of trade, ideas, or common geopolitical interests have repeatedly forged significant bonds of economic, political, or ideological community on an international level.

Human communities were therefore nothing new in 1500. What was new was the increasing scale and com-

plexity of these fundamental forms of human social organization in the centuries that followed.

BASIC COMMUNITIES— A TALE OF TWO CITIES

You can see an old-fashioned face-to-face human community in the strees of Siena, Italy, a Renaissance survival complete with cathedral, town hall, and a round central piazza lined with outdoor cafes. This hill town about an hour's train ride from Florence preserves such medieval traditions as the *palio*, a reckless horse race through its cobbled lanes that draws hordes of tourists every summer. The paintings around the walls of the town hall celebrate the unification of Italy in the nineteenth century. The pictures in the cathedral glorify the medieval God whose praise is still sung every Sunday.

Visit Siena in winter and you will see a friendly, traditional style of life. The regular evening stroll gives residents a chance to stop and chat along the narrow streets. Children are loved, cared for—and disciplined. Old people who have known each other all their lives stand and talk around the farm machinery at the weekly open-air market. Everyone knows everyone, and the life of the city goes on much as it did centuries ago, when Siena rivaled Florence as a center of commerical wealth and Renaissance culture.

You can see a very different sort of community in the city of Chengdu in Central China today—a community in the grip of drastic, dynamic change. Wander a block or two from your modern hotel and you will find yourself in the middle of the old China, with its tiny open-fronted shops, grandmothers squatting on their stools, kids swarming through the alleys, and old men playing cards in the inexpensive outdoor tea shops along the river.

Without ever leaving your hotel, however, you can see the new Chengdu emerging. Down in the hotel coffee shop, young men in white shirts and ties and polished shoes and sharply creased slacks sit over their morning coffees—with cellular phones glued to their ears. Up the broad central boulevards of Chengdu, factories and fashionable condo blocks with trendy Western names are shooting up everywhere. Chengdu is a boomtown, a community generating new patterns of life rooted in modern get-and-spend capitalism, yet still recognizing the importance of such traditional values as respect for age and family.

How long an Italian hill town may be able to defend its traditional way of life while angling for tourist business, how long a Chinese boomtown can preserve family values while plunging headlong into a modern world built on competitive individualism, remains to be seen. What is sure is that there are much larger communities than these basic face-to-face units in our world today—and that the future may belong to these mega-communities that span the globe.

INCREASING SCOPE AND INTERACTION OF COMMUNITIES

In many ways, this unprecedented expansion in the scope and interaction of human communities over the past five hundred years has in fact been the defining characteristic of modern world history.

Such growth was of course quite visible in earlier periods. Throughout the first five thousand years of history, a trend toward larger communities and more extensive and elaborate webs of relations between them may be detected. Families, clans, foraging bands, agricultural villages, and pastoral nomads were all small communities relating in relatively simple ways to other groups. Cities, nations, empires, long-distance trade, and the spread of missionary religions all represented substantial expansion in the size of communities or in the complexity of interaction between them. In the last few centuries before the beginning of the modern period, vast zones of culture emerged in parts of Europe, Asia, Africa, and the Americas. These large regional communities were composed of peoples sharing common Christian or Muslim religious beliefs, shaped by powerful Chinese or Indian influences, or determined by a common geographical frame of West African grasslands or Andean mountain terrain.

What happened after 1500, then, was essentially the acceleration and intensification of long established historical trends. But the result was something quite unexpected. Western imperial expansion, as previously noted, carried the influence of a single community of nations around the world. And through the channels of communication and interaction thus established, all the peoples of the earth came to influence each other to a degree unmatched in earlier times. The result was to create at least the possibility of a single global community encompassing all the diverse peoples of the earth.

THE GRIP OF OLDER COMMUNITIES

From intercontinental empires and the world market to international organizations and global economic interdependence, from cultural imperialism to global cultural community, the peoples of the world were thus drawn steadily closer over the modern centuries. From the vantage point of our times, these trends may seem to point to still greater closeness to come. But there have also been forces working to retard and even reverse this historic trend. The interaction of these two opposing tendencies, of an ongoing thrust toward global unity with persisting loyalties to older, narrower communities would generate much of the history of the modern era.

All the older forms of community survived into the new age of increasingly global history. Many of the populations of the earth still lived in village communities well into the twentieth century. Allegiance to the independent nation-state remained perhaps the most powerful of all community loyalties. And most people were still much more likely to see themselves as part of a religious, ethnic, or class-based community than as members of a broader "human community" encompassing all the peoples of planet earth. These older communities would interact and often conflict with the broad drift toward global community defined above. They would thus contribute significantly to the taut and troubled course of modern history.

The grip of the older, established communities, from face-to-face local groups to much larger communities based on such established cultural forces as shared religion, ethnicity, or nationality, remains very strong. Newspapers in the 1990s frequently include grim stories highlighting the divisive force of these deeply felt loyalties. You might thus read over your morning coffee about the return of a Croatian family to its home in an area of the former Yugoslavia seized by Serb rebels a few years ago and recently recaptured by Croatian forces. You would not need to understand the tangled national rivalries of the region to recognize the passion in the returning refugee's declaration that the Serbs who have occupied his home for the last four years and have just been driven out "can f___ off back to Serbia and stay there."

Similar expressions of the strength of these older loyalties are everywhere. In Africa, rivalry between Hutus and Tutsis at the University of Burundi divides a campus and causes dozens of deaths among faculty and students. In the Near East, a bomb planted on a bus by Palestinian extremists kills a number of Israelis. In India, Islamic guerrillas fighting for the right of the Muslim province of Kashmir to secede from primarily Hindu India have held—and beheaded—Western hostages.

Similar if less sensational instances of divisive allegiances to historic communities may be found in the West as well. Conflicts between Basque nationalists and the rest of Spain, between Protestants and Catholics in Northern Ireland, and between black and white citizens of the United States, all have deep historical roots and a real potential for splitting whole nations.

THE DRIFT TOWARD GLOBAL COMMUNITY

No one should underestimate the power of national, religious, ethnic, and other basic human communities deeply rooted in all our histories. Nevertheless, there are communities in our world that link rather than divide people, that tend toward unity rather than diversity. And these have power too.

A cultural community forged by enthusiasm for the same Western popular art and culture is the youthful international audience for rock music. The morning newspaper detailed the profound disappointment of a group of Siberian fans when a British "glam rock" band was unable to honor its commitment to tour three Siberian cities because its drummer broke his arm. The huge crowd gathered to meet them at the airport in Omsk reflected the region's loyalty to this now long out-dated form of rock entertainment. Glam rock had fascinated generations of Siberian yough since the 1970's, "the era when Gary Glitter roamed the earth," and perhaps the last time a Western rock group came that way.

The global reach of the new popular music is not, however, a simple matter of pervasive Western influence. Significant strains of this youth-galvanizing art form and its related culture include Caribbean reggae, West African high life, and, stretching it only a little, the karaoke bars of East Asia. Paris rocks to the music of bands from French-speaking West and Central Africa, and hip young Americans tune in to South African "township music" on their college radio stations. Many fans believe that the creative potential of what is usually called *world music* has only begun to be felt on the global rock scene.

Rock music and the dances and drugs, costumes and customs that go with it have thus created a remarkable international youth culture. This community of the young has not taken a significant political stance since the 1960s. But its passion for Madonna and Michael Jackson, Bob Marley, Sunny Ade, and Ladysmith Black Mambazo—as we will see in the second volume of this book—is a powerful unifying force nonetheless. Nor would anyone who remembers the sixties be surprised to see this community of the young once again take a hand in the world's affairs.

On the foundations laid by the developments of the first 5000 years of history, the peoples of the next 500 years have laid the foundations for an unparalleled global community. It was not a conscious effort. Neither defenders of older societies nor imperialist conquerors would have any idea of the new global order that might result from their struggles. Nevertheless, as the year 2000 rushes toward us, it is even possible to postulate the emergence, in the not too distant future, of a single unitary global culture, a world community sharing common social values, economic systems, political institutions, taste and mores. For some, such a new world order would be a paradise of peace and global prosperity after millennia of conflict. For others, such a climax of world history would be a nightmare of uniformity and conformity after centuries of rich pluralism of peoples and cultures.

Both predictions, however, depend on the continuance of the basic trend toward greater interdependence, increasing mutual influence, and in the end a single global culture. Neither the history of the first five millennia of human history nor that of the last five hundred years make such a continuing trend at all certain. Most people in the world of 1500 were thoroughly committed to smaller traditional communities and had no sense of "the human race" as a whole at all. Most of the five or six billion people who will see the year 2000 dawn will be equally focused in their views. Still, a drift toward global community does seem to emerge from a study of the human story. It may indeed be the central theme of global history as we understand it today.

SUMMARY

The world was facing a decisive change in human history around the year 1500. From that time on, a world of cultural pluralism would give way to a slow but accelerating drift toward a single global order.

By 1500 a number of complex and tenacious cultural zones had evolved around the world. Many of these centered on powerful empires, on religious hegemonies, or on other cultural foci that gave them a strong sense of cultural uniqueness and of allegiance to their own way of life.

The major civilizations around the world had also developed a rough parity of power by 1500. This approximate equality in strength, coupled with the substantial geographical barriers between many of them, had enabled each to maintain its separate identity for hundreds or thousands of years.

This strategic balance, however, was on the verge of being upset as modern history began.

The rise of one among the world's most powerful civilizations, that of Christian Europe, would lead to the establishment of a globe-girdling system of intercontinental empires over the next few centuries. And these initial ties would in turn generate a genuinely global integration of human cultures. By the twentieth century this globalization of history would be well under way.

But the crucial turning point had come five centuries earlier, when the cultural pluralism of 1500 began to feel the strength of the new forces that would in time convert many worlds into one.

Loyalty to older, narrower communities—nations, religions, and others—would remain strong throughout this period. These traditional allegiances would resist absorption into a larger, common culture. Nevertheless, for better or for worse, the five centuries after 1500 would produce at least the possibility of a single global community of peoples for the first time in human history.

SUGGESTED READING

BARRACLOUGH, G., ed. *The Times Atlas of World History*. London: Times Books, 1978. The basic geographical reference for global history, with emphasis on relationships and dynamic elements.

CURTIN, P. D. *Cross-cultural Trade in World History*. Cambridge: Cambridge University Press, 1984. Long-distance trade and the resulting "trade diasporas" as factors in human history.

DRIVER, H. E., ed. *The Americas on the Eve of Discovery*. Englewood Cliffs, N.J.: Prentice Hall, 1964. Readings on Amerindian cultures at the end of their independent development.

HUCKER, C. O. *The Traditional Chinese State in Ming Times, 1368–1644*. Tucson: University of Arizona Press, 1961. Short description of Chinese society during the dynasty that faced the first significant contact with Europeans.

JONES, E. L. *The European Miracle: Environments, Economics, and Geopolitics in the History of Europe and Asia*. Cambridge, England: Cambridge University Press, 1981. Europe's advantages at the beginning of the modern age, from climate and coastline to governments that fostered economic development.

JULY, R. W. *A History of the African People*. New York: Scribner's, 1970. See chapters 3–7 for the centuries immediately preceding the European intrusion and for a brief overview of initial contacts.

KNAPTON, E. J. *The Emergence of the Modern Era, 1450–1650*. New York: Scribner's, 1961. One of many brief surveys of Europe on the eve of expansion.

LANGER, W. L. *An Encyclopedia of World History*. Boston: Houghton Mifflin, 1972. Standard chronological reference.

SAUNDERS, J. J., ed. *The Muslim World on the Eve of Europe's Expansion*. Englewood Cliffs, N.J.: Prentice Hall, 1966. Collection of sources on the Muslim zone around 1500.

STAVRIANOS, L. S. *The Global Rift: The Third World Comes of Age*. New York: William Morrow, 1981. Five centuries of the history of Asia, Africa, and Latin America, with emphasis on the economic impact of the First World on the Third, especially since World War II.

————. *The World Since 1500: A Global History*. Englewood Cliffs, N.J.: Prentice Hall, 1982. Second volume of Stavrianos's readable and informed text.

THOMAS, H. *A History of the World*. New York: Harper & Row, Pub., 1979. Emphasis on technology and material culture. Two-thirds of the book deals with the period since 1500.

UNESCO History of Mankind (6 vols.). New York: Harper & Row, Pub., 1963. Multiauthor, multivolume survey of world cultures, drawing more widely on non-Western scholars and scholarship than some.

WOLF, E. R. *Europe and the People without History*. Berkeley: University of California Press, 1983. An arthropologist's eye and Marxist economic analysis of the global impact of capitalist imperialism on non-Western peoples since the fourteenth century.

THE WORLD IN BALANCE

Modern world history is the story of the merging of the histories of the world's diverse peoples into a single human story. In 1500, however, that globalization of history lay in the unthinkable future still.

The world of the fifteenth and sixteenth centuries remained a world of separate zones of culture. Regional societies, great empires, and some of the most impressive civilizations the world has seen shared the earth at the beginning of the modern period. In the first six chapters we will explore each of these zones of culture in turn.

In so doing, we will try to establish a firm sense of the geographical, historical, and cultural identity of each of the main regions and powers. Such a sense of the major cultural zones will be essential when, in later chapters, the global nature of our

modern history compels us to skip about rather casually among the continents and cultures.

We will begin, then, with the comparatively familiar continent of Europe around 1500—the tidy little world from which Columbus sailed. It is a colorful, half-legendary time for Western people, an age of Renaissance art and swashbuckling cavaliers, of queens in jeweled gowns and popes in splendor. Between Columbus's first voyage in 1492 and the conquest in 1521 of Aztec Mexico, the first non-Western empire to fall to Western arms, Leonardo da Vinci painted the *Mona Lisa*, Isabella of Castile and Ferdinand of Aragon completed the unification of Spain, Henry VIII became king of England, and Martin Luther nailed his Ninety-five Theses on the church door at Wit-

tenberg. This Europe, the Western World of the centuries around 1500, will be our starting point.

We will then proceed eastward across the double continent of Eurasia—four fifths of which is Asia—into much less familiar realms. First there will be the great Islamic empires of the Muslim center of Eurasia. By 1500 the faith of Muhammad the Prophet, starting six centuries later, had spread much farther than Christianity had. Mosques were built, the *Koran* read, and the Muslim Law obeyed from West Africa to Southeast Asia. But the jewels of the Islamic world in the early sixteenth century were the three wealthy and powerful central Eurasian empires of Ottoman Turkey, Safavid Persia, and Mogul India. The achievements of this Muslim heartland must, then, concern us here.

Farther still to the east, we will encounter the ancient, immense empire of China and the dynamic island nation of Japan. The Chinese emperors ruled by far the largest country in the world, whose population was many times that of any European nation. They had been doing so, at least intermittently, since before the time of Christ. Chinese civilization, with its Confucian philosophy and its centralized government of scholar-bureaucrats, had shaped the cultures of much of the rest of East Asia as well. Of these satellite cultures, vigorously evolving Japan—the Japan of the warlord shoguns—will particularly concern us.

Civilization, however, had also grown up outside the world island of Eurasia. There were impressive kingdoms on the grasslands of West Africa and even in the dense forests of the Guinea Coast. On the other side of the continent, trading states flourished along the East African coast, part of the network of trade that bound the nations around the Indian Ocean into a single community of commerce. To understand these cultures, we will poke through the Bazaars of Timbuktu and the mysterious ruins of Great Zimbabwe.

The New World—as the Europeans called it—also had its highly developed societies in 1500. When Columbus and his successors reached those shores, the most impressive of all Latin American empires had recently emerged: the Aztec predominance in Mexico and the Inca Empire of Peru. We will look at those American empires as they were before the Europeans fell upon them with fire and sword. A glimpse of the canals and pyramids of Aztec Tenochtitlán, or the golden temples of Inca Cuzco, was enough to convince even the Spanish conquistadores that high culture was not a European monopoly.

Civilization itself, finally, was not the only viable human option at the beginning of the modern age. As the preceding volume of this book tried to emphasize, the majority of the world's peoples have lived through most of history in tiny agricultural villages, or have survived by herding cattle or sheep or by hunting, fishing, and gathering vegetable food from nature's bounty. Most of the earth's inhabited land was still populated by these peoples in 1500, including most of Africa, the Americas, and Australia. The accomplishments of these preurban cultures deserve our attention here as much as the more flamboyant achievements of the builders of cities and empires.

The varied world of many cultures and civilizations of 1500 was thus something none of us has ever seen. It was a world in balance.

For a last few centuries around 1500, genuine cultural pluralism prevailed. Many civilizations, many cultures lived together on the surface of the globe in a rough equilibrium. Let us take a last, long look, then, at this world of separate cultures and regional hegemonies, the world all our forebears knew back to the beginning of history. That roughly balanced world deserves our attention for the sake of its own accomplishments. And it was out of this pluralistic world that our own astonishing five-hundred-year epoch of world history evolved—the period of the birth of global culture.

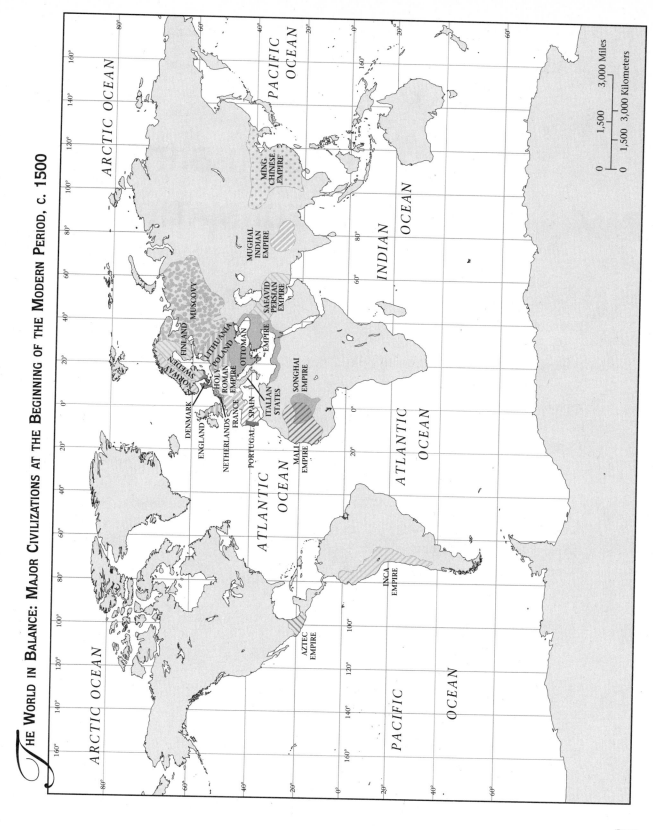

The World in Balance: Major Civilizations at the Beginning of the Modern Period, c. 1500

ARCTIC OCEAN

PACIFIC OCEAN

MING CHINESE EMPIRE

MUGHAL INDIAN EMPIRE

SAFAVID PERSIAN EMPIRE

MUSCOVY

FINLAND

LITHUANIA

POLAND

OTTOMAN EMPIRE

SWEDEN

NORWAY

HOLY ROMAN EMPIRE

DENMARK

ENGLAND

NETHERLANDS

FRANCE

PORTUGAL

SPAIN

ITALIAN STATES

MALI EMPIRE

SONGHAI EMPIRE

INDIAN OCEAN

ATLANTIC OCEAN

ATLANTIC OCEAN

INCA EMPIRE

AZTEC EMPIRE

PACIFIC OCEAN

ARCTIC OCEAN

0   1,500   3,000 Miles

0   1,500   3,000 Kilometers

CHAPTER 25

EUROPE'S REBIRTH AND REFORMATION

THE NEW WEALTH

REMEMBERING THE RENAISSANCE

The folk memory of a people is a strange thing. It filters, distorts, obliterates, remembers what it will, and expunges what it wants to forget. Much of what folk memory preserves it transmutes into fiction—ancedotes, folk tales and songs, romantic plays and novels, and, most recently, film. The result is a communal dream of the past, a golden age of handsome pasteboard men and beautiful unreal women living fairytale lives in a world far more interesting and exciting than our own. Nobody, popular myth-history assures us, ever went to bed bored for lack of a date in Good Queen Bess's glorious days.

From the Renaissance, the first age of modern Western history, we remember the splendors.

The English remember Henry VIII—"Bluff Prince Hal"—wassailing in his banquet hall, or Queen Elizabeth's thousand gowns, each more gorgeous than the last. For Italians, the names that have survived from those vanished centuries conjure up a glittering time—names such as Lorenzo the Magnificent, who ruled Florence when that city was the queen of the Italian Renaissance. Spanish people honor the memory of Ferdinand and Isabella, who unified their country and sent Columbus on his famous voyages. Their neighbors across the Pyrenees remember chivalric Francis I, with his long, aristocratic nose and many mistresses, the champagne king of France. And Germans still revere the moral splendor of Martin Luther, defying authority for the principles he believed in.

We all remember the artistic splendor that survives from the Renaissance—Leonardo's battered but still deeply moving *Last Supper*, Michelangelo's panorama of the creation of the world on the ceiling of the Sistine Chapel in Rome, or Cellini's dazzling golden salt cellar, an amazing sculptural group fit to grace an emperor's table.

We are less likely to know the source of the money that bought the thousand gowns or paid for Cellini's splendid salt cellar. The faceless clerks and bureaucrats who ran Lorenzo the Magnificent's banks or translated King Henry's imperious will into action have faded from the collective memory. Few today can cite the theological arguments behind Luther's ringing declaration, or even name the wars in which the famous heroes fought and so many thousands died in those gory centuries.

We will try here to preserve the memory of the banners and the trumpets. But we must look also at more pedestrian aspects of the life of that Western reawakening that goes by the twin labels of Renaissance and Reformation.

THE WESTERN WORLD 500 YEARS AGO

By most definitions, the Western world today encompasses not only a widespread Atlantic community of nations including most of Europe and North America, but also allied countries as far afield as Israel and Australia. Five hundred years ago, however, the West was Europe only, a cramped little cluster of nations occupying the western one fifth of Eurasia. It was neither the oldest nor the most impressive of world civilizations.

Geographically, Europe was divided by mountains and rivers, its margins chopped up into peninsulas and islands. The Ural and Caucasus mountains and the Black Sea cut it off from Asia, the Mediterranean from Africa. The Atlantic Ocean lay between Europe and the Americas, continents whose very existence was unknown to Europeans before 1492.

Some of the major modern states had already assumed a rough approximation of today's boundaries by 1500. England and France, Spain and Portugal, even Poland and a truncated version of Russia were all there. Some other areas that would later become unified nations were still disunited regions. Germany was "the Germanies," Italy "the Italian states," the Netherlands a loose confederation, and Switzerland a collection of cantons. Austria presided loosely over the Holy Roman Empire, meaning mostly the three-hundred-odd German states. The Scandinavian countries of Sweden, Norway, and Denmark, on the other hand, were temporarily united in 1500. The Ottoman Empire of the Turks included among its provinces many of today's Balkan countries as well as chunks of southern Russia.

This half-familiar collection of countries was inhabited mostly by peoples speaking Indo-European languages of the Romance, Germanic, or Slavic varieties. Almost all Europeans were Christians, Roman Catholic in the west and Greek Orthodox in Eastern Europe. The monarchs who governed all the larger states claimed to rule by divine right, and the immense Christian religious establishment generally supported this claim.

The society over which these secular and religious authorities presided was as strictly hierarchical as any in the civilized world. A landowning, militarily trained aristocracy dominated the countryside and collected as courtiers and counselors around the princes of Europe. A secondary elite of merchants and leading guild artisans ran the many cities of the continent. Most Europeans, however, like most people everywhere, were peasant farmers living in small villages in the countryside. They ranged in legal status from abject serfs—in bondage to the land—in much of central and Eastern Europe to relatively prosperous tenants and freeholders in Western Europe. All, however, were subordinate to the landed aristocracy who constituted Europe's most prestigious social class.

The lands and peoples of Europe had two thousand years of recorded history behind them in 1500. Western civilization, one of the last Eurasian urban cultures to emerge, had first taken shape in the city-states of ancient Greece, then had swollen to imperial scale in the days of the Roman *imperium*. Europe's Mediterranean phase had ended with the period of internal decay and nomadic invasions that brought Rome down in the fifth century A.D. A new European culture had developed, however, rooted in barbarian vigor and Christian faith. Its political center was north of the Alps, in England, France, and the Germanies. This medieval culture had reached its apogee in the twelfth and thirteenth centuries, the age of the cathedral builders. It was the collapse of this second European civilization that opened the way for the emergence of a third—the vigorous new culture of the modern West.

THE RENAISSANCE ECONOMIC REVIVAL

Europe around 1500 was engaged in pulling itself out of the deep trough occasioned by the crumbling of the Christian Middle Ages during the preceding couple of centuries. The great fourteenth-century plague called the Black Death and the depopulation and long economic depression that resulted had been major causes of this medieval collapse. So had the Mongol conquest of Russia, the Hundred Years' War between France and England, the Turkish seizure of Constantinople and invasion of southern Europe, and the civil wars that wracked a number of European nations. The temporary division and spiritual decay of the Roman papacy had put the cap on this continent-wide catastrophe.

The worst period ran from the middle 1300s to the mid-1400s. Thereafter the long recovery was clearly under way. But it had been a major disaster in Europe's history.

A few figures may clarify the scope of the debacle and the strength of the recovery that began modern European history. The population of Europe was more than 70 million in 1300, at the height of the commercial revolution of the High Middle Ages. The Black Death struck

for the first time in 1347, and by 1400 the population had tumbled to some 45 million. By 1500, however, there were again almost 70 million Europeans, and by 1600, as Europe paused on the brink of the great population explosion of modern times, almost 90 million.

As a result of this revived demand and the expanded supply of labor to meet that demand, the economy of Europe began to grow once more in the fifteenth and sixteenth centuries. Agriculture expanded as more mouths to feed led to a renewed assault upon waste and marginal lands. More soil was brought under the plow than at any time since the High Middle Ages. Improved mining technology, particularly in the extraction of precious metals, significantly increased the amount of silver and gold available for coinage. This in turn put more money in circulation and contributed to both economic growth and inflation.

With coins again available and demand high, trade and handicraft industry boomed once more. Renewed eco-

The spirit of Western business enterprise is vividly embodied in this portrait of a banker of the early 1500s by the Flemish painter Jan Gossaert. The watchful eyes, tightly pursed lips, quick pen, and the soberly expensive clothes all reflect the character of the age that forged the first truly global market in the history of the world. (Jan Gossaert [Mabuse] Flemish, c. 1478–1532, "Portrait of a Merchant." Date: c. 1530. Wood, 0.636 × 0.475 [25 × 18-3/4 in.]. National Gallery of Art, Washington. Alisa Mellon Bruce Fund 1967)

nomic growth began in the Mediterranean trading cities of Italy, which enjoyed access to the luxury products of Asia. The commercial cities of the German Hanseatic League, the manufacturing and trading towns of the Netherlands, and great European metropolises such as Paris and London were soon reintegrated into the golden network of commercial exchange.

The medieval commercial revolution of the twelfth and thirteenth centuries and the Renaissance economic revival of the fifteenth and sixteenth laid the foundations of modern capitalism in the West. Key features of the new capitalist economy included private ownership of the means of production (as opposed to feudal land-holding in return for military service), production for the market (rather than for mere subsistence, as on the medieval manor), and widespread use of money and credit (by contrast to simple bartering of goods). Other important elements of early capitalism were the development of business law, larger economic organizations, and freedom of economic choice by the individual.

Among the technical innovations that advanced the system from the eleventh to the sixteenth century were expanded minting of coins, double-entry bookkeeping, loans at interest, maritime insurance, bank checks and letters of credit, and above all the joint-stock company, which pooled the capital of many businessmen in a single venture.

Cities were the center of all this business activity. Florence, the most famous of Renaissance cities, had in 1472 some 270 wool merchants' shops, 84 cabinetmakers' establishments, 54 stonecutters' workshops, 44 goldsmiths' shops, and 33 banks. It was not a large city by Asian standards—less than two and a half square miles, with a population of between 50 thousand and 70 thousand. But it was a bustling, vital metropolis, straddling the Arno River in the hills of northern Italy. Woolen cloth, banking, and finance were the core of its prosperity, and the Florentine florin was a gold coin good anywhere in Europe, the dollar of its day. Run by an oligarchy of business wealth, beautified by churches, and distinguished by the palaces of its great financial and commercial families, Florence became the first center of Renaissance art as well as a center of the revived Renaissance economy.

SOURCES OF THE CAPITALIST SPIRIT

The sources of this resurgent spirit of business enterprise are much debated. Both the medieval revival of trade and towns and the subsequent Renaissance resurgence of the commercial economy involved more than the mechanical interaction of supply and demand. There was a new spirit abroad in these centuries, a set of attitudes that had much to do with the rise of modern capitalism in the West.

Qualities that made for success in business, contemporaries and modern historians agree, included industry, thrift, orderliness, rationality, sobriety, and a willing-

ness to defer pleasure in order to pile up wealth to invest in still greater wealth-making potential. Some scholars have suggested that the cultures of some subgroups in Western society, such as Jews and early Protestants, may have fostered the sort of hard-working, meticulous character that did well in the evolving capitalist society. It should be remembered, however, that the medieval and early modern capitalists of Italy and the Netherlands—for two instances—were Catholic, and that a vigorous spirit of enterprise flourished even in the scattered cities of Orthodox Russia before the Mongol invasions.

Another attempt to explain the spirit of early merchant capitalism stresses the acquisitive impulses that contemporary moralists condemned as greed. In this view, capitalists owned the means of production but did not contribute to the process of producing goods. They paid workers as little as possible for their labor and then sold the product wherever they could get the best price for it. Merchants were thus parasites, contributing nothing to the wealth of nations while making a good living for themselves. Profit was certainly a prime motive, and traders normally seek to "buy cheap and sell dear." Some historians, however, believe that the charge of parasitism ignores the real contributions merchant capitalists made in bringing raw materials and labor together, in taking goods where there was a demand for them, in the risks they took, and in the spirit of enterprise they displayed.

This emphasis on the capitalist spirit of enterprise, finally, may apply most convincingly, not to the High Middle Ages or the earlier Renaissance, but to the sixteenth and seventeenth centuries. By this time, business people in some parts of Europe may have been more clearly aware of the way the free market worked. They may also have seen competition, not as something to be controlled by guild and government regulation, but as both a legitimate and efficient way of supplying society's needs while providing good profits for traders. Some of the free-market ideas that Adam Smith would propound in the eighteenth century may thus have been at least hazily felt somewhat earlier in modern history.

MONEY, POWER, AND CULTURE

The moneyed aristocracy were certainly among the greatest names of this fifteenth- and sixteenth-century economic revival. There were towering self-made men among them, such as the French tycoon Jacques Coeur, who in his prime negotiated with princes as an equal—and then died broke. There were business dynasties such as the plutocratic Fugger family of Austria, who published an international business newsletter for the far-flung branches of the family firm that was a precursor of today's financial press. Most famous of all, however, was the Medici banking family of Florence.

Generations of the Medici built the family fortune during the fifteenth century, Florence's Renaissance

LONDON

London in Shakespeare's day. London Bridge, old St. Paul's cathedral, and other landmarks show in this view, which is centered on the Thames river. The Globe Theater, where Shakespeare's plays were performed, shows in the lower left, on the near side of the river with a flag flying over it. What part do you think the river flowing through the center of the picture played in the evident prosperity of the city along its banks? (Library of Congress)

prime. At its height, Medici enterprises included branches in all the major Italian cities—Rome, Milan, Venice, and others—as well as beyond the Alps, in London, Bruges, Lübeck, Avignon, and elsewhere. The Medici were primarily bankers, processors of woolen cloth, and manufacturers of silk, but they dealt also in sugar and cotton, spices, tapestries, rare manuscripts, and they even provided singers from all over Europe for the papal choir.

As the richest bankers in Florence, the Medici soon became the uncrowned political bosses of the city. As the acknowledged rulers of the Florentine Republic, they manipulated the Italian balance of power to keep peace among all the other independent states of the peninsula. In the sixteenth century they became dukes of Florence, popes of Rome, and queens of France—a glittering dynasty of titles and power built on Renaissance money.

As early as the fifteenth century, furthermore, the Medici millions had been put at the service of Renaissance art and culture. The most famous of the clan, Lorenzo the Magnificent (1449–1492), was also the family's most renowned patron of the arts. Under Lorenzo de' Medici, poets like Angelo Poliziano and philosophers like Marsilio Ficino graced the halls of the Medici palace. Artists like Michelangelo learned their craft by sketching ancient Roman statues collected in the Medici gardens. Lorenzo was himself a poet, whose carnival songs are still anthologized in collections of Italian verse.

Self-made men like Jacques Coeur and self-made families like the Medici showed how far brains and ambition could carry a person in the Renaissance business world. Lorenzo the Magnificent—millionnaire, political leader, poet and patron of the arts—also illustrates the multifaceted type we call the Renaissance man.

RENAISSANCE LADIES AND CULTURE

But there were Renaissance women too. The condition of upper-class Renaissance women at least seems to have been considerably better than that of their medieval predecessors. A few medieval ladies may have been idealized and loved from afar. But some Renaissance ladies were educated and highly cultured, and the admiration they engendered seems to have been based on these genuine accomplishments rather than on the hazy mystique of troubadour romanticism.

Many aristocratic Renaissance women studied Latin, read ancient religious writings, and plunged eagerly into the literary classics of ancient Rome that were the heart of Renaissance intellectual life. Ladies such as Michelangelo's platonic friend Vittoria Colonna, the talented Este sisters, and the famous daughters of England's Sir Thomas More were widely admired for their learning. There were celebrated women poets, such as Christine de Pisan and Louise Labé in France, and women painters, such as Artemisia Gentileschi.

One of the most famous of Italian Renaissance women was Isabella d'Este, "the first lady of the world." Raised in her father's cultivated court at Ferrara, she was married young to the hunting-and-fighting duke of Mantua. She ruled the court at Mantua with grace, firmness, and discriminating culture while her husband enjoyed ruder pleasures elsewhere. Learned in Latin and Greek, a lover of Vergil and other Roman poets, Isabella became a major collector of ancient sculpture, vases, bronzes, coins, and medals. She had her walls decorated with paintings by living Renaissance artists, and she patronized Renaissance poets. Like Lorenzo de' Medici and other patrons of her day, Isabella d'Este thus channeled significant portions of the wealth of the age into the culture that would earn that era its distinctive place in the history books.

THE NEW RULERS

THE RENAISSANCE REVIVAL OF PRINCELY POWER

During the European Dark Ages following the fall of Rome—roughly the period 500–1000—most of the genuine power in medieval Christendom was in the hands of the feudal aristocracy whose forts, keeps, and finally castles provided what protection there was in an anarchic age. Many of the kings from whom the feudal nobles held their vast estates were do-nothing rulers with little actual authority.

However, during the High Middle Ages—the eleventh, twelfth, and thirteenth centuries—strong kings emerged once more in Europe. Monarchs such as William the Conqueror of England and Philip Augustus of France strove to convert the fiction of royal power into a reality. For a time, at the apogee of medieval civilization, they had in fact tamed if not broken the feudal nobility. They had also expanded the territories under their own direct rule and begun the slow process of reassembling administrative machinery to govern their nations.

The medieval collapse of the fourteenth and earlier fifteenth centuries had brutally interrupted this slow evolution of the European nation-states. In the later fifteenth and sixteenth centuries, however, strong rulers took up the task of their medieval predecessors once more. Europe would remain a divided region, unlike such huge contemporary empires as Ming China and Mogul India. But some of the separate European nation-states would become aggressive political powers capable of challenging their larger imperial rivals around the world.

The new rulers who made this possible were the royal monopolists of power of the later 1400s and the 1500s, the "new monarchs" of the Renaissance.

Like the strong rulers of the Middle Ages, the new monarchs suppressed rebellions and brought ambitious nobles—"overmighty subjects," as they called them—sharply to heel. They sought to smother local autonomy under a blanket of nationwide royal power, exercised through centralized bureaucracies and hired armies of mercenaries. They asserted with renewed passion their medieval divine right to rule and bolstered it by comparing their authority to that of ancient Roman emperors.

The new monarchs found support for these efforts in the commercial cities that were the heart of the contemporary economic revival. As in the Middle Ages, the business communities of the towns believed that only centralized royal power could provide the peace and order within which business could flourish. Townsmen were therefore willing to pay taxes (within reason), provide trained officials, give legal recognition of royal authority, and generally underwrite the growth of central government once more. In later medieval deliberative bodies like the English Parliament, the French Estates General, and the Spanish *Cortes*, this upper-middle-class stratum of society joined the nobility and high churchmen in providing advice and voting funds for medieval monarchs.

Several generations of strong kings and queens were involved in this restoration of royal power in the major European nations. In England, there were Henry VII, Henry VIII, and the famous Queen Elizabeth; in France, Louis XI, Francis I, and Henry IV, the first Bourbon; in Spain, Ferdinand and Isabella, Charles V, and the great Philip II—to limit ourselves only to the most successful.

There were differences from country to country, as the following pages will indicate. In each case, however, the basic pattern was the same. All these nations experienced a rebuilding of centralized national political institutions under the aegis of royal claims to sovereignty. There was more behind Elizabeth's dazzling thousand gowns than the national wealth that paid for them. There was the political power that they represented—and that their shrewd display enhanced—as well.

FRANCE: THE SPIDER AND THE KNIGHT

The road to the restoration of royal power in France began, properly speaking, when Joan of Arc set the crown on the head of Charles VII at Reims in 1429, reaffirming the legitimacy of the French monarchy then reeling under English assault. The Hundred Years' War dragged on for another quarter of a century, however, and it was not till the accession of Louis XI (1461–1483) that royal authority really began to grow once more in the ravaged French nation.

King Louis, nicknamed "the Spider" for his Machiavellian intrigues, took up in the later fifteenth century the centralizing labors begun by Philip Augustus and Saint Louis in the thirteenth. Louis was superstitious, conniving, merciless, and so totally unchivalrous that he preferred bribing his enemies to besting them in the field. Nevertheless, he left France more powerful, wealthy, and unified than it had been since the High Middle Ages.

Louis's most famous struggle was with that archetypal overmighty subject, the chivalrous duke of Burgundy, Charles the Bold. Duke Charles was killed in battle by the Swiss, who were subsidized by the French king. By the end of his reign, Louis XI had brought almost all the major regions of modern France to heel.

Louis ignored other centers of power, such as the *parlements* (regional law courts) and the Estates General, France's embryonic Parliament, while laboring assidu-

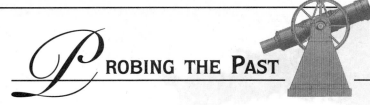

PROBING THE PAST

"To take the emancipation of women as a vantage point is to discover that events that further the historical development of men, liberating them from natural, social, or ideological constraints, have quite different, even opposite, effects upon women. The Renaissance is a good case in point. Italy was well in advance of the rest of Europe from roughly 1350 to 1530 because of its early consolidation of genuine states, the mercantile and manufacturing economy that supported them, and its working out of postfeudal and even postguild social relations. These developments reorganized Italian society along modern lines and opened the possibilities for the social and cultural expression for which the age is known. Yet precisely these developments affected women adversely, so much so that there was no renaissance for women—at least, not during the Renaissance. . . . Women as a group, especially among the classes that dominated Italian urban life, experienced a contraction of social and personal options that men of their classes . . . did not. . . . I found the following criteria most useful for gauging the relative contraction (or expansion) of the powers of Renaissance women and for determining the quality of their historical experience: (1) the regulation of female sexuality as compared with male sexuality; (2) women's economic and political roles, that is, the kind of work they performed as compared with men, and their access to property, political power, and the education or training necessary for work, property, and power; (3) the cultural roles of women in shaping the outlook of their society, and access to the education and/or institutions necessary for this; (4) ideology about women, in particular the sex-role system displayed or advocated in the symbolic products of the society, its art, literature, and philosophy.

Joan Kelly's classic essay, "Did Women Have a Renaissance?," well illustrates the new women's history, which frequently revises traditional views of the past. This excerpt outlines Kelly's challenge to the traditional belief that upper-class women at least were better educated, more influential, and more widely admired in the Renaissance than they had been earlier.

What do you think of the author's "criteria" for rating women's status and quality of life? Is it your impression that "female sexuality" has commonly been more restricted than male sexual activity? Are differences in the economic and political roles of the two sexes common in many societies? Can you think of any examples of "ideology"—here meaning commonly held beliefs—about women's "nature" in our own times?

Joan Kelly-Gadol, "Did Women Have a Renaissance?" in Renate Bridenthal, Claudia Koonz and Susan Stuard, eds., Becoming Visible: Women in European History, 2nd ed. (Boston: Houghton Mifflin, 1987), p. 176.

ously to make the central administration ever more efficient. Within his growing realm, he actively sought the support of the burghers of the towns by encouraging foreign trade and new industries and by appointing bourgeois advisers. The augmented wealth of the land filled the royal treasuries and paid for an expanded royal standing army, another source of strength for the monarchy.

No one wept when Louis the Spider died. But he left France strong enough to survive the crises that almost immediately confronted the nation.

The first of these problems was the long series of foreign wars that began in the 1490s and lasted through the 1550s. The great national enemy during this period was the powerful Austrian house of Habsburg—Holy

Roman Emperors of the Germanies, rulers of the Netherlands, kings of Spain, and a power in the Italian states. France's most celebrated royal champion in the half-century struggle that followed was Francis I (1515–1547), the most brilliant, knightly, and mercurial of French Renaissance rulers.

The dashing Francis fought four wars with the immensely powerful Habsburg Charles V, mostly over the wealth of Renaissance Italy, where both had dynastic claims. The wars cost both sides dearly in lives and treasure. But they did preserve France from encirclement by Habsburg power and established the basic frontiers of the French nation.

When he was not leading his armies on the battlefield or dallying with his mistresses, Francis I also directed the continued strengthening of France's central government. A natural autocrat, he increased the power of his royal council and centralized the royal revenues under a single treasury. By so doing, he helped prepare France for an even more brutal challenge than the Habsburg wars: the bloody religious civil wars of the second half of the century.

The wars of religion in France that raged from the 1560s through the 1590s were partly the result of sectarian passions unleashed by the Protestant Reformation, which triggered the initial clashes between the French Protestant sect called the Huguenots and the Catholic League. Rivalry for the tottering throne of France, however, led two ambitious noble houses to assume leadership of the two factions—the Guises of the Catholic extremists and the Bourbons of the Huguenots. Half a dozen civil wars laid the nation waste through the later sixteenth century.

A strong hand took control once more at the end of the sixteenth century when Henry IV restored the authority of the monarchy and founded the powerful Bourbon line. But the Bourbons had something to build on—the foundations of modern French power laid by Louis the Spider and Francis I.

SPAIN: THE GOLDEN CENTURY

Ferdinand and Isabella are best known to Americans as the sovereigns who financed Columbus. In Spanish history, however, they are the rulers who expelled the last of the Moorish conquerors of Spain, unified the country, and made the new kingdom one of the great powers of Europe.

The marriage of Ferdinand of Aragon and Isabella of Castile in 1469 led to the unification of the two largest portions of Spain, to which lesser territories were added by conquest during their reigns. By driving the last Muslims from Granada and using the notorious Spanish Inquisition to expel all Jews from the country, the "Catholic Kings," as they were called, strengthened the new nation by religious uniformity—though these brutal policies cost them some of their most industrious subjects. By assert-

ing Italian territorial claims, negotiating a French alliance, and marrying their children into the royal houses of England and the Holy Roman Empire, the founders of Spanish unity made their country perhaps the most powerful in Europe. And when, after long negotiations with Queen Isabella, Columbus sailed in 1492, he laid the foundations for a Spanish New World empire that would grow in the following century into the largest in the world.

The *siglo de oro* ("golden century"), as the sixteenth century is called in Spanish history, owed much of its glitter to that American empire. But subsequent Spanish monarchs Charles V (grandson of Ferdinand and Isabella) during the first half of the century and his son Philip II during the second half played central roles in European affairs as well.

Charles V (1516–1556), Holy Roman Emperor as well as king of Spain and lord of the Netherlands and large parts of Italy, Mexico, Peru, and other lands beyond the seas, was easily the most powerful of European rulers. His armies fought Turks, Protestants, and American Indians as well as his bitter rival Francis I of France. In pursuing his ambitious foreign policy, Charles strained the resources of even his vast empire.

Still, Charles V further strengthened the unity of Spain. Building on the royal council established by Ferdinand and Isabella, he created a structure of governing councils, which would grow to twelve in number under Philip II. All these Spanish sovereigns were hard-working rulers: they read reports, presided over councils, and decided government policies themselves rather than delegating authority to ministers of state. The policies they chose—especially their war policies—were not always wise. But Spain was more united and more rigorously governed for their labors.

Philip II (1556–1598) harbored even vaster ambitions. A fervent Catholic, he made Spain the sword and shield of the Counter-Reformation. He was also an autocrat by instinct, determined to impress his will on the enormous Spanish domains. The Spain of Philip II had the best armies in Europe and the largest revenues, especially from the Netherlands and the Americas. With the Spanish colossus towering over the West, it looked to rival rulers as if one of the European kings might at last lay a single hegemony upon the whole Western world.

It did not happen, however. The Protestant powers—the England of Elizabeth, the Huguenots in France, and Spain's rebellious Netherlands—allied themselves against Spain in a cause that was as much political as religious. Philip won some great victories, such as the naval battle of Lepanto against the Ottoman Turks, but his greatest military efforts led to defeats. His most famous naval expedition was the attempted invasion of England that climaxed in the humiliating destruction of the Spanish Armada in 1588. His attempt to crush the Protestant revolt in the Netherlands ended, after forty years of bloodshed, in the independence of the Dutch Republic in 1609.

The result of these long wars, furthermore, was to reduce the immensely wealthy Spanish Empire to poverty, to turn its ascendancy into decline. Spain's golden century ended, and from the seventeenth century on, the nation of Ferdinand and Isabella, Charles V, and Philip II was to be an apathetic backwater.

ENGLAND: BLUFF PRINCE HAL AND GOOD QUEEN BESS

Tudor England would become for later generations of English-speaking people the very incarnation of "merrie England." Bluff Prince Hal and Good Queen Bess—Henry VIII and Elizabeth I—are perhaps the best known of all British sovereigns. And for such homely things: every English schoolchild knows that Henry VIII had six wives and threw chicken bones on the floor, that Queen Elizabeth's courtiers spread expensive capes over mud puddles for her, and that the queen herself wore a bright orange wig! The travails of nations and the achievements of sovereigns are so easily replaced by trivia in the folk memory of peoples.

One of the most successful of the Tudors was the founder of the line, Henry VII (1485–1509)—about whom fewer folk memories survive. Shakespeare brought him on at the end of *Richard III* to bring a happy ending to the Wars of the Roses, England's late medieval civil war, by defeating his arch-villain Richard III. In the light of later scholarship, Richard looks less like a villain, and Henry less a military hero and much more the architect of Tudor England's domestic tranquility and prosperity.

After his victory at Bosworth in 1485, the first Tudor monarch determinedly avoided further military adventures. Instead, he signed trade treaties advancing the cause of English commerce. He furthered domestic peace—and defended the Tudor dynasty—by firmly suppressing a number of rather inefficient conspiracies aimed at reopening the Wars of the Roses. In general, he maintained the "splendid isolation" from European entanglements that was to become England's peacetime trademark.

Henry VII, like the new monarchs elsewhere in Europe, strengthened royal power, using a large royal council and a system of local magistrates called justices of the peace to govern the country. His parliaments were amenable to royal influence, and Henry was his own first minister. When he died, he left the treasury full, the nation at peace, and a popular prince to rule after him as Henry VIII.

Henry VIII (1509–1547), far more famous than his father, is seen by many historians as rather less successful as a ruler. He gave over his earlier years to fun and frolic, hunting, wenching, and an occasional war. He left the real affairs of government during those youthful years to one of the most powerful royal ministers in English history, the intelligent and arrogant Cardinal Wolsey. The latter half of the reign was filled with more serious business for the aging monarch: more wars, the Reformation, and an increasingly desperate effort to provide an heir for the English throne. The wars were, as always, costly. The decision to take Reformation England out of the Roman church—because the pope refused to grant the king a politically necessary divorce—divided the nation religiously. And Henry's six marriages not only failed to produce a healthy male heir but were almost all personal disasters as well.

Yet Henry VIII lived in English memory as a powerful and even admired ruler. This was partly due to the labors of others. Wolsey in the first half of the reign managed affairs with some success. An innovative official named Thomas Cromwell strengthened and professionalized the royal bureaucracy during the 1530s. But Henry VIII himself contributed to the growth of central government by making use of Parliament as often as he could, especially when he was establishing his authority as head of the Protestant church in England. The Parliament, a bicameral assembly of burghers, gentry, and noblemen, was traditionally summoned to vote on taxes. But Parliament also passed laws and sought to influence royal policies—a practice that would have crucial consequences in the next century.

Queen Elizabeth I (1558–1603), finally, was the new monarch par excellence, arguably the most successful of any Renaissance ruler. Of all periods of English history, the Elizabethan Age still kindles the warmest feelings in English hearts.

Princess Elizabeth, a slender, athletic, extremely intelligent young woman, received an ideal Renaissance education in Latin, Greek, and modern languages, in history and Scripture. As Henry VIII's second eldest child, shunted back to third in line for the throne by the complex politics of the period, she also had a very practical education in political intrigue—and the fine art of political survival. She came in 1558 to a royal throne shaken by a decade of misgovernment, religious fanaticism, and economic problems. She proceeded to give England forty-five years of strong government, moderate religious policies, and unexampled prosperity.

Elizabeth was a prudent ruler, avoiding costly wars, seeking religious compromise rather than religious crusades, working through her appointed ministers, and dealing firmly with an increasingly vocal Parliament. She was well served by lifelong royal counselors such as Lord Treasurer Burghley and veteran warriors such as Sir Francis Drake. She was less well supported by dashing younger cavaliers such as the Earl of Essex and Sir Walter Raleigh, whose ardent ambitions got in the way of common sense. Elizabeth herself preferred guile to force. She was a past mistress of public relations, alternately charming and terrifying her friends and her enemies, her ministers, courtiers, and subjects.

The later years of Elizabeth's long reign were graced by a scintillating galaxy of poets and playwrights,

Queen Elizabeth I, looking every inch the Renaissance monarch—something she did very well. This famous "Armada Portrait" by Marcus Gheeraerts is dense with the symbols of the great queen's wealth (jewels, lace, and velvet), royal power (the crown at the left, her hand resting on the great globe itself), and historic accomplishment (the sinking of the Spanish Armada, shown in the picture, upper right). Do modern political leaders also like to project pictorial images associating them with symbols of power and victory? (George Gower [1540–96]. "Elizabeth I—The Armada Portrait." The Bridgeman Art Library)

of whom Shakespeare was only the best known. But these years—the 1580s and 1590s—also saw increasing political intrigue at court. Moreover, religious extremism, both Protestant and Catholic, emerged in the nation, and the exhausting conflict with Philip II at last drew England into the wars of religion.

Religious extremists found Elizabeth hard to live with, and young men eager for war called her timid. But they called her Gloriana to her face. The whole nation was dazzled by her splendid court and costumes and cowed by the stamp of an indignant royal foot. And she has been Good Queen Bess ever since—England's greatest and best-loved ruler.

THE RENAISSANCE OF WESTERN ART

THE HUMANIST MOVEMENT

Genuine golden ages are often times of violent conflict; the age of Confucius was also the age of the Warring States in ancient China, and the Periclean Greeks seem to have been almost constantly at war. Golden ages are also not infrequently materialistic times, much concerned with getting and spending the wealth that pays for their culture. Nor are ethical standards always at their highest during such periods, as our own artistically and scientifically brilliant yet morally bewildered century makes clear.

The European Renaissance was as violent, materialistic, and morally questionable as any of the above. But it did leave a cultural legacy that would shape the intellectual and artistic life of the West for the next three centuries at least.

The word *renaissance* means "rebirth," and the age was so called by it's own leading intellectual lights, the classical scholars of Renaissance Italy. They thought of their era as one of cultural rebirth, a revival of the wisdom and art of what was for them Europe's greatest age—the ancient world of Periclean Greece and Augustan Rome. The legacy of ancient Rome especially enthralled them. They did a splendid job of imbuing Renaissance culture with Latin literature and Roman history and mythology. Indeed, it is almost impossible to read Renaissance literature or look at much Renaissance art without some knowledge of ancient Rome.

The study of classical culture, in contrast with the study of things divine, was known in the Renaissance as *humanism*. The men who began to read the Latin classics seriously again after a thousand years were called humanists. They were a varied lot of classical scholars—teachers and writers, poets and philosophers, pious Christians and libertines. The first of them, the fourteenth-century Italian poet Petrarch, wrote Renaissance love poems and medieval meditations on death with equal enthusiasm. The most famous sixteenth-century humanist, Erasmus, was equally admired for his editions of the New Testament and for his worldly satires on every aspect of Renaissance life, including the sins of organized religion.

The humanists as a group performed one great service for the modern West. They recovered much of our Western heritage of ancient Greek and Latin literature, lost and moldering in forgotten corners of obscure monastic libraries, unhonored and unread. They also attempted, with more modest success, to "civilize" the sword-swinging medieval nobility by a strong infusion of ancient culture. They did not produce the race of Platonic philosopher-kings they hoped for. But they did produce the first really literate aristocracy Europe had had for ten centuries—a first step at least toward matching the more cultivated courtier classes of the Muslim East or China's Confucian scholar-bureaucrats.

Perhaps the most celebrated product of humanist studies was Niccolo Machiavelli, the founder of modern political thought. Machiavelli, well read in Latin literature and history, was also an experienced Florentine diplomat. He fused his knowledge of past and present statecraft in one of the most famous of Renaissance books: *The Prince*. This shrewd, cynical, and brutally realistic commentary on the political style of Renaissance rulers has made the name Machiavelli synonymous with devious political intrigue ever since.

ART IN THE AGE OF LEONARDO AND MICHELANGELO

In some areas, Renaissance culture was neither a rebirth nor a revival, but an original creation of the highest order. Among these areas of artistic innovation, Renaissance painting stands out—particularly when we compare it with the brilliant but clearly derivative development of Renaissance architecture and sculpture.

Renaissance Italian architecture was strongly influenced by the Roman ruins that seemed to be everywhere. The architects had no use for the barbarous style of architecture they were the first to call "Gothic." Instead, Brunelleschi's fifteenth-century dome on the cathedral at Florence and Michelangelo's sixteenth-century one on Saint Peter's in Rome are both modeled on the dome of the Roman Pantheon built by the Caesars.

Renaissance sculpture also showed powerful classical influences. Michelangelo, who called himself a sculptor, learned his trade from Roman statuary, and his own early works included Bacchuses and satyrs. His mature statues of *David* and *Moses*—big-boned, heavy-muscled, with strong features hacked out of the marble—are Old Testament figures, but they look more like Greek or Roman heroes than medieval saints.

Renaissance painting, however, was unique to the age that produced it. No doubt this is partly because there was simply no ancient painting available for copying at that time. But Renaissance painting was also an expression of the creativity of that turbulent time. The epoch that discovered new continents, initiated the Scientific Revolution, and spawned the Reformation was almost bound to produce some striking breakthroughs in the arts as well.

The essence of the Renaissance revolution in the graphic arts was what Renaissance painters themselves frequently called *life-likeness*. Fidelity to nature, or Renaissance naturalism, meant reproducing what the eye actually saw as convincingly as possible. To this end, the artists of the time developed new techniques that would become standard in art schools from that day on. Detailed sketches from nature, study of shadows and highlights, attention to pose, costume, and setting, concealing of brushstrokes, revealing character—all were part of the new approach. The science of perspective became a mania with some Renaissance artists. And anatomically accurate figure drawing—the special achievement of Renaissance painting—became a necessity.

Yet each Renaissance painter had his own distinctive style. They were towering individualists all, and it is their uniquenesses and eccentricities of treatment that define their greatness.

Leonardo da Vinci, the eternally restless, many-sided Renaissance mind, was as interested in science and

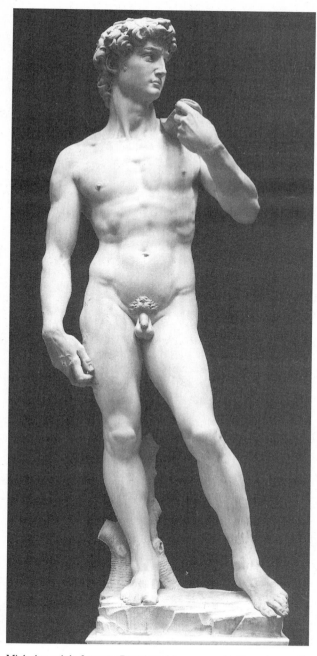

Michelangelo's famous <u>David</u>, looking as much like a hero of classical myth as like a biblical shepherd boy. Michelangelo's Renaissance immersion in the Greco-Roman tradition, his sixteenth-century spirituality, and his awesome skill with a chisel all show in this gigantic statue. Note particularly the powerful hands, the watchful glance, the realistically rendered musculature, and the thoroughly conventionalized hair. (Art Resource)

mechanical inventions as he was in art. Experimenting endlessly with everything from pigments to composition, he has left us only a handful of finished paintings.

Leonardo's mural of *The Last Supper* depicts the disciples turning toward each other, hands, features, angle of head and trunk expressing their horror as the terrible question runs round the table: "Is it *I* who will betray my Lord?" His portrait of a distinguished patron's wife, the *Mona Lisa*, is perhaps the most famous Western painting in existence. The endlessly debated Mona Lisa smile illustrates one of Leonardo's most delicate and distinctive techniques, the use of "smoky" shadows to define the subtle modeling of the lady's cheeks.

Michelangelo Buonarotti may have thought of himself as a shaper of stone above all, but his paintings on the ceiling of the Sistine Chapel in the Vatican—recently restored to their original brightness—have earned him a place among the greatest painters as well. These scenes from Genesis, running from the Creation of the world to the story of the Flood, are a long parade of heroic Renaissance figures, their heavy limbs and bulging muscles far larger than life size. The most famous of all these scenes is the moment when a white-bearded Jehovah reaches out to pass the gift of life into the limp finger of a just-created Adam—a figure handsome enough to double for Apollo in any classical fresco. That moment in pigment on the Sistine ceiling, combining ancient and medieval inspirations in a uniquely Renaissance way, has for centuries defined the creation of the race in the imagination of Western humanity.

Raphael's seraphic Madonnas and Titian's Renaissance portraits, many of them with the burnished, copper-colored "Titian hair," are also part of our artistic legacy from the Renaissance in Italy. The meticulous bourgeois realism of the Dutch school of Jan and Hubert van Eyck, who produced thoroughly believable portraits of thoroughly believable businessmen, belongs to the artistic heritage of those centuries too. So do Peter Paul Rubens's lush pink goddesses and swirling composition, and the Spanish paintings of El Greco, with their flamelike elongated heads and sour colors.

For the next three hundred years, from 1600 to 1900, Western artists would accept the standards and imitate the techniques of the Renaissance masters. Even on a global scale, the work these masters produced at the dawn of modern history is fit to stand with that of any age and continent.

LITERATURE IN THE AGE OF SHAKESPEARE

The innovative, creative spirit that infused Renaissance art also shaped Renaissance literature.

Literature in the living languages of modern Europe appeared in substantial quantities for the first time during these centuries. The influence of Latin literary forms, Roman mythology, and even the ideas and styles of ancient writers was present in these Italian, French, English, and other literatures. But new forms, new stylistic devices, and great writers of daunting originality flourished in these Renaissance national literatures as well.

Italy, which led Europe into the new age in so many other areas, also had its share of literary pioneers. Francesco Petrarch, the first humanist, was one of the early masters of poetry in the Italian tongue. His collection of love poems, collected as *Sonnets to Laura*, was set to music and sung in Italian taverns during his own lifetime and influenced Renaissance poetry in a number of languages for two hundred years thereafter. His fourteenth-century contemporary Giovanni Boccaccio produced in the *Decameron* perhaps the most famous short-story collection in Western history. In particular the bawdy tales among them were read, enjoyed, and imitated throughout Europe.

Sixteenth-century France produced a number of famous writers in the French language, but none so celebrated as the risqué Rabelais and the profound and skeptical Montaigne. François Rabelais, a former monk, wrote a single unique work of fiction, the multivolume adventures of the most famous of giants, *Gargantua,* and his son *Pantagruel.* Their raw and gaudy adventures satirized all aspects of Renaissance life, including the monasteries from which the author had fled. Michel de Montaigne, a cultivated Renaissance gentleman of the later sixteenth century, invented a whole new literary form to express his thoughts on life and the world—the essay. His three volumes of *Essays* on everything from friendship and education to cannibals and coaches were full of quotes from the wise ancients, but fuller still of the coolly penetrating insights of Michel de Montaigne.

A final flowering of Renaissance literature came in the last two decades of the sixteenth century and the early years of the century that followed, in the England of Elizabeth. The "nest of singing birds" of later Elizabethan times included poets and playwrights such as Edmund Spenser, Sir Philip Sidney, Christopher Marlowe, and of course William Shakespeare.

Spenser's long epic poem *The Faerie Queene* and Sidney's "novel" *Arcadia* mixed medieval knights, classical mythology, magic, adventure, love, and deeper allegorical and symbolic meaning in uniquely Renaissance literary productions. Christopher Marlowe, the Elizabethan bohemian who died young in a tavern brawl, wrote the most admired English plays before Shakespeare. His *Tamburlaine the Great, Doctor Faustus,* and other heroes are all giants of ambition, aspiring to more than human achievements—and struck down like their creator for their arrogant presumption.

William Shakespeare is generally regarded as the most prodigious talent ever to write in English. His three dozen plays—*Richard III, A Midsummer Night's Dream, Romeo and Juliet, Julius Caesar, Macbeth, Hamlet, King Lear, The Tempest,* and the rest—have enriched the Western imagination with a galaxy of living characters. And if you are asked to identify a "familiar quotation," guess Shakespeare and the odds are you will be right, for his poetry has become part of the language. His plots are borrowed, his ideas seldom original, but his words are often perfect, and his characters are still the greatest challenge any actor can face. Will Shakespeare's work, said his friend and fellow playwright Ben Jonson, was "not of an age, but for all time!"[1] So far this estimate has proved accurate: More than three and a half centuries after his death, Shakespeare's plays are still on view any night of the year in the great cities of the English-speaking world.

THE REFORMATION OF RELIGION

THE DECLINE OF THE WESTERN CHURCH

The Renaissance began in the fourteenth century and ended somewhere in the sixteenth. But during the sixteenth century it overlapped with another major subdivision of Western history, the Reformation. This great upheaval in the Christian church began not in Italy but in Germany and spread rapidly across northern Europe. The Protestant revolt produced some powerful religious ideas, kindled a great Catholic Counter-Reformation, and led to a wave of terrible religious wars. It is sometimes referred to as Europe's last great age of faith—the last time Western people were willing to die, and to kill, in large numbers for their religious beliefs.

The powerful personality of Martin Luther, the German monk who started it all, looms over the Reformation. Yet it is sometimes said that if Martin Luther had never lived, some sort of reformation of religion must nevertheless have taken place. For the Roman Catholic church was in deep need of reform long before Luther nailed his Ninety-Five Theses to the church door in Wittenberg in 1517.

The Roman church was still wallowing in the aftermath of its great late-medieval collapse as the sixteenth century began. The Babylonian Captivity—the period when the popes lived at Avignon and were widely regarded as tools of the French kings—and the Great Schism—which produced two and then three claimants to Saint Peter's seat—had left the papacy badly demoralized. The popes of the later fifteenth and early sixteenth centuries were more concerned with Renaissance art, humanistic literature, Italian politics, and luxurious living than they were with religion. They were members of worldly, ambitious families such as the Florentine Medici and the Spanish Borgias. The Borgia pope Alexander VI, and especially his son Cesare and his daughter Lucrezia, made

---

[1]Ben Jonson, "To . . . Mr. William Shakespeare: And what he hath left us," in Shakespeare's *Complete Works*, ed. Hardin Craig (Chicago: Scott, Foresman and Company, 1961), p. 48.

Martin Luther, in a picture by the celebrated German artist Lucas Cranach. Something of the warmth and geniality of Luther's later years show here, but there is still the haunted look of the young Luther about the eyes, a hint of the spiritual torment in which the Protestant Reformation was born. Contrast the simple air and clothing of the founder of the Reformation with the worldly splendor of Renaissance rulers like Queen Elizabeth—and of Catholic Counter-Reformation churches like St. Peter's. (New York Public Library Picture Collection)

the papacy a springboard for a series of military campaigns, intrigues, and even murders that shocked Europe. The Medici pope Leo X, a son of Lorenzo the Magnificent, is reputed to have greeted the news of his accession with an exultant "God has given us the papacy—let us enjoy it!"[2]

Worldliness and corruption seemed to many to have infected all levels of the church. Simony (buying and selling of offices), nepotism (appointment of relatives to office), clerical concubinage, clerical ignorance, pleasure-loving monks, and high-living cardinals all made ecclesiastical corruption a byword in Europe—and a stench in the nostrils of the pious.

This decadence had stimulated a number of revolts during the century before Luther came on the scene. Jan Hus in the Holy Roman Empire, John Wycliffe in England, Girolamo Savonarola in Italy, and other popular preachers and reformers had defied the Church in the fif-

teenth century. All had been stigmatized as heretics; all had died for their beliefs.

Then came Luther.

MARTIN LUTHER: HERE I STAND

Martin Luther (1483–1546) was a disturbed young man when he entered the Augustinian order of monks in the summer of 1505. Raised by pious middle-class German parents in the duchy of Saxony, he turned his back on law school and entered the cloisters in the grip of a full-fledged religious crisis.

Like other deeply believing Christians of his time, young Luther was convinced that he was a sinner, hated by God, doomed to hellfire. The Church taught that two things earned a person salvation: faith in Christ and a life of Christian good works. Luther tried a number of Christian works. Entering a monastery was a great work of Christian commitment. He also confessed his sins repeatedly, mortified the flesh with fasting and flagellation, and in the service of his order undertook a pilgrimage to Rome, where he was duly horrified by the worldliness of the papal court and cardinals. He remained, however, convinced of his own sinfulness, his own damnation.

Seeking a deeper understanding of Christian faith, the unhappy monk had meanwhile become a professor of theology, lecturing on Scripture at the University of Wittenberg. He found himself increasingly dissatisfied not only with the official doctrine of salvation through faith *and* works, but with such Church practices as worship of the relics of saints and the sale of indulgences—papal pardons for sins—to raise money for the Church's good works.

In the mid-1510s Martin Luther's rebellious spirit boiled over. While preparing lectures on Saint Paul, he at last found certainty of his own salvation in a new doctrine: belief in salvation through *faith alone*, rather than faith and works. This belief became the cornerstone of Protestantism. Then in 1517, Luther launched the Reformation itself by publicly proposing Ninety-Five Theses (arguments) against the efficacy of purchased indulgences.

The rest of Luther's tumultuous life grew from these two challenges to orthodoxy. He developed other radical doctrines. The only certain source of religious truth, he said, was the Bible—not the Bible plus the accumulated wisdom of popes, Church councils, and Church tradition. Priests had no special powers: all true believers were priests and had as much direct access to God as clergymen could claim. The Roman pope, he finally dared to declare, had no control over him or anyone else: the pope had usurped power; he was, in fact, the Antichrist foretold of old.

When defenders of the orthodox faith spoke or wrote against him, Luther confuted them in print or in public debate. When Pope Leo X at last excommunicated the troublesome German monk, the rebel publicly burned the bull of excommunication. When a council called at

[2]S. Harrison Thompson, *Europe in Renaissance and Reformation* (New York: Harcourt, Brace, and World, 1963), p. 453.

Worms by the Holy Roman Emperor Charles V outlawed him, Luther answered that he could not compromise his principles: "Here I stand—I cannot do otherwise."[3]

It was a road of defiance taken by more than one doomed heretic before him. But Luther found many supporters for his rebellion—not all of them impelled by purely religious motives. There were German princes eager to get their hands on the wealth of the German church. There were those who sought to use Luther's crusade to justify their own revolt against the Holy Roman Emperor. There were nationalistic noblemen and knights, angry that German money was building Roman churches or lining the pockets of Italian churchmen. There were peasants who used Luther's name to support their insurrections against the out-of-date manorial exactions imposed upon them by their lords.

Luther accepted the support of German princes and noblemen, rejected that of peasants, and miraculously came through unscathed. Lutheran churches were set up in many North German states, then in Scandinavia. Henry VIII, after authoring an early tract against the Lutheran heresy, took England's religious establishment out of the Roman church for political reasons—and made himself its head. Religious turmoil spread through Europe, and it looked for a while as though all Roman Catholic Christendom might revolt against the pope.

The mature Luther was a barrel of a man, the gaunt cheeks of his tortured youth comfortably padded by the solid German meals prepared by the nun he married. Earthy and eloquent, equally skillful at writing hymns, theological treatises, polemical invective against his foes, and translations of Holy Writ, he was a powerful propagandist for his cause. Absolutely convinced of his own rightness and righteousness, he epitomized the ideological true believer of modern times. Like Robespierre in the French Revolution or Lenin in the Russian one, Luther made his ideas a force in modern history.

JOHN CALVIN: BUILDING THE NEW JERSUALEM

The most famous reformer of the generation after Luther was John Calvin of Geneva (1509–1564), who rose to eminence in the 1530s. Calvin was a very different sort of person from Martin Luther. A cultivated Frenchman, trained in humanism and law as well as theology, Calvin was more famous for his lucid logic and shrewd organizing mind than for eloquence or passion. With his thin face, hollow eyes, and long goat beard, he came much closer to the popular image of the religious fanatic than the hearty German monk did.

In the city-state of Geneva in the Swiss Alps, Calvin set up a Protestant theocracy and preached a militant faith

that inspired Protestants all over Europe. His doctrines differed from Luther's more in emphasis than in substance. Calvin put special stress on the omnipotence of God. He set the predestination of each human soul to heaven or hell at the center of his theology. His theocratic state of Geneva was dominated by the Calvinist pastors, and the pastors in turn by the iron will of John Calvin. His great book, the *Institutes of the Christian Religion*, was read by Protestants everywhere, and his Geneva became the sixteenth-century Protestant ideal of a Christian community.

Life in Geneva was rigorous, filled with sermons and narrowly restricted by puritanical moral legislation. Calvin's theology was inflexible, a grim vision of a world divided into the saved and the damned, with the pope as Antichrist and Calvinist Protestants as the builders of a new Jerusalem on earth. This view, and the fervor it produced, became the crusading faith of religious revolutionaries all across Europe. It spread to the Huguenots in France and to the Dutch Reformed church in the rebellious Netherlands, to English Puritans and Scottish Presbyterians. It would leave a mark as deep as Luther's on Protestantism, both in northern Europe and in the New England colonies of America.

The long-range impact of Calvinism extended even beyond the sphere of religion. Calvinism may have inspired the taut, rigorous drive that made Calvinist Huguenots and Puritans the most successful businessmen in France and England, respectively. Calvinist religiosity may thus have been an important cause of the growth of capitalism in the West.

Because of their opposition to popes, archbishops, and bishops in the Church, Calvinists frequently opposed hierarchy in the state as well. Calvinism could thus be seen as an influence on the emergence of democracy in the Netherlands, in England, and in the New England colonies. Through colonial town meetings and elected assemblies, Calvinism may even have contributed to the birth of the American republic two centuries later.

In his own time, however, John Calvin was a prophet of religious revolt, and it is as such that he looms largest in Western history.

THE CATHOLIC REFORMATION

The Roman Catholic church, meanwhile, had mounted a massive Reformation of its own. Led by a pious new breed of pope, the Church launched a powerful counterattack against the Protestant revolt that had already carried the North German states, England, and Scandinavia out of the Roman fold.

The organizer of the Counter-Reformation was Pope Paul III (1534–1549). During his pontificate the papal court was reformed and Catholic reformers gained commanding positions in the Church, from which they and their successors were able to guide the Catholic Reformation for the rest of the century.

---

[3]Roland H. Bainton, *Here I Stand: A Life of Martin Luther* (New York: New American Library, 1950), p. 144.

St. Peter's cathedral in Rome, looking much as it does today, in a painting by Giovanni Panini. The Counter-Reformation attempt to awe Christians into a renewal of faith in the Roman Catholic church by the sheer splendor of its architecture is nowhere better illustrated than in St. Peter's. The painting itself reveals the powerful continuing influence of the Renaissance passion for perspective. (Giovanni Paolo Panini, "Interior of St. Peter's. Rome" Canvas, 60-3/4 × 77-1/2 [1.544 × 1.970] National Gallery of Art, Washington, D.C. Alisa Mellon Bruce Fund 1968)

To deal with the Protestant threat more directly, Pope Paul refurbished the medieval Inquisition and established the board of censors known as the Index of Forbidden Books. He also recognized a militant new order, the Society of Jesus. This order of friars was organized in 1540 by a former Spanish knight—and future saint—named Ignatius Loyola. The Jesuits, as the friars were known, were to become the Church's most militant agents, the shock troops of the Counter-Reformation, as well as one of the greatest missionary orders in Church history.

Pope Paul also called the Council of Trent, one of the most important of all Church councils, which met off and on for twenty years during the 1540s, 1550s, and 1560s. The Council of Trent carried the reforming impulse from the papal center to the Catholic church as a whole. Decrees of the council provided stiff penalties for immorality and corruption among the clergy. The council founded new seminaries in order to create a better-educated priesthood. Trent also reaffirmed the traditional Catholic views on all the theological points the Protestants had challenged. From Trent, then, the Roman church entered the second half of the century better prepared for battle and full of renewed fervor for the fray.

THE WARS OF RELIGION

The result of the clash of religious sects was a bloody period in European history. These wars of religion brought the age of the Reformation to a violent climax.

Europe's religious wars began in the early 1500s with revolts such as the Protestant Peasants' War in Germany and the Catholic Pilgrimage of Grace in Henry VIII's England. They petered out in the early 1600s in the Thirty Years' War in central Europe and the English Puritan Revolution. The height of violence, however, occurred from the 1560s to the early 1600s. During this period, the Dutch Revolt pitted Calvinist Protestants against Spanish Catholics, the wars of religion in France set Huguenots against the Catholic League, and the Anglo-Spanish naval war blazed from the English Channel to the Spanish colonies in the New World.

During the great religious wars of the latter half of the sixteenth century, the religious passions of Luther's and Calvin's day exploded in decades of propaganda broadsides, revolutions, wars, atrocities, and assassinations. Protestant mobs vandalized and sometimes looted Catholic cathedrals. The Inquisition broke and burned human bodies. Luther was willing to execute Anabaptists—the radical fringe of the Protestant movement—and Calvin to martyr the religious eccentric Servetus. But Protestant violence was more than matched by the long-established repressive machinery of the Roman church.

By the early 1600s on the Continent and the middle of the century in Puritan England, the fires of religious zeal kindled by Luther a century before had burned themselves out. Europeans turned from fruitless crusades to secular state building and modern science. The second half

The legend:
- Lutheran
- Anglican
- Calvinist Control or Influence
- Anabaptist
- Roman Catholic
- Eastern Border of Western Christianity

300 MILES

300 KILOMETERS

of the seventeenth century would be the Age of Louis XIV—and of Isaac Newton.

THE WORLD HAD A PROBLEM

The age of the Renaissance and Reformation—to give it its full name—was a tumultuous time for Europeans. Europe, recovered from the collapse of late medieval times, was wealthy—and hungering for more. The kingdoms of the West were strong, contentious, armed, and dangerous. The Reformations, Protestant and Catholic, had rekindled the crusading Christian faith of the High Middle Ages.

The rest of the world, blissfully unaware of the powerhouse that was building up at the western end of Eurasia, went on with its own getting and spending, its own wars and politics, its own artistic and religious impulses. But by 1500 the West was already reaching out. The Europeans were already appearing among other peoples around the globe. They offered their goods for sale on the rialtos of western India. They thrust deeper into the islands and forests of the New World, swords in one hand and crosses in the other. The world, though it did not know it yet, had a problem on its hands: the rise of the West.

SUMMARY

Money, politics, art, and religion all exhibited a renewed dynamism in the Europe of the Renaissance and Reformation.

During the fourteenth and fifteenth centuries in Italy, the later fifteenth and sixteenth centuries in Europe north of the Alps, the European commercial economy bloomed once more. Recovering from the wars, plagues, and depression of later medieval times, Renaissance trade made immense fortunes for business families like the Medici of Florence. The Renaissance business revival also completed the work of the commercial revolution of the High Middle Ages in laying the foundations of the dynamic capitalist economy of modern Europe.

Royal power also revived during these early modern centuries. Italian Renaissance despots and the "new monarchs" of other European nations took up the work of building strong central governments for the major European powers. Louis the Spider and chivalric Francis I in France, Ferdinand and Isabella and Philip II in Spain, Henry VII, Henry VIII, and Queen Elizabeth in England all helped build powerful nations in western Eurasia.

Renaissance art and literature established cultural patterns that would influence Western culture through most of modern history. From da Vinci to Shakespeare, they would provide models and inspirations for painters and poets for the next three or four centuries.

The Protestant Reformation and the Catholic Counter-Reformation, finally, revitalized Western Christianity, though at considerable cost in Western lives. Militant Protestant reformers like Luther and rigorous Puritans like Calvin successfully challenged the accumulated abuses of the Catholic church. The popes responded by reforms—and a renewed militance—of their own. The religious conflicts that resulted ravaged Europe through the later sixteenth century and left Western Christendom divided between a Catholic south and a Protestant north.

All told, this brilliant, bloody age generated a renewed European vitality that contributed powerfully to the wave of overseas empire building that also began during this era of Western rebirth.

SUGGESTED READING

ASCH, R. G., and A. M. BIRKE. *Princes, Patronage, and Nobility: The Court at the Beginning of the Modern Age c. 1450–1650.* London: Oxford University Press, 1991. Solid collection of essays on this undervalued but key political institution.

BAINTON, R. H. *Here I Stand: A Life of Martin Luther.* New York: New American Library, 1978. Standard, scholarly, clearly written, with a strong sense of the times. See also J. D. Tracy, ed., *Luther and the Modern State in Germany* (Kirksville, Mo.: Sixteenth Century Journal, 1986), a collection of recent essays on the political implications and consequences of Luther's ideas.

BERENSON, B. *The Italian Painters of the Renaissance.* Ithaca, N.Y.: Cornell University Press, 1980. Seminal studies by the founder of modern connoisseurship. For a more recent overview, see J. Beck, *Italian Painting of the Renaissance* (New York: Harper & Row, Pub., 1981).

BOUWSMA, W. J. *John Calvin: A Sixteenth Century Portrait.* New York: Oxford University Press, 1988. Sees the Reformation leader as a divided personality, reflecting the deep cultural divisions of his century.

BRAUDEL, F. *Capitalism and Material Life, 1400–1800.* New York: Harper & Row, Pub., 1973. A trailblazing French historian's stimulating account of the economic realities of the earlier modern West.

BRUCKER, G. A. *Renaissance Florence,* rev. ed. Berkeley: University of California Press, 1983. Government, politics, and the social order. See also H. Baron's classic study of the relations between Renaissance humanism and politics, *The Crisis of the Early Italian Renaissance: Civic Humanism and Republican Liberty in the Age of Classicism and Tyranny* (Princeton: Princeton University Press, 1966).

DAVIES, R. T. *The Golden Century of Spain, 1501–1621.* New York: Macmillan, 1954. Old but standard history of Spain when it was the greatest power in the Western world. For a student-oriented summary of the latest findings, see A. W. Lovett, *Early Habsburg Spain, 1517–1598* (New York: Oxford University Press, 1987).

DICKENS, A. G. *The Counter-Reformation.* New York: Norton, 1979. Solid, vividly illustrated survey.

EISENSTEIN, E. L. *The Printing Press as an Agent of Change in Early Modern Europe* (2 vols.). Cambridge: Cambridge University Press, 1980. Challenging assertion of the larger cultural impact of printing.

ELTON, G. R. *The Tudor Revolution in Government.* Cambridge: Cambridge University Press, 1959. Much debated, pioneering study of governmental changes in one of the most important of the "new monarchies."

GOLDSTONE, J. A. *Revolution and Rebellion in the Early Modern World.* Berkeley: University of California Press, 1991. Thoughtful study of major upheavals from Europe to Asia.

HOGREFE, P. *Tudor Women: Commoners and Queens.* Ames: Iowa State University Press, 1975. Profiles of women of the English Renaissance, from the guilds to the court.

KRISTELLER, P. O. *Renaissance Thought: The Classic, Scholastic, and Humanist Strains.* New York: Harper & Row, Pub., 1961. One of a number of collections of papers by a leading authority on Renaissance intellectual history.

MATTINGLY, G. *Renaissance Diplomacy.* Baltimore: Penguin, 1964. Standard account of the evolution of interstate relations in Europe at the beginning of modern history.

MONTAIGNE, M. *Selections from the Essays*, trans. D. M. Frame. Arlington Heights, Ill.: Harlan Davidson, 1973. A chance to browse through one of the finest minds of the Renaissance.

NEALE, J. E. *Queen Elizabeth I.* New York: Doubleday, 1957. Still the best life of Britain's most famous ruler.

OZMENT, S. *When Fathers Ruled: Family Life in Reformation Europe.* Cambridge: Harvard University Press, 1983. Sees companionate marriage and warm family life in the age of the Reformation; part of the ongoing debate over marriage and family life in earlier modern history.

SHAKESPEARE, W. *The Complete Works of Shakespeare*, ed. Hardin Craig. Chicago: Scott, Foresman, 1961. The finest writer in English brings the beginning of the modern age to life. His Renaissance men and women, even when they are disguised as ancient Romans or medieval kings, speak with the lusty voices of his age.

SPITZ, L. W. *The Protestant Reformation, 1517–1559.* New York: Harper & Row, Pub., 1985. Old-fashioned narrative history, stressing the contributions of Luther and other leading personalities. A. McGrath, *The Intellectual Origins of the European Reformation* (New York: Basil Blackwell, 1987), emphasizes continuity between late medieval and Reformation religious thought. H. J. Hillerbrand, ed., *Radical Tendencies in the Reformation: Divergent Perspectives* (Kirksville, Mo.: Sixteenth Century Journal, 1988) offers a useful collection of papers on the social dimensions of the radical Reformation, by East German and American scholars.

CHAPTER 26

THE MUSLIM EMPIRES

THE ABODE OF ISLAM

THE MUSLIM WORLD: FROM TIMBUKTU TO MALACCA

Europe in 1500 had a truly amazing future. But the present, and indeed the immediate future as well, belonged to Europe's far more powerful neighbor, the vast "Muslim center" of the Old World.[1]

The Arab prophet Muhammad (570?–632) had called himself the Messenger of God. The message he preached of salvation through submission (*Islam* in Arabic) to the will of God (*Allah*) had spread far across Eurasia and Africa by 1500. The mosque and the minaret, the Koran, the Muslim Law, and mystic Sufi holy men were found everywhere from West Africa to Southeast Asia, from the steppes of Russia to the Indian Ocean. It was a vast terrain, almost four times as far from end to end as Europe was and well worth a brief geographical survey before we turn to its history.

The heart of the Islamic world was in the Middle East, where civilization itself had been born. The chief Muslim holy city was Mecca, in Arabia, where Muhammad had first preached. The splendid capitals of the medieval Arab Empire had been Damascus and Baghdad, the capitals of Syria and Iraq, respectively, today. The mountains and plateaus of Turkey, Iran, and Afghanistan were Muslim too, as were the dry steppes of central Asia. Much of the history of Islam before and after 1500 took place in this area of desert and oases, chilly uplands and stubbly grasslands.

In Africa, ancient Egypt, the fertile strip along the Mediterranean shore, and the sun-bleached Sahara were all Muslim. So were the grasslands of the Western Sudan and the trading cities down the East African coast. In Europe, Islamic armies had overrun most of the Balkan states and pushed up into southern Russia. Farther to the east, they had traversed the snowy passes of the Hindu Kush and flooded down into northern India. Muslim merchants and Sufi missionaries had penetrated even the trop-

ical islands of Southeast Asia—Indonesia is mostly Muslim today—and carried the word of the Prophet as far east as the Philippines.

The range and diversity of the Islamic world was thus far greater than those of Christendom. Arabs, Berbers, and black Africans, Turks and Persians, Slavs, Mongols, Indians, and Southeast Asians all heard the call to prayer five times a day and prostrated themselves toward Mecca.

The great cities of the Islamic sphere dazzled European visitors. From the gold marts of Timbuktu to the silk and spice bazaars of Malacca, from the imperial Constantinople of the Ottomans to the dawning splendor of Mogul India, sixteenth-century Islamic culture was one of the glories of the globe.

A TRANSREGIONAL ZONE

Islam in 1500 was not merely a regional culture, like Christian Europe or China's East Asian sphere of influence. It was a transregional culture, encompassing portions of three continents. It must qualify as one of the very few intercontinental hegemonies to emerge before the rise of Western imperialism.

The Islamic impact on its zone, furthermore, was much deeper than the Western impact on its emerging colonies would be for several centuries. The Islamic religion—the youngest of the major world religions—had imposed itself deeply upon the lives of all the peoples it touched.

The faith of Islam included an immense body of Muslim law and Islamic tradition that affected every aspect of life. Political organization and business dealings, relations between the sexes, family life, and a multitude of other matters were matters of religious concern. All were regulated according to the teachings of the Prophet and the body of tradition that had grown up about his life and work.

Conquest by Muslims or conversion to Islam through the influence of merchants or missionaries brought other cultural influences into a community. As each new region was absorbed, Muslim scholars and Sufi preachers, artists, architects, and artisans, poets and musicians would be summoned to grace the courts of newly converted local rulers. Mosques would be built, Sufi centers and colleges would spring up, and *qadis* (judges) would sit in every marketplace, settling disputes and decreeing punishment for crimes on the basis of the Muslim Law.

---

[1]I borrow this usage from the innovative Tufts University world history program, and from Professor Lynda Schaffer, from whom I first heard it.

Nor were these merely scattered islands of Islamic civilization. Each sector was bound by ties of commercial exchange to all the rest of the Muslim zone. Muslim merchants carried luxury goods along the caravan trails of Eurasia and northern Africa, plied the sea lanes of the Indian Ocean and the Southeast Asian archipelago. Muslim holy men, scholars, and administrators traveled these same routes, seeing large parts of the Old World without ever leaving Islam. It was "a cohesive, growing, and self-replenishing network of cultural communication" that created "a self-conscious, cosmopolitan sense of being loyal citizens of the Abode of Islam (*Dar al-Islam*) taken as a whole."[2]

To understand the power and brilliance of this huge Muslim zone at the beginning of modern history, we will have to look both forward and back from the pivotal period around 1500. We will have to go back several centuries to note the emergence of powerful new peoples as leaders of the Islamic world, particularly the Seljuk and Ottoman Turks. And we will have to survey the history of three great Muslim states in the sixteenth century: Ottoman Turkey, Safavid Persia, and Mogul India, the core of Islamic greatness in early modern times.

A DIVIDED REALM

For a clear vision of Muslim achievement, then, we must briefly go back as far as A.D. 1000, to the time of the decadence of the first Muslim state, the far-flung empire built and ruled by the Prophet's own people, the Arabs.

During the first three centuries after Muhammad's death in 632, the Arabs had been ruled by *caliphs*, or "successors to the Prophet," of the Omayyad and Abbasid dynasties. These religious and secular rulers had established an impressive Islamic predominance across North Africa and the Middle East, with a touch of southern Europe thrown in. The culture of Abbasid Islam in the ninth and tenth centuries easily outshone that of Christendom, and the power and wealth of the caliphs of Baghdad dwarfed those of any Western ruler.

By the eleventh century, however, the political authority of the Arab Empire had collapsed into disorder from Spain to Afghanistan. The western subdivisions of the empire, located around the Mediterranean, had largely seceded to form independent Muslim states. Of these, Egypt dominated much of the Levantine east end of the Mediterranean, while Moorish Spain was a scintillating center of medieval culture at the other end. In Asia, the eastern regions of the Arab Empire, still nominally ruled by the Abbasids, in fact disintegrated into a series of hegemonies established by marauding nomad converts to the faith. The most important and long-lasting of these were the Seljuk Turks and the Mongols.

The Seljuks were herders of the steppes, mongoloid peoples speaking an Altaic language that originated somewhere north of China. Led by tribal chieftans and military adventurers, they drifted south from the steppes into the Muslim Middle East, converted to Islam, and became the new military arm of Islamic expansion. By 1000, officers of the Turkish guard at Baghdad were making caliphs, as Praetorian guardsmen had once made Roman emperors, while Turkish chiefs ruled the Persian countryside.

For a brief two centuries—less in some parts of their domain—the Seljuk Turks brought some unity to the Islamic Middle East. But it was at best a tenuous unity. The Seljuks were soldiers and tribute gatherers, not administrators. Their regime was little more than the sort of traditional tribal confederacy that was the highest form of social organization on their native steppes. They fought constantly among themselves. At the same time, enemies came against them repeatedly, from Europe and from Asia.

Their Christian enemies were the Byzantine emperors at Constantinople and the western European Crusaders. In their prime, Seljuk armies conquered Palestine and administered shattering defeats to the hitherto strong Byzantine armies, Christendom's easternmost bastion against Asian conquest. But they were unable to conquer Constantinople, and Europe remained beyond their reach. A major counterattack came in the eleventh and twelfth centuries in the form of the Crusades. Worried by Turkish victories over Constantinople and angered by high-handed treatment of Christian pilgrims in Jerusalem, crusading armies of medieval knights seized Jerusalem and held it for a century. The famous Seljuk prince Saladin recaptured the city. But the Seljuk predominance was already weakening, and in the thirteenth century an immensely more powerful enemy appeared out of Asia.

The Mongols of Genghis Khan surged out of the east in the 1200s, built the world's largest empire up to that time, and as quickly faded from the scene. In their glory, however, they were unstoppable. The Mongol cavalry crushed the Seljuks in the 1240s, took and pillaged Baghdad in the 1250s, killing the last figurehead Arab caliph in the process. For a hundred years, the Mongol Ilkhans ruled the Muslim Middle East. Even less skilled at the art of government than the Seljuks, however, the Mongols brought no more real unity to Islam. They too feuded among themselves, levied tribute, and kept fear of the conqueror alive in the hearts of the conquered.

Through these troubled late-medieval centuries of secession and conquest, however, Islamic culture survived, persevered, and prospered. The Seljuks encouraged the further development of the Muslim legal system, especially the essential local authority of the *qadi*. In the end even the Mongol Ilkhans accepted conversion to Islam. And the cosmopolitan cultural and commercial links endured, binding the farthest ends of this politically divided realm.

---

[2]Ross E. Dunn, "The Challenge of Hemispheric History (1000–1500 A.D.)." Paper presented before the American Historical Association (San Francisco: December 28, 1983).

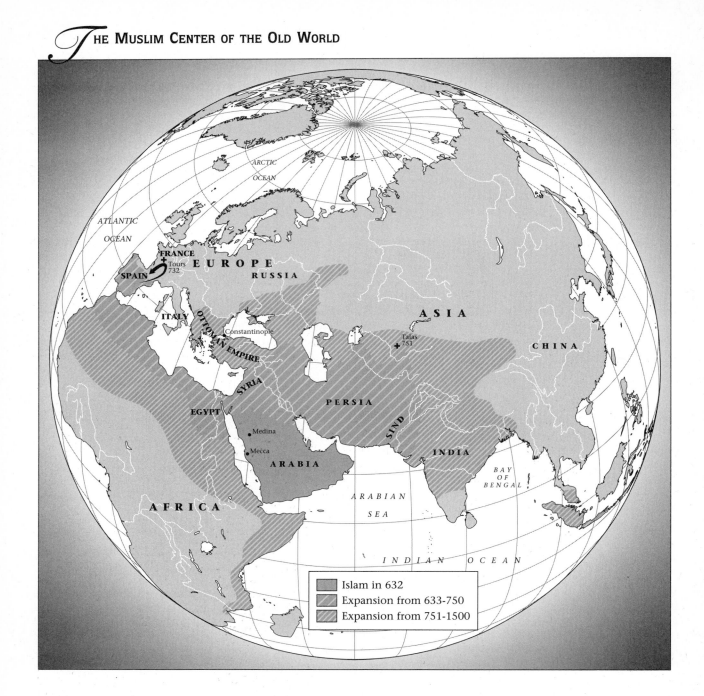

▨	Islam in 632
▧	Expansion from 633-750
▨	Expansion from 751-1500

A RESURGENCE OF ISLAMIC POWER

Political unity was never to come again for the immense and still-growing expanse of Muslim lands. Like the Christian world, Islam was to be fragmented into many nations. But at the beginning of the modern period, the Islamic peoples enjoyed a sudden dazzling resurgence of power.

This revival of Muslim greatness stretched through the sixteenth century, much of the seventeenth, and even beyond in some places. It was led and dominated by three great Muslim empires—those of the Ottoman Turks around the Mediterranean, the Safavids in Persia, and the Mogul dynasty of northern India. All were peoples of Turkish or Mongol background. All were great empire builders and presided over opulent and cultured courts. All three stand out in the history of Islam.

Around these three empires, Muslim steppe nomads in central Asia, Muslim Kingdoms in West Africa, and Muslim enclaves in Southeast Asia made a formidable Islamic presence. Together, they make Islam central—and not only in a geographical sense—to the history of the time.

THE MUSLIM DYNASTIES: OTTOMANS, SAFAVIDS, MOGULS

THE OTTOMAN EMPIRE: THE GHAZI PRINCES

The Ottoman Turks, like the Seljuks before them, were nomadic clans from the steppes who had drifted down into the Middle East, converted to Islam, and became militant champions of their new faith. Their leaders became military captains and petty princes, carving out little principalities for themselves along the borders of the medieval Byzantine Empire. They were thus lords of the marches on the frontier between Islam and Orthodox Christianity.

Osman (or Othman) I, the founder of the Ottoman dynasty, rose to prominence early in the fourteenth century. He was a *ghazi*, a fighting frontier lord, the Muslim equivalent of a Christian crusader. He won victories, and eager swords from all across the Muslim world flocked to join him in his repeated attacks on what was left of Byzantine power in the Middle East.

Whatever defeats they sustained elsewhere in their long history, the Byzantines, heirs of Roman power in the Middle East, had always been able to fall back behind the huge walls of Constantinople, "the city protected by God" and ride out the storm. On Constantinople, therefore, the Ottomans fixed their eyes. It took them a hundred and fifty years from the days of Osman the *ghazi*, but in the end they succeeded where all others had failed.

They first gobbled up all that remained of the Byzantine lands on both sides of the straits that divided Europe from Asia. Then, in the 1450s, Muhammad II—the Conqueror, as he came to be called—moved against Constantinople itself.

Muhammad mounted the biggest cannon in the world against the impregnable walls. He portaged a whole fleet overland to gain a strategic advantage on the Byzantine fleet in the Golden Horn, the harbor of Constantinople. In the spring of 1453 the Turks broke through. The last Christian emperor of Byzantium—the eightieth in the line since the Roman emperor Constantine—died on the walls. Sultan Muhammad rode in triumph into the city that had been the eastern frontier of Christendom for a thousand years.

Under Muhammad and his immediate successors, especially Selim the Grim in the early sixteenth century,

The Ottoman sultan Muhammad II enters Constantinople as conqueror in 1453. After a thousand years as Christian Europe's most powerful bastion against Asiatic invasion, the Byzantine Empire thus fell to the latest champions of Islam, the Ottoman Turks. This romantic nineteenth-century painting stresses the color and pathos of the moment, emphasizing the oriental costumes, banners, scimtars, and the crescent of Islam, as well as the fallen defenders in the foreground. Fifteenth-century Muslims saw the capture of Constantinople as a great victory for Allah and for God's chosen people, the followers of the Prophet Muhammad for whom the sultan was named. (Painting by Berj. Constant)

the power of the Ottomans spread far across the Muslim center and into Christian Europe. Like the other empire builders of the age, they utilized the new technology of gun-powder and artillery with devastating effect. Their fluttering pennons and flashing scimitars drove deep into the Balkans and swung north above the Black Sea into the Ukraine. Southward from Constantinople (now Istanbul), they imposed unity by force upon Mesopotamia and parts of Persia, the Levant, Arabia. They conquered even Egypt, whose military ruling class, the Mamelukes, had once stopped even the Mongols in their tracks.

By 1500, then, the former *ghazi* princes ruled a considerable swath of territory, extending from southeastern Europe around the eastern end of the Mediterranean, from their capital at Istanbul. It was to this tradition and this heritage that Suleiman the Magnificent, the most renowned of all the Ottomans, was born at the beginning of the sixteenth century.

SULEIMAN THE MAGNIFICENT

Under Sultan Suleiman the Magnificent (1520–1566), the Ottoman Empire became a world power. The Ottomans absorbed new territories in Europe, Asia, and Africa. They put fleets to sea from the Mediterranean to the Indian Ocean. They played the game of power politics with the leading European rulers and dominated the Muslim center as no one had since the Arab caliphs of Baghdad.

Suleiman himself fought a dozen major campaigns, spent a total of ten years in the field, and died in his seventies at the head of his troops. He reclaimed most of the old Omayyad lands along the coast of North Africa and conquered more of western Persia. He advanced still farther into eastern Europe, overrunning Hungary, invading Austria, besieging and barely failing to take Vienna, the capital of the Holy Roman Empire.

Suleiman's commanders on the Mediterranean raided the southern coasts of Italy and France and fought the Spanish fleet to a standstill. In the Indian Ocean, Ottoman squadrons battled the Portuguese on the sea routes to India. On the sea as on land, Ottoman power dominated the heart of the Old World.

By the time he died, Suleiman the Magnificent ruled all or part of what is today Hungary, Yugoslavia, Greece, Albania, Romania, Bulgaria, and southern Russia; Turkey, Iran, Iraq, Syria, Lebanon, Jordan, and Israel; Saudi Arabia, Egypt, Lybia, Tunisia, and Algeria—among others. Unlike the Seljuks and the Mongols, furthermore, the Ottoman sultan really ruled his immense realm. The Ottoman Empire of Suleiman—Suleiman the Lawgiver, as his own people called him—was a far cry from the loose confederations of *ghazi* times. It was a centralized state with an administrative system second to none in that half of the Old World.

Sultan Suleiman's empire did not draw its administrative personnel from a single social class, like the European bourgeoisie or China's gentry of scholar-bureaucrats. The Ottoman administrative system built upon three groups who already had important functions in society: the *qadis*, the *timariots*, and the *ghulam* system.

The *qadis*, the traditional Islamic judges, had been assigned administrative functions at the village level as far back as the Arab Empire, and they fulfilled similar functions under the Ottomans. The *timariots* were the old *ghazi* cavalry. Rewarded for their military service by tax revenues from recently conquered villages, they also provided police power and protection for these towns. The *ghulam* system was the Turkish practice of appointing men who were nominally slaves to high positions of civil and military authority in the land. Delegating power to slaves avoided any problems of insubordination, since slaves had no rights against their masters. Christian converts to Islam were incorporated into this system in the fifteenth century, becoming the famous Janissary Corps of elite soldiers and civil servants.

These three groups staffed an impressive administrative structure. At its head was the grand vizier, nominally a slave, but in fact the sultan's right hand. The vizier presided over the royal council, or *divan*, with its many secretaries, scribes, and subordinate bureaus. The provinces of the empire were run by local governors called *pashas* in the cities, *begs* in the countryside. At the local level, *qadis* and *timariots* performed their traditional functions. Janissaries were seeded through the whole system in key administrative and military posts from the capital to the farthest border provinces.

Sophisticated European visitors much admired the empire of Suleiman the Magnificent. Official merit was recognized and corruption punished, they said, as they were not in Europe. Public charity cared for the needy, schools prospered, and the sultan's armies were ever victorious. It was an idealized picture, but there was much truth in it.

Suleiman himself had a clear sense of his own place in the world. "I am God's slave," he caused to be inscribed on a public monument, "and sultan of this world."[3] Ruling in splendor from Istanbul on the Golden Horn, the Grand Turk, as Westerners called him, was the most powerful of Muslim rulers and more powerful than almost any Christian king.

SAFAVID PERSIA: THE SHIITE KINGDOM

Persia, the Muslim power due east of the Ottoman Empire, was no upstart *ghazi* state. In 1500 the Persians already had two thousand years of history behind them. Many dynasties had ruled there since Cyrus the Great founded the first Persian empire in the sixth century B.C. Ever since the Arab conquest in the seventh century A.D., Persia had become in many ways the cultural heart of Islam, producing theologians, scholars, and poets in profusion as well as leading schools of art.

Persia had also managed to civilize—and Islamicize—one after another of its subsequent conquerors and foreign rulers. The Seljuk Turks in the eleventh century, the Mongols in the thirteenth, and the terrible Tamerlane and his descendants in the fifteenth had all been schooled in ancient Persian ways. Politically, however, Persia had remained weak and often fragmented among its conquerors.

Persians had not entirely lost control of their own destiny. Turks and Mongols might conquer, but cultivated

---

[3]Halil Inalcik, *The Ottoman Empire: The Classical Age, 1300–1600,* trans. Norman Itzkowitz and Colin Imber (New York: Praeger, 1973), p. 41.

Persian viziers did much of the governing for them. Persian taste guided one rude warrior after another into magnificent building, lavish patronage of the arts, and Islamic piety. Then, in 1500, a native Persian dynasty seized power once more and set Persian history on an odd new path.

Shah Ismail (1500–1524), the first of the Safavids, was thirteen years old when his devoted religious followers, the *kizilbashi* ("Red Caps") swept him into power. He reunified Persia and gave the nation a Persian ruling house, initiated a great age in Persian history—and fueled a religious rift in the Islamic world that persists to the present day.

The Safavids were Shiites, members of Islam's largest minority sect. Regarded as heretics by the Sunnite majority of Islam, the Shiites rejected the traditional leadership of the caliphs, the acknowledged successors to the Prophet. Shiites insisted that only someone directly related to Muhammad—that is, a descendant of the third official caliph, Ali, who had been Muhammad's cousin and son-in-law—could be the true head of Islam. Such a rightful heir to the Prophet, furthermore, would be an *imam*, a real spiritual head of the faithful—not a mere secular ruler, as most caliphs had tended to be.

Shiites had been martyred for this heterodox faith for centuries. In Safavid Persia they found a homeland of their own at last.

Young Ismail, surrounded by Sufi holy men, swept to power on a wave of religious enthusiasm. He was hailed as shah—secular ruler—and *imam* in Tabriz, the red caps of his supporters thronging about him. By seizing power in Persia, however, Ismail drove a religious wedge into the heart of Islam. To the east and north lay the Sunnite Muslims of India and central Asia; to the west and south, those of Ottoman Turkey, Arabia, Egypt, and North Africa. Even more dangerous, Shiite Persia, with its *imam* emperor and its crusading zeal, exerted a powerful attraction on Shiite minorities elsewhere in the Middle East.

As in Reformation Europe at the same time, the sixteenth century saw savage persecutions and wars of religion in the Muslim Middle East. The Sunnite champion was the Ottoman colossus, Persia's neighbor to the west. The Safavids compelled Persian Sunnites—who were actually in the majority in the early days—to accept Shiite formulations of the faith on pain of death. The Ottomans martyred Shiites, whom they saw as potential rebels, in large numbers. And the armies of the Safavid shah and the Ottoman sultan met repeatedly on the battlefield throughout the century.

In the early days especially, the Ottomans generally had the better of it, adding substantial chunks of Persian territory to their already swollen empire. This is perhaps not surprising, since Ottoman armies were early equipped with firearms and artillery, while Ismail's soldiers were capable of charging bare-chested into battle, calling upon the sanctity of the *imam* to protect them. Around 1600, however, the Safavids produced a ruler who would have considerably more success—the great Shah Abbas.

SHAH ABBAS OF ISFAHAN

Shah Abbas I (1587–1629) is in fact generally considered the greatest of all the Safavids. A dark-complected, masterful, immensely energetic man, Abbas, like Ismail before him, came to the throne young, at seventeen. But he reigned much longer than Ismail, and his forty-odd years in power were one of Persia's golden ages.

Shah Abbas came to a throne threatened by encroachment from both sides—by Ottomans occupying western provinces and Uzbek peoples pressing down from central Asia. He made a temporary peace with the Turks, drove the Uzbeks out of the northeast—and then began to prepare for war on better terms with the Ottomans. By the turn of the century, he had replaced an army of religious enthusiasts with a new military arm composed of paid soldiers trained in the European style. He even armed his new troops with artillery made by English cannon founders he had welcomed for the purpose. Thus equipped, he pushed the Ottoman Turks back out of his western provinces at last.

Shah Abbas also streamlined the royal administration along Western lines. He gladly received European traders and opened diplomatic relations with Western nations. He typically used these Western contacts for his own purposes, however, as when he cooperated with a British naval squadron in forcing the Portuguese out of the strategic island of Hormuz at the mouth of the Persian Gulf.

For his own people, the greatest of the Safavids built roads, dug canals, erected caravansaries to encourage trade. He imported skilled artisans from other lands to expand Persia's ancient store of handicraft manufacturing industries. He fostered the pilgrim trade in Persia by building shrines. But he also distanced himself from the Shiite fanaticism of the *Kizilbashi* and was far more tolerant of other faiths than Ismail had been.

The jewel of Shah Abbas's Persia was the new capital he built at Isfahan. This ancient town, centrally located for administrative purposes and closer to the Persian Gulf for trade, was soon humming with new industry as Abbas imported artisans and built huge bazaars. Isfahan grew in time to a city of half a million souls, with 160 mosques, 50 religious colleges, 275 public baths—and 1800 caravansaries! The shah's palace, the imperial mosque, the roofed bazaars, the royal gardens within and outside of the city were things of beauty. Wealthy homes had lovely gardens of their own, and the poor found public charities ready to hand.

Like many masterful men, Abbas could tolerate no rivals, not even potential successors. His failure to prepare his heirs left Persia with a series of much less capable rulers after his passing. But during the four decades of his reign, the nation prospered, art and culture flourished, and even European travelers admired the Sophy, as they called him, as much as they did the Grand Turk.

Mogul India: A Rabble of Adventurers

A journey eastward from Safavid Persia would have brought a sixteenth-century traveler into the third of the great Islamic empires—the realm of the Moguls, comprising most of what is today Pakistan, northern India, and Bangladesh. Mogul India, like Safavid Persia and Ottoman Turkey, was a major exemplar of the transnational, transregional civilization of early-modern Islam.

Two towering individuals shaped the Mogul achievement: Babur, the founder, and Akbar the Great, the true architect of the empire. They were in a sense the Ismail and Shah Abbas of sixteenth-century India.

Like Ismail, Babur (1483–1530) came to precarious power as a youth. He was only eleven when he inherited the throne of the unstable central Asian kingdom of Ferghana, north and west of India. Half Turk, half Mongol, Babur claimed descent from Tamerlane, who had himself sacked Delhi around 1400.

Babur turned to the conquest of northern India only when the fortunes of war and politics had deprived him of hope for a central Asian empire. In the middle 1520s, when he was already in his forties, he and his Mogul tribesmen descended through the Afghan passes of the Hindu Kush, India's ancient invasion route along the Northwest Frontier.

He was an exceptional man. Athlete, warrior, poet, and composer of his own memoirs, Babur was relatively humane in an age of massacres. He was also capable of extraordinary heroism, of diabolical practical jokes, and, in the last fateful decision of his life, of remarkable self-sacrifice.

The small army he led down into the Punjab was a typical rabble of central Asian adventurers. But Babur also trundled artillery along in his train, with Turkish gun crews and a mounted force trained in Turkish cavalry tactics. The Mogul realm, like that of the Ottomans, would be a "gunpowder empire." And Babur, like other famous conquerors, earned at least half his victories through skillful preparation.

The India Babur entered was, like Persia, one of the world's oldest civilizations. Highly developed urban culture had existed for perhaps four thousand years in the Indus and Punjab valleys, where the ancient cities of Harappa and Mohenjodaro rose and fell many centuries before Athens or Rome were dreamed of. The Indian subcontinent as a whole had developed a cohesive culture based on the Hindu religion and the caste system. It was a land of highly developed arts and crafts, many rich commercial cities, and countless peasant villages.

Political unity, however, had been rare in India. Only under the Mauryas (322–185 B.C.) and the Guptas (A.D. 320–540) had a single centralized political order been imposed on most of the vast triangular land mass between the Himalayas and Ceylon (Sri Lanka). Even when there was political power in India, it focused where the Moguls would build theirs—along the wide, brown, sacred river Ganges in the north.

In Babur's time, India had collapsed into a particularly messy period of political division. An earlier Muslim regime in the north, the Delhi Sultanate, had crumbled away. Many petty rajas vied for power in the resulting vacuum, imposing extortionate taxes on the people and allowing their armies to live off the land. Lesser princes and nobles felt no loyalty to greater ones. The villagers, who had seen so many invaders stream down from the mountains, remained indifferent to the outcome of any war.

Babur thus arrived at an auspicious time. His artillery, cavalry, and personal heroics combined with this disunity and widespread apathy to give him a series of astonishing victories over larger hosts. Neither the traditional Indian elephant cavalry nor the famous chivalry of the Rajput princes could stop the invader from the north. His first great victory at Panipat in 1526 gave him a kingdom in India. Subsequent triumphs expanded it into a brief and glittering empire.

Then suddenly, still in his forties, worn out by a lifetime of struggle, Babur was dead. According to a perhaps apocryphal account, his oldest and best-beloved son had fallen deathly ill, and Babur offered Allah his own life for that of the young man. In a few months, the youth was healthy once more and the emperor had passed away.

The Three Lives of Akbar the Great

For the next half century Babur's newly won empire struggled to survive. Then, in Babur's grandson Akbar, the true builder of the Mogul order came at last.

Akbar the Great (1556–1605) reigned for half a century and became for later generations in northern India a figure of legendary benevolence and accomplishment. The greatest and strangest of the Moguls, he lived three very different lives, one after another, each stranger than the last.

Yet another young heir to an unsteady throne, Akbar led an irregular, self-willed life of hunting and revelry during his youth, leaving the conduct of affairs to an overbearing but loyal minister of state. So petulantly pleasure-loving was the young Akbar, and so irregular was his style of life, that he apparently refused to trouble himself even to learn to read. In fact he remained unlettered all his life, an illiterate wise man at the center of one of Islam's most sophisticated courts.

Outbreaks of anarchic violence reaching even into his court finally jolted the young emperor into an awareness of his duties. He reportedly hurled the aristocratic murderer of a royal minister from the battlements of the palace with his own hands—and plunged straightaway into his second life, that of a leader of armies and a rebuilder of empire.

Akbar was an aggressive general, famous for incred-

The Mogul palace at Delhi, built in the early seventeenth century by Shah Jehan. The huge size of the palace complex—roughly half a mile by a third of a mile—and its sumptuous marble buildings provided a fitting center for what was perhaps the most magnificent capital city in the world. Its central hall, two stories high and 375 feet long, impressed even the later European historian of architecture James Ferguson as "the noblest entrance to any existing palace."

ibly rapid marches that repeatedly caught his enemies off guard. He aimed not only to reassemble the fragments of the empire his grandfather had won, but to achieve a predominant position in all India. He reconquered the north, going well beyond Babur's conquest to rule from Gujurat in the west to Bengal in the east, from the mountains of Kashmir in the north down into the Deccan, the triangular peninsula of southern India. He thus made the Muslim Moguls heirs of the Hindu Guptas and the Buddhist Mauryas as unifiers of India.

But Akbar was more than a conqueror: he was a pacifier and a conciliator. He humbled the fierce Rajput *rajas* and then made them his vassals and partners in rule, even going as far as to marry a Rajput princess. He launched a Hindu policy, offering equal rights to the Hindu majority among his subjects and opening up high places in his government to highcaste Indians.

He provided, finally, for a centralized administrative system superior to anything northern India had seen since Gupta times a thousand years before. He divided his realm into a dozen provinces and appointed governors for each. He chose provincial officials from all classes and castes, organized them in thirty-three graded ranks, paid them in cash, and promoted them on a merit basis. He organized the crucial land tax efficiently, fixing a system that lasted for hundreds of years.

Meanwhile, a middle-aged Akbar had undergone another crisis and entered the third of his lives—that of a religious mystic and founder of a new faith. He had listened for many years to the discussions of holy men of various faiths at his court—Muslims and Hindus, Buddhists, Jains, and even Jesuit Christian fathers. By 1580 he had abandoned orthodox Islam in favor of a new cult, an attempt at a universal religion with himself as its prophet. He called it the Divine Faith.

There was a practical side to Akbar's new religion, since the cult transcended the divisive pull of Islam and Hinduism and focused religious veneration upon the head of the state. But we may grant him a higher sincerity too when he preached his universal religion:

> O God, in every temple I see people that seek Thee;
> in every language I hear spoken, people praise Thee;
> if it be a mosque, people murmur the holy prayer;
> if it be a Christian church, they ring the bell for love
> of Thee. . . . it is Thou whom I seek from temple
> to temple.[4]

Akbar's Divine Faith did not extend far beyond official circles, nor did it long outlast his lifetime. But its

---

[4]Steven Warshaw and C. David Bromwell, with A. J. Tudisco, *India Emerges* (Berkeley: Diablo Press, 1974), p. 60.

overarching tolerance for all religions contrasted strikingly with the bloodshed of Protestant–Catholic and Shiite–Sunnite wars in other parts of Eurasia in early-modern times.

Akbar was a great builder and patron of the arts, a man of broad intellectual and spiritual concerns, and a powerful organizer of empire. Like Asoka in ancient India, he comes as close as any earthly monarch to meeting Plato's criteria for a true philosopher king.

ISLAMIC CULTURE: THE GARDEN OF OMAR KHAYYÁM

THE CITY AND THE VILLAGE

The wealth of the Grand Turk, the Sophy of Persia, and the Moguls of India was proverbial in Europe. When they were not fighting, they traded with each other and with the Christian West. All three of the empires of the Muslim center, as we have seen, encouraged crafts and manufacturing. By establishing peace and order, they maximized the potential for both economic and creative endeavor.

In Islamic Asia, as in Christian Europe, wealth gravitated to the cities. Istanbul, Isfahan, and Delhi were among the great urban centers of the world.

The metropolises of the Muslim Middle East and of Muslim-controlled India were divided by occupation and by religion. As in Europe, artisans and merchants were organized into guilds, and all practitioners of the same trade had their shops in the same section of the city. There were more likely to be devotees of other religions in the Muslim city than in the West, however: Jews and Christians in Middle Eastern cities, Hindus, Jains, Sikhs, and others in Indian ones coexisted, though they kept to their own quarters of the city. There might also be a foreign quarter for merchants from other places. In India, the many Hindu castes, which were also occupational and religious groupings, were firmly segregated by ancient Indian custom.

The governors, judges, and police commanders who ruled the city, however, were almost always Muslims. In the teachings of the Prophet, they could usually find warrant for a religious forbearance that Christian Europeans sadly lacked. The bloody feuds of Shiite and Sunnite were thus rather the exception than the norm in the Islamic world. Even the intermittent wars with Christians or Rajputs were affairs of high policy or wild border raiders—not the concern of civilized city dwellers. In the Muslim metropolis, the Christian merchants had their quarter, the Hindu administrator his high place in government. In the polyglot middle parts of Asia, diversity was simply a fact of life.

The village was much more likely to be homogeneous, however. Villages in the Middle East and in South Asia were physically like villages everywhere: small collections mostly of stone- or mud-walled huts, surrounded by scanty croplands or pasturage. Because Middle Eastern land was less fertile than much of Europe, farm animals were often lean and hungry, and the people burned dung rather than wood. Monsoon India was much wetter, and the Ganges and other streams from the Himalayas provided ample irrigation in the north. Yet villages were meager places, dusty and muddy by turns, and usually poor, even in the subcontinent.

The typical Muslim village was solidly patriarchal. It was run by a headman, and each large household was headed by the father of the family. The authorities expected the headman to keep his village peaceful and productive, the heads of families to be responsible for all their kin. In a period of imperial order, royal armies or authorities from nearby cities would control the lives of villagers. In less orderly times, roving bands of nomads in the Middle East or warring local *rajas* in India would be their masters.

WOMEN IN THE MUSLIM WORLD

The condition of women also had its distinctive features in Islamic lands. Muhammad had allowed polygamy for those who could afford more than one wife, and sixteenth-century Islam was as thoroughly male-dominated as any section of the globe. Muslim women were generally required to wear the veil and to live their lives in a world of women, cut off from the larger world of men by screens, curtains, and high walls. Bare-faced European women, particularly those wearing the low-cut gowns of Renaissance and later times, seemed shockingly immodest to Muslims.

On the other hand, women in the Islamic world enjoyed property rights, control of their own income, and the right to divorce their husbands—none of which was possible, except in exceptional cases, in Christian Europe. Women in the Middle East especially made substantial contributions to the economy, performing farm labor or supervising it on their husband's lands, herding flocks, or weaving many of the famous Persian rugs that found such a large market in the West. Others were shopkeepers, street venders, and artisans of other sorts.

In Islamic countries as elsewhere, there were also women who wielded great power. This was most commonly done from behind the scenes: it is much harder to find famous female rulers in the Muslim center than in either Christian Europe or Confucian China. But through political intrigue, especially in the intricate and often critical politics of the royal harem, Muslim women could exert immense influence upon the course of events from "behind the veil."

Some Muslim women, finally, firmly rejected seclusion and the harem life. The golden age of Ottoman power, in particular, produced a number of women widely recognized for their talents and contributions to Ottoman society.

Many of these talented women were intellectuals privately educated by intellectual fathers. There were writers, musical composers, and gifted calligraphers among them. There were also a number of celebrated women doctors, including some attached to the court of Suleiman the Magnificent himself. In addition, women of the aristocracy sometimes organized and ran charitable foundations.

LITERATURE AND LEARNING: THE INFLUENCE OF PERSIA

A Book of Verses underneath the Bough,
A Jug of Wine, A Loaf of Bread—and Thou
   Beside me singing in the Wilderness—
Oh, Wilderness were Paradise enow![5]

These, among the more commonly quoted lines of English verse, are actually a translation from the twelfth-century Persian poet and astronomer Omar Khayyám. Through such poetry, we have direct access to a very different side of Islamic society, a world of sophisticated skepticism rather than religious devotion. *The Rubáiyát of Omar Khayyám* introduces us to a seductive Middle Eastern world where fine wine warms the spirit in spite of the Prophet's prohibition of alcohol, and where all women do not lead secluded lives behind veils and screens.

If the Ottoman Empire was the most powerful of the Islamic states at the beginning of the modern age, Persia was still the cultural heart of the Muslim world. Persian literature, Persian painting, Persian dress and manners, and the Persian language were common among cultured Muslims from Istanbul to Delhi. What Italy was to Renaissance Europe, Persia was to the Muslim center—the predominant force in literature and the life of the mind.

Paradoxically, Persia's own major contributions to literary culture in particular came not under the Safavids, but under the Turkish and Mongol rulers of the later medieval centuries. The Mongol Ilkhanate of the thirteenth and fourteenth centuries produced Persia's most celebrated historical writing, as well as eminent works in astronomy, botany, medicine, philosophy, and theology. This earlier period also produced a vital literature of Sufi mysticism and romantic poetry. Omar Khayyám wrote under the Seljuks, but the Mongol period saw the writing of Sadi of Shiraz, widely admired as Persia's greatest poet as well as a famous Sufi. Under the descendants of Tamerlane in the fifteenth century, Hafiz, also of Shiraz, revived something of Omar's spirit in his odes to springtime and rose gardens, wine and youth, blending Muslim mysticism with a melancholy skepticism that Omar would have understood.

Persian literature of the Safavid sixteenth century, by contrast, was far less vital and original. The puritanical narrowness of the Shiite clerics smothered both the passionate mysticism of the Sufis and the worldly lyricism of the poets. Safavid scholarship had little originality. Safavid poetry sank into a morass of elaborate "poetic diction" and complex verse forms, more a challenge to the professional writer than a pleasure to the reader.

At this time, however, Persian influence spread east and west across the Muslim heartland of Eurasia.

The Ottomans took their theology from the Arabs and borrowed geographical ideas from Europe, but they reserved their highest respect for the history and poetry of their mortal enemies in Safavid Persia. Ottoman scholars wrote exhaustive commentaries on the Persian classics, and Ottoman poets copied them, both in the Persian language and in Turkish. Thus the distinctive mixture of mysticism and romanticism that had taken shape in Persia lived on, in the writing of Persia's greatest foe.

Persian culture was also massively transplanted to India under the Moguls, especially Akbar the Great. Persian architecture and painting, language and literature spread not only across heavily Muslim northern India but down into the Hindu south as well. Educated Rajput princes spoke Persian in polite society, dressed in the Persian style, lounged in Persian gardens. Persian poetry was read in the summer palaces of Indian Kashmir as enthusiastically as it was on the Golden Horn at Istanbul. It was probably read in both places with more appreciation than it could any longer command in the puritanical Persia of the *Kizilbashi*. But then, Omar Khayyám of Khorasan had scarcely expected immortality:

Ah, my Beloved, fill the Cup that clears
Today of past Regrets and future Fears:
   Tomorrow—Why, Tomorrow I may be
Myself with Yesterday's Sev'n thousand Years.[6]

THE LUMINOUS POWER OF ART

No Muslim nation has left us sculpture or painting like that of Renaissance Europe—living human beings, ready to step down from their pedestals or out of their great gilt frames. The artistic genius of Islam lay elsewhere—in Arabic calligraphy and the decorative arts, in glass, ceramics, and textiles, in the exquisite art of the miniature, and perhaps above all, in architecture, the art of mosques and palaces.

Painting of human or divine figures was frowned upon by Islamic theology as conducive to idolatry, or as an attempt to usurp God's creative function. Yet some lovely figure painting was done in the Ottoman, Safavid, and Mogul empires—on a small scale and for private consumption.

The art of miniature painting flourished first in Persia, as did so much else, and spread from there to the neighboring Turkish and Indian realms. Small in size

---

[5]*The Rubáiyát of Omar Khayyám,* trans. Edward Fitzgerald (New York: Three Sirens Press, n.d.), p. 175.

[6]Ibid, p. 177.

A Persian miniature dating from around 1600. The subject is the archetypal father-son combat of Sohrab and Rustem, based on a tenth-century epic poem, the <u>Shah Nameh</u> of Firdusi. The integration of martial figures, flowery setting, and script in a charming composition is typical of the elegant Muslim art of miniature painting. Effective decorative patterning was a key element in Muslim art from its earliest days. (Leaf from the Shah-namah by Firdausi, "Combat of Sohrab and Rustem." The Metropolitan Museum of Art, Gift of Alexander Smith Coderan, 1913. [13.228.16])

(Indian miniatures average less than a foot square), these works usually depicted group scenes—famous victories, royal courts, popular festivals—or illustrated well-known myths or famous poems. Simply drawn, delicately colored figures often move against a flat background of trees and flowers. At the court of Akbar, Mogul painters did some striking portraiture: lightly shaded, oddly luminous likenesses of shahs and Muslim saints in silks and turbans. But the classic Persian miniature depicted legendary heroes in action, royal weddings, or emperors in splendor against abstract backgrounds of bright verdure or

arched gates and rectangular walls, all glowing like jewels with color and exquisite detail.

The Muslim world's most admired graphic art, however, was calligraphy. Ever since the days of the Arab caliphates, Arabic script has been widely used to decorate mosques, ceramics, metalwork, and textiles, as well as in gorgeous copies of the Koran. Indeed, the universal use of Arabic lettering for religious, commercial, and other purposes helped to bind Muslims of all nations into a single cosmopolitan community.

The decorative potential of Arabic script filled much of the gap created by the taboo on pictures or sculpture in public places. Verses from the Koran mingled with interwoven abstract patterns to produce a peculiarly Muslim blend of aesthetic pleasure and religious piety. The living word of Allah and the luminous power of art thus mingled in the work of the skilled Arabic calligrapher.

ARCHITECTURE: THE MOST BEAUTIFUL BUILDING IN THE WORLD

But in the days of the Muslim resurgence, as in the original golden age of the Arab Empire, architecture was the most dazzling triumph of Islamic art.

The rulers of the three great Islamic empires lived in a style suitable to the proverbial Oriental potentate. Some of the palaces they built as settings for their elaborate court life survive as evidence of those splendors.

The Topkapi Palace in Istanbul—now a museum—is the example most familiar to travelers. Its sumptuous interiors, polychrome or dazzling blue in color, are brilliant with beautifully woven carpets and glazed tiles in

The Taj Mahal at Agra, built by the Mogul emperor Shah Jahan in the early 1600s in memory of his favorite wife, the Mumtaz Mahal. Exquisite in design and setting, the Taj Mahal is one of the jewels of Mogul—and of Islamic—architecture. It also illustrates the subtle interplay of simple masses found in some of the best Muslim building. (Monkmeyer Press)

VOICES FROM THE PAST

> "It should be known that differences of condition among people are the result of the different ways in which they make their living. . . . Some people live by agriculture, the cultivation of vegetables and grains; others by animal husbandry, the use of sheep, cattle, goats, bees, and silkworms, for breeding and for their products. Those who live by agriculture or animal husbandry cannot avoid the call of the wide fields, pastures for animals, and other things that the settled areas do not offer. . . . Their social organization and co-operation for the needs of life and civilization, such as food, shelter, and warmth, do not take them beyond the bare subsistence level, because of their inability (to provide) for anything beyond those (things). Subsequent improvement of their conditions and acquisition of more wealth and comfort than they need, cause them to rest and take it easy. Then, they co-operate for things beyond the bare necessities. They use more food and clothes, and take pride in them. They build large houses, and lay out towns and cities for protection. This is followed by an increase in comfort and ease, which leads to formation of the most developed luxury customs. . . . They build castles and mansions, provide them with running water, build their towers higher and higher, and compete in furnishing them (most elaborately). They differ in the quality of the clothes, the beds, the vessels, and the utensils they employ for their purposes. "Sedentary people" means the inhabitants of cities and countries, some of whom adopt the crafts as their way of making a living, while others adopt commerce. They earn more and live more comfortably than Bedouins, because they live on a level beyond the level of bare necessity, and their way of making a living corresponds to their wealth."

The eminent British twentieth-century global historian Arnold Toynbee saw the four-teenth century Arab historian Ibn Khaldun (1332–1406) as the most profound student of world history before modern times. The <u>Muqaddimah</u> or "Introduction" to Ibn Khaldun's <u>Universal History</u> quoted here goes far beyond traditional chronicle history in attempting to explain as well as to narrate events.

In this passage, the Arab historian tries to show how the lifestyles of both bedouin farmers and herders on the one hand and sedentary urban civilization on the other are products of "the different ways in which [people] make their living." Does this explanation seem to you to reflect the historic experience of the Arabs themselves? Can you see the author as describing the universal experiences of other peoples as well? Does this excerpt describe the spread of urban civilization today?

Ibn Khaldun, <u>The Muqaddimah: An Introduction to History</u>, trans. Franz Rosenthal, ed. N. J. Dawood (Princeton: Princeton University Press, 1967), pp. 91–92.

---

floral or leaf designs. Equally splendid, however, are the palaces of the Mogul rulers of India, particularly the Red Forts of Delhi and Agra and the great Akbar's palaces at Fatehpur Sikri. The Fatehpur Sikri complex, built of white marble and red sandstone, enclosed by multilevel galleries and arcades with rows of bell-topped towers in mingled Muslim and Hindu styles, epitomizes the splendid lives of the Moguls. The pleasure gardens of Shalimar in Calcutta and Kashmir, in the foothills of the Himalayas, remind us that these sophisticated Muslim monarchs were only a few generations removed from the open steppes and still enjoyed life in the out-of-doors.

Religion, however, remained central to the life of Islam, as the great mosques built during these centuries testify. The first mosques had been in the open style of the Arabs—a large courtyard, a prayer hall with a decorated *mihrab* (alcove) facing Mecca, and tall, slender towers called minarets from which the faithful were daily called to prayer. Two new styles in particular emerged in later times, retaining the basic elements but clothing them in striking new forms.

One of these was the "four-*ivan*" style developed in Persia, featuring four open-ended vaulted halls focusing on a central court or prayer hall. The huge Mosque of Shah Abbas in Isfahan illustrates this form on a colossal scale, its intricately vaulted surfaces rich with tilework and mosaic. Sumptuous carpets, hanging lamps, and ornate *mihrabs* made such imperial mosques fitting sanctuaries for the God who had smiled upon Islam.

It was the Ottoman Turks, however, who developed the more familiar style of huge domes and slender minarets that most Westerners associate with the architecture of the mosque. The dome does go further back, beginning with the earliest of Islamic monuments—the gold-sheathed Dome of the Rock, built by the Arabs in Jerusalem. But it was the Ottomans, impressed by such awesome Roman domes as that over Hagia Sophia in Constantinople, who made the central dome the core of the architectural design of the mosque.

After surrounding Hagia Sophia itself with minarets, Ottoman architects proceeded to erect similar buildings of their own. These included such wonders as the Mosque of Sultan Suleiman in Istanbul and the Mosque of Selim at Adrianople. These mountainous accumulations of domes and half domes had multigalleried minarets at all four corners and vast courtyards filled with trees and walks, hospitals, caravansaries, the tombs of saints, and other pious structures. They broadcast the greatness of their builders—and their faith in Allah—to the world.

A final brief word must be reserved for the last resting places of the saints and potentates of the Islamic world—for the artistry of Muslim tombs.

There was nothing gloomy about these monuments to the mighty dead, beautifully domed and often set in flowering gardens. The azure dome of Tamerlane's mausoleum at Samarkand looms over walls and towers of exquisite glazed brick and carved marble. The garden where Omar Khayyám lies buried—in the shadow of the tomb of a Muslim saint—blooms with a profusion of blossoms that would have brought a smile to the poet's lips. And the blue reflecting pools, the dazzling white domes, and minarets of the tomb built by the Mogul Shah Jahan for his empress in the early 1600s make the Taj Mahal at Agra quite possibly the most hauntingly beautiful building in the world.

SUMMARY

The Muslim center of the Old World included parts of all three continents of this half of the inhabited globe. North Africa, Balkan Europe, the Middle East, South and Southeast Asia were among the regions dominated by followers of the teachings of Muhammad around 1500.

The Arab Empire that had established this Islamic hegemony during the earlier Middle Ages had declined and fragmented in later medieval times. First the Seljuk Turks and then the Mongols had replaced the original followers of the Prophet as the predominant people in the central portions of this sprawling Islamic world. Whether ruled by Arabs, Persians, Seljuks, Mongols, or the array of African kings and South and Southeast Asian rajas, these Muslim peoples enjoyed a powerful cultural, commercial, and religious unity.

Around 1500, finally, three new empires rose to power in the heart of this Muslim zone.

The Ottoman Turks conquered the Byzantine Empire and the Arab states of the Near East and North Africa. The Ottoman sultan, Suleiman the Magnificent, was the most powerful ruler in the western half of the Old World, revered among his own people and respected in Christendom. To the east, meanwhile, the new Safavid dynasty seized power in Persia. Safavid Persia became the militant center of Shiite Islam, a sect as divisive in the Muslim world as Protestantism was in Western Christendom.

Still farther to the east, the Muslim Moguls conquered northern India. Under Akbar the Great, Mogul wealth, administration, and culture gave India another golden age—its last before the coming of the Europeans.

During the centuries of shifting rule in Islam, Muslim culture produced beautiful poetry, painting, Arabic calligraphy, and religious architecture. Persia was the recognized cultural center of the Muslim zone. But the mosques of the Ottoman sultans and the Taj Mahal in Mogul India also revealed the artistic brilliance of the Islamic world at the beginning of modern history.

SUGGESTED READING

ARJOMAND, S. A. *The Shadow of God and the Hidden Imam*. Chicago: University of Chicago Press, 1984. Theoretical study of the political influence of Shiite Islam on Iran in medieval and modern times.

ARNOLD, T. W. *The Preaching of Islam*. London: Luzac, 1935. Old survey of twelve centuries of Muslim expansion.

AZIZ AHMAD. *Studies in Islamic Culture in the Indian Environment*. Oxford: Clarendon Press, 1964. Includes studies of Mogul times.

BABUR, Z. M. *Memoirs of Babur* (2 vols.), trans. J. Leyden and W. Erskine. Oxford: Oxford University Press, 1921. The Mogul founder's own extraordinary account of his life.

Cambridge History of Iran (7 vols.). Cambridge, England: Cambridge University Press, 1983. Includes both later Abbasid and Safavid times, presented in the thorough and scholarly style of all the Cambridge histories. For a one-volume treatment of this powerful dynasty, see R. Savory, *Iran under the Safavids* (New York: Cambridge University Press, 1980).

GRUBE, E. J. *The World of Islam*. New York: McGraw-Hill, n.d. A beautiful collection of photographs of all forms of Muslim art, from calligraphy to mosques.

HODGSON, M. G. S. *The Venture of Islam: Conscience and History in a World Civilization* (3 vols.). Chicago: University of Chicago Press, 1974. An interpretive account of Islamic history and beliefs. For a briefer introduction, see H. A. Gibb, *Mohammedanism: An Historical Survey* (New York: Oxford University Press, 1970).

INALCIK, H. *The Ottoman Empire: The Classic Age, 1300–1600*. London Weidenfeld and Nicolson, 1972. Rise of the Ottoman power through the century of Suleiman the Magnificent.

MOOSVI, S. *The Economy of the Mughal Empire, c. 1595*. New York: Oxford University Press, 1987. Impressive quantitative study of the Indian economy under Akbar.

PARRY, V. J. "The Middle East, 1453–1574," in D. Johnson, ed., *The Making of the Modern World*. London: Ernest Ben, 1971. Brief account of the Ottoman realm around 1500.

PICKTHALL, M. M. *The Meaning of the Glorious Koran*. New York: New American Library, 1953. Readable translation of the Muslim holy book.

SAUNDERS, J. J., ed. *The Moslem World on the Eve of European Expansion*. Englewood Cliffs, N.J.: Prentice Hall, 1966. Primary sources on the Muslim center.

SMITH, V. *Akbar the Great Mogul*, 2nd ed. Oxford: Clarendon Press, 1927. Still the standard biography.

SPEAR, P. *A History of India*. Baltimore: Penguin, 1965. A solid survey of Indian history, with sections on the reigns of the Moguls.

WADDY, C. *Women in Muslim History*. London: Longman, 1980. An overview, somewhat thin on the early modern period. The first chapter of S. H. Mirza's *Muslim Women's Role in the Pakistan Movement* (Research Society of Pakistan, Punjab University, 1969) includes some discussion of women poets and other leading spirits of the Mogul period.

CHAPTER 27

MING CHINA AND ITS SPHERE

THE CONFUCIAN ZONE

EAST ASIA: THE WORLD BEYOND THE MOUNTAINS

The hardy, not to say foolhardy, sixteenth-century traveler who wanted to go beyond the Muslim center of Eurasia into the farthest East would have found the last leg of his journey much harder than anything before. Trade routes were no longer what they had been in the Classic Age of the Roman and Han Chinese empires, or even in the more recent period of Mongol rule across Eurasia, when Marco Polo had made the trip. And basic geography had always cut East Asia off from the rest of the double continent.

The lands and peoples of East Asia were isolated from the world by some of the most formidable barriers in nature. To the north lay barren deserts and the forbidding steppes of Siberia. In the west, the mountains of the Pamir Knot, the Tibetan Plateau, and the five-mile-high wall of the Himalayas barred the way. Southward, the mountains and dense jungles of mainland Southeast Asia were all but impenetrable. Still farther to the east, the Pacific Ocean stretched—forever, as it must have seemed in 1500. In addition, the sheer size and wildly varied geography of China itself, with its huge river valleys—especially the Yellow River in the north and the Yangzi in central China—made the East Asian giant an impossible country to know.

Within these protecting and isolating barriers, an almost entirely mongoloid population had created a number of centers of civilization over the preceding three thousand years. But by far the largest and oldest civilization in the Far East was that of imperial China.

The unity of the East Asian world, then, was not like that of either the reborn West or the Muslim center. East Asia was not a system of feuding states with a rough parity of power, like the great powers of Europe. Nor did a common religion, producing cultural similarities among its adherents, bind this part of the globe as it did the Muslim zone. It was rather the historic predominance of a single great nation, warping the history and shaping the culture of all its neighbors, that made the East Asian world a distinct region of Eurasian civilization.

China in 1500 was the largest country in the world, larger in area and population than all of Europe. The very presence of this colossus, with its impressive Confucian civilization and its unified bureaucratic government, had awed the other peoples of the Far East since before the time of Christ. China, vast in its power and influential in its culture, was the great historic fact that imposed cultural unity on the East Asian world.

CHINA AND ITS SPHERE OF INFLUENCE

China's sphere of influence included a considerable number of peoples around the frontiers of the Chinese Empire. There were steppe nomads to the north, beyond the Great Wall, in Mongolia, Manchuria, and elsewhere, sometimes half Sinicized but always a military threat. There were the two peninsular societies of Korea to the northeast and Vietnam in the southwest, both significantly shaped in China's image by 1500. And there was the island kingdom of Japan, which had been accepting some Chinese influences and rejecting others for more than a thousand years.

Chinese influence has in fact waxed and waned over all its huge area of cultural and political predominance down the centuries. When powerful, aggressively expansionist dynasties ruled in China, its influence was all but inescapable. This had been the case particularly after the Qin unification, during the Han (206 B.C.–A.D. 220), and again after the Sui reunification, during the Tang (618–906). Over the half-dozen centuries before 1500, however, China's influence had declined, especially under the embattled Song dynasty (960–1279) and during the century of Mongol rule (1264–1368).

By that time, however, the pervasive impact of Chinese civilization had been felt everywhere in East Asia. The Chinese language and its characters, the classical writings attributed to Confucius, and some Chinese-style central government had appeared in a number of neighboring lands. Buddhism, originating in India, had reached China first and been passed on in Chinese forms to Korea, Japan, and elsewhere. Whether they paid formal tribute to the Son of Heaven in Beijing or not, the peoples of East Asia owed a great deal to the land the Chinese called the Middle Kingdom and thought of—understandably—as the true center of the world.

At the beginning of the modern period, a good case could certainly be made for the superiority of China's historic accomplishment. In Europe, Marco Polo's admiring descriptions of the China of Kublai Khan were still read. It was golden dreams of the wealth of Cathay and Cipangu (Japan), as well as of India and the Spice Islands, that drew the Europeans across the oceans. It should be remembered, after all, that it was the West that felt the need of the East: East Asia seems to have been satisfied with what it had of wealth and culture.

A look at the East Asian world, then, will illustrate again the plurality of successful civilizations that prevailed around the world on the eve of the Western predominance. And it will demonstrate once more how unlikely the emergence of such a single predominant power in a world of many impressive cultures really was.

 # THE MING DYNASTY

THE PIG EMPEROR: ZHU YUANZHANG

The Chinese Empire, the vast central expanse of East Asia, had been unified off and on since Qin and Han times, contemporaneous with ancient Rome in the West. But the Roman Empire fell, and Europe has never been unified since. The Han dynasty in China, by contrast, was by no means the last to rule a united China. In fact, a regular pattern of the rise and fall of central government in China had established itself in the so-called dynastic cycle.

According to this pattern, recognized by Chinese historians since the Zhou dynasty, a particular dynasty ruled China only as long as it enjoyed the Mandate of Heaven, the Chinese equivalent of what was called divine right in Europe (or the will of Allah in Muslim lands). When a regime became corrupt, neglected the ceremonial worship of ancestors and the gods, and oppressed the people, Heaven withdrew the mandate to rule. Divine displeasure was manifested through weak and divided government, flood, famine, rebellion, and foreign invasion, climaxing in the overthrow of the regime and the rise to power of a new dynasty. The latter stages of this cycle were clearly manifested in the fall of the Mongols and the rise of the Ming dynasty in the later 1300s.

The inefficiency and internecine strife of the later Mongol Khans had left dikes untended, the realm ill-governed. In the resulting storm of natural catastrophes and civil discord, the dynasty foundered and fled northward, to the Mongolian steppes from which they had come. The immense expanse of China, as so often before in its history, was surrendered to marauding bandits, rebellious peasants, secret societies, and feuding warlords struggling to see which of them would be granted the divine mandate.

But thoughtful Chinese had long since decided that peace, prosperity, and order required political unity under a duly certified Son of Heaven. In the end, then, autocratic order did emerge from anarchy. There was a winner, and once his supremacy was demonstrated, the nation accepted the new dynasty with gratitude for the end of the crisis. Thus began a new cycle in the long history of China.

The founder of the Ming dynasty (1368–1644) must have seemed an unpromising beginning to the cultured gentry and scholarly Confucian bureaucrats who ran the provinces and staffed the new government, as they had done for many centuries. Zhu Yuanzhang (1368–1398) was, to put it mildly, a man of the people.

Born of dirt-poor peasant parents, Zhu had been successively a novice in a Buddhist monastery (where he learned to read and write), a beggar, a bandit, and finally a rebel leader. He had a swinish face—he was called the Pig Emperor in later chronicles—was paranoically suspicious, and could be extremely cruel, especially in his later years. But he also had a great capacity for organization, decision making, and plain hard work. He called his dynasty Ming, meaning "brilliant"—and he did his best to make it so.

Zhu Yuanzhang inaugurated a more rigorous personal autocracy than China had seen before. Building on the foundations laid down by the Mongols—who, as foreign rulers, had also had to rule by fiat—Zhu took as much actual power as possible into his own hands. A workaholic, he plowed through piles of official memorials every day. At court, disloyal or inefficient officials were beaten publicly with bamboo as examples to their peers. In the countryside, a system of neighborhood responsibility for labor service and security set neighbors to watching neighbors. Part of the founder's legacy to the Ming dynasty was thus an unprecedented degree of imperial power.

But Zhu's thirty-year reign also saw a number of more positive accomplishments. He provided some economic relief for the peasants after the devastation of the civil wars and introduced a more efficient system of taxation. He constructed many schools; reinstituted the civil-service examinations, which had been virtually ignored by the Mongols; and restored Confucianism—the closest thing to a state religion the secular Chinese have ever had—as the nation's official philosophy.

The Ming founder built on a grand scale, especially at his capital at Nanjing, which he made perhaps the largest walled city in the world. While medieval Europe sank into the chaos of the Black Death, the papal schism, and the Hundred Years' War, China thus found unity under a strong dynasty once more.

YONGLE AND THE PRECIOUS SHIPS

A strong founder has normally been essential to dynastic success in China. Equally important, however, has been the part frequently played by a powerful successor as consolidator and sustainer of the newly established regime. Zhu Yuanzhang was followed on the dragon throne—after a brief power struggle—by perhaps the most powerful of the Ming rulers: the Yongle emperor (1403–1424).[1]

As the consolidator of the Ming, Yongle embarked upon such sizable public works as the renovation of the Grand Canal linking central and North China. He moved whole populations into war-devastated areas to develop these regions once more. He built more schools, honored at least the letter of Confucian doctrine, and commissioned huge scholarly projects for the preservation of Chinese literary culture.

Yongle also moved the capital back to Beijing, the ruined Mongol center in North China. He rebuilt the city on a still grander scale, ringing it with fourteen miles of forty-foot walls. The new Beijing was centered in the administrative section called the Imperial City and the red-walled Forbidden City, where the emperors were to live thereafter in a paradise of palaces and gardens.

Yongle's most startling enterprise, however, was the launching of an unprecedented series of overseas expeditions. These were the voyages of the Precious Ships, as they are called in Chinese history.

Between 1405 and 1433, a total of seven great fleets of seagoing junks carrying tens of thousands of men sailed from China to explore southern and western seas. Under the command of a shrewd Muslim court eunuch named Zheng He (1371–1433), these huge armadas nosed their way through the islands of Southeast Asia, touching at the rich seaports of western India. They went on to the Persian Gulf and Arabia, up the Red Sea, and down the coast of East Africa. Giraffes, ostriches, and zebras were brought back from Africa. The kings of Ceylon and Sumatra were brought to Beijing in chains. Tributary relations were established with scores of nations. Then, less than sixty years before Columbus inaugurated the great age of European expansion, China's overseas expeditions ceased as abruptly as they had begun.

They were the largest maritime ventures in human history up to that time, some of them involving more than sixty great ships and almost thirty thousand men and traversing thousands of miles of distant seas. The Precious Ships that were the backbone of the fleets were up to four hundred feet long and featured four decks, watertight compartments, and the seaworthiness for which the junk has always been known. They navigated with the help of compasses and detailed sailing instructions accumulated over the centuries in South Chinese trading ports such as Canton (Guangzhou). They were an impressive demonstration of the scale on which China might have operated at sea if this had been its chosen field of endeavor.

But the great maritime ventures of Yongle were also

extremely costly. In addition, they were the special project of the court eunuchs and hence were opposed by the scholar-bureaucrats, who were the eunuchs' great rivals in Beijing. Furthermore, China's land frontiers soon preoccupied the Ming emperors. It is also probably fair to say that the emperors of China, with their vast heartland empire, had little sense of the potential importance of seapower in the world.

GOVERNMENT AND SOCIETY: MANDARINS AND PEASANT MASSES

The majority of later Ming emperors were competent men; the latest did not even attain that level. But for two centuries after the founder and the sustainer of the dynasty, the Chinese system of government carried even mediocre rulers, giving China the domestic tranquility all nations crave. A look at Chinese government in general, and at the Chinese economy and society in early-modern times, is thus more important here than more names and dates of emperors.

Despite the augmented, sometimes arbitrary powers of the emperor, the organization chart of Chinese government looks much the same under the Ming as it had for centuries previous. Central government fell traditionally into three main divisions: civil administration, the military, and the board of censors. Civil government was carried out through the ancient six ministries for defense and justice, revenues and public works, personnel matters and religious rites. The imperial army, consisting of almost five hundred guards and garrison units of more than five thousand men each, sounded more impressive than it was: in an unwarlike society, under an unaggressive dynasty, the troops got comparatively little practice. The censors, finally, were young officials chosen for integrity and courage, who inspected all bureaus and subdivisions of government and reported corruption and treason directly to the palace.

Ming China, a nation the size of the United States today, was divided into 15 provinces, approximately 160 prefectures, 235 subprefectures, and 1200 counties. Each province had civil and military administrators, each lower subdivision its prefect, subprefect, or county magistrate, plus a few clerks to carry out the paperwork.

The backbone of this administrative system were the scholar-bureaucrats, or *mandarins*, as Europeans came to call them. Chosen by a graded system of nationwide examinations on the Confucian classics, this highly educated ruling class came largely from the landowning gentry. There were problems, of course. The civil service could do little about weak emperors or feuds between officials and court eunuchs. Nevertheless, it seems fair to say that the Chinese government was the closest approximation of a real meritocracy to be found anywhere in the world in 1500.

Much local government was still undertaken on a

---

[1] Reign names like "Yongle" (he was born Chengzu) are commonly used by Western historians as if they were personal names, and will often be so used here.

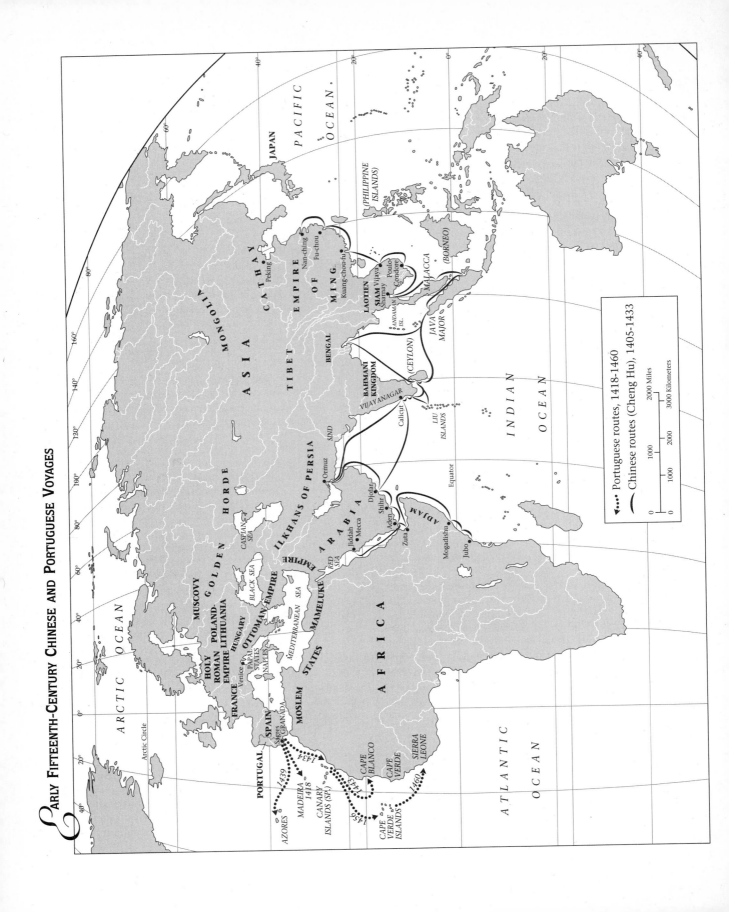

EARLY FIFTEENTH-CENTURY CHINESE AND PORTUGUESE VOYAGES

ARCTIC OCEAN

Arctic Circle

MUSCOVY

GOLDEN HORDE

HOLY ROMAN EMPIRE
POLAND-LITHUANIA
HUNGARY
FRANCE
PAPAL STATES
Venice
NAPLES
OTTOMAN EMPIRE
BLACK SEA
CASPIAN SEA
MEDITERRANEAN SEA

SPAIN
GRANADA
PORTUGAL
Sagres

MOSLEM STATES

MAMELUKE EMPIRE
RED SEA
Jiddah · Mecca
Aden
Zeila
Shihr
Dhofar
ARABIA

ILKHANS OF PERSIA
Ormuz
SIND

AFRICA

AZORES
MADEIRA
CANARY ISLANDS (SP.)
CAPE VERDE ISLANDS
CAPE BLANCO
CAPE VERDE
SIERRA LEONE

1439
1434
1445
1450
1460

ATLANTIC OCEAN

MONGOLIA

ASIA

CATHAY

TIBET

BENGAL

VIJAYANAGAR
BAHMANI KINGDOM
Calicut
(CEYLON)
LIU ISLANDS

INDIAN OCEAN

Equator

Mogadishu
Jubo
ADJAM

JAPAN

Peking
Nan-ching
Fu-chou
Kuang-chou-fu

LAOTEN
SIAM
Shamay
Vijaya
Poulo Condore

MALACCA

(BORNEO)

JAVA MAJOR

ANDAMAN ISL.

(PHILIPPINE ISLANDS)

PACIFIC OCEAN

▶···· Portuguese routes, 1418-1460

—— Chinese routes (Cheng Hu), 1405-1433

2000 Miles
3000 Kilometers
1000
2000
1000
0
0

voluntary basis by prestigious local gentry, especially degree holders, who had passed at least some of the Confucian examinations. These educated landed families organized everything from repairing roads and irrigation ditches to maintaining local schools and temples. Demands upon the peasant masses were limited, consisting of land taxes at harvest time and a variety of compulsory labor.

The Ming centuries were a prosperous time economically. North China, ravaged by the Mongols—who turned large parts of it into hunting parks—was restored to agricultural use under the Ming. Central China, especially the fertile Yangzi valley, produced a prodigious rice crop and flourishing commercial cities such as Nanjing and Hangzhou. The south, finally, remained the most populous and prosperous section of the country, and trade became highly developed at ports such as Canton. From the political capital at Beijing in the north to the economic heartland in the south, from the rice bowl of the Yangzi valley to the endless chilly plains of Xinjiang in China's Far West, the Middle Kingdom of the sixteenth century flourished on a scale unmatched elsewhere.

In many ways, Chinese society under the Ming looked rather like the China of 1900—the China into which Mao Zedong, China's preeminent twentieth-century leader, was born.

At the top of Ming Chinese society were the landholding classes, though they were more likely to be middle-rank gentry than the huge landholders of earlier centuries. The nation's recognized leaders were the holders of the chief offices of state, with their titles and protocol, their silken robes, ink brushes, long, thin beards, and long fingernails. At the bottom society, the vast peasant majority worked diligently along the carefully maintained canals and irrigation ditches fed by China's great rivers. Rich black mud and dully gleaming rice paddies, wide straw hats, and slow-moving water buffalo filled the days of most of the hundred million Chinese of 1500.

WOMEN IN TRADITIONAL CHINA

Women constituted perhaps half this huge population, and as usual, we know less about them than we would like. There were no great empresses during the Ming period, as there had been in Han and Tang times and would be again under the Manchus. There was an important minority of highly educated women, ranging in social background from court aristocracy and country gentry to imperial concubines, famous courtesans, and Buddhist and Daoist nuns. Some women served as midwives, herb doctors, spirit mediums, silkworm farmers, and tapestry embroiderers. The great peasant majority of women lived lives as limited as the lives of their husbands—the life of unremitting labor that undergirded the wealth of all nations in 1500.

Most women in traditional China were expected to marry and to produce a male heir to carry on the religious ceremonies that bound the living family to the spirits of their ancestors. Because women could not perform these rites of veneration for ancestors, daughters were believed to be inferior to sons.

Young women in traditional China were instructed in the basic female virtues, including fidelity, chastity, and obedience, in a series of moral tales about honored women who had demonstrated these qualities. One such story recounts the heroism of a daughter of the Chan clan who, captured by bandits with her father and brother, won their freedom by offering herself to the bandit chief. As soon as her loved ones were safely away, however, the young woman hurled herself into a nearby river and drowned. She thus both saved her father and brother and preserved her own womanly honor.

Growing girls of the better classes were required to submit to the painful process of footbinding, intended to produce tiny deformed feet. These both made it clear that they were wealthy enough not to have to do any active work and produced a stiff, swaying walk that Chinese men found attractive. Marriages were arranged by older relatives and marriage brokers, who considered family interests much more important than the personal inclinations of the bride and groom. Once she had married and borne sons to perpetuate the family, however, a woman could exercise great authority, expecting to be consulted by both her husband and her children on all matters of importance concerning the household. A strong-willed matriarch could thus come to dominate several generations of a large extended family in Ming China.

A LAND OF SAGES CONFRONTS THE BARBARIANS

When the first Portuguese traders and Jesuit missionaries arrived in China at the end of the sixteenth century, they tended to be impressed by what they saw. Jesuit accounts described China in idealized terms as a land of sages lacking only the Christian Gospel to make it perfect.

In fact, under the Ming emperors of the fourteenth, fifteenth, and sixteenth centuries China, enjoyed another enviably long spell of political stability, relative peace, and general prosperity. The secular cast of mind typical of China spared the Chinese the religious tumults of the Christian West or the Muslim Middle East. The nation's economic well-being was quite comparable even to that of Renaissance Europe, with its new prosperity. And China's central government avoided the endemic warfare of fifteenth- and sixteenth-century Europe.

As mentioned, the Ming emperors built the vast new palace area of Beijing called the Forbidden City. A visit to the Forbidden City of Beijing today is inevitably very touristy. You drift with crowds through spacious courtyards, climb broad staircases you've seen in the movies somewhere, and peer into dimly lit palaces and temples.

But even surrounded by Western faces and flashing Japanese cameras, you can get a sense of the Ming achievement.

There is a wonderful symmetry and space to these imperial precincts. The very repetition of red pillars, gilded decorations, and the same sculptured mythic beasts rising from every upward-curving pagoda roof-line reveals a powerful presiding intelligence. It is hard to think of the Forbidden City as home, even to the "lord of ten thousand years." But it is a fitting memorial to the power he once wielded as master of the Middle Kingdom, the largest empire in the sixteenth-century world.

The Ming period actually gave traditional Chinese culture what became its final formulation. It was the civilization of Ming China that the Manchu invaders of the seventeenth century would inherit and carry on down into the early twentieth century. It was a massively conservative system of society, heavily oriented toward the past and more famous for stability than for progress. And it had the misfortune to settle into its final, fixed form just when the reborn West was launching into the most dynamic period of Western history.

In hindsight it is easy to condemn China for its rigidity and traditionalism in the face of the coming challenge. Through sixteenth-century Chinese eyes, however, the first Europeans to find their way to South China must have seemed like only moderately subtle barbarians, with their passion for money, their rampant militarism, and their religious fanaticism. What, indeed, did the West have to offer that was better than stability, prosperity, and peace?

 # SATELLITE CIVILIZATIONS

THE MIDDLE KINGDOM AND ITS NEIGHBORS

Chinese preeminence, one of the great facts of East Asian life since Han times, continued to be widely recognized under the Ming dynasty. China's political and military power was not as great as it had been under the Han and Tang emperors. But tribute continued to flow into the Middle Kingdom, and China's cultural influence was perhaps greater in 1500 than it had ever been.

The tributary system exemplified China's unique relationship to the East Asian world it dominated. As tributary states, lesser Asian rulers—from tribal chieftains in Manchuria to the emperor of Vietnam—acknowledged the supremacy of the Son of Heaven in Beijing. In return, these lesser potentates got letters patent certifying their right to rule their own lands, a seal to use on official documents, and an intermittent flow of pious exhortations to rule in a true Confucian spirit. More important, perhaps, they got some military protection, the right to trade in the vast Chinese market, and permission to send missions to study the immensely admired Chinese way of life.

Three or four examples of the satellite civilizations that resulted will make clear how great China's influence was. Such an overview will also indicate how vigorous other East Asian cultures were on the eve of European intrusion.

INFLUENCE ON KOREA, VIETNAM, AND MANCHURIA

Korea, the peninsular land north of China—or, more accurately, due east of Beijing—is often cited as the model of a Chinese-style Confucian society. Partially Sinicized in earlier centuries, briefly absorbed into the Mongol Empire, Korea emerged as an independent nation once more just before 1400. General Yi, the founder of the new Korea, was, however, strongly proChinese. Yi quickly dispatched the obligatory tribute to the new Ming dynasty, and under his descendants, Korea proceeded once again to import Confucian culture, ideals, and governmental structures wholesale.

Korea was soon divided administratively into provinces and smaller subdivisions on the Chinese model. China's six ministries and board of censors blossomed in miniature in the new Korean capital at Seoul. The Chinese system of Confucian education and state examinations for civil-service posts became still more firmly rooted. Indeed, the fifteenth century was actually a golden age of Confucian scholarship—in the neighboring tributary nation of Korea.

Vietnam, the peninsular country south of China, had a rather rougher long-term relationship with the Middle Kingdom. In the end, however, China's influence played a crucial part here too.

Governed as part of South China for nearly a thousand years, from Han times till the collapse of the Tang, Vietnam gained its political independence in the tenth century—and at once proceeded to send formal tribute to the Son of Heaven to the north. In the centuries that followed, the Vietnamese bitterly resisted Chinese attempts to reimpose their rule by force of arms, fighting off both the Mongols and the Mings. At the same time, however, the Sinification of Vietnam continued apace.

During the fifteenth century especially, the Le dynasty modeled Vietnamese government very closely on that of Ming China. The southern nation was divided into thirteen provinces and subdivided into prefectures, counties, and smaller units. A graded system of bureaucratic government, centered in the new Vietnamese capital at Hanoi, was imposed on the land. Chinese culture, dress, and styles of life were cultivated at the court in Hanoi, and the royal chronicles of Vietnam were dutifully compiled in the Chinese style—and in the Chinese language.

This pervasive Chinese influence in Vietnamese ruling circles did have the unfortunate effect of cutting the monarchs off from the masses, who retained their traditional Southeast Asian codes and folkways. But the Chi-

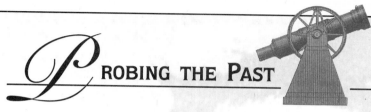

PROBING THE PAST

"In the written and collected memory of T'an-ch'eng as it was stored in the biographical sections of the Local History, the highest standards were demanded and claimed. This was even truer for women than for men, and the dissemination of these biographies of "Honorable and Virtuous Women" was one of the important ways that the local worthies—acting in full accord with the stated values of the government—sought to impose their views of correct female behavior. By this they meant, in general, the behavior of women toward their husbands, for of the fifty-six T'an-ch'eng women's biographies printed in the 1670s, only three were of unmarried women, and of these three two were betrothed and about to be married. The virtues fostered were those of chastity, courage, tenacity, and unquestioning acceptance of the prevailing hierarchy—unto death if necessary: fifteen of the listed women had committed suicide, and in thirteen of these suicides the motive was loyalty to a deceased husband or to avoid rape, which would shame both wife and husband. In contrast to the suicides for vengeance, or out of anger, which Huang Liu-hung had criticized so strongly, these suicides (if by childless women) were considered morally "correct," as they showed the depth of the woman's reverence for her husband. . . . Such suicides were not restricted to members of elite families who had been educated in the neo-Confucian ideals of loyalty: one woman Liu, who killed herself after her husband's death from illness, was a carpenter's daughter; her husband was a farm laborer; another was married to a small trader who traveled back and forth between the market towns of Li-chia-chuang and Lai-wu."

◆◆◆

Jonathan D. Spence, one of the most admired modern historians of China, has written several intriguing books for the intelligent general reader. The Death of Woman Wang (1978) offers a look at life in a peasant village in the seventeenth century—early Manchu times chronologically but so far below the level of high politics that we are really dealing with traditional Chinese life as inherited from the Ming period. In the present extract, T'an-ch'eng was an obscure county in northern China; Huang Liu-Hung a scholarly local official whose handbook on the duties of the magistracy included illustrative accounts of local events.

What qualities were expected of "Honorable and Virtuous Women" in T'an-ch'eng? Do you think of these qualities as virtues? What would the citizens of T'an-ch'eng think of the sexual mores and divorce rate of the United States today?

Jonathan D. Spence, The Death of Woman Wang (New York: Viking Press, 1978), pp. 99–100.

nese model also gave Vietnam a government concerned with public works, the patronage of culture, and other valuable features of the Chinese way in 1500.

Northeast of China, another and rather less likely example of the transforming impact of Chinese influence appeared somewhat later, in the sixteenth century. This was the militarized Manchurian state that was to play such a significant part in China's future.

Southern Manchuria, northeast of Beijing, had been part of China under the Han, and the Ming dynasty exercised a loose suzerainty over the area. Chinese emperors sent certificates of authority and honorific awards to Manchu tribal chiefs and accepted their daughters into the imperial harem. Chinese settlers moved into Manchuria, establishing Chinese towns among the seminomadic tribes and exerting a slowly growing cultural influence on their leaders.

But Manchuria lay north of the Great Wall, China's main line of defense against restless steppe invaders. In this no-man's-land beyond the Wall, the unaggressive Ming emperors found the Manchu difficult to control. Then, in the later 1500s, a leader arose who was able to unify the tribes into a roughly centralized state—which suddenly became a threat to China itself.

The new leader in the north was a restless chieftain named Nurhachi. Nurhachi (1559–1626) built state power in Manchuria through a combination of negotiation and warfare, strategic marriages, and tribal alliances. He converted the region from a clan-based society to a bureaucratic state by means of a system of military units called *banners* run by appointed commanders. But he also drew heavily on Chinese models and Chinese personnel. China's six ministries were soon duplicated at the Manchurian capital of Mukden, and literate Chinese-settler administrators were recruited to run the Manchu banners.

In the next century, the Middle Kingdom would regret the strength and order its cultural exports had given to the new Manchurian state. In the 1600s, the Manchu banners would break through the Great Wall itself and come flooding south to overwhelm the ancient civilization that had been their teacher. The establishment of what became China's last historic dynasty was surely facilitated by the influence of Chinese culture on the society of the Manchus before the conquest.

INDEPENDENT JAPAN: LAND OF THE SAMURAI

The island empire of Japan, stretching northeastward from the coast of Korea, some 120 miles offshore, had absorbed the Chinese model early in its history. A unified Japanese government had first emerged in the sixth century, with a capital at what is today Kyoto in southern Honshu, the large central island of the group. During the formative centuries that followed, Japan had gone to school—like so many others—to the great Tang empire. Japan had copied Tang government institutions, learned the Chinese written language, accepted Chinese Buddhism and Chinese costume and customs.

When the Tang empire fell, shortly after 900, however, Japan had turned inward to shape over the centuries a distinctively Japanese lifestyle and society.

What actually developed were two cultures. At the imperial capital, the Heian culture flourished. Political power slipped away from the imperial government and into the hands of feuding court families. At the same time, however, these courtly Japanese aristocrats cultivated a unique elegance and sensitivity in their personal lives. They developed in their pavilions and palaces a delicate, sensual, and highly aesthetic style of living, delighting in poetry, sophisticated fiction, and the fine art of love.

In the Japanese countryside, however, another culture entirely was growing up. This was the virile, violent

A Japanese Buddhist temple complex. The turned-up pagoda roof lines and the giant statute of Buddha meditating behind the tree on the right recall Chinese influences in earlier centuries. Notice also the lightness of the architectural lines, the openness and airiness of the Japanese center of worship. (New York Public Library Picture Collection)

lifestyle of the *bushi*, the warrior, with his *bushido* code of Japanese chivalry. From about 1200 on, the bushi—under the more familiar label of *samurai*, "one who serves"—became the real arbiters of Japan's destiny.

From the thirteenth century through the sixteenth, then, Japan underwent a progressive political disintegration. At the top, this process was precipitated by the rise of a military commander called the *shogun*. Appointed by the emperors, nominally as military leaders against barbarian invasion from the northern islands, the shoguns in fact became the feudal overlords of the samurai—and much closer to the true rulers of Japan than the emperors were.

The two early shogunates were those of Kamakura and of the Ashikaga family. The Kamakura shogunate (1185–1333) dominated Japan from a separate court at the city of Kamakura in central Honshu, far to the east of the imperial capital at Kyoto. The Ashikaga shogunate (1336–1603) saw the warriors move into Kyoto itself while the feudal lords of the countryside filled the land with war.

Even at their strongest, the shoguns of these medieval centuries were only paramount feudal lords, never wielders of centralized state power. And even at the top there was conflict—between shoguns and emperors who tried to assert their own long-dormant authority, between rivals for the imperial throne in Kyoto or for the shogunate itself. With central authority thus in disarray, actual power devolved increasingly upon the greatest of the warrior nobles, landed magnates called *daimyo*, or "big names."

In the fourteenth century—about the time that Europe's medieval synthesis was collapsing—Japan's "centralized feudalism" also slid over the brink into the anarchy of the Japanese dark age. For two and a half centuries, central political authority was almost totally lacking in Japan.

Political breakdown, however, was not accompanied by economic decline. Japanese agriculture actually became more productive during these centuries. New strains of rice, new farm tools, and more farm animals helped increase Japanese population. Trade expanded, especially with Ming China. The Chinese, however, let very few Japanese into the Middle Kingdom, largely because of the reputation of the Japanese as pirates and brawlers.

By 1500 Japan had thus drifted far from the Chinese model of earlier centuries. While centralized government run by scholarly bureaucrats prevailed on the mainland, the island kingdom had fallen into hopeless anarchy, ravaged by soldiers whose power extended only a short distance beyond their castle walls.

The contrast between the Confucian mandarin of China and the feudal samurai of Japan could scarcely have been greater. The Japanese equivalent of Europe's medieval knights had their code of chivalry too, prescribing such ancient warrior virtues as courage, pride, and loyalty to one's overlord. The samurai was expected to reject wealth, live a hard, strenuous life on the battlefield, and be prepared for death at any moment. Defeat

meant certain death by decapitation. Dishonored, the samurai was expected to commit suicide like an antique Roman, by disemboweling himself with his sword in the ritual of *seppuku*. The shogun, as supreme military commander, was seen as the perfect embodiment of these warrior virtues.

They were inspiring qualities for "those who served" in a war-torn age. The samurai, it was said, let go of his life as easily as a cherry blossom falls from the branch in spring. This oddly poetic warrior ideal would live on long after the age that engendered it had passed away. The militant spirit of the age of samurai predominance, from the thirteenth through the sixteenth centuries, would survive and impose itself upon much of the history of modern Japan.

The Europeans who appeared in Japanese waters in the sixteenth century would find their muskets much more welcome than their missionaries. In the nineteenth and twentieth centuries, they would discover that Japan's bushido tradition, equipped with big guns and battleships, could be a formidable rival indeed.

CHINA AND JAPAN: CONTRASTING CULTURES

CULTURAL DIFFERENCES

A central feature of East Asian history in later modern times would be the conflict between China and Japan. In the nineteenth and twentieth centuries particularly, China's majestic preeminence in East Asia would be challenged by the vigorous, adaptable Japanese. Some of the crucial differences between these two great peoples go back to the cultures that had evolved in China and Japan by 1500, the very beginnings of modern times.

In China, as we have seen, the Ming period saw a final reformulation of the ancient cultural patterns that would survive through the Manchu centuries into the present one. In Japan, whose civilization had begun to emerge more recently, the period of the Kamakura and Ashikaga shogunates saw the first formulation of much of the ethos and artistic tradition that would dominate the modern Japanese spirit. This final section, then, will concentrate on the culture of these two pivotal East Asian nations at the beginning of the modern age.

The most striking thing about the two is the range of differences between them.

Ming China remained, like the China of earlier centuries, an astonishingly secular society, especially by contrast with the religious bent of Hindu India, the Muslim center of Eurasia, or Europe in the Reformation. China was also distinguished by its passion for the culture of the word. It was as profoundly literary a society as any in history, as the intellectual developments of the Ming period make clear.

Japan, by contrast, was as devoted to religion, especially to various forms of Buddhism, as the Hindu, Muslim, or Christian cultures further to the west. The other major aspect of Japanese culture between 1200 and 1600, however—the ethic, art, and literature of the samurai military tradition—makes an equally striking contrast with the literary culture of China—a contrast between sword and pen that is also to be found within the Muslim and Christian worlds.

In stressing these differences, one runs the risk of undermining the larger notion of a single East Asian civilization shaped primarily by the pervasive influence of the Middle Kingdom. In reading what follows, then, it will be useful to remember how much of Japanese culture, from Buddhism to painting to written language, was, after all, derived from China. We may also ask ourselves if there is not a distinct, if ill-defined, East Asian flavor even to the differences between the two national cultures. The samurai and the mandarin may have their parallels in other cultures, but both are distinctive products of the East Asian world.

Ming Culture: Fisherman's Flute to Golden Lotus

Ming China was firmly committed to the Neo-Confucian philosophy that had taken shape during the Song dynasty. Buddhism, once so influential in China, was banished to the provinces by Ming times. Under the Ming, hundreds of Confucian schools sprang up to train local collections of scholars and students. And the great Hanlin Academy was established at the capital to undertake, under imperial patronage, truly staggering scholarly projects in the tradition of the Confucian sages. An often cited example is the great *Encyclopedia* produced around 1400 under the most famous of the Mings, Yongle. This immense collection of major Chinese works of the past on history and geography, government and ethics, occupied the labors of 2000 scholars and ran to more than 1100 volumes.

The most influential Confucian philosopher of the period was Wang Yangming, a learned official and military commander who experienced a moment of philosophical enlightenment like that of a Buddhist saint. Wang urged self-cultivation as the road to sagehood, but stressed particularly the close relation between right knowledge and moral action. We do not really *understand* the doctrine of reverence for elders and ancestors, he urged, unless we are so convinced of it that we do *in fact* revere them. Knowing and doing are one.

The most famous Ming painters—nature artists in the great Song tradition—blended literary skills into their painting. These "literati" of China's Southern school were poets as much as they were painters, and they frequently added a clearly literary dimension to pictorial art.

Executed in the ancient Chinese way, with brushes and ink on hangings or hand scrolls made of paper or silk, these pictures project a sense of reality that would have impressed a contemporary Renaissance artist. Qiu Ying's *Fisherman's Flute Heard over the Lake* vibrates with the reality of leaves and bark, rock and water, a tree-shrouded house on the near shore and misty mountains far off beyond the lake. Tang Yin's *Ink-Bamboo* projects the same sense of reality in the simple shadow of a bamboo branch seen across a window. Other Ming painters went beyond realism, manipulating nature to suit their personal aesthetic canons. They turned mountains into startling architectural forms, or trees into abstract patterns against the sky.

Ming drama also combined art forms and stressed authorial artistry. Here again there was a Southern style, reflecting the increasing importance of the prosperous and populous South in Chinese history.

Ming dramatists produced plays composed of dozens of scenes, highlighted by flute music and songs. The most famous Ming playwright, Tang Xianzu, created a series of dream plays. His *Dream of Han Tan*, for instance, is the story of a young man who dreams an entire future for himself and awakens vividly aware of the brevity of this earthly existence—a popular Renaissance European theme as well. These subtle dramas, many of them written by scholarly men, were intended to win the plaudits of fellow sophisticates rather than the cheers of a mass audience.

There was, however, a large popular readership for the stories and novels of the period. Printed on the woodblock press and read by a growing audience of literate common folk, these Ming fictions drew on both history and fantasy for their subjects.

Some of the most famous of Chinese novels date from this period. The universally popular *Romance of the Three Kingdoms* fictionizes the struggles of three rivals for the throne of the dying Han dynasty, while *All Men Are Brothers* recounts the exploits of a band of Robin Hood bandits in the closing years of the Northern Song. *Monkey*, by contrast, is the story of the pilgrimage of a real Chinese Buddhist monk to India—accompanied in this version by a mischievous, magical monkey hero assigned by Buddha himself to protect the holy man in his wanderings. *The Golden Lotus*, finally is a thoroughly erotic novel, still hard to find in uncensored English.

It is a range as wide and human as the age itself. On a smaller scale, the same may be said of the short stories of writers such as Ling Mengqi. Ling's tales of Chinese kings and generals, scandalous Buddhist monks and Daoist sages, strange lands, demons and ghosts, comic incidents, exotic revenges, and properly filial offspring bring the whole of the Ming to life.

JAPAN: FROM THE PURE LAND TO LADY NIJO

The thought and art of contemporary Japan focused rather more starkly on two dominant themes: religion and war. But the Japanese expressions of these two ancient concerns of the human race are as rich and vivid as the whole broad spectrum of life revealed in Chinese culture.

Religion in Japan still meant, in part, reverence for the ancient spirits of nature worshiped at simple Shinto shrines. But the shrines were presided over by shamans who were also frequently Buddhist monks. And two forms of Buddhism were even more widespread in Japan than they had been in the preceding Heian period: the Pure Land sect and Zen meditation.

Believers in the Pure Land—the Western Paradise or heaven of popular Buddhism—believed like many Christians that simply to call with a believing heart upon the Enlightened One was to find salvation. Zen Buddhism, by contrast, required a rigorous monastic life and a personal quest through daily meditation, and only serious adepts were likely to take it up. Masses of common people flocked to the Pure Land and other sects in those violent times. Samurai and great nobles were drawn to the demanding self-discipline of Zen.

Intense vitality and astonishing anatomical realism are main features of Japanese Buddhist sculpture during these centuries. Buddha figures such as the fifty-foot meditating *Buddha of Kamakura* retain traditional poses and proportions, the calm round face and lowered lids, the conventionalized swooping folds of the robe. But the ferocious figures of temple guardians at holy places are carved or cast in metal with an almost supernatural realism. The bulging lifelike muscles and swollen tendons, the menacing gestures, the snarling mouth, bared teeth, and glaring eyes have a ferocity that reflects the savage side of that age of endemic warfare and samurai supremacy. These figures also, incidentally, reflect a mastery of human anatomy that no Renaissance European sculptor could better.

Religious and military themes mingle also in the literature of the early shogunates.

Courtly literature in prose and poetry continued to weave its delicate spell even at the court of figurehead emperors. But now the *Confessions of Lady Nijo*, after detailing her love affairs, conclude with her retirement to a Buddhist convent and a life of chanted prayers and religious rites. The most uniquely Japanese literary development of the period, the *No* drama, reveals a deep sense of the mystery of life behind the gorgeous *No* costumes, the masks, the stylized gestures and choral songs. The typical *No* play features gods and demons, warriors, women—and lunatics.

Warrior tales of the Kamakura period hail the great battles, ingenious ruses, and famous victories of heroes such as the celebrated Yoshitsune, the most famous samurai of them all. But even the great Yoshitsune came to a tragic end, betrayed and driven to ritual suicide by his own brother. Even in their hero tales, the Japanese of the age of the bushido code never forgot the brevity of life and honored above all things the warrior's willingness to cast his own life away.

It was a strange culture and a strange age, at least from a Western perspective. It was an era of seemingly endless warfare, of severed heads and *seppuku*. It was also the period that developed the delicate formality of the traditional Zen tea ceremony, the rich symbolism of Japanese flower arrangement, and the austere beauty of the sand and stone gardens of old Kyoto. The samurai spirit of blazing temple-guardian eyes and flashing swords also found expression in the stillness of Zen meditation and the calm formality of pouring a cup of tea.

The greatness of China was recognized across East Asia in 1500, and even Europeans had heard of the wonders of Cathay. The formidable talents of the Japanese would be a few centuries in emerging to the astonished gaze of Western people.

SUMMARY

The ancient Middle Kingdom of China continued to dominate East Asia as the modern age began. Cut off from the rest of the Old World by formidable geographical barriers, the world's largest nation exercised a degree of preeminence at its end of Eurasia unmatched by any state in either the Muslim or the Christian zones.

Under the Ming dynasty, China recovered thoroughly from the Mongol conquest of the later Middle Ages. The powerful fifteenth-century Ming emperor Yongle even sent out fleets of junks across island Southeast Asia and the Indian Ocean to the Middle East and East Africa more than half a century before the Portuguese crossed the Indian Ocean the other way. Under the less spectacular later Mings of the sixteenth century, China's unique Confucian administrative system and prosperous society took on the forms that would prevail in the Middle Kingdom until the Europeans at last forced their way into China hundreds of years later.

The scattered satellite cultures around the Middle Kingdom were closely modeled on Ming China. These sister civilizations in 1500 included the Koreans, the Vietnamese, and even the half-settled Manchurians, who in the seventeenth century would become China's last conquerors before the Europeans came. But the most dynamic of China's neighbors, the island kingdom of Japan, which had owed so much to China in earlier times, developed along contrasting lines in the later medieval and early modern centuries. In Japan, not scholar-bureaucrats but soldiers (samurai) were the leading social class. And strong central government came to Japan in 1600, not through a divine-right monarchy, but through the victory of the samurai overlord, the shogun.

Chinese culture during the Ming period featured a continuing national commitment to Confucianism, as well as exquisite landscape painting and a range of popular literature from drama to romance. In Japan, Zen and Pure-Land Buddhism flourished, and the bushido warrior code of the samurai found its natural home in a war-torn age.

SUGGESTED READING

BARY, W. T., et al. *Sources of Chinese Tradition.* New York: Columbia University Press, 1960. Useful collection of primary source materials, ancient and modern.

BRAZELL, K. trans. *Confessions of Lady Nijo.* Stanford: Stanford University Press, 1973. Scholarly but readable translation.

BUCK, P., trans. *All Men Are Brothers* (2 vols.). London: Methuen, 1957. Translation of the classic Ming novel. See also A. Waley's *Monkey,* an abridged version of *Journey to the West* (London: Allen and Unwin, 1942.)

CAHILL, J. *Parting at the Shore: Chinese Painting of the Early and Middle Ming Dynasty, 1368–1580.* New York: Weatherhill, 1978. Ming art, continuing the great tradition of the Tang and Song.

COOPER, M., ed. *They Came to Japan—An Anthology of European Reports on Japan.* Berkeley: University of California Press, 1965. Outsiders' views of Japan starting from the sixteenth century.

FAIRBANK, J. K. *East Asia: Tradition and Transformation.* Cambridge: Harvard University Press, 1973. The best one-volume account of the history of China, Japan, Vietnam, and Korea.

GALLAGHER, L. J., trans. *China in the Sixteenth Century: The Journals of Matteo Ricci.* New York: Random House, 1953. A European view of Ming China.

HALL, J. W., and T. TAKESHI, eds. *Japan in the Muromachi Age.* Berkeley: University of California Press, 1977. Highly praised collection of papers on all aspects of Japan in the Ashikaga shogunate, from politics and economics to religion and culture.

HUANG, R. *1587, A Year of No Significance: The Ming Dynasty in Decline.* New Haven: Yale University Press, 1981. Readable and fascinating immersion in the life of late Ming China. For the decline and fall of the dynasty, see L. A. Struve, *The Southern Ming, 1644–62* (New Haven: Yale University Press, 1984).

HUCKER, C. H. *The Traditional Chinese State in Ming Times, 1368–1644.* Tucson: University of Arizona Press, 1961. Brief but highly recommended analysis. See also Hucker, ed., *Chinese Government in Ming Times: Seven Studies* (New York: Columbia University Press, 1969) and, on the Confucian examination system, I Miyazaki, *China's Examination Hell: The Civil Service Examinations of Imperial China,* trans. C. Schirokauer (New York: Weatherhill, 1976).

KEENE, D., ed. *Twenty Plays of the Nō Theater.* New York: Columbia University Press, 1970. Collection of classic Japanese drama, with drawings to illustrate this highly visual art form.

NEEDHAM, J. *Science and Civilization in China.* Cambridge: Cambridge University Press, 1954–. A multivolume work still in progress. Volume 4 discusses the Precious Ships, Ming marine design, and technology generally.

REISCHAUER, E. O. *Japan: The Story of a Nation,* rev. ed. New York: Knopf, 1970. Excellent one-volume account by a leading authority and former ambassador to Japan.

SANSOM, G. *The Western World and Japan.* New York: Knopf, 1950. A good and readable survey of relations between Japan and Europe.

SCHIROKAUER, C. *A Brief History of Chinese and Japanese Civilizations.* New York: Harcourt Brace Jovanovich, Inc., 1978. Particularly good on the cultural history of the two great powers of East Asia.

SIMKIN, C. G. F. *The Traditional Trade of Asia.* London: Oxford University Press, 1968. Includes the westward probes of Yongle.

TSUNODA, R., et al., eds. *Sources of the Japanese Tradition.* New York: Columbia University Press, 1960. Valuable collection of materials.

YANG, L. "Female Rulers in Imperial China," *Harvard Journal of Asiatic Studies,* vol. 23 (1960–1961). Suggestive discussion of the institution and functions of the dowager empress as ruler. On the more traditional place of women, see R. Willier, "Confucian Ideal of Womanhood," *Journal of the China Society,* vol. 13 (1976).

CHAPTER 28

From Songhai to Great Zimbabwe

WEST AFRICA

THE UNKNOWN LAND

Much closer to Europe than the far reaches of Asia lay the third part of the Old World and the second largest of continents—Africa. And yet, surprisingly, Europeans were just beginning to make contact with many African peoples as the modern period began.

The history of some parts of Africa had been closely interwoven with that of Europe and Asia for many centuries. Africa had been linked by trade and cultural exchange to the Middle East since Egypt and Mesopotamia were the only two centers of civilization in the world. North Africa had interacted with southern Europe since Carthage battled Greece and then Rome for mastery of the western Mediterranean. East Africa had long been part of the Indian Ocean commercial community: African coastal cities exchanged goods with India, Southeast Asia, and even China, usually through Arab or Indian intermediaries.

But neither Europeans nor Asians had much knowledge of what lay behind the coastal lands of Africa. The whole interior of the continent was *terra incognita*— "unknown land"—on traders' maps. European charts sometimes showed Africa breaking off abruptly somewhere around the equator, or curving round to the east to link up with southern India, making the Indian Ocean an inland sea like the Mediterranean.

The reality was a great, roughly tapered continent traversed by broad climatic bands running east to west: the green Mediterranean coastal belt, the Sahara Desert, the grasslands of the Sudan, the dense rain forests of the Guinea Coast and the Congo, then more grassy savannas, more deserts, and the plains and hills of South Africa. Broadly speaking, it was Africa south of the Sahara— black Africa—that was unknown to outsiders. And it was over the wide expanses of this region that political growth and development were mushrooming in the centuries around 1500.

The Portuguese, who in the later fifteenth century first sailed around Africa, found a number of highly developed states on the far side of the continent. The most impressive of them were the empires of the Western Sudan and the trading cities of East Africa. Some of the antecedents of these kingdoms and city-states went back to the tenth century and before. But there were newer kingdoms in the rain forests of the Guinea Coast and down the Congo River basin too. New names thus began to appear on European maps: Songhai, Kano, Benin, Ife, Kilwa, the kingdom of Kongo, and, centuries later, the most mysterious of them all—Great Zimbabwe, "where the stone houses are."

In 1500, then, Africa south of the great desert was a world unto itself, living by its own rhythms, growing according to its own patterns of social evolution. A look at some of the emerging states of sixteenth-century Africa will reveal striking similarities with Eurasian civilizations—and striking differences as well.

THE SUDANNIC EMPIRES: SONGHAI

The Sudanic belt—grasslands dotted with trees—just south of the Sahara had produced a number of African nations during Europe's Middle Ages. Among these, the Kanem-Bornu states went back to the tenth century, the Hausa city-states to the twelfth. The westernmost portions of the Sudan had, however, been most prolific in new nations between 1000 and 1500. The most important of these kingdoms were Ghana, Mali, and finally Songhai.

Ghana and Mali had developed successively as the largest kingdoms of the Western Sudan in the centuries before 1500. The kings of these states had built their power on the villages of the grasslands. But their wealth had come from trade. Muslim merchants from north of the Sahara had brought salt, manufactured goods, and other things to exchange for gold and slaves from the forest lands south of the Sudan. The Sudanic kings of Ghana and Mali had been the middlemen, managers of the marketplaces of West Africa's commercial cities between the desert and the forest.

Typical Sudanic trading states had thus developed. They were hereditary monarchies with black elites of the powerful Mande people—known later in the West as the Mandingo—and resident communities of Muslim Arabs and Berber merchants. Appointed officials and standing armies held these states together. Differences of religion and culture divided them: Mande elites became increasingly Islamicized and lived in walled capitals and trading cities such as Timbuktu, while the majority of the people

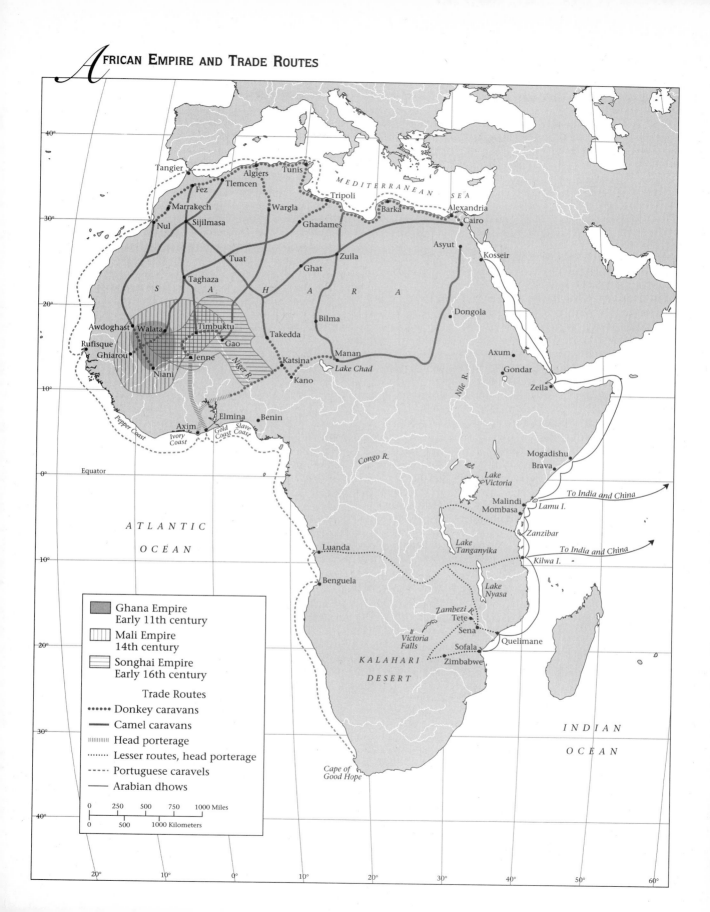

AFRICAN EMPIRE AND TRADE ROUTES

MEDITERRANEAN SEA

Tangier
Fez
Algiers
Tlemcen
Tunis
Marrakech
Nul
Sijilmasa
Wargla
Tripoli
Barka
Alexandria
Cairo
Ghadames
Tuat
Zuila
Asyut
Kosseir
Taghaza
Ghat

S   A   H   A   R   A

Bilma
Dongola

Awdoghast
Walata
Timbuktu
Takedda
Manan
Axum
Gondar
Rufisque
Ghiarou
Gao
Katsina
Lake Chad
Zeila
Niani
Jenne
Kano
Niger R.

Nile R.

Pepper Coast
Axim
Elmina
Benin
Ivory Coast
Gold Coast
Slave Coast

Equator

Congo R.

Mogadishu
Brava

Lake Victoria

Malindi
Mombasa
Lamu I.
To India and China

ATLANTIC OCEAN

Luanda

Lake Tanganyika

Zanzibar
To India and China
Kilwa I.

Benguela

Lake Nyasa

Zambezi R.
Tete
Sena
Quelimane

Victoria Falls

Sofala
Zimbabwe

KALAHARI DESERT

INDIAN OCEAN

Cape of Good Hope

Legend

Ghana Empire Early 11th century

Mali Empire 14th century

Songhai Empire Early 16th century

Trade Routes

- •••• Donkey caravans
- —— Camel caravans
- ||||||| Head porterage
- ······ Lesser routes, head porterage
- ----- Portuguese caravels
- —— Arabian dhows

Scale:
0   250   500   750   1000 Miles
0   500   1000 Kilometers

remained animists and lived in agricultural and pastoral communities scattered across the grasslands. There were also feuds over the royal succession and endemic rebelliousness among conquered peoples—problems in imperial cultures everywhere.

In the latter part of the fifteenth century, the third and greatest of this West African succession of empires emerged: the kingdom of Songhai.

In the days of Mali's greatness, the Songhai peoples dominated the Niger River between its big bend and its juncture with the Benue River in what is today Nigeria. They were farmers and river boatmen. As river navigators, they provided a vital link between the Malian heartland and the empire's eastern provinces. Though subjects of the kings of Mali, the rulers of Songhai—whose capital of Gao was a great trading city too—chafed under foreign domination. In the second half of the fifteenth century, the royal Sonni line of Songhai produced a ruler who could focus this resentment and make it pay: the soldier-king Sonni Ali (1464–1492).

The kingdom of Mali had grown weak and weary by the later fifteenth century. Its kings wasted the wealth of the land and could not hold the provinces against rebellion and foreign invasion. In his nearly thirty years on the throne of Songhai, Sonni Ali battered Mali, the erstwhile superpower of the Western Sudan, into a second-class nation, a petty Sudanese state that soon became part of an even larger Songhai Empire.

The founder of Songhai power was a hard man. He looted Timbuktu and was particularly harsh with resident foreigners, the Berbers and Arabs from north of the Sahara. His followers were drawn from the animist majority of the population, and though he was a nominal Muslim himself, Sonni Ali had little respect for mosques and Islamic scholars.

By the time of his death—in 1492, the year Columbus sailed—Sonni Ali's empire controlled the economic heart of West African commerce—the three great trading centers of Timbuktu, Gao, and Jenne. Under his successors, Songhai grew until it commanded the largest sweep of West Africa ever ruled by a Sudanic kingdom.

The most effective of those who followed Sonni Ali was the man who destroyed the ancient Sonni dynasty. He also restored what was in essence the old Muslim Mande elite of Ghanaian and Malian times. His name was Askia Muhammad (1493–1528), and he would become known as Askia the Great.

Askia Muhammad had been one of Sonni Ali's generals. He rebelled against the old man's heir, however, and established his own dynasty at the end of the fifteenth century. Like Sonni Ali, he was a fighter and an empire builder, and he completed the edifice of Songhai power that his predecessor had begun. He was also an administrative reformer, dividing the enlarged empire into a number of provinces for more efficient governance. He spread the fame of Songhai farther abroad by making a triumphant royal pilgrimage to Mecca and establishing closer relations with the Muslim states of North Africa and the Middle East.

Askia Muhammad's seizure of the throne meant the return to power of the urban elite of Islamicized Mande and northern merchants who had dominated Ghana and Mali. These wealthy, sophisticated communities provided the Songhai Empire with most of its administrators, generals, traders, and thinkers, as they had done for the earlier Sudanic powers. They gave continuity to this succession of West African empires for more than five hundred years.

Under Askia the Great, Muslim culture flourished as never before in West Africa. He encouraged the building of mosques and schools. Muslim universities at Timbuktu and Jenne drew scholars and poets from distant places. Under Askia, Songhai was thoroughly integrated into the cosmopolitan world of Islamic peoples that stretched from West Africa to Southeast Asia.

The fortunes of Songhai, the greatest of West African kingdoms, never stood higher than in the days of Askia Muhammad. But worse days were coming for the empire of the grasslands—indeed, before the end of the great king's reign.

Blind in his old age, Askia was deposed in 1528 by his own rebellious sons. His successors strove to carry on in his tradition and that of Sonni Ali, but the second half of the century saw rebellion and invasion by neighboring princes sweep over Songhai. And in 1590, the rulers of Songhai faced an invasion unlike anything they had ever confronted before.

The new invaders were Moroccans who had successfully crossed the Saharan barrier into the Sudan in force. They were armed with muskets and artillery, and the bow-and-arrow soldiers of Songhai soon learned that such weapons introduced a new and chilling dimension into the ancient art of empire building.

The Moroccan invaders, fresh from victories over the Portuguese along the shores of the Mediterranean, crushed the armies of Songhai also in the field. Like the Alomoravids of earlier centuries, however, they did not succeed in establishing their own power south of the Sahara. They merely plunged the Western Sudan into prolonged chaos, a condition from which West Africa would scarcely emerge before the coming of the Europeans in much greater force centuries later.

THE HAUSA STATES: KANO

If you can only locate three countries on your mental map of Africa, they should probably be ancient Egypt, wealthy South Africa—and Nigeria. Sprawling across the inner angle of West Africa, straddling the Y of the Niger and Benue rivers, the developing nation of Nigeria today has the resources, including oil, and the population—about a quarter of the people of black Africa live in Nigeria—to become one of the great powers of the continent. In the past, too, more than one of Africa's historic civilizations flowered in the area of modern-day Nigeria. Among these, the Hausa city-states were particularly prominent in later medieval and early modern times.

Hausaland, in the central Sudan just east of Songhai, encompassed much of the well-watered, thickly populated plateau of northern Nigeria. The Hausa people, black Africans speaking an Afro-Asiatic language akin to that of Egypt, apparently migrated south from the expanding Sahara into the fertile region between the two rivers and Lake Chad to the northeast before the year 1000. They found in their new home a region capable of supporting an expanding agricultural people, with enough excess population to build prosperous cities. By the fourteenth century, then, clay-walled towns had sprung up among their scattered farmsteads. Within the walls, farmers heaped their produce for sale in the marketplaces. Weavers and dyers of cotton cloth, leatherworkers, blacksmiths, coppersmiths, and other artisans plied their crafts. And merchants began to gather, including growing numbers of Arabs and Berbers from north of the Sahara. By 1500, such cities as Kano and Katsina were regular stops on the trans-Saharan caravan routes, and Hausa products were being sold as far away as southern Europe.

The city-states of Hausaland never united into a nation or an empire like Ghana, Mali, or Songhai. Like the city-states of Renaissance Italy or ancient Greece, however, the states of central Sudan found lack of political unity no handicap to economic and cultural development. Behind their fifteen-foot walls and iron-bound gates, Hausa merchant and craft communities grew wealthy enough to replace those of Timbuktu and the other trading cities of Songhai as that empire declined toward the end of the sixteenth century. The elites of the Hausa cities accepted a modified Muslim religion and developed a written language based on Arabic. They built many mosques and established schools where their children studied reading, writing, arithmetic, ethics, government, and the Islamic faith.

Kano, eight or nine miles in circumference, with a population of perhaps 75,000—approximately the size of Renaissance Florence—by 1600, was the best-known of the Hausa states. The most famous of Kano's kings, the fifteenth-century ruler Muhammad Rimfa (1463–1499), illustrates the achievements of which this cluster of Sudannic states was capable.

According to the *Kano Chronicle,* this exemplary monarch expanded the city's walls and its caravansaries, enlarged and restructured the army, and reorganized the government, promoting talented slaves rather than hereditary aristocrats to positions of authority. He welcomed Islamic scholars to his capital and presided over a harem of a thousand queens and concubines. Sitting under swaying ostrich fans to listen to the learned Algerian Muhammad al-Maghili read his famed treatise on *The Obligations of Princes,* Muhammad Rimfa represented one more center of urban civilization in the western part of Africa.

THE KINGDOMS OF THE GUINEA COAST: BENIN

South of the Songhai Empire and the Hausa city-states lay the rain forests of the Guinea Coast. The forest peoples who dwelt there had learned agriculture and ironworking centuries earlier, at the time of the great Bantu migrations. But the culture of the forest remained one of agricultural villages, loosely linked by clan and tribal ties, until the last few centuries before 1500. Then larger states appeared there too, in the deep woods and mangrove forests between the grasslands and the sea.

Little is known about the states of the Guinea Coast of West Africa—Ife, Oyo, Benin, and others—in these early years. They kept no written records themselves, and few Muslims from the north or Europeans coming by sea penetrated the dense rain forests. From oral traditions, scattered European accounts, and some archaeological remains, it is possible, however, to piece together something of this new zone of state building and even urban culture.

The forest peoples of West Africa may have been significantly influenced by more sophisticated societies not in the Western but the Eastern Sudan. Egyptian influences on the powerful Yoruba people of Nigeria, for example, have been suggested. The source of the wealth to support the new cities of the Guinea Coast is also open to conjecture. Probably, however, it came primarily from trade in such forest products as pepper, ivory, and, later, especially slaves.

Limited by the thick jungles, the kingdoms of the forest belt tended to be smaller than those of the open savannas, over which conquering armies could sweep with ease. They may, however, have been commensurately tightly knit and well organized. The Guinea kingdoms were the work of African peoples skilled in arts and crafts, immensely self-confident, and particularly talented at political organization. Certainly their achievements in these areas were impressive when the Europeans first encountered them in the late 1400s.

Perhaps the most famous of the Guinea Coast states was the kingdom of Benin, located in what is today Nigeria, at the great inner angle of Africa.[1]

Benin was probably an offshoot of the earlier Ife culture. Ife produced some of the continent's most beautiful terra-cotta and bronze sculpture as early as the twelfth and thirteenth centuries but is otherwise little known.

---

[1] The present Republic of Benin lies to the west of the original kingdom.

The walled city of Benin shows in the distance behind two subjects of the <u>oba</u> (king) in this picture by a Dutch artist. A sense of African plenty and of foreign exoticism is conveyed by the costumes, especially the headgear, and by the tropical products and vegetation. The city in the background, however, reflects the artist's Dutch background more than the reality of Benin. (Library of Congress)

Benin seems to have taken shape sometime in the fourteenth century and to have been flourishing in the fifteenth, when the first Europeans arrived.

They found a kingdom 250 miles across lying just west of the mouth of the Niger. The city of Benin was a walled metropolis three miles long with broad avenues and houses in tidy rows, very unlike the close-pressing huts of many African villages. There was a huge palace with many courtyards and long galleries decorated with brass plaques and statues.

Crops grew luxuriantly in the cleared land around the city. Prosperous Benin merchants traded as far away as the Sudan. Benin's carvers of ivory and wood and casters of brass were as famous as those of Ife had been.

The political system was a complex one centering in a political and religious leader, the *oba* (king). But a good deal of power was also dispersed among the *Iyoba* (queen mother), the crown prince, a group of leading noblemen or palace chiefs, and the town chiefs outside the capital. The kingdom was divided into provinces with appointed governors, and there was a standing army with a supreme commander and an enviable reputation for winning.

Ewuare the Great (ca. 1440–1473) was busy building an empire of his own when Portuguese ships first touched at his main port of Gwatto in the 1470s. Ewuare was reputed to have added more than two hundred villages to his domain. Yet he and the other *obas* of Benin had a reputation for mild and beneficent rule, to which European observers would testify in the centuries that followed—even as they themselves proved less than benevolent intruders into African affairs.

CENTRAL AND EAST AFRICA

THE KINGDOM OF KONGO

The rain forest of Africa flows east along the Guinea coast, then south and east again across the Congo River basin. Just south of the mouth of that jungle river, fifteenth-century Portuguese explorers found a flourishing African nation—the kingdom of Kongo.

The Congo River winds some 2700 miles through the deep forests of modern Zaire, draining the whole central portion of Africa. It is one of the continent's greatest rivers, comparable in importance to the Nile and the Niger, the Senegal and the Zambesi. The Portuguese, exploring slowly down the western side of Africa in preparation for da Gama's voyage to India fifteen years later, reached the mouth of the Congo in the 1480's. Africans who came down to the river to trade told the foreigners that the king of all that region lived a week's journey to the south. On a later voyage, the Europeans made the journey.

What they saw when they emerged from the footpath through the jungle did not impress them as Benin had, or as Timbuktu had impressed Arab travelers. Mbanza, the capital of Kongo, was a dusty African town of straw houses built around a central square. The gates of the royal enclosure were guarded by armed men and trumpeters. There was a great baobab tree where the king of Kongo meted out traditional justice to his people, as King Alfred or Saint Louis had done in Europe centuries before.

Yet from this simple center, a kingdom the size of Belgium or the Netherlands was effectively governed.

Kongo was a developed agricultural society, depending most heavily on a variety of palm trees from which the people made oil, wine, bread, and the fibers they used for everything from clothing to the roofs of houses. The people of Kongo were also stock raisers and worked both iron and copper.

The political organization of this country was based on the immemorial village but was articulated all the way up to the national level. Each village had its head, chosen locally on a matrilineal basis, headship descending through the female side. Villages were grouped into districts, each run by an official appointed from above. The districts in turn were grouped into the six large provinces that constituted the nation of Kongo.

The king was in theory an absolute monarch, governing according to traditional law through a small but centralized bureaucracy in Mbanza. Unlike the rulers of West Africa, the king of Kongo had no standing army, depending instead upon a universal military-service obligation to rally all the men of the kingdom at need. Taxes and tribute were collected by provincial governors, and cowrie shells from an island off the coast were used as coinage. The throne was not directly hereditary: the ruler was chosen by a board of electors, like the Holy Roman Emperor of the Germans.

Kongo was only one of a number of central African countries emerging about this time, but it was more strongly centralized than most. It was an awkward time to be emerging, just as the imperial expansion of the West was getting under way. Like Japan in later centuries, however, Kongo responded positively, even enthusiastically to the coming of the Europeans. The people of Kongo absorbed some European technology, and Christianity spread among the elite.

After the technicians and the missionaries, however, would come the slavers, and with them a considerable decline in the popularity of things European.

THE RIDDLE OF GREAT ZIMBABWE

On archaeological maps of the African interior, there is a blob-shaped area, inland from the coastal cities of East Africa, north of the Limpopo River and south of the Zambesi, usually labeled "Stone Buildings" or "Where the Stone Works Are." Much of this area is in the modern state of Zimbabwe, and the heart of it is the ruined city known today as Great Zimbabwe, for which the new nation is named.

Great Zimbabwe is one of the mysteries of the African past—"perhaps," says one authority, "the greatest riddle in the whole of African history."[2]

It was an impressive stone city, stretching over rocky hilltops and the valley below. There were huge walls, a sprawling palace, conical towers, and a looming fort and temple on the hill beyond. It is a remarkable sight—so remarkable that the first Europeans to see it, in the nineteenth century, assumed it to be the work of ancient

---

[2] Roland Oliver, "The Riddle of Zimbabwe," in Roland Oliver, ed., *The Dawn of African History* (London: Oxford University Press, 1961), p. 53.

(a)

(b)

(a) This commemorative head of a sixteenth-century Benin queen-mother was made of a copper alloy with an iron inlay. It features an up-swept hairstyle covered by a cap of coral beads. (The British Museum) (b) This ivory pendant, carved in exquisite detail and only six and a half inches high, was worn on the belt of the oba of sixteenth-century Benin. The crown is carved in the form of tiny Portuguese heads, a symbol of the royal alliance with the Europeans during the early days of the Western intrusion. ([a] Queen Mother Head Benin. Reproduced by courtesy of the Trustees of the British Museum #38365 [MOPM]; [b]F. L. Kennet; used in Coons, Many Peoples, One Country)

Contemporary Africans at the ruins of Great Zimbabwe, now crumbling and overgrown with forest. This mystery city of East Africa was a flourishing metropolis centuries before Europeans arrived. Probably at its peak between 1000 and 1500, this African Kingdom remains one of the world's true "lost civilizations." (Photo Researchers, Inc.)

Phoenician traders, or perhaps even King Solomon's famous African mines.

Instead it was almost certainly the capital of an African trading empire linked to the commercial cities of East Africa. Bits of Chinese porcelain and glass beads that came from India or Southeast Asia show that this great city of the African interior was linked by commerce to the trading community of the Indian Ocean. When the Portuguese sailed up the distant coast around 1500, there were Arab traders in Sofala, probably the main port for Zimbabwe, and in the interior also. But Great Zimbabwe itself, much of it built perhaps two to five hundred years earlier, was no longer an imperial capital in 1500: its great days were already shrouded in the past.

The empire of the Bantu-speaking Karanga people whom the Portuguese discovered in that part of East Africa in the sixteenth century may have been an offshoot of the earlier Zimbabwe empire. The Karanga kingdom of Zimbabwe was a remarkable state in itself, probably larger than today's Zimbabwe. It had a traditional god-king with a huge court, a powerful queen mother, and nine main wives, all of whom had their own courts. A centralized bureaucracy ruled the nearer districts; appointed governors ran the farther provinces. This government hierarchy maintained order among a diversity of tribes, collected tribute for the royal coffers and conscripts for the royal army. The people cropped the land, herded cattle, made fine textiles, mined and smelted gold. They also traded gold and ivory for luxuries from India and China.

But the capital of the Karanga empire, two hundred miles to the north of Great Zimbabwe, was built of wood and thatch. The splendors of their precursors, the builders of the earliest stone city in the south, can only be guessed at now.

You can rebuild Great Zimbabwe in your mind's eye today. From the hilltop Acropolis, you can look down over broken walls and tumbled boulders to the towering grey stone bastions of the Great Enclosure. Imagine all that space between you and those distant walls filled with buildings, crowded streets, the life of that lost African world.

Stretch the causeway across what was then a marsh, rebuild the stone houses, fill the streets with teeming thousands and the air with Bantu voices. Hear the rattle of bullock carts, the clop of donkeys' hooves—you will see both today on the roads around Masvingo. Set drums to beating somewhere, add the clang of ironsmiths' hammers and work songs rising from the labors of a prosperous people long ago.

The wind will blow the sounds away, a blink of the eye sweep the city into ruins once more. But you can still look at the spreading iron spear points those people hammered out, the stone birds they carved at Great Zimbabwe seven centuries ago. And the sense of vanished grandeur will be with you long after you have left these monuments to the birds and lizards who guard ruins everywhere, from ancient Greece to far Peru.

AFRICAN SOCIETY AND CULTURE

AFRICAN SOCIETY

African society south of the Sahara was thus evolving rapidly beyond—or away from—village culture as the modern age began. From the grasslands to the rain forests, kingdoms were springing up across the second largest continent. Royal councils, appointed governors, hierarchies of officials much like those of Eurasia appeared. Though many of these administrations lacked the key Eurasian element of literacy and written records, they were able to govern countries as large as the nations of Europe quite effectively.

Structured societies containing an established nobility and an important, frequently Muslim, merchant class developed above the older village organization. Villages still based their social structure on family and clan, age groups, and traditional sex roles. But the court of the East African Karanga people, with its aristocracy and its concubines, its powerful official class and its even more powerful queen mother, had more in common with the courts of Europe or Asia than it did with the African villages it ruled.

QUEENS OF THE MARKETPLACE

This early modern Africa of articulated societies and evolving kingdoms differs strikingly from the nineteenth- and twentieth-century image of Africa as "backward" or "underdeveloped." As Africanists have pointed out, Western imperial conquest probably contributed significantly to the later "underdeveloping" of the second largest continent. Other factors, including the Industrial Revolution, would presently give the West an advantage that made all other cultures, including that of Africa, look at least materially less impressive. For now, it will suffice to note that the Africa of Songhai, Kano and Benin, Kongo and Zimbabwe was a continent on the move, the home of dynamic societies as full of change and development as other major centers of civilization five hundred years ago.

The many roles of women in this Africa of emerging nation-states illustrates vividly the nature of those changing times.

Women were at least as important as men in the subsistence economy of the African village, for they dominated the traditional hoe culture on which many villages depended. Women were important in the political and social organization of village Africa too. Leaders of women's age-set organizations were also the recognized authorities on such aspects of village life as peacemaking and price scales. Women held important religious positions as mediums, diviners, and faith healers.

But women also participated significantly in the new political and economic hierarchy of the evolving kingdoms of Africa. They shared power as queens, queen mothers who were co-rulers, chiefs, and subchiefs. They were sometimes the recognized magistrates of their districts. In the economic sphere, the famous West African women's trading network was probably already emerging. This pattern of female domination is still to be found in West Africa, where powerful women merchants reign as queens of the marketplace.

By 1500, however, some of these high-status positions were being undercut by the spread of Islam in Africa. Womens's religious roles were undermined by the more

limited part granted women in the new religion. Still later, women's political roles would frequently be ignored by Europeans who were unused to the complexity of African political organization and sought a single "chief" with whom to exchange gifts and negotiate trade treaties.

Altogether, then, the varied roles played by African women exemplify the transitions that Africa was undergoing in 1500—and the changes that were still to come.

The emerging Africa of five hundred years ago, like the modernizing African states of today, already had an impressive cultural achievement to show. The balance of this chapter will therefore deal with African culture on the eve of the European intrusion—the inner lives of Africans before the rise of the West began to change the lives of peoples everywhere.

THE LIFE OF TIMBUKTU

The very names of some towns have the power to stir wanderlust in any red-blooded reader, names like Samarkand and Zanzibar . . . and Timbuktu. During its heyday, from the thirteenth to the sixteenth century, Timbuktu would certainly have repaid the effort necessary for a visit.

Timbuktu today is a dusty little market town in the West African state of Mali. It still enjoys the location that once made it great, on the southern edge of the Sahara and only eight or nine miles north of the big bend of the Niger. But it is hard to imagine it as the splendid center of trade and culture it was in the days of the Mali and Songhai empires.

Fortunately, we do not have to depend on imagination. We have archaeological remains, as well as the vivid descriptions of Timbuktu as it looked to such experienced Muslim travelers as Ibn Batuta in the fourteenth century and Leo Africanus in the sixteenth. And the reconstitution of the life and spirit of this city perhaps more than any other brings us in contact with the courtly culture of the Sudanic kingdoms.

Around 1500, Timbuktu was a walled city of perhaps 25,000 people, a mixed population of Muslim and animist, black Sudanese, Berber, and Arab. In the market squares of Timbuktu, salt from the Sahara and copper, cloth, and metal weapons and tools from the Mediterranean and Europe were all on sale. They were exchanged for the products of the south—ivory, ebony, ostrich plumes and cola nuts, black slaves and gold.

Leo Africanus paints a vivid picture of the city in the days of Askia the Great. Then as now, market women dominated the food marts. And since the desert had not pressed as far south five hundred years ago as it has today, there was plenty of food grown around Timbuktu, a region of cattle and grain and sweet well water. The merchants, Leo assures us, were all very rich, and skilled artisans wove excellent linen and cotton cloth. The houses were unimpressive, thatched roofs on whitewashed wattle-and-daub walls. But there were some impressive brick

The West African metropolis of Timbuktu as seen by a European artist in the nineteenth century. Note the towering Sankoré mosque on the horizon and the metropolitan sweep of this city of the Western Sudan even in its decadence. This picture was drawn from a rooftop, where much of the life of Arab and North African cities still goes on today. Does the architecture of this sun-bleached land south of the Sahara remind you of buildings in any part of the United States?

Metal sculpture from Benin. Attention to intricate detail and a combination of smooth and carefully worked surfaces distinguish this vivid image of Bini rulers. Note the elaborate detail, especially in the clothing worn by the oba. (Benin Figures. Late 17th Century. Bronze. 17 × 14 inches. The British Museum, London)

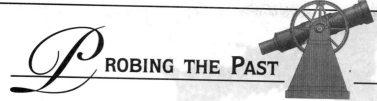

PROBING THE PAST

"*Because most societies in Africa south of the Sahara were oral, even if they used writing marginally, historians who study them must confront the question of the validity of oral traditions as sources for history. To go by our experience of what sources survived orally in Europe, for example, in the nineteenth century, is to go wrong. For centuries all data felt to be socially important were written down; only trivia remained unrecorded. Thus, in his survey of oral tradition Ernst Bernheim cited only song and tale, saga, legend, anecdote, geflügelte Wörter [popular sayings], and proverbs. Quite a contrast with Africa, where all the principal political, legal, social, and religious texts were transmitted orally. Indeed, for every functional type of written source in Europe one can find an equivalent oral source in Africa. For instance, most African courts had archivists, who learned by rote the royal genealogy—which legitimized the position of the ruler—and the history of the state—which was its unwritten constitution. Typically, when such an oral civilization moves to become literate, the first items recorded are the texts felt to be most important, just as the first printed book in Europe was the Bible. When Sultan Njoya of the Bamum in the Cameroons invented a script, the first materials written down were the royal chronicle and a code of the customary law and the local pharmacopoeia.*"

The distinguished African historian Jan Vansina here explains the value of oral traditions, passed on from generation to generation, as sources for African history. What contrast does Vansina see between the sort of orally transmitted materials commonly collected in the West (folk songs and children's games would be good examples) and those available to historians studying traditional Africa? When would you expect Africans to begin to forget their oral history? Are orally transmitted "documents" any more likely to contain errors than written ones? Would an oral archivist who got the king's genealogy wrong be likely to keep his job long?

Jan Vansina, "Once Upon a Time: Oral Traditions as History in Africa," in Felix Gilbert and Stephen R. Graubard, eds., <u>Historical Studies Today</u> (New York: W.W. Norton & Co., 1972), p. 414.

mosques, and the old stone palace of Mansa Musa, the most famous of Malian kings, was still there.

Askia the Great, the sixteenth-century patron of Muslim culture, surrounded himself with scholars, doctors, *qadis* (judges), and *imams* (holy men) of his faith. The Sankoré mosque, with its typically pyramidal West African tower, was the center of the most famous university in the Sudan, where learned men taught Muslim law and medicine, Islamic religion, philosophy, and government. The king supported many of these scholars, both native-born and foreign, from his own purse. Manuscripts and books in Arabic, the universal language of the Muslim world, were imported from the Mediterranean. Books, said Leo Africanus, fetched a better price in the markets of Timbuktu than any other merchandise.

The spirit of this city of merchants and mosques, courtiers and scholars was the open, cosmopolitan spirit of a wider Islamic world. But there were other aspects of the culture of the new African kingdoms that were distinctively their own. None of these achievements of African genius has aroused more admiration than the art of one of the forest peoples to the south of Songhai—the famous Benin bronzes.

THE BENIN BRONZES

The widely used term *Benin bronzes* is in fact a bit of a misnomer. For one thing, they originated not in Benin but in Ife to the north. Benin sculpture includes ivory carving and terra-cotta objects as well as metalwork—and the metal in question is usually brass, not bronze. An artistic phenomenon, however, this art of the West African forests truly is.

Ife was the religious center of a whole section of the Guinea Coast, its famous oracle consulted by many Yoruba peoples. The earliest of all the organized forest states appeared at Ife, probably around 1050. Perhaps as early as the twelfth century, a uniquely naturalistic style of sculpture began to be produced there.

Most African sculpture, like that of most Amerindian peoples, was abstract and symbolic. It made little effort to depict human beings or animals realistically, as Greco-Roman or East Asian Buddhist art frequently did. But the Ife heads, most of them brass or terra-cotta, were strikingly lifelike. The patterns of parallel grooves running over some of the faces may represent ritual scarification, but they also heighten the sense of form and contour brilliantly. There is a lofty serenity to some of these idealized but thoroughly convincing African heads that no later African work could match.

Nevertheless, the techniques of metal casting and other sculptural skills did pass to neighboring peoples, including the new kingdom of Benin. And in Benin especially, the result was an array of carved ivory and cast brass that has impressed the world since it first went on display in the West in the present century.

It was perhaps the technical facility revealed by the "bronzes" in particular that first stirred Western viewers. These works were first produced as early as the twelfth century, though their great period is dated from the sixteenth—just in time for the Portuguese to be properly impressed. The castings were made by the classical lost-wax process and are extremely delicate work, no more than two or three millimeters thick. Authorities have compared these sculptures with the metal work of Benvenuto Cellini, the most celebrated bronze caster of the Italian Renaissance.[3]

But once more, as in the art of so many lands, it is the work itself that moves us in the end. A metal rooster, fat and strutting, displays an elegantly formalized patterning of feathers that may remind us of the scales of ancient Chinese dragons. A famous sixteenth-century ivory mask, once part of the royal regalia of a king of Benin, stares at us with deep liquid eyes beneath heavy lids out of the yellowed bone.

In Benin sculpture the naturalism of Ife has been replaced by an exaggerated emphasis on lips and nose and by an increasing stylization, especially of ears, eyes, costume. Yet the life of the people who made them glows from the dark metal of an ancestral head, the smooth skin contrasting with the royal cap and choker of coral beads, the strong features radiating vitality. One is reminded of something even older than Chinese dragons—of the bronze head, cast more than two thousand years before Christ, of Sargon of Akkad, the first of the historic empire builders. This *oba* of West Africa, whose likeness once stood on the altar of a temple in Benin City, was a builder of nations too.

---

[3]Earlier Western art experts, unable to believe that such delicate work had been done in the African rain forests, credited Renaissance Europeans, ancient Greeks, or even artists from mythical Atlantis.

SUMMARY

Kingdoms had sprung up in many parts of Africa south of the Sahara by 1500. On the grasslands of the Western Sudan, the Songhai kingdom of Sonni Ali and Askia Muhammad followed in the imperial tradition of Ghana and Mali. In the rain forests of the Guinea Coast, Benin and other kingdoms sprang up, impressing the first European mariners as the empires of the Sudan had earlier Arab caravans. The institutional complexities of the kingdom of Kongo in central Africa were less visible to early European visitors. And the civilization of Great Zimbabwe had largely faded by the time outsiders came to marvel at its mysterious stone ruins.

Much of Africa had thus moved beyond village culture by the time Europeans began to sail regularly along its shores. The complexity of evolving African society south of the Sahara was well illustrated by the varied roles played by women in the society: from faith healer to subsistence agriculturalist, from queen-mother to queen of the marketplace.

African culture flourished during the centuries around 1500. Cities like Timbuktu shared in the cosmopolitan interregional culture of the Muslim world, with its mosques, scholars, sophisticated courts, and merchant wealth. Among the most impressive artistic accomplishments of the age are the Benin bronzes and the more naturalistic—but not more artistically impressive—sculpture of Ife.

SUGGESTED READING

AJAYI, J. F. A., and I. ESPIE, eds. *A Thousand Years of West African History.* Ibadan: Ibadan University Press, 1965. A scholarly Nigerian view. See also J.D. Fage, *An Introduction to the History of West Africa,* 3rd ed. (Cambridge: Cambridge University Press, 1962).

BOVILI, E. W. *The Golden Trade of the Moors.* London: Oxford University Press, 1958. The commercial side of the important northern influence on West Africa.

CANTON-THOMPSON, G. *The Zimbabwe Culture: Ruins and Reactions.* London: Oxford University Press, 1931. A classic study of the archaeology of Zimbabwe. For a more colorful treatment, see R. Summers, *Zimbabwe: A Rhodesian Mystery* (New York: Tri-Ocean Books, 1963).

CHITTICK, N. "Kilwa and the Arab Settlement of the East African Coast," *Journal of African History,* vol., 1, no. 1 (1960). On the trading emporium of East Africa.

DAVIDSON, B. *The African Past: Chronicles from Antiquity to Modern Times.* Boston: Little, Brown, 1964. Primary sources.

EGHAREUBA, J. *Short History of Benin,* 3rd ed. Ibadan: Ibadan University Press, 1960. A handy survey of the most celebrated of the kingdoms of the West African forest peoples. See also R. E. Bradbury, *The Benin Kingdom and the Edo Speaking Peoples of Southwestern Nigeria* (London: Oxford University Press, 1957).

GIBB, H. A. R., ed. and trans. *Ibn Battuta: Travels in Asia and Africa* (2 vols.). New York: Cambridge University Press, 1958–1962. Famous Arab traveler and his observations on the western Sudan. See also Leo Africanus, *The History and Description of Africa* (3 vols.) (London: Hakluyt Society, 1896).

HILTON, A. *The Kingdom of Kongo.* New York: Clarendon Press, 1985. Kongo from the fifteenth century through the seventeenth century, including the early impact of Portuguese penetration. On family life and social customs, see G. Balandier, *Daily Life in the Kingdom of the Congo: From the Sixteenth to the Eighteenth Century* (New York: Meridian Books, 1968).

HUNWICK, J. O. "Songhay, Bornu, and Hausaland in the Sixteenth Century," in J. F. A. Ajayi and M. Crowder, eds., *History of West Africa* (New York: Columbia University Press, 1972). A brief, scholarly survey.

LEBEUF, A. "The Role of Women in the Political Organization of African Societies," in D. Paulme, ed., *Women in Tropical Africa* (Berkeley: University of California Press, 1960). Female power on all levels, from African queens and queen mothers to the village level, with a historical dimension.

OLIVER, R., and J. D. FAGE, eds. *The Cambridge History of Africa* (8 vols.). Cambridge: Cambridge University Press, 1975. Solid and scholarly. For a shorter treatment by these two leading authorities, see Oliver and Fage, *A Short History of Africa* (Baltimore: Penguin, 1962).

OLIVER, R., and G. MATHEWS, eds. *History of East Africa.* Oxford: Clarendon Press, 1963. Includes essays on the period before European intrusion began. For an archaeological perspective, see J. S. Kirkman, *Men and Monuments on the East African Coast* (London: Luterworth Press, 1964).

SEGY, L. *African Sculpture Speaks,* 4th ed. New York: Da Capo Press, 1975. Excellent overview, with emphasis on religious purposes and regional styles. For a subtler aesthetic analysis, see D. Williams, *Icon and Image: A Study of Sacred and Secular Forms of African Classical Art* (New York: New York University Press, 1974).

SUDARKASA, N. *Where Women Work: A Study of Yoruba Women in the Marketplace and in the Home.* Ann Arbor: University of Michigan Anthropological Papers, 1973. Good study of West African market women, with some account of the historical evolution of their role.

VANSINA, J. *Art History in Africa.* New York: Longman, 1984. Sophisticated analysis of African genres and styles.

———. *Kingdoms of the Savanna.* Madison: University of Wisconsin Press, 1966. By a leading American Africanist.

CHAPTER 29

THE AZTECS AND THE INCAS

Kingdoms Beyond the Seas

A Separate World

East Asia and Africa south of the Sahara were comparatively isolated patches of the Old World, sundered by distance and geographical barriers from other developed societies. All of the Old World, however, was totally cut off from an even more isolated zone of habitation: the linked continents of the Americas. It is to the remarkable political and cultural achievements of the New World that we must turn in order to complete our survey of the globe the Europeans scarcely knew as modern history began.

Geographically, it was a separate world indeed. The two huge continents of North and South America, the narrow isthmus of Central America between, and the archipelagoes of the Caribbean contained all the geographical forms of the world of Eurasia and Africa. The Rockies and the Andes were the New World equivalents of the Alps and the Himalayas. The great plains of western North America and the Argentine pampas matched the savannas and steppes of Africa and Asia. The deserts of Chile and the American Southwest were as forbidding as any Sahara or Gobi. Nor were the Niger, the Danube, and the Yangtze more impressive rivers than the Mississippi and the Amazon.

The differences were cultural ones. For there were striking differences, as well as impressive similarities, in the ways people lived on opposite sides of the globe. The Atlantic and Pacific oceans were far more cultural than geographical barriers in 1492.

Twenty Centuries of History

Culturally, it seems fair to say, the range of development was much greater in the New World than it was over most of the Old. The closest parallel is perhaps with Africa. In Africa, as in the Americas, some people lived in cities, paid taxes and tribute, and organized their lives according to the will of distant governments. Many others in both

places, however, still lived and died in isolated villages, obeying only the traditional mores and taboos of the tribe, clan, and village elders.

We will be concerned here only with the Amerindian kingdoms of the Incas and the Aztecs as they were around 1500. But the fact that a vast spectrum of preurban cultures also flourished in the Americas should not be forgotten. These preurban cultures may explain some features of the Mexican and Peruvian empires. They certainly explain much of the attitude of superiority Europeans developed from the beginning toward pre-Columbian Americans.

In fact, civilization had emerged in the New World as early as it had on the mainland of Europe, in Mycenean Greece—in the first millennium B.C. The huge and astonishingly realistic Olmec stone heads of Mexico were as old as the golden mask of Agamemnon. Highly developed cultures, built around religious ceremonial centers rather than true urban areas, had been rising and falling in Middle and South America for two thousand years before Columbus came. Larger political states—kingdoms and conquest empires—had also emerged, though this is harder to demonstrate because of the general lack of written records over most of the Americas. But of the artistic brilliance of cultures like that of Teotihuacán in Mexico (ca. 200 B.C.–A.D. 700) and the Mochica in Peru (A.D. 300–700), and of the intellectual brilliance of the Classical Maya of Middle America (A.D. 300–900), there can be no doubt.

It was on a foundation of twenty centuries of cultural evolution, then, that the great civilizations of the Aztecs in Mexico and the Incas in Peru were built—both, as it happens, not long before 1500. These were the American empires the European conquerors found, and the ones to be dealt with in the pages that follow.

The Aztecs: Warrior Lords of Mexico

The Meaning of Quetzalcóatl

Of all the ancient gods of Mexico, none aroused more reverence and awe in the hearts of Mesoamericans than that incarnation of divine spirit they called Quetzalcóatl, the

Amerindian Empires on the Eve of the Spanish Conquest

ATLANTIC

OCEAN

GULF
OF
MEXICO

Oxitipan
Tuxpan
Tenochtitlán
TLAXCALA
Coatza-
coalco
Querétaro
Chichén Itzá
Uxmal

TARASCANS

Petlatlán
Acapulco
Oaxaca
Mitla
Chiapa
Comitán
Ayotlán

MAYAS

Tikal

Copan

*Indefinite
Eastern
Frontier*

CARIBBEAN SEA

Orinoco R.

THE
CHIBCHAS

Pasto

Quito

Manta

Tumbez

Moyobamba
Cajamarca
Chimu
Huanuco

INCAS

Machu Picchu
Cuzco

*Lake
Titicaca*
Tiahuanaco
Cochabamba

Arequipa

Amazon R.

CHINCHAS

Equator

PACIFIC

OCEAN

Iquique
Tarija

Atacama

Tucumán

Copiapó
Coquimpu

Catamarca

Maule R.

ARAUCANIANS

Aztec Empire (approximate area)

Inca Empire (approximate area)

0   500   1000 Miles

0   500   1000 Kilometers

feathered serpent. The god of merchants, god of priests and learning, lord of the wind, lord of the "dawn house" (the planet Venus), the once and future god who sailed off across the sea promising to return, he held a high place in the pantheon of many Indian cultures.

This hybrid divinity, a plumed serpent, often bearded, having the fangs of a great cat, was worshiped far back in the history of civilization in Middle America. Gargoylelike, barbarically abstract heads of the plumed serpent projected from the walls of the Temple of the Sun at Teotihuacán as early as the first or second century A.D. In the 900s, Quetzalcóatl in human form was believed to have led the famous Toltecs into the lands of the Maya, where temples were built to him under the name of Kukulcan. And in the 1500s, he was so revered among the Aztecs that when the Spanish appeared out of the east in the very month foretold for his return, Moctezuma's armies refrained from the violence with which they would otherwise have greeted such an invasion, lest they raise their hands against divinity.

Quetzalcóatl was many things to many peoples, yet a core of identity persists in the plumed serpent for perhaps fifteen hundred years. In this core of continuity and these multiple meanings of the god of the merchants, god of the wind, god of the dawn house, we have a vivid symbol of the unity within multiplicity that characterizes the whole sweep of Mesoamerican history. In the following sections, we will look first at the common core of this unified Mesoamerican culture. Thereafter, we will turn to the last and by far the best-known of the many distinctive cultures that have risen and fallen here under the volcanoes of Mexico: the brilliant, blood-colored splendor of the Aztecs.

Mesoamerican Society

Geographically, Mesoamerica is a chain of upland valleys and mountains running between strips of coastal lowlands from Mexico down the length of Central America. Here, by the first millennium B.C., civilization in the New World had begun with the development of maize and other food crops and the resulting growth in population density and social sophistication. Olmec culture, the mother culture of Mesoamerica, had taken shape in the Caribbean lowlands, and the most renowned of Middle American societies, that of the Mayans, had also flourished there. But the influence of both had extended into the high plateaus between the mountains also. With the emergence of the metropolis of Teotihuacán in the upland plateau of central Mexico, the Mesoamerican cultural heartland shifted to the high valleys, and Mexico, at the northwestern end of the isthmus, became its power center.

By the year 1000 of the Christian calendar, the classical Mesoamerican civilization of the Mayans and the great city of Teotihuacán had passed away. But the cycles of civilization continued in the area now occupied by Mexico, Guatemala, Honduras, and neighboring states. A well-developed Mesoamerican culture had clearly emerged, one with a capacity for recovering from periodic disasters and for absorbing conquerors comparable to that of India or China.

Mesoamerican culture was built on an agricultural base of maize, beans, chilis, and squash, which supported a comparatively dense population of several million people. Mesoamerican societies were as hierarchical as any in the Old World. Besides the farming majority, they supported many sorts of artisans, a powerful priesthood presiding over large ceremonial religious centers, a fierce warrior caste, and merchants who circulated goods over hundreds of miles. Mesoamericans also had elaborate mythologies and cosmological theories, mathematics and astronomy, and, in some places, forms of writing.

Amerindians in this part of the New World were learning the art of effectively governing large empires. They continued to conduct human sacrifices—a fading practice elsewhere on the globe. They also suffered periodic influxes of less-settled, skin-clad Indians from the north, attracted as Goths were to Roman Europe or Mongols to China by the seductive charms of civilization.

The most successful of these earlier northern barbarian invaders were the Toltecs, who came to be revered in later days as a race of golden-age heroes. But there was an even more formidable name yet to come down from the north: the Aztecs, future conquerors of all Mexico.

The Rise of the Aztecs

Aztec codices (folded scrolls of picture writing) and information collected by the Spaniards after the conquest tell us a great deal about the history of this last of Mesoamerican Indian civilizations. These sources chronicle, reign by reign, the rise and transformation of a half-savage people into great conquerors and rulers during the two centuries preceding the descent of the Europeans upon their coasts.

As late as the fourteenth century, the Aztecs were a small, warlike people, one of the many uncultivated Nahuatl-speaking groups to drift down into Mexico from what is today the United States. They had been nomadic for centuries, following their priests and their god Huitzilopochtli in search of a vaguely promised land in the south. They found it on a muddy island in Lake Texcoco in the high Valley of Mexico, where around 1325 they began to build the city that became Tenochtitlán, the amazing Aztec capital the Spanish found when they arrived in their turn in 1519.

In the early days, the Aztecs were a rude folk, living largely by hunting, by gathering lake creatures, and by trading with the more developed peoples around them. They were said to be given to stealing the daughters of their neighbors for wives, as the most ancient Romans had done, and to forms of human sacrifice that even the

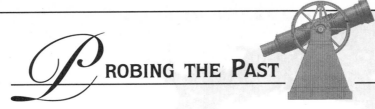

PROBING THE PAST

"Purely materialistic attitudes display a lack of comprehension not merely of Mesoamerica, but of other civilizations of the ancient world, whose basic concepts and motivations are so remote from our own.

To illustrate this point one might reverse the situation and consider the sheer bewilderment that would have afflicted the votaries of Huitzilopochtli if they had suddenly been told that their destinies were no longer subject to the dictates of their familiar gods, but that they were to be governed instead by a parliamentary democracy or by a dictatorship of the proletariat. The teaching of Jesus, the victorious Man-God, whose church was the patrimony of a resplendent priest-ruler, was far less alien to native thought; however, even Christian doctrines were hard for the friars to expound, and endless misconceptions ensued, such as the adoration of the cross as a deity in its own right.

The grip of scientific materialism on the modern mind is so firm—regardless of individual political sympathies—that contemporary man can barely comprehend the mystico-religious approach to life of his own medieval forebears, let alone of their Mesoamerican counterparts. The Spaniards, notwithstanding their preconceived notions, were better equipped to understand this mystico-religious native outlook. A parallel between Spanish and Aztec attitudes has often been noted; typical was Cortés himself, filled with a fervor to convert the heathens to Christ and to save them from Hell, but intent upon extracting, on their road to salvation, every ounce of gold that they possessed.

Such attitudes were not alien to the Aztecs, who conquered in the name of their gods but levied tribute on a transnational basis in exchange for the privilege of doing homage to Huitzilopochtli."

Nigel Davies, an authority on the development of pre-Columbian Mesoamerica, has tried to see "Mesoamerican motivations as a part of human history rather than as an isolated phenomenon." Here he compares the "mystico-religious approach" of the Aztecs with that of the Spanish invaders—and contrasts both with the philosophical materialism of our own century.

Do you agree with Davies' comparisons between the two sixteenth-century peoples? In what ways do you think twentieth-century historians might be <u>less</u> able to understand sixteenth-century Mesoamericans than contemporary Europeans were? Are there aspects of Aztec society that modern historians might be better equipped to understand precisely because of their "materialistic" concerns?

Nigel Davies, <u>The Toltec Heritage: From the Fall of Tula to the Rise of Tenochtitlán</u> (Norman: University of Oklahoma Press, 1980), pp. 17–18.

sacrifice-prone Mesoamericans found disgusting. Small in numbers and regarded as primitive, the Aztec clans were at first oppressed by their civilized neighbors and generally looked down upon.

But the rich mud of their island home and the environing shores produced lavish quantities of corn, beans, and chilis, and the Aztecs managed to acquire enough brides to produce a rapid growth in their population. They were also fierce warriors, in demand as mercenaries and allies in the frequent wars of the Mexican uplands. And they seem to have been very quick learners indeed, picking up techniques of political intrigue, alliance making, and empire building from the developed zone of urban culture in which they had settled.

Their resulting rise was as rapid as any we have recorded. Wielding bows and arrows—the Toltec had apparently fought primarily with the atlatl, or spear-thrower—and swinging wooden swords edged with razor-sharp obsidian, the Aztecs stepped into the power vacuum left by the disintegration of the older Toltec hegemony.

They began by freeing themselves from persecution by their neighbors in the Valley of Mexico and ended by conquering them. Under kings with names like Izcoatl (Obsidian Serpent) and Moctezuma (Angry Lord) I, they made warfare a paying proposition, imposing their will by force and collecting tribute over a sphere that extended far beyond the valley of central Mexico. Under more philosophically inclined leaders such as Netzahualcóyotl and his son Netzahualpilli in the fifteenth and early sixteenth centuries, they reared great temples, palaces, and gardens, cultivated such arts as astronomy and eloquence, and ruled severely but impartially over a wide swath of Mexico.

THE AZTEC EMPIRE

The Aztecs made much of their alleged descent from the legendary Toltecs, and they certainly learned a good deal from the surviving Mayan city-states they conquered in Yucatán. But the hegemony they established in the fifteenth century bore the unique mark of their own society and temperament.

Aztec society was dominated by priests and warriors. Most people were now settled farmers, but all men were liable for the military service necessary to keep subject peoples in awe. Though they did not have money, the Aztecs developed a system of market exchange, even in small provincial cities, that was superior to that of the Mayans. Food flowed into the huge market squares of Tenochtitlán from a hundred miles around. Jade, gold, and silver, feathers and skins, honey, cacao, and other valued luxury items came in tribute from an empire of five million people settled over much of the area of modern Mexico.

Like the contemporary West African kingdoms, the Aztecs had succession problems. Their kings too were not directly hereditary, but were chosen from the males of the more prestigious lineages. The Aztecs compensated for this, however, by considering their monarchs not only as essential intermediaries between the people and their gods, but increasingly as gods themselves, like the pharaohs of ancient Egypt.

As rulers, Aztec kings were able to impose a system of enforced alliances or appointed governors on some sixty provinces and subject peoples. A large scribal bureaucracy kept records of the flow of tributes and the endless wars. Warfare was necessary to maintain Aztec supremacy—and to supply prisoners of war for sacrifice to Huitzilopochtli at his gigantic pyramid temple in Tenochtitlán.

Aztec nobles, high priests, and kings lived in spacious stone houses built in the Mesoamerican style. These flat-roofed buildings were doorless—rigorous laws made thievery rare—and had cool patios and gardens filled with flowers, fruit trees, and pools. The fabled halls of Emperor

Moctezuma, emperor of the Aztecs, is shown here in an idealized European rendering. Unrealistic combinations of Western artistic taste, hazy traditions about the New World (lots of feathers!), and a vaguely conceived Aztec city reveal a European sense of the impressive New World culture they were destroying. (Library of Congress)

Moctezuma impressed even the European conquerors with their size, cleanliness, and grandeur.

The average Aztec family had little share in such splendors. Like peasants the world around, they were taught to keep their places and respect their betters. The new order required not only military service but payments to the state in produce and labor. Some peasants were serfs; others were slaves.

Most Mesoamericans, however, lived under the Aztecs as their ancestors had before the conquest. Men worked in the fields, using simple wood and stone tools. They had no beasts of burden to help, since no large domesticatable animals had survived the hunting stage in Middle America.

Women spun and wove cloth made of cotton and other vegetable fibers into the short pants and long mantles or capes worn by men and the long skirts and blouses the women themselves wore. The women also spent many hours a day—as many Indian women still do—grinding corn by hand to make the tortillas that, with beans and chili, were the mainstay of the Mesoamerican diet.

It is hard to associate the sturdy, broad-faced, hardworking people of the surviving codices and paintings with the splendors—and the horrors—of the priestly-military elite who ruled over them, or with the towering, blood-drenched pyramid on the great plaza of Tenochtitlán.

THE INCAS:
EMPIRE OF THE ANDES

A LAND AND PEOPLE DIVIDED

The Andes change color through the day. Driving down through the mountains toward the coast, you crawl like an insect among ridges and peaks that are dark blue in the morning, gray slashed with green and ocher in the dry cold noon, and red in the sunset, sliding through violet and purple toward the dark. The precipitous surge and fall of that miles-high world of angled rock, plunging gorges, and bare, isolated valleys far above the timberline make hard enough driving on a narrow modern road. The thought of traveling through this world before the age of modern transport—let alone living and building here—can kindle an impulse of respect in the most cynical modern spirit.

To unify such a realm in any but the loosest cultural sense would require both immense labor and a kind of genius rare in history. As far as we know, it happened only once before the coming of the conquistadores—in the days of the Sapa Incas, rulers of the largest empire in the history of pre-Columbian America.

Pan-Andean cultural unity was of course achieved long before the Incas conquered the Andes. As in Mesoamerica, the Amerindians of what is today Peru and portions of neighboring nations had perfected a thoroughly workable style of life, with sophisticated forms of art and social organization, centuries and even millennia earlier.

Agriculture was widely practiced. Potatoes were the upland staple, though corn, beans, and various squashes were common here as in Mexico. Hills and mountainsides were terraced, irrigation canals and ditches spread water over arid lowland valleys, and fertilizing was common. Ceremonial centers and even some true cities featured large stone temples and palaces. Many crafts were practiced, including the ancient ceramic and textile industries and more metal working than in Middle America. Society was acquiring the habits of specialization and hierarchical class divisions characteristic of urban civilization everywhere.

But the Andes divided and subdivided Peru and the peoples who lived there as the mountains and the high central plateaus divided Mexico. If anything, the world's longest mountain range did a more thorough job of breaking up the western side of South America. Peru's rocky spine effectively separated the tropical rain forests of the interior from the coastal deserts along the Pacific. Ecologically, these three zones—jungle, mountains, arid coastland—contrasted as sharply as any in the world. In addition, the ridges and jagged crests subdivided the uplands and the coastal lowlands into many narrow val-

leys—and separate valley societies—with only the most difficult communication between them.

The economy reflected these geographical and ecological divisions. Amerindian peoples pastured llama and alpaca herds and cultivated potatoes in the higher altitudes. They raised corn in the hills below, took fish from the sea, and gathered coca and other tropical products from the other side of the mountains, where the rain forests of the Amazon basin began. Each separate people, scattered among mountains or hills or forests, also had its unique traditional patterns of ceramic and textile design. Each had a style of life suited to its ecology and its traditions.

To overcome some of these problems rooted in environmental differences, Andean peoples had long since learned to trade with one another, exchanging the produce of one region for that of another. Another solution was to send out "colonies" for seasonal harvesting in a different zone, or even for permanent exploitation of crops available only in a neighboring area. Thus whole regions of this rugged corner of the world attained at least a degree of economic unity. In some cases, as among the areas conquered by the Mochica, there was regional political unity as well.

There had been significant efforts to impose hegemony over even larger tracts of pre-Columbian Peru. During the second half of the first millennium A.D., several sizable empires had divided most of Peru among them. These were the conquest empires of Huari in the north and Tiahuanaco in the south, both flourishing from approximately 600 to 1000, and the Chimu state. The latter flowered somewhat later in the northwestern coastal areas earlier organized by the Mochica.

As in Mesoamerica, a key factor behind the rise of these larger political units was the increase in population caused by improved agricultural techniques. The people seem to have needed some higher authority than the usual clan and family structure to deal with the more complex problems of life in their overcrowded valleys. Arguments over water use, landownership, and the conflicting traditional rights of neighboring villages could most effectively be settled by a superior governmental power. And there was never a shortage of ambitious chiefs, priests, and warriors eager to establish such a higher power.

But there was more to come than the successful regional empires of Huari, Tiahuanaco, and Chimu. There was pre-Columbian America's most impressive political achievement—the pan-Andean imperium of the Incas.

PACHACUTI INCA AND THE UNIFICATION OF THE ANDES

The Incas were the ruling house of a small kingdom that rose in the upland mountain-ringed valley of Cuzco perhaps as early as A.D. 1200. It was not until 250 years later, however, that a great conqueror came to the throne and became the real founder of the Inca Empire.

The historically significant rulers of Inca Peru thus number no more than half a dozen, from the emergence of the empire around 1450 to its fall to the Spanish in 1532. And the greatest of these Inca empire builders was the first, the famous Pachacuti.

Pachacuti Inca (1438–1471) seized power during a disastrous war with a powerful neighboring people. He first overthrew his father, who had retreated before the enemy, and then executed his brother, who had been so successful against the foe as to seem a threat to Pachacuti's authority. In the process of achieving and assuring his throne, the new ruler also defeated the foreign enemy who had made his rise possible. He then capped his achievement by enlisting his defeated neighbor's armies for a great campaign of conquest up and down the Andes and across the coastal lowlands as well. Pachacuti Inca and his highly competent heir Topa Inca extended their domain north into what is today Ecuador, south as far as the middle of Chile, and inland to include half of Bolivia and even a corner of Argentina.

Topa Inca's successor added little to the empire, and two of Topa's grandsons fought a civil war over the throne, a conflict that was just ending when Pizarro appeared. But the Incas had already earned their place in history. The empire they had assembled was the most impressive—and, among scholars of a later age, the most controversial—in the New World.

THE INCA EMPIRE

The peoples who lived under the Inca emperors found their lives changed significantly by their new rulers. For in their comparatively short tenure of power, the Incas demonstrated an unsurpassed skill at social and political organization.

The Inca Empire stretched for 2500 miles down the western side of South America, over some of the most difficult terrain in the world. The population may have run as high as six or eight million. To unite this realm and the divided peoples who lived there, the Inca rulers established an awesome hierarchy of officials.

The empire was divided into quarters, each of which was further divided into provinces. There was an appointed or hereditary *curaca,* or leader, for every 10 families, and again for every 50, 100, 500, 1000, 5000, and 10,000. There were appointed governors for each of the quarters. There were officials in the central government in Cuzco charged with special functions, from transportation to the military. And all this vast bureaucracy was run by people whose most complicated record-keeping device was the *quipu,* a tangle of knotted strings that served as an all-purpose aid to memorizing both statistics and events!

The great king, or Sapa Inca, at the top of this society lived in splendor in Cuzco. He never wore the same elaborate royal regalia twice, was carried about in a golden litter to a chanting of hymns, and was generally believed to be descended from the Sun, who was one of the chief gods in the Inca pantheon.

The millions of Inca subjects were expected to provide tribute in produce and were compelled to perform long hours of labor for the state. They were regulated by government edict in everything from care of crops and herds, craftwork, and construction to marriage and religion. In return, the Inca government attempted to provide defense, justice, transportation and communication facilities, food distribution from government granaries in times of scarcity, and at least minimal care for widows and orphans, the old and the sick.

To some scholars this sort of government intervention right down to the village level looks like benevolent welfare-state socialism. To others, it smacks of nothing more than modern totalitarianism. It was neither, of course. The Incas had neither the ideology nor the modern administrative machinery for such ventures. What they did do was provide rigorous government and vigorous prosperity at a cost of rigid regulation, compulsory labor, and occasional military intervention or deportation, sometimes moving whole peoples from one part of the empire to another.

In the context of the times, the price was perhaps not as high as it might seem to a later age. And the Incas, as we shall see, used their power for some of the more impressive works left by our predecessors on this planet.

PARALLEL CULTURES OF MEXICO AND PERU

COMMON BASE, PARALLEL EVOLUTION

Like the civilizations of China and Japan, those of the Incas and Aztecs were very different from each other. The Incas, like the Chinese, demonstrated remarkable skills in the arts of social organization, whereas both the warlike Aztecs and the Japanese of the age of the samurai made martial vigor central to their societies.

As with the cultures of China and Japan in the centuries around 1500, we will therefore note more differences than similarities between the Aztecs and the Incas. Yet these Amerindian civilizations will turn out to have much in common. From sun worship and temple pyramids to a highly developed social morality, Mexico and Peru reveal a distinctive substratum of shared ideas, attitudes, and cultural forms.

Since there is no evidence of cultural contact of any significance between them, however, these similarities are not a matter of cultural diffusion—the influence of one society upon another. They must instead reflect parallel evolution out of a common American cultural base. Such parallel evolution accounts for a substantial proportion of

The Pyramid of the Sun dominates the ceremonial site at Teotihuacán, near Mexico City. Approximately 750 by 250 feet at its base, this gigantic structure is precisely oriented to face the point on the horizon where the sun sets on the day each year when it passes closest to the zenith overhead. (Art Resource)

the basic similarities among peoples around the world as different cultures find their way to similar solutions to the problems they all share.

TENOCHTITLÁN: HEARTS FOR THE GODS OF MEXICO

Tenochtitlán was the center of the Aztec world, and its great central square the ideological core of Aztec life. It is to that vast plaza with its looming temples that we must go, then, if we would understand the source of the throbbing energy and the grim rigor of spirit that made the Aztec achievement possible.

In their later years at least, the once barbaric Aztecs mastered many of the traditional Mesoamerican arts and sciences. They possessed considerable knowledge of astronomy, mathematics, and a form of picture writing. They also had great skill in engineering, architecture, and sculpture in stone, and a distinctive style of painting featuring flat colors, heavy outlines, and lively cartoonlike figures. As the ancient Romans learned from the Greeks, or the Arabs from the peoples they conquered, so the Aztecs acquired a sophisticated high culture from their predecessors.

The uniqueness of the Aztecs lay not in art or science, however, but in the rigor of their morality and the extravagance of their religion.

Aztec children were taught from their earliest years to fear the gods, respect their elders, stand firm in battle. They learned to avoid vice and injustice, work hard, and accept punishment with humility. Courage, self-discipline, justice, and piety were preeminent Aztec virtues. Both parents and a widespread system of village education taught all children these virtues, as well as a trade and the necessary military skills. An equally widespread system of law courts punished misdeeds so rigorously—death for stealing more than four ears of corn—that crime seems to have been all but eliminated among the Aztecs.

Women's rights were limited but real in Aztec Mexico. Most women were married, and polygamy was not uncommon. Women had legal rights, however, could sign contracts, divorce their husbands, and remarry. Some girls were trained to be priestesses in special schools. Here they studied religion, ritual, and the handcrafting of feather vestments to be worn in religious ceremonies.

Religion had a powerful grip on all Aztec people. Like other Mesoamericans, the Aztecs were animists. They felt the closeness of the supernatural in earth and rain, the stars and the forests, the sharp edge of the obsidian blade and the burning of the fire. They personified these felt presences in anthropomorphic gods and goddesses, whom they often depicted as hybrid combinations of animals, such as Quetzalcóatl, the feathered serpent with a jaguar's teeth. There were two sorts of divinities: nature gods worshiped by farmers—for example, "your lordship, the corn"—and the great gods of the state, headed by the ancient Aztec sun god, Huitzilopochtli.

In the measured judgment of most historians, it was an intensely felt need to placate the great Huitzilopochtli, the all-devouring Mexican sun, that drove the whole brilliant, brutal machinery of the Aztec state.

Human sacrifice has been practiced at one time or another almost everywhere, usually in order to acquire supernatural powers—or to placate them. The Aztecs believed that the sun above, source of all life, required constant feeding on human hearts. Their unending wars, their stoic warrior ethic, the empire itself was from this perspective but an elaborate way of gathering food for the sun. As long as blood continued to darken the pyramidal temple of Huitzilopochtli on the great plaza—as long as fresh-plucked hearts were held up to the sky—so long would the sun shine, the crops flourish, and the Aztecs rule.

The conquistadores were vastly impressed by the lake city of Tenochtitlán, the Venice of the New World, with its "great towers and . . . buildings rising from the water, and all built of masonry,"[1] with green jungles and purple volcanoes behind it. Five square miles in area, its population perhaps as high as 100,000, it was larger than Renaissance Florence. The streets were swept clean daily; even human waste was thriftily hauled away by canoe to be used as fertilizer. The temples, plazas, palaces, and market squares, the sculptured walls, pleasant gardens, and aromatic trees were like something out of a fairy tale to the Spanish intruders.

And then they saw the racks of skulls, thousands upon thousands of them, at the foot of the temple stairs. Europeans, who burned people alive in their own countries to please their God, were, of course, unconvincing champions of humanitarianism. We can lament the destruction of that Venice of the Americas, all gone today beneath the hum and roar of Mexico City. But it is hard to regret the cessation of the rise and fall of that razor-edged obsidian blade, the swiftly probing hand, and the still-pumping lump of flesh thrust up against the sun.

CUZCO: THE KING'S HIGHWAY

But there was another way of worshiping the great central fire, and another kind of culture to be built upon this primal human religion. Two thousand miles south and east, the Inca way evolved, producing its own uniquely American cultural forms.

The Incas and their subjects, like most peoples in history, were polytheistic. They believed in a creator god, Viracocha, who had made all things in heaven and earth, including human beings fully equipped with their tribal languages, traditional music, and textile patterns. Viracocha, however, did not rule the universe: he left that to his chief assistant, Inti, the sun, who was believed to be the ancestor of all the Incas.

The moon, various stars, and Mother Earth were also gods and had earthly responsibilities as patrons of

crops, herds, and trades. Numinous power also clustered about many earthbound objects, from the tombs of ancestors to the boundary stones of fields. Even a heap of rocks along the road might be worth a prayer, and might give strength to the traveler.

Religion was as well organized as everything else in the empire of the Incas. There were shrines and temples at the village and provincial-city level as well as at the mountain capital of Cuzco. Priests and priestesses performed rituals and sacrifices punctually. The sacrifices, unlike those in Mesoamerica, were normally guinea pigs or llamas.

Inca priestesses—the "Chosen Women" and "Virgins of the Sun" held a unique place in Inca culture. Selected as girls from their home villages, they were carefully educated in religion, weaving, and ceremonial duties. Chosen Women might become wives for nobles, officials, or the Inca himself. The Virgins of the Sun devoted their lives to religious duties at sun temples in every province. They were among the best educated and most admired women in the empire.

The subjects of the Incas were not as advanced in mathematics and had not invented writing, as Mayans and Aztecs had. But they had made some practical advances. They had domesticated the llama as a beast of burden—a considerable advantage, even though a llama could carry no more than a hundred pounds. They had also learned a good deal more about working metals, edging and pointing their tools with bronze instead of with hard stones such as obsidian.

Women in Inca Peru spun and men wove gorgeous textiles out of cotton (on the coast) or alpaca and llama wool (in the highlands), using almost two hundred different dyes. Ceramicists crafted amazing pots in the Mochica and Chimu traditions, some shaped like animals or gods, some sculptured to resemble particular individuals—a striking form of pot portraiture. They worked in bronze and copper, silver and gold, using gold especially for jewelry, for dishes for noble tables, and for idols and the decoration of temples.

These crafts, like so much else in Inca society, were also organized for large-scale production. Textiles and ceramics especially were mass-produced according to standard patterns in sizable workshops.

But it is in their great public works that this most organized of New World societies excelled. The Incas were above all else great builders.

Inca stonework was probably the best in the Americas, despite the greater flamboyance of Mesoamerican architecture. Inca artisans cut, polished, beveled, and fitted stones with an unexcelled precision. Much of their best work was done at Cuzco, where royal palaces, noble mansions, and the great Temple of the Sun provided a challenge suited to their talents.

The Inca capital was a huge city, containing an estimated 100,000 to 300,000 people. The population of Cuzco represented all the varied populations of the empire, and each was required to wear his or her own brightly colored native costume. The palaces of the Incas

---

[1]Bernal Díaz del Castillo, *The Discovery and Conquest of Mexico,* trans. Irving A. Leonard (New York: Grove Press, 1950), p. 190.

Machu Picchu, the cloud-draped city in the Andes fifty miles from the Inca capital of Cuzco. Poking through the roofless ruins of this walled city on a mountain top 8000 feet high, you cannot help but be impressed with the genius and determination of this Native American people, and with the ancient South American civilization of which the Inca Empire was the final flowering. (A. Minaev/ United Nations Photo)

and of the noble heads of great clans were complexes of low buildings built around many courtyards, with gardens and storehouses for the clan treasures. There was a great public square for religious ceremonies. And there was the Coricancha, the Temple of the Sun, some of whose walls may be seen in Cuzco today serving as foundations for a Spanish colonial church.

The greatest of all Inca engineering feats, however, was the famous royal highway through the Andes. There were apparently almost 9500 miles of it, up and down and across one of the world's highest mountain ranges. The roadway was graded, smoothed, frequently paved with stone, and walled where it ran along the edge of a precipice. There were hostels and way stations for the runners who carried the royal post. There were hundreds of bridges over gorges and rivers. All of it was built, cared for, cleaned of falling rock, and repaired when heavier slides carried whole sections away, by the corvée labor of the peasants. Amazingly, much of this royal road was kept up by local villagers long after the fall of the Incas who built it, so strong a sense of social responsibility had the Inca regime instilled in its people.

To see Inca building today, one must go by train, bus, and foot up to Machu Picchu, the famous "lost city" in the clouds north of Cuzco. Here, framed by mist-draped crags high above the valley floor, yellow grass sprouts among the beveled stones, and the characteristic trapezoidal doors open on roofless rooms. The labor, the skill, and the organizing will that shaped this masonry and set it in its place so perfectly that a knife blade still cannot be inserted between the blocks testify to the unique genius of the Incas.

It is perhaps easy to discount the cultural achievements of the Aztecs and the Incas. They would fall so easily, so rapidly, to handfuls of European adventurers. They were the first great victims of the Western imperialism that is in so many ways the defining feature of our era. And their accomplishments are so completely gone today, so totally a matter of artifacts in museum cases and lonely ruins in distant jungles or mountain peaks.

The same, however, might be said of ancient Egypt and Mesopotamia, of medieval Byzantium or old Baghdad, yet we do not revere these splendid cultures less for having fallen to the universal fate. The canals of Tenochtitlán and the royal highway of the Incas were among the most impressive of human achievements in the year 1500. They are further evidence of the rich variety, the breadth and depth of the world's many civilizations at the beginning of the modern period of history.

SUMMARY

In the Americas, as in Africa, urban cultures had emerged much earlier than we are used to thinking. This was so in two areas in particular: Mesoamerica and the Peruvian Andes. Here many of the arts of civilization had been practiced for two thousand years when the first Europeans broke in upon this independent stream of social evolution shortly after 1500.

In both Mexico and Peru, techniques of imperial government were evolving rapidly. In the northern zone of civilization, the vigorous and militaristic Aztecs fought their way to power among the peoples of the high valleys of central Mexico in the fourteenth and fifteenth centuries. Initially regarded as northern barbarians, the Aztecs rapidly mastered a range of traditional Mexican skills, from settled agriculture and city building to diplomacy and bureaucratic administration. By 1500 they governed the largest empire in Mesoamerican history.

The largest of all pre-Columbian American empires, however, was that of the Incas, which emerged in the fifteenth century in Peru. Pachacuti Inca, the founder of Inca power, demonstrated amazing skill at imposing centralized authority on the historically and geographically divided peoples of northwestern South America. Over a realm of high mountains, coastal plains, and interior jungles, a structured government exacted labor and obedience and provided services ranging from defense to social welfare.

In both of these highly developed urban-imperial societies of the New World, arts and ideas flourished. They shared a variety of common elements, from sun worship and temple pyramids to a strong sense of social morality. There were, however, striking differences between them.

The Aztecs enforced rigorous moral standards and martial vigor. Their central religious ceremony, human sacrifice on the altar of the sun, was believed necessary to guarantee continued prosperity to the empire. The Incas, though neither literate nor as mathematically inclined as the Mesoamerican peoples, developed other skills. They worked metals on a larger scale and were probably the most expert builders with stone in the Americas. The astonishing Inca royal road through the Andes was one of the great feats of engineering—and social discipline—of the age.

SUGGESTED READING

ANTON, F. *Women in Pre-Columbian America.* New York: Abner Schram, 1973. Good pictures, thorough commentary on Amerindian women before the Europeans came.

COLLIER, G. A., and others, eds. *The Inca and Aztec States, 1400–1800: Anthropology and History.* New York: Academic Press, 1982. Varied collection of ethnohistorical studies of these peoples before and after Spanish conquest.

DAVID, N. *The Aztecs: A History.* New York: Putnam, 1974. A good solid account of the Aztecs.

DE LA VEGA, G. *Royal Commentaries of the Incas and General History of Peru* (2 vols.), trans. H. V. Livermore. Austin: University of Texas Press, 1966. Primary source, perhaps too sympathetic to the Incas.

DRIVER, H. E., ed. *The Americas on the Eve of Discovery.* Englewood Cliffs, N.J.: Prentice Hall, 1964. Useful book of readings, including the developed urban-imperial cultures of the New World.

FURST, J. L., and P. T. FURST. *Pre-Columbian Art of Mexico.* New York: Abbeville Press, 1980. Large format, impressive photographs.

HASSIG, R. *Aztec Warfare: Imperial Expansion and Political Control.* Norman: University of Oklahoma Press, 1988. Analyzes Aztec military tactics and imperialistic motives, questioning the central role of religion.

LÉON-PORTILLA, M. *Aztec Thought and Culture: A Study of the Ancient Nahuatl Mind.* Norman: University of Oklahoma Press, 1963. Cultural history of a people often considered—like the ancient Romans—less cultured than some of those they conquered.

MCADAMS, R. *The Evolution of Urban Society: Early Mesopotamia, Prehistoric Mexico.* Chicago: University of Chicago Press, 1965. Illuminating example of comparative history and of the cultural evolutionist analysis that prevails among students of pre-Columbian America.

MÉTRAUX, A. *History of the Incas.* New York: Pantheon, 1969. Scholarly summary.

NASH, J. "Aztec Women: The Transition from Status to Class in Empire and Colony," in M. Etienne and E. Leacock, eds., *Women and Colonization: Anthropological Perspectives.* New York: Praeger, 1980. Marriage and work before and after the conquest.

SAHAGÚN, B. DE. *General History of the Things of New Spain* (12 vols.), trans. and ed. A. O. J. Anderson and C. E. Dibble. Santa Fe: School of American Research, 1950–1969. Basic primary source for the Aztecs.

SALOMON, F. *Native Lords of Quito in the Age of the Incas.* New York: Cambridge University Press, 1986. Uses Spanish colonial records as well as archaeological and anthropological evidence to analyze this Amerindian society at the time of the Inca conquest.

SILVERBLATT, I. "Andean Women in the Inca Empire," *Feminist Studies,* vol. 4, no. 3 (1978), pp. 36–61. Social status and labor contribution of women in the Inca Empire.

SOUSTELLE, J. *The Daily Life of the Aztecs on the Eve of the Conquest,* trans. P. O'Brian. New York: Macmillan, 1962. Social history.

VON HAGEN, V. W. *The Aztec, Man and Tribe.* New York: New American Library, 1958. Older, but by a leading authority on pre-Columbian American civilization.

———. *The Incas: People of the Sun.* Cleveland: World Pub. Co., 1961. Well-written description of the society of this most impressive of Andean empires.

WOLF, E. J. *Sons of the Shaking Earth.* Chicago: University of Chicago Press, 1959. Evocative portrait of preconquest Mexico.

CHAPTER 30

PREURBAN PEOPLES

Alternate Styles of Life

Images: Beastmen and Cannibals

Europe was only one among many highly developed cultures at the beginning of modern history. There were polities in the Muslim center of Eurasia, in the Far East, in Africa, and in the Americas that rivaled the European nations in power, wealth, or splendor, in artistic brilliance or spiritual profundity. Islam had spread much farther than Christianity in half the time. China had united a population larger than all Europe's under a central government—something Europe has not managed to this day. No Western monarch could point to a road like the royal highway of the Incas. The Western sense of superiority was thus little more than an ethnocentric illusion in 1500.

But there was more to the non-European world than Istanbul and Isfahan and Delhi, Beijing and Kyoto, Timbuktu and Cuzco and Tenochtitlán. There was a *pre*urban world out there too. To this world, where cities, kingdoms, and empires had not yet appeared, all the urban-imperial peoples of the globe felt immensely and intrinsically superior. And always had.

Muslims called them pagans, Chinese called them barbarians. To sixteenth-century Europeans, these peoples who had neither cities nor countries, written laws nor visible religious institutions were only marginally human. They called such people savages, beastmen, or even anthropophagi, a reference to their allegedly common proclivity for cannibalism.

As recently as the earlier part of the present century, the peoples of the West were still calling them backward and primitive, barbarous and heathen. Today we use words such as *underdeveloped, developing,* and *preurban*—and still too often tend to mean *precivilized.*

What they were in fact were people who for a variety of reasons, including their own free choice, had not followed the same lines of cultural evolution as their cousins within the city walls. A closer look at this preurban—or nonurban—world will complete this overview of the earth's peoples at the beginning of modern history.

Theories: Levels of Culture

The following survey will be couched in terms of levels of culture. It is important at the outset to assert clearly that this terminology refers to *chronological order* of development and is not intended to impute superior value to more recent cultural developments.

Recent anthropological and archaeological research indicates that people like those who scavenge the barren wilderness of the Kalahari Desert of southern Africa today may get a more than adequate diet. They get it, furthermore, by working about half as many hours per day as a farmer or a factory worker does, and they do not have to pay taxes or serve in anybody's army. They also do not have modern medicine, social security, books, television sets, or Saint Peter's cathedral—but these are, after all, in considerable part a matter of taste.

Without implying any superiority to the urban civilizations we have examined thus far, then, let us remind ourselves of the other chronological levels of cultural development that shared the world with the urban-imperial peoples in 1500.

The oldest existing culture, it will be recalled, was that of the hunting and gathering peoples who had evolved with the race over several million years of prehistory. Because hunting and gathering could feed only small populations, and because the technological sophistication of these people was not great, they had retreated before later comers, into the cold north, the deep forest, or deserts such as the Kalahari. Yet large parts of several continents were still populated, however thinly, by such peoples at the beginning of the sixteenth century.

The most recent basic way of life to emerge, the nomadic-herding mode, had developed only a few thousand years before. Nomadism evolved when peoples too weak to claim a share of good agricultural land—or disdaining the hard work involved—retreated to the fringes. On deserts or steppes, they found food and water sufficient to feed animals as long as the herds were kept on the move. In their endless migratory round, many of the nomad peoples had become tough, well-organized, highly mobile—and historically a serious threat to the more settled peoples around them.

The most widespread preurban style of life, however, was that of the agricultural village. The Neolithic Revolution, which had begun in the Middle East around

PREURBAN PEOPLES OF THE WORLD IN 1500

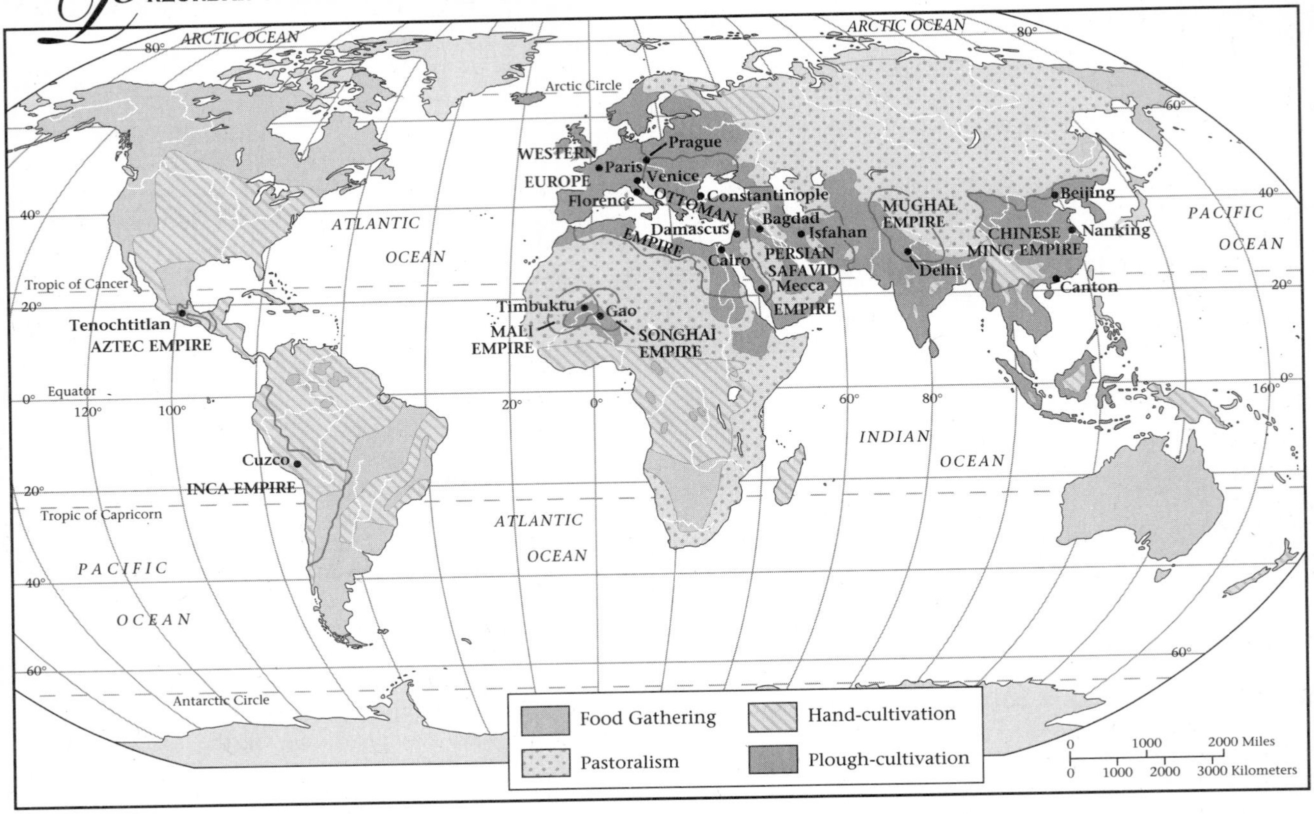
ARCTIC OCEAN
ARCTIC OCEAN
Arctic Circle
WESTERN EUROPE
Prague
Paris
Venice
Florence
Constantinople
OTTOMAN EMPIRE
Damascus
Bagdad
Isfahan
Cairo
PERSIAN SAFAVID EMPIRE
Mecca
MUGHAL EMPIRE
Delhi
CHINESE MING EMPIRE
Beijing
Nanking
Canton
ATLANTIC OCEAN
PACIFIC OCEAN
Tropic of Cancer
Tenochtitlan
AZTEC EMPIRE
Timbuktu
Gao
MALI EMPIRE
SONGHAI EMPIRE
Equator
Cuzco
INCA EMPIRE
Tropic of Capricorn
PACIFIC OCEAN
ATLANTIC OCEAN
INDIAN OCEAN
Antarctic Circle
Food Gathering
Hand-cultivation
Pastoralism
Plough-cultivation
0 1000 2000 Miles
0 1000 2000 3000 Kilometers

8000 B.C., had spread slowly around the world, bringing with it agriculture, the domestication of animals, ceramics, weaving, and many other skills. It was from the settled villages that larger towns, walled cities, and empires slowly developed.

The city, however, proved a Frankenstein's monster to the village culture that had spawned it. Urban centers turned neighboring villages into a hinterland, more distant ones into provinces. They put once free peasants to work on irrigation canals, temples, palaces, pyramids, and the Great Wall of China. But there were a great many farming villages in the world, and in 1500 many of them remained unabsorbed by the urban-imperial peoples of the earth.

The following sections, then, will offer a brief montage of hunter-gatherers, nomadic herders, and agricultural-village societies around the world. Masters of parts of Europe, much of Asia, Africa, and South America, and all of North America and Australia, these preurban peoples still owned a very large tract of the globe at the beginning of the modern period.

PREURBAN PEOPLES OF THE OLD WORLD

EUROPE'S STEPPE FRONTIER

The Old World, for all its ancient cities, had its share of preurban societies too in 1500. Europe, Asia, and Africa were by no means entirely parceled out among the kingdoms we have examined in earlier chapters.

Europe, one of the smallest of continents, had few hunters and gatherers outside of a handful of reindeer hunters in northern Scandinavia. It would have been hard to find agricultural villages that were not integrated one way or another into the European system of landed estates, urban markets, and national economies. But there were still migratory populations in Europe, sheepherders who made the rounds of southern Italy or moved back and forth between France and Spain. There were, above all, the nomads of eastern Europe's steppe frontier.

Nomadic herders of cattle and horses, sheep and goats had been drifting into Europe from central and East Asia for thousands of years. Indeed, the settled populations of the European nations—Greeks and Romans, Celts, Slavs, Germans—were Indo-European nomads who had come that way. The most recent waves, however, were mongoloid peoples such as the Golden Horde who had conquered Russia in the thirteenth century. For a time, Russia had been a khanate of the Mongol Empire, and the rest of eastern Europe, with the Ottoman Turks pressing up from the south, looked very much at risk.

The Mongols, at least, had ceased to be a serious threat by 1500. The Golden Horde was gone, and the mongoloid nomads who remained on the southern steppes of Russia were capable of destructive raids but no longer of permanent conquests. Europe's steppe frontier was in fact on its way to pacification and eventual absorption by the growing Russian state.

THE BORDERLANDS OF ASIA

Asia, the largest of all the continents, had also developed some of the largest civilized states. The Persian Empire at its height, India during its periods of unity, and above all China brought many millions of Asians within the purview of urban-imperial civilization. Smaller trading states had developed in southern India and Southeast Asia, and clones of the Chinese Empire in Korea, Vietnam, and elsewhere. But there were still large tracts of Asia in which the older ways of life survived.

There were hunting-and-fishing peoples in the islands of Southeast Asia and in northeastern Asia as well, from Kamchatka to the Bering Strait. There were villages of hunter-gatherers in the hills of India, animists still, living entirely outside the ancient Indian system of caste, cities, and major religions. Once more, however, the nomads of the Eurasian steppes were the most important remaining representatives of the preurban world.

China, India, and Persia, like Europe, had suffered repeatedly from nomadic invasions launched from the sparse grasslands and barren deserts north of their frontiers. Indo-European barbarians called Aryans had conquered India in ancient times. The Mongols had overwhelmed and ruled all China, as they had Russia, in more recent centuries. Huns and Xiongnu, Kushans, Turks, Tatars, and many others, they had been a clear and present danger for many centuries. And they were there still in 1500.

The whole vast sweep of northern Asia—the region constituting most of the modern Russian state—was given over to pastoralism wherever the land would support it. Living north of the empires of southern Asia, subject only to their own transient confederations, these steppe nomads still loomed as a threat to the urban cultures of the warmer south. Even China, the world's largest urban-imperial state, was to undergo one more barbarian conquest.

AFRICA FARTHER SOUTH

Africa south of the Sahara had its share of cities and kingdoms in 1500, as we have seen. The northern coasts had long since been integrated into the civilization of the Mediterranean, the east-coast ports into that of the Indian Ocean. Now the Sudanic empires and the kingdoms of the Guinea coast, the Congo, and elsewhere were evolving rapidly. Most of the second-largest continent, however, was still occupied by hunter-gatherers, nomadic pastoralists, and unaffiliated village agriculturalists at the beginning of the modern period.

The Sahara, from the Atlantic across to the Red Sea, belonged to the bedouin and the camel. Cattle herders occupied much of the Sudanic belt, and many of them acknowledged none of the new kings who had risen among them. Cattle raisers also moved on the plains of East Africa, from the Nile almost to the Cape of Good Hope.

Agricultural villages unaffiliated with any of the new kingdoms were common in the rain forests of West and central Africa. Hoe culture and root crops were more likely to be the heart of their economy, rather than the plowed fields and grains that predominated in Eurasia. Hand cultivation could not support the population that plowed lands could, and so there were fewer cities in Africa. And the lack of cities meant a simpler style of life.

Simplest of all, of course, were the lives of Africa's hunter-gatherers, mostly Pygmies and Bushmen. These primordial peoples were still to be found in the forests of central Africa and on the dry southern savannas and the Kalahari Desert of southwest Africa. Grubbers in the arid earth or killers of elephants in the steaming rain forest, these peoples preserved humankind's oldest lifestyle in its pristine state.

These preurban African majorities were organized into societies based on tribe, clan, and family, like preurban peoples in other parts of the world. Traditional sex roles and age groups with assigned responsibilities further structured the world of the villagers, the herders, and the hunters. A common language group and cultural pattern strengthened felt relationships between some villages but had not yet crystallized into kingdoms or empires. Animists, tellers of tales, producers of some haunting art, they lived by local taboos, worshiped local gods.

Big, however, is not necessarily beautiful, and there is no way at all to tell whether these small peoples of unorganized Africa were more or less happy than peasant farmers who paid taxes to the Yongle Emperor or to Queen Elizabeth.

Preurban Peoples of the Americas and Oceania

The Rest of Latin America

In all of the Americas in 1500, there were only two great empires: the Aztec Empire in Middle America and that of the Incas running down the west coast of South America. Legend would fill both continents with El Dorados, but the facts were otherwise. All the rest of what would become Latin America belonged to isolated agricultural villages, hunter-gatherer peoples, and peoples who combined these sources of sustenance in varying proportions.

Agriculture predominated in Central America and the Caribbean islands and in the tropical forests of Brazil. On the Central American isthmus and in the Caribbean, maize—Indian corn—and manioc fed most people. In the isolated villages of the Amazon rain forests, manioc and other root crops, cultivated by hand, were the main means of subsistence.

Hunting and food gathering were common in eastern Brazil and down the long sweep of Argentina. Here the lifestyle of the earliest humans flourished undiluted by cultivation of the soil or domestication of animals. People hunted game, fished the sea and the rivers, gathered nuts, berries, roots, and shellfish, as all their ancestors had done since the first mongoloid migrations from the north.

These Amerindian populations of Central and South America included some chiefdoms, hereditary rule without any of the other paraphernalia of an urban-imperial culture. But most were much more loosely organized socially. Most of these peoples apportioned responsibilities by age and sex and claimed ties by virtue of family and clan relationships and vaguer tribal affinities. Here as in Africa, common language and culture had not yet led to any more structured political organization outside the empires discussed above.

A more rigid political order was coming, of course. The Portuguese came among them offering axes for brazil-wood, and the Spanish in their iron shirts and helmets pressed down the rivers looking for El Dorado.

Stone Age North America

North America in 1500 had no urban societies at all: the entire continent was given over to preurban forms of social organization. Metal was worked here and there, but mostly for articles of adornment rather than for tools. Hoes, axes, arrowheads, fishhooks, knives were all still made of stone

or bone, the shafts of spears, bows, and other long tools out of wood. To all intents and purposes, it was a Stone Age world.

This is not to say that a monotonous sameness prevailed across the immensities of what are today two of the world's largest nations, the United States and Canada.

It looks simple enough on a map. Across the thickly wooded eastern two thirds of the United States and southern Canada, a modest village hoe-culture prevailed. Down the Pacific coast from Alaska to California and eastward across the great plains of the United States and northern Canada, hunting and fishing outweighed all other means of subsistence. Nowhere were true cities or organized kingdoms yet to be found.

Yet even in this preurban world, there was a considerable variety of cultural forms. The famous Pueblo Indian culture was rearing its multistory "apartment houses" against the red cliffs of the American Southwest—as close to towns as you can get without the marketplace and municipal institutions. In the East, the mound-building societies of the Mississippi culture were erecting their temple-mounds, probably topped with wooden buildings, from the coast to the Mississippi, trading their metalwork and exquisite eggshell pottery over large sections of the country, and probably creating chiefdoms that combined a number of neighboring villages. Before the sixteenth century was over, the celebrated Iroquois Confederacy would link half a dozen great North American tribes by a "covenant chain" of agreements, a central council, and a central sacred fire in a political association that pushed deceptively close to true empire.

In differing degrees, this range of social forms prevailed all across the New World. Nevertheless, beyond Mesoamerica and the Andean highlands, the Americas were still entirely in the hands of preurban peoples.

Once more, these were not inferior peoples. The English settlers who first established Britain's claim to the New World, at Jamestown Island in Virginia in 1607, were helpless in the wilderness. Half of them died the first year, and the rest survived only on the charity of the Indians, who offered maize and fish and a little technological help for their future conquerors.

Aboriginal Australia and the Islands

There is a romantic aura about some of these peoples of the jungles, grasslands, and the sea, at least when seen from a Western perspective. And nowhere did the Western imagination create a more romantic image for the preurban peoples of other parts of the globe than in the far Pacific.

Western people did not actually begin to penetrate Australia and the Pacific islands until rather well along in their unprecedented imperial expansion—not in any numbers until the eighteenth century. Before that, these unknown watery regions were spattered with hypothetical

"*After the creation of the earth, all the other animals withdrew into the places which each kind found most suitable for obtaining therein their pasture or their prey. When the first ones died, the Great Hare caused the birth of men from their corpses, as also from those of the fishes which were found along the shores of the rivers which he had formed in creating the land. Accordingly, some of the savages derive their origin from a bear, others from a moose, and others similarly from various kinds of animals; . . . their villages each bear the name of the animal which has given its people their being—as that of the crane, or the bear, or of other animals. . . . These first men . . . whom hunger had weakened, inspired by the Great Hare with an intuitive idea, broke off a branch from a small tree, made a cord with the fibers of the nettle . . . and thus they formed a bow [and arrows] with which they killed small birds. After that, they made* viretons *[crossbow arrows], in order to attack the large beasts; they skinned these, and tried to eat the flesh. But as they found only the fat savory, they tried to make fire, in order to cook their meat. . . . The skins of the animals served for their covering. . . . They invented a sort of racket [snowshoe], in order to walk on this [snow] with more ease; and they constructed canoes, in order to enable them to cross the rivers, . . . These men, . . . while hunting found the footprints of an enormously tall man. . . . This great colossus, having wakened, said, "My son, why art thou afraid? Reassure thyself; I am the Great Hare, he who has caused thee and many others to be born from the dead bodies of various animals. Now I will give thee a companion." Here are the words that he used in giving the man a wife: "Thou, man," said he, "shalt hunt, and make canoes, and do all things that a man must do; and thou, woman, shalt do the cooking for thy husband, make his shoes, dress the skins of animals, sew, and perform all the tasks that are proper for a woman.*"

James Axtell, a prize-winning American ethnohistorian, studies preurban Native American cultures through a critical reading of Jesuit and other early colonial descriptions. The present extract, taken from the Memoir of the seventeenth-century French Canadian missionary, trader, and government agent Nicolas Perrot, presents an Ottawa Indian account of the creation and early history of the human race. As Axtell points out, this means "explaining the origins of society as they know it." Can you find here explanations of the Ottawa's totemic belief in animals sacred to each village? (Note that the greatest of the gods, the Great Hare, is also named for an animal.) How does the legend explain Ottawa technology? Traditional Ottawa sex roles?

James Axtell, ed., The Indian Peoples of Eastern America: A Documentary History of the Sexes (New York: Oxford University Press, 1981), pp. 180–181.

islands on the maps—islands often grimly labeled, like Asia and Africa on older maps, "Here Be Cannibals."

Oceania, comprising the continent of Australia and the scattered island groups of Melanesia, Micronesia, and Polynesia, was in fact the last refuge of European dreamers as recently as the present century. Who indeed has not dreamed of a South Sea island in the sun? Books, films, travel posters spread the image to this day.

There was in fact some truth to both these mythic images of the South Seas. There were certainly many islands in the sun. And there were some cannibals too.

The great migrations that peopled the islands of the South Pacific were over well before 1500. Many of the small atolls—ring-shaped islands surrounding a central lagoon—were inhabited by then. So were most of the mountainous, tropically forested volcanic islands, such as Tahiti and Hawaii. From New Guinea and New Zealand to Hawaii and Easter Island, millions of square miles of ocean had been occupied and settled by preurban peoples centuries before the Europeans came.

The people of the islands lived by fishing and by cultivating root crops and tree crops, especially the ubiquitous coconut. Though their great migrations were over, they were still famous seafarers, the "Vikings of the Pacific." Their long double canoes could navigate hundreds of miles of ocean between one island group and another to exchange goods, either as gifts or on a commercial basis. There were hereditary chiefdoms on some of the islands, and even tributary relationships that, once more, verged on more complex political structures.

On the continent of Australia, finally, some of the least developed of human societies flourished, apparently quite happily, as they had for thirty thousand years.

The australoid Aborigines were Old Stone Age hunters and gatherers, like many Indians of North America, in 1500. Theirs was the oldest of preurban cultures—the migratory life of people who lived off game and fish, fruits, roots, and nuts in their seasons—and the entire continent was given over to it. They had no higher form of social organization than the hunting band of two or three dozen, no arts more complex than body paint, no theologies more elaborate than the myths and legends of the Dream Time before history began. They had no villages, no houses, no clothes.

Yet the Aborigines had already survived in this minimalist mode for something like six times as long as the oldest of urban-imperial societies. Some of them still live that way today, literally and quite cheerfully hand to mouth.

There was a darker side to the preurban paradise of Oceania on the eve of European conquest, of course. Australian Aborigines and Polynesian islanders both fought wars as bloody—in proportion to their numbers—as those of more developed societies. And there was ritual cannibalism in some of these islands in the sun.

Dancing the mask in today's Nigeria. An Ighogho mask-dancer seeks to protect this African village from smallpox and other contagious diseases. Years of training and a sacred initiation have traditionally gone into the preparation of masks, dancers, and the ritual itself. As in early modern times, such performances have a variety of social functions in modern African villages. (Eliot Elisofon Archives, National Museum of African Art, Smithsonian Institution)

 ## PREURBAN CULTURE

DANCING THE MASK

As we have noted, the preurban world also had its intellectual and artistic culture. For a slightly deeper penetration of the art and thought of these dwellers beyond the frontiers of the world's major civilizations, we will look a little more closely at two significant instances. We will see what an African mask and an Amerindian ball game can teach us about the worldviews and central values of Africa south of the Sahara and pre-Columbian North America.

Africa is a huge continent with many and diverse populations, and generalizations about an "African" worldview are as dubious as generalizations about a single "European" or "Asian" view of the world. Nevertheless, efforts have been made to summarize the religious views in particular that predominated in the African villages south of the Sahara before the two great world religions of Islam and Christianity reached them.

Recent studies of the indigenous religious life of Africa tend to focus on a profound sense of unity in African life. They stress the continuity of nature and humanity, land and people, the individual and the group, the living and the dead. More commonly than not, this faith is called *animism*—a religion that sees a common *life* in all things.

There is, African animists seem to feel, a spiritual vitality in everything around them. Mountains, streams, wells, trees, the animals they kill, and the plants they grow all live as people do, and many communicate with them as people do with each other. Africans and the world they inhabit are thus, in a deep spiritual sense, one.

The individual is also one with the group, or groups, of which he or she is a part. The family and the clan, the age group into which one is born, the village community as a whole form a living network of relationships. This network absorbs people at birth, nurtures them all their lives, and determines their destinies. The individual is part of the community, as he or she is of nature.

There are, finally, fundamental ties binding the generations, living and dead. The spirits of ancestors are with the living still, to guide, warn, or haunt them as their actions warrant. Past and present, life and what we call death thus merge in the mind of the African animist into a seamless web of spirituality surrounding us all.

Much African art seems to focus on this fundamentally religious vision of the world. It is an art made for religious purposes—an art of fetishes and nature spirits, ancestor worship and magic. Like the art of the medieval cathedral, it has no other object but to enhance the numinous experience of being in the presence of the divine.

The African mask, perhaps the most successful African sculptured form, expresses these spiritual themes with unsurpassed intensity. African masks clearly illustrate the continuity of the clan and the people. They are made according to strict tribal traditions, and every West African can tell a Senufo from a Mande mask, the shaman's mask from that of the men's secret society. Carved in wood, painted, decorated with raffia, cowrie shells, and colorful beads, these masks have a life of their own—the vivid, sometimes fearful life of the spirit they personify.

It may look like a finished art product, strikingly carved and intricately decorated, hanging on the wall of a museum. But an African mask is never really experienced until it is seen in motion—in performance—worn by an African dancer as part of the ceremonial activity it was made for.

The art and ritual of "dancing the mask" is still taught over long periods of secret initiation in sacred groves around small villages in the interior of Africa. Dancing the mask still expresses the deep African feeling of oneness, of identity among the dancer, the mask he wears, and its indwelling spirit. It is this spiritual presence that possesses the dancer when he presses the wood against his face, feels the leather thongs behind his head and the raffia mane spreading over his shoulders. And it is this spiritual presence that possesses him as he sees through narrow slits the familiar village faces, the hard-packed earth of the dancing place, as they appear in the distorting and exalting vision of the spirit of the mask.

THE RITUAL BALL GAME

Culture is a complicated thing, and that of the Native American peoples, like that of village Africa, involved some unique elements. One of these was the ritual ball game.

A ballcourt in the Mayan sacred center of Chichén Itzá in Yucatan, Mexico, as it looks today. In later Aztec versions, as in ancient Roman gladiatorial contests, the losers of the ritual ball game might pay with their lives for their defeat. (D. Donne Bryant Stock Photography)

Ancient peoples of many lands, from classical Greece and Rome to Celtic Britain, engaged in rough competitive team sports involving balls. In the urban-imperial parts of the pre-Columbian Americas, a Great Ball Court was a common feature of both Toltec and Aztec towns. The ball court at Chichén Itzá was huge, a walled enclosure 270 feet long and 25 feet high. In these Mexican versions of the great game, hard rubber balls were hurled through stone rings in a violent competition, which may have climaxed with the ritual sacrifice of the losers.

Among the preurban peoples of North America, the game was played without a ball court or human sacrifice—but it played an important part in the lives of these peoples too.

The Iroquois, the Cherokee, and other Native American peoples played a ball game using rackets from which evolved the modern game of lacrosse. In this version, teams of players raced up and down a field using long-handled rackets to carry, toss, catch, or deposit a ball in their opponents' goal. Teams from rival tribes sometimes numbered as many as a thousand, with goals set miles apart and games lasting several days.

But there was much more to these contests than competitive sport. Since a winning strategy involved knocking rival players out of the game by breaking limbs or even by killing them, the ball game was often seen as good training for warfare: The Cherokee called it "the little brother of war." Because of the rigorous training, skill, stamina, and courage required, Native American ball games were also considered important tests of character and manhood. Perhaps most important, there was clearly a religious dimension to the game, which was often surrounded by mystic rites and ritual dancing.

The ball game as played by the Cherokee of the southeastern United States well illustrates these religious elements. Like other Amerindian peoples, and like the African village people already discussed, the Cherokee believed themselves to be part of the natural world and strove consciously to live in harmony with other natural creatures—animals, plants, and earth itself. Long and rigorous training for the game thus involved, not only physical exercise, but also invoking the spirits of the natural world. Instead of an athletic coach, the village shaman presided: praying to the spirits of powerful, swift, or tough animals and plants (the eagle, the deer, the catgut, and other tough-fibered plants); forbidding tabu foods such as the timorous rabbit; and "going to water"—the nearest river—with individual players to call upon "the long man," as the river was conceived, to strengthen them for the coming ordeal. The game itself was preceded by a full night of dancing, invocations, and the ritual "scratching" of the competitors with turkey claws until their legs, arms, and bodies ran with blood. There followed an early morning hike of several miles to the playing field, final prayers to all the forces of the living world, and the game began. Needless to say, the losers immediately demanded a rematch!

THE COMING CATASTROPHE

Europeans had learned from Arab legend that the equator was a "burning line"—so hot that the sea boiled, ship's tar melted, and sails and rigging caught fire under the blazing sun. Green weed would foul your hull there, and crocodiles as big as whales rolled in the waves, waiting to devour you. The burning line was one of many barriers, like the ice of the polar north or the unmeasured expanse of the Ocean Sea itself, that penned Western people into their narrow end of Eurasia.

In 1500, Europeans were just embarking upon an unparalleled expansion, a drive toward all horizons that would breach all barriers, real or imagined. From the poles to the burning line, the whole earth suddenly lay open to them.

Three-quarters of the land surface of that earth was populated by animists, makers of stone tools, societies based on family, clan, and scattered chiefdoms. When the grim-faced men with iron helmets and firearms, sailing ships, and military discipline came among such peoples, they would have little chance.

Isolation, tropical diseases, or the sheer fact that they had little that the Westerners wanted would protect them for a long time. They would fight for the lands they inhabited, however thinly. And an Apache or a Zulu could frequently be the equal of a conquistador or a redcoat, man for man. But the society of the hunter, the herder, the village tiller of a meager earth was not equal in strength to the society of the invader.

Three quarters of the earth belonged to the preurban peoples in 1500. Almost none of it belongs to them today.

SUMMARY

Most of the population of the earth had been brought under centralized government and integrated, however loosely, into the urban-imperial culture by 1500. Geographically speaking, however, most of the planet was still inhabited by practitioners of earlier forms of social organization. Agricultural villagers, pastoral nomads, and hunting-and-gathering peoples were still thinly scattered over all of Australia and North America, most of Latin America and Africa, and parts of Asia and Europe as well.

In the Old World, Europe still had its pastoral herders who moved with the seasons, as well as a broad steppe frontier to the east. All of northern Asia was inhabited by such pastoral nomads, and there were pockets of hunter-gatherers here and there as well. In Africa, desert bedouins survived on the inhospitable Sahara, nomadic cattle-herders were common in East Africa, and Pygmy and Bushman hunter-gatherers were still to be found in rain forests and in the far south. In addition, many African agricultural villages still remained free of higher governmental jurisdiction.

In the New World, Latin America's two urban-imperial cultures alone represented the more complex social forms. Preurban agricultural villages were common in Central America and the Caribbean, in western Brazil, and in the eastern United States and Canada. Hunting, fishing, and the seasonal gathering of vegetable foods fed the populations of northern and western North America, of eastern Brazil, and the Argentine stem of South America.

In Oceania, finally, the peoples of the islands and the isolated continent of Australia did without cities and empires entirely. Islanders farmed and fished, Australian aborigines hunted and gathered as their ancestors had done.

These hunters, herders, village farmers—historically looked down on by peoples who had built cities and empires—had nevertheless survived for five thousand years, since the first cities rose in Mesopotamia. In the centuries after 1500, however, these older cultures would be largely absorbed or destroyed by the most successful of all urban-imperial cultures, that of the imperialistic West.

SUGGESTED READING

BERNAI, I. *Mexico before Cortez: Art, History, Legend.* Garden City, N.Y.: Doubleday, 1963. Amerindians of the Valley of Mexico; illustrated.

BERNDT, R. M., and C. H. BERNDT. *The World of the First Australians: An Introduction to the Traditional Life of the Australian Aborigines.* Chicago: University of Chicago Press, 1964. A good study of this much studied preurban—and preagricultural—people of the Australian outback.

COON, C. S. *Caravan: The Story of the Middle East,* rev. ed. New York: Holt, Rinehart & Winston, 1961. Ecological frame and cultural forms of pastoral societies from North Africa to Pakistan.

DENEVAN, W. M., ed. *The Native Population of the Americas in 1492.* Madison: University of Wisconsin Press, 1976. Balanced estimate of Native American populations.

DOCKSTADER, F. J. *Indian Art in America: The Arts and Crafts of the North American Indian,* 3rd ed. Greenwich, Conn.: New York Graphic Society, 1966. Useful introduction to the rich variety of Amerindian art in the northern continent.

DRIVER, H. E., ed. *The Americas on the Eve of Discovery.* Englewood Cliffs, N.J.: Prentice Hall, 1964. Useful collection of readings on pre-Columbian North and South America.

————. *Indians of North America,* 2nd ed. Chicago: University of Chicago Press, 1969. Topical survey of all aspects of Native American culture, from horticulture and crafts to marriage and religion.

ELKIN, A. P. *The Australian Aborigines,* 3rd ed. Garden City, N.Y.: Anchor, 1964. An older but still solid account.

FAGE, J. D., and R. OLIVER, eds. *Cambridge History of Africa: Vol. III, 1050–1600.* New York: Cambridge University Press, 1975. Includes preurban populations as well as the African empires, kingdoms, and city-states.

FENTON, W. N. *The False Faces of the Iroquois.* Norman: University of Oklahoma Press, 1987. Religious rites and world views of the powerful Indian confederation, by the leading authority.

HALLET, R. *Africa to 1875: A Modern History.* Ann Arbor: University of Michigan Press, 1970. Excellent general history, with coverage of this period.

KRADER, L. *Social Organization of the Mongol-Turkic Pastoral Nomads.* The Hague: Mouton, 1963. Historic Mongols and other steppe-dwelling nomads are discussed.

OLIVER, R. A. *The African Middle Ages: 1400–1800.* New York: Cambridge University Press, 1981. Regional organization; by a leading authority.

STEWARD, J. H., ed. *Handbook of South American Indians* (7 vols.). Washington, D.C.: Bureau of American Ethnology, 1946–1959. A standard source.

————. *Theory of Culture Change.* Urbana: University of Illinois Press, 1955. Old but standard formulation of the theory of local evolution of culture, requiring no influences from more "developed" cultures to bring about change. Applied here to Latin America, but also applicable to many societies outside Eurasia.

WAUCHOPE, R., ed. *Handbook of Middle American Indians* (15 vols.). Austin: University of Texas Press, 1964–1975. Authoritative.

THE WORLD
OF INTERCONTINENTAL EMPIRES

The world had seen empires before, but never empires like these.

Empire building goes back to the dawn age of human civilization. The city-states of ancient Mesopotamia spawned several empires large enough to encompass the entire Tigris-Euphrates valley, and Egypt for a time extended its power around the southeastern corner of the Mediterranean. During the classic age that followed, empires established in Roman Europe, the Persian Middle East, northern India, and Han China linked all Eurasia commercially. Later periods saw the emergence of other empires across Eurasia, as well as in parts of Africa, Middle America, and South America. Empire building has thus been a basic pattern of territorial organization from the beginning.

During the centuries immediately preceding the great age of European conquests, there were two particularly astounding waves of interregional empire building in the Old World. The expansion of Islam, beginning in the seventh century, created a loose religious and cultural hegemony that stretched from Spain to Southeast Asia and reached well down into Africa as well. And the amazing conquests of the Mongols in the thirteenth century absorbed much of Eurasia, from Russia to China, into a single vast empire, the largest the world had ever seen.

The Mongols had fallen away by 1492. Islam, though still expanding, had long since fragmented into a number of feuding nations no more politically united than Christian Europe. But a third great surge of interregional empire building began just before 1500—the rise of the West.

Western imperialism would be similar to earlier waves of imperial outreach in the past in some fundamental ways. Like earlier empire builders, Europeans frequently employed military force to impose their will upon other peoples. Like earlier empires, Europe's imperial predominance also commonly took on a political form, converting formerly independent peoples into colonies ruled by Europeans. As in the past, Western political and military power led to economic exploitation, ranging from favorable trade agreements to the massive extraction of natural resources, exploitation of cheap local labor, and large-scale investment—all of greater benefit to Westerners than to indigenous populations. As had frequently happened in the past, finally, military, political, and economic hegemony led to a growing intellectual and social influence by Western society on non-Western societies, a process frequently described as "cultural imperialism."

All these features of Western imperial expansion would have been familiar enough to anyone aware of Persian, Roman, Indian, Chinese, Islamic, West African, Peruvian, Mexican, and many other forms of imperialism. But there were unique elements in this new wave as well.

One essential feature was the medium upon which Western imperialism depended from the beginning: sea power, and the resulting mastery of the world's oceans.

This led in turn to a second distinguishing characteristic: the intercontinental reach of the new European empires. By bridging the oceans, European empires brought continents and peoples thousands of miles apart under common Western rule.

The greatest consequence of Western imperialism, finally, may have been to trigger a genuinely global interaction for the first time in human history. The European intercontinental empires, by bringing all the peoples of the world into much closer contact than ever before, fostered an increasing amount of mutual interaction—cultural, economic, demographic, even ecological—including as much influence of the conquered on the conquerors as the other way around.

The next few chapters, then, will deal with the history of the world in the age of European intercontinental empires—roughly the four hundred years from the sixteenth through the nineteenth centuries. European imperialism is only one of the main strands of modern global history, yet it runs like the proverbial scarlet thread through the history of these centuries, affecting all the other strands.

European global expansion began around 1500 with the Spanish *conquista* of South and Central America and the Portuguese commercial penetration of Brazil, the coasts of Africa, India, and points farther east. The great conquest continued after 1600 when the North Atlantic powers—Britain, France, and the Netherlands—began to carve out overseas empires for themselves, especially in North America and the Caribbean, in India and Southeast Asia. After 1700 came a series of significant imperial adjustments, including the ebbing of Dutch imperial vigor and a duel between Britain and France that ended in the 1760s with Britain's emergence as the greatest of global empire builders.

The nineteenth century, finally, climaxed with the New Imperialism that began around 1870. In a few decades thereafter, European imperialists, making use of the new technology of the Industrial Revolution, reduced almost all of Africa to colonial status and transformed much of Asia into protectorates or spheres of influence. By 1900, the Western hegemony of the world was essentially complete.

For most of this period, however, there was another history besides that made by European soldiers, traders, missionaries, and proconsuls of empire. The great conquest is the unifying factor, but it was by no means the whole story of the four centuries between 1500 and 1900.

In the Far East, China was conquered by the Manchus, and the last of the Chinese dynasties was established in Beijing during the seventeenth century. During the 1600s also, feudal Japan fell under the centralizing Tokugawa shoguns, who dominated its history until the nineteenth century. Much of Asian history, however, especially during the latter part of this period, is a story of decline, withdrawal, and turning inward. Tokugawa, Manchu, Mogul, and Ottoman emperors were soon past their first vigor, no match for the Western onslaught.

In the Americas and in Australia, conquered and colonized by Europeans, these centuries saw a double transformation. These three continents evolved politically from dependencies of European imperial powers into a number of independent nations. But they were nations ruled and increasingly populated by Western peoples, and the resulting process of Westernization continued apace after political independence. By the end of the nineteenth century, then, Australia and both the Americas had been dramatically transformed along essentially Western lines.

Europe itself, finally, underwent remarkable changes during the seventeenth, eighteenth, and nineteenth centuries. The powers of the royal rulers of European nation-states grew during the age of absolutism that began in the 1600s. The wealth of the European economies increased amazingly, particularly with the coming of the Industrial Revolution in the later 1700s. New ideas spread through the West in these centuries, particularly the ideas of the Scientific Revolution and the social and political views of the Enlightenment. During the 1700s and the 1800s, science contributed fundamentally to the industrial development of Europe, while the ideologies spawned by the Enlightenment led to an astounding series of political revolutions across the Western world. By 1900, then, technological advance, democratic institutions, social reform, and nationalistic foreign policies had swept Europe to the brink of what is in many ways the most astonishing of centuries—our own.

The age of intercontinental empires was therefore a time of great change in the global picture. It saw the rise to genuinely worldwide predominance of one of the world's great civilizations, an event unprecedented in history. It saw the decay of the great empires, the transformation of whole continents. It saw the establishment and spread of radical new ideas and the creation of a technological capacity unparalleled in human experience.

Granted, many peoples—in the interiors of Africa, central Asia, and South America, for instance—remained unaffected and even unaware of these phenomenal changes. But in the century that began in 1900, they too would feel the impact of the new conditions for world history that had been laid down in the earlier modern centuries. By that time, too, the greatest change of all was clearly discernible, even in its earlier stages: the birth of a genuinely global community, a world order that reached far beyond Western hegemony and pointed toward even more astonishing changes still to come.

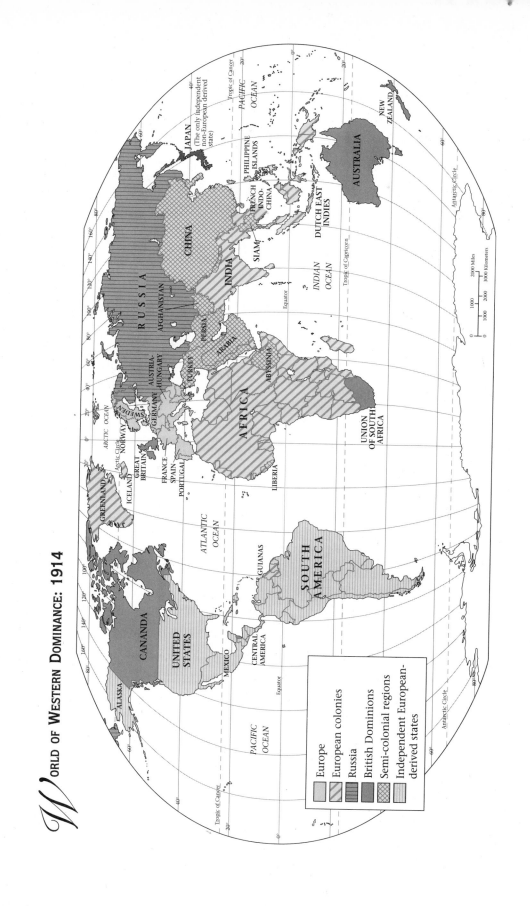

WORLD OF WESTERN DOMINANCE: 1914

Legend:
- Europe
- European colonies
- Russia
- British Dominions
- Semi-colonial regions
- Independent European-derived states

Labels on map:

ALASKA
CANANDA
UNITED STATES
MEXICO
CENTRAL AMERICA
GUIANAS
SOUTH AMERICA
GREENLAND
ICELAND
GREAT BRITAIN
NORWAY
SWEDEN
FRANCE
SPAIN
PORTUGAL
GERMANY
AUSTRIA-HUNGARY
TURKEY
RUSSIA
AFGHANISTAN
PERSIA
ARABIA
ABYSSINIA
LIBERIA
AFRICA
UNION OF SOUTH AFRICA
INDIA
CHINA
SIAM
JAPAN (The only independent non-European derived state)
PHILIPPINE ISLANDS
FRENCH INDO-CHINA
DUTCH EAST INDIES
AUSTRALIA
NEW ZEALAND

PACIFIC OCEAN
ATLANTIC OCEAN
ARCTIC OCEAN
INDIAN OCEAN

Tropic of Cancer
Equator
Tropic of Capricorn
Arctic Circle
Antarctic Circle

0   1000   2000   3000 Kilometers
0   1000   2000 Miles

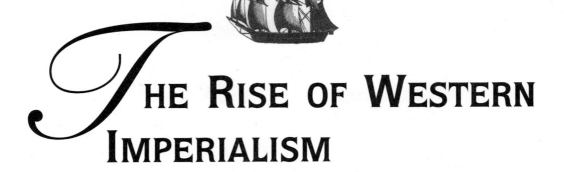

CHAPTER 31

THE RISE OF WESTERN IMPERIALISM

MEANS AND MOTIVES

SHIPS, COMPASSES, AND GUNS

There was an explosion of white foam under a ship's bow, a scream of gulls overhead, and the gliding shadow of a great fish beneath a sliding wave. Above all, there would be the buffeting of the wind about Chinese, Arab, European cheeks, about bare brown Polynesian shoulders or the frozen beards of Vikings. The sea and sea creatures, the push of the wind, and the voyagers who roamed the oceans of the world are all essential elements to the now half-forgotten romance of the sea. But the key to this daring chapter in the long human venture is the ship itself, and to ships we must turn as we begin the story of the farthest voyagers of all.

Boats of papyrus and balsa wood, triremes and double canoes, Venetian galleys, Viking dragon ships, Arab dhows, and Chinese junks have all carried human beings to violent adventure, dazzling wealth, or the loneliest of deaths on the vast blue reach that covers most of the surface of the globe. We who have so easily conquered the air in a single century must make an effort of the imagination to empathize with those of our ancestors who at such cost learned to ride freely on the waters.

Europeans were not the first to venture out upon the oceans of the world. But between the fifteenth and the nineteenth centuries, Western humankind mastered the seas as no other peoples had. And by mastering the sea, they opened a watery road to the conquest of all the mainlands and islands of the earth.

The European sailing ships of Columbus's time were not the largest vessels in the world. Any of the huge seagoing junks that China's Yongle Emperor sent east across the Indian Ocean could have carried all the crews of the four ships of Vasco da Gama that crossed the Indian Ocean the other way sixty-five years later. But the Portuguese caravels of the years around 1500—and the Spanish galleons of the later sixteenth century—had advantages that no other vessels could match. And in the seventeenth century, Europeans began to build huge trading vessels themselves. These "East Indiamen," intended for the round trip to the Far East, could carry 1600 tons of cargo and as many as a thousand passengers and crew.

It was not size, however, that primarily distinguished Western ships of the age of sail. A major innovation was a new combination of the sails themselves. This mix of medieval European square sails and Arab lateen (triangular) ones made it possible for Europeans to develop unprecedented skill at tacking—sailing across or even into the wind. European ships thus became the most maneuverable of sailing vessels, ideally suited for exploring—or for fighting.

European vessels also employed an impressive array of navigational aids for their time. Some of these devices were borrowed, like the magnetic compass, developed first by the Chinese. Some were ancient instruments, like the astrolabe, used for measuring the altitude of the sun above the horizon, and hence the ship's latitude north or south of the equator. There were sand glasses for measuring time, sounding leads for assessing the depth of the water, and the original "log"—a piece of wood flung over the stern at the end of a knotted cord—for estimating speed at sea, and hence longitude east or west.

Improvements in map making also gave Europeans an advantage. Many of the detailed coastal charts drawn by explorers and traders were extremely accurate. The technique of the Mercator projection made it possible to represent the curved surface of the earth on a flat map—a valuable aid for a people embarking on what became a global venture. By the end of the sixteenth century, only a hundred years into the great conquest, Europeans had charted the coasts of all the continents except Australia, which was added more slowly over the next two centuries.

To excellent ships and unexcelled navigational equipment, finally, Western overseas venturers added a range of weaponry that gave them a powerful advantage wherever they went. The cannon and firearms of European infantry—harquebuses, muskets, and larger powder-and-shot weapons—gave Western soldiers the edge over even the best non-Western troops not so equipped. Above all, the broad spectrum of artillery mounted on European ships made them likely victors in any naval conflict. With rows of cannon lining gun decks and firing in unison to produce devastating broadsides, the ships of European countries soon became the acknowledged rulers of the waves.

It was with these ships that the European empire builders advanced against the world. During the centuries of the so-called Old Imperialism—from the later 1400s to the later 1700s—they imposed their will on peoples of distant continents in an unprecedented manner.

GOD, GOLD, AND GLORY

The means for this first stage of the great conquest were thus clearly there by the time Columbus began to importune Queen Isabella to invest in an attempt to reach the East by sailing west. The motives also had developed among these restless, aggressive peoples of Eurasia's western fringe. Columbus's own dreams embodied most of them.

Wealth was certainly the primary motive for many, as it was one of Columbus's great bargaining points with the king and queen of Spain. Gold and silver, silks and spices, and later the valuable products that could be grown (like sugar) or caught (like furs or fish) in foreign parts all drew the makers of the Old Imperialism to far places.

And they made money too. Columbus may have died a disillusioned man, but the silver and gold that Spain extracted from the Americas over the next century made that nation Europe's richest and most powerful. Vasco da Gama brought home spices enough from India to pay for his long voyage many times over. Many a Dutch or English fortune was founded on a timely investment in the East India Company of Holland or Britain.

Gold was clearly a prime cause of the Old Imperialism. But God also inspired many of these world conquerors. Christopher Columbus himself, after all, claimed that he—like Saint Christopher—was carrying the Light of the World across the water.

The Iberian nations were old Crusaders; Ferdinand and Isabella had in fact just expelled the last of the Moors from Spain when the great overseas conquest began. The sixteenth century was also the century of the Protestant Reformation and the Catholic Counter-Reformation. It was a religiously charged time that saw Jesuits set out to save souls in China and South America as well as in Protestant lands. Seventeenth-century English Puritans and Dutch Protestants were heavy investors in overseas expansion, and their objectives also included the spread of Christianity as well as the extraction of profits from the heathen.

Gold, God, and, dubious as it may seem, glory stand as the three main causes of European empire building in the early centuries. The glory sought was the sort of public adulation and eternal fame that champions of European chivalry had fought and died for on European battlefields for centuries. The conquistadores of all Western nations were soldiers of a society where soldiering was the most respected of professions, honor the greatest virtue. They wanted crowds to cheer them, crowned heads to honor them with knighthoods and titles, poets and historians to immortalize them. For such insubstantial honors, men such as Hernando Cortes and Sir Walter Raleigh would risk their lives—and sometimes get their hearts' desires.

Money and what it would buy, converts for the Christian God, and a meed of glory to warm a soldier's heart—these were the taut springs that drove the men who manned the remarkable ships of the Western world.

All of these motives, in one form or another, could be found among others of the world's peoples. But in Europe there was a competitive diversity of peoples that perhaps stimulated these passions beyond the normal. There was a freedom for merchant investors, filibustering soldiers, missionary orders, and ambitious princes that was not so common in the centralized empires of the East. Even the most autocratic European rulers, such as the kings of Spain or France's Louis XIV, allowed much of the exploring, trading, and conquering overseas to be done by ambitious private citizens, thereby multiplying the impact by the number of competitors.

China's vast armadas of Precious Ships were an imperial venture and could be stopped forever by a memorial from the Son of Heaven. It is hard to imagine any force powerful enough to restrain the motley hordes of Western conquerors, lusting after golden idols and cargoes of spices, converts beyond the burning line, and immortal glory when they sailed home again.

THE LONG REACH OF THE WEST

The beginning of this great conquest is sometimes called the Age of Discovery. Literally, of course, it was nothing of the sort. Europeans were not scaling Mount Everest, reaching the North Pole, or otherwise going where no human ever had before. Most of the lands they reached were thoroughly inhabited, possessing ancient cultures of their own. But these voyagers did run risks, suffer hardships, and accomplish feats of seamanship and exploration deserving all the honor that posterity has heaped upon them. Storm-swept or becalmed, wracked by hunger and thirst, scurvy and malaria, beset by foreign foes, rival merchants, and the priesthoods of other faiths, they plunged with desperate courage into perils few of us can clearly imagine.

Many of these men were also brutal, treacherous, blind with greed and prejudice. They were, after all, the aggressors, the invaders, and as savage as intruders into other peoples' lands have always been. But savagery and treachery, avarice and prejudice have never been rare on this earth. The courage, ingenuity, and accomplishment of these travelers of distant seas have been in rather shorter supply.

With both sides of the picture clearly in mind, then, let us proceed to a brief overview of some of the more famous voyages of the three centuries between 1492 and 1776—the centuries of the Old Imperialism.

The Portuguese were the pioneers, pushing methodically down the coast of Africa until Vasco da Gama's epochal voyage of 1497–1499 from Lisbon around the Cape of Good Hope and on to the Malabar Coast of India and back. Thereafter, Portuguese and later Dutch merchants thrust still farther east, through Southeast Asia and around to China and Japan. Portugal thus became the first European nation to push her way into the East, shoulder Arab traders aside, and establish a Western trading empire in Asia.

The Spanish were later into the game, though Christopher Columbus sailed five years before da Gama's climactic Portuguese voyage. Columbus died probably believing he too had reached the East, though Spain had little profit to show for it. But he blazed a trail that more martial Spanish captains followed. Vasco de Balboa crossed the Isthmus of Panama and looked on the Pacific in 1513. In the years 1519–1521, Ferdinand Magellan, sailing under the Spanish flag, commanded an expedition that crossed the Atlantic, the Pacific, and the Indian oceans, circumnavigating the globe for the first time in human history.

Hernando Cortes discovered and conquered Aztec Mexico in the 1520s, and Francisco Pizarro did the same to Inca Peru in the 1530s. The Portuguese Cabral had stumbled upon the eastward bulge of Brazil in 1500 and claimed this vast region for his king. But the rest of the continent was circumnavigated, criss-crossed, and claimed by Spanish conquistadores during the sixteenth century. The Amazon was traced from its Andean headwaters to its Atlantic mouth, and in the far south Cape Horn was rounded. Spanish missionaries and explorers traversed the deserts of the southwestern United States and worked their way up the California coast.

Most of North America, however, was explored by French and English seekers, mostly after 1600. The French settled thinly across eastern Canada and probed down the Mississippi to its mouth. The British founded thirteen colonies down the east coast, from New England and New York to Virginia, the Carolinas, and Georgia. The French, the English, and the Dutch as well soon established profitable sugar colonies in the Caribbean. The Dutch were also for a time established in eastern North America, from Hudson's Bay in Canada down to New Amsterdam—New York after the British came.

Australia alone remained unexplored by Westerners. Chinese voyagers may have touched its shores several hundred years before the first European could have. But its northern and western coasts were charted by Dutch mariners in the seventeenth century, and the famous captain James Cook explored its eastern margins in the eighteenth. Cook and the gallant French explorer Antoine de Bougainville also explored many of the island groups of Oceania, including such paradises as Tahiti and Hawaii.

The peoples of the West were suddenly everywhere. Their pale, sweaty faces showed at the courts of East Asian emperors and the *maharajas* of India, around the smoky campfires of Indian *sachems* along the Mississippi, and at the dark slave pens of West Africa. Their little vessels were dwarfed by the great rivers—the Congo, the Amazon, the Mississippi, and the Ganges—and all but vanished in the vastness of the three oceans. Their numbers were swal-lowed up in the teeming cities of Asia or lost in the barren deserts, deep woods, or triple-canopy rain forests of Africa, Australia, and the Americas. But they were everywhere nonetheless. And they would not go home.

THE OVERSEAS EMPIRES, 1500–1800

THREE CENTURIES OF CONQUEST

It was the crash of their great guns that a startled world most vividly remembered. The Chinese had developed gunpowder weapons long before the Europeans did. In 1453, the Ottoman Turks mounted the largest cannon in the world against the walls of Constantinople. But Western gunnery had distanced that of all other peoples by 1500, and Western ships were thereafter converted into floating gun platforms lined with huge "ship-killing" artillery. "They have guns with a noise like thunder," a Ceylonese source wrote of the first Portuguese to come that way, "and a ball from one of them, after traversing a league, will break a castle of marble."[1]

Explorers, missionaries, merchants, soldiers all played important parts in the establishment of the European predominance. But the final arbiter was most often military force.

The first three hundred years of the conquest that resulted, from the end of the fifteenth century through most of the eighteenth, will be outlined in the sections that follow. The climactic phase of Western imperialism—the nineteenth century—will be dealt with in a later chapter.

Century by century, the pattern was something like this. The sixteenth century was the age of Iberian overseas expansion. During this period, the Portuguese set up a primarily commercial empire in the East that encompassed trading posts in Africa, India, and Southeast Asia, an outpost in South China, and a huge territory in Brazil. Spanish power established an even vaster settlement empire in the West, centering in Middle and South America and the Caribbean and extending into North America and across the Pacific to the Philippines.

The seventeenth century was the century of the interlopers, the age in which the North Atlantic powers challenged the monopoly of intercontinental empire enjoyed by the Iberian nations. This was the golden age of the Netherlands, when Dutch traders drove into the Far East, South Africa, and North America. France in the age of Louis XIV established an elaborate edifice of colonies, commercial relations, and mercantilist policies especially in Canada, the Caribbean, and India. The British staked

---

[1] C. M. Cipolla, *Guns, Sails and Empires: Technological Innovation and the Early Phases of European Expansion, 1400–1700* (New York: Pantheon Books, 1966), p. 107.

guzmā. mchv acā.

The Spanish conquest in the New World was a bloody business, as this picture shows. The Aztecs, a warlike people themselves, met their match in the conquistadores from Spain. Western beards, shown here, amazed the Amerindian peoples almost as much as the horses and firearms of the invaders. (The Bettmann Archive)

their claims to colonies in what would become the eastern United States, and in the Caribbean and India also.

There were thus five European powers with holdings on four other continents and many islands by the end of the seventeenth century. In the eighteenth there came a settling out, and a global duel for imperial supremacy. The Dutch gave ground, as the Spanish and Portuguese had before them. And the British shouldered the French aside to emerge as the greatest of European empire builders.

Let us look now in a little more detail at the intercontinental empires established by each of the European imperial powers in these centuries and at the struggle for empire that climaxed the period of the Old Imperialism.

PORTUGAL IN ASIA

When Vasco da Gama reached Calicut on the Malabar Coast of India in 1498, the Arab merchants who were already established there sneered at the goods he laid out for sale. "They spat on the ground," one who sailed with him reported, "saying, 'Portugal, Portugal!'"[2] It was war from the beginning between the Portuguese invaders and the Arabs who had dominated the trade of the Indian Ocean for centuries. The architect of Portuguese victory,

[2]E. G. Ravenstein, ed., *A Journal of the First Voyage of Vasco da Gama* (London: Hakluyt Society, 1898), p. 68.

and of the Portuguese commercial empire that resulted, was one of the greatest of the European empire builders, Affonso de Albuquerque (1453–1515).

Albuquerque, governor-general of the Portuguese Indies in the early sixteenth century, seems to have been a man with an intuitive understanding of the proper deployment and use of sea power to seize and defend key points in Portugal's monopoly of Eastern trade. Instead of basing his operation in far-off Lisbon, Albuquerque captured the wealthy and readily defended island city of Goa off India's west coast to serve as his headquarters. He established a series of lesser bases down the western side of India and others on islands at the entrances to the Red Sea and the Persian Gulf. With Portugal's bases in East Africa, what had once been the Arabian Sea thus became a Portuguese lake.

At the same time, Albuquerque pushed on into Southeast and even East Asia. He seized the rich Southeast Asian commercial center of Malacca on the strait between Malaya and Sumatra through which all Asian trade had to pass. And he dispatched other Portuguese vessels north and still further east to set up a trading port at Macao in South China, just downriver from the great Chinese entrepôt of Canton (Guangzhou).

Portugal thus bestrode crucial waterways and coastlines from East Africa to South China. The profits in silks and spices that had once gone to Arab middlemen now lined the purses of Portuguese merchants. And the little medieval kingdom of Portugal stood taller than ever before in the affairs of Europe.

The Portuguese crown defended this monopoly with savage rigor. European vessels that dared intrude were sunk, their crews thrown into the sea. Muslim spice ships—and sometimes Muslim pilgrim ships bound for Mecca—shared a similar fate. Arab dhows were gutted to the waterline, Arab traders swallowed up by the sea that had once been theirs—brutal evidence of a policy of frightfulness unsurpassed by any Mongol horde or Aryan conqueror of the past.

For a time, at least, it worked. In the later sixteenth century, however, the Portuguese monopoly crumbled. Portugal's failure to establish close ties with local *rajas* and increasingly rigorous policy of religious repression in Goa and elsewhere weakened its position. The smallness of Portugal itself and the comparatively few people Lisbon could put into the Far East further limited Portuguese strength. When the North Atlantic powers—the Dutch, French, and English—burst onto the eastern seas in force around 1600, Portuguese power dwindled rapidly.

SPAIN IN LATIN AMERICA

The conquistadores of Spain followed a different path to a very different empire. These military adventurers first occupied the Caribbean islands, including the large central island of Cuba. They then probed westward to the mainland of Mexico, south to Peru and beyond, and north to the American Southwest, the Gulf Coast, and Florida. Both the conquest and the organization of Spanish America were models of the vigor—and the cruelty—of the great conquest.

The conquest of Aztec Mexico in the 1520s by Cortes and a few hundred ambitious, out-at-elbows swordsmen is one of the bloodiest epics of the *conquista*. Cortes burned his ships behind him, followed the rumors of a great city on a lake in a high valley beyond the coastal jungles—and found his El Dorado. The Spanish first occupied Tenochtitlán as Emperor Moctezuma's guests. When they converted him into a puppet ruler, the Aztecs revolted and drove them from the city, killing a third of their number in one terrible night. Reinforced at the coast, and supported by a number of other Amerindian peoples who had suffered under the Aztecs, Cortes returned to Tenochtitlán in 1521, captured it, and destroyed it. Aztec power was broken; Spanish rule soon replaced it.

Francisco Pizarro's seizure of the still larger Inca Empire in Peru was an even more unlikely—and equally brutal—feat of arms. Pizarro followed his rumors to Peru with less than two hundred men. But the Inca Empire was just emerging from a bloody civil war, and the Spanish capture of the Inca Atahualpa himself in 1532 further demoralized the ruling elite. The story of that ambush in the village square at Cajamarca, and of the subsequent ransoming and murder of Atahualpa, is another of the gory romantic legends of the New World conquest.

The Europeans had profited from the fact that the realms of the Aztecs and the Incas were both conquest empires that had earned the resentment of their subject peoples. The Europeans, however, wreaked far greater havoc among the Amerindians than any native conquest ever had. Spain had conquered the most heavily populated areas in the Americas. But Western weapons, forced labor in fields and mines, and perhaps above all, unfamiliar diseases to which the Indians had no immunities, reduced the population drastically. It was, in fact, to replace declining Indian labor forces—and to prevent further decimation of their numbers—that African slaves began to be imported soon after the conquest.

Few of the conquistadores enjoyed the fruits of their victories for long. Balboa was executed for treason. Pizarro was killed in a power struggle with his own lieu-

The fall of the Inca Empire was essentially accomplished by one bold and ruthless stroke: the seizure of the Inca Atahualpa himself by Francisco Pizarro and his Spanish freebooters at Cajamarca in 1532. The essence of the larger confrontation between these two peoples is conveyed even in this simple drawing. Note the weapons and means of transport employed by the two sides, the seizure of the Inca by a soldier and a priest, and the broadly sketched city on the horizon, evidence that the Western conquerors were aware that they were destroying, not "primitive savages," but a civilized society with roots as ancient as their own.

tenants. Cortes was called back to Spain, heaped with honors—and firmly deprived of his New World kingdom.

Instead, Spanish lawyers and bureaucrats were sent out to govern the new Spanish Empire in the king's name. The aging conquistadores grudgingly settled down to raise cattle and run gold or silver mines with Indian slave labor. Their descendants would run plantations worked by black slaves from Africa. But the colonial cities that grew up on the ruins of Tenochtitlán and Cuzco were dominated by the new imperial bureaucracy, the paper-shuffling administrators of New Spain (Mexico), New Granada (Peru), and the other divisions and subdivisions of the huge Spanish settlement empire in the Americas.

THE DUTCH EMPIRE

The sixteenth century belonged to the empire builders of Spain and Portugal. The most successful European overseas empire of the seventeenth century, however, was that of the Netherlands. In some ways, indeed, the Dutch seaborne commercial empire was the most efficient of all those established during the period of the Old Imperialism.

The architects and operators of the Dutch Empire were not soldiers like Cortes and Pizarro, or even royal administrators like Albuquerque. They were the solid, stolid Dutch burghers who stare unsmilingly out of their Rembrandt portraits at us. A dull and unromantic lot, one might think—certainly not given to burning their ships behind them or following rumors of El Dorado. But in the seventeeth century, the Dutch East and West India companies dominated trade with the Far East and siphoned off much of the commercial profit from other European colonies in the New World as well.

The Dutch brought to their far-flung trading empire centuries of business experience, manufacturing skills, and accumulated capital. Their ships and their seamanship were acknowledged to be the best. Their trade goods were carefully selected to suit their customers—sultans and *rajas* in Asia, European colonists in the Americas. At need, they could be as ruthless and unscrupulous as any in the great imperialist venture. For a hundred years, they profited exceedingly in the global marketplace that they themselves did so much to create.

The Dutch East India Company shouldered its way into the Spice Islands of Southeast Asia around 1600, expelling first the Portuguese and then the fledgling British East India Company. They paid much more attention than the Portuguese had to the local sultans, giving them the goods they wanted, signing treaties with them, avoiding both rank piracy and religious persecution. From the company's capital at Batavia in Java, they soon controlled not only the European spice trade but much of the profitable regional commerce of Southeast Asia as well.

The Dutch West India Company, meanwhile, set up its trading posts in the Caribbean and in North America,

especially along the Hudson River in what would be New York State. Settlers from French, English, and Spanish colonies often preferred trading illegally with the Dutch at New Amsterdam—later New York City—or Curaçao in the Caribbean to dealing with their own more expensive and less efficient compatriots.

For a golden century, hardheaded Dutch merchants handled most of Europe's imperial carrying trade, coasted Australia, settled in South Africa, and took their profits home to build tall houses in Amsterdam and commission Rembrandt or Vermeer to paint their pictures. Then sheer lack of numbers caught up with them, as it had with the Portuguese. Exhausting foreign wars further weakened them. The British expelled them from North America in the later seventeenth century. Dutch predominance survived in the East Indies, but the center of European imperial activity in Asia shifted to the richer pickings of India, where England and France were the prime contenders.

COLBERT AND THE FRENCH EMPIRE

The French were the great organizers of empire. The foremost European exemplars of royal absolutism in politics and mercantilism—government regulation—in economics, seventeenth-century France also took the lead in royal supervision of colonies overseas. It was, as will be evident, a mixed blessing.

In the earlier seventeenth century, French overseas adventures were largely undertaken by daring individuals or by groups outside royal control. Like Spanish conquistadores or Dutch merchants, French fur traders and Jesuit missionaries in Canada, French plantation owners in the West Indies, and French East India Company traders in India had to depend on their own resources and work closely with indigenous peoples. Jesuits, trappers, and traders in the Great Lakes region of North America were better than any other Europeans at living and working with the Native American tribes, learning their languages, marrying and settling among them. In India the French, like the Dutch and English, depended on treaties with and the protection of Indian princes.

In the second half of the seventeenth century, however, the all-encompassing power of Louis XIV and the tidy organizing mind of his first minister, Jean-Baptiste Colbert, reorganized France's overseas holdings. Mercantilistic policies, which most early-modern European governments followed, involved official encouragement and regulation of all branches of the economy—agriculture, handicraft industry, domestic and foreign trade. Under Colbert's direction, colonies overseas became a crucial element in developed French mercantilism.

Colonies provided tropical and other products unavailable in France. They offered a market for French manufactured goods. And they were expected to give plenty of carrying trade to the French merchant marine.

Colbert undertook to increase the population of New World settlements and to establish military strongholds there to strengthen French colonies against their English rivals. The French East India Company was heavily financed by the French crown.

By the early 1700s, then, there were French trading and settlement colonies in eastern Canada, their capital at Quebec; in Louisiana at the mouth of the Mississippi; and in West Indian islands such as Martinique and Guadeloupe. There was also a growing French commercial presence in India, headquartered at Pondichéry on the southern coast of the subcontinent. France, the most powerful nation in Europe under Louis XIV, was determined to take a leading role in the building of intercontinental empire as well.

ENGLISH ENTERPRISE AND THE ENGLISH EMPIRE

The second man to circumnavigate the globe was an Englishman. Sir Francis Drake, with a single ship, the *Golden Hind,* accomplished the feat in 1578–1580, sixty years after Magellan's expedition. Drake's vessel sailed up the Thames laden to the gunwales with stolen treasure and golden memories. He spent six hours telling Queen Elizabeth about it:

> So the voyage lived again, more wonderful than the jewels and bullion in the room. . . . the worst storm since Noah, the great Indians, the flying fish which the dolphins had hunted . . . the sophisticated rajahs of the Spice Islands—the wonders and perils of the world, its seas so much wider than the great Columbus had believed, its lands so rich in the surprising inventions of the Almighty.[3]

Queen Elizabeth's swashbuckling soldiers and sea dogs, men such as Sir Francis Drake, Sir John Hawkins, and Sir Walter Raleigh, founded no lasting colonies for England. But their raids on Spanish holdings and their dreams of English empire launched Great Britain on what became the most extravagantly successful career of imperial conquest in world history.

British empire building in the next century laid the groundwork at least for the great English venture into intercontinental power.

The beginnings were not promising. Britain's first surviving American colony in Virginia suffered from the climate and their own helplessness in the wilderness, then from Indian massacres, and for years from financial losses before the colonists discovered in tobacco a crop that would pay. The Dutch ousted early English traders from Southeast Asia, so that they had to fall back on the then less profitable Indian trade.

But English merchants were thirsty for profits. English political history in the revolutionary seventeenth century produced religious exiles in need of new lands to settle in. And the English kings after mid-century proved more willing to encourage colonial development. By the early 1700s, then, Britain's overseas holdings were as widely dispersed as those of the Netherlands or France.

Great Britain's major settlement colonies were across the Atlantic in North America and the Caribbean. These included colonies inhabited by Puritan nonconformists in New England, planter settlements in Virginia and surrounding territories, and the plantations of the Lesser Antilles, Jamaica, and the Bahamas. Typically, these colonies were founded by commercial companies having little royal support. In time, however, royal governors were appointed and mercantilistic regulations imposed on England's growing American empire.

The British East India Company was also a private venture. It never had the government support accorded its French and even its Dutch rivals. In the early eighteenth century, however, British traders were well established on the coast of India, having developed bases at Bombay in the northwest, Calcutta in the northeast, and Madras on the southeastern shores of peninsular India.

The English had good relations with the Mogul emperors and were protected by them. As the Mogul Empire declined, however, the British East India Company found it increasingly necessary to fight its own battles. In the middle 1700s, the company would do just that—with spectacular results.

THE STRUGGLE FOR GLOBAL HEGEMONY

By 1700, then, the Dutch, with too small and embattled a base at home, were losing momentum everywhere to their larger rivals. Spain and Portugal were rapidly declining into backwaters, their overseas empires no longer expanding and much less profitable. In the 1740s, 1750s, and 1760s, therefore, Britain and France fought each other across two oceans and three continents for imperial supremacy.

The War of the Austrian Succession in the 1740s and the Seven Years' War in the 1750s and 1760s, in both of which England and France chose opposite sides, provided occasions for conflict between the two nations overseas. Hostilities raged in North America and India, as well as in the Caribbean and on the west coast of Africa. The Indian and American encounters, however, determined the outcome of the struggle.

In India, the French had the advantage in the early years; they even temporarily overran the English settlement at Madras. Thereafter, however, the conflict resolved itself into a feud between the two extraordinary governors of the French and British East India companies, Joseph Dupleix and Robert Clive. Dupleix, by extending judicious French military support to local princes in

[3]George Malcolm Thomson, *Sir Francis Drake* (London: Futura Publications, 1972), p. 154.

southern India, had the English base at Madras once more surrounded and in imminent danger of extinction. But Clive, who had worked his way up from genteel destitution through the British India Company, was both a skilled military commander and a superior politician. Instead of Madras, it was the French capital at Pondichéry that fell, and with it all serious hope for a French empire in India.

In North America also, the French began strongly, thanks again to close ties with the indigenous population. With the help of Indian allies, they pushed down the Mississippi Valley, seeking to link up their Canadian colonies with their settlement in Louisiana. They might thus box the British in against the Atlantic shore and at the same time lay out a mid-American empire for themselves. An expedition sent to dislodge them—in which a Virginia colonist named George Washington futilely warned the British commander to beware of French-and-Indian hit-and-run tactics—was cut to pieces in the forest.

But the English prime minister, William Pitt, rose to the challenge to become one of Britain's most famous war leaders. His grand strategy, his choices of leaders and targets all seemed to work like a charm. Clive swept to victory in India. French settlements in West Africa and the West Indies fell to British forces. And in Canada, British armies captured Quebec high on its impregnable bluffs overlooking the St. Lawrence, and then Montreal. All French Canada fell into British hands.

With Britain's victories in India and Canada, English supremacy was unquestionable. Britain had taken a great step forward on the phenomenal march to world empire that would distinguish its history in the following century.

In 1763, when a peace signed at Paris settled the fate of Native Americans and East Indians who had never heard of the City of Light, Western power was entrenched around the world. Europeans held as much of North and South America as they had yet had time to occupy, and the rest was pretty clearly theirs for the taking. They had bases and seaports around the coasts of Africa south of the Sahara, though they had as yet scarcely penetrated inland. They had a number of ports on both coasts of India and had compelled or bought profitable alliances with *rajas* all across the subcontinent. They owned the Caribbean and were masters of the island portion of Southeast Asia.

They had been rudely repulsed from Japan, had made little progress in China, and were only beginning to explore Australia and Oceania. Huge expanses of the interiors of Asia, Africa, and the Americas—protected by difficult geography, disease to which Europeans had no immunity, and other factors—remained to be penetrated. But they would be penetrated in time. A beginning had thus been made in the greatest conquest the world had ever seen.

 ## CONSEQUENCES: THE MODERN WORLD SYSTEM

ASIA AND AFRICA: SPICES AND SLAVES

There were missionaries eager for converts and young men mad for glory among these Western imperialists. But there were probably more who went out to the far places of the earth, as a chronicler who marched with Cortes put it, "to grow rich as all men desire to do."[4] And like empire builders from one end of history to the other, Europeans brought home many things from conquered lands. Asia, Africa, North and South America all paid their tithes to Europe during the early modern centuries.

Asia was the first objective, and the first to pay. The original goal of the Western voyagers had been to find a sea route to the spices and luxury goods of the Far East that would be cheaper and surer than the overland routes controlled by other peoples. First the Portuguese, then the Dutch, French, and English broke into the trade of the Indian Ocean and Southeast Asia, and soon they were its masters.

In the holds of caravels and lumbering East Indiamen (large merchant ships), Europeans brought home silk, tea, porcelain, and spices such as pepper, cloves, and cinnamon from China; cottons and precious stones from India; coffee from Arabia and the Middle East; drugs, saltpeter for gunpowder, indigo dye—the list is almost endless. Europe's consumption of pepper doubled in the first half of the sixteenth century. In the seventeenth, coffee and tea became national drinks in Europe. Indian cotton would spawn a whole new industry in Britain and trigger the Industrial Revolution. The long-range consequences of Asian imports were even more incalculable than their immediate impact.

On the way to Asia, European vessels had to sail around the second-largest continent—Africa. They found profitable commodities here too: pepper and cloves, gold and ivory—and, above all, slaves. Cheap labor became Africa's primary contribution to the burgeoning wealth of the West.

Perhaps twelve million Africans were bought from slave-raiding African peoples—who of course redoubled their activities once they realized they could get a good price from the Europeans. The victims were transported not to Europe but to the Americas, where they made a very substantial contribution to the labor force of the New World. They thus became part of the famous triangular trade route linking Europe, Africa, and the Americas: man-

---

[4]Bernal Díaz, quoted in Robert Knecht, "The Discoveries," in Douglas Johnson, ed., *The Making of the Modern World,* Vol. I (New York: Barnes and Noble, 1971), p. 14.

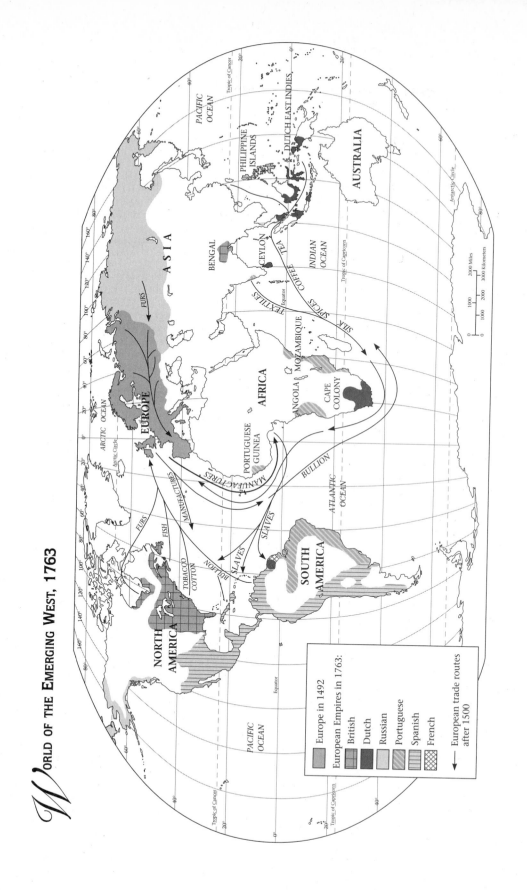

World of the Emerging West, 1763

Europe in 1492
European Empires in 1763:
British
Dutch
Russian
Portuguese
Spanish
French
European trade routes after 1500

451

ufactured goods to Africa, slaves to the Americas, and agricultural products such as sugar, molasses, and rum back to Europe.

The enslaved Africans who did reach the New World had survived a brutal ordeal. Seized in their inland villages by slave-raiding warriors, they had been roped in long lines and led sometimes hundreds of miles to the coast. After weeks or months in dank dungeons or open pens, they had been crammed into the holds of European slave ships for the westward journey. The horrors of the "middle passage"—Africa to the Americas—were worse still. Broken by disease, filth, brutal treatment, and the shock of the experience, between a tenth and a quarter of the two hundred Africans crowded into a typical slave ship might die.

Those who survived, however, actually made important contributions to the colonial societies of which they became involuntary members. Their skilled hands and sweating backs harvested the crops, built the plantation houses, raised the children, and served the food of Latin American and North American planters. In Latin America particularly, they learned and practiced many urban trades. They also brought African skills to the New World. It was from enslaved West Africans, as one British planter reported, that the colonists "found out the true way of raising and husking rice"—a major money crop in Britain's southern colonies.[5]

THE AMERICAS: SUGAR AND SILVER

The North American colonies paid tribute to their European rulers in such commercial goods as ships' stores and timber, furs, codfish, tobacco, and sugar. French fur trappers in the sun-dappled quiet of Canadian forests, English fishing vessels laboring in heavy seas off New England or the Newfoundland banks, sweating slaves bending under the watchful eyes of European overseers in the tobacco fields of Virginia or the sugar plantations of the West Indies were also profitable parts of these sprawling European intercontinental empires.

Timber, furs, sugar, fish—it was a stodgy and unromantic contribution compared with the spices and precious stones from the East or the black gold from Africa. Yet by 1776 the North American and Caribbean settlements were probably the most profitable of all the European colonies around the world.

The simplest and most avidly sought form of profit from conquered lands overseas, however, was the silver and gold of Middle and South America. First as booty ripped from the walls of Inca temples, later as ore from mines in Mexico, Bolivia, and elsewhere, hundreds of tons of gold and thousands of tons of silver were shipped across the Atlantic.

All of it was originally destined for the coffers of Spain, but much of it ended up in other hands. Some of it was seized by English or French pirates and privateers. More flooded out over Europe as payment for Spain's huge debts or in salaries and supplies for the armies of Europe's greatest power in the sixteenth century. Much of it, finally, was siphoned off to more industrious peoples like the Dutch, who produced all the good things that Spanish *caballeros*—officers and gentlemen all—were too proud to soil their hands in manufacturing for themselves.

The flood of silver and gold replenished a continent poor in precious metals. It also led to a century of inflation, doubling or tripling prices over the 1500s in various parts of Europe. The new wealth—and the accompanying inflation—benefited the commercial classes, who profited from high prices. But inflation hurt the old nobility who lived on fixed revenues from land. It also hurt the peasantry, many of whom were expelled from their farms to make way for more profitable sheepwalks as their landlords strove to keep up with inflation.

The great influx of precious metals also left Europe with its most enduring memories of that first great surge of intercontinental empire building—memories of real-life El Dorados found beyond the burning line.

THE MODERN WORLD SYSTEM: THE CORE

As we noticed in Chapter 24, the relations between nations and peoples often make more sense when they are analyzed in terms of *world systems*. In a world system, the usually more developed nations of the economic and political *core* shape and exploit a fringe of less developed peoples called the *periphery*. Immanuel Wallerstein and others see the *modern world system* as the archetypal example of this sort of intricate, changing, yet centrally important structure of international relations.[6]

The modern world system, which emerged at the end of the fifteenth century, was built around the economically developed core of Western Europe. Specially, as we have seen, it was the economic and political power of a half-dozen Western European "Atlantic powers" that forged the new world system. These nations—Spain and Portugal, the Netherlands, France, and England—poured a vast accumulation of capital into the development of overseas possessions and global commercial networks. They set the terms of trade, the rules under which business would be carried out, wherever their seagoing caravels and galleons and East Indiamen carried them. In many of these places, they also exercised political control over the lands they penetrated, converting a growing portion of the New World particularly into European colonies.

As we have seen, relations between the members

---

[5]Quoted in Peter H. Wood, *Black Majority: Negroes in Colonial South Carolina from 1670 Through the Storo Rebellion* (New York: Norton, 1974), p. 61.

[6]Immanuel Wallerstein, *The Modern World System* (New York: Academic Press, 1974–).

of the European core changed over the early modern centuries. The Iberian powers, Spain and especially Portugal, declined in importance, becoming part of semiperiphery of only partially developed states. The Netherlands became the world's most successful global trader in the seventeenth century, but followed Spain and Portugal into second-class status in the eighteenth. Britain and France, meanwhile, dueled for hegemonic power, the preminent position in the world economy, and Britain emerged victorious in the later 1700s.

THE MODERN WORLD SYSTEM: THE PERIPHERY

The most important regions of the early modern world system's periphery were Latin America, the Caribbean, and—Wallerstein points out—Eastern Europe, which was also economically underdeveloped. In the eighteenth century, India, West Africa, much of the declining Middle East, and a still backward Russia were also sucked into the world system dominated by Western Europe.

In all these areas, the impact of the world system was felt in many ways. The peoples of the periphery commonly contributed not capital but labor to the system. Laboring on the plantations and in the mines of the New World or weaving textiles in Asia, they fed the growing demand of an increasingly wealthy Western European core. Enslaved Africans and Native Americans dragooned into forced labor illustrate the fundamental role of the periphery in the modern world system.

The primary products of the periphery were raw materials and agricultural goods. Gold and silver, sugar and fish, brazilwood, ebony, cotton, and species were all of central importance to the new economic network. Indian cotton fabrics and Chinese porcelain still found markets in Europe. But by the eighteenth century, Europeans had learned to make elegant "china" themselves and to weave enormous amounts of cotton on machines unheard of in India. Inexorably, an industrializing Europe would convert the rest of the world into raw material suppliers for the peoples of the Capitalist core.

Life on the periphery of the system was affected in many ways by the emerging new world order. To feed the hoppers of the world system, small-scale subsistence production was replaced by large-scale export production. Economic diversity gave way to an economy geared to the demands of the world market, and particularly of the European core. Traditional political and social structures were also weakened by intrusive foreign power (as in India) or replaced entirely by centralized foreign rule (as in Latin America). Ancient religious faiths were challenged (in Asia) or driven underground (in the Americas).

The transforming presence of the world system was thus very great among the peoples of the periphery. the Mayans of Mexico, for instance, remembered the coming of their Spanish conquerors in a series of vivid metaphors.

The ships with their billowing sails looked to them like "mountains rising out of the sea on clouds." And they lamented:

> On that day, a cloud arises,
> On that day, a mountain rises,
> On that day, a strong man seizes the land,
> On that day, things fall to ruin. . . .[7]

GLOBAL IMPACT: THE COLUMBIAN EXCHANGE

In the long run, however, the broader global impact of Europe's intercontinental imperialism would prove even greater than its commercial value to Europe. During the period of the Old Imperialism, there began a great reshuffling of plants, animals, and peoples, a series of economic and political realignments, that would truly transform the world.

Basic ecological changes were initiated by Europeans eager to exploit their new overseas holdings to the maximum. Europeans transplanted such profitable plants as sugar and coffee and cotton, as well as basic grains such as wheat and large domesticated animals such as horses, cattle, and sheep, from Europe and Asia to the Americas. From the New World they carried potatoes, corn, tobacco, and other crops to the Old. Native American food crops alone would come to feed a large part of the world's population in centuries to come.

Populations also began a shift more dramatic than any since the great prehistoric migrations that had peopled the continents tens and hundreds of thousands of years before. The major population changes in these early centuries of the Western hegemony came in North and South America. Here European germs brought deadly diseases—including malaria, measles, bubonic plague, and above all smallpox—to which the original Amerindian population had no inherited immunities. The result was a catastrophic decline in Native American populations, running perhaps as high as 90 percent in such areas as Mexico, the Caribbean islands, and Peru.

Particularly in South America, however, most of the Native American population did survive. To them were added millions of Europeans settlers and enslaved Africans. This mix of peoples created the most diverse population pattern anywhere in the world. It was a diversity that would grow even more in later centuries.

The profitable exchanges of goods undertaken by Europeans during these centuries had a larger economic impact too. They created the first genuinely worldwide market in human history, inaugurated a global division of labor, and pointed toward the global economic integration and interdependence of later centuries.

Europe contributed manufactured goods to this emerging global economy, Asia contributed luxury

---

[7]Quoted in Charles Gallenkamp, *Maya: The Riddle and Rediscovery of a Lost Civilization* (Harmondsworth, England: Penguin, 1981), p. 205.

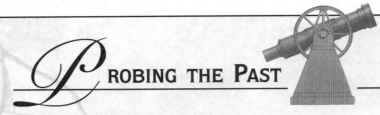

PROBING THE PAST

"*It is contended here that most entities usually described as social systems—"tribes," communities, nation-states—are not in fact total systems. Indeed, on the contrary, we are arguing that the only real social systems are, on the one hand, those . . . small . . . subsistence economies not part of some regular tribute-demanding system and, on the other hand, world-systems. These latter are to be sure distinguished from the former because they are relatively large; that is, they are in common parlance "worlds." More precisely, however, they are defined by the fact that their self-containment as an economic-material entity is based on extensive division of labor and that they contain within them a multiplicity of cultures.*

It is further argued that thus far there have only existed two varieties of such world-systems: world-empires, in which there is a single political system over most of the area, . . . and those systems in which such a single political system does not exist. . . . We are using the term "world-economy" to describe the latter.

Finally, we have argued that prior to the modern era, world-economies were highly unstable structures which tended either to be converted into empires or to disintegrate. It is the peculiarity of the modern world-system that a world-economy has survived for 500 years and yet has not come to be transformed into a world-empire—a peculiarity that is the secret of its strength.

This peculiarity is the political side of the form of economic organization called capitalism. . . . Capitalism as an economic mode is based on the fact that the economic factors operate within an arena larger than that which any political entity can totally control. This gives capitalists a freedom of maneuver that is structurally based. It has made possible the constant economic expansion of the world-system, albeit a very skewed distribution of its rewards."

Immanuel Wallerstein is one of the best known of modern globalists. His three-volume study of <u>The Modern World-System</u> has stimulated vigorous debate among scholars and has made such terms as "core" and "periphery"—for the European center and the exploited colonies and other outlying subdivisions of the system—common among global historians.

An economic historian, Wallerstein defines his world-system as a structure based on a global division of labor manipulated by an exploitative capitalist core that dominates political and social as well as economic institutions. He believes that such a system took shape with the intercontinental empires and the world market in the sixteenth century.

What does Wallerstein mean by "world" in "world-system"? What two types of world-system does he see? How does the failure of a single world-empire to emerge benefit capitalism? Can you imagine a modern world-system based on something other than economic relations—on culture, perhaps, or on ecology?

Immanuel Wallerstein, <u>The Modern World - System I: Capitalist Agriculture and the Origins of the European World-Economy in the Sixteenth Century</u> (New York: Academic Press, 1974), p. 348.

exports, Africa labor, and North and South America raw materials and plantation products.

The heaviest flow of goods was across the Atlantic, between Europe and the Americas, where Europeans settled in large numbers and were soon producing the things that Europeans at home wanted. Africa, in return for a large drain in labor, got more European manufactured goods than it had had before and, perhaps most important, American agricultural imports, including Indian corn, which was soon growing in many parts of Africa.

The meagerest exchange was between Europe and its ancient trading partner, Asia—due, as in ancient times, to the fact that Europe produced little that the highly developed civilizations of Asia wanted or needed. This too would change, however, for in later centuries the European Industrial Evolution would flood the Far East, like the rest of the world, with Western manufactured goods.

The global power balance, finally, shifted dramatically between 1500 and 1800. As we have seen, in 1500 the most powerful nation in the world was certainly China. The most dynamic expanding culture was probably that of the Muslim center of Eurasia. In Africa and the Americas, independent centers of empire were developing in the Western Sudan, Mexico, and Peru. Pluralism prevailed, and Europe was by no means the greatest of world civilizations.

As 1800 approached, all this had clearly changed. European power had destroyed the American empires, and the African kingdoms had declined in a welter of internecine conflict. The Western nations, meanwhile, had repulsed and outflanked the Islamic lands, transformed the Indian Ocean from a Muslim to a European lake, replaced Muslim power in Southeast Asia with European power. The rulers of India were being slowly sucked into the maw of European dependency. Everywhere except East Asia, the weight of Western political predominance was being felt as the eighteenth century drew to a close.

The famous philosopher Voltaire, perhaps the most alert of all eighteenth-century observers of his own time, stated a great truth very casually in his "Remarks on History" of the middle 1700s:

> The silver on which we take our meals, our furniture, our needs, our new pleasures, all these remind us every day that America and the Great Indies, and consequently all the parts of the whole world have been reunited for almost two and a half centuries by the labors of our fathers.[8]

Few people outside the Western world—indeed, few Westerners—could have estimated so accurately the dimensions of the European predominance. That predominance was growing, warping the old world of many cultures into a new shape and placing the West at the world's center. Since the world had never *had* a single political, economic, or cultural center before, this represented a very significant change indeed.

---

[8]François Marie Arouet de Voltaire, "Remarques sur l'histoire," *Oeuvres Historiques,* ed. René Pomeau (Paris: Gallimard, 1957), p. 44.

SUMMARY

The Western conquest of the world that began around 1500 is a saga of adventure and brutality, raw greed and raw courage, to match any that history has seen.

The ships, navigational aids, and weapons the European peoples deployed in these opening centuries of the great conquest were among the most advanced of their time. Their motives, however, were not new: a thirst for gold, for converts to their religion, and for the military honor that could only be earned in war. These were old ambitions, though particularly developed in the West at the beginning of modern history. Southern Europeans—Spanish and Portuguese, often with Italian navigators—set the pace in the sixteenth century. In the seventeeth, northern European nations—England, France, and the Netherlands—took the lead in empire building. By the eighteenth century, Britain emerged as the greatest Western imperial power of all.

The Portuguese, led by daring commanders like da Gama and the brilliant imperial organizer Albuquerque, pushed eastward to India, Southeast Asia, and beyond. They established a cruelly enforced monopoly over the sea trade of the Indian Ocean. The Spanish probed westward. Colum-bus discovered a "New World," and Cortes, Pizarro, and their fellows conquered much of South and Middle America, looted the realms of the Aztecs and Incas, and established a continental empire.

The Dutch were the most successful of all the seventeenth-century empire builders. They established trading posts in North America, the Caribbean, South Africa, Southeast Asia, and even East Asia. By the eighteenth century, however, British and French commercial enclaves in India and settlement empires in North America and the Caribbean made them the prime contenders. After the wars of the middle 1700s, British triumphs in India and Canada made her master of the greatest of overseas empires.

From their overseas holdings, Europeans brought home spices, silk, cottons, slaves, gold and silver, codfish, sugar, tobacco, and much more. The impact of the so-called Old Imperialism was, however, even greater on the rest of the world. Plants, animals, and human populations were shuffled around the globe on the little European sailing ships. The beginnings of a genuine global economy emerged, and the world power balance began decisively to tilt toward the West.

SUGGESTED READING

BANNON, J. F., ed. *The Spanish Conquistadors: Men or Devils?* New York: Holt, Rinehart & Winston, 1960. A book of essays on the "black legend" of Spanish cruelty in the Americas.

BOXER, C. R. *The Christian Century in Japan, 1549–1650.* Berkeley: University of California Press, 1967. The impact of Western religion on samurai Japan, by a leading authority on the Old Imperialism.

———. *The Dutch Seaborne Empire, 1600–1800.* New York: Knopf, 1965. The Dutch golden age overseas, and their relative decline thereafter. See also J. Van Goor, ed., *Trading Companies in Asia, 1600–1830* (Utrecht: HES, 1986), which focuses on Dutch traders in what is today Indonesia.

———. *The Portuguese Seaborne Empire, 1415–1825.* New York: Knopf, 1969. An outstanding account of the oldest of the European intercontinental empires.

———. *Women in Iberian Expansion Overseas 1415–1815.* New York: Oxford University Press, 1975. Brief account of Spanish and Portuguese women in Asia, Africa, and the New World.

CARRINGTON, C. E. *The British Overseas: Exploits of a Nation of Shopkeepers.* Cambridge: Cambridge University Press, 1950. Uncritical but still useful survey of the history of the British Empire.

CIPOLLA, C. M. *Guns, Sails, and Empires.* New York: Minerva Press, 1965. Material explanations of the great conquest.

CROSBY, A. W. *The Columbian Exchange: Biological and Cultural Consequences of 1492.* Westport, Conn.: Greenwood Press, 1972. Classic account of the larger results of European contact with the New World. See also his more recent *Ecological Imperialism: The Biological Expansion of Europe, 900–1900* (Cambridge, England: Cambridge University Press, 1986), which seeks to demonstrate that European colonists brought so many animals, plants, and microorganisms with them that they radically restructured the ecosystems of much of the rest of the world.

CURTIN, P. D. *The Atlantic Slave Trade: A Census.* Madison: University of Wisconsin Press, 1969. The impact of the trade on Africa, by an authoritative Africanist and an expert on intercontinental trade. See also Curtin's *The Rise and Fall of the Plantation Complex: Essays in Atlantic History* (New York: Cambridge University Press, 1990) on this agricultural system using forced labor in medieval and early modern times.

FLINT, V. I. J. *The Imaginative Landscape of Christopher Columbus.* Princeton, N.J.: Princeton University Press, 1992. Columbus's view of the rest of the world before he set sail—and how it shaped his view of the world he found.

FRANKE, W. *China and the West.* Oxford: Blackwell, 1967. Interaction between the Western world and the most isolated of Eurasian civilizations. See also G. F. Hudson, *Europe and China: A Study of Their Relations from Earliest Times to 1800* (Boston: Beacon Press, 1961).

HAMILTON, E. *American Treasure and the Price Revolution in Spain, 1501–1650.* Cambridge: Harvard University Press, 1934. Seminal study of one of the major consequences of the Old Imperialism.

ISRAEL, J. I. *Dutch Primacy in World Trade, 1585–1740.* New York: Oxford University Press, 1989. Global role of the small trading nation that once dominated world trade.

LÉON-PORTILLA, M., ed. *The Broken Spears: The Aztec Account of the Conquest of Mexico,* trans. L. Kemp. Boston: Beacon Press, 1961. The other side of Cortes's victory. For an eyewitness account by a Spaniard, see B. Diaz del Castillo, *The Discovery and Conquest of Mexico,* trans. A. P. Maudslay (New York: Grove Press, 1956).

LEVENSON, J. R., ed. *European Expansion and the Counter-Example of Asia, 1300–1600.* Englewood Cliffs, N.J.: Prentice-Hall, 1967. Approaches the question of why European imperialism took place by looking at Asia, which did not reach out to other continents.

MCALISTER, L. N. *Spain and Portugal in the New World, 1492–1700.* Minneapolis: University of Minnesota Press, 1984. The most comprehensive recent account.

MORISON, S. E. *Admiral of the Ocean Sea: A Life of the Admiral Christopher Columbus* (2 vols.). Boston: Little, Brown, 1942. Still the standard life of Columbus, with vivid detail and a seaman's appreciation.

PAGDEN, A. *Spanish Imperialism and the Political Imagination.* New Haven: Yale University Press, 1990. Social theory generated in Spain and Spanish America during the period of Spanish rule.

PANIKKAR, K. M. *Asia and Western Dominance.* New York: Harper & Row, Pub., 1954. An Indian perspective on the great conquest.

PARRY, J. H. *The Age of Reconnaissance: Discovery, Exploration and Settlement, 1450–1650.* New York: New American Library, 1963. Excellent standard work on the most active years of the Old Imperialism. See also Parry's collection of source materials, *European Reconnaissance: Selected Documents* (New York: Harper & Row, Pub., 1968).

———. *The Spanish Seaborne Empire.* New York: Knopf, 1966. Another standard work by a leading interpretor of the great conquest. For good recent studies of two important areas of Spanish domination, see O. H. K. Spate, *The Spanish Lake* (Minneapolis: University of Minnesota Press, 1979), and K. A. Andrews, *The Spanish Caribbean: Trade and Plunder, 1530–1630* (New Haven: Yale University Press, 1978).

—————. *Trade and Dominion: The Overseas European Empires in the Eighteenth Century.* New York: Praeger, 1971. Survey and analysis of the first imperial system fully assembled.

SALE, K. *The Conquest of Paradise.* New York: Knopf, 1990. Critical analysis of cultural and ecological effects of the European conquest.

THORNTON, J. *Africa and Africans in the Making of the Atlantic World, 1400–1680.* New York: Cambridge University Press, 1992. Trailblazing study, challenging orthodox views of African underdevelopment, African slavery, and the role of Africans in the New World. For new perspectives on Africans in the Americas, see S. W. Mintz and R. Price, *The Birth of African-American Culture: An Anthropological Perspective* (Boston: Beacon Press, 1992).

TRACY, J. D., ed. *The Political Economy of Merchant Empires: State Power and World Trade, 1350–1750.* Cambridge, England: Cambridge University Press, 1991. Essays on the relative importance of government sponsorship, military advances, and business organization in the global expansion of European trade.

TRIGGER, B. G. *Natives and Newcomers: Canada's "Heroic Age" Reconsidered.* Kingston, Ontario: McGill-Queen's University Press, 1985. Reexamination of the early colonial period, giving the Indians an important place in the narrative.

TUDOROV, T. *The Conquest of America: The Question of the Other,* trans R. Howard. New York: Harper & Row, Pub., 1984. Challenging structuralist reading of Spanish perception of the Aztecs. See also I. Glendinning, *Ambivalent Conquests: Maya and Spaniard in Yucatan, 1500–1570* (New York: Cambridge University Press, 1987), a subtle analysis of the conflicting motives and adaptations of Spanish missionaries and Native American peoples.

WALLERSTEIN, I. *The Modern World System.* New York: Academic Press, 1974– . This challenging and widely debated synthesis is now into its third volume and the nineteenth century.

CHAPTER 32

Absolutism and Enlightenment in Europe

THE EUROPEAN STATE SYSTEM

PALACES, PERIWIGS, AND PHILOSOPHY

From a broad overview of the world of intercontinental empire, we turn now to a closer look at some of the major regions of the globe in the centuries before 1900. We begin, because of its significance as well as its familiarity, with the Western world.

Europe in the seventeenth and eighteenth centuries conjures up a pleasantly homogeneous collection of images. Periwigs and knee breeches come to mind, or low-cut gowns and lace. Carriages, chandeliers, stately homes, and baroque palaces. Playing fountains, elegant facades—and the Hall of Mirrors at Versailles. We have to think a minute to call up beggars and the plague years, women hanged for witchcraft, debtors' prisons, and Hogarth's vivid depiction of the London slums, *Gin Lane*—all as much a part of the seventeenth and eighteenth centuries in Europe as the formal gardens of France or the stately homes of England.

In many ways, it was an in-between period for Europe. It was the climax of the age of kings and queens, hereditary aristocrats, and the power of churchmen if not of religion. It was also, however, a transition to a startling new age of popular ideological revolutions, unprecedented industrial growth, and the predominance of Europe's middle classes over the old aristocracy.

We are dealing in this chapter, then, with the middle period of modern Western history. During the Renaissance and Reformation, Europe had rediscovered its classical past, survived its medieval religious hangover, and moved on into modern history. Over the next two centuries, from 1600 to the late 1700s, the earlier modern period came to a climax and the seeds of later modern history were planted. The seventeenth and eighteenth centuries saw a continent that was already imposing its will on so much of the world evolve politically, economically, and culturally toward the revolutionary crises that would impose new directions on the West in the decades around 1800.

Seen as a part of global history, this middle period of modern European history accomplished two things. It significantly strengthened the power of Europeans to impose their will upon the rest of the world. It also saw the development of ideas and trends that, exported to the world at large over the following two centuries, would drastically transform the way many other peoples thought and lived.

With this larger impact as background, the pages that follow will outline the increasing power of European thrones in the age of Louis XIV and Peter the Great. They will also examine the expanding wealth of the West in the days of the Dutch burghers we have already met and the Bank of England that will be with us from this time onward. Finally we will explore intellectual currents, which played an equally important role, from the Scientific Revolution to the Enlightenment.

To many contemporaries, the splendor of Louis XIV's great palace at Versailles was the ultimate symbol of that age of royal triumph. But the mocking smile on the lips of the liberal philosopher Voltaire—or the legendary apple that fell in Isaac Newton's garden—may in the long run have done more to shape the history of centuries to come.

A BALANCE OF POWERS

There were five great powers in Europe during the 1600s and 1700s. Three of them—Britain, France, and Austria—were established states with roots deep in the Middle Ages. The other two, Prussia and Russia, were new monarchies shouldering their way to the fore. Much of the history of this age was made by these powerful nation-states and the competitive dynasties that ruled them.

The most powerful and admired of European nations was France, particularly during the long reign of Louis XIV, in the latter half of the seventeenth and the early eighteenth centuries. Enjoying a balanced agricultural, commercial, and industrial economy, a large population, a strong royal government, and a high culture that was the most imitated in Europe, Bourbon France was by common consent the greatest of European states.

The other great power of western Europe was Great Britain. Britain was on its way to commercial, naval, and imperial preeminence during these centuries. Wracked by a long revolution in the seventeenth century, the island nation emerged after 1688 as Europe's major liberal

power, the possessor of a strong Parliament and a constitutionally limited monarchy.

The long-standing power of central Europe was the Holy Roman Empire, centered in Austria and ruled by the oldest of European dynasties, the Habsburgs. Because the Austrian Habsburgs had never been able to convert their feudal suzerainty over several hundred central European principalities, duchies, free cities, and other units into a modern centralized monarchy, their authority outside Austria was sometimes shadowy. Austria's eighteenth-century enlightened despots would strengthen that power, however, and the Habsburgs would continue to govern a large multinational realm, including Slavic, Italian, Magyar, and other peoples as well as the German states.

The second power in central Europe was the aggressive new state of Brandenburg-Prussia. This divided principality in North Germany, partially incorporated in the Holy Roman Empire, was actually on its way to replac-

ing Austria as the greatest of the German states. The ambitious Hohenzollern dynasty depended on Prussia's hardworking Junker aristocracy to staff the highly efficient Prussian civil service and to officer the redoubtable Prussian army. Frederick the Great would do much for both these institutions in the eighteenth century, and both would carry the Hohenzollerns and their country far in centuries to come.

The largest power in eastern Europe, and on the continent as a whole, was Russia. Unfortunately, Romanov Russia was also the most underdeveloped of all the major European powers. Cut off from the rest of the continent by the vast East European plain, by Byzantine influences, and by two centuries of Mongol rule, Russia had not shared in early modern Europe's dynamic growth. The Romanov czars expanded their territorial holdings far across Asia and shoved their way determinedly into European affairs during the seventeenth and eighteenth centuries. But Russia remained a poverty-stricken land of serfs and ill-disciplined ancient nobility despite all that heavy-handed eighteenth-century autocrats like Peter the Great and more subtle ones like Catherine the Great could do.

There were other large nations and many smaller ones in this politically fragmented continent. The Mediterranean states that had played central roles in the fifteenth and sixteenth centuries—Renaissance Italy and the Iberian empire builders, Spain and Portugal—had declined to sleepy backwaters. The Netherlands, as we have seen, enjoyed a golden century of commercial and imperial power in the 1600s, only to settle for well-scrubbed but second-class-power status thereafter. In northern Europe, Sweden was the strongest of the Scandinavian states, taking a leading part in the terrible Thirty Years' War and fighting a long duel with Peter the Great's Russia before sinking back into comparative obscurity. Poland, large and powerful enough to march on Moscow in the early seventeenth century, was partitioned off the map of Europe by more powerful neighbors in the later eighteenth century.

Five powerful nations and dozens of lesser states thus continued to divide the western end of Eurasia among them. Their traditional rivalry bred a series of bloody wars, including the Thirty Years' War (1618–1648), the four wars of Louis XIV (1667–1714), and the mid-eighteenth-century cluster of wars centering in the War of the Austrian Succession and the Seven Years' War (1740–1763).

European rulers fought one another for dynastic rights and territory in Europe and for commercial rights and colonies overseas. They fought to maintain—or to upset—the balance of power, the rough parity in war-making potential that alone guaranteed that no one power would ever come to dominate all Europe politically. The West thus jealously defended the political divisiveness that made Europeans among the most fiercely competitive of the world's peoples. If unity has eluded Europeans down the centuries, it is at least partly because they have resisted it tooth and nail throughout their history.

ABSOLUTISM AND ENLIGHTENMENT

The royal rulers of seventeenth-century Europe acquired more power over their peoples than their medieval or Renaissance predecessors had ever exerted. Governing through larger and more efficient bureaucracies than Europe had known since ancient times, these seventeenth-century monarchs came to be known as *absolute* rulers, so unquestioned was their authority. The absolutists of the seventeenth century in fact elevated hereditary monarchical government to a peak of power and paved the way for the even stronger republican governments of more recent centuries. The most powerful of all the power brokers of the 1600s were perhaps Prussia's Great Elector, Frederick William; Russia's most powerful czar, Peter the Great; and above all Louis XIV, the Sun King of France.

The seventeenth century was thus a time of hard-driving nation builders, brutal wars, and royal splendor. European kings and queens in the eighteenth century retained the expanded authority and the enlarged administrative systems of their absolutist predecessors. But some of them added an ostentatious new concern with the welfare of their subjects that earned for these monarchs the label *enlightened*. This concern was sometimes genuine, at least with regard to selected afflictions of their subjects. It was also sometimes a cloak for increasing state revenues or a means of decreasing the likelihood of popular rebellion. And it was sometimes merely a matter of royal vanity. But the eighteenth-century "enlightened despots" were at least a straw in the great wind blowing toward the democracies and welfare states of later centuries. Among the most celebrated examples of enlightened despotism were Frederick the Great of Prussia, Catherine the Great of Russia, and Maria Theresa and her son Joseph II of the Holy Roman Empire.

A look at Europe's great powers under the absolute monarchs of the seventeenth century and the enlightened despots of the eighteenth follows.

 # THE GREAT POWERS

FRANCE UNDER LOUIS XIV: I AM THE STATE

No ruler of the age embodied the spirit of royal absolutism as did Louis XIV (1643–1715), for whom the age is sometimes named. Who but the Sun King, the Grand Monarch, could have interrupted a diplomat's pompous references to the French state with an impatient but quite accurate *"l'état, c'est moi"*—"I am the state"—and have historians nodding sagely ever since?

Louis erected his edifice of power on the state-building efforts of powerful French rulers of the first half of the seventeenth century. Henry IV, the chivalric White Plume of Navarre, had ended France's long religious civil wars and established the Bourbon dynasty on the throne. The powerful and thoroughly secular Cardinal Richelieu had strengthened royal power and laid the foundations of Louis's new structure of administration. But it was Louis himself, during his reign of more than seventy years, who supervised the building of that structure.

Building royal power meant undermining local and regional power centers, and this Louis did with a will. The old independent-minded French aristocrats were turned into tame courtiers at Louis's court. Town officials became royal appointees. Royal regulations were imposed upon medieval guilds. Provincial courts called *parlements* were compelled to rubber-stamp royal decrees. The Estates General, France's embryonic Parliament, became a dead letter by virtue of never being summoned to meet during Louis's long reign.

The Sun King himself, Louis XIV, posed in seventeenth-century splendor, from huge wig to high red heels, against an appropriately Roman backdrop. Hyacinth Rigaud's portrait catches much of the magnificence of Europe's absolute monarchs in what has been called the Splendid Century. Though Louis XIV was able to combine hard work with symbolic splendor and ceremony, the lives of his eighteenth-century successors would be swamped by sumptuous living. (Art Resource)

In place of medieval regional autonomy, centralized royal institutions grew up. Central councils presided over by the king formulated government policies. Powerful royal ministers such as the Marquis de Louvois, minister of war, and above all Jean Baptiste Colbert (1619–1683), chief minister for finances and many other matters, elaborated and applied these policies. A centralized administrative system of agents called *intendants* then implemented them in the provinces, collecting taxes and army conscripts, regulating the economy, and providing at least some government protection in the countryside.

Perhaps the most impressive achievement of absolutism under Louis XIV, however, was the elaborate system of mercantilist regulation of the national economy developed by Colbert. The traditional goals of mercantilism were to increase national production, secure a favorable balance of trade in the goods produced, and thus guarantee a flow of payments in gold and silver bullion

into the country. Bullion, in the mercantilist view, constituted true national wealth. It could also be readily taxed by the state—an additional incentive not lost on Louis's administrators.

Under Colbert, then, an intricate structure of monopolies, chartered companies, protective tariffs, controls on wages, prices, and product quality, and colonial regulations was established to achieve these ends. All major powers practiced mercantilistic regulation of their economies. But few did so as efficiently and wholeheartedly as Louis and his first minister, Colbert.

Louis's war minister, Louvois, presided over the worst fruit of royal absolutism: the four wars fought during Louis's long reign.

They were clearly dynastic wars fought to secure lands Louis claimed for his wife (the Spanish Netherlands—Belgium today), for his grandson (Spain itself), or in his own right (the Rhineland). Louis's immense power and matching ambition elevated France to the position—enjoyed by Spain during the preceding century—of Europe's greatest power, threatening to impose its predominance upon the continent.

The result—as in Philip II's day—was a series of alliances against Louis XIV. Most of them were led by William of Orange, ruler first of the Netherlands and then of Great Britain, a comparatively liberal ruler in an age of absolutism. Louis's ambitions were finally frustrated in the early 1700s, when a Europe-wide conflict called the War of the Spanish Succession prevented the Sun King from uniting the throne of France with that of Spain and all its possessions overseas.

The symbol of Louis's predominance was the biggest palace in Europe, built at Versailles, outside Paris. Versailles provided a regal setting for the most admired of absolute monarchs, a world of formal gardens, glittering fountains, and acres of stately architecture. Here Louis and his ministers, mistresses, and courtiers paraded in their ermines and velvets, living in a style befitting the Grand Monarch, the incarnation of sovereignty whose only fitting symbol was the Sun.

PRUSSIA AND AUSTRIA: NATIONS OF BUREAUCRATS AND SOLDIERS

Frederick William (1640–1688) pulled his new nation of Brandenburg-Prussia together out of the ashes of the Thirty Years' War, which centered in the German states. This bloody conflict began as a last flare-up of the European wars of religion and ended as a struggle for territory involving England, France, Spain, the Holy Roman Empire, and a number of other powers. Perhaps a third of the population of the German states was killed, wolves prowled the streets of deserted villages, and German development was retarded for generations. It is perhaps not surprising, then, that Frederick William chose to base the new power he built from the rubble on what must have seemed the prime essential of his violent age: military strength.

The Great Elector's twin goals—and those of his successors in Brandenburg-Prussia—were to link up the scattered Hohenzollern holdings into a united block of territory stretching across North Germany, and to impose the royal will upon the resulting nation. The Prussian army won him powerful allies, as well as more territory. The army also helped bring his new lands to heel, imposing royal authority upon free cities and the medieval assemblies of his expanding realm.

Frederick William found a second ally in the Prussian nobility, the hardheaded Junkers. Unlike the frequently rebellious aristocrats of many countries, the Prussian Junkers cast their lot with royal absolutism. They staffed the Hohenzollern bureaucracy and made it arguably the best in Europe. They officered the army. They ran their landed estates efficiently too, thus building the country's agricultural wealth. From Frederick William's day to Bismarck's, the Junkers would be synonymous with Prussian power.

Russia's most famous state-builder, Peter the Great, is here depicted in armor like a king of an earlier time—a vivid evocation of his determination to strengthen Russia militarily. The emperor's huge size, legendary capacity for eating and drinking, great physical strength, and harshly pragmatic attitude are less clear in this elegant portrait. (PH Archives)

Frederick II the Great (1740–1786) was Prussia's greatest enlightened despot—and its greatest royal general. He ended up, in fact, with a greater reputation as a war-maker than as a reformer. A Frenchified lad who resisted Hohenzollern militarism and loved poetry and playing the flute, Frederick hardened in later years into Prussia's most brilliant military commander.

As an enlightened despot, he wrote volumes of philosophy and history, sponsored reforms of the judicial system, and encouraged religious toleration. He called himself the "first servant" of the state and seems genuinely to have believed that only absolute power in royal hands could bring a better life for his people.

He most captured the imagination of Europe in a more typically Hohenzollern role, however: as a general and a state builder. He fought a long duel with the Habsburg empress Maria Theresa and her allies during the mid-century War of the Austrian Succession and the Seven Years' War. While England and France were using these wars to fight for colonies overseas, Prussia and Austria battled for territory in central Europe. And in the end, by inspired generalship and at considerable cost to his beleaguered homeland, Frederick did detach a sizable chunk from Austria and attach it to the Kingdom of Prussia.

Maria Theresa (1740–1765) and her son Joseph II (1765–1790), rulers of Europe's oldest great power, were the most dedicated enlightened innovators of all rulers of major powers. A pious Catholic, Maria Theresa nevertheless forced reforms upon her Church. A firm believer in the Habsburg dynasty's power and destiny, she nonetheless drastically reformed both the central and provincial administration of the empire.

Her son Joseph, both more ambitious and more enlightened, sponsored legal reform, religious toleration, and comparative freedom of the press. Above all, he worked to improve the lot of the peasants by introducing tax reforms for them and eliminating vestiges of serfdom. Unfortunately, Joseph's autocratic style of implementing these innovations alienated his subjects so thoroughly that little was actually accomplished.

Soldiers and bureaucrats were thus the keys to central European power in the seventeenth and eighteenth centuries—and particularly to the rise of Prussia, the core of what would become modern Germany.

RUSSIA'S WINDOW ON THE WEST

In Russia, on Europe's eastern frontier, Peter the Great and Catherine the Great faced problems of modernization rather than of unification. But they, like Frederick William and Frederick the Great, depended on royal absolutism and military force to achieve their objectives.

Peter I the Great (1682–1725) built on the centralizing efforts of earlier Russian rulers such as Ivan the Great in the fifteenth century and Ivan the Terrible in the sixteenth. Ivan III the Great had reduced the other Russian princes who had survived the reign of the Mongols to vassal status under Muscovy in the 1400s. Ivan IV the Terrible had imposed a rough form of central government by terror on the growing eastern European nation in the 1500s. Peter the Great, the most colorful and autocratic of all the czars, sought to turn his still medieval country into an up-to-date absolutist regime by sheer energy and hamfisted force of will in the decades around 1700.

Six feet four inches tall and massively built, given to violent rages and symbolic gestures such as chopping the old-fashioned beards off his noblemen with his own hands, Peter was the stuff of which legends are made. His determination to redesign Russia on the model of western Europe divided his country between Westernizers and Slavophiles—admirers of the West and lovers of old Russian ways—for the next two centuries. But he did make Russia a great power—and the most rigidly autocratic of all European states.

Under Peter I, royal power was felt more heavily by more people than ever before in Russian history. A new structure of state-service nobility, in which one's title depended on service in the bureaucracy or the army, gradually superseded the anarchistic old *boyar* aristocracy. The Russian Orthodox church was taken over by a royal appointee, its ancient monasteries confiscated to fill the royal treasuries. Taxes, military conscription, and forced labor were heaped on the Russian peasantry, and serfdom actually increased in Russia in the eighteenth century.

Peter's accomplishments, however, were as prodigious as his tyrannies. He built the huge bureaucracy that would be Europe's largest, both in czarist and communist times. He created a powerful army, founded the Russian navy, and fought long wars with the Turks in the south and the Swedes in the north. The latter conflict won a slice of Baltic seacoast that gave the largely landlocked country a crucial "window on the West" through which trade and Western influences would flow henceforth. Peter made himself an emperor and built himself a great new capital on this conquered land—St. Petersburg, the Leningrad of twentieth-century Russia.[1]

Peter the Great found his country hopelessly medieval and only half European. He left it, if not modern or yet Westernized, at least a recognized great power and more rigorously centralized than it had ever been before.

Catherine the Great (1762–1796), Russia's most celebrated enlightened despot, was actually not Russian at all. She was a German princess married to an ineffectual young czar who soon died, leaving the throne to his shrewd young widow. Catherine brought the reforming ideas of the European Enlightenment with her to the endless steppes and dark forests of Russia. She also proved to be another of Russia's most colorful rulers, entertaining her court indiscriminately with philosophical letters from Voltaire and her long line of stalwart lovers.

Reforming ideas, unfortunately, did not find a congenial environment in Europe's most unbending autocracy. The Legislative Commission Catherine convened produced no enlightened legislation. Her Charter of Nobility merely strengthened the nobles' control over their serfs. In the end, she made more of a mark in history by crushing a famous peasant uprising—Pugachev's Rebellion— by acquiring Russia's share of Poland in the partitioning of that unfortunate state, and by conquering more lands from the Turks.

By the end of the eighteenth century, then, Russia had thrust its way into the councils of Europe's great powers—and had laid the foundations of the global power of the Soviet Union of the twentieth century.

ENGLAND'S CENTURY OF REVOLUTION

Most of Europe's seventeenth- and eighteenth-century monarchs, enlightened or not, were dedicated absolutists. But there was another line of political development to be detected in the 1600s and 1700s. This was the much rarer liberal line of governmental evolution best illustrated by the rise of Parliament and constitutional monarchy in Great Britain. And if royal absolutism pointed ahead to the more authoritarian governments to come, constitutional monarchy would lead in time to the mass democracies of more recent centuries.

There were other comparatively liberal governments in this period, most importantly that of the Netherlands. But Britain would be the primary early proving ground for democracy in the West, and its Parliament the mother of representative institutions around the world.

The seventeenth century was England's century of revolution.

A series of foreign rulers—the Scottish Stuart dynasty—who tried to impose absolute monarchy on England without understanding English traditions undoubtedly helped to precipitate the English Revolution. So did the survival of the strong Tudor Parliament, which served as a rallying point for the enemies of absolutism. So, finally, did unfinished business from the previous century: unresolved Reformation tensions, simmering discontent with the autocratic Tudor style of governance, and the rise of a prosperous and self-confident English gentry class and a merchant middle class ready to defend its interests.

In the seventeenth century, then, resistance to the crown developed among several groups of English people. Puritan Protestants opposed immorality at the royal court and feared creeping Catholicism in the Anglican church. Thrifty merchants resented courtly extravagance and high taxes. Above all, solid country squires rebelled at favoritism shown to a handful of royal courtiers, at the abridgment of their own rights in Parliament, and at the high-handedness of James I and his successors in the Stuart line.

---

[1]In 1991, Leningraders voted to rename their city St. Petersburg—and to try to make it a genuine "window on the West" once more.

Catherine the Great—German by birth, Russian by royal marriage, French by cultural preference—epitomized the cosmopolitan spirit of the Enlightenment. The sophisticated empress looks appealingly human in this picture. As a girl, she loved horseback riding and reading; as a ruler, she was proud of military victories, governmental reforms, and "edicts for improving the life of the people." (Photographie Bulloz)

In the 1700s, the cabinet system and the office of prime minister both emerged. The chief royal advisers and heads of the royal administration became a cabinet, or council of leading members of Parliament. They were led by a prime (first) minister, who was the head of the majority party in the House of Commons. Parties themselves also took shape: a conservative Tory faction and a more liberal Whig party. Each group was bound by ties of family connection, political interest, and governmental principles. And the competition of these parties of elected politicians determined to an increasing degree the policies of England.

Elections were still far from democratic: Only a handful voted, usually on the basis of property ownership. The kings remained very powerful. But a start had been made on a road that would lead over the next two centuries to genuine democracy in Britain.

THE WORLD OF THE RISING MIDDLE CLASSES

THE BOURGEOISIE ON THE BRINK

If the politics of the age of absolutism and enlightened despotism was still dominated by the old aristocracy, the economics of these centuries remained solidly in the hands of the middle classes. Much of the present section, on the economic and social trends of the age, will thus be concerned with that famous historical cliché, the rising middle classes, now closing rapidly in on their blue-blooded rivals.

In much of Europe, the closeness of the contest was by no means apparent in the 1600s and 1700s. In many places, the dominant aristocracy seemed to establish a lock on high places in royal courts and royal governments, in churches, armies, and diplomatic corps, and other top spots in European society. In central and eastern Europe especially, aristocrats bought increased authority over the peasant majority of the population in return for acknowledging the absolute power of the monarchy over the nation as a whole. Since the middle classes in middle and eastern Europe tended to be bureaucratic servants of the state rather than independent merchants, there was really no contest. Aristocratic social prestige remained high all over Europe, and the social-climbing tradesman, or "bourgeois gentleman"—a contradiction in terms—remained an object of satire.

In western Europe, however, the middle classes were actually doing very well indeed. Thriving on the commercial and imperial expansion of the Atlantic powers, the upper bourgeoisie grew wealthier than ever before. In government, middle-class administrators such as Colbert did much of the work of absolutist government.

Through the first half of the century, this opposition took the form of famous court cases and courtly scandals, running battles in Parliament, and finally armed revolt. A Puritan country squire named Oliver Cromwell defeated the royal armies in battle, beheaded the second Stuart king, Charles I, in 1649, and ruled the country as Lord Protector for the next decade. Charles II was restored to power in 1660, but his successor, James II, was expelled for good in 1688. A parliamentary faction then imported a new king from the Netherlands: William of Orange, strong Protestant and archenemy of royal absolutism, who with his Queen Mary Stuart became England's first constitutional monarch.

The Glorious Revolution of 1688 gave Parliament a large share in governing the country, including the power to control royal revenues and the rights to free elections and debate. The eighteenth century saw the slow evolution of parliamentary power, especially the authority of the elected House of Commons, though the hereditary House of Lords remained powerful too.

The solid middle classes who continued to guide Europe's economic expansion during the middle-modern centuries challenged the skills of painters like Jan Vermeer. His picture of a Woman Holding a Balance reveals some of the calm strength and dignity of this woman and her class. Notice also the composition of the painting, achieved largely by light and shadow, focusing on the woman's thoughtful face and competent hands. (Jan Vermeer, "A Woman Weighing Gold." Canvas. 16-3/4 × 15 [0.425 × 0.380] National Gallery of Art, Washington, D.C. Widener Collection 1942)

Merchants ran the government of the Netherlands and sat in the increasingly powerful Parliament of Britain. And despite the jeers of their betters, bourgeois citizens were also increasingly well-educated, self-confident—and willing to criticize the fecklessness and unearned privileges of their traditional social superiors.

The great upheavals that were about to transform Europe—the French Revolution of 1789 and the Industrial Revolution that would begin in Britain about 1760—would further enhance the fortunes of the bourgeoisie. But those fortunes were already well advanced. Thanks to a great surge of money power in the 1600s and 1700s, western Europe's middle classes were strongly positioned to take advantage of what was to come as this middle period of modern European history drew to a close.

EUROPE'S NEW PROSPERITY

The prosperity of the commercial middle classes took different forms in different parts of western Europe. Dutch burghers and shipmasters built on a tradition of trade and seamanship that went back to the Middle Ages. In the sev-

enteenth century, as we have seen, the Netherlands dominated the carrying trade of all Europe and was a leading producer of manufactured goods, as well as perhaps the most successful of the new empire builders. In the eighteenth century, British merchants profited from Europe's largest free-trade zone after the union of England and Scotland. They also benefited from the West's solidest financial institution, the Bank of England, as well as from extensive foreign trade and Britain's own triumphant empire. French merchants had western Europe's largest population to supply. They also had the West's most elaborate mercantile system, and a sizable empire too, at least until France's imperial duel with England ended in 1763.

In western European countries especially, capitalist institutions and governmental supports for business growth were thus widespread. Joint-stock companies pooled capital for large-scale commercial projects, and stock exchanges facilitated investment. Mercantilistic governments provided subsidies, monopolies, protective tariffs, and other forms of encouragement for business. Europe's bourgeoisie might be mere tradesmen to the old aristocracy, but they were among the world's richest businessmen too.

Industrial production remained largely in the hands of city guilds or peasants engaged in cottage industry. Peasants spun and wove wool into cloth, made wine, and otherwise processed the fruits of their lands and labors. Guild artisans still made most of the useful objects Europeans needed, from shoes and barrels to books and jewelry. Some of the heavier industries—mining and metallurgy, shipbuilding, cannon foundries, and printing presses—used elaborate machinery containing intricate combinations of pulleys, screws, and other mechanisms for multiplying force. Waterpower and windpower, however, remained all that the West—and the world at large—could muster beyond the labor of animals and human backs to do the world's work.

THE POPULATION EXPLOSION

The demographic history of Europe took an astonishing and decisive turn around the middle of this period. After stalling in the seventeenth century, population growth turned decisively upward in the middle decades of the eighteenth. We must rely largely on estimates—hard statistical evidence is rare this early—but Europe's total population may have risen by as much as 80 percent between 1730 and 1830. It was, in fact, the beginning of the greatest population explosion in the world's history.

Explanations for this initial take-off are complex and sometimes contradictory. One likely cause for the new numbers, however, is clearly the agricultural revolution of the early 1700s.

Agricultural improvements in the eighteenth century included advances in fertilizer and the rotation of crops to increase production, and stock breeding to develop heav-

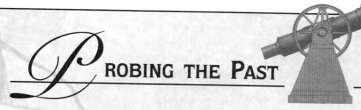

PROBING THE PAST

"Material life, *consisting of very old routines, inheritances and successes, is there at the root of everything. Agriculture for example—the way of life of most people throughout the world before the eighteenth century (and even beyond that critical threshold)—goes back thousands of years before the fifteenth century, when this book begins. This is true of corn, rice, maize, the domestication of animals and basic cookery; that is, of some of man's longest-lasting early practices. Elementary tools are as old as cultivated plants, and the same can almost be said of the still fairly simple tools that increased or facilitated physical effort: lever, lathe, pedal, crank and winch. It is equally true of windmills and watermills, which were twelfth-century revolutions in the Western world. The expression* material life *will therefore be deliberately used throughout the book to denote repeated actions, empirical processes, old methods and solutions handed down from time immemorial, like money or the separation of town from country. It is an elementary life but neither entirely passive nor, above all, completely static. It has moments of acceleration and occasionally of surprise: new plants become acclimatised, techniques improve and spread, changes occur in processes employed by blacksmiths, weavers and, still more, by miners and shipbuilders. These changes take place slowly but steadily. Money and towns play a continually increasing part and some innovations are of decisive importance.*"

France's Fernand Braudel, one of the most admired historians of the twentieth century, is renowned for his breadth of vision, his originality, and the concreteness of his writing, which makes his work quite accessible to the general reader. His first book, on The Mediterranean and the Mediterranean World in the Age of Philip II (1949) set a new standard for supranational regional history. His global range is such that in two pages of the present work on "transportation," he can sweep through Russia, Argentina, Turkey, Persia, China, the Philippines, and the Guinea coast of Africa.

Braudel's approach to the economic history of earlier modern times differs from Wallerstein's (see Chapter 31) in its emphasis on material culture, a source of historical understanding only recently explored by the "new history" of the later twentieth century. What does Braudel mean by "material life"? He uses agriculture as a prime example: Does peasant life really change from century to century? What technologies clearly do see major changes during the period under consideration here? What technologies and technological changes affect your life as a twentieth-century American student?

Fernand Braudel, Capitalism and Material Life, 1400–1800, trans. Miriam Kochan (New York: Harper & Row, Pub., 1967), p. xii.

ier beef cattle or pigs. Enclosure of village lands and advanced techniques of land management helped make such improvements possible. These agricultural developments came in areas where there were already large enough concentrations of population to make worthwhile the work involved and the cost of the improvements. Thus the new agricultural revolution was initially limited to parts of England and France, to the Netherlands, the Rhineland, and northern Italy—all of which were regions with large cities to be fed.

Once the agricultural revolution was in train, however, it contributed substantially to further population growth. More food could feed more people. Life expectancies therefore increased, more people lived to reproduce, and a cycle was set in motion that would multiply the population in the next few centuries.

Most Europeans were still desperately poor. Serfs in central and eastern Europe and tenants in western Europe were at the mercy of their landlords or masters. Even free peasants who owned their own land, which many of them did in France and some in England, still lived within reach of starvation in years of bad harvest. Excess rural population, no longer needed on more efficient farms, clogged the cities seeking nonexistent work. Living on black bread and little else in the best of times, sinking easily into total destitution, crime, or the endemic violence stimulated by cheap rum and gin, these early generations of the population boom had little to be grateful for. They too, however, would have their part to play in the history of Europe's next era, the impending age of revolutions.

THE CONDITIONS OF WOMEN

Women, as usual, played many parts in this period. At one end of the scale, there were poverty-stricken peasant women even in such prosperous countries as France. Bent and wizened, made old and ugly by years of field labor and a level of childbearing "close," as the demographers say, "to the biological maximum," such women could look sixty—and be in their twenties. At the other extreme, there were the court ladies, the salon hostesses, royal mistresses such as *mesdames* de Pompadour or du Barry, charming or regal in their velvets and laces, their high-piled wigs and winking diamonds. In between there were many middle-class women, well if not ostentatiously dressed, thoroughly respectable, managers of households or businesses, readers of novels as well as Scripture.

Scattered generalizations may be made about these women of the Age of Reason. They were normally married (as were most men), and married by their parents with property and other material considerations in mind—though this may be as good a recipe for a happy union as marrying for looks or personality, as some would do in later centuries. Within the family, women remained at least formally subordinate to their husbands. All married women were expected to bear and rear children, who were still valued, both as free labor and as a form of old-age insurance for their parents. In addition, women of the peasant, servant, and other working classes had hard physical labor to do all their lives.

Nevertheless, there does seem to have been some improvement in the feminine condition, particularly during the eighteenth century. There were a number of successful women rulers, including Queen Anne of Great Britain, the empresses Maria Theresa and Catherine the Great, and two other Russian rulers. Managing a great house or even a solid middle-class home, with its many servants and other supernumeraries, was a challenge as it had always been. There were celebrated women novelists such as Mademoiselle de Scudéry in the seventeenth century and women painters such as the famous portraitists Elizabeth

Vigée-le Brun and Adelaide Labille-Guyard at the court of Marie Antoinette. Extraordinary women shone in the salons; ordinary women, in western Europe at least, found it easier to move freely in society and felt less stigma in remaining "spinsters."

Women played significant roles in the high politics of seventeenth-century France in particular. Aristocratic ladies were leading intriguers at the Bourbon court. During this period, they also founded the first French *salons*, centers for discussion and the arts. The wives of imprisoned princes were leaders in the Fronde, the tangled revolutionary upheaval that ravaged French cities at midcentury. Less aristocratic women rioted in the streets of French towns during this tumultuous and confused time.

Laws still curtailed the legal rights of women; women's education was still distinctly limited; and marriage and family were still important parts of most women's lives. But social and cultural areas formally closed to women were beginning to open up to them. Like other unprivileged groups in Western society, women were on the verge of at least a beginning of emancipation by 1800.

 # THE AGE OF REASON

THE SCIENTIFIC REVOLUTION

The cultural life of this middle period of modern European history has a distinctly cerebral cast. The bubbling creativity of the Renaissance that preceded this era and the passion of Romanticism that followed it bracket Europe's great Age of Reason. It was a period of scientific discovery and social philosophizing, of both courtly and bourgeois art and literature, of dry wit and stinging satire.

The Scientific Revolution of the sixteenth and seventeenth centuries provided the intellectual underpinnings for much of the cultural life of the Age of Reason.

The physical sciences, as we have seen, flourished in many cultures, including those of China, India, the Islamic center of Eurasia, and the Mayans in the New World. Europe's last significant contribution had come among the ancient Greeks. Hundreds of years before Christ, Greek thinkers reasoned their way to the globular shape of the earth, calculated the distances of the sun and the moon mathematically, developed Archimedean physics and Euclidean geometry. They also classified biological organisms and at least urged an empirical approach to medicine.

The Greco-Roman period, however, left one great error to bedevil later scientific understanding: the astronomer Ptolemy's geocentric (earth-centered) theory of the structure of the universe. It was in correcting this error that the sixteenth-century astronomer Copernicus launched the Scientific Revolution.

Nicolaus Copernicus, a Polish churchman who made astronomy his hobby, first propounded the heliocentric (sun-centered) theory in a book *On the Revolutions of the Heavenly Spheres* in 1543. In Copernicus's view, the sun was the center, the earth merely one of a number of planets. The earth, he said, spins around the sun and rotates on its own axis at the same time, giving the illusion that the universe itself is moving around us. Copernicus retained some of the creaky old machinery of the Ptolemaic system, including circular orbits, "eccentrics," and "epicycles" to explain anomalies of planetary motion, and a "sphere of the fixed stars" beyond that of the farthest planet. But the Polish astronomer had made the great breakthrough: the Scientific Revolution is sometimes called the Copernican Revolution in his honor.

Scientists of many lands built on these foundations over the century and a half after 1543. The German mathematician Johannes Kepler proposed the three laws of planetary motion—including the key recognition that

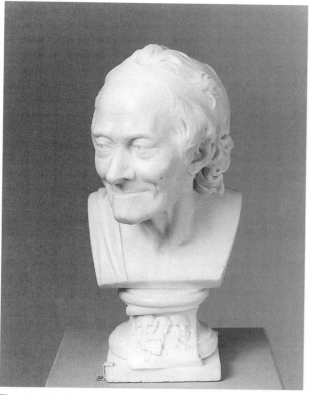

The most celebrated mind of the Enlightenment was that of Voltaire, shown here in a bust by Jean Antoine Houdon. The skeptical, satiric spirit of the age perhaps shows best in the hooded eyes of the king of the philosophes. Can you see why the leaders of the French establishment could find such a sardonic personality disturbing? (Jean Antoine Houdon. "Bust of Voltaire," 1781. Marble. 20.25 x 9.25 x 9 inches. The Fine Arts Museums of San Francisco. Gift of Mr. and Mrs. John Magnin, 61.31)

planets move around the sun in elipses rather than circles. The famous Italian astronomer and physicist Galileo Galilei built the first astronomical telescope and observed for the first time the mountains on the moon, sunspots, the rings of Saturn, the moons of Jupiter, and the stellar composition of the Milky Way. Galileo is also celebrated for such terrestrial discoveries as the law of the acceleration of falling bodies and the principle of the pendulum.

The mind that tied all this into a coherent scientific picture of the universe was that of the English mathematician Sir Isaac Newton. The linchpin of Newton's theory was the law of universal gravitation: every particle of matter in the universe, from planets in their orbits to falling bodies here on earth, attracts every other particle of matter with a force called gravity. This gravitational force, Newton declared in his *Mathematical Principles* of 1687, varies directly with the sum of their masses and inversely with the square of the distance between them.

Copernicus, Galileo, Newton, and the other makers of the Scientific Revolution gave the West—and the world—a new technical language and a new approach to truth. Empirical observation and mathematical calculation replaced ancient authority and abstract logic as the road to understanding the world. Science and its jargon became the core of a new Western world view.

During the seventeenth and eighteenth centuries scientific explanations, based on empirical observation or experiment and on mathematical analysis of the results, gained wide acceptance in Europe. Simplified layman's explanations of the world according to Newton popularized the new discoveries and the empirical-mathematical approach to truth that had produced them. Scientific societies were organized in England, France, Italy, and elsewhere. In the Enlightenment of the eighteenth century, amateur dabbling in science acquired the sort of prestige among the aristocracy and even the middle classes that dabbling in literature and art had enjoyed in the Renaissance.

The Scientific Revolution was the beginning of several centuries of progress in pure and applied science that would dwarf all earlier scientific advances. It was also the basis for the equally revolutionary social thought that began during these centuries.

THE ENLIGHTENMENT

"My trade," the eighteenth century's most famous intellectual is supposed to have said, "is to say what I think."[2] Voltaire was a *philosophe*, one of the intellectual leaders of the French Enlightenment, the climax of the Europe-wide Age of Reason. A writer of poetry, fiction, drama, history, popular science, political philosophy, and much, much more, François-Marie Arouet, known as Voltaire

[2]Evelyn Beatrice Hall, *Life of Voltaire,* 3rd ed. (New York: G. P. Putnam, 1926), p. 145.

(1694–1778), was celebrated as much for his radical critique of the society of his time as for his literary brilliance. Of his many books, none is more widely known and imitated than *Candide* (1759), a picaresque, satirical novel about a naive young man who manages to encounter hypocrisy, injustice, and folly in every country and every class of eighteenth-century society.

Voltaire's contemporary, Jean Jacques Rousseau (1712–1778), was a wild man among the coolly witty philosophes, stressing emotional sincerity rather than satirical wit and urging the superiority of the natural world to artificial modern society. Rousseau was given to passionate declarations like "Man was born free, and everywhere he is in chains," which influenced such later revolutionaries as Robespierre.[3]

The French *Encyclopedia,* edited by Denis Diderot and Jean d'Alembert, used this apparently neutral form as a cloak for more subtle attacks on the "old regime," as the society of this age was later called. The influence of such works, particularly in the hands of the educated French bourgeoisie, was inexorably subversive, undermining faith in the major social institutions of the time.

Enlightened philosophes were thus not system builders, like Aristotle or Thomas Aquinas; they were social critics, the most vigorous Europe had known for centuries. Voltaire and his colleagues attacked the churches of their day—Catholic and Protestant—as nests of superstition, fanaticism, and useless logic-chopping. They condemned the European aristocracy as mere decorations rather than pillars of society, daring to suggest that merit might be more important in determining a person's true value than inherited social position. And if kings and queens were less vigorously assaulted, it was primarily because the philosophes hoped to work through duly enlightened despots to build a more rational and more just world.

On the positive side, these same often satirical social critics found hope in the Scientific Revolution that a better society was possible once human reason was set to solving social problems. They pointed out that before Copernicus, Galileo, and Newton began to probe, the natural world had seemed as confused and unsystematic as the social world still did in the eighteenth century. Another century or two of determined *social*-scientific inquiry, they believed, would uncover "natural laws" as valid in society as the laws of planetary motion or the law of gravity were in the material world.

Indeed, such natural laws of history and society seemed to come to light before the end of the Age of Reason itself. John Locke, a British political thinker writing at the time of the English Revolution of 1688, insisted that all people have natural rights, including liberty, equality, and property. In the middle 1700s, the Baron de Montesquieu's monumental *Spirit of the Laws* argued that within governing institutions there were political principles such as "checks and balances" that, properly applied, would guarantee just and virtuous government. And in 1776 Adam Smith, the father of modern economics, declared in his *Wealth of Nations* that the road to prosperity lay in accepting the law of supply and demand as it functioned naturally in the free market economy.

It was a period of revolutionary social thought that seemed to shed a dazzling new light on the way human society works. This Enlightenment critique challenged such ancient social principles as divine-right monarchy, the alliance between church and state, and the hierarchy of unequal classes on which developed societies had been built since ancient Babylon. In the shorter term, the subversive attacks of the philosophes fueled the fires of the impending American and French revolutions. In the longer run, Enlightenment confidence in the possibility of building a better society on the basis of radical social theories spawned all the revolutionary ideologies of the next two centuries, from Jeffersonian liberalism to Leninist socialism. This Enlightenment faith in reason underlies the social engineering and big government, as well as the more revolutionary creeds, of our own time.

COURTLY AND BOURGEOIS ART

By and large, literature and the arts during the 1600s and 1700s tended to suit the tastes of the two most prominent elements in the society of those two centuries: the courtly aristocracy and the rising bourgeoisie.

Courtly art produced baroque and classical styles rooted in the art of the Renaissance and the Catholic Counter-Reformation, as well as in the traditional culture of ancient Greece and Rome.

The baroque style emerged first as Catholic church art, intended to awe the faithful into acceptance of religion through the sheer grandeur of churches such as the new Saint Peter's in Rome. But secular rulers of the seventeenth century soon saw that the same baroque qualities of rich color, vitality and movement, gilt, glass, light, and sheer scale could awe their subjects into submission to absolute monarchy also. Many a palace, church, and monastery in between were built with these religious or political ends in view.

The classical style in art went back to the Renaissance, which had emphasized classical Greek and especially Roman models. The more restrained classical approach in painting, architecture, and sculpture differed from the baroque in many ways. It stressed balance, not movement; drawing, not color; simplicity, not complex-

---

[3]Jean Jacques Rousseau, *The Social Contract,* trans. Maurice Cranstan (Baltimore: Penguin Books, 1968), p. 49.

ity. In literature this approach resulted in the French classical drama at the court of Louis XIV, where writers such as Racine and Corneille shaped powerful emotions to the formal precision of hexameter verse.

In all areas, classical art and literature sought guidance in rules and in models. Rules for painting, writing, even acting were made available in books and taught in academies. The models were provided by the "old masters"—Greek, Roman, and Renaissance—in every art.

Aristocratic taste responded to the dry wit and worldly wisdom of La Rochefoucauld's maxims or the poetry of Alexander Pope. Phrases like "A little learning is a dangerous thing," "Fools rush in where angels fear to tread," and "We are so accustomed to disguising ourselves before others that we end by disguising ourselves from ourselves" became part of the temper of the times.

Aristocrats also loved the romantic novels of Mademoiselle de Scudéry, who earned wealth and fame and in the process created a national rage for her delicate mapping of the "tender passions." And the comedies of Molière, France's greatest comic dramatist, showed the court of the Sun King how to laugh at all the pretensions of their age.

Gentlemen and gentlewomen with classical educations and a part to play at royal courts felt right at home with classical art and baroque magnificence. But solid Dutch burghers, aggressive French bourgeois citizens, and middle-class merchants in England had entirely different tastes in art. These middle-class tastes also found expression in the arts of the 1600s and 1700s.

Painters such as Rembrandt van Rijn could depict the merchant oligarchs of the Netherlands—*The Syndics of the Cloth Guild,* say—with the sober dignity and seriousness of purpose this business elite saw as their great virtues. The French artist Jean Baptiste Chardin could paint a Parisian housewife cutting bread, or a family offering *Grace before Meat* with a simple strength that universalized these aspects of everyday bourgeois life.

In England, the most striking manifestation of middle-class taste was the development of the English novel. In Daniel Defoe's *Robinson Crusoe,* for instance, the bourgeois virtues of industry, ingenuity, common sense, perseverance, and piety that enable Robinson to conquer his island glorified the virtues with which middle-class Europeans were mastering the material world of their own time. Samuel Richardson's early novel *Pamela* deals in a realistic if sentimental way with so commonplace if reprehensible an event as the attempted seduction of a servant girl. It also focuses on Pamela's concern with her proper place in society, with marriage and the security it brings, and with such old-fashioned virtues as chastity and honor—a psychologically realistic portrait that the different values of a later age should not obscure.

A cynical Voltairian aristocrat might sneer at the subtitle of *Pamela—Virtue Rewarded.* For the Protestant or Catholic middle ranks of society, however, God still did reward staunch adherence to the middle-class virtues. Art in such novels, such paintings, was merely mirroring life as these middle-class people saw it.

THE SALON

The center of the cultural life of the Enlightenment was a unique social institution known as the *salon.* A word or two on this living heart of the Age of Reason will serve to close this look at Europe in the middle of the modern period. In particular, the preeminent part played by women in the salon deserves special attention here.

The salon of the seventeenth and eighteenth centuries was not so much a place—an elegant drawing room—as it was a social occasion. The typical salon was a weekly "at home" bringing together witty, cultured people in the drawing room of a witty, cultured, and fashionable hostess. Seventeenth-century salons such as that of the Marquise de Rambouillet featured literary people in particular; eighteenth-century gatherings such as those at Madame Necker's or *chez* Julie d'Espinasse added science, philosophy, and even political reform to the intellectual fare. In both centuries, the salon brought the aristocratic ruling class and the leading intellectual lights of the age together, advancing intellectual careers and civilizing the aristocracy in the process.

The central role in the salon was of course that of the hostess. Salon hostesses of the 1600s tended to be more aristocratic, like the Marquise de Rambouillet, who designed her own mansion and entertained the literary giants of her day in almost regal splendor. In the 1700s, the social tone became at least marginally less aristocratic—Madame Necker's husband was a mere banker, after all, though for a short time first minister to Louis XVI. But most of the hostesses had some things in common. They tended to be well off if not overwhelmingly wealthy; to be older rather than young; to be single, separated, or widowed rather than married; and to have a large talent for getting people to talk well.

Intellectually, the salon hostess cultivated range more than depth. She had to know enough to guide conversations on everything from the latest play in Paris to German philosophy, from Newton to political reform. She also had to develop such managerial skills as the ability to curtail the bore, encourage the timid, and cut off the potentially explosive argument. She moved with ease and confidence among the best minds of her age, creating among the chandeliers and mirrors an island of intellectuality where ideas could grow, pass from mind to mind, and produce the unique culture of the Age of Reason.

SUMMARY

Politically, Europe was dominated during the seventeenth and eighteenth centuries by its powerful monarchs. In the long run, however, the rise of bourgeois money power and the intellectual breakthrough of the Enlightenment would prove even more important in Western history.

Five great powers and dozens of smaller states divided Europe among them during the 1600s and 1700s. The first of these centuries saw the great strengthening of governmental power under royal absolutists like Louis XIV. The following century saw the rationale for royal government shift from simple divine right toward public service and enlightened rule.

Two German-speaking nations, Prussia and Austria, dominated central Europe. Austria was old and established; under Maria Theresa and Francis Joseph, it was the most enlightened of European monarchies. Prussia was aggressive, efficient, militaristic; under rulers like Frederick the Great, it was the most rapidly growing of the great powers.

Russia, the sprawling backward giant of eastern Europe, emerged as a major power for the first time under Peter the Great and Catherine the Great. France under Louis XIV was the seventeenth-century model of a modern absolutist state, his court at Versailles the ultimate symbol of royal power. And Britain, after a century of revolutionary turmoil and overseas empire building, emerged as the wave of Europe's future: constitutional government with a strong commercial base.

The rise of Europe's commercial bourgeoisie was another major trend of these centuries. In western Europe particularly, middle-class merchants and handicraft manufacturers dominated the economy and, supported by mercantilistic governments, developed the wealth of the Continent. In the eighteenth century, the population also took off, beginning the greatest demographic expansion in history.

The intellectual life of the West was shaped by the Scientific Revolution of the sixteenth and seventeenth centuries and by the Enlightenment of the eighteenth. Scientists from Copernicus to Newton began the great modern expansion of our understanding of the material universe. Philosophes like Voltaire and Rousseau turned the resulting confidence in human reason toward a critique of traditional society that called all inherited institutions into question and proposed the creation of a brave new world.

The arts of the time reflected both courtly and bourgeois cultures. Baroque splendor and the classical emphasis on rule and order suited the ruling aristocracy. Dutch painting and the English novel appealed to middle-class audiences with their solid morality and their comfortable middle-class subjects. Presiding over the exciting cultural and intellectual life of these two centuries, the salon hostess epitomized the age as a whole: cultivated, witty, autocratic, forward-looking, and elegant.

More violent times were coming as the eighteenth century drew to a close.

SUGGESTED READING

ANDERSON, M. S. *Europe in the Eighteenth Century, 1713–1783.* London: Longman, Green, 1976. An excellent introduction.

AUCHINCLOSS, L. *False Dawn: Women in the Age of the Sun King.* New York: Doubleday, 1984. Profiles of leading seventeenth-century women, illustrating women's influence in the court, the church, culture, and in other areas.

BERNIER, O. *The Eighteenth Century Woman.* Garden City, N.Y.: Doubleday, 1981. Profiles of famous women of the Enlightenment century, from Madame de Pompadour to Abigail Adams.

CAMDEN, C. *The Elizabethan Woman.* New York: Elsevier, 1952. Focuses on marriage and social life.

COLE, C. W. *Colbert and a Century of French Mercantilism.* Hamden, Conn.: Archon, 1964. Scholarly analysis of the policies of the most famous of mercantilists. See also E. F. Heckscher's interpretive and controversial *Mercantilism,* 2nd ed. (New York: Macmillan, 1962).

CRANKSHAW, E. *Maria Theresa.* New York: Viking, 1969. Life of one of the more enlightened of the enlightened despots.

DARNTON, R. *The Literary Underground of the Old Regime.* Cambridge, Mass.: Harvard University Press, 1982. The book trade, from hack writers and book dealers to the reading public.

FRASER, A. *The Weaker Vessel: Woman's Lot in Seventeenth-Century England.* New York: Knopf, 1984. Vignettes from top to bottom of society.

GAY, P. *The Enlightenment.* New York: Simon & Schuster, 1974. Authoritative and insightful. See also the thoughtful analysis by one of Europe's most admired intellectual historians, E. Cassirer, *The Philosophy of the Enlightenment* (Princeton: Princeton University Press, 1951). For samples, see C. Brinton, *The Portable Age of Reason Reader* (New York: Viking, 1956).

HELD, J., and D. POSNER. *Seventeenth and Eighteenth Century Art.* Englewood Cliffs, N.J.: Prentice Hall, 1972. Well-illustrated survey. See also G. Bazin's provocative volume on *The Baroque* (New York: Norton, 1978).

HILL, C. *The Century of Revolution, 1603–1714.* New York: Norton, 1982. Survey of British history in the century of the Puritan Revolution by a leading authority, with a socioeconomic slant. See also D. Hirst, *Authority and Conflict: England, 1603–1658* (London: Arnold, 1986), a thoughtful and up-to-date history of the English Civil War, coming to terms with revisionist views.

————. *God's Englishman.* New York: Harper & Row, Pub., 1972. Oliver Cromwell, flinty revolutionary, military dictator, and ideologue. See also C. V. Wedgewood's highly readable *Oliver Cromwell,* 2nd ed. (London: Duckworth, 1973).

MADARIAGA, I. DE. *Russia in the Age of Catherine the Great.* New Haven: Yale University Press, 1981. Authoritative, with a range that goes beyond standard political treatments to economic, social, and intellectual developments.

MASSIE, R. K. *Peter the Great: His Life and World.* New York: Knopf, 1981. Stresses the role of Peter's dominating personality in shaping the history of his time. For a range of views on the controversial emperor, see M. Raeff, ed., *Peter the Great Changes Russia* (Lexington, Mass.: Heath, 1972).

MOBIUS, H. *Woman of the Baroque Age.* Trans. B. C. Beedham. Montclair, N.J.: Schram, 1984. Scholarly, profusely illustrated history of European women in the seventeenth and eighteenth centuries.

PARKER, G. *The Military Revolution: Military Innovation and the Rise of the West, 1500–1800.* New York: Cambridge University Press, 1988. Military developments and their contributions to Western expansion overseas. See also M. S. Anderson, *War and Society in Europe of the Old Regime, 1618–1789* (New York: St. Martin's Press, 1988), a concise but wide-ranging study of evolving military institutions and their place in Western society.

RAEFF, M. *The Well-Ordered Police State: Social and Institutional Change through Law in the Germanies and Russia, 1600–1800.* New Haven: Yale University Press, 1983. A noted Russian historian sees parallel developments in the evolving governments and elites of central and eastern Europe.

RAGNILD, H. H. *Europe in the Age of Louis XIV.* New York: Norton, 1979. Good overview of main currents of French and European history in the age of the French predominance.

RITTER, G. *Frederick the Great.* Berkeley: University of California Press, 1968. Scholarly studies of Prussia's most intriguing eighteenth-century ruler.

SOREL, A. *Europe under the Old Regime.* New York: Harper & Row, Pub., 1964. Stimulating brief interpretation of Europe before the French Revolution. See also W. Doyle, *The Ancien Regime* (Atlantic Highlands, N.J.: Humanities Press, 1986), a brief theoretical and historiographical exploration of the "old regime" as a concept.

SPENCER, S. I., ed. *French Women and the Age of Enlightenment.* Bloomington: Indiana University Press, 1984. Solid collection of essays on women in society, politics, and above all culture.

WESTFALL, R. S. *Never at Rest: A Biography of Isaac Newton.* New York: Cambridge University Press, 1980. Thoroughly researched and authoritative.

WOLF, J. *Louis XIV.* New York: Norton, 1968. Thorough political biography.

CHAPTER 33

ASIAN EMPIRES IN DISARRAY

DISINTEGRATION OF THE MUSLIM CENTER

THE END OF ASIAN PREEMINENCE

While Westerners were exploding in all directions out of their end of Eurasia, the eastern four-fifths of the double continent was undergoing a very different process. While Europe was dynamic, aggressive, and expansionist, much of Asia sank into lethargy and decline or simply turned inward, away from the perils of the new age. It was a startling reversal of what had been the norm more often than not: the preeminence of the East in Eurasian history.

Europe had only twice matched the cultural achievements of the major Asian civilizations over the five thousand years of history before 1500. During Greek and Roman times (roughly 500 B.C.–A.D. 500) Europe had been one of the great global centers of urban culture. The same had been true during the High Middle Ages (approximately 1100–1350). For most of the rest of the time, however, Asia had clearly led in the building of complex societies, large empires, civilized arts and ideas.

Evidence for Asian preeminence is not hard to find. History and civilization began in the Near East. All the Eurasian world religions originated in Asia, not Europe. All but one of the greatest Eurasian empires before 1500 were built in Asia. Trade between East and West almost always drained gold out of Europe because Asians disdained European manufactured items as inferior, while Europeans continually coveted the superior workmanship of the East.

At the beginning of modern times, the situation was pretty much normal. The power of the Ottoman Turkish Sultan Suleiman the Magnificent cast a vast and terrifying shadow over Europe. The new empires of Safavid Persia and Mogul India were wealthy and cultured centers of civilization. Ming China was still by far the world's largest nation, busy working out the final parameters of traditional Chinese culture. Feudal Japan hovered on the edge of unification under the shoguns. Asia, in short, was thriving in the sixteenth century.

By the eighteenth, the picture looked very different. During this middle period of modern history, Asia could legitimately be described as losing ground, while Europe forged ahead.

This cultural retreat, or relative decline, took different forms in different parts of Asia during the 1600s and 1700s. The following pages will look first at predominantly Islamic West and South Asia—the Ottoman, Safavid, and Mogul empires—where the Muslim center failed at last and slid into decline. The chapter will then examine the Manchu conquest of China, the Tokugawa unification of Japan, and the long centuries of intensified isolation that subsequently enveloped both lands.

Throughout, emphasis must fall on the consequences of this decay and withdrawal of the great civilizations of the East. From this decline came the weakened and intensely conservative traditional Asia into which Westerners would finally force their way in large numbers in the nineteenth century. The imposition of the Western hegemony on the largest and most populous of continents was thus facilitated by the relative decline of the East during these centuries of the rise of the West.

THE OTTOMAN EMPIRE RETREATS

Under Sultan Suleiman the Magnificent (1520–1566), the Turkish Empire had attained its greatest extent, stretching from the Persian Gulf to the Atlantic, from Hungary in the north to Egypt in the south. The wealth of the Ottomans was legendary, the efficiency of their government proverbial. And though the sultans at Istanbul made alliances with European rulers in the tangle of Renaissance power politics, the terror of the Turkish scimitar hung heavy over Europe as a whole.

Within five years of Suleiman's death, the situation began to change. The naval battle of Lepanto (1571), a great victory of Spanish and Italian galleys over the fleets of the Ottomans, effectively ended Turkish expansion in the Mediterranean. In the Balkans, too, the Ottoman Empire would make few gains thereafter. In the east, the Ottomans faced the Safavid dynasty of Persia in a series of ultimately indecisive wars during the late 1500s and the earlier 1600s. On all sides, the Ottoman advance was blunted and turned. After one final expansive effort in the later seventeenth century, this halt to Turkish expansion turned into a disastrous retreat.

A series of energetic grand viziers of the Kiuprili family mounted the Ottoman Empire's last great offensives

The luxury of the court of the Ottoman Empire is clear from this photographic portrait of "the sultan's favorite," taken in the imperial harem. Notice the water pipe—in which Middle Easterners most commonly smoke tobacco—the lavishly embroidered robes, the sumptuous overstuffed sofa and inlaid table. But note also that the camera which took this picture was a Western invention, and that it had penetrated here to the very heart of the sultan's palace at Istanbul.

in Europe in the 1660s, 1670s, and 1680s. Turkish arms were victorious from Crete to Hungary, and in 1683 Muslim troops for the last time laid siege to Vienna, the capital of Austria and its German Holy Roman Empire. But Vienna held. The siege was broken by a combined force of German and Polish troops led by the celebrated Polish king John Sobieski. Thereafter, the tide turned relentlessly against the once great power on the Golden Horn.

In the century following the failure of the last siege of Vienna, the Austrian Habsburgs and the Romanov czars of Russia proved more than a match for the Ottomans in eastern Europe. The Habsburgs took a substantial chunk of the northern Balkans, including Hungary and Transylvania, away from the Turks. The Russians, particularly under Catherine the Great in the later eighteenth century, pushed down to the northern shores of the Black Sea in the Crimea. They even forced the straits linking the Black and Mediterranean seas, bringing Istanbul itself temporarily within range of Russian naval guns. By 1800, Russia seemed quite capable of overwhelming Turkey entirely.

That Russia did not achieve this goal during the nineteenth century was due more to pressure from other European powers than to the dwindling strength of the Ottomans. Turkey was throughout the nineteenth century "the sick man of Europe," ghoulishly observed by Western powers waiting for their shares of the once vast Ottoman inheritance.

The internal decay of the Ottoman Empire was less spectacular but no less inexorable than its decline as a great power. The two were closely related, of course. Turkey's domestic conservatism and decline were reflected in its failure to keep up militarily with the advances of its powerful Western rivals. Turkey, whose big guns had once breached the walls of Constantinople, fell far behind in field artillery during the seventeenth and eighteenth centuries. Its fleets clung to old-fashioned ramming and boarding tactics long after Europeans had turned their naval vessels into floating gun platforms capable of demolishing their foes without ever boarding them at all. The famed Janissary troops, allowed to marry and mingle with ordinary citizens, soon lost their fighting edge and became a sort of Turkish Praetorian Guard, deeply involved in the court politics of Istanbul.

Indeed, corruption sapped the vigor of the entire Ottoman political system in the seventeenth and eighteenth centuries. Weak sultans more interested in enjoying than in running the empire surrendered authority to their grand viziers. Some of these chief ministers were effective rulers, like the Kiuprili clan mentioned above, but all of them used power to feather their own nests. *Begs* and *pashas* in the provinces and provincial cities followed this example. Military commanders who could no longer be rewarded with new conquests milked the sultan's own subjects instead. A regime envied in sixteenth-century Europe for efficiency and justice became by the nineteenth a byword for corruption.

Economic problems also afflicted the aging empire. There were some advances, notably the great increase in cash-crop agriculture and food production brought about by the introduction of corn and tobacco from the Americas. But manufacturing, dominated by a conservative guild system, did not keep up—a fatal mistake as the Industrial Revolution began in Europe. Fortunes were made in money lending and through political chicanery, but solid economic progress was neglected.

Division also beset the multinational Ottoman Empire. Various nationalities and religious groups made special arrangements with Istanbul. Greek Orthodox Christians, Jews, Armenians, and others were in effect ruled by their own authorities under the sultan. This tolerance, a virtue in the days of Suleiman, became a decided drawback as later sultans lost the respect of those they ruled.

By the early 1800s, the possibility of fragmentation of the empire was thus as real as that of Russian conquest. Russia had already declared itself official protector of the Christian subjects of the Ottomans. All the southern provinces, from Morocco to Egypt and Arabia, were autonomous or independent. Early in the nineteenth century, the Balkan states of Serbia and Greece successfully rebelled against their Turkish overlords.

The sun that rose over Istanbul still glinted on the masts and spars of the many ships thronging the Golden Horn, flooded the courts of splendid palaces, gilded the domes and minarets of ancient mosques. But the sultans

were weak, European traders were many and rich, and the spirit of the Western Enlightenment was penetrating even this far east by the year 1800 of the Christian calendar.

SAFAVID PERSIA BECOMES A COCKPIT

Safavid Persia had reached its apogee, as we have seen, slightly later than Ottoman Turkey, under Shah Abbas I (1571–1629). Abbas ruled an empire the size of present-day Iran, large enough to fill a sizable chunk of the western United States today. Under Abbas, the Safavids turned back both Ottoman and central Asian invasions. They also made their capital, Isfahan, one of the most beautiful cities in the world.

The century following Abbas's death, however, was not so splendid.

The seeds of Safavid decay were perhaps planted deep in the brilliant Persian dynasty from the beginning. The warrior tradition of *ghazi* princes smouldered always beneath the cultivated surfaces of beautiful Isfahan, finding violent expression in the many wars of the Safavid period. The militant Shiite spirit was central to the national

ASIAN EMPIRES OF THE EIGHTEENTH AND NINETEENTH CENTURIES

Map legend:
- Ottoman Empire, 1699
- Mogul Empire, 1700
- Manchu Empire, 1796
- Territory lost to Russia
- Territory lost to Austria-Hungary
- Territory lost to Britain
- Dutch territory
- Territory lost to France
- Boundry of Islamic Zone, 1699

ATLANTIC OCEAN
GREAT BRITAIN
British
Dutch
NETHERLANDS
AUSTRIA-HUNGARY
RUSSIA
Black Sea
Caspian Sea
OTTOMAN
Mediterranean Sea
EMPIRE
Serbia (Independent, 1804)
Greece (Independent, 1830)
SINKIANG
Extent of China in 1664
CHINA
MOGUL EMPIRE
PACIFIC OCEAN
INDIAN
OCEAN
British
Dutch
DUTCH EAST INDIES
British
Dutch

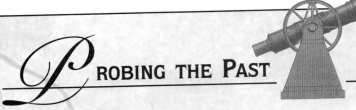

PROBING THE PAST

"*The Ottoman Empire was in an even more disadvantageous position, for the secularist and rationalist ideals of enlightened despotism which inspired and strengthened Russian administration had a precisely opposite effect in Turkey, where official identification with Islam and true religion made secularism as suspect as Christianity itself. Yet Russian and Austrian successes, French theorists, and (after 1789) French actions too, all presented Ottoman officials with a challenge increasingly difficult to dodge. If Allah ruled the world, why did he award victory to Christian dogs, untrue even to their own faith? Within the frame of Moslem piety there was no intellectually satisfactory answer to this question, for from Islam's early days Allah's favor and success in battle had been closely linked.*

The result, therefore, was that among a small but important educated class, secret doubts and inner uncertainty gained ground, yet were denied any straightforward overt expression by the fact that to remain a Turk at all a man had to remain Moslem; and the Sacred Law of Islam, massive and imposing, remained totally incompatible with the secularist rationalism of the European enlightenment. . . .

Head-on collision could only be escaped by systematically neglecting the new ideas swarming out of France, and many Ottoman officials doubtless were able to live out their lives in blissful and more or less deliberate ignorance. Yet such an elementary defense against subversive ideas was barely tolerable in a state that desperately and increasingly required drastic military and administrative reform if it were to survive at all.

The decay of the Ottoman Empire, in short, set in sharply and decisively after the mid-eighteenth century."

Professor William H. McNeill of the University of Chicago, the dean of American world history studies today, is perhaps best known for his Pulitzer Prize-winning study of <u>The Rise of the West</u> (1963). In this excerpt from <u>Europe's Steppe Frontier,</u> however, he looks at the decline of what had been one of the great powers of the East, the Ottoman Empire.

Professor McNeill emphasizes the conflict of modern Western ideas with Islamic beliefs. What effect does he think the former had on educated Muslims? How does he think Western military victories affected the conflict of ideas? Why does he see Muslim efforts to ignore these subversive doctrines as counterproductive in "a state that desperately . . . required . . . military and administrative reform"?

William H. McNeill, <u>Europe's Steppe Frontier, 1500–1800</u> (Chicago: University of Chicago Press, 1964), pp. 189–190.

identity of Safavid Persia from the days of the founder Ismail, but that spirit also made the Shiite state an outlaw among the Sunnite majority of Muslim lands. The intrusion of Europeans, finally, was encouraged by even the great Abbas, who wanted their technological and military skills. But those same Western powers would contribute largely to the collapse of the empire into a cockpit of feuding peoples in the eighteenth and nineteenth centuries.

The long wars between the Shiite Safavids and the Sunnite Ottomans turned against Persia after Shah Abbas's death. His successors retired to their harems and the sophisticated pleasures of Isfahan. But persecution of Sunnite minorities in Persia still exploded from time to time. And the English and Portuguese who had competed for influence and trade in Persia were joined in the later seventeenth century by French, Dutch, Spanish, and Russians, the last a particular threat due to Russia's location just across Persia's northern border.

In the early eighteenth century, a Sunnite rebellion in Afghanistan severed the eastern portions of the empire from Persia. In the 1720s, Afghan invaders overthrew the Safavids and precipitated an orgy of massacres and persecutions in Isfahan and elsewhere. Persian independence was restored by the militant Nadir Shah in the 1730s, and this great Persian war leader soon overran both Afghanistan and northwestern India, compelling even the Indian Moguls to pay ransom. But Afghanistan then produced its own great general, and the whole area of modern Iran, Afghanistan, and Pakistan sank into a welter of unending wars.

Moving dexterously around the fringes of the carnage, vying for influence and encouraging the combatants, were the advance guard of European imperialism. Europeans sold the guns and powder on which all sides depended. Russians pushed down from the north: there were Cossack raids in the 1660s, Peter the Great seized Persian territory in the 1720s, and a long competition with Britain for spheres of influence in Iran filled the following century. The British, meanwhile, pressed for Persian trade and considered influence at Isfahan essential for protecting their growing imperial involvement in India.

Shahs of Iran signed treaties, accepted subsidies and advisors, and continued their squabbles with their Afghan rivals on into the nineteenth century. What had once been a great empire, skillful at manipulating client princes, became itself increasingly a puppet of European powers.

MOGUL INDIA CRUMBLES

Akbar the Great (1542–1605), the most celebrated of the Mogul emperors, had ruled not only most of modern India but also today's Pakistan, Bangladesh, and part of Afghanistan. As noted in Chapter 26, Akbar's toleration of other Indian faiths and his cultivation of Indian civilization made him popular with the majority of Hindu Indians as well as with his Muslim subjects.

After his death at the beginning of the seventeenth century, there was Muslim power in India still, but never a ruler as popular. And even the political power of Islam in India would disintegrate drastically in the eighteenth century.

The most powerful Mogul ruler of the 1600s was in fact the least popular of all the Moguls: Aurangzeb (1658–1707). Aurangzeb imprisoned his own father and thrust three brothers aside to seize the throne. He reigned long, sometimes cruelly, and generally intolerantly. He persecuted the Hindu majority, pulling down Hindu temples and making it increasingly difficult for any but Muslims to rise in his service. He carried on the military tradition of the Moguls by driving deep into the south, until at his death the Mogul realm encompassed almost the whole of the subcontinent.

Aurangzeb's long reign, contemporary with that of Louis XIV in Europe, was rendered illustrious in seventeenth-century eyes by these many victories. It was also unique in its effort to cut back on courtly magnificence and expenses. But the emperor's reputation for violence and unscrupulousness tarnished all the rest. The traditional history of the Indian countryside attributes everything glorious and admired from these centuries to Akbar the Great, everything dark and terrible to the reign of Aurangzeb.

After 1700, disintegration advanced rapidly. The decay of Mogul power carried India, so seldom politically united, rapidly back to the more familiar plurality of feuding states. And from political disintegration, the subcontinent drifted more rapidly than any other part of the Muslim center into the imperial orbit of the expanding West.

A prime center of discord even during Aurangzeb's time were the Marathas, the Hindu hill people of the Deccan plateau to the south. United by the famous Hindu leader Sivaji in the seventeenth century, the Marathas fought a long guerrilla war against the Moguls. Another center of Indian power lay among the Sikhs in the Northwest. A warrior people like the medieval Rajputs, the Sikhs rejected caste and priestly hierarchy, got along with Muslims, and soon had their own state in the Punjab.

Foreign pressure also mounted on the Moguls. Nadir Shah's Persian invasion in the 1730s resoundingly defeated Mogul armies and looted Delhi itself. Subsequent attacks by Afghan rulers further weakened the hold of the once mighty dynasty.

The greatest long-term threat, however, came from the growing numbers of Europeans gathering in trading cities and isolated forts around the fringes of India. By the eighteenth century, the field had narrowed to the British and the French, and after 1763 the British, victorious in the Seven Years' War, were effectively alone in the field.

We have noticed the beginnings of Great Britain's Indian empire above. The British East India Company came to trade in the 1600s. Its officers became involved in princely politics in order to protect their interests. They ended in the 1700s by leading armies of *sepoy* Indian troops and signing political alliances with almost all the important *nabobs* (local governors) and independent *rajas* on the subcontinent.

In the 1790s the British crown assumed dual directorship with the company. By 1800 British dependencies stretched the length of the Ganges Valley, across northern India from the fringes of the Punjab to Bengal, and down the east coast to the southern tip of the subcontinent.

The once mightly Moguls now had little more than formal claim on the allegiance of their governors and subordinate princes. Most Indian potentates received British "advisors" at their courts, depended on British-officered *sepoy* regiments, and traded liberally in silks and cottons and spices, indigo and precious stones with Britain. The crown and the company in London still railed against political entanglements and costly wars. But in fact the company's "servants" had become the most powerful single force in India as the nineteenth century began.

THE FAR EAST TURNS INWARD

EAST ASIA CUT OFF FROM THE FLOW OF HISTORY

The story of East Asia during the seventeenth and eighteenth centuries is rather different from that of the Muslim center of Eurasia. Both Manchu China and Tokugawa Japan were in many ways very successful dynasties. But China under its Manchu conquerors and Japan under the unifying Tokugawa shogunate both sought to isolate themselves from the outside world during this period. The result of their efforts to cut East Asia off from the flow of history was a slowing of social change and a relative decline by comparison with the dynamic culture of the West.

The next two sections will outline the Manchu conquest in the earlier 1600s and the following century and a half of stability but relative stagnation in China. The following sections will sketch the resurgence of centralized government in Japan under the Tokugawa shoguns around 1600 and the deliberate isolation of the island kingdom that followed. Throughout, the emphasis will fall on the turning inward of these two great civilizations in their last centuries of independent development.

The degree of East Asian isolation, as we shall see, was astonishingly complete. As late as the 1790s, when the British Empire already spanned the world, a British envoy to China was ferried upriver to Beijing under a broad banner identifying him as a "Barbarian Bearing Tribute."[1] The Manchu emperor of that time, who was an extremely cultivated person, had only the haziest fairy-tale impression of Britain in the reign of George III as a sea kingdom somewhere far away to the west.

THE MANCHU CONQUEST OF CHINA

The Ming dynasty, which had replaced a regime of Mongolian conquerors in the fourteenth century, fell to a wave of Manchurian invaders in the seventeenth. The end of the Ming era was preceded by the familiar symptoms of dynastic decline: weak emperors, corruption at court and in the administration, drought, famine, and peasant rebellion. The Mandate of Heaven, China's equivalent of the divine right to rule, had clearly been withdrawn by the early 1600s.

Into this decaying order plunged the vigorous new Manchu armies from the north. Nurhachi (1559–1626), the founder of the Manchu state, had welded the Manchurian tribes into a powerful force, combining Chinese bureaucracy with his own system of military organization. The Manchu banner armies, named for the colors

of their distinctive standards, were built on companies of three hundred men and included Mongol and Chinese units as well as Manchurians. A total of sixteen banner-man armies—275 companies—participated in the invasion of China two decades after Nurhachi's death.

The conquest was prepared and led by two of Nurhachi's sons, Abahai and Dorgon, between the 1620s and the 1640s. Their success in this unlikely project—victory over a nation twenty times their size—was facilitated by a late-Ming peasant rebellion and by the collaboration of a Ming general. The last Ming emperor committed suicide in a capital beset by peasant rebels, and the Ming commander at the Great Wall opened the gates to the Manchu invaders. The Manchu, or Qing ("Pure"), dynasty was formally proclaimed in 1644.

South China held out longer, as it had against the Mongols. Chinese generals carved out short-lived kingdoms for themselves in the south. Port cities and seagoing resistance forces fought to the end. But by the 1680s, all China was in the hands of the invaders from the north. The Mandate of Heaven had passed, as it usually did even in this most stable of nations, in blood and violence.

The Qing dynasty (1644–1912) was to be China's last. Autocratic and conservative in domestic affairs, the Manchus of the seventeenth and eighteenth centuries also brought growth, prosperity, and further expansion of China's already vast realm. It was only after 1800 that, with sickening suddenness, the decline began.

Two great and long-lived Manchu emperors divide the history of the century and a half between 1644 and 1800 between them: the Kangxi emperor in the seventeenth century and the Qianlong emperor in the eighteenth. Between them these two Chinese rulers outlived three Louis in France, the later Stuarts and the first three Georges in Britain, and almost the entire rise of the Hohenzollerns in Prussia. And their accomplishments were at least as great.

Kangxi (1661–1722), the longest-reigning emperor in Chinese history, was the ideal monarch. A vigorous outdoorsman, hunter, and leader of armies, like his Manchu ancestors, he was also a Chinese scholar and intellectual and an administrator of endless industry and rigor. At the end of his sixty-year reign, the northern invaders were firmly seated on the throne of China.

Kangxi ruled firmly and fairly, plowing through huge quantities of official reports daily. He preserved most of the Ming structure of government, pairing Chinese provincial governors with Manchu banner-men, combining continuity with the new leadership. He cut taxes and forbade further confiscation of Chinese lands by Manchus once pacification was complete.

As commander in chief of the armies, Kangxi first completed the conquest of South China and then turned his attention to expanding Chinese power westward, into central Asia. He defeated the western Mongols, an ancient threat to China. He turned back the Russian Cossacks,

---

[1]Roy MacGregor-Hastie, *The Red Barbarians* (London: Pan Books, 1961), p. 11.

point men for Russia's own expansion eastward to the Pacific. He imposed a pro-Chinese Dalai Lama in Tibet.

As a scholar, Kangxi sponsored a famous dictionary, yet another gigantic encyclopedia, and an official history of the preceding dynasty. He patronized artists and philosophers. He had himself painted, surrounded by art objects, with a Chinese landscape painting and his own portrait on the wall behind him.

A contemporary of Aurangzeb in India and Louis XIV in Europe, Emperor Kangxi combined the Mogul's military prowess with the Sun King's dedication to the art of governance. He has been called not only the longest-reigning but the most successful of Chinese emperors.

Qianlong (1735–1796), Kangxi's grandson, led the Middle Kingdom to new levels of political strength, size, population, prosperity, and international power. Since many of the accomplishments of his reign represent the apogee of the dynasty, they will be developed at length in the survey of Qing society that follows.

Qianlong's personal contribution was particularly visible in his magnificent style of life and his extensive foreign conquests. Under his direction, Manchu Chinese armies pushed westward, as they had in Han, Tang, and Mongol times. Chinese sovereignty was expanded once more across the wastes of central Asia as far as the towering Pamirs.

At home, prosperity and government revenues grew, so that Qianlong was able to live in as grand a style as any European monarch. He built immense palaces and undertook magnificent royal progresses across the empire. His patronage of literature and learning produced a famous collection, *The Complete Library of Four Treasuries,* which amounted in the end to 36,000 volumes!

Qianlong's suspicious nature and absolutist bent led him to censor as well as to sponsor scholarly activity, and he suppressed any book he deemed anti-Manchu. But his splendid style cloaked a work schedule as relentless as Kangxi's, beginning before dawn and exhausting his secretaries. Qianlong piously abdicated in 1796 rather than reign longer than his illustrious grandfather. But his powerful personality continued to dominate the government until death finally stilled his fierce energies in the last year of the century.

THE QING DYNASTY: DEVELOPMENT AND DECLINE

The power of the Manchus, in numbers a small percentage of the population they had conquered, was imposed on China in a number of ways. Manchu garrisons were stationed strategically across the country. Large tracts of land were set aside to provide revenues for the Qing emperors and for Manchu bannermen. Manchus were forbidden to marry Chinese; Manchu women were discouraged from binding their feet in the Chinese style. All Chinese men, by contrast, were required to shave all but a single braided pigtail from their heads, a symbol of accep-

tance of the overlordship of the Manchus, who wore their hair this way.

The political organization of China, however, has often been described as a dyarchy, a dual Chinese-Manchu government—and in many ways it looks more Chinese than Manchu. The trend of a historically autocratic government toward royal absolutism, begun under the Mongols and the Ming, continued under the Qing. Manchu emperors made all major decisions and many minor ones personally. But all important imperial bureaus were headed by two officials, one Manchu and one Chinese. Government boards were half Manchu and half Chinese in membership. As noted above, Chinese provincial governors were matched with Manchu governors-general.

Below the provincial level, however, all officials remained Chinese. Local magistrates and village headmen were chosen on the basis of local prestige, as in earlier periods. For the average peasant, to whom the Son of Heaven had always been a half-mythical being in a far-off capital, foreign rule can have made little difference.

One thing many must have noticed over most of the 1600s and 1700s, however, was the flourishing state of the economy under the Manchus.

Agriculture was basic, as it had always been in China. New types of rice, improvements in irrigation and fertilization, and new crops such as corn and sweet potatoes boosted food production dramatically. Traditional handicraft industries grew steadily—pottery, silk, cotton, mining, and metalwork—practiced by ancient guilds in many parts of China. Domestic trade reached new highs, and foreign trade, though comparatively small, produced an inflow of gold and silver steady enough to warm the heart of a European mercantilist.

A further result of economic prosperity was a continuing growth in population, which probably doubled over these two centuries to approximately 300 million by 1800. Some of these teeming millions began to emigrate to Southeast Asia, the core of the overseas Chinese minorities of later centuries. Others, unable to leave, felt the growing pressure of population on even a burgeoning food supply. This Malthusian problem for all modern states was noticed by a Chinese scholar about the time that Parson Malthus detected it in late eighteenth-century Britain.

A final testimony to the success of the Qing emperors during the 1600s and 1700s was the further expansion of the empire. The Manchus brought Manchuria and its suzerainty over Korea with them to China. Once and for all they broke the power of the Mongols, the last of the great steppe nomads, by conquering Inner Mongolia and opening Outer Mongolia to Chinese commercial exploitation. They reconquered and finally incorporated the huge western lands of Xinjiang into the empire. They set up a protectorate over Tibet, garrisoned central Asia all the way to the Pamirs, and collected tribute from Vietnam, Burma, and other East and Southeast Asian states.

Yet in many ways even the greatest of the Manchus

were inward-looking and conservative. As is so frequently the case, the seeds of their ultimate decline were there from the beginning.

To prove themselves more Chinese than the Chinese, the Manchu emperors encouraged the most conservative Confucianism. They stressed China's total self-sufficiency and supremacy, depicting their empire as the one truly civilized land in a barbarous world. Since they did not need the rest of the world, they did nothing to build a navy or a great merchant marine; the nation that had put huge fleets to sea in the fifteenth century was now left far behind in shipbuilding and naval development. Scholars and literatti also had no use for mechanical things, and so the nation that had invented printing, gunpowder, and the compass slid steadily further behind in industrial development also.

Contact with the West, reestablished under the later Mings, developed uncertainly and then declined under the Manchus. Jesuit missionaries were welcomed at court in the seventeenth century, mostly for their skills in Western arts and sciences. But later missionaries, who refused to compromise their opposition to Chinese traditional ancestor worship and the veneration of Confucius, were proscribed in the 1720s. Trade developed relatively freely in early Manchu times but was narrowly limited to a section of the southern port of Canton in the later 1700s. Manchu emperors might enjoy learning to play exotic instruments such as the clavichord or dressing up a few court ladies in colorful Western costumes, but they saw little importance in European trade.

When the great decline in Manchu fortunes began around 1800, the Middle Kingdom would pay dearly for having ignored the chance to learn more valuable things from the West while there was time.

THE TOKUGAWA SHOGUNS SEIZE POWER IN JAPAN

The Japanese islands were much more open to foreign influences than China was in the early part of this period. In Japan also, a strong new dynasty came to power in the seventeenth century—not foreign conquerors but the unifying Tokugawa shoguns. But in Japan too, an increasingly conservative regime had rejected foreign influences and turned inward before the seventeenth century was over.

Japan, which had learned so much from China in centuries past, was initially much more willing than the Middle Kingdom to deal with the West. From this interaction came a transformation of Japanese feudalism and the reemergence of a strong government—which, paradoxically, proceeded to turn its back upon the West once more.

In the sixteenth century the wealthier Japanese barons, or *daimyo*, were glad to have Portuguese and later English, Dutch, and other merchants come with their goods. To attract the traders, some *daimyo* welcomed Jesuit and other missionaries, who were soon making more converts in Japan than in China. Most important of all in that war-torn age, Western muskets and cannon transformed the art of war in samurai Japan. Firearms gave the military edge to *daimyo* who could build companies of musketeers, artillery, and the huge new castles needed to resist these military innovations in the hands of others.

The suppression of feudal warfare and the political reunification that followed were the work of a series of three of these *daimyo* barons clever enough to exploit both the old feudal rules and the new military circumstances to their own advantage.

Their names were Oda Nobunaga, Hideyoshi, and Tokugawa Ieyasu. These three men shared a knack for manipulating the new weapons with tactical daring. They were also masters of the traditional methods of feudal alliance-building through distribution of rewards, political marriages, and political intrigue. All three first moved to establish themselves as protector of the ceremonial emperor at the old capital at Kyoto, then turned to overcoming opposition from rival nobles in the countryside.

Oda Nobunaga (1534–1582) established a powerful *daimyo* alliance in the large central island of Honshu, moved on to Kyoto, and overthrew the Ashikaga shogunate, by then moribund and ripe for dispatching. Hideyoshi (1536–1598), a rude peasant who had risen to general's rank under Nobunaga, is usually considered the real unifier of Japan. Hideyoshi expanded Nobunaga's baronial connection to include all the chief *daimyo* in the island empire. He disarmed the peasantry, encouraged trade with the West, and dreamed megalomaniacal—and fruitless—dreams of conquering China itself. Tokugawa Ieyasu (ruled 1603–1616), a vassal of Hideyoshi's, outfought all rivals for his master's legacy at the great battle of Sekigahara in 1600 and was officially named shogun three years later.

Under Ieyasu and his son and grandson, the Tokugawa shogunate was firmly established. They would wield power for the next two and a half centuries (1603–1868). Like the Manchu emperors of China, the Tokugawa shoguns were in many ways a very successful dynasty. But the Tokugawa, like the Manchus, made what became the fatal conservative error of trying to turn their back upon the roaring tide of change.

Typical of this tendency was the great event of the immediate postcentralization period: the closing of Japan to Western influences.

By the early 1600s there were Portuguese, Spanish, English, and Dutch merchants in Japan. There were Jesuit and Franciscan missionaries and almost a third of a million Christian Japanese. There was much more interaction between the two cultures in Japan than in China: Jesuits learned the Zen tea ceremony, and fashionable Japanese wore crucifixes and smoked tobacco.

But the seventeenth-century Tokugawa shoguns grew suspicious of European imperialist ambitions. They began to see Christianity as a subversive ideology. Then official persecution set off a short-lived Japanese Christian revolt in one section of the islands. The government reacted with massive martyrdoms that destroyed all but a tiny underground remnant of Christianity in Japan.

Traders also became suspect. One Western trading power after another was expelled, until by the 1640s—a century after the first Portuguese had arrived—only a single Dutch trading post on an island in Nagasaki harbor remained to connect Japan with the Western world.

The fundamental conservatism of the Tokugawa shogunate extended to domestic as well as foreign affairs. Determined efforts were made throughout the seventeenth and eighteenth centuries to revive such traditional elements of Japanese culture as the samurai virtues, class structure, and the agrarian pattern of life.

The most famous such effort to turn the clock back was made by the eighteenth-century shogun Yoshimune (1716–1745). Yoshimune was a model of ancient Japanese rectitude. He issued many decrees on moral and social behavior and urged simplicity, decency, and the military code of the samurai upon his people. Yoshimune's economic reforms, intended to favor agriculture at the expense of trade, succeeded in triggering a major commercial depression, but this has not damaged his reputation as one of the most virtuous of the shoguns.

THE TOKUGAWA SHOGUNATE: TRANSFORMATION AND TENSION

The Tokugawa shogunate actually saw an odd amalgam during its first two centuries: an intensely conservative, still semifeudal political regime presiding over a boom-ing urban, commercial economy. Out of this unlikely combination evolved the unique culture of Tokugawa Japan.

The political system of the Tokugawa shoguns was built on the feudal order out of which they had risen. Tokugawa "centralized feudalism" was a structure of power based on the huge landholdings of the shoguns and the substantial allotments of the puppet emperors and the shogun's vassal *daimyo*. The rest of society was fixed by law in a rigid system of classes—peasants forbidden to leave the land, samurai prohibited any but military or administrative careers. There was government support for the traditional agrarian economy. There was also repeated legislation against conspicuous consumption by people of the lower classes. The Tokugawa thus seemed totally dedicated to preserving old Japan in amber, an unchanging perfection in a changing world.

In fact, however, the Japanese islands were in the grip of rapid economic progress during these centuries. The resulting population growth, urban development, and cultural innovation had few points of contact with the conservative ideals of the Tokugawa shoguns.

Agriculture, encouraged by the government, developed steadily. Acreage under cultivation doubled under the impact of new fertilizers and seeds, double cropping, and other improvements in agricultural techniques. The increase in the amount of food available led in turn to considerable growth in population, from perhaps 18 million in 1600 to 30 million in the eighteenth century.

The growth of trade, though it was largely domestic, was even more spectacular, constituting a commercial revolution in Japan during the seventeenth century. Low taxes, a lack of government intervention, and the gen-

In stately halls like this one in Kyoto, sixteenth- and seventeenth-century daymo received supporters and petitioners in splendor. The great noble's chair would be placed on the raised platform to the right. Incense might be burned in the open alcove at the far right, while behind the two central panels of the four in the center of the picture, guards would lurk. The painted screens and high, carved ceilings reflect the exalted status of the builders of the powerful Tokugawa shogunate in the decades around 1600. (Werner Forman Archives)

eral lack of interest in business on the part of the country's feudal and Confucian rulers left merchants free to grow as fast as they could. Urban development also contributed by concentrating large numbers of customers for merchants and artisans. Edo—later called Tokyo—reached a population of a million, and the commercial port of Osaka half that. The shoguns required the *daimyo* aristocracy to establish residences in Edo, the samurai collected there and in other cities, creating a growing demand for food, handicraft manufactures, and the luxury trades.

Out of these transformations and tensions in an island kingdom largely cut off from the world, a distinctly Japanese national character evolved. Buddhist and bushido traditions, love for art and culture going back to Heian times, the success-worshiping values of the new commercial world, and the pleasures of urban life mingled in Tokugawa Japan. The result was a Japanese temperament combining aesthetic sensibility with a martial sense of duty, a compulsive determination to live up to ancient standards, and an intense drive for personal success.

It was a character that could cling doggedly for hundreds of years to the outdated feudal ideals of the Tokugawa—and then throw itself with equal passion into the modernization and Westernization of Japan in the later nineteenth century. In the seventeenth and eighteenth centuries, however, it was the past that prevailed as Japan turned inward once more to shape its own soul in isolation from the larger world.

 # CULTURES OF A TWILIGHT AGE

A BACKWARD GLANCE

Only the narrowest Western vision could see cultural unity in the rich and varied civilizations of Asia. Even at the broadest stereotypical level, there is little similarity to be found among the crusading passions of Arabic Islam, the otherworldly acceptance of Hindu India, the scholarly humanism of the Confucian tradition, and the taut soldier's code of the samurai. The "Asia" that produced the Blue Mosque in Istanbul, Angkor Wat in Cambodia, and the Great Wall of China is surely more of a cultural smorgasbord than a unity.

During these centuries of decline and inward turning, however, a single note is struck again and again across the diverse cultures of the world's largest continent. It is a tone that may be described perhaps most simply as a backward glance.

The great cultures of the East were all firmly in place by early-modern times. They had evolved and changed since their foundations had first been laid down centuries or millennia before. But they were essentially accomplished by the seventeenth and eighteenth centuries. We speak of "traditional India," "traditional China" from then on, of civilizations whose main outlines are fixed and clear.

What remained was to comment on, to revive, to echo the great achievements of the past. In an Asia where the great centers of civilization were either crumbling away or withdrawing, that was precisely what happened.

New religions did not emerge—only sects. New art modeled itself upon old art, or otherwise reacted to the old masters. Philosophers were much more likely to be commentators on the ancient sages than original thinkers. The sciences were left with a shrug to the Westerners, who, as many Asians saw it, vulgarized everything they touched with the crudest of practical applications.

It was a culture of the twilight, art, and ideas conceived by ancient civilizations whose day was drawing to a close. A few examples of this culture of traditional Asia's waning centuries follow.

MUSLIMS AND HINDUS RETURN TO THE SOURCE

The Wahabi sect that emerged in the deserts of Arabia in the middle of the eighteenth century has at first glance little of a twilight feel about it. Flinty Arab fundamentalists, the Wahabis look more like Puritans building the new Jerusalem than a people at the end of an age. Their fundamentalist rigor was actually more than a backward glance: it was a wholehearted rush into the past, a pell-mell plunge back to Islam's beginnings.

The founder of the Wahabi sect, Muhammad ibn' Abdul-Wahab (1691–1787), preached a return to the teachings of the Koran and the Law, the most authentic Sunni traditions of the Prophet. Muslims, he declared, should live as Muhammad had taught them to, and nothing should come between the believer and submission to those fundamental teachings. With rigor worthy of a Martin Luther, Abdul-Wahab rejected all that had come since. The insights of Islam's golden age under the Arab caliphs, the mystical visions of the Sufis, all the accumulated wisdom of the Islamic community since Muhammad had to be rejected. Veneration of Muslim saints, broad interpretation of the Muslim Law, unsanctioned habits such as the drinking of wine—all were cast aside in that long, eager backward reach to the sources of Islam.

Deep in the desert fastnesses of Arabia, in the very area where the Prophet had once walked the earth, the Wahabis lived their vigorous, puritanical faith. Abdul-Wahab accepted the patronage of the ambitious house of Saud—the rulers of Saudi Arabia today—and Wahabism spread rapidly across the peninsula. Wahabis soon dominated both the Muslim holy cities of Mecca and Medina, and pilgrims carried word of the new sect back with them to all parts of the Islamic world.

An Egyptian invasion of Arabia put an end to the worldly expansion of the Wahabi movement. But the reputation and influence of the desert sect spread to pious

Muslims as far away as Ottoman Turkey and even India. The Wahabis were *living* as Muslims had in the days of the Prophet! Forbidding as its puritanical rigor might be, this fundamentalist return to the source could not but be appealing in a bewildering time when history seemed to be slowly turning its back on the followers of Allah.

The Rajput painting of seventeenth- and eighteenth-century India, in its very different way, also cast that long, wistful backward glance.

The Rajput painters are normally considered artists in a popular tradition, to be contrasted with the sophisticated realism of the art of the Mogul courts. They actually worked at the courts of provincial princes in central India or in the foothills of the Himalayas. They painted many subjects in a variety of styles. But in both subject and style, there is once more that sense of turning back to the great traditions of the past.

Popular Rajput subjects, for instance, included the heroic deeds of Rajput warriors in earlier centuries; passages from the ancient Indian epics, the *Mahabharata* and the *Ramayana;* and episodes from the timeless myths of Vishnu and Shiva. Rajput artists also painted scenes to illustrate musical modes and the many forms of love—but the latter at least was also a well-established Hindu tradition.

Style, essentially ahistorical, is a harder thing to read in historical terms. But there are elements of earlier schools in the work of most of these painters of the lesser courts. There is a refusal to change, to keep up with the first European influences creeping into the art of the great *rajas*. There is in the painting of one court in Rajastan, where the divine lovers Krishna and Radha were particularly revered, a twilight loveliness that transcends time and space, "a fragile elegance and a wan, neurasthenic refinement that are like an echo of the beauty of Ikhnaton's queen,"[2] the swan-necked Nefertiti—doomed too, like the art of the Rajput princes.

HAN LEARNING AND GENROKU CULTURE

Chinese thought and art had always managed a delicate balance of traditionalism and originality. Under the Manchus, culture seemed to career off to wild extremes, reacting with jarring extravagance to a powerfully felt sense of past greatness and present inadequacy.

Some aspects of Chinese culture continued largely as before. Confucius continued to be revered, sumptuous palaces to be built, immense quantities of traditional chinaware to be produced by government works for export. But scholarship exhibited the odd dichotomy indicated above: there was passion for "Han learning," the wisdom of two thousand years before, yet this same period saw a wave of literary detective work that actually challenged the authenticity of some of the most admired Confucian

---

[2]Benjamin Rowland, *The Art and Architecture of India* (New York: Penguin Books, 1981), p. 350.

classics. Painters were divided into two rather different camps: the "orthodox," who followed stylistically in the footsteps of their predecessors, and the "individualists" and "eccentrics," who reacted violently against all earlier schools. Orthodox painters did beautiful work in traditions that went back to the Song. The eccentrics produced wildly assymetrical or whimsical paintings drawn with blunted brushes or—in one case—even with bare hands!

Imitation, however, was probably more common than iconoclasm in this ambivalent preoccupation with the past. The most famous work of literature produced in Manchu times was also China's most loved novel, Cao Xuehqin's *Dream of the Red Chamber*. It is the story of a great family in decline. Generational conflicts, powerful female characters, and the intricate life of a traditional Chinese family combine against a background of social decay and profound Buddhist and Daoist devotion. *The Dream of the Red Chamber* thus offers a moving vision of yet another Eurasian culture of the twilight centuries.

Two geishas, skilled and cultured Japanese courtesans of two centuries ago, go through their dressing ritual in this colored Japanese workblock print by Kitagawa Utamaro, a famous eighteenth-century artist. Utamaro was widely admired for his depiction of beautiful women. (Kitagawa Utamaro. "Oiran Yososoi Seated at Her Toilet." Woodblock. 14-4/5 × 19-15/16 inches. The Metropolitan Museum of Art, Rogers Fund)

Tokugawa Japanese culture has its aristocratic casting back to better times too. In particular the court of the figurehead emperor at Kyoto continued to develop a delicate sensibility that harked back centuries to Japan's medieval Heian culture. The shoguns trumpeted the virtues of more recent samurai times. But in Japan, almost uniquely, there was also a surge of originality and vigor under the Tokugawa. It appeared in the new commercial cities, especially in Edo and Osaka, and its finest flowering came in the half century around 1700. It is usually called Genroku culture.

Genroku culture blossomed most brilliantly in the urban subculture of playboys and prostitutes, popular entertainment, gambling, and bohemianism. It created *haiku* poetry, *kabuki* theater, and the Japanese print—an array of cultural innovation that would distinguish any age.

Haiku verse, with its deceptive simplicity—seventeen syllables arranged in three lines—deliberately leaves much to the reader's imagination. Typically a series of images drawn from nature is presented in order to stir up a unique complex of associations and echoes in the mind of each reader. Evocative, haunting, sometimes funny, *haiku* can stimulate a sense of spiritual depth as great as that of a misty Song landscape. *Haiku* verse has tempted not only Japanese, but foreigners in many languages since.

Kabuki theater, which attracted wildly enthusiastic crowds in Tokugawa Edo, has proved less readily exportable. Begun by a troop of women actors and dancers in the early 1600s, *kabuki* evolved into a popular form of pageantry with gaudy costumes, dazzling scenery, and extravagant passions unleashed in traditional stylized movements. In time, male actors took over the productions. But the most admired of these actors were always the ones who, through a lifetime of training, specialized in playing the female parts.

The Japanese print, finally, is familiar to every Western admirer of the work of Toulouse-Lautrec and other nineteenth-century French painters who were profoundly influenced by the Japanese form. Done in four colors, these wood-block prints were the quintessence of Genroku culture. Beginning as illustrations for "pillow books" (sex manuals), wood-block prints developed as pictures of famous courtesans, theatrical scenes, and representations of city life. These eighteenth-century Japanese prints breathe the sophistication of the very unfeudal pleasure capitals of Tokugawa Japan.

SUMMARY

While Western power grew, the great empires of the East either declined or withdrew into isolation during the seventeenth, eighteenth, and early nineteenth centuries. For the first time, Asia lost the position of parity with or superiority to Europe that the larger continent had enjoyed throughout history.

In the Middle East, the Ottoman Empire ceased to be a threat to Europe, lost territory to Austria and Russia, and sank into political corruption and industrial decay. In Persia, the endless Shiite wars led to fragmentation, the successful secession of Afghanistan, and increasing British and Russian influence in Isfahan. Mogul India also felt the divisive force of religious difference—in this instance, Hindu revolts against Muslim persecution—and the pressure of growing European power, which climaxed in the ascendency of the British East India Company after the defeat of the French in 1763.

In East Asia, powerful new dynasties dominated both China and Japan in the seventeenth century. But both the Manchu emperors and the Tokugawa shoguns adopted isolationist policies toward the West, which, in the long run, did not pay. The long-lived emperors Kangxi and Qienlong led China to renewed power and still greater prosperity under the Manchus. But their intense Confucian conservatism and their rejection of Western influences left China ill prepared for the unprecedented Western onslaught that was to come in the nineteenth century.

The Tokugawa shogun Ieyasu, who seized power in 1600, brought an end to centuries of civil strife. He and his successors presided over a prosperous economy and a sophisticated urban culture. But the Tokugawas also preached conservative *bushido* traditions and expelled the Europeans who had found a foothold in their country.

In withdrawal or decay, Asia drew heavily on its past artistic and intellectual achievements during these centuries. Thus, Arab Muslims turned to Wahabi fundamentalism, and Rajput painters drew on India's ancient myths and epics for themes and subjects. Manchu Chinese culture went to extremes of conservatism and eccentricity. Only in Japan did cultural development take a dynamic new direction, in the sophisticated urban art and literature of Genroku culture.

SUGGESTED READING

ADSHEAD, S. A. M. *China in World History.* New York: St. Martin's Press, 1988. Relations between China and the rest of the world, from ecology and trade to the exchange of ideas.

BELLAH, R. N. *Tokugawa Religion: The Values of Pre-Industrial Japan.* Glencoe, Ill.: Free Press, 1957. Religion and value systems in traditional Japan.

DAVIS, F. *The Ottoman Lady: A Social History from 1718*

to 1918. New York: Greenwood, 1986. Analysis of the life-styles of upper class women under the later Ottomans.

EASTMAN, L. *Family, Field, and Ancestors: Constancy and Change in China's Social and Economic History, 1550–1949.* New York: Oxford University Press, 1988. Readable introduction to recent research and scholarly controversies on China's changing society from Ming and Manchu times to the coming of Communism.

HABIB, I. *Agrarian System of Mughal India, 1556–1707.* New York: Asia Publishing House, 1963. Agricultural land holding.

IRVINE, W. *Later Mughals* (2 vols.). Calcutta: M. C. Sarkar and Sons, 1921–1922. Old, but still useful. For the completion of the story of the decline of the dynasty, see J. Sarkar's scholarly *Fall of the Mughal Empire* (4 vols.) (Calcutta: M. C. Sarkar, 1932–1950).

KAHN, H. L. *Monarchy in the Emperor's Eyes: Image and Reality in the Ch'ien-lung Reign.* Cambridge: Harvard University Press, 1971. Perhaps the greatest ruler of Manchu China.

KEENE, D. *World within Walls: Japanese Literature of the Pre-Modern Era, 1600–1867.* New York: Holt, Rinehart & Winston, 1976. Authoritative and elegantly written history of Japanese literature in the Tokugawa era. For haiku poetry, see H. G. Henderson, *An Introduction to Haiku* (Garden City, N.Y.: Doubleday, 1958).

KESSLER, L. *K'ang-hsi and the Consolidation of Ch'ing Rule, 1661–1684.* Chicago: University of Chicago Press, 1976.

LANE, R. *Masters of the Japanese Print—Their World and Their Work.* Garden City, N.Y.: Doubleday, 1962. Japan's most imitated contribution to the graphic arts.

LEWIS, B. "Some Reflections on the Decline of the Ottoman Empire," in C. M. Cipolla, ed., *The Economic Decline of Empires.* London: Methuen, 1970. Interesting reflections on the economic aspects of Ottoman decline.

LUDDEN, D. *Peasant History in South India.* Princeton: Princeton University Press, 1985. A thousand years of slow social change in agrarian life, 900–1900.

MARUYAMA, M. *Studies in the Intellectual History of Tokugawa Japan,* trans. M. Hane. Princeton: Princeton University Press, 1974. A monument of Japanese scholarship.

METZGER, T. A. *Internal Organization of Ch'ing Bureaucracy.* Cambridge: Harvard University Press, 1973. The final formulation of China's traditional administrative system.

NAQUIN, S., and E. S. RAWSKI. *Chinese Society in the Eighteenth Century.* New Haven: Yale University Press, 1987. Thoroughly researched synthesis of Chinese society in the last century before decline set in, noting early signs of the government's weakening grip on distant provinces.

QURESHI, I. H. *Administration of the Mughal Empire.* Karachi: University of Karachi Press, 1966. Scholarly description of India's last central government before the imposition of British rule.

SANSOM, G. *The Western World and Japan.* New York: Knopf, 1950. Includes the sixteenth-century period of initial penetration and the seventeenth-century expulsion of the Westerners. See also C. R. Boxer's *The Christian Century in Japan* (Berkeley: University of California Press, 1951).

SARKAR, J. *History of Aurangzib* (5 vols.). Calcutta: M. C. Sarkar, 1928. Old but irreplaceable piece of solid scholarship on the greatest of the later Moguls.

SAUNDERS, J. J. "The Problem of Islamic Decadence," *Journal of World History,* vol. 7 (1963), pp. 701–720. Consideration of the broad pattern of decline across the Muslim center.

SMITH, R. J. *China's Cultural Heritage: The Ch'ing Dynasty, 1644–1912.* Boulder, Colo.: Westview Press, 1983. The final formulation of traditional Chinese culture under China's last dynasty.

SPEAR, P. *Twilight of the Mughals.* Cambridge: Cambridge University Press, 1951. The Mogul Indian Empire in the shadow of Western imperialism.

SPENCE, J. D. *The Search for Modern China.* New York: W. W. Norton, 1990. Monumental study of Qing times.

STOIANOVICH, T. "Factors in the Decline of Ottoman Society in the Balkans," *Slavic Review,* vol. 21 (1962), pp. 623–632. Failure of Ottoman rule in southeastern Europe.

TOTMAN, C. *Politics in the Tokugawa Bakafu, 1600–1843.* Cambridge: Harvard University Press, 1967. Japanese politics from the reimposition of central authority to the eve of the Meiji reform.

TS'AO HSUEH-CHIN. *The Dream of the Red Chamber,* trans. and abridged by Chi-chen Wang. Garden City, N.Y.: Doubleday, 1929. China's most celebrated novel, and one of the richest and most sophisticated. A complete translation in five volumes by David Hawkes is now appearing under the title of *The Story of the Stone* (Baltimore: Penuin, 1973–).

WALTHALL, A. *Social Protest and Popular Culture in Eighteenth Century Japan.* Tucson: University of Arizona Press, 1986. Focuses on a decade of popular protest—the 1780s—in Tokugawa Japan.

CHAPTER 34

TURMOIL IN AFRICA

NEW NATIONS IN AFRICA

NEW STATES SOUTH OF THE SAHARA

If ancient empires were crumbling in Asia, in Africa new states were rising, particularly in the later eighteenth and nineteenth centuries. Yet Africa, like Asia, would face the overpowering weight of Western expansion before the nineteenth century was over. And like the declining Asian empires, Africa's new states would be ill prepared to meet that challenge. The rise of new centers of power in Africa and the failure of these structural changes to prepare the continent for what was coming will be the primary themes of this chapter.

Until quite recently, Africa was widely imagined— by outsiders—to have been a continent without a history. The grass-roofed huts of Tarzan's Africa were believed to house primitive folk living much as they had since prehistoric times. We have already seen how mistaken this view of an unchanging Africa was for earlier periods. "To know nothing is bad," goes a West African proverb; "to learn nothing is worse"—and Africans, like other peoples, had in fact been learning, growing, changing throughout their history.[1] In modern times, the age of change par excellence, the pace of social transformation accelerated among African peoples as it did elsewhere. And these changes began well before the Western invasion of the continent in the nineteenth century.

In the present chapter we will first survey the emergence of a number of new states in Africa south of the Sahara, from the Muslim-ruled Sokoto Caliphate of the Western Sudan to the Zulu military regimes in South Africa. We will then look at broader political and economic developments and at traditional African society and culture under the pressure of these changes. Finally, we will glance ahead to estimate the part both changes and continuities played in Africa's response to the impending wave of Western expansion we call the New Imperialism.

[1]Richard W. Hull, *Modern Africa: Change and Continuity* (Englewood Cliffs, NJ: Prentice Hall, 1980), p. 82.

THE JIHAD STATES OF THE WESTERN SUDAN: THE SOKOTO CALIPHATE

A *jihad*, it will be remembered, is a holy war, a Muslim crusade. The eighteenth and nineteenth centuries may seem a bit late for religious crusades, yet the grasslands of the Western Sudan did in fact see a great wave of Islamic crusading and the emergence of a series of Islamic *jihad* states during the early 1800s.

Muslim merchants and an Islamicized urban elite had played key roles in the life of the earlier empires of the Western Sudan. The farmers and herders who formed the bulk of the population of these states, however, had remained staunchly animist, invoking the spirits of nature and revering their ancestors. The fall of Songhai to Moroccan invaders around 1600 both destroyed the last of these empires and weakened the influence of Islam. For the next two centuries, West African society remained fragmented in small political units, while African Muslims gradually adapted their religion to that of their animist neighbors. Then, in the later eighteenth century, a Muslim reform movement erupted across West Africa. Demanding a return to the true faith, these religious purifiers reached for the political power to achieve their goal.

Half a dozen *jihads* founded as many new Muslim states, most of them over the century between 1770 and 1870. The most militant leaders were the Fulani people, zealous Muslims, many of them Islamic scholars or teachers who lived and taught in the towns of the Western Sudan.

One of the most important of these Islamic revolutions took place in the Hausa states, the ancient and long prosperous city-states of what is today northern Nigeria. Here in 1804 the Fulani scholar Usman dan Fodio (1754–1817) led a religious revival and then a political revolt that spread like a prairie fire from one to another of these Muslim trading cities. In half a dozen years, the Muslim revolutionaries had seized power in the Hausa states and had begun to weld them into the empire known as the Sokoto Caliphate with a population of several million people.

The goal of the Fulani rulers of the new empire was a theocratic state governed by its *imams,* religious leaders who would both purify and enforce the faith of the Prophet Muhammad. They established a strongly centralized state in which dan Fodio and his successors took the titles of sultan and "king of the Muslims."

A West African sultan's palace in the modern state of Niger, a French colony in the later nineteenth and first half of the twentieth century. Compare the architectural style with that of the mosque at Jenne and with that of Timbuktu shown in Chapter 28. Such structures, built of local materials and featuring thick walls and small windows, are both ecologically viable and havens of coolness and shade under the blistering African sun to this day. (Diane Rawson/Photo Researchers, Inc.)

In the Sokoto Caliphate, the formerly independent Hausa states were headed by emirs appointed by the sultan in Sokoto City, the new capital the Fulani built for their empire. Officials multiplied, both at the sultan's court and in the emirates. In addition to appointing the emirs, the sultan issued special commissions to provincial aristocrats, whose power thus balanced that of the official governors. The emirs in their turn often gave their slaves, who had no independent source of power beyond their masters' favor, extensive administrative authority over free citizens. Taxation, meanwhile, grew heavier at all levels of government; funds were needed to pay for endless military campaigns against the exiled Hausa aristocracy striving to reconquer

power. In the name of religion, in short, a thoroughly modern structure of state power took shape on the African savannas in the first half of the nineteenth century.

Other Muslim *jihad* states also emerged, ranging from the small principality of Futa Toro, founded in 1776, to the sprawling Tokolor Empire established by al-Hajj Umar in 1862. Founded by scholars and warriors, these new nations were committed both to religious reform and to military crusades to spread the faith. To achieve these thoroughly traditional ends, however, the builders of the *jihad* states organized stronger, more centralized, and more thoroughly bureaucratized governments than Africa had seen before.

African Muslims prostrate themselves outside the great mosque at Jenne, in modern Mali. They have washed their hands, faces, and feet before prayers, as the shoes behind the bowing figures indicate. The parked bicycles give a modern touch to this ancient ritual. The influence of Islam on Africa, however, can scarcely be exaggerated. In the nineteenth century, it inspired the builders of the <u>jihad</u> states, and even today, knowledgeable Africans will tell you, the faith of the Prophet continues to spread, village by village, across the continent. (United Nations)

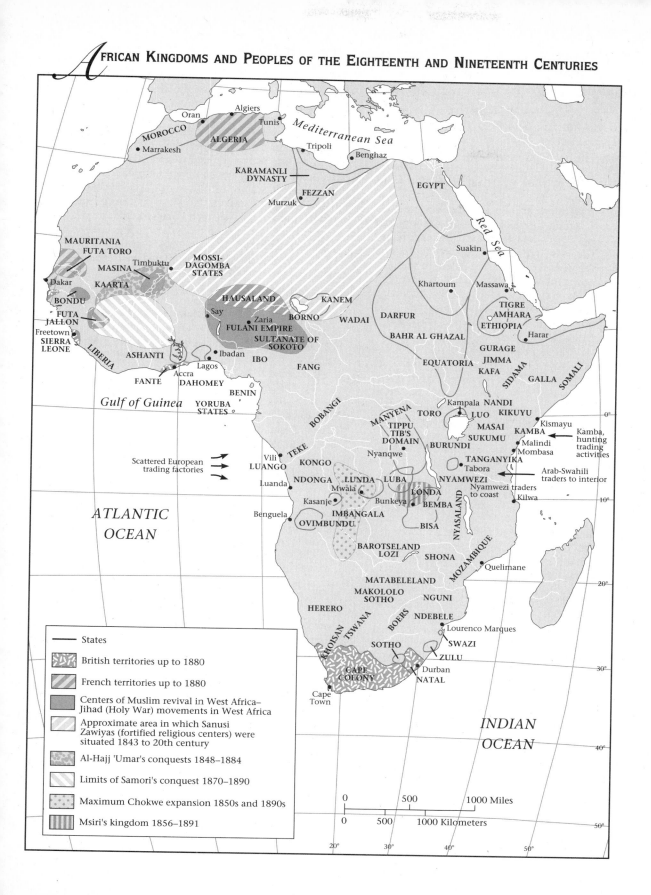

African Kingdoms and Peoples of the Eighteenth and Nineteenth Centuries

Oran
Algiers
Tunis
Mediterranean Sea
MOROCCO
ALGERIA
Tripoli
Marrakesh
Benghaz
KARAMANLI
DYNASTY
EGYPT
FEZZAN
Murzuk
Red Sea
MAURITANIA
FUTA TORO
Suakin
MASINA
Timbuktu
MOSSI-
DAGOMBA
STATES
Khartoum
Massawa
Dakar
KAARTA
HAUSALAND
KANEM
TIGRE
AMHARA
ETHIOPIA
BONDU
Say
Zaria
BORNO
WADAI
DARFUR
FUTA
JALLON
FULANI EMPIRE
SULTANATE OF
SOKOTO
Harar
Freetown
SIERRA
LEONE
BAHR AL GHAZAL
GURAGE
ASHANTI
Ibadan
IBO
FANG
EQUATORIA
JIMMA
KAFA
JIMMA
SIDAMA
GALLA
SOMALI
LIBERIA
Lagos
Accra
FANTE
DAHOMEY
BENIN
YORUBA
STATES
Gulf of Guinea
Kampala
NANDI
Kismayu
BOBANGI
TORO
LUO
KIKUYU
KAMBA
Kamba,
hunting
trading
activities
MANYENA
MASAI
TIPPU
TIB'S
DOMAIN
SUKUMU
Malindi
Mombasa
Scattered European
trading factories
Vili
TEKE
Nyanqwe
BURUNDI
LUANGO
KONGO
TANGANYIKA
Tabora
Arab-Swahili
traders to interior
Luanda
NDONGA
LUNDA
LUBA
NYAMWEZI
Nyamwezi traders
to coast
Mwala
LONDA
Kasanje
Bunkeya
BEMBA
Kilwa
Benguela
IMBANGALA
OVIMBUNDU
BISA
*ATLANTIC
OCEAN*
BAROTSELAND
LOZI
SHONA
MATABELELAND
MAKOLOLO
SOTHO
NGUNI
HERERO
NDEBELE
Lourenco Marques
KHOISAN
TSWANA
BOERS
SWAZI
SOTHO
ZULU
CAPE
COLONY
Durban
NATAL
Cape
Town
MOZAMBIQUE
Quelimane
NYASALAND

*INDIAN
OCEAN*

Legend

States

British territories up to 1880

French territories up to 1880

Centers of Muslim revival in West Africa–
Jihad (Holy War) movements in West Africa

Approximate area in which Sanusi
Zawiyas (fortified religious centers) were
situated 1843 to 20th century

Al-Hajj 'Umar's conquests 1848–1884

Limits of Samori's conquest 1870–1890

Maximum Chokwe expansion 1850s and 1890s

Msiri's kingdom 1856–1891

0   500   1000 Miles

0   500   1000 Kilometers

CENTRALIZED MONARCHIES OF THE WEST AFRICAN RAIN FOREST: THE ASHANTI CONFEDERACY

In the West African forest belt stretching south from the grasslands of the Western Sudan to the swamps and lagoons of the Guinea coast, other strong centralized states developed during the later eighteenth and nineteenth centuries. Of these, perhaps the best known was the Ashanti Confederacy, located in what was then called the Gold Coast, today's Ghana.

The Ashanti were one of the Akan-speaking peoples of the rain forest region. Eighteenth-century leaders had unified several neighboring peoples into the Ashanti Kingdom. Acquiring firearms, trading in gold, and raiding the villages of other peoples for slaves, the rulers of the new kingdom grew powerful. By 1800, they had absorbed neighbors still farther afield into the Ashanti Confederacy, an African state that in the nineteenth century included 150,000 square miles of tropical forest and grassy plains centered in the capital city of Kumasi.

To hold such a large area together, the Ashanti kings forged a powerful monarchical ideology and a substantial bureaucracy of royal servants. Taking the title of *asantehene*, "king of the Ashanti state," they claimed to rule by virtue of the "golden stool," a royal throne believed to have fallen from heaven. A victorious national army and an elaborate annual festival further focused loyalty on the sovereign.

Sources of administrative strength included a traditional council, originally composed of the kings of the confederacy's member states, which was gradually replaced by an ad hoc advisory council chosen by the *asantehene* himself. The hereditary chiefs of leading clans and subject peoples were deprived of authority over their own people, which was delegated instead to appointed palace officials and proconsuls. Other royal officials took charge of the profitable mining and slave businesses, both royal monopolies. Muslims from the north served as scribes and treasurers in the Ashanti state.

With a disciplined army and a large taxable population under rigorous royal control, the Ashanti Confederacy dominated the region. Only the restraining power of British coastal settlements established for commercial purposes limited the expansive power of this black African kingdom.

There were other such centralized states in the forests of West Africa. These included the kingdoms of Dahomey and Oyo, the latter tracing its civilization back to the medieval culture of Ife. But no other was as widely known, admired, and feared as the Ashanti Confederacy.

EXPANDING POWERS OF EAST AFRICA: EGYPT AND ZANZIBAR

Another pattern of political growth developed in East Africa during the nineteenth century. From Egypt and Ethiopia in the northeast to the island kingdom of Zanz-ibar off the coast of what is today Tanzania, aggressive African states expanded rapidly down the eastern side of the continent. And here too, territorial expansion was often accompanied by a calculated process of state-building and the beginnings of modernization.

The earliest case was that of Egypt's Muhammad Ali Pasha (1769–1849), who came to Egypt in 1800 as a mercenary in the service of the Ottoman emperor and ended his life as the founder of a ruling dynasty in what was nominally a province of the Ottoman Empire. Over almost half a century of power in Cairo, Muhammad Ali crushed the Mamelukes, the country's long-established military ruling class. He also conquered both Syria in the Near East and the area up the Nile which is today's nation of Sudan. Neither of these conquests lasted; but in preparing for his military campaigns, the pasha undertook some important changes in Egypt.

Among Muhammad Ali's domestic reforms were important irrigation projects, the encouragement of industry, and a more efficient system of taxation. Some of these innovations were scuttled by the British, who feared his growing strength in the area. Nevertheless, Muhammad Ali Pasha's tenure of power on the Nile did set Egypt on the long road to modernity.

In the middle of the nineteenth century, Arab Sultan Sayyid Said (1806–1856), who in the late 1830s moved his capital from Oman on the Arabian peninsula to the African island of Zanzibar, built a large commercial empire on the East African mainland. Trading particularly in ivory and slaves, Sayyid Said reached far into the interior of Africa. He enormously increased the profitability of the web of trade routes he found there by expanding the volume of commerce, by scattering Arab merchants along the trails to collect customers for his caravans, and by signing agreements on tolls and protection with local chiefs. He also imported Indian experts to organize his finances and turned Zanzibar itself into the world's largest exporter of cloves.

THE REBIRTH OF ETHIOPIA

The most successful of these East African expansions, however, was that of the ancient monarchy of Ethiopia. Here the Christian descendants of the long-vanished empire of Axum had survived in their mountain fastnesses for fifteen hundred years. There had been later flowerings of Ethiopian culture, notably in the thirteenth century, when the unique churches of King Lalibela were carved from the living rock of volcanic mountains. By 1800, however, foreign incursions and domestic division had left the nation little more than a loose coalition of princes with a figurehead king. Then in the later nineteenth century, a series of three rulers reversed this trend toward disintegration with spectacular consequences.

The first of these reforming monarchs, King Theodore, laid out an elaborate program of modernization only to fall victim to a quarrel with Britain, which dispatched a military expedition in 1868. His successor Yohannes IV faced several foreign foes before falling in battle with the Sudanese in 1889. Only under the third in this vigorous line, King Menelik II (1889–1913) did Ethiopia, like Egypt, set out on the long, slow path of development often called modernization.

Prince of the autonomous Ethiopian state of Shoa, Menelik II had also served an apprenticeship in government under Yohannes before himself succeeding to the title of *negusa nagast,* "king of kings." From the beginning, Manelik's goals included reestablishing both the authority of the king of kings over the princes and Ethiopian suzerainty over neighboring peoples who had once been tributary states. He was also thoroughly aware of the menace of further European incursions like that which had destroyed King Theodore. To accomplish his aims, however, he found it necessary to begin the modernization of his ancient land by borrowing skills from the West he feared.

Menelik thus imported both Western technicians and Western guns. He built bridges and roads, and, with the help of his European experts, introduced the beginnings of Western postal and educational systems and financial institutions. From his new capital at Addis Ababa, he ruled a united nation by the end of the nineteenth century.

Menelik II's achievements in international affairs were equally impressive. Through a combination of force and diplomacy, he succeeded in imposing his own authority on neighboring peoples. And in 1896, at the high tide of Europe's New Imperialism, Ethiopia's large and well-armed military shattered an Italian invasion at the great battle of Adowa. "If powers at a distance come forward to partition Africa," the Ethiopian emperor had declared,

"I do not intend to be an indifferent spectator."[2] He had been as good as his word.

EMERGING NATIONS OF CENTRAL AFRICA: BUGANDA

Another area in which centralized and expanding states had begun to emerge by the nineteenth century was the Central African *interlucastrine* region. This was the area "between the lakes," a string of African lakes running from Victoria down to Nyasa, comparable in size and importance to the Great Lakes of North America. Of the new states to emerge in this area, Buganda on Lake Victoria was the wealthiest and most powerful.

The builders of Buganda lived in what is today Uganda. Winning independence from their once-powerful Bunyoro overlords as early as the seventeenth century, the *kabakas,* or kings, of Buganda had doubled the size and significantly strengthened the government of their emerging state by 1800. Though the *kabaka's* own title was hereditary, during the eighteenth century the rulers of Buganda took the crucial step of replacing most other hereditary titles with appointive ones. The king's chief minister, his council, and most of his subsidiary chiefs thus came to hold their positions only by royal patent.

In the nineteenth century, the Central African kingdom took advantage of its location to become the interior anchor of the Zanzibar trading system established by Sultan Sayyid Said. At the same time, the kings of

---

[2]Robert W. July, *A History of the African People* (New York: Charles Scribner's Sons, 1970), p. 338.

The ceremonial tomb of the "Three Kings," ancestors of a twentieth century kabaka of Buganda, in modern Uganda. In earlier centuries, sacrifices were made at such shrines in honor of the royal dead. In the twentieth century, the widows of the deceased monarchs came daily to lament their passing until the kingdom itself was abolished by the new government in the 1960s. (Diane Rawson/Photo Researchers, Inc.)

Buganda purchased quantities of firearms from Arab merchants and incorporated still more of the surrounding populace into their expanding empire. Buganda thus became the greatest of the new nations of the interlucastrine region.

THE ZULUS AND THE MFECANE STATES OF SOUTH AFRICA

Zululand today is a small enclave 10,000 square miles in area on the east coast of the Republic of South Africa. The Zulus who live there trace their ancestry to one of a number of Nguni-speaking peoples who had reached southern Africa by the fifteenth century. Their arrival marked the end of the great Bantu migrations and came only a short time before the first Portuguese vessels touched there on their way to India. The Zulus and other Nguni peoples were thus well established when the first Dutch settlers—the ancestors of the nineteenth-century Boers (today's Afrikaners)—arrived around 1600. For the next two hundred years, the two peoples, black and white, lived side by side, herding cattle, sheep, and goats, raising corn, and occasionally raiding each others' settlements to burn crops and steal stock. Then, in the 1800s, as the Boers began to carve out a state for themselves, the Zulus emerged as the dynamos of change and of state building among the black inhabitants of southern Africa.

The original impetus for Zulu expansion seems to have been ecological and demographic. The fertile, disease-free South African plateau produced a steady growth in population, which by 1800 had generated land hunger and conflict among the Nguni peoples. Endemic warfare in turn fostered tighter military and civil organization replacing the loose clan federations of earlier centuries. Troubled times and an evolving society, finally, opened the way for the most famous African soldier and state builder of the century—Shaka (1787–1828), the "African Napoleon" and founder of the Zulu nation.

The illegitimate son of a war-loving Zulu chief, Shaka revealed little of his innovative genius until he inherited leadership of the Zulus himself in 1817. Throughout his career, he like his father remained above all a military leader. Like state builders elsewhere in Africa—as well as in such European nations as Prussia and Russia—Shaka developed new political institutions primarily as a means of strengthening his army. Both his military and political innovations, however, had far-reaching consequences.

To strengthen his troops, Shaka built upon a reform with which others had already experimented: the conversion of the younger Zulu age grades into permanent military regiments. Shaka's regiments, or *impis,* however, were rigorously trained, rigidly disciplined, and endlessly drilled. Kept under arms for many years, they became experienced and effective forces of veteran fighters. Shaka also revolutionized African tactics by replacing the long throwing spear with the *assegai,* a short stabbing spear

used at close quarters by troops advancing in tight formation behind tall cowhide shields. And his "cow's horns" battlefield deployment, with flanking units (the "horns") closing behind their foes, added still further to the effectiveness of his armies. Thus trained, armed, and deployed, operating not as individual warriors seeking personal glory but as groups under officers' orders, Zulu *impis* swept to victory after victory.

As a political organizer, Shaka also showed both shrewdness and rigor. Claiming divine kingship, he made his soldiers completely dependent on him for food—the cattle they won in battle—for clothing, weapons, and for their very lives, since any failure of courage or any act of disobedience was punishable by death. The Zulu nation,

Shaka Zulu, the "African Napoleon," equipped for war. Proverbial for bravery, brutality, organizational skill, and tactical brilliance, the founder of the Zulu nation is still honored by his people in South Africa. This foreign rendering gives only the most general impression of the towering Zulu warrior. Nevertheless, the picture does seem to hint at least at the fury of an impi charge, the terror of the mfekane that Shaka loosed across the southern stem of Africa. (Nathaniel Isaacs)

VOICES FROM THE PAST

"The reason why a man is allowed to have a number of wives is that he may have a lot of women to work for him, is it not?
—Yes, that is one reason, and another is that they may have a large family. . . .

Is it a good thing to make women work for the men? Is it not better for the men to work?
—[The king laughed.] Husbands work as well as the wives, except in the case of a king or chief. . . .

And any man . . . who has a number of wives lets the wives work in the fields?
—The wives do the planting, and the servants do the cutting wood, and so on.

Is it not enough for the women to bear children, and do the housework? Why do you let them do this work instead of the men, who are stronger and better able to do it?
—The housework is done by the grandmothers, and the children are looked after by the elder children, while the women are working in the gardens . . .

Is it considered a disgrace for a man to do a woman's work by tilling and so on?
—No, not a disgrace at all, but sometimes when men do see a man hoeing, they chaff [kid] him, and ask him why he does that work when his wives can do it. It is not man's ordinary work."

This is a fragment of a British colonial interrogation of the captured Zulu king Cetywayo in Cape Town, South Africa, in 1881. Originally published by the Government Commission on Native Laws and Customs, the interview was apparently an attempt to expand Western understanding of the culture of the once powerful kingdom of Zululand. As we read it a century later, however, the transcript seems to reveal the basic social beliefs of Victorian English people as much as it does those of the Zulus.

Would you say that the interrogator has as strong a view of what constitutes legitimate work for women as Cetywayo does? What evidence can you see of a traditional African division of labor much more complex than the model the Western questioner wishes to explore? Do you think Cetywayo is dodging the issue in his final response, or does his statement about men kidding other men sound psychologically convincing to you?

Cetywayo kaMpande, A Zulu King Speaks, eds. C. de B. Webb and J. B. Wright (Pietermaritzburg, South Africa: University of Natal Press, 1978), p. 73.

furthermore, grew rapidly as Shaka incorporated the youth of each new conquered people into his army, converting each new levy into Zulus too, equally dependent on the king. A precocious Zulu nationalism was thus created, which outweighed—and outlasted—the fear of their leader's iron discipline. "Who are the Zulu?" demanded Shaka:

They are parts of two hundred unruly clans which I had to break up and reshape, and only the fear of death will hold them together. The time will come when they will be as one nation. In the meantime, my very nature must inspire them with terror.[3]

---

[3]E. A. Ritter, *Shaka Zulu* (London: Hamilton and Co., 1955), p. 319.

By the time of his death in 1828, Shaka's word was law to half a million Zulus spread over 80,000 square miles of South Africa. And a national feeling had been born that is still a political force in the region today.

Shaka was a violent man who died by assassination, struck down by his own brothers. Some of his best commanders had already broken with him, seceding with their regiments to spread both the violence and the discipline Shaka had fostered all across the southern stem of Africa. His former officers also took Shaka's military and political innovations with them, establishing new states wherever they settled. In addition, the Zulu diaspora inspired other peoples to adopt similarly rigorous new social structures to defend themselves against the *mfecane*, the "time of troubles" that shook South Africa in the first half of the nineteenth century.

Shaka's successors ruled the Zulu people for half a century, fighting the hardy Boers and winning battles against the British as late as the 1870s, before falling victim to superior European firepower in 1880. It was yet another example of the flexibility and growth of which African political organization was capable in that last century before the Western conquest.

 ## POLITICAL AND ECONOMIC CHANGES

STRUCTURAL TRANSFORMATIONS

Beneath this turbulent history of wars and dynasties, deeper currents of change were also flowing. Politically and economically, Africa seemed to be undergoing—or at least beginning—significant structural transformations during the nineteenth century. The preceding pages illustrated some of those trends. The following sections will survey them in general terms, including political innovations and economic developments, as well as the impact of foreign influences during the last generations before the renewal of Western imperial expansion washed over Africa.

Throughout, we will again notice the vigor with which Africa seemed to be adapting to this era of change and challenge. At the same time we will emphasize the turbulence itself, the upheaval which those troubled times brought to Africa. For the political and economic innovations and foreign influences to be surveyed here inevitably clashed with older established African institutions. The result was a tumultuous and disturbing age, the beginning of a cultural upheaval that in some ways continues today.

STATE BUILDING AND STATE POWER

As we have seen, in the early nineteenth century, rulers in several parts of Africa embarked upon programs of state building, or expansion of state power, without parallel on

that continent since the fall of the Songhai Empire two hundred years earlier. These leaders included such varied types as the Muslim reformers of the Western Sudan, hereditary monarchs in Central and East Africa, and military conquerors in South Africa. Some general patterns of governmental reform and restructuring were, however, common to many of these emergent powers.

Almost all, for instance, aimed at strongly centralized monarchies. Hereditary rulers built upon traditional attribution of divinity to monarchs, which could provide a strong foundation for claims to enhanced and expanded powers. At the same time, however, they were quick to set aside the element of reciprocal obligation traditionally owed by rulers to the ruled. Rulers also commonly rejected requirements that they consult with councils of elders, subordinate chiefs, or other groups whose countervailing power had once limited the authority of African kings.

Strong central governments entailed the growth of bureaucratic structures, and this too was a feature of these new states. Emperors, kings, and other rulers governed through increasingly elaborate hierarchies of appointed officials, some concentrated at the royal court, others dispatched to execute the royal will in distant parts of the kingdom. Increasingly, efficiency in the royal service, rather than hereditary right or other traditional criteria, determined appointment and promotion. Even royal slaves, completely dependent upon their masters, sometimes held high administrative posts and rose to wealth and power. And as with bureaucracies everywhere, their numbers grew: the Guinea coast kingdom of Oyo, for instance, boasted 15,000 royal officials by the end of the eighteenth century.

It is even possible to detect in some of these new politics the equivalent of a modern sense of national feeling. Some of the new or expanding states drew strength from such preexisting factors as a common language or shared ethnic or clan loyalties. Such allegiances, sometimes dismissed as "tribalism," could in fact involve millions of people, more than some European nationalities could claim. In other places, such as Christian Ethiopia or the Muslim states of West Africa, religion helped to unify a nation and to justify government policies. In still other states, like those of the Zulus in South Africa, efforts were made to expand existing systems of lineage and clan to absorb newly conquered peoples into a unifying structure of loyalties.

All such efforts to create deeper allegiances went beyond anything attempted earlier in Africa. For Mali, Songhai, and other early African empires, like premodern imperial powers in many places, had seldom sought to assimilate the various peoples they ruled into a common framework of cultural affiliation.

EVOLVING COMMERCIAL NETWORKS

Commercial exchange also evolved in many parts of Africa during the nineteenth century. The majority of Africans remained farmers, herders, and intermittent food gatherers, completely self-sufficient but producing little surplus for sale outside their own villages. But trade did play an increasingly important part in the lives of other Africans as the century advanced.

Long-distance trade had of course existed for many centuries in West Africa and in the coastal trading cities of East Africa. Even in these areas, however, commercial exchange both expanded and changed in this period. In most of Central, South, and inner East Africa, there had been little beyond local trade before 1800. In these regions, a narrow but expanding flow of commerce developed after that date.

A fundamental change was the passing of the slave trade, which had afflicted both coasts and had extended its tentacles far into the African interior ever since European slave traders had made slave raiding a profitable business in the sixteenth century. The eighteenth-century Enlightenment, however, and the accompanying wave of humanitarian concern had led growing numbers of West-

Tippu Tip, the venerable nineteenth-century merchant prince of East Africa, is shown here in a drawing by a contemporary Western artist. By simplifying the clothing and accoutrements and emphasizing the face, the sketch artist has given us a vivid impression of this African trader whose shrewd, sad eyes had seen a lot of the seamier side of human nature while he accumulated the wealth and power that made him a legend in his own time. (British Library Reproductions)

Desert nomads like these still travel the invisible trails of the Sahara today, as in this late nineteenth-century picture. Here a caravan has been stopped by a Tuareg sentinel, who must report their presence to his superior before the travelers can continue their journey through the land of the Tuaregs. The bleached bones in the lower right serve as a grim reminder of the perils confronting these restless desert peoples who have been living on the dangerous edge of civilization for thousands of years. (Albert Richter)

ern people to see slavery as a social evil. The economic imperatives of capitalism may also have made free labor seem more flexible and efficient. Whatever the reasons, over the course of the nineteenth century, one Western nation after another outlawed first the trade in slaves and then slavery itself. And in the later 1800s, the British navy in particular began to hunt down slavers of all nationalities and repatriate slaves found in their holds to the continent if not the region of their birth. First in West Africa, then in East Africa, the trade in human flesh thus finally ended.

Commercial exchange among Africa, Europe, and the Americas did not, however, end with this winding down of the large-scale export of African labor. New West African export items included timber, peanuts, kola nuts, and palm oil, the latter used to lubricate the new machinery of the Industrial Revolution. East Africa exported luxury products like ivory and cloves as well as a continuing flow of slaves, for which there was still a market in Asia, particularly in the Middle East. In return, Africans imported light cotton cloth from Europe or India, mass-produced utensils, alcoholic beverages, and increasing quantities of firearms, despite the efforts of Europeans to curtail exports of the latter to Africa.

Especially on the coasts, where foreign merchants had long established commercial enclaves, this "legitimate trade"—as contrasted with the trade in slaves—grew through the century. On the African side, the lucrative export trade was often a royal monopoly. African kings thus forbade foreign merchants to go directly to local markets, requiring them instead to deal only with royal officials. The latter, though sometimes legally slaves of the king, could become exceedingly wealthy through the administration of such commercial monopolies.

Elsewhere, an energetic new commercial class emerged. Individuals even of lower-class origins rose to commercial prominence on both coasts. Thus the East African Arab-Swahili merchant Muhammed bin Hammad, known to Europeans as Tippu Tip, constructed a vastly profitable string of trading posts reaching deep into Central Africa. Dealing in slaves as well as ivory, Tippu Tip became the virtual ruler of an inland trading empire, though he always insisted that he was "merely a merchant." Similar rags-to-riches stories could be found in other parts of the continent as African traders competed vigorously and often successfully with the Europeans who gathered ever more thickly on their coasts.

INTERACTION WITH OUTSIDE FORCES

As throughout its history, Africa in the nineteenth century was thus by no means isolated from the outside world. Despite the tendency of Europeans to see it as the "unknown continent" because much of it was not yet on Western maps, Africa continued to relate to the other two continents of the Old World particularly.

Politically, the Ottoman Turkish Empire still claimed parts of North Africa, and Muhammad Ali, even while he built his power base in Egypt, remained nominally the viceroy of the emperor in Constantinople. The sultan of Zanzibar, as we have also seen, moved his capital from Oman in southern Arabia to the East African island from which he expanded to the African coast and beyond. Also during the earlier nineteenth century, at least some European penetration of the continent occurred. In the 1830s, the French crossed the Mediterranean to begin the occupation of Algeria, in North Africa. In that decade also, the long-established Boer settlers in South Africa, pressured by the British, began the Great Trek into the interior to found the new European enclaves of the Transvaal and the Orange Free State. The vast bulk of the world's second largest continent remained under African control before 1870, but the political presence of these intruders was a reality with which some Africans at least had to deal even in the early 1800s.

Both Muslims and Christians sought converts in Africa with increasing determination in the nineteenth century. We have already noted the emergence of the

Islamic *jihad* states, mostly in the first half of the century. In the second half, expanding networks of Christian missionaries would play a significant part in Europe's imperial penetration of Africa.

All this foreign activity had its impact on Africans, stimulating economic, political, and cultural changes. By and large, however, as one authority put it, "the scope and nature of these changes" remained as late as 1870 "matters for African decision and initiative."[4] Only at the end of the century did Western power begin to determine the course of African history.

TRADITIONAL CULTURE IN AN AGE OF TRANSITION

SOCIETY AND COMMUNITY

Nineteenth-century African views of society and corresponding patterns of social relationships seem to reflect the time of transition that was already under way. An older, more egalitarian view was still preserved in many places, as it is today. In others, sharper distinctions between social classes had clearly emerged, though they were still softened by an older African sense of community.

Village cultures, particularly in areas of ethnic homogeneity, tended to distinguish between people on traditional grounds, in terms of sex and age group. Different African peoples assigned different social roles and attributed different qualities to men and women, to the old, the mature, and the young. Despite these divisions of labor, women could and did work outside the home. The Traditional Laws of the Yoruba of what is today Nigeria, for instance, declared that though "it is accepted that the husband is the breadwinner," nevertheless "whenever a wife has an independent job of her own from which she could earn some money, she may be expected to . . . contribute to the maintenance of the family."[5]

In such traditional societies, status rather than class was the foundation of the ranking system. Where levels of material wealth were uniformly low, distinctions on the basis of material possessions were much less important. Social status meant honor, respect, and social privilege and was assigned to heads of families or clans, to age rather than youth, and to such spiritually powerful professionals as diviners, rainmakers, and priestesses. In these traditional cultures also, an older worldview still prevailed. The individual was seen as part of the community, soci-

[4]John E. Flint, "Introduction," *The Cambridge History of Europe*, Vol. 5, *From c. 1790 to c. 1870* (London and New York: Cambridge University Press, 1976), p. 11.

[5]Quoted in R. O. Ekundare, *Marriage and Divorce under Yoruba Customary Law* (Ife, Nigeria: University of Ife Press, 1969), p. 25.

ety as embedded in nature, and the natural world itself as part of a larger spiritual order of things.

By contrast, in areas where political and economic changes and outside influences had begun to transform African society, this older view was beginning to change.

Where royalty or rich merchants towered over ordinary people, there were ample grounds for distinguishing one class from another. Where wars of conquest had had their effect, aristocrats were often ethnically distinct from the rest of the population, the heirs of a conquering people. Ordinary peasants, herders of cattle, or cultivators of crops comprised most of the middle range of such a structured society. But there were also often castes or whole villages dedicated to specialized crafts, from ironworking to weaving. There was also likely to be a substantial unfree portion of the population. Technically slaves, these servile elements ranged from field hands and house servants to concubines and even administrative personnel who could wield great power. Despite their unfree status, such people typically felt little of the stigma that was heaped upon slaves in some places.

Moreover, even in these more hierarchically structured societies, traditional attitudes fostered a sense of community. Lineage and clan membership still softened the impact of class differences. Poor relations could confidently call upon more fortunate kinsmen for material help at need. And professional *griots,* or praise-singers, reminded rich and poor alike of the deeds of their celebrated ancestors, veneration for whom bound them all in a larger unity.

ART AND LIFE

Traditional arts also continued to flourish in nineteenth-century Africa. Indeed, more than any other aspect of African life, the arts tended to preserve the traditions on which the older African order was based and to integrate ancient beliefs with daily life.

Among the traditional arts still widely practiced were distinctive forms of sculpture, literature, music, and dance. Carvers of wood, storytellers, players of drums, flutes, and stringed instruments, and dancers and dance troupes were common in various parts of Africa. In the twentieth century, the work of these practitioners of ancient arts would be collected, analyzed, applauded, and imitated in the West. In the nineteenth century, it was still part of the daily lives of the African people. Fetishes and masks were still the dwelling places of spirits, bards still celebrated ancestral glories, and music accompanied work and play, weddings, births, and deaths.

But the arts also adapted to the evolving political and economic order. In kingdoms and empires like those of West Africa, artists might be sequestered in palace courtyards, reserving the secrets of their crafts for their royal masters. Rich merchants who could afford to hire a *griot* for a traditional family feast combined the honor-

ing of their ancestors with a chance to impress their less affluent kin. On the other hand, singers and dancers had in some places the traditional right to satirize and lampoon as well as to praise the rich and powerful. This privilege they sometimes used as a sharp-edged tool of social criticism, exposing the vanity of the new rich or challenging the untraditional policies of kings.

DEVELOPMENT OR DISINTEGRATION?

It was a turbulent time of change in Africa. What, however, was the overall impact of these changes on traditional African society? The result, it may be suggested, was a combination of strengths and weaknesses that had the cumulative effect of leaving Africa unprepared for the European onslaught to come.

On the political side, the growth of centralized bureaucratic government in some parts of Africa was certainly a move toward stronger states. At the same time, however, these changes undermined hereditary elites and traditional ethnic and clan loyalties. Appointed officials

This forceful sculpture of an <u>oba</u> of Benin echoes styles developed in earlier centuries. Later sculpture from this part of Africa became less naturalistic and more conventionalized, emphasizing emblems of rank like the high necklace of coral beads worn even in the twentieth century by these rulers on ceremonial occasions—though by then the <u>obas</u> were part of the structure of indirect rule in the British colony of Nigeria. (The Mansell Collection Limited)

thrust aside hereditary chiefs and ritual priests. Innovative leaders like Shaka warped age groups into full-time military forces and destroyed their role in traditional society.

Economic changes also had complex and not always beneficial consequences. Wealth channeled into the service of threatened African states, as in the revived Ethiopian kingdom, could pay for the beginnings of a modern infrastructure and an accumulation of weapons to defend at least one corner of Africa against foreign invasion. This very accumulation of wealth, however, could also undermine older ways. Both royal trade monopolies and the rise of commoners to great wealth flew in the face of ancient African systems of family ownership and collective use of the means of production.

There had of course been powerful monarchs and rich merchants in Africa before. The more common these became, however, the more subversive they were of older institutions.

Increasing—and increasingly intense—African relations with the outside world brought their share of problems too. Muslim rulers might bring better government, Christian missionaries new skills or medical knowledge. But both Christians and Muslims now sought to uproot older African religions, which both saw as "pagan," down to the village level. In medieval Ghana or early modern Songhai, Islam had been the faith of an urban elite only, leaving the rural majority to the animist faiths of their forefathers. But the Fulani rulers of the new empires of the Western Sudan worked zealously to destroy paganism and to spread a purified Islamic faith to all their subjects. In the colonial order to come, Christian missionaries would further intensify this assault on traditional beliefs.

These political, economic, and ideological changes had one final paradoxical weakness: they were coming too slowly. The drift toward stronger political units, the concentration of wealth, even the spread of a more militant religious faith were simply not proceeding rapidly enough to prepare the continent to face the assault of Western peoples among whom these sources of strength were already well developed. Changes that might have produced a stronger, richer, more militant Africa had time to get under way in the nineteenth century, and to undermine the old order. But they did not have time to produce a new society. The peoples of Africa were thus no better prepared than were the decaying empires of Asia to confront the New Imperialism that swept over them all at the end of the nineteenth century.

SUMMARY

In a variety of ways, many parts of Africa were evolving rapidly in the nineteenth century. New nations were emerging, and political and economic changes were occurring that challenged much of Africa's traditional culture.

New kingdoms and empires arose from the grasslands of West Africa through the lakes region of Central Africa to the South African plateau. Muslim crusaders built *jihad* states in the Western Sudan; the Ashanti Confederacy grew in the rain forests back of the Guinea coast; and Buganda emerged on the shores of Lake Victoria. The Christian kingdom of Ethiopia revived in the northeastern highlands, while Shaka and the Zulu *impis* shook South Africa.

Resulting political changes focused on the growth of strong central government. Economically, commerce expanded as the slave trade gave way to "legitimate trade." Foreign influences intensified, challenging traditional African attitudes and institutions.

Africa on the eve of the last great wave of Western imperialism was thus in the throes of changes that, given time, might have materially strengthened the continent. But lacking such time left Africa as ill prepared for what was to come as the declining empires of Asia.

SUGGESTED READING

BEN AMOS, P. *The Art of Benin.* London: Thames and Hudson, 1980. Informed analysis of style and social context.

BOAHEN, A. A. *African Perspectives on Colonialism.* Baltimore: Johns Hopkins University Press, 1987. Stimulating summation of the African view that the continent was actually developing rapidly before Western imperialists imposed underdevelopment on their colonies.

EDGERTON, R. B. *Like Lions They Fought: The Zulu War and the Last Black Empire in South Africa.* New York: Free Press of Macmillan, 1988. Perceptive analysis of the tactics, motives, and social backgrounds of British and Zulu military leaders and fighting men.

ETTIS, D. *Economic Growth and the Ending of the Transatlantic Slave Trade.* New York: Oxford University Press, 1987. Scholarly evaluation of the

British campaign against the slave trade, seen here as a consequence of moral concern rather than a form of imperialism.

HAY, M. J., and M. WRIGHT. *African Women and the Law: Historical Perspectives.* Boston: Boston University Press, 1982. Papers on the legal position of African women in the nineteenth and twentieth centuries.

HULL, R. W. *Modern Africa: Change and Continuity.* Englewood Cliffs, N.J.: Prentice-Hall, 1980. Excellent concise overview.

KIWANUKA, S. *A History of Buganda.* Oxford: Clarendon Press, 1971. Widely cited survey.

LAST, M. *The Sokoto Caliphate.* London: Longman, 1967. Good introduction to this model jihad state of the Western Sudan.

MARKS, S., and A. ATMORE, eds. *Economy and Society in Pre-Industrial Africa.* New York: Longman, 1981. Essays in scholarly analysis.

MAYLAM, P. *A History of the African People of South Africa: From the Early Iron Age to the 1970s.* New York: St. Martin's Press, 1986. Class-based analysis of the repression of black South Africans.

OMER-COOPER, J. *The Zulu Aftermath.* London: Longman, 1965. Standard treatment of the *Mfecane* states.

ROMERO, P. W., ed. *Life Histories of African Women.* London: Ashfield Press, 1988. Reconstructed lives of African women, including a number from the nineteenth century.

SAGAY, J. O., and D. A. WILSON. *Africa—A Modern History (1800–1975).* New York: Holmes & Meier, 1978. Profusely illustrated; the first third deals with the period under consideration here.

VANSINA, J. *Art History in Africa.* London and New York: Longman, 1984. Expert analysis by a leading Africanist.

WILKS, I. *Asante in the Nineteenth Century.* New York: Cambridge University Press, 1975. A standard account.

CHAPTER 35

Europe's Age of Revolutions

THE FRENCH REVOLUTION

BREAKTHROUGHS

Europe in the nineteenth century has one of the least exciting images of any time and place. One thinks of frock coats and Queen Victoria. One imagines a world reeking of cultural smugness, moral hypocrisy, and overstuffed bad taste. Was this not the century that tried to deny sex, glorified imperialism, and prepared the way for World War I—the greatest war the world had seen up to that time? Much of the cultural history of the present century may be seen as a rejection of everything the preceding century stood for, a violent disowning of our most recent Western past.

It will not work. The nineteenth must, in fact, rank as one of the most important of all centuries, not only in Western history but in the broader historical evolution from regional cultures through intercontinental empires to genuinely global history.

If we begin the historical nineteenth century a bit earlier, in the later 1700s, we see that the period stands out in two areas especially. It is the era that saw the evolution and dissemination of the new social ideologies spawned by the Enlightenment and the French Revolution. And it is the century of Europe's industrialization, beginning with the Industrial Revolution in Great Britain.

These two seminal trends originated in western Europe, especially in Britain and France, and spread slowly east, reaching Russia in full force only at the very end of the century. They became the most important Western exports to the rest of the world in the climactic New Imperialism of the later 1800s. They would also be the central shaping forces in the history of the twentieth-century world in which we live. These two main currents—industrial development and ideologies—make the nineteenth century second only to our own in modern world history.

There will be room for a number of things in the following pages, from Napoleon and Bismarck to the most notorious prostitute in Paris and Sunday in the park with Seurat. But again and again we will find ourselves circling back to these twin focuses of the century: industrialism and ideology, the steam engine and the ballot box.

STORMING THE BASTILLE

Participants in the Paris mob that attacked the Bastille on July 14, 1789, did not know that they were making history.

The Bastille had been built as a fort and converted to a prison and was notorious as a place of incarceration for political offenders—Voltaire himself had once languished there. To the mob that surrounded its huge towers and creaking drawbridge that July morning, it was primarily a potential source of weapons to use against the royal troops who had been gathering in Paris over the past two weeks to control just such political violence as this.

A deputation from the crowd demanded the weapons and were refused. When some of the mob broke into the courtyard, they were fired on and scores were killed. When the governor of the prison finally yielded up the keys in return for guarantees of safety, he and a number of his officers were cut to pieces by the vengeful *sans-culottes,* the outraged rabble of Paris. Seven prisoners were freed: four forgers, two madmen, and a sex offender.

Next day the mob came again—to begin the dismantling of the Bastille itself. The prison was leveled, the keys sent to George Washington across the Atlantic in fraternal greetings. July Fourteenth became France's Fourth of July—the French Independence Day.

The storming of the Bastille revealed the will of the French people to defy their ancient kings and take their political destinies in their own hands. Most important, however, it was a symbol—and ideological revolutions live on symbols. When word of the attack was carried to Louis XVI, he gasped, "It's a revolt!" "No, Sire," he was answered more gravely, "it is a revolution."[1] It is as a symbol of governmental tyranny and popular revolution that the Bastille has entered the language of modern ideological conflict.

The French Revolution looms much larger in Western history than the American Revolution, which preceded it. The revolution in France, the greatest power in Europe, was the archetypal assault on the old order of kings, aristocrats, and priests that had prevailed on that continent since the Middle Ages. It introduced a cycle of revolt, Europe's Age of Revolutions, that would last for more

---

[1]Robert Ergang, *Europe from the Renaissance to Waterloo* (Boston: D.C. Heath, 1954), p. 657.

The attack on the Bastille, July 14, 1789, France's Independence Day. The actual events of that day may not have been so dramatic, but the symbolic significance of the fall of this royal prison to a mob of angry Parisians was not lost on Europe. The fact that the people in arms liberated only seven prisoners, none of them political offenders, did not dim the luster of this potent act of political defiance. (Hulton Deutsch Collection Limited)

than half a century, from 1789 through the Europe-wide Revolutions of 1848. Its causes, stages, and consequences therefore deserve a few pages here.

CAUSES OF THE FRENCH REVOLUTION

The complex causes of the French Revolution included some deep-seated social problems, subversive ideas, and a cluster of devastating political and economic crises.

Social discontent in France revolved around an anachronistic social structure. This social order gave special privileges to half a million aristocrats and church-men and denied them to 23 million members of the "third estate"—the rest of the population. Under this system, the urban poor languished in poverty and frequent hunger in city slums, free peasants grumbled at forced labor and other feudal survivals, and an increasingly aggressive and wealthy bourgeoisie resented the tax exemptions and unearned prestige of the nobility. The nobility clung to their feudal privileges and challenged both the absolute power wielded by the weak heirs of Louis XIV and the demands of the rising middle classes.

Even France's kings helped bring on the revolution. Louis XV (1715–1774) lived for pleasure for most of his sixty-year reign and predicted with a sigh that after him

would come the Deluge. Louis XVI (1774–1792), a well-meaning but weak-willed man, dithered through most of his decade and a half of power—and reaped the whirl-wind.

The subversive literature of the Enlightenment fur-ther undermined the old order by creating a negative public image of the kings, aristocrats, and clergymen who ran it. Voltaire and his colleagues depicted the clergy as worldly and bigoted, the aristocracy as foppish and feck-less, and the monarchy itself as bearing ultimate respon-sibility for a society far gone in rot and decay. The French philosophes supported a Lockean notion of natural human rights, which contrasted sharply with the traditional priv-ileges claimed by the aristocracy and the Church. The rad-ical critique of the Enlightenment thus contributed sig-nificantly to the coming of the revolution.

In the late 1780s a series of linked economic and political crises swept France to the brink of revolution. Bad harvests and industrial depression sent mobs of bread rioters into the streets of French cities and gangs of hungry peasants roaming the countryside, burning and looting. At the same time, a financial crisis, rooted in military expen-ditures and in the tax exemptions of the nobility and the church, brought the government to the edge of bankruptcy. When all efforts at reform failed him, Louis XVI in desperation summoned an antique political assembly, the Estates General, to meet in the spring of 1789 and vote him the taxing power he needed to save the nation from economic and political collapse.

From that point on, things spiraled out of control. The representatives of the third estate—the 23 million—came up to the Estates General with long lists of popular grievances, shrugged off royal leading strings, and announced their intention to undertake a sweeping reformation of the state. The Paris mob stormed the Bastille. In the fall, another mob, composed mostly of Paris women, marched on Versailles demanding bread and returned with the royal family as virtual prisoners. In between these colorful scenes, the work of the revolution got under way.

COURSE OF THE REVOLUTION

This archetypal ideological revolution unfolded in four clearly definable stages over a violent decade, 1789–1799. The first and most creative phase of the French Revolution lasted for more than two years, 1789–1791. It produced France's bill of rights—the Declaration of the Rights of Man and the Citizen, including the ideals of Liberty, Equality, and Brotherhood. It formulated a written constitution replacing royal absolutism with limited constitutional monarchy. It saw the surrender of the feudal privileges of the nobility and the nationalizing of the French Catholic church and its vast wealth.

France was now roughly on a par with Britain across the Channel. For many enlightened French, this was quite far enough. But not for others, notably the members of the radical Jacobin clubs and their leader Maximilien Robespierre (1758–1794), a dedicated revolutionary known to his admirers as the Incorruptible. During the second stage of the revolution, the year of the constitutional monarchy (1791–1792), the revolt split into two main factions. The Jacobins and other extremists pushed for the establishment of a republic, while moderates such as the Girondins attempted instead to make the limited monarchy work.

Meanwhile, war hawks among the revolutionaries beat the drums for a great crusade to liberate all Europe from kings and priests. In so doing, they played into the hands of reactionary governments, who were looking for an excuse to extinguish the spirit of rebellion before it spread. In the spring of 1792, then, the Austrian Habsburgs led an invasion of France to rescue Louis XVI and his queen, Marie Antoinette, a Habsburg princess.

The third phase of the French Revolution was the notorious Reign of Terror (1792–1794). During this period of a little less than two years, Robespierre and the Jacobins ruled the beleaguered country through the Committee of Public Safety and the guillotine. Under Robespierre's ideologically impassioned rule, the king and queen were executed, the monarchy itself abolished. Many

nobles were also guillotined and their lands confiscated. Attempts were made to abolish the church altogether. Considerable numbers of revolutionaries, too moderate or too anarchistically radical for the Jacobins, also died under the slanting blade of the guillotine.

At the same time, the Jacobins turned the tide of war against the Austrians and their allies. By declaring that the nation now belonged to its people, they mobilized modern nationalism for the first time. Huge revolutionary armies of enthusiastic volunteers drove the invaders out of France and even occupied the Netherlands and the Rhineland. The Committee rallied all the resources, labor, and energies of the nation for this patriotic effort, which is thus sometimes seen as a precursor of the "total wars" of the twentieth century.

But the Square of the Revolution reeked with the blood of traitors, and even revolutionary Paris sickened of the carnage. In the summer of 1794, Robespierre and the Jacobin junta in their turn went under the knife, and the Reign of Terror was over.

The long, grimy final phase of the French Revolution was the rule of the Directory (1794–1799), a grubby period of ideological reaction and political opportunism. Genuine radicals were rooted out, while political careerists got rich. The war was prosecuted with zeal, not for the cause, but for loot, fame, and personal advancement. French armies led by one young general in particular—Napoleon Bonaparte—won famous victories, first and most brilliantly in Italy, then still farther afield, against the British in Egypt. And when General Bonaparte returned from the Battle of the Pyramids, a cabal of Directory politicians tried to use him as a front for their own power.

NAPOLEON CONQUERS EUROPE— AND MEETS HIS WATERLOO

But Napoleon Bonaparte (1769–1821) had a vision of his own destiny. A coup in 1799 made Napoleon first consul of France. His armies and a seemingly unending string of victories over the great powers of Europe did the rest.

This one-time Corsican artillery officer had learned from brilliant French military innovators. He had risen rapidly in the wide-open revolutionary years, when careers were made by talent rather than by aristocratic names. Napoleon used new light artillery brilliantly and maneuvered with great rapidity over European roads built by generations of enlightened despots. He had the huge, now thoroughly seasoned armies of the French Revolution at his disposal. And he had a rare genius for military command that puts him on any short list of the greatest generals of all time.

For a decade and a half, Napoleon Bonaparte ruled a larger European empire than anyone since ancient Rome. He crowned himself emperor of the French in 1804. By 1810 he, his family, and his generals ruled directly or indirectly over a collection of states that

Napoleon the Man of Destiny never looked more portentous than in this picture by the French revolutionary painter Jacques-Louis David. The young general is shown about to lead his troops over the Alps into Italy, where his dazzling victories would prepare the way for his rise to the imperial throne of France and to mastery of most of Europe. To add a historic dimension to this patriotic image, the artist has inscribed below Napoleon Bonaparte's name the fading name of Hannibal, the great African general who had led his armies across the Alps to ravage Roman Italy two thousand years before. (Jacques Louis David/Art Resource)

stretched from Spain to the frontiers of Russia, from the English Channel to the toe of Italy. Wherever his armies went, furthermore, Napoleon spread the ideals of the French Revolution. At home he was France's enlightened despot at last, streamlining institutions and modernizing laws with military efficiency.

It looked almost as if Europe might find the unity it had enjoyed in Roman times, under a child of the French Revolution.

But Europe's old regime fought back tenaciously against the "Corsican upstart." Britain, safe on its islands, would not make terms. Napoleon's invasion of Russia in 1812 was a fiasco—his first major setback. He had beaten three coalitions of great powers, but in 1813 a fourth defeated him at Leipzig, in the epochal Battle of the Nations. Temporarily exiled from Europe in 1814, Napoleon returned the following year for the miraculous Hundred Days that ended in 1815 at Waterloo.

It was the end of a great adventure—and the beginning of something even greater. For the revolution and its general had seeded Europe with radical ideas, images, and memories that would bear startling fruit for much of the coming century.

THE INDUSTRIAL REVOLUTION

ENERGY REVOLUTIONS

While the drama of the French Revolution and the epic of Napoleon were running their course across the English Channel, events that would prove even more significant were taking place in Britain: the Industrial Revolution.

In the narrowest sense of the term, the Industrial Revolution was the transformation of European industrial production between 1760 and 1830. In a broader sense, the Industrial Revolution continues to this day, a long unfolding of new technologies from steam to petroleum to nuclear power, from the locomotive to the microchip. The nineteenth century, the steam-engine age, may look primitive from the perspective of our age of space exploration, electronics, and computer technology. But the technological breakthrough of the later 1700s was crucial to all that came afterwards.

To accomplish anything at all—to feed, clothe, house ourselves, to build a pyramid or a skyscraper, to read a book or play a tune—human beings must have access to one thing: *energy*. The amount of energy available to us for all purposes, however, is strictly limited by the sources of energy we have at our disposal. Three stages in the exploitation of energy may be distinguished.[2]

For most of our evolution as a species, it will be remembered, we were hunters and gatherers. Our Paleolithic ancestors depended entirely upon the animals and plants they could collect in the course of each day. If our accomplishments were limited over those endless generations, it was because we could in this way accumulate only enough energy to support a tiny population from day to day.

Around ten thousand years ago, in the Middle East, the Agricultural Revolution began. Our Neolithic forebears learned to cultivate grain, domesticate animals, and thus feed substantially larger populations. Cities and empires developed, with large classes freed from primary energy gathering for more specialized tasks as priests and soldiers, merchants and craftspeople, artists and bureaucrats.

Nevertheless, the sources of energy at our disposal remained strictly biological, and a ceiling was thus placed on human achievement over the next ten thousand years,

---

[2]I follow here Carlo Cipolla, *The Economic History of World Population* (Baltimore: Penguin Books, 1982), chaps. 1 and 2.

including the five millennia of recorded history. An acre of wheat could only support so many human beings, an acre of pasturage only so many bullocks to labor for their human masters.

Then, a mere two hundred years ago, came the Industrial Revolution. For the first time, nonbiological energy sources were exploited in substantial quantities. Coal came into widespread use first, then oil and its derivatives, then hydroelectric power, and finally nuclear energy in our own time. Such alternatives as solar and geothermal energy are still to be adequately developed.

The energy locked up in these sources was immensely, indeed incalculably greater than the energy in acres of wheat, laboring oxen, or toiling human backs. With this extra energy, we have doubled our life spans, redoubled our population over and over, and built the push-button world of skyscrapers and jetliners we live in today.

How did this material transformation of human life come about—and why, out of all the centuries, did it happen when it did?

CAUSES OF THE INDUSTRIAL REVOLUTION

Attempts to explain the Industrial Revolution of the later 1700s no longer focus on a single central factor such as inventions or investment capital. Instead, a complex combination seems necessary to explain so momentous an event. Commonly cited among the components of the chemical mix that made the Industrial Revolution possible are resources, labor, demand, capital, technology, and entrepreneurship.

Natural resources, especially coal and iron, were essential. So was a substantial labor force free from agricultural labor. An increased demand from a growing population is often cited, as is capital accumulation to pay the huge initial cost of tooling up for industrial production. Invention undoubtedly played a part, though in the more systematic form of an ongoing process of technological development. Perhaps most important, there was the role of the entrepreneur, the catalytic agent that brought all the other elements together, added a touch of factory management and marketing skills—and made the Industrial Revolution happen.

ENGLAND AND THE AGE OF STEAM

The cultural milieu within which this combination first developed was Great Britain in the 1760s. Britain had resources in the iron and coal of the Midlands "black country." The British had surplus labor produced by the eighteenth-century Agricultural Revolution. They had immense amounts of capital from empire and trade, and a growing population to provide the requisite demand. And Britain had a vigorous middle class, including both skilled technicians and aggressive entrepreneurs.

The process began in textile manufacturing, notably the new cotton industry, which was more willing to inno-

vate than the older, more hidebound woolens business. In the cotton industry, small steam engines bred the factory system, embryonic assembly lines, and rapidly accelerating production. From textiles the new approach spread to heavy industry, transportation, and other central elements of the industrial economy. And from Great Britain the new technology spread to western Europe, North America, and on around the world. It is spreading still, its transforming effects greater even than the ideologies spawned by the French Revolution.

"Steam," they said in the nineteenth century, "is an Englishman." The importance of steam was summed up in a remark made by the well-known entrepreneur Matthew Boulton. Boulton had just finished showing a visitor around the Soho Manufactury, where he and James Watt produced the first industrial steam engines. "I sell here, Sir," Boulton told his guest, "what all the world desires to have—Power!"[3]

MAIN CURRENTS OF THE NINETEENTH CENTURY

PATTERNS: REVOLUTIONS AND POLITICAL CHANGE

In the two central sections of this chapter, we will look at the complicated history of nineteenth-century Europe in two ways. The present section will survey some of the main currents of the century in Europe as a whole. The section that follows will go over the same period country by country, offering a cavalcade of European nations in what was in some ways Europe's golden age.

The overall patterns of the political and economic history of Europe will provide us with a skeleton upon which we can hang what follows.

The first half of the nineteenth century—once the French and Industrial revolutions are accounted for—is a short one, historically speaking. It covers the period from 1815 to 1848, from Waterloo to the midcentury revolutions of 1848. In political terms, this was, in fact, Europe's Age of Revolutions, when Europe was as tormented by ideological revolt as the Third World has been since World War II.

At the time of Napoleon's defeat in 1814 and 1815, a great international conclave was held at Vienna to draw up a peace settlement after twenty years of Napoleonic wars. The goals of the Congress of Vienna, however, included not only a lasting peace but also a massive attempt to turn the historical clock back to the old regime, to the way things had been before 1789. To this end, pre-Napoleonic "legitimate" dynasties were restored to power,

---

[3]H. W. Dickinson, *Matthew Boulton* (Cambridge: Cambridge University Press, 1937), p. 73.

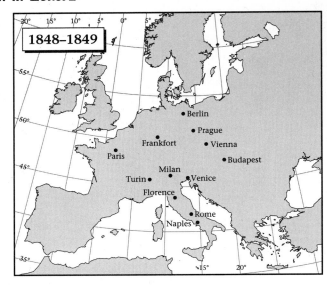

established churches were reestablished, and the old hereditary aristocrats were encouraged to reclaim their leading places in society everywhere. The primary architect of this Vienna settlement was the intensely conservative Austrian foreign minister, Prince Metternich. Metternich would lead the forces of European reaction for the next thirty-odd years.

You cannot, however, set history back like a clock. Reaction only bred more revolution—three and a half decades of it between 1815 and 1848.

The revolutions of the 1820s were largely on the southern and eastern fringes of the Continent, in European backwaters such as Spain, the Italian states, Greece, and Russia. The revolutions of 1830, however, carried the spirit of revolutionary change into the heart of western Europe, to France again and to Belgium and a number of the German states as well as to Italy and elsewhere.

The revolutions of 1848–1849, finally, saw the great floodtide of the movement—and its ebb. The "springtime of the peoples" in 1848 saw rebellion in France, Austria, Prussia and other German states, various Italian states, and elsewhere. Another French king was overthrown in Paris. The Habsburg emperor and Metternich himself were driven from Vienna by a revolution spearheaded by students and workers. The pope was expelled from Rome by a revolutionary upheaval. "If someone had said, 'God has been driven from heaven and a republic proclaimed there,'" the Russian anarchist Bakunin remarked of those amazing days, "everyone would have believed it and no one would have been surprised."[4]

---

[4]P. H. Noyes, *Organization and Revolution: Working-Class Associations in the German Revolutions of 1848–1849* (Princeton, N.J.: Princeton University Press, 1966), p. 57.

In 1849 the great tide turned. France got a new monarch to replace its deposed king, the Austrian emperor and the Roman pope returned, backed by bayonets, and the old order was apparently restored once more all across Europe.

Once again, however, pressures for change doggedly forced their way to the surface in Europe—peacefully this time, through continuing reform movements. And rulers, weary of revolutions, began to make concessions. By 1900 all the great powers except Russia had constitutions, elected legislatures, even bills of rights—and France was an established republic at last. Much more power remained in the hands of central and eastern European monarchs than was the case in western Europe. But the revolutionary agenda of the first half of the century had finally been achieved—through reform rather than revolution.

The second half of the century saw other major developments besides the victory of the liberal ideals of the French Revolution, however.

Nationalist movements achieved amazing triumphs in the third quarter of the nineteenth century, which saw the creation of two new great powers in Europe. In 1859–1860, Italy was united at last under the king of Piedmont and the guiding hand of his prime minister, Count Cavour. In 1870–1871, the German Empire unified all the German states except Austria under the Prussian house of Hohenzollern. The new nation, immediately recognized as the greatest power in Europe, was a monument to the greatest diplomat of the century, Prussia's Otto von Bismarck.

The last quarter of the nineteenth century, finally, saw a diversity of trends. Socialism, labor unions, and other developments advanced the cause of Europe's industrial workers during these decades. But this period also saw the beginnings of the rise of big business as we know it today. In addition, this was the period of the climax of the New Imperialism and the firm establishment of Western hegemony over the world. It was also, however, the period that paved the way to World War I—the beginning of the end of Europe's global supremacy.

The nineteenth century was certainly one of Europe's greatest ages. International wars were few and brief within Europe itself. The Industrial Revolution made Europe richer than any people had ever been before. Political and social reform built toward the healthier, freer, more egalitarian Europe of today.

But golden ages are not placid ones, and the nineteenth century was, as this outline has tried to indicate, far more than waltzes and bustles, Victorian smugness, and tea in the afternoon.

THE BIRTH OF THE MODERN IDEOLOGIES

It was, as indicated above, an age of ideological agitation unmatched by any in European history. It was, in fact, the century that saw the emergence of all the revolutionary social ideas that have transformed the world in our own century.

Karl Marx, the most influential of all the nineteenth-century ideologues, does not look much like the prophet of World Revolution in this picture. Though the great global upheaval he foresaw never came, Marx's theories inspired revolutionaries around the world. Born in Germany, Marx was driven to seek political asylum in other parts of Europe and died in London, where he did most of his writing. (New York Public Library Picture Collection)

A list of the radical seeds that were sown in the last century would have a distinctly contemporary ring to it. The first ideologically based student movement erupted in Germany just after 1815. The Italian freedom fighter Garibaldi pioneered the art of revolutionary guerrilla warfare in the 1830s, 1840s, and 1850s, while anarchists brought terrorist bombs to the streets of European cities in the last decades of the century. The women's movement began to make significant numbers of converts in the later 1800s, and the labor movement made substantial headway about this time also. The first stirrings of modern anti-imperialism were felt in the colonies. And so on down a considerably longer list.

Three great ideological trends, however, informed most of these demands for change in nineteenth-century Europe, as they have in the twentieth-century world as a whole: liberalism, nationalism, and socialism.

Nineteenth-century political *liberalism* built on the ideas of the seventeenth-century English thinker John Locke and of French Enlightenment philosophes such as Montesquieu and Rousseau. Liberals believed in Lockean "natural rights" to liberty and equality. They further asserted Locke's contract theory of government—government by consent of the governed—as put into practice in revolutionary France and America. Liberals were thus militantly opposed to hereditary aristocracies, divine-right monarchies, and political oppression in all its forms. They demanded freedom of speech, the press, and religion; equality of economic opportunity and equality before the law; constitutional government, elected legislatures, and bills of rights.

Liberalism had an economic dimension as well, however. Here liberals drew on the theories of Adam Smith, whose *Wealth of Nations* had come out in the revolutionary year 1776. Nineteenth-century liberals believed with Smith in natural laws governing the operation of the economy. These included the key law of supply and demand, which guaranteed that goods would be produced to meet any substantial demand, and that prices, wages, profits, and other aspects of the economy would best be regulated by natural market forces. Another basic liberal economic principle was the law of accumulation, which declared that the wealth of nations would grow steadily if supply and demand were allowed to operate freely. Liberal economists therefore opposed mercantilistic regulation of the economy and fought in particular for free trade—another of the great crusades of the first half of the century.

In some ways *nationalism* blazed even more brightly than liberalism across the nineteenth-century sky. Nineteenth-century nationalists built on the teachings of the eighteenth-century German cultural nationalists who preached the importance of each people's national spirit. They also drew on the model of the French Revolution, which had unleashed powerful patriotic energies, both in France and in nations conquered by Napoleon. Nationalists in the nineteenth century dedicated their energies to unifying divided peoples such as the Italians and the Germans. Or they labored to win national self-determination for oppressed minorities such as the eastern European, mostly Slavic peoples ruled by the Austrian, Russian, and Ottoman emperors. Later in the century, however, nationalism turned chauvinistic. It began to be used to justify the aggressive or expansionist policies of German or French or British governments in the eyes of their peoples.

Nationalists believed that common language and literature, history and custom welded a people into a larger whole—the nation. Some of them believed in a Folk Soul or Folk Spirit uniting a people spiritually. Many saw a national character that they shared with their fellow nationals: Frenchmen were naturally more civilized and artistic than other peoples, Germans more philosophical or scientific, Britons better at government and more practical, and so forth.

These apostles of nationality preached their patriotic creed in terms of native soil and blood—the black earth of Russia, for instance, or German or Anglo-Saxon blood. They expressed their loyalty with reverence for such concrete symbols as the national flag or the national anthem. They wept when the French Tricolor or the British Union Jack passed by, and they sang the "Marseillaise," "Britannia Rules the Waves," or "Germany over All" with passion.

The last of the major isms to develop was *socialism*. Socialism could claim few antecedents in earlier centuries. Socialists sought a solution to a uniquely nineteenth-century problem, after all: the problem of widespread working-class poverty in the middle of the Industrial Revolution. The new industrial order was producing more goods and services than the world had ever seen before. Yet the laborers who worked in the factories and mines lived in slums, worked long hours under brutal conditions, and were subject to malnutrition, disease, and early death. The socialist solution to this very genuine problem was, quite simply, the transfer of the means of production—the new mines and mills, railroads, banks, and the rest—from private ownership to ownership by the workers themselves.

Several sorts of socialism emerged in the nineteenth century. Utopian socialists urged a rejection of the Industrial Revolution itself and a return to small-scale handicraft production, preferably in small communities in the healthy countryside. Inspired by prophets such as Charles Fourier, Utopians did, in fact, establish a number of socialist country communes—as their successors do, here and there, to this day.

The most influential socialist theorist, however, was clearly Karl Marx (1818–1883), some of whose followers came to call themselves communists in later years. Marx rejected Utopianism as naive. He preached a more violent creed of working-class revolution against the capitalist entrepreneurs and investors who owned the new technology.

According to Marx's widely influential theory, all history had been a chronicle of class struggles between patrician and plebeian, lord and serf, guild master and journeyman. The present class struggle between the proletarians (workers) and their capitalist bosses would lead to a great world revolution. This final class war would end class struggle forever by putting the means of production in the hands of the working people once and for all. In the little tract called *The Communist Manifesto,* which he and his lifelong collaborator Friedrich Engels wrote in 1848, Marx urged the workers of the world to unite, overthrow the bourgeois-capitalist order everywhere, and establish the workers' paradise. Marx's theories helped to structure the state-socialist, one-party nations of Eastern Europe, East Asia, and elsewhere during much of the twentieth century.

The form of socialism that predominated in Western Europe, however, has been the more moderate type known as social-democratic or (in Great Britain) Fabian socialism. Social democrats drew some ideas from Marx, others from other socialist writers. But they firmly rejected revolution in favor of reform. Social democrats were more practical than the Utopians, more constitutionally minded than the revolutionary Marxists. They were willing to work with labor unions and liberal allies, using the free press and the ballot box to gain their ends. The socialist parties of Western Europe today are of this practical, reform-minded social-democratic sort.

Nineteenth-century ideologues of whatever stripe lived a hard life. Often censored, imprisoned, or driven into exile, they survived on dreams of coming revolutions and utopian futures. And though history seldom bore out their predictions in any detail, they did have a powerful impact on the history of their century—and on ours.

THE SPREAD OF THE INDUSTRIAL REVOLUTION

The economic development of preindustrial societies into modern, economically productive states has been high on the world's list of concerns since the new nations of Africa and Asia began to emerge after World War II. The first developing society, however, was Europe itself. And the European experience has influenced the development planning both of those who hold Europe up as a model and of those who reject the Western example totally.

The most striking elements in the continuing nineteenth-century evolution of the Industrial Revolution were the mid-century drive toward unrestricted freedom of competition and the countertrend of the later 1800s toward industrial combination—the startling phenomenon we call big business today.

The middle half of the nineteenth century, from the 1820s to the 1870s, was the heyday of free competition in the simplest sense of the term. Liberal entrepreneurs persuaded many governments that mercantilistic regulation of

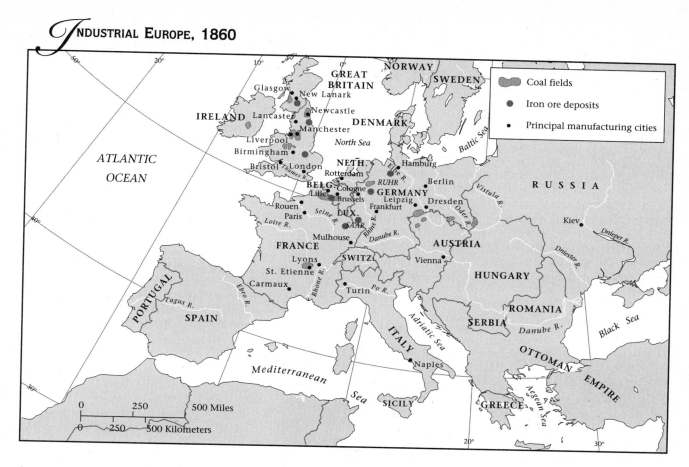

the economy was a handicap rather than a help to the new technology of the Industrial Revolution. Free trade, freely negotiated contracts between capital and labor, and a decline in government regulation of all sorts resulted.

By mid-century, competition between rival nations, between old and new industries, between countless small or middle-sized producers of the same good or service was widespread in Europe. Cloth making, coal mining, transportation all saw hundreds and even thousands of freely competing firms at work. "Competition," it was widely said, "is the life of trade and the law of progress."

In the last quarter of the century, however, there came a change. It was not a return to government regulation—that would not come on a large scale until the present century. It was rather the rigorous curtailment of free competition by businessmen themselves. These limits on competition were the result of large-scale business combinations—the sort that American law would come to call "combination in restraint of trade."

The move toward monopoly combination that began in the 1870s was in part a defensive measure in the face of the sheer brutality of the fang-and-claw competition of the age. During the periodic depressions particularly, unregulated competition hurt all competitors and drove many into

bankruptcy. Under such circumstances, many business leaders began to think that combination, not competition, might be the life of trade and even the law of survival. The result was the most amazing flower of nineteenth-century economic development: the rise of big business.

Some aggressive industrialists merged with or bought out either competitors or related industries to produce giant new corporations. Thus Albert Krupp, the German steelmaker, bought up coal and iron mines, ore boats, and even industries which used his steel. When complete, the Krupp family's industrial empire included machine-tool plants, railcar manufactures, a shipyard, and the arms industries for which his descendants would be most famous.

Another form of combination did not go to the length of actual corporate merger, but simply resorted to working agreements called *cartels*. Cartels, which might be national or even international in scope, fixed prices, assigned quotas, or divided up the market in ways that effectively eliminated competition. A shipping cartel organized first in Britain, for instance, expanded to include major steamship lines in Germany, France, the Netherlands, and even Japan. This single group came close to setting ocean fares and freight rates on the sea-lanes of the world.

This was the trend as the twentieth century got under way, and it has remained a main current of Western economic history since. Big business controls more of the Western world's economic activity today than big government ever has.

AN EVOLVING SOCIETY

The structure of society in an industrializing, increasingly ideological Europe of course differed in some striking ways from European society under the old regime. But there were notable similarities with the past as well. And there were indications of movement in directions that have a very familiar ring to citizens of our own century.

Over much of nineteenth-century Europe, the landed nobility remained the most prestigious class, and the peasants—freeholders, laborers, even serfs—the most numerous. The medieval guilds at last expired, but many small shops remained, producing by hand everything from bread to shoes. Even the most progressive cities still had many more narrow, cobblestoned streets than modern boulevards, and any country lane still led to peasant villages.

The most noticeable new class in Western Europe, and to increasing extent in central Europe as well, was the new work force created by the Industrial Revolution. The proletariat, as this group came to be called, was drawn in immense numbers to the new industrial cities by work in mills, mines, railway yards, and other elements of the new industrial society. Men, women, and children worked twelve- and fourteen-hour days and lived jammed into malodorous, unsanitary, disease-ridden slums. Frequently unemployed and normally underpaid and resentful, the proletariat was widely feared as a dangerous element in the population, social dynamite ticking toward an explosion.

The predominant class in Western Europe, finally, consisted more and more of the industrial, commercial, and financial middle classes, who profited from the new industrial order. Britain was a "nation of shopkeepers" and proud of it. In France, the *haute bourgeoisie* of industrial and financial magnates pushed to the fore. Middle-class liberal politicians and journalists worked to advance the interests of this emergent elite. And the brownstone front in London and the Paris town house—the homes of the middle class—grew more and more crowded with the

Gustave Doré, one of the best-known illustrators of the 1800s, here captures the urban misery of a London slum. The working people of the great city are shown wandering in the streets or leaning out of tenement windows to catch a breath of sooty air. How has the artist conveyed a sense of the grimness of slum life? (Art Resource)

material possessions that were the sign and seal of bourgeois success.

Sheer numbers, finally, distinguished the society of nineteenth-century Europe as of so many other parts of the world. The accelerating population explosion turned the 200 million Europeans of the early 1800s into 450 million by 1914. Population growth seems to have been due, as usual, to a combination of causes: increased supplies of food, thanks to agricultural technology; younger marriages; the conquest of some diseases; and improvement in sanitation. Most of the new population flooded into the cities, and for the first time since the fall of the Roman Empire, cities of half a million, a million, and more appeared in Europe.

It was a contentious, crowded, vigorous society that took shape in that Europe of a century ago, a society many of whose problems would not be solved until our own time.

WOMEN CHALLENGE THE SYSTEM

The multiple conditions of women remained as diverse as ever, but there seems to have been a new twist: an image of womanhood that would prove a hard cross for subsequent generations of Western women to bear.

Peasant women still handled chores as well as housework and child rearing, and rallied to the fields at harvest time. Many poor girls and women, like many men, were personal servants or salespeople in shops or eating houses, and prostitution flourished in the mushrooming cities. Petty-bourgeois women often ran the shop, and aristocratic ladies supervised large households, as they had in past centuries.

Some new lines of work opened up for women, however. Female proletarians shared their husbands' grueling lives in the mills and even in the mines, perhaps suffering more for the lower wages they were paid. But a number of more respectable professions opened up to women, including positions as governesses, elementary schoolteachers, nurses (toward the end of the century), and, for the talented, writing. Novelists such as the three Brontë sisters and Jane Austen, George Eliot and George Sand, and poets such as Elizabeth Barrett Browning and Christina Georgina Rossetti established a place for women at the top of the world of letters.

In the latter part of the nineteenth century, the organized movement for female emancipation emerged in Europe. As early as the 1840s, Utopian socialists had preached female equality, and by mid-century some liberals also spoke up for political rights for women. During the later decades of the century, women in fact gained improved legal status: married women got control of their own property, for example, and divorce became easier. Contraception began to liberate some women from the burden of large families. Women were admitted to universities and invaded formerly all-male professions such as medicine. They were also increasingly prominent among radical and revolutionary groups in countries such as Russia and France. In England they organized a vigorous, sometimes violent campaign to get the right to vote—the "suffragette" campaign that finally led to women's suffrage after World War I. It was the first wave of a women's movement that still continues.

Most women of all classes, however, still married and reared children. And it was in the nineteenth century that this ancient women's occupation acquired the special luster it was to enjoy for more than a hundred years thereafter, down to our own time. Middle-class women were even urged to do nothing else *but* serve as companions for their husbands and mothers for their children—both of which were now believed to be tasks requiring much tact, training, character, and intelligence. Women who aspired to the other professions just opening up to them were told that they were too "fine" for such crude masculine concerns as business, medicine, or politics.

They were, as the saying went, "put on a pedestal" to be worshiped by their men—who meantime went on running the world. The descent of women from this pedestal would require another psychic revolution in our own century.

 ## THE CAVALCADE OF NATIONS

BRITAIN IN AN AGE OF REFORM

The archbishop of Canterbury and several other hoary-headed statesmen woke Princess Victoria up in the middle of the night to tell her the news. At the age of seventeen, she had inherited the throne of the largest empire in the world. After they left, Victoria wrote by candlelight in her journal: "I shall do my utmost to fulfil my duty toward my country. I am very young, but I am sure that very few have more desire to do what is fit and right than I have."[5]

The year was 1837. She would rule the British Empire for the rest of a long and prosperous century, and few would ever accuse her of doing anything that was not "fit and right." She would become the living symbol of the Victorian Age, the century when Brittania ruled the waves and the sun never set on the British Empire. A central achievement of that prosperous and progressive century was the growth of democratic institutions in Britain's "age of reform."

The domestic history of Britain in the nineteenth century is in fact usually presented as a chronicle of social and political reform. Queen Victoria (ruled 1837–1901) presided over a parliamentary government that was able to change with the times, to meet the needs of a rapidly

[5]Quoted in Giles St. Aubyn, *Queen Victoria: A Portrait* (New York: Atheneum, 1992), p. 57.

"*It is vain to expect virtue from women till they are, in some degree, independent of men; nay, it is vain to expect that strength of natural affection, which would make them good wives and mothers. Whilst they are absolutely dependent on their husbands they will be cunning, mean, and selfish, and the men who can be gratified by the fawning fondness of spaniel-like affection, have not much delicacy, for love is not to be bought. . .*

But what have women to do in society? I may be asked. . .

Women might certainly study the art of healing, and be physicians as well as nurses. And midwifery, decency seems to allot to them. . . .

They might, also, study politics, and settle their benevolence on the broadest basis; for the reading of history will scarcely be more useful than the perusal of romances, if read as mere biography; if the character of the times, the political improvements, arts, etc. be not observed. In short, if it be not considered as the history of man; and not of particular men, who filled a niche in the temple of fame. . . .

Business of various kinds, they might likewise pursue, if they were educated in a more orderly manner, which might save many from common and legal prostitution. Women would not then marry for a support, as men accept of places under government, and neglect the implied duties; nor would an attempt to earn their own subsistence, a most laudable one, sink them almost to the level of those poor abandoned creatures who live by prostitution. . . . How much more respectable is the woman who earns her own bread by fulfilling any duty, than the most accomplished beauty!—"

Mary Wollstonecraft (1759–1797), an eighteenth-century writer, teacher, and radical intellectual, was also a pioneer feminist crusader. Inspired by the French Revolution and its ringing assertions of the "Rights of Man," she produced her own <u>Vindication of the Rights of Woman</u> in 1792.

Wollstonecraft's social vision, like that of other Enlightenment radicals, saw human unhappiness and vice as consequences of faulty social organization. What does she here suggest caused the women of her time to be "cunning, mean, and selfish"? What jobs beyond that of wife and mother does she believe women could perform in society? What is Wollstonecraft's view of the history books available in her day?

Mary Wollstonecraft, <u>Vindication of the Rights of Woman</u> (London: J. Johnson, 1792), pp. 321–322, 337–338, 340.

evolving industrial society. Politicians of various persuasions, from the Liberal William Gladstone to the Conservative Benjamin Disraeli, both guided and responded to the wishes of a growing electorate to produce the model of a functioning nineteenth-century Western democracy—social change through the ballot box.

Parliamentary reform bills extending the right to vote to one group after another provided the skeleton of Britain's age of reform. The great Reform Bill of 1832 gave new industrial cities such as Manchester and Bir-mingham—and the business middle classes everywhere—representation in Parliament. Disraeli's reform bill of 1867 granted the suffrage to factory workers, Gladstone's bill of 1884 awarded it to farm laborers, and the 1918 bill climaxed the women's suffrage movement by giving the vote to most women.

Other reform measures included laws designed to render the new industrial system more livable. Laws regulating women's working conditions and child labor were passed, as were factory-safety acts and legislation limiting the length of the working day. Public education began in Britain in the later nineteenth century. During the years before World War I, a Liberal government enacted such socialistic measures—as they then seemed—as the beginnings of public health service and old-age pensions.

There was tension, of course—the massive and sometimes violent demonstrations connected with the Reform Bill of 1832, the (failed) Chartist movement of the 1840s demanding universal manhood suffrage, and the women's campaign for the suffrage in the 1890s and early 1900s. But the system proved flexible and strong enough to contain and channel all such pressures. Change came comparatively peacefully, through the democratic process.

FRANCE'S CENTURY OF REVOLUTION

Social change came also to France, the other more liberal member of the great powers. But in France, change came as much through revolution as through reform.

Revolutionary barricades went up in Paris four times between the late 1700s and the later 1800s: in the great revolution of 1789, in 1830, in 1848, and in the destructive Paris Commune of 1871. New forms of government were established by force five times between 1815 and 1914: three monarchies—the restored Bourbons, the constitutional monarchy of Louis Philippe, and the empire of Louis Napoleon after 1848—and two republics, the Second and the Third, the latter lasting until 1940. Only the French civil service, a centralized structure of administration rationalized and strengthened by Napoleon I, provided basic continuity in government.

Political change thus came to France revolution by revolution. The restored Bourbons felt it expedient to grant France a constitution and a two-house legislature in 1814. Bourgeois voting and political predominance came with Louis Philippe, "the middle-class king," in 1830. Universal manhood suffrage made a brief appearance under the Second Republic, was permanently established by the Third in 1875. Women, however, did not vote till the 1940s. Other social reforms also lagged in the land that had given birth to the Enlightenment. But change did come, and nineteenth-century France saw no more revolutions after 1871.

BISMARCK AND GERMAN UNIFICATION

Chancellor Bismarck, chief minister of the king of Prussia, looked at the faces of this key committee of the legislature with undisguised disdain.

The liberals in the Prussian legislature opposed Bismarck's demand for tax hikes to further strengthen the feared Prussian army. These politicians seemed to think that their endless discussions and disputes determined what the Prussian monarchy was going to do. Looking the assembled political leaders in the eye, Bismarck let them have a dose of hard-boiled realism. "The great issues of

the day," he declared, will not be decided "by speeches and resolutions, but by blood and iron!"[6]

Bismarck, Germany's "iron chancellor," would prove the truth of his tough, grim view of history as architect of German unification and as the greatest statesman in Europe during the second half of the nineteenth century.

The Austrian Habsburgs had dominated the German states since the Middle Ages. The Prussian Hohenzollerns had been challenging that predominance since Frederick the Great's long feud with Empress Maria Theresa in the mid-eighteenth century. In the nineteenth century, Prussia added to its efficient administration and its powerful army a dynamic, rapidly growing industrial machine and close economic relations with other industrializing North German states. Finally, shortly after the revolutions of 1848, the Prussian king William acquired a chief minister who was also the greatest diplomatic manipulator of his age: Otto von Bismarck (1815–1898).

Bismarck, a huge, powerfully built Junker with an incongruously high-pitched voice, was the architect of modern Germany. He was no ideological nationalist, but an old-fashioned royal minister, loyal to the interests of the house of Hohenzollern. He was also not the master planner of later legend. He was rather a brilliant opportunist and manipulator, playing his diplomatic cards as they fell and winning far more often than he lost.

Bismarck demonstrated the power of the Prussian army in the brief Danish War of 1863 and defeated Austria itself handily in the Austro-Prussian War of 1866. He then rallied all the rest of the German states in a war of revenge against their common enemy, the victorious Franco-Prussian War of 1870–1871. Intoxicated with their triumph over the French emperor Napoleon III, the German princes gathered in Louis XIV's great Hall of Mirrors at Versailles in the spring of 1871 to swear allegiance to the king of Prussia, now Emperor William I of the new German Empire.

Bismarck proceeded to guide the destinies of the new united Germany for the next twenty years. Austria, meanwhile, labored through a sea of troubles, political and otherwise.

AUSTRIA'S POLYGLOT EMPIRE

Austria's besetting political problem between 1815 and 1914 was that of growing and conflicting nationalisms within its multinational empire. Inspired by ideologues to take their German, Italian, Hungarian, and various forms of Slavic background very seriously, the peoples ruled from Vienna demanded so much autonomy that in the wake of World War I the empire itself would be fragmented and destroyed.

---

[6]Quoted in René Albrecht-Carrié, *Europe Since 1815: From the Ancient Regime to the Atomic Age* (New York: Harper, 1962), p. 108.

Austria also industrialized in the nineteenth century, though not as impressively as Prussia or the new German Empire, which was second only to Great Britain among European industrial states by 1900. Austria and the new Germany both established elected legislatures, though each was elected by limited suffrage and neither had great power. But the central difference between them lay in their reactions to the new ideology of nationalism. The German Empire, however reluctantly, became the embodiment of Europe's most powerful national feeling, and prospered mightily. The Austrian Empire necessarily fought nationalism to the death—and perished thereby.

ITALIAN UNIFICATION

You can see heroic paintings of Garibaldi in half the courthouses in Italy, leading his Red Shirts to victory all across the nation he helped to found. This deification by the Italian state is an ironic end to the career of one of the greatest revolutionaries and guerrilla fighters of the nineteenth century.

The new kingdom of Italy was a more or less pure and certainly enthusiastic product of the new nationalism. Divided like Germany into many small principalities since the Middle Ages, Italy after 1815—again like the German states—was dominated by Austria. For half a century, from the Congress of Vienna to the revolutions of 1848, Italian nationalists such as the ideologue Giuseppe Mazzini and the guerrilla leader Giuseppe Garibaldi worked to overthrow Italy's petty despots and expel the Austrian power that supported them. Garibaldi led rebel forces in 1830, in 1848, and finally in the victorious years 1859–1860.

Success, however, came only when the cause of Italian liberation and unification was taken up by Piedmont, the northernmost, most industrially developed, and most liberal of Italian states. Piedmont's prime minister, Count Camillo di Cavour, threw his boundless energies, his diplomatic skill, and his country's small but efficient army into the struggle in the 1850s. Cavour negotiated an alliance with France for a brief war against its ancient enemy, Austria. Behind this screen of military action in the north, well-organized rebellions in much of Italy and a brilliant campaign by Garibaldi in the south freed the peninsula of its Austrian puppet rulers. Then in a plebiscite the Italians voted for unification as a constitutional monarchy under the royal house of Piedmont.

RUSSIA RESISTS CHANGE

If modern Italy was the creation of the new isms—nationalism, liberalism, industrialism—czarist Russia was the slowest of the powers to recognize these forces. The Russian Empire was the most determined hold-out against all the nineteenth-century ideologies, as well as the most underdeveloped industrially of all Europe's great powers. Despite the best that Peter and Catherine the Great had been able to do in the preceding century, Russia remained socially and economically backward. It had a minuscule middle class, a large serf population, and a medieval Russian Orthodox religion that had yet to come to terms with the Enlightenment, let alone Darwinian evolution.

Furthermore, because of the success of absolutist rulers such as Peter and Catherine, Russian autocracy was absolute. The czars depended on a horde of bureaucrats, a sinister secret police known as the Third Section, and regiments of Cossacks for riding down street demonstrations or punishing troublesome villages.

The history of Russia between 1815 and 1914 is a story of few and tentative concessions to modernity followed by brutal repression of "Westernizers" who sought reform or turned in desperation to revolution. The reforming czar Alexander II (1856–1881) abolished serfdom, instituted some local self-government, and undertook other, more modest reforms. But after his assassination—for not going far enough—repression was once more the order of the day. The Russia to which Marxism came at the end of the century was thus a land in which revolution seemed to many the only hope at all for change.

THE CLIMAX OF EUROPEAN CULTURE

MOODS: ROMANTICISM AND MATERIALISM

It may seem foolhardy to label any period in the ongoing history of a living society as the climax of its cultural achievement. The nineteenth century was, however, the last period in which there flourished a distinctively *European* culture, free of major foreign influences, a model for colonial art and thought around the world. In this sense, at least, the life of the European spirit in the 1800s may be said to constitute the historic climax of European culture.

Two overarching worldviews dominated European cultural life during that century: romanticism and materialism. Romanticism flourished during the first half of the century and enjoyed a revival in the late 1800s. Materialism predominated during the second half of the century.

These broad views of the world, or *Weltanschauungen,* were articulated less precisely than the ideologies were; they were more a matter of assumption, perspective, or attitude. But they did impart tone and feeling to the life of the Western mind. They determined public attitudes toward arts, sciences, ideologies, and indeed society itself. These sweeping worldviews may thus have been more important to European culture in this climactic period than more precisely expressed artistic insights or scientific theories.

The romantic movement, best known for its artistic expressions, was actually a broad-gauge cultural rebellion. Romantic poets, painters, composers, and other leaders of the movement certainly thought of it as an artistic revolt. It was a demand for movement, color, emotion in the arts, and a rejection of the rigidity and aridity of classicism. It was an enthusiasm for exotic new subject matter, from medieval knights and Renaissance adventurers to Turkish harems and simple peasant cottages. It was a call for freedom, the liberation of the romantic ego from the rules of the academies and the models of the ancients and the old masters.

It was also, however, the beginning of a broad sense of cultural alienation and of a sweeping rebellion against the tyranny of human reason itself. Both of these broader aspects of the romantic revolt have persisted down to our own time.

The romantics' feeling of alienation from the dull, crass bourgeois-philistine society they lived in was very powerful. It led them to turn from society to nature, to draw strength and solace from woods and flowers, from the Alps, the sea, the wild west wind. This romantic sense of alienation drove some artists to flee the West entirely, to explore North Africa, the Middle East, or even the South Seas. And many who were not artists came to feel that they too were out of sympathy with their own time, strangers in their own land.

The romantic revolt against reason has become an even more fundamental part of Western consciousness. Romantics thought that the Enlightenment and the Scientific Revolution provided only thinly cerebral, emotionally unconvincing explanations for things. Since Plato and Aristotle, Western culture had defined humanity as the *rational* animal; now the romantics turned away from reason to glorify the emotions instead.

Love, beauty, suffering, human will, dreams, drugs, enthusiasm for such allegedly nonrational beings as peasants, savages, and children, a fascination with supernatural phenomena, mystic intuitions of God—nonrational elements flooded the romantic consciousness. "All theory, my friend, is gray," said Goethe's *Faust:* "but green is life's glad golden tree."[7] Wordsworth went even further in condemning human reason:

> Our meddling intellect
> Misshapes the beauteous forms of things;
> We murder to dissect.[8]

The physical sciences, however, produced some notable advances in the 1800s. As new trends in the arts had fostered the romantic worldview in the first half of the century, progress in the sciences encouraged the materialist *Weltanschauung* in the second half.

During this period scientists learned more than ever before about the nature of matter. The modern theory of the atomic and molecular structure of matter, the cellular construction of living matter, the germ theory of disease,

Darwinian evolution, and much more first came to light at this time. The prestige of the sciences and the scientific method rose once again, especially after the appearance of Charles Darwin's epochal *Origin of Species* in 1859, as it had in the wake of Newton's *Principia* nearly two centuries before. And with science came materialism, which found more followers than ever before.

This was not the crude commercial materialism that delights in owning material possessions. It was the more profound philosophical materialism that denies the existence of anything *but* matter.

For this school of thought, God was a myth, the human soul an illusion, humanity itself simply a somewhat more complicated ape. Claiming to be realistic rather than sentimental, hard-boiled rather than tenderhearted, materialists turned from religion to science, from poetry to economics. They agreed with the German philosopher Friedrich Nietzsche that God was dead, and with Auguste Comte, the founder of modern sociology, that if there was anything left to worship, it was rational humanity itself.

Romanticism and materialism colored the thought of their respective half centuries. Early cultural nationalists were romantics, revolutionaries of the heart; Bismarck and Cavour, who unified their countries, were hard-boiled realists, manipulators of armies and masters of diplomatic chicanery. Utopian socialists were romantic, back-to-nature communards; Marx was an atheist, a materialist, and a worshiper at the shrine of hard economic facts.

Wordsworth's heart leaped up when he beheld a rainbow in the sky. Bazarov, the materialistic young antihero of Turgenev's *Fathers and Sons,* cuts up frogs for medical experiments.

ART AND THE IMAGE OF THE AGE

The arts in this divided age have one overwhelming thing in common: a fascination with the age itself, which fostered a longing to portray that age in words or pictures much as it really was.

Romantic painters, with their love for nature and for people who lived close to it, may have made their sowers and harvesters a bit more bronzed and husky, their countryside a little greener, their ocean bursting into spray a touch more sublime than nature managed. But John Constable surely got the farm wagons right in his *Hay Wain,* or Jean-Francois Millet the heave and strain of his laboring *Quarriers.* And if J.M.W. Turner's seascapes please us as abstract explosions of color, they also give a vivid impression of real sea and sky ablaze with sunset light.

The realist and even many impressionist and postimpressionist painters of the latter half of the century are more likely to show us around the city and the suburbs, the world of the triumphant bourgeoisie. One can wash up at the basin in front of the mirror in the morning with Mary Cassatt (*La Toilette*), spend Sunday in the park with Georges Seurat (*La Grande Jatte*), go dancing at the

---

[7]Johann Wolfgang Goethe, *Faust, Part One,* trans. Philip Wayne (Baltimore: Penguin Books, 1949), p. 98.

[8]William Wordsworth, *The Thorn,* iii.

British artist J. M. W. Turner's <u>Keelmen Heaving in Coals by Moonlight</u> illustrates the nineteenth-century's rediscovery of light and color—concerns that would link romanticism with the modernist movement of the twentieth century. Can you see how the picture is more "about" light than about its alleged subject—loading coal onto ships? (Joseph Mallord Turner. <u>Keelmen Heaving in Coals by Moonlight</u>. Canvas. 36-1/4 × 48-1/4 [0.923 × 1.288]. National Gallery of Art, Washington, D.C. Widener Collection 1942)

Moulin de la Galette with Auguste Renoir, the bourgeois artist par excellence, or visit the *Moulin Rouge* with the dwarfish nightclub painter Henri de Toulouse-Lautrec. One might end the evening with the urbane Édouard Manet, having a drink at *Bock's* and visiting the celebrated prostitute *Olympia,* her small body reclining a bit stiffly on the bed, an unconvincing flower over her left ear.

The prose and poetry of the nineteenth century also offer up the age in living, breathing, sometimes exhausting detail. Jane Austen's novels of English society bring the world of the country gentry convincingly before us, with their provincial balls and journeyings, their endless concern with property and marriage, family life, common sense, and human individuality. Charlotte Brontë's *Wuthering Heights* takes us deep into the labyrinthine twists and turns of two tormented human hearts, showing us two passionate lives led in a bleak northern English world of harsh winds and hardened souls.

The urban realities are there too, in the immense canvases of the century's fiction. The many socially realistic novels of Honoré de Balzac give us all Paris in the first half of the century, those of Émile Zola all France in the second half. We can visit the malodorous slums of London with Charles Dickens, explore the unfamiliar world of the Russian serfs in Ivan Turgenev's *Sportsman's Sketches,* or probe with the Norwegian dramatist Henrik Ibsen the corruption behind the frock coats, frilly bodices, and formal manners of the bourgeois drawing room.

The spirit of the age is here, too, the surging emotions of nineteenth-century writers and artists. Aurore Dupin, France's most famous woman of letters, astonished her contemporaries by taking the male name of George Sand, dressing as a man, smoking cigars, and writing some of the century's best-selling novels. Her love affairs with fellow writers and with the composer Chopin were as notorious as her novels like *Indiana* were famous. George Sand hurled herself into everything she did with the passion for life she described to a friend: "To live! how wonderful, how lovely. . . . To live is to be in a state of constant intoxication! To live is happiness! To live is Heaven!"[9]

But there is always the awareness of the physical realities of nineteenth-century life. When Balzac describes the boardinghouse where *Old Man Goriot* lives, we see every crack and knickknack, we hear the very boardinghouse conversation over dinners a century and a half ago. When Zola takes us through *les Halles,* the vast, heaped, crowded, noisy food markets of old Paris, we can smell the rotting vegetables, see the bloom on the fruit that Paris housewives thumbed and dropped into their shopping bags a hundred years ago. Even the most Romantic poet of the nineteenth century had an eye for concrete detail that many a more modern writer might envy. Keats shows us summer woods as real as Balzac's boardinghouse as he wanders

> Through verdurous glooms and winding mossy
>   ways . . .
> The murmurous haunt of flies on summer eves.[10]

The flies would never have been there in an Elizabethan sonnet; they might dominate the picture in a twentieth-century production. In the nineteenth, they were simply there, part of the richness of that European cultural climax.

[9]Quoted in Bonnie S. Anderson and Judith P. Zinsser, *A History of Her Own: Women in Europe from Prehistory to the Present* (New York: Harper Collins, 1988), p. 170.

[10]John Keats, "Ode to a Nightingale," in Arthur Quiller-Couch, ed., *The Oxford Book of English Verse* (Oxford: Clavendon Press, 1939), p. 743.

Summary

A century of radical change in Europe began in the later 1700s, with the French Revolution (1789–1799) and the Industrial Revolution, which got under way in England in the 1760s.

The French Revolution was rooted in the deep social dislocations of the old regime and in the radical social critique of the Enlightenment. The Revolution accelerated through a series of stages, which would be followed by later upheavals. Its most immediate outcome was the rise of Napoleon Bonaparte, the "man on horseback" who restored order and directed the new energies unleashed by the Revolution into the conquest of much of Europe. The key long-term consequence was the beginning of more than half a century of ideological revolutions in Europe.

The harnessing of steam power to work industrial machinery was at least as revolutionary an event. The Industrial Revolution, resulting from the coming together of a number of social, economic, and natural elements, put vast new energy sources at the disposal of the human race. The capacity to exploit these nonbiological forms of energy multiplied the economic output of the Western World many times over in the century that followed.

The main currents of nineteenth-century history flowed from these eighteenth-century beginnings. Between 1815 and 1848 Europe was swept by its age of revolutions, most of which failed but were followed by decades of reform. The third quarter of the century was highlighted by the unification of two new European great powers, Germany and Italy. The fourth quarter saw the rise of big business and of the labor movement and the resurgence of overseas empire building known as the New Imperialism.

It was an age of intensely felt revolutionary ideologies: liberalism, nationalism, socialism, and their offshoots. It spawned industrial corporations and cartels that dwarfed any earlier forms of economic organization. It was a century of expanding population, middle-class predominance, increasing pressure from the proletariat, and the birth of the modern women's movement.

The European nations related to these general trends in a variety of ways. Britain and France emerged as the most liberal of the European powers—the former through reform, the latter through successive revolutions. Bismarck unified Germany and saw it become an industrial colossus second only to Britain. Austria lost its preeminence in central Europe and much of its hold on its non-German national minorities. Italy, unified by dashing activists like Garibaldi and the shrewd Count Cavour, was more liberal but not as powerful as Germany was. Russia remained the most economically backward and politically autocratic of Europe's great powers.

The cultural history of nineteenth-century Europe was dominated by romanticism, originating in the arts, and by materialism, rooted in the progress of the sciences. Romantic alienation and materialistic atheism would spread further still in the twentieth century. The arts vividly reflected the social history of the age, from realistic fiction and romantic poetry to painting of all schools.

Suggested Reading

APPLEWHITE, H. *Women in the Age of the Democratic Revolution.* Ann Arbor, Mich.: 1990. Essays on women's role in the revolutions of the late 1700s and early 1800s.

BARTLETT, C. J., ed. *Britain Pre-Eminent: Studies in British World Influence in the Nineteenth Century.* London: Macmillan, 1969. The unique position of Britain, mother of Parliaments and master of the world's largest empire, in the days when steam was an Englishman and Britannia ruled the waves.

BEALES, D. *The Risorgimento and the Unification of Italy.* New York: Barnes & Noble, 1971. Balanced survey of the nationalist movement in Italy and its consequences.

BEST, G. *War and Revolution in Europe, 1770–1870.* New York: St. Martin's Press, 1982. Sees the French Revolution as intensifying warfare by mobilizing the masses, and Prussian military leaders adding technical and organizational efficiency to further increase the destructiveness of modern warfare.

CHURCH, C. H. *Europe in 1830: Revolution and Political Change.* Boston: Allen and Unwin, 1983. Good brief summary of the revolutionary year across Europe.

CIPOLLA, C. *The Economic History of World Population,* 6th ed. London: Penguin, 1975. Brief but brilliant account of the roots of modern achievement in basic energy sources.

COATES, W. H., and H. V. WHITE. *The Ordeal of Liberal Humanism.* New York: McGraw-Hill, 1969. European intellectual history in the nineteenth and twentieth centuries, organized around the liberal mainstream. See also R. W. Grant, *John Locke's Liberalism* (Chicago: University of Chicago Press, 1987), on Locke's liberal political theory and its place in the liberal tradition.

DOYLE, W. *Origins of the French Revolution.* Oxford: Oxford University Press, 1980. Good place to begin on the historical debate over causes of the great upheaval. See also R. W. Greenlaw, ed., *The Social Origins of the French Revolution: The Debate on the Role of the Middle Classes* (Lexington, Mass.: Heath, 1975).

EISELEY, L. *Darwin's Century.* New York: Doubleday, 1958. The evolution of evolutionism. For its impact, see J. C. Greene, *The Death of Adam* (Ames: University of Iowa Press, 1959).

FURST, L. *Romanticism in Perspective,* 2nd ed. Atlantic Highlands, N.J.: Humanities Press, 1979. Clear interpretative analysis, putting the movement in its historical setting. For a selection of representative writings, see H. Hugo, ed., *The Romantic Reader* (New York: Viking, 1975).

HEILBRONER, R. *The Worldly Philosophers,* 5th ed. New York: Touchstone, 1980. Eminently readable treatment of economists and economics in the tradition of Adam Smith.

KOHN, H. *Nationalism: Its Meaning and History,* rev. ed. New York: Van Nostrand, 1965. Concise summary of evolution and meanings of the most influential modern ideology. For a critical analysis, see B. C. Shafer, *Nationalism: Myth and Reality* (New York: Harcourt, Brace and World, 1955).

LANDES, D. S. *The Unbound Prometheus: Technological Change and Industrial Development in Western Europe from 1750 to the Present.* Cambridge: Cambridge University Press, 1969. The long view of the Industrial Revolution, convincingly presented. See also S. Pollard, *Peaceful Conquest: The Industrialization of Europe, 1760–1970* (New York: Oxford University Press, 1981).

LONGFORD, E. *Queen Victoria: Born to Succeed.* New York: Harper & Row, 1964. Admired life of the long-lived queen. For a more recent—and more negative—view, see S. Weintraub, *Victoria: An Intimate Biography* (New York: E. P. Dutton, 1987).

LUKACS, G. *Essays on Realism,* trans. D. Fernbach. Cambridge, Mass.: MIT Press, 1983. Studies of the other main current of nineteenth-century art and thought, by an eminent Western Marxist.

MARX, K., and F. ENGELS. *Basic Writings on Politics and Philosophy.* Boston: Peter Smith, 1975. A good sample of the work of the founders of Marxism. For expert commentary, see G. Lichtheim, *Marxism: An Historical and Critical Study* (New York: Columbia University Press, 1982), or E. Wilson's less authoritative but extremely readable *To the Finland Station* (New York: Farrar, Straus & Giroux, 1972).

MARKHAM, F. *Napoleon.* New York: New American Library, 1963. Good life of the greatest general of modern times. See also O. Connelly, *Blundering to Glory: Napoleon's Military Campaigns* (Wilmington, Del.: Scholarly Resources, 1987), suggesting that persistence and drive, rather than "genius," lay behind the French general's unparalleled string of victories.

MILL, J. S. *Essential Works of John Stuart Mill.* New York: Bantam Books, 1961. Includes important works of the quintessential nineteenth-century liberal. See also his *On the Subjection of Women* (Cambridge, Mass.: MIT Press, 1970).

PALMER, R. R. *The Age of the Democratic Revolution.* Princeton: Princeton University Press, 1980. Controversial but influential thesis of a wave of democratic revolutions sweeping across the Western world. P. K. Liss's *Atlantic Empires: The Network of Trade and Revolution 1713–1826* (Baltimore: Johns Hopkins University Press, 1982) traces a web of commerce linking the imperial powers and their colonies—and the role of traders in colonial revolts against imperial rule.

PFLANZE, O. *Bismarck and the Development of Germany.* Princeton: Princeton University Press, 1963. Challenges older views; widely accepted.

POSTGATE, R. *Story of a Year: 1848.* Westport, Conn.: Greenwood Press, 1975. Colorful chronicle of the revolutionary year. On the significance of the "springtime of the peoples," see M. Kranzberg, ed., *1848: A Turning Point?* (Lexington, Mass.: Heath, 1959).

REYNAL, M. *The Nineteenth Century.* Geneva: Skira, 1951. European painting in the 1800s, beautifully illustrated.

RUDÉ, G. *The Crowd in History, 1730–1884.* Atlantic Highlands, N.J.: Humanities Press, 1981. Revealing analysis of the allegedly "faceless mob" by a pioneering student of revolutionary crowds.

SUTHERLAND, D. M. G. *France, 1789–1815: Revolution and Counterrevolution.* New York: Oxford University Press, 1986. Solid survey of the revolutionary period in Paris and the provinces, with attention to problems of interpretation. See also J. F. Bosher, *The French Revolution* (New York: W. W. Norton, 1988), which rejects Marxist and other sociohistorical explanations for a combination of traditional emphasis on leaders—including Louis XVI—and attention to the political culture of the masses, presented here in a very negative light.

TILLY, L. A., and J. W. SCOTT. *Women, Work, and Family.* New York: Holt, Rinehart & Winston, 1979. About women in England and France. On women in Germany, see J. C. Fout, *German Women in the Nineteenth Century: A Social History* (New York: Holmes & Meier, 1983). See also E. Riemer and J. Fout, eds., *European Women: A Documentary History, 1789–1945* (New York: Schocken, 1980).

CHAPTER 36

THE AMERICAS FROM COLONIES TO COUNTRIES

The United States Takes Shape

A Century of Change

While Europe evolved astonishingly from the later eighteenth through the nineteenth century, the Europeanized New World across the Atlantic was in some ways even more dramatically transformed. The Americas had already changed drastically during the colonial period (roughly 1500–1800). During the century and a quarter after 1776, the former colonies would undergo as total a transformation in a half dozen generations as the world has ever seen.

Politically, this period saw what had once been English, Spanish, Portuguese, and other colonies become independent nations—the two countries of Canada and the United States in English-speaking North America and a score of new nations in Latin America to the south. Economically, almost all of these new countries were affected to some degree by the Industrial Revolution, and one among them—the United States—had developed the world's most dynamic industrial economy by 1900.

The Thirteen Colonies

From sea to shining sea, North America was a thinly settled continent during the period of European colonization. Most of the land, of course, was still inhabited primarily by Amerindian peoples during the colonial centuries. The Spanish claimed much of western North America and the Gulf Coast; the French, Canada and the Mississippi Valley; the Russians, the far Northwest. But a scattering of Spanish missions, French fur traders, and the odd Russian Cossack scarcely diluted the life of the indigenous population over most of the continent.

Only in one place were Europeans thick on the ground in the seventeenth and eighteenth centuries. In the English settlements along the east coast, European farms, villages, and cities steadily displaced the Indians who had lived there in 1600. Here on the Atlantic seaboard was born the expansive society that in the nineteenth century would sweep to the Pacific.

The thirteen English colonies differed from one another in important ways. The rocky New England hills of Massachusetts, Connecticut, and Rhode Island bred Puritan clergymen in the early days, flinty Yankee storekeepers, and whaling captains in later centuries. The middle colonies, including bustling New York, New Jersey, and the Quaker haven of Pennsylvania, were the breadbasket of the colonies, producing grains such as wheat and barley. The balmier southern colonies, from Maryland and Virginia down through the Carolinas to Georgia, were the plantation territories, owned by debonair American equivalents of English country squires, worked by black slaves, and producing large cash crops of tobacco and rice for export.

But the thirteen colonies, penned in between the Appalachian Mountains and the sea, had important elements in common too. They had a large population, perhaps two and a half million by 1776—a third of the population of Great Britain itself. They also had a relatively homogeneous society, the Indians having been pushed westward out of English-settled areas, the African slaves thoroughly segregated in the southern plantations. It was in some ways a more prosperous society than that of Europe, thanks to the large amounts of land available for the taking. It was almost certainly a more mobile society, in which the ability to do a job came to count for more than family background. It was even a comparatively well-educated culture, especially in the North, where the first European settlers had been dedicated Protestants, the "people of the Book."

Most important, perhaps, the thirteen English colonies were all used to a significant amount of self-government from the beginning. In Latin America, military commanders and royal officials dominated the *conquista* and the colonies. In English North America, by contrast, all the settlements had assemblies of freemen who debated and determined their own affairs. New England town meetings and colonial legislatures were part of the fabric of colonial life. Royal governors and mercantilistic regulations would run afoul of these colonial assemblies throughout the later colonial period. After 1776 this tradition of self-government would provide the model—and the experience—that would bring the world's largest republic into existence in the United States.

The American Revolution

The American Revolution may be seen a dozen different ways: as a patriotic struggle for freedom, as an economic revolt against mercantilism, as an ideological clash, as a theater of towering personalities, as part of a larger "age of democratic revolutions" around the North Atlantic, as the first of what would later come to be called national liberation struggles, and on and on. In a global perspective, the primary significance of the American Revolution is perhaps twofold. It revealed the fragility of the political structure of the European intercontinental empires. Its aftermath, however, demonstrated the tenacity of Western society, culture, and interrelations once the Western predominance was firmly established beyond the seas.

Even in retrospect, the Revolution seems to have come on with remarkable suddenness.

In 1763, Britain had won the Seven Years' War and stood mistress of the greatest of all the European overseas empires. The American colonies were the jewel of that empire—productive, populous, and full of promise. Almost immediately, however, the British government began an ill-considered series of mercantilist measures. These reforms were designed to increase government revenues from America after the expense of the recent war, much of which had been fought in defense of the colonies. They were also intended to tighten up London's hold on those cities, villages, and farms three thousand miles away.

Mercantilist economic regulation was not new, of course, and the measures did not seem extreme to the royal ministers who proposed them. Taxes on sugar and coffee and tea, stamp taxes on printed matter, and attempts to wipe out smuggling seemed legitimate enough in Britain—but they outraged the colonists. Decisions to quarter troops in the colonies and finally to reorganize colonial governments in order to destroy the power of their assemblies aroused violent opposition.

The colonies responded to a decade of such measures with a series of ingenious—and increasingly subversive—organizations of their own. Like contemporary radicals and revolutionists in Europe, they were endlessly inventive. They held colonial congresses and set up committees of correspondence to coordinate the activities of the colonial leadership. Some of them collected weapons and organized the riotous Sons of Liberty and the paramilitary Minutemen.

A roster of talented leaders emerged during those dozen years of crisis from 1763 to 1775. These included the aging but still witty Enlightenment intellectual Ben Franklin of Philadelphia, the passionate spokesman Sam Adams of Boston, and his determinedly anti-British cousin John Adams. The new colonial leadership also included a group of Virginia gentlemen, among them the orator Patrick Henry, the young lawyer Thomas Jefferson, and the most impressive of the Virginians, the planter and sometime soldier George Washington.

By the spring of 1775, subversive organization and mob violence had triggered military retaliation. Troops dispatched to seize arms caches in two villages west of Boston confronted colonial militia, and the shot heard round the world was fired on the village green at Lexington.

It was more than a year, however, before the leaders of the colonial revolt, assembled at the Second Continental Congress in Philadelphia, made the break official. On July 4, 1776, Jefferson's Declaration of Independence was formally promulgated, with its ringing Lockean assertion

That all men are created equal, that they are endowed by their Creator with certain inalienable Rights, that among these are Life, Liberty, and the pursuit of Happiness.

That to secure these rights, Governments are instituted among men, deriving their just powers from the consent of the governed. . . .

Or, as a veteran put it, "What we meant in going for those redcoats was this: we always had governed ourselves, and we always meant to. They didn't mean we should."[1]

And so they fought. For six long years, ragtag regiments of summer soldiers fought armies of British regulars and Hessian mercenaries up and down the fifteen-hundred-mile strip of land, much of it still wilderness, between the Appalachian Mountains and the Atlantic. The colonial troops were ill trained, ill equipped, inexperienced, and given to desertion around harvest time. The Continental Congress could not supply their armies properly. Most of the colonial population was lukewarm or indifferent, and many were loyal to Great Britain. Freezing at Valley Forge, retreating from many defeats, the Revolution looked much less noble and romantic close up than it has in many a Fourth of July oration since.

But the British were an ocean away from home, the colonials frequently fighting in familiar fields and hills. There were some timely and heartening victories. The snowy midnight crossing of the Delaware to catch the Hessians unaware at Trenton is as much a part of American folklore as the grim winter at Valley Forge. Much more important was the surrender of "Gentleman Johnny" Burgoyne's army, invading from Canada, at Saratoga. On the strength of the Saratoga victory, Ben Franklin was able to negotiate the crucial French alliance that sent arms, money, and a French expeditionary force commended by the young Marquis de Lafayette to America.

Above all, perhaps, there was General George Washington (1732–1799). Six feet two, pale-skinned and blue-eyed, he looked good on a horse. He was a prudent man, not imaginative, but resolute once he had decided on action. This single-minded resolution, combined with a southern planter's reserve and a natural dignity, made Washington a perfect symbol for the cause he led, as later for the nation he governed.

Washington was no Napoleon: he seldom commanded ten thousand men (Napoleon could marshal hundreds of thousands), won few battles, and rather wore his

---

[1]George Brown Tindall, *America: A Narrative History* (New York: W. W. Norton, 1984), p. 203.

enemies out by patience than out-generaled them. British problems and the French alliance were crucial to his final success. And yet when all is said and done, Washington kept armies in the field for six long years. And when the bands struck up at Yorktown in 1781, the song they played was "The World Turned Upside Down"—for it was a British army, the last of any size left in the colonies, that laid down its arms.

The Development of Democracy

The nation that evolved over the three quarters of a century after 1781 saw itself as a new beginning in human history. The great seal of the United States proclaimed a *novus ordo seclorum,* a "new ordering of the ages." In a global context, the rise of the United States of (North) America is perhaps better seen as a new surge of Western power—and as a main road toward the climax of the Western hegemony of the world in the twentieth century.

It was, in any event, a spectacular achievement. Three aspects of the growth of the United States between the Revolution and the Civil War will be examined here: the evolution of political democracy, economic growth, and imperial expansion across the continent.

The fruit and in many ways the most important political achievement of the new country was the United States Constitution, the oldest such document in the world today.

After a decade of groping for political stability under the wartime Articles of Confederation, the thirteen United States set a constitutional convention to work, again at Philadelphia, in 1787. Balancing the interests of large and small states, fear of tyranny against the need

for unity, the resulting Constitution created a strong yet flexible central government for the new republic.

Executive authority was put in the hands of an elected president with appointed officials and an army and navy at his disposal. Lawmaking power was vested in a two-house legislature balancing the claims of more and less populous states. There was an appointed but independent federal judiciary. The first ten amendments provided a Bill of Rights protecting the people against governmental encroachments on their liberties as citizens.

The power of this grudgingly accepted central government grew steadily in the hands of the men who filled the offices thus defined for the next few decades. Washington, the first president (1789–1797), brought immense prestige and even a modestly imperial style to the presidency. Alexander Hamilton, the first Secretary of the Treasury, strengthened the crucial power of the government in financial matters, and John Marshall, Chief Justice of the Supreme Court from 1801 to 1835, emphasized the authority of federal laws over those of the states. The new national capital built at "Washington City" after the turn of the century and strong national leaders such as presidents Thomas Jefferson (1801–1808) and Andrew Jackson (1829–1836) also contributed to the power of the central government in the new country.

At the same time, however, the democratic base of the Republic grew apace. Major spokesmen for popular sovereignty included Jefferson, with his faith in the American "yeomanry," the solid landowning farmers he regarded as the backbone of the nation. A more rudely democratic spokesman was Andy Jackson. A westerner and one of the few heroes of the War of 1812, Jackson

George Washington presides over the last day's deliberations at the Constitutional Convention of 1787. The United States Constitution, built on European liberal ideas, became itself part of the evolving Western liberal tradition. Does the picture seek to convey an impression of passionate political radicalism, flag-waving patriotism, or responsible discussion? (New York Public Library Picture Collection)

became a champion of the "common man," whether he owned land or not, and a vocal opponent of effete eastern aristocrats. In such a climate, taxpayer suffrage and even universal manhood suffrage spread rapidly, till almost all adult males could vote in America by 1850.

There were limitations to all this political democratization, of course. Millions of black slaves and Native Americans had no part in the political process in the first half of the nineteenth century. The entire female half of the population would remain disfranchised throughout the 1800s. The democratic ideal, however, was firmly established. Its own logic—and rhetoric—would in time carry it to virtually universal application, in the United States as across the Western world.

ECONOMIC GROWTH AND TERRITORIAL EXPANSION

Economic growth was also a striking feature of American history throughout the nineteenth century.

The United States had some distinct economic advantages over the Old World. These included free land in virtually unlimited quantities, which became available as rapidly as it could be taken from the sparsely distributed Indians. The United States also had at its disposal the unmeasurable natural resources of a continent that stretched westward for thousands of miles. Another advantage was a rapidly growing population, rising from less than 4 million at the time of the first census in 1790 to more than 30 million at the beginning of the Civil War—an eightfold multiplication in three generations.

A final advantage, once more, was a relatively open and mobile society, in which it was comparatively easy to move from place to place or up and down the social scale. Particularly in the expanding American West, it was what you could *do,* not who you *were,* that counted. Most people did not make fortunes or rise from rags to riches. But there were enough poor-boy millionaires and shirt-tail western senators to make getting ahead a virtue and a genuine possibility in the United States.

The American economic "miracle," as similar surges elsewhere would be labeled in the twentieth century, was a jumble of lusty work songs and sharp dealings in land, of technological innovation and public-be-damned private enterprise. Its all-encompassing justification was, quite simply, success. That it had. From the Erie Canal boom to flush times in Alabama to the California gold rush, there seemed to be no end to opportunity for Americans.

To bumper crops and burgeoning mines, furthermore, was added the unprecedented eruption of the Industrial Revolution. Crossing the Atlantic from Britain almost as quickly as it crossed the Channel to Europe, the new potential for multiplied industrial production caught the United States at precisely the right moment in its accelerating economic growth. British investment capital, technology, and large numbers of European immigrants all made their con-

tributions. The steam engine in the North brought an industrial boom to New England just as the cotton gin made cotton the king of the southern agrarian economy.

This was, finally, the age that saw the beginning of a tremendous American imperial expansion. Westward "the star of empire," as the Manifest Destiny advocates called it, did inexorably move.

The new United States was ideally positioned for old-fashioned empire building in 1776. The most powerful political entity in North America, it had nothing between it and the Pacific but untended European colonies and weakened Indian confederations and tribal groupings. Through wars, cash payments, diplomatic maneuvers, and the irresistable westward push of population, the United States laid claim to all of North America south of Canada and north of the Rio Grande by the middle of the nineteenth century.

The Louisiana Purchase brought the huge middle swath of the continent into the Union in 1803. Texas, after it revolted from Mexico, was annexed to the United States in 1845. The Oregon Territory was secured through negotiation with Britain in 1846. California and most of the rest of the West were seized after the Mexican War in 1848. These, with smaller acquisitions in Florida and along the Mexican and Canadian borders and the purchase of Alaska from Russia in 1867, multiplied the size of the United States as its population and economic production grew.

Expansion was a heady tonic for the young nation. There was talk of further growth north and south, "from Panama to Hudson's Bay." President James Monroe's Doctrine (1823), originally proposed by the British to protect their commercial interests in Latin America, declared the entire Western Hemisphere closed to Old World colonization—but not, as it later turned out, to American imperialism south of the border. With American clippers racing to China in the 1840s and 1850s and Admiral Perry opening Japan to American influence in the mid 1850s, a global role for the new country seemed assured.

Then at mid-century, calamity struck the United States with the devastating fury of what seemed to Americans of those days the Lord's own terrible swift sword.

CIVIL WAR: UNITY AFFIRMED

The American Civil War (1861–1865) had been building for decades beneath the bustling enthusiasm of the new nation. The "irrepressible conflict" was rooted in part in the differing economic interests of the plantation South and the rapidly industrializing North. There was also a southern sense of decreasing political power as new western states undermined the influence of the region that had produced the "Virginia dynasty" of post-Revolutionary presidents. In the end, however, the central issues were the South's insistence on maintaining its "peculiar institution" of slavery even if it meant seceding from the Union—and the North's determination that the Union must be preserved at all costs.

There were 4 million black slaves in the United States in 1860, mostly in the South and mostly field hands. But some were artisans or factory workers, and in Louisiana there was even a mulatto aristocracy set apart from both white and black. Slave importation had ended in 1808, but important elements of West African cultures had survived among the descendants of these forced African immigrants. Slave were strong family people and hard workers. But they were still property, to be bought and sold like farm animals; and their resentment sometimes exploded in violent revolts such as Nat Turner's rebellion in Virginia. Slowly, slavery also began to touch the conscience of the nation.

Antislavery abolitionist societies in the North crusaded for the total abolition of the peculiar institution in the decades before the Civil War. The "underground railway" smuggled runaway slaves north to Canada and freedom. Free-Soilers fought with rifles to keep new states such as Kansas free of slavery. Harriet Beecher Stowe's sociologically unconvincing but morally powerful *Uncle Tom's Cabin* moved the nation, and abolitionist John Brown's bloody raid on Harper's Ferry shocked it. Senators and congressmen thundered and maneuvered, seeking to avoid what to many seemed the ultimate catastrophe: southern secession from the Union.

But no crusade or compromise could cut the Gordian knot. The United States, said Abraham Lincoln, could not long endure half slave and half free. "The crimes of this guilty land," John Brown declared on the day he was hanged, "will never be purged away, but with blood."[2]

When Lincoln was elected president in 1860, the southern states began to secede and to organize themselves into the Confederate States of America. In the spring of 1861, southern troops fired on a U.S. fort on an island in Charleston harbor, South Carolina, and the Civil War was begun.

Both sides entered the war confident of victory. The Union under President Lincoln had three quarters of the free population, two thirds of the railways, four fifths of the industry, and most of the nation's wealth. The Confederacy under its hastily elected president, Jefferson Davis, had many of the most experienced military commanders, the patriotic and tactical advantage of fighting in defense of its own soil, and the powerful card of cotton exports, with which it hoped to win crucial support from European textile manufacturing nations such as Great Britain.

Southern generals did, in fact, more than compensate for superior northern numbers in the early years of the war. Robert E. Lee, "Stonewall" Jackson, and the brilliant cavalry commander J.E.B. "Jeb" Stuart repeatedly outmaneuvered and reversed northern advances. Later in the struggle, however, Lee met his match in generals such as the implacable Ulysses S. Grant and William Tecum-

Abraham Lincoln, perhaps America's most admired president, is shown here without the familiar beard. A shrewd politician beneath his legendary folksy stories, Lincoln presided over the costly effort that preserved the Union and freed the slaves. Often described as homely, the tall, gangly Lincoln made a good impression as an orator and debater "on the stump" addressing large outdoor crowds. (Library of Congress)

seh Sherman. And the South, for all its dash and valor, never had a monopoly on courage.

Above all, the North had President Abraham Lincoln (1861–1865). Tall and gaunt, his hair and beard ill combed and his eyes somber and hollow, Lincoln cut an unprepossessing figure in his stovepipe hat and habitual suit of solemn black. But he was a skillful manipulator of people and patronage, a speaker whose eloquence can move us still, and a man in whom confidence in his cause—the salvation of the Union— combined with an immense compassion for all who suffered in that time of national trial.

The war Lincoln fought to a successful conclusion was the bloodiest in the history of the United States, before or since. The basic Union strategy was to blockade the South by sea and cut it off from the West before invading, destroying the southern armies, and ending the secession. Lee and the southern generals fought to defend territory and strove mightily to win victories—especially on northern soil—that might bring them foreign help. In the end, it was the northern strategy that worked.

[2]Stephen B. Oates, *To Purge This Land with Blood: A Biography of John Brown* (New York: Harper & Row, Pub. 1970), p. 351.

Labrador
Sea

Hudson's
Bay

DOMINION OF CANADA

NEWFOUNDLAND
(with Labrador)
1949

NEW
BRUNSWICK
1867

PRINCE EDWARD
1873

**BRITISH
COLUMBIA
1871**

**ALBERTA
1905**

**MANITOBA
1870**

**ONTARIO
1867**

QUEBEC
1867

NOVA
SCOTIA

VANCOUVER

**SASKATCH-
EWAN
1905**

(UPPER CANADA)

(LOWER CANADA)

(MARITIME PROVINCES)

(to Mass.)

Lake Superior

St. Lawrence R.

**OREGON
COUNTRY
1846**
(By treaty with Great Britain)

Lake Michigan

Lake Huron

L. Ontario

L. Erie

ATLANTIC

OCEAN

LOUISIANA

PURCHASE

1803

UNITED STATES

IN 1783

THIRTEEN

ORIGINAL

STATES

**MEXICAN
CESSION
1848**

**TEXAS
ANNEXATION
1845**

**GADSDEN
PURCHASE
1853**

1810–1813
Acquired by treaty
with Spain, 1819

Tropic of Cancer

MEXICO

Gulf of Mexico

PACIFIC

OCEAN

Caribbean
Sea

0   500   1000 Miles

0   500   1000 Kilometers

- - - - - Present-day state boundaries

Dates in Canadian provinces show
admission to dominion

160°   155°

60°   70°   160°   150°   140°

64°30'

H A W A I I

20°

ALASKA
PURCHASE
1867

50°

PUERTO
RICO
U.S.

U.K.

VIRGIN IS.

Territory, 1898;
50th state, March 1959

49th state, January 1959

U.S. territory, 1898;
commonwealth since 1953

Acquired from
Denmark, 1917

16°

Lee's greatest effort carried him as far north as Gettysburg, Pennsylvania, where in July 1863 Pickett's famous charge carried across a long and bloody mile to the crest of Cemetery Ridge, to break at last in the acrid powder smoke and the crash of Union guns—and fall away. It was the high tide of the Confederacy—the high tide and the turn.

Ahead lay even bloodier battles in the West and South, and Sherman's notorious scorched-earth march southeast to Atlanta and then on to the sea. Ahead too was the awesome silence at Appomattox, where Lee laid down his arms in 1865—and the last shot, less than a week later, when a mad actor put a bullet through President Lincoln's brain.

Six hundred thousand men had died. The Union was preserved, the slaves freed. A nation "conceived in liberty and dedicated to the proposition that all men are created equal" had survived its most terrible ordeal.

THE GILDED AGE

The four decades between the Civil War and the emergence of political reformism at the end of the century were perhaps the grubbiest in the history of American politics. Economically, however, the nation boomed as never before. And U.S. expansive energies continued to manifest themselves, filling the American West and reaching out beyond the seas for a share of the world's trade and empire.

After the war to save the Union, the nation as a whole turned its back on political crusades and sank into a period of corruption and cynical disregard for the public welfare seldom matched in its history. Ineffectual presidents, state machines, big-city bosses, and legislators who cheerfully peddled their votes to big business dominated the political scene between Lincoln's death in 1865 and Teddy Roosevelt's accession in 1901.

In the South, the old white aristocracy soon re-emerged. Blacks, freed without land, were reduced to sharecropping, working for landowners for a never sufficient share of the crops they grew. Hooded terrorists such as Ku Klux Klanners and a series of Jim Crow laws reduced blacks to second-class status at best, segregated, discriminated against, and denied even the basic right to vote.

Farmers' organizations did agitate for reform, and labor unions painfully took shape during the later nineteenth century. Some big-city bosses seem to have served the useful purpose of giving immigrants and other otherwise neglected citizens a bit of patronage in return for their votes. By and large, however, it was a dismal time politically.

Economically, however, the nation grew even faster than it had before the war. Resources were still seemingly limitless, and the population was doubling every quarter century. Vast amounts of capital were available, much of it from Europe, and technological advance was accelerating. What now amounted to a national faith in rags-to-riches entrepreneurship drove the nation to still greater efforts. Under such circumstances, the economic success of the continental republic was perhaps not surprising.

But it was certainly dazzling. In the decades after the Civil War, railroads stretched from sea to sea, till the United States had more miles of track than all Europe combined. The output of U.S. factories tripled from 1877 to 1892 alone. By the end of the century, the United States was both the world's leading agricultural producer and the world's leading manufacturer.

As in Europe, big business developed in the United States at this time. The railroads were the first huge corporations, hiring armies of workers and buying up great expanses of western lands. The names of financial giants such as J. Pierpont Morgan and industrial empire-builders such as Andrew Carnegie, the steel king, and John D. Rockefeller of Standard Oil became household words. Master organizers and employers of skilled managers, they learned to cut waste, buy and build in depressed times, and pyramid their holdings. Ruthless competitors, willing to use rebates, stock watering, and other shady or illegal devices, they became greater monopolists than their European contemporaries.

To muckraking reformers, these "robber barons" were symbols of monopoly capital and industrial exploitation. To admirers and would-be imitators, they were embodiments of what Americans were already thinking of as the American success story.

The climax of the westward expansion and the beginning of the nation's reach for empire overseas added to the sense of Yankee progress. It was a gaudy, giddy time, and they called it, if not a true golden age, at least a gilded one.

SOCIETY: PROBLEMS OF THE GROWING NATION

Socially speaking, the whole of the nineteenth century in the United States is perhaps best described by that most overworked of historical clichés, an age of contrasts.

Fourth of July speakers tirelessly reiterated that the great republic was the homeland of freedom, equality, opportunity, and hope. Equally impassioned—if rather less numerous—radicals pointed out that these great gifts were distributed quite unevenly among the classes, races, sexes, and other groups that made up the nation. And there was significant truth in both views.

The oldest Americans had essentially no share at all in the benefits of the new democratic-industrial state. Defeated in endless petty wars, betrayed by one broken treaty after another, Native Americans were chivied into "Indian territories" and "reservations" farther and farther west and on increasingly barren tracts of land. Here they lived according to what was left of their old ways, infected by whiskey and guns, tempted either to surrender to the lure of the conqueror's world or to rebel futilely against it.

Black Americans, still clustered very largely in the South, also had little or no part in American growth and self-government. A few blacks did move north to begin building a genuine black bourgeoisie in cities such as Chicago. Others began to construct a base for black advancement in the South itself through educational institutions such as Hampton Institute in Virginia and Tuskegee Institute in Georgia. A start was thus made, though in the nineteenth century it was no more than that.

Another frequently victimized group comprised the millions of new immigrants who poured into the country, primarily in search of economic opportunity but also to escape even more rigidly hierarchical societies in the Old World. Most of these newcomers were still Europeans, still mostly from northern and western Europe. Some, however, were East Asians, Chinese, and Japanese, many recruited across the Pacific to help build the western end of the transcontinental railroad—while Irish immigrants built the eastern end.

Whether they came to lay rails, to farm the endless western plains opened up to homesteaders, or to practice European trades in the ghettos of eastern cities, the newest comers were likely to be cheated, exploited, and discriminated against. They would typically require a couple of generations to achieve even an uneasy integration into their new country.

Farmers in the United States also had their share of problems in the latter part of the nineteenth century. Declining crop prices, unprotected markets, deflation, and mortgage debt ground them down year after year. Extortionate railway rates and an unfortunate surge of droughts, floods, and blizzards around 1890 added to their miseries. Many farmers were driven into bankruptcy, others into militant farmers' organizations such as the Grange or to radical agitators like "Sockless" Jerry Simpson, "Cyclone" Davis, and Mary E. Lease, who urged farmers to raise "less corn and more hell."

American labor also organized during the closing decades of the century, forming embattled unions, staging strikes that were often suppressed by hired strikebreakers or even the National Guard. Waves of unemployment in the depressions of the last quarter of the century added to the bitterness of laboring people. Organizations such as the Knights of Labor and the American Federation of Labor and leaders such as the AFL's Samuel Gompers could boast few victories in the 1880s and 1890s. Genuine improvement for factory workers, as for farmers, lay two generations ahead, in the New Deal of the 1930s.

THE INDEPENDENCE OF AMERICAN WOMEN

Women's lives, finally, were as varied in North America as in Europe. Recent research has reminded us of the brutal lives of women in New England mills in the earlier 1800s and in the sweatshops of New York's garment district around 1900. We have learned that pioneer women went west not only with their husbands and children, but on their own or as heads of families. Middle-class American women seem to have earned a particular reputation, especially toward the end of the century, for independence of mind and forthright strength of character. They toured Europe alone, or ran mission stations on isolated Pacific atolls. Europeans found them rather *too* independent; Asians found them inscrutable.

As in Europe, American women were likely to be involved in social causes, from the abolition of slavery to the emancipation of women themselves. They broke into the professions on this side of the Atlantic too, and were soon demanding the vote. There were many women writers in the United States, from Harriet Beecher Stowe before the Civil War to the reclusive poet Emily Dickinson and the great novelist Edith Wharton after it.

But American middle-class women also found themselves considered too fine and delicate for politics, business, science, and other careers deemed suitable only for the ruder clay and more rational heads of men. In America even more than in Europe, descending from this unsolicited pedestal would be a problem for the following century.

 # LATIN AMERICA EMERGES

THE LATIN AMERICAN COLONIES

The Iberian colonies in the Western Hemisphere were a century older and many times larger than the English colonies on the east coast of North America. Portugal's Brazilian colony alone, occupying half of South America, was almost as large as the continental United States. Spanish America included the rest of South America, the Central American isthmus and most of the Caribbean, Mexico, and much of what is today California, Texas, and Florida, with the Southwest and the Gulf Coast in between. By contrast with Britain's compact strip of colonies—a fraction of the future United States—these continental expanses of colonial territory to the south must have strained any early-modern European government.

The population of colonial Latin America was also much more complex than that of the British colonies that would come to master North America. To the large numbers of Amerindians who survived the brutalities of the conquest, the victorious Europeans added masses of African slaves. The result was a tripartite population, like that of colonial North America but less rigidly segregated—caucasoid, mongoloid, and negroid mingling as they did nowhere else in the world.

This demographic pattern was further complicated by powerfully felt social divisions. There were, in the first place, two groups of Europeans. The peninsulars, primarily officials sent out from Spain or Portugal to govern

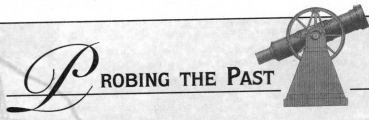

"*From the conditions of frontier life came intellectual traits of profound importance. The works of travelers along each frontier from colonial days onward describe certain common traits, and these traits have, while softening down, still persisted as survivals in the place of their origin, even when a higher social organization succeeded. The result is that to the frontier the American intellect owes its striking characteristics. That coarseness and strength combined with acuteness and inquisitiveness; that practical, inventive turn of mind, quick to find expedients; that masterful grasp of material things, lacking in the artistic but powerful to effect great ends; that restless, nervous energy; that dominant individualism, working for good and for evil, and withal that buoyancy and exuberance which comes with freedom—these are traits of the frontier, or traits called out elsewhere because of the existence of the frontier. Since the days when the fleet of Columbus sailed into the waters of the New World, America has been another name for opportunity, and the people of the United States have taken their tone from the incessant expansion which has not only been open but has even been forced upon them. He would be a rash prophet who should assert that the expansive character of American life has now entirely ceased. Movement has been its dominant fact, and, unless this training has no effect upon a people, the American energy will continually demand a wider field for its exercise.*"

———————— ◆◆◆◆ ————————

The American republics, although part of the Western World, also saw distinct differences between their own national characters, cultures, and destinies, and those of Europe. An exponent of American uniqueness was the turn-of-the-century historian Frederick Jackson Turner (1861–1932), who, in a widely influential essay of 1893, urged the special significance of the frontier experience for the United States.

What qualities of character did Turner feel were encouraged by life on the frontier? Elsewhere in the essay, Turner describes the frontier zone as "an area of free land" tempting "American settlement westward." Does "free" here mean uninhabited, available free of charge, or what? Do you think that America's "expansive character" has continued to demand "a wider field for its exercise" during the century since Turner wrote?

Frederick Jackson Turner, "The Significance of the Frontier in American History," in George Rogers Tayler, ed., The Turner Thesis Concerning the Role of the Frontier in American History, rev. ed. (Boston: D. C. Heath, 1956), pp. 17–18.

the colonies, were the ruling elite in the colonial period. *Criollos,* European-descended Latin Americans born in the colonies, composed the provincial aristocracy of mine and plantation owners who would inherit power when the colonies broke free in the nineteenth century.

A final subdivision with a long future were the *mestizos,* Latin Americans of mixed racial background, descended primarily from European and Indian ancestors. This vigorous group belied every racial stereotype of the evils of "race mixing." Minor officials, petty tradesmen, and the like in colonial times, when they were discrimi-

nated against, they would emerge as the dominant cultural and political force in twentieth-century Latin America.

This vast expanse and complex population were administered through most of the colonial period in three colonial jurisdictions. These were the viceroyalty of New Spain (from California and Texas through Mexico to Central America), the viceroyalty of Peru (Spanish-speaking South America), and the Portuguese colony of Brazil. Viceroys, captains general, bishops, and other high-ranking officials were sent out from Spain and Portugal to govern, primarily in the interests of the crown. These men, many of whom were bureaucrats with little firsthand knowledge of the huge territories they administered, necessarily depended on local people and lower-ranking officials for the real work of running the colonies.

There were no town meetings or colonial assemblies to resist the authority of the Crown in Latin America, as there were in British North America. But there were the *audencias,* judicial boards whose members also served as advisers to viceroys and sometimes resisted misguided viceregal policies. At the local level there were small town councils usually dominated by the *criollo* elite. And there were local representatives of the Crown, minor officials often more interested in lining their own pockets than advancing any policies, royal or *criollo.*

This system, modeled on continental European absolutism and attempting to govern an area twice as large as all Europe put together, can be presented in a uniformly glum light. Top-ranking officials, who were sent out for short terms and whose primary allegiance was to the Crown, were too often stodgy bureaucrats uninterested in and ignorant of the colonies they ruled. Many of the local officials were extremely corrupt, and mercilessly exploited the conquered Amerindian villages under their jurisdiction. *Criollo* landowners and even Jesuit and other missions built their own little empires of wealth and power on the labor of large numbers of Indians or black slaves.

There is also the prevailing sense of the Latin American colonies being a cultural and social backwater during the seventeenth and eighteenth centuries. Spain and Portugal themselves had declined to second-rate powers after the sixteenth century; their colonies may be seen as the dusty provinces of decaying metropolises.

A more positive view of much of the colonial experience can also be taken, however. The neglect of the colonies by weakened and impoverished mother countries in the seventeenth century may be seen as a form of benign neglect that allowed local people to solve local problems. And in the eighteenth century, the Bourbon kings of Spain in particular embarked upon a campaign of enlightened reforms that had very positive effects. These included efforts at administrative, legal, and financial reform, as well as encouragement of agriculture and local industry and the building of churches and schools. Thanks at least in part to these manifestations of the spirit of the European Enlightenment, there seems to have been a surge of genuine prosperity toward the end of the colonial period, in the later eighteenth and early nineteenth centuries.

Colonial Latin America remained a sprawling region of isolated villages, backcountry plantations, and provincial cities. Sleepy plazas were ringed by dusty colonial baroque churches and palaces. Indians drowsed, *mestizos* hustled, and colonial gentlefolk in last year's European fashions strolled in the late-afternoon shade.

It was indeed a backwater. But in many ways it was a backwater that worked.

THE SPIRIT OF REVOLT

Into this somnolent world on the far side of the Atlantic a new spirit intruded around 1800—the spirit of revolution.

Social, economic, and political resentments had been building up for centuries among a variety of colonial groups. Conquered Indians resented the conquest and all the subsequent oppression. Black slaves were never reconciled to slavery. *Mestizos,* cut off by prejudice from all other communities, envied the power of their fathers' European world and resented the oppression of their mothers' non-European people. *Criollos,* the chief builders of the colonial economy, saw no justice in the privileged social position and the political authority enjoyed by peninsular judges, bishops, military commanders, captains general, and viceroys.

In the late eighteenth century, the subversive intellectual influences of the Enlightenment made themselves felt along with the enlightened reforms of the Bourbons. Satirical Voltairian attacks on foppish aristocrats and worldly churchmen applied as well in the New World as in the Old. Rousseauian talk of government by popular consent had as much appeal to colonials in South America as in North America.

Simón Bolívar, most famous of the liberators of Latin America. Something of the great freedom-fighter's deep humanity comes through in this bust. The disciple of Rousseau who swore in his youth to liberate his country felt, as he wrote to a former teacher, a compelling passion for "liberty, justice, greatness and beauty." (PH Archives)

Then revolt broke out, in the 1770s in Britain's North American colonies and in the late 1780s in France itself. Under such circumstances, some sort of revolution in Latin America, where there were as many grounds for discontent as in either North America or Europe, is surely not surprising.

The most oppressed rebelled first—Indians in South America and black slaves in the Caribbean.

Tupac Amaru, who claimed descent from the Incas, was Jesuit-educated and wealthy. Nevertheless, he led a 1780 revolt of the brutally exploited Indians of the Peruvian Andes that briefly liberated Bolivia and parts of Peru and Argentina. Toussaint L'Ouverture, grandson of an African king, was a Haitian slave who had made his own fortune. Inspired by the French Revolution, he launched a ten-year rebellion against the French planters in Haiti (1791–1801). Tupac Amaru was captured and executed, many thousands of his followers slaughtered, his insurrection suppressed. Toussaint L'Ouverture freed Haiti but was betrayed to his enemies and died in a French prison. But the flame had been lit, in both South America and the Caribbean, and it would not go out.

LATIN AMERICAN WARS OF INDEPENDENCE

Ironically, it was not the North American or French Revolution that triggered Latin America's fifteen years of revolutionary upheaval, but the great empire-builder Napoleon Bonaparte. Napoleon conquered both Spain and Portugal in the early 1800s and put puppet kings on their thrones. Even royalists in the Latin American colonies turned against these usurping monarchs in Madrid and Lisbon.

Three major wars for independence ran their long and often bloody course between 1810 and 1824. There was a revolution in Mexico, pioneered by Father Hidalgo; another in northern South America, led by Simón Bolívar; and a third in southern South America, under the leadership of José de San Martín.

Mexican independence was declared in 1810 by a reforming village priest named Father Miguel Hidalgo y Costilla in the hamlet of Dolores, a hundred miles north of Mexico City. Hidalgo's Sunday sermon on September 16, 1810, before a congregation of poor *mestizos* and Indians gave the revolution its battle cry, the famous *grito de Dolores:* For Freedom and the Virgin of Guadalupe—Death to the Spaniards!

After this inspirational beginning, however, ill-armed and often poorly led hordes of Indians and *mestizos* made little headway against Spanish troops. Father Hidalgo himself was captured and shot. In 1820, however, a liberal revolution in Spain had the paradoxical effect of stimulating wealthy Mexican *criollos* to revolt—against the spreading infection of liberalism from the mother country! At their head was a rich and calculating man—and a formerly successful military commander *against* Hidalgo's rebellion—named Augustín de Iturbide. Iturbide

joined the rebels he had once fought, and in 1821 he led a victorious coalition army into Mexico City. Mexico, and with it all of Central America, was liberated at last.

Simón Bolívar (1783–1830), the liberator of northern South America, was an eloquent, dramatic man with a flair for grand schemes and public triumphs. Born to wealthy parents in Caracas, raised by tutors steeped in Rousseau, well traveled in Napoleonic Europe, Bolívar felt himself destined for revolutionary leadership. A rare combination of intellectual and man of action, he was widely read in the Enlightenment and totally committed to freedom in all its forms. He freed his own slaves, promoted members of all classes and races, and tried to persuade his fellow *criollos* to distribute land to peasants and emancipate their slaves.

Bolívar's fifteen-year revolutionary career began with his participation in an abortive insurrection in Caracas in 1810, stimulated by the Napoleonic conquest of Spain. There followed a period of repeated setbacks and exiles in various Caribbean islands—including liberated Haiti. Victories began to come when Bolívar organized the interior of Venezuela and forged an alliance with the *llaneros,* the wild herders of the Venezuelan grasslands. He liberated neighboring Colombia first, then swung back to free Venezuela in 1821. Ecuador came next, and the three territories were thereupon united in the short-lived Republic of Gran Colombia.

Thereafter, Simón Bolívar presided over the freeing of Bolivia and Peru. But here the way had already been paved by the liberator of the south—San Martín.

José de San Martín (1778–1850) was a career military officer from Argentina, and a much quieter, more self-effacing man than the mercurial Bolívar. Tall and dark, courteous and simple in his habits, San Martín was a rigorous disciplinarian who cared for the welfare of his troops. He was also a skilled organizer and a general with a rare gift for grand strategy. He clearly ranks with Bolívar as one of the two great leaders of the Latin American revolutions.

Argentina had been in turmoil for years over the same sort of antimercantilist, free-trade issue that had agitated the North American colonies. Napoleon's invasion of Spain led leading citizens of Buenos Aires to declare their independence of the French emperor's puppet ruler in Madrid in 1810.

San Martín took service under the new regime and soon set to work on his grand strategy. The center of Spanish power in South America was in Peru, and San Martín proposed to attack that power base by a great flanking movement across the Andes and north through Chile. Practically single-handed, he organized a military expedition, led his Army of the Andes over the towering mountain barrier, and crushed the Spanish troops in Chile with a series of striking victories in 1817 and 1818. Thereafter he moved with greater caution north to Peru, maneuvered his way into Lima, and then sought an alliance with Bolívar for a final blow at the Spanish military in Peru.

A famous "meeting of the liberators" in Ecuador in 1822, however, revealed personal and political differences between the two men that were too great to bridge. San Martín therefore graciously stood aside, and it was Bolívar's troops who dealt Spanish arms in the Americas a final resounding defeat in the Battle of Ayacucho—Latin America's Yorktown—high in the Andes in 1824.

The independence of Brazil came much more quietly in 1822. The liberation of this largest of Latin American colonies occurred several years after the Portuguese royal family fled to Rio to escape Napoleon. During this period Brazil had gained valued rights, including the right whose denial by the Crown had exercised so many of the colonies—free trade. When an 1820 revolution in Lisbon threatened to countermand these new privileges, events were set in motion that brought full independence to Brazil with a minimum of violence. Alone among the new Latin American nations, Brazil was a constitutional monarchy—under the crown prince of the Portuguese ruling house—rather than a republic.

Paraguay and Uruguay, located between Brazil and Argentina, attained their freedom in a tangle of politics between their powerful neighbors. By 1824 all the Latin American states except a few small colonies around the Caribbean had won their independence. A saga of colonial revolt that began a half century before, in 1776, was ended.

NEW COUNTRIES: THE REIGN OF THE CAUDILLOS

The Latin American revolutions had been more protracted and much more costly in lives and property than the revolt of the thirteen colonies. It had been much closer to a social revolution, pitting *criollos* against peninsulars, and sometimes Indians and *mestizos* against the European power structure as a whole. But the result was no more a social transformation south of the Rio Grande than north of it.

Royal authority had been replaced by republican constitutions in most places, peninsular officials by a *criollo* ruling class, and mercantilistic regulation by free trade. But the basic economic and social structure of the region remained largely as it had been before, as we will see presently.

There were some political changes, however—not all of them for the best. There were, in the first place, a number of other wars and revolutions in the decades following the Wars of Independence. Some of these later conflicts led to major transfers of territory from one new state to another. Other clashes led to the fragmentation of some of the newly independent nations. Still others created a chronic political instability within the new countries.

Major Latin American wars of the nineteenth century included the lopsided struggle between the United States and Mexico (1846–1848), which cost Mexico 40 percent of its territory. Another such conflict was the

Paraguayan War (1864–1870), in which Argentina, Brazil, and Uruguay ravaged Paraguay in a struggle that cost 300,000 lives. The War of the Pacific (1879–1883), finally, saw Chile emerge as a major power in Latin America by winning a nitrate-rich northern region also claimed by Argentina and Bolivia.

Among the most important fragmentations of new nations was that of the United Provinces of Central America, which split into half a dozen Central American countries. Bolívar's Gran Colombia was divided into Venezuela, Colombia, and Ecuador. Uruguay also managed to make good its secession from southern Brazil.

Revolutions were common within the new nations of Latin America. Regionalism, which led to the Civil War in the United States, was equally prevalent in the new states to the south. There also, the hinterlands tended to resist the encroaching power of the industrializing cities. Such circumstances led to frequent civil wars and changes of government by force.

Central to this chronic political instability and endemic military conflict was a political phenomenon common almost everywhere in Latin America—the rise of *caudillismo,* the reign of the *caudillo.*

All these new countries had emerged from the Wars of Independence with constitutions, political parties, and civil liberties—at least on paper. In fact, however, political power usually devolved upon local strong men called *caudillos.* These backcountry military chiefs seem frequently to have embodied traditional sources of authority in the countryside: they owned large estates, concluded marriage alliances, performed and received favors. But they also reflected the breakdown of central authority and the burgeoning power of the gun, which were among the by-products of the revolutions. *Caudillos* were above all commanders of military force and beneficiaries of the popular respect for courage and strength that was bred into these descendants of the conquistadores.

Most of the *caudillos* were thus local warlords who championed the autonomy of the regions against the centralizing efforts of the new capital cities. Sometimes, however, a *caudillo* would seize national power himself, bringing the violence and crudity of the backwoods to the center of national life. Examples included the dictatorship of Bolívar's lieutenant José Páez (1830–1848) in Venezuela after the liberator's death; the brutal regime of Manuel de Rosas (1829–1832) and his equally ruthless and Machiavellian wife, Dona Encarnación, in Argentina; and the inept rule of General Santa Anna in Mexico (1834–1855).

As military dictators, *caudillos* were frequently brutal; as country people, many of them were unlearned, even—in the eyes of more polished Latin Americans—barbarous. Secret police, organized mob violence, land confiscations, and executions were notorious adjuncts of many of these dictatorships. On the other hand, *caudillos* were sometimes quite popular with the poor. They shared the values and prejudices of peons and gauchos, and they saw to it that at least some of their patronage filtered down to the village level.

By the end of the century, however, *caudillo* rule was giving way to a new bourgeois class of progress-minded centralizers. These were the architects of the substantial economic advances of the end of the century, to which we now turn.

ECONOMIC PROBLEMS: HACIENDAS AND DEPENDENCY

Nineteenth-century Latin American economic history is normally divided around 1880. During the half century between independence in the 1820s and the 1870s, the typical Latin American country remained a hacienda economy of separate regions and *caudillo* politics. From the 1880s on, exports and foreign dependency increased, and with these economic changes the authority of central governments and port cities.

Through most of the century, then, the central Latin American economic institution remained the hacienda, the huge plantation or ranch operated by a *criollo* landowner with Indian, *mestizo,* or black labor. Slavery was abolished earlier in South America than in North America—as early as the 1810s and 1820s in Argentina, Mexico, and Central America. Throughout Latin America, however, Indian and *mestizo* workers remained peons, landless laborers bound by unending debt to their masters. The Wars of Independence brought little change to the life of the European-descended hacienda aristocracy, or to that of the laborers on West Indian sugar plantations, Argentine ranches and wheat fields, and in Bolivian mines.

From the 1880s through the early decades of the twentieth century, however, foreign exports increased phenomenally. These exports were largely agricultural products and minerals: sugar, bananas, coffee, wheat, meat, and wool, as well as silver, copper, lead, and tin, all boomed as export products. Swelling profits from the sale of commodities like these stimulated great increases in foreign investment in Latin America and in Latin American imports of foreign manufactured goods. Argentina, Uruguay, and other progressive countries also used some of their earnings from exports for railways, roads, schools, and other reforms. Commodity exports looked to some like the road to progress for Latin America.

Actually, as recent scholarship has stressed, increases in exports also increased the dependency of Latin American countries on more developed nations—Britain especially in the nineteenth century, the United States in the twentieth. The nations of the south borrowed their capital and bought their manufactured goods overseas, while their own industrial production scarcely developed. The end of the century saw boom times for the merchants of port cities and for the landed producers of export products, but the average Latin American worker earned little more in 1900 than in 1800.

In politics too, it sometimes seemed as if the more things changed, the more they stayed the same. Regionalism declined, thanks to the new transportation and communications nets and to the increasing power of large cities. The local power of the *caudillo* thus diminished, and with the loss of his regional base, the chances of his seizing national power also declined.

Yet military rule, political violence, and corruption remained almost as common after 1880 as before. The rough-and-ready *caudillo* was replaced by a spit-and-polish professional military officer—but the latter still felt an obligation to intervene in politics. The goals of the new juntas—Order and Progress—might have a more disinterested ring than the blatant self-aggrandizement of the *caudillo,* but civil government and civil liberties still failed to develop. Corruption at the lower levels of government, finally, remained as common in South America as in North America in the later 1800s.

SOCIETY: TRADITION AND CHANGE

The social life of Latin American cities continued to be that of provincial Europeans, even after modern buildings and electric trolley lines made their appearance. For most of the century, *criollos* simply replaced peninsular Spanish or Portuguese aristocrats in the baroque palaces or churches around the plazas. Polished merchants or professional people or crude *caudillos* and their hangers-on were now the governors, judges, officials, and presidents. And Paris or London fashions, European plays only a year or two out of date still dominated the social and cultural life of urban elites.

The life of the backcountry hacienda went on as it always had. There was a big house with its self-sufficient workshops and stores, barns and corrals; villages of peons on poorer land up the hillside; and the endless acres of cropland or pasturage that belonged to the patrón, the patriarchal owner of the estate. The landed families all knew and married each other, in the way of country families everywhere. The villages had their own social integrity, based on shared labor and communal decision making. And there was frequently a personal bond between peon and patrón that transcended the peasant's eternal debt at the hacienda store—a relationship not rare in backcountry areas around the preindustrial world.

The condition of women in Latin America, finally, in some ways worsened in the century after independence. But there were the beginnings of more promising trends as well.

LATIN AMERICAN WOMEN

Colonial European standards continued to be urged on Latin American women in the nineteenth century. Religious piety, sexual chastity and fidelity, and obedient dependence on fathers or husbands were enjoined upon

*L*ATIN AMERICA, 1828, AFTER THE WARS FOR INDEPENDENCE

them from childhood. Domestic duties filled most of their adult lives, and laws passed by liberal bourgeois regimes sometimes actually increased the husband's power over his wife and her property.

In the later nineteenth century, however, some women escaped the seclusion of the household for work in the larger world. Admittedly, the work often turned out to be brutal sweatshop labor in the new factories of the Industrial Revolution. Few though these were, they were often glad to have women, who would work more cheaply.

A more promising direction was the increase in education for girls in some countries. In relatively progressive nations such as Mexico and Argentina, women began to find work as schoolteachers themselves.

There was even a nascent feminist movement in Latin America in the last decades of the century. Women schoolteachers took the lead in organizing feminist societies and editing women's journals. Feminists worked diligently for the social and intellectual advancement of women and tried to defend their sisters from economic exploitation.

One of the most famous Latin American writers— and a leading proponent of education for women—the Argentine Domingo Sarmiento, declared that "the level of civilization of a people can be judged by the social position of its women."[3] By that standard, Latin America was

---

[3]Benjamin Keen and Mark Wasserman, *A Short History of Latin America* (Boston: Houghton Mifflin, 1980), p. 241.

no more civilized than the rest of the world in the nineteenth century. But there were harbingers, at least, of things to come.

PROVINCIAL CULTURE

PROVINCES OF THE WESTERN WORLD

The transformation of the Americas from colonies to countries was slower and more difficult in the cultural realm than in any other area of national development.

An armed revolt and paper constitution could bring political independence. Economic dependency on Europe might drag on, but at least the makers of economic policy now included Americans as well as their European trading partners. Enthusiasm for Old World ways and fashions might continue, but distinctively American social types, Yankee and *criollo,* began to take shape under the influence of New World conditions.

A distinctive American high culture, however, was very slow to develop. Both in the colonial era and during the first century of independence, the art, literature, and intellectual currents of the New World exhibited a character that may best be defined as provincial. American culture, North and South, was like that of a distant province of a more sophisticated metropolitan center. Europe was still the cultural heartland of the Western world; the Americas, culturally speaking, were its provinces.

The provincial nature of American culture during this transitional period came out in several ways. In part, the former colonies remained cultural colonies simply because much of their high culture was clearly derived from the artistic, literary, and intellectual life of Europe. Thus the Americas felt the impact of the eighteenth-century Enlightenment in late-colonial times and nineteenth-century European romanticism in the early-national period, though the forms of both were modified to suit the New World cultural milieu.

American culture was also provincial in its lack of sophistication, and in an occasional air of backwoods crudity that was sometimes quite calculated but nonetheless reflected American realities. This seems to have been particularly true of North America, where a rich vein of "frontier culture" runs from Ben Franklin's *Almanac* and fur cap to Mark Twain's Mississippi days and Jack London's Yukon.

There is, finally, a provincialism that consists simply in a vigorously artistic anatomizing of what constituted the rather far-off and exotic provinces of the Western world. In seeking to understand themselves, Americans—perhaps Latin Americans especially—revealed a distant backwoods world to Europeans.

This world of Indians and gauchos, rain forests and

pampas, mining camps and great rivers, was far stranger than any province of the old country, no matter how colorful and old-fashioned. New World intellectual concerns, with *caudillismo* or the "barbarism" of their own life, with transcendentalism or the abolition of slavery, were even more exotic. The books that brought this world and these concerns to vivid life were provincial simply in that their subject matter was the provinces of the considerably expanded Western world of the nineteenth century.

Let us look first at the provincial culture of the United States in the colonial era and the nineteenth century, and then at the cultural life of Latin America over the same period.

AMERICAN CULTURE: SONG OF MYSELF

The continuing cultural development between 1600 and 1900 of the new United States and the British colonies from which the new nation was born was a striking combination of European influences and American originality. The influences, not surprisingly, were strongest during the colonial centuries; the originality emerged more strongly during the middle and later decades of the nineteenth century.

The most powerful cultural influence on the British colonies in the seventeenth century was the Calvinist Protestantism that had brought most of the New England settlers there in the first place. Puritan religiosity infused the simple white boxes and pointed steeples of New England churches, the passion of Cotton Mather's sermons, the lyrical intensity of Anne Bradstreet's poetry. This puritanical religious dimension might be partially transmuted into taut Yankee business sense in the next century—as it was among Puritans, Huguenots, and Dutch burghers in Europe. But moralism and religiosity remained important tonal elements in American culture in later centuries.

The most important eighteenth-century European influence all over the North American colonies was the Enlightenment. Benjamin Franklin was not the only colonist to embrace the new interest in science. The political ideas of the Enlightenment found an interested audience among the increasingly disgruntled colonists. John Locke's belief in natural rights and government based on a social contract, Montesquieu's theory of checks and balances in government, and other political beliefs of Europe's Age of Reason influenced the thinking of Franklin, Thomas Jefferson, the Adamses, and other architects of the new American nation.

Europe's Age of Revolutions in the first half of the nineteenth century was an age of fermenting ideas in the new United States. Abolitionism, the crusade against liquor, rights for women, the Mormons and other new sects, utopian socialism imported directly from Europe—all made converts in the United States. These American social movements had a heavier religious and moralistic tone than the liberalism, nationalism, and socialism of the

Old World. But these American ideological gropings also stirred passions and provided background at least for more radical enthusiasms to come.

The later nineteenth century, furthermore, saw more and more individuals and schools of thought whose work was unique, whose concerns were distinctly those of the far fringes of the Western world. The two most strikingly American schools of thought were transcendentalism and pragmatism. Both originated in the intellectual center of the young United States—New England. But they illustrated two strikingly dissimilar aspects of the American mind.

Ralph Waldo Emerson, essayist, poet, and eager proponent of transcendentalism, urged confidence in our own instincts, an inner understanding that transcended reason, authority, even observation. William James, the philosopher who championed pragmatism the most ardently, declared that truth was really a matter of the *usefulness* of an idea, of its "cash value" to us. Emerson's view reflected the spiritual dimension of American thought, which went back to the Puritans, whereas James expressed the practical, this-worldly aspect of the American experience, with its emphasis on getting the job done.

Much of the cultural contribution of the young United States, however, was the work not of schools of thought such as transcendentalism or pragmatism, but of one-of-a-kind individuals.

There is much of the European romantic in the American poet and short-story writer Edgar Allan Poe and in the fiction writers Nathaniel Hawthorne and Herman Melville. Other aspects of their work, however, have few parallels in the Old World. In his obsession with death and beauty, Poe exceeded most European romantics who held similar predilections. Hawthorne's flair for allegory and his immersion in the New England past, Melville's combination of seafaring and symbolism, have no obvious sources in Europe. "The Raven," *The Scarlet Letter,* and *Moby Dick* are all uniquely individual productions.

In the decades after the Civil War, novelist Henry James—William's brother—probed a uniquely American experience in novels such as *The Portrait of a Lady* and *The Ambassadors:* the rediscovery of Europe by Americans, who pitted their strength and provincial innocence against the Old World's sophistication and deeper knowledge of life. Mark Twain, meanwhile, went the other way, exploring the depths of the provinces in the small towns of the American South and West, and produced the novel Ernest Hemingway would call the best ever written by an American: *Huckleberry Finn.*

Among later nineteenth-century American poets, Emily Dickinson stands out in one way, Walt Whitman in another. Dickinson, living a reclusive life in a small New England town, never seeing either Europe or the Far West, came closer than anyone else of her time to capturing glints of the infinite in a few brief, crystalline lines.

Walt Whitman, frequently hailed as America's greatest poet, celebrated the democratic heart of the nation and with equal fervor sang his "Song of Myself" in the lush, earthy, exultant lines of his *Leaves of Grass.*

Any attempt to characterize American thought and literature before 1900 would surely include moralism, from the Puritans to Hawthorne; humor, from Ben Franklin to Mark Twain; and interest in the special North American experience, from the rather unconvincing Indians of Longfellow's *Hiawatha* and Cooper's *Last of the Mohicans* to realist William Dean Howells's chronicle of a nineteenth-century robber baron, *The Rise of Silas Lapham.* But perhaps the outstanding feature of the culture of the new country was an almost exaggerated individualism, a democratic passion for common things, which could find greatness in a runaway slave, a whaling ship, or a slant of light in a New England afternoon.

LATIN AMERICAN CULTURE: GAUCHOS AND INDIANS

The culture of Latin America was also a self-consciously provincial one in these colonial and early-national periods.

The intellectual life of the Spanish and Portuguese colonies was in some ways more religious than that of the English-speaking colonies to the north. But it was a Counter-Reformation Catholic faith rather than a Protestant one, Jesuits its most ardent spokesmen instead of Puritan preachers. The hundreds of churches scattered over the southern continent were not simple New England boxes, but elaborately ornamental baroque cathedrals thick with marble and statuary, color and gilding and rich decoration. The greatest Latin American poet of the seventeenth century was a nun, Juana de La Cruz—who, like her Puritan counterpart Anne Bradstreet, was known as the Tenth Muse.

The Inquisition, still busy in the New World as in parts of the Old, seriously inhibited the spread of the Enlightenment in Latin America. The enlightened despotism of the Spanish Bourbons, however, did lead to an upsurge in scientific studies, particularly in Mexico. Mexico's famous School of Mines taught much more than that—geography and geology, astronomy, mathematics, and other sciences. Jesuits even labored to reconcile the rationalism and empiricism of Descartes, Bacon, and Newton with Catholic theology. On the historical side, an interest in the Indian past developed very early: missionary fathers and Indian informants were collaborating on chronicles of the Aztecs and Incas as early as the sixteenth century.

The nineteenth century saw a continuing approximation of the cultural history of the Old World unfolding in the new Spanish- and Portuguese-speaking nations. The romantic movement in particular stirred a parallel upheaval across the Atlantic. But Latin American romanticism had especially strong liberal-nationalist overtones. It also exhibited a powerful concern with such strictly Latin American matters as their conquistadore and Indian past and the gauchos and *caudillos* of their own century. Mexico and the ABC countries of South America—Argentina, Brazil, and Chile—produced especially powerful literary and historical cultures in the 1800s.

Condemnation of their own Spanish ancestors was common among the Latin American writers and thinkers of the nineteenth century. The Chilean author Francisco Bilbao, writing under the influence of French liberal and socialist ideas, depicted the conquistadores as feudal Catholic holdovers from the Middle Ages. He saw these founding fathers as the source of the slavery, ignorance, and economic backwardness he detested in his own time.

The Indian past was also condemned as barbarous by some, particularly in Argentina. Others, however, especially in Brazil and Mexico, glorified the ancient Indian cultures, seeing them as their true American heritage. Thus in *Prophecy of Cuauhtémoc,* a poem of powerful romantic imagery, the Mexican Ignacio Rodriguez Galván summoned up the ghost of a martyred Aztec king to lead Mexico to new greatness.

Concerned more directly with present problems was the poetry and fiction of young liberal romantic writers who had been swept up in the opposition to the postindependence *caudillo* dictatorships. Esteban Echeverría, the moving spirit behind Argentine romanticism, was also a liberal and a utopian socialist who was driven into exile by the Rosas regime. Echeverría's grim little masterpiece, *The Slaughterhouse,* a realistic yet symbolically intended account of the torment and death of a young man of character and culture in a slaughterhouse reeking of carcasses, guts, and blood, thus figuratively condemned the Buenos Aires dictatorship in a series of vivid images.

Attitudes toward the lawless gaucho, *vaquero,* or *llanero* horsemen of the plains and the backcountry were more varied. Some, like the Argentine romantic leader Domingo Sarmiento, saw the gaucho as the base of *caudillo* power and a symbol of the nation's barbaric past. Others praised the gaucho as the symbol of a wild, free life that was being steadily undermined by the spread of bourgeois urban culture. Jose Hernandez's epic poem *The Gaucho Martin Fierro,* written in the racy language of the Argentine pampas and strongly influenced by gaucho folk songs, condemned officialdom, the military, and civilization generally and glorified the outlaw life of the vanishing gaucho breed.

Groping for a sense of national identity once national independence had been achieved, Latin American writers and thinkers, like their North American counterparts, turned defiantly to the exploration of their own frontier world. They approved of some aspects of what they saw—their Indian past, and frequently the fading gaucho present—and disapproved of others, such as the brutal *caudillo* dictatorships. Whatever their attitude, the result was a vivid depiction of these westernmost provinces of the Western world.

SUMMARY

During their first century of political independence, the new nations of the Western Hemisphere remained in many ways provinces of the Western world. Both North and South America moved toward a broader future. But both were still rooted in their colonial pasts during the nineteenth century.

The English colonists of eastern North America were numerous, socially mobile, and accustomed to self-government. Attempts to tighten the mercantilistic ties that bound the colonies to the mother country led the generation of Washington, Jefferson, and the Adamses to break those ties entirely in the Revolutionary War (1776–1781). The new nation had its troubles, but strong early leadership and a flexible constitution, combined with the immense resources of the continent, led to a prosperous, increasingly democratic, and territorially expansive first half century.

The Civil War (1860–1865) nearly tore the nation in half, but determined leadership by Lincoln and superior Northern firepower both saved the Union and freed the slaves. The last four decades of the century, however, were a gilded age of political corruption and disregard for the interests of farmers, blue-collar laborers, blacks, Indians, and immigrants. The latter half of the century nevertheless saw substantial additions to the nation's wealth and territory.

By contrast, the Latin American colonies of Spain and Portugal had a much larger admixture of Amerindians and a less rigidly segregated black African component. Colonial rule in Middle and South America permitted much less self-government; but during the later eighteenth century, Enlightenment reform brought many improvements and a surge of prosperity. The Wars of Independence began with ill-fated revolts by the most oppressed: blacks and Indians. Between 1810 and 1824, however, Bolívar in Venezuela, San Martín in Argentina, and the rebellion instigated by Father Hidalgo in Mexico liberated most of Latin America, and Brazil achieved its independence from Portugal.

The governments of the new Latin American republics, however, remained autocratic, though the new leaders were gun-toting local *caudillos* rather than appointed European administrators, and revolutions were far more common. Economically, the new countries were nearly as dependent on European capital, manufactured goods, and markets for their commodities as they had been as colonies. Prosperity and progressive reforms were found only in a few nations, such as Argentina and Uruguay.

Culturally, North and South America remained provincial in their involvement with European intellectual movements and in their concern with their own exotic provincial worlds of Amerindians and gauchos. North America did produce two original schools—transcendentalism and pragmatism—and a number of rugged individualists in literature. Latin American writers explored their colonial and precolonial past and their often rough frontier present, seeking a sense of national identity that would not emerge until the next century.

SUGGESTED READING

AXTELL, J. *The Invasion Within: The Contest of Cultures in Colonial North America.* New York: Oxford University Press, 1985. Acclaimed analysis of Native American, British, and French cultures in conflict during the colonial era. See also J. Hemming's *Amazon Frontier: The Defeat of the Brazilian Indians* (Cambridge: Harvard University Press, 1987), which chronicles the impact of military repression, loss of land, disease, alcoholism, and other consequences of Western intrusion into Amazonia on the Indian population.

BREEN, T. H. *Puritans and Adventurers: Change and Persistence in Early America.* New York: Oxford University Press, 1980. Society and settlement in colonial North America, especially Massachusetts and Virginia.

BROWNLEE, W. E. *Dynamics of Ascent: A History of the American Economy,* 2nd ed. New York: Knopf, 1979. A good summary of recent views on the causes and course of American development. On industrial development in particular, see T. C. Cochran, *Frontiers of Change: Early Industrialism in America* (New York: Oxford University Press, 1981).

BURNS, E. B. *The Poverty of Progress: Latin America in the Nineteenth Century.* Berkeley: University of California Press, 1980. Stimulating essay on the theme that economic advance was limited to Latin American elites, seldom trickling down to the masses.

FLEXNER, J. T. *George Washington* (3 vols.). Boston: Little, Brown, 1968–1972. Standard account of the revolutionary commander and first president of the United States; makes him more interesting than most of the cliches about the father of his country.

FREYRE, G. *The Mansions and the Shanties: The Making of Modern Brazil,* trans. H. de Onis. New York: Knopf, 1963. A classic study of Brazilian social and racial relations. See also E. Viotti da Costa, *The Brazilian Empire: Myths and Histories* (Chicago:

University of Chicago Press, 1985), which examines key aspects of Brazil's history from independence in the 1820s to the emergence of the republic in the 1880s.

GENOVESE, E. *Roll, Jordan, Roll: The World the Slaves Made.* New York: Random House, 1976. Perhaps the best of a number of important books debating the nature and consequences of black slavery in the United States.

HALPERIIN-DONGHI, T. *The Aftermath of Revolution in Latin America.* New York: Harper & Row, Pub., 1973. Discusses Latin American history—particularly social and cultural—after the heroic days of the revolutions.

HARTZ, L. *The Founding of New Society: Studies in the History of the United States, Latin America, South Africa, Canada, and Australia.* New York: Harcourt, Brace, and World, 1964. Comparative evolution of new societies in the European intercontinental empires.

LANG, J. *Conquest and Commerce: Spain and England in the Americas.* New York: Academic Press, 1975. A comparative study of the empires of the two biggest winners in the New World.

LAVRIN, A., ed. *Latin American Women: Historical Perspectives.* Westport, Conn.: Greenwood Press, 1978. Includes accounts of women in the colonial period. See also C. R. Boxer, *Women in Iberian Expansion Overseas, 1415–1815* (New York: Oxford University Press, 1975).

LOCKHART, J., and S. B. SCHWARTZ. *Early Latin America: A History of Colonial Spanish America and Brazil.* New York: Cambridge University Press, 1983. Valuable synthesis of modern research on the interaction of Iberian and Amerindian cultures.

LYNCH, J. *The Spanish-American Revolutions, 1808–1826.* New York: W. W. Norton, 1973. A thoroughly scholarly survey. On causal factors, see R. A. Humphreys and J. Lynch, eds., *The Origins of the Latin American Revolutions, 1808–1826* (New York: Knopf, 1965).

MASUR, G. *Simón Bolívar,* 2nd ed. Albuquerque: University of New Mexico Press, 1969. The best biography. On San Martín, see J. C. J. Metford's brief but still useful *San Martín the Liberator* (London: Longmans, Green, 1950).

MERK, F. *Manifest Destiny and Mission in American History.* New York: Knopf, 1963. The United States version of the Western world's imperialistic conviction of its right to rule and its global civilizing mission. See Merk's *History of the Westward Movement* (New York: Knopf, 1978) on the transcontinental conquest.

MIDDLEKAUFF, R. *The Glorious Cause: The American Revolution, 1763–1789.* New York: Oxford University Press, 1982. A good overview of the big picture.

MILLER, P. *The New England Mind* (2 vols.). Cambridge: Harvard University Press, 1983. A classic on the Puritan mentality. On post–Civil War cultural trends, including pragmatism, see B. Kuklick, *The Rise of American Philosophy* (New Haven: Yale University Press, 1977) and J. Martin, *Harvests of Change: American Literature, 1865–1914* (Englewood Cliffs, N.J.: Prentice Hall, 1967).

NORTON, M. B. *Liberty's Daughters.* Boston: Little, Brown, 1980. Women's role in the American Revolution. For women's emancipation in the later nineteenth century, consult E. C. Dubois, *Feminism and Suffrage: The Emergence of an Independent Movement in America* (Ithaca: Cornell University Press, 1978).

OATES, S. B. *With Malice toward None.* New York: Harper & Row, Pub., 1978. Life of Lincoln, the most internationally admired of American presidents.

PORTER, G. *The Rise of Big Business, 1860–1910.* Arlington Heights, Ill.: Harlan Davidson, 1973. Survey of the dynamic economic expansion of the Gilded Age. For a dazzling example, see R. Chernow's *The House of Morgan.* (New York: Atlantic Monthly Press, 1990). On the labor movement in the United States seen in the broadest context, see H. G. Gutman, *Work, Culture, and Society in Industrializing America* (New York: Random House, 1977).

RANDALL, J. G., and D. DONALD. *Civil War and Reconstruction,* 2nd ed. Boston: Little, Brown, 1973. Older, but perhaps still the best one-volume account.

ROUT, L. B., JR. *The African Experience in Spanish America, 1502 to the Present Day.* Cambridge: Cambridge University Press, 1971. Has useful chapters on both the colonial and nineteenth-century periods. See also H. S. Klein, *African Slavery in Latin America and the Caribbean* (New York: Oxford University Press, 1986).

SLATTA, R., ed. *Banditos: The Varieties of Latin American Banditry.* New York: Greenwood Press, 1987. Essays on bandits and their popular images as possible symptoms of peasant social discontent.

STEIN, S. J., and B. H. STEIN. *The Colonial Heritage of Latin America.* London: Oxford University Press, 1970. Interpretive examination of colonial influences on later Latin American republics.

WHITAKER, A. P., ed. *Latin America and the Enlightenment.* Ithaca, N.Y.: Cornell University Press, 1961. Cultural influences during colonial times. See also M. Pícon-Salas, *A Cultural History of Spanish America from Conquest to Independence,* trans. I. Leonard (Berkeley: University of California Press, 1962), an eminently readable survey.

WOOD, G. S. *The Creation of the American Republic, 1776–1787.* New York: W. W. Norton, 1972. Frequently cited overview of transformation of thirteen colonies into one nation.

CHAPTER 37

THE CLIMAX OF WESTERN IMPERIALISM

THE NATURE OF THE NEW IMPERIALISM

INTO THE HEART OF DARKNESS

The English poet Rudyard Kipling called it "the white man's burden." The Russian revolutionary socialist V. I. Lenin defined it as "the highest stage of capitalism." The distinguished Indian historian Kavalam Madhava Panikkar explained it as "the dominance of maritime power over the land masses." But Joseph Conrad, sea captain turned novelist, experienced it viscerally while nursing a rusty river steamer up the Congo into what he called the *Heart of Darkness:*

> Going up that river was like travelling back to the earliest beginnings of the world, when vegetation rioted on the earth and the big trees were kings. An empty stream, a great silence, an impenetrable forest. The air was warm, thick, heavy, sluggish. . . . On silvery sandbanks hippos and alligators sunned themselves side by side.

And then:

> . . . houses on a hill, others with iron roofs, . . . A jetty projected into the river. . . .
> . . . A heavy and dull detonation shook the ground, a puff of smoke came out of the cliff. . . . They were building a railway.

Finally, halfway up the hill toward the company station:

> A slight clinking . . . made me turn my head. Six black men advanced in a file, toiling up the path. They walked erect and slow, balancing small baskets full of earth on their heads, and the clink kept time with their footsteps. . . . I could see every rib, the joints of their limbs were like knots in a rope; each had an iron collar on his neck, and all were connected together with a chain whose bights swung between them, rhythmically clinking.[1]

[1] Joseph Conrad, *Heart of Darkness* and *The Secret Sharer* (New York: New American Library, n.d.), pp. 102–103, 79, 80.

Sometimes it takes a novelist to capture the reality of things.

The great revival of Western expansion we call the New Imperialism, running from around 1870 to perhaps 1914, was one of the most astonishing aspects of nineteenth-century world history. The New Imperialism was particularly surprising because during most of the preceding hundred years, imperial expansion had been widely seen as a losing proposition by European statesmen. This feeling was generated by the loss of Europe's most highly developed colonies in the New World between the 1770s and the 1820s, when revolutions cost Britain, Spain, and Portugal their American colonies and France was prevailed upon to sell its substantial sweep of middle North America to the new United States. "Colonies," the philosophe and statesman Turgot declared in a famous aphorism, "are like fruits which cling to the tree only until they ripen."[2]

Still, large parts of the world either remained in European hands or were strongly influenced by European traders, missionaries, and others. For example, there were British holdings in India, Canada, and Australia; the French West Indies and France's conquest of Algeria in 1830; and the Dutch settlements in South Africa and continuing Dutch preeminence in island Southeast Asia. The former colonies in the Americas, furthermore, though politically independent, continued to be ruled by people of European descent and culture and remained closely bound commercially, socially, and intellectually to the Old World.

Then, around 1870, the Western peoples launched a startling new wave of imperial aggression against the rest of the world, an explosion of Western conquest that would dwarf the achievements of preceding centuries.

MOTIVES OF THE NEW IMPERIALISTS

The causes of the New Imperialism have frequently been presented in the most simplistic and unconvincing way. The imperialists themselves claimed that Western colonialism was, in Kipling's phrase, "the white man's burden"—a moral obligation to spread the benefits of a "higher" Western civilization to a backward world. Par-

[2] F. Lee Benns, *European History since 1870* (New York: Appleton-Century-Crofts, 1950), p. 13.

ticularly since the collapse of the European overseas empires after World War II, on the other hand, enemies of imperialism have depicted it as exploitation pure and simple, a cloak for Western capitalist looting of a helpless world. As with most major historical events, however, the New Imperialism seems to have been the product of a considerable variety of factors—economic, political, humanitarian, and even psychological.

As the exploitation theorists emphasize, economic causes played a large part in the new wave of overseas expansion. The Industrial Revolution created new and complex economic and technological demands that in many cases could best be met by the extension of European power into distant parts of the world. One of the most obvious of these needs was the demand for natural resources—many of them exotic commodities such as rubber, manganese, and oil—to feed into the vast hopper of the new industrial machine. There was also a demand for cheap labor, especially as European wages went up in the later nineteenth century. "Coolie" overseas labor would work much more cheaply than unionized Western workers and was therefore hired in large quantities to extract, process, and ship the resources of far-off lands back to Europe.

Another economic motive for expansion was the need for more customers for the fantastic production of the newly industrializing West: new colonies meant new markets for Western goods. The immense profits piling up in Europe also sought new investment areas and often found them in the underdeveloped world. Building a trunk railway line across Asia or Africa could bring in 30 percent interest on an investment, whereas a modest spur line in Europe returned less than 5 percent.

Political and military motives also played a part in empire building. The need for naval bases or coaling stations for the new steam navies and merchant marines could lead Western powers to seize key harbors or islands. Many strategic straits and strips of land with geopolitical value were targets for annexation. Political determination to outmaneuver a European rival could impel Western governments to acquire large territories having no detectable economic value at all.

Besides economic and political causes, humanitarian impulses—however wrongheaded some of them may look now—did in fact play a significant part in the New Imperialism. Protestant and Catholic missionaries thronged to the "mission fields" in Africa and Asia in unparalleled numbers. The flag often followed them, for governments were compelled by pious public opinion to support the spreaders of the Gospel in their good work.

Antislavery societies—formed after the Europeans themselves had given up slavery—urged Western governments to do whatever was necessary to suppress Arab slavers in the nineteenth century. And tidy-minded proconsuls of empire really did go out into what was for them the Heart of Darkness to spread European law, education,

and medicine—as well as taxes and compulsory labor—south of the Sahara and east of Suez.

Finally, totally irrational psychological drives may have been at work beneath all of these expressed motives for imperial expansion. A simple but powerful sense of Western superiority, rooted in nineteenth-century progress, prosperity, and racist theories of the biological superiority of caucasoid humanity, was clearly part of the psychological equipment of most imperialists, for instance.

It has also been suggested that instinctive aggessiveness, revealed at home in a range of activities from sports to politics and business competition, may have helped cause imperialism. Europeans may have taken up arms against Zulus and Afghans for the pure primordial joy of "smashing 'em good." Even so simple a human psychological impulse as hero worship was perhaps better met by cavalry charges against the Apaches or skirmishes in the Khyber Pass than by portly politicians fighting election campaigns at home.

Political, economic, humanitarian, and psychological, the motives behind the New Imperialism were thus manifold. To all of these it might be well to add a final reminder that imperial conquest of other peoples is, after all, one of the great givens of history. A pattern of human behavior that can be traced back to the third millennium before Christ perhaps doesn't require too elaborate a scaffolding of explanation in our own day.

MEANS: THE WORLD DOWN THE BARREL OF A MAXIM GUN

The awesome success of the New Imperialism probably requires more explanation than the motives for its undertaking. And here, at least, there is some agreement among the experts.

The new wave of Western aggression may have succeeded in part because of the powerful *esprit* of Western military forces, a total self-confidence generated by many triumphs and by the arrogant sense of racial superiority mentioned above. Another factor was almost certainly the greatly improved governmental organization and efficiency of post-Enlightenment Western administrative machinery. But the major cause of Western supremacy admits of little argument. Once again, the technology of the Industrial Revolution is at the heart of the matter.

Nineteenth-century European empire builders now faced Ashantis and Uzbeks with massed repeating-rifle fire. They confronted the junks and sampans of Eastern potentates with ironclad warships. They reduced the most impregnable strongholds of ancient kingdoms with heavy artillery and explosive shells. For a few brief decades a hundred years ago, the West had a technological advantage over the rest of the world that made Western Foreign Legions and thin red lines, Western Marines and gunboats well nigh invincible.

There were many differences among cultures, as

even the smuggest Victorian had to allow. But the difference that mattered, as a cynical commentator perceptively suggested, was that Western peoples had Maxim guns and other peoples didn't.

FORMS OF IMPERIAL CONTROL

To most people *empire* means colonies—something like the original thirteen American colonies, perhaps, with royal governors and redcoats. The New Imperialism, however, was a good deal more complicated than that. In fact it took several characteristic forms.

Some of the bastions of Western power overseas were colonies, of course. In a fully developed colony, European administrators set up centralized governmental structures in major cities. They also fanned out through the backcountry, scattering isolated "district officers" among the villages as agents of the new authority. European armies policed the newly acquired region. Marching up and down like Roman legions across Gaul, they often had to carry out several punitive expeditions before the new order was accepted.

A protectorate, by contrast, provided a form of control that was much less than total—and much less expensive. Here the key institution was the European *resident* or *advisor* to the local potentate. The traditional ruler accepted the advice of the European resident on any matter of concern to Europeans—trade, investment, missionary efforts, and the like. Otherwise, he ran his country in his own way. In return, the local sultan or shah or *raja* got financial aid, protection, and perhaps European support in his wars. The European resident was also supported by armed force, of course—commonly a naval squadron, which could patrol a large area and guarantee a number of protectorates.

The sphere of influence, finally, provided a still more diffuse and limited form of European control. The main objective here was almost always economic penetration. Western personnel took over a single institution—say, the customs service—or a limited area, such as a strip of land for a railway or the right to exploit mineral deposits. Spheres of influence commonly developed in regions where European rivals were evenly matched in strength; each would exercise an influence over an agreed-upon portion of the territory in question. The expense to European governments was minimal, the potential for exploitation and development often quite substantial.

There were, of course, many combinations of these three—colony, protectorate, sphere of influence—and bastard versions of each form. The internal imperialism to be discussed in a later section is not a matter of *overseas* empire building at all, but of absorbing neighboring peoples—a form of imperialism as old as civilization.

There are, finally, those who see any economic relationship in which one party gets the better of another—that is to say, most economic relationships—as forms of imperialism. This concept of informal imperialism will be discussed under the twentieth-century rubric of *neo-imperialism*—though, again, it is anything but new.

Let us turn now, however, to a chronicle of the final phase of the great conquest—the New Imperialism of the later nineteenth century.

 ## THE SCRAMBLE FOR AFRICA

FIRST THE TREATIES, THEN THE TROOPS

The partitioning of nine tenths of the world's second largest continent among the colonial powers of Europe during the last quarter of the nineteenth century was a transfer of sovereignty to rank with the Iberian seizure of South and Central America in the sixteenth century or the Mongol conquest of much of Eurasia in the thirteenth. It was initially accomplished with minimal bloodshed, although holding the Africans in line, even for a few decades, sometimes turned out to be a very bloody business indeed.

The "scramble for Africa" by competing European powers was carried out by politicians and diplomats in Europe and by explorers, missionaries, military commanders, economic developers, and others in Africa itself.

Interest in the unknown interior of the "dark continent" was aroused initially by a handful of colorful individuals. Explorers poking about in search of the source of the Nile and other wonders kindled romantic enthusiasm at home. Increasing numbers of missionaries like Dr. Livingston carried Western religion and medicine into Africa and came back urging government intervention against the slavers.

In Europe, crowned heads and prime ministers began to concern themselves with Africa. Speeches were made about spreading the benefits of French civilization, defending Britain's lifeline to India, acquiring a "place in the sun" for Germany. There was public talk of developing the mineral wealth of inner Africa, suppressing the slave trade, expanding European commerce, and other issues. International conferences were held in Belgium (1876) and Berlin (1884) to lay down acceptable ground rules for carving up the continent.

On the African earth itself, it was first the treaties, then the troops. In the 1870s and 1880s, expeditions set out for the interior from the string of European settlements that had been scattered along the coasts since the heyday of the Old Imperialism. These handfuls of government officials or agents for trading companies negotiated treaties with Muslim monarchs and paramount chiefs, including the rulers of many of the newly evolving states we have explored in an earlier chapter. In return for gifts, protection, and other benefits, African rulers thus accepted a European overlordship that many of them only partly understood.

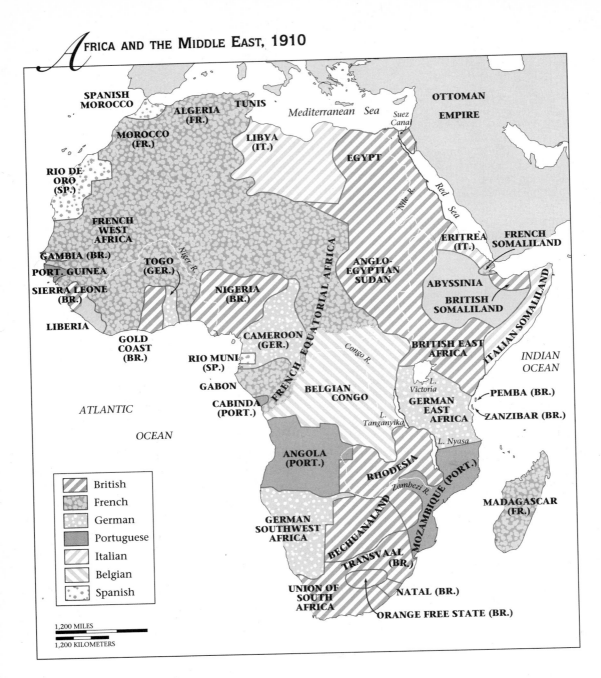

Africa and the Middle East, 1910

Legend:
- British
- French
- German
- Portuguese
- Italian
- Belgian
- Spanish

1,200 MILES
1,200 KILOMETERS

The misunderstandings were thrashed out later, during the sometimes savage fighting of the 1890s and the early 1900s. The larger states of inner Africa resisted initial penetration. Other African peoples revolted later against the increasingly heavy hand of Western rule.

Recent scholarship suggests that we should not exaggerate the European mastery of the situation. Local rulers often knew the local situation much better than the intruders did and made quite advantageous terms, at least in the short run. In the early 1830s, after a dozen years of mounting British pressure on the Ashanti of West Africa, the Ashanti princess Akyaawa Yikwan negotiated a key peace treaty that brought her people a vigorous revival of trade and postponed foreign rule for most of the rest of the century.

Rarely, however, was either resistance or diplomacy successful for long. The courage of the Africans was great, and their numbers often greater than those of the intrud-

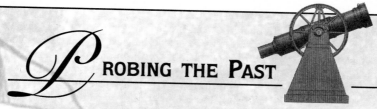

PROBING THE PAST

"It will be clear to the reader (and will become clearer still throughout the many pages that follow) that by Orientalism I mean several things. . . . Orientalism is a style of thought based upon an onto-logical and epistemological distinction made between "the Orient" and (most of the time) "the Occi-dent." Thus a very large mass of writers, among whom are poets, novelists, philosophers, political theorists, economists, and imperial administrators, have accepted the basic distinction between East and West as the starting point for elaborate theories, epics, novels, social descriptions, and political accounts concerning the [East]. To speak of Orientalism therefore is to speak . . . of a cultural enter-prise, a project whose dimensions take in such disparate realms as the imagination itself, the whole of India and the Levant, the Biblical texts and the Biblical lands, the spice trade, colonial armies and a long tradition of colonial administrators, a formidable scholarly corpus, innumerable Orien-tal "experts" and "hands," an Oriental professorate, a complex array of "Oriental" ideas (Oriental despotism, Oriental splendor, cruelty, sensuality), many Eastern sects, philosophies, and wisdoms domesticated for local European use—the list can be extended more or less indefinitely. . . . It is not the thesis of this book to suggest that there is such a thing as a real or true Orient (Islam, Arab, or whatever). . . . On the contrary, I have been arguing that "the Orient" is itself a constituted entity, and that the notion that there are geographical spaces with indigenous, radically "different" inhab-itants who can be defined on the basis of some religion, culture, or racial essence proper to that geo-graphical space is equally a highly debatable idea."

◆◆◆

Edward W. Said's influential study of <u>Orientalism</u> seeks to expose the origins, charac-ter, and fallacies of the Western image of the Orient—"the East," especially the Near East. Born in Palestine, now a professor of comparative literatures at Columbia University, Said is uniquely positioned to analyze Western stereotypes of the mysterious world "east of Suez."

Said defines orientalism as "a style of thought": Who does he believe has propagated orientalist ideas? What qualities does orientalism attribute to Asians and Asian societies? How do you think Said would react to an effort to define "the Western World" in terms of sweeping generalizations, stereotypes, and images?

Edward W. Said, <u>Orientalism</u> (New York: Random House, 1979), pp. 2–4, 322.

ers. But a single Maxim machine gun could make num-bers and courage suddenly irrelevant. From Egypt to the Cape, from the tree-studded grasslands of the Western Sudan to the green hills of East Africa, European organi-zation, discipline, ruthlessness, and firepower carried the day.

BRITAIN AND INDIRECT IMPERIALISM

Great Britain's holdings in Africa comprised colonies and protectorates north, south, east, and west.

In North Africa, the Conservative prime minister Disraeli and the Liberal Gladstone between them estab-lished a British protectorate over Egypt, despite the bitter opposition of the French, who had just completed the Suez Canal on Egyptian territory. Then trouble arose with a Muslim religious leader called the Mahdi farther up the Nile, and a famous British colonial officer known as "Chi-nese" Gordon was defeated and killed at Khartoum. British troops responded by pushing up the river, crush-ing the Mahdi's followers at the Battle of Omdurman, and establishing British authority in what became the Anglo-Egyptian Sudan.

In South Africa, the British faced two tenacious

rivals: the Zulus, one of history's great warrior peoples, and the rugged Dutch settlers called Boers. Both were defeated, though at great cost. By 1914 Britain controlled the whole region, rich in gold, diamonds, and farmland. They divided it into the three colonies of Northern and Southern Rhodesia and the Union of South Africa.

On the Guinea Coast of West Africa, British colonies included Nigeria and the Gold Coast (Ghana today), isolated enclaves in the huge French-controlled bulge of West Africa. In East Africa, the British held what are today Uganda and Kenya, reaching from the Sudan to the coast. The western colonies were acquired by treaties with paramount chiefs, the eastern ones through British trading companies and a protectorate over the sultan of Zanzibar.

Almost everywhere in Africa, the British pursued a policy of indirect rule. They left traditional authorities in power at the local level, at least insofar as this was commensurate with British commercial interest and basic values. They intervened to maintain law and order and to support trading companies, railroad builders, and missionary activities. But local chiefs and *emirs* ruled in most matters and were even allowed to keep a substantial chunk of the taxes they collected to support the colonial regime.

AN EXTENSION OF FRANCE OVERSEAS

A very different policy was followed by the French in Africa. French colonies were concentrated in the Mediterranean Muslim lands of Tunisia, Algeria, and Morocco, in the great westward sweep of Saharan and Sudanic Africa, and on the huge East African island of Madagascar—twice the size of the British Isles. All were run as if they were provinces of the French nation.

French penetration of North Africa began as early as the 1830s with the bloody conquest of Algeria, due south of France across the Mediterranean. Tunisia was occupied late in the century at the urging of Jules Ferry, France's leading proponent of empire, and Morocco was made a protectorate after a tense dispute with Germany in the early 1900s. Meanwhile, French troops had pushed south across the Sahara, east along the Senegal River from the Atlantic, and north up the Niger into western Sudan. They overcame with considerable difficulty the prolonged resistance of Muslim rulers such as Samori, a Mande leader and heir of the great Mande Sudanic kingdoms of medieval and early-modern times. Madagascar, finally, proved a quagmire for the French. France's intrusion provoked violent revolts and a long pacification campaign, which climaxed in the deposition and exile of the last queen, Ranavalona III, and the declaration of a French colony in the late 1890s.

Because these areas were seized only after prolonged fighting and were ruled for some time by military commanders, a rigidly centralized system of government was established. All of French West Africa—an area roughly the size of the United States—was ruled by a single government in Dakar. French proconsuls did not negotiate with local chieftains or leave the largest share of government in their hands, as the British did. French officials regarded traditional local rulers as subordinates and summoned them to French offices to give them orders.

Arab children in North Africa would soon be memorizing French classical tragedy in their schools. Black Africans from the western Sudan would be studying in Paris—all part of the effort to create an integrated empire that was in every sense an extension of France overseas.

OTHER POWERS SEEK THEIR PLACES IN THE SUN

The main area of British colonial control in Africa ran north and south in a broken strip from Cairo to the Cape of Good Hope. The primary French zone was the whole of northwestern Africa—the states of the Maghreb, French West Africa, and French Equatorial Africa, reaching from the Atlantic to the frontiers of the Anglo-Egyptian Sudan. Most of the rest of Africa beyond these two great blocks was soon absorbed by other European powers, jostling and shoving for their share of the dwindling continent. The

Ceremonies celebrating the opening of the Suez Canal in Egypt in 1869, which provided a short route for shipping from Europe to Asia. Built by French engineers, the canal would later be taken over by the British and only became Egyptian in the 1950s. Such monumental undertakings were major accomplishments of the new industrial technology—and of the New Imperialism of the nineteenth century. (The New York Public Library Picture Collection)

most important of these other exploiters of Africa were Belgium, Germany, Portugal, and Italy.

The Belgian king Leopold hired the journalist-turned-explorer Henry Stanley to sign treaties with chiefs all across the dense rain forest of the Congo Basin in central Africa. This gigantic Belgian colony, almost ten times the size of Belgium itself, became a major copper producer—and a byword for colonial cruelty to native peoples.

Germany, filled with national pride and expansive vigor after the unification of 1870–1871, demanded its "place in the sun" rather late. But the new nation soon had three large colonies: Cameroons, at the hinge of West Africa; an East African territory that is today Tanzania; and a southern colony bordering South Africa and composed largely of desert—modern Namibia. The genocidal suppression of the Maji-Maji rebellion in Tanzania became another of the horror stories of the great conquest.

Portugal expanded ancient holdings into the two large colonies of Angola and Mozambique on opposite sides of the stem of South Africa. The new nation of Italy set out with much vigor but mixed success to acquire North African territories. Italians seized the desert sprawl of Libya between French Tunisia and British Egypt, and the northeastern strip of Somaliland on the Red Sea and the Indian Ocean. Italian efforts to conquer Ethiopia, however, met disaster when an Italian army was destroyed at Adowa by the Ethiopians in 1896.

As the twentieth century began, then, only Ethiopia remained a truly independent African state. All the rest had come under the control, direct or indirect, of the relentlessly expanding West.

THE EXPLOITATION OF ASIA

LOANS AND RIGHTS OF WAY

In Asia—the four fifths of Eurasia east of the Dardanelles—Europeans confronted a very different situation from that prevailing in Africa. The East, the original home of civilization, had for thousands of years been dominated by powerful Asian empires and complex urban societies. These Asian cultures had successfully resisted or effectively absorbed many invaders over the centuries.

Over much of the East, then, the more direct and brutal methods that had worked in Africa had less application. Military conquest and the establishment of a full-scale colonial administration did happen in Asia, but less often. More common was the protectorate, more common still the sphere of influence.

In Asia, imperialism was thus much less a matter of pith helmets and pacification campaigns. More often it was a dignified affair of bank loans or railway rights of way, of European officers retraining royal armies or European bureaucrats taking over crucial departments of someone else's government.

The gunboats played their part, of course, patrolling the coasts of China or "opening up" Japan. There were savage struggles to hold India during the Mutiny of 1857 or to conquer chunks of mainland Southeast Asia. But much of the work of imposing the will of the West upon the East was done in meetings between Europeans themselves, in which they agreed to respect each others' "interests" in other peoples' countries.

There were fewer misunderstandings of the sort that might occur with a paramount chief in West Africa. Highly literate, if not always strong-willed, Asian sovereigns knew very well what they were getting into when a treaty was finally presented for their signature. There was simply very little that they could do about it. The benefits of a modernized army or a big loan were too great to be resisted. And the gunboats were always there.

GREAT-POWER COMPETITION IN THE MIDDLE EAST

This was notably the pattern in the Middle East, where France and Germany, Russia and Britain all jockeyed for strategic position and long-range profits.

France was first into the Middle East, in the days of Napoleon's eastern campaign just before 1800. The French victory at the Battle of the Pyramids, which broke the once-feared Mamelukes, attracted respectful attention all across the aging Ottoman Empire. French stock—and interests—rose higher with the opening of the Suez Canal by a French company in 1869. The British pushed the French out of Egypt in the 1880s, but Paris simply turned farther east, investing and building influence in Syria and Lebanon.

Germany developed a close relationship with the center of Ottoman power in Istanbul. German banks lent large sums to Turkey, and German officers worked to modernize the Turkish army. There were negotiations for a German consortium to build railroads in the Ottoman Empire. As the British talked of a Cape-to-Cairo line, the Germans dreamed of a Berlin-to-Baghdad railway with stops in Vienna and on the Golden Horn. Direct trade between the throbbing industrial heartland of Germany and the Far East via the Persian Gulf seemed a distinct possibility to William II, whose father had founded the German Empire in 1870, and who himself dreamed of a larger German empire overseas in the 1890s.

British and Russian imperial interests, finally, clashed in Iran and Afghanistan. These warring fragments of ancient Persia lay athwart the land route to British India—and along expanding Russia's southern frontier. Military commitments were therefore made by London and St. Petersburg to shahs and emirs in Teheran and Kabul. Russia continued to expand in central Asia, and Britain fought several Afghan Wars. Soon after 1900, however, an understanding between the two European powers

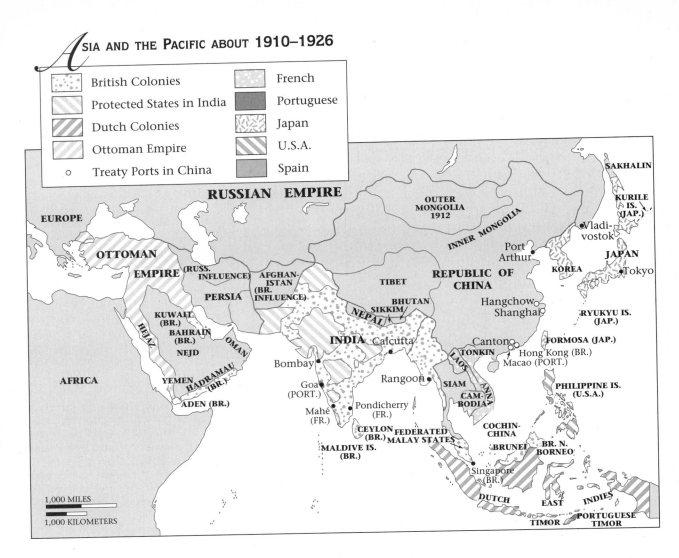

ASIA AND THE PACIFIC ABOUT 1910–1926

Legend:
- British Colonies
- Protected States in India
- Dutch Colonies
- Ottoman Empire
- ○ Treaty Ports in China
- French
- Portuguese
- Japan
- U.S.A.
- Spain

divided Iran into three spheres of influence: a Russian zone in the north, including Teheran and ancient Isfahan; a British zone in the south, dominating the Persian Gulf; and a large neutral zone in between.

Thus Western governmental efficiency and industrial development began to filter into the ancient Muslim center of Eurasia. With these influences, however, came increasing political and economic dependence on the West.

BRITAIN AND FRANCE IN INDIA AND SOUTHEAST ASIA

The British in South Asia and the British and French in Southeast Asia were the primary participants in the great drive for a more formal colonial empire east of Suez.

In British India, the subcontinent that constitutes the bulk of South Asia, imperialism took the form of the intensification and systematization of the British supremacy established there in the preceding century. This process was particularly accelerated by the Indian Mutiny of 1857.

The mutiny was a consequence of the increased British presence in India in the nineteenth century. Unpopular policies included the dispossession of some Indian princes of their states, campaigns by Christian missionaries against Hindu religious customs, and a tightening up of restrictions on the Indian officials in the employ of the British East India Company, which still ruled India under parliamentary supervision. The famous incident that triggered the great revolt by Indian troops, the greasing of cartridges with pig and cow grease, affronted the most ancient religious taboos of both Hindus and Muslims. In the resulting carnage, hundreds of British men, women, and children were slaughtered—as were thousands of Indians, whose villages were put to the torch by vengeful British soldiers.

After the suppression of the mutiny, the British government took over sole responsibility for governing almost the entire subcontinent. A number of small princedoms continued to exist on sufferance, but a royal viceroy and thousands of British civil servants henceforth guided the colony's destinies. Schools, railroads, harbor facilities were built, and serious attempts were made to root out such unacceptable religious practices as *suttee*, in which Hindu widows burned themselves on the funeral pyres of their husbands as a display of devotion. India entered the twentieth century as the most glittering jewel in Queen Victoria's crown.

In Southeast Asia, Britain and France found themselves in uneasy competition as they established colonies on the western and eastern sides of the Indochinese peninsula. France pushed into Vietnam as early as the 1860s and subsequently established a protectorate over Cambodia and Laos. Expanding eastward from India, the British invaded and occupied Burma; other British expansionists pushed north from the key port of Singapore up the Malay Peninsula.

In the middle was Siam—Thailand today—the sole remaining independent state in mainland Southeast Asia. An agreement between Britain and France left Siam as a buffer between them. With the islands of today's Indonesia Dutch since the seventeenth century and the Philippines in American hands from 1900 on, Thailand remained, like Ethiopia in Africa, an isolated peak of independence in a sea of expanding Western power.

THE OPENING OF JAPAN

Even East Asia, which had flourished so long in comparative isolation from the rest of Eurasia, was in the end sucked into the maelstrom of the New Imperialism. Ancient China became the largest victim yet of Western expansion. And Japan became the first major Asian convert to Western technology—and to Western-style imperialism.

The Meiji Restoration of 1868 was one of the decisive events of modern Japanese history. Its immediate cause was the shattering of Japan's traditional isolation by the West—in this case by the United States.

The Tokugawa shogunate, two and a half centuries old by the middle of the nineteenth century, was an institution—and a dynasty—on its last legs. The Tokugawa clan no longer produced strong leadership capable of meeting crises decisively. Students of Japan's past had already begun to examine the traditional role allotted to the hereditary emperors, a position of religious and ceremonial importance but completely lacking in political power, and to speculate on restoring political authority to Japan's Son of Heaven.

It was at this point that an American fleet appeared. Commodore Matthew Perry arrived with a U.S. naval squadron, including three steam frigates, in 1853, instructed to "open" Japan to diplomatic and commercial exchange. The American ships with their massive artillery much impressed the Japanese. After months of bitter disputes in Japanese ruling circles, Japan signed its first unequal treaty with the United States—and soon after with other Western countries. By these treaties, Japan's rulers agreed to receive Western merchants and diplomats and to allow them special rights in Japan not to be granted Japanese in other countries.

In 1868, in the aftermath of these concessions, a group of outraged *daimyo* compelled the last shotgun to resign—and passed political authority not to a new shogun but to the sixteen-year-old emperor, Mutsuhito. Known to history by his reign title—the Meiji ("Enlightened Rule") Emperor—Mutsuhito ruled Japan until his death in 1912 and saw his country rise from victim to victor, from an isolated island nation in East Asia to world power.

The architects of the restoration of imperial power moved the imperial capital from old Kyoto to the shogun's former capital of Edo—renamed Tokyo—and set to work preparing Japan to resist Western penetration in an entirely new way. To this end, they engineered an amazing transformation of their country.

Like Peter the Great in eighteenth-century Russia, this nineteenth-century Japanese emperor and his allies consciously set out to Westernize Japan from the top. Japanese students were sent abroad to learn, foreign experts brought to Japan to teach. Western methods of education and systems of transportation and communications were introduced. Industry, agriculture, banking were all modernized. Above all, Japan's military was updated, the old samurai class deposed, and a modern war machine created, from a steam navy to Western-style uniforms.

Forty years after Perry, Japan was ready to try its new power. In 1894–1895 the Japanese routed their ancient mentor, China, in the Sino-Japanese War. In 1904–1905 they decisively defeated one of the European great powers in the Russo-Japanese War—the first time in this age of the New Imperialism that a Western nation had lost to an Asian country.

From these victories Japan got Korea, the Liaotung Peninsula in North China—and a new status in the world. In the century that followed, the Japanese would play an expanding role in the first age of global history.

THE OPEN DOOR TO CHINA

The destiny of China was final proof of how thoroughly the world was turned upside down by the unprecedented power and unappeasable drive for dominion exhibited by the modern West.

British naval vessels bombarding Canton. This ancient port city in south China surrendered under a rain of shells and rockets—typical prelude to the extraction of unequal treaties from the helpless imperial government in Beijing. "Gunboat diplomacy" was a prominent feature of Western imperial expansion and economic hegemony in many parts of the world in the nineteenth century. (The Bettmann Archive)

For more than two hundred years, European traders in the Middle Kingdom had been confined to a small section of the port of Canton (Guangzhou) and to the nearby Portuguese port of Macao, in South China. Jesuits might teach European painting styles or techniques of casting cannon in Beijing, but they were not allowed to proselytize much for their faith. When a British ambassador showed up at the capital in the 1790s, he was graciously received and firmly turned away.

Then in the 1800s, Europeans seemed to burst into China from all directions, shattering its immemorial isolation forever.

China was brutally punished in four wars during the nineteenth century. Britain's Opium War (1839–1842) broke out over Chinese attempts to curb opium smuggling by Britain from British India into China. British naval bombardment, against which the Chinese could do little, compelled the emperor to sign the first of many unequal treaties. China was forced to open a number of ports to Europeans and grant Britain its first slice of Chinese territory, the island of Hong Kong.

A second war (1856–1860), fought by the British and French against China, began with more naval action and climaxed with the temporary seizure of Beijing itself. More "treaty ports" were opened up by the resulting agreements, and more diplomatic concessions made. The

Japanese next humiliated the Chinese in the Sino-Japanese War, forcing them to open still more ports to the world and beginning a round of Chinese territorial concessions to foreign imperialist powers.

A final Western invasion, involving not only British and French forces but also U.S., German, and Japanese troops, resulted from the Boxer Rebellion (1899–1900). This revolt was a desperate effort by mobs of Chinese peasants to destroy the by then ubiquitous Western presence in their country. The Boxers were summarily suppressed by a small international expeditionary force—which also brushed aside the Chinese army and took Beijing again in the process.

This disastrous century for the ancient Middle Kingdom was made worse by violent civil discord. The terrible Taiping Rebellion of the 1850s and 1860s was inspired partly by traditional peasant discontents. But it was led by a Christian convert who mixed hazy Christian fundamentalism with Confucian social idealism—and ravaged the land for fifteen years.

At the highest level, China was also divided by the mounting Western pressure. Two factions of officials formed. There were those who favored following the Japanese road and learning modern methods from the West. There were others, including the indomitable Empress Ci Xi, who clung to old methods and prayed to the old gods in this moment of crisis. By and large, the latter prevailed—with unfortunate results for China.

During the last sixty years of the century, then, the Chinese Empire was opened up with a vengeance to Western imperialism. China was forced to open its seacoasts and its great rivers to Western merchants, large areas of its hinterlands to Christian missionaries, and its capital to Western diplomats and embassies. The Chinese government accepted the right of extraterritoriality: all these foreigners could live according to their own laws in China. Beijing also agreed to most-favored-nation clauses, which granted to all foreign countries every concession made to any one of them.

From the 1870s on, furthermore, China surrendered its ancient claims to tributary states in East and Southeast Asia: Vietnam to France, Burma to Britain, concessions in Xinjiang to Russia and in Korea to Japan. In the 1890s the Chinese gave up important slices of China proper to the outsiders: Canton to France, the Shandong Peninsula to Germany, the Liaotung Peninsula to Russia (later passed on to Japan), and coastal territories across from Liaotung and Hong Kong to Great Britain.

Europeans also secured rights to build railways, develop minerals, and otherwise exploit Chinese land. By 1900, Western troops were stationed in China to guard all these concessions, Western gunboats patrolled the coasts and rivers of China, and the Chinese customs service was run by an Irishman.

China's curse and China's preserver during much of this terrible time was the last of its great rulers, Ci Xi (1835–1908). An imperial concubine who clawed her way to power in 1862 and ruled through a series of feckless males through most of her life, Ci Xi was, practically speaking, the last of the Manchus.

In her later years especially, the Dowager Empress—the Old Buddha, as she was called behind her back—was a rigidly conservative, hopelessly superstitious, imperious old woman, determined to make no concessions to the ways of the Western barbarians. She suppressed efforts at reform, pinned much of her hope on a revival of the faithful scholarly bureaucracy, and even supported the Boxers.

Ci Xi built all her hopes on China's immense past, and she lost. Had she been willing to learn, as the Japanese were, China might have been saved many humiliations. On the other hand, a weaker person, less supremely confident in the rightness of all things Chinese, might well have presided over the destruction of the dynasty—perhaps of her country as a whole—half a century earlier.

Driven from her capital by Western armies as the Boxer Rebellion collapsed in a chaos of bloody reprisals in 1900, Ci Xi survived to return to power and make final terms with her enemies. We have photographs of her surrounded by Western diplomatic wives, her aged face a mask of powder and paint, her clawlike fingers glittering with rings. Even in defeat she is the Old Buddha still, a grizzled hawk among doves.

 # INTERNAL IMPERIALISM

PACIFYING, SETTLING, CIVILIZING

While Europeans partitioned Africa and imposed their will on Asia, another form of imperial expansion was coming to a climax also—the internal imperialism of Western nations whose territorial claims included large portions of the earth's surface still occupied by non-Western peoples. The pacifying, settling, and "civilizing" of such territories had, of course, begun with the first contact between Europeans and non-European peoples. But in several huge areas, this process reached a climax in the later nineteenth century.

Regions that thus came under definitive Western control in this climactic age of the New Imperialism included the Russian Far East, the American Far West, and the British continental colony of Australia. A number of similarities may be noted between these and other areas of internal colonization.

The first comers tended to be peoples from the fringes of the conquering society—mountain men in the American West, Cossacks in Siberia, beachcombers in Oceania. Traders and missionaries frequently followed, beginning the long job of transforming the material and spiritual lives of the peoples thus invaded. Then came farmers, driven by a hunger for land—American homesteaders, Russian peasants, Australian sheepherders—pushing the indigenous populations off their thinly settled territories.

Most of these native peoples were living at a much earlier stage of social evolution than their conquerors. Nomadic Amerindian hunters on the American Plains, nomadic mongoloid pastoralists in much of Russian Asia, wandering Aborigine hunters and gatherers in the Australian Outback were thus overcome relatively easily.

The population of many of these native peoples fell drastically as a consequence of Western intrusion. Typically, these huge casualties were not the direct result of military action by the West. Maoris and Plains Indians, for instance, proved to be powerful antagonists. Drastic declines in population were rather the result of Western disease to which the natives had no immunities, and of starvation as they were driven from the lands where they had gained a livelihood.

Always, however, Western technology lay at the root of the destruction of these preurban peoples. Ships and railways, plows and barbed wire, and everywhere the increasingly devastating firepower of Western weapons destroyed not individual lives alone, but whole societies.

RUSSIA'S EASTWARD EXPANSION

Russian eastward expansion across Eurasia paralleled the American westward movement. It was a slower and more deliberate advance, and one that covered even greater dis-

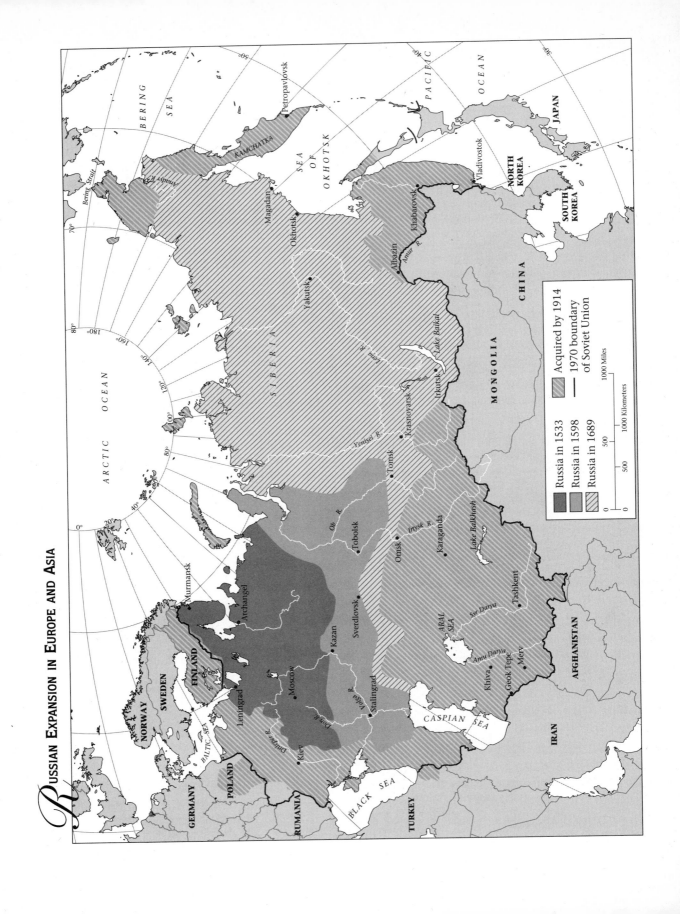

Russian Expansion in Europe and Asia

BERING SEA

PACIFIC OCEAN

ARCTIC OCEAN

SEA OF OKHOTSK

JAPAN

NORTH KOREA

SOUTH KOREA

CHINA

MONGOLIA

AFGHANISTAN

IRAN

TURKEY

RUMANIA

POLAND

GERMANY

NORWAY

SWEDEN

FINLAND

BALTIC SEA

BLACK SEA

CASPIAN SEA

ARAL SEA

Lake Balkhash

Lake Baikal

SIBERIA

KAMCHATKA

Petropavlovsk

Magadan

Okhotsk

Anadyr

Bering Strait

Yakutsk

Khabarovsk

Albazin

Vladivostok

Irkutsk

Krasnoyarsk

Tomsk

Omsk

Karaganda

Tashkent

Merv

Geok Tepe

Khiva

Tobolsk

Sverdlovsk

Kazan

Stalingrad

Moscow

Kiev

Leningrad

Archangel

Murmansk

Lena R.

Yenisei R.

Ob R.

Irtysh R.

Syr Darya

Amu Darya

Volga R.

Don R.

Dnieper R.

Amur R.

Legend:
- Russia in 1533
- Russia in 1598
- Russia in 1689
- Acquired by 1914
- 1970 boundary of Soviet Union

Scale: 1000 Miles / 1000 Kilometers / 500 / 500 / 0

tances. But the result was the same: the imposition of a Europe-based culture upon the thinly scattered non-European populations who had once been masters of a substantial portion of the earth's surface.

Prior to 1500, the northern Eurasian steppe had been the homeland of the world's most extensive and formidable nomadic peoples. Semimilitarized, highly mobile, and frequently predatory in their attacks on the urban-imperial cultures to the south, these pastoral nomads were the most dangerous barbarians. The days of the great nomadic offensives in the West ended, however, with the Russian defeat of the Golden Horde in the fifteenth century. And from the sixteenth century on, the Russians themselves began to push relentlessly into central and East Asia.

The first Russians to cross the Ural Mountains—the traditional boundary of European Russia—were the Cossacks. These bands of free-living horseriders were semi-nomadic pastoralists themselves, as well as hunters, marauders, and sometime soldiers of the czar. Skilled navigators as well as horseriders, the Cossacks followed a network of rivers eastward across Siberia, reaching the Pacific shortly before 1650.

In 1689, a hundred years before the first British ambassador arrived in Beijing, Russia signed a treaty with Manchu China delimiting their mutual frontier. Some Russians even crossed the Bering Strait to Alaska and worked their way down the Pacific coast into California long before the United States existed to claim it.

Russia's eastward movement was punctuated by a series of southward thrusts toward its Asian rivals south of the steppes. In the eighteenth century, especially under Catherine the Great, Russian armies pushed south against the Ottoman Empire to the Black Sea. In the nineteenth century Russian troops fought their way into the mountainous Caucasus, between the Black and Caspian seas. They also overwhelmed the crumbling Muslim khanates of central Asia, east of the Caspian. In the Pacific Far East, Russia pressed south along the Amur River frontier with Manchuria, acquiring the site of its great Pacific port at Vladivostok.

Obtaining land, however, was not occupying it. Modern Russia expanded till it stretched for six thousand miles, a quarter of the way around the world. But most of this land was a vast frontier, only beginning to be settled by Russians in the nineteenth century.

The Cossacks had come in the seventeenth century as fur trappers and marauders. Traders, officials, and tax collectors soon followed, and a number of penal colonies were established in the wilderness. A few landowners took their serfs into western Siberia as early as the eighteenth century. In the nineteenth, increasing numbers of peasants moved east on their own, seeking free land to cultivate. After the emancipation of the serfs in 1861, peasants began to pour into the east, a migration facilitated by the opening of the Trans-Siberian Railway in the 1890s. Three and a half million colonists thus took land in the east during the two decades before 1914.

The impact of Russian eastward migration was in many ways not as devastating as the American colonization of the West or the contemporary British occupation of Australia. Russians had known Turko-Mongol peoples for centuries and felt little racial superiority, and Russian peasants did not expect to live much better than Tatars or Mongols. There was none of the genocidal destruction of native societies that would mark the internal expansion of other continental nations.

Nevertheless, there were inevitable conflicts—and the subject peoples inevitably lost. Cossack depredations made the warning "The Cossacks are coming" feared by Mongol tribes all across Siberia, and official tribute-gathering was almost as burdensome. Tribal resistance to conquest would last for decades in the Caucasus Mountains, and central Asian nomads preyed on Russian caravans well into the nineteenth century. Russian Orthodox settlers hated and feared Islam in central Asia, and there were bitter feuds over irrigation water in those dry regions.

The czarist exploitation of the minority peoples of the empire was angrily condemned by the Bolshevik revolutionaries who took over Russia in 1917. But the work of Europeanization, begun in a haphazard way in czarist times, continued in the Soviet Union through most of the twentieth century.

AMERICA'S WESTERN EXPANSION

When the Europeans began to push their way into North America, there were perhaps a million Amerindians living north of the Rio Grande. Culturally speaking, they were far from homogeneous. In the varied environments of the northern continent, a variety of Native American cultures had been evolving for thousands of years. There were thus hundreds of different tribal societies, including nomadic hunters, agricultural villagers, and some few, like the Mound Builders or the Pueblo Indians, pushing to the edge of settled town life. During the colonial period itself, loose confederacies east of the Mississippi bound tens of thousands of Indians for purposes of peace, war, and trade.

Almost all Indians, however, remained Stone Age toolmakers. Most were organized primarily on the basis of clan and tribe. All were worshipers of animist gods, ghosts, and nature spirits. Like African animists, they frequently believed in the Great Spirit who was the author of all things.

The destruction of these societies took several hundred years. But the process accelerated significantly in the later eighteenth and the nineteenth centuries, reaching a climax during the American westward movement of the half century after the Civil War.

By 1776, the two and a half million English settlers on the east coast substantially outnumbered all the Indian nations on the continent—and their hostility to the

Far from the world of gunboat diplomacy, the Amerindian population of the United States still lived much as their pre-Columbian ancestors had. But Western firepower easily shattered aboriginal societies like these around the world. Photography, however, did preserve a unique record of the culture of such peoples. (Western History Collections, University of Oklahoma Library)

Indians was well demonstrated. American land hunger and refusal to mix with the alien culture of the indigenous population thus set a juggernaut in motion. Rolling westward, the expanding United States dislocated, defeated, fragmented, and finally destroyed all the major Amerindian cultures from the Atlantic to the Pacific.

Disease, warfare with Europeans, and involvement in European wars had broken the back of the eastern Indian confederacies before 1800. Even the League of the Iroquois, which for two centuries had bound a half dozen large tribes into a loose but powerful unit capable of treatment as an equal with Dutch, French, and English colonies, was divided and broken during the American Revolution.

After the Revolution came mounting pressure for Indian "removal" from all the lands east of the Mississippi. This was accomplished by force during the Jacksonian 1830s. Indians such as the Southern Cherokee were rounded up and headed west along the infamous Trail of Tears to Oklahoma, leaving many dead along the road to exile.

After 1865 the restless westward thrust of Americans—gold seekers and other miners, cattlemen, sheepherders, and farmers—shattered the buffalo-hunting Indian tribes of the Plains as they had the woodland confederacies of the East. Their weapons were technological and bureaucratic. Repeating rifles and pistols, railroads, barbed wire, and the steel plow defeated the nomadic "wild Indians" in the field.

The destruction of the Indian cultures was completed by treaties that were never kept, reservations that were always the worst land, exploitative Indian agents, land speculators, and other parasites. The final enemy of traditional Indian society, ironically, turned out to be government reformers who claimed to be the friends of the "vanishing red man." It was these reformers who set out to introduce Indians to private property, modern education, and integration into American society—which meant the disintegration of their own.

The North American tribes had responded to the inexorable advance of the Europeans in many ingenious ways. The woodland Indians acquired firearms, organized large confederations such as those of the Iroquois and the Creeks, and played the power game with the invaders as long as they could. Plains tribes such as the Cheyenne, the Sioux, and the Apache acquired the horse from the Spanish and became as mobile and fierce a nomadic people as any Mongol or Indo-European people of earlier centuries. Defeated once more by the cavalry and the virtual extermination of the buffalo herds upon which they subsisted, the demoralized Amerindian remnants took up religious movements like the Peyote Cult or the Ghost Dance, until even these were declared illegal.

The westward march of the frontier line, a measure of advance and expansion for most Americans, was a measure of the defeat and disintegration of Amerindian culture in North America. For the real first comers, it was all a Trail of Tears.

AUSTRALIA CONQUERS THE OUTBACK

Other sparsely settled areas nominally controlled by Western peoples were also occupied and their indigenous populations subjugated in the course of the nineteenth century. Dutch and English settlers seeking land and gold pushed deeper into South Africa. Canadians moved westward across their even larger swath of North America, as their Yankee neighbors did. Latin Americans, especially in Mexico and the Andean regions, began to suck the withdrawn and silent Indian populations back into the economic life of the nation—meaning mostly peonage.

The most sweeping instance of Europeanization within a colony, however, came in Oceania, particularly on the continent of Australia and the large islands of New Zealand and Tasmania.

Oceania was the last part of the globe to be reached by the expanding peoples of the West. Explored in the eighteenth century and colonized in the nineteenth, the relatively simple societies of the far Pacific were quickly swept up in the cresting wave of the New Imperialism.

Whalers, sealers, traders, missionaries, and a variety of beachcombers and castaways moved among the thousands of South Pacific and Southeast Asian islands in the nineteenth century. Many were shocked at the customs of these paradise islanders, which in some societies included cannibalism, headhunting, and endemic warfare. But the Westerners brought their own afflictions: guns to intensify warfare, liquor, and, as everywhere, diseases to which Polynesians, Melanesians, and Micronesians had no immunities. These material misfortunes, plus Western government and European religion, slowly but surely undermined the integrated cultures of the South Seas.

In Australia and New Zealand, the process was more direct and violent.

Criminals came early to the Antipodes, as to Russian Siberia. A British penal colony was established at Botany Bay in New South Wales, southeastern Australia, in 1788. In the nineteenth century came sheepherders, cattle ranchers, and wheat farmers. Beginning at mid-century, a series of gold rushes began that once again drew adventurers and other dubious frontier types. Railway lines were built and Europeans spread into the arid Outback, the scantily watered interior of the continent.

There were perhaps 300,000 Aborigines scattered over the Outback, living by hunting and gathering, as the earliest humans had. Their technology was that of the Old Stone Age, their social organization based on the hunting band. They had neither clothes nor settled habitation, nor indeed any substantial accumulation of worldly goods at all.

The aboriginal inhabitants were a nuisance to the frontier farmers, ranchers, and miners. Deprived of their own hunting grounds, they killed the ranchers' stock. To British settlers they seemed dirty, lazy, uninterested in acquiring European skills or in working for the newcomers.

The struggle was one-sided, seldom documented, and deadly for the Aborigines. They were driven off their lands by European sheep and cattle, killed by European diseases, the Border Police, the settlers themselves. The government finally herded them into "reserves," where some still live. Many more have joined the society of the conqueror.

The pattern in New Zealand differed in that the fiercely warlike Maoris made much more of a fight of it. In the face of increased demand for their land, they united under a single Maori king for the first time in their history. Around mid-century, settlers launched a series of wars aimed at destroying the emerging Maori polity before its strength grew. This they succeeded in doing, seizing vast acreages in the process. The Maori, like the American Plains Indians, took refuge in religious ecstasies—and slowly learned to adapt.

On the large island of Tasmania, off the coast of Australia, no adaptation was allowed. Tasmanians also fought the invaders, killing both herds and herdsmen. In 1830 a series of mass manhunts began, intended to exterminate the aboriginal population. Five hundred out of five thousand survived. The last of these native Tasmanians died in 1876.

The great conquest thus completed the destruction of the preurban peoples who once shared the world with the rest of us.

Populations may creep back upwards. In Australia today there are almost as many people who claim aboriginal descent as there were in 1800. There are at least half as many North American Indians as there were in Columbus's time. The Muslim peoples of Russian Asia are actually among the fastest growing of Russia's populations.

What has gone are the cultures that these people once built for themselves. Destroyed by new governments, new religions, and new values, or preserved here and there in the amber of reservations, reserves, homelands, and other protected areas, these alternate ways of life are among the most striking casualties of the great Western conquest of the rest of the world.

CLIMAX OF THE MODERN WORLD SYSTEM

AN EVOLVING SYSTEM

As we have seen in earlier chapters, the global economy that had emerged in the 1500s both grew and changed over the modern age. In the later eighteenth and the nineteenth centuries, the modern economic world system was fully developed and evolving according to clearly established patterns.

During the late 1700s and the 1800s, three separate zones defined the system. A growing *core* dominated the world system economically and politically. A *semiperiphery* provided a source of skilled labor—and sometimes a buffer between the core and the exploited periphery. The rapidly expanding *periphery,* finally, provided relatively unskilled, often coerced labor and contributed basic commodities—agricultural products and raw materials—to the system.

As earlier, the modern world system had an important influence upon all its members in the 1800s. Historians vigorously debate the extent of this impact, but few question its reality. Economic factors may not be as central to human affairs as some world systems theorists have asserted. As critics have suggested, local factors and forces may well have shaped the history of "peripheral" peoples more decisively than the world system did. But the influence of the global economic system was surely an increasingly important element in history. And by the end of the nineteenth century, those involved in the modern world system included virtually all the peoples of the earth.

CORE AND PERIPHERY

We will emphasize here the two key elements in the system: the controlling core and the periphery it controlled. Both changed significantly from the later eighteenth century to the end of the nineteenth.

The core of the world system both lost and gained members between 1700 and 1900. Some members of the original core—Spain, Portugal, England, France, and the Netherlands—faded into semiperipheral status. These included Spain and Portugal, the original founders of the modern world system in the 1500s, and the tiny Netherlands, the center of the world economy in the 1600s.

New economic powers, however, soon thrust their way into the core. The first of these was the United States, the world's most productive economy by 1900. Two other economic powerhouses also played increasingly important parts in the global economy. The first was Germany, politically unified and Europe's biggest industrial power after 1871. The second was Japan, which began its drive to modernization in 1868 and was Asia's most productive economy by 1900. As a result, New York, Berlin, and Tokyo now commanded as much labor and paid for as much of the periphery's commodity exports as British pounds or French francs did.

The zone of labor and commodity exports called the periphery also continued to expand. The original key peripheral zones had been Latin America, the Caribbean islands, and parts of Eastern Europe. To these the eighteenth century had added India, the Middle East, West Africa, and a still underdeveloped Russia. The nineteenth century, finally, saw East Asia (excluding Japan), South-east Asia, the rest of Africa, and the far-flung archipelagos of the Pacific added to the global periphery.

GLOBAL IMPACT OF THE WORLD SYSTEM

The impact of overseas empire and world trade on the nations of the core could be political and military as well as economic. As we have seen in this and earlier chapters, the core nations profited exceedingly from their commanding position in the world economy. Even while they grew rich on the rewards of foreign commerce and conquest, however, they also competed bitterly with one another. As William Pitt, British prime minister during the decisive struggle with France in the mid 1700s, said, "When trade is at stake, it is your last retrenchment; you must defend it or perish."[3]

The impact of the modern world system on the peoples of the periphery, as we have seen, could also be very great. The demands of core markets could warp and restructure the economies and societies of peripheral peoples. During the period of the old imperialism, for instance, European development changed the basic terms of global trade. Europe learned to manufacture goods of higher quality and technical sophistication—goods that Asians and other non-Westerners coveted. As a result, the West was no longer compelled to pay cash for the products of China, India, and other developed civilizations that had long disdained European goods. By the nineteenth century, the situation was reversed as non-Western peoples clamored for the products of the Western industrial revolution.

During this period also, European demand changed. Instead of seeking small but high-value luxury products—spices, gems, precious metals—the European market more and more demanded bulk goods. Cotton, peanuts, palm oil, rubber, coffee, tea, cocoa, copper, petroleum—there was no end to the cargos that flowed into the core from the ends of the earth. The peasantries of the world thus found themselves abandoning subsistence farming to tend export crops or labor underground in mines, using their wages to buy food they had formerly grown for themselves.

The Western imperial hegemony is already fading in former colonies around the world. Grand Bassam, once a busy port in Ivory Coast, French West Africa, is now a quiet place for the citizens of Abidjan, Ivory Coast's shiny new capital, to sightsee on a Sunday afternoon. In Zanzibar, you can swim off a tiny white beach in the shadow of a broken fort, crenellations thick with vines, half a projecting round tower fallen into the sea, almost all that is left of a vanished imperial presence.

Elsewhere, emerging nations make imaginative use of their colonial heritage. In Singapore, the dazzling new market capital of Southeast Asia, the imperialist name

---

[3]Quoted in J. H. Plumb, *England in the Eighteenth Century (1714–1815)* (London: Penguin, 1950), p. 71.

of Sir Stamford Raffles is a highly honored part of the past. The remodeled Raffles Hotel draws hordes of very well-heeled tourists, and the tiny country's top-ranked airline proudly offers travelers "Raffles Class" luxury accommodations. In Shanghai, central China's booming economic heart, the colonial buildings along the harborfront Bund have been kept up and are now being leased to Western companies again—sometimes to the same firms that lost them to Mao's revolutionaries fifty years ago!

As we will see, the imperial legacy lives on in subtle and sometimes not-so-subtle ways. But much of that violent clash of cultures is fading into the common past of a world whose history is increasingly all of a piece.

SUMMARY

The resurgence of overseas empire building we call the New Imperialism brought almost all of Africa and large parts of Asia under Western domination, as well as immense tracts of Russia, North America, and Australia.

The motives of the New Imperialists were neither economic exploitation alone nor civilizing impulses pure and simple. The causal factors at work included a varying mixture of economic, political, humanitarian, and even psychological drives and interests. The elements that made possible so vast a conquest in the generation or two after 1870 included superior Western organization, esprit, and, above all, firepower. The resulting unprecedented global hegemony took several forms, including full-scale colonies, protectorates, and spheres of influence.

The "scramble for Africa" was the most dramatic theater of imperial expansion at the end of the nineteenth century. There European powers negotiated treaties with local chiefs and other rulers all over the continent, and frequently sent in troops later to enforce the new agreements. France's African colonies, mostly in West Africa, were tightly governed as extensions of metropolitan France. Britain's holdings in all parts of Africa were generally run on a system of delegated authority called indirect rule. Germany, Belgium, Italy, and other countries also seized parts of Africa.

In Asia the resistance of long-established and populous urban-imperial cultures was strong. As a result, protectorates and spheres of influence were more common, though there were important new colonies and some old ones as well. Among the areas that came under Western control were British India, German-dominated Turkey, and the British and French colonies on mainland Southeast Asia. Japan was also "opened" to Western trade and influence, and China became the hapless victim of European gunboat diplomacy from the Opium War to the Boxer Rebellion.

Control of areas already claimed by Western peoples often led to the destruction of indigenous pre-European cultures. Russian Siberia was less violently pacified than some other areas. The Amerindian peoples of the United States and the Australian Aborigines, however, were largely destroyed as independent societies.

By the turn of the century, then, the great conquest had reached its climax with a Western hegemony that was—for the first time in history—genuinely global in scope.

SUGGESTED READING

BAUMGART, W. *Imperialism.* New York: Oxford University Press, 1982. Comparative study of British and French forms of the New Imperialism.

BETTS, R. F. *The Scramble for Africa.* Lexington, Mass.: Heath, 1972. A range of interpretations of the causes and nature of the New Imperialism in Africa. See also R. Oliver and G.N. Sanderson, eds., *The Cambridge History of Africa*, Vol. 6, *From 1870–1905* (New York: Cambridge University Press, 1985), which provides the latest research on the scramble for Africa.

———. *The False Dawn: European Imperialism in the Nineteenth Century.* Minneapolis: University of Minnesota Press, 1978. Authoritative overview.

CHAUDHURI, N., and M. STROBEL. *Western Women and Imperialism: Complicity and Resistance.* Bloomington: University of Indiana Press, 1992. Collection of studies on women's roles in empire building, suggesting that they played larger and more varied roles than commonly assumed. See also L. E. Donaldson, *Decolonizing Feminisms: Race, Gender, and Empire Building* (Chapel Hill: University of North Carolina Press, 1992), on women in imperialist literature.

CLAYTON, A. *France, Soldiers, and Africa.* Elmsford, N.Y.: Pergamon, 1988. The military role in French imperial expansion in Africa and in France's continuing influence in the area from the 1830s to the 1980s. On another aspect of French imperialism in Africa, see G.W. Johnson, ed., *Double Impact: France and Africa in the Age of Imperialism* (Westport, Conn.:

Greenwood Press, 1985), which features essays defining interaction and mutual influences in many areas, from economics to art.

FAIRBANK, J. K. *Trade and Diplomacy on the China Coast: The Opening of the Treaty Ports.* Cambridge: Harvard University Press, 1953. A classic example of gunboat diplomacy.

FERGUSON, R. B., and N. L. WHITEHEAD, eds. *War in the Tribal Zone: Expanding States and Indigenous Warfare.* Santa Fe, N.M.: School of American Research Press, 1992. Impact of imperialism on warfare in areas inhabited by pre-urban peoples.

GORDON, D. C. *The Moment of Power.* Englewood Cliffs, N.J.: Prentice Hall, 1970. An excellent analysis of Britain's imperial supremacy. For examples of British imperialism in various forms and in widely separated regions, see D. Kennedy, *Islands of White: Settler Society and Culture in Kenya and Southern Rhodesia, 1890–1939* (Durham, N.C.: Duke University Press, 1987), which provides a psychohistorical investigation of the society constructed by white settlers in black Africa; W. Golant, *The Long Afternoon: British India, 1601–1947* (New York: St. Martin's Press, 1975), an impressionistic survey from the perspective of the rulers of the evolving Indian colony; and L. Marcus and P. Sutton, eds., *This Is What Happened: Historical Narratives by Aborigines* (Canberra: Australian Institute of Aboriginal Studies, 1986), a sometimes historical, sometimes magical Aborigine account of the Western conquest.

HEADRICK, D. R. *The Tentacles of Progress: Technology Transfer in the Age of Imperialism, 1850–1940.* New York: Oxford University Press, 1988. British technology exported to the colonies.

HIBBERT, C. *The Great Mutiny: India 1857.* London: Penguin, 1980. The rebellion that shook the British hold on India—and ended by tightening that grip. See also W.G. Broehl, *Crisis of the Raj: The Revolt of 1857 through British Lieutenants' Eyes* (Hanover, N.H.: University Press of New England, 1986), which contains contemporary impressions of the great revolt from those who had to face it.

KENWOOD, A. G., and A. L. LOUGHEED. *The Growth of the International Economy, 1820–1920.* London: Allen and Unwin, 1983. Valuable overview of a complicated subject. See also L. E. Davis and R. A. Huttenback, *Mammon and the Pursuit of Empire: The Economics of British Imperialism* (New York: Cambridge University Press, 1988) on the role of economic forces in the growth of the largest Western empire.

KINROSS, P. BALFOUR, LORD. *Between Two Seas.* London: Murray, 1969. One of the great enterprises of the New Imperialism—the building of the Suez Canal.

LANDES, D. S. *Bankers and Pashas.* Cambridge: Harvard University Press, 1980. Good example of the subtler forms of the New Imperialism, here economic exploitation of Egypt by the French.

MACKENZIE, J. M., ed. *Imperialism and Popular Culture.* Manchester, U.K.: Manchester University Press, 1986. Films, magazines, music hall, and other popular expressions of imperial spirit in Britain.

MANGAN, J. A., ed. *Making Imperial Mentalities: Socialization and British Imperialism.* Manchester, U.K.: Manchester University Press, 1990. Papers on the shaping of imperialist attitudes.

MARKS, S. G. *Road to Power: The Trans-Siberian Railroad and the Colonization of Asiatic Russia, 1850–1917.* Ithaca: Cornell University Press, 1991. Relates the epic construction project to the building and retaining of an empire.

MAY, E. *Imperial Democracy.* New York: Harper & Row, Pub., 1973. American imperialism. On American westward expansion, see the new *Oxford History of the American West,* edited by C. A. Milner, et al. (New York: Oxford University Press, 1994), and for a sample of the new western social history, with its emphasis on the conquered rather than the conquerors, P. N. Limerick's *The Legacy of Conquest* (New York: W. W. Norton, 1987).

PORTER, A. N., ed. *Atlas of British Overseas Expansion.* New York: Simon & Schuster, 1991. Maps give a good sense of the immensity of the British imperial outreach.

SPATE, O. H. K. *Paradise Found and Lost: The Pacific Since Magellan.* Minneapolis: University of Minnesota Press, 1988. Final volume in a monumental history of the Pacific basin, with stress on European impact.

STOECKER, H. *German Imperialism in Africa.* Atlantic Highlands, N.J.: Humanities Press, 1986. Solid survey of Germany's attempt at African empire building.

WALLERSTEIN, I. *The Modern World-System III: The Second Era of Great Expansion of the Capitalist World-Economy, 1730–1840s.* San Diego: Academic Press, 1989. The founder of world-systems analysis outlines the economic history of the Europe-dominated world of the eighteenth and early nineteenth centuries, stressing growth and change of the global economy.

WESTNEY, D. E. *Imitation and Innovation: The Transfer of Western Organizational Patterns to Meiji Japan.* Cambridge: Harvard University Press, 1987. Readable, detailed picture of the beginnings of Japanese modernization.

THE WORLD TORN
BY WAR AND REVOLUTION

Future historians may well consider the first half of the twentieth century to have been a step backward in the global drift of history.

The great wars and major revolutions that swept the globe between the early 1900s and mid-century pitted so many nations and peoples against each other—and against themselves—that it is hard to see the period as an advance in the global venture. The two world wars certainly seem to show the world at its most violently divided. The lengthy revolutions in some of the world's largest nations and the rise of cruelly authoritarian governments in many countries seem to reflect the inability of twentieth-century people to live together, even in well-established nations, without inflicting savage injuries on one another.

Yet these traumas, and the glimmerings of peace and material progress sandwiched here and there among them, were also in their way indications of a global future. Over those four or five decades, the major events, trends, achievements, and

even disasters were, after all, increasingly global in scope. Even a cursory overview will reveal the extent to which the peoples of the world, once so isolated in their many cultures, had become thoroughly interdependent by the first half of the twentieth century, and historically involved with one another as never before.

World War I, fought mostly in Europe between European armies, was part of the ancient chronicle of continental rivalries that has darkened the history of that strife-torn region of the globe. But non-Europeans also fought in that war, and there were battles beyond the continent. Certainly the causes and consequences of the conflict were global in scale.

The economic history of the earlier part of the century focused still on booms and busts in Western stock markets, fields, and factories. But by the early 1900s, *Western* included North American and other European-settled regions too. The ties of empire, furthermore, linked the economic health of Africa, Asia, and Latin America to the prosperity of the

1920s and the Great Depression of the 1930s in Europe and America.

The earlier decades of the twentieth century also saw the longest and bloodiest ideological revolutions since the Reformation and the Age of Democratic Revolutions around 1800—and unlike those earlier European upheavals, these were global affairs. The Russian revolutionary transformation under Lenin and Stalin, the Chinese civil war that climaxed with Mao's victory, the long and bloody Mexican Revolution all served as models, inspirations, or warnings to whole regions. At least in part because of these revolutions, anti-imperialist rebelliousness fermented in many parts of the globe.

The brutal decade of the 1930s was the age of ideological tyranny and aggression in Europe—the age of Hitler and Stalin. But it was also the decade of Japanese militarism and imperialism resurgent in the Far East, of continuing civil war in China, of Mussolini's invasion of Africa, and much more. The 1930s were brutal years around the world, not just in the West.

World War II was beyond doubt a global conflict. Its theaters of war included Europe, Asia, Africa, and large sections of the Atlantic and Pacific oceans. Major combatants included great powers of all the inhabited continents except South America. No part of the globe escaped the conflagration unscathed. It may seem perverse to cite the ruins that littered half the world in 1945 as evidence of the globalization of history. Yet this would seem to be exactly what the global rubble did, unhappily, demonstrate. Confronted with wave after wave of violence that girdled the globe, the survivors found it hard not to recognize, however ruefully, that they all lived on the same planet—that in the future what happened in one part of the world would have to be of concern to all the world's peoples.

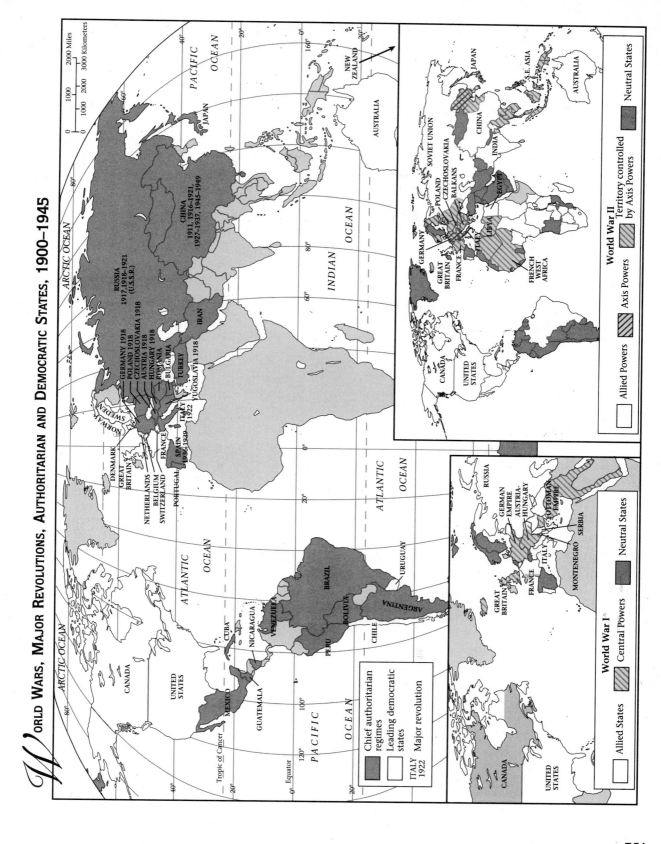

World Wars, Major Revolutions, Authoritarian and Democratic States, 1900–1945

Chief authoritarian regimes

Leading democratic states

ITALY 1922 — **Major revolution**

RUSSIA 1917,1918–1921 (U.S.S.R.)
GERMANY 1918
POLAND 1918
CZECHOSLOVAKIA 1918
AUSTRIA 1918
HUNGARY 1918
ROMANIA
BULGARIA
TURKEY
YUGOSLAVIA 1918
IRAN

CHINA 1911, 1916–1921, 1927–1937, 1945–1949

ITALY 1922
SPAIN 1936,1939
FRANCE
PORTUGAL
SWITZERLAND
BELGIUM
NETHERLANDS
GREAT BRITAIN
DENMARK
NORWAY
SWEDEN

MEXICO
GUATEMALA
NICARAGUA
CUBA
VENEZUELA
PERU
BOLIVIA
BRAZIL
CHILE
ARGENTINA
URUGUAY

CANADA
UNITED STATES

JAPAN
AUSTRALIA
NEW ZEALAND

ARCTIC OCEAN
PACIFIC OCEAN
ATLANTIC OCEAN
INDIAN OCEAN

Tropic of Cancer
Equator

2000 Miles
3000 Kilometers
1000
2000
1000
0

World War I

Allied States

Central Powers

Neutral States

RUSSIA
GERMAN EMPIRE
AUSTRIA-HUNGARY
OTTOMAN EMPIRE
SERBIA
MONTENEGRO
ITALY
FRANCE
GREAT BRITAIN
CANADA
UNITED STATES

World War II

Allied Powers

Axis Powers

Territory controlled by Axis Powers

Neutral States

SOVIET UNION
JAPAN
CHINA
S.E. ASIA
INDIA
POLAND
CZECHOSLOVAKIA
BALKANS
GERMANY
GREAT BRITAIN
FRANCE
ITALY
EGYPT
LIBYA
FRENCH WEST AFRICA
AUSTRALIA
CANADA
UNITED STATES

CHAPTER 38

THE WORLD OF THE WESTERN HEGEMONY

EUROPE AND NORTH AMERICA

TURN OF THE CENTURY

As the beginning of a new century approaches across the 1990s, the turn of the present century acquires an almost mythic quality. To many of us, products of the turbulent twentieth century, those years around 1900 may call up vivid, quaint, perhaps oddly comforting impressions.

That was the world of Queen Victoria, after all, when Britannia ruled the waves and the Empire on Which the Sun Never Set. It was the *belle époque* in France, with cafes under the trees along the Paris boulevards and chorus girls dancing the cancan at the Moulin Rouge. In the United States, the turn of the century is perhaps remembered most pleasantly as lemonade on the long front porch, with the music of a mandolin floating up a tree-lined street. But it was also glittering dinners at Delmonico's or the Waldorf in New York and the smells and color and foreign babble of Hell's Kitchen. South of the border, trolleys and electric wires were going up in Buenos Aires, and the gauchos were gone from the pampas.

Over most of Asia and almost all of Africa, Western imperial rule was a firmly established fact of life. Pith helmets and parasols kept the African sun from vulnerable European faces while blacks labored on coffee plantations and in copper mines to produce the things Western people prized.

In Asia, the Dowager Empress Ci Xi still ruled in China, the Meiji emperor in Japan. In the Middle Kingdom, the turn of the century calls up violent images of superstitious Boxers charging into Western machine guns in a frantic effort to fling the modern world bodily out of their ancient land. In Japan, by contrast, Tokyo's main street, the Ginza, looked like any European boulevard in 1900, all brick and gas lamps; Western clothing was required at court; and the Christian calendar was used in a Buddhist-Shinto state.

Life was changing at all levels and almost everywhere. In Britain, a man's home was his castle and patriarchy reigned—but women's suffrage demonstrators were already marching in the thousands, demanding the right to vote. In China, elderly ladies still paraded across the land on Buddhist pilgrimages, carrying incense from one shrine to the next—while young women in Shanghai dressed in Western clothes and talked to men in public! In India, good Hindu wives confined their interests to home and family—yet some of those same women would join their husbands in militant street demonstrations against British rule before the twentieth century was well along.

By way of introduction to our own century, an overview of that turn-of-the-century world follows. We will look first at some of the independent nations of the globe during those years between the 1890s and the outbreak of World War I in 1914. Thereafter we will survey that very substantial portion of the world that was not independent at all as the twentieth century began.

BRITAIN AND FRANCE: EUROPE'S LIBERAL POWERS

Europe was still the center of a Westernizing world in 1900, the greatest concentration of political power, wealth, and military might on earth. The most prescient pundit or politician would have been astonished to be told that this European predominance, centuries in the building, was almost over.

Within fifty years the European hegemony would have faded. It would give way in the second half of this century to a world of superpowers and global blocs in which a divided Europe would play an important but no longer central part. In the 1890s, however, with what looked like half the exotic peoples of the earth paying homage to Queen Victoria, no one could have foreseen what was to come.

Some of Europe's half-dozen great powers of 1900 were the same as those of 1800. Great Britain, France, and Russia were still territorially the nations they had been. Others differed drastically from their counterparts of a century before. In 1860 the separate Italian states had found unity for the first time since ancient Rome, in the new nation of Italy. Austria had lost its German territories and had had to share power with Magyar leaders in the Austro-Hungarian Dual Monarchy after 1867. And in 1871 Prussia had absorbed most of the German-speaking lands of the former Holy Roman Empire into the German Empire.

As the nineteenth century wound down and the twentieth began, all these nations had their share of problems. We will look first at the two liberal powers of Western Europe.

British difficulties in the years around 1900 included the Boer War, continuing Irish agitation for home rule, an increasingly militant campaign for women's suffrage, and growing German economic and naval competition.

The revolt of the rugged Boer farmers in South Africa was eventually crushed, though it required the deployment of hundreds of thousands of British troops and the invention of the concentration camp, all of which cost the British severely in international esteem. A solution to the long demand for self-government by the Irish Catholics—England's oldest colony—was deferred until after World War I. The same was true of the demand for the vote for women, which swelled into a national crusade under the leadership of Emmeline Pankhurst and her daughters in the 1890s. The dynamic industrial economy of the new German Empire, finally, was growing much more rapidly than Britain's; German goods were shouldering Britain's out of international markets; and the expansion of the German navy made British admirals yearly more nervous. About these problems, little or nothing could be done.

Not all of Great Britain's difficulties, however, were judiciously deferred or dealt with at such cost. In Britain, twenty years of primarily Conservative rule gave way in 1906 to a Liberal predominance in parliament that was to carry through World War I. The usual spate of reforms accompanied Liberal supremacy in the world's oldest parliamentary democracy. These reforms ranged from the beginnings of national health insurance and retirement benefits to constitutional limitation on the power of the hereditary House of Lords to veto legislation passed by the elected House of Commons.

The most colorful politician of the Liberal period before World War I, the fiery Welsh orator David Lloyd George, even pushed through a government budget specifically aimed at redistribution of wealth from rich to poor through taxes on income and inheritance and other devices. To the liberal-minded, at least, the democratic parliamentary system seemed to be working well enough as the fatal summer of 1914 rose over the horizon.

France, just across the Channel, was in theory even more liberal than Britain. After all, the Third Republic, created in 1871 in the aftermath of the fall of Emperor Napoleon III in the Franco-Prussian War, had dispensed with even a figurehead monarch. France was the only republic among the European great powers in 1900, and despite serious difficulties, the French also seemed to be making democracy work.

Many of France's problems were the legacy of its past—of the century-long series of revolutionary upheavals since 1789 and its more recent humiliating defeat by the Germans in 1870. Politically, the nation was torn by feuds between defenders of the republic and those who longed for the good old days when kings, aristocrats, and priests still ruled French society. The famous Dreyfus case brought this conflict to a head during the later 1890s and the early 1900s.

Alfred Dreyfus, a Jewish army captain falsely accused of selling military secrets to the Germans, was finally exonerated, brought back from the Devil's Island penal colony, and even awarded the Legion of Honor. But the outcome came only after years of violent confrontations between liberals and republicans on the one hand, and virulently anti-Semitic supporters of the Church, the aristocracy, and "the honor of the army" on the other.

France's industrial economy did not grow as rapidly as Germany's, but its overseas empire was much larger. French irridentist sentiment still demanded the recovery of the "lost provinces" of Alsace and Lorraine, taken by Germany in 1871. But no opportunity for a rematch with the powerful rival across the Rhine presented itself convincingly—until 1914.

GERMANY AND ITALY: THE NEW NATIONS

One of two new nations established in the second half of the nineteenth century, the German Empire fared notably better in many ways than the kingdom of Italy.

The shadow of Bismarck stretched across turn-of-the-century Germany, though the Iron Chancellor himself had been in uneasy retirement since 1890. The master diplomat of the second half of the century was widely recognized as the architect of the Hohenzollern German Empire. He had managed to preserve the nation's autocratic royal government while creating the most advanced system of social legislation in Europe. He had presided over the new Germany's remarkable surge of industrial growth and had quietly assembled the majority of its overseas colonies in Africa and Oceania. And he had managed to keep peace among the powers for twenty years in the bargain.

After Bismarck, what was there for Kaiser William II (ruled 1888–1918) to do? In fact, the young emperor who retired the great chancellor in 1890 accomplished little—but he did it very noisily indeed.

William II's public clamoring for a place in the imperial sun added few colonies to Germany's total. His aggressive naval buildup only made the British nervous enough to seek an anti-German alliance with France. German industrial growth continued with astonishing speed in the years before World War I, however. And it was a commonplace that the army of Bismarck and Frederick the Great was far and away the best in Europe.

The new Italy was more democratic than the new Germany, but it was never able to play a role in European affairs comparable to that of the powerful German Empire. Italy's economy was handicapped by poor agricultural land and industrial underdevelopment, especially in the south, and by an exploding population that put constant strain on the nation's limited productive capacities. Internationally, the newly unified country suffered a series of rebuffs and setbacks in these years. These misfortunes climaxed in its defeat by the Ethiopians at Adowa in 1896. A humiliating reverse for Italy's imperial aspirations, it was not erased in Italian minds by the seizure of the large Saharan colony of Libya in the early 1900s.

Nevertheless, political and social reforms did highlight Italy's history in the early twentieth century. The country's economic and international problems had bred all sorts of passionate ideological commitments, from socialism and anarchism to nationalism and imperialism. Italy's leading politician during the decade before World War I, Giovanni Giolitti, manipulated these isms more than he shared them. But he was nevertheless responsible for a great expansion of the suffrage, encouragement of the labor movement, and a good deal of social legislation intended to alleviate the hard lot of the poor.

AUSTRIA AND RUSSIA: DYING DYNASTIES

If the two new nations of Germany and Italy were a study in contrasts, the long-established Habsburg and Romanov monarchies of Austria-Hungary and Russia had much in common. Both Austria and Russia were ruled by well-meaning if not brilliant autocrats. Both were vast peasant states in which hereditary aristocrats still played a central role. Both had problems with minority nationalities, and neither was as developed industrially as it should have been. Both, finally, had an eye on the Balkan lands of the crumbling Ottoman Empire to the south. This rivalry would inexorably draw these two quite similar ancient states into a fatal face-down in 1914.

The aged Emperor Francis Joseph (1848–1916), Europe's longest-reigning ruler after Queen Victoria, had little imagination but a great deal of experience and a strong sense of obligation to govern. His empire had really been two realms since 1867—an Austrian empire and a Hungarian kingdom, united by a common ruler. Austrian Germans and Hungarian Magyars were the majority populations of this polyglot medieval survival, but there were also millions of Czechs, Slovaks, Yugoslavs (including Serbs), Poles, Ukrainians, Rumanians, and others under Francis Joseph's rule. Many of these peoples had been inflamed by nationalistic zeal by dedicated nineteenth-century ideologues. Parading, demonstrating, and disrupting imperial and provincial legislatures, these minority nationalities demanded the autonomy that in the end would pull the empire apart.

A prime source of the nationalistic virus in Austria-Hungary was the small neighboring Balkan state of Serbia. Freed from the Ottoman Empire in the later 1800s, the Serbs were eager to unite with fellow Yugoslavs in the Habsburg realm to form a Greater Serbia. Both the Serbs and the Austrians lusted after the Ottoman provinces of Bosnia and Herzegovina—Serbia for nationalistic reasons, Austria to frustrate these ambitions. When the Austrians annexed the provinces in 1908, the two countries came very close to war. Conflict was avoided, however—or, more accurately, postponed.

Nicholas II (ruled 1894–1917), czar of all the Russias, was that perennial downfall of embattled authoritarian regimes, a weak autocrat. Like Charles I in seventeenth-century England or Louis XVI in eighteenth-century France, the last of the czars meant well. But he did not like politics, and he left the country largely in the hands of rigorously authoritarian people such as Procurator Pobedonostsev, head of the holy synod of the Russian Orthodox church, and Minister of the Interior Plehve, head of the notorious Third Section, the czar's secret police. These officials, remembering all too vividly the assassination of the reforming emperor Alexander II in 1881, made no concessions to any ism. They dealt with popular discontent by sowing the land with police and secret agents and by suppressing strikes and student demonstrations with force. They also embarked upon a vigorous campaign to Russify the empire's minority nationalities—Finns and Poles, Baltic Germans, Jews, Armenians, and other conquered peoples.

Paradoxically, however, a major source of trouble was not the reactionary measures of Pobedonostsev and Plehve but the progressive industrializing policies of the czar's minister of finance, Sergei Witte. Witte encouraged industrial growth, mining, oil production, and the building of the Trans-Siberian Railway—and in so doing increased the size of Russia's discontented industrial work force considerably. Such progressive industrial policies, furthermore, did nothing to address the problems of the nation's peasant majority, who, though no longer serfs, still languished in poverty and ignorance as the century turned.

Internal repression and progress that was no progress combined with Russia's ignominious defeat in the Russo-Japanese War to trigger Russia's first twentieth-century rebellion—the Revolution of 1905. The widely hated Plehve was assassinated by a revolutionary terrorist in 1904. On Bloody Sunday in January 1905, a priest named Gapon led thousands of striking workers to the Winter Palace in St. Petersburg to plead for a constitution and better working conditions; they were met by withering rifle fire that killed hundreds in the snow. Within months, strikes paralyzed the economy, nationalistic and other riots flared, and there were even mutinies in the armed services.

Nicholas II responded with what looked like concessions. The October Manifesto promised more freedom and an elected legislative assembly. The assembly, called the Duma, actually met off and on during the decade between the Revolution of 1905 and World War I. In fact, however, the government emasculated both these reluctant concessions to the spirit of liberal reform. The Manifesto was never treated as a binding constitution by the czar, and the powers of the Duma were limited so thoroughly that it never became a true Russian parliament. The little-known Russian revolutionary leader, V. I. Lenin, living in exile in Switzerland in 1905, declared grimly that the struggle against the czar was "only beginning."[1]

---

[1]Louis Fischer, *The Life of Lenin* (New York: Harper & Row, 1964), p. 49.

Turn-of-the-century rulers liked to sit for official portrait photographs, often surrounded by their families, as their predecessors had sat for portrait painters. A famous picture of Emperor Nicholas II and the Russian royal family shows only one smiling face, that of one of the czar's four daughters. The saddest faces of all are those of Alexandra, Nicholas's German empress, and of the imperial heir, Crown Prince Alexis, a tragic little boy afflicted with hemophilia, the shadow of death already draping his thin features.

With the sole exception of Queen Victoria, all the crowned heads mentioned in the last three sections had one unhappy characteristic in common. They were all the last of their lines. Though none of them would have believed it in 1900, Europe's long age of kings and queens had less than twenty years to run as the nineteenth century ended and the twentieth began.

THE UNITED STATES: THE NEW GREAT POWER OF THE WEST

Things looked better for the world's republics. Flourishing above all in the New World, elected governments, for all their limitations, had greater potential for survival than the European monarchies. The United States in particular enjoyed an impressive political renaissance in the decades around 1900. It was called Progressivism, and it was the first of the great waves of reform that would sweep across the United States during the twentieth century.

The Populist reform agitation of the 1890s, the militance of farmers, and the struggles of organized labor all contributed to the emergence of the Progressive movement. So did a fastidious genteel tradition of disgust at the crooked politics and vulgar greed of America's urban political bosses, corrupt legislators, and new-rich industrialists over the decades since the Civil War. A major source of the Progressive revolt, finally, was a turn-of-the-century surge of investigative reporting by journalists and popular historians called muckrakers. The muckrakers published blistering indictments of the methods and morals of the self-made millionaires of the Gilded Age, yesterday's "captains of industry," now dubbed "robber barons" in the popular press.

Beginning on the state and local levels, Progressive reform stressed increased democracy, challenges to political bosses and party machines, and greater efficiency in government. Progressives also emphasized regulation of big business through such measures as trust-busting—the breakup of corporations so big that they constituted "conspiracies in restraint of trade." The movement also sought some social legislation, including labor laws, tried to help the poor generally, and renewed the struggles for women's rights and "temperance," the outlawing of alcoholic beverages.

During the first two decades of the twentieth cen-

Theodore Roosevelt and the Panama Canal—a triumph for TR's "big stick" imperialism. The drawing shows him complete with cowboy hat, the "Teddy" bear, which was named for him, and the familiar features that made him a cartoonist's delight. When the waterway opened in 1914, it joined the Suez Canal as one of the two most important canals in the world. (Library of Congress)

tury, the Progressive movement produced two of the most active and influential presidents in American history: the Republican Theodore Roosevelt (1901–1909) and the Democrat Woodrow Wilson (1913–1921).

They were two very different men. Moustached, big-toothed, roly-poly Roosevelt, the endlessly energetic exponent of vigor in all things, was a vivid personality. A self-made outdoorsman (he had been a sickly child), a national hero as leader of the Rough Riders in the Spanish-American War, and an aggressive reforming governor of New York, Teddy Roosevelt was one of the most popular of presidents. Woodrow Wilson, leaner and far less bumptious in style, a southern preacher's son and former reforming president of Princeton University, took a loftier moral tone. They ran against each other in the crucial election of 1912, Roosevelt preaching a more moderate New Nationalist version of progressivism, Wilson a more liberal New Freedom. Both were eloquent orators in their very different styles, both turned out to be skillful politicians, and both were pioneers of twentieth-century reform politics in America.

Roosevelt busted some trusts—including Standard Oil—regulated the worst abuses of the railroads, meat-packers, and others, and passed some legislation designed to improve working conditions in factories. He was an early conservationist, nationalizing large chunks of wilderness and other natural resources to save them from private developers for the nation as a whole. He was no radical, however, and his progressivism was directed rather toward equalizing competitive opportunities for all than toward government care for the unfortunate.

Wilson also began relatively conservatively. During his first term he reformed the tariff in the direction of free trade, stabilized the banking system by establishing regional Federal Reserve banks, and set the Federal Trade Commission to regulating interstate commerce. In 1916, however, he was caught up in a new surge of Progressive reform activity, including credit for farmers in need of loans, an eight-hour working day for factory hands, and other social legislation.

In general, the United States was more conservative in social reform than Europe was—and it still is. But Teddy Roosevelt, Woodrow Wilson, and the Progressives set the nation on a path of active government intervention on behalf of the governed that would lead most of the Western world to some form of the welfare state by the second half of the century.

The other side of the American coin in 1900 was the rise of American imperialism.

American overseas expansion was for many simply a natural extension of the continental expansion of the nineteenth century. Indeed, the United States had already purchased Alaska from the Russians (1867) and taken over Hawaii from its last queen, annexing the islands in 1898. American traders had in fact been jostling Europeans in the "China market" on the far side of the Pacific for the better part of the preceding century.

The Spanish-American War of 1898, however, not only added the Philippines to the scattered Pacific holdings of the United States, it began several decades of aggressive U.S. intervention in the affairs of Middle America and the Caribbean. Teddy Roosevelt encouraged a Central American revolution and then acquired what became the Panama Canal Zone from the victorious revolutionaries in 1903. Woodrow Wilson intervened twice in the great Mexican Revolution that began in 1911. The U.S. Marines also landed to calm troubled regimes and make the Caribbean safer for foreign investors in Nicaragua, Haiti, and elsewhere.

Roosevelt called it the Big Stick; Wilson described it as instruction in democracy; critics labeled it Dollar Diplomacy.[2] In fact, the motives seem to have been a familiar Western imperialist mix of vested economic interests, a missionary zeal for spreading stable democratic government, strategic concerns, and a sense of cultural superiority. Imperial intervention by the United States, as by the other powers, kindled bitter resentment. The Philippines in particular, far from expressing gratitude for liberation from Spain, launched an insurrection against their

---

new American rulers that took years to suppress and cost the United States as much in international approval—and self-esteem—as the Boer War did the British.

For Americans, then, the twentieth century began with a mixture of domestic reforms and foreign wars that would become familiar as the decades passed.

ASIA AND LATIN AMERICA

CHINA: SELF-STRENGTHENING THAT FAILED

China around 1900 was at the depths of its century-long decline. It is hard to recognize, in that spectacle of late-Manchu decay, either the ancient empire of the East or the new China of the present day.

Following a disastrous series of mid-century conflicts—wars with Britain and France, the Taiping Rebellion—China had embarked upon a decades-long program

The "Old Buddha," Dowager Empress Ci Xi, symbol and sustainer of China's ancient civilization. Her defiance of changing times and Western power left China almost helpless at the turn of the century. During her last years, "Old Buddha" lived a secluded life amid the fading splendors at the Forbidden City in Beijing. (Library of Congress)

---

[2]Teddy Roosevelt made the West African proverb, "Speak softly—and carry a big stick" one of his trademarks.

"*The maintenance of general peace and the possible reduction of the excessive armaments which weigh upon all nations present themselves in existing conditions to the whole world as an ideal toward which the endeavors of all governments should [be] directed. . . .*

"*In the course of the last twenty years . . . the longing for general appeasement has grown especially pronounced in the consciences of civilized nations; and the preservation of peace has been put forward as an object of international policy. It is in its name that great states have concluded between themselves powerful alliances.*

"*It is the better to guarantee peace that they have developed in proportions hitherto unprecedented their military forces, and still continue to increase them, without shrinking from any sacrifice.*

"*Nevertheless, all these efforts have not yet been able to bring about the beneficient result desired—pacification.*

"*The financial charges [furthermore] strike at the very root of public prosperity. The intellectual and physical strength of the nations' labor and capital are mostly diverted from the natural application, and are unproductively consumed. Hundreds of millions are devoted to acquiring terrible engines of destruction, which, though to-day regarded as the last work of science, are destined to-morrow to lose all their value in consequence of some fresh discovery in the same field. National culture, economic progress, and the production of wealth are either paralyzed or checked in development.*

"*It appears evident that if this state of things were to be prolonged it would inevitably lead to the very cataclysm it is desired to avert, and the horrors whereof make every thinking being shudder in advance.*

"*To put an end to these incessant armaments and to seek the means of warding off the calamities which are threatening the whole world—such is the supreme duty to-day imposed upon all states.*"

◆◆◆◆

The ringing denunciation of war and demand for disarmament printed here was issued by Count Muraviev, foreign minister of the Russian Empire in 1898, in the name of Nicholas II, the last czar. What reasons does the Russian diplomat give for hoping for a world without wars, a future history in which the nations will disarm and agree to discuss their differences rather than fight over them? From your general knowledge of the history of the century since 1898, did the nations in fact behave as Muraviev hoped? Do disarmament negotiations and other international discussions aimed at keeping the peace continue? Do you think they may be more successful in the twenty-first century than they have been in the twentieth?

Charles Morris, The Wonderful Century 1800–1900: Its History and Progress (Chicago: H. J. Smith, 1899), pp. 620–621.

of "self-strengthening." This rather desultory campaign, presided over by the immensely conservative Dowager Empress Ci Xi (1835–1908), focused first on modernizing the Chinese military, then on encouraging the growth of merchant wealth in order to further strengthen the nation. The aim was to adopt a few Western techniques while retaining the essence of China's ancient civilization.

It had not worked. A new round of Western imperialism had seen Europeans seize control of a number of traditionally Chinese tributary states in the later nineteenth century and force concessions of leases and development rights to territories on the Chinese mainland. In 1895 Japan—which had flung itself much more wholeheartedly into Westernization—had humiliated China in the Sino-Japanese War. In 1900 the Boxer Rebellion had brought Western armies back to Beijing with China's armies being swept aside once more in the process, and had left the nation saddled with a huge indemnity and even more Westerners.

At the beginning of the twentieth century, then, China was filled with tumultuous dispute over more drastic reforms, about educational changes and constitutions, even about revolution. And now the debate focused on the core of the Chinese system: on the ancient Confucian administrative system that had served the nation so well for so long, and on the Manchu monarchy itself.

Ci Xi's clawlike hand still moved to frustrate any reform that touched her own power. When the impressionable young Guangxu emperor attempted the Hundred Days reform campaign after the SinoJapanese War, she choked it off, executing some of the reformers and driving others into exile in Japan. When a constitution was actually drawn from her reluctant fingers after the Boxer debacle, she certainly had reservations as strong as any czar's about granting actual power to even quasi-democratic institutions.

Change, however, had to come to the battered Middle Kingdom. It would come only after Ci Xi's death, when the Chinese Empire was plunged into the longest revolution of the twentieth century, not to know peace again until 1949. And by that time, China would have yielded its customary primacy in East Asia to a much more enthusiastic Westernizer—the island kingdom of Japan.

JAPAN: THE NEW GREAT POWER OF THE EAST

Japan at the turn of the century was a nation in rapid and vigorous transition. "Restore the Emperor and expel the Barbarian" had been the cry of the Meiji reformers of thirty years before.[3] The first objective had certainly been accomplished; but by 1900, Western "barbarian" influences were everywhere in the new Japan.

The Meiji Emperor (1867–1912), whose restoration to full power in 1868 had begun Japan's spectacular modern development, still ruled in 1900. Politically and economically, the land he ruled was a very different place from the Japan that Commodore Perry had "opened" in the 1850s. And Japan's aggressively imperialistic foreign policy was already setting the expansionist pattern that nation would follow throughout the first half of the twentieth century.

Politically, Meiji Japan had developed a complex constitutional structure that amounted to rule through the

---

[3]Ruth Benedict, *The Chrysanthemum and the Sword: Patterns of Japanese Culture* (Boston: Houghton Mifflin, 1946), p. 76.

cooperation and competition of separate and often rivalrous elites. The emperor himself enjoyed great respect and the power to appoint officials up to and including the prime minister—though he customarily delegated this responsibility to a group of elder statesmen. The political parties of the Diet, the Japanese legislature, passed laws and voted on the budget in a very Western way, but had little of the power exercised by a British-style parliament, whose leader was also the political leader of the nation. The imperial bureaucracy, led by brilliant if conservative Tokyo Law School graduates, also had a good deal of authority in the nation. The army and the navy, finally, had great prestige because of their victories: the military had no civilian superiors in Japan except the emperor himself.

It was a complicated political system, one that could easily have evolved in more than one way. In the twentieth century it moved in two directions—toward military control in the first half of the century, toward a business-dominated democracy in the second half.

Economically, Japan was in the middle of a boom in 1900, and that surge of economic growth accelerated into the new century. Between 1900 and 1940, Japan's exports of raw materials would triple and its overseas sales of manufactured goods would multiply a dozen times. Its population would also explode once more, from 44 million in 1900 to 78 million in 1940, absorbing at least some of its economic gains. But the direction toward mushrooming growth was clear—and impressive.

The heart of Japan's expanding industrial, commercial, and financial economy was the small group of super-rich business families known as the *zaibatsu*. These equivalents of the German Krupps or the American Rockefellers included such powerful industrial dynasties as the Mitsubishi, Mitsui, Kawasaki, and half a dozen other major firms.

Expanding to control a spectrum of ventures from mining and manufacturing to shipping and commerce, *zaibatsu* clans such as Mitsui and Mitsubishi may, in fact, have been the biggest privately owned corporations in the world. They made Japan's economic growth possible. They also had a powerful say in politics, thanks to close ties with the bureaucracy and—as in Europe and America—to substantial contributions to the campaign funds of political parties.

During the turn-of-the-century decades, finally, Japanese imperialism was a central factor in Far Eastern affairs. Japan's decisive victories over the world's two largest land empires—China in 1895 and Russia in 1905—astonished the world. Just as the United States regarded the Western Hemisphere as its bailiwick, so Japan clearly saw the Far East as its own back yard. It was not unlikely that these two dynamic, expansive nations on opposite sides of the Pacific would themselves come to blows sooner or later.

In 1900 the Western imperial powers tried with

some success to limit Japan's gains from its initial victories. But there was no question that modernizing Japan was the most powerful nation in Asia—and there was no clear notion just how far the Japanese might go in the century just beginning.

LATIN AMERICA: ECONOMIC DEPENDENCY

In Latin America, the economic and political trends of the late nineteenth century reached a climax around 1900. Efforts at reform were much less pronounced than in North America, and no comparable burst of imperial expansion was generated in the south. Altogether, Latin America was characterized much more by continuities with the 1800s than was the case north of the Rio Grande.

Economic dependency was perhaps the most striking carry-over from the nineteenth century. The Latin American republics continued to depend on the export of agricultural products—beef, wheat, coffee, bananas, and others—and of natural resources such as nitrates, copper, tin, and oil to pay for their economic growth. These nations also depended on Europe and North America for imported manufactured goods and for capital to build the fine new streets of Mexico City, Buenos Aires, and Rio de Janeiro.

The results of development through economic dependency, recent scholarship suggests, were far from uniformly good. One obvious consequence was to strengthen the grip of the hacienda—which produced the raw materials for export—on the countryside, and the hold of the export merchants on the growing cities. By contrast, domestic industrial development languished, unable to compete with manufactured goods from Europe and the United States. Progress thus remained skin-deep, a matter of hacienda agriculture and industrial underdevelopment capped by shiny new cities, railroads, and other modern amenities and by imported luxuries for the wealthy few who could afford them.

The *mestizo* and the Indian masses, in contrast, remained poor and illiterate. Deprived of their land by hacienda power, sucked into monocultural plantation labor or mining for export, many Latin Americans could no longer even feed themselves through subsistence farming.

It was a box into which other parts of the world were also sinking, and these regions would sink deeper as the twentieth century advanced. This global division of labor fostered by Western economic predominance was, in fact, to be one of the prime features of twentieth-century world history.

The histories of several of the major Latin American nations during the decades around 1900 illustrate these aspects of life in the other half of the hemisphere. Mexico in the north and the ABC countries of South America—Argentina, Brazil, and Chile—will all be glanced at briefly from this point of view.

MEXICO AND THE ABC POWERS: PROGRESS AND POVERTY

Mexico, ruled by the modernizing but brutal dictator Porfirio Díaz from 1876 to 1911, epitomized most of these turn-of-the-century trends. The Díaz dictatorship, which began as a popular constitutional regime, had by 1900 become government by and for large landowners, high churchmen, foreign investors, and growing numbers of generals and government officials. There were rewards, of course. British, United States, and other foreign capital, combined with Mexican export profits, and operating in the stable social environment produced by repression, had crisscrossed the nation with railroads and made Mexico the world's third largest oil producer and a leader in other mineral and agricultural products as well. But massive land grabs by speculators and hacienda owners, decline in production of ancient food staples such as maize and beans, and widespread peonage left the majority of Mexicans deep in poverty.

Elections were routinely rigged under Díaz, political opposition jailed, peasant discontent suppressed by backcountry policemen called *rurales,* and strikers attacked and even killed by troops. Government intellectuals called the *Cientificos* ("Scientifics") pointed proudly to zooming production figures and insisted that economic strength must precede political democracy. As the century turned, however, there was growing opposition to the aging Díaz among peasants, proletarians, the liberal middle classes, and nationalistic opponents of foreign economic predominance. Mexico had little in the way of a progressive reform movement, but it would have its revolution—one of the most significant in Latin American history.

At the other end of Latin America, Argentina illustrated many of these same unhappy trends. But Argentine history also revealed the beginnings of both political freedom and radical agitation as the twentieth century began.

Argentina in 1900 was ruled not by a towering individual like Díaz, but by a loose political coalition called the Generation of 1880 (after the period when they came to power), or sometimes simply the Oligarchy. The Oligarchy meant—once more—government by wealthy landowners, export merchants, and foreign capital, especially British. Huge exports of meat and wheat from the rolling pampas made Buenos Aires a modern metropolis and built railways and processing plants. It also led to the usual expropriation of the Indians, land grabs, and peon labor. Argentina's economic boom, the wonder of the south, made it the most industrially developed nation in Latin America. But most of the new wealth stayed in Buenos Aires, where even the hacienda owners now moved to share in the good life.

Politically speaking, Argentina's Oligarchy was more flexible than the Díaz regime far to the north, and even intermittently liberal. In Argentina, undue church influence was curtailed, education was encouraged, labor unions were made legal, and some political dissent was even tolerated. The principal opposition was the so-called Radical party, really a rather moderate middle-class movement whose major achievement was to induce the Oligarchy to grant the nation universal manhood suffrage in 1912. But there were genuine radicals in Argentina too. Socialists and labor-union leaders, many of them European immigrants, were able to organize massive strikes and win a ten-hour-day law early in the 1900s.

Thanks to such piecemeal reforms, Argentina would escape anything like the revolutionary storm that was building in Mexico. And despite the problems of dependency, Argentina was one of the most industrially developed nations outside the Europe–North American axis as the century got under way.

Brazil, Argentina's enormous neighbor to the north, was as strikingly divided, economically, politically, and culturally, as any Latin American land in 1900.

Rio de Janeiro was being rebuilt around its perfect harbor and its trademark, Sugarloaf Mountain, into one of the most beautiful and modern cities in the world. Its new corporate offices, banks, and broad avenues matched anything in Europe or North America. The Brazilian "backlands," by contrast, were dark with the poverty of Indians and blacks who had been slaves until 1888, with the feudal power of great landowners, with rampant banditry, and with exotic religious cults that were sometimes cruelly suppressed for their radical social views.

The Brazilian monarchy, headed by a Portuguese prince, had been overthrown as recently as in 1890. The alliance of landowners, businessmen, and progressive military officers who had engineered the coup had soon split, and power had fallen largely into the hands of the richest Brazilian landowners, the coffee planters. Brazil produced three quarters of the world's coffee in the early 1900s, and the coffee interests—with the help of foreign bankers—ruled the huge new republic in the decades before 1914.

Foreigners controlled the large banking, transportation, and export-trade businesses. Brazilians—including, however, many new immigrants—built a bustling light-industrial sector, particularly in textiles. In the mills, a Brazilian working class developed—again, composed largely of recent European immigrants. Among these workers, labor unions and socialist agitation began, despite police repression.

Chile, Argentina's long, string-bean neighbor across the Andes to the west, was the third of Latin America's ABC powers. Like the others, it was in many ways a textbook case of the common Latin American mix of progress and poverty.

Chile's economy was dominated by nitrate and copper production, mostly in the northern territories seized from Peru in the War of the Pacific in the early 1880s.

The nitrate kings of the north, the owners of the railways, and other economic leaders were British; Germans were powerful in the south. An effort at government stimulation of a Chile-controlled industrial sector had ended with the overthrow of the would-be reformers in the 1890s. Thereafter, foreign capital and foreign influence continued unimpeded into the new century.

Politically, this was the period of Chile's parliamentary republic. Under this regime, the center of power was not in the presidential palace but in the Chilean legislature, where factions representing landowners, priests, business, and foreign interests managed the nation. It was a fundamentally conservative government, but a constitutional and parliamentary one. Growing numbers of factory workers and miners, labor organization, and the beginnings of socialist parties were exerting pressure for social reform. By the time of World War I, factory legislation had begun to be passed in Chile too.

One way to compare the development of North and South America at the beginning of the twentieth century would be to say that the southern equivalent of the U.S. Gilded Age of gaudy corruption and sometimes impressive economic growth continued unabated in Latin America after 1900. Certainly the southern republics had little to parallel the Progressive movement or the reform leadership of Roosevelt and Wilson in the early 1900s.

One might also point out that despite economic growth in some areas, Latin America had not by the turn of the century developed anything like the huge industrial machine of the United States. And it was this productive capacity that would enable the United States not only to escape European economic domination but to rival and then surpass Europe as an exploiter of economic opportunities in other lands—including Latin America—in the twentieth century.

THE WESTERN EMPIRES AND COLONIAL RESISTANCE

THE VIEW FROM SHEPHEARD'S HOTEL

It is to the great Western intercontinental empires themselves, finally, that we must come at the end of this overview of the world at the beginning of the twentieth century.

Shepheard's Hotel in Cairo would have been the ideal place for a Westerner to sit and contemplate the world as the nineteenth century drew to a close. Cairo was centrally located—geographically in Africa, yet in local color and mood thoroughly east-of-Suez. It was also anomalous, like so much of the New Imperialism: nominally ruled by a *khedive* who was officially subject to the Ottoman sultan, turn-of-the-century Egypt was in fact governed by Lord

Cromer, the British resident in Cairo. It was, finally, properly exotic and mysterious, thick with bazaars and mosques, a few miles' ride from the Pyramids.

The view from the terrace at Shepheard's—over a cold sherbet, say—would have been horses and carriages, pith helmets, starched frocks, and Western uniforms. For this most famous hotel in imperial Cairo faced the Ezbekiyeh Gardens in the heart of the European section. The imitation French architecture around the square, obsequious waiters in red sashes and *kepis*, urgent multilingual *dragomans* (guides or interpreters) eager to show you the wonders of the pharaonic past could give the Western tourist a lordly sense of being the master of all he surveyed. But there were only 25,000 Europeans in Cairo, and almost half a million Egyptians.

A short walk from the Ezbekiyeh would put one in the heart of the real Cairo, in all its exotic profusion. Arabs, Turks, Copts, water carriers, sherbet sellers, mule wagons, camels, *fellahin* in from the villages, bedouin in from the desert jostled and jeered and bargained and shouted. Shimmering silken robes mingled with the black gowns and veils of women, the *tarboosh* and the Syrian shawl. The streets were narrow and winding, with Arabesque latticing and carved gates, protruding second stories, whitewashed walls, narrow courtyards, and the clutter and din and clutching hands of the bazaars. At the end of every street, gleaming above the immense vitality of the city, rose the domes and minarets of a mosque.

This section will be concerned largely with what one could see from the terrace at Shepheard's, with the new world order the imperialists were building. But while we watch the changes come, we should remember that the other, older world was there all the time—and that it is there still.

THE RESISTANCE

The major intercontinental empires of a hundred years ago were among the most amazing human institutions ever constructed. But the view from Shepheard's Hotel omitted one crucial element, which must be included if the history of the world in the next century is to make any sense: resistance.

The rest of the world did not take kindly to the Western predominance. Even in the face of ironclads and Maxim guns, the other peoples of the globe resisted Western aggression. It was a disorganized, usually hopeless resistance, but it was a beginning. Within a long half century, it would emerge triumphant.

The colonial wars and revolts, the reform movements and embryonic nationalist groups of the late nineteenth and early twentieth centuries were of two types. We may call them traditional and progressive.

The large majority of these anti-imperialist movements were traditionalist rebellions. They were rooted in ancient religions or long-established social structures and political loyalties. Such revolts could mobilize large numbers of ill-organized and poorly equipped native peoples against the new order of things imposed upon them from without. Almost always, they failed.

A few of these nineteenth-century movements, however, were the work of Westernized minorities in colonial areas. These people recognized the necessity of learning some of the organizational, technological, and military

The savagery of the struggle for empire was nowhere more horrifyingly illustrated than in the "Indian Mutiny" of 1857. The rebellious Sepoy troops had killed their officers and slaughtered civilians, sending a thrill of terror through the handful of British colonials who presided over hundreds of millions of Indians. Determined on exemplary punishment and hoping to spread terror in their turn, the victorious British troops in some places executed captured rebels by lashing them across the barrels of field artillery—and firing. (Painting by Vasili Vasilevitch Vereshchagin)

skills developed by the West if they were ever to expel the Westerners from their homelands. This approach was progressive not in any moral sense, but simply in that it reflected a determination to master the latest technical advances in order to use them against their inventors. It was an approach that had a much more successful future in the century that began in 1900.

There were prototypes for both these forms of resistance to Western imperialism as early as the 1850s. The Indian Mutiny was a traditionalist rebellion that resulted in an intensification of the British grip on India. The opening up of Japan in that same mid-century decade, however, set the Japanese on a crash course of modernization that enabled that nation not only to escape Western imperialism but to join the ranks of the imperialists by the end of the century.

A brief survey of some of the major revolts will at least give some idea of the variety and extent of the resistance even at the high tide of the great conquest.

KHARTOUM AND THE LITTLE BIG HORN

Continent by continent, it was a violent picture. And there were many similarities between the anti-imperialist movements of one colony and those of another.

In Africa the British faced two rebellions in their Egyptian protectorate, the Mahdist movement in the Sudan in the 1880s and 1890s, as well as wars with the Zulus and the Matabele in South Africa and with the fierce Ashanti in the West African Gold Coast (today's Ghana). The French had to deal with rebellions in Tunisia and Madagascar and with insurrections in French West Africa. These latter included a long resistance by the Mande, who in earlier centuries had built some of the most impressive kingdoms of the Western Sudan.

The Germans were challenged by indigenous peoples in almost all their African colonies after 1900. Their savage repression of the Maji-Maji revolt (1905–1907) in what is today Tanzania has lived as one of the most brutal assertions of Western supremacy. The Portuguese, the Belgians, and the Italians also confronted armed resistance in Africa in the late nineteenth and early twentieth centuries.

In Asia the British experienced determined opposition when they invaded Burma in the 1880s, and terrorism in both eastern and western India. The French met decades of armed defiance all over French Indochina. One of their most persistent opponents was the guerrilla Ham Nghi, who fought them from the colony's mountain spine in the 1880s. There were revolts against the Dutch in Java and Sumatra. A bitter guerrilla movement was directed against the American occupation of the Philippines at the turn of the century. The Boxer Rebellion of 1899–1900 in North China, as we have seen, sought the destruction of all Westerners of whatever nationality in that country.

The final stages of United States and Russian continental expansion involved bitter fighting. Russian troops pushing south into the Caucasus faced decades of savage resistance from fierce mountaineers under Shamil, "destroyer of the unbeliever." There was a widespread revolt in Muslim central Asia against the Russian authorities as late as World War I.

The expanding United States, as noted above, faced recurrent resistance all across the North American continent and overseas as well. In the eastern United States, the most celebrated nineteenth-century fight was probably that of the Seminoles in Florida, who refused to take the Trail of Tears. In the West, the raids of the horseriding Plains Indians also took decades to suppress. In the Philippines, the 1900 insurrection cost tens of thousands of Filipino lives.

Religion provided the impetus and inspiration for many of these resistance movements, including Islam in Africa, the Middle East, and Russia; Hinduism in India; the Ghost Dance among the American Plains Indians; and peasant polytheism in China. Other movements were tribal in origin, such as the resistance of the Mande, Ashanti, and Zulu people in Africa and that of the Moros in the Philippines. Sometimes traditionalist revolts fought doggedly in defense of traditional rulers, such as the emperors in Cambodia and Vietnam.

Modernizing or progressive rebellions were most common in Asia, where structured government, urban environments, and all the skills necessary for a changeover to Western ways already existed. Two of the most striking such modernization movements were the Persian Revolution of 1905 and the Young Turk revolt in 1908. Both were directed against antiquated indigenous governments that seemed likely to surrender their countries to the Europeans. Both movements aimed, with some success, to modernize their nations sufficiently to withstand further Western aggression.

A peaceful modernizing movement with a long future was the Congress party, organized by professional people in India in 1885. In the next century Indian leaders such as Gandhi and Nehru would rise in this party and lead the country to independence after World War II. As we shall see, Mahatma Gandhi's nonviolent methods were rooted deep in Hindu traditions, but his goals included a great deal that was thoroughly Western.

With spears and machetes and rifles, with ancient prayers and traditional battle cries, they resisted. With what Western technology and bits of Western ideology they could muster, they strove to expel the foreigners. Homekeeping Europeans could shrug off such manifestations of discontent. It was not quite so easy for the soldiers of empire to ignore.

General "Chinese" Gordon and General George Custer had very little in common besides their unhappy fates. Gordon died at Khartoum in the Sudan at the hands of the Mahdi, Custer at the Little Big Horn in Montana, cut down by Sitting Bull's Sioux. Such victories for the resistance were rare. But the spirit of resistance was not.

IMPERIALISM AND THE DRIFT TOWARD GLOBAL UNITY

THE IMPACT OF THE WEST ON NON-WESTERN CULTURES

The New Imperialism had a much more important transforming influence on the rest of the world than the Old Imperialism had had, an impact that was already becoming apparent by 1900. In many parts of the world, this second, more intense and penetrating wave of Western conquest inaugurated a process of social change sometimes called Westernization, sometimes simply modernization.

Distinctions can be drawn, but the overall pattern is evident, however we label it. The new and more pervasive Western presence led to the breakdown of many traditional cultural modes, forms of social organization, and patterns of belief. The advance of the West also stimulated the global adoption—and adaptation—of many economic, social, and political institutions, of ideological and technological forms derived from Western theory and practice.

This transformation would continue after the fall of the Western intercontinental empires. It would make a crucial contribution to the larger pattern of global exchange of goods, institutions, and ideas that would distinguish the twentieth century even more than the nineteenth. In itself, however, this great wave of Westernization that began in the later 1800s is an amazing historic development.

Many instances of far-reaching regional influences from a single dynamic center could be adduced as precedents. Islam had transformed cultures wherever it spread. The cultural weight of India had reshaped South and Southeast Asian societies. China's immense continuing presence had done the same throughout East Asia. But the global reach and the sheer rapidity of the Western impact resulting from the New Imperialism make Westernization a unique and awesome case.

MATERIAL IMPACT OF IMPERIALISM

Materially, the New Imperialism thrust its way into other people's cultures as the Old Imperialism seldom had. A European trading post on the shores of Africa or Asia, an isolated missionary or fur trapper in the Amazon rain forest or the Canadian wilderness could, as we have seen, make a significant difference in the lives of other peoples. Increases in slave raiding or spice cultivation, the introduction of the iron ax or the horse were not negligible forces for social change. But the changes the new wave of Western intruders brought dwarfed all earlier material influences.

The makers of the New Imperialism exploited and developed colonial regions with unmatched thoroughness and intensity. They reaped harvests, tapped trees, dug mines, drilled for oil from Brazil to Borneo. They unrolled barbed wire, strung up telegraph lines, laid rails, constructed harbor facilities. They built processing plants and even manufacturing plants in the colonies to turn raw materials into something closer to the use objects the Europeans, the Americans, or their other customers wanted.

Westerners themselves came in increasing numbers. They came partly to administer and garrison the new colonies. But they also came to manage the new economies and to operate the new technology thus translated beyond the seas. They came as advisors to governments or businesses in old countries in the Middle East or new ones in Latin America. And wherever they came, more and more local people were hired to do the necessary physical labor of remodeling the world.

The material impact was vast, cumulative, and accelerating. Irreplaceable natural resources—Congo copper, Arab oil—began to be drained from the land. Patterns of agriculture were drastically changed. Cash crops replaced subsistence farming until populations that formerly fed themselves came to depend on imported food for sheer survival.

Local industries were ruined by the competition of cheap Western machine-made alternatives. The Indian cotton industry was the world's leader in the seventeenth century. It was driven to the brink of extinction by the cotton mills of Manchester and Birmingham in the nineteenth.

Native peoples were often uprooted and forced into new patterns of life. The bright lights of cities built by Europeans lured African villagers away from their old lives and into new ones that were often rootless and demoralizing. European laws were forced on local people by fiat of colonial administrators. European customs spread with the temptation of jobs and contracts that went to those who accepted European ways.

Everywhere, Western supremacy was flaunted in the shining new facilities—mines and factories, government houses, transportation networks—and the nice homes and private clubs of the European quarters of town. Asians and Africans whose only contact with Westerners was to gawk at the viceroy's palace in passing, to scrub the floors of an engineer's home, or to take his children out to play could not help but be impressed.

Envious, resentful, filled with righteous wrath or a burning desire to live as these intruders did, the victims of this climactic phase of the Western conquest were drawn as by a great magnet in directions their ancestors could not have imagined.

CULTURAL IMPACT OF IMPERIALISM

Intellectually and spiritually, the influence of the West on the rest of the world was perhaps even more astonishing.

Ancient traditional religions, systems of ethics, scientific ideas, political theories, and styles in art had mostly

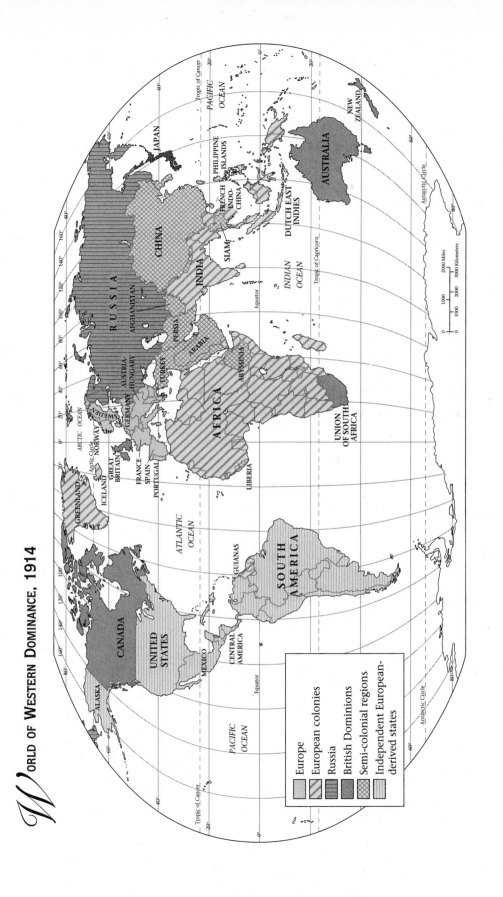

World of **Western Dominance**, 1914

Legend:
- Europe
- European colonies
- Russia
- British Dominions
- Semi-colonial regions
- Independent European-derived states

survived the Old Imperialism. Tolerant Eastern potentates had cheerfully added Christian priests to Muslim, Buddhist, and other holy men at their courts. Wandering missionaries had half-converted considerable numbers of "rice Christians," who were drawn to missions in time of famine and easily fitted Western divinities into their traditional pantheons.

But with the permeating impact of the New Imperialism, old systems of ideas and values began to melt away. It was the beginning of a process that continues today—a process that one expert on twentieth-century non-Western societies has described as "the most totally pervasive example of what historians call cultural diffusion in the history of mankind."[4]

Some of the fundamental features of Western culture—in the intellectual sense of the term—thus spread around the world. European languages, for example, were so widely taught and accepted that they remain the languages of former colonial elites today, decades after independence. Thus, French still flourishes in what was once French West Africa, as English does in India.

Western Christianity spread more widely and deeply than ever before in Asia and Africa as unprecedented numbers of missionaries flooded the non-Western world. Much of the southern half of Africa is Christian today, and there are Christian enclaves from the Middle East to Southeast Asia. China was governed by a Christian—Chiang Kai-shek—in the earlier twentieth century, and the presidents of the independent African states of Tanzania and Ivory Coast in the last third of the century were Catholics, Julius Nyerere and Felix Houphouet-Boigny, respectively.

Perhaps more important, the new ideologies of nineteenth-century Europe were broadcast among non-European peoples.

European liberal beliefs were introduced slowly through the gradual democratization of at least some colonial governments. European nationalist notions were seized upon more eagerly as the clamor for independence grew. Though they took the form of anti-imperialist agitation, colonial nationalism soon developed the same preoccupations with national culture, character, mission, and the rights to self-determination that had animated nationalism in the West. Even European socialism, an ideology designed for industrially developed nations with large proletariats, spread to colonial dependencies as the new century advanced. Socialism, especially in its Marxist form, would thus be adapted to the needs of peasant populations in countries having quite limited industrial sectors, most importantly China.

But the most valuable of all Western intellectual contributions to the life of the world was undoubtedly Western science and technology. Western schools run by colonial governments or religious missions began to teach the world according to Newton and transmit technology on the Manchester model. Students from the colonies picked up such up-to-the-minute ideas as Darwinism or the relativistic social theories of modern sociologists and anthropologists in the universities of their imperial masters—and found these notions as disturbing to their Buddhist or Hindu sensibilities as they were to Christian beliefs. Soon elites in other cultures everywhere were compromising traditional religious or philosophical beliefs in order to come to terms with the latest insights of the all-conquering West.

The spread of Western ideas, as well as Western material skills, would direct the course of non-Western development long after the Western structure of political power had collapsed. The pervasiveness of Western techniques and theories would make modernization a continuing feature of Third World history long after the great conquest had given way to the great liberation.

ECONOMIC INTEGRATION

By the eve of World War I—the historic end of the nineteenth century—the Industrial Revolution and the New Imperialism had combined to produce a genuinely integrated global economy for the first time in history. The exchange between Europe and the rest of the world that had appeared under the Old Imperialism now expanded enormously, evolving into something much more elaborate and all-encompassing. By 1914 a network of commerce, communication, investment, and industrial development linked nations and colonies in all parts of the world.[5]

The web of trade was now centered not only in Europe but also in North America. The leading commercial nations were Britain, Germany, the United States, France, the Netherlands, and Belgium. Established trade routes linked all the continents of the globe. The busiest arteries of trade, however, were not between Europe and its colonies but between the two great centers of industrial and commercial development, Europe and North America.

The importance of international commerce in the global economy had also increased greatly. In 1800 only 3 percent of the gross national product of the world was exchanged beyond national frontiers. In 1914 the figure was 33 percent. Fully a third of all the goods produced flowed into the trade routes and sea lanes of the world at the beginning of the twentieth century.

Those routes had themselves improved unimaginably over the intervening century. For land transport, the railway had been invented during the interim and had rapidly eclipsed beasts of burden and vehicles drawn by animals as a conveyor of trade goods. By 1914 Europe

[4]Paul Harrison, *Inside the Third World: The Anatomy of Poverty* (New York: Penguin Books, 1979), p. 48.

[5]These economic links can be effectively observed in the maps of Geoffrey Barraclough, ed., *The Times Atlas of World History* (London: Times Books, 1978).

Early twentieth-century Egyptian water carriers filled their pigskin bags in the Nile and sold the water in the streets of Egyptian towns and cities. The basic technology involved went back to the days of the pharaohs, and the street-vender's chant, "May Allah reward me!" was as old as Islam. (The Bettmann Archive)

Europe, especially in Russia; lesser amounts of francs financed projects in North and South America, Sudanic Africa, and the Ottoman Empire. And so it went down the line, bankers in London and Paris, New York and Berlin financing much of the large-scale business activity of the world.

This integrated world economy was clearly orchestrated and run by the West, in the interests of Western peoples. Frequently the new web of exchange, investment, and production warped the economies of non-Western nations. Many Latin countries and African colonies, as noted above, became monocultural commodity producers, catering to the international market rather than to domestic needs. For good or ill, however, a global pattern was established that continues to the present day.

THE POPULATION EXPLOSION AND URBANIZATION

The population explosion, which Parson Malthus had noticed at the end of the eighteenth century, was in full swing during the nineteenth. The growth and movement of population in the 1800s is another important dimension of the process of global integration stimulated by the Western hegemony of the world.

Statistics are still questionable or nonexistent for much of the world for this period, but informed estimates indicate a global population of 900 million at the beginning of the century, 1.65 billion at the end of it. In the broadest terms, a world population of considerably less than a billion around 1800 had advanced to well over a billion and a half by 1900.

Regional populations in 1900 ran roughly as follows: Asia, 935 million; Europe, 425 million; Africa, 120 million; North America, 100 million; South America, 45 million; and Australia, 5 million. In round terms, well over half the people in the world lived in Asia, another quarter inhabited Europe, and the remaining one fourth were scattered unevenly over the other four continents.

Several of the reasons for the global population explosion are closely tied to the Industrial Revolution and the New Imperialism. In Europe and North America, technological improvements in agriculture, new jobs in industry, better plumbing, higher standards of cleanliness, and medical advances certainly contributed. Western industrial and agricultural enclaves in the colonial world also fed and provided jobs for more people, and thereby lengthened life spans.

There was also an unprecedented amount of population *movement* in the nineteenth century. A major flow of migrants took place from Europe to the other three Europe-dominated continents of North and South America and Australia. The new immigrants came sometimes for political or religious freedom, as in earlier centuries. Germans and others fled political repression after the Revolutions of 1848, while Jews sought to escape eastern

and the United States were crisscrossed by a mesh of rail lines. Railroads had been built through the Alps and over the Andes, and transcontinental lines spanned the United States, Canada, Russia, and India.

The steamship had also all but replaced sailing vessels for most long hauls. Metal steamers with ten and twenty times the carrying capacity of earlier shipping now dominated the sea lanes of the globe. The Suez and Panama canals allowed ships to pass between Asia and Africa and between North and South America, lopping many hundreds of miles off their voyages.

A less visible but equally important force binding the peoples of the world into an increasingly integrated economy was the web of investment, again centered in Europe with a secondary center in the United States. Great Britain had twice the foreign investments of second-ranked France, with Germany, the Netherlands, and the United States following.

Britain's heaviest investments were, once more, not in its colonies but in the United States and the self-governing Dominion of Canada. Thereafter, the pound was deployed most widely in India, Australia, Latin America, and South Africa—a truly global reach. Most of France's smaller total was invested elsewhere in

European pogroms. More commonly, however, immigrants came for economic reasons. They came for cheap land, or to get rich quick in a gold rush, or simply because there were more opportunities to get ahead in the growing, less class-bound societies of Australia, Argentina, or the United States.

There were substantial movements of population from and to other continents, however. Emigrants from India continued their ancient drift down into Southeast Asia and Sri Lanka. But Indians also moved the other way, across the Indian Ocean to East Africa, where they came to outnumber European settlers, to dominate business, and probably to accumulate more money than even the Europeans. Chinese, feeling the population pinch in that swollen country, spread both southwest into Southeast Asia and east across the Pacific to the western United States. These overseas Chinese became a powerful element in the business life of Southeast Asia and the Pacific, though in the United States many of them became manual laborers or opened small businesses in the segregated Chinatowns of American cities.

Migration from the countryside to the city, finally, was a central feature of the demographic history of the nineteenth century. The magnet, of course, was the insatiable demand of the new industries for factory hands, miners, transportation workers, and all the service personnel that the new urban environment required. Many of the new cities that resulted mushroomed out of nowhere, called into existence by mineral deposits, transportation hubs, market demands, or investment decisions in faraway board rooms.

From London and Paris to St. Petersburg, from New York and Buenos Aires to Calcutta and Hong Kong, metropolitan centers grew. These cities were soon more numerous and larger than the most impressive urban complexes of earlier ages. They were also as unsanitary, disease-ridden, and dangerous as any cities in history. Whole families crowded into a single room; entire tenement buildings shared a single toilet. Men, women, and children might suffer from malnutrition or, because all three groups participated in the labor force, from work-related ailments. Workers were often unemployed and sometimes violent. Huge fires were common, devouring miles of rickety tenements before they burned themselves out.

And still the people came, drawn by jobs or rumors of jobs, by the bright lights of gas-lit streets, the excitement of the metropolis. Middle- and upper-class citizens shook their heads, wondering how human beings survived in the East Ends, the Left Banks, the Hell's Kitchens of the world. In fact, many were trapped, far from their home counties or their home countries. There were others, however, who wouldn't have gone back to the monotony of the provinces if you had paid them. It was a pattern of accelerating urbanization that would continue to be a central feature of global history for another hundred years at least.

SUMMARY

The world at the beginning of the present century was in the grip of rapid and accelerating change.

Europe was in its golden afternoon, still the most powerful continent in the world, but entering the century that would end that predominance. British problems included the Boer War in Africa, Irish demands for independence, German competition in the commercial world, and the suffragette movement at home. France survived the Dreyfus case and the larger struggle between republican liberals and conservative supporters of an older social and political order.

The new Germany of Bismarck and William II was militarily master of the continent, had an advanced welfare system, and was rapidly overtaking the British industrially. The more liberal new nation of Italy, economically underdeveloped, nevertheless followed the path of reform in 1900. Conservative Austria and reactionary Russia both had huge backward peasant populations, militant minority nationalities, and conflicting interests in the Balkans.

Across the Atlantic, the United States experienced a great surge of political reform in the Progressive movement, led at the national level by the rival politicians Teddy Roosevelt and Woodrow Wilson.

South of the Rio Grande, the Latin American republics continued to be economically dependent on Europe—and increasingly on North America. Unlike most of the *caudillos* of the nineteenth century, turn-of-the-century authoritarian governments often did bring basic if badly distributed progress to their countries.

Beyond the Pacific, China seemed on the verge of collapse, battered by wars and revolutions. Japan, by contrast, had already developed a more efficient government, *zaibatsu* big business, a powerful military machine, and soaring imperialistic ambitions of its own.

The Western intercontinental empires were at their height in 1900. Britain and France had the largest, but older powers like Spain, Portugal, and the Netherlands still had overseas holdings, as did newcomers like Germany, Belgium, Italy, the United States, and Japan. However, the colonies were never willing victims, and rebellions were frequent.

Westernization, meanwhile—the restructuring of traditional non-Western societies along modern Western lines—became endemic in the new century as peoples around the world coveted Western material advantages. Non-Western peoples also absorbed the languages, religions, ideologies, and other cultural achievements that had originated in Europe.

The Western hegemony created by the overseas expansion that climaxed in the New Imperialism had a profound global impact. Global integration was advanced immeasurably by the creation of new or expanded intercontinental empires in the last decades of the nineteenth century. The economic demands of the Industrial Revolution now affected the entire world. The new styles of life that resulted also led to an unprecedented global population boom and to massive intercontinental migrations.

SUGGESTED READING

BARRATT-BROWN, M. *The Economics of Imperialism.* Harmondsworth: Penguin, 1974. A good place to begin on this aspect of intercontinental empire.

CHAPMAN, G. *The Dreyfus Case: A Reassessment.* Westport, Conn.: Greenwood Press, 1979. An able critique of France's great turn-of-the-century crisis.

COCHRAN, T., and W. MILLER. *The Age of Enterprise: A Social History of Industrial America.* New York: Harper, 1961. Older but still recommended for coverage of big business in the age of the robber barons. See also E. Kirkland, *Industry Comes of Age, 1860–1897* (New York: Holt, Rinehart & Winston, 1961), and F. L. Allen, *The Big Change: America Transforms Itself, 1900–1950* (New York: Harper, 1962).

DARLING, F. C. *The Westernization of Asia.* Cambridge, Mass.: Schenkman, 1980. Transformations of South, Southeast, and East Asian cultures.

EKIRCH, A. *Progressivism in America.* New York: New Viewpoints, 1974. Good survey of the American Progressive Movement. Equally solid is W. O'Neill, *The Progressive Years* (New York: Dodd, Mead, 1975).

ETIENNE, M., and E. LEACOCK, eds. *Women and Colonization.* New York: Praeger, 1980. Anthropological analysis.

EVANS, R. *The Feminists: Women's Emancipation Movements in Europe, America, and Australasia 1840–1920.* New York: Barnes & Noble, 1977. Good comparative study. See also W. O'Neill, *Everyone Was Brave: The Rise and Fall of Feminism in America* (Chicago: Quadrangle Books, 1969), a widely commended summary of American feminism on the road to the suffrage amendment.

HALE, O. J. *The Great Illusion, 1900–1914.* New York: Harper & Row, Pub., 1971. Europe at the turn of the century—and on the eve of the Great War. See also B. Tuchman, *The Proud Tower* (New York: Bantam Books, 1972).

HENDERSON, W. O. *The Rise of German Industrial Power, 1834–1914.* Berkeley: University of California Press, 1975. Expert presentation of the economic growth that accompanied Germany's political unification and military achievements in the later nineteenth century. But see also L. L. Farrar, Jr., *Arrogance and Anxiety: The Ambivalence of German Power, 1848–1914* (Iowa City: University of Iowa Press, 1981).

HUGHES, H. S. *Consciousness and Society: The Reorientation of European Social Thought, 1890–1930.* New York: Random House, 1961. Perceptive interpretation of major shifts in the tone and content of European thinking after the turn of the century.

LAVRIN, A., ed. *Latin American Women: Historical Perspectives.* Westport, Conn.: Greenwood Press, 1978. Essays including studies of this period.

MACPHERSON, W. J. *The Economic Development of Japan, c. 1868–1941.* London: Macmillan, 1987. Very brief survey of Japan's economic modernization from the Meiji Restoration to World War II.

MANNONI, O. *Prospero and Caliban.* London: Methuen, 1964. Controversial psychohistorical analysis of settler and native reactions to their relationship.

MAY, E. *Imperial Democracy: The Emergence of America as a Great Power.* New York: Harcourt, Brace and World, 1961. Outline of America's surge to international prominence even before World War I.

OHLIN, B. *Interregional and International Trade.* Cambridge: Harvard University Press, 1935. The world market as shaped by the New Imperialism.

PURCELL, V. *The Boxer Uprising: A Background Study.* Cambridge: Cambridge University Press, 1963. Best book on the rebellion.

SCHORSKE, C. E. *Fin-de-Siecle Vienna: Politics and Culture.* New York: Knopf, 1980. A crucial time and place for the evolution of modern culture, subtly evoked and analyzed.

TANNENBAUM, E. R. *1900: The Generation before the Great War.* Garden City, N.Y.: Anchor Books, 1976. Well-illustrated book capturing the tenor of life on the eve of the "century of total war."

CHAPTER 39

WORLD WAR I

CAUSES OF THE FIRST WORLD WAR

Assassination at Sarajevo

Nationalism, Economics,
and Militarism

Imperial Rivalries

THE COURSE OF THE WAR

Leaders and Campaigns

Trench Warfare and Total War

European Colonies and the War

Non-European Powers and the War

CONSEQUENCES OF THE WAR TO END WAR

Casualties: Ten Million Dead

A Bad Peace and a Shaken Society

Growing Empires and New Powers

New Visions: The League of Nations

![wagon icon] CAUSES OF THE FIRST WORLD WAR

ASSASSINATION AT SARAJEVO

For many historians, the twentieth century began with two pistol shots on a sun-drenched, crowded street in the ancient Balkan city of Sarajevo. The man who pulled the trigger was a slightly built nineteen-year-old terrorist named Gavrilo Princip, an agent for a Slavic nationalist organization called Union or Death, popularly known as the Black Hand. The chief victim was the archduke Francis Ferdinand, heir to the throne of Austria-Hungary. The consequences of those two shots, fired on June 28, 1914, were the terrible guns of August, the beginning of the greatest war in human history up to that time.

Around that moment in Sarajevo—the excited crowds, the open cars approaching, the man with the plumed helmet and bemedaled chest, the woman in the wide summer hat—swirled a maelstrom of events, deeper causes, and incalculable consequences.

The Black Hand was centered in neighboring Serbia—the core of the postwar nation of Yugoslavia—and was dedicated to the unification of all Yugoslav ("South Slav") peoples into a Greater Serbia. The prime enemy of Slavic unity, as Serbian nationalists saw it, was the Austro-Hungarian Empire. Hence the choice of the Habsburg heir as a symbolic victim. Hence also Austria's violent response to this act of terrorism: accusation, ultimatum, and, a month after the assassination, declaration of war upon Serbia.

Bad news for little Serbia, whose government probably had no part in the crime, and whose dreams of becoming the Prussia of South Slav unification were thus drastically reversed. But worse news for Europe as a whole—and disturbing news for the world at large.

The great powers of Europe in 1914 were locked into two opposing alliances. These treaty obligations were in some cases several decades old. The main coalitions were the Central Powers, Germany and Austria, on the one hand, and the *Entente* ("Understanding") or simply the Allies, comprising primarily Great Britain, France, and Russia, on the other. Established to keep the peace or to defend the legitimate interests of the members, these rival alliances were now to prove a deadly snare, sucking one power after another into a widening war that would quickly engulf all Europe.

Thus Serbia had a patron among the great powers, the Russia of Nicholas II, which announced that it would mobilize in support of its little Slavic brother. Habsburg Austria's strongest ally, William II's Germany, gave Vienna a diplomatic blank check, promising support for whatever action the Austrians took against Serbia. Tension thus mounted through July.

Russia's ally—and Germany's archenemy—France meanwhile seized the opportunity to put diplomatic pressure on Berlin. Britain hesitated, hoping to exercise a moderating influence on the increasingly belligerent powers. But when Germany's elaborate war plans led German armies to violate Belgian neutrality on their way into France, London honored its commitments to the *Entente* and declared war on the Central Powers. The guns of August thundered over the Continent.

Bad news for Europe, but strange news also for a larger world that had become used to the monolithic granite face of European mastery. For the peoples of the globe were now about to see that pale, enigmatic effigy of the world-conquering West cracked and fissured by the greatest war in history.

Gavrilo Princip's Browning revolver put a bullet into the Duchess Sophy's stomach and blew a gouting hole in the side of Archduke Francis Ferdinand's neck. But the terrorist of Sarajevo did a great deal more than kill the unhappy royal pair. His were truly shots heard and felt around the world.

NATIONALISM, ECONOMICS, AND MILITARISM

As is usual with such historic disasters, there were deeper causes for World War I. Among those most often cited are rival nationalisms, economic competition, and militarism—what would later be called an arms race.

Nationalism, perhaps the most powerful of the nineteenth-century European ideologies, had turned chauvinistic in the latter part of the nineteenth century. French patriots dreamed of revenge on Germany for France's humiliating defeat in the Franco-Prussian War of 1870. Russian nationalists aspired to a pan-Slavic sphere in eastern Europe—dominated by Russia, of course. And the tan-

"*For Riezler there was no question of a rational principle which would allow or make desirable the peaceful coexistence of nations, large and small. He not only fell back on a Hobbesian philosophy of war of all against all, but he even proclaimed the theory that the eternal struggle—not for survival, but for world domination—was the supreme aim of all nations. Riezler went as far as to use the precise term for his wordy circumscription—"world domination"—as the supreme prize in the political struggle. . . . He pleaded for the supremacy of German Kultur in the world, endorsing the Kaiser's view that the world should one day be healed by German ideas and methods. Like Max Weber, Riezler saw in Germany's economic expansion the impulse to German Weltpolitik [global policy] and the basis for greater political expansion . . . , making Germany so powerful that, in the interest of her Weltpolitik, she would have the opportunities of victory in "any possible constellation," that she could deter any possible combination of all her adversaries and rivals in the world. . . . Thus, as a matter of fact, it was not an irrational fate which made war inevitable, but the German ideology, ill-disguised philosophically as the permanent struggle of all nations until the domination of the world was achieved by German Weltpolitik for the German Empire.*"

German revisionist historian Dr. Imanuel Geiss here revives the oldest Allied version of the origins of "the Kaiser's war" by asserting that German aggressiveness was the prime cause of World War I. Geiss's analysis, however, is much more subtle than the wartime nationalism that led the Allies to blame the Germans for the conflict.

Here the author outlines the views of an influential German advisor to the German government, the patriotic liberal writer Kurt Riezler. Riezler's convictions reflected the popular "social Darwinism" of the time, which saw history as a struggle among individuals, classes, and nations for "survival of the fittest." Do you see any truth in this theory? Do you see dangers in it? Can you suggest other forms of national competition besides war?

Imanuel Geiss, "The German Weltpolitik and Weltanschauung as a Cause of the War." In Brison D. Gooch, ed. Inter-preting European History, 2 vols. (Homewood, Ill.: Dorsey Press, 1967), Vol. 2, pp. 303–304.

gled and conflicting nationalisms of the Balkans—Magyar, Czech, Slovak, Serbian, Greek, and others—had already kindled two brief Balkan Wars (1912–1913) before World War I even began. National feeling was thus a Europe-wide problem; when the war began, people danced in the streets of Paris and Berlin, Vienna and St. Petersburg.

The central economic rivalry in Europe at the beginning of the twentieth century was the competition between Europe's two leading industrial powers, Great Britain and the German Empire. Britain had first developed the new industrial-power sources and forms of economic organization of the Industrial Revolution in the later eighteenth century. For a hundred years, "steam," as the popular

saying went, was "an Englishman." After the unification of Germany in 1871, however, that nation's already formidable industrial potential had flowered astonishingly. By the turn of the century, Germany's dynamic new industrial plant was pushing past Britain's now antiquated technology to lead Europe in production. Such competition bred bad blood and lent a note of practical national interest to the patriotic fervor of nationalists on both sides.

Militarism was a problem long before nuclear weapons made atomic-age weaponry the transcendent national issue it would become. The new technology and the new wealth of the Industrial Revolution made huge, mechanized military machines affordable even in peacetime. Large military expenditures were soon being built into national budgets, millions of young men conscripted into national armies to be prepared for war if war should come.

Militarism gave special prominence to military leaders—to Germany's famous General Staff, for example, or to admirals in Britain. Arms races also inevitably developed. The most famous of these was the rivalry in fleet construction between a Germany eager for a slice of overseas empire and a Britain determined to maintain its naval preeminence over any conceivable foe. "All this," as a prominent historian of the period pointed out half a century ago, "was done in the name of peace, for it was argued that the best insurance against war was national preparedness."[1] In the end, however, Napoleon's shrewd remark that you can do anything with bayonets except sit on them proved more to the point than slogans about preparedness.

IMPERIAL RIVALRIES

But there were still other sources of friction besides the fundamentally European conflicts created by alliances, nationalism, economic competition, and militarism. There was in addition a nexus of intercontinental issues created in large part by the colonial rivalries of the New Imperialism.

Some of the causes already cited were partially rooted in the renewed scramble for overseas territories after 1870. Chauvinistic nationalism fed on imperial conquest. Naval buildups were clearly related to establishing, maintaining, and defending empires beyond the seas.

Specifically, colonial disputes made alliances between imperial rivals such as Britain and France (in Africa and Southeast Asia) and Britain and Russia (in Persia and Afghanistan) particularly difficult. But more divisive imperial competition developed in the early twentieth century between powers on opposite sides in 1914, and these colonial rivalries help to explain the feuds that led to war.

Germany and Britain, for instance, faced significant areas of conflict in both Africa and the Middle East. Britain objected to Germany's rapid establishment of colonies in Southwest Africa (Namibia today) and especially in Tanganyika (Tanzania) in East Africa. The British were also made nervous by Germany's cultivation of the Ottoman Turkish sultan, seeing the German dream of a Berlin-to-Baghdad railway as a threat to Britain's lifeline to India at Suez. The British were especially incensed when William II sent an encouraging message to Britain's rebellious subjects in South Africa during the Boer War.

France's resentment of Germany, rooted in the Franco-Prussian War, was considerably exacerbated by German competition for Morocco. Disagreements over this remaining strip of North African coast produced the two Moroccan crises of 1905 and 1911. The French were

[1]F. Lee Benns, *European History since 1870* (New York: Appleton-Century-Crofts, 1938), p. 325.

also disturbed at the German development of a colony in the Cameroons, which thrust up into the solid block of French West Africa and French Equatorial Africa.

Germany, for its part, grew increasingly angry over these same conflicts. German imperialists and militarists felt that the sprawling British imperial presence blocked German expansion around the world. They believed that France's victory—with British support—in the two Moroccan crises, climaxing in a French protectorate over the area, represented signal diplomatic defeats for Germany. These setbacks would have to be compensated for at the next opportunity.

Czarist Russia, the great power of eastern Europe, also had its share of frustrated imperial aspirations. Russia's ambitions to take control of the Turkish straits from the enfeebled Ottomans was of long standing. Russia felt an increasing need to control the entrance to the Black Sea, where lay Russia's only seaports not closed by ice for a large part of the year. Here, however, Russia's ambitions conflicted with Germany's hopes for German predominance in Turkey.

The Balkan tinderbox itself was part of this larger, extra-European picture. The Balkans and the tensions that divided them were after all part of the legacy left by the decay of the once glorious Ottoman Empire. Russia's support of these new Slavic nations against their old Muslim overlord intensified the feeling that led Turkey to join the Germans and the Austrians in what was then called the Great War.

Conflicts south of the Mediterranean and east of Suez thus played their part in bringing on World War I. These areas, and regions still farther afield, would be importantly involved in the war itself. And the world as a whole would be vitally affected by what Woodrow Wilson would hail as the War to End War.

 # THE COURSE OF THE WAR

LEADERS AND CAMPAIGNS

The world has supped so full of horrors in this century that the "frightfulness" of the War of 1914–1918 may no longer shake us as it shook the generations who fought the Great War. It is perhaps hard for people who have grown used to the notion of a nuclear holocaust to empathize with a time that could still see submarine warfare as cowardly piracy and machine guns and barbed wire as atrocities. We have gotten used to the grisly photographs of no-man's-land, and to disturbing verses written by young men who would soon become part of some forgotten battlefield.

As for the impact of the Great War on the world—the very phrase Lost Generation has become a cliché, and the Peace of Versailles has no more resonance than the Congress of Vienna. Nevertheless, an effort must be made to bring both the war and its consequences back to life. Both have left their marks upon all our lives.

The leaders were as varied a lot as the nations they led. The Allies were for the most part the democracies: Britain under the charismatic Welsh reformer David Lloyd George; France under the belligerently nationalistic Georges Clemenceau, sometimes called the Tiger; and the United States under the preacher's son turned Progressive reformer, Woodrow Wilson. But the Allies also included Russia, the most unrelentingly autocratic of the powers, under Nicholas II, and imperialistic Japan, thrusting its way to prominence in the Far East.

The key leaders of the Central Powers in 1914 were thorough autocrats but were otherwise totally different. William II, the German emperor, was an aggressive expansionist who liked to pose, moustache bristling, going over war maps with his generals. Aged Francis Joseph, the Austro-Hungarian emperor, was so opposed to war that he had to be tricked into signing the declaration of war against Serbia by a fake telegram reporting a Serbian invasion.

A traditional way to approach the war these men made is in terms of the great offensives that marked the coming of each new year. A list of some of the more famous of them may stir faint echoes of forgotten heroism. For there was heroism amid the horrors of the Great War.

In 1914, for instance, there was a race to Paris as a new generation of Germans strove to emulate their grandfathers' quick victory in 1870—and failed. This was followed by a race to the sea, French and Germans striving to outflank each other until they reached the English Channel and could go no farther. There was the Gallipoli campaign of 1915, aimed at opening the Turkish straits into the Black Sea—the very name a symbol for futile loss of life.

There was the great German offensive at Verdun in 1916, when Frenchmen fell in unthinkable numbers for the ringing watchword "They shall not pass"—and the Germans did not. There was the colossal British offensive on the Somme, also in 1916, weeks of carnage that began with so many tens of thousands of British casualties in a twenty-four-hour period that it has been described as the blackest day in the history of the British army. There was Caporetto in 1917, the debacle on the Italian front that was Hemingway's *Farewell to Arms*. There was the last great heave of the Kerensky offensive in Russia, again in 1917, which turned beaten Russian soldiers against their own officers, and against the politicians who had sent them off to the front once more.

After such offensives, all sides were exhausted and reeling by 1917. There were mutterings of peace in Austria and even in Germany. There were riots in Italian munitions factories, mutinies in ten divisions of the French army, and revolution in Russia. But 1917 was also a year of startling reversals and renewed hope for both sides, and these developments built toward the climactic battles of 1918.

A British naval blockade, imposed from the beginning of the war, led Germany to respond with something new—a massive submarine campaign against all shipping attempting to reach the British Isles. Both the blockade and the submarine campaign were having their effect by 1917. But the undersea war had an unfortunate side effect: it so outraged neutrals trying to trade with Britain that in 1917 it led Woodrow Wilson to bring the United States

Women at war. These members of Britain's Women's Auxilliary Army Corps (WAAC) served as military drivers in World War I, the first conflict to make significant use of the automobile. Here they pose in uniform with one of the vehicles they drove for the British forces in France. As WAACs, as army nurses, and as war workers on the home front, women played an important part in the Great War. (The Illustrated London News Picture Library)

(a)

(b)

At the left, French tanks roar toward the front, "eager to strike a blow at the foe." At the right, a shattered tank lies in the mud near Cambrai. Intrigued wartime readers had to have the mechanism of the new weapon explained to them, including "the wide caterpillar tread which . . . ran over the . . . sprocket wheel [and] laid itself down as an ever-renewing road for the monster above" and "the turret from which a deadly fire was directed upon the enemy." But a German shell had broken the sprocket and the tread, leaving the tank a "stationary target" to be destroyed. (Keystone View Co. of N.Y.)

into the war on the Allied side—a major setback to German hopes of victory.

This pivotal year, however, also saw the abdication of the Russian czar, the subsequent seizure of power by the Bolsheviks, and their decision to pull battered Russia out of the war unilaterally. Thus if the Central Powers faced the long-run threat of huge American reinforcements, in the short run Germany could all but close down its eastern front and concentrate its forces for crushing offensives in the west.

This Generals Hindenburg and Ludendorff tried to do in the summer of 1918. Three mighty German assaults hurled the Allies back dozens of miles and came as close to breaking through to Paris as Germany ever came. But France's Marshal Foch, enjoying for the first time a unified supreme command of the Allied armies, and reinforced by waves of fresh American troops, stemmed the German tide. As a cold, wet autumn settled over Europe, the war ground to a halt. An armistice was declared on November 11, 1918. The biggest, bloodiest, and, as it increasingly seemed to contemporaries, most pointless war in the history of the world was over.

TRENCH WARFARE AND TOTAL WAR

An analysis in terms of leaders and campaigns is traditional for great wars. But it is probably not the best approach to this one.

Studies of World War I have generally recognized it as a war of position rather than a war of movement. In military terms, it was a war in which defensive capabilities outperformed offensive ones, so that neither side could achieve significant breakthroughs. In human terms, the result was trench warfare: four dehumanizing years of living and dying half buried in the earth, wet, cold, frightened, and bombarded by the most barbarically ingenious combinations of metal and chemicals the Western mind could invent.

This description applies best to the western front in France. Here the trench lines stretched from Switzerland to the English Channel and moved scarcely at all between late 1914 and early 1918. On the eastern front in Russia, the lines typically swayed back and forth, enormous Russian drives bogging down in a sea of casualties and finally reeling backward in defeat. In northern Italy too—after Italy joined the Allied cause in 1915—advances by one side were likely to be followed by regrouping and successful counterattacks by the other.

Everywhere, the machinery of modern warfare made its true potential felt for the first time in Europe. New weapons were flung into the fray one after another in hopes of achieving a breakthrough: submarines, tanks, airplanes, poison gas. But the most brutally efficient killers were the staples: repeating rifles, barbed wire and machine guns, artillery capable of lobbing explosive shells for miles and burying whole trenches full of soldiers when they hit. The "sacrifices" that patriotic orators liked to make speeches about were, as American novelist Ernest Hemingway put it, "like the stockyards at Chicago if nothing was done with the meat except to bury it."[2] The war was a meat grinder, reducing generations of European youth to hamburger in the mud of Flanders fields.

The other great fact about the war was that it involved national commitment to an extent seldom even approached before. To keep millions of men fed, clothed, armed, and supplied with munitions sufficient for four years of firing at each other over hundreds of miles of front lines required an unparalleled effort by the populations involved. World War I thus became the first total war in history.

Governments took control of national economies as they had never dared do in peacetime. Government boards allocated raw materials, controlled transportation, regulated wages and prices, rationed food and other essentials. All able-bodied males were liable for conscription into the armed services.

Many women went into the war plants to produce the shells and guns their husbands and sons would use. Almost a million English women worked in munitions factories, and well over half a million French women. Others replaced men drafted for the war in other facto-

ries, on farms, as railway conducters, milk deliverers, and in many other jobs.

New taxes, war loans, and a massive increase in the national debt of the warring countries were additional costs. A continual drain of food, fuel, clothing, and other essentials from the home front also resulted. Russians froze through icy northern winters, Germans went hungry, Austrians starved. Total war thus ravaged European economies even as it strengthened European governments.

This total mobilization of all the resources of great modern states was in its way as striking a feature of the Great War as the raking machine-gun fire and billowing clouds of mustard gas that turned European battlefields into no-man's-lands. And it would leave as long a legacy in battered economies and in governments with newfound powers.

EUROPEAN COLONIES AND THE WAR

"World War I," one historian of the great debacle has written, "was really a vast global enterprise—Europe became an enormous cauldron into which men and resources from Asia, Africa, and America were poured."[3] The war was, in fact, also fought outside of Europe, by peoples from other

---

[2]Ernest Hemingway, *A Farewell to Arms* (New York: Scribner's, 1957), p. 185.

[3]Jack C. Roth, *World War I: Turning Point in Modern History: Essays on the Significance of the War* (New York: Alfred A. Knopf, 1967), p. 105.

(a)   (b)

No-man's-land, the endless miles of shell-torn, blood-soaked earth between the armies. On the left, "No Man's Land Near Lens, France," where "hardly an inch of ground has not been blasted over and over again by explosive shells." On the right, "Germans Dead in the La Basse Area," where "the dead lay thick, bodies without heads, without arms or legs, human flesh plastered by the explosions of shells against and actually into the walls [of the trenches.] The dead lay for days, decomposing under the feet of the living." (Keystone View Co. of N.Y.)

War production booms. The industrialized nations of the West turned their formidable energies to manufacturing immense quantities of rifles and artillery, bullets and shells, helmets, gas masks, tanks, planes, warships—the hardware that made the War to End War the bloodiest in human history. Here women munitions workers move casually through endless rows of shells, their fuses still in place, which will soon be on their way to the battle fronts of Europe. (Imperial War Museum, London)

parts of the globe, and involved extra-European ambitions, resources, and conflicts that had little to do with an assassination at Sarajevo. These larger dimensions of the Great War must be surveyed briefly if the worldwide impact of the struggle is to be understood.

Global involvement in World War I took several forms. Germany had colonies, which of course became targets for the Allies, who controlled the oceans of the world. The Allies also drew upon their own overseas empires for military and support personnel. And important powers from as far away as the Middle East, the Far East, and North America became directly involved in the conflict. World War I thus deserves its global label.

German colonies in East Asia, Oceania, and Africa were cut off from German reinforcement or support by British sea power, and most of them fell easily. The easternmost of the Allies, Japan, laid siege to Germany's base on the Shandong Peninsula of North China and soon captured it. British colonial forces from Australia and New Zealand rolled up German island holdings in Oceania. The Boers, who had fought Britain so recently, now led the imperial forces that overran German Southwest Africa, and Anglo-French colonial troops took Germany's West African possessions. Only in East Africa, in Tanganyika, did a skillful and prolonged German defense require years of fighting before a German colony was yielded to the Allies—in this case, Britain.

The European Allies, meanwhile, drew heavily upon their own overseas possessions to augment their forces in Europe. Large numbers of Indian troops fought in the British lines on the western front, and many Africans served in French armies. Both Chinese and Indochinese coolie labor worked behind the Allied lines in Europe in support of the war effort. The bloody Gallipoli campaign to open the Turkish straits was carried out almost entirely by Australian, New Zealand, Indian, and French colonial troops. Indian units also performed yeoman service for the British elsewhere in the Middle East.

The Germans thus lost their empire in the Great War. The British and the French, by contrast, profited immensely from theirs. Either way, colonial peoples far from Europe were significantly affected.

Non-European Powers and the War

Besides these imperial contributions, the war drew in a number of independent non-European powers. Of these, Turkey, Japan, and the United States were the most importantly involved.

Germany's great influence in Istanbul and the long rivalry between the Ottoman Empire and Romanov Russia brought Turkey into the war on the side of the Central Powers in 1914. It was a disastrous miscalculation for the Ottomans. Turkish troops held heroically at Gallipoli. But British soldiers and rebellious Arab sheiks—urged on by the romantic British agent Lawrence of Arabia—chewed into the Ottoman Empire from the south. By war's end, this Middle Eastern campaign had detached large sections of Arabia, Palestine, and Mesopotomia from the dwindling Ottoman domain.

Japan also entered the war—on the Allied side—in 1914, and much more successfully than Turkey. The

Japanese shrewdly exploited Allied support and European preoccupation on the other side of the world to advance their own imperial interests in the Far East, above all in China. After seizing Germany's bases in Shandong and on a Pacific island or two, Japan turned its attention to pressuring the new Chinese republic—established in 1911—into accepting what amounted to protectorate status under Japan. The Twenty-one Demands of 1915, which embodied this claim to imperial suzerainty, had little to do with the war, but they would be the basis for continuing Japanese pressure on China for decades to come.

The United States was the last and most important of the major extra-European participants to enter World War I. The United States had insisted on neutrality through the early years of the war, though Americans sold huge quantities of essential supplies to the Allied side. It was Germany's unrestricted submarine war on shipping destined for Allied shores, along with other manifestations of German resentment, that impelled President Wilson to declare war in 1917.

It was not till the spring and summer of 1918 that a significant number of American troops could be thrown into the struggle. They came at a propitious time, however, to help stem the climactic German offensives of 1918. And as the Germans slowly retreated that last fall of the war, the continuing arrival of fresh American troops undoubtedly helped to convince the German high command that the war was lost.

A famous cartoon of the time showed American doughboys debarking in France with the inspiring remark, "Lafayette, we are here!" There is little warrant for the notion that the United States was repaying a debt of honor that went back to the Revolutionary War when American armies went to Europe in 1918. If it was not a significant echo of the past, however, that first dispatch of U.S. troops to western Europe was certainly a harbinger of things to come. American soldiers would be back for World War II and again for the Cold War. World War I thus saw the beginning of a U.S. military involvement in Europe that would last for most of the rest of the century.

CONSEQUENCES OF THE WAR TO END WAR

CASUALTIES: TEN MILLION DEAD

A German slogan in the Great War has a resonance of the Crusades of a simpler age: *Gott mit Uns*—God Is on Our Side. For their part, the Allies unleashed a flood of propaganda charging that the Central Powers were twentieth-century barbarians—the Hun come again to Europe—and claiming that the Allied struggle was a war to save civilization. Woodrow Wilson, widely hailed in war-weary Europe as a savior from beyond the seas, called it a "war to make the world safe for democracy" and even "the war to end war."

In the outcome, the Great War scarcely seemed to reflect any divine intent, did not make the world safe for either civilization or democracy, and certainly did not put an end to war. It did, however, have significant consequences, on both a European and a global level.

One thing the war produced on an awesome scale, of course, was casualties. At least ten million men in uniform were shot, bayonetted, poisoned, or blown to pieces, and perhaps half that many noncombatants died in the war zones. Millions more were hurt but not killed: Europe after the war was full of walking wounded—armless, legless, blinded, or broken-spirited men who could never seem to get their lives together again.

The figures are numbing. During the worst periods of the war, for instance, the Russians took a quarter of a million casualties *a month*. The casualties in the battle of Verdun alone reached three quarters of a million; in the battle of the Somme they ran well over a million. Whole school classes of English, French, German, and other young men marched off to the front en masse. There, according to one eyewitness, they could look forward to about three more months of life. Statistics like these have shaped the twentieth century's attitude toward one of the most common of human occupations—the making of war—from that day to this.

A BAD PEACE AND A SHAKEN SOCIETY

Efforts to estimate the further impact of the war on Europe alone fill volumes. Diplomatically, politically, economically, and in many other ways, the Great War left a smoldering scar across the continent.

Perhaps most obvious, the map of Europe was significantly altered by the war and by the peace the Allies imposed. All three of the great central and eastern European autocracies that began the war were gone by the end of it, the Romanovs overthrown by revolution in 1917, the Hohenzollerns and the Habsburgs toppled in 1918. Communists clung to power in Russia, and fledgling republics struggled to be born in Germany and Austria as the victorious Allies met in Paris to dictate peace terms. The peace treaties further modified the political map, recognizing the fragmentation of the Austro-Hungarian Empire and the independence of several minority nationalities who had seceded from the collapsing czarist Russian Empire. The result was a band of new or enlarged eastern European countries running from the Baltic Sea through Poland to the Balkans.

The terms imposed upon Germany by the Treaty of Versailles in 1919 left a bitter political legacy. Worked out in detail by platoons of technical experts, this and the other peace treaties, each dealing with a separate Central Power, reflected uneasy compromises among the three principal Allied war leaders: France's vengeful

WORLD WAR I AND THE TERRITORIAL RESTRUCTURING OF EUROPE, 1914–1926

Legend:

— Political boundaries, 1914
— Boundaries of 1926
----- Boundary between Austria and Hungary
----- Greatest advance by Central Powers
••••• Greatest advance by Allies
✦ Battle sites

Allied and Associated Powers
Central Powers and their allies
Neutrals
Allied Occupation Zone (Rhineland)
Demilitarized areas (Rhineland, "The Straits")

Clemenceau, Britain's pragmatic Lloyd George, and the perhaps unrealistically idealistic President Wilson. Most important, however, the Versailles Treaty reflected the determination of the British and the French to destroy the German power that had held all Europe in awe since Germany's unification half a century before.

The Versailles peace thus required Germany to acknowledge its "war guilt" publicly and imposed fantastic reparations, by which Germany was to pay for the war it had allegedly caused. The treaty compelled Germany to disarm so thoroughly that it would never again be a threat to its neighbors, stripped it of its overseas colonies, and generally strove to reduce the new German

republic to a second- or third-class power. The Germans signed because they had to, seething inwardly at the injustice of the dictated peace. If the Allies had set out to provide Hitler with a list of causes upon which to build his political career, they could not have done a better job.

More subtle social and economic changes also resulted from the war—not all of them as unpromising for the future as the diplomatic and political consequences sketched above.

Economically, the greatest change was that Europe was left deeply in debt. European investment capital had helped start other nations on the road to industrial development, so that much of the world was in Europe's debt in 1914. The enormous costs of the war, however, had absorbed all this foreign credit and had forced the combatants to borrow huge sums in their turn, particularly in the United States, to pay for supplies and war material. The Allies' war debts were, in fact, impossible to pay, like the reparations imposed on the Central Powers, and the two would contribute to the disastrous economic fluctuations of the interwar period.

Some social groups, though, had done well because of the war. Skilled workers had earned good wages in defense plants. Women had taken a big step toward more flexible patterns of life through their work in war industries. In some places, as in England, women had been widely admired for their war service—British women got the vote on the strength of it.

Aristocrats and middle-class people in general, however, came out of the Great War shaken in status and self-confidence. Hailed as the pillars of the prewar social order, these groups were now widely blamed for the war and all its horrors. The postwar militance of working-class people, plus the menacing power of the newly established Communist Russian power to the east, made many in Europe's ruling classes wonder how long their supremacy might last.

GROWING EMPIRES AND NEW POWERS

In the world at large, however, World War I unleashed some wild new dreams indeed. There were new powers moving in the larger world after 1919, new aspirations and new institutions with a genuinely global focus. They were signposts toward a future that would have astonished the most prescient thinker only a few years before.

Expanded empires and emergent world powers were among the more striking larger consequences of the Great War. The peace settlements provided for yet more European protectorates and for colonial possessions enlarged by colonies confiscated from Germany in Africa and the Far East, and from the lands of the rebellious Arab princes of the former Ottoman Empire. Britain got Tanganyika; France acquired German West Africa; the Republic of South Africa received German Southwest Africa; and Japan got Shandong. The modern Middle East—with the crucial exception of Israel—came into being at this time, its southern tier of Arab states from Iraq through Syria and Lebanon to Palestine mostly under the control of Britain or France.

Even in this apparent display of imperial business-as-usual, however, there were differences. The new territories were not taken as of right, in the old way, but mandated to the care of European powers by a new international organization called the League of Nations. Some of these territories, at least, were intended for ultimate independence once they had been adequately "developed." The League at least seemed to be taking seriously some of the more idealistic New Imperialist rhetoric about civilizing missions and grooming for independence.

There was more than rhetoric that was new after 1919, however. Three rising world powers shouldered their way further into the international arena in the aftermath of the war. All three were influenced by Europe, and one was half European geographically, but all were part of an emerging global challenge to the established European hegemony of the world.

Japan, as noted above, had used the war to further advance its imperial ambitions in the Far East. The Japanese had seized Germany's Chinese holdings and after the war refused to return them to China. Japan's Twenty-one Demands on China, requiring changes in that nation's government and policies that, if accepted, would have made China virtually a Japanese protectorate, did in fact gain some reluctant acceptance from Chinese officials. Japan used this measure of acquiescence as the basis for further aggression against China during the interwar years.

Militarily powerful and victorious in three consecutive wars—two of them involving European nations—Japan was also East Asia's most successful trading and manufacturing nation. By 1919 Japan had thus established the trajectory that would determine its rise to greatness over the rest of the century.

The new Union of Soviet Socialist Republics—still "Russia" to most people—looked much less like a winner in 1919. But the Soviet Union also had an astonishing future ahead of it.

Russia's non-European dimension—three quarters of its territory and much of its population were Asian—had been noted long before the twentieth century. The Bolshevik Revolution, however, put the country in the hands of militant ideological enemies of much that the rest of Europe stood for, from capitalism and democracy to imperial hegemony. The Russia of 1919, still bleeding from World War I, now swept by civil strife, seemed little threat to European predominance. But Joseph Stalin was already prowling in the wings, and the willingness of the Russian Communists to use government power ruthlessly to build up the nation was already amply demonstrated. The Soviet Union too would play a global role in the emerging century.

The United States, finally, stepped definitively onto the stage of world history in World War I. Any attempts to hastily step off again would prove impossible.

The richest nation in the world by the turn of the century, the United States emerged even richer from the war, thanks to European borrowing and to booming American war industries. The United States had also demonstrated in 1917 and 1918 that it could commit its youth to a major war if the nation's interests and ideals were involved. America's President Wilson, whose idealistic Fourteen Points aimed to settle all the world's problems, was for a time hailed as a Messiah on both sides of the Atlantic.

Unaccountably to many, however, the United States drew back from the role thus thrust upon it in 1919. America refused even to join the League of Nations—Wilson's brainchild—and withdrew into fastidious isolation from the difficulties of the rest of the world. It would take another great war to propel the United States to the position of world leadership it would occupy during the second half of the century. But that direction too was laid down by the war of 1914–1918 and by America's part in it.

New Visions: The League of Nations

There was, finally, a powerfully felt and growing hope for a larger and more just world order in 1919—one no longer dominated by European intercontinental empires.

Indians and Africans who had fought in Europe and Chinese and Southeast Asians who had served behind the lines went home with an image of the all-conquering Europeans that was rather different from the one they had once had. Woodrow Wilson's talk of "national self-determination of peoples," which had created the new nations of eastern Europe, seemed equally applicable to the colonies of Asia and Africa. V. I. Lenin's revolutionary charge that imperialism was a stage in the evolution of capitalist oppression had a great appeal to Westernized

Asians particularly, as did his call for worldwide revolt. A ferment of new visions and new ideas, none of them conducive to continuing European predominance, was thus abroad in the world after the war.

Most impressive, perhaps, the peace conference at Paris, inspired and urged by Wilson, created a new international forum for such global aspirations: the League of Nations. Even after the United States rejected its own president's dream, the League seemed to point to a different worldwide order. Its Council of permanent and rotating members was empowered to plan for world peace and an end to aggression, by European empire-builders as well as by others. Its Assembly gave equal voting strength to all the nations of the world—and most of them were not European. The League of Nations was affiliated with other global organizations, such as the World Court, which also seemed a sign of things to come.

The League had little actual power and would founder after two difficult decades of existence. But it was a beginning, at least, toward recognition of a global system that could conceivably transcend even the interests of the great powers, European or otherwise.

The heritage of the worst of wars thus far was therefore not all danger and depression. The new powers, new visions, new institutions unleashed by that unprecedented conflict pointed down the generations to a wholly unexpected future for the world.

Summary

World War I was triggered by the assassination of the heir to the Austrian throne by a Balkan terrorist. Larger causes, however, turned this local conflict into a global catastrophe. These deeper causes included entangling diplomatic alliances, nationalistic passions, economic competition, and massive military build-ups. Imperial rivalries also helped to create the conflicts of interest and the international tensions that led to World War I.

The Great War, as it was called, was the bloodiest in the history of the world up to that time. Major offensives by both the Allies—Britain, France, Russia, Italy, and later the United States—and the Central Powers—Germany and Austria—repeatedly failed. Trench warfare—a war of position featuring a horrifying array of new weapons, from planes and submarines to machine guns and poison gas—slaughtered millions in a four-year war of attrition. Total commitment was also required on the home front, where governments gained new powers, and economies were drained in the long struggle.

The war also involved non-European peoples. The German colonies overseas were lost, and the British and French colonies participated in the war. Turkey, Japan, and the United States also entered the war, the last two gaining significant imperial and economic benefits from their part in the struggle.

The results of World War I included 10 million dead and many millions more maimed or mentally shattered. Governments were toppled in Germany, Austria, and Russia, and resentments were kindled, especially among the Germans, that would have long-range repercussions. Economies were destabilized by Europe's immense war debts. Middle-class self-confidence was shaken, and the class conflicts seem to have intensified.

On the international scene, the British and French empires were strengthened, and the United States, the Soviet Union, and Japan emerged as world leaders. Perhaps most striking, the League of Nations was created—the first political organization to seek genuinely global participation, and a symbol at least of the growing globalization of history.

SUGGESTED READING

BAILEY, T. A. *Woodrow Wilson and the Lost Peace.* Chicago: Quadrangle Books, 1963. Wilson, Versailles, and the peace that paved the way for the next great war.

BALDWIN, H. *World War One.* New York: Harper & Row, Pub., 1962. Military history by a distinguished military analyst.

FALLS, C. B. *The Great War.* New York: Putnam, 1959. Well-constructed presentation by a gifted military historian.

FELDMAN, G. D. *The Army, Industry, and Labor in Germany, 1914–1918.* Princeton: Princeton University Press, 1966. The impact of total war on basic institutions on the home front. See in this connection M. Ferro, *The Great War, 1914–1918* (London: Routledge & Kegan Paul, 1973), stressing social and economic elements.

FUSSELL, P. *The Great War and Modern Memory.* New York: Oxford University Press, 1977. The literary image of World War I and its impact on modern consciousness.

GILBERT, F. *The End of the European Era, 1890 to the Present.* New York: W. W. Norton, 1979. Broad and detailed assertion of the view that European centrality in the world was destroyed by World War I. See also E. Fischer, *The Passing of the European Age* (Cambridge: Harvard University Press, 1943).

HORNE, A. *The Price of Glory: Verdun, 1916.* London: Penguin, 1979. Detailed account of one of the great offensives that failed.

KEEGAN, J. *The Face of Battle.* New York: Vintage Press, 1977. Contains vivid descriptions of combat at Agincourt, Waterloo, and the Somme in World War I.

LAFORE, L. *The Long Fuse: An Interpretation of the Origins of World War I.* New York: Harper & Row, Pub., 1971. The causal chain, reaching back into the nineteenth century, that led to the first total war of the twentieth.

MARWICK, A. *War and Social Change in the Twentieth Century: A Comparative Study of Britain, France, Germany, Russia and the United States.* New York: St. Martin's Press, 1975. The transforming effect of both world wars on modern societies. See also J. Williams, *The Home Fronts: Britain, France, and Germany, 1914–1918* (London: Constable, 1972).

NICOLSON, H. *Peacemaking 1919.* Boston: Houghton Mifflin, 1933. A diplomatic history of Versailles by an expert.

REMARQUE, E. M. *All Quiet on the Western Front,* trans. A. W. Wheen. New York: Fawcett Crest, 1958. Vivid fictional evocation of trench warfare.

TUCHMAN, B. *The Guns of August.* New York: Macmillan, 1962. Moving narrative of the coming of the war.

WOHL, R. *The Generation of 1914.* Cambridge: Harvard University Press, 1979. The ideas and attitudes of the generations that survived the war in Europe.

CHAPTER 40

THE WEST BETWEEN THE WARS

TRENDS OF THE TWENTIES AND THIRTIES

FLAPPERS AND FELLAHIN

The stillness that settled over the battlefields of the Great War in November of 1918 triggered a variety of responses around the world. There was exultation in the streets of victorious nations, bitterness among the losers, dull indifference in the eyes of the maimed, the shell-shocked, the walking wounded. On one thing, however, there was general agreement: it was a different world after the war.

In the United States a new freedom emerged in the 1920s, projecting a vivid image of bobbed hair and short skirts, bathtub gin and wailing saxophones. In Europe young moderns got their new dances from across the Atlantic and daringly crossed the Channel by airplane. Older people imitated younger ones, and everybody seemed to drive fast cars.

This is an essentially middle-class image of the age, of course: Kansas farmers, Sicilian peasants, blue-collar workers at Ford's or Krupp's had no cars and would never fly in an airplane. But the prosperous bourgeoisie was the heart of Western society still, their lifestyle glorified in magazines and films and admired by many who could not afford to share it. Their image reflects the ideal and much of the reality of the glossy new world of the West after the war.

Most of the rest of the world evidently did not share in this era of automobiles and airplanes that gave a hard-edged new meaning to that overworked adjective *modern*. As we have seen, there were shiny modern cities in South America, but Indians were still making pre-Columbian pottery in the jungles. Modern metropolises were emerging in Africa and the Middle East, but many Arabs were bedouin still, and village Africa was almost entirely intact south of the Sahara. People in Western business suits still swayed along in rickshas in Singapore and Shanghai, and Tokyo's handful of new earthquake-proof skyscrapers towered over a city of bamboo and paper. Yet change would come to these seemingly changeless regions too, just as it did to the Western world, between World Wars I and II.

It will take three chapters to survey the startling, sometimes horrifying trends of the 1920s and 1930s. The sections immediately following will outline the events of the Jazz Age and the Depression decade in the West. The next two chapters will deal with special features of the period in various parts of the globe: with the great revolutions that shook Russia, China, and other nations, and with the development of new forms of dictatorship in Germany, Japan, and elsewhere.

A typical American flapper might glory in change and newness, in art-deco modernity for its own sake. Egyptian *fellahin* laboring in the black earth along the Nile, as their ancestors had done since the beginning of history, might never have heard of the modern world at all. But time and change—not always for the better—would come to both of them between that stillness on the November battlefields of 1918 and the roar of Stukas rising into the dawn of September 1, 1939.

THE WORLD ECONOMY IN TROUBLE

It is hard to find two decades that seem to contrast more strikingly than the 1920s and the 1930s. The twenties were frivolity and fun; the thirties were a decade of agonizing social concerns, of taking stands and building brave new worlds. Most vividly, the twenties seem to mean prosperity, boom times; the thirties brought the Great Depression, the biggest economic bust in modern Western history.

On the economic side, however, the contrast seems in fact to have been rather less striking. This is particularly so when the two decades are examined from a global perspective.

The world as a whole seems to have suffered in the 1920s from a vast overproduction, a wartime buildup that could not find peacetime demand to sustain it. Commodity producers in Latin America and in the European colonies of Africa and Asia thus suffered from declining prices through much of the twenties. So did farmers in the United States, coal miners in Britain, and other primary producers within the West.

There were other economic problems as well. There was a postwar depression as hordes of demobilized soldiers swarmed into a job market that was already shrinking because of the end of wartime demand. Inflation soon followed in some parts of Europe, devouring the savings of middle-class citizens in Germany particularly.

Even the apparent prosperity of much of the population of the United States, Europe, and other Westernized

Ford motor cars, symbol of the new affluence of the 1920s, were produced by assembly-line methods that put them within reach of Americans of relatively modest means. On Ford's movable assembly line, the chassis of a car like this required only two man-hours of work to produce. Automobiles, however, were still something of a status symbol, as the house in the background of this picture indicates. (The Bettmann Archive)

lands such as Australia and Canada had an unreal quality about it. The United States, the world's most productive nation before the war, now its foremost trader and exporter of capital as well, was actually responsible for much of the apparent economic health elsewhere. The profits of booming American business, widely available to bolster flagging economies across the West, maintained a material well-being that was in large part artificial.

The central international role of the United States was illustrated most importantly in the nagging problems of reparations and war debt that haunted the twenties.

World War I had left even such prewar economic giants as Great Britain deeply in debt to the United States. To pay these war debts, all the Allies depended on the reparations payments from Germany prescribed by the Treaty of Versailles. But Germany, hard hit by the Great War, the inflation of the 1920s, the French occupation of the industrial Ruhr, and other problems, simply could not meet its reparations payments. To handle these obligations, Germany therefore borrowed heavily—from the United States.

Money thus flowed ponderously in a great circle, from the United States to Germany as loans, to the Allies as reparations, and thence back to the United States as war debts. It was a dubious procedure at best. When the American economy began to stagger, it would bring the economies of much of the world down in ruins.

The prosperity of the 1920s has thus been exaggerated in modern memory. The economic misery of the 1930s scarcely could be.

The world depression of 1929–1939 began with the collapse of the American stock market and was sustained by the long years of American economic paralysis that followed. American financiers, hard hit at home, soon cut back on their loans to Europe, putting the fragile structure of European prosperity also under pressure. The failure of Austria's central bank two years after the Wall Street crash triggered a similar wave of economic disaster across the continent. As the depression deepened all across the West, finally, the commodity producers of the rest of the world began to feel the effects of the new poverty of their best customers. Prices of agricultural goods and raw materials, weak through the twenties, spiraled downward in the thirties. By the middle of that bleak decade, much of the world was thus locked in the grip of the Great Depression.

Political and economic leaders tried many expedients during the 1930s to reverse the spiral, prime the pump, get the laws of supply and demand working once more. In the end, paradoxically, it would take another world war to create sufficient demand to get the world economy moving again. In the meantime, as we will see below, the political and social repercussions of the Great Depression were felt all across the Western World.

TECHNOLOGY IN THE AGE OF FORD

Economic dislocation was thus a continuing feature of Western history between the wars, rather than a characteristic of the 1930s only. There were other areas also in which main trends carried on through these two apparently contrasting decades. One crucial aspect of Western life in which change would continue throughout the entire century was technological advance.

In every area, from industrial production, transportation, and communication to modern entertainment, the West and selected areas of the rest of the globe felt the impact of technological change throughout the 1920s and 1930s. The United States had become the recognized leader in many fields of technological development by this time, but the major nations of Europe were not far behind.

The rise of the twentieth century's two main sources of industrial energy, hydroelectric power and petroleum, had actually begun around the turn of the century. Electric lighting and electric railway trains were common in the West by the twenties and thirties. Petroleum production, which had been only 20 million tons at the turn of the century, reached a quarter of a billion tons by the end of the thirties. Refined petroleum products powered ships, automobiles, and airplanes throughout the interwar years.

Technological improvement included key developments in both heavy industry and large-scale agriculture. The industrial assembly line, pioneered by Henry Ford, the American automobile manufacturer, was soon speeding up production in many other industries as well. In agriculture these decades were the age of the tractor. In the United States there were 160,000 tractors already at work in the fields in 1919; by 1939 there were a million and a half of them.

The central innovation in transportation during the twenties and thirties was, of course, the automobile. In Britain the number of cars in use multiplied twelve times between 1923 and 1938; in France, twenty times. And in the United States, forty times as many people had cars—almost 50 million of them—by the end of the 1930s as in the early 1920s, in spite of the depression. Railways remained important, airplanes rare except for military purposes. But the car was king of the road, retiring the working horse in city after city across the West after thousands of years of faithful service to humankind.

Communications, revolutionized by the telegraph in the nineteenth century, was revolutionized again by the telephone in the early part of the twentieth. But it was in the mass media of communications that the interwar decades saw major breakthroughs, particularly in the development of radio and film. Before World War I, radio was used primarily between ships at sea, where wireless communication was essential, and "moving pictures" were little more than an arcade game. Between 1920 and 1940, tens of millions of radio sets came into use in homes across America and Europe, and gaudy art-deco movie theaters blossomed in every city.

The impact of the automobile on the social life of the West, of the telephone on business and government, of radio and film on popular culture as well as in the hands of a Hitler or a Franklin Roosevelt is almost incalcula-

These victims of the Great Depression might as easily be British or German as Americans. Even solid American family men were reduced to free food at public soup kitchens during the dark days of the global economic collapse. What do you see in the faces of these men? Can you imagine one of them driving the Ford car shown in an earlier picture in this chapter? (AP/Wide World Photos)

"*By the 1920s it had become clear that in most industrial countries the proportion of women workers relative to numbers of women in their populations was stagnant or falling. . . .*

As a result of increased world competition, there was a drastic drop in the manufacture of cotton and new synthetic materials in industrial countries, hence there was a parallel drop in the numbers of women textile workers including weavers, the original female industrial elite. . . .

By the late 1920s many . . . industries were adopting a speed-up of operations based on time and motion study. Women workers were badly affected since they were mainly employed on repetitive mass production work. . . .

Apart from the extra work involved, increasing productivity per worker simply meant putting more people out of jobs. It was because of the fears of unemployment that women still resisted limitations on their hours of work as they had in England in the 1870s. In 1921 in New York there was a famous revolt against the ban on women working at night by women proofreaders, linotypists and monotypists. . . . Various states were legislating on terms and conditions of women's work. Several introduced new restrictions. Ostensibly, as in the past, these were humanitarian. But in a time of shortage of jobs, women were naturally suspicious that such new measures were intended to give preference to men in jobs. . . .

What happened when minimum wage legislation was directed to eliminating the lower woman's wage . . . was shown in Canada. There only women were felt to need this protection and no minimum wage regulations were applied to men. Coupled with high male unemployment, this meant that by 1933 men were being brought in at wages below the local minima fixed for women."

Sheila Lewenhak, a widely traveled British labor historian who took her degree from the London School of Economics, here develops some of the factors that led to the actual decline of the number of Western women working in industry during the decades between the two world wars.

How does Lewenhak see declines in particular industries affecting the numbers of women involved in industrial production? What part did new policies by industrial management play? How did reformers seeking to protect women by regulating their hours, conditions of work, and minimum wages contribute to declining female employment in industry?

Sheila Lewenhak, <u>Women and Work</u> (New York: St. Martin's Press, 1980), pp. 206, 208–211, 213.

ble. And the takeoff time for all these social and technological revolutions was the period between the wars.

If the first half of the nineteenth century was the age of steam, then the early decades of the twentieth may well be described as the age of electricity—and Henry Ford.

CLASS CONFLICT

The Bolsheviks who seized power in Russia in 1917 confidently expected workers' revolts to follow in other countries—the world revolution Marx had predicted. Despite

abortive starts in places as widely separated as Germany and China, this did not happen. Nevertheless, there was a good deal of talk about class conflict during the 1920s. And during the 1930s, such conflicts seemed to threaten the very fabric of Western society as never before.

There had, of course, been industrial violence before, particularly since the beginning of the Industrial Revolution. But with the Soviet Union intermittently championing proletarian revolt in the twenties, and then with the entire capitalist system apparently on the verge of collapse during the Great Depression of the thirties, socialist agitation and class consciousness reached new highs.

Deprivation and suffering among factory laborers, miners, transportation and construction workers, and others of the blue-collar labor force were in fact very great during the world depression. Unemployment, hunger, illness, a sense of injustice and oppression, and a willingness to respond with strikes, political organization, and even violence spread through working-class neighborhoods in many Western countries during the thirties.

Hitler in Germany and Roosevelt in the United States were able to defuse these class divisions in their very different ways. Other Western nations muddled through on a combination of the dole and worker hopelessness. But the tensions between the classes were certainly as great as they had ever been before, and greater than they have been since.

WOMEN'S EMANCIPATION

The conflict between the sexes, by contrast, seems to have been less of a public issue than before the war or in later decades. As we have seen, Western women had begun to demand legal, educational, economic, and political parity with men in the nineteenth century. They had made some progress, breaking into some male-dominated professions and crusading for social reforms, including women's rights. Early in the new century, women in some Western nations had secured the right to vote—in Australia and some Scandinavian countries shortly after 1900, in Britain, the United States, and Weimar Germany just after World War I. During the war, furthermore, many middle-class women had joined their poor sisters in working outside the home in war industries.

It was a heady era of progress for women on many fronts. But it drew to a close around 1920—the beginning of the period under consideration here.

Women's emancipation in the 1920s took such social and apparently frivolous forms as shorter skirts, cosmetics, public drinking, and smoking. There was also an apparent increase in sexual freedom as women broke through the famous double standard, indulging in pre- or extramarital sex almost as casually as men did. Social emancipation, however, was not accompanied by economic independence. Women found their opportunities for work outside the home set back twice during this period. Immediately after World War I, "the boys came marching home"—and reclaimed the jobs women had taken over during the conflict. A decade later, as the world depression closed factories and shops, women were first fired as they had been last hired.

Most Western women, however, remained housewives. Women were still effectively excluded from large-scale participation in traditionally male professions. And the new women voters did not vote as a bloc or put any significant number of women into office. The idealism of the women's movement seemed to have spent itself in the great effort for women's suffrage in the decades around 1900. For most of the rest of the first half of the twentieth century, other causes would preoccupy socially concerned women as well as men in the Western world.

LOCARNO, DISARMAMENT, AND THE DREAM OF PEACE

One of these causes during the 1920s and 1930s was the peace movement, as it subsequently came to be called. The dream of peace among nations had flickered before, of course, even in the frequently contentious West. The Roman peace was widely admired as one of Rome's greatest gifts to Europe. Medieval churchmen at least tried to negotiate occasional "truces of God" in a world of feudal violence. The humanist Erasmus, the philosopher Kant, and other modern thinkers had written tracts urging peace on heads of state. International meetings around 1900 had labored to create agencies such as the World Court that might defuse disputes between nations before they erupted into war.

The huge casualties and immense destructiveness of World War I, however, galvanized a much wider range of Western public opinion to attempt to prevent similar holocausts in the future. The greatest single achievement of those who dreamed that the First World War might really be the last war was, of course, the League of Nations. In addition, the 1920s saw a series of diplomatic agreements and disarmament conferences intended to prevent future wars.

The Locarno treaties of 1925, signed by most of the major European powers, tried to guarantee peace through agreements to negotiate all disputes. The Kellogg-Briand Pact of 1928, signed originally by the United States and France, then by more than twenty other countries, formally renounced war as an instrument of national policy. The League itself responded to some of the totalitarian aggressions of the 1930s with investigations and denunciations—though to little practical effect, as we shall see.

Disarmament negotiations focused on the world's navies, the preeminent long-range weapons systems in those days before intercontinental bombers and ballistic missiles. Agreements were reached by the five major naval powers to freeze naval tonnage at a fixed ratio, to limit base strength, and even to scrap some "capital ships"—battleships and heavy cruisers. But discussions on limiting land forces bogged down throughout the 1920s in endless disputes concerning definitions of offensive weapons, methods of comparing various sorts of armies, and other matters too technical for any but a League subcommittee to understand.

The lay public had its say in the 1930s as some powers grew more bellicose, crises multiplied, and the chances of war mounted. Particularly in Britain and the United States, young people petitioned, argued, and demonstrated against war policies. Some even took the famous "Oxford oath" first adopted by students at Britain's premiere university: under no circumstances would they take up arms to fight for their country. But the winds of war were already rising, and there were plenty of other young people in Germany, Japan, and elsewhere who were ready and eager to take up arms.

The following section will look at the period a little more closely, in a regional and even a national focus. It will also illustrate more concretely some of the broad trends sketched above, the main currents of two decades that were building, whether they knew it or not, toward the biggest war of all.

THE WESTERN DEMOCRACIES BETWEEN THE WARS

JAZZ AGE AMERICA

The United States in the 1920s was Jazz Age America. And thereby hangs a problem. How seriously can you take an age that is named for its popular music? At least the Renaissance was named for its serious culture! But the 1920s were fun times for many Americans, and perhaps it won't hurt to pay a little attention to fun once in a while. There were grimmer times coming.

By 1920, the enthusiasms of the Progressive Era had clearly run their course. Teddy Roosevelt and Woodrow Wilson, the war to make the world safe for democracy, and Wilson's last, most quixotic crusade, the League of Nations, were all consigned to the trash bin of history. "The business of America is business," the new breed declared. It was okay to get rich again, and practically everybody seemed to be doing it.

There were weaknesses even in the American economy—the twenties were still hard times for farmers—but the overall economic trend was intoxicatingly upward. Per-capita income more than doubled between 1914 and 1929. Consumer luxuries such as wristwatches, washing machines, vacuum cleaners, and even automobiles became increasingly common. Technological advances such as the telephone, radio, phonograph, and movie were particularly widespread in America.

There were those who resisted the onward march of progress, of course. Fundamentalist Protestants defended established moral values and the "old-time religion." Intellectuals and literati sneered at the Babbits who ran America—doltish businessmen with little culture and less sensitivity, named for the central character in a novel by Sinclair Lewis. And many people lamented the passing of the front porch as a social center and its replacement by the automobile, symbol of freedom to youth, "petting parlors on wheels" to disapproving elders.

"Nothing to fear but fear itself!" Franklin and Eleanor Roosevelt seemed to embody a new self-confidence that many Americans found heartening even in the depths of the Great Depression. The ebullient public image displayed here gave credence to the president's confident assertion that his generation had "a rendezvous with destiny." (The Bettmann Archive)

"Flaming youth," "modern youth," "the younger generation"—the young people of the American 1920s embodied all the vitality and foolishness of the decade. They drank too much, drove too fast, cut their hair and their skirts too short, invented endless fads and new dances every year. They adopted a brassy black style of popular music called jazz and took the gaudy, improvident lifestyle of novelist Scott Fitzgerald and his glamorous wife, Zelda, as their ideal. For the giddy middle-class American youth of the 1920s, it was always New Year's Eve and no tomorrow.

FDR AND THE NEW DEAL

Tomorrow came, of course—a morning-after like few in modern history—in the wake of the New York Stock Market crash of October 1929.

The causes of the Crash of '29 included unwarranted speculation, overcapitalized business ventures, shaky banks, lack of adequate government regulation, and plain fraud. The Great Depression that filled the next decade in America was rooted in deeper problems, however. Continuing hard times for farmers, miners, and others carried over from the twenties. Saturation of middle-class markets for big-ticket items such as autos and houses, a top-heavy income distribution that gave a third of the income to 5 percent of the population, and a "depression psychology" that paralyzed investment for years also contributed to the disaster.

The result was the terrible downward spiral of depression. Business bankruptcies threw people out of work. Unemployed people could not buy goods. More businesses thus closed, throwing yet more people into the ranks of the jobless. And so it went, spiraling down into a seemingly bottomless pit.

It is ancient history now, like scratchy old phonograph records or jittery black-and-white movies. But it was an unbelievable nightmare then.

"Brother, can you spare a dime?" Hoovervilles—tin-and-tarpaper shacks flung up on ash heaps at the edges of cities. Men wrapped in newspapers, sleeping on park benches. Hollow-eyed women and dirty-faced children watching the dry, dead earth of their farms blow away.

One and one-half million Americans were out of work in 1929. Thirteen million were jobless in 1933.

Yet American democracy survived the decade. The survival expert who carried the nation through was an improbable upstate New York patroon with an aristocratic cigarette holder, a mellifluous voice, and a contagious certainty that "all we have to fear is fear itself"—and a man who could not get out of his wheelchair unaided. His name, perhaps the best-known in twentieth-century American politics, was Franklin Delano Roosevelt—FDR to headline writers everywhere. An unbeatable politician who was elected president four times—twice as many as any other—and who guided the nation through both the Great Depression and World War II, Franklin Roosevelt (1933–1945) stands with George Washington and Abraham Lincoln on the very shortest list of America's greatest presidents.

At Roosevelt's side throughout the presidential years was his wife, Eleanor, who thereafter became America's most admired woman in her own right. They made an unlikely couple at first glance. Franklin was a handsome, ambitious assistant secretary of the navy and an aggressive governor of New York—condemned to a wheelchair for life by a shattering attack of polio in 1921. Eleanor was plain and shy, the ugly-duckling daughter of an equally aristocratic family. Yet they forged one of the most effective political partnerships in U.S. history. Eleanor Roosevelt was FDR's eyes and ears, his physical presence where he could not go to hearten the people, and a militant champion of social causes.

Roosevelt was a man of action rather than an intellectual, and it was action that the nation wanted in 1933. "I pledge myself," he declared during his first campaign, "to a new deal for the American people. . . . This is more than a political campaign; it is a call to arms."[1] After three

[1]James T. Patterson, *America in the Twentieth Century* (New York: Harcourt Brace Jovanovich, 1976), p. 158.

grinding years of waiting for the business cycle to turn up again, for the laws of supply and demand to pull the country out of the trough, Americans were finally ready for government involvement in the economy to a degree they had never tolerated before. The result was wave after wave of reform legislation through the 1930s—and a transformed America.

There was relief for the hungry, public-works projects for the unemployed, loans to help people keep their homes, regulation for Wall Street, insurance for banks, devaluation for the dollar. The Civilian Conservation Corps (CCC) and the Works Progress Administration (WPA) put hundreds of thousands of people to work on government-sponsored projects. The Agricultural Adjustment Act (AAA) raised farm incomes by encouraging cuts in production. The Tennessee Valley Authority (TVA) began the integrated development of an entire region of the country on the basis of cheap electricity and irrigation. The Wagner Act strengthened the bargaining position of labor unions as never before in America. Social Security at last brought national old-age pensions, begun decades before in Europe, to the United States.

Roosevelt's foreign-policy credentials were impeccably liberal also. He broke a conservative Republican front against the Bolsheviks by extending diplomatic recognition to the Soviet Union—and American businessmen as solid as Henry Ford were soon cheerfully trading with Communist Russia. FDR announced a new policy of nonintervention south of the border, a Good Neighbor Policy that at least looked like a significant change from the days of Dollar Diplomacy and sending in the Marines.

Most important, by the end of the thirties Roosevelt was clearly aware of the international danger posed by the rise of aggressive totalitarian regimes in Germany, Italy, Japan, and elsewhere. His efforts to prepare Americans for the possibility of a new world war were handicapped by general disillusionment with the last one. But his estimate of Axis intentions would prove all too accurate as the decade ended.

Franklin Roosevelt could not stop the world depression—it took World War II to do that. But he carried America through it without recourse to totalitarian tyranny and with a renewed sense of national purpose and dignity. And he set the United States at last on the road other Western nations had already taken toward the welfare state—that precarious balance of capitalistic economy, democratic government, and socialist concern for the basic social and economic needs of the people.

BRITAIN MUDDLES THROUGH

In Europe, democratic governments and capitalist economies survived best in Britain and France, in Scandinavia (Norway, Sweden, and Denmark in particular), in the Low Countries (the Netherlands and Belgium), and in such isolated pockets as Switzerland and Czechoslo-

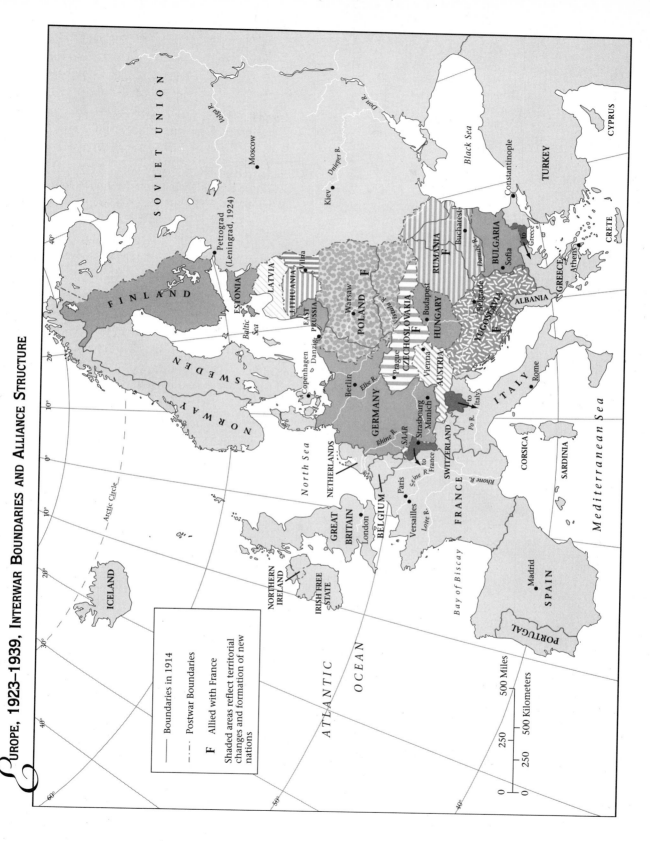

EUROPE, 1923–1939, INTERWAR BOUNDARIES AND ALLIANCE STRUCTURE

SOVIET UNION

Moscow

Volga R.

Dnieper R.

Don R.

Kiev

Petrograd
(Leningrad, 1924)

FINLAND

ESTONIA

LATVIA

LITHUANIA

Baltic Sea

**EAST
PRUSSIA**

Danzig

Riga

POLAND **F**

Warsaw

Vistula R.

CZECHOSLOVAKIA **F**

Prague

**RUMANIA
F**

Bucharesti

Danube R.

Black Sea

BULGARIA

Sofia

**YUGOSLAVIA
F**

Belgrade

ALBANIA

GREECE

Greece

Athens

Constantinople

TURKEY

CYPRUS

CRETE

NORWAY

SWEDEN

Copenhagen

North Sea

Berlin

Elbe R.

**GERMANY
F**

HUNGARY

Budapest

AUSTRIA

Vienna

Munich

to Italy

Po R.

ITALY

Rome

SWITZERLAND

Strasbourg

SAAR

to France

Rhine R.

Seine R.

FRANCE

Paris

Versailles

Loire R.

Rhone R.

NETHERLANDS

BELGIUM

**GREAT
BRITAIN**

London

**NORTHERN
IRELAND**

**IRISH FREE
STATE**

ICELAND

*ATLANTIC
OCEAN*

Bay of Biscay

CORSICA

SARDINIA

Mediterranean Sea

SPAIN

Madrid

PORTUGAL

Arctic Circle

— Boundaries in 1914

--- Postwar Boundaries

F Allied with France

Shaded areas reflect territorial
changes and formation of new
nations

500 Miles

500 Kilometers

0   250   500

0   250   500

60°

40°

30°

20°

10°

0°

10°

20°

40°

50°

40°

601

vakia. In much of the rest of Europe, as we will see, very different tides were flowing. For now, however, it is the interwar experience of liberal capitalist Western Europe that concerns us, particularly that of the two major western European powers, Britain and France.

Great Britain between the wars managed to muddle through. But its circumstances were sadly reduced, its imperial and commercial predominance undermined, and its empire increasingly unstable.

Economically, Britain had lost a quarter of its overseas trade and had been replaced as the greatest foreign investor by the booming United States. The British industrial plant, so vigorously challenged by Germany before the war, remained dated and slow to recover. British workers, particularly in badly depressed industries such as coal mining, were frequently on strike. The great miners' walkout of 1926 turned into the famous general strike of that year, shutting down almost the entire economy for ten days and leading to violent confrontations between blue-collar strikers and middle- and upper-class Englishmen fearful of Bolshevik plots.

When the Great Depression came in the 1930s, Britain handled it no better than other western European countries. The United Kingdom had no FDR to rally the nation against the rising tide of bankruptcies, layoffs, and poverty. A series of more or less ineffectual Conservative leaders cobbled together an array of half measures, from reluctant devaluation of the pound to an inadequate dole intended merely to keep the unemployed from starving.

Politically, Britain was dominated by a succession of unmemorable Conservative-party governments between 1919 and 1939. Perhaps the most important feature of British political life between the world wars, however, was the emergence of Labour—Britain's socialist party—as the Conservative party's major rival. The Liberals, meanwhile, declined to third-party status. It was a net shift to the left in British politics. But this shift, despite two Labour governments in the interwar period, would have little effect on Britain's national life until after World War II.

The British Empire also showed the strains of Britain's anomalous new position in the world. In India, an independence movement led by Mahatma Gandhi and the Congress party gained momentum. Closer to home, England's oldest colony, Ireland, was at last granted its freedom after a brief rebellion in 1916 and a bloody British struggle with the terrorists of the Irish Republican Army in the years around 1920. Northern Ireland, however, with its heavy Anglo-Protestant population, remained part of Britain—and a source of friction for the rest of the century.

A more positive adjustment to new realities was the creation of the British Commonwealth of Nations by the Act of Westminster in 1931. By this act, some of Britain's largest and oldest colonies, including Canada, Australia, and South Africa, gained complete political independence under the symbolic headship of the British crown, while still benefiting from "imperial preference" in trade.

Most of Britain's overseas territories remained colonies in 1931, including huge, populous India. But a road to voluntary and mutually profitable association was opened by the Commonwealth, and dozens of former colonies have followed it since.

The Maginot Line, the complex of science-fiction super-trenches with which France prepared to defend itself between the wars. Pictures like this, showing the underground electric railway which linked up the hundreds of miles of fortifications, reassured the French that they would be ready for "the next time." Fixed defensive bastions like this, however, would prove no defense at all against the highly mobile offensive capability of the blitzkrieg the Germans would hurl against France in 1940. (Imperial War Museum, London)

FRANCE'S MAGINOT-LINE MENTALITY

France, the other large democracy of Western Europe, survived two even more undistinguished decades between the two wars. And here, as across the Channel, there was a sense of better times behind, of indecision and no clear line of movement into the future.

There were some advantages to being French. The world depression came late to France and was not felt as fiercely. The braking effect of a substantial admixture of peasant farmers, old-fashioned artisans, and petty-bourgeois shopkeepers saved the French economy from the violent oscillation between 1920s boom and 1930s bust that looked so stark in America. The number of unemployed in France never much exceeded half a million, compared with three million in Britain.

Like Great Britain, the French republic had its first socialist government in the interwar years, in the 1930s. French socialism was as constitutional and committed to democracy as the British Labour party was. But the French Left was as fragmented as most democratic politics were in Europe, where the multiparty system prevailed. French socialist power thus depended on an alliance between two separate socialist parties and the French Communists, who at that time were committed to following Moscow's line. Only in the mid-thirties, when Moscow urged all communists to seek a united front with socialists and liberals, could the French Left form a coalition capable of holding power for even a brief time.

For most of these two decades, then, conservatives dominated French politics as they did politics in Britain. Right-wing splinters even flirted with totalitarianism in France. The far-right Cross of Fire veterans' party had a quasi-fascist image, including uniforms, extremist language, and an enthusiasm for street confrontation. But the Cross of Fire never really came close to power in that nation of peasants and shopkeepers.

French foreign policy in the 1920s and 1930s was also conservative and increasingly defensive in tone. France's overriding preoccupation was with the threat of revived German power across the Rhine and with the more distant menace of Bolshevism in eastern Europe. French leaders moved aggressively if imprudently in the 1920s, occupying the industrial Ruhr district in order to squeeze reparations payments out of Germany. The result was severe economic damage, to France as well as to Germany, and a negotiated settlement.

In the thirties the French spent years and hundreds of millions of francs building an elaborate string of steel-and-concrete fortifications facing Germany—the notorious Maginot Line. While Hitler prepared to fight the next war with highly mobile panzer divisions, France braced itself to fight the last one over again in the grimly defensive spirit of Verdun.

This backward-looking, defensive, Maginot-Line mentality in fact characterized much of French history between the wars. American tourists might enjoy Paris in the springtime, and there was still no better place to be an expatriate. But there was little sense of grandeur along the Seine, and no Napoleons in sight as France's next time of testing came on inexorably.

THE COMMONWEALTH COUNTRIES: CAPABLE OF COPING

The United States and Europe were the heart of the Western World, as they would be throughout most of the twentieth century. But there were more Western worlds than one by this time. A look at two other areas of Western culture will therefore be necessary to complete this overview.

The nations of the British Commonwealth, scattered around the world geographically, were as much a part of this new, expanded twentieth-century West as the United States was. Domestic autonomy had been granted to Canada, Australia, and New Zealand in the nineteenth century, to South Africa around 1900, soon after the Boer War, and to Ireland around 1920, following the Irish "troubles." The formal grant of independence and equality under the British crown in 1931 completed what had begun a century before—the creation of a British family of nations around the globe.

The nations of the Commonwealth were for the most part as democratic as any in the world, possessing representative legislatures, bills of rights, and lively traditions of political and social reform. South Africa, which contained a huge, totally disfranchised black majority, was the great exception to this tendency.

Economically, most of the Commonwealth countries had been outgrowing their original roles as suppliers of agricultural products and raw materials in return for manufactured goods from the mother country. They continued to produce large quantities of beef, wheat, mutton, wool, gold, diamonds, and other valuable commodities. But the South African mining industries and Australian manufacturing grew apace, and Canada became one of the major manufacturing nations of the world during these decades.

All the nations of the British Commonwealth suffered in the world depression. But all survived it without draconian political measures, as they would survive World War II. For the most part, then, the Commonwealth countries entered the second half of the century as leading examples of successful Western nations, capable of coping with the worst this century could dish out.

THE LATIN AMERICAN NATIONS: VOICES FOR IDEALS

The Latin American nations, like the Commonwealth countries, were in most ways as much a part of the Western World as the United States or Europe. Like the predominantly English-speaking nations of the British Commonwealth, this score of mostly Spanish- and Portuguese-speaking republics shared a dominant European heritage, here overlaid upon strong Amerindian and African-American traditions. Though Latin America escaped participation in both world wars, it was affected by them, by the depression, and—as we shall see in later chapters—by global trends toward revolution and authoritarian government in the interwar years.

By and large, the twenties were better times, the thirties considerably worse in Latin America, as for most of the Western World. Here, however, general trends stretching over both decades will be stressed.

Economically, a major change was the takeoff of a domestic manufacturing capacity in some of the more developed Latin American states. This change was partly the result of the high prices charged for North American and European manufactured goods. These prices were particularly hard for Latin Americans to pay during the depression, when the prices of their exports of agricultural products and raw materials declined rapidly. All this led some Latin Americans to try to produce at home what they could not afford from abroad.

In part also, the building of new manufacturing plants and the nationalizing of foreign-owned extractive industries was a deliberate policy stimulated by national pride and by a growing awareness of Latin America's relative technological underdevelopment. The result, in any case, was genuine growth in consumer-goods manufacturing—notably in textiles—in Argentina, Brazil, and other nations, and of the oil industry in Mexico, Venezuela, and Andean states such as Peru.

Politically, there was also some striking evidence of progress between the wars, both in political performance and in ideals and social services.

Conservative and military elements did remain prominent in government during the period, but in the 1920s, at least, revolutionary seizures of power dwindled greatly. Some sectors of the civil service, such as the agencies dealing with public utilities and those concerned with irrigation projects, tended especially to be more modern and professional and less exploitative.

Outside groups pressured governments to enact reforms. Liberal, middle-class parties urged more democracy, as did students at Latin America's large universities. The growing working class, reinforced by a new influx of European immigrants bringing socialistic ideas and no tradition of subservience to Latin American establishments, demanded attention to the needs of working people. Furthermore, many Latin Americans of all classes, disturbed by the U.S. military interventions of the early years of the twentieth century, strongly resented foreign influences of all sorts in their countries.

Some genuine though limited progress resulted from the pressures generated by these new groups and by idealistic political impulses. Mexico and the ABC countries—Argentina, Brazil, and Chile—significantly expanded the role of their governments in providing social services for their people. Advanced labor codes regulating hours and conditions of work were passed in some countries. Even some of the more reactionary autocrats prided themselves on educational reforms. Mexico's nationalization of foreign oil wells in the 1930s exemplified a wave of government moves aimed at limiting foreign participation in Latin American economies.

Many of these reforms never reached the peons in the countryside, and others were never put into practice at all. Foreign capital continued to be needed, so that in the end, patriotic fervor frequently gave way to pragmatism, or to a desire for a share of the profits.

Nevertheless, much was accomplished. Domestically owned industries were at last beginning to grow, government's responsibility to the people was broadening, and twentieth-century social idealism had no more ardent spokesmen than in Latin America.

SUMMARY

The decades between the two world wars of this century are often contrasted. The 1920s are seen as the Jazz Age of prosperity, flappers, and fun; the 1930s, as the depression decade, the red decade, the decade of unemployment, suffering, and ideological commitment. In fact, the two decades had much in common. Overproduction, worldwide throughout the period, led to poverty among commodity producers in both developed and underdeveloped societies. Technology further transformed the Western world, bringing widespread use of automobiles, telephones, electrical appliances, radios, and moving pictures.

Tensions increased between social classes, and the appeal of socialism reached a century-long high during the 1930s.

The women's movement, however, languished or turned to new forms of social equality. Efforts to guarantee world peace included the League of Nations, a series of naval disarmament agreements, and student demonstrations.

A country-by-country survey of the West between the wars reveals a variety of national styles and developments. Politically, the United States in the 1920s was in a slump between strong presidents; economically, however, the United States sustained half the Western world. The depression decade in America was dominated by the powerful personality of Franklin D. Roosevelt and the New Deal. Britain muddled through both decades, surviving class tensions and massive unemployment, and even showing some of its old political flair in the establishment of the British Commonwealth of Nations. France was deeply conservative, building international alliances and the Maginot Line against foreign enemies, and escaping the worst of the depression because of its old-fashioned economy. In both Britain and France, however, socialist political parties chalked up their first national political victories.

The Commonwealth countries—especially Canada, Australia, and New Zealand—evolved as a loose family of self-governing nations. Their economies became increasingly independent, and Canada became one of the world's leading industrial nations. The Latin American republics also continued their development toward economic independence and revealed new tendencies toward political reform and social welfare. The depression, however, brought increased poverty and a resurgence of authoritarian regimes in Latin America.

SUGGESTED READING

ALLEN, F. L. *Only Yesterday.* New York: Harper & Row, Pub., 1972. Social and cultural trends of the 1920s; lively reading.

BANNER, L. W. *Women in Modern America: A Brief History.* New York: Harcourt Brace Jovanovich, 1974. Brief but very readable history of American women and American attitudes toward women in the twentieth century. See also W. H. Chafe, *The American Woman: Her Changing Social, Economic, and Political Role, 1920–1970* (New York: Oxford University Press, 1972) for a scholarly survey.

BOTHWELL, R., et al. *Canada, 1900–1945.* Toronto: University of Toronto Press, 1987. Useful synthesis of twentieth-century Canadian history.

BULMER-THOMAS, V. *The Political Economy of Central America since 1920.* New York: Cambridge University Press, 1987. Stronger on the economic than the political side.

BURNS, J. M. *Roosevelt: The Lion and the Fox.* New York: Harcourt Brace Jovanovich, 1970. Positive assessment of Franklin D. Roosevelt as leader and political tactician.

GREENE, N. *From Versailles to Vichy.* Arlington Heights, Ill.: Harlan Davidson, 1970. Complicated narrative of French political life from victory in World War I to defeat in World War II.

HUGHES, T. P. *Networks of Power: Electrification in Western Society, 1880–1930.* Baltimore: Johns Hopkins University Press, 1983. Social consequences of the first half-century of electric power in Europe and North America.

KINDLEBERGER, C. P. *The World in Depression, 1929–1939.* London: Allen Lane, 1973. The larger picture; good for Europe in particular.

MELMAN, B. *Women and the Popular Imagination in the Twenties: Flappers and Nymphs.* New York: St. Martin's Press, 1988. Psychosocial investigation of the multiple meanings of the popular image of the free-wheeling young woman of the 1920s.

NUNN, F. M. *Chilean Politics, 1920–1931: The Honorable Role of the Armed Forces.* Albuquerque: University of New Mexico Press, 1970. Balanced and thorough.

POTASH, R. A. *The Army and Politics in Argentina, 1928–1945.* Stanford: Stanford University Press, 1969. Compares the traditional power of the military with the equally traditional role played by students in politics.

REES, G. *The Great Slump: Capitalism in Crisis.* New York: Harper & Row, Pub., 1971. The big picture of the depression. On the American stock market crash that triggered the global collapse, see J. K. Galbraith, *The Great Crash* (New York: Avon, 1980).

SCHLESINGER, A. M. *The Age of Roosevelt.* Boston: Houghton Mifflin, 1957. Balanced but generally approving analysis of the New Deal. For a variety of views, see F. Freidel, ed., *The New Deal and the American People* (Englewood Cliffs, N.J.: Prentice Hall, 1964).

SONTAG, R. *A Broken World, 1919–1939.* New York: Harper & Row, Pub., 1971. Excellent overview of this complex and many-sided era.

TAYLOR, A. J. P. *English History, 1919–1945.* Oxford: Oxford University Press, 1965. Quick-witted and critical. For social history of the period, see R. Graves and A. Hodge, *The Long Weekend* (New York: W.W. Norton, 1963).

CHAPTER 41

$\mathcal{T}$HE LONG REVOLUTIONS

THE SPREAD
OF IDEOLOGICAL REVOLUTION

THE MYSTIQUE OF THE REBEL

A visit to Lenin's tomb was part of any trip to Moscow during the Cold War years. The tomb itself—a squat rectangular building dwarfed by the Kremlin wall behind it—was not particularly impressive. But the location in Red Square, the heart of the Soviet empire, was. So were the silent guards, rigid in their long coats, marching on and off duty with that slow, implacable Red Army goose step. Above all, you could not help but be impressed by the endless line of Soviet citizens, who had come to see the embalmed body of the founder of the Soviet state. The queue stretched all across the vast square and often up a side street, an endless file of silent citizens in dark clothes.

The Soviet state is history now, of course. The line is gone; the guards stroll around looking bored. There are rumors that Lenin's body may be removed: One story has it that the corpse may be acquired by a socialist archive in Western Europe; another is that a German entrepreneur wants to take it on tour. But for most of the twentieth century, Lenin was honored as the greatest revolutionary of his time, the Russian Revolution itself hailed as the wave of the global future.

The twentieth century may well be the most revolutionary of centuries. Certainly the rebel has become a stock figure of our times. We all know him—or her: young, committed to a great cause, challenging the established order of things. Some of us may in fact *be* this archetypal rebel, heading for the barricades once more.

The twentieth century did not, of course, invent rebellion, or even rebellion for a good cause. The literature and legendry of many peoples include versions of Jesse James or Robin Hood, stealing from the rich and giving to the poor. There were social dimensions to peasant revolts in such nations as China two thousand years ago. And modern ideological rebellions aiming at major social transformation go back to the eighteenth-century age of democratic revolutions in the West—back to the sixteenth century if you count the great wars of religion. But seldom have revolutions of all sorts played such a part in history—particularly in global history—as in the present century.

During the period between World Wars I and II, as we have seen, social and cultural revolutions transformed European and American lifestyles and even reached as far as Japan. Artistic rebels, as we shall see in a later chapter, reshaped literature, painting, architecture, music. Popular Freudianism told sophisticated people that rebellion against inhibiting conventions was good for their emotional health. Young people rebelled against older people, women against the double standard. And all of these revolutions have continued since, becoming part of the fabric of our lives.

The major political and economic revolutions that will be dealt with below, however, have had a special place in history. These great revolutions of the first half of the twentieth century reached far beyond the Western world to set global history as a whole moving in new directions.

THE CENTRAL ROLE
OF IDEOLOGY

The forms of rebellion—even of political revolt—are many and varied, and they are as old as history. As far back as our records run, there have been peasant rebellions, palace coups, civil wars between claimants to the same throne, feuds between factions within the same city. But the ideologically based revolution, inspired by new social ideas and envisioning a totally new social order, is a modern phenomenon.

There are elements of ideological revolt in this sense in the English Civil War of the 1600s, a good deal of it in the American Revolution and particularly the French Revolution of the later 1700s. There was an epidemic of ideological revolution in Europe between 1815 and 1848. It was only in our own century, however, that revolution based on liberalism, nationalism, and socialism and their variants swept beyond the confines of the West into the larger world.

Until quite recently, at least, liberalism has perhaps been the weakest of the major modern ideologies in its impact on twentieth-century revolutionaries. Liberal convictions, political and economic, were most potent among rebels between 1776 and 1848. By 1900, many liberal objectives had been achieved in the West. Outside Western Europe and America, demands for democracy and free trade often seemed less than central to the felt needs of insurrectionary peoples. The rhetoric of freedom was still widely heard, but it tended to mean something different to twentieth-century revolutionists around the world.

Nationalism, particularly in the form of anti-imperialism, has been much more of a driving force behind the revolutions of this century. Resentment of foreign rule, or of foreign economic domination, has been the primary motive behind many popular struggles for independence since 1900. The European intercontinental empires would be shattered by nationalistic rebellion against foreign domination after World War II. Powerful currents of nationalistic feeling flowed also in the great Mexican and Chinese revolutions of the earlier twentieth century, to be dealt with below.

Marxist revolutionary socialism, however, has perhaps been more visible than any other ideology in the revolutions of the present century. This is in a way ironic, because Marxism was originally conceived as a doctrine for rebellious proletariats in developed industrial countries, whereas most twentieth-century revolutions have come in primarily peasant countries such as Russia, China, and Mexico—the subjects of the present chapter. As a consequence, Marxist ideologues have had to do some recasting of theory to suit the needs of their preindustrial constituency (as in Mao's China) or have had to impose the new order by force (as in Stalinist Russia). But Lenin's turn-of-the-century thesis that imperialism was an extension of capitalism overseas would appeal to revolutionary cadres around the world for most of the rest of the century.

The impact of ideology is much more complex than formulations such as "rebellions for a cause" might indicate. Like the religious motives of earlier times, ideological impulses are frequently mixed with other motives, from political ambition and social resentment to economic needs and desires. But the part played by visions of brave new worlds built on a bedrock of ideas has nonetheless been central. Liberals, nationalists, and socialists, whose influence on the West has been so great over the past two centuries, have been reshaping the world as well during the last hundred years.

SCOPE AND SCALE OF THE LONG REVOLUTIONS

Between 1911 and 1949, great ideological revolutions shook some of the largest nations in the world: Russia, the largest in territory; China, the largest in population; and Mexico, one of the largest on both counts in Latin America. During this same period between the wars, less violent but nonetheless ideologically based independence movements gathered force on the Indian subcontinent—second only to China in population—and in many parts of Africa, the second largest continent.

There would be many revolutions in the second half of the century as well, but these would tend to be in rather smaller corners of the globe, in places such as Vietnam,

Algeria, and Cuba. These revolutions were significant because of their frequency, cropping up again and again around the globe in the decades after World War II, and because of the part they played in the Cold War. But the big revolutions came in the first half of this century, especially during the years between the wars.

The Russian, Chinese, and Mexican revolutions had much in common. They were based on Western ideologies and visions of social justice, and they anticipated a better social order. They became models for later generations of rebels in other parts of the world. But perhaps most impressive, they had *scale* in common.

They were fought over hundreds of thousands of square miles by millions of people. Their casualty totals dwarf those of the English, French, and American revolutions of earlier centuries. They changed the lives of hundreds of millions. And they dragged on, sometimes for decades, before a new social order was at last established, a new regime firmly in place.

For the historian, sheer length is perhaps the most striking feature. How long can a revolution be, after all, before it becomes a kind of violent social evolution, consuming whole generations in its quest for a brighter tomorrow?

There was heroism enough for any lover of courage in the face of terrible adversity. There were horrors to turn the sternest of us queasy at the unending violence. There was, finally, social change—though not always the change dreamed of by the founders, many of whom had long been in their graves when the consummation came.

The long revolutions of the years between the wars are historic monuments of our century. They have given us crusaders such as Madero and Gandhi, men of violence such as Pancho Villa, founders of new nations such as Lenin and Mao, transformers of whole societies by force, such as Stalin. They gave the world new powers—the Soviet Union and the People's Republic of China—which would play central parts in the history of most of the rest of the century.

Idealistic young rebels—and millions of other men and women—fell in hecatombs to bring these things to pass. The long revolutions are their monuments too—and their story.

REVOLUTIONS ON THREE CONTINENTS

RUSSIA: LENIN AND THE BOLSHEVIKS

Russia was unique, even in relatively conservative and undeveloped Eastern Europe. Its huge population of peasants, the eternally suffering *muzhiks,* were sunk in poverty and ignorance. Its fairy-tale aristocracy lived the life of the American antebellum South, of Versailles before the Bastille fell, with town mansions and vast estates, lavish balls, and sleigh bells jingling through the Russian night. Its divine-right emperor was a figure out of the Middle Ages, convinced that God had sent him to rule his people. And so he did, with the help of repressive Cossack regiments and the largest bureaucracy and the most notorious secret police in the Western World.

In the nineteenth century, revolutionary rumblings had become endemic. Decembrist plotters in 1825, nihilist rioters in the 1860s, and Narodnik terrorists in the 1870s and 1880s had all failed. Then, at the turn of the century, this revolutionary tradition produced its final flower: the generation of Lenin.

It was a rebellious generation whose many voices demanded change of the new czar, Nicholas II (1894–1917). Local peasant disturbances were at a new high around 1900. Workers in the growing numbers of factories and railway lines brought the industrial strike to Russia. Middle-class professional groups urged change less noisily. Students were demonstrating again. And underground, a tangle of feuding revolutionary groups demanded a more violent solution to the nation's long-standing problems.

There were two main revolutionary organizations, one of them divided into two factions. The older of the two major groups was the Social Revolutionary party—the SRs. Heirs of the Narodniks of the preceding generation, they were convinced that the oppressed peasants would one day rise up to overthrow the man they still called the "dear father czar." The newer group, Russia's first Marxists, insisted that the new and still relatively small Russian industrial proletariat was the wave of the revolutionary future. This group called themselves the Social Democratic party, or SDs, though their revolutionary predilections made them very different from the constitutional reform-minded Social Democrats of Western Europe.

The SDs split into two factions in the early 1900s: the Mensheviks and the Bolsheviks, the "Minority" and "Majority" factions. The split was a matter of tactics, not goals. The Mensheviks urged a large, inclusive party that would take in supporters having a broad range of viewpoints and degrees of involvement in the cause. The Bolsheviks insisted on a relatively small, tightly knit party of disciplined, full-time revolutionaries. The leader of the Bolshevik wing was a man named Vladimir Ilich Ulyanov, known to history by his alias of Lenin.

Lenin (1870–1924) was a school administrator's son from the Volga region of eastern European Russia. A student demonstrator in his youth, he was an early convert to Marxism. His older brother had been hanged for plotting to assassinate the czar in the 1880s, and Lenin himself spent time in Siberia for organizing subversive "study groups" among Russian workers. With his wife and comrade, Nadezhda Krupskaya, he had in the 1890s followed the common path of nineteenth-century ideological revolutionaries of many persuasions—exile, first in Berlin and London, finally to Switzerland. There he lived, wrote, schemed, and organized through the opening years of the new century.

He was, said one who knew him, "a man of iron will, of indomitable energy, who combined a fanatical faith in the movement and the cause with no less faith in himself. . . . "[1] He looked old even in youth, with his rapidly receding hairline, broad forehead, narrow Tatar eyes, and small moustache. His fellows in the underground called him the Old Man, honored him for his skill in ideological debate, his strong will, and his twenty-four-hours-a-day commitment to his cause. Many followed him into the Bolshevik faction when the party split in 1903. They were still with him in 1917, when their hour came at last.

THE REVOLUTIONS OF 1917

There is no question of the dedicated revolutionary zeal of Lenin and his colleagues. There is no doubt either, however, that they did not bring down the czar in 1917. World War I did that.

Lost wars stimulated domestic upheavals three times during the last sixty years of Romanov rule in Russia. The pounding Russia took on its own soil in the Crimean War of the 1850s kindled the nihilist rebelliousness—and led to the reforms—of the 1860s. Russia's humiliating defeat by Japan in 1905 led to the revolution of that year and to the political concessions that gave Russia its first legislative assembly, the Duma. In the same way, it was the terrible punishment Russia took in World War I that triggered both the February and October revolutions of 1917. The Russian revolutionaries rode and to some degree guided the whirlwind. They did not conjure it up.

Romanov Russia's creaky economy, dilapidated administration, and military backwardness made it the least prepared of all the great powers to meet the challenges of total war in 1914. The nation's huge peasant armies were poorly led, trained, and equipped, their human-wave assaults costly and futile in a modern war. The meager railway system and inefficient administration denied the troops supplies and kept casualties from getting back to medical help. Cities swollen with war workers ran out of food, fuel, even housing in the long Russian winters.

The government of the last czar was a carnival of inefficiency and corruption. Nicholas II himself was at the front with the troops, further complicating the desperate efforts of his generals. Empress Alexandra, trying to preside at St. Petersburg, came increasingly under the influence of the "monk" Rasputin, whose ability to ease the suffering of her hemophiliac son Alexis, heir and hope of

[1] Bertram D. Wolfe, *Three Who Made a Revolution: A Biographical History* (Boston: Beacon Press, 1948), p. 258.

Lenin orates to a Russian crowd in Red Square, Moscow, in the darkest days of the civil war that followed the 1917 revolutions. A committed activist, Lenin believed that revolutions were "the locomotives of history," and that seizing power to effect social change was the point of revolutions. (The Bettmann Archive)

the dynasty, mesmerized her into thinking he had been sent by God to guide Russia's divine-right rulers in their hour of peril. In fact, Rasputin, an unscrupulous peasant faith healer almost totally ignorant of foreign affairs, devoted himself to debauchery, influence peddling, and promoting the fortunes of his equally unworthy cronies.

Under such external pressures, a government so thoroughly rotted within simply could not stand. Lenin was still in exile in Switzerland when it fell.

The February Revolution that brought down the czarist monarchy was guided by liberal Duma politicians and generals who recognized the hopelessness of the military situation. In the depths of that winter of 1916–1917, with mobs surging through the streets of the capital, this group went to Nicholas and persuaded him to abdicate for the good of the country. The nation, they said, would not follow him further.

Nicholas resigned, first in favor of his young son, and then of his brother. But the momentum of the revolution quickly swept the Romanovs aside, and a republic was declared. The new provisional government of Duma leaders, basically liberal in composition, was headed by Alexander Kerensky, leader of a prolabor party in the Duma. This regime, which ran Russia for less than a year, was the nation's one historic hope for Western-style democracy before 1990.

The great failing of the Kerensky government, however, was its inability to break radically enough with the past. Kerensky could not bring himself to take Russia out of the war that had already brought the Romanovs down. He launched one more vast offensive in the summer of 1917. When this last effort failed, the provisional government followed the czarist one into oblivion.

By this time, Lenin was back in Russia to pick up the pieces. The Bolshevik leader had hastened home after the fall of Nicholas II and devoted himself to organizing a second revolt against the "bourgeois liberal" Kerensky regime. An effort in June misfired. But in October, after the catastrophe of the Kerensky offensive, the time was ripe at last.

Beaten soldiers were streaming home that winter of 1917–1918, some of them mutinying, many bringing their rifles with them. The cities were hungry, cold, overcrowded, bitter. The provisional government was in disarray. The peasants were restless, the workers ready to strike.

The Bolsheviks were everywhere, plotting with the disaffected, haranguing mobs in the streets in order to intensify the disaffection. Lenin's bald head and short, choppy gestures became familiar in St. Petersburg. At this crucial juncture, the revolutionary who had devoted his life to Marxism had more sense than to try to explain the master's theories to the mob. "Land!" he shouted into the sea of upturned faces, land for the peasantry at last. "Bread!" for the starving cities. "Peace!" and an end to the hopeless carnage. Land, bread, and peace did the job.

The fighting took place in the cities and was generally brief. Kerensky was driven from St. Petersburg into a long American exile. The walled Kremlin in Moscow fell after a bloodier battle. In other cities, Bolsheviks led workers' militias and squads of mutinous sailors from the Russian navy in quick seizures of power. The grip of the provisional government, never strong, was easily broken. The Bolshevik revolutionaries took their place, with Lenin at the head of the new government.

It was then that the Bolsheviks—soon renamed the Communists—showed what they were made of. For the great Bolshevik achievement lay not in seizing power but in holding on to it.

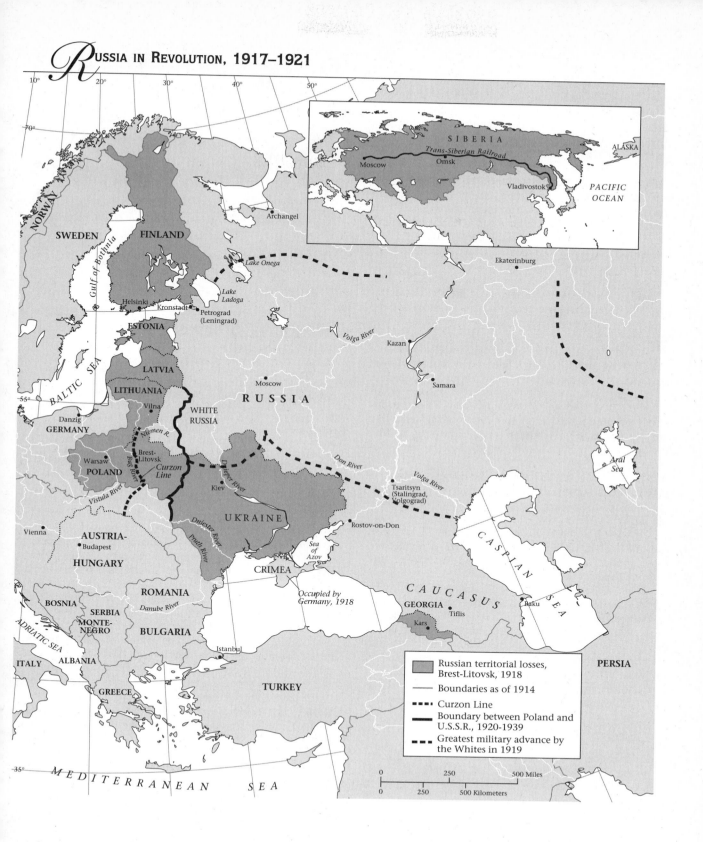

Russia in Revolution, 1917–1921

SIBERIA

Trans-Siberian Railroad

Moscow Omsk

Vladivostok

ALASKA

PACIFIC OCEAN

Archangel

NORWAY

SWEDEN FINLAND

Gulf of Bothnia

Lake Onega

Ekaterinburg

Helsinki *Lake Ladoga*

Kronstadt

Petrograd (Leningrad)

ESTONIA

Volga River

Kazan

BALTIC SEA

LATVIA

LITHUANIA

Vilna

Danzig

GERMANY

Moscow

RUSSIA

Samara

WHITE RUSSIA

Niemen R.

Warsaw

Brest-Litovsk

Bug River

POLAND *Curzon Line*

Dnieper River

Kiev

Don River

Volga River

Tsaritsyn (Stalingrad, Volgograd)

Aral Sea

Vistula River

Vienna

AUSTRIA-

Budapest

HUNGARY

Dniester River

Prutl River

UKRAINE

Rostov-on-Don

Sea of Azov

CAUCASUS

CASPIAN SEA

BOSNIA

SERBIA

MONTE-NEGRO

ADRIATIC SEA

ITALY ALBANIA

ROMANIA

Danube River

CRIMEA

Occupied by Germany, 1918

GEORGIA

Tiflis

Kars

Baku

PERSIA

BULGARIA

GREECE

Istanbul

TURKEY

Russian territorial losses, Brest-Litovsk, 1918

Boundaries as of 1914

Curzon Line

Boundary between Poland and U.S.S.R., 1920–1939

Greatest military advance by the Whites in 1919

MEDITERRANEAN SEA

Through the late teens and early twenties, the new Russian Communist government was beset by enemies on every side. So-called White Russian armies loyal to the czar took the field against the Reds. Subject nationalities—the Baltic states, Poland, and others—rebelled. Invading German armies forced a costly peace upon the new government. The newly independent Poles invaded Russia from the west, Russia's imperial rival Japan from the east. Allied forces—British, French, American—angry at Russia's separate peace and afraid of the Bolshevik virus, established beachheads in Russia and provided logistical support for its enemies. Thus surrounded and attacked from all sides, the Bolsheviks fought back with an ingenuity, energy, and ruthlessness that finally carried the day.

Lenin threw a government together. He called for a constitutional convention, then dissolved it when peasant voters gave a majority to his revolutionary rivals the SRs. He hastily nationalized large sectors of the Russian economy, less for doctrinaire reasons than to mobilize the nation's resources for civil war. And he jerry-built the first Red Army to fight it.

Lenin's right hand in the struggle was a relatively recent convert to bolshevism named Leon Trotsky. A thin, bespectacled, wild-haired intellectual, shrewd theoretician, and brilliant orator, Trotsky became the unlikely architect of the new Red Army. Roaring about Russia in his famous armored train, haranguing the troops or terrifying them by rigorous punishment for slackness or failure, Trotsky made a major contribution to the Bolshevik victory.

It was a costly triumph. The largest nation in Europe, already ravaged by the worst war in Western history, bled for more long years in the Russian Civil War. Red and White terrors rivaled each other in ferocity. Lenin himself was shot and badly wounded by an SR terrorist. Even the sailors, once the most dedicated of revolutionaries, rebelled at last, and Trotsky had to turn the Red Army on them in their turn.

The idealistic American journalist John Reed, who was in Russia in 1917, wrote a widely read account of the October Revolution called *Ten Days That Shook the World*. It took more like five years than ten days, and it was the retention rather than the seizing of power that earned the Bolsheviks their place in history. Nevertheless, they won. When Lenin, weakened by his immense exertions and his injury, died in 1924, the members of the renamed Communist party were the masters of Russia.

THE STALIN REVOLUTION

After the immense strains of a decade of war and revolution, the 1920s saw a relaxation and a falling off of zeal in Russia—before the revolutionary drive was renewed once more in the Stalinist 1930s.

During the twenties, the Communist New Economic Policy actually represented a retreat on the economic

Joseph Djugashvili, then known as "Koba," later as "Stalin" ("Steel")—the future dictator as young revolutionary. Stalin, who encouraged the belief that he had been Lenin's right-hand man in Russia, was actually not a central figure in the revolutionary underground. Arrested five times, he did however serve his share of time in czarist prisons and Siberian exile. These mug shots from czarist police files reveal something of the young Georgian rebel who in later years would himself condemn millions of Soviet citizens to considerably grimmer prisons and labor camps. (Culver Pictures, Inc.)

front. Land was left in the hands of individual peasant proprietors; small businesses were left to entrepreneurs. Efforts to encourage revolution in other lands through the Communist International, or Comintern, had little success.

The great event of the twenties was a quiet power struggle in the Communist party after Lenin's death. And the winner was not one of the Old Man's close associates in prerevolutionary days—not even the brilliant late convert Trotsky—but a stolid, hard-working Bolshevik from the south called Joseph Stalin.

Stalin—real name Dzhugashvili—was the son of a heavy-fisted cobbler from Georgia, in the bandit-haunted mountainous Caucasus region. After a brief seminary education he had become a convert to Marxism and a revolutionary organizer, preaching his new faith to railway workers and serving several terms in prison and in Siberia. While Lenin and Trotsky were arguing the party's future in Switzerland, Stalin was organizing "expropriations" at home—bank robberies to acquire funds for the party in Russia. Lenin never knew him well, added him to the party's Central Committee as an afterthought, and would no doubt have been astonished to learn that half a dozen years after his death, Stalin would be hailed everywhere as "the Lenin of today."

Stalin's rise to power was a triumph of political savvy, hard work, and the organization-man mentality. He was secretary of the Communist party in the twenties, and he made that post the real center of power in Russia. Running the party machine, he came to know its leaders—who the idealists were, who the opportunists, who needed what and how to get it. Neither a great Marxist theoretician nor a spellbinding orator, he had a much more valuable skill—a talent for manipulating power blocs. By the end of the decade Stalin ruled Russia. His rivals had either joined the chorus of support for "the Lenin of today" or, like Trotsky, were on their way to exile abroad.

As the 1930s came on, then, Stalin set out to win his own niche in history—by taking up the revolution once more. His chosen front was economic development, his method a series of Five-Year Plans for unprecedented economic growth in the most backward of the world's great powers.

Russia's long effort to catch up economically with Western Europe had begun in Peter the Great's time two hundred years before. The reforming czar Alexander II in the 1860s and 1870s and turn-of-the-century financial minister Witte had nudged the process on. But World War I had shown how far behind Russia still was: it had been the first to collapse under the strains of modern, mechanized war. Feeling surrounded by capitalist enemies—especially after the Civil War, with its foreign interventions—the Communists had particular reason to strengthen the nation's economy. And Karl Marx seemed to show them the way: through government control, central planning, and collective effort, Russian Communists hoped to succeed where czarist Russia had failed.

During the 1930s the first three Five-Year Plans did, in fact, transform and in key areas expand the Russian economy beyond the wildest dreams of Peter the Great. The Russian government assumed control of industry, agriculture, finance, and trade in the Soviet Union. Government planning commissions worked out schedules of growth for each region, each sector of the economy. Resources were allocated, quotas decreed for every sector, every factory and farm, every worker at his or her desk, lathe, or tractor.

In industry the results were spectacular. Great hydroelectric projects, huge dams, steel mills, tractor factories went up. Whole industrial complexes sprang from the empty steppes. Production goals were reached and surpassed. If there were questions about some of the statistics, the achievement was nonetheless genuine. In a capitalist world still reeling under the hammer blows of the Great Depression, Russia's achievement was particularly impressive.

Agriculture was collectivized under government control. Private farms were merged into large state farms owned by the government, or into farms run collectively by the peasants. Modern agricultural methods and centrally located government machine-tractor stations were introduced to improve production. The increased output was to be used to feed the industrial cities and sold abroad for vitally needed foreign capital. Advances on the agricultural front, however, were slower and much more costly than in the industrial sector, as we will see.

Nevertheless, as World War II came on, Stalin could claim convincingly to have carried Russia's long revolution to something of a climax. Communist-party rule was unquestioned in the vast one-party state, and state socialism had become a reality in the largest nation in the world.

What this transformation of society had cost the country will be deferred to the following chapter, which considers the rise of authoritarian government between the wars. For Stalin had also made Russia the largest totalitarian state in the world.

MEXICO: VILLA, ZAPATA, AND THE VIOLENT DECADE

The Mexican Revolution, a beacon in Latin America, was longer than the Russian Revolution and in some ways more complex than the Chinese. Like the Russian upheaval, the revolution in Mexico began with an abdication under pressure and ended with a massive attempt at a social transformation of the nation in the 1930s. In between, however—as in China—a host of conflicting leaders, armies, and parties competed for power in the bloodiest revolution in Latin American history.

Porfirio Díaz, Mexico's heavy-handed *caudillo* dictator for thirty-five years, was eighty years old in 1910. He had brought the country economic development in the usual Latin American way, through export sales of agricultural and mineral products, especially oil, which was controlled by British and American capitalists. But 90 percent of Mexico's *mestizos* and Indians were still desperately poor peons on the ranches or haciendas of a handful of wealthy landowners. Workers on the foreign-owned railways and in the mines and oil wells, which were becoming more numerous, were equally poverty-stricken. The population was 80 percent illiterate, miserably unhealthy, and kept in line by brutal rural police and federal troops.

Yet there was little opposition. A few middle-class liberals muttered about democracy. Workers occasionally struck and were suppressed. There were bandits in the hills. Otherwise the country was calm. The aging *caudillo's* regime seemed impregnable.

Then in 1910 began a cycle of revolution that would last, in one form or another, for thirty years. The first decade of revolt turned Mexico into a cauldron of violence. The next twenty years saw the establishment of a new revolutionary elite in power—and climaxed in a wave of social reform that paralleled and in some ways outdistanced the contemporary New Deal in the United States. At a time when much of Latin America was turning sharply to the right under a renewed surge of "personalist" dictatorships, Mexico's revolutionary achievement was remarkable indeed.

The names of most of the leaders who made this revolution—Madero, Villa, Zapata, Obregón, Cárdenas, and others—are not household words outside Latin America, as names such as Lenin, Stalin, and Mao have become. But the name of Cárdenas, at least, should surely be added to that list—though he stands closer in means and aims to Franklin Roosevelt than to Joseph Stalin.

Some of the rest of Mexico's revolutionary leaders, such as Zapata and Pancho Villa, have become popular folk heroes in Mexico. Others, such as General Huerta in the early years, were very much the ruffians that preacherly President Wilson across the border called them. But even the revolutionaries who succumbed to the temptations of power, such as the Northern Dynasty of presidents who ruled between 1915 and 1934, were at least efficient organizers who took some steps to help the Mexican masses.

The violent decade that took the lives of some two million Mexicans began almost casually with outbreaks of revolutionary activity against the aging Díaz in 1910. Three very different men led this diverse opposition. Francisco Madero was a slightly built, highly idealistic leader of middle-class reformers. In 1910 he broke the somnolence of Mexican politics by calling for free elections across the nation. Pancho Villa was a bandit chief from the north, a flamboyant incarnation of Mexican macho spirit and an instinctive cavalry leader. Villa led a motley horde of *vaqueros* (cowboys) in revolt in the large, arid northern province of Chihuahua. And Emiliano Zapata was a peasant horse and mule dealer in the mountainous southern province of Morelos. About this same time, he mobilized a guerrilla force to compel the redistribution of some of the local land among his long-suffering Indian and *mestizo* neighbors.

With pressure gathering on all sides, the long-pampered and inefficient Díaz regime suddenly showed its weakness. The government began to crumble. Porfirio Díaz himself abruptly packed up and left for Europe, and Mexico became a battleground for the violent forces thus unleashed.

There is no space here to follow the gaudy, bloody tale of the next decade—roughly 1910–1920—in any detail. The frail Madero was hailed as the Apostle of Democracy, elected president, and murdered by survivors of the Díaz regime who still hoped to recover power. Zapata carried his "land to the peasants" crusade all the way to Mexico City, shared the limelight for a time with Villa, was forced back into Morelos, and finally was killed by troops under a flag of truce. Pancho Villa, after a colorful, bloody time of plundering, was driven back to his bailiwick in Chihuahua, took to killing gringos so as to precipitate U.S. intervention in the chaos, and had a fine time riding rings around General Pershing's expeditionary force. He was finally murdered by a personal enemy in the early 1920s. All three lived on as Mexican folk heroes; none had done much for Mexico.

Meanwhile, a succession of leaders from the dry, spacious northern provinces that abut the American Southwest came to the fore. This succession of powerful men, the Northern Dynasty, in time established a reasonably stable regime that at least preached some concern for the welfare of the Mexican people.

They were not saints. Perhaps the worst was General Huerta, a drunken warlord who briefly ran central Mexico from the bars and brothels of Mexico City. A self-aggrandizing politician from the old Díaz days named Carranza succeeded Huerta. Seeking popular support, Carranza at least left Mexico the Constitution of 1917, the most liberal in Latin America and a model for later revolutionaries throughout the southern half of the hemisphere. This document promised land to the peasants;

Emiliano Zapata, champion of the peasants of southern Mexico. One of the most popular leaders of the Mexican Revolution, Zapata became a legend after his violent death. His battle cry of "land and liberty" led to the burning and looting of many plantations during the bloodiest years of the Mexican Revolution. (North Wind Picture Archives)

decent hours and wages as well as unions for workers; equal pay for women; and at least the possibility of nationalization of the property of the reactionary Mexican Catholic church and of exploitative foreign capitalists.

The United States intervened twice in this turmoil, in 1914 and 1916, to protect American lives and property and to teach Latin Americans how to choose leaders of a higher moral caliber, as Wilson unctuously put it.

During the 1920s and 1930s the Mexicans emerged from the bloodbath of the preceding decade and put together a remarkable compromise regime that realized some of the exalted promises of the Constitution of 1917.

CÁRDENAS AND THE PRI

The instrument that brought Mexico order out of chaos and some measure of social justice was a unifying, centralizing political party. Known as the PRI, or Party of the Revolutionary Institutions, this organization combined all the nation's new leadership cadres—the military, the bureaucracy, business interests and intellectuals, and now the labor unions and the peasantry—in a single structure that would run Mexico for the next fifty years.

It was essentially a one-party system, and more socialistic than anything ever seen north of the Rio Grande. But no less a democrat than Franklin Roosevelt was willing to declare a Good Neighbor Policy toward Cárdenas, the Mexican leader who carried the social revolution furthest in the 1930s.

The twenties saw two other leaders from northern Mexico—a one-armed, self-proclaimed socialist general named Obregón and his handpicked successor, the "Maximum Chief" Calles—lay down the party's basic structure and smother the last flames of revolution. These men organized the party and the basic PRI alliance of ruling elements. They made a beginning, at least, at land redistribution, supported some colorfully corrupt labor leaders against foreign business interests, and began a long and brutal struggle with the Mexican church. Too long in the saddle, these middle-aged revolutionaries also lined their own pockets in the process of rebuilding Mexico.

In 1934, however, the PRI leadership chose for the next president the last and most admired of all the leaders of Mexico's long revolution: Lázaro Cárdenas. Cárdenas was an Indian, young and vigorous, a tireless activist, and an instinctive politician. A friend to socialists, peasants, and workers, he was willing and able to defy the North American colossus and get away with it. He carried the revolutionary drive for social justice further than many believed possible.

Cárdenas was as much an organizer as he was an idealist. He kept the military on his side by letting generals alone—and won over the troops by military reforms. He earned the allegiance of much of the business community by supporting industrialization by Mexican rather than foreign investors. He replaced corrupt old revolu-

tionaries with young radicals eager to make a social revolution of their own. He supported a huge new labor union and an even larger peasants' union, bringing new spokesmen for these groups into the PRI.

With this massive base of support, Cárdenas redistributed twice as much land to the tillers as all his predecessors had, some to private holders and some to collective farms. He supported workers' demands and raised their standard of living. He also supported Mexican entrepreneurs, who for the first time began to produce sufficient quantities of manufactured goods to break the ancient cycle of dependency on foreigners. And he astonished the world by nationalizing the American- and British-run oil industry, thus breaking the back of foreign exploitation of this key Mexican resource. Britain and the United States, preoccupied with the looming Nazi threat in Europe, bit the bullet.

There were failures, of course. The nationalized oil industry, deprived of foreign capital and technological know-how, almost expired in the early years. Mexico suffered throughout the period from a lack of technological skills, even as Mexican art became world-famous. And of course the PRI, for all its social conscience, continued to suppress any serious political opposition with a firm hand.

But when Cárdenas retired in 1940, Mexico was in crucial ways a different country from the Mexico of Porfirio Díaz. Its thirty-year revolution would be a banner and a beacon to many of the Latin American republics to the south.

CHINA AND THE LEGACY OF SUN YIXIAN

The longest of all the long revolutions was the Chinese Revolution of 1911–1949, which began a few years before World War I and ended several years after World War II, in the hectic early years of the Cold War. These four decades include only the military phase of the longest revolution, leaving out the revolutionary transformation of Chinese society that followed the Communist victory of 1949. But these social and economic changes too were prepared by the forty years of political and military struggle to be traced here.

China's twentieth-century revolution—like all the movements to be dealt with in the remainder of this chapter—was triggered by contact with the West. In the case of China, it was the catastrophic encounter that ended the nineteenth century. It was Western victories that destroyed the Manchu dynasty by revealing its weakness. Westernized Chinese leaders fought the subsequent revolution, and their Western ideologies determined China's future direction. Whether the Nationalists or the Communists won, the new China would thus be significantly shaped by Western influences. There *was* no Confucian candidate.

The three great leaders of this long revolution were all world figures in their time: Dr. Sun, the founder, and Jiang Jiehi and Mao Zedong, who fought for his legacy.

"What is the standing of our nation in the world? In comparison with other nations we have the greatest population and the oldest culture, of four thousand years' duration. We ought to be advancing in line with the nations of Europe and America. But the Chinese people have only family and clan groups: there is no national spirit. Consequently, in spite of four hundred million people gathered together in one China, we are in fact but a sheet of loose sand. We are the poorest and weakest state in the world, occupying the lowest position in national affairs; the rest of mankind is the carving knife and the serving dish, while we are the fish and the meat. Our position now is extremely perilous; if we do not earnestly promote nationalism and weld together our four hundred million into a strong nation, we face a tragedy—the loss of our country and the destruction of our race. To ward off this danger, we must espouse nationalism and employ the national spirit to save the country."

This statement from Sun Yixian's <u>Three Principles</u> develops one of the fundamental ideas introduced by the founding father of the Chinese Revolution: the importance of nationalism, the sort of national feeling that had begun to animate Western peoples more than a century before, for the success of any emerging nation. Dr. Sun, like earlier European prophets of this ideology, saw national character as rooted in racial stock, language, shared ways of life, and common beliefs, all of which he thought the Chinese people possessed.

What basic forms of loyalty to social groups does Sun Yixian detect in traditional China? Why does he believe the Chinese must develop a larger allegiance to their country as a whole? Does he believe that the Chinese do in fact have much to be proud of in their past? In China's long revolution, the Nationalists were eventually defeated by the Communists: did this mean the abandonment of nationalism in China?

Sun Yixian, <u>The Three Principles of the People</u> (Taipei, Taiwan: China Cultural Service, 1987), pp. 4–5.

In forty years, in a country the size of the continental United States and several times as populous, many other leaders rose and fell, many more rebellious banners were raised and struck down than can even be touched on here. But the central thread of Sun Yixian's legacy and the long duel between Jiang and Mao does give coherence and direction to the story of this longest and bloodiest of twentieth-century revolutions.

Bullied by foreign imperialists and deeply divided over how far to go in learning from the West in order to defeat the West, China was dissolving into a hopeless confusion of conflicting theories, ambitions, and factions as the twentieth century began. The mandate of Heaven had clearly passed from the battered Manchus: but to whom?

Old realities and new influences collided in turn-of-the-century China. Established court politicians such as the military leader Yuan Shikai, powerful provincial generals, the perennially dangerous Chinese secret societies, and the

eternally exploited, increasingly restless peasant masses would play important parts in the coming struggle, as such groups had in the past. New groups with equally important roles included the overseas Chinese community, many of them wealthy merchants scattered over Southeast Asia, the western Pacific, and even the Untied States; the growing numbers of Western-educated Chinese students trained in Japan, Europe, or the United States, or at the new Chinese university in Beijing; and the emerging Chinese proletariat, exploited products of the rapid industrialization of great Chinese cities such as Shanghai.

Among the better-educated of these groups, at least, Western ideas ranging from Darwinian evolution to nineteenth-century political ideologies circulated freely around 1900. Magazines and journals, clubs and discussion groups flourished, spreading the new ideas and debating their application to China's multiplying problems. Out of the tangle, two basic tendencies evolved: a reformist campaign for a constitutional monarchy, which reached even into court circles, and a revolutionary demand for a Chinese republic, which found support among radical students and insurrectionary organizations.

The reformers had their day first. In a final effort to save the Manchu dynasty, the Dowager Empress Ci Xi uncharacteristically acquiesced in a series of changes in the old order that were far more drastic than any thus far. In the early years of the twentieth century, then, the nationwide system of Confucian civil-service examinations, which had served the empire for the better part of two thousand years, was abolished. Provincial legislative assemblies were introduced, and then a national assembly in Beijing. Plans were laid for a gradual transition to a constitutional monarchy like those in Europe or Japan.

The result was to provide more issues for debate as the old Confucian-educated ruling class saw themselves being phased out, and new arenas to debate those issues—the new assemblies. Feuds broke out between the powerful Yuan Shikai and the regent for the three-year-old emperor who succeeded Ci Xi in 1908. A rash of abortive popular insurrections made the weakness of the monarchy even clearer. By 1911, the hour of the republican revolutionaries had come.

Sun Yixian (1866–1925) was the best-known revolutionary proponent of a Chinese republic, both in China and abroad. Born of peasant stock near Canton (Guangzhou) in the cosmopolitan south, he was a thoroughly Westernized Chinese. He had studied at a Christian mission school in Honolulu, read for his medical degree in the British colony of Hong Kong, established his first revolutionary organization in Westernized Japan. He had even made a special visit to his native hamlet to break the village idols, a gesture symbolic of his rejection of the old China.

Sun had been to the United States and Europe and was well-known among the wealthy overseas Chinese community. He had been involved in secret-society uprisings in South China. He had developed the charismatic personality and the ability to bring rival factions together that would earn him the title of Father of the Chinese Revolution.

Sun Yixian's legacy to those who followed him was also fully assembled by the time of the Revolution of 1911. That legacy took the form of his famous—and highly flexible—Three Principles of the People.

The Three Principles are usually stated as nationalism, democracy, and socialism. By nationalism Sun meant opposition to the Manchus as well as to Western imperialists. By democracy he intended civil rights for all Chinese and constitutional government modeled in part on that of the United States. The socialist (more literally, "people's livelihood") plank was a rather undeveloped economic principle derived not from Marx or any other Western socialist but from the then-popular theories of the American land-tax crusader Henry George, who saw a single tax on land as a panacea for many social ills.

In the broadest sense, these three principles summed up all the European ideological development of the century following the French Revolution. These sweeping social ideals, suitably modified by a much longer indigenous tradition of social thought, would now begin the twentieth-century transformation of China.

Sun Yixian would work for the last fifteen years of his life (like Lenin, he died in his fifties) to make the Chinese republic a democratic reality. Generalissimo Jiang Jiehi would become the maximum leader of China's Nationalist party through the 1920s, 1930s, and 1940s. Chairman Mao Zedong would organize and lead China's Communist party and would rule the nation through the 1950s and 1960s and into the 1970s. The Three Principles that were China's inheritance from Dr. Sun thus sum up much of the nation's history since.

WARLORDS AND STUDENT REBELS

The Republic came quickly. Within three years of Empress Ci Xi's death in 1908, the demoralized empire finally collapsed in a welter of peasant rice riots, student agitation, army revolts, court intrigues, and revolutionary outbreaks led by Dr. Sun's own organization, the United League. Sun, like Lenin, was out of the country when the monarchy fell. After many abortive uprisings elsewhere in the nation, a local army revolt at Wuhan in the Yangzi Valley of central China in the fall of 1911 snowballed into a far-reaching repudiation of Manchu rule. Sun, who was in the United States rallying support for the cause, read about the revolution in a Denver newspaper. He hurried home in time to be proclaimed first president of the new Republic of China in January of 1912.

But the long revolution in China, like those in Russia and Mexico, rather began than ended with the collapse of the old regime. The diehard supporters of the old order, however, had their innings first.

Like Madero in Mexico, Sun was rather a symbol of the revolution than a ruler. Knowing that he had neither the power nor the support to govern a nation still sliding toward anarchy, he shrewdly used his new position to win to the republican cause the one man who could govern the country. Yuan Shikai was the most powerful survivor of the old order—court official, famous general and military reformer, currently prime minister of the constitutional monarchy still hanging on in Beijing. In return for a promise of the presidency of the new republic, Yuan engineered the dissolution of the monarchy. In the spring of 1912 Sun stepped down and Yuan became the second president of the Chinese republic.

Yuan Shikai, however, was thoroughly a product of the old China. He accepted the newfangled foreign title—and at once began to intrigue to establish himself as first emperor of a new Chinese dynasty.

But the old order was finished in China. Sun opposed Yuan's plans; local rebellions again broke out, and some of the president's own generals refused to suppress them. With the outbreak of World War I in 1914, Japan further embarrassed the new regime, first by seizing Germany's possessions in Chinese Shandong, then by imposing the notorious Twenty-one Demands on China itself.

These imperialistic demands included acceptance of Japanese political, military, and financial advisers, further economic penetration by Japan, and recognition of a paramount position for Japan in Manchuria and elsewhere in the north. Such concessions would have made the enormous continental empire little more than a protectorate of the island kingdom. Yuan, hoping for Japanese support for his dynastic ambitions, accepted most of the proposals—and turned the nation definitively against himself. His dream of an imperial restoration frustrated, Yuan died in 1916.

With the passing of the old order's strong man, China, as so often before in its long history, fell apart. A facade of republican government continued at Beijing, but its authority was minimal. Military cliques claimed some power in North and in South China. Sun Yixian set to work to reorganize his faction, now dubbed the Guomindang, or Nationalist party. But real authority quickly fell into the hands of the local power brokers in the provinces, most of them military leaders with private armies who became known as *warlords*. Through the late teens and early twenties, the anarchy of the warlord era prevailed.

Chinese warlords, like the regional *caudillos* of nineteenth-century Latin America, were typically aggressive military commanders with strong and sometimes colorful personalities. Many were former generals or bandits, and they ruled their territories by force. Their armies were strengthened by modern weapons and by the mobility made available by railways and river steamers. They lived off the revenues of cities or seaports, by taxing or plundering the peasants, and sometimes on subsidies from foreign powers. They were quick to voice the new slogans about democracy, patriotism, and the people's welfare—and they were an unmitigated plague on the land.

But there was a new force too during this time—the Chinese student movement—and it grew in influence. These young products of the new school system, Westernized yet bitter enemies of Western exploitation of China, took seriously the ideological legacy that the warlords degraded. The students became the leaders in the hurricane of national outrage that exploded in the spring of 1919—the famous May Fourth Movement.

The May Fourth Movement was a nationwide wave of strikes and demonstrations against foreign exploitation—and the Chinese weakness that made such exploitation possible—launched by the students at Beijing University. Triggered by the refusal of the Versailles Peace Conference to require the Japanese to return Shandong to China, the movement focused on a repudiation of Japan's Twenty-one Demands of five years before.

The student organizations were severely punished for their patriotic defiance of authority. But their cause triumphed. Workers' strikes, merchants' boycotts of Japanese goods, and public outrage drove the current cabinet in Beijing to resign and forced the Chinese government to refuse to sign the Treaty of Versailles.

Students also took a leading role in China's New Culture Movement, a sweeping reassessment of the nation's ancient cultural heritage and a search for new directions for China. American pragmatist John Dewey, British pacifist and philosopher Bertrand Russell, Indian writer and Nobel laureate Rabindranath Tagore, and others toured the land lecturing to the new clubs and student groups. Chinese cultural and intellectual innovators of all sorts published in the new journals that spearheaded the New Culture Movement.

The most important new direction of the 1920s in China, however, was a turning away from Japanese, American, and other earlier influences and a new interest in Communist Russia. From postrevolutionary, pre-Stalinist Russia came antiimperialist assurances, political and military advisors, and the doctrines of Marx and Lenin. Marxism-Leninism explained imperialism in simple terms: it was a consequence of Western capitalism. Leninism offered the Bolshevik model of tightly knit organization and discipline in challenging the weak government in Beijing and the foreign exploiters still present everywhere in China.

In 1920 a small group at Beijing University began to study Marxism seriously. In 1921 the Chinese Communist party was organized at Shanghai. Among the organizers was a former Peking University student named Mao Zedong.

Jiang Jiehi versus Mao Zedong

Some Russian Communists were still working for the world revolution that had failed to materialize after World War I. They were realistic enough to realize, however, that the only force strong enough to pose a threat to the Chinese government in Beijing was not the handful of Communists who organized in 1921, but Sun Yixian's Nationalist party, the Guomindang. To the Nationalists, therefore, they offered not Marxism but practical help in organizing the Guomindang as a disciplined Bolshevik-style party. The Russians also sent military advisors to retrain the Nationalist army under the superintendent of the military academy, a younger officer named Jiang Jiehi.

Jiang Jiehi (1886–1975), a patriotic, ambitious soldier with training in both Japan and Russia, was soon carving out a central position of power for himself. Jiang's landlord background and the elitist military tradition of the samurai that he had absorbed in Japan had left him with little sympathy for either democracy or socialism. At the Whampoa Military Academy near Canton he trained a generation of officers to unify their country—and to support their teacher in the power struggles to come.

Sun Yixian died in 1925. The party he had founded

Chairman Mao. Dismissed as a "Red bandit" by Generalissimo Jiang Jiehi, Mao Zedong "swam in the peasant sea" and defeated Jiang, to become the revolutionary ruler of the world's most populous nation. Some of his most important later economic experiments, however, would prove costly failures. (The Bettmann Archive)

continued to build its power in the south. Then in 1927 the Guomindang armies, supported by Russian advisors and arms and led by Jiang Jiehi, moved out of South China in the long-awaited Northern Campaign to unify the nation. Scores of warlord armies capitulated or joined the host as it advanced. Propagandists spread out ahead of the troops, convincing many that Jiang was the man who could restore the one indisputable political necessity for peace and prosperity in China: unity.

Soon most of the country was his. The Beijing government dithered, would fall the following year. Meanwhile, Jiang had what must have seemed a secondary problem to deal with: the divisive disagreements that kept cropping up between his Nationalist followers and the new Communist cadres in the Guomindang.

The Chinese Communist party, founded largely as a student group, had found many recruits among factory and railroad workers in rapidly industrializing cities such as Canton and Shanghai. Russian advisors, however, had urged the Chinese Communists to join the Nationalists in their drive to overthrow the Beijing government. This they had done. But the alliance was purely one of convenience, and in 1927 the victorious Jiang Jiehi decided to destroy these potential enemies within the Guomindang.

He struck swiftly and without warning. Trapped in the cities where they had gathered to organize the workers, the Communist cadres were slaughtered. Their enclaves of proletarian support, isolated in that vast peasant country, were surrounded and crushed, and with them the Communist party in China. Or so it seemed.

Handfuls of the routed Reds escaped to the countryside, fled to the villages. Among the few who had already sought to organize the peasant masses was a now considerably more mature Mao Zedong (1893–1976). A man of peasant stock himself and a former student Communist from Beijing, he never forgot the devastating lesson of the debacle of 1927. In 1926 he had espoused the orthodox Marxist view that "the industrial proletariat is the leading force in our revolution"; but by 1928 he was pointing out that the communist cadres "have sprung from the agrarian revolution and are fighting for their own interests . . . "[2] No matter what Marx or Lenin said about the vanguard role of the industrial proletariat, in China it was the peasantry, with its incalculable numbers and ancient grievances, that would be the wave of the revolutionary future.

Jiang went on to capture Beijing in 1928. Mao established a Communist base in the interior, in the hills of Jiangxi Province. Here, like Zapata in Mexico, he began to divide large estates among the peasants, to provide education and some health care, and to teach a modified version of Marxist socialism. This Jiangxi Soviet became the model for the basic Maoist tactic thereafter—a tactic as old as guerrilla warfare—which he called "swimming in the peasant sea."

Jiang, established as head of the Chinese republic after 1928, tried to provide for the economic and social development of China too. He had married an American-educated woman named Soong Mei-ling, who, as Madame Jiang Jiehi would become an immensely valuable voice for Jiang in the United States over the years. The Generalissimo, as the Western papers called him, thus acquired important American support. But he was also closely tied to Chinese banking families, and he depended on cronies and clients to help him run the country—all important political creditors to be repaid with favors and promotions.

The nation had been badly damaged by the warlord era, and now it faced an even graver foreign threat—a renewal of Japanese imperialist pressure in the 1930s. Thus surrounded by problems, China's foremost general nevertheless found time to launch a series of so-called "antibandit" campaigns to rout the Communists out of Jiangxi in the early thirties. Not till 1934 did Jiang succeed in dislodging Mao from his hills, and then only by completely surrounding the area and burning his way in through the villages.

Perhaps 100,000 Communists escaped the tightening noose. Led by Mao and his right-hand man Zhou Enlai, the survivors of the shattered Jiangxi Soviet fled

---

[2]Mao Tse-tung, *Mao Tse-tung: An Anthology of His Writings,* ed. Anne Freemantle (New York: New American Library, 1962), pp. 59, 90.

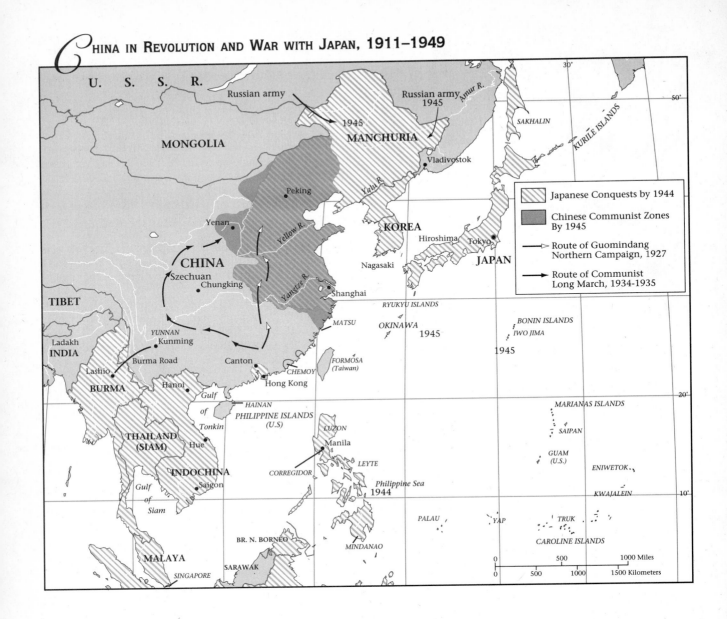

once more, this time north and west, pursued by the Nationalist armies. The perilous and costly year-long march that followed took them some 6000 meandering miles to a new sanctuary in the northern province of Shaanxi. Only a few thousand of them made it.

In Chinese Communist history, this is the Long March. The terrible casualties, the desperate river crossings, the frozen mountain passes that Mao's followers traveled through on their northern march have been immortalized in every art since the Communist victory in 1949. In the mid–1930s, however, as Mao and his remnant bands settled into the caves of their new Shaanxi base, ultimate victory must have looked very far away indeed.

MAO'S VICTORY

Jiang Jiehi had failed to destroy the "Red bandits." But he had much worse problems in the 1930s. In 1931 the Japanese had seized the industrializing northern province of Manchuria. In 1937 they launched a major invasion of China proper. By 1939 most of eastern China was in their hands, and Jiang Jiehi had retreated to the interior, to what became his wartime capital of Chongqing.

Confronted with this massive foreign threat, many Nationalist leaders urged that the final destruction of Mao's Communists be postponed for the duration. The Communists themselves organized guerrilla warfare

Soldiers like these Chinese Red Army troops survived the Long March and went on to fight the Japanese invaders of North China. Mao Zedong, a peasant himself, had a knack for mobilizing peasant soldiers like these and keeping them together throughout China's long revolution.

against the Japanese occupying forces in North China, thus strengthening their image as patriots. In a dramatic development, some of Jiang's own officers virtually kidnapped him and compelled him to sit down and negotiate a truce with the Communists so that both might concentrate on the war with Japan. Throughout the Second World War—1941–1945 in Asia—this uneasy armistice between the two rivals prevailed.

Jiang was China's recognized ruler, meeting in the larger Allied summit conferences with the rest of the Big Five—Roosevelt, Churchill, Stalin, and the Free French leader Charles de Gaulle, most of whose country was also occupied by the enemy. Mao, meanwhile, built up his Red Army, strengthened his peasant support, and nicked away at the Japanese. Jiang failed to expel the invaders, and as his Chongqing government grew more autocratic, corrupt, and inefficient, many Chinese who were not peasants began to wonder if Mao might not after all be a viable alternative to the Generalissimo.

When World War II ended in 1945, then, things at long last began to go Mao's way. In the last days of the war, the Soviet Union declared war on Japan and quickly liberated large chunks of North China. Though Stalin had not approved of Mao's peasant-based communism—had even apparently expelled Mao from the Communist International for a time—the Silent Man in the Kremlin now moved to help the Chinese Communists. Liberated territories and captured weapons were turned over to Mao's forces, not to Jiang's. Mao was left stronger than ever as the final confrontation approached.

As the later 1940s passed, furthermore, Jiang Jiehi's American friends began to lose patience with him. Envoys from the United States demanded that he clean up the cor-

ruption in his government. Like his Russian advisors in the 1920s, his American mentors in the 1940s urged him to work with the Communists to unify the country.

Rivalries and suspicions that went back twenty years were not so easily erased, however. Within a couple of years after the defeat of Japan, clashes between Nationalist and Communist troops had escalated again to full-scale civil war. And this time Mao was on the offensive. Jiang's retreat into the South became a rout, and the roads were littered with abandoned American military hardware.

By 1949 Jiang had withdrawn from the mainland altogether to the large offshore island of Taiwan (Formosa), where he was to survive as president of a Chinese mini-republic protected by an American fleet for the rest of his life. Mao, meanwhile, stood before a crowd of hundreds of thousands in Beijing's Tiananmen Square to announce the new People's Republic of China—which he also would rule until his death.

Jiang's career was essentially over in 1949. But Mao's had only reached the halfway point. The social revolution he would bring to China, the military clashes with India and the United States in Korea, and the disastrous social experiments of his later years all lay in the future in 1949.

Mao's round, smiling face and slicked-back hair and the wart on his chin were unfamiliar to a world used to Jiang's handsome graying visage. But one thing, at least, became clear quite soon. China, after a half century of chaos, had found unity once more—this time under a man who was as much a child of twentieth-century Western ideologies as he was a product of the ancient land he ruled.

Colonial Challenges to Western Predominance

Emergence of Westernized Anti-Western Movements

Across the European intercontinental empires that sprawled over Asia and Africa, rebellious impulses also flickered and flared up during the two decades between the wars. They produced no great revolutions like those in Russia, China, and Mexico. But they did keep alive the spirit of resistance that had been born during the New Imperialism and that would bear fruit at last during the Great Liberation after World War II.

Most of the colonial struggles of the intervening period were not military insurrections, like the resistance of earlier decades. The peoples of Africa and Asia had learned that force was not the answer when dealing with Westerners, who were, for that time at least, the masters of the new technological warfare. Instead, the resistance tended to take political form within the institutional framework made available under colonial governments.

The new leaders of this simmering revolt against the West were now almost uniformly Western-educated. Most had studied in mission schools. Many had gone on for further training in Europe or America. They were people who knew the imperialists well, spoke their languages, and understood the rules of the political game as it was played by their colonial rulers. Many of them had also spent time in Western jails, but this too they were able to turn to their advantage as leaders of unfree peoples.

The Asian and African independence movements they led were for the most part at early stages of development during the 1920s and 1930s. They were preoccupied with such basics as defining goals, which might range from reform of the colonial administration through autonomy within the empire to complete independence. There was also the problem of gathering in adherents—not so easy when Western training had cut many leaders off from their own people. Finally, there was the matter of how best to organize for effective opposition. This last raised a number of very practical questions. Were study groups a good place to begin? Was it time to move on to a political party? Was terrorist activity necessary?

All the anti-imperialist movements were primarily nationalist in content and tone. They drew heavily on the nationalist movements of nineteenth-century Europe for the basic idea of nationhood, but they were indigenous movements in terms of their characteristics, sought-after rights, and sense of destiny.

A detailed survey of these movements would yield nothing but a bewildering array of organizations, issues, small struggles won or lost. It is the slow gathering of forces we need to be aware of here in the colonial world, the preparation for the great liberation to come. With this in mind, we will trace in some detail the growth of one of the greatest of these movements—the Congress party of Gandhi's India—and attempt a few sweeping generalizations about the independence organizations among African peoples during this period.

India: Gandhi and the Congress Party

India during the early decades of the twentieth century was still the India of the Raj—the period of British supremacy—and the jewel in the crown of the British Empire. Paradoxically, if perhaps understandably, it was here that the most successful of anti-British independence movements evolved.

British rule had brought some distinct benefits to India. British engineers had built tens of thousands of miles of railroads, roads, and canals across the subcontinent, stimulating business activity and a new surge in the growth of India's traditionally bustling commercial middle classes. Pressured by Indian demands, the British took steps toward Indian self-government. Indians were admitted to higher positions in the colonial administration, including the English viceroy's advisory council. Provincial legislatures—elected by propertied elites—were introduced. Formal education was made available for more people than ever before, and Oxford and Cambridge were opened to the talented sons of India's *rajas* and urban wealth. There were attempts to improve public health in that huge and in places densely crowded stretch of Asia.

But British rule, for all its benefits, had cost Indians dearly. The new transportation networks, for instance, benefited the English economy more than the Indian, facilitating Britain's extraction of a third of India's raw materials and India's receipt of two fifths of her imports from Britain. The Western concept of private property, which undermined traditional family ownership and government claims on land, made some Indians very wealthy—and others poorer than they had ever been. Western education undermined India's traditional culture. Even Western health measures brought new problems by stimulating the disastrous population growth of twentieth-century India. And despite "steps toward" independence, genuine freedom still seemed very far away.

The Indian National Congress, or Congress party, had been organized in 1885 by a group of moderate middle-class reformers, mostly lawyers, teachers, and journalists. They had won important reforms from the British. At the same time, a Hindu renaissance of arts and letters had kindled a renewed pride among educated Indians. Around the turn of the century, a burst of nationalist violence that led to repressive measures by the British had further encouraged Indian nationalism and opposition to foreign rule.

But India still seemed an unlikely candidate for a

popular nationalistic independence movement as World War I drew to a close. The isolation of its countless tiny villages, the traditional lines of social cleavage between the castes, the Hindu-Muslim split, the lack of a common language, and the great distance between the well-off, Western-educated leadership and the Indian masses looked like insuperable obstacles.

The man who bridged these gaps was Mohandas K. Gandhi (1869–1948), who became known to the world as Mahatma Gandhi, the Great Soul of India.

Raised by pious, well-to-do Hindu parents, young Gandhi was shipped off to London to study law. Isolated for years in a London slum, he pored over a potpourri of spiritual sources, from the ancient Hindu *Bhagavad-Gita* (Song of God) and the Christian Bible to nineteenth-century prophets such as Tolstoy and Thoreau. His first campaign for the oppressed came not in India but in South Africa, where he was sent as a young man by his Indian law firm. Here he took up the cause of the Indian contract laborers who worked as peons in the South African gold mines. The success of the peaceful protests he organized there brought him home to India to a hero's welcome from the Congress party.

Gandhi's message and methods were set from the time of his return during World War I. Building upon the ancient Hindu principle of *ahimsa* (nonviolence), he organized a series of nonviolent demonstrations, first for reform in the administration of the Raj, then for Indian independence. He went repeatedly and peacefully to jail for his cause, frequently turning imprisonment into victory by embarking upon prolonged hunger strikes. As his reputation as a spiritual leader grew, he abandoned his Western clothing and lifestyle entirely, dressed in a traditional Indian costume of homespun, and lived the life of a Hindu guru of an earlier age.

The principles he championed were an odd mix of ancient and modern. He urged a return to the simplest of ancient Indian ways of life. His campaign to get Indians to reject British manufactured cloth and spin cotton at home on the old-fashioned spinning wheel put that homely implement on the Indian flag. At the same time, however, he was a firm believer in Western notions of human equality, rejecting India's traditional caste distinctions and preaching the equality of women with men. In Gandhi, then, the Indian National Congress found at last a leader who could bridge the many gaps that divided Indians and who could build a genuine sense of Indian national identity.

The English tongue—ironically—gave him the national language his country needed. His eclectic religious studies made it easy for him to work with Muslims as well as Hindus. His firm rejection of caste turned the lowest of the low from "untouchables" into "children of God," in Indian parlance. Above all, his common touch, his guru garb and manner, his endless traveling among the villages enabled him to bridge the immense abyss that separated the cosmopolitan Congress leaders, with their

Mahatma Gandhi, Indian Congress party leader, shown here with his famous spinning wheel. Gandhi's unique blend of Western savvy and Indian spirituality made him the foremost leader of the independence movement in Britain's largest colony. Can you imagine the Mahatma in a Western business suit, of the sort he wore studying law in Britain or organizing his first protests in South Africa? (AP/Wide World Photos)

London-cut suits and lovely homes in Calcutta or Bombay, from the Indian masses in their uncountable mud-walled villages across the land.

Gandhi manipulated the foreign press with as much skill as he moved the hearts of other Indians. Colonial police and soldiers overreacted to nonviolence—or to the riots that sometimes accompanied nonviolent demonstrations—and generated public support for Gandhi abroad, even in Britain. Viceroys learned to negotiate with him—when they were not locking him up. The thin, bespectacled little man in white homespun became as familiar to newsreel watchers between the wars as FDR or Hitler. For many in the West as well as for hundreds of millions of Indians, Mahatma Gandhi stood out as the only living saint in a darkening world.

In the end, dealing with a basically democratic imperial power, Gandhi and his nonviolent protests prevailed. In 1947, in the anti-imperialist aftermath of World War II, Great Britain let his people go.

Gandhi was shot in 1948 by an Indian fanatic who

was outraged at the Mahatma's efforts to calm the terrible Hindu–Muslim rioting that accompanied independence. It was a violent death for a supremely nonviolent man. Nor was Mahatma Gandhi the last Indian leader who would fall victim to the religious differences that still divide that great nation.

AFRICA: THE ANTI-IMPERIALISTS ORGANIZE

The condition of colonial Africa between the world wars was quite different from that of India. Ten times the size of the subcontinent, Africa had only a little over half its population—fewer than 200 million people in 1940. Most of Africa remained less urbanized, less literate, less politically sophisticated, and less rich in roads, railways, and other modern facilities. Most of Africa also seemed much further from independence than India under the Raj.

There were some signs of changing colonial attitudes during the 1920s and 1930s, however, which would work to the advantage of the second largest continent in its restless quest for freedom.

The upsurge of political idealism that accompanied the founding of the League of Nations and the peace and disarmament conferences of the interwar years affected colonial policies too, even in Africa. The German colonies—most of which were African—were turned over to the victors after World War I as mandates, territories to be governed as much in the interests of the indigenous peoples as for the colonizing Europeans, with regular reports required. Britain's policy of indirect rule through traditional local authorities evolved in the direction of a conscious policy of "preparing Africans for independence" at some admittedly hazy future date. French centralization, which envisaged no future separation of metropolitan France from its overseas territories, nevertheless welcomed African leaders to French educational institutions and political life, where they obtained the skills they would later use against French rule.

In general, African colonies were more peaceful and produced more profits and taxes during these twenty years than at any time since their acquisition during the scramble for Africa at the end of the preceding century. Despite low commodity prices on the international market, there were revenues. Some of these were channeled into modest programs of economic development, health, and education. An air of relatively benevolent rule and an impression of slow but measurable advances along Western lines prevailed over much of Africa.

As in India, however, the impression was in many ways deceptive. Tensions were real, and the seeds—in some places, the fact—of militant revolt quite vigorously present.

Westerners saw Africa much as they did Latin America and much of Asia—as a source of raw materials. They utilized cheap African labor to siphon off the cotton of Egypt, the copper of the Congo (Zaire), and the gold of South Africa. They put black or Arab Africans to work on the farms of European settlers in East or South Africa, or along the Mediterranean shores of North Africa. The African middle class was much smaller than that of India, and African economic development proceeded much more slowly.

As for the "civilizing mission" of the colonizers and the preparation for independence that some claimed to be undertaking—there was, at best, much less evidence of it than in India. In all of French West Africa, an area roughly the size of the United States, there were no more than eighty high schools; Nigeria was the only British African colony that boasted more than a dozen secondary schools. British indirect rule left local authority in the hands of traditional chiefs, but it did little to advance the few Western-educated Africans beyond clerk status in the colonial administration. French direct rule gave some Africans more power in the colonial government—but only those who were thoroughly transformed by total immersion in the French way of life.

Under these circumstances, then, anti-imperialist sentiments, some openly nationalist movements, and even a handful of armed resistance groups persisted in Africa between the wars.

Violent resistance was confined largely to North Africa. Here Islam's long feud with Christendom still simmered, leading to intermittent turbulence. Resistance by desert sheiks and tribes flared up during the 1920s, particularly in French Morocco and in Italy's new colony of Libya.

The Christian European predominance established in the Middle East and North Africa during the nineteenth century, meanwhile, stimulated a pan-Islamic cultural revival. Centered at the Al-Azhar University in Cairo, this intellectual revival of Islamic consciousness sent student militants back to their homelands all over Mediterranean and Sudanic Africa. In the 1930s these highly educated Muslim militants were organizing modern nationalist political parties to work for independence from the European rulers.

South of the Sahara, open independence movements were fewer, violence almost nonexistent.

African student organizations set up at British or French universities were a fertile source of dreams and plans for African independence, and the students would bring these dreams home with them. The pan-African ideal of African independence and unity, preached primarily by African Americans such as the flamboyant Marcus Garvey and the scholar W.E.B. Du Bois, also found eager converts among African students.

In Africa itself, reform-minded African nationalist organizations were set up in the British West African colonies of the Gold Coast (Ghana) and Nigeria and in East Africa in Tanganyika (Tanzania). These groups typically made modest demands. But they used modern Western techniques of organization and newspaper journalism to spread their ideas among Africa's now growing urban populations.

In French West Africa, particularly in Senegal and the Ivory Coast, African politicians affiliated themselves with the more radical political parties of metropolitan France in order to work for colonial reform. In the 1930s they began to join the French Socialist and Communist parties and to dream even wilder dreams of autonomy and independence.

It was a comparatively quiet time in Africa south of the Sahara. But it was a deceptive calm. The students of the 1920s and 1930s—men such as Kwame Nkrumah, Jomo Kenyatta, Leopold Senghor, and others—would become the leaders of the great liberation movements of the tumultuous years after World War II.

Over Africa as a whole, in fact, it was seeding time, when ideas were planted and nurtured in some extraordinary young minds. The harvest would come with the great liberation of mid-century.

SUMMARY

The twentieth century may have been the most revolutionary of centuries. Modern ideological revolutions—drawing on liberal, nationalist, revolutionary socialist, and anti-imperialist visions of a new social order—have been overthrowing governments around the world since before World War I. The most impressive of these upheavals, however, involving millions of people and taking decades to run their course, sprang up in the first half of the century in Russia, Mexico, and China.

The Russian Revolution of 1917 came as the climax of a century of agitation against the political autocracy and economic underdevelopment of czarist Russia. It was the immense pressures of World War I on an underdeveloped country that overthrew the last Russian czar. Lenin and his Bolshevik cadres thus seized power in a crumbling nation with relative ease. But it was in retaining power that they revealed their true capacities, successfully turning back attacks by the forces of czarism, rival radical groups, rebellious minority nationalities, and foreign intervention during the civil war.

Lenin in his last years made some concessions to capitalism so that Russia might recover from the war and the civil struggle. Stalin, however, worked his way into power in the late 1920s and plunged the nation into a new economic revolution in the 1930s. Heavy industry was vastly expanded under Communist state socialism. Agriculture was also largely collectivized, but production still dropped drastically owing to peasant resistance to socialization.

Mexico also underwent a major revolution, beginning about 1910 and climaxing in the 1930s. The revolt against the Díaz regime began with the liberal bourgeois Madero movement and the popular insurrections of Villa and Zapata. The revolution expanded into a bloody nationwide struggle that cost many lives and led to anarchic destruction. Under the Northern Dynasty of political leadership, however, progressive one-party rule was imposed on Mexico in the 1920s. And under the charismatic Indian leader Cárdenas in the 1930s, significant democratic and socialist reforms were achieved.

The Chinese Revolution was the largest and longest of them all, the military phase alone beginning before World War I and lasting until after World War II. China's ancient monarchy collapsed soon after the death of the autocratic Empress Ci Xi in 1908. The new Republic of China became little more than an arena in which rival political leaders and warlords struggled for power for the next forty years.

Dr. Sun Yixian left the feuding revolutionaries his Three Principles—nationalism, democracy, socialism—to guide them in the reconstruction of China. Of these, democracy did not really take hold in the war-torn peasant nation. Nationalism was championed by Generalissimo Jiang Jiehi, who succeeded Sun and ruled China from the late 1920s through the 1940s. Socialism, or "people's welfare," became Marxist state socialism in the hands of the Communist leader Mao Zedong. The struggle between Jiang and Mao, complicated by the Japanese invasion and by World War II, ended in 1949 with Jiang driven off the mainland to the island of Taiwan, and Mao triumphant in Beijing.

Within the European empires, finally, resistance to Western hegemony laid the foundations for the future end of Western colonialism. The Congress party in India and the arrival of a new generation of Westernized African leadership both pointed toward liberation in later decades.

All three of these long revolutions provided models and inspiration for other upheavals around the world in the second half of the twentieth century.

SUGGESTED READING

ANTONIUS, G. *The Arab Awakening.* New York: Capricorn, 1965. Standard, sympathetic account of the new aspirations triggered by World War I.

ASCHER, A. *The Revolution of 1905: Russia in Disarray.* Stanford: Stanford University Press, 1988. First volume of a major account of the revolution, interpreted here as Russia's last chance for liberal reforms before 1917.

CHAMBERLIN, W. H. *The Russian Revolution, 1917–1921.* New York: Grosset & Dunlap, 1965. An older but still standard account. See also E. H. Carr, *The Russian Revolution: From Lenin to Stalin* (New York: Free Press, 1979), by a leading authority and L. Schapiro, *The Russian Revolutions of 1917: The Origins of Modern Communism* (New York: Basic Books, 1984).

CHI, H. *Warlord Politics in China 1916–1928.* Stanford: Stanford University Press, 1976. One of a number of good descriptions of warlordism in China.

CHOW, T. *The May Fourth Movement: Intellectual Revolution in Modern China.* Stanford: Stanford University Press, 1967. Informed analysis of the intellectual upheaval that proved to be the seedbed of social action.

COCKCROFT, J. *Intellectual Precursors of the Mexican Revolution, 1900–1913.* Austin: University of Texas Press, 1968. Another instance of intellectual dissent preceding action—a repeated pattern in the West since the Enlightenment.

EASTMAN, L. E. *The Abortive Revolution: China under Nationalist Rule, 1927–1937.* Cambridge: Harvard University Press, 1974. An essential study of the period of Jiang Jiehi's domination of China.

ERIKSON, E. *Gandhi's Truth.* New York: W. W. Norton, 1969. Psychohistorical examination of the India leader by a leading exponent of psychohistorical biography. See also B. R. Nanda, *Gandhi and His Critics* (New York: Oxford University Press, 1985), refuting critics of Gandhi's character and tactics.

FAIRBANK, J. K. *The Great Chinese Revolution, 1800–1985.* New York: Harper & Row, Pub., 1986. Up-to-date overview of China in transition by the dean of America's Chinese historians.

FITZPATRICK, S. *The Russian Revolution 1917–1932.* New York: Oxford University Press, 1982. Recommended analytical overview, from the 1917 revolutions through the first Five-Year Plan.

HARRISON, J. P. *The Long March to Power: A History of the Chinese Communist Party 1921–1972.* New York: Praeger, 1972. Richly detailed narrative of the rise of the Chinese Communists.

HART, J. M. *Revolutionary Mexico: The Coming and Process of the Mexican Revolution.* Berkeley and Los Angeles: University of California Press, 1987. Analysis of social groups in revolutionary Mexico, from peasants and industrial workers to Mexican elites and foreign businessmen.

KNIGHT, A. *The Mexican Revolution* (2 vols.). New York: Cambridge University Press, 1986. Comprehensive account, stressing regional over national issues and political rather than economic causes.

PATTABHI SITARAMAYYA, B. *History of the Indian National Congress* (2 vols.). Bombay: Padma Publications, 1946–1947. The party of Gandhi and Nehru, from its foundation.

REED, J. *Ten Days that Shook the World.* New York: Random House, 1960. Gives a reporter's colorful view of the October Revolution. See also R. A. Medvedev, *The October Revolution,* trans. G. Saunders (New York: Columbia University Press, 1979), an interpretive account by a dissident Soviet historian, suggesting that early victories for democratic socialism were betrayed by Lenin's policies.

SCHAPIRO, L. *The Life of Lenin.* New York: Harper & Row, Pub., 1964. By a scholar with a broad background in both Russian history and the other ideological movements and leaders of the interwar years. In addition, see R. Service's account of the earlier years, *Lenin: A Political Life* (Bloomington: Indiana University Press, 1985).

SPENCE, J. D. *The Gate of Heavenly Peace: The Chinese and Their Revolution, 1895–1980.* New York: Viking, 1981. Authoritative overview of a century of change. For an equally expert and even longer perspective, see J. K. Fairbank, listed above.

UHALLY, S. *Mao Tse-tung, a Critical Biography.* New York: New Viewpoints, 1975. Good life of one of the great revolutionaries of the twentieth century.

WOLFE, B. D. *Three Who Made A Revolution.* Boston: Beacon Press, 1956. Lenin, Trotsky, and Stalin, underground and in exile, before 1917; readable and intriguing.

WOMACK, J. *Zapata and the Mexican Revolution.* New York: Knopf, 1968. Perhaps the most admired of the Mexican revolutionary leaders, sympathetically portrayed.

CHAPTER 42

THE TOTALITARIANS

THE FLIGHT FROM FREEDOM

New-Style Dictatorships
Sources of Authoritarianism
Defining Totalitarianism

TOTALITARIANISM IN EUROPE

Italy: Mussolini and Fascism
Germany: Failure of the Weimar Republic
Hitler in Power
Nazism and the Holocaust
Russia: Sources of Communist Tyranny
Stalin's Iron Age

AUTHORITARIANISM IN ASIA, EUROPE, AND LATIN AMERICA

Japan: The Failure of Zaibatsu Liberalism
Rise of the Militarists: The Day of the Assassins
A Great Authoritarian Tide

THE FLIGHT
FROM FREEDOM

NEW-STYLE DICTATORSHIPS

In the mythology of our decades—the flaming twenties, the rebellious sixties—the thirties are the depression decade, the red decade, the low, dishonest decade of appeasement. If we were painting them, the thirties would be gray, greasy storm clouds rolling in, with cracks of lightning advancing from a black horizon. It was a time when many of the best lacked all conviction, while the worst were full of passionate intensity.

The Great Depression accounted for much of the grimness of those years, of course: soup kitchens, bread lines, the dole. So did the continuing long revolutions in many parts of the world: nonviolent Indians clubbed into the dust, Chinese slaughtering Chinese on the endless Long March north. The advance of the second global conflict of the century across that numbing decade, as we shall see, did its part to darken those years: Italian planes strafing Ethiopian roads, German bombers over Spanish villages, a baby screaming in the rubble of Shanghai after the Japanese planes had passed.

But there was an even more immediate source for the savage image of the decade. It was the political brutality of the new-style dictatorships that gave the thirties much of their tone and color in our collective memory. For this was the decade of Adolf Hitler and Joseph Stalin, of secret police, party purges, slave camps, death camps. Stalin's Iron Age, one author called it; others lamented—but did nothing to stop—the March of the Swastika. It did indeed seem like a reversion to an earlier, crueler time, a new iron age.

The brutal years did not begin in 1930. Mussolini's march on Rome, the Red and White terrors in Russia, street fighting in Germany went back to the 1920s. But the thirties were the climax, the decade that redefined the jackboot and seemed to put half the world into the hands of old-style authoritarian governments, a new wave of militarism, and—newest, most shiny-modern, and grisliest of all—the totalitarians.

SOURCES OF AUTHORITARIANISM

One of the most disturbing things about the upsurge of autocratic, authoritarian, and just plain tyrannical governments was that earlier twentieth-century people seemed to welcome them with open arms. It was not enough, some astute observers pointed out, to blame everything on the gangster mentalities at the top of many of the new regimes, or on the odious machinery of enforcement they commanded. Too many of the new dictators enjoyed widespread popular support among the peoples they tyrannized. There were too many cheering crowds lining the advance of Nazis or Fascists to power, too few tears shed for lost liberal institutions—it could not all be blamed on the Gestapo.

To many, it looked like what social psychologist Erich Fromm diagnosed as a flight from freedom. The nineteenth century had seen the steady advance of liberal political institutions across the Western world. The early twentieth seemed to be witnessing a widespread rejection of freedom, a disillusionment with democracy. Confronted with economic and social challenges too great for its fragile new liberal institutions, the world seemed to be turning back to cruder, more brutal beliefs in blood and violence, in irresistible force and omnipotent leadership.

The problems of modernization or of recovery from the depression, it appeared, were too difficult to be handled by the majority votes of demoralized and battered peoples. The cult of the leader was the only answer. Let the SS, let the commissars, let the new samurai do it.

The new leaders themselves, not surprisingly, took up the theme with enthusiasm. From the bully pulpits of new authoritarian states around the world, they jeered at the decadence of democracy, the failure of capitalism, the physical weakness and moral corruption of the Western World. They contrasted the flabbiness and degeneracy of the liberal West with their own virility, discipline, and strength. "Today," Mussolini declared with total confidence, "the liberal faith must shut the doors of its deserted temples, deserted because the peoples of the world realize that its worship . . . will lead, as it has already led, to certain ruin."[1]

---

[1]Benito Mussolini, *The Political and Social Doctrines of Fascism,* trans. Jane Soames (London: Hogarth Press, 1933), p. 9.

Major Powers and Nations with Overseas Territories, 1919–1939

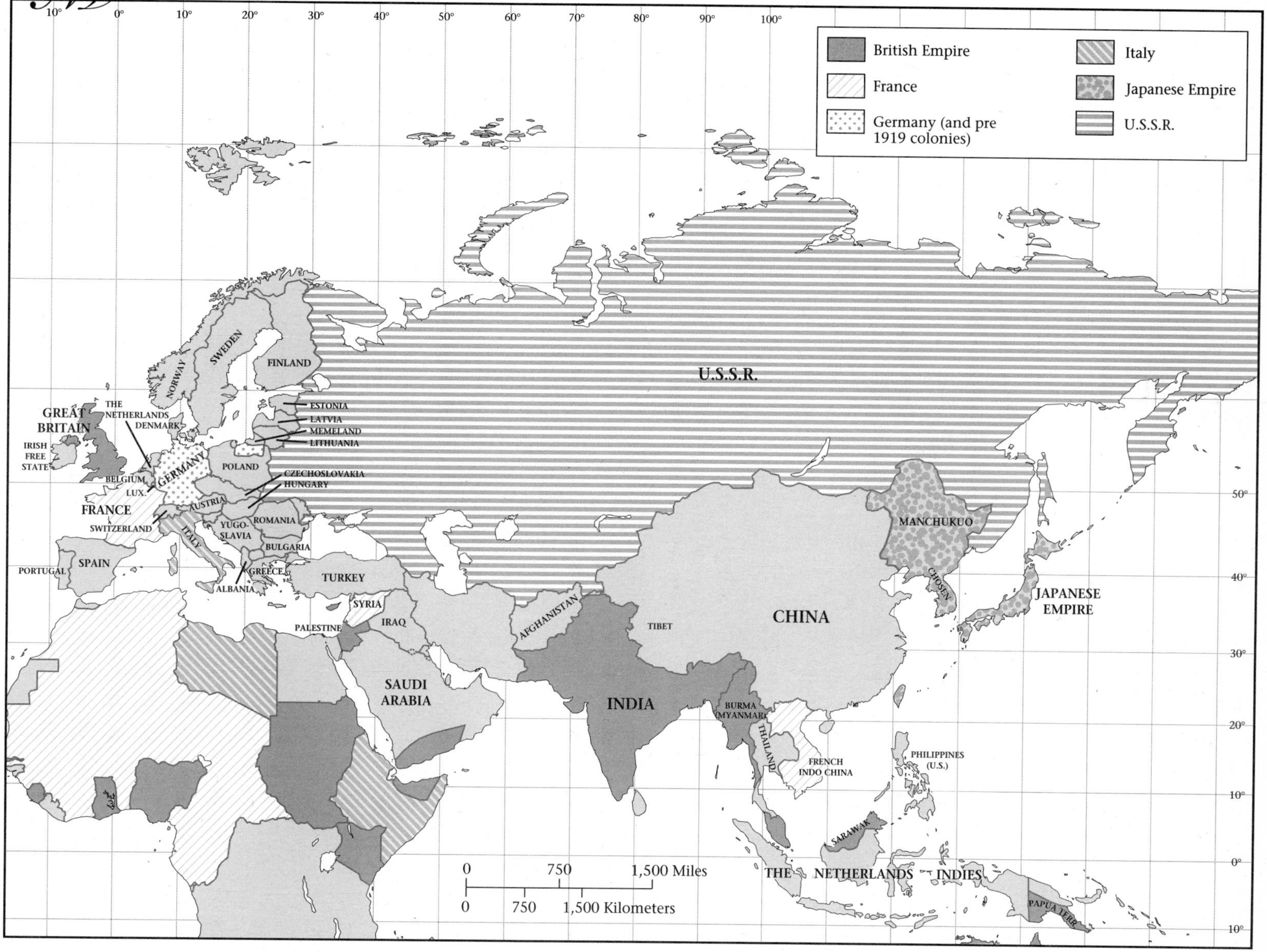

British Empire
France
Germany (and pre 1919 colonies)
Italy
Japanese Empire
U.S.S.R.
GREAT BRITAIN
IRISH FREE STATE
THE NETHERLANDS
DENMARK
NORWAY
SWEDEN
FINLAND
ESTONIA
LATVIA
MEMELAND
LITHUANIA
POLAND
GERMANY
BELGIUM
LUX.
FRANCE
SWITZERLAND
AUSTRIA
CZECHOSLOVAKIA
HUNGARY
ROMANIA
YUGO-SLAVIA
BULGARIA
ITALY
ALBANIA
GREECE
PORTUGAL
SPAIN
TURKEY
SYRIA
PALESTINE
IRAQ
SAUDI ARABIA
AFGHANISTAN
U.S.S.R.
TIBET
CHINA
INDIA
BURMA (MYANMAR)
THAILAND
FRENCH INDO CHINA
MANCHUKUO
CHOSEN
JAPANESE EMPIRE
PHILIPPINES (U.S.)
SARAWAK
THE NETHERLANDS INDIES
PAPUA TERR.
0 750 1,500 Miles
0 750 1,500 Kilometers
10° 0° 10° 20° 30° 40° 50° 60° 70° 80° 90° 100°
50° 40° 30° 20° 10° 0° 10°

> "*We have assumed that ideologies and culture in general are rooted in the social character; that the social character itself is molded by the mode of existence of a given society; and that in their turn the dominant character traits become productive forces shaping the social process. . . .*
>
> *With regard to Fascism [in Italy] the same principle of explanation was applied: the lower middle class reacted to certain economic changes, such as the growing power of monopolies and postwar inflation, with an intensification of certain character traits, namely, sadistic and masochistic strivings; the Nazi ideology [in Germany] appealed to and intensified these traits; and the new character traits then became effective forces in supporting the expansion of German imperialism. In both instances we see that when a certain class is threatened by new economic tendencies it reacts to this threat psychologically and ideologically; and that the psychological changes brought about by this reaction further the development of economic forces even if those forces contradict the economic interests of that class.*"

The German psychiatrist Erich Fromm, transplanted to America in the 1930s, wrote a number of books analyzing society from a psychoanalytic perspective. This excerpt is from one of his best-known works, Escape from Freedom. Although the book deals with both the Reformation era and modern democratic societies, it is best known for its attempt to explain the motives that led millions of people to turn their backs on political freedom and accept enthusiastically such authoritarian regimes as those of Mussolini and Hitler.

Do you think the complex pattern of psychological and economic forces Fromm delineates here provides a convincing explanation for the flight from freedom? Can you think of other reasons why people might have accepted authoritarian rule? Can you point to an economic explanation for popular acceptance of the new regimes?

Erich Fromm, Escape from Freedom (New York: Avon Books, 1941), pp. 324–325.

To liberal analyst and totalitarian critic alike, it looked very much, in the depths of the brutal years, as though liberalism was dead, authoritarianism and totalitarianism the wave of the future.

DEFINING TOTALITARIANISM

Not all the new dictatorships were of the sort normally described as totalitarian, but the most notorious and powerful of them were. It will therefore be worthwhile to spend some time answering a rather subtle question: What exactly is totalitarianism?

This distinctive twentieth-century ism may be defined most simply as an attempt at total control of society by government. Totalitarian states have attempted to achieve this end by building on the commitment and discipline of ideologically based political parties. Totalitarian rulers have maintained their power over the less committed majorities of their people through two other instruments particularly well developed in our time: bureaucracy and technology.

The party, with its uniforms and parades, its access to power and the perquisites of office, its inspiring ideals and sense of driving purpose, brought many into the totalitarian fold. The omnipresent bureaucracy carried the power of the totalitarian state into the lives of all its citizens as never before. And technology, from propaganda to military and police power, from microphones to machine guns, was always there to deal with doubters and dissenters. The result was a regime that tried to impose the will of new leaders and new elites, and the ideologies they preached, on whole populations. The new order subverted all other institutions and ideas, sucking all classes and groups, all ages and both sexes into the new Leviathan state.

A number of explanations have been offered for the rise of this new Leviathan. The economic, social, and political challenges of modernization, the strains of the Great Depression, the humiliations of imperial domination or military defeat certainly played a part. The sheer faceless power of the modern state with its endless hierarchies of officials, all of whom can claim that they were just following orders, helps to account for the iron grip of the system once it is established. The hypnotic grasp of modern ideologies, comparable to the power of religion in earlier centuries, surely underlies the new phenomenon—indeed distinguishes it most clearly from the authoritarian regimes of earlier centuries. And there have been some psychological explanations that seek to pinpoint a totalitarian personality, predisposed by family structure, child-rearing methods, and other distinctive cultural forms to accept, indeed to long for, autocratic control in society and the state.

Seen as a cast of mind rather than a form of government, totalitarianism involves total commitment to the cause, complete submergence of the individual in the group, unquestioning obedience to the authority of the party or the leader. From this sort of commitment, moral and emotional, comes a sense of inner harmony and collective strength. The petty ego of the individual, submerged in the larger whole of the group, swells with pride, strength, joy, disciplined purpose.

That is at least an attempt to understand the hearts that beat beneath the grim gray uniforms, the minds behind the fixed adoring eyes. More material concerns, such as the arrogance of a uniform, a living wage in a depression-ridden country, and the career ladders open only to party members, perhaps help explain the lure of totalitarianism too.

So much for deeper explanations of the jackboot in the face. Now for a look at some historical realities.

TOTALITARIANISM IN EUROPE

ITALY: MUSSOLINI AND FASCISM

The first totalitarian state was neither Hitler's nor Stalin's, but Benito Mussolini's Fascist Italy, which began to take shape when Mussolini came to power in 1922. *Il Duce*— the Leader—his Fascist party, and his reorganization of Italy along totalitarian lines became the models for later totalitarian and authoritarian regimes in the 1930s.

Mussolini began his career as a left-wing syndicalist before World War I. As such, he preached the syndicalist gospel, urging local socialist organization, mass revolution, and the subsequent abolition of the state—a far cry from the Fascist regime he would presently erect in Italy. After the war, however, Mussolini was caught up in Italian demands for "unredeemed" territories held by Austria and Yugoslavia. He changed his ideological stripes and became an ardent nationalist.

Mussolini organized the Fascist party in 1919 and turned violently against his former socialist comrades. His strong-arm squads of militantly nationalistic war veterans, the black-shirted *squadristi,* were soon breaking up Socialist-party meetings, smashing left-wing presses, raiding the headquarters of industrial and agricultural unions. In so doing, Mussolini won the support of many factory owners and large landowners—the very people he had fought in the prewar years.

In 1921 and 1922, Italy's democratic constitutional

Mobilizing the youth for war. These young Italians were taught early to accept military discipline and prepare to fight for the Duce, the Fascist cause, and a new Roman Empire around the Mediterranean. In the 1930s, all Italian boys over the age of eight were required to have military training. The youth organizations of all the totalitarian states sought to instill a similar spirit of combat-ready commitment in the younger generation.

monarchy went through a paralyzing governmental crisis. As would happen a decade later in Weimar Germany, no party or coalition of parties could form a government that could command a majority in the Italian legislature. Nobody, in short, was in charge in Rome.

During this tense period, the Fascist *squadristi* moved from attacking socialists and unions to seizing control of whole towns. When a Fascist march on Rome itself was announced, Italy's constitutional monarch, Victor Emmanuel III, capitulated and asked Mussolini to form a government.

Thereafter, through massive propaganda campaigns, roughly engineered electoral victories, constitutional "reforms," and an occasional assassination, Fascist power was institutionalized in Italy. Mussolini would be the Leader for the next twenty years, the senior if not the strongest of Europe's totalitarian rulers.

On the political side, totalitarianism in Italy meant the suppression of all rival parties and the submission of a single list of candidates—prepared by the Fascist leadership—to the voters. Elected officials of provinces and towns were abolished and replaced by appointed *podestàs*. Mussolini was given authority to make law by decree, and in time the legislature was abolished in its turn.

The Italian economy also came under at least nominal party control. An elaborate system of "syndicates" and "corporations" was set up, each representing labor, business management, and the government, each concerned with a particular branch of industry, agriculture, trade, finance, or the professions. This "corporative" economic system was run from the top. It forbade strikes and pushed steadily for higher production, and not incidentally for higher profits. Labor unions and free enterprise were alike suppressed as outmoded survivors of the liberal past. Tourists, however, were always pleased to see that in Fascist Italy the trains ran on time.

The rest of society also came under the more or less vigilant eye of the party. Politically untrustworthy individuals were taken up by the secret police and bundled off to the Lipari Islands off the coast of Sicily. The press was censored, education regulated, social and cultural organizations dominated by the Fascists. Children's and youth groups, from the Sons of the Wolf to the Young Fascists, were given their first uniforms and set to drilling at an early age. "Everything in the state," trumpeted Mussolini, "nothing outside the state, nothing against the state!"[2]

Il Duce was a dictator much photographed, usually on balconies reviewing his troops or his Fascist party, unmistakable with his big jaw and increasingly solid belly. It has been suggested that he was not as massively in control as he seemed. His grab for political power in the twenties may have been almost forced upon him by the restless militance of his *squadristi* Black Shirts. The corporative economic organization, at its fullest development in the thirties, looks to some historians suspiciously like a front for big-business domination of the Italian economy.

Nevertheless, the model was established. Mussolini himself may have hit upon a profound political truth of those merciless years when he declared: "Never before have the nations thirsted for authority, direction, order as they do now."[3]

GERMANY: FAILURE OF THE WEIMAR REPUBLIC

One of the greatest challenges of any attempt to deal with the Nazi period in German history is, quite simply, to explain how it could have happened. How could the Germans, best known in the nineteenth century for philosophy and music, then for science and industry—one of the most civilized of European peoples, in short—have produced the twelve-year Nazi nightmare? How could so many have gloried in it, defended the regime vigorously to foreigners who "didn't understand the *Führer's* policies" even as the shattered glass of *Kristalnacht* tinkled in the streets?

The origins of Nazism are frequently traced to the notable success of autocracy in German history—and the equally notable failures of democracy. It is a good place to start.

The rise of the Hohenzollern dynasty and of Hohenzollern Prussia to mastery of all Germany was rooted in such autocratic institutions of centralized state power as the Junker bureaucracy and the Prussian army. National heroes such as Frederick the Great and Bismarck had been strong men, depending on "blood and iron" to advance the interests of the state. Liberalism, by contrast, had never really taken hold, even in the nineteenth century. The Student Union Movement of the early 1800s, the German contribution to the Europe-wide Revolutions of 1848, had dramatically failed in their objectives. So, as we will see directly, had Germany's third liberal experiment, the Weimar Republic of the 1920s. By 1933, then, liberalism and democracy meant weakness, authoritarianism meant strength to most Germans—and at that time, they desperately needed strength.

The debacle of World War I is another commonly cited cause of the Nazi triumph in Germany. The failure of German arms was a terrible shock to the psyche of a people who had regarded themselves as the greatest power in Europe for fifty years, who had not lost a war since Napoleon's day. The manner of their defeat also—their armies still in the field, strangled by a British naval blockade, tricked by an armistice that somehow turned into an

[2] F. Lee Benns and Mary Elizabeth Seldon, *Europe, 1914–1939* (New York: Appleton-Century-Crofts, 1965), p. 226.

[3] Ibid.

abject surrender—left many Germans feeling betrayed. The harsh Versailles peace terms, stripping Germany of lands, colonies, and military forces, and imposing huge reparations and the unspeakable war-guilt clause, outraged and embittered many Germans. Anyone who would denounce Versailles, give Germans a scapegoat for defeat, and promise victories to come could surely expect a great outpouring of support in Germany.

The political and economic problems of the Weimar Republic (1919–1933), which succeeded the defeated German Empire, also proved fertile breeding grounds for totalitarian sentiment.

In November of 1918, Kaiser William II was persuaded to abdicate for the good of the nation—as the Russian czar had been before him—by his own generals. Hindenburg and Ludendorff knew, if the German people didn't, that their armies could fight no more. The leading party in the Reichstag, the Social Democrats, thereupon took the lead in establishing a German republic.

The German Constitution adopted at Weimar in 1919 was, in fact, one of the most liberal in the world, providing for democracy, civil liberties, rights for women. It opened the way for a vigorous opposition press and the brilliant cultural life that distinguished Weimar Germany in the 1920s. The liberals and socialists who ruled through most of that decade were parliamentarians, labor leaders, and constitutional reformers.

Yet within fifteen years, political attacks from left and right and the economic buffeting of alternating inflation and depression had virtually paralyzed the new government—and opened the way for the rise of Adolf Hitler.

Political attacks from the left came first, with the rebellion of a communist group called the Spartacists in 1919, followed by other abortive left-wing plots in the early 1920s. The Spartacists were suppressed, their leaders Rosa Luxemburg and Karl Liebknecht murdered while in custody. Right-wing attempts to seize power included an army revolt called the Kapp putsch and, in 1923, Hitler's futile Beer Hall putsch in Munich—which cost the Nazi leader no more than a few months in prison.

Through the rest of the decade, Communists, Nazis, and other political extremists organized paramilitary cadres and fought each other in the streets. Right-wing terrorists assassinated government officials—and generally got off with light sentences. The democratically elected government seemed helpless to do anything about it.

The economic ups and downs of the twenties and early thirties were equally disastrous for the new regime. Inflation unparalleled in modern times ravaged Germany in the early 1920s. The value of the German mark plunged from four to the dollar in 1914 to four billion to the dollar in 1923, wiping out the savings of Germany's once prosperous middle classes. After a brief respite, the Great Depression whipsawed the economy from the other side.

Germany, hardest hit of all the European nations, had six million unemployed in the early 1930s.

The Nazis would promise peace in the streets and renewed prosperity, and although what they delivered was the peace and prosperity of the police state, many battered Germans would vote for them. For the Nazis did not seize power, as the Communists and Fascists had: They were voted into office.

Hitler's victory in 1933 climaxed a three-year political crisis, rooted in the Great Depression, that had made many Germans feel that democracy was unworkable in their country. The coalition of Social Democrats and centrist parties that ruled in 1930 fell apart over the problem of how to deal with the depression. Attempts to organize other coalitions of left- and right-wing parties in the Reichstag also failed, because of the refusal of Social Democrats to work with Communists and because of a similar rejection of the Nazis by old-fashioned German conservatives. Between 1930 and 1933, therefore, President von Hindenburg had to invoke emergency powers to govern at all, conferring authority on a series of conservative chancellors who had no majority support in the Reichstag.

Elections were held frequently during those three years, as those in government tried desperately to find a majority that could get the system working again. But the party that gained most rapidly as the depression deepened and the paralysis of democracy became clearer was the Weimar Republic's greatest enemy, Adolf Hitler and his National Socialist, or Nazi, party.

Who supported Hitler? Masses of statistics and elaborate theories have been advanced about the "people behind" the Nazi demagogue, but the point is still being argued. Students supported him noisily and gave him thumping majorities in university straw votes. Big business contributed to his war chest, but gave as much or more to other, more respectable conservative groups. Major support, however, seems to have come from lower-middle-class Germans—shopkeepers, civil servants, old-fashioned artisans—and from farmers; all these groups suffered from the depression. And a great ground swell of support came from embittered nationalists of all classes.

In large part, fear put Hitler in power. Fear of urban unemployment, of collapsing farm prices, of middle-class loss of status, of communism, of foreign humiliations, of governmental paralysis—all contributed to Hitler's meteoric rise. The convicted putschist of 1923 got 2.6 percent of the vote in 1928. In 1930 the Nazi total jumped to 18.3 percent. In 1933 the Nazis were the nation's most popular party, commanding 37.3 percent of the vote.

At the beginning of 1933, then, with Hitler clearly the nation's best vote-getter, the politicians around the aging Hindenburg persuaded him to appoint the Nazi leader chancellor of Germany. Like the politicos who made Napoleon first consul of France, they thought they could use the strident, vulgar little man with the ridiculous moustache for their own purposes.

HITLER IN POWER

Adolf Hitler (1889–1945) was not German but rather Austrian by birth. Failed art student, one-time Munich bohemian, wounded and decorated soldier in World War I, he had found his true career in the extremist politics of the Weimar Republic. He had joined a nationalist sliver group called the National Socialist German Workers party and had quickly come to dominate it, thanks to his fiery oratory and superpatriotic doctrines. As mentioned, the failure of the Beer Hall putsch in 1923 cost him some months in prison, but he spent the time assembling his credo in a famous book, *Mein Kampf* (*My Struggle*), and emerged as the idolized *Führer* (Leader) of the Nazi party.

Hitler preached German greatness, the superiority of Aryan or Teutonic racial stock, and the coming splendor of the Fatherland. He condemned the Versailles treaty, the Communists, and sometimes the very rich. He blamed Germany's troubles increasingly on the Jewish segment of the population, convenient targets of European persecution for centuries and a pathological fixation of Hitler's. He developed a high-pitched but electrifying speaking style and a natural flair for the dramatic—uniforms, swastika banners, night rallies, parades, marching songs. Once in power, he also demonstrated a knack for shrewd political tactics and ruthless manipulation of people.

During the first six months of 1933, the new chancellor made himself absolute ruler of Germany.

Hitler took advantage of an attempt to burn down the Reichstag building in Berlin, probably undertaken by a feebleminded Dutch Communist, to begin his assault on the structure of the Weimar Republic. Apparently genuinely fearful of a Communist power play, he suspended all civil liberties and arrested the German Communist leadership. Riding the crest of this victory, he held a quick election and won a Reichstag majority large enough to vote the chancellor special powers to make laws on his own authority for the next four years.

Thus strengthened, Hitler turned against the parties. He already had the Communists in jail. He now outlawed the Social Democrats, claiming they also were too far to the left. Then he talked all the other conservative and nationalist parties except the Nazis into dissolving voluntarily in order to promote unity on the right—in other words, to give the Nazis a free hand. Finally, in June 1934, he purged his own party of potential rivals in the gory Night of the Long Knives, when his elite SS troopers seized and executed hundreds of Nazi and other leaders deemed undependable by the Leader.

During the rest of the decade, Hitler turned Nazi Germany into the archetypal totalitarian state. Political and economic institutions, religion, education, recreation, and all other aspects of national life came under the centralized control of the party and its *Führer*.

Totalitarian political structures quickly replaced those of Weimar democracy. All parties except the Nazis having been suppressed, the Reichstag became a rubber

Adolf Hitler addresses the Nazi Party faithful. Hitler's insistence on the Führerprinzip or "Leadership principle" was most vividly validated for most by his hypnotic speaking style. Always intense, as here, he built to shrill climaxes which swept his hearers up in his vision of German greatness and his own destiny to lead his people. Equally effective with beery Rathskeller audiences and the rapt crowds that thronged a stadium, Hitler stormed to power on a wave of passionate words.

stamp for the Leader's decisions. The elected governors of the German states were replaced by appointed *Statthalters.* Everywhere, in provinces and towns, power passed into the hands of Nazi strong men called *Gauleiters.*

Totalitarian economic organization also evolved rapidly. In the 1920s Hitler had preached power to peasants, artisans, and shopkeepers, the traditional salt of the German earth. In the 1930s, however, he forged a monolithic alliance of big government and big business with which to run the German economy. Huge cartels were put in charge of industry and agriculture. Massive programs of public works (including the Autobahn highway system) and military rearmament (in defiance of the Versailles treaty) put much of the labor force back to work. At the same time, rigid controls were slapped on wages and prices, small businessmen lost operational control of their businesses, and labor unions were abolished.

The Nazi apparatus reached into every aspect of German life. The Protestant churches were merged into a single German Evangelical church under Nazi control; a concordat gave the party a say in the appointment of Catholic bishops and forbade priests to speak out on political issues. Nazi doctrines were taught in public schools while university professors were being discharged. Books were burned for presenting views the Nazis disapproved of. All professional, social, or cultural associations and clubs were politicized—Nazified—or abolished.

Young people were quickly enrolled in the Hitler Youth and the League of German Maidens, which replaced the traditional Boy and Girl Scout type of hiking and camping organization. Workers got free Strength-through-Joy vacations in the healthy countryside, which also strengthened them for future military service. Women were piously urged to stick to home and church—and produce children for the Fatherland.

Under Hitler's leadership Germany quickly pulled out of the depression, boosted production to new highs, and put almost everyone back to work. Hitler unilaterally rejected the Versailles treaty, rapidly built the most powerful army in Europe, and announced a new German empire—the Thousand-Year Reich. Germans stood tall again, proud of their country, contemptuous of the capitalist democracies still floundering in the depths of the Great Depression all around them.

NAZISM AND THE HOLOCAUST

There was, of course, a price to be paid. The Germans bought their strong leadership, economic revival, and national pride at the expense of what must be a good candidate for the most brutal tyranny in European history.

Nazi propaganda glorified the leadership. Actually the Nazi elite seems to have been a heterogeneous group of adventurers and opportunists having few ideological or other principles and a strong attachment to showy wealth and conspicuous displays of power. Their military organization and early victories, their talk of commitment and building new worlds clothed them in a myth of efficiency, invincibility, and glamour that they did not deserve. In fact, the system seems to have survived as long as it did, not through monolithic unity and discipline, but on the basis of a rough balance of feuding factions—the Nazi apparatus versus the old bureaucracy, the *Führer's* SS Corps versus the German army—and the clashing ambitions of individual Nazi leaders.

In the area of police repression, however, the Nazis were acknowledged masters.

The chief instruments of the Nazi terror were the *Schutzstaffel* (SS), the Leader's black-uniformed private troops, and the Gestapo, the Nazi secret police. The SS, originally Hitler's bodyguard, later an elite military force, were publicized as the perfect Aryans, blond, blue-eyed embodiments of Teutonic racial superiority. They purged the party for Hitler in the early 1930s and ran the concentration camps—the death camps—of the later 1930s and the 1940s. The Gestapo worked much more in the shadows, as a secret political police. It was they who made the after-midnight arrests and ran the most feared torture chambers since the days of the Spanish Inquisition.

Millions of human beings died in Hitler's concentration camps—political dissidents, resistance fighters from conquered countries, social "misfits" such as homosexuals, and particularly "inferior" racial groups such as Slavs, gypsies, and, above all, Jews.

Hitler defined the Jewish "race" as the greatest threat to the German people, blaming them for their success in business and the professions, for Versailles, for the depression, and for weakening the blood of the German "master race" through "interracial" marriage. Once in power, Hitler passed discriminatory laws against them, expelling them from government service, confiscating their property, compelling many to emigrate. Riotous pogroms were organized against them, including *Kristalnacht,* the Night of the Broken Glass, when the windows of Jewish homes and businesses were shattered in cities all over Germany.

In the later 1930s Jews were herded into concentration camps. In the early 1940s, after the outbreak of World War II, the Final Solution to the Jewish problem got under way. This was the methodical extermination of the Jewish population of Germany and German-occupied Europe. This Holocaust was undertaken at first rather haphazardly with machine guns. Then at camps like Dachau, Belsen, and Auschwitz, the process was systematized in specially constructed gas chambers, followed by cremation of the corpses. Six million European Jews of both sexes and all ages and conditions of life were worked, starved, stripped, gassed, robbed of rings and the gold in their teeth, and trundled off to the crematoria.

The deliberate savagery and the racial dimension of the Holocaust have earned it a unique place in the history of the twentieth century. In fact, it was almost certainly the largest deliberately instigated massacre in history.

A mass grave at Belsen concentration camp. Victims of the totalitarian death camps were required to surrender their clothing and any remaining possessions before being shot or gassed. Though most victims were cremated at the death camps, horrifying finds like this, coupled with the skeletal survivors rescued from some camps, brought home the horror of Nazism to the world more forcefully than any other experience of the totalitarian and wartime years. (The Bettman Archive)

Western people sometimes feel a certain superiority to other human beings. We shudder piously at the horrors of the Assyrian warfare state, at the piles of skulls the Mongols left in their wake, or the obsidian blades of the Aztecs lancing down. Whenever so tempted, we would perhaps do well to remember such Western atrocities as the fires of the Inquisition—and the gas chambers of the Final Solution.

RUSSIA: SOURCES OF COMMUNIST TYRANNY

The sources of Stalinist totalitarianism in Soviet Russia reach further into the historical past than the roots of Nazi totalitarianism. But Communists tended to be more serious about their ideology than Nazis; hence there are ideological origins for Soviet totalitarianism too. As in Germany, finally, the circumstances of the 1930s helped to define the pattern of party dictatorship as it developed in Stalinist Russia.

Historically, relatively rigid authoritarianism went far back in Russian history—to Byzantine and Mongol models, to the heavy-handed rule of autocrats such as Ivan the Terrible in the sixteenth century and Peter the Great in the eighteenth. Even conservative nineteenth-century western Europeans were shocked at the absolute power of the czars, who ruled a vast peasant nation through a huge bureaucracy, secret police, and military repression, all justified by the traditional divine-right doctrines of the Russian Orthodox church. Some twentieth-century historians would see Communist Russia as little more than a continuation of this Russian autocracy, but with an even larger bureaucracy, a more efficient secret police, and Marxist dogma in place of Orthodox rationalizations of power.

But there were distinctive ideological sources of Stalinist tyranny too. Marx had had little to say about the political organization of the classless utopia of the future. But Lenin, seeking to impose discipline on disputatious Russian ideologues and half-educated proletarians, had developed the key political principles of the *vanguard party* and *democratic centralism*. Communists thus early came to believe that their party was the vanguard of the advancing proletariat—and that the workers themselves, unable to understand Marxist subtleties, must be brought to accept this party leadership through slogans and indoctrination. Bolshevik leaders came to believe also that ideological disputes within the party must in the end give way to discipline and obedience. Democratic debate within the party was all very well while policy was being hammered out. Thereafter, however, central authority must prevail, and all must close ranks behind the leaders.

Lenin dominated the party and the people by force of will and intellect, and by the sheer weight of his success. Stalin, lacking charisma or a brilliant record of revolutionary achievement, used the older political skills of manipulation and force. But Stalinist totalitarianism has been traced by many to the Leninist doctrine of democratic centralism.

The immense pressures of the 1930s also help to explain the regression of the Soviet Union to autocracy and terror under Stalin. The strains of the first Five-Year Plans, which attempted to achieve in a few years a level of economic development that had taken other nations generations to accomplish, might alone account for draconian measures. The Communist fear of "capitalist encirclement" and especially of Hitler, who denounced the threat of international communism as he built up his own nation for war, impelled the Russian leadership to look for internal enemies and drive their people to work still harder.

To these external pressures we must add the desire of the party and its leader to increase their power. The Soviet Communist party of the 1930s was no longer the scattering of underground or exiled revolutionaries living on dreams and ideology that it had been under Lenin. Stalin's party was a bureaucracy of *apparatchiks* ("machine men"), much less ideological and much more career-oriented. Stalin himself was the super *apparatchik*—a wooden orator and a plodding thinker, but skilled at organizing and

political maneuver. Extremely ambitious and completely ruthless, he seems, especially in his later years, to have been a pathologically suspicious man as well.

The party wanted to increase its power, individual *apparatchiks* to advance their careers, by expanding Communist control into more and more areas of life. Stalin wanted to ensure his own power and to eliminate potential rivals or enemies of his programs. And so, after the lull of the 1920s and the New Economic Policy came the Five-Year Plans of the 1930s—and the sweeping totalitarianization of Russian society.

STALIN'S IRON AGE

Like Nazism, Communism could boast of successes in the thirties. As in Germany, unemployment was virtually eliminated as the state made work for every man and most women in the Soviet Union. Agriculture suffered severe setbacks, in part because of peasant resistance to collectivization. But at least the farms were collectivized and could now develop on a centralized, socialized basis. State-owned heavy industry grew rapidly, overall industrial production expanding at the phenomenal rate of 15 or 20 percent a year. Even allowing for doctored Stalinist statistics, it was an impressive achievement.

Western admirers who came to Russia in the 1930s to "see the future" were duly impressed by the new indus-

Russian peasants march off to their newly collectivized fields in 1931, bearing a banner demanding the expropriation of the <u>kulaks.</u> Not all peasants responded this enthusiastically to Stalin's collectivization of agriculture. Nor did productivity on these collectively operated farms ever match that of the privately owned farms of the non-Communist West. (AP/Wide World Photos)

trial cities, the huge dams and factories, the showcase Moscow subway with its dazzling cleanliness and its marble statues. They were sometimes even allowed a glimpse of beefy workers lolling on the pebbly beaches of the Black Sea as a reward for exceeding their quotas.

But there was more to Communism than the Moscow subway and Black Sea vacations, as there was more to Nazism than Autobahns and Strength through Joy. In some ways, Soviet totalitarianism made Hitler's version look like a ramshackle collection of improvisations. Politically, economically, socially, culturally, the Communists either met less institutional resistance or were driven by ideological compulsions to more sweeping measures. The total impact of the party on Russian life was commensurately greater.

Politically, party control was unquestioned from the moment Lenin dissolved the constitutional convention in 1918. Stalin gave the nation a shiny new constitution in the 1930s, and elections were held—but in a one-party state there was only a single list of candidates to vote for. And the Soviet Union was a one-party state: Since the Communists were the vanguard of the people, what other party was needed? The real power structure was thus the highly autocratic one of the Communist party.

The economy under Stalin reversed Lenin's New Economic Policy. State planners now allocated resources and set quotas; government-appointed managers ran factories and the huge new farms and directed trade, transportation, and all other aspects of the economy. The small-time New Economic Policy entrepreneurs were squeezed out of business. Comparatively well-off peasants, called *kulaks,* were expropriated outright, and almost all private farms were collectivized. Half the new collective farms were owned by the state; the others, collectively owned by the peasants who worked them, depended on the state for farm machinery and fertilizer and sold their crops to the state at fixed prices. Only tiny private plots and a few peasant markets remained outside governmental control.

Communists dominated the huge bureaucracy engendered by so much government involvement in the economy. Commissars shared command with military officers in the armed services. In any line of work, from science to the arts, Communist-party membership was the way to get ahead.

The Communists, as Marxists, were materialists—atheists in matters of religion—and the role of the Orthodox church as a pillar of the old order made it a natural target. Many churches were closed, atheism was taught in the schools, and museums of church abuses dotted the landscape. Education aimed at producing hardworking and obedient Soviet citizens, and courses on Marxism-Leninism were required. Communist children's and young people's organizations, beginning with the Young Octobrists and climaxing with the Komsomol, for people in their teens and twenties, filled the new generation with veneration for Marx, Lenin, and Stalin, "the Lenin of today."

Joseph Stalin looks up after signing a death warrant. Feeling himself surrounded by traitors, "the Silent Man in the Kremlin" lashed out pitilessly at "enemies of the people." At the height of the purge trials of 1937 and 1938, it has been estimated that Stalin signed "forty or fifty death warrants as part of his office routine" each day. (Sovfoto/Eastfoto)

As the 1930s advanced, the world outside began to become dimly aware of the human cost of Soviet achievements, and of the brutality of which this version of totalitarianism was capable.

The tip of the iceberg was the public "purge trials" of leading Communists in the later 1930s. Once-revered party leaders, highly placed economic managers, famous generals were accused of crimes against the state. The charges included sabotaging the Five-Year Plans, plotting with Trotsky (then in exile overseas) or with capitalist foreign agents, voicing antiparty ideas, or simply failing to meet assigned quotas. More shocking still, the accused confessed to these crimes, some of which seemed very unlikely even to sympathetic Western observers, and were duly executed.

Only slowly did the more submerged depths of the Stalinist terror come out. The peasants, it gradually became clear, had resisted collectivization more vigorously than expected, burying their grain and slaughtering their animals rather than surrendering them to the collective. The *kulaks* among them had been sent off to labor camps in the Russian north, where many had died. Other peasants who resisted had had their grain dug up and carried off without compensation. This rigorous government response, coupled with bad weather and small harvests for a couple of years in the early thirties, had cost the lives of millions.

In the later thirties, the secret police added substantially to the human cost of Stalinism. Large numbers of less prominent people, charged with industrial sabotage, spying, or Trotskyite tendencies, were dealt with by the GPU (formerly the Cheka, later the NKVD, the KGB, and other secret police agencies) without benefit of public trials. For these officially defined enemies of the state, the knock on the door after midnight was followed by months of imprisonment without trial, rigorous interrogation, years of struggling to survive in a forced labor camp, or simply a bullet in the back of the neck at the end of a long dark corridor. Tens of millions were sent off to work camps in Siberia or the Soviet arctic, and millions more were executed.

Stalin, who had none of Hitler's flair for the dramatic, made few public speeches. Western journalists called him the Silent Man in the Kremlin. But his machinery for destroying enemies of the state was at least as efficient as that of his archenemy ranting at him across the width of Poland.

AUTHORITARIANISM IN ASIA, EUROPE, AND LATIN AMERICA

JAPAN: THE FAILURE OF ZAIBATSU LIBERALISM

Japan, like Germany, moved from a period of troubled liberal government in the 1920s to one of strident nationalism, militarism, and renewed imperial expansion in the 1930s. If European-style totalitarianism did not develop in Japan, political tyranny and violence certainly did. The militarist Japan that joined the Axis alliance with Nazi Germany and Fascist Italy was no unworthy partner to those two totalitarian powers of the West.

From about the time of World War I through the 1920s, the major political parties in the Japanese Diet enjoyed an enhanced share of political power among the complex system of elites that ran the country. Party leaders established close ties with leading bureaucrats and resisted rare imperial efforts to intervene in favor of one party or the other. The army and navy, though continuing to get large cuts of the budget for the mechanization of the armed forces, were generally prevented during the 1920s from undertaking further imperial adventures. The politicians in the Diet pursued policies of economic expansion instead, investing huge quantities of time and money in establishing close commercial ties with China.

Party power in the 1920s brought mixed results. From a liberal standpoint, laws providing for universal suffrage, legalized labor unions, and health insurance for factory workers were all to the good. The influence of *zaibatsu* big businesses, however, made itself felt in the

Diet, producing both crackdowns on radicals and government corruption.

Outside the Diet, military leaders and nationalists generally resented the unaggressive tone of Japan's politicians toward Europeans and Americans. And the peasant majority of Japanese, who did not share in *zaibatsu* prosperity during the 1920s, grew even more bitter when the World Depression of the 1930s further ate away at their already dwindling incomes. With little support from the liberal end of the spectrum and mounting unhappiness in such conservative quarters as the armed services, the peasants, and patriots generally, the political parties rapidly lost control in the 1930s.

RISE OF THE MILITARISTS: THE DAY OF THE ASSASSINS

No single leader masterminded the military monopolization of power in Japan in the 1930s. The armed forces were frequently rivals with one another, and there were factional feuds within the leadership of the army itself. What happened was a tangled web of conflicting intrigues punctuated by outbursts of violence that left political-party rule a shambles, the nation in the grip of a wave of chauvinistic passion, and the army rampaging through China.

The decline of party influence began with the totally unauthorized seizure of most of Manchuria from China in 1931 by units of the Japanese army. The annexation was engineered by a cabal of young army officers who ignored civilian orders from Tokyo to cease and desist until their objective was accomplished. Brought to trial for insubordination, the officers were hailed as national heroes by many Japanese; like right-wing assassins in Weimar Germany, they got off with light sentences. The "liberated" areas, meanwhile, were reorganized as the Japanese puppet state of Manchukuo.

From this beginning at the start of the decade, Japanese military arrogance and power grew by leaps and bounds through the 1930s. Other superpatriotic young officers began to raid the headquarters of the political parties, to attack wealthy *zaibatsu* executives, and finally to assassinate important politicians, including the prime minister.

In 1936 a group of junior officers with hundreds of troops under their command seized downtown Tokyo itself, occupied government buildings, and murdered a number of prominent officials. The rebellion was quickly suppressed with the help of the navy, and one of the army factions was disgraced. But the military leadership as a whole was only strengthened, since civilian authorities thereafter lived in fear of a second and more successful military coup.

By and large, the Japanese people supported the military. The failure of civilian authorities to clean up corruption, cut ties with the *zaibatsu,* or substantially alleviate the suffering of masses of peasant farmers undercut their moral position. Many were glad to see military men emerge as the new political leaders. The average Japanese, after all, had little knowledge of left-wing radicalism and did not object when censorship, arrests, and other forms of persecution cut into radical ranks. The ideological void was easily filled by nationalistic propaganda and renewed assertions of absolute loyalty to the emperor.

Young Emperor Hirohito himself, ironically, had more than once stood up to the military. But by 1937, when another "incident" led to a full-scale Japanese invasion of China, there was nothing much even he could do to control the nation's new militaristic masters.

A GREAT AUTHORITARIAN TIDE

Public attention focused on the major totalitarian and militaristic powers in the interwar years, particularly on Nazi Germany and Fascist Italy. But there were many other examples around the world of the disturbing flight from freedom that some critics noticed.

In Europe, many of the nations in the east and the south proved fertile ground for authoritarian regimes during these two decades. The Mediterranean peninsular states of Europe's southern fringe (Spain, Portugal, Italy, Greece) and the band of Eastern European states from the Baltic (Estonia, Latvia, Lithuania) through Poland and Austria to the Balkans (Hungary, Rumania, Yugoslavia, and others) all flirted with or fell to authoritarian regimes.

Many of these were new countries, most of them poor and technologically underdeveloped. Almost all were dominated in 1920 by antiquated social groups and institutions—traditional monarchies, established churches, landowning aristocracies. The strains of economic modernization, the poverty of both urban and peasant masses, the political demands of affluent middle classes, and the increasing appeal of various ideologies—liberalism, nationalism, socialism, communism, anarchism, and fascism—all contributed to tension and disorder in these areas.

In these unstable circumstances, the appeal of authority, direction, and order was obvious. The two groups who most vigorously exploited fear of anarchy or social revolution to create authoritarian regimes were military leaders and fascist ideologues. In some places, military strong men such as Marshall Pilsudski in Poland and Admiral Horthy in Hungary ruled with an iron hand. In other countries, uniformed proto-Fascist parties such as Rumania's Iron Guard or Austria's Fatherland Front broke heads, persecuted Jews, assassinated liberals.

In Latin America, the relatively good times of the 1920s turned definitively sour when the World Depression hit, drastically depressing the commodity prices on which the southern republics still depended heavily. In the early 1930s, more than half the twenty independent nations of Latin America responded to the resulting pressures with revolutions. The regimes that came to power followed a familiar pattern. Outside of Cárdenas's Mexico and a few other examples, military leaders, conservatives, and nationalists triumphed again and again.

The result for the major Latin American powers, such as Argentina and Brazil, was by no means uniformly bad economically. But the politics of the new regimes were almost always extremely undemocratic.

Thus Argentina's Radical party, which governed the country during the 1920s with policies that ranged from moderate to liberal, was overthrown by a military coup in 1930. The Conservative Republic, as the regime that ruled for the next dozen years is called, accelerated the growth of Argentine industry from small-scale workshops to much larger factories employing hundreds of workers. The new industry was capable of supplying much of the country's needs for manufactured goods without having to depend on foreign imports—a net gain for the economy.

Politically, however, democracy clearly lost ground under the Conservative Republic. The so-called *Concordancia,* an alliance of militarists, nationalists, and conservatives, rigged elections and suppressed political opposition in Argentina as vigorously as any nineteenth-century *caudillo.*

Brazil's maximum leader for fifteen years after he seized power in 1930, and again from 1951 to 1954, was the nationalistic military leader Getúlio Vargas. This long-lived dictator proved to be a skillful administrator who encouraged the growth of domestic industry and, most important, took great strides toward unifying the huge country under the central government in Rio de Janeiro. To accomplish this, Vargas both undermined the independent power of the separate Brazilian states and considerably expanded the functions of the central administration.

Besides these administrative reforms, however, Vargas frequently exercised dictatorial powers. He governed by censorship and decree, outlawed opposition political parties, and even deployed military force when necessary. Again, stability and progress were bought at the cost of stunted political liberties.

Some of the smaller Latin American states suffered from more brutal "personalist" dictators, building mass power on the traditional basis of personal followings and personal favors, during the hard times of the 1930s and beyond. The Somoza family seized power in Nicaragua in the mid-thirties and were soon constructing a successful modern sector of the economy while savaging all political rivals. Rafael Trujillo did a brilliant job of modernizing the island republic of Santo Domingo—and turned it into the "dry guillotine" of the Caribbean in the process.

Across the world in the Middle East, much the same sort of procedure was noticeable. Modernizing autocrats such as the Pahlavi shahs of Iran might expand oil output and even sprinkle some schools and hospitals across the land. But political tyranny, extending to imprisonment, torture, and death for enemies of the authoritarian regime, was the perhaps exorbitant price the nation was asked to pay.

Everywhere during those gray, hard, often despairing years, democracy seemed like a lost cause. The strains of modernization, resurgent conservatism, the appeal of ideologies such as nationalism and communism, and the impact of the Great Depression proved too much for many fragile experiments in self-government. A swelling totalitarian tide seemed to be rising around the world.

SUMMARY

While the liberal West struggled with its problems and while China and Mexico labored through their long revolutions, other nations succumbed to the totalitarian, militaristic, or otherwise authoritarian dictatorships of the brutal years. In the 1920s, 1930s, and 1940s, powerful and often cruel authoritarian regimes ruled in such major powers as Germany, Russia, Italy, and Japan, and in many smaller nations as well. The most powerful of these governments are often described as totalitarian, vesting total power in a single highly ideological party and appealing to the total commitment of party members to the cause, the movement, and its leader.

The prototype totalitarian state was Fascist Italy under Mussolini. *Il Duce* seized power from Italy's enfeebled liberal government in the 1920s. He created a regime characterized by one-party rule, economic centralization, and militarism.

Hitler's Nazi party rose to power in 1933, capitalizing on German resentment of the Versailles peace, disillusionment with democracy, and economic collapse. Once in power, Hitler, like Mussolini, suppressed free elections and free enterprise, as he remilitarized his country. He bailed the nation out of the depression with his public works and rearmament programs, and he unilaterally abrogated the Versailles Treaty. He also introduced Gestapo secret-police terror and SS death camps, massacring six million Jews and millions of others deemed biologically inferior to the "master race."

Stalin brought Communist party power to a climax in Russia in the 1930s. The new regime built on the czarist tradition of authoritarian rule but developed the bureaucracy, the army, and the secret police far beyond czarist models. Stalin's party dictatorship did modernize much of the Russian economy and boost production dramatically. At the same time, however, Communist policy decisions and deliberate repressions cost the lives of millions of Russians—officially classified as enemies of the working class—in Stalinist work camps and prisons, or in the famines of the early 1930s.

In Japan, resentment of an unaggressive parliamentary regime and of *zaibatsu* big business allowed the militarists to dominate affairs in the 1930s. Through assassinations and the threat of a military coup, Japanese generals and admirals cowed civilian authorities into accepting increasingly nationalistic, imperialistic, and reactionary policies.

A great authoritarian wave seemed to be sweeping over the world. One-party rule, military dictatorship, and other forms of autocratic government rose to power in many East European, South American, and Middle Eastern nations. Under the pressure of great economic and political problems, people seemed to be turning their backs on democracy.

SUGGESTED READING

ALLEN, W. S. *The Nazi Seizure of Power.* New York: Franklin Watts, 1973. Nazi rule comes to a single German town, a convincing microcosm of the nation.

BERGER, G. M. *Parties Out of Power in Japan: 1931–1941.* Princeton: Princeton University Press, 1977. Highly recommended survey of Japanese political history under militarist dominance in the 1930s.

BULLOCK, A. C. *Hitler: A Study in Tyranny.* New York: Harper & Row, Pub., 1964. Perhaps the best life of Hitler. See also J. C. Fest, *Hitler,* trans. R. and C. Winston (New York: Harcourt Brace Jovanovich, 1974).

CHAMBERLIN, W. H. *Russia's Iron Age* (2 vols.). Boston: Little, Brown, 1934. The trauma of the first Five-Year Plan, described by one who was there.

CONQUEST, R. *The Great Terror: Stalin's Purge of the Thirties.* New York: Collier, 1973. Causes, nature, and consequences of the Stalinist terror.

DANIELS, R. V. *The Stalin Revolution: Fulfillment or Betrayal of Communism?* Boston: Heath, 1965. Essays debating economic modernization, political terrorism, and other aspects of Stalin's impact on Russia.

FINER, H. *Mussolini's Italy.* Hamden, Conn.: Archon, 1974. Solid analysis by a political scientist.

FROMM, E. *Escape from Freedom.* New York: Farrar and Rinehart, 1941. Psychiatric diagnosis of Western humanity's fear of the responsibilities of freedom in the first half of the twentieth century.

HOFFMAN, P. *German Resistance to Hitler.* Cambridge: Harvard University Press, 1988. Best introduction to a much discussed subject, with some emphasis on the military leaders who opposed the Führer.

KIRKPATRICK, I. *Mussolini: A Study in Power.* New York: Hawthorn Books, 1964. A diplomat's analysis, and the most detailed account of the first totalitarian.

KOEHL, R. L. *The Black Corps: The Structure and Power Struggles of the Nazi SS.* Madison: University of Wisconsin Press, 1983. Convincing outline of the growth, internal feuds, and impact of Hitler's notorious "political soldiery."

MARRUS, M. E. *The Holocaust in History.* Hanover, N.H.: University Press of New England, 1987. Historiographical discussion of the genocide of the 1940s. For a more impassioned account, see L. S. Dawidowicz's *War against the Jews* (London: Weidenfeld and Nicolson, 1975). W. E. Mosse's *Jews in the German Economy: The German-Jewish Economic Elite, 1820–1935* (New York: Clarendon Press, 1987) presents a statistically based account of Jewish business and social achievements, depicting Jews not as fringe elements but as leading participants in German society and economic growth.

MEINECKE, F. *The German Catastrophe.* Boston: Beacon Press, 1963. A renowned German historian's view of Germany's twelve years of totalitarianism.

MORRIS, I., ed. *Japan 1931–1945: Militarism, Fascism, Japanism?* Boston: Heath, 1963. Japanese "isms" during this age of authoritarian predominance.

NAGY-TALAVERA, N. M. *The Green Shirts and Others: A History of Fascism in Hungary and Rumania.* Stanford: Hoover Institution, 1970. Fascism in Eastern Europe. See also H. Seton-Watson, *Eastern Europe Between the Wars, 1918–1941,* 3rd ed. (Hamden, Conn.: Archon, 1962).

NOLTE, E. *The Three Faces of Fascism,* trans. Leila Vennewitz. New York: Holt, Rinehart & Winston, 1966. Two places where fascism triumphed (Italy and Germany) and one where it failed (France); a complex and original appraisal. See the essays in H. A. Turner, Jr., ed., *Reappraisals of Fascism* (New York: Franklin Watts, 1975), and D. Muhlberger, *The Social Basis of European Fascist Movements* (New York: Methuen, 1987), studies of the roots of fascism in countries where fascists eventually seized power and in others where they failed.

ROGGER, H. and E. WEBER, eds. *The European Right: A Historical Profile.* Berkeley: University of California Press, 1965. The rise of authoritarian right-wing parties across Europe, in a series of essays.

SOLZHENITSYN, A. I. *The Gulag Archipelago 1918–1956* (3 vols.), trans. T. P. Whitney. New York: Harper & Row, Pub., 1974–1978. Personal testimony of the labor camps and prisons of Stalinist Russia, collected by a leading Soviet exile novelist, who was there himself.

TANNENBAUM, E. R. *The Fascist Experience: Italian Society and Culture, 1922–1945.* New York: Basic Books, 1972. Life in a society dominated by the slogans and institutional structures of *il Duce's* regime.

TUCKER, R. C., ed. *Stalinism: Essays in Historical Interpretation.* New York: W. W. Norton, 1977. Essays by leading experts on the nature and significance of the Stalinist period.

ULAM, A. B. *Stalin: The Man and His Era.* New York: Viking, 1973. Stalin as a political manipulator. See also R. C. Tucker, *Stalin as Revolutionary* (New York: W. W. Norton, 1973), a much-debated psychohistorical portrait of the "Silent Man in the Kremlin."

YACK, B. *The Longing for Total Revolution: Philosophic Sources of Social Discontent from Rousseau to Marx and Nietzsche.* Princeton, N.J.: Princeton University Press, 1986. Sophisticated, controversial analysis of revolutionary philosophical assumptions about true human nature and modern society, the latter seen as impeding the emergence of authentic humanity.

CHAPTER 43

World War II

CAUSES OF THE SECOND WORLD WAR

THE BIGGEST WAR IN HISTORY

It does not look like so much in the old news photographs, really. Moonscapes of ruins pall after a while. Dead bodies on a beach are either a scattering of small dark blobs—from a distance—or, close up, an anonymous young face with its chin in the sand, helmet spilling forward, a tangle of expensive equipment, and perhaps one arm stretched out, fingers stiffening just short of an unused rifle.

Even smoke boiling up over St. Paul's, a bloodied German family stumbling from its ruins, or soldiers with odd-shaped hand grenades charging up what had been a street in Stalingrad are only pictures, after all. "Smoke Break in Malayan Jungles" or unshaven tankers in the Sahara, "'Thumbs Up' after Rommell"—it all seems very far away somehow, as unreal as Verdun or Gettysburg. Or Agincourt or Jericho, for that matter.

Even at the time, it could sound a bit hysterical on the radio: "On land, on the sea, and in the air, we are hitting them, we are hitting them today. . . . " Or so low-key and understated as scarcely to merit the to-do, as in a letter from the front.

> What can one say about combat that has not been written time and time again. It is confusion, noise, but mostly hard work. . . . Then when one reaches some objective, one digs in, and so it starts all over again. . . . [1]

What it was, quite simply, was the biggest war in human history.

It was a war of immense offensives, catastrophic defeats, stunning victories—all the adjectives are apposite. A war that saw whole armies annihilated in set-piece battles, nations toppling like tenpins in a few days, cities reduced to rubble too hot to touch in a few unthinkable hours. A war in which a single battlefront in Russia could stretch for 1800 miles—roughly the distance from New York City to the Rocky Mountains. A war in which uncountable millions of soldiers went slogging into the noise, the confusion, the hard work, the digging in and moving on . . . or not.

It was the biggest and most thoroughly global war in all the human venture. It was six years and a day of escalating carnage, from the German invasion of Poland on September 1, 1939, to the Japanese surrender on the battleship *Missouri* in Tokyo Bay on September 2, 1945.

On one of those days, the sergeant quoted above settled to a forest floor in Germany so naturally that the men behind him thought he had "seen something" and ducked for cover. A few minutes later the platoon commander crawled up to try to administer first aid, and died there. As, no doubt, did the men who killed them. As tens of millions of others did in the biggest war.

LONG-RANGE CAUSES: DEPRESSION, VERSAILLES, AND THE STATE SYSTEM

Given what has been said about the nature of totalitarian governments, it is easy to see World War II as a splendid illustration of the "devil theory" of history—aggressive dictators on one side, democracies on the other. Certainly, Germany, Italy, and Japan were aggressive, militaristic, and expansionist in the 1930s. On the other hand, Stalin's Russia was as totalitarian as Hitler's Germany, and "Uncle Joe" was on the Allied side. Britain still headed the largest empire in the history of the world in 1939. Even the United States, few as its holdings were outside the continent, had made itself so unpopular meddling in the affairs of the Latin American republics that some of them would not side with America against the Nazis.

A related approach having much appeal because it seems to carry a message for our time is to see the cause of the war as Allied appeasement of Axis aggression. Again, there is much truth in this view, as will be apparent when we follow the grim sequence of crises down the thirties to the final confrontation over Poland in 1939. Yet this approach also is incomplete, for it does little to explain why the Axis powers were aggressive and expansionist in the first place.

Deeper, longer-range causes for the Second World War include the World Depression, the Versailles peace after World War I, and perhaps some deeply disturbing features of the global political order.

---

[1] Personal correspondence from John Calvin Kreamer to Ross Kreamer, Belgium, January 22, 1945.

The Great Depression certainly accounted in significant part for Hitler's rise to power and for the decline of party government in Japan. Military expenditures were also a good way for Hitler and other totalitarian leaders to put people back to work in a hurry. Perhaps most important, however, the depression left the Western democracies badly weakened in the 1930s. Preoccupied by domestic problems, divided class against class by the new poverty, and unsure of their own future, democratic leaders found appeasement and the avoidance of the confrontation as natural as aggressive rhetoric was to the heads of militarized totalitarian states.

Confrontations there were in plenty—and many of them went back to the unsatisfactory peace settlement signed at Versailles in 1919. The Versailles peace divided the great powers into two camps: the satisfied and the unsatisfied, the supporters of the settlement and those who demanded revisions. Britain, France, and the United States—to the extent that the United States involved itself at all—supported the treaty as signed. Germany, Italy, Japan, and the Soviet Union were among the major revisionists.

Germany and Soviet Russia had emerged from World War I as pariahs among the nations. Germany had been saddled with war guilt and reparations, stripped of its colonies and armies. The Soviet Union had lost large portions of czarist territory in the collapse of 1917–1918 and felt surrounded by capitalist enemies after the civil war that followed. Italy and Japan had seen their imperial ambitions frustrated by the Versailles settlement and by the diplomacy of the postwar period.

The revisionist powers, in the time-honored style of great powers, seized every opportunity to modify the settlement in their favor—and in so doing drew steadily closer to another great war.

There is, finally, the obvious, which it sometimes takes a certain amount of intellectual boldness to state:

> There is a larger view . . . according to which both [world] wars reflect fundamental shortcomings of a brilliant but flawed civilization that could not settle its differences without periodic blood baths. Nothing in the 1919 settlement had changed the basic division of . . . the world into separate sovereign states that recognized no higher authority than national interest. . . . Some would argue that until the state system is replaced by a world government, there can be no lasting peace.[2]

In a rapidly shrinking world, these differences would clash more frequently and more violently in the twentieth century than ever before. The state system itself and the system of international anarchy it generated would

thus make world wars a more likely occurrence in our time than in any previous one.

Though they didn't know it, then, revisionist dictators demanding justice and defenders of the international status quo pointing to the sanctity of treaties, militarists and appeasers, aggressive politicians, and peoples who were simply too busy with the depression to care about the international situation all in their different ways contributed to the coming of the biggest war in history.

ITALIAN AND JAPANESE AGGRESSION

A string of international crises led up to the final explosion. Each crisis pitted revisionists against defenders of the peace, authoritarian states against those that were at least less so. The result was a series of totalitarian and militaristic aggressions met with such tepid responses on the part of relatively democratic states as to give the word *appeasement* a bad taste ever since.

At first the confrontations seemed far off and exotic to the Western powers that still claimed to run the world. Japanese aggression in China, Italy's latest plunge into Ethiopia, even a civil war in Spain—land of bullfighters and sunny poverty—did not seem like central concerns to Western democracies struggling for their economic lives. Then it was much, much closer—but still involving unfamiliar names and places: the Rhineland, *Anschluss,* the Sudetenland, the Polish corridor. . . . And then the Panzers were revving up their motors, the Stukas roaring into the dawn.

But at first it was distant thunder on a horizon half a world away. Japan in Asia, Italy in Africa first broke the peace so dubiously established in 1919.

Japan attacked China first in 1931, in Manchuria, and again, in an all-out invasion, in 1937. In both instances Japan's military leaders instigated the aggression while its own civilian government, the Chinese army, and the nations of the world did little but wring their hands in dismay.

Japan had been developing Manchuria, the old Manchu homeland northeast of the Great Wall, as a center of grain, coal, and iron production for decades. A campaign by Jiang Jiehi to regain the political and economic initiative there, plus the revival of Russian power in the Far East under Stalin, aroused the concern of imperialistic Japanese fearful of losing their foothold in Manchuria. In 1931 a handful of Japanese officers stationed in the area staged an attempt to sabotage the Japanese-run railway and used it as an excuse to seize control of the whole region, rechristen it Manchukuo, and install a Manchu puppet there.

Reactions to this first major act of aggression on the decade-long road to World War II were illuminating. The Japanese officers used their trials for insubordination as platforms to explain their patriotic motives, and—as we have seen—were hailed as national heroes in many quar-

[2]Robert O. Paxton, *Europe in the Twentieth Century* (New York: Harcourt Brace Jovanovich, 1975), p. 428.

ters. In the end it was the current prime minister and cabinet who resigned in disgrace. Jiang Jiehi, preoccupied with his annual campaign against Mao's first base in Jiangxi, could do nothing. The League of Nations appointed a commission of inquiry. When the commission very mildly rapped Japan's knuckles over the incident, Japan simply withdrew from the League. Japan kept its new colony, and was soon expanding its influence into the neighboring provinces of China.

All-out invasion did not come until 1937. By that time Jiang had been compelled by popular opinion—and his own Guomindang colleagues—to make common cause with Mao, now installed in Shanxi, against Japanese power in the north. This united front, encouraged by the Soviet Union, threatened to reverse the Japanese expansionist drive. Another "incident," this one at the Marco Polo Bridge near Beijing, gave Japan the excuse Japanese generals sought for a full-scale invasion of China.

Over the next few years Japan's mechanized, highly trained and motivated army and navy dominated China's coasts, rivers, and harbors, occupied many Chinese cities, and conquered most of China's east coast. Jiang Jiehi's government, accompanied by large numbers of Chinese fleeing the sometimes savage behavior of the Japanese troops, retreated up the Yangzi Valley into the interior to establish a wartime capital at Chongqing.

Jiang's scorched-earth policies as his troops retreated, Mao's guerrilla attacks, and the primitive logistics and transport systems in the interior of China soon turned the triumphant Japanese advance into a grim occupation. But despite strongly worded protests from the United States and some modest continuing Soviet aid, little was done for China. The United States, in fact, went on selling Japan such basic war materiel as iron and oil right up until 1941.

Italy invaded Ethiopia in 1935, halfway between Japan's aggression in Manchuria and its massive invasion of China proper. Confronted with Italy's African venture, the Western democracies once more reacted inadequately, and the aggressors carried the day.

Mussolini, the oldest of the totalitarian rulers, apparently felt that the younger generation of Fascists needed a great adventure, the party as a whole a new shot of glory. Italy also needed more space to resettle the growing numbers of the unemployed. And Ethiopia, which adjoined Italy's colonies in the Horn of Africa and was the last country on the African continent without a colonial overlord, seemed a logical answer to his needs.

An incident between Italian and Ethiopian troops at an unused water hole on a disputed frontier gave Mussolini his excuse. The Ethiopian king, Haile Selassie, offered to submit the dispute to arbitration. Mussolini responded with shelling, aerial strafing, and mustard gas. The Ethiopians fought a gallant fight, but they could not match the weaponry of the civilizers from the north. By the spring of 1936, King Victor Emmanuel had been proclaimed emperor of Ethiopia.

The international outcry this time was considerably greater. The League of Nations voted economic sanctions against Italy, and the French and British governments worked through diplomatic channels. But the sanctions did not include oil, the one essential that, cut off, could have stopped Italy's war machine in its tracks. And the British and the French were still trying to keep Italy, their ally in World War I, from drifting into Hitler's orbit. So the aggressors rolled on.

THE SPANISH CIVIL WAR

During the years 1936–1939, the Spanish civil war gave the self-proclaimed champions of liberty in the world another chance to stand up for freedom. Again, they left the field to the totalitarian powers. It was, by all accounts, the most heart-rending lost cause of a decade that was littered with them.

Spain during the early thirties seemed to be going against the trend of that authoritarian decade—replacing a dictatorship with a budding democracy. In 1930 it had been a European backwater, afflicted by many of the problems of its former colonies overseas: arrogantly wealthy landlords and poverty-stricken peasants, a reactionary and influential Catholic church, and a military-officer caste habituated to interfering in government. In addition, a modest amount of industrial development had created a small, overworked, and underpaid proletariat, a happy hunting ground for anarchists, syndicalists, and communists. Regional nationalisms also flourished, particularly in Catalonia and among the Basques.

Conflicts among these groups had flared up in 1930 as the world depression added to the pressures building within the nation. In a few hectic months, both the most recent military dictator and then the monarchy itself were swept away. A shiny new Spanish republic thus set to work in 1931 to design itself a constitution and begin some desperately needed reforms.

Five years of rather modest social change—redistribution of some large estates among peasants, anticlerical legislation, autonomy for Catalonia—only deepened the divisions in Spanish society. A seesawing series of elections further divided the nation without determining who was to have power.

In July of 1936, then, a self-styled Nationalist movement headed by General Francisco Franco took up arms against the Spanish republic. Within a few weeks Franco had occupied half the country, the south and west. But the Republic held the capital of Madrid and the industrialized east, including Catalonia. For the next three years, the Spanish Republic and the Nationalist rebels fought each other in a gory civil war that cost half a million lives. Symbolically, the Spanish civil war also became to many a political morality play, a struggle between good and evil for the soul of the Western World.

Franco's Nationalist coalition included militarists, landlords, strong Catholics, and Spanish nationalists. The Republic was supported by liberals, peasant anarchists, worker syndicalists, Catalonian nationalists, anticlericals, and communists. But it was the foreign friends of the Spanish contenders who determined all their destinies.

The liberal powers, Britain and France, trying to avoid escalation of a local conflict into a general war, urged noninvolvement and an embargo on arms shipments. Hitler and Mussolini, however, seeing a brother-in-arms in Franco, sent him tens of thousands of Italian troops and Germany's Condor Legion, the bombers of Guernica. Of the great powers, only the Soviet Union, fearful of German rearmament under a militant anticommunist such as Hitler, sent advisors, money, and weapons to the republic.

Large numbers of idealistic young people, however, came to Spain as volunteers to fight for the Spanish Republic and try to stop the further spread of fascist totalitarianism. They agreed with John Donne's warning quoted in Ernest Hemingway's novel of the Spanish Civil War, *For Whom the Bell Tolls*, about the funeral bell tolling in Spain: "Never send to ask for whom the bell tolls: it tolls for thee." But the members of the International Brigade, the Abraham Lincoln Brigade, and the rest were going to fight in a lost cause; they were going, in the words of a film made long afterwards, *To Die in Madrid*.

Franco won. What was left of the volunteers, and many Spaniards too, fled across the Pyrenees. The bell went on tolling.

GERMAN AGGRESSION

Of all the totalitarian leaders, the most successful and in the end the destroyer of the peace was Adolf Hitler.

Having unilaterally revised the Versailles treaty and begun German rearmament on a vast scale, Hitler was soon demanding modifications of the territorial arrangements of central Europe. A passionate nationalist as well as a racist, he insisted that all German-speaking areas had a right to be reabsorbed into the new German Reich. He also talked about what he called *Lebensraum*—"living space"—for the dynamic and growing German people, meaning a resumption of Germany's historic tendency to push eastward, into the lands of the Slavs.

As steps toward these nationalistic goals, Hitler embarked on a series of aggressive moves in the heart of Europe, against Austria, Czechoslovakia, and Poland. As a preliminary step, however, he remilitarized the Rhineland in 1936.

This German frontier zone between Germany and France was to have remained free of troops so as to discourage border clashes between the two traditional ene-

A famous cartoonist's comment on the destruction of Poland in 1939 by her totalitarian neighbors. David Low's caricature of Hitler and Stalin shows the two former archenemies greeting each other with a sardonic parody of the insults they had once exchanged so vigorously. There was, however, no love lost between the two authoritarian rulers, who were at war with each other within two years. (New York Public Library Collection)

mies. But this also left Germany open to French invasion. In March 1936, Hitler therefore sent 35,000 German soldiers into the Rhineland, unilaterally revising an international agreement once more and materially strengthening his hand against the liberal Allies. It was his first international aggression. His armies were not ready for war, had apparently even been ordered to withdraw if confronted with force. But the French did not confront them, and the German troops stayed.

In March 1938 Hitler absorbed Austria into the Third Reich. Some of Austria's German-speaking population did, in fact, support what Hitler was doing across the border, and there was an aggressive Austrian Nazi party. Many other Austrians, however, wanted to maintain their historic independence, even of a Germany headed by the Austrian-born Hitler. Nevertheless, the German *Führer* browbeat Austria's leaders into accepting a Nazi chancellor, then dictated a "request" for German troops to "maintain order" in the shaken country. The German army marched in, to be greeted by cheering crowds, and the *Anschluss*—"unification"—of Germany and Austria was completed. Hitler now ruled a country of 80 million Germans—equal to the populations of Britain and France combined, and well over half the population of the United States.

In later 1938 and early 1939, he took over Czechoslovakia. Claiming that that country's German-speaking minority in the Czech Sudetenland was being mistreated. Hitler demanded the surrender of this territory to Germany. France and Russia both had treaty alliances with the Czechs, and Britain supported them publicly. But

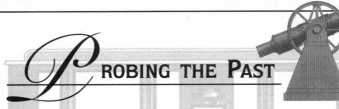

PROBING THE PAST

"*On 30 January, 1933 . . . Hitler became Chancellor. . . . He changed most things in Germany. He destroyed political freedom and the rule of law; he transformed German economics and finance; he quarreled with the churches; he abolished the separate states and made Germany for the first time a united country. In one sphere alone he changed nothing. His foreign policy was that of his predecessors, of the professional diplomats at the foreign ministry, and indeed of virtually all Germans. Hitler, too, wanted to free Germany from the restrictions of the peace treaty; to restore a great German army; and then to make Germany the greatest power in Europe from her natural weight. . . .*

This is not the accepted view. Writers of great authority have seen in Hitler a system maker, deliberately preparing from the first a great war which would destroy existing civilization and make him master of the world. In my opinion, statesmen are too absorbed by events to follow a preconceived plan. They take one step, and the next follows from it. The systems are created by historians, as happened with Napoleon; and the systems attributed to Hitler are really those of Hugh Trevor-Roper, Elizabeth Wiskemann, and Alan Bullock."

This paragraph from the celebrated British historian A. J. P. Taylor's <u>Origins of the Second World War</u> illustrates revisionist history at its most daring. Taylor challenged the orthodox view of the struggle as "Hitler's war," depicting Hitler as more of a blunderer than a would-be world conqueror and insisting that blame for the war should be apportioned among other statesmen as well, including British Prime Minister Neville Chamberlain. Taylor's interpretation remains controversial to this day.

Do you have the impression that most, if not "virtually all" Germans supported Hitler's foreign policy in the 1930s? Do you think historians and biographers like those listed in the last sentences might have seen a "system" in Hitler's policies where no master plan existed?

A. J. P. Taylor, <u>The Origins of the Second World War</u> (Harmondsworth, England: Penquin Books, 1963), pp. 96–98.

Hitler again blustered and threatened until the British and French leaders once more agreed to a settlement giving Hitler what he wanted. This final concession, agreed to by British prime minister Neville Chamberlain at Munich in September 1938, made the name of that city synonymous with the bankrupt policy of appeasement.

Most of Europe, however, heaved a sigh of relief: the dead of the First World War were only twenty years in their graves by that time, and many then living remembered. In March 1939, meanwhile, German troops marched into Prague, and most of the rest of Czechoslovakia became a German protectorate.

In September 1939 Hitler moved against Poland, and Europe went to war again at last. Rectification of a dubious Polish-German frontier, the return of the German-speaking port of Danzig to Germany, and a German railway across the Polish corridor that separated Danzig from the Reich were the diplomatic demands that kindled this final crisis. In a broader perspective, the invasion of Poland looked very much like a continuation of the *Drang nach Osten,* Germany's historic drive into Slavic Eastern Europe.

By way of preparation, Hitler astonished Europe by negotiating a nonaggression treaty with his most vocal opponent—Joseph Stalin. The Nazi-Soviet Pact of August 1939 was a triumph of practical self-interest over ideology on both sides. It gave Hitler a free hand in Poland and allowed Stalin further time to prepare for future conflict with his aggressive rival. A secret codicil also agreed on the division of Eastern Europe between them.

Britain and France had given ringing guarantees of

Polish rights and territorial independence as the crisis came to a head. Hitler, understandably, did not believe them. A week after the signing of the Hitler-Stalin Pact, German troops invaded Poland.

World War II had begun.

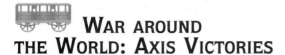

WAR AROUND THE WORLD: AXIS VICTORIES

THE FIRST GLOBAL WAR

World War I had involved much of the world, one way or another, but most of the fighting had been in Europe, and most of the casualties and destruction were borne by Europeans. World War II, by contrast, was in every sense a truly global war—perhaps the first such conflict in world history.

The two great alliances of nations that confronted each other were clearly intercontinental. The major Axis powers were two European nations and one powerful Asian one: Germany, Italy, and Japan. Bound by a series of treaties in 1936 and 1937, including the Anti-Comintern Pact against the Soviet Union, the so-called Rome-Berlin-Tokyo Axis involved mutual recognition of one another's spheres of interest and future conquests in Europe and Asia.

The Allied Big Five—Britain, France, the Soviet Union, China, and the United States—included two purely European powers (though both had large overseas empires), one transcontinental Eurasian power, one purely Asian nation, and one North American state. Growing slowly from the Franco-British declarations of war on Germany in 1939 through the German invasion of Russia and the Japanese attack on the United States in 1941, this alliance was soon locked in combat with the Axis over much of the world.

Europe, Asia, North Africa, and Oceania were all major battlefields. The war was fought on many seas and islands, from the North Atlantic to the South Pacific, from Crete to Okinawa. Military planners—and armchair strategists at home—filled world maps with colored pins, and everybody learned to pronounce names they had never even seen before, let alone heard spoken over their radios.

The globe was thus divided into theaters of war where the two grand alliances battled for strategic islands, patches of desert, cities in the northern snows. The casualties and the destruction were spread around the globe much more widely than ever before. And when victory finally came, it centered in Berlin and Tokyo, two capitals on opposite sides of the world.

THE GERMAN BLITZKRIEG

World War I was a war of position: there was little change in the trench lines, and the armies swayed agonizingly back and forth, going nowhere. Generalities may suffice to give a sense of that terrible conflict. World War II, by contrast, was a war of movement: armies advanced hundreds of miles, fleets struck across even greater distances. Some narrative, then, will be necessary to give a proper sense of this story.

The war began with stunning Axis victories: Hitler's *Blitzkriegs* and the Phony War sandwiched in between.

The first *Blitzkrieg*—"lightning war"—struck into Poland in September of 1939. German motorized Panzer divisions rolled across the frontier, preceded by waves of bombing planes, at 5:00 A.M. on September 1. Western Poland was overrun in two weeks. Soviet Russia, Hitler's ally of one month, then stabbed into the hapless land between them, and Warsaw, Poland's last stronghold, fell before the month was over. It was Germany's first demonstration of what modern mechanized warfare could be like, not in defense, as in the First World War, but on the offense.

The so-called Phony War followed through the winter of 1939–1940. The Soviet Union, triumphant in Poland, turned next on its northern neighbor Finland. But Soviet armies, which had just lost half their officer corps to the purge trials, became bogged down in a sideshow David-and-Goliath struggle with the Finns. The British and the French had declared war on Germany in September. With Poland gone, however, there was little they could do to keep their pledge to defend it. Both Western European powers seemed content to defend themselves, the French in particular barricading themselves behind the steel-and-concrete ramparts of the Maginot Line. They were thoroughly prepared, thanks to massive military outlays during the 1930s, to fight the 1914 war over again. But that was not what was in the cards in 1940.

The reporters who had dubbed the winter lull the Phony War changed their tune when spring came, and with it another *Blitzkrieg*.

Hitler, seeking air and naval bases for himself and intending to cut Britain off from a prime source of foodstuffs, struck suddenly into Scandinavia in April 1940. In a plot so outrageous few thriller writers would attempt it, he dispatched "Trojan-horse" troop ships disguised as freighters and ore barges to pour Germans onto the docks in Denmark and Norway. Denmark, overwhelmed, capitulated. Norway fought—and lasted one month to the day.

The Low Countries came next. Determined to outflank the Maginot Line from the north—the Channel side—Hitler attacked the Netherlands, Belgium, and Luxembourg in May. While their troops flooded over the borders, the Germans made skillful use of paratroopers and brutal bombing of civilian centers to seize key cities well behind the lines. Little Luxembourg fell in one day, the Netherlands lasted five. Belgium, bolstered by desperate French and British help, held out for two and a half weeks. By the end of May it too had fallen.

In June, it was France's turn. But the British were thrust aside first.

The collapse of Belgium exposed the British Expe-

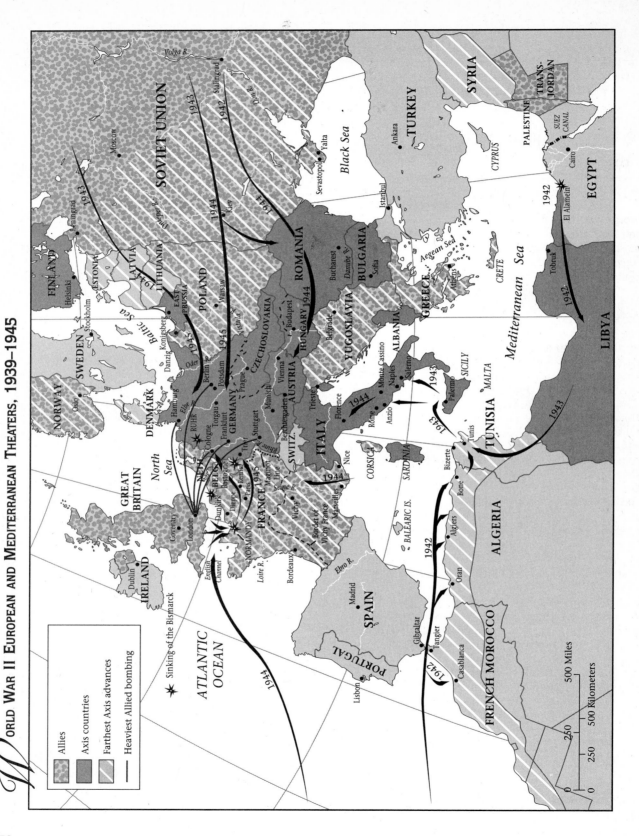

WORLD WAR II EUROPEAN AND MEDITERRANEAN THEATERS, 1939–1945

Allies
Axis countries
Farthest Axis advances
Heaviest Allied bombing
✳ Sinking of the Bismarck

ATLANTIC
OCEAN

IRELAND
Dublin

GREAT
BRITAIN
London
Coventry
North
Sea
English Channel

NORWAY
Oslo

SWEDEN
Stockholm

DENMARK
Hamburg
NETH.
BELG.
Brussels
Dunkirk
Dieppe

FINLAND
Helsinki
Leningrad
1943

SOVIET UNION
Moscow
Volga R.
Stalingrad
1942
Don R.
1943
1943

ESTONIA
LATVIA
LITHUANIA
EAST PRUSSIA
Dnieper R.
Kiev
1944

Baltic Sea
Danzig
Königsberg
Oder R.
Warsaw
POLAND
1945
1945

GERMANY
Berlin
Potsdam
Torgau
Prague
CZECHOSLOVAKIA
Frankfurt
Cologne
RUHR
Stuttgart
Munich
Vienna
AUSTRIA
Berchtesgaden
SWITZ.
1945

FRANCE
Paris
Seine R.
Maginot Line
Loire R.
Bordeaux
Vichy
Border of
Vichy France
NORMANDY
Bastogne
Rhine R.
Nice
Marseilles
1944
1944

SPAIN
Madrid

PORTUGAL
Lisbon

Gibraltar
Tangier

FRENCH MOROCCO
Casablanca
1942

ALGERIA
Oran
Algiers
Bone
1942

TUNISIA
Tunis
Bizerte
1943

BALEARIC IS.

CORSICA
SARDINIA

Elbe R.
HUNGARY
1944
Budapest
YUGOSLAVIA
Belgrade
ROMANIA
Bucharest
Danube R.
BULGARIA
Sofia

ITALY
Florence
Rome
Anzio
Naples
Monte Cassino
Salerno
1944
1943

ALBANIA
GREECE
Athens
1943

SICILY
Palermo
MALTA

Mediterranean Sea

Black Sea
Sevastopol
Yalta

TURKEY
Ankara
Istanbul

Aegean Sea
CRETE

CYPRUS

SYRIA

TRANS-
JORDAN

PALESTINE
SUEZ CANAL
Cairo

EGYPT
El Alamein
1942

Tobruk
1942

LIBYA
1943

500 Miles
0   250   500

500 Kilometers
0   250   500

650

dictionary Force on the continent to disaster. Pressed back against the sea at Dunkirk in early June, the bulk of the British troops were evacuated with the help of a flotilla of private yachts and sailboats. But the "miracle" of Dunkirk was nonetheless a military disaster: the British had been hurled out of Europe.

The German armies, meantime, swung south and west around the end of the Maginot Line and drove for Paris—the great race they had been unable to win in the 1914 war. Before the month of June was out, gray-uniformed German infantrymen were goose-stepping up the Champs-Elysées. Hitler danced a little jig as he received the French surrender—in the same railway car where the Germans had been forced to accept the armistice in 1918.

More than half of France was occupied by the Germans for the remainder of the war. The rest of the country was governed by a puppet French government set up in the south.

THE BATTLE OF BRITAIN

The next phase of the war, 1940–1941, saw the fighting still focused on the western end of Eurasia, in the Battle of Britain and the overrunning of eastern Europe. In this phase too the Axis was generally victorious, though not quite as uniformly as in the lightning thrusts of the preceding year.

Hitler turned his attention particularly to Britain in 1940 and 1941—and met his first setback. Like Napoleon before him, he abandoned plans to invade the British Isles directly because he lacked flat-bottomed barges to transport sufficient troops for the operation. He turned instead to the twentieth century's armory of new war machines—to planes and submarines.

He tried first to break the British by massive bombardment from the air, pounding cities such as Coventry and London with tons of high explosives in almost nightly air raids. Londoners slept in the subways and came up to smoke and ruin. But the Royal Air Force took an unexpectedly heavy toll of the attackers. The rolling oratory of the new prime minister, Winston Churchill, rallied the British people. And Britain did not surrender.

Thereafter the Germans settled down to a submarine siege of the islands, as in World War I. The goal was to cut Great Britain off from overseas supplies, either from the Commonwealth countries or in the form of increasing aid from the United States. For a while it looked very much as though that aim might be accomplished: during the first year after Dunkirk, the Germans sank 1400 merchant ships in Atlantic waters.

Still, the British did not yield—and the United States began to provide increasingly open support for the last fighting democracy left in Europe. Under a "lend-lease" arrangement Franklin Roosevelt negotiated an aid package that beefed up the British navy, and he announced that although he would not send American boys to fight overseas, the United States could and would become "the arsenal of democracy." In the summer of 1941 Roosevelt and Churchill met secretly at sea to sign an idealistic statement of mutual aims, the Atlantic Charter.

Frustrated in the West, the armies of the totalitarian powers were much more successful in Eastern Europe. During 1940 and 1941, Hitler and Mussolini were mopping up the Balkans, Stalin the Baltic states.

Besides Finland and Poland, former czarist territories lost to Russia in World War I included the states of Estonia, Latvia, and Lithuania on the Baltic Sea. Stalin now seized his chance to reabsorb them into the Soviet Union. Hitler, meanwhile, with some help from Mussolini, overran the countries of the Balkan peninsula. Some—Hungary, Rumania, Bulgaria—were forced to join the Axis alliance. Others—Yugoslavia and Greece—were conquered, though bands of guerrillas remained active in the rugged mountains of both countries.

By the middle of 1941, after almost two years of fighting, the Axis tide was still at its flood. Then, in the latter half of 1941, German and Japan made their biggest mistakes of the war.

BARBAROSSA AND PEARL HARBOR

In June 1941 Hitler launched his biggest offensive thus far—and made his largest error of judgment: the invasion of Russia. He seems to have been motivated by simmering disagreements over the spoils of war—especially the division of the Balkans, where Russia's interest went back to the pan-Slavism of the nineteenth century. The German ruler therefore decided on Operation Barbarossa. Named for the famous medieval German warrior-emperor, Barbarossa was planned as a quick campaign to break Russia as the German armies had so many others in those two years.

The invasion began in late June 1941, and in six months Hitler's armies had swept over half of European Russia. By December, German troops were fighting in the suburbs of both of Russia's historic capitals, Moscow and Leningrad (St. Petersburg).

But neither city fell. Long supply lines, the slow Soviet retreat that left only scorched earth behind, and the crushing cold of a Russian winter slowed Hitler's impetuous drive to a crawl, as they had Napoleon's in 1812. Meanwhile, the Soviet Union's newly built factories in and beyond the Ural Mountains farther to the east remained comparatively safe and productive, grinding out war materiel. And supplies from Britain and the United States began to arrive by sea, through Murmansk in the far north.

There were horrendous battles yet to come in Russia. But by the beginning of 1942, Hitler had reached his limits in the east, as he had in the west. Neither Britain on its tight little offshore islands nor Russia on its endless eastern plains would fall. And by that time a third great power was coming against him—the United States.

An American battleship sinks in the smoke and flame of Pearl Harbor on Sunday morning, December 7, 1941. The United States lost 2400 men and most of its Pacific fleet in the Japanese surprise attack. Ask any American old enough to remember that morning what they were doing when they heard the news, and the odds are they will remember, even half a century later. (National Archives)

While Hitler was knifing into Russia, on the other side of the globe, Japan was carrying Axis victories to a climax by overrunning almost all the Western colonies in the Far East during 1941 and 1942. In so doing, however, the Japanese made the other biggest Axis error of judgment: bringing the United States into the war.

Japanese imperialists and militarists, now thoroughly in charge of Emperor Hirohito's government, saw a golden opportunity for renewed empire building in the East while the Western imperial powers reeled from Hitler's blows. By the end of 1941, the Japanese had planned a coordinated series of attacks. The first to be hit were the British colony of Hong Kong off the South China coast—and the two American colonies of the Philippine Islands in Southeast Asia and the Hawaiian Islands in the central Pacific.

Hawaii, too far away for invasion, was nevertheless hit first from the air so that the American Pacific fleet based there, at Pearl Harbor, could be destroyed. On a quiet Sunday morning—December 7, 1941—carrier-based Japanese planes swept in low over the islands. Shouting into their microphones the prearranged signal for success, *Tora! Tora! Tora!*—Tiger! Tiger! Tiger!—they zoomed along Battleship Row and inland over the airfield, raining down bombs. They sank eight battleships and ten other vessels, leaving the most powerful Western naval squadron in the Pacific dead and smoldering in the water.

Through the following winter and spring of 1942, Japanese forces conquered the American Philippines, British Hong Kong, Malaya and Burma, and much of the Dutch East Indies. They had forced the French to yield to them de facto control of French Indochina—Vietnam, Cambodia, Laos—and absorbed the last independent Asian kingdom, Thailand. In so doing they cut the famous Burma Road, the supply line from British India to China, and brought victory in the long Chinese struggle within sight at last.

The summer of 1942 was thus the highwater mark for Japan in Asia, just as Germany was reaching its limits in Europe. And Japan's error in attacking the United States was already beginning to show.

WAR AROUND THE WORLD: ALLIED TRIUMPH

THE ALLIED COUNTERATTACK: NORTH AFRICA AND ITALY

The years 1939 to 1941 were a period of almost unbroken Axis victories. From 1942 through 1945, the initiative shifted to the Allies, and with it the rising tide of victories.

In 1942 the United States, Britain, and the Soviet Union formed what Churchill, with eighteenth-century grandiloquence, called the Grand Alliance. France's government-in-exile under General de Gaulle and what remained of Jiang Jiehi's China were lesser partners. The larger nations of the British Commonwealth joined them, and many other countries around the world found it prudent to cast their lot at least nominally with the Allied cause. The Big Three in particular—Roosevelt, Churchill, and Stalin—met repeatedly through the rest of the war to plan grand strategy and reaffirm their determination to make no terms with their adversaries, to accept only unconditional surrender.

The world's biggest industrial machine, that of the United States, now went into high gear. Factories and men, idle and rusting through the depression, went back to work with a rush. As in World War I, many women took jobs formerly held by men now absorbed by the armed forces. Huge quantities of war supplies were conveyed across the Atlantic to Britain and Russia in the teeth of the German submarines and planes.

In Europe, a massive coordinated air attack was launched against Germany. British and American bombers hit German bases, industrial complexes, and cities, the Americans by day and the British by night. In the Pacific, reinforcements arrived. British raiders began to strike back at the Japanese in the jungles of Southeast Asia. And the U.S. Navy began to raise and repair most of the shattered hulks the Japanese had left behind in Pearl Harbor.

The first major Allied victories, however, came on battlefields not even mentioned yet—in North Africa and Italy.

The deserts of North Africa had been the site of a seesaw tank war between the British and the Germans since 1940. The turning point of the struggle—and one of the turning points of the war—came in the Battle of El Alamein in the fall of 1942. General Montgomery's victory over General Rommel, Germany's celebrated "Desert Fox," saved Egypt and the Suez Canal, Britain's lifeline to the East.

Thereafter the British drove the Germans and their Italian allies out of Egypt and pushed on into Libya, Italy's major North African colony and an Axis stronghold in Africa. In the meantime, an Anglo-American force had landed in the French colonies of Morocco and Algeria and easily overwhelmed the Germans and the collaborationist French forces there. By the spring of 1943, the last Axis armies in North Africa had surrendered.

Hitler had not only been stopped but also had been rolled back. And new Allied victories followed in Italy, later in 1943.

American and British forces leaped from North Africa across the narrow waist of the Mediterranean, first to the island of Sicily, off the toe of the Italian boot, and then to the mainland of Italy itself. The great southern metropolis of Naples fell in the autumn of 1943. The impact of these combined defeats in Libya, Sicily, and southern Italy, furthermore, were sufficient to bring about the fall of Mussolini in July and the surrender of Italy in September of that year.

The German armies in Italy fought on, and the battle for the peninsula turned into a grinding struggle that would drag on through the rest of the war. But one of the Axis powers, at least, had given up. And by the end of 1943, the war had turned against the Axis elsewhere as well.

STALINGRAD AND D DAY

The years 1943 and 1944 were years of mounting pressure on the Axis, major breakthroughs for the Allies. In Europe these were the years of Stalingrad and D Day; in the Far East, the island-hopping war that brought American forces within reach of Japan.

The Battle of Stalingrad, like that of El Alamein, is generally considered a major turning point in the war. The Germans, unable to take either Leningrad in the north or Moscow in the center of European Russia in 1941, had swung south in 1942. They had aimed a great offensive at Russia's huge Baku oil fields and at Stalin's name-city on the Volga. Again, they reached the suburbs but never managed to take the city. The Russians defended Stalingrad street by street, house by house, room by room: "We have fought during fifteen days for a single house," a German officer recorded in his diary,

> with mortars, grenades, machine guns and bayonets. Already by the third day fifty-four German corpses are strewn in the cellars, on the landings, and the staircases. . . . From story to story, faces black with sweat, we bombard each other with grenades in the middle of explosions, clouds of dust and heaps of mortar . . . fragments of furniture and human beings. Ask any soldier what half an hour of hand-to-hand struggle means in such a fight.[3]

The Russian counteroffensive at Stalingrad ringed the German besiegers, lined up field artillery almost hub to hub, and pulverized the now trapped German forces. What remained of the German Sixth Army surrendered in February 1943—a greater disaster than Dunkirk was to the British.

The Russians thereafter launched a series of tremendous offensives on the longest battlefront in a world at war. They attacked summer and winter, even in the Russian snows. By the spring of 1944, the last German forces were staggering out of Russia. Before the year was ended they had been driven out of Poland and the Balkans too, and most of Eastern Europe had been overrun by Russian armies.

---

[3]William L. Langer, et al., *Western Civilization,* vol. II (New York: American Heritage/Harper & Row, Pub., 1968), p. 789.

The spring of 1944 had worse news for Hitler in the west, however. In June 1944 came D Day, the invasion of France.

The Russians had long been urging the opening of a "second front" that would take some of the German pressure off their own armies. On June 6, 1944, they got it, when Operation Overlord, under the overall command of American general Dwight Eisenhower, breached Hitler's Fortress Europe from the west. The largest invasion fleet in history—3200 warships, transports, and landing craft—crossed the English Channel from Britain to materialize at dawn off the Normandy coasts. Within twenty-four hours they had put a quarter of a million American, British, and Canadian soldiers ashore, and the battle for Western Europe had begun.

France and Belgium were liberated by the end of 1944, despite a powerful German counterattack in Belgium in the fall, the Battle of the Bulge on all the military maps. In spite of setbacks, then, United States and British troops opened 1945 camped on the Rhine, ready to invade Germany itself.

ASIA AND THE PACIFIC WAR

On the other side of the globe, where the world is mostly water, other landings on equally inhospitable shores were advancing the Allied cause in the Pacific. The Japanese offensive in the Pacific had actually ground to a halt as early as 1942—about the time of the critical German and Italian reversals at El Alamein and Stalingrad. In the east, it was the linked battles of the Coral Sea, Midway, and Guadalcanal that turned the tide.

After their initial victories in Hawaii, Hong Kong, and Southeast Asia, the next likely Japanese targets were the big island of New Guinea and the thinly populated continent of Australia. When they began to move in this direction, from bases already seized in the Solomon Islands, American aid was rushed to these archipelagoes.

Here, in the beautifully named Coral Sea, between Australia and the Solomons, a U.S. naval force intercepted a large Japanese fleet in May 1942, and for the first time in the war won a major victory in this half of the world. In June the U.S. Navy met and defeated another big Japanese naval detachment, this one far to the north, approaching Midway Island, east of Hawaii. Both victories were won by the navy's carrier-based air arm—like Pearl Harbor itself, strong evidence of the crucial part air power would play in naval combat throughout the war.

There was, however, some bloody foot slogging left to do—in the jungles of Southeast Asia and on the islands of Oceania.

In Southeast Asia—the so-called China-Burma-India theater of war—Japanese military power was stretched to its thinnest. By overrunning Burma and cutting the Burma Road in 1942, the Japanese had temporarily severed the line that allowed supplies to reach

U.S. Marines raise the American flag on Iwo Jima during the bloody battle to take the island against determined Japanese resistance. This picture, by Associated Press news photographer Joe Rosenthal, came to symbolize Marine fighting prowess in World War II. (AP/Wide World Photos)

beleaguered China, Japan's original and always central target. But when Japanese forces pushed still deeper into northeastern India, they were turned back by British, American, Indian, and other allied troops and forced off the subcontinent in 1943.

The war in this corner of the globe thereafter centered in the steaming jungles and precipitous mountains of Burma. Allied road builders carved a new highway through the rain forest while groups of irregulars with colorful names like Wingate's Raiders and Merrill's Marauders were keeping the Japanese off balance. Weakened by tropical diseases, mired in the monsoon rains, and handicapped by long and uncertain supply lines, the Japanese gradually gave ground. The British pushed east and south, capturing Rangoon and Mandalay and gradually retaking their former colony.

America's westward drive from island to island across Oceania began with the bloody Battle of Guadalcanal in the Solomons in the latter part of 1942. The first of many amphibious landings put U.S. Marines ashore on a jungle island defended by deeply entrenched and determined Japanese. Major air and sea battles roared overhead and in the surrounding waters, and the Japanese launched repeated counterattacks to recover lost ground. The back-and-forth struggle ended with U.S. forces in control, but it was a hard-won victory. Guadalcanal established a pattern of bloody island campaigns that seldom varied thereafter.

The Americans in the South Pacific spent most of 1943 recovering from the losses sustained in the defeats

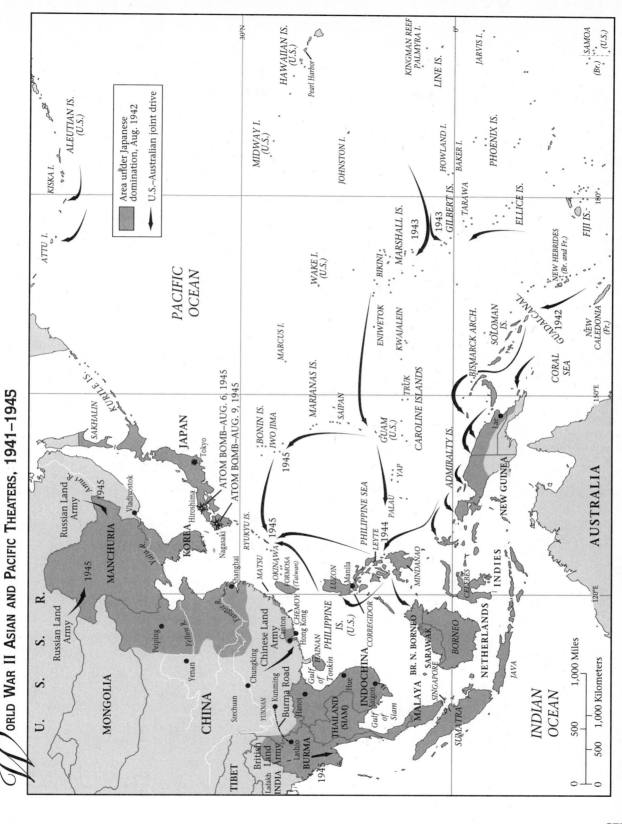

World War II Asian and Pacific Theaters, 1941–1945

Legend:
- Area under Japanese domination, Aug. 1942
- U.S.–Australian joint drive

U. S. S. R.

MONGOLIA

MANCHURIA

CHINA

TIBET

INDIA

BURMA

THAILAND (SIAM)

INDOCHINA

MALAYA

BR. N. BORNEO

SARAWAK

BORNEO

NETHERLANDS INDIES

SUMATRA

JAVA

CELEBES

AUSTRALIA

NEW GUINEA

JAPAN

KOREA

Tokyo

Hiroshima

Nagasaki

ATOM BOMB—AUG. 6, 1945

ATOM BOMB—AUG. 9, 1945

Shanghai

Peiping

Yenan

Chungking

Kunming

Hanoi

Hue

Saigon

Canton

Hong Kong

Amoy

Szechuan

YUNNAN

Burma Road

Lashio

Ladakh

Vladivostok

SAKHALIN

KURILE IS.

ALEUTIAN IS. (U.S.)

KISKA I.

ATTU I.

PACIFIC OCEAN

INDIAN OCEAN

HAWAIIAN IS. (U.S.)

Pearl Harbor

MIDWAY I. (U.S.)

JOHNSTON I.

WAKE I. (U.S.)

MARCUS I.

BONIN IS.

IWO JIMA

MARIANAS IS.

SAIPAN

GUAM (U.S.)

YAP

PALAU

TRUK

CAROLINE ISLANDS

ENIWETOK

KWAJALEN

MARSHALL IS.

BIKINI

GILBERT IS.

TARAWA

ELLICE IS.

HOWLAND I.

BAKER I.

KINGMAN REEF

PALMYRA I.

LINE IS.

JARVIS I.

PHOENIX IS.

SAMOA (Br.) (U.S.)

FIJI IS.

NEW HEBRIDES (Br. and Fr.)

NEW CALEDONIA (Fr.)

CORAL SEA

SOLOMON IS.

GUADALCANAL

BISMARCK ARCH.

ADMIRALTY IS.

Lae

PHILIPPINE SEA

PHILIPPINE IS. (U.S.)

LUZON

Manila

CORREGIDOR

MINDANAO

LEYTE

OKINAWA

FORMOSA (Taiwan)

HAINAN

RYUKYU IS.

MATSU

QUEMOY

Gulf of Tonkin

Gulf of Siam

SINGAPORE

Russian Land Army

Chinese Land Army

British Land Army

Amur R.

Ussuri R.

Yalu R.

Yangtze R.

Yellow R.

1945

1945

1945

1945

1945

1945

1945

1943

1943

1944

1942

500   1,000 Miles

500   1,000 Kilometers

655

Red flag over a gutted Berlin. Russian soldiers raised their banner over the Nazi capital in May 1945. The immense offensives of the Red Army had, in Churchill's words, "clawed the guts" out of Germany's military machine on the long road from the suburbs of Moscow to the center of Berlin. (Sovfoto/Eastfoto)

German forces back out of Eastern Europe, conquering Hitler's small Axis allies there and liberating the countries that had resisted him. In the latter effort they received important help from partisan leaders such as Marshal Tito in Yugoslavia.

The American, British, French, and Allied forces, meanwhile, after containing the German counterattack in Belgium, pressed in on Germany from the west. The last line of defense, the so-called West Wall, was outflanked and breached, the Rhine was crossed at several places, and the Allies poured into Germany.

From the east, the Russians did the same. With Hitler's eastern European satellite states firmly in their hands, Soviet forces swept into eastern Germany. Under Marshal Zhukov, defender of Moscow and victor of Stalingrad, the Russians drove for Berlin. In the spring of 1945, Russian soldiers swarmed into the half-ruined capital of the Thousand-Year Reich.

Hitler, in his Berlin command bunker, hands shaking, face twitching as the thud of explosions shook his city, took poison. His body was burned by faithful officers. All across the country, battered German armies gave up. The unconditional surrender of all surviving German forces was signed a week after the fall of Berlin, on May 9, 1945— V–E Day, for Victory in Europe, in American parlance.

A famous photograph shows Russian soldiers plant-

The Japanese surrender on the deck of the American battleship Missouri in Tokyo Bay in September 1945. General MacArthur stands at the microphone on the right. Japan's unchecked military successes going back to the Sino-Japanese and Russo-Japanese wars of 1895 and 1905, respectively, thus ended after half a century. (Library of Congress)

and victories of the first year of the Pacific war, and in regrouping their forces for a major offensive. Then, with ships, planes, and U.S. Marines available in sufficient quantities, and General Douglas MacArthur in overall command, America launched a series of costly but successful amphibious attacks on the Japanese-held islands that formed the outer perimeter of its Asian empire. Through 1944 and 1945, coral atolls and jungle islands such as Tarawa, Saipan, Iwo Jima, and Okinawa became the sites of hard-fought American victories. The Philippines were also invaded and retaken by MacArthur's troops.

Everywhere the Japanese fought with the courage of their samurai ancestors. But 1945 found American arms poised to attack the Japanese home islands themselves.

ALLIED VICTORY: BERLIN TO TOKYO

Nineteen forty-five was the last year—the year of unconditional surrender.

In Europe, the Russian Red Army had driven

ing the red hammer-and-sickle banner of the Soviet Union high on a gutted tower of the German Reichstag. Below them, the wreckage that was left after years of American and British bombing fades into the smoke of the last battle of Berlin.

The fall of Japan was very different. It came after an exclusively aerial bombardment—a further graphic demonstration of the power of attack from the air.

From newly captured island bases, U.S. bombers began to visit the same sort of mass destruction on Japan that Europe, mainland Asia, and Oceania had already suffered. Through the first three quarters of 1945, high-explosive and incendiary bombs gutted large sections of Japanese cities, including Tokyo. Then in August, the war's most terrible secret weapon was deployed against two Japanese urban complexes, Hiroshima and Nagasaki. Atomic bombs destroyed most of both cities—in a matter of minutes. With the majority of its armed forces still intact and occupying foreign lands from Southeast Asia to China, Japan surrendered unconditionally to the Allies.

The surrender document was signed on the deck of the American battleship *Missouri,* anchored in Tokyo Bay, on September 2, 1945—V–J Day. There was no more than a gentle roll on the water, and the hands that signed the document were steady.

But one aspect of that scene was quite similar to the Berlin where the red flag fluttered. The city that ringed the harbor, like Hitler's shattered capital, was a bombed-out ruin as the biggest war drew to a close.

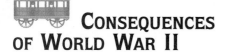 ## CONSEQUENCES OF WORLD WAR II

TOTAL WAR

World War II, even more than World War I, required a total commitment from the societies that fought it. To mobilize, equip, and support modern mechanized forces of millions of men, the great powers had to put immense political, social, and above all economic power into the hands of their central governments.

On the political side, this could mean significant increases in the authority of governing officials, even in democratic countries. Government censorship—or self-censorship by the press—of war news was universal, as were the combatants' propaganda campaigns to convince people on all sides that theirs was the righteous cause. Even in a country with an established tradition of civil liberties like the United States, 100,000 Americans of Japanese ancestry were interned for the duration on no better grounds than fear and racial prejudice. In Germany, it was after the beginning of the war that the systematic extermination of six million Jews and several million Slavs and other "inferior races" began.

WOMEN AT WAR

The biggest war in history swept up women as well as men. The heavy bombing of cities, to be discussed below, took its toll on civilians of both sexes, killing and injuring millions of women around the world. Conquering armies preyed on women as they always had, raping, looting, and destroying their homes and families. Women fought back, joining partisan guerilla bands in conquered lands or serving with underground resistance movements. Their heroism was widely testified to after the war. "The average 'life' of a female liaison officer," a leader of the French resistance remembered, "was no more than a few months."[4]

Perhaps the most striking social consequence of the war, as in World War I, was the movement of large numbers of women out of the home and into war plants or even into the armed services themselves. In the United States alone, more than 200,000 women served in special units of the U.S. Army, Navy, Marines, and Coast Guard, and six million worked in munitions factories. Some 40 percent of all American aircraft workers were female, a fact that permanently altered old-fashioned notions about the ability of women to acquire mechanical skills. Rosie the Riveter was a label that symbolized another step toward an equal place for women in the Western world.

The most striking area of increased government involvement in national life was, as in World War I, the economic sphere. Once more, governments allocated raw materials for war industries; regulated wages and prices; set labor policies, generally excluding strikes for the duration; and gave priorities to military production. For the totalitarian states, including the Soviet Union, this could make little difference to peoples already habituated to official control of the economy. Western nations that had hesitated even at some of the welfare legislation of earlier decades, however, were much more willing to accept a strong government role after this wartime experience.

CASUALTIES AND DESTRUCTION: FIFTY MILLION DEAD

Not surprisingly, a total war fought with what were then the most up-to-date technological tools available produced vast ruin and unmatched casualty figures.

Years of fighting between huge armies in western Russia and in eastern China cost millions of lives. But the most impressive material destruction, and the most astronomical casualty figures, came with the bombing of cities. Industrial cities, with their heavy concentration of defense plants, transportation junctures, and military facilities, were clearly essential to the enemy's war effort. It was also believed that a rain of destruction from the sky might break an opponent's will to fight on, thus hastening vic-

[4]Henri Michel, *The Shadow War: Resistance in Europe, 1939–1945* (London: Corgi Books, 1975), p. 189.

tory. As a result, lavish expenditures of money, scientific ingenuity, labor, and lives were poured into this key feature of the biggest of all wars.

The Japanese in China, the Italians in Ethiopia, and the Germans in Spain showed what could be done from the air before World War II properly got under way. In the early years of the war itself, German bombers began the practice of terror bombing in Warsaw, Amsterdam, Coventry, and London.

But as the war advanced, American and British bombing raids more than matched these German efforts. High explosives and incendiary bombs rained over German and Japanese cities. As many as 100,000 people may have died in a single incendiary raid on Tokyo; the notorious Dresden raid cost hundreds of thousands of lives in one night. And in a fraction of a second, in a single flash of light brighter than a thousand suns, Hiroshima was turned into as close an approximation of hell as twentieth-century humanity has thus far managed to achieve.

Total casualties in the greatest and most destructive of ways can only be estimated. Fifty million is a figure frequently advanced.

A million is a hard number to comprehend. As an aid to the imagination, you might note that by the time it sees print, the book you hold in your hand will perhaps contain a quarter of a million words. Multiply that by four, and that again by fifty. Imagine each word as a small white cross on an endless field of green—the military cemeteries of Europe are meticulously cared for—and you will be on your way to appreciating World War II.

PEACE NOT YET

As in 1918, there was dancing in the streets in 1945. And as on that earlier occasion, the celebrations—where celebrations were in order—proved to be premature.

There was the wreckage to clean up, dislocated populations to resettle, defeated nations to occupy, shattered economies to rebuild. There was, in short, a large part of the world to raise from the ashes.

Even more unexpected was the almost immediate breakdown of the Grand Alliance that had defeated the Axis during the postwar period. First Europe and then much of the world was soon divided into two rapidly rearming camps, one headed by the greatest of Eurasian powers, the Soviet Union, the other by the North American colossus, the United States. The Cold War was under way—a global confrontation that would last for four decades.

Peace was clearly not yet at hand in 1945, and the tensions and conflicts that surfaced then were of historic significance. World War II was, in fact, central to the history of the twentieth century. Its origins go back to the main currents of the first half of the century. Its consequences have in many ways dominated the history of the second half, as subsequent chapters will indicate.

A historical event, however, is more than the sum of its consequences. World War II was a chunk out of the lives of millions.

Some of the people in the old black-and-white photographs are still alive and can tell you about it. Solid burghers over a drink in a nice German living room will tell you how the thunder of the incoming planes shook the ground, how their numbers darkened the sun. A polite old man at the Ground Zero Arch in Hiroshima will explain for the millionth time what he was doing when it happened—and what happened then. Others—men, women, children—died soon after the old photographs were made: "Young Serviceman Celebrates the Night before His Ship Sails"; "Young Mother and Child Wait to Board the Train to Dachau." World War II is all their stories, their part in the unbelievable, sometimes unspeakable, human venture into history.

SUMMARY

World War II, the most terrible of all wars thus far, resulted from the usual tangle of causes. These included the dissatisfactions and ambitions of the more authoritarian powers—Germany, Japan, Italy, and Russia—and the weakness of the leaders of the liberal West—notably Britain, France, and the United States. Through the 1930s, a series of international crises in East Asia, North Africa, and several European countries built toward a final confrontation over Poland in 1939. Hitler's invasion of that country finally led Britain and France to declare war on Germany, beginning the second global conflict of the century.

The war began with a Nazi *Blitzkrieg* of Poland, undertaken in alliance with Communist Russia. After a winter lull, Hitler launched a second series of lightning invasions, this

time in Western Europe, resulting in the defeat of France, Belgium, the Netherlands, and most of Scandinavia. German efforts to overwhelm Britain by air and submarine attacks failed, however.

The totalitarian alliance made two crucial errors in 1941. Hitler's armies invaded Russia, only to be stopped at the very outskirts of Moscow. The Japanese attacked the Pacific colonies of the battered Western powers, including those of the United States. The Soviet Union and the United States were thus brought into the war against the Axis powers.

The tide turned in favor of the Allies in 1942. In that year the British stopped the Germans short of the Suez Canal in Egypt, the Russians destroyed a besieging German army at Stalingrad, and the United States shattered two Japanese fleets in the Pacific and began to regain a foothold in the islands. Allied troops also invaded Italy, which became the first Axis power to surrender.

By 1944 the Russians were driving the Germans back across Europe, and the Japanese were in retreat in the Far East. A huge invasion fleet put American, British, and Canadian armies ashore in France. Hitler's Germany was crushed between advancing Russian and Anglo-American forces in 1945. In the Pacific, an American island-hopping campaign put their bombers within range of Japan, and two atomic bombs finally forced the last Axis partner to surrender in August 1945.

SUGGESTED READINGS

BERGAMIN, D. *Japan's Imperial Conspiracy.* New York: Morrow, 1971. Japanese expansionism in Asia.

CHURCHILL, W. S. *The Second World War* (6 vols.). Boston: Houghton Mifflin, 1948–1953. The war as it looked to the great war leader; resounding prose.

CRAIG, W. *Enemy at the Gates: The Battle of Stalingrad.* New York: E. P. Dutton, 1973. The bloody turning point in southern Russia.

DEAKIN, F. W. *The Brutal Friendship: Mussolini, Hitler, and the Fall of Italian Fascism.* London: Weidenfeld and Nicolson, 1962. Relations between the two most aggressive European totalitarians. On Hitler's relationships with Japan, see J. M. Meskill, *Hitler and Japan: The Hollow Alliance* (New York: Atherton, 1966).

EISENHOWER, D. D. *Crusade in Europe.* New York: Da Capo, 1977. Military operations in Europe, as seen by the American commanding general.

FEIS, H. *Churchill, Roosevelt, Stalin.* Princeton, N.J.: Princeton University Press, 1967. The Big Three, in a balanced presentation.

HERSEY, J. *Hiroshima.* New York: Knopf, 1946. The famous book about the first atom bomb, as experienced by those who were under it. For a more typical example of the air war, see M. Caidin, *The Night Hamburg Died* (New York: Ballantine, 1960).

HOUGH, R. *The Longest Battle: The War at Sea, 1939–1945.* London: Weidenfeld and Nicolson, 1986. Authoritative military history of the naval side of World War II.

KEEGAN, J. *Six Armies in Normandy: From D-Day to the Liberation of Paris.* New York: Viking, 1982. Vivid account of three crucial months of fighting in France in the summer of 1944.

LEVIN, N. *The Holocaust: The Destruction of European Jewry, 1933–1945.* New York: Crowell, 1968. Hitler's Jewish policy, escalating to the Final Solu-

tion. For a searing case study, see O. Friedrich's anatomy of the Auschwitz death camp, *The End of the World: A History* (New York: Coward, McCann and Geoghegan, 1982).

LIDDELL HART, B. H. *History of the Second World War.* New York: Putnam, 1970. Military history of the war by a famous military historian.

MAUMONT, M. *The Origins of the Second World War.* New Haven: Yale University Press, 1978. Diplomatic encounters along the road to war. A more controversial treatment is A. J. P. Taylor's *The Origins of the Second World War* (London: Hamish Hamilton, 1961), which contends that Hitler had no plan for war and lays much of the blame on the British and French.

OVERY, R. J. *The Air War, 1939–1945.* London: Europa, 1980. Pioneering synthesis of scholarly research on the contributions of the world's air forces.

READ, A., and D. FISHER. *The Deadly Embrace: Hitler, Stalin, and the Nazi-Soviet Pact, 1939–1941.* New York: W. W. Norton, 1988. Diplomatic history of the ill-fated alliance, suggesting that Stalin was less Hitler's dupe than is often assumed.

TAYLOR, T. *Munich: The Price of Peace.* New York: Doubleday, 1979. Insightful examination of a diplomatic crisis whose resolution has become synonymous with appeasement.

THOMAS, H. *The Spanish Civil War,* rev. ed. New York: Harper & Row, Pub., 1977. Perhaps the best account of this much discussed "little war."

TOLAND, J. *The Rising Sun: The Decline and Fall of the Japanese Empire.* New York: Bantam Books, 1970. A Japanese perspective on the war.

WRIGHT, G. *The Ordeal of Total War, 1939–1945.* New York: Harper & Row, Pub., 1969. Excellent overview, with attention to the home front and to broader intellectual and social consequences.

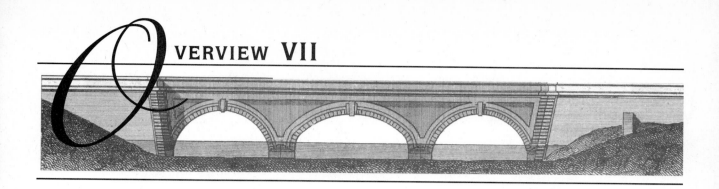

THE GLOBALIZATION
OF HISTORY

◆━◆━◆

The twentieth century since the time of Christ—approximately the fifty-fifth since civilization was born in ancient Mesopotamia—is in some ways a climactic age. Our century has produced so many *most* and *biggest* things in the long human story: the most people, the longest lives, the biggest wars, the biggest cities, the most polluted environment, the most material wealth. The list of records is endless. From the perspective of the past, our century is certainly the climax of much that has gone before.

From the perspective of the future, however, ours may be seen as a century not of climaxes, but of beginnings.

There are innovations in science and technology, to be sure; we have almost come to expect them as a matter of course. But there have been beginnings also in major assaults on age-old social problems, from poverty to pestilence. There have been breakthroughs in mass culture, in large-scale social organization, and in much else. In our war-ravaged century, there has been a more widespread commitment to peace than ever before.

Above all, ours is perhaps the first century of genuinely global history. Many aspects of the history of the second half of the century especially have shown the destinies of all peoples of the world to be in a number of important ways inextricably bound up together.

Thus the two great armed camps that squared off against each other in the Cold War were thoroughly intercontinental from the beginning. The Soviet Union, the leader of one side in the conflict, was the interregional power par excellence, sprawling across Europe and Asia. The United States, the leader of the other side, loomed as the powerhouse of the Americas. Major Cold War confrontations came in Europe, in Asia, in Latin America, in Africa—in every part of the world.

The Great Liberation of European colonies that followed World War II was as global as the intercontinental empires themselves had been. The result was to create a new international bloc, the Third World of developing nations. Again, it is a global designation for a reality that transcends any one region, continent, or cultural tradition.

In the second half of the twentieth century, the industrially developed "have" nations of the world were no longer limited to Europe, or even to Europe and North America. Fabulously rich oil sheikdoms, the evolving industrial powers of Japan and the East Asian rim, Australia, South Africa, the relatively affluent ABC powers (Argentina, Brazil, Chile), and other success stories of Latin America have all revealed the worldwide spread of technology and wealth.

The Third World, the world of village people and traditional cultures, has had its own global history since the liberation. Its problems of economic underdevelopment and dependence on industrial states, its oscillation between political instability and dictatorship, and its struggles with disease, illiteracy, overpopulation, famine, and new and old ways in conflict have been no respecters of boundaries or hemispheres.

In the latter part of the twentieth century, furthermore, a truly global culture, bridging the gap between rich and poor nations, has begun to take shape for the first time in history. From American television to Indian religion, from Russian ballet to the wood carving of Africa and Oceania, the world today feasts at an unparalleled cultural smorgasbord, the foundation perhaps of the global civilization of tomorrow.

On the basis of this emerging planetary culture, finally, global organization has advanced at an extraordinary pace. From the Hague world-peace conferences around 1900 through the United Nations of 1945 to the thousands of global organizations, associations, and agreements that bind us all today, we have advanced to a point from which the dim outlines of a new world order are at least partially visible.

Tomorrow, then, will almost certainly be a global matter. We will either survive together, citizens of a slowly, no doubt painfully reorganizing globe, or we will perish with our planet. We will learn to live together in some sort of reasonably harmonious relationship, or we will expire together, starved by overpopulation or the exhaustion of our resources, choking on our own wastes or incinerated in a global firestorm of our mutual kindling.

The second half of the twentieth century in particular has thus been an age of genuinely global history—perhaps the first of many. As such, it is rather a beginning than an end, a new dawn rather than a climax to human history.

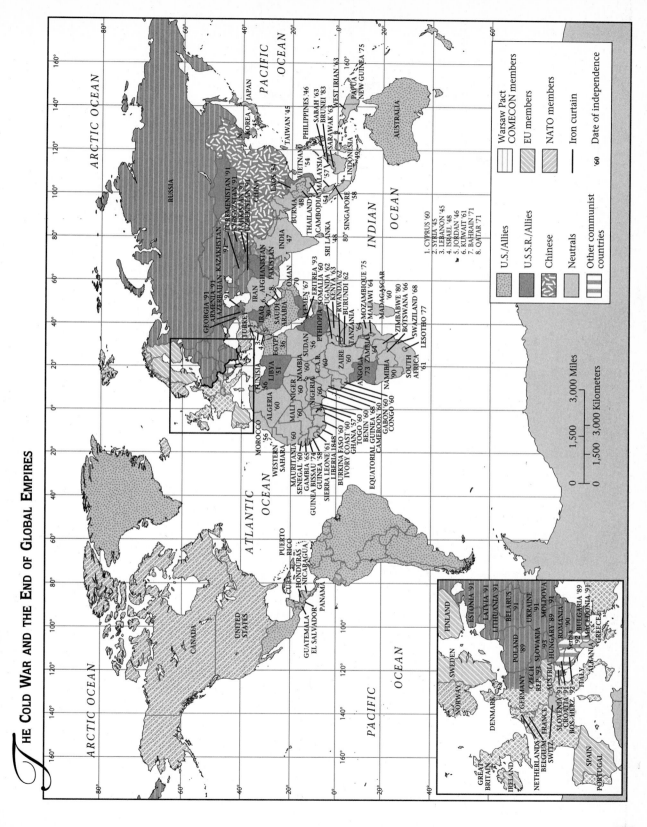

The Cold War and the End of Global Empires

CHAPTER 44

THE COLD WAR

THE POSTWAR WORLD

A WORLD IN RUINS

Every American heard stories after the war. Personal anecdotes, newspaper editorials, vivid journalistic accounts—in those last pretelevision years—of what it was like "over there."

A six-foot man, a laconic U.S. Air Corps major said, could see from one side of Hamburg to the other. Graphic photographs showed what had once been the bustling modern Japanese city of Hiroshima, now

> four square miles of reddish-brown scar . . . range on range of collapsed city blocks, with here and there a crude sign erected on a pile of ashes and tiles ("Sister, where are you?" or "All safe and we live at Toyosaka") . . . and in the streets a macabre traffic—hundreds of crumpled bicycles, shells of streetcars and automobiles, all halted in mid-motion.[1]

Some of the people who thought they were "all safe" were beginning to notice burns that did not heal, skin turning patchy, hair falling out.

Britain had "austerity"—more grim, gray years of shortages and digging out of the ruins. In China, a renewal of the long civil war of the interwar years soon convulsed the land once more. From the Far East to central Europe, hollow bellies and empty eyes told a common story of starvation, disease, and human misery.

The world was hungry for peace in 1945. Ironically, the settlement that followed led directly to a new conflict—the long and painful confrontation known as the Cold War.

THE PEACE SETTLEMENT

There was no great gathering of diplomats and heads of state to rearrange the world after World War II, as there had been at Vienna and Versailles after Europe's last two major military conflicts.

The Big Three met one last time later in 1945, at

---

[1] John Hersey, *Hiroshima* (New York: Bantam Books, 1959), p. 86

Potsdam in defeated Germany, but they were strangers already. Roosevelt was three months dead, and a feisty but not overly informed President Truman spoke for the United States. Winston Churchill was defeated for reelection in Britain during the conference itself, and Labour-party leader Clement Atlee brought a very different perspective to the meeting. Only Joseph Stalin had been there before.

The Grand Alliance, deprived of a common enemy, rapidly came apart at the seams. Peace treaties were signed with the lesser Axis partners, and eventually with Japan, but not with Germany. Some of the most important consequences of the war simply happened, evolving out of provisional or temporary military agreements that hardened into long-lasting historic realities.

The territorial rearrangements that followed World War II were less complicated than those after World War I, but the dislocation of populations was much greater.

The chief postwar transfer of territory in Europe involved the westward shift of Poland's frontiers. This shift allowed Russia to keep gains made from the period of the Hitler-Stalin Pact and compensated Poland with a substantial slice of German territory. Even more significant, however, was the division of Germany itself into four separate zones of military occupation. The American, British, and French zones coalesced into the German Federal Republic (West Germany), while the Russian zone evolved into the German Democratic Republic (East Germany). The two Germanies, allied to the rival power blocs of the United States and the Soviet Union, yet never dismissing the possibility of reunification, would be key pieces in the jigsaw puzzle of postwar Europe.

Similarly tangled and unpremeditated territorial settlements occurred in the Far East. The Soviet Union declared war on Japan in the last days of World War II and quickly occupied Manchuria and the northern part of Korea. Manchuria was turned over to the Chinese Communist armies, who thus were strengthened for their final drive to power in China. The Soviets established a provisional government in the northern part of Korea, but the United States sponsored a new government in the southern part of the former nation. Once more, reconciliation between the two proved impossible, and the peninsula entered the postwar period as the two nations of North and South Korea. Within five years the United States would be plunged into a war in Korea, thanks to this division.

A lone survivor bicycles through the ruins of Nagasaki, Japan, destroyed by an American atomic bomb in August 1945. The wreckage of many other great cities, leveled by more conventional explosives and incendiary bombs, littered Europe and Asia at the end of World War II. For decades afterward, the devastation caused by the atomic bombs dropped on Japan would symbolize the horror of modern technological warfare to peoples around the world. (The Bettmann Archive)

World War II generated as many as 25 million refugees, perhaps half of them Germans expelled from the Slavic countries of Eastern Europe. Resettlement was undertaken by the victorious Allies through displaced-persons camps and through an International Refugee Organization. Frequently, however, the refugees themselves settled things with their feet, spreading outward in a great postwar diaspora to West Germany and Britain, the United States, the Commonwealth countries, Latin America, and Palestine.

The United States, finally, occupied Japan in 1945. The vigorous program of demilitarization and democratization that the United States embarked upon at this time, coupled with Japan's rapid economic recovery, transformed that country in an amazingly short time. Here, at least, the postwar settlement led to an apparently stable and satisfying outcome.

POSTWAR RECOVERY

Economic recovery for the nations of Western Europe proceeded at first with agonizing slowness. The destructiveness of the war and a series of harsh winters in the mid-1940s slowed things appreciably. The loss of important overseas markets to the United States during the war and the growing rift between the United States and the Soviet Union after the war also contributed to economic sluggishness at the outset. In 1948, however, at the urging of U.S. Secretary of State George Marshall, the nations of the West inaugurated a massive European Recovery Plan combining European cooperation and self-help with substantial American aid.

Food, oil, coal, steel, farm equipment, trucks, electrical gear were soon pouring into Europe. The Europeans themselves negotiated an end to mutually destructive tariffs, balanced their budgets, brought inflation under control, and increased their share of foreign trade. By the 1950s, led by a booming West Germany gripped by what came to be called an "economic miracle," European production and commerce were surpassing prewar levels. Equally important, a successful model for continued economic cooperation had been created among the nations of Western Europe.

Two broad and somewhat contradictory currents transformed the politics of the western half of the continent during the postwar years: the rejection of organized communism and the acceptance of some socialist ideas and reforms.

Domestic Communist parties enjoyed a temporary wave of popularity and electoral success in the years immediately after World War II. Their prestige was heightened by their important role in wartime resistance movements against Nazism. Postwar economic dislocation also brought some votes to the far left. Thanks to vigorous campaigns by conservative leaders such as Charles de Gaulle of France and Alcide de Gasperi in Italy, however, the Communists were defeated in key election campaigns. They soon lost the potential for power they had briefly enjoyed.

Socialist ideas, by contrast, did better in Europe after the war. In Britain, the Labour party under Atlee unceremoniously unseated the great war leader, Tory Winston Churchill, in 1945. Atlee at once proceeded to nationalize large sections of the British economy, including coal mining, iron and steel production, and public transportation. In most Western European countries, government welfare programs were expanded significantly after the war, creating for the first time what British Labourites called cradle-to-the-grave security—the real birth of the modern welfare state.

In Eastern Europe, the Soviet Union played the central economic role filled by the United States in the west. There was, however, a basic difference; whereas the United States had grown richer during the war, the Soviet Union had been one of the most war-ravaged of the combatants. In the immediate aftermath of the war, the Soviets used Eastern Europe primarily as an economic resource for their own recovery. Not only East Germany but also Hitler's former allies in the Balkans were stripped of industrial and other resources. Close trade relationships were established, and joint economic ventures set up, both of which tended to work to the Soviets' benefit. The Russians seemed to be trying hard to encourage most of Eastern Europe to depend on them for manufactured goods, while serving as their source of agricultural products and other commodities.

After Stalin's death in 1953, there was some backing away from too rigid an insistence on the Soviet model in Eastern Europe. Agricultural collectivization, for instance, was cut back in some places, never implemented in others. There was a new stress on consumer goods, in the Soviet bloc as well as in the Soviet Union. Nevertheless, cut off by the Cold War from American aid and from lucrative exchange with the West, hampered by rigid ties to Soviet needs, to Marxist economic theories, and to the Soviet economic model, the Eastern bloc did not achieve even a modest level of economic development until the 1960s.

China had been locked in a brutal war with Japan for eight years by 1945, and had been torn by civil war, as well as by intermittent Japanese intervention, through most of the preceding quarter of a century. Nor did the end of World War II signify an end to China's agony. Under American pressure Jiang Jiehi might clink glasses with Mao Zedong for the photographers; but both men knew that their long duel was not finished. Recovery was thus not possible in China. The war was not over yet.

Recovery was quite possible, however, for China's great East Asian rival, Japan. Japan's war was definitely ended—and ended, as it turned out, in a way that opened the road to decades of even more impressive development for the most Westernized of Eastern nations. During the half-dozen years of the American occupation that followed the surrender in Tokyo Bay, the democratic tendencies that had been submerged by militarism in the 1930s surfaced once more. As in Germany, this second exercise in representative government "took" as the first had not, and in a few years Japan became as stable a working democracy as any in the world.

The Japanese industrial economy also revived with remarkable rapidity, though the nation's impressive economic development over the preceding century made this less surprising than the triumph of democratic institutions. The occupation also imposed some land reform, helping the most miserable of the peasant population, who had not shared in Japan's earlier modernization. By the early 1950s, then, Japan, like West Germany, was embarking on an economic miracle that would contribute substantially to the Western boom years that were coming.

THE UNITED NATIONS

A peace settlement of sorts had thus been made, and recovery from the war was underway before the end of the 1940s. Even more encouraging, a substantial step had been taken toward keeping the peace in the future: the organization of the United Nations.

The U.N. began as a war-time alliance against the Axis—a cause to which most of the world had nominally pledged itself by 1945. A United Nations Relief and Rehabilitation Administration was set up as early as 1943 to provide basic material necessities to liberated zones as the Allied armies advanced. At the Yalta Conference of the Big Three in early 1945, Roosevelt devoted much time to plans for a postwar United Nations Organization, which would both guarantee international peace and open up the world to freer economic exchange.

In the spring of 1945, with Germany and Italy defeated and Japan reeling, representatives of fifty countries met at San Francisco to design a new global organization to replace the League. The United Nations Organization, to be permanently headquartered in New York, was the result.

Like the League of Nations that preceded it, the United Nations had two central deliberative bodies to deal with major international issues, plus a number of special committees concerned with social, cultural, and humanitarian matters.

The most powerful element in the U.N. was the eleven-member Security Council. Five of its members were guaranteed permanent seats: the United States and the Soviet Union, the two most powerful countries in the world; Britain and France, holders of the world's largest empires; and China, the most populous country on earth. Each of these recognized great powers, furthermore, had the right to veto any item of business if it felt that its vital interests might be adversely affected. This special position of the great powers represented a realistic assessment of the fact that some nations *were* politically, economically, and militarily "more equal" than others. It was also necessary simply to get all the major powers into the organization.

The General Assembly grew in time to represent all the nations of the world. This larger body had less power than the Security Council. But it did provide an international forum in which the smallest country could air its grievances, and in which the collective feelings of the entire international community could be expressed by votes on large issues.

The U.N.'s many subagencies and committees concerned themselves with the social ills of the world at large. Under the broad umbrella of the Economic and Social Council were grouped such agencies as the World Health Organization, the United Nations Educational, Scientific, and Cultural Organization, the International Labor Organization, the International Trade Organization, and the Food and Agricultural Organization. In years to come these international bodies would mount campaigns to alleviate hunger, control major infectious diseases, bring literacy to the unlettered, and deal with a wide variety of other problems.

As established in 1945, the U.N. was dominated by the United States, which could normally depend on the votes of its European allies and of the nations of Latin America, where U.S. economic influence was strong. This situation would change over the years, as the Soviet Union acquired satellites of its own and as former colonial territories thronged into the U.N. with no predilection to support the Western powers that had once been their masters.

Global economic problems also preoccupied the Allies as World War II drew to a close. They held less formal, more specialized meetings in order to deal with some long-standing economic difficulties and to avoid some of the postwar economic dislocations that had afflicted the world after World War I.

Key decisions were reached at the Bretton Woods Conference, held in New Hampshire in 1944. Two long-lasting international economic organizations came out of this conference; the World Bank and the International Monetary Fund.

The World Bank—officially the International Bank for Reconstruction and Development—would supply loans to poor nations to help them develop their economies. The original function of the International Monetary Fund was to prevent drastic devaluation of major currencies. Later, however, it became essentially a lender of last resort to underdeveloped nations.

Like the United Nations, the Bretton Woods agreements originally did much for American interests. For the next quarter of a century, European currencies were pegged to the dollar at a highly favorable exchange rate. But Bretton Woods also stabilized key aspects of the international economy between the later 1940s and the early 1970s—a boon to all concerned.

Subsequent international compacts brought order to both Western and Eastern European economies—notably the Common Market in the West and COMECON in the East.

Regional improvements also surfaced during and after the war. During the war years Brazil, Argentina, and some of the other southern republics continued to build domestic industry beyond the small workshop stage. The mid-1940s saw the signing of a series of hemisphere-wide agreements at Mexico City. Rio de Janeiro, and Bogotá. These treaties created the Organization of American States, provided for mutual hemispheric defense, promised an end to intervention by one government in the internal affairs of any other, and encouraged economic collaboration and aid.

THE BEGINNINGS OF THE COLD WAR

THE SUPERPOWERS: THE USA VERSUS THE USSR

Peace after the biggest war was thus more or less established, recovery under way, and a new international organization created. But conflict was not yet banished from the earth. And even as these steps toward peace were being taken, the foundations of the Cold War were being laid down.

The leaders of the two global alliances that confronted each other in the wake of World War II were the United States and the Soviet Union.

It is as easy to point out similarities between these two nations as it is to point out their differences. By the 1980s, both were huge nations, with large populations—250 million for the United States, 270 million for the Soviet Union—and vast natural resources. Most important, perhaps, both countries had been expanding throughout their modern history. Russia pushed eastward from the forests around Moscow and the Kievan steppes, America westward from its New England hills and tidewater South. Each had grown to a prodigious size and become the dominant power in half the globe—the United States in the New World, the Soviet Union in the Old.

Historic differences, however, were even more important. Russia's political tradition has historically been autocratic, from the legacy of the Byzantine emperors and Tatar khans, through the heavy-handed authoritarianism of Peter the Great, to the totalitarian regime of Joseph Stalin. Russia had the most autocratic royal government and the largest bureaucracy in Europe in the nineteenth century, long before communism came on the scene.

America's history, by contrast, has always included a strong element of representative government, from the colonial legislatures through the federal Constitution. In the nineteenth and twentieth centuries, the United States developed an increasingly democratic suffrage and a competitive party system. Americans are thus used to voting and to demanding their rights; Russians, to a strong hand on the helm.

The economic development of the two nations also differed significantly. Americans have been a prosperous

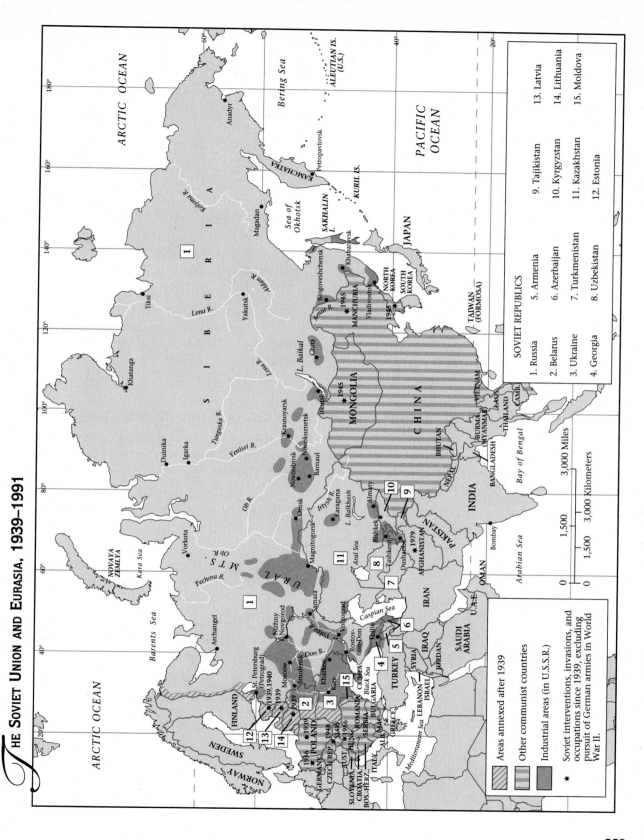

THE SOVIET UNION AND EURASIA, 1939–1991

and in many ways a progressive people. Russia, by contrast, was technologically backward and economically underdeveloped through most of its modern history. Peter the Great's attempts to modernize his country were paralleled by Stalin's efforts two hundred years later.

One further historic difference should be cited: the deep roots of free enterprise in the United States and the Russian tradition of government intervention in the economy.

The United States inherited the Western European entrepreneurial pattern of economic development that went back to the commercial revolution of the medieval West. Free enterprise and large private corporations dominated America's economic history from the beginning.

Russia's commercial middle class, by contrast, had been small and comparatively undeveloped since commercial Novgorod gave way to czarist Moscow in Russia's late-medieval struggle for power. From Peter the Great to Stalin, therefore, Russia's economic growth had largely been the result of government initiatives, subsidies, and regulation. Like autocratic government and economic underdevelopment, government involvement in industry and commerce went back a long way in Russia.

By the mid-twentieth century, finally, the Soviet Union and the United States had developed a number of conflicting national interests and attitudes that would contribute significantly to the shape of the Cold War.

Russian interests—under the czars as under the Communists—had for centuries included a need for warm-water ports, which would give the world's largest nation commercial and naval access to the world's oceans. Russia had also had a history of feuding with the Germans that went back to medieval wars with the Teutonic Knights and climaxed with two German invasions of Russia during the present century. Any Russian government was therefore likely to feel a strong national interest in a weak Germany. A divided Germany and the string of puppet governments that Stalin established in Eastern Europe after World War II satisfied these strategic needs admirably.

The United States, meanwhile, developed a historic set of strongly felt national interests of its own, most of them economic. From the beginning of U.S. history, New Englanders were traders, southern planters exporters. America's late-nineteenth-century foray into empire building fits this pattern to a considerable degree. American interventions in Latin America and the Dollar Diplomacy of the earlier twentieth century were also rooted in these crucial economic interests. So, almost certainly, was some portion of America's position in the Cold War.

It has also been suggested, however, that Americans tended more than most peoples to see themselves as a crusading nation with a message for the world. This tendency may be traced back to colonial New England, many of whose settlers came to build a Protestant New Jerusalem in America. The founding fathers of the American Revolution claimed to be building a *novus ordo seclorum*, a "new order of the ages." A sense of "manifest destiny" carried Americans across the continent in the nineteenth century, and they fought their global wars in the twentieth century to "make the world safe for democracy." The Cold War had thus been seen by many Americans not as a conflict of interests but as a morality play on a world stage.

An important aspect of Russia's attitude toward itself and its place in the world, by contrast, was the notorious Russian inferiority complex. The Russian's sense of cultural inferiority went back to the days of Peter the Great. It was reinforced by the post 1917 Soviet Communist fear of "capitalist encirclement." Cold War efforts by the United States to "contain" what U.S. leaders perceived as Soviet ambitions by surrounding the U.S.S.R. with a ring of hostile alliances and bases only intensified this sense of inferiority and persecution. It was a feeling that could lead the Soviet Union to strike out, or to cling doggedly to a course of action that was not always justifiable in purely practical terms of national interest.

The two most powerful countries in the world, maintaining sharply contrasting worldviews and possessing national interests that could easily bring them into conflict, thus faced each other across a prostrate Europe in 1945.

POSTWAR GAINS OF THE SUPERPOWERS

Both the United States and the Soviet Union came out of World War II with substantial material advantages: territorial gains for the Soviets, economic ones for the Americans. Both sought to expand these gains still further during the immediate postwar years. In so doing, the two superpowers prepared the way for the decades of Cold War that followed.

Despite the heavy damage the Soviet Union sustained in World War II, territorial rewards were very impressive indeed. For the first two years of the war, Russia fought on the German side. During this period, the U.S.S.R. acquired parts of Finland, the Baltic states of Estonia, Latvia, and Lithuania, a broad slice of eastern Poland, and some areas in the eastern Balkans, notably Bessarabia, a long-disputed section of eastern Romania. All these areas were incorporated directly into the Soviet Union.

From 1941 on, Stalin fought on the side of the Allies against Hitler. Rolling back the German armies in 1944 and 1945, the Red Army occupied most of the rest of Eastern Europe. And Stalin made it clear to his major allies that he would insist upon "friendly" governments in countries located between the Soviet Union and Germany henceforth. In the case of Hitler's former satellites—Hungary, Rumania, Bulgaria, and of course Russian-occupied East Germany—the Western Allies could hardly object to the establishment of strongly pro-Russian governments.

In countries where Communist guerrillas had led the resistance against the Germans—as in Yugoslavia and Albania—it was difficult to deny these partisans the right to set up governments that would be natural allies of the Soviet Union. In countries that had allied with the West but had been overrun by the Nazis—Poland and Czechoslovakia—the Soviets proceeded more slowly, promising free elections but offering every aid to Communist candidates that the Red Army and the Soviet security services could provide. The result, however, was the same; further expansion of the growing Russian sphere of influence in Eastern Europe.

American gains from the war were less obvious but just as real. As we have seen, these gains amounted to further improvement of America's already paramount economic position in the world. While European nations were blowing up each other's factories, the American industrial machine was revving up to fill the gap. By war's end, the gross national product of the United States had nearly tripled, whereas those of its European continental competitors had nose-dived. During the war, American enterprise had also pushed into markets and resource areas formerly controlled by Europeans in Latin America, the Middle East, and Africa.

While the Marshall Plan was helping Europe to recover economically and compelling Europeans to begin serious economic integration, it was also benefiting the American economy. Aid took the form of American products, and this helped to carry the United States over the nervous period of conversion to peacetime production. Aid also enabled recovering Europe to buy necessary manufactured goods—again, mostly from the United States. Postwar economic settlements, finally, strengthened the dollar against European currencies, enabling American firms to invest very cheaply in European industry.

Altogether, American business came out of the war thriving. For a continuation of this trend, it was important that as much of the world as possible remain open to American enterprise after the war. Thus, as the Soviet Union swiftly established an Eastern European sphere of influence, the United States was pushing its way even into the older zones of Western European imperial hegemony elsewhere in the world. The Soviets were building closed zones of influence for themselves, America was pushing for an open world in which it expected to prosper. Out of the momentum generated by their respective World War II advances, then, came increasingly tense confrontations between the two superpowers.

CONFLICTS AFTER THE WAR

Western objections to the Soviets' emerging sphere of influence became particularly loud only in the case of the two Eastern European states that had been among the most lamented victims of Hitler's aggression a decade earlier: Poland and Czechoslovakia.

In Poland a British-sponsored government-in-exile was rudely shunted aside by a Moscow-sponsored one. Evidence accumulated that the Russians had also massacred thousands of aristocratic Polish army officers during the war. There were less substantiated charges that the Red Army had deliberately halted its advance in order to allow a Warsaw rebellion by supporters of the "London Poles" to be crushed by the Germans.

The takeover in Czechoslovakia in 1948 was an open Communist coup. It involved the seizure of public buildings by Czech Communists, who thereby forced liberal president Eduard Beneš to cancel an impending election. And it climaxed with the "suicide" of the country's foreign minister, Jan Masaryk, while he was in the custody of the new regime.

The territorial division of Europe was completed by the division of Germany itself into two nations—the front-line states of the Cold War—in the heart of central Europe. As we noted above, Germany had initially been divided simply for purposes of military occupation and administration into four zones—American, British, French, and Russian. Because of its importance, Berlin, located deep within the Soviet sector, was also broken up into four military administrative districts. As the Western Allies and the Soviets found it increasingly difficult to get along, these lines hardened. The Western zones were merged and eventually became the Federal Republic of Germany, one of the major Western powers. The Soviet zone became the German Democratic Republic, the westernmost of the Soviet satellites. Berlin remained a zone of conflict and testing in the middle of East Germany.

As these events unfolded, the United States responded with a series of economic, diplomatic, and military moves of its own. The basic policy formulated in Washington was one of limiting Soviet efforts to enlarge Soviet influence or the new Russian empire. As early as 1946, George Kennan, head of the U.S. State Department's policy-planning staff, had described America's policy toward the Soviet Union as "a long-term, patient, but firm and vigilant containment of Russian expansive tendencies. . . ."[2] The first result of this "containment" policy was to create a massive concentration of power, anchored in Europe but reaching around the globe, with which to counter Soviet expansive tendencies.

In 1947 President Truman enunciated a new diplomatic principle of American behavior, the Truman Doctrine. He promised United States help "to support free people who are resisting attempted subjugation by armed minorities or by outside pressures." He referred in the first instance to Greece and Turkey, both of which were fearful of Soviet pressure from the north. By implication, however, the United States was offering aid to any gov-

---

[2]"The Sources of Soviet Conduct," *Foreign Affairs,* 25 (July 25, 1947), pp. 566–582.

ernment threatened by Soviet expansion or by Communist rebels anywhere in the world.

Two years later, in 1949, the key American military alliance came into existence: the North Atlantic Treaty Organization. The NATO treaty guaranteed mutual Western action against any further Russian expansion into Europe. It also stationed American troops in Europe as part of a Western European NATO army in order to block any further Soviet move.

In later years the United States supported similar mutual security arrangements in the Middle East, in Southeast Asia, and elsewhere, all aimed at curtailing the further spread of Soviet power. American military bases in Europe, the Middle East, and East Asia brought the U.S.S.R. within range of American bombers, listening devices, spy planes, and other forms of military pressure.

The Soviet Union reacted by beefing up its own power in Eastern Europe. Economically, a series of bilateral treaties between the U.S.S.R. and its satellites was followed in 1949 by COMECON, an Eastern European equivalent of the Western European Common Market—which followed soon thereafter. Militarily, the U.S.S.R. expanded its army, hastened to develop an atomic bomb of its own, and in 1955 set up the East-bloc military alliance known as the Warsaw Pact to confront the Western NATO alliance.

What Churchill called an Iron Curtain thus divided Europe and the world in the middle of the twentieth century. With World War II barely into the history books, the globe was once more divided into two armed camps, the antagonists girding themselves for the complex, involuted struggle known, again in a Churchillian phrase, as the Cold War.

CONFRONTATIONS AROUND THE WORLD

CONFLICT IN CENTRAL EUROPE

With the world divided once more, international confrontations were inevitable during the decades that followed World War II. The Cold War spawned conflicts in Europe and wars in Asia. It led to American intervention in Latin America and to Soviet repression of insurrectionary tendencies in Eastern Europe. More rarely—but even more dangerously—Cold War tensions led to facedowns between the two superpowers themselves.

In Europe, the first dramatic confrontation between the United States and the Soviet Union was the Berlin blockade of 1948–1949. This dangerous encounter grew out of a dispute over a currency reform introduced in the Western zones of occupied Berlin—part of a series of moves that the Soviets interpreted as an effort to make

Berlin a showcase for West German economic recovery. In hopes of forcing the Western Allies out of the old German capital entirely, the Soviets closed all roads and railways across Russian-occupied East Germany into Berlin. The Allies, however, took up the challenge. They proceeded to supply the Western zones of the city entirely by air for almost a year, until the Russians ended their blockade. The Berlin airlift was widely hailed in the West as an indication of Western, and particularly American, resolution to resist any further expansion of Soviet power.

In 1961, however, the Soviets stirred up a new crisis by building an amazing wall dividing the city of Berlin in half in order to close off an embarrassing and debilitating drain of East German emigrants into booming West Germany. In the long run, the Berlin Wall became a propaganda victory for the West, looming as a dramatic symbol of the economic and political failures of the East. In the short run, however, America's inability to prevent the building of the Wall looked like a distinct setback for the West.

By contrast, the Yugoslav defection from the Stalinist system represented a clear net loss to the new Russian East European empire. Heavy-handed Soviet efforts to reshape Yugoslavia economically and militarily in the image of Stalin's Russia had alienated the Yugoslav Communists. The expulsion of Marshall Tito, Yugoslavia's partisan hero and postwar ruler, from the ranks of international communism proved to be the straw that broke the Russo-Yugoslav alliance. The Yugoslav comrades responded by rallying around their leader. Tito became the chief international spokesman for the new doctrine of "many roads to socialism"—the view that each Communist country should choose its own path to the classless society rather than blindly following the Soviet model. For the next thirty years, Tito played a neutral role with consummate skill—accepting aid from Washington and Moscow alike—and enjoying an honored place among nonaligned Third World countries as well.

REBELLION IN EASTERN EUROPE

On both sides of the Iron Curtain there were tensions, discontents, and occasional rumbles of insubordination over the years. When this happened, both Russian and American governments were capable of taking a firm stand with their allies and client states.

In Eastern Europe, continuing postwar poverty and the economic discontents that resulted from collectivization of agriculture, harsh industrial working conditions, and shortages of consumer goods all bred bitterness. This resentment focused on Soviet exploitation of satellite economies and on the Russian presence generally. Nationalism was also a factor, impelling the peoples who had fought Ottoman Turks, Habsburg Austrians, and Hitler's Germany—not to mention each other—to turn against Stalinist Russia as well.

The "airlift" that broke the Berlin blockade of 1948. United States Air Force transport planes discharge cargoes of flour, milk, and other supplies at Templehof Airport in West Berlin. A more positive image than the atomic bombs over Japan, the supplying of an isolated city by air for many months also revealed the enormous potential of technology as a force in modern history. (Library of Congress)

The first of a series of rebellions behind the Iron Curtain exploded in 1953 with demonstrations in Czechoslovakia against the Soviet-supported government in Prague. In East Germany, a workers' revolt flared briefly, producing scores of deaths in the streets and hundreds of executions thereafter. Vivid photographs of German youths hurling rocks at Russian tanks symbolized to many Westerners the nature of the Eastern alliance.

In 1956, three years after Stalin's death, an anti-Stalinist reaction stimulated new challenges to Soviet control in Poland and Hungary, both nations with strong nationalistic and anti-Russian traditions. In both countries, the lead in demanding concessions was taken by anti-Stalinist Communists who had earlier been punished for defending national roads to the classless society. Wladyslaw Gomulka in Poland, returned to power by noisy demonstrations, cut back on compulsory collectivization of peasant farms and on police repression, announced a new emphasis on consumer goods—and got away with it.

Hungary in 1956 went much further—and didn't get away with it. Imre Nagy had attacked forced collectivization, police power, and shortages of consumer goods earlier in the 1950s. Recalled to power by strikers, demonstrators, and rioters in October 1956, Nagy watched mobs topple Budapest's huge bronze statue of Stalin, tear down Russian flags, and attack secret policemen in the streets. He announced the withdrawal of Soviet troops and a return to multiparty democracy.

The Soviet Union responded with a massive military intervention. As many as twenty-five hundred tanks poured into Hungary, shelling thousands of buildings and killing several thousand Hungarians. Hundreds of thousands more fled abroad to exile.

The 1960s, which saw a surge of youthful dissent around the world, also sparked discontent in Eastern Europe. In 1970, Poles demonstrated against Gomulka, grown authoritarian in his later years, and forced his ouster. Romanian Communists refused to lock their national economy into COMECON, the Soviet-centered Eastern European version of the Common Market. But the major anti-Russian revolt of the decade was the Prague Spring in Czechoslovakia in 1968.

Sources of tension in Czechoslovakia, one of the most highly developed industrial societies in Eastern Europe, included worker resentment of grinding industrial discipline. Equally important, however, were the demands of a new generation of technical experts and government administrators for the freedom to make decisions on a pragmatic basis rather than on the basis of party ideology. In 1968 a repressive older regime was replaced by a new Communist leadership headed by a more liberal party man, Alexander Dubcek. Dubcek cut back on police repression, abolished censorship, called for popular expressions of differing opinions, and unleashed a wave of popular demands for change, including multiparty democracy and withdrawal from the Warsaw Pact.

The Soviets responded with a military occupation of Czechoslovakia by half a million Soviet and other Warsaw Pact troops. Dubcek and the new leadership were removed from power. Years of sedition trials followed that heady moment of rebellion in Prague in the spring of 1968, and more refugees crossed the frontiers.

Stalin's head, broken from his toppled statue, lies in the streets of Budapest at the height of the Hungarian revolt of 1956. Such attacks on symbols of Soviet rule in Eastern Europe would be matched by attacks on statues of Lenin and other Communist leaders in the Soviet Union itself during the Gorbachev years three decades later. (The Bettmann Archive)

Yet another major defiance of Soviet-sponsored Communist rule came in the 1980s—once more in Poland. In 1980 the Polish economy, with an unfavorable balance of trade and a huge debt to Western banks, was in especially bad condition. Polish workers compounded these problems by opposing new price hikes with an unprecedented series of strikes, plant occupations, and demands for a new labor union independent of the Communist party. Again a pressured party backed off, allowing not only an independent union—called Solidarity—but also more freedom of religion, an end to censorship, release of some political prisoners, and pay raises.

One reform that no Communist government seemed able to tolerate, however, was the existence of any strong center of power rivaling its own. In 1981, then, the Polish Communist party chose as its new head the tough general Wojciech Jaruzelski. And in December of that year, Jaruzelski abruptly imposed martial law on the country, smashed Solidarity, and arrested its leaders or drove them underground. No Soviet intervention was required.

REVOLUTION IN LATIN AMERICA

In Latin America, meanwhile, the postwar period saw a return to the sort of American intervention that had flourished in the first decades of the century. Peasants south of the Rio Grande had long lived with poverty and exploitation, both by their own landowners and military juntas and by the foreign businesses that drew substantial profits out of Central and South America. In the twentieth century, U.S. business replaced European enterprise as the primary developer—and exploiter—of Latin American countries. And in the second half of the century, Soviet patronage and Marxist doctrines inspired a new generation of revolutionaries to challenge the status quo. Nationalistic anti-Yankee feeling and communist ideology thus combined to produce a series of violent confrontations over the decades following World War II.

The Central American republic of Guatemala offered a textbook case of this familiar Latin American syndrome. Dirt poor and dominated by the United Fruit Company, Guatemalans elected a reform-minded—and strongly anti-American—president named Jacobo Arbenz in 1952. Arbenz proceeded to redistribute land to peasants and to nationalize foreign holdings with minimal compensation—including hundreds of acres of United Fruit Company property. Worse yet from a Cold War perspective, there was a well-organized Communist party in Guatemala that cheered Arbenz on. The U.S. Central Intelligence Agency (CIA) thereupon sponsored and equipped a Guatemalan revolution against Arbenz. The president was overthrown, his Communist allies imprisoned or driven into the hills, and a Cold War victory quietly chalked up for the CIA.

Perhaps the most striking case of U.S. political intervention in the affairs of its Latin American neighbors during the Cold War, however, was Washington's long-running feud with Fidel Castro's Cuba—a Communist state and Soviet ally less than a hundred miles off the coast of the United States.

In 1959, Castro, a young Cuban lawyer turned revolutionary, led a ragged guerrilla movement to victory over the dictatorial pro-American government of Fulgencio Batista. Relations between Cuba and the United States soured rapidly after Castro's seizure of power. The charismatic leader's rejection of Cuba's heavy economic dependence on the American market for Cuban sugar, his nationalization of American industry and property, and his turn to the Soviet Union for trade and aid led to the ill-fated Bay of Pigs scheme. President Dwight Eisenhower organized and John Kennedy launched an invasion of Cuba by fifteen hundred CIA-trained Cuban exiles in the spring of 1961. Kennedy, however, refused to provide open air cover for the covert operation, and Castro's popular support and military organization proved much stronger than expected. Almost all the invaders were captured, and no grass-roots rebellion emerged, as the CIA had believed it would.

Fidel Castro in the Sierra Maestra. The bearded Cuban guerrilla leader opposed not only the Batista dictatorship in his own country, but also U.S. predominance in the Caribbean. To many Latin Americans, Castro symbolized not communism but opposition to the vast economic and political predominance of the United States in the Western Hemisphere. In the 1990s, however, an aging Castro defended communism after Eastern Europe and the Soviet Union itself had abandoned it. (AP/Wide World Photos)

The Cuban missile crisis later the following year (to be dealt with later) originated on the island but was carried on over Castro's head, as a military confrontation between the United States and the Soviet Union. Thereafter, affairs settled down to a long-term feud.

The United States imposed diplomatic nonrecognition and an economic boycott on Cuba, and persuaded most of the Organization of American States to go along with these measures for a number of years. Castro became active in the disputes which from time to time divided the leaders of international communism and the nonaligned nations. At the same time, however, Cuba served as a base for revolutionary attempts to overthrow governments in other Latin American countries. Some of these were notorious tyrannies, such as Nicaragua under the Somozas. Others, however, were progressive democracies, such as the Venezuela of Romulo Betancourt. The United States reacted by providing counterinsurgency training for threatened Latin American states and won a proxy victory of sorts when Castro's right-hand man, the charismatic Che Guevara, was killed leading a guerrilla band in Bolivia in 1967.

A much discussed—if less decisive—instance of American interference was the covert support apparently given to the military revolt that overthrew Latin America's first elected Communist ruler, Salvador Allende, in Chile in 1973. Chile, one of the influential ABC powers of South America (Argentina, Brazil and Chile), was a functioning democracy with strong leftist parties, ongoing land-reform programs, and a good deal of socialized industry when Allende was elected president in 1970. By 1973 the Marxists' drive to give Chile state socialism by democratic means had brought economic chaos, a turmoil encouraged by official U.S. disapproval. In September 1973 a military coup overthrew Allende, who died in an attack on the presidential palace, as did several thousand of his Chilean supporters. The Pinochet military regime that followed was widely condemned for brutal political repression, though it did restore Chilean economic prosperity.

The actual degree of U.S. involvement in Allende's overthrow remains disputed. The CIA does appear to have sent funds to "destabilize" the Communist government, particularly early in Allende's administration. The coup, however, was probably the work of the Chilean military officers who subsequently established themselves in power—a familiar enough political syndrome in Latin America.

In the 1980s, the United States once again intervened in Central America in revolutionary turmoil. This latest upsurge of political turbulence in Central America began in the later 1970s and reached a first climax with the overthrow of the Somoza dictatorship by the Sandinista rebels in Nicaragua in 1979. United States leaders at that time saw the new regime as a liberal one, likely to improve the lot of the peasantry without abandoning their newly won democracy. Washington therefore offered diplomatic recognition and even some aid to the Sandinistas.

In the early 1980s, however, the militantly anticommunist government of President Ronald Reagan saw the new Nicaragua in a very different light. By that time, too, circumstances had changed significantly in the area. There was an active guerrilla movement in neighboring El Salvador and a faction-torn Communist regime on the small Caribbean island of Grenada. Castro's Cuba seemed to be supporting the revolutions in all three small countries, and Reagan insisted that the Soviet Union was in fact behind it all.

Through the early 1980s, therefore, President Reagan moved to extinguish the revolutionary fires that appeared to be building in Central America. The United States put heavy pressure on Cuba and Nicaragua to stop supporting the guerrillas in El Salvador. American aid for El Salvador included substantial military support. The CIA organized an anti-Sandinista guerrilla movement of disaffected Nicaraguans and supported their efforts to topple the new regime. Then in 1984 the U.S. military seized Grenada, overthrowing the divided Communist government there and capturing or killing a number of Cuban engineers and military advisors in the process.

As in Eastern Europe, so in Central and South America, a basic pattern of conflict thus seemed firmly established. To many, the Cold War seemed like a fact of life that would continue for the forseeable future.

WAR IN ASIA

In addition to these intermittent rebellions in East Europe and revolutions in Latin America, the postwar decades also saw outbreaks of open warfare in East Asia.

Here China's long civil war came to an end in the late 1940s with victory for the Mao Zedong's Communists. Guerrillas challenged Western authority in Malaya and Burma, the Dutch East Indies, and the Philippines in the years immediately after the war. There was a largely American war in Korea in the 1950s and a French struggle in its colony of Vietnam about the same time. In the 1960s the United States launched its own escalating intervention in Vietnam, a bloody conflict that dragged on into the 1970s. And in the latter decade, the Soviet Union sent an army into Afghanistan.

Some of these struggles were fundamentally anti-imperialist rebellions, with or without a veneer of Marxist-Leninist rhetoric. The extent to which these wars were rooted in the Cold War, however, make the Vietnamese and Korean struggles and the Soviet intervention in Afghanistan part of the story of the Cold War.

The French Vietnamese war fits only tangentially into the broader pattern of Cold War conflict. The large majority of the Vietminh guerrillas who fought their former French overlords from shortly after World War II until 1954 were simply Vietnamese anti-imperialists. But their leader, Ho Chi Minh, and many of his cadres were Marxists as well as Vietnamese nationalists, and the Communist government they established in North Vietnam was welcomed as a Soviet ally.

The Korean War was more clearly part of the larger Cold War picture. The ancient Korean nation, divided along the thirty-eighth parallel into American and Soviet zones of liberation after World War II, had in less than five years evolved into two countries. Both the Soviets' ally in North Korea, Kim Il Sung, and America's protege, Syngman Rhee, strongly favored reunification—each under his own rule, of course. It was North Korea that acted, invading South Korea in the spring of 1950.

There was no evidence of Soviet instigation of the affair, but a North Korean victory could be seen as another gain for the communist alliance headed by the Soviet Union. President Truman therefore responded by sending U.S. occupation troops from Japan, under General MacArthur, to Rhee's aid. The American forces, however, were operating under U.N. auspices with modest contingents from other U.N. members in what was officially described not as a war but as a "police action"—all very typical of the increasingly involuted patterns of the Cold War.

Militarily, the Korean conflict turned into a seesaw struggle up and down the rugged peninsula. In the beginning the well-prepared and well-armed North Koreans almost drove the South Koreans and their American supporters into the sea. MacArthur then recovered, surprised the enemy with large amphibious landings behind North Korean lines, and drove the aggressors back across the thirty-eighth parallel. He did not stop there, however, but pushed on north, overrunning much of North Korea and pressing too close to the Chinese frontier along the Yalu River. The Chinese Communists therefore intervened in their turn, sending massive "volunteer" regiments across the Yalu to help the North Koreans. The front finally stabilized close to the thirty-eighth parallel, where a truce was eventually signed in 1953—a nonpeace to end the nonwar in Korea.

Within a decade the United States was again drawn into a war in Asia, this time in Vietnam. The United States had declined to commit military force to help France keep its Vietnamese colony. Washington was, however, willing to put a large military force into the field to prevent the overthrow of a pro-Western government in South Vietnam, as in South Korea, but the outcome in Vietnam was very different.

Within a few years of Ho Chi Minh's victory over France and his establishment in power in Hanoi, guerrillas appeared in the jungles of South Vietnam. Their goal was the overthrow of the Saigon government headed by the pro-French Ngo Dinh Diem and his ambitious family. Diem was undemocratic and authoritarian, and the initial guerrilla revolt seems to have been the work of South Vietnamese chafing under his rule.

The United States sent advisors and supplies to help Diem resist what American leaders saw as communist imperialism. North Vietnam sent supplies and then troops to support the South Vietnamese guerrillas, and in time essentially assumed command of the war. The Soviet Union, and to a lesser extent China, supplied war materiel to North Vietnam.

The United States and North Vietnam, however, were involved far more deeply than other nations. By the later 1960s, the war had become primarily a contest between the North Vietnamese army and a half-million-man U.S. Expeditionary Force, each side with its own South Vietnamese auxiliaries. Several unpopular Saigon governments were overthrown apparently with U.S. connivance. The Americans carried open warfare into the neighboring states of Cambodia and Laos, which North Vietnam had been using as supply routes to the south. The war cost perhaps a million lives and resulted in brutal devastation in the villages of Vietnam.

In the end, the unpopularity of the long war in the

United States led to the withdrawal of its troops in 1973. In 1975 North Vietnamese armies overran the south, and soon thereafter South Vietnam was absorbed into a single unified Vietnam ruled from Hanoi, as in precolonial times.

In the broad perspective of Asian history, Vietnam's reemergence as an important second-level power in Southeast Asia was perhaps to be expected. From the point of view of the Cold War, however, the outcome was a clear setback for the West.

Besides Korea and Vietnam, a third major locus of Asian conflict clearly linked to the Cold War was Afghanistan. This mountainous, sparsely populated Middle Eastern land on the southern frontier of the U.S.S.R. became the target of a major Soviet military incursion at the end of the 1970s.

Afghanistan had experienced Russian incursions and influence for centuries. Most recently, a Soviet-supported regime in Kabul, the Afghan capital, had pushed modernization—and secularization—too far and too fast for the deeply conservative, notoriously combative Muslim villagers. By the end of the 1970s, a guerrilla revolt led by Muslim fundamentalists threatened to topple the pro-Russian government of Afghanistan. In a swift airborne assault late in 1979, therefore, Soviet troops occupied the capital and engineered a coup that left their own former client ruler in Kabul dead and a new and apparently more moderate pro-Soviet leader in his stead.

The rebellion, however, remained to be crushed—no easy task in the mountains of Afghanistan. Like the American war in Vietnam, Russia's new Afghan war pitted modern firepower against guerrillas who swam in the peasant sea. Although between two and three million Afghans were driven into exile in Pakistan, this war also proved difficult for the superpower to win. In the end, as we shall see, the Soviets would "declare victory" and withdraw their troops, leaving a friendly government in power in Kabul that would soon fall to the rebel armies still unbroken in the countryside.

CONFRONTATION BETWEEN THE SUPERPOWERS

The most dangerous conflicts for the world, however, were the Cold War confrontations between the United States and the Soviet Union. Armed with a nightmarish array of science-fiction weaponry, the two superpowers repeatedly seemed to threaten the futures of all peoples with their willingness to risk "Mutually Assured Destruction" in defense of their conflicting interests and ideals. And the tensest of these threatened conflicts was almost certainly the Cuban missile crisis of 1962.

For most of the 1950s, Stalin's Soviet successor, Nikita Khrushchev, and U.S. President Dwight Eisenhower managed to avoid major clashes, allowing their nations to recover from the tensions of the Stalin and Truman years.

Then in 1960 the Russians shot down an American U-2 spy plane over the heart of the Soviet Union. When President Eisenhower refused to apologize for this violation of Soviet air space, Khrushchev walked out of a U.S.-Soviet summit meeting in Paris. It was the beginning of a very tense period in Russo–American relations.

President John F. Kennedy came to office in 1961 with an image of youth and vigor and a campaign promise to end alleged Soviet superiority in weapons development—the so-called missile gap. Kennedy's first year, however, saw a jarring series of American setbacks. At a new summit meeting in Vienna, Kennedy apparently failed to impress Khrushchev with his vigor and determination. The CIA-organized invasion of Fidel Castro's Cuba failed as the invading Cuban exiles were mopped up on the beaches of the Bay of Pigs. And in beleaguered Berlin later that same year, the Berlin Wall went up—a challenge that went unanswered by the United States. Kennedy was thus put in the position of having to prove that he could prevent the Soviets from working their will in the world.

Kennedy's chance came the following year, in the Cuban missile crisis of October 1962. Khrushchev, it seems, was also under pressure at home to prove himself as tough with the Americans as Stalin had been. American missile strength was, in fact, rapidly outdistancing that of the Soviet Union in the early 1960s, and the technological superiority of the West revealed by the U-2 rankled the Soviet leader's Kremlin colleagues. Khrushchev therefore followed up the American humiliation at the Bay of Pigs by responding to Castro's pleas for more support by secretly stationing Soviet missiles in Cuba—only ninety miles away from the American mainland across the Florida straits.

When U-2 reconnaissance photos of Cuba revealed the new Soviet installations, Kennedy took the United States to the brink of war with the Soviets in order to get them out. The American president rallied the Organization of American States and as many Western European allies as he could, put the U.S. military on alert—nuclear bombers in the air, missiles ready to fire—and established a naval blockade around the island of Cuba. More Soviet missiles were already on their way. Kennedy declared that they must be called back, and that those already in place must be removed or face American military action. Privately, he offered assurances that there would be no more invasions of Cuba, and even that some American missiles aimed at the Soviet Union would be redeployed elsewhere.

For a tense week, the world was on the edge. Then the Soviets agreed to remove their weapons from the Western Hemisphere, and the crisis passed. But it left Soviet military leaders determined to overtake the United States in missiles and nuclear warheads—a goal they would achieve in the years that followed that most perilous of Cold War confrontations.

THE END OF THE COLD WAR

COEXISTENCE AND DÉTENTE

Over four decades, then, the Cold War brought the world rebellions, revolutions, wars, and the threat of confrontation between the superpowers. The Cold War also, however, turned out to be much more subtle and complicated than a survey of these open clashes might suggest. The forms of conflict, the contending parties, even the terms of engagement and the goals sought grew immensely complex over the years. And in the end, the conflict terminated—dramatically enough, but without the final showdown many had feared.

One form the Cold War did *not* take was direct military engagement between the principals: the United States and the Soviet Union. There were proxy wars, as we have seen, involving American or Russian client states, revolutions supported by one side or the other, or other forms of conflict in which one or both superpowers became involved. There were near misses, most notably the Cuban missile crisis, but the balance of nuclear terror prevented military conflict between the Soviet Union and the United States.

There was, however, a wide range of nonmilitary contention between the two. There were propaganda broadsides aimed at their own people, at each other, and at "world opinion." There was espionage of all sorts, from the most sophisticated electronic gear to old-fashioned spying. There was intense technological and economic competition, ranging from the battle to see who could produce the most tungsten or toothbrushes to the race to the moon. And there was, of course, the unending arms race, to which we will turn presently.

Accompanying these varied forms of competition, however, were repeated attempts to improve relations between America and the Soviet Union. These efforts included a broad spectrum of political, economic, cultural, and military moves by the two sides. Under such rubrics as "coexistence" or *détente*, these efforts provided a counterpoint of hope that the world could avoid a third global war in the twentieth century.

A number of summit meetings occurred between the two states and a great many consultations between foreign ministers, ambassadors, and other lesser officials of the two governments. Direct electronic communications between the White House and the Kremlin were set up for easy and quick discussions when problems arose. Trade relations, while fluctuating with other aspects of the relationship, repeatedly provided a splendid opportunity for America to market its habitual agricultural overproduction and for the Soviet Union to import lifesaving quantities of grain when chronically inefficient Russian collectivized agriculture failed to produce. Western Europe also developed lucrative trade connections with Eastern Europe and with the Soviet Union in particular.

Cultural exchanges were another part of the long-term effort to improve international understanding. American audiences got a chance to see Russian ballet, famous since czarist times, and Soviet audiences enjoyed American jazz groups. Educational meetings were frequent, as were exchanges at larger international meetings of all sorts.

Above all, agreements were negotiated limiting arms development in the two superstates—though this proved in the long run perhaps the most difficult problem of all for the two armed camps.

POLYCENTRISM IN THE BLOCS

Over the years after Stalin's death, the configurations of the two international alliances also changed. While leaders—and true believers—on both sides continued to talk about the "socialist camp" and the "free world" as if the lines were as clear and hard as they had been under Truman and Stalin, both sides, in fact, tended to fragment—and each side to intrigue for support on the other side of the Iron Curtain.

Thus Marshal Tito broke with Stalin in 1948 and took Yugoslavia out of the Soviet orbit. Little Albania, its mountain fastnesses even farther removed from the Soviet Union than Yugoslavia, also broke ideologically with Moscow—and found a new patron in Beijing. Rumania, Czechoslovakia, Hungary, and other satellite countries often pushed for more trade with the West than the Soviets approved of. North Korea and North Vietnam, never satellites in the classical sense, apparently started their wars with their southern neighbors without either instigation or prior approval from the Soviet Union.

Most important, Mao's China broke with the Soviets in 1959–1960. Ideological differences partly explain the split. Mao's People's Republic of China saw itself in 1960 as more uncompromisingly Marxist than the Soviet Union under Khrushchev. A history of Russian imperialism in the Far East and continuing border disputes between the U.S.S.R. and Communist China also help to account for the break. Soviet high-handedness, China's refusal to be treated like a junior partner, and perhaps most important, the long frontier between thinly populated Russian Siberia and China's land-hungry hundreds of millions all contributed to the sudden chill between the Cold War partners.

The result was a great schism in the Communist world as early as 1960. The Soviets called home their technical advisors and canceled their aid programs to underdeveloped China. Trade between the two nations dwindled, border garrisons were beefed up. Moscow and Beijing competed around the world for the allegiance of other Communist parties. Propaganda organs in both cap-

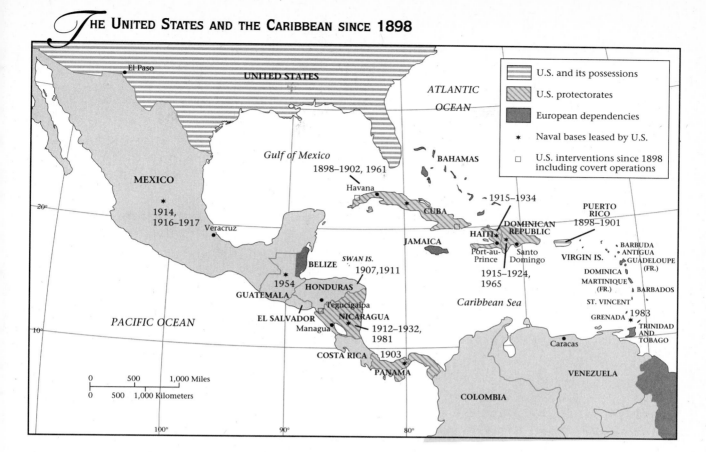

The United States and the Caribbean Since 1898

Legend:
- U.S. and its possessions
- U.S. protectorates
- European dependencies
- ★ Naval bases leased by U.S.
- ▢ U.S. interventions since 1898 including covert operations

itals dealt more harshly with each other than with the common capitalist foe. Attempts to patch things up after Mao's death in 1976 eased the strain somewhat, but China's increasingly good relations with the United States—and its ancient sense of its own importance in the world—made any return to monolithic Soviet leadership extremely unlikely.

On the Western side, Europe's rapid recovery from the war, as we noted in an earlier section, soon transformed the Western European countries from economic dependents of the United States to economic rivals. As a result, some American allies felt increasingly free to develop independent foreign policies of their own, even toward communist countries.

France under the strongly nationalistic President de Gaulle, for example, broke with the North Atlantic Treaty alliance and established its own nuclear strike force. The ultraconservative de Gaulle became one of the first Western leaders to trade freely with Communist China and the U.S.S.R. West Germany, first under socialist chancellors like Willy Brandt and later under the conservative government of Helmut Kohl, explored avenues of rapprochement with East Germany and developed its own policy toward the Soviet Union, though without ever backing away from the crucial NATO alliance. The Western coalition, in short, became much looser than it had been in the early years. It was always much freer than the Soviet system, loose as that became over the years.

THE ARMS RACE AND DISARMAMENT

Despite hopes for détente and weakening alliances, however, the United States and the Soviet Union continued the most dangerous form of Cold War competition throughout the postwar decades: the unending—even accelerating—arms race.

Popular discussion of the subject tended to distinguish between conventional and nuclear forces, as will be seen in the following paragraphs. In fact, however, the two are closely related. The Western allies, for example, stressed the deployment of nuclear weapons where they could not muster the troop strength to win a conventional war—as in Western Europe, where they felt outnumbered and outgunned by the Warsaw Pact. In actual combat, however—as in Vietnam or Afghanistan—both superpowers preferred to commit their troops rather than to use nuclear weaponry—a decision only partially determined by the guerrilla tactics of the opposition.

The arms race began on the conventional side. In the 1940s the Red Army had overrun Eastern Europe. Under NATO, the United States and its allies established a multinational Western European army, which included large American contingents, to defend Western Europe against any further Soviet expansion. The Soviets responded in the 1950s with the Warsaw Pact and a Russian-led Eastern European army that, built with conscription, was soon larger than the NATO force.

The United States, meanwhile, had been seeking to counter the Soviet Union's massive land power in Europe by surrounding that country with a ring of American alliances and bases. After NATO in 1949 came the Southeast Asia Treaty Organization (SEATO) in 1954, the British-run Baghdad Pact in the Middle East in 1955, and its replacement, the Central Treaty Organization (CENTO) in 1959. By 1960 hundreds of U.S. bases were scattered through thirty countries around Russia's perimeter, from West Germany to Japan. The American Seventh Fleet patrolled the far Pacific, the Sixth Fleet the Mediterranean, and others the Indian Ocean, the North Atlantic, and most of the seven seas. Soviet advantages in Europe—still the heart of the conflict—were thus offset by a ring of U.S. bases and allies.

Increasingly, however, the two superpowers came to depend on a range of awesome new weapons involving nuclear warheads delivered by air. The aspect of the arms race that most terrified the world was the multiplication of these weapons and their potential for global destruction. The arms race was hectic, ever changing, and so expensive that it warped and drained the economies of both great powers.

The United States maintained its monopoly of the original Hiroshima atomic bomb—based on atomic fission rather than fusion—for only five years, until the Soviets exploded their first test bomb in 1949. In 1952 the United States exploded the first H-bomb—the vastly more destructive hydrogen or thermonuclear bomb, based on fusion. The Russians tested their first H-bomb the following year.

Emphasis then shifted to delivery systems—ways of depositing these terrifying explosives on enemy military installations and cities. By the mid-1950s American Strategic Air Command B-52 bombers had an intercontinental range, as did their Soviet equivalents. The United States, however, had four times as many of these intercontinental bombers as did the Russians.

Then in 1957 the Soviet Union tested the first long-range ballistic missile—a rocket-powered bomb that used its motor to establish a ballistic path and then followed this arching trajectory over thousands of miles to deliver a nuclear warhead without any airplane at all. The race to build intercontinental ballistic missiles was on. The United States rapidly overtook the Soviets in the field; by the time of the Cuban missile crisis in 1962, America had more than four hundred targeted missiles to Russia's one hundred, as well as two thousand nuclear warheads to Russia's two hundred.

Through the 1960s the race went on. The United States pioneered in the arming of nuclear-powered submarines with nuclear missiles—an undersea force almost impossible to find and destroy, and one soon emulated by the U.S.S.R. Other new devices included antiballistic missile systems (ABMs) intended to protect cities and missile installations from nuclear attack, and multiple independently targeted reentry vehicles (MIRVs), rockets that could carry several warheads instead of one.

In the 1970s and early 1980s came cruise missiles, which skimmed the treetops, thus slipping in under enemy radar detection systems. There was talk of using disease as a weapon, and of manufacturing neutron bombs that would cause very little damage while killing large numbers of people. Early in the 1980s President Reagan began to urge the development of a new defensive capability, using the potential of satellites, lasers, and other "Star Wars" weapons as an ultimate defense against surprise attack. But it was hard to imagine that any weapon could be truly "ultimate" in this seemingly unending competition.

International treaties were negotiated, and some signed, to control the escalating arms race. The first Nuclear Test Ban Treaty was signed by President Kennedy and Russia's Khrushchev in 1963. Two Strategic Arms Limitation Treaties (SALT I and SALT II) were signed in 1972 and 1979, though the second was never ratified by the U.S. Congress. In 1985 arms negotiations began again between the two superpowers, this time focusing on President Reagan's "Star Wars" initiative and on the Soviets' long arms buildup of the 1970s.

As in the disarmament discussions between World Wars I and II, there were technical disputes over definitions and equivalents, over what to count and how. Questions of verification of compliance also came up, and each side accused the other of violating agreements already in force. Since neither side was willing to give up a nuclear advantage, treaties were hard to negotiate. In the end, many years of dickering seemed to have done little to slow what to many began to look like a race to Armageddon.

Then, with a suddenness that astonished the world, the rigid global structure of the postwar settlement and the implacable Cold War conflict itself began to dissolve.

THE COLLAPSE OF THE SOVIET BLOC

In 1985 a new sort of Communist leader maneuvered his way to leadership of the Soviet Union. Mikhail Gorbachev saw his country confronted by a plethora of problems, from a stagnant economy to a draining intervention in Afghanistan. Vigorous yet flexible, Gorbachev was willing to break with the postwar policies, domestic and foreign, which he saw as responsible for the nation's difficulties. The reforms that he set in motion in 1985, as we shall see in a later chapter, further unraveled the fabric of Soviet society and weakened the structure of the Soviet state. Then, with dramatic suddenness, Soviet economic and political disarray combined with Gorbachev's flexibility to trigger both the collapse of Russia's East European satellite empire and the end of the Cold War itself.

From month to month through the astonishing year 1989, newspaper headlines around the world chronicled the stunning collapse of the Soviet hegemony of Eastern Europe. "Upheaval in the East" intoned *Le Monde* in Paris, and "The People Rise!" blared West Germany's *Die Zeit*. The cover of *U.S. News & World Report* trumpeted a "Communist Meltdown—The Crumbling Iron Curtain—The Soviet Economy in Ruins," while *Time* saw it as "The Big Break—Moscow Lets Eastern Europe Go Its Own Way." The nightly news on television was a sea of moving faces, East Europeans pouring across frontiers to the West or surging up the streets of their own capitals demanding the resignations of their Communist governments. Placards called for democratic elections, agitators urged free-market economic reforms, and everyone seemed to want

the Soviet troops garrisoned on their soil since World War II to pack up and leave.

To the amazement of a watching world, the East European peoples had their way. The borders opened: the governments toppled. First in Poland and Hungary, then in hard-line states like East Germany and Czechoslovakia, finally in the less developed Balkan nations of Rumania and Bulgaria, Soviet puppet regimes disappeared one by one. The opening of the Berlin Wall, symbol of a divided Europe for three decades, convinced most observers that Soviet domination of half the continent had effectively ended.

The Soviet reaction to these popular revolts was of course crucial to the success of the anticommunist opposition movements. Gorbachev would in fact garner the Nobel Prize for Peace in 1990 in large part for the decisions he made when the 1989 upheaval swept across the Soviet bloc. The Soviet leader actually had to some degree fostered popular unrest by encouraging fellow Communist rulers to follow his example and attempt the sort of political and economic reforms he was endeavoring to

The Berlin Wall begins to come down early in 1990. First opened to free passage late the preceding year, this grim barrier dividing the eastern and western sectors of Berlin was chopped up and sold for souvenirs over the months that followed. Here East German border guards and crowds of civilians watch as the work of demolition gets under way in the shadow of the Brandenburg Gate, Berlin's traditional victory symbol in the center of the city. (German Information Center)

"*The circumstances of the immediate post-Revolution period—the existence in Russia of civil war and foreign intervention, together with the obvious fact that the Communists represented only a tiny minority of the Russian people—made the establishment of dictatorial power a necessity. . . .*

Let it be stressed again that subjectively these men probably did not seek absolutism for its own sake. They doubtless believed—and found it easy to believe—that they alone knew what was good for society and that they would accomplish that good once their power was secure and unchallengable. . . .

Now the outstanding circumstance concerning the Soviet regime is that down to the present day this process of political consolidation has never been completed and the men in the Kremlin have continued to be predominantly absorbed with the struggle to secure and make absolute the power which they seized in November 1917. They have endeavored to secure it primarily against forces at home, within Soviet society itself. But they have also endeavored to secure it against the outside world. For ideology, as we have seen, taught them that the outside world was hostile and that it was their duty eventually to overthrow the political forces beyond their borders. . . .

Today the major part of the structure of Soviet power is committed to the perfection of the dictatorship and to the maintenance of the concept of Russia as in a state of siege, with the enemy lowering beyond the walls. And the millions of human beings who form that part of the structure of power must defend at all costs this concept of Russia's position, for without it they are themselves superfluous."

George Kennan, American diplomat, distinguished historian, and influential authority on Soviet affairs, is credited with having decisively shaped the U.S. Cold War policy of "containment" of Soviet expansionism. Though well aware of other factors besides ideology behind the U.S.S.R.'s Cold War stance, Kennan here presents a view that interweaves ideology and power as the roots of Russian hostility toward the Western powers.

Does Kennan's interpretation of the motives of the founders of the Soviet Union sound convincing? Would you say that Kennan's view of how history happens stresses political rather than economic forces? Can you see how different views of history could lead to different interpretations of what was for both a crucial contemporary problem?

George F. Kennan, "The Sources of Soviet Conduct," in Norman A. Graebner, ed., The Cold War: Ideological Conflict or Power Struggle? (Boston: D.C. Heath, 1963), pp. 30–31.

---

achieve in the Soviet Union. Some Western analysts felt that Gorbachev had really little choice but to acquiesce to the anticommunist forces. The Russian leader needed an end to Cold War spending and the infusion of substantial Western economic aid to make his policies of "restructuring" the U.S.S.R. succeed. To achieve these goals, he had to convince the West that the U.S.S.R. no longer constituted a threat, even to its East European neighbors.

It was probably for such reasons, then, that Gorbachev reversed the interventionist policies that had maintained Soviet domination of East Europe for half a century. He first urged other Communist leaders to meet their peoples halfway with progressive reforms. And when such offers failed to placate the mobs of angry demonstrators, Soviet garrison troops stayed in their barracks while Communist governments collapsed. Within months, many Red Army units were on their way home, unceremoniously dismissed by the countries they had once dominated.

The "Revolutions of 1989" across Eastern Europe were as dramatic as the Europe-wide "Revolutions of 1848," though considerably less bloody. The wave of revolts thrust up a bewildering array of new leaders, from the internationally known labor union leader Lech Walesa in Poland to the avant-garde playwright Vaclav Havel in Czechoslovakia, both former political prisoners who within a year became heads of state. The major villain of the upheaval was Rumania's Nicolae Ceausescu, the only Communist leader to unleash the state security police on his own people. "Nothing short of death," Western journalists opined in November 1989, "is expected to nudge this dinosaur, in office since 1967, toward reform."[3] Two months later, in a still murky combination of palace coup and popular revolt, Ceausescu was overthrown and shot.

Perhaps the most dramatic change of all, however, came in the center of Europe, where the two sides in the Cold War had confronted each other most directly from the beginning. In 1990, the newly liberated German Democratic Republic—East Germany—voted to merge with the Federal Republic—West Germany—re-creating a united German nation after forty-five years of division. From a Soviet security perspective, the reemergence of the powerhouse that had twice invaded Russia in this century was the greatest blow yet. Gorbachev, however, accepted German reunification also—in return for desperately needed economic aid from the new German republic. West German Chancellor Helmut Kohl, who had

---

[3]*Time*, November 6, 1989, p. 50.

orchestrated this remarkable coup, had his reward in December 1990, when he was elected to head the first government of the united Germany.

PHASING OUT THE COLD WAR

As the 1990s began, then, the armed forces of NATO no longer had a European foe to fight. The Soviet bloc had collapsed, and a politically democratic, economically dynamic Germany dominated Europe. The Soviet Union, by contrast, had retreated from Eastern Europe and was itself sliding into economic and political turmoil.

It had been a costly conflict for both the Soviet Union and the United States. Both nations had had to support needy and sometimes greedy allies and to send their troops into other countries to advance or defend their Cold War interests. Both sides in what was widely seen as a conflict of ideologies had also had to sacrifice some of their most loudly trumpeted ideals in the heat of the conflict. Free-world nations had sometimes abandoned civil liberties to root out sympathizers with the ideological enemy, as in the United States during the anticommunist campaigns of the 1940s and 1950s. Nations that claimed to be "workers states" had suppressed labor unions, as the Polish government had endeavored to crush the Solidarity labor movement in the 1980s.

Ideals, blood, and treasure had thus all been squandered lavishly by both sides. But the great schism that had divided the Western world, indeed the globe itself, came to an end in the final decade of the twentieth century.

SUMMARY

Peace was patched together after World War II without a great international peace conference. But the falling-out of the victorious Allies left much of Europe and Asia divided between zones of American and Soviet influence. Economic recovery came with surprising rapidity, especially to the Western nations, and the United Nations embodied a renewed commitment to international organization. But the Cold War brought conflict to the postwar world on a scale as global as the peace and the recovery.

Some aspects of the histories of the United States and the Soviet Union made rivalry between them likely if not inevitable. These two large and populous nations had different political traditions and patterns of economic development. They had differing interests and very different ideological points of view. The United States came out of World War II with a stronger global economic position than ever before, the Soviet Union with a sphere of influence in Eastern Europe.

The Cold War involved economic and technological competition between the two superpowers. It led to rival military alliances and economic organizations. It impelled the United States to take covert action against revolutions in Latin America; the Soviets to employ direct military force to suppress rebellions in its satellites in East Europe. It sent American troops into Korea and Vietnam and Russian ones into Afghanistan. And it fueled an accelerating arms race that at least once, over Cuba in 1962, came close to plunging the world into nuclear war.

Efforts to achieve coexistence or détente continued, including trade agreements, summit meetings, and disarmament talks. The authority of both superpowers over their respective camps weakened, and each side sought to lure members of the other alliance into at least a neutral stance. The increasingly expensive and unthinkably dangerous arms race between the two superpowers continued, although treaties limiting nuclear forces were negotiated. Then, after forty years of conflict on all fronts, the Cold War ended as suddenly as it had begun. The emergence of a new and more flexible leader, Mikhail Gorbachev, to power in the Kremlin and the economic and political deterioration of the Soviet Union, which proved greater than anyone had realized, were apparently the precipitating causes. At the end of the 1980s, Gorbachev reversed the policies of his predecessors, abandoning the Soviet empire in Eastern Europe, permitting the unification of the two Germanies, and seeking closer relations with the United States and Western Europe as his own country slid into chaos.

SUGGESTED READING

BARNET, R. J. *The Giants: Russia and America.* New York: Simon & Schuster, 1977. The superpowers of the later twentieth century locked in global confrontation.

CALDWELL, L. T., and W. DIEBOLD, JR. *Soviet-American Relations in the 1980s: Superpower Politics and East-West Trade.* New York: McGraw-Hill, 1981. Recognizes the complexities.

CALVOCORESSI, P. *World Politics since 1945,* 4th ed. London: Longmans, 1982. Valuable overview.

DAVISON, W. P. *The Berlin Blockade.* Princeton, N.J.: Princeton University Press, 1958. Anatomy of a crisis—arguably the most dangerous of the immediate postwar years.

DE PORTE, A. W. *Europe between the Superpowers: The Enduring Balance.* New Haven, Conn.: Yale University Press, 1979. Valuable assessment of the European situation since 1945.

DINERSTEIN, H. S. *The Making of a Missile Crisis.* Baltimore: John Hopkins University Press, 1976. The Cuban missile crisis in perspective.

GADDIS, J. L. *Strategies of Containment.* New York: Oxford University Press, 1983. Balanced account of American policies in the Cold War.

GARTON ASH, T. *We the People: The Revolution of '89.* London: Granta Books, 1990. Brilliant firsthand account of the East European revolts by a journalist who knew the revolutionaries. See also W Echikson, *Lighting the Night: The Revolution in Eastern Europe* (London: Sidgwick and Jackson, 1990), another concerned journalist's account, featuring encounters with rank-and-file rebels as well as leaders.

GRAEBNER, N. A., ed. *The Cold War: Ideological Conflict or Power Struggle?* Lexington, Mass.: Heath, 1976. Excellent collection of contrasting views.

HERRING, G. C. *America's Longest War: The United States and Vietnam, 1950–1975.* New York: Random House, 1979. Perhaps the best survey. Views critical of United States intervention include F. Fitzgerald, *Fire in the Lake: The Vietnamese and the Americans in Vietnam* (New York: Random House. 1973), and D. Halberstam, *The Best and the Brightest* (New York: Fawcett Crest, 1973).

HOROWITZ, D. *The Free World Colossus,* rev. ed. New York: Hill and Wang, 1971. Sees the United States as an actively counterrevolutionary force in the world, rather than as merely containing Soviet expansionism. Among those stressing American economic globalism are such revisionists as W. A. Williams, *The Tragedy of American Diplomacy,* 2nd ed. (New York: Dell, 1972). Accounts emphasizing Soviet expansive tendencies as a prime cause of the confrontation include H. Feis, *From Trust to Terror: The Onset of the Cold War, 1945–1950* (New York: W.W. Norton, 1970).

JOHNSON, H. *Bay of Pigs.* New York: W.W. Norton, 1964. The failure of the United States-sponsored effort to overthrow Castro.

KALDOR, M. *The Disintegrating West.* London: Allen Lane, 1978. Divisions in the Western camp. For essays on ideological divisions in the Communist camp, see W. Laqueur and L. Labedz, eds. *Polycentrism: The New Factor in International Communism* (New York: Praeger, 1962).

MCDOUGALL, W. A. *The Heavens and the Earth: A Political History of the Space Age.* New York: Basic Books, 1985. The first three decades of the "space race" between the U.S. and the U.S.S.R.

MEDVEDEV, R. *China and the Superpowers,* trans. H. Shokman. New York: Basil Blackwell, 1986. A Russian dissident historian looks at China's place in the Cold War and its split with the Soviet Union.

SVITAK, I. *The Czechoslovak Experiment, 1968–1969.* New York: Columbia University Press, 1971. Events leading up to Soviet intervention in 1968.

ULAM, A. *Expansion and Coexistence: The History of Soviet Foreign Policy, 1917–1967,* 2nd ed. New York: Holt, Rinehart, 1974. Clear and concise analysis; perhaps the best single volume on the whole course of Soviet foreign policy from the revolution to the Cold War.

ZINNER, P. E. *Revolution in Hungary.* New York: Columbia University Press, 1962. The Hungarian revolt of 1956 and its suppression by the Soviets.

CHAPTER 45

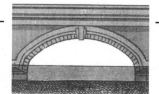

THE END OF THE WESTERN EMPIRES

FREEDOM AND CONFLICT IN THE THIRD WORLD

NEW NATIONS AROUND THE WORLD

Sooner or later, the pattern was everywhere much the same. There would be parades, speeches, flags. There would always be soldiers, very spit-and-polish usually, and large, enthusiastic crowds. Quite commonly, since these were usually tropical countries, everybody would be perspiring freely.

The European speeches would come first, grave and measured, with talk of obligations discharged and of responsibilities and friendship to come. Then the pale faces would settle down at the back of the speakers' platform, and Asian, African, or Arab faces would take their places at the rostrum.

The climax was always the same. There would be the anthem of the European power, a salute to the old flag—British, French, Dutch, American—fluttering down the pole. Then guns would boom, and to the martial strains of some still unfamiliar national song a new flag, the symbol of a new nation, would rise into the blue.

Even a brief survey of the European empires that crumbled, the major new nations that emerged during the decades after World War II, will give some sense of the scope of this movement.

Great Britain granted independence to many of its colonies in Asia and Africa. In South Asia during the 1940s and 1950s, British India, Pakistan, and Ceylon (Sri Lanka) were liberated, as were Burma (Myanmar) and Malaya in Southeast Asia. In the Middle East, British termination of the Palestine mandate led to the foundation of the new nation of Israel. In Africa, perhaps the most important British colonies to gain their freedom during the 1950s and 1960s were the Gold Coast (Ghana) and Nigeria in West Africa and Kenya and Tanganyika (Tanzania) in East Africa.

France, whose empire was second only to Britain's in size, more reluctantly liberated a number of territorial holdings in both Asia and Africa. In Asia, French Indochina—North and South Vietnam, Laos, and Cambodia—emerged from French rule as four separate nations. In

Africa, Algeria led the way to freedom, to be followed by all the colonies of French West and French Equatorial Africa.

Lesser Western imperial powers also surrendered their overseas colonies, usually unhappily. The Dutch East Indies, the Belgian Congo, and the American Philippines were all freed after the war. As late as the 1970s, some imperial holdouts in South Africa were at last liberated, including the large Portuguese colonies of Angola and Mozambique.

By the 1980s, only isolated enclaves of Western imperial control remained, usually by mutual consent, as in British Hong Kong. The major, much-resented exception was the powerful and wealthy state of South Africa, still governed by transplanted Europeans in spite of its large black African majority; but in the early 1990s, apartheid was phased out there too.

The great liberation dramatically transformed the global political picture. A total of ninety new countries emerged between the mid-1940s and the 1990s. Well over a billion people—a third of the earth's population—gained their independence of foreign rule.

Whatever the flags and ceremonies that heralded the emergence of each of these new nations, the magic word "Freedom" was sure to crackle out over the microphones again and again, to be emphasized with pounding fists, to be repeated in the jubilation that would fill the streets of the new capital on into the night. The Swahili word, used in various East African colonies, was *uhuru*. *Uhuru!* became a kind of symbol for what was granted—or taken—in these ceremonies repeated in one new country after another across Asia and Africa, particularly during the first two decades after the war.

CAUSES OF THE COLLAPSE OF THE INTERCONTINENTAL EMPIRES

World War II opened the floodgate of the great liberation in several ways. Most obviously, perhaps, the biggest of all wars seriously undermined the imperial vigor of the one-time *pukka sahibs* of the world. The war sapped the ability of some imperial powers to hold their empires in subjection any longer. Neither France nor the Netherlands, battered by Germany, could muster the power to maintain their former colonial ascendancy in the postwar world.

In other cases, this decline in imperial strength was

The British armed forces pull out of India. The modern buildings in the background were part of Britain's legacy to its huge colony. The departure of the troops was a product of the determination of former colonies everywhere to guide their own destinies. What evidence of the transforming influence of the West do you see in this picture of the world the Western imperialists left behind them? What other aspects of the colonial legacy might not show in such pictures? (AP/Wide World Photos)

really more a failure of will, or even an outright rejection of the whole imperial mystique. The British Labour party, sweeping into office on a postwar electoral tide, had for years opposed imperialism. The Labourites were only too happy to undertake what the Conservative Winston Churchill had sworn he would never do—preside over the dismantling of the British Empire.

Even as World War II was weakening the colonial powers, it was encouraging their colonies to move against them. Perhaps it was the example of the Japanese, so easily overwhelming British, French, Dutch, and American troops from Hong Kong to the Dutch East Indies, that stirred the colonial peoples. The Japanese yoke did not prove to be any great improvement, but when they left, the Japanese sometimes left weapons behind—with suggestions for using them. When the Europeans reasserted their supremacy with rude force, their nothing-has-changed attitude further estranged their former subjects. This attitude, for example, strengthened the resolve of the Vietnamese to win their independence from France.

World War II also produced a basic new set of power relations in the world—one that was essentially favorable to the independence of overseas colonies. The war had put global supremacy in the hands of the two superpowers. Despite their differences, neither the United States nor the Soviet Union aspired to old-fashioned colonial empires. Both of them, in fact, opposed such colonial holdings on ideological grounds.

Finally, there were new winds of opinion blowing over the world in the decades after World War II. Idealistic statements about freedom in wartime documents such as the Atlantic Charter of 1941 and the United Nations Charter in 1945 were expressions of a libertarian point of view that was generally hostile to the holding of colonial peoples in bondage. There was also a widespread practical conviction that, in the end, almost all colonies would have to have some kind of independence. Europeans might see autonomy as still generations away, but colonial leaders thought in terms of a few years at most. The difference was one of timing and method; the eventual achievement of freedom was inevitable.

Under such circumstances, then, it is not surprising that the great empires began to come apart almost as soon as World War II ended.

PATTERNS OF THE LIBERATION STRUGGLE

The leaders of the various movements for colonial emancipation tended to be both Westernized and charismatic. As Western-educated people, they could deal effectively with their European rulers. The internationally known poet Léopold Senghor of French West Africa and Kwame Nkrumah of the British Gold Coast colony (today's Ghana), educated in France and in Britain and the United States, had no trouble dealing effectively with Westerners. As charismatic figures, flamboyant personalities such as Sukarno of the Dutch East Indies (Indonesia) and saintly ones such as Mahatma Gandhi in India could move their own people to action.

The strength of many colonial revolts also resided in powerful independence parties put together by the new colonial leadership. These intensely nationalistic organizations were strongly centralized in the person of the leader. They helped to overcome regional, religious, tribal, or other differences within the colony, to articulate common demands, and to mobilize mass support for challenges to colonial authority. After independence was achieved, however, these parties tended to become a stronger focus for loyalty than the new nation itself. In some places, they became the core of one-party governments.

In some of the emerging nations, as we shall see, bitter and sometimes long-drawn-out revolutions were fought before independence was achieved. In general, however, a relatively low level of violence—by comparison, say, with the long revolutions of the first half of the century—accompanied the great liberation. This was, in fact, a striking feature of the final disintegration of Europe's huge intercontinental empires.

A New Imperialism?

Violence, however, has not been absent from the Third World in recent decades. And there are those who suggest that imperialism also has not vanished with the collapse of the political empires of the Western Europeans.

Sources of conflict included the persistence of foreign economic exploitation of these former colonies in Africa and Asia even after the Western political presence was withdrawn. Another source of contention was to be found in precolonial claims and quarrels among Third World peoples themselves—old conflicts reemerging after emancipation. Much of the resulting bloodshed was from revolutionary violence within the new nations. But wars were also fought between the new developing nations, sometimes with a violence that matched that of the superpowers.

Throughout the postwar decades, there were great differences in wealth and material well-being between the less economically and technologically developed nations of the Third World and the wealthy industrial powers of North America, Europe, and the East Asian Pacific rim. The underdeveloped countries, many of them in the Southern Hemisphere, were thus immensely dependent on the developed countries of the north for trade, aid, and investment capital. This situation was extremely profitable for the developed nations, but the relationship often distorted the economies of less developed states, which had to produce what the wealthier nations wanted if they were to get the capital they needed for development.

This situation was often described—by its victims—as *neo-imperialism,* a new imperialism based entirely on economic hegemony. Lenin, after all, had defined the essence of earlier imperialism as "the highest stage of capitalism"—economic exploitation with a political and ideological superstructure. Third World radicals, whether they had read Lenin or not, often voiced this view in bitter attacks on foreign investors as exploiters of their countries, and on their own rulers and elites for doing business on a neo-imperialistic basis.

Western multinational corporations, experts from the World Bank or the International Monetary Fund, and others might see development in terms of production statistics, expanding cities, and social and cultural modernization. Third World radicals identified with the peasantry and village culture and urged expenditures for social services rather than for industrialization or expanded exports. When their own ruling classes sided with—and profited from—neo-imperialism, some radicals became revolutionaries. Violent revolts and bloody repressions often followed.

Revolutionaries of this sort might sound like communists to Western leaders, but the springs of their revolts were more often in the genuine differences between North and South than in the ideological disputes between East and West.

Regional and Traditional Sources of Conflict

There were, however, other reasons for war and revolution that had little or nothing to do with neo-imperialism. There were causes rooted deep in the past and vendettas that were still powerful enough to move people to violent action—and sometimes to draw in the great powers too.

China's sense of centrality in East Asia, for example, and the Iranian desire to reassert Persian primacy in the Middle East went back to a time when most European social organization was still based on the village and the clan. Tribal politics was still important in parts of black Africa and could lead to internecine conflict.

Perhaps most important, however, was the power of ancient religions, particularly the drive of a resurgent Islam. As many as a third of the member states of the United Nations could claim some degree of Muslim predominance. The postwar revival of that crusading faith contributed to clashes with other religions and ideologies from North Africa to Southeast Asia. The conflicts between Pakistan and India, the Iranian Revolution, and the long series of Arab-Israeli wars were all manifestations of this reborn spirit of *jihad* (holy war). Communists, Western powers, and Muslims of differing sects have all suffered at the hands of the new Muslim militance. And the lives of growing numbers of Muslims have been transformed by this resurgence of an ancient faith.

THE WINDS OF CHANGE IN AFRICA

GHANA AND ALGERIA: TWO ROADS TO LIBERATION

Africa, the second largest continent, was also the most completely colonized in 1945. Nor were the European imperialists who were established there in any hurry to grant the demands of independence movements in Africa.

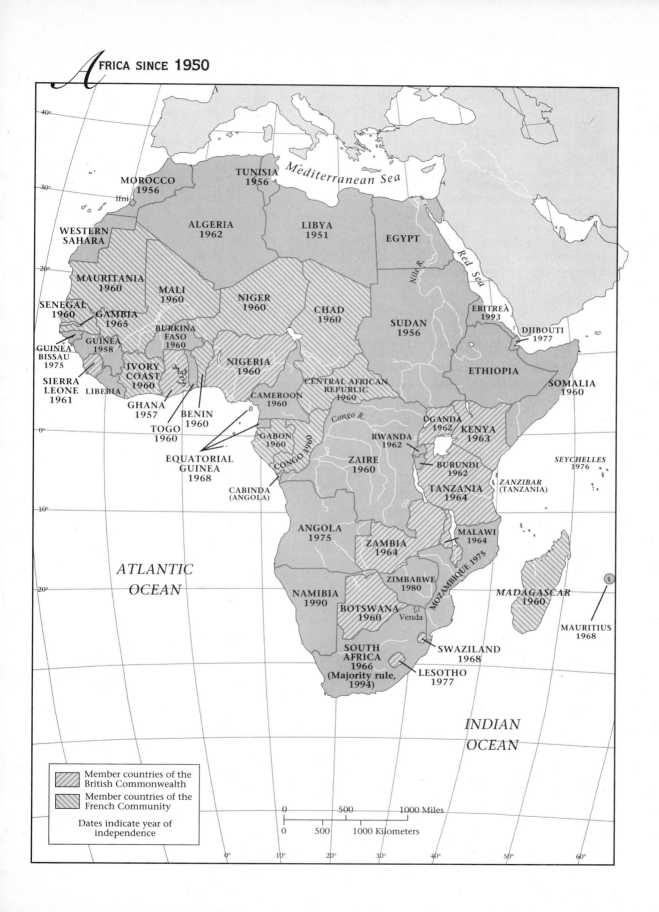

Africa since 1950

MOROCCO 1956
Ifni
TUNISIA 1956
Mediterranean Sea
WESTERN SAHARA
ALGERIA 1962
LIBYA 1951
EGYPT
Red Sea
Nile R.
MAURITANIA 1960
MALI 1960
NIGER 1960
CHAD 1960
SUDAN 1956
ERITREA 1993
DJIBOUTI 1977
SENEGAL 1960
GAMBIA 1965
BURKINA FASO 1960
GUINEA BISSAU 1975
GUINEA 1958
NIGERIA 1960
CENTRAL AFRICAN REPUBLIC 1960
ETHIOPIA
SOMALIA 1960
SIERRA LEONE 1961
LIBERIA
IVORY COAST 1960
GHANA 1957
BENIN 1960
TOGO 1960
CAMEROON 1960
UGANDA 1962
KENYA 1963
EQUATORIAL GUINEA 1968
GABON 1960
CONGO 1960
ZAIRE 1960
RWANDA 1962
BURUNDI 1962
SEYCHELLES 1976
CABINDA (ANGOLA)
Congo R.
TANZANIA 1964
ZANZIBAR (TANZANIA)
ANGOLA 1975
ZAMBIA 1964
MALAWI 1964
MOZAMBIQUE 1975
NAMIBIA 1990
ZIMBABWE 1980
MADAGASCAR 1960
MAURITIUS 1968
BOTSWANA 1960
Venda
SWAZILAND 1968
SOUTH AFRICA 1966 (Majority rule, 1994)
LESOTHO 1977

ATLANTIC OCEAN

INDIAN OCEAN

Member countries of the British Commonwealth
Member countries of the French Community
Dates indicate year of independence

0   500   1000 Miles
0   500   1000 Kilometers

Most African colonies, however, were not much more than half a century old, having been seized during the scramble for Africa in the late 1800s. Vigorous campaigns for independence began to bear fruit in the middle 1950s, with the liberation of Ghana in West Africa. By the end of the 1970s, almost all of Europe's African colonies were free.

Kwame Nkrumah, the leader of the emancipation movement in Britain's Gold Coast colony, was one of a brilliant postwar generation of African leaders that included Léopold Senghor and Sékou Touré in French West Africa, Jomo Kenyatta and Julius Nyerere in British East Africa, and Gamal Abdel Nasser in Egypt. Like them, Nkrumah was part of the new elite of Western-educated Africans, having lived and studied for years in both the United States and Britain.

The Gold Coast colony to which Nkrumah returned late in the 1940s was already agitated by economic tensions and anti-imperialist sentiment. African farmers and workers believed they had not shared fairly in the war-stimulated boom in commodity prices. Strikes in the largest city, Accra, African boycotts of British goods, and criticism of the colonial administration were spreading. Turning his back on the older, more moderate African nationalist organization, Nkrumah set up his own Convention Peoples party (CPP) in 1949.

Nkrumah's CPP demanded drastic change—not administrative reforms in the colonial government but immediate independence—freedom now! Through the militant party newspaper in Accra, vigorous organizing in the villages, and his own charismatic personality, Nkrumah mobilized widespread support for the independence of the Gold Coast. Under this pressure, the British drastically accelerated plans for selfgovernment, filling the colonial cabinet with Africans and holding elections for a parliament. In 1957 Nkrumah's labors were rewarded by independence for the Gold Coast—now renamed Ghana for the ancient West African empire—and by his election as first president of the new nation.

The other major British West African colony, Nigeria, achieved its independence three years later, and Britain's remaining West African colonies received their freedom soon thereafter. The black star on Ghana's national flag, as magazines pointed out at the time, had been the morning star of African independence.

The Africans of the much larger West and North African territories controlled by France gained their freedom in two very different ways. The black African peoples of the Western Sudan and the Guinea Coast won independent statehood much as the British colonies did, through political organization and shrewdly applied political pressure, as did some of the North African Arab populations of French colonies. But in the North African territory of Algeria in particular, France's colonial subjects had to fight for their freedom.

Most of French West and French Equatorial Africa was sun-bleached Sahara or tree-scattered Sudanic pas-tureland in 1945, thinly populated by Arab, Berber, or black-African peoples, almost empty of Europeans. The fertile Mediterranean shores to the north, however, had been supporting complex civilizations since ancient Carthage. Here in the Maghreb—Morocco, Algeria, Tunisia—French *colons* had been settling in large numbers for over a century, ever since the French conquest began in the 1830s. Here in the mid-1950s, within months of the end of their bloody Vietnam conflict, the French became embroiled in a second long and brutal colonial struggle—this one in Algeria.

Algeria was politically integrated into the mother country across the Mediterranean. Many of its million or so French settlers had lived in Algeria for generations. But *colon* economic exploitation and political domination fanned the flames of anti-imperialist resentment among the Arab and Berber majority of Algerians. In 1954 the National Liberation Front (FLN) began a campaign of terrorism and guerrilla struggle to oust the French. The French poured in 500,000 troops and resorted to bombing villages, stripping the countryside, and treating prisoners brutally. A *colon* vigilante force indulged in random violence, outdoing the FLN terrorists at their own game.

By the time the struggle ended in 1962, a million Algerian Arabs had been killed. France itself had been painfully divided. General de Gaulle, called back to power and granted virtually dictatorial powers to end the anarchy at home and the long war in Africa, proved himself more a statesman than a nationalist by acceding at last to Algerian demands for freedom.

Conflict in Kenya

East Africa differed from most of West Africa in that its fertile upland farm country had drawn much larger numbers of European settlers. These British farmers, who had taken over the best agricultural land from native Africans, resisted independence—and black rule—as vigorously as Algerian *colons* did. And for some years after World War II, the British farmers in the Kenya colony especially continued to have their way.

Two strikingly dissimilar factors turned the tide against the settlers around 1960. One was an upsurge of terrorism by the Mau Mau, a secret society that sprang up within the dominant Kikuyu people of Kenya. The other was one man—Jomo Kenyatta, a Kikuyu with a London Ph.D., who became the leader of his people in their struggle.

Kenyatta's Kenya African National Union (KANU) party pushed vigorously for independence. The Mau Mau depredations, considerably exaggerated in the press, nevertheless led to many thousands of arrests, which further increased African resentment. Kenyatta had no connection with the superstitious Mau Mau, though he was imprisoned for refusing to disown them. Between them, however, these two quite different manifestations of Kikuyu

Jomo Kenyatta, leader of the Kenya independence movement and its first president, was a tall, regal-looking, London-educated Kikuyu. Like other leaders of African liberation struggles, Kenyatta combined Western training with charismatic popular appeal. (The Bettmann Archive)

power did convince the British to move more rapidly toward freedom for Kenya. In 1963 Kenya became an independent nation, the tall, impressive Jomo Kenyatta its first president.

Other British East African colonies also achieved their liberty in the 1960s. In many ways the most notable of these was Kenya's neighbor to the south, Tanganyika, which became the country of Tanzania under the young African Catholic socialist, Julius Nyerere. Outside of Kenya, however, *uhuru* came without violence. Agitation and organization by leaders such as Nyerere and Kenyatta prodded the colonial administration, and freedom came more rapidly on this side of Africa too.

CONGO CRISIS

The worst explosion of violence set off by independence movements in Africa south of the Sahara came in the immense central African colony of the Belgian Congo—the future country of Zaire.

The Congo was totally unprepared for freedom when it came with startling suddenness in 1960. The Belgians had lavished much time and money on developing the hugely profitable copper mines of the Congo's Katanga Province. But they had done almost nothing at all to educate an African elite, train African civil servants, or otherwise prepare residents of almost a million square miles of rain forest and bush villages for life in the modern world. Then, at the first exploratory outburst of anti-imperialist feeling in the Congo, the Belgian government

turned its back on the whole imperial venture. Fearful of becoming mired in the sort of colonial warfare that had entangled the French, the Belgians announced the independence of the Congo colony and left the arena to the Africans.

An arena it was through the early 1960s, as Congolese and foreign elements battled for supremacy. The main contenders were Patrice Lumumba, a radical with a broad vision of national unity—and Communist connections; Moise Tshombe, suave ruler of Katanga Province—with close ties to Belgian mining interests; and General (then Colonel) Joseph Mobutu, the military strongman who came out on top in the end. Outside forces involved in the escalating Congolese chaos included the Belgians, who sent troops in to protect their nationals; the United Nations, which authorized several African members to send in armed forces to hold the country together; and various colorful and brutal white mercenary troops, who fought for the highest bidder.

The Congo crisis of 1960 revolved around Tshombe's attempt, supported by the Belgian mining combine, to detach the mineral-rich province of Katanga from the new country. To keep from losing this key source of national wealth, Lumumba, the nation's newly elected prime minister, called for help, first from the United Nations, then from the Soviet Union. At this point, however, a coup led by Colonel Mobutu overthrew Lumumba—and then turned him over to his archenemy Tshombe. Meanwhile, intertribal violence flared in many parts of the country as village people settled ancient rivalries with modern weapons.

In the end Lumumba was murdered, probably by Katanga secessionists. Tshombe was overthrown in his turn, and the Katanga secession was ended by U.N. troops. General Mobutu emerged as the strongest of the strongmen and ruler of the new country, which he renamed Zaire.

THE LONG STRUGGLE IN SOUTH AFRICA

"The wind of change," British Prime Minister Harold Macmillan admitted during an African tour in 1960, "is blowing through this continent. . . ."[1] Those winds blew less briskly in southern Africa, however, than in any other part of the continent—indeed, than in almost any other part of the colonial world.

The liberation of the two Portuguese colonies of Angola and Mozambique was linked to the politics of their Portuguese masters. During the postwar years, Portugal was governed by the autocratic Salazar regime, a holdover from the 1930s which offered no concessions, either to liberalism at home or to anti-imperialism in the colonies. It was only in 1974, when Salazar's equally autocratic suc-

---

[1]Speech of February 3, 1960, in *Vital Speeches of the Day* (March 11, 1960).

cessor was overthrown in Portugal, that Angola and Mozambique were granted their independence as well.

The two Rhodesias—named for the celebrated nine-teenth-century British South African imperialist Cecil Rhodes—reached independence almost a decade and a half apart. Northern Rhodesia won independence as Zambia, ruled by its black African majority under mild-mannered Kenneth Kaunda, as early as the mid-1960s. Southern Rhodesia, with its copper mines and determined English settler community, clung to minority white rule until the end of the seventies. It took an international boycott and a long struggle by two separate guerrilla groups—Robert Mugabe's Zimbabwe African People's Union and Joshua Nkomo's Zimbabwe African National Union—to win majority African rule in the new state of Zimbabwe in 1979.

But no amount of international pressure, guerrilla assault, or domestic resistance seemed to shake the grip of European settlers in the Republic of South Africa. There the winds were blowing all the other way during the post-war decades, for this was the period that saw the imposition of the system of *apartheid* on South Africa.

The colonial and precolonial history of South Africa is a complex story of peoples, rights, and freedoms in conflict. Occupied by only a thin scattering of bushmanoid hunters and pastoralists and Bantu-speaking farmers in 1500, the southern tip of Africa has since been overrun by successive waves of Zulu, Dutch, and British settlers, with admixtures of Southeast Asian slaves, Indian contract workers, and others.

Though British colonists have dominated the state economically in this century, the Dutch-descended Afrikaners have held political power. However, a great many more indigenous Africans live in South Africa than European-descended people of any description. The economic and political position of the black Africans, bushmanoid peoples, Indians, and other "colored" peoples had always been drastically inferior to that of the Europeans. But at the end of World War II the ruling Afrikaner Nationalist party set out to codify that inferiority in a system of discriminatory racial legislation reminiscent of the old Jim Crow laws in the American South.

Apartheid means "apartness," and the physical separation of the ethnic communities was clearly one purpose of the apartheid laws passed in the years around 1950. Europeans, black Africans, Asians, and others were to live in separate areas, be educated in separate schools, work at different jobs, find recreation in separate places. Marriages between Europeans and others were made illegal. Black Africans had to carry passes in white areas.

But it was, of course, more than a matter of separation. Black Africans were confined to the least productive lands, the least pleasant living places; the best jobs were closed to them; they could not be elected to parliament. Apartheid meant separate and *un*equal, and all Africa knew it.

For decades after the imposition of apartheid, then,

South Africa was caught up in a tragic, brutal confrontation, a struggle of guerrillas and counter-insurgency, of border raids and military incursions. South Africa was pitted against a handful of states on its borders—from Tanzania in the east to Angola in the west—all poor, many politically authoritarian. Facing a black continent that was ideologically united against the racist regime in Pretoria, South Africa nevertheless generally won.

South Africa's developed economy lured poverty-stricken neighboring black states such as Botswana and Mozambique into signing treaties with the South African government. The South African military knifed repeatedly into the territories of more belligerent antagonists such as Angola, shooting up guerrilla camps in spite of Angola's Cuban garrisons. Foreign trade and investment from Western nations such as the United States helped keep South Africa rich and powerful—and provided jobs in industry for many black laborers, as Pretoria never tired of pointing out.

In the end, it was not possible for an apartheid regime to survive forever in a black continent. And as the twentieth century moved into its final decade, as we shall see, liberation came to the southern tip of Africa as well.

Asia in Arms

Israel and the Arab World

One of the most complex colonial situations was in the Middle East. There anti-imperialist feeling and growing pan-Arab nationalism had led the British to give up control of Egypt and Iraq during the 1930s, though Britain retained control of the crucial Suez Canal. During World War II, Arab princes in the region established the Arab League, which, with British support, compelled the French to liberate Syria and Lebanon in the mid-1940s. In the 1950s, however, a nationalist revolt in Egypt overthrew the pro-British king of that country, and in 1956 the new Egyptian military ruler, Gamal Abdel Nasser, nationalized the Suez Canal.

The most explosive colonial problem in the Middle East, however, had to do with the British mandate of Palestine and the emergence of the modern state of Israel. This strip of Arab land along the eastern end of the Mediterranean Sea, the site of the ancient Hebrew kingdom of David and Solomon, had been the focus of the Jewish nationalist movement called Zionism since the nineteenth century. Encouraged by a British statement of support during World War I, Jews had begun to emigrate from Europe to Palestine in the 1930s. After World War II, survivors of the Nazi Holocaust poured into the British mandate, determined to establish a homeland.

The Palestinian Arab population, strongly supported

by the Arab League, resisted these incursions. As violence spread across Palestine, the British attempted to work out a compromise, and the new United Nations voted for a partition of the area between Arabs and Jews. In the spring of 1948, however, Jewish leaders in Palestine, citing the U.N. resolution and depending on strong American support, announced the formation of the new state of Israel. The surrounding nations of the Arab League at once declared war, determined to expel the Jewish immigrants and reclaim all Palestine for its Arab inhabitants.

The 1948 Arab–Israeli War, the first of a series, looked to be stacked in favor of the Arab countries. But the Arab princes competed among themselves and were not as familiar with modern weaponry as the Jewish immigrants from Europe and America were. The Israelis, fighting for their existence as a state, unified and determined, not only defended themselves but expanded beyond the U.N. partition line, creating an even larger Jewish nation for the Arabs to deal with.

For the surrounding Arab countries, Israel has been a bitter problem ever since. This problem has been considerably exacerbated by the large number of Palestinian refugees—a million in 1948—who were not absorbed by the neighboring Arab countries and continued to demand the return of Palestine.

The new nation of Israel thus fought no less than five wars with the Muslim states surrounding it during the thirty-five years between 1948 and 1982. Militarily speaking, the earlier of these Arab–Israeli encounters were clear Israeli victories. More recent conflicts, however, proved costly and led to few detectable gains.

The 1948 war with which Israel's history began left the new nation larger than even its founders had expected. The 1956 war, fought by a secret alliance of Israel, Britain, and France against Nasser's Egypt over the Suez Canal, saw more Israeli military successes, though heavy international pressure forced the alliance to evacuate their conquests. The 1967 "Six Day War" was Israel's most smashing success, leading to the conquest of the Sinai from Egypt, the Golan Heights from Syria, and the West Bank from Jordan.

After the 1967 war, however, the leading role in the struggle against Israel was taken over by Palestinian refugee guerrilla organizations. Under the leadership of the Palestine Liberation Organization (PLO), the Palestinians stepped up border raids and terrorist attacks inside Israel. Israeli counterterrorist activities and harsh treatment of Arabs living within Israel's borders cost Israel some international support from this time on.

Later Israeli wars were less successful. The 1973 "Yom Kippur War," so-called because the Arabs attacked Israel on that Jewish holiday, led to Egyptian reconquest of part of the Sinai. Thereafter, peace initiatives by Egypt's new leader, Anwar Sadat, coupled with mediation by U.S. President Jimmy Carter, resulted in a peace treaty and the return of still more conquered territory.

Israel's invasion of Lebanon in 1982, finally, did result in defeats for both Syria and the PLO. But Israel's effort to establish a strong client regime in Beirut failed, and the Israelis eventually withdrew from Lebanon with little but a puppet Christian army in southern Lebanon to show for this latest war with its Arab neighbors.

STRUGGLE FOR POWER IN THE MIDDLE EAST

Despite postwar Pan-Arab sentiment favoring Arab unity, the Muslim rulers of the Middle East proved to be among the more contentious of the world's leaders. Domestic discord further aggravated the tensions and sporadic violence that made the region one of the world's hot spots.

Two centers of conflict in the 1980s were Iran, power center for the militant Shiite sect, and Iraq under Saddam Hussein.

Iran had been divided into British and Russian zones of influence as late as World War II. Russia had attempted after the war to reach out for paramount influence through a strong local Communist party and the presence of the Red Army in the north. The main result of this effort, however, was to drive the shah of Iran firmly into the arms of the West. A strongly nationalist premier named Muhammad Mossadegh attempted to seize control of the nation's Western-run oil industry but was overthrown by a coup engineered by the American CIA.

For the next quarter of a century Iran was an American ally, ruled by a modernizing shah who spent his oil money to build up his country to something of its ancient preeminence in the Middle East. He left to his notorious secret police the suppression of both radical opposition and resurgent Islam. In 1979 it was the Muslim *mullahs* who pulled him down, mobilizing huge crowds of militant demonstrators to demand the shah's overthrow and to welcome an exiled spiritual leader, the Ayatollah Ruhollah Khomeini, in his place.

Militant Shiite followers of the Ayatollah, like the *Kizilbashi* supporters of Shah Ismail in the sixteenth century, were soon running the nation and shaking up the Middle East. Following Khomeini's dictum that "the legislative power in Islam is limited to God alone," the *mullah* leaders purged both American sympathizers and Russian-leaning Marxists.[2] The Ayatollah's supporters embarked upon a national effort to build an "Islamic republic," a theocracy operating according to the religious and social principles of the Koran and Islamic Law. Women appearing in public were veiled once more, and religious minorities and leftist students alike suffered brutal persecution under the new regime.

In 1980 the new government came into conflict with

[2]Ruhollah Khomeini, *Islamic Government,* in Nikki R. Keddie, *Roots of Revolution: An Interpretive History of Modern Iran* (New Haven: Yale University Press, 1981), p. 207.

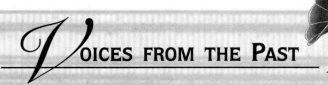

VOICES FROM THE PAST

"India was in my blood and there was much in her that instinctively thrilled me. And yet I approached her almost as an alien critic, full of dislike for the present as well as for many of the relics of the past that I saw. To some extent I came to her via the West and looked at her as a friendly Westerner might have done. I was eager and anxious to change her outlook and appearance and give her the garb of modernity. And yet doubts rose within me. Did I know India, I who presumed to scrap much of her past heritage? . . .

I stood on a mound of Mohenjo-daro in the Indus Valley in the northwest of India, and all around me lay the houses and streets of this ancient city that is said to have existed over five thousand years ago; and even then it was an old and well-developed civilization. "The Indus civilization," writes Professor Childe, "represents a very perfect adjustment of human life to a specific environment that has endured and forms the basis of modern Indian culture."

I read her history and read also a part of her abundant ancient literature and was powerfully impressed by the vigor of the thought, the clarity of the language and the richness of the mind that lay behind it. The mighty rivers of India attracted me . . . and the Ganga, above all the river of India, which has held India's heart captive and drawn uncounted millions to her banks since the dawn of history. The story of the Ganga . . . is the story of India's civilization and culture, of the rise and fall of empires, of great and proud cities, of the adventure of man and the quest of the mind which has so occupied India's thinkers. . . .

These journeys and visits of mine, with the background of my reading, gave me an insight into the past. And gradually . . . a sense of reality began to creep into my mental picture of India and the land of my forefathers became peopled with living beings, who laughed and wept; loved and suffered; and . . . built a structure which gave India a cultural stability which lasted for thousands of years."

Jawaharlal Nehru, the author of this account of his quest for the soul of India, was a Western-educated intellectual who became a leading anti-British agitator and first president of an independent India. Note how Nehru's study of India's past inspired his national feeling in the present.

What evidence of the Indian leader's involvement in Western culture do you see? What aspects of his own country's past does he remember with pride? How does Nehru's view of his people's culture compare with your own view of American history, national character, and achievements? Can you see value to citizens of both countries in these patriotic self-images? Can you see dangers?

Jawaharlal Nehru, The Discovery of India (New York: John Day, 1946), pp. 38–40.

the United States when a group of Muslim student militants seized the American embassy and held it—and its personnel—for more than a year of increasing tension.

The Ayatollah's militance disturbed a number of Arab powers almost as much as it did the United States. Khomeini, like Persian Shiites of earlier centuries, talked extravagantly of unleashing a *jihad*, or holy war, against the "corrupt" Sunni states around him. The particularly pious Sunni state of Saudi Arabia, keeper of the holy places at Mecca and Medina, was much disturbed.

But it was Iran's neighbor Iraq that responded with force to the Ayatollah's challenge. This Muslim nation, which also used the Persian Gulf to export large quantities of oil, was run by the Ba'athist Party—dedicated to pan-Arab nationalism and to "Arab socialism," heavily dependent on an alliance with the Soviet Union, and ruled by the brutal and aggressive Saddam Hussein. Saddam, apparently seeking to take advantage of disarray in Iran resulting from Khomeini's Islamic revolution, determined to settle outstanding disputes, including a conflict over the Shatt-al-Arab waterway, by military force. Iraq's strike into Iran late in 1980 at first promised a quick success, thanks to superior equipment and military leadership. But the Iraqi invasion bogged down in a human sea of Iranian fanatics willing to die for the Ayatollah's *jihad*. The war dragged on for years, shifting back to Iraqi territory and escalating to involve attacks by both sides on shipping in the Gulf—a threat to the world's oil supply that gave Western powers a special stake in the conflict. Then, in 1988, Khomeini decreed an end to the slaughter and soon thereafter he died. The more moderate regime of Ali Akbar Rafsanjani, which succeeded the Ayatollah, seemed willing and even eager to come to terms with the West.

INDIA VERSUS PAKISTAN

Conflict along religious lines also haunted the subcontinent of India during and after its liberation from British rule. After independence, differences between Hindus and Muslims led to a long series of disputes between the new nations of India and Pakistan.

The Indian Congress party, led by Mahatma Gandhi and Jawaharlal Nehru, had spearheaded the struggle for Indian independence during the interwar years. Gandhi and the Congress party, however, were Hindus, spokesmen primarily for India's 350 million practitioners of that faith. But there were 100 million Muslims in India too. The chief spokesman for this huge minority was Muhammad Ali Jinnah, head of the colony's Muslim League.

When the newly elected British Labour government began to negotiate the final liberation of the subcontinent in the 1940s, bitterness between Hindus and Muslims was wildly inflamed. Rioting flared, civil war threatened, and in the end the huge colony was partitioned. Two nations, Hindu India and Muslim Pakistan, thus came into existence in 1947.

Freedom, however, only exacerbated the rioting between the two religious communities. Some 15 million Hindu and Muslim refugees abandoned their villages and headed for the new frontiers. More than half a million died violently or by starvation and exposure on the road. Gandhi himself was assassinated by a Hindu extremist who hated the Mahatma for his efforts to curb violence between Muslims and Hindus.

During the following decades, three wars were fought between India and Pakistan. Two were over the lovely, high-mountain northwestern Indian province of

Pandit Nehru, leader of India's Congress party, speaks before a women's organization in Bombay. His wife, Kamala (seated), shares the platform as she shared his struggle, including arrest and imprisonment in the cause. Nehru, an aristocrat and a man of great personal charm, was an effective speaker and negotiator at all levels, and with British as well as with Indian people. (Library of Congress)

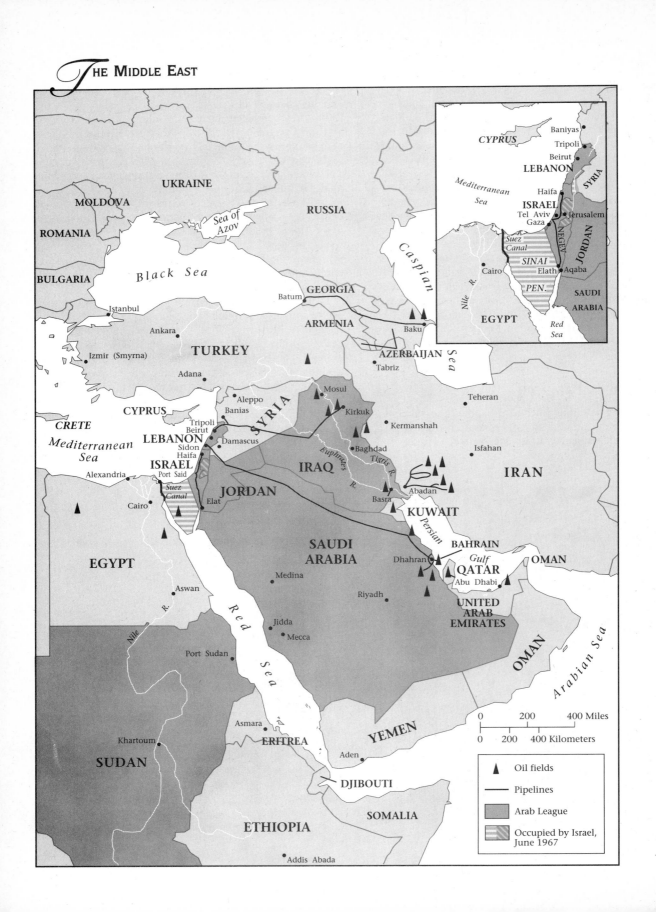

THE MIDDLE EAST

UKRAINE

MOLDOVA

ROMANIA

BULGARIA

Black Sea

Istanbul

Ankara

Izmir (Smyrna)

TURKEY

Adana

Aleppo

Banias

Sea of Azov

RUSSIA

GEORGIA

Batum

ARMENIA

AZERBAIJAN

Tabriz

Caspian Sea

Baku

Teheran

Mosul

Kirkuk

Kermanshah

SYRIA

Tripoli

Beirut

Damascus

Euphrates R.

Baghdad

Tigris R.

Isfahan

IRAN

CRETE

CYPRUS

LEBANON

Sidon

Haifa

ISRAEL

Port Said

Mediterranean Sea

Alexandria

Suez Canal

Elat

JORDAN

IRAQ

Basra

Abadan

KUWAIT

Persian Gulf

BAHRAIN

Dhahran

QATAR

Abu Dhabi

OMAN

Cairo

SAUDI
ARABIA

Medina

Riyadh

EGYPT

Aswan

Nile R.

Jidda

Mecca

UNITED
ARAB
EMIRATES

OMAN

Red Sea

Port Sudan

Arabian Sea

Asmara

ERITREA

YEMEN

Khartoum

SUDAN

Aden

DJIBOUTI

ETHIOPIA

SOMALIA

Addis Abada

Inset map

CYPRUS

Baniyas

Tripoli

Beirut

LEBANON

Mediterranean Sea

Haifa

ISRAEL

SYRIA

Tel Aviv

Gaza

Jerusalem

NEGEV

JORDAN

Suez Canal

Cairo

SINAI
PEN.

Elath

Aqaba

SAUDI
ARABIA

EGYPT

Nile R.

Red Sea

Legend

▲	Oil fields
—	Pipelines
	Arab League
	Occupied by Israel, June 1967

0   200   400 Miles

0   200   400 Kilometers

Kashmir, whose population has a Muslim majority. Despite these wars of 1947–1948 and 1965–1966, the area remains disputed and torn by guerrilla violence.

A third clash, in 1971, was over the isolated northeastern territory of East Pakistan. This portion of divided Pakistan, almost entirely surrounded by Bengal India, felt exploited and oppressed by the central government in West Pakistan. East Pakistan finally rebelled and, with Indian help, founded the independent state of Bangladesh. During the prewar repression and the conflict itself, casualties mounted over the million mark, and 10 million refugees fled into India.

WAR IN SOUTHEAST ASIA

Religion counted for less, politics for more in the struggles for independence—and after independence—in East and Southeast Asia. Ceylon achieved independence in 1948 with minimal difficulties and changed its name to Sri Lanka in 1972. Burma, however, freed the same year, was at once faced by revolts led by two distinct groups of Communist guerrillas and by various ethnic minorities, struggles that would drag on for years. In 1990, after a military coup, Burma also changed its name—to Myanmar.

The Malay Peninsula faced both Communist-led revolts and ethnic rivalries so serious that independence there was postponed for a decade. British troops stayed on until the Communist guerrillas were defeated. Ethnic and cultural differences between the Malay peoples of the peninsula and the overseas Chinese majority in the great commercial center of Singapore proved harder to deal with. In the early 1960s, the colonial union between the two areas was therefore dissolved, and once more there were two nations where one colony had been: the country of Malaysia (most of the Malay Peninsula plus portions of island Southeast Asia) and the immensely prosperous little city-state of Singapore.

By far the bloodiest struggle for independence in Asia—and the most violent aftermath—was that in French Indochina. This conflict between French armies numbering up to half a million and Vietnamese guerrilla forces under Ho Chi Minh dragged on from 1945 until 1954, producing large casualties for the Vietnamese—and defeat for the French.

Ho Chi Minh, the revolutionary leader, was a Vietnamese nationalist, a Communist, and a militant anti-imperialist. In 1945 Ho had declared the independence of Vietnam as soon as the Japanese left. The French, however, had no intention of surrendering their colonies, and French colonial authorities broke up Ho's provisional government, reestablished the old order, and prepared to suppress any terrorist activities that might result.

Ho and his right-hand man, General Giap, led a determined guerrilla struggle for most of the next decade. Like Mao Zedong's troops in China during the interwar years, Ho Chi Minh's soldiers were farmers by day, fighters by night. The paddies, the jungles, and the mountains were Ho's real country, the cities the centers of French control. In 1954 the French finally tried to break the stalemate by luring Ho's guerrillas out into the open with a prize too rich to ignore: the powerful, isolated French fortress of Dien Bien Phu. The guerrillas took the bait, but they came with prudence, skill, and artillery. They surrounded Dien Bien Phu and crushed it.

That same year, at a peace conference in Geneva, the French let Indochina go. Ho Chi Minh, however, was deprived of the full spoils of victory. He got only North Vietnam. South Vietnam, Cambodia, and Laos—the other subdivisions of French Indochina—were freed under their own governments, and the Saigon regime remained a center of Western influence. The seeds of future struggle—including America's Vietnam War—were thus sown by the peace settlement that got the French out of Southeast Asia at last.

CHINA AND ITS ANCIENT SPHERE

In the struggle for predominance in East Asia, China had to face—and accept—the challenge of one spectacular rival. As the dust of World War II and the Chinese civil war settled, Japan, the third most productive nation in the world after the two superpowers, was the dynamo of the Far East. But Japan's imperialistic ambitions seemed to have expired with the samurai spirit in the smoke of the war.

The People's Republic of China, by contrast, concerned itself from the moment of Mao Zedong's victory with reestablishing the Middle Kingdom's ancient frontiers and old influence, at least insofar as circumstances allowed. Most of China's energies also went into domestic affairs: the staggering task of bringing something resembling a modern quality of life to one quarter of the world's population. But Mao and his successors also found time to remind their neighbors that the old imperial giant was still there.

In 1950, the year after winning control of China, Mao sent the Chinese Red Army to occupy the high, thinly populated plateau of Tibet, which had been dominated by China in earlier centuries. Manchuria, Inner Mongolia, and other large areas were also firmly incorporated into the new China. In 1962 China fought a brief border war with India to readjust some mutual frontiers in the Himalayas; similar disputes were settled peacefully with Burma, Nepal, and Pakistan.

A major continuing territorial dispute was with China's former Communist ally, the Soviet Union, over the region along the Amur River border northeast of Beijing. A crucial sticking point in China's relations with the United States was America's support for the Chinese Nationalist regime on Taiwan, an ancient part of China that in Chinese thinking had to be reabsorbed sooner or later into the Middle Kingdom. And in 1984 Britain negotiated the return of its colony of Hong Kong, the rich gateway to South China, to Chinese sovereignty by 1997.

Much of China's foreign policy, in short, had nothing to do with ideology, but simply to do with reestablishing the Chinese imperial position in the Far East. China's involvement with Korea and Vietnam, two peoples who had in earlier centuries been the Middle Kingdom's most successful satellite cultures outside of Japan, illustrated this basic Chinese concern.

In both these countries, as we have seen, China supported northern Communist regimes in wars against large American armies defending governments established in the south of the two peninsulas. But in both cases China's concern was modified by the fact that both North Vietnam and North Korea were much closer to the Soviet Union than to their former overlords in Beijing. Only in this complex context of past Chinese preeminence and present Russo-Chinese rivalry can China's ambiguous role in the Korean and Vietnamese conflicts be understood.

China had no part in North Korea's invasion of South Korea, and the Chinese did not intervene in the struggle until American troops pushed close to China's own frontier along the Yalu River. Then, probably preferring a small Korean neighbor to an outpost of American power, Beijing entered the war and pushed the Americans back as far as the former frontier with South Korea before a truce was signed.

During America's long struggle on the Indochinese peninsula, China did supply North Vietnam with some aid. But Ho Chi Minh depended primarily on the Soviet Union for war materiel, and Chinese support was apparently always lukewarm.

Then, in the mid-1970s, while South Vietnam fell to the North Vietnamese, Cambodia and Laos were also overrun by their own Communist-led guerrillas. In 1977 Cambodia (renamed Kampuchea and ruled by the brutal Khmer Rouge regime) tumbled into a new civil war—and was then overrun by North Vietnamese troops. Laos also quickly came within Hanoi's orbit.

In 1978, then, the People's Republic of China seized upon the mistreatment of overseas Chinese in Vietnam as a cause for conflict and sent a "punitive" expedition across Vietnam's northern border. The ancient rivalry between the two thus flamed into the open once again. The brief incursion also demonstrated that China could attack a Soviet client state in Asia with impunity. The short Chinese incursion into Vietnam thus served as one more reminder of China's historic primacy in East Asia.

SUMMARY

The decades after World War II saw the collapse of the vast intercontinental empires constructed by Europeans over the preceding five centuries.

The causes of this collapse included the resentment against foreign domination and economic exploitation that had been building for generations in the colonies. These feelings were strengthened by the encouraging spectacle of Japanese victories over Westerners, by European weakness of will and resources after the war, and by the fact that both the United States and the Soviet Union opposed old-fashioned territorial imperialism.

The great liberation that followed the war was violent in some places, as in Vietnam and Algeria; it was relatively peaceful elsewhere, as in most British colonies. A third of the world's population thus gained political independence. Asia and Africa thereafter joined Latin America in the vast bloc of politically free but economically underdeveloped countries known as the Third World.

The freedom struggles of the new nations were followed by other conflicts on the two largest continents. Some of these conflicts were traceable to the economic dependency of poor nations on rich ones. Others went back to precolonial political or religious rivalries that reasserted themselves after the passing of the colonial era.

In the Middle East, Israel fought a long series of wars with its Arab neighbors. Muslim militance and the rivalry of Middle Eastern rulers led to a number of armed clashes. In Asia, Hindu India and Muslim Pakistan fought repeatedly. And in East Asia, China reasserted its primacy by limited interventions in Korea and Vietnam, as well as by the occupation of Tibet and continuing disputes with the Soviet Union over their mutual frontier.

SUGGESTED READING

ALI, A. A., and G. N. S. RAGHAVAN. *The Resurgence of Indian Women.* New Delhi: Radiant Publishers, 1991. Indian Women in the liberation struggle and the new India.

BETTS, R. F. *Uncertain Dimensions: Western Overseas Empires in the Twentieth Century.* Minneapolis: University of Minnesota Press, 1985. The Western empires on the eve of dissolution.

BURKE, S. M. *Mainsprings of Indian and Pakistani Foreign Policies.* Minneapolis: University of Minnesota Press, 1974. Authoritative. See also his *Pakistan's Foreign Policy: An Historical Analysis* (London: Oxford University Press, 1973).

CROSS, C. *The Fall of the British Empire, 1918–1968.* London: Hodder and Stoughton, 1968. Sweeping overview of the decline of the largest of the overseas empires.

DARBY, P. *Three Faces of Imperialism: British and American Approaches to Asia and Africa, 1870–1970.* New Haven: Yale University Press, 1987. Contrasts Anglo-Saxon approaches to the underdeveloped world.

DUPUY, T. N. *Elusive Victory: The Arab-Israeli Wars, 1947–1974.* New York: Harper & Row, Pub., 1978. Comprehensive, detailed survey, excluding only the Lebanon incursion of the early 1980s.

EMERSON, R. *From Empire to Nation: The Rise of Self-Assertion of Asian and African Peoples.* Cambridge: Cambridge University Press, 1960. Excellent overview of the great liberation from the colonial perspective.

FEUER, L. *Imperialism and the Anti-Imperialist Mind.* Buffalo, N.Y.: Prometheus, 1986. Sweeping essay, urging that Western feelings of guilt over imperial exploitation contributed significantly to the collapse of the Western empires.

FIELDS, K. *Revival and Rebellion in Colonial Africa.* Princeton: Princeton University Press, 1985. African resistance to the Western-imposed social order. See also M. Crowder, ed., *The Cambridge History of Africa,* Vol. 8, *From 1940 to 1975* (New York: Cambridge University Press, 1984), which chronicles the high hopes of the liberation movements and their sometimes disillusioning aftermaths.

GILIOMEE, H., and R. ELPHICK, eds. *The Shaping of South African Society.* Capetown: Longmans, 1979. Essays on the complexities of South Africa's situation. On two crucial elements in the problem, see J. Suckling, et al., *The Economic Factor of External Investment in South Africa* (London: Africa Publications Trust, 1975).

HOWE, S. *Anticolonialism in British Politics: The Left and the End of Empire, 1918–1964.* Oxford: Clarendon Press, 1993. The contribution of European opposition to the collapse of the empire.

HUNTINGTON, S. P. *Political Order in Changing Societies,* New Haven: Yale University Press, 1969. Broad analysis.

KAHIN, G. M., ed. *Governments and Politics of Southeast Asia.* Ithaca: Cornell University Press, 1964. Triumphs and troubles of the great liberation in this corner of Asia.

KEDDIE, N. R. *Religion and Politics in Iran: Sh'ism from Quietism to Revolution.* New Haven: Yale University Press, 1983. Religious background to the overthrow of the shah and the resulting tumult in the Middle East. See also his *Roots of Revolution: An Interpretive History of Modern Iran* (New Haven: Yale University Press, 1981).

KUMAR, R. *The History of Doing.* London: Verso, 1993. Illustrated history of Indian women's movements during the nineteenth and twentieth centuries.

LEGUM, C., et al. *Africa in the 1980s: A Continent in Crisis.* New York: McGraw-Hill, 1979. Outlines international relations and economic dependency.

LENCZOWSKI, G., ed. *The Political Awakening in the Middle East.* Englewood Cliffs, N.J.: Prentice-Hall, 1970. Nationalism and anti-imperialism in the ancient Muslim center of the Old World. For the life of an outstanding liberation leader in the region, see J. Lacoutre, *Nasser* (New York: Knopf, 1973).

MENON, V. P. *The Transfer of Power in India.* Princeton: Princeton University Press, 1957. A scholarly account. See also R. Suntharalingham, *Indian Nationalism: An Historical Analysis* (New Delhi: Vikas, 1983), a synthesis of scholarship on the complex political, social, and economic causes of the emergence of national feeling in India under British rule, and J. M. Brown, *Modern India: The Origins of an Asian Democracy* (New York: Oxford University Press, 1985), which offers a penetrating study of India's evolution toward democracy under British rule.

QUANDT, W. B., F. JABBER, and A. M. LESCH. *The Politics of Palestinian Nationalism.* Berkeley: University of California, 1975. On this vexing question of a homeland for the Palestinian refugees, see also views strongly critical of Israel, including E. W. Said, *The Question of Palestine* (New York: Random House, 1980).

TINKER, H. *Men Who Overturned Empires: Fighters, Dreamers, and Schemers.* Madison: University of Wisconsin Press, 1987. Profiles of leaders of the national liberation struggles, including Nehru, Jomo Kenyatta, and Ho Chi Minh.

WALLERSTEIN, I. *Africa: The Politics of Independence.* New York: Random House, 1963. Good on the liberation of Africa. See also A. A. Mazrui, *Protest and Power in Black Africa* (London: Oxford University Press, 1972), and V. LeVine, *Political Leadership in Africa* (Stanford: Hoover Institution, 1967), on the post-emancipation elites.

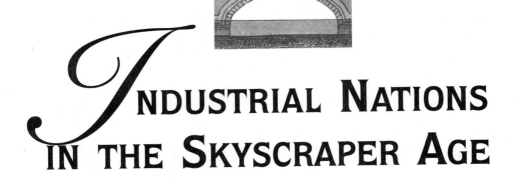

CHAPTER 46

INDUSTRIAL NATIONS IN THE SKYSCRAPER AGE

STRATEGIES OF PROGRESS: THE USA IN THE AMERICAN EPOCH

POWER STRUCTURES, EAST AND WEST

There were two sorts of political power structure in the North during the decades after World War II. There were important similarities between them, as social scientists often pointed out. But the differences were real too—and important enough to have generated the Cold War itself.

The most striking similarity was that governments on both sides of the Iron Curtain were performing a great many more services for the governed than governments ever had before. Even in the free-enterprise West, public education, health care, housing, paved roads, streetlights, water and sewers, public transportation, police and fire protection, mail delivery, and a thousand more amenities of modern life were generally provided by national, state or provincial, and local governments. In the state-socialist countries of the East bloc, nationalized economies and central planning meant that all the office staffs of Western private business were government employees too—making big government even bigger.

Capitalist and communist thus had a basic pyramid of bureaucratic power in common. The significant political difference between them, however, lay in the degree to which the citizens were free of and could regulate the behavior of that power structure.

Western democratic governments came in several varieties. There were multiparty systems, common in Western Europe, in which coalitions of parties governed. There were also two-party versions, especially in English-speaking countries, in which two major parties competed for office.

Looked at another way, there were parliamentary and presidential systems. In the parliamentary pattern, modeled on the British House of Commons, executive and legislative power were merged, the prime minister and his or her cabinet representing the majority party—or coalition of parties—in the elected legislature. A presidential system, such as the varied versions to be found in the United States and France, put much more authority in the hands of a chief executive, who was elected separately and who could be of a different political party from the majority in the legislature.

All Western democracies, however, had two things in common: elected rulers and civil liberties. Periodic elections required political leadership to account to the people for its stewardship. Civil rights limited political repression and prescribed the basic freedom to complain about the way things were going and to organize political opposition to change them. In combination, the freedom to speak one's mind and the requirement that politicians stand for periodic reelection gave the governed at least some control over their governments.

One-party states, especially those infused with a strong ideological component, put power in the hands of a single, usually autocratically run party. With the destruction of most of the fascist states in World War II, almost all the surviving one-party states of the North were Communist—the Soviet Union and its East European allies.

In Communist countries, dispute over public policy was confined to party members, especially to those in the upper echelons. Elections were held, but since the ballot contained only the names of party-approved candidates, there was little genuine choice and very little public check on the policies and politics of rulers.

These politically authoritarian systems were strengthened by the lack of most of the civil liberties valued in the West. Freedom of the press, of speech, of the right to organize politically was seldom to be found east of the Iron Curtain. In Russia the brutal repressiveness of the Stalin years seemed to recede after his death in 1953. But dissidents were still routinely exiled to the provinces or incarcerated—sometimes in insane asylums, on the grounds that serious opposition to life in the workers' paradise must indicate serious mental disorder.

A survey of these varied—and variously successful—strategies for progress in the global North from the 1940s to the 1990s follows.

POSTWAR PROBLEMS AND PREDOMINANCE

The United States, between victory in World War II and triumph in the Cold War, was the world's wealthiest and most powerful nation. Both of its chief defeated World War II foes, West Germany and Japan, as well as the once-predominant imperial powers of Western Europe, Britain and France, accepted America's leadership in the post-war period. Much of the rest of the earth fed the hoppers of U.S. industry with their raw materials, enriched America with trade or investment profits, or accepted American largesse in return for political or military commitments of one sort or another.

A distinguished historian called it the American Epoch.[1] Europeans talked about the *Pax Americana*—the American Peace—and some complained about American economic predominance and the "cocacolazation" of their ancient cultures. American influence was certainly greater than it had ever been before.

American political history during the latter part of the twentieth century breaks down into decades. There were the tense Truman years immediately after the war and the conservative and prosperous Eisenhower 1950s. There were the colorful sixties, the turbulent, liberal, affluent Kennedy–Johnson years. There were the economically depressed, self-interested seventies, a time of less distinguished presidents. And there were the eighties and early nineties, the Reagan–Bush years, which tried to turn the country back to conservatism with a degree of success that stunned American liberals.

The United States had no ruins to dig out of after World War II and only a few hundred thousand war dead to mourn. In 1945 the United States had the most powerful army in the world, a two-ocean navy, and sole possession of the most devastating weapon ever devised, the atomic bomb.

America's industrial economy was the most productive in history, and its agricultural sector would soon learn that it could feed half the globe. With Europe and Japan temporarily out of the running, the entire world was open to American exports and overseas investments. American democratic government was stable, even if the Republicans did some chafing under the long Democratic control of the federal government by the late Franklin Roosevelt.

Roosevelt's successor, bustling, sharp-tongued Harry Truman (in office 1945–1952), was to all appearances a very ordinary hack politician from Missouri, chosen as vice president merely to balance the ticket, now suddenly confronted with some of the most critical decisions in American history. But Truman managed the early years of the Cold War with vigor. He pushed on with the New Deal program, stressing full employment, higher wages, government subsidized public housing, more Social Security benefits, aid to education, even a new campaign for civil rights for black Americans. And when in 1948 he ran for a second term on this expanded New Deal platform, he astonished everyone by winning.

The international tensions of the Truman years, however, generated domestic divisions as well—most dis-turbingly the wave of anticommunist witch hunting dominated by the ambitious Senator Joseph McCarthy.

The Communist victory in China, the Korean War, the speed with which the Russians built an atomic bomb, and allegations that spies had sold U.S. atomic secrets to the Soviets all contributed to this burst of witch hunting and scapegoating in the early 1950s. Senator McCarthy, generally condemned since as a demagogue seeking to advance his own career, seized upon the theory of an all-powerful "international communist conspiracy" to explain a wide range of disturbing phenomena, from the New Deal to the Cold War.

McCarthy's wild charges ruined careers and smeared reputations, especially in the foreign service, with accusations of communist sympathies or affiliation. American courts convicted a handful of Russian agents, and two government employees, Julius and Ethel Rosenberg, were executed for giving atomic secrets to Russia. In general, however, McCarthy and his allies offered little evidence to support their charges. In the hysteria of the time, charges were enough.

McCarthy finally overreached himself by claiming that the U.S. Army was full of reds. Censured by the Senate, he faded from the political scene while the fires he had kindled expired in the calmer atmosphere of the Eisenhower years.

Dwight Eisenhower (1952–1960), the first Republican president since the New Deal, was a broad-faced Kansan who had become famous as the commanding general of the Allied armies in Europe in World War II. He knew very little about politics, preferred playing golf to reading position papers, and depended heavily on his cabinet, a body dominated by conservative big businessmen.

Nevertheless, as a self-styled progressive Republican, Eisenhower legitimized the New Deal simply by not moving to repeal it. He even made a few modest contributions himself, further expanding Social Security benefits and committing the country to the Eisenhower highway program, which in subsequent years crisscrossed three million miles of America with superhighways. During Eisenhower's second term he reluctantly sent troops into Arkansas to enforce a crucial 1954 Supreme Court decision requiring racial integration of American schools. Here, and in the 1956 Montgomery, Alabama, bus boycott led by the young Rev. Martin Luther King, Jr., began what would become the most successful crusade of the decade of crusading that followed.

THE TURBULENT SIXTIES

The 1960s combined the social excitement of the 1920s and the political commitment of the 1930s in the most tumultuous American decade of the century. Two Democratic presidents presided: John Kennedy as inspiration, Lyndon Johnson as technician. But much of the demand

---

[1]Arthur S. Link, *American Epoch: A History of the United States since the 1890s* (New York: Alfred A. Knopf, 1955).

The most successful demonstrator during the turbulent American 1960s was Dr. Martin Luther King. He is shown here with his wife, Coretta King, and other leaders of the black civil rights struggle in the United States, marching on Montgomery, Alabama, in 1965. Such nonviolent protest demonstrations caught the imagination of the world and brought a significant amount of political and social liberation for black Americans. (The Bettmann Archive)

for change welled up from below, particularly from the most rebellious younger generations in American history.

John Kennedy (1960–1963) was a handsome young Irish-American millionaire from Boston, the first Catholic president, and the embodiment of the youth and energy that America seemed to want in 1960. In fact, he accomplished little, at least in domestic affairs. He combined a tax cut and a little Keynesian fine-tuning of the economy to produce a new boom after a late-Eisenhower recession. He committed the United States to a race with the Russians to put the first human being on the moon. But his more substantive reforms were stalled by a conservative Congress, and he had neither the patience nor the political know-how to push them through.

Then in the fall of 1963, Kennedy was shot by a neurotic young man named Lee Harvey Oswald. The new president, Lyndon Johnson (1963–1968), had all the political skills Kennedy lacked, and he used the national grief over the assassination to propel a final flood of New Deal–style reforms through the Congress and into law.

Medical insurance for elderly Americans, aid to education, public housing, aid for rural poor whites in Appalachia, aid for depressed, often largely black inner cities, and a hundred lesser reforms were passed. So was the most sweeping civil rights bill in U.S. history, an act that outlawed racial discrimination in all public places, in employment, and in other aspects of American life.

Domestic reform was Johnson's strong suit; his major contribution to American foreign policy was the disastrous involvement in Vietnam. As a reformer, however, Lyndon Johnson's administration was the real climax of the New Deal wave of social change begun thirty years before.

Much of the excitement of 1960s America, however, was the work of the demonstrators and agitators, most of them youthful, who swarmed the streets of the nation.

Young Americans demanded a freer, more human educational system, further relaxation of already relaxed sexual mores, freer use of drugs other than alcohol, and other youth-oriented changes. In addition, a host of ad hoc youth organizations launched campaigns against unequal treatment for black Americans, against the "pockets of poverty" still left in affluent America, and against the Vietnam War.

Martin Luther King, Jr., spearheaded the struggle for civil rights for black Americans. A young black minister from Atlanta, King developed and applied the Gandhian principles of "nonviolent direct action" through marches, pickets, sit-ins, and other forms of protest to gain public and government support for black rights. In 1963 he led hundreds of thousands of black and white Americans on a peaceful March on Washington, and in 1964 his efforts were recognized by the Nobel Peace Prize. King was assassinated in 1968, but he had already done more than anyone else to create the climate of opinion that made possible the landmark civil rights legislation of the sixties. These laws and court decisions of the Kennedy–Johnson years forbade racial discrimination in employment, education, housing, transportation, voting, and office-holding.

The other great reform causes of the decade fared less well. Lyndon Johnson declared a War on Poverty, but his efforts to eradicate it fell far short of success. By 1968, John Kennedy's younger brother Robert had been converted to the cause of peace in Vietnam. But he too fell to an assassin's bullet, and peace was finally achieved by the Republican who was elected that year, Richard Nixon.

Over these two very different decades, it should be stressed, the United States flourished economically as never before in its—or anybody else's—history. The gross

The leaders of the last major surge of liberal reform in the New Deal tradition, John Kennedy and Lyndon Johnson, are shown here with their wives, Jackie Kennedy and Lady Bird Johnson. Presidents Kennedy and Johnson would dominate the electoral politics of the 1960s in America. (The Bettmann Archive)

national product was valued at something over $200 billion in 1945; by 1970 it was pushing the trillion-dollar mark, a fivefold increase. The United States in 1970 had 6 percent of the world's population—and reputedly consumed well over half the world's production. Both the calm of the Eisenhower years and the turbulence and social reform of the Truman and Kennedy–Johnson administrations were thus supported by unprecedented economic growth.

THE CONSERVATIVE YEARS

Things changed during the demoralized and depressed 1970s. The U.S. withdrawal from Vietnam, followed by the communist victory there, shook American self-confidence badly. The Arab oil-price hikes of the seventies staggered the economies of all nations, including that of the United States. And the political debacle of Richard Nixon left the country reeling and adrift by the middle of the decade.

Republican President Richard Nixon (1968–1974), former vice president under Eisenhower and an established anticommunist politician, succeeded Johnson at the end of the 1960s. Nixon's foreign-policy record was impressive, including the revival of American relations with China. But his overreaction to massive, sometimes violent political demonstrations led him to countenance a series of undercover schemes that violated the civil rights of those who opposed him, from street-radicals to the leadership of the Democratic party. In the end, Nixon, his vice president, and a number of his cabinet members

and other key officials resigned under fire, many of them serving prison terms as well.

Of Presidents Gerald Ford (Republican) and Jimmy Carter (Democrat), little need be said except that both were honest. But the deepest recession of the postwar period thus far continued during their presidencies, and foreign affairs did not go well. In 1980 a former actor and two-term governor of California named Ronald Reagan was elected president—the most conservative man to serve in the White House in fifty years.

Reagan tried to repeal large chunks of the liberal legislation of the preceding half century. He sought to cut welfare payments, replacing expensive government programs with volunteer aid, and to cut taxes, putting more money in people's pockets to stimulate national economic recovery. But he also launched the most expensive armament program in U.S. history, pyramiding the national debt beyond anything seen in peacetime before. Nevertheless, economic recovery came on with a rush in the middle of the 1980s. And Reagan's religious supporters, calling themselves the Moral Majority, preached vehemently against such manifestations of the spirit of the sixties as sex without marriage and legal abortion and urged more religious emphasis in the schools.

Ronald Reagan was reelected by a landslide in 1984, and the boom years rolled on. But there were those who noted that, while production figures rose and aggressive entrepreneurs and wheeler-dealers did well under the Republican administration, other Americans did not share commensurately in the long economic resurgence. The per capita incomes of the middle classes scarcely rose, though this was less visible because both husband and wife now commonly brought home paychecks. The income gap between rich and poor, or between white and black citizens, however, grew quite visibly wider. Homeless people and beggars in the streets remained a troubling social presence throughout the 1980s and on into the 1990s.

Reagan's vice president, George Bush, was elected to succeed him in 1988. By that time, however, deep economic problems were apparent. The long boom gave way to a recession. The national debt continued to soar despite efforts to control the budget, and even President Bush, elected on a pledge not to raise taxes, had to admit that this would have to be done. Savings-and-loan institutions failed in record numbers, and a series of widely publicized trials of Wall Street manipulators and crooked bankers tarnished the reputation of this latest generation of success stories.

THE CLINTON YEARS

The resulting discontent led to the election of a Democrat, the little-known, relatively liberal governor of Arkansas, Bill Clinton, in 1992. Clinton, his politically active wife Hillary, and his vice president Al Gore, a leading environmental reformer, dedicated their efforts to restoring the nation's faith in government. Clinton sought to build a foundation for strong government by cutting the budget deficits inherited from the Reagan–Bush years and by committing the United States to free-trade agreements

through the revised General Agreement on Tariffs and Trade (GATT) and the new North American Free Trade Agreement (NAFTA). Many Democrats, however, feared that the global market would cost Americans jobs.

The centerpiece of the Clinton drive for renewed government activism was an ambitious new health plan aimed at giving all Americans comprehensive health care comparable to that found in other developed industrial nations. Despite the dedicated efforts of Hillary Clinton, however, voter fears of high cost and bureaucratic control prevented congress from enacting a health plan. Scandalous personal allegations about the president further weakened the administration. At the midterm elections of 1994, Republicans swept to power in the Congress and in most state governments.

The newly elected Republican congressional representatives in particular seemed passionately dedicated to taking up Reagan's antigovernment crusade. They sought to cut taxes, chop government programs, shrink the bureaucracy, return power to the states, and generally reduce the role of the federal government in the lives of Americans. Their leader, Speaker of the House of Representatives Newt Gingrich, was better known for his slashing attacks on political adversaries than for constructive legislation. But his militance and that of his followers suggested that America's conservative years might not be over yet.

STRATEGIES OF PROGRESS: WESTERN EUROPE AND EAST ASIA

GERMANY: FROM ECONOMIC MIRACLE TO REUNIFICATION

West Germany, the major European loser in World War II, was soon back among the leaders. The Federal Republic became the most successful economic performer among Western European nations and a notably successful democracy as well.

Forged from the Western zones of occupation, West Germany had most of the population and resources of the prewar Reich. With a new capital at Bonn, the new nation soon revived the democratic spirit of Weimar without its deep divisions and weaknesses. West Germany was fortunate too in its leading statesmen in the early decades. The conservative Christian Democratic chancellor Konrad Adenauer, former anti-Nazi mayor of Cologne, guided West Germany through its first fifteen years with skill and dignity. The first Social Democratic chancellor, Willy Brandt, who made his reputation as mayor of West Berlin, eased tensions with the Soviet bloc and kept the door open for future reunification with East Germany.

The Federal Republic's economic miracle, mean-

The conservative resurgence of the 1980s was personified in the United States by President Ronald Reagan. Here, "the great communicator" makes a forceful point without losing the geniality that made him so successful a campaigner. Reagan's ideological successors were the aggressive younger conservatives who came to control the Congress in the mid-1990s. (The Ronald Reagan Library)

while, startled the world. It was built on billions of dollars of Marshall Plan aid, millions of German refugees from Eastern Europe and "guest workers" from other countries, and on the proverbial hard work and technical skills of the German people as a whole. The architect of the achievement was Adenauer's free-enterprise economic minister Ludwig Erhard, but there was a good deal of judicious government support for the upwardly mobile economy too.

West Germany, like Japan, had a serious problem in its lack of oil, and as a result its economy was shaken by the global recession of the 1970s and early 1980s. Overall, however, the Federal Republic of Germany, like Japan, was one of the pillars of the Western world in the 1980s.

To cap these achievements, finally, West German leaders engineered an astonishing diplomatic coup in 1990. As the Soviet bloc collapsed in Eastern Europe, the two German states, led by West German chancellor Helmut Kohl, were reunited into a single German nation.

The dream of national unification had burned strongly in Germans on both sides of the Cold War divide. When popular pressure forced the opening of the Berlin Wall in November 1989, champagne corks popped from the Rhine to the Elbe, and crowds from East and West Germany fraternized enthusiastically. Kohl, a big, burly, beer-drinking German with one of the shrewdest political heads of his time, moved quickly to take advantage of the situation. While his gifted foreign minister, Hans-Dietrich Genscher, soothed the nervous apprehensions of the Soviets and the Western Europeans, Kohl used the political and economic weight of West Germany to draw East Germany toward union.

In the spring of 1990, East Germany's first free elections since Hitler's rise to power resulted in victory for the chancellor's supporters in the east. The two nations were politically joined in the fall of 1990, and in reunited Germany's first elections, held in December 1990, Helmut Kohl emerged as the new nation's first head of state.

The years that followed, however, were not a happy time in the newly united Germany. The cost of rebuilding the East German economy along capitalist lines proved much greater than expected. Large numbers of Eastern European immigrants flooded into Germany in search of jobs and refuge from troubles in their homelands, stirring up violent antiforeign agitation among Germans.

In the long run, the new Germany would surely continue West Germany's role as the economic powerhouse of Europe. But Kohl was re-elected chancellor by a whisker in 1994, and his party's long domination of German politics could not last forever.

WESTERN EUROPE: PROSPERITY AND COMMUNITY

Both Britain and France had some wrenching readjustments to make after the war. The loss of the two largest intercontinental empires, the loss of primacy in international affairs to the United States and the Soviet Union, and the dawning realization that their defeated foes, Germany and Japan, were rapidly outdistancing them economically were not easy blows to absorb over the postwar decades. Both nations, however, played major roles in the formation of a new Europe during the second half of the twentieth century.

Britain, under Labour leader Clement Attlee, led postwar Western Europe into the comprehensive system of social services known as the welfare state in the later 1940s. Expanded unemployment insurance, old-age pensions, public-housing estates, new middle-class universities, and above all the much-debated British public health service provided cradle-to-grave security for Britons. Soon all Western European nations had similar systems of social welfare for their citizens.

Another fundamental change in postwar Western Europe was a much larger role for government in the direction of a national economy—a trend in which France took an early lead. This system involved nationalization of leading banks, insurance companies, utilities, and mines on the one hand, and a deliberate policy of channeling investment into strong private industries in order to direct economic development on the other. Other European nations used other methods, but everywhere the new "welfare capitalism" included government participation in economic development to supplement the driving force of capitalist competition.

Two postwar French statesmen, Jean Monnet, and Robert Schuman, were the architects of another major transformation in Western Europe's economic life during the 1950s and 1960s: the birth of the European Community (EC). Built around a tariff union popularly called the Common Market, the EC coordinated the economic policies of a growing number of Western European nations—twelve as the 1990s began, with a lengthening line of countries eager to join. The Community was directed by a Commission and a Eurobureaucracy headquartered in Brussels, and by a largely advisory European Parliament meeting in Strasbourg, France. The organization guaranteed free trade between members and a common tariff policy toward outsiders. In addition, the EC and its affiliated institutions regulated the production of coal, steel, and atomic power and encouraged common policies on many matters, from migrant labor to social security. It was a daring experiment that led to unprecedented productivity, trade, and prosperity for all the member nations.

The world recession of the 1970s and 1980s, however, hurt the Western European countries also. Interestingly enough, it was Great Britain, which had led Europe into the welfare state thirty years before, that now set a new trend—toward conservative retrenchment.

Tory leader Margaret Thatcher, first elected prime minister in 1979, faced her very substantial industrial problems with a strongly conservative program. She cut back on services, turned some nationalized industries back

Britain's prime minister for over a decade, Margaret Thatcher became known as the "Iron Lady" for her uncompromisingly conservative stands on many issues. She fought hard battles with British labor unions, with the Common Market's "Eurocrats," and with all Soviet rulers before Gorbachev, and led her country to victory against Argentina in a brief war over the disputed Falkland Islands. (PH Archives)

to the private sector, and accepted massive unemployment in order to trim Britain's labor bill and make the nation internationally competitive again. Nor was the "Iron Lady" alone in her conservative crusade. The United States in the Reagan years, West Germany under Kohl, Canada, and other nations joined in the rightward drift of the 1980s. Even France's new Socialist president, François Mitterand, after a renewed burst of nationalization and expanded services, had to turn to a Thatcher-style austerity in the middle of the decade.

President Mitterand, unable to match the economic might of West Germany, made his own country a leading political advocate of European unity, thus striving to keep France abreast of its one-time foe and postwar partner in European leadership. Prime Minister Thatcher, after serving a record three consecutive terms, fell from power in 1990, rejected by her own party in part over her refusal to make the United Kingdom a fully committed member of the booming European Community. Her successor, John Major, though personally popular, lacked Thatcher's powerful personality and faced a resurgent Labor party which looked likely to win the next election. In France, President Mitterand's power also declined after a dozen years in office. Beset by political scandals, he and his Socialist party were defeated by conservative Jacques Chirac in 1995.

Similar problems confronted many Western European governments too long in power. Besides France's Social-

ists, socialist parties in Sweden and Spain looked likely to fall. Whereas conservative governments in both Britain and Germany looked unlikely to be returned to office, both conservative Christian Democrats and Socialists faced angry voters in Italy. There crusading judges risked Mafia assassination to expose the graft and corruption that infected both parties. A media magnate named Silvio Berlusconi swept into office in 1994 at the head of a right-wing coalition pledged to clean up politics—only to fall from power in a welter of corruption charges himself.

Western Europe did increase its economic unity in 1992, opening borders to the free flow of capital and labor as well as goods. Hopes for greater political unity and for Europe-wide social reforms failed, however, rejected by European voters opposed to bureaucratic control and defensive of their separate national traditions.

JAPAN: THE NEW ECONOMIC SUPERPOWER

Japan emerged in the postwar decades as the most economically powerful nation in the world after the United States.

Democratic political institutions established during the American occupation guided Japan's destinies effectively. The conservative Liberal Democratic party won most elections, despite vigorous opposition led by the Socialist party. Neither violent student demonstrations in the 1960s nor some nasty political scandals in the 1970s and again at the end of the 1980s put any serious strain on the system.

Economically, Japan boomed. The economic miracle of its recovery from the war was only the beginning. The Japanese were early leaders in a system of government guidance of business firms into profitable export markets. This system—sometimes wryly called Japan, Incorporated—plus a hardworking and loyal work force, a frugal population willing to save and reinvest, and the sheer energy and drive of the people made Japan a tough competitor for the older exporting nations.

In the 1990s, millions of automobiles clogged Japan's own roads, virtually everyone had a television set, and Japanese bullet trains were a world's wonder. Tokyo was larger than New York and had a worse smog problem than Los Angeles. Japan was home to the world's largest banks and was both the world's leading creditor nation and the largest provider of foreign aid for less-developed nations.

Japan had its problems. These included the need to import almost all natural resources, an extremely serious pollution problem, and repeated requests from trading partners for "voluntary" limits on Japanese exports—a serious difficulty for a country that prospered by trade. For defense, the island nation still depended above all on America's "nuclear umbrella." But Japan's remarkable postwar success augured well for an equally thriving future.

In the early 1990s, finally, Japan faced a double

Japan's emergence as one of the most productive industrial nations in the world is clearly illustrated in this robot-run Japanese factory. "Japan, Incorporated" was at the cutting edge of technological development in many fields in the 1990s. (The Bettmann Archive)

crisis—its deepest economic recession since the "economic miracle" that followed World War II and the first political defeat for its long-time ruling party, the conservative Liberal Democrats. The resulting combination of economic disarray and political confusion was further exacerbated by the terrible Kobe earthquake of 1995. For the time being, at least, Japan's self-confidence seemed badly shaken. The island nation's global economic role, however, seemed ensured for the long-term future.

THE EAST ASIAN RIM: SOUTH KOREA TO SINGAPORE

The string of nations curving down the eastern end of Eurasia into Southeast Asia provided the greatest success story of postwar Third World history. The so-called "tigers," South Korea, Taiwan, Hong Kong, Singapore, all became productive and prosperous new nations, following Japan in moving from the Third World to the First World. In the early 1990s, China joined them in an unprecedented surge of economic growth.

South Korea recovered from the devastation of the Korean War of the 1950s. Ruled first by military men, then, thanks partly to the pressure of student demonstrations, becoming more democratic, the Republic of Korea also developed economically from the 1960s on. By the 1990s, industrial growth and export trade made the southern half of the Korean peninsula an enclave of prosperity on the Asian mainland. Farther south along the China coast, the island republic of Taiwan had also recovered spectacularly from the painful years when Jiang Jiehi's armies, defeated by Mao Zedong, fled to the island from the mainland in 1949. Autocratically

ruled, first by Jiang and then by his heirs, "free China" became another beehive of East Asian productivity, its citizens far more prosperous than their fellow Chinese in the People's Republic.

Still farther down the coast of China, Hong Kong, a small island with mainland territories across the bay, remained a British crown colony—and a crucial gateway to the world for Communist China. Chock-a-block with skyscrapers and some of the world's most elegant hotels, Hong Kong epitomized the success of modern business methods in the East. Nervously contemplating the colony's scheduled reversion to mainland Chinese rule in 1997, many of Hong Kong's residents talked of taking their British passports and their skills and leaving. But the economic importance of this crucial entrepôt made the continuing prosperity of Hong Kong highly likely. At the southern tip of Malaysia, finally, the city-state of Singapore achieved the fastest economic growth of any nation between the 1960s and the 1990s. Lee Kuan Yew, for thirty years prime minister of this burgeoning community of overseas Chinese, created a model state. More than half the population owned their own homes. Connected to the outside world by one of the great national airlines and the world's busiest harbor, Singapore also showed what could be done with energy and brains.

All these small countries combined cheap labor with foreign capital, domestic drive with ingenuity, to build up light industry and commerce in order to give them a competitive edge. Then, in the 1990s, the backward communist nations of China and Vietnam also opened up to capitalism and began to grow economically at double-digit rates. Strengthened by a second generation of "tigers"—Thailand, Indonesia, and Malaysia—the East Asian rim became the fastest growing economic zone in the world.

PEOPLES OF PLENTY: FROM CANADA TO ISRAEL

Scattered around the world, mostly in the global North, there were other nations, smaller in size or population, whose inhabitants were also among the later twentieth-century's peoples of plenty. Most of these affluent countries were European, or were nations dominated by European-descended populations.

Some of these smaller rich nations had higher per capita incomes than the United States. Switzerland, a world banking center, and Sweden, one of Europe's most highly developed welfare states, both combined capitalist productivity with the benefits of developed welfare states. Sweden in particular was also known for its extensive foreign aid to less-developed peoples.

In North America, Canada had been a major industrial power for much of the century. The huge northern nation depended heavily on trade, especially on massive agricultural exports to China and Russia. Canada also traded extensively with, and imported capital from, its even wealthier neighbor to the south, the United States.

Australia, the other continental nation of the older British Commonwealth, encouraged immigration and foreign investment, especially from the United States and Britain, developed its mineral resources, and inaugurated major water projects to irrigate its arid Outback. As the century drew to a close, Australia also took an increasing part in the economic life of East and Southeast Asia.

Israel benefited from the latest Western technology and from a highly skilled and motivated population, including many immigrants from Europe and America. The Jewish state also received large amounts of foreign aid from the United States and West Germany. Israel thus became the most developed nation in the Middle East, achieving an economic growth rate of over 10 percent annually throughout its early decades.

All these developed countries suffered from the economic downturn and politically unsettled conditions of the 1990s. Recession racked both Australia and Canada, and both Australia's socialists and Canada's conservative governments went down to jolting electoral defeats. Even in the worst of times, however, few of their citizens would have traded places with the peoples of the global South.

DEVELOPMENT AND DISASTER: THE U.S.S.R. AND THE COMMUNIST BLOC

SOVIET ACHIEVEMENTS— AND UNSOLVED PROBLEMS

The Soviet Union emerged as the second most powerful nation in the world during the second half of the twentieth century. Politically, however, the U.S.S.R. of the post-Stalin decades remained repressive, a one-party state with none of the freedoms common in the West. And economically, the huge country's problems seemed to grow decade by decade.

Joseph Stalin had ended his life in a new wave of state terror, rapidly refilling the prisons and work camps after the heroic fervor of the Great Patriotic War against Germany. His passing in 1953 left no one capable of filling his shoes. But two strong personalities did rise above the sea of faceless *apparatchiks* to guide the nation through the next three decades: Nikita Khrushchev (1956–1964) and Leonid Brezhnev (1964–1982).

Both Khrushchev and Brezhnev were older men, party men, products of the Stalinist pyramid of power established in the 1930s. Both shared final authority with influential colleagues during their rule, and both depended on the machinery of the state and the Communist party.

Both, finally, had to face the same recurring problems with the United States and the Eastern European satellites, agriculture, consumer goods, and Soviet dissidents.

Nikita Khrushchev's major political achievement was destalinization, the famous Russian Thaw of the middle 1950s. Soon after Stalin's death in 1953, the current head of the secret police was unceremoniously executed. Soon most of the vast secret-police-operated forced-labor camps, the notorious Gulag, were closing down.

In 1956 Khrushchev, by then recognized as the winner of the almost bloodless struggle for power that followed Stalin's passing, read a famous "secret speech" to the Communist leadership. In it he denounced Stalin's personality cult and blamed the purges, the camps, the pounding the U.S.S.R. had taken early in World War II, and other misfortunes on the late Great Leader.

The Thaw did not last long. A few books, such as Alexander Solzhenytsin's labor-camp novel *One Day in the Life of Ivan Denisovitch,* ripped the lid off the brutality of earlier years. Then the government clamped on the censorship again, and dissidents were soon being harassed and imprisoned once more. But their numbers were far fewer now, and the great fear engendered during Stalin's Iron Age would not recur.

Other things did not go as well for Khrushchev. His campaign to deal with Russia's perennially flagging agricultural production by opening vast tracts of virgin Siberian lands to the plow did not solve the problem. The spirit of the Thaw spread to the satellites and triggered a revolt in Hungary in 1956. Khrushchev had to send in the tanks, thereby undermining his—and the Soviet Union's—new liberal image. He built up Russia's nuclear-missile armory from a small beginning, but he was still so far behind the United States that he had to back down to Kennedy over the Cuban-missile crisis of 1962. In 1964, reeling from the Soviet split with China, the retreat before American power, and another bad harvest, Khrushchev was quietly and painlessly forced to retire by his colleagues in the Kremlin.

His successor, beetle-browed Leonid Brezhnev, handled problems with methodical pragmatism. He dealt with a bad harvest by buying American grain, with a lack of high tech by contracting with French and Italian companies to build him a plant in the Soviet Union. He had no use for dissenters, sent some to labor camps, some to jail, some into foreign exile.

Brezhnev did, however, build up the nation's nuclear arsenal till it rivaled America's. He expanded the conventional armed forces in Europe and on the Chinese frontier in the East. He met rebelliousness in Czechoslovakia in 1968, reacting as Khrushchev had in Hungary—by sending in troops. He even indulged in a foreign adventure or two, including the Soviets' long, drawn-out intervention in Afghanistan, which began in 1979.

Overall, however, Brezhnev kept things on an even keel. He established détente with President Richard Nixon that lasted through most of the 1970s. His failing health in the early 1980s and eventual demise in 1982 seemed to end an era of predictability and stability in Soviet-American relations.

But there was more to Russian history from the 1950s through the 1970s than Communist party politics. During these years, the Soviet Union also faced a growing number of economic and technological problems.

As in the Stalin period, the Russia of Khrushchev and Brezhnev did best on large-scale projects. The Soviet Union forged ahead in heavy industry, replacing the United States as the world's leading producer of steel, coal, and oil. Most impressively, the U.S.S.R. was a pioneer in space exploration. A Russian was the first into space in an orbiting earth satellite in 1961. And if U.S. astronauts won the race to the moon, Soviet cosmonauts held the records for long periods aloft, conducting experiments in space for months at a time.

Agriculture remained the Soviet Union's largest economic bottleneck, requiring the labors of up to half of Russia's work force (compared with 5 to 10 percent in the West). Partly because of peasant inefficiency and recalcitrance in the face of compulsory collectivization, partly because of several bad harvests, inadequate grain supplies frequently required the Soviets to buy large amounts of grain overseas. A winter visitor, browsing empty market shelves in Moscow in the 1980s, would soon come upon Soviet citizens lining up to buy grapes from a peasant woman selling them at sky-high prices on a snowy street corner.

Beyond the problems of particular sectors, however, the Soviet economy as a whole apparently suffered from a crushing paralysis rooted in the system of central planning and state control itself. Neither the Soviet Union nor any other communist country matched the increasing affluence or the quality of life attained in Western Europe, North America, or other free-enterprise societies around the world. A structure of bureaucratic control, assigned production quotas, and fixed prices subsidized inefficiency and discouraged independence, innovation, and entrepreneurial energy. There was little of the cyclic unemployment of capitalist societies, and nobody needed to work very hard; but the results were commensurately poor. Consumer goods were often unavailable and frequently shoddy; housing remained in short supply; transport and communications were at Third World levels. When the multiplying costs of the Cold War were added to the inefficiency of the system, the Soviet economy declined drastically in the Brezhnev years.

THE GORBACHEV REVOLUTION

Two old men from the Khrushchev–Brezhnev generation succeeded Brezhnev briefly in the early 1980s. But the subsequent accession of relatively young, vigorous, and thoroughly informed Mikhail Gorbachev in 1985 seemed like

Mikhail Gorbachev, who took the helm in Moscow in 1985, reflected a new, more sophisticated style of Soviet leadership. Even Britain's arch conservative Margaret Thatcher thought she could "do business" with Gorbachev. And, in fact, the Gorbachev years saw the winding down of the Cold War, the end of Soviet domination of Eastern Europe, and the reunification of Germany on essentially Western terms: the West had done some very good business with Gorbachev indeed. (The Bettmann Archive)

a real turning point in Russian history. At age 54, Gorbachev spoke for a post-Stalin generation more flexible and open than any previous generation of Russian leadership.

The new Soviet leader's initial attempts to solve the nation's problems emphasized two tactics: *glasnost,* or "openness," in discussing problems, and *perestroika,* or "restructuring" of Communist institutions to effect change. What this modest program for change mainly succeeded in doing, however, was something very different. Half-way solutions merely exacerbated shortages, bottlenecks, black marketeering, and confusion. And the new tolerance for free expression unleashed a torrent of demands for much more radical changes than the leadership had ever contemplated.

Under the mounting pressure of lengthening lines in front of shops and angry voices in the streets, many changes in fact came about. The Communist party relinquished its monopoly of power, and hundreds of local parties and other independent organizations sprang up across the country. The government was reorganized, leaving much power in Gorbachev's hands as president of the U.S.S.R., but also creating a freely elected and sometimes rebellious legislature. Economic radicals demanded a complete abandonment of the planned economy and a return to private property and capitalist competition, though Gorbachev proceeded more slowly with economic than with political changes. A number of the constituent republics, including the Baltic states of Lithuania, Latvia, and Estonia, demanded vastly increased autonomy or threatened outright secession from the Soviet Union. Meanwhile, as we have seen, the Soviet Union abandoned the Cold War and the East European satellite states.

Factions emerged to the left and right of the leader who had launched the drive for change. On Gorbachev's left were rivals like the liberal Boris Yeltsin, elected president of the huge Russian Republic, which included half the population of the Soviet Union. Yeltsin demanded the devolution of almost all powers to the republics, which would reduce the central government in Moscow to a figurehead regime, and urged free-market reforms. Conservatives, including the Communist party, military leaders, the KGB (secret police), and the entrenched managers of the state-run economy, by contrast, fiercely demanded a return to the iron fist to deal with what seemed to them a disintegrating society.

The Yeltsin Years

In August of 1991, the balance between these two conflicting forces seemed to shift dramatically. An attempted right-wing coup, threatening to topple Gorbachev, failed in the face of popular opposition, and drove Gorbachev into the arms of the reformers led by Boris Yeltsin.

The world followed the events of those three days in August with shock, amazement, and renewed hope. A group of inept Communist conspirators, leaders of the army, the interior ministry, and the KGB, detained Gorbachev in his vacation home in the south and announced that he was ill and would be replaced by his hard-line vice president. But reformers in Moscow and St. Petersburg and plain Soviet citizens tired of being pushed around refused to accept the new leadership. Yeltsin became the hero of the hour by climbing atop a tank and denouncing the coup. Troops refused to fire on protesting crowds, Gorbachev was released, and the conspiracy collapsed.

The coup that failed brought down the last vestiges of the Soviet system. Communist party headquarters across the country were padlocked, the Baltic states were allowed to secede, and the centralized Soviet Union was reorganized as a loose confederation of sovereign republics. At Christmas 1991, Gorbachev officially resigned as president of the defunct Soviet Union. Boris Yeltsin, as president of the Russian republic, was the most powerful individual in the Commonwealth of Independent States, which replaced the U.S.S.R.

The Yeltsin years were a time of tumult and confusion in the former Soviet Union. The fragmentation of the one-time superpower continued until fifteen separate countries, loosely linked in the Commonwealth of Independent States, had replaced the once monolithic Soviet state. Despite Western aid, steps toward capitalist reform, and its own vast population and natural resources, Yeltsin's Russia sank into economic chaos. Russians suffered grievously from unemployment, inflation, "robber baron"-style profiteering, and an unprecedented crime wave. Boris Yeltsin proved less democratic than many had hoped: the hero who had defied the tanks at the time of the anti-Gorbachev coup sent tanks himself to shell the parliament building when it defied his authority.

Late in 1994, finally, the Russian president dispatched the Russian army into the tiny autonomous republic of Chechnya to prevent its secession from Russia. What was intended as a demonstration of Yeltsin's strength and a reassertion of Russia's place as a great power turned into a bloodbath, which exacerbated his unpopularity at home. Angry Russian generals and reactionary nationalist leaders like the flamboyant Vladimir Zherinovsky began to look like possible successors to Boris Yeltsin. If this were to happen, democracy in Russia would be the most consequential casualty of the Chechnya intervention.

Eastern Europe: From Slow Growth to Revolution

Eastern Europe did not reach the levels of productivity or per capita income achieved in Western Europe. But industrial productivity did rise, and compared to Soviet Russia, such nations as East Germany, Hungary, and Czechoslovakia were doing very well.

The standard that East Europeans used to judge their progress, however, was not the U.S.S.R. but Western Europe, which was rapidly becoming the most populous center of affluence on the globe. As the years passed, Eastern Europeans increasingly resented the political authoritarianism, economic inefficiency, and technological backwardness of the Soviet bloc.

As we have seen, the year 1989 was the year of the East European revolutions. First came the Polish government's decision to recognize and deal with the long outlawed Solidarity movement, followed by Hungary's recognition of the rebels of 1956 as national martyrs. In the summer of 1989, East European frontiers began to open and refugees poured into Western Europe by the tens of thousands. With autumn came the opening of the Berlin Wall and the fall of the East German Communist government. This was closely followed by the delicately managed and equally bloodless "Velvet Revolution" in Czechoslovakia, propelling an avant-garde playwright named Vaclav Havel to the presidency of his country. At Christmas time, even Nicolae Ceausescu's rigidly autocratic Rumania exploded. The megalomaniacal Rumanian ruler died before a firing squad, perhaps as much a victim of a coup by his fellow Communist rulers as of the popular revolution surging through the streets.

LOOMING PROBLEMS: DEVELOPMENT AND NATIONALISM

Popular revolutions thus overthrew unpopular Communist governments all across Eastern Europe. A good case could be made, however, that the hardest part still lay ahead as the 1990s began.

Under the leadership of hastily organized dissident groups like East Germany's New Forum or Czechoslovakia's Civic Forum, the successful revolutionaries embarked upon the difficult process of political and economic transformation. As in the aftermath of Europe's earlier waves of revolution in 1830 and 1848, new constitutions, free elections, and other democratic political changes were a first order of business. At least as important, however, the new regimes sought to dismantle the inefficient and unproductive structure of state-run industry and replace it with a free-market system. To effect the transition, they hoped for as much aid from well-off Western countries as possible.

These goals would not be easily achieved. In some places, political leaders linked to the Communist past managed to hang on to power into the new, more democratic era. Everywhere, economic transformation would inevitably impose great hardships on East European populations. Inefficient, uncompetitive factories would have to close, throwing many people out of work. Formerly subsidized prices would rise until there was sufficient economic demand to motivate increased production. Everywhere, people unused to the rigors of capitalism would have to learn to work under the competitive pressures that made free-enterprise states so productive.

Another general problem also loomed threateningly as the former Communist nations sought to come to terms with the new freedom and the impending hardships of the 1990s. Nationalistic passions, long held in check by the internationalism of class-based Marxism, flared up in many parts of this traditional hotbed of conflicting nationalisms. Czechs and Slovaks soon fell out in democratic Czechoslovakia. Rumanians beat up Hungarians in the northern Rumanian province of Transylvania, while Hungarians grumbled about recovering their "lost" province—of Transylvania.

THE RUNNING SORE OF BOSNIA

The worst casualty of the collapse of communism in Eastern Europe was the bloody disintegration of the multinational state of Yugoslavia. During the upheaval following the Revolutions of 1989, Yugoslavia's most developed constituent republics, Croatia and Slovenia, seceded and sought economic integration with Western Europe. Slobodan Milosovich, nationalist leader of the majority Serbian population, supported Serbian minorities demanding independence from Croatia and from the Muslim region of Bosnia. The latter soon became the site of a long-drawn-out civil war.

Across that mountainous little country, villages were torn apart by brutal guerrilla strife. Evidence mounted of what came to be known as "ethnic cleansing"—mass expulsions of Bosnians from their homes, systematic rape, brutal imprisonment, and outright massacres. The Cold War was barely over, and already southern Europe was torn by the first hot war since 1945.

An arms embargo was imposed on all sides, the United Nations sent in "peacekeepers," and NATO launched occasional air strikes. American policymakers urged support for the Bosnians, while Western European leaders feared the spread of the conflict to neighboring Balkan areas. Alone of the great powers, Russia tended to support the Serbs. In 1995, however, a successful Croatian offensive and NATO air strikes seemed to turn the tide against the Serbs.

THE SOCIETY OF THE GLOBAL NORTH

THE CITYSCAPES OF THE TWENTIETH CENTURY

The cover of the *New York Times Magazine* shows a man in a hard hat sitting on an orange girder, his feet dangling into space. Far enough below to dim its outlines, dull its hue, is the top of the nearest skyscraper. Beyond and still farther below, block after block, mile after mile, the vertical world of New York City spreads under a glistening haze.

It is a world of narrow man-made canyons, of concrete and brick, glass and asphalt, jammed with cars, streaming with millions of people. It is a world so new that a word has had to be coined to describe representations of it: not a landscape, but a cityscape. It is a world built by human hands whose skyline is dominated by the imperial splendor of the skyscraper.

The drawbacks of city life in the later twentieth century were not to be ignored, indeed could not be ignored by anyone who lived there. The daily devouring of irreplaceable resources, from petroleum products to aluminum cans, by a city of several millions boggled the imagination. So did the mountains and sluices of waste the modern city generated, and the pollution darkening the waters around it, thickening the air above it. The millions themselves—double-digit millions of people in metropolises

The skyscrapers of Manhattan dwarf towers of earlier centuries. Built for the most part by great business corporations, these many-storied structures were as typical of the twentieth century as the palaces and temples of earlier centuries were of their times. There were slums, pollution, and poverty below these skyscrapers, but there was grandeur in them too. (AP/Wide World Photos)

selves—double-digit millions of people in metropolises such as Tokyo and Mexico City—put their own immense strain on the system. They required food, housing, schools, jobs, police protection, garbage collection, help for the poor, care for children, care for the growing numbers of the elderly.

Yet the role of the urban complex remained central. The twentieth-century metropolis, with its concentric rings of suburbs and its links by rail and road and air with other cities, was as much the core of the modern industrial state as the walled city was of the urbanimperial state of ancient times. The uniquely vertical skyline of the twentieth-century city—originating in the United States, found in the 1990s on every continent—was an instantly recognized symbol of the technologically based wealth and power of the global North.

In the second half of the twentieth century, modern cities were to be seen in every part of the world, but they clustered most thickly in the Northern hemisphere, particularly in the north temperate zone—in North America, Europe, and East Asia, especially Japan. Urban culture and the power and affluence that went with it were thus heavily concentrated in what came to be known as the global North, in contrast with the less affluent, less urbanized lands of the South.

Both the First World and the Second World—as the American and Soviet zones in the Cold War were sometimes called—were parts of the global North in terms of basic technological development. U.S., Japanese, and European industrial plants were much more advanced than those of Eastern Europe. But both the towers of the Man-

hattan skyline and the housing blocks marching out a main road in Moscow looked very different from the village streets of the Third World.

THE NEW TECHNOLOGIES

Much of the technological progress made by the North, beginning in the 1950s, manifested itself in improved—or at least interestingly varied—lives for large segments of the population. This was particularly so in the West, where consumer demand largely determined what got developed and manufactured. From basics such as frozen foods, clothes washers, central heating, and air conditioning to luxuries such as stereo equipment, video recorders, and electronic arcade games, the buying public got its share of the latest technology in capitalist countries.

Much of the applied science of the age, however, was the preserve of the specialist or the large institutional user, from government and big business to the general hospital and the airline. In such areas as space exploration and nuclear weaponry, the Soviet Union was also a world leader in the postwar decades.

The peoples of the global North thus created a dazzling new material culture for themselves during the third quarter of the twentieth century. Thousands of later-twentieth-century people walked around with remarkable artificial limbs or electronic pacemakers regulating the beating of their hearts. Decent hygiene, diet, exercise, wonder drugs, and hospital technology doubled the human life span. In industry and government, steady progress in computer technology, robotics, electronics, biological neering, and energy science continued to reshape the world around us.

In the decades after World War II, regularly scheduled jumbo jets linked the cities of the world, till there was virtually no place more than a day away from anywhere else, and millions flew the friendly skies of the world every year. Artificial satellites orbited the earth, beeping back a spectrum of information ranging from weather reports to newscasts from the other side of the world—straight to the home television screens of countless viewers.

In 1961 the Russian cosmonaut Yuri Gagarin became the first human being to orbit the earth in an artificial satellite. In 1969 an American, Neil Armstrong, became the first to set foot on the moon. In the mid-1970s Soviet spacecraft landed on Venus, and American ones sent back vivid photographs from the surface of Mars. The peoples of planet earth grew quite blasé about angle shots of the rings of Saturn and fly-bys of the moons of Jupiter. For the developed nations of the North, at least, it seemed as if even the sky was no longer the limit.

THE HELICOPTER ECONOMY

The economies of the nations of the North also exhibited a tendency to rise at an unprecedented rate during the decades after World War II.

The free-enterprise nations of the West did do a certain amount of nationalizing of major industries, from transportation to steel, during the postwar years. But they retained a solid core of privately capitalized corporations, and with them the stimulus of competition as an incentive to produce and sell. By and large, it worked very well, providing an engine of economic growth that flooded the Western world with goods and services.

The Western capitalist economy was no longer the fang-and-claw economic jungle of the nineteenth century. The major corporations themselves imposed order—and controlled competition—as efficiently as any medieval city guild in a wide variety of fields, from oil and automobiles to air travel and fast foods. Government also regulated the conduct of business, laying down rules for everything from environmentally polluting by-products to employment practices. Western governments also provided support for industry, agriculture, export trade, and other sectors of the economy by tightening or loosening credit, guiding industry into areas having a strong export potential, and even sharing the cost of research and development.

Such economic "fine tuning" helped. So did the advantages of cheap immigrant labor and raw materials from the global South. The result was an economic boom of unprecedented proportions through the 1960s and into the 1970s.

In 1973, however, and again in 1979, the oil producers' international cartel, OPEC, drastically hiked the price of petroleum, the single most important source of energy for Western industry. Meanwhile, economic feuds

between such rich nations as the United States and Japan intensified. In the 1970s and early 1980s, these and other factors combined to produce the deepest recession since the Great Depression of the 1930s. Despite an upturn of the business cycle in the later 1980s, the population as a whole never recovered the prosperity of the postwar years.

Consumer goods, however, remained much harder to come by in the East bloc than in the West. The differences grew more pronounced with the passing decades. In the West, the goal was the "helicopter economy"—rising as economic production had never risen before. In the East, it was hard to find a good pair of shoes or an apartment, let alone anything electronic.

TOWARD A ONE-CLASS WORLD?

The distribution of the good things also remained a problem for the nations of the North in the later twentieth century, as it had since the beginning of the Industrial Revolution. Capitalist countries preached equality of opportunity rather than economic parity for all people. Because of the great prosperity of the West over most of the time since World War II, the majority of the citizens of its countries enjoyed a vastly improved standard of living. By the 1960s, cars, television sets, decent housing, paid vacations, and other perquisites of the new wealth were commonplace.

In addition, capitalist countries generally supplied a safety net of public services for all, paid for by tax money. It included such welfare measures as unemployment insurance, public health care, old-age or retirement benefits, and much more.

Even among these postwar "people of plenty," however, there were striking economic disparities. Women, ethnic minorities, immigrant workers, among others were all paid less than other segments of the population. Some even slipped through the welfare state's safety net and suffered grievously during economic downturns. Beggars and homeless people were still to be found in some of the world's richest cities in the 1990s.

The Communist Eastern European countries had made an outright commitment to economic equality, at least in Marxist theory. But slogans such as "From each according to his ability, to each according to his need" had a rather hollow ring in the real world of the Soviet bloc. In the Soviet Union itself, even before World War II, the state had adopted piecework, quotas, and other incentives to production that set successful "shock workers" off from the rest of the work force.

In the early postwar years, the Yugoslav heretic Milovan Djilas declared in print that a "new class" of party leaders, government bureaucrats, industrial managers, scientists, generals, and others had come to dominate Communist society.[2] The new elite, like the old cap-

---

[2]Milovan Djilas, *The New Class: An Analysis of the Communist System* (New York: Praeger, 1957).

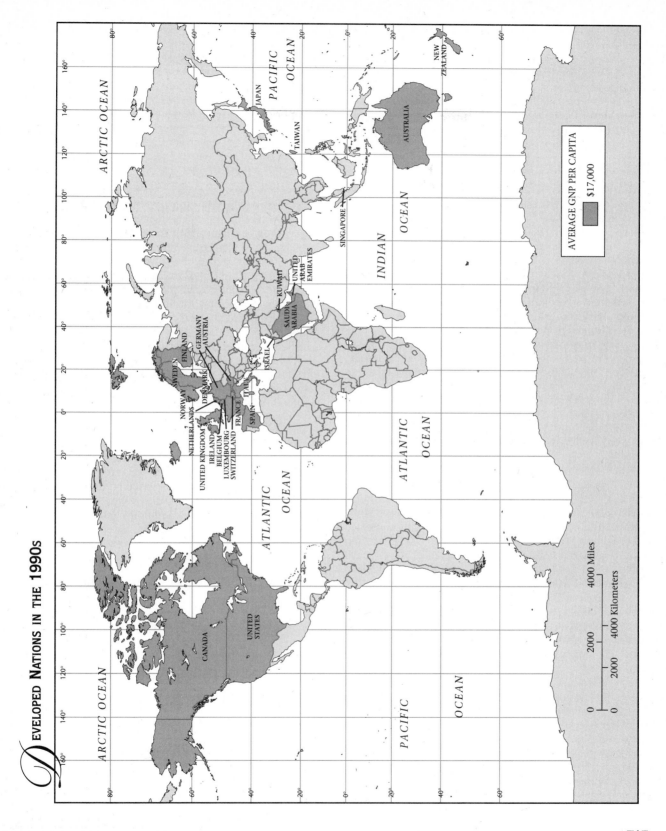

Developed Nations in the 1990s

ARCTIC OCEAN

PACIFIC OCEAN

NEW ZEALAND

JAPAN

TAIWAN

AUSTRALIA

SINGAPORE

INDIAN OCEAN

KUWAIT

UNITED ARAB EMIRATES

SAUDI ARABIA

GERMANY

AUSTRIA

FINLAND

ISRAEL

SWEDEN

ITALY

DENMARK

FRANCE

SPAIN

NORWAY

NETHERLANDS

UNITED KINGDOM

IRELAND

BELGIUM

LUXEMBOURG

SWITZERLAND

ATLANTIC OCEAN

CANADA

UNITED STATES

ARCTIC OCEAN

PACIFIC OCEAN

ATLANTIC OCEAN

AVERAGE GNP PER CAPITA	
	$17,000

4000 Miles

4000 Kilometers

2000

2000

0

0

italist one, garnered a larger share of the material rewards than less exalted comrades ever could.

When the East European Communist regimes crumbled in 1989, the East joined the West in pursuit of economic productivity through free-market incentives. During the transition period, these long-suffering peoples slid still further into the economic basement. By the mid-1990s, however, Poland, Hungary, and the Czech Republic seemed to be developing vigorous free-market economies.

THE LIBERATION OF WOMEN

During the postwar decades, many women once more took up the crusading spirit of the turn-of-the century women's suffrage movement—this time primarily in the economic sphere. Again, the results were striking.

In the immediate aftermath of World War II, "Rosy the Riveter" seemed to be content to return to the nineteenth-century ideal career for women—as wives and mothers. What came to be called the "feminine mystique" praised these time-honored social roles, as it urged longer dresses, frillier fashions, and a more feminine image on the female half of the population.

The turmoil of the 1960s, however, stirred the women's movement to life again. In the following decade, women's organizations such as the National Organization for Women (NOW) in the United States began a campaign to overcome the remaining forms of discrimination against women.

Women in the 1970s and again in the 1990s ran for and won election to political office in unprecedented numbers.

The main thrust of the revitalized women's movement, however, was economic. Women demanded equal pay for equal work, promotion of more women to executive levels in business, larger representation in the ranks of the professions. In some of these areas, at least, they seemed to be making progress in the last decades of the century. More than half the married women in the United States worked outside the home, and it was no longer difficult to find successful women as role models in all spheres of life.

In Eastern Europe, women had long been integrated into the economy, a measure as much of the need for labor as of ideological commitment. Child care for working women was widely available. Some professions were thoroughly integrated: most of the doctors in the Soviet Union were women.

But women in the Soviet bloc were expected to do a day's work at the factory or office and then come home and get supper for the family.

Recent studies reveal both progress and problems in the world of women and work. Throughout the developed world, women remain less well paid, more likely to get stuck in dead-end jobs, and still most likely to do the housework in addition to work outside the home. Yet these differences seem to be decreasing in industrialized states. More education for women and laws requiring equal treat-

ment raised women's remuneration to three-quarters that of men, and the gap seems likely to continue to narrow.[3]

Around the world in the later twentieth century, meanwhile, family size decreased, divorce rates rose, and the number of single mothers grew. These changes in family size and structure seemed to be due to such factors as the need for both parents to work to maintain a high standard of living, the abandonment of the family by husbands, or the departure of husbands to work in distant cities.

YOUTH IN REVOLT

In the later twentieth century, young people also thrust their way into popular consciousness. The revolt of the younger generation of the 1960s highlighted the emergence of youth as a force in history. But the development of a distinct youth culture went back very far, at least to the 1920s.

The subculture of the young transcended national boundaries, class lines, and most other traditional divisions in the societies of the global North. It was a subculture with its own shifting kaleidoscope of manners and mores, its endlessly new clothing styles, haircuts, dances, music, drugs and fads, folk heroes, and other enthusiasms. Particularly after World War II, it was a consuming society, supporting whole industries from blue jeans to phonograph records. It was also frequently a culturally rebellious group, rejecting the values and beliefs of older generations, determined to "do their own thing."

In the 1960s the youth culture turned political. The youth revolt of the sixties took many forms. Young people in Japan opposed their government's conservative policies and the military alliance with the United States. In America they mobilized for educational reform, for civil rights for black Americans, against poverty, and against America's role in the Vietnam War. In Western Europe it was educational reform, ban-the-bomb, Yankee-Go-Home; in East Europe it was demands for an end to secret-police terror, for democracy, for more consumer goods—and Russky-Go-Home!

The demonstrations, marches, sit-ins, occasional violence, and general noise of the youth movements of the 1960s were unprecedented in scale. Nor were they without effect. Youth movements helped shape the history of those years, from the chaos of the Chinese Cultural Revolution to the American withdrawal from Vietnam, from more relaxed social mores to more rigorous regulation of industrial pollution.

PROBLEMS OF THE 1990S

As the last decade of the twentieth century advanced, the developed industrial societies of the global North seemed to many to have lost their way. Economic, polit-

[3]See H. Kahne and J. Z. Giele, eds., *Women's Work and Women's Lives: The Continuing Struggle Worldwide* (Boulder, Colo.: Westview Press, 1992).

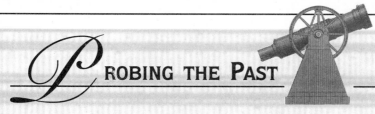

PROBING THE PAST

"*Everything helps to confirm this hierarchy in the eyes of the little girl. The historical and literary culture to which she belongs, the songs and legends with which she is lulled to sleep, are one long exaltation of man. It was men who built up Greece, the Roman Empire, France, and all other nations, who have explored the world and invented the tools for its exploitation, who have governed it, who have filled it with sculptures, paintings, works of literature. Children's books, mythology, stories, tales, all reflect the myths born of the pride and the desires of men; thus it is that through the eyes of men the little girl discovers the world and reads therein her destiny.*

The superiority of the male is, indeed, overwhelming: Perseus, Hercules, David, Achilles, Lancelot, the old French warriors Du Guesclin and Bayard, Napoleon—so many men for one Joan of Arc.

The goddesses of pagan mythology are frivolous or capricious, and they all tremble before Jupiter. While Prometheus magnificently steals fire from the sun, Pandora opens her box of evils upon the world.

Reality confirms what these novels and legends say. If the young girl reads the papers, if she listens to the conversation of grown-ups, she learns that today, as always, men run the world. The political leaders, generals, explorers, musicians, and painters whom she admires are men; certainly it is men who arouse enthusiasm in her heart."

Even in the Western nations with the strongest traditions of freedom, some groups felt oppressed in the twentieth century. Feminists urged that patriarchy—domination of society by the male sex—was still a real and painful problem for women. As they saw it, the socialization process that perpetuated patriarchy warped the attitudes of both little girls and little boys. In this passage, the leading French intellectual Simone de Beauvoir links this process to childish impressions of history.

What effect does de Beauvoir think history as taught has on a young girl's view of the relative importance of men and women in the world? Note that the historical (and journalistic) accounts mentioned here focus on individuals—history as the story of "great white men." Do you think a type of history that emphasized social trends or material culture would be less male-centered?

Simone de Beauvoir, The Second Sex, trans. H. M. Parshley (New York: Random House, 1974), pp. 324–326.

ical, social, and even psychological problems abounded in North America, Europe, and Japan. We will look at some of these problems in a global perspective in a later chapter. An impressionistic overview will, however, be useful here.

By 1995, both the major Western nations and the rising industrial states of the East Asian rim had emerged from the latest economic recession. Some economists, as we will see, thought that the world stood on the brink of another long boom like that of the postwar decades. But the psychological, social, and political consequences of the downturn of the 1970s and 1980s remained potent

forces, contributing to ongoing tensions whose outcome none could predict.

Reviving economies filled stores with electronic gadgets and streets with shiny new cars—indeed, there had been plenty of both even during the twenty lean years since the oil crunch of 1974. Yet homeless people still slept in the park across from the White House in Washington, Russian engineers peddled junk in Moscow flea markets, and even the buskers in the Paris Metro had a lean and hungry look. Drugs, crime, and random violence tore at the social fabric everywhere, making once well-ordered European cities unsafe at night and turning American inner cities into war zones where teen-agers mowed each other down with automatic weapons fire.

Solid middle- and working-class citizens, mired in neither poverty nor criminal behavior, faced gnawing economic insecurities of their own. Middle-management and white-collar staff as well as blue-collar workers feared "downsizing" and "steamlining" that might put them out of work while it made their companies more competitive. These once self-confident and solid citizens now faced declining living standards, children they could not afford to send to college, and retirement without savings. In Eastern Europe, the dream of political and economic freedom seemed to have produced skyrocketing prices, disappearing jobs, graft, corruption, and a world run by self-serving politicians, profiteers, and gangsters.

Only five years away from the end of the millennium, many citizens of the world's most prosperous nations seemed to have little faith in their future.

SUMMARY

The United States was the predominant power in the world of the later twentieth century, enjoying prosperity much of the time and consuming a substantial portion of the produce of the world at large. Political stability prevailed, whether under liberal administrations such as those of Truman, Kennedy, and Johnson, or under conservative regimes such as those of Eisenhower, Nixon, Reagan, and Bush.

In Europe, Germany loomed as the richest nation, carrying on in its prewar tradition of industrial skill. Britain and France pioneered such advances as the welfare state and European economic integration, while Western Europe as a whole benefited from the Common Market and the evolving European Community. Japan and other nations of the East Asian Pacific rim, meanwhile, forged a productive new center of economic growth at the other end of Eurasia. Other highly developed nations, not all of them in the geographical north, included Canada, Australia, and Israel.

The Soviet Union became the second most massive producer of such basics as steel and oil, but fell drastically behind in agriculture, consumer products, and other areas. Between 1989 and 1991, revolts toppled governments and forced drastic political and economic changes all across the communist bloc of East European states.

The material achievements of what is sometimes called the global North—the developed nations of Europe, North America, Japan, and other areas—were truly spectacular during the later decades of the twentieth century. High technology was the secret, a continuation of the Industrial Revolution that produced a range of marvels from frozen foods and television to space science and nuclear power. Free enterprise—with some government fine-tuning—produced more goods and services for Western peoples than any people had ever enjoyed. State socialism in communist countries was considerably less successful, and the system collapsed in chaos as the last decade of the century began.

Social inequalities remained in the most affluent societies in history. Other problems of the end of the century included crime, collapsing families, and widespread discontent with the state of society.

SUGGESTED READING

BARONE, M. *Our Country: The Shaping of America from Roosevelt to Reagan.* New York: Free Press, 1990. Monumental political history of the United States from the 1930s through the 1980s.

BEER, S. H. *British Politics in the Collectivist Age.* New York: Knopf, 1965. British institutions in the age of the welfare state.

BIALER, S. *Stalin's Successors: Leadership, Stability, and Change in the Soviet Union.* New York: Cambridge University Press, 1980. Important, especially on the Brezhnev years. On Khrushchev, see a perceptive Russian analysis by R. A. Medvedev and J. A. Medvedev, *Khrushchev: The Years in Power* (New York: Columbia University Press, 1976).

CARRÉ, J. J., et al. *French Economic Growth.* Stanford: Stanford University Press, 1976. Government central planning in a developed capitalist state. See also S. Mazey and M. Newan, eds., *Mitterand's France* (New York: Croom Helm, 1987), a collection of essays analyzing Mitterand's socialist government.

CHAFE, W. H. *The American Woman: Her Changing Social, Economic, and Political Roles, 1920–1970.* New York: Oxford University Press, 1974. Good survey of the period between the suffrage movement at the beginning of the century and the renewed militance of the 1970s.

CRAIG, G. A. *The Germans.* Eminently readable profile of postwar Germany by a well-known historian of that country. Also see H. A. Turner, *The Two Germanies Since 1945* (New Haven: Yale University Press, 1987) for a concise summary of the political evolution of the Federal Republic and the Democratic Republic, carrying the story down to within a few years of the latter's absorption by the former.

DUNN, R., ed. *Democracy: The Unfinished Journey.* Oxford: Oxford University Press, 1992. Essays on the history and present advantages of democratic government, with some emphasis on interaction with economic forces.

HEIDENHEIMER, A. J., H. HEDO, and C. T. ADAMS. *Comparative Public Policy: The Politics of Social Choice in Europe and America.* New York: St. Martin's Press, 1975. Draws distinctions between the social policies of these two major centers of democratic capitalist society.

HUGHES, H. S. *Sophisticated Rebels: The Political Culture of European Dissent, 1968–1987.* Cambridge: Harvard University Press, 1988. A leading historian of European social thought surveys recent social movements, from the youth revolt of the 1960s to contemporary environmentalist Green parties, Soviet dissidents, and others.

IKE, N. *Japanese Politics: Patron–Client Democracy.* New York: Knopf, 1972. Postwar political structure. See also N. Thayer, *How the Conservatives Rule Japan* (Princeton: Princeton University Press, 1969), on the long conservative tenure of power.

LAPIDUS, G. W. *Women, Work, and Family in the Soviet Union.* New York: M. E. Sharpe, 1982. Contrasts significant female contribution in the workplace with continuing inequality elsewhere in society. F. du Plessix Gray's *Soviet Women: Walking the Tightrope* (New York: Doubleday, 1990) contains perceptive insights gleaned from interviews by a Western writer of Russian ancestry.

LAQUEUR, W. *Europe since Hitler.* London: Penguin, 1982. Survey by a leading European historian. On Europe's postwar resurgence, see R. Mayne, *The Recovery of Europe, 1945–1973* (Garden City, N.Y.: Anchor Books, 1973).

LEWIN, M. *The Gorbachev Phenomenon: A Historical Interpretation.* Berkeley and Los Angeles: University of California Press, 1988. Puts the Gorbachev reforms into a context of other attempts at changing Soviet Russian society. For Gorbachev's years in power, see a thoughtful account by two journalists, D. Doder and L. Branson, *Gorbachev: Heretic in the Kremlin* (New York: Viking, 1990).

LEWIS, A. *Portrait of a Decade: The Second American Revolution.* New York: Random House, 1964. Narrative of the American civil rights movement, by a reporter who covered it. See also the life of the movement's charismatic leader in D. Lewis, *King: A Critical Biography* (New York: Praeger, 1970). On other aspects of the tumultuous 1960s in America, see M. Dickstein's counter-culturally oriented *Gates of Eden: American Culture in the Sixties* (New York: Basic Books, 1977), and L. M. Baskir and W. A. Straves, *Change and Circumstance: The Draft, the War, and the Vietnam Generation* (New York: Knopf, 1978), on the antiwar movement.

MOWAT, R. C. *Creating the European Community.* New York: Barnes & Noble, 1973. The forging of Europe's unexampled economic institutions in the years after World War II.

OPHULS, W. *Ecology and the Politics of Scarcity.* San Francisco: Freeman, 1979. Ecological concern in the United States, a nation more concerned than most about saving the environment.

PATRICK, H, and H. ROSOVSKY, eds. *Asia's New Giant: How the Japanese Economy Works.* Washington, D.C.: Brookings Institution, 1976. Articles on Japan's economic challenge to the older developed nations.

REISCHAUER, E. O. *The Japanese.* Cambridge, Mass.: Belknap Press, 1977. By the leading authority and former United States ambassador to Japan.

SCHLESINGER, A. M., JR. *A Thousand Days.* Boston: Houghton Mifflin, 1965. The Kennedy years in the United States, by a historian who also served in the government. On the social legislation of the Kennedy-Johnson years, see G. Steiner, *State of Welfare* (Washington, D.C.: Brookings Institution, 1971) and P. Marris and M. Rein, *Dilemmas of Social Reform* (Chicago: University of Chicago Press, 1982).

SULLEROT, E. *Women, Society, and Change.* New York: McGraw-Hill, 1971. Women in Western Europe after World War II. For comparisons between the British and American women's movements, see O. Banks, *Faces of Feminism* (New York: St. Martin's Press, 1982).

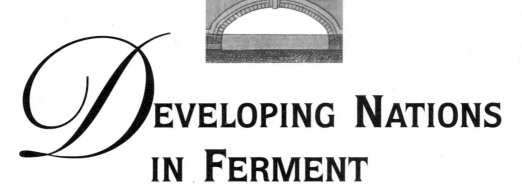

CHAPTER 47

Developing Nations in Ferment

THE POLITICS OF DEVELOPMENT: ASIA

POWER STRUCTURES: MILITARY RULE, ONE-PARTY RULE—AND REVOLUTION

The new nations of Africa and Asia, like the older Third World countries of Latin America, tended to alternate between authoritarian regimes and revolutionary upheaval. The authoritarian governments were normally either one-party systems or ruled by military strongmen.

A one-party regime would often emerge soon after independence, built on the loyalty of the people to the party that had won the colony its independence. Frequently, however, this party of national liberation would, with the passage of time, no longer deserve the people's support. Failure of grand schemes for development was often the cause of this loss of popular support, but flagrant corruption and high living—considered unsuitable in a tribune of the people—was an even stronger source of disillusionment.

At this point, a military cabal would usually make use of the other major institution that could command disciplined support—the army—to overthrow the party in power. Such military juntas might, or might not, prove more honest, but they generally lacked the skills needed to run a civilian government, let alone the economic and technical knowledge necessary for nation building. Thus the country was often no more likely to progress under the military than under one-party rule.

The one-party states with the most capacity for staying in power were those ruled by socialist or communist parties. Such regimes, however, also had their liabilities. They sometimes turned to the ideologically justified but impractical policies mentioned above, subsidizing benefits for their people that the country was not yet rich enough to afford. Such countries also frequently had to face the hostility of powerful capitalist nations like the United States.

A small number of democratic governments emerged in the Third World. A more common alternative to authoritarianism, however, was revolution. Coups and rebellions, guerrilla wars in the back country and terror-

ism in the cities were widespread across the underdeveloped world. The two great Cold War adversaries also frequently provided moral or material support for the contestants—the United States most commonly for military regimes or the rare democracy, the Soviet Union for one-party governments or guerrilla movements. This outside involvement further complicated Third World politics.

The world grew used to media reports of corruption, military dictatorship, single-party authoritarianism, guerrilla attacks, and "death-squad" repression in the global South. In mitigation, it should be pointed out that these really were very new nations, most of them dating only from the period since World War II. Poverty also might account for many of the difficulties, a poverty rooted in a global economy largely beyond the control of Third World nations.

Underlying all these political gropings for direction, however, there did seem to be a fundamental concern: a search for a viable strategy of economic development, for the modernization of these premodern peoples. Politics throughout the global South was thus fundamentally the politics of development. It is this thread that will unite most of the examples cited below.

CHINA'S LONG ROAD TO DEVELOPMENT

China's domestic history after the end of its long civil war in 1949 was determined by the Communist party leaders who won that war. For the first quarter century of that period, this meant rule by the leader of the Chinese Revolution, Mao Zedong, or in his later years by the group of revolutionary ideologues who gathered around his iron-willed wife, Jiang Qing. Throughout the years from mid-century to the middle of the 1970s, Mao's round, smiling face and receding black hairline, Mao's "thoughts" in the famous little red book, and Mao's revolutionary legend dominated Chinese life even more than Stalin's personality cult had towered over Russia in his heyday.

The Chinese Communist party and a wide variety of other mass organizations—from the All-China Federation of Trade Unions to the Young Communist League and the All-China Federation of Democratic Women—gave the Communist leadership an unparalleled capacity to mobilize China's hundreds of millions for mass action. Harsher measures were also used to control the nation. Ideological dissenters were given peasant labor that would

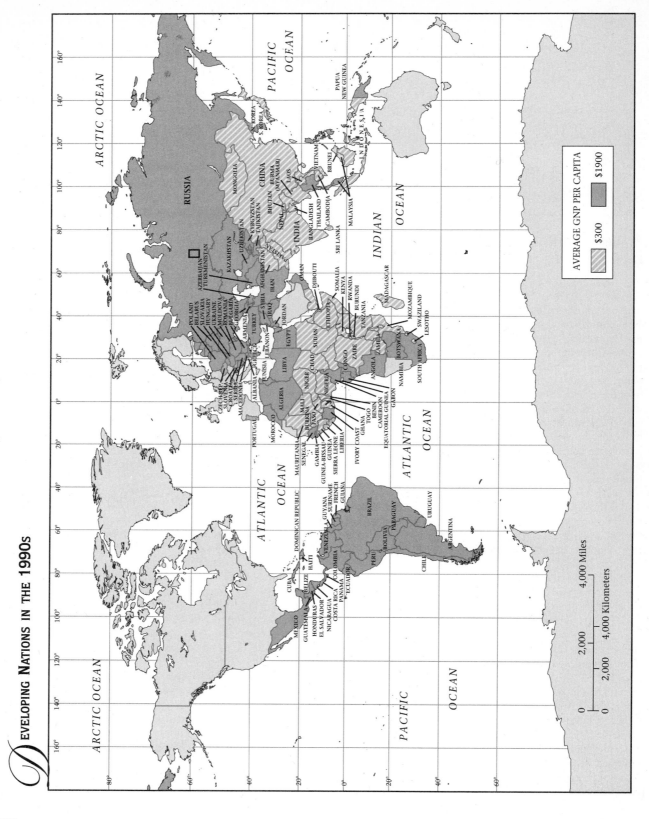

Developing Nations in the 1990s

ARCTIC OCEAN

PACIFIC OCEAN

ATLANTIC OCEAN

INDIAN OCEAN

RUSSIA

CHINA

INDIA

MONGOLIA

KOREA
KOREA

PAPUA NEW GUINEA

BRUNEI
VIETNAM
BURMA (MYANMAR)
LAOS
THAILAND
CAMBODIA
MALAYSIA
BANGLADESH
BHUTAN
NEPAL
SRI LANKA
PAKISTAN
AFGHANISTAN
KYRGYZSTAN
TAJIKISTAN
UZBEKISTAN
TURKMENISTAN
KAZAKHSTAN
AZERBAIJAN
ARMENIA
GEORGIA
IRAN
IRAQ
SYRIA
JORDAN
LEBANON
TURKEY
OMAN
DJIBOUTI
SOMALIA
KENYA
RWANDA
BURUNDI
TANZANIA
ETHIOPIA
SUDAN
EGYPT
MADAGASCAR
MOZAMBIQUE
SWAZILAND
LESOTHO
SOUTH AFRICA
BOTSWANA
NAMIBIA
ANGOLA
ZAMBIA
ZAIRE
CONGO
GABON
CAMEROON
EQUATORIAL GUINEA
BENIN
TOGO
GHANA
IVORY COAST
NIGERIA
NIGER
CHAD
LIBYA
ALGERIA
MALI
BURKINA FASO
MOROCCO
MAURITANIA
SENEGAL
GAMBIA
GUINEA-BISSAU
GUINEA
SIERRA LEONE
LIBERIA
PORTUGAL
TUNISIA
ALBANIA
MACEDONIA
SERBIA
CROATIA
SLOVENIA
BOSNIA
CZECH REP.
POLAND
BELARUS
SLOVAKIA
HUNGARY
UKRAINE
MOLDOVA
ROMANIA
BULGARIA

MEXICO
GUATEMALA
HONDURAS
EL SALVADOR
NICARAGUA
COSTA RICA
PANAMA
BELIZE
CUBA
DOMINICAN REPUBLIC
HAITI
VENEZUELA
GUYANA
SURINAME
FRENCH GUIANA
COLOMBIA
ECUADOR
PERU
BOLIVIA
PARAGUAY
BRAZIL
URUGUAY
ARGENTINA
CHILE

AVERAGE GNP PER CAPITA

$300	$1900

4,000 Miles
0   2,000   4,000 Kilometers
0   2,000   4,000

proletarianize their thinking. Hundreds of thousands, as Mao himself admitted, were "liquidated" in the early years, and more hundreds of thousands, as his successors charged, died during the Cultural Revolution of the 1960s. Most of the time, however, a combination of persuasion and party control was adequate to move the world's largest nation along the paths laid out for it by its new rulers.

Those paths could take some colorful turns as they followed the sometimes erratic thoughts of Chairman Mao and the more moderate insights of those who succeeded him. Early land reforms were soon followed by loose collectivization of agriculture on large peasant-owned farms. Nationalization of heavy industry and government Five-Year Plans followed the familiar Russian model. But in the later 1950s Mao announced a Great Leap Forward involving tightly organized communal farms and small-scale backyard industry on the local level. Peasant discontent with the loss of their private plots and with the compulsory group living, plus a series of bad harvests, led to widespread starvation and a pulling back from some of the extremes of this Maoist reform.

During the later 1960s, however, the aging Mao decreed a new campaign, the so-called Great Proletarian Cultural Revolution, which came very close to shaking the system to pieces. Mao, his young wife—film actress Jiang Qing—and their allies in Beijing apparently felt that the People's Republic was drifting away from its ideological roots, settling into old bureaucratic ways, and losing its revolutionary zeal. The Cultural Revolution mobilized millions of young people in the new Red Guard units to denounce bureaucrats, compel self-criticism by any and all—up to and including Mao's old comrades in the top leadership—and to reassert the primacy of Marxist-Maoist thought.

The result was a reign of terror that had nearly paralyzed the country by 1968. Large numbers were hounded to death by local vigilantes or killed in clashes between rival factions, including rival gangs of Red Guards. In the end, the Chinese Red Army had to be called upon to regain control.

In the long run, however, pragmatism won the day. By the early 1970s, practical men such as Mao's old colleague Zhou Enlai had even arranged a rapprochement between China and Richard Nixon's America. And after Mao's death in 1976, the pragmatists seized power under another old revolutionary—and victim of the Cultural Revolution—Deng Xiaoping. Under the diminutive but bustling Deng, the new leadership actually brought to trial and convicted Mao's widow and her allies, the now condemned Gang of Four, for the follies of the Great Leap Forward and the excesses of the Cultural Revolution.

China had broken its close relationship with the Soviet Union as early as 1959–1960. After the middle 1970s, the pragmatic new leaders sought closer economic ties with Western nations, including the United States and Japan, in order to help modernize China. In many places,

capitalist incentives were introduced to encourage increased production.

Genuine progress resulted. Though general living standards remained at Third World levels, foreign investment and joint ventures with foreign firms stimulated growth rates comparable to those of East Asian "tigers" like South Korea and Taiwan. The People's Republic was able to feed its one billion citizens, and some of its cities were sprucer, its domestic industry developing. A rigorous birth-control program was introduced to deal with what was perhaps the nation's number one problem, massive overpopulation.

In the later 1980s, however, economic changes and increasing contact with Westerners stimulated renewed demands for both political democracy and action against the corruption that had accompanied economic growth. The culmination of these demands for further reform came in the spring of 1989 in Beijing. There student demonstrations in Tiananmen Square gained the support of a large segment of the population of the nation's capital and sparked sympathy demonstrations in other cities. Deng and the rest of the older Communist leadership, however, refused to open up the political process and finally sent in tanks to clean out the demonstrators. Hundreds were killed in what came to be known as the "Tienanmen massacre," and political freedom was once again suppressed throughout China.

In the mid nineties, China thus seemed to be entering a period of uncertainty. Deng's age and ill-health made his passing inevitable. The key question, then, was whether his successors would continue the economic policies that were transforming China—whether a new generation of leaders might be more liberal politically—and how China's hundred's of millions would respond to the inevitable strains and pressures of change.

INDIA: THE WORLD'S LARGEST DEMOCRACY

India was the second largest Asian nation from the late 1940s on, and made significant progress under the leadership of a strong national party and charismatic leadership. But there were crucial differences between the two Asian giants. India's economic growth was somewhat slower, but its politics were democratic, its charismatic leaders elected by those they ruled.

The Republic of India was governed for most of the four decades after independence in 1947 by a "dynasty" of father, daughter, and grandson: first by Gandhi's disciple Pandit Nehru, from 1947 till his death in 1964, then by Nehru's daughter Indira Gandhi (no relation to the Mahatma) from 1966 until her assassination in 1984 and finally by her son Rajiv Gandhi for most of the next half-dozen years, until he too died at the hands of an assassin. Their problems were many, their successes significant in this context of endless difficulties.

India, seldom united over its long history, had to

be welded into a nation before it could be governed. Institutionally, at least, Nehru accomplished this by compelling all the surviving *rajas* of the so-called princely states to accept absorption into the new country. Mrs. Gandhi had the harder task of melding the subcontinent's many peoples, languages, traditions, and religions into some approximation of a citizenry. This she at least began to do by a combination of personal appeal, political manipulation, and occasional use of force. Rajiv Gandhi, a reluctant politician, had less success in dealing with political corruption, religious and ethnic violence, and multiplying economic problems.

Attempts to develop the country economically encountered similar difficulties. The Indians tried a wide variety of methods to encourage development, from Five-Year Plans to foreign investment, from foreign aid (from both Russia and America) to the agricultural technology of the Green Revolution. In overall production, India achieved a respectable rank somewhere between that of the leading Western and Eastern European nations.

The best efforts of Nehru and the Gandhis, however, repeatedly foundered on India's greatest problem: its burgeoning population. As Nehru said, it was necessary for India to run very hard simply to keep up with the needs of the millions who were added to its citizen body every year. The country thus remained a sprawling land of poverty-stricken and in many cases illiterate villages, and the gap between those masses and the wealthy residents of Calcutta or Bombay was perhaps even greater in the 1990s than it was in the 1940s.

Politically, "the world's most populous democracy" managed to preserve a democratic system despite political corruption and violence. There was a short period of "emergency dictatorship" by Indira Gandhi in the 1970s. There were periods of anarchic violence triggered by ancient religious differences, most notably the conflicts between Hindus and Muslims in the 1940s and those between Hindus and the movement for Sikh autonomy and Tamil independence that cost Mrs. Gandhi her life in 1984 and her son and successor Rajiv his in 1991.

ARAB NATIONALISM AND ISLAMIC RESURGENCE

Islamic militance, Arab nationalism, and the dark gleam of oil determined the history of a wide swath of Asia and North Africa in recent decades. Politically speaking, the Muslim nations followed different paths. Some, like Iran under the shah and the oil-rich giant Saudi Arabia, remained anachronistic absolute monarchies in the later twentieth century. Others became military dictatorships, such as Pakistan under General Zia or Libya under the colorful Colonel Qaddafi, often accused of being a patron of international terrorism. Egypt was dominated for decades by a series of former military men of considerable political skill, including the nationalist leader Gamal

Abdel Nasser and the internationally admired Anwar Sadat, the first Arab leader to sign a peace treaty with Israel. Two leaders of the Ba'athist Arab Nationalist party came to power, Saddam Hussein in Iraq and Hafez Assad in Syria, and were soon locked in an intense rivalry, like so many of the Arab rulers.

The vast reservoirs of oil that stretch from Iran to the far end of the Sahara gave these recently emancipated sheiks and colonels a powerful new economic role in the world. They used some of their wealth to feud with each other or with their non-Muslim neighbors from Israel to India. Much of it went into lavish living and foreign investments—the petrodollars that flooded the banks of the West. Some of their oil wealth, however, did go into providing agricultural projects, education, health care, decent roads, and housing for the sometimes scanty but rapidly growing populations of these arid lands.

Another powerful force that helped to shape the history of the Middle East was Arab nationalism. Kindled by the anti-imperialist movements of the first half of the century, pan-Arab feeling resembled in some ways the pan-Slav or pan-German movements of the 1800s. All Arabs were brothers, Arab nationalists believed, no matter what country they lived in. The score of postliberation Arab states stretching from Morocco to Iraq were often denounced as products of imperialistic European machinations. For Arabs who believed in the spiritual unity of the "Arab nation," the great enemy was Israel, condemned for occupying Arab land and oppressing its Palestinian Arab minority. In 1990, Iraq's ambitious nationalist ruler Saddam Hussein violated the principles of Arab nationalism by occupying the neighboring Arab state of Kuwait. He then, however, invoked loyalty to the Arab nation when an international military coalition led by Israel's great patron the United States moved to prevent Saddam's bid for leadership of the Arab world. The humiliating defeat that followed, as we shall see, left many Arabs further embittered at the United States, Israel, and the West.

Islamic religious fervor was also at a new high in the later 1990s. This dynamic element kindled some sensational violence. In 1965, Indonesian Muslim fundamentalists, encouraged by the Indonesian army, rose in righteous indignation against local Communist cadres and their atheistic gospel, slaughtering hundreds of thousands of them. In 1979, the Iranian Muslim followers of the Ayatollah Ruhollah Khomeini overthrew their autocratic modernizing shah. Soon they had instituted a religious reign of terror of their own, decimating student radicals and religious minorities alike and holding the U.S. Embassy and its personnel hostage for more than a year in the early 1980s.

The early 1990s saw a new wave of militance led by Islamic fundamentalists in many lands. Moves toward peace with Israel led by the Palestinian nationalist Yassir Arafat were challenged by fundamentalist *fedayeen* organizations like Hamas, who continued to kill Israelis and defy Arafat. In Algeria, fundamentalists denied free elec-

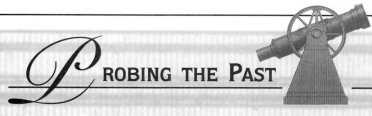

"*In the hundred years that preceded the Islamic revolution Iranian women had slowly and tenaciously fought for equality. They gained access to education in 1910, the abolition of the veil in 1936, the vote in 1962, a curb on the unequivocal male right to divorce and custody of children in 1973, free abortion on demand in 1974, and a ban on polygamy and a right to alimony after divorce in 1976. The ban on polygamy and free abortion on demand were significant steps. . . . However, the devout and less wealthy women equated sexual freedom with immorality, imperialism and corruption. . . .*

Access to paid work became more of a loss than a gain for many women who often supported an idle husband as well as their children on meagre incomes. The process of modernisation had, in many instances, displaced male labour by cheaper female labour without leading to alternative jobs for men. Unemployment, however, did not significantly erode the absolute control of fathers and husbands over the household; in many cases it merely intensified the subordination of women. Those women who worked in factories did have direct access to their wages, but the substantially larger group working in the informal sector as servants, washerwomen and cleaning ladies often had their pay negotiated by, and paid to, their male relatives. In all cases the women continued to do all the domestic work. Hence, many impoverished working class women felt that they had lost the honour and dignity bestowed on them by their religion without gaining any material benefits in return. As a result the advocates of domesticity for women found a large support base among the poor and working classes. . . .

Khomeini, on his return in 1979, exploited this situation and embarked on an intensive campaign to drive women back to the sphere of domesticity."

This passage comes from a paper first presented at a New Delhi conference of sociologists and anthropologists concerned with the place of women in modernizing Asian societies. Haleh Afshar is an authority on the changing position of women in the Muslim society of Iran.

The Pahlavi dynasty overthrown by the Ayatollah Khomeini in 1979, though a repressive autocracy, had sought to "modernize" the country by introducing Western values and practices. Why did some pious Muslims oppose the abolition of polygamy and the legalization of abortion? What economic changes made jobs for women outside the home less popular than a Westerner might expect?

Haleh Afshar, "Behind the Veil: The Public and Private Faces of Khomeini's Policies on Iranian Women," in Bina Agarwal, ed., <u>Structures of Patriarchy: State, Community, and Household in Modernizing Asia</u> (London: Zed Books, 1988), pp. 228–229.

tions by nationalist army leaders launched a savage campaign of assassination against modernized Algerians and resident foreigners. In many Islamic countries, meanwhile, people who had been moving toward Western ways turned back toward Islamic customs, costumes, and fervent worship. Muslim fundamentalism, even more than Arab nationalism, seemed to be carving out a widening gap between Islam and the West.

ASIA IN THE 1990S: MOUNTING TENSIONS

As the century entered its final decade, mounting tensions still threatened to erupt into open conflict in many parts of Asia. In East Asia, southern Asia, and the Middle East, internal tensions and civil strife mounted.

China, having reestablished its massive political and military preeminence in East Asia, concentrated on domestic development in the 1980s and 1990s. Catching up with Japan economically posed a long-term challenge for China after the death of Mao Zedong in 1976. The suppression of student demonstrations in Beijing in 1989 brought international condemnation but threatened little slowing of China's economic resurgence. Wealthy little Hong Kong, bound by treaty to pass from British to Chinese rule in 1997, blanched at the thought of facing an iron fist similar to that which had crushed the students in Tienanmen Square. There seemed to be a good chance, however, that Hong Kong's value as an economic gateway to the West might exempt it from the rigors of Communist repression.

At China's northern frontier, meanwhile, South Korea's rapid economic growth also led to student demands for still more political freedom and even for reunification with Communist North Korea. When that nation's ageing dictator Kim Il-Sung, died, however, a stand-down with South Korea and the United States began.

In South Asia, India also faced international tensions on two frontiers. In the far northern region of Kashmir, guerrilla revolt flared and rivalry with Pakistan threatened to explode into war once more as the 1990s began.

In the far south, Indian troops were actually deployed to the island republic of Sri Lanka (Ceylon) in the later 1980s to block efforts by nationalist Tamil guerrillas to overthrow the government. Indian intervention, however, proved less than successful, and the civil war in Sri Lanka dragged on into the 1990s, when Tamil terrorism spread to India itself. In the spring of 1991, a Tamil suicide bomber assassinated Rajiv Gandhi, leaving India wracked by corruption and violence.

Between China and India, the Southeast Asian state of Kampuchea (Cambodia) also threatened to slide back into anarchy when North Vietnam's occupying troops were withdrawn in the late 1980s. A loose alliance of guerrilla forces at once accelerated their efforts to overthrow the government the North Vietnamese had left in place. The most aggressive of the rebels were the Khmer Rouge, notorious for turning Kampuchea into the "killing fields" of the 1970s. Peaceful elections were held under U.N. sponsorship in the early 1990s, but fears of renewed violence or dictatorship persisted.

Some of the most disturbing threats of conflict, however, emerged in the Middle East.

In the late 1980s, Israel, after repelling so many external attacks, proved unable to control a Palestinian uprising called the *Intifadah* in the occupied territories of Gaza and the West Bank of the Jordan River. Here stone-throwing youths confronted Israeli soldiers, and as months of attempts at suppression turned into years, world opinion began to turn against Israel. In the early 1990s, even the United States, Israel's oldest and staunchest ally, urged discussions with the Palestinian Liberation Organization and supported peace talks between the Israelis, their Arab neighbors, and representatives of the Palestinians. In 1994,

Israel signed a peace treaty with Jordan and granted the Palestinians at Gaza and part of the West Bank autonomy under the former terrorist chief, Arafat.

Most explosive of all, however, was the oil-rich region around the Persian Gulf. Here Iraq's Saddam Hussein, victorious but deeply in debt after his long war with Iran, sought once more to advance his interests by a swift military stroke. Literally overnight, his troops occupied the little neighboring state of Kuwait, giving him control of its vast oil resources to add to his own. A world that ran on oil, however, reacted more forcefully than the Iraqi ruler had expected. President George Bush took the lead in rallying global opposition. The United Nations voted a stringent embargo to isolate and drain Iraq economically. Hundreds of thousands of American fighting men and women poured into Arabia to protect that nation—and its oil—from further Iraqi expansion, and military units from Britain, France, and such rival Arab nations as Egypt and Syria joined the coalition. In a rapid and thoroughly high-tech military campaign in the opening months of 1991, the U.S.-led alliance expelled Saddam's troops from Kuwait and devastated Iraq itself. The larger significance of this "Gulf War" will be examined in the next chapter. Its immediate impact on the Middle East and the Arab world, however, was to intensify political instability and anti-Western feeling.

THE POLITICS OF DEVELOPMENT: AFRICA AND LATIN AMERICA

BLACK AFRICA'S STRUGGLE

In Africa south of the Sahara, political instability and autocratic one-party or military rule alternated in a bewildering kaleidoscope, punctuated by bloody flashes of rebellion. Economically, some of these countries prospered on a combination of commodity exports and foreign aid and investment; others seemed to settle deeper into poverty.

For black Africa, life after the great liberation was a struggle in many ways more difficult than the victorious fight for independence had been. In French-speaking West Africa, for instance, close economic relations with France enabled such liberation leaders as Félix Houphouët-Boigny of the Ivory Coast and Senegal's Léopold Senghor to lead their new nations to relative prosperity. There were paved roads there, bright lights, marketplaces full to bursting, and new skyscrapers in the great African cities of Abidjan and Dakar. But landlocked inner African Sahel states such as Mali, Niger, and Chad remained dusty, poverty-ridden backwaters.

In the former colonies of British East Africa, two of the continent's best-known liberation leaders, Jomo Kenyatta of Kenya and Julius Nyerere of Tanzania, provided an interesting contrast in development styles. Kenyatta opened his doors to Western capital, while Nyerere preached self-reliance and socialism—and got aid from European socialist countries and China. Kenya, with a considerable colonial head start in development, grew more rapidly, building some industry and an East African metropolitan center in Nairobi. Nyerere's Tanzania provided water, food, some education and health care for his people first—and was on the edge of bankruptcy by 1990.

African countries generally were among those hardest hit by declining world prices for the commodities they produced and rising costs for things they consumed—particularly oil. Terrible famine added to the travail of a number of African nations in the 1970s and 1980s. Drought, government mismanagement, devastating civil wars, and the increasingly rapid spread of the desert into areas bordering the Sahara all contributed to the disaster. In Ethiopia, the Sahel countries, and elsewhere, hundreds of thousands died and whole districts were depopulated by starvation.

The greatest struggle of all persisted in the Republic of South Africa, whose all-white Afrikaner Nationalist party government continued through the postwar decades to deny the black majority more than a token share of power.

Blacks organized to demand equal treatment during the postwar period, particularly after the implementation of apartheid policies in the early 1950s. But demonstrations and strikes were suppressed, sometimes violently, as in the Sharpeville massacre of 1960 in which scores of Africans were shot down. White radicals who called for racial compromise were placed under house arrest. Black resisters were imprisoned, among them the militant Nelson Mandela and Nobel Peace Prize winner Albert Luthuli; some, like student leader Steve Biko, died under suspicious circumstances while in custody.

South Africa tried separate-but-equal segregation of blacks in so-called homelands—but the territories assigned to the blacks were generally poor lands that were economically dependent on surrounding white South Africa. In the 1980s the republic took steps toward allowing some non-Europeans a modest part in the political process. But black terrorism had by that time been added to the unpalatable mix, and for a time there seemed to be no way out of the impasse.

AFRICA IN THE 1990S: HOPES, FEARS— AND A MAJOR BREAKTHROUGH

In the late twentieth century, conflict in Africa south of the Sahara continued to take the form of civil strife rather than international wars. Struggles between traditionally rivalrous peoples within a new nation, military intervention in politics, and the ambitions of political leaders all undermined the stability of the new regimes. The contin-

Nelson Mandela, South Africa's first black president, raises a defiant fist. President Mandela's powerful personality won the respect of blacks and whites alike as he carried his country through a tense time of transition. (A/P) Wide World Photos)

uance of Western rule in South Africa and the Cold War involvements of East bloc nations in other parts of the continent added to the brew.

The world paid little heed to these endemic clashes south of the Sahara. Revolutionary struggles and open war came and went in Ethiopia, Somalia, Sudan, in Angola and Mozambique in the south, in Liberia, Ghana, and other parts of West Africa. The Western nations seldom noticed unless a major famine erupted in the war zones, as in Ethiopia and Sudan, or unless Western people were directly involved, as in South Africa. Western involvement, when it did come, took more positive forms than it had in earlier centuries. Substantial international famine relief campaigns were repeatedly launched in the 1980s and 1990s. And South Africa's apartheid policies of racial segregation led to the increasing isolation of that nation, including its exclusion from capital markets, normal trading channels, and even international athletic competition.

The end of the Cold War and the Soviet Union's turn inward to deal with its own domestic problems, meanwhile, led to the withdrawal of international Communist support for revolutionary regimes from Angola to Ethiopia. If internal rivalries still threatened to explode in a number of countries, from Kenya to the Ivory Coast, at least rival great powers no longer fueled the fires of revolt and repression.

Clan and ethnic rivalries still tore individual African nations apart. In Rwanda in the middle 1990s, for instance, the long-running feud between the majority Hutu people and the dominant Tutsi minority blew up into a horrendous civil war. Hutus massacred perhaps half a million Tutsis, and the Tutsis responded with a military offensive that turned hundreds of thousands of Hutus into starving refugees in neighboring lands.

A major African breakthrough, meanwhile, came in the Republic of South Africa. At the end of the 1980s, a new president, F.W. de Klerk, offered peace to the black African militants who had resisted apartheid for so long. He repealed the racial laws of apartheid, legalized the outlawed African National Congress, and in 1990 freed the ANC's leader, Nelson Mandela, after three decades in prison.

Under the remarkable leadership of Mandela, the South African freedom fighters negotiated a plan for free elections and an interim regime that would protect the interests of white South Africans. In the spring of 1994, black and white citizens lined up together at polling places for an election that produced South Africa's first black president, Nelson Mandela.

Many problems remained, from widespread black poverty and a soaring crime rate to the need to encourage foreign investment and trade. But the immense potential of Africa's wealthiest and most powerful nation now linked to the rest of the continent by a black African government gave hope of better times to come.

LATIN AMERICAN REVOLUTIONS

The Latin American nations were also engulfed in struggles of many kinds during the later decades of the twentieth century. Efforts at accelerated economic development, governmental reform, and even social revolution were all prominent parts of their postwar history. The Cuban slogan, *Venceremos!*—"We Shall Overcome!"— summarized much of the spirit, if not always the results of this Latin American ferment.

Development became an all-devouring passion south of the Rio Grande in the decades after World War II. In its name, poor people supported and middle-class businessmen frequently tolerated strong governments of left or right that promised development in return for submission to authoritarian rule. Central planning, import-substitution industries, diversification of industrial and agricultural production, continued construction of such essential infrastructures as the new postwar highway systems—all contributed to Latin American economic growth. In some places social services proliferated, though

the gulf between rich and poor still remained great in the southern republics.

The 1960s were the boom times. By the early 1970s two large Latin American nations, Brazil and Mexico, ranked with some European countries in overall production. Even in these successful cases, however, poverty remained endemic in the villages where most Latin Americans lived. This poverty of the domestic market choked off the boom in the 1970s and 1980s.

Economic failures stimulated an increasingly radical ideological opposition to the status quo in Middle and South America. This new revolutionary spirit flourished particularly among university students inspired by Fidel Castro's Cuban Revolution, among some Catholic priests preaching a new gospel of social reform called liberation theology, and among radicalized peons and urban workers. The resulting wave of radical agitation and revolutionary activity ranged from university strikes to urban terrorism to guerrilla warfare. It led to the election of Marxist presidents in Guatemala and Chile and to renewed bitterness toward North American and European influence. It also led to a strong countercurrent of reaction, which in several cases was at least as violent as the radical wave that had called it forth.

An early manifestation of the new demand for change was the decade-long personal dictatorship of Juan and Eva Peron (1946–1955) in Argentina. Peron drew his support from the growing Argentine urban working class, the *descamisados* ("shirtless ones"), whom he gave higher wages, social services, and retirement benefits. The magnetic Evita, a former actress, worked for women's emancipation and services for the poor. The Perons, however, also rigged elections, feuded with the Catholic church, and tended to ignore the problems of the peasantry. Three years after Evita's death in 1952, Peron was overthrown by the military.

The most flamboyant and influential revolution in the region during this period, however, was that led by Fidel Castro in Cuba. During his decades of rule in the island country, Castro ran a one-party Communist government. But though many middle-class Cubans fled, the peasant population remained loyal to the revolution, and in many ways benefited from it.

Economic growth was not exuberant under the *Venceremos* regime. Early efforts to diversify the country's one-crop sugar economy did not succeed, and Castro came to depend on selling sugar to the Soviet Union, as his predecessor Batista had on selling it to the United States. A United States-sponsored economic boycott further stunted Cuba's development.

Despite this lack of economic growth, Castro forged ahead with the most elaborate set of social services offered by any of the southern American republics. He built public housing and schools for the poor and provided health care and retirement pensions. A weak economy and impressive social services were thus combined, thanks to substantial economic aid from the Soviet Union—at least until the Soviets' own political changes and economic problems led to drastic cut-backs in the 1990s.

The most recent surge of revolutionary social experimentation in Latin America occurred in the Central American republic of Nicaragua. Here the brutal Somoza dictatorship was overthrown in 1979 in a bloody insurrection that involved practically every social class and political faction. The victorious revolutionary regime, called the Sandinistas (after a martyred revolutionary leader) represented a range of anti-Somoza views, from socialist and middle-class liberal to the liberation theology of some of the priests who took part. A variety of changes were instituted in the early 1980s, from socialization of important parts of the productive economy to literacy and public-health campaigns.

Like most revolutionary juntas, however, the Sandinistas had a low tolerance for political opposition. And by accepting help and encouragement from Cuba and the U.S.S.R., they incurred the enmity of the militantly anti-communist Reagan administration in the United States. Charges that the Sandinistas were supporting a guerrilla movement in neighboring El Salvador led Washington to organize an anti-Sandinista partisan force inside Nicaragua. This constituted a further drag on an economy that was already being asked to support new social services for Nicaraguans. At the end of the 1980s, however, a free election led to the fall of the Sandinistas and the choice of a pro-American candidate, Violeta Chamorro, as president.

LATIN AMERICA IN THE 1990S: PROBLEMS AND PROSPECTS

A regional revolution that attracted fewer headlines was the resurgence of democratic government and free-market economic growth in many Latin American nations during the 1980s and early 1990s.

Where authoritarian regimes, frequently military dictatorships, prevailed in the 1950s, elected civilian governments came to power in the 1980s. Older democracies like Mexico and Venezuela were thus joined by the largest South American countries, Argentina and Brazil, as the military gave way to civilian leadership. By 1995, only a single unelected ruler remained in power in Latin America—Fidel Castro.

The new leaders of the 1990s, furthermore, seemed to be following the emerging trend in Third and Second World economic policies as well. Breaking with a pattern of protective tariffs and government direction of Latin American economies that went back to colonial times, these popular rulers turned to free-trade and free-market forces to solve their economic problems. Both Mexico and Brazil, Latin America's leading industrial powers, moved vigorously in this direction. They began at once to lower tariffs, sell off government-run industries to the private

sector, trim government spending, and curb the inflation that was Latin America's particular bane. In 1993, the North American Free Trade Agreement—NAFTA—opened Mexico to further economic stimulation from the United States and Canada, while South American trade treaties opened borders elsewhere in the New World.

Such rapid changes cost many jobs and led to much suffering. In the long run, however, these reforms might enable Latin America to follow the East Asian rim from the Third World into the First World.

THE SOCIETY OF THE GLOBAL SOUTH

VILLAGE PEOPLE: ASIA, AFRICA, LATIN AMERICA

A Third World village is a cock crowing while it is still dark outside, or perhaps a *muezzin* calling to predawn prayers. It is close-set houses made of wattle and daub, clay brick, roughly whitewashed plaster over stone, roofs of thatch, palm leaves, tile, or tin. It is hard-packed earthen paths and streets, bare feet, sandals, a bike or two. It is water from a village well, vegetables from the back garden, chickens underfoot, goats, sheep, perhaps a sacred cow wandering at will.

It is dirt under your fingernails, in the cracks of your skin, sunshine, insects, and a sore back by noon. It is women slapping wet clothes against the rocks in a stream and laying them out on the grass to dry. It is kids in school uniforms hopping off the school bus at the crossroads, books swinging in straps or satchels, and racing into town. It is dried-up old people without teeth, kids with untreated umbilical hernias, overworked young women ready to drop at the end of the day, young men away in the city, trying to find work.

Village people are three quarters of the human race, three and a half billion out of the more than five billion of us who swarm over this planet today. They live mostly in Asia, Africa, and Latin America—the three continents of the global South, the world south of the north temperate zone. They are for the most part non-Western peoples, dwellers in hot lands who wear clothing unlike that worn by Americans, Europeans, or the average Japanese.

There are important exceptions: underdeveloped China is not in the geographical south, fully developed Australia is. But by and large, the global South is where village people live.

They may live in an ancient civilization like that of India or China, temporarily relegated to the unfamiliar category of "backward" or "underdeveloped" by the West's sudden leap ahead in industrial technology two centuries ago.

They may be citizens of a new nation, such as Nigeria or Zimbabwe, building from scratch, only decades old, even its name a recent acquisition, all its uncertain history still ahead.

They may be residents of a middle-level developing country such as Venezuela, Mexico, and increasingly China, with resources, cheap labor, and some industry to give them the long-run hope of an industrialized future, with regular elections and a land-reform program that works.

Plenty of books will tell you about their problems: overpopulation, disease, malnutrition, unemployment, illiteracy, one-crop economies, political authoritarianism or instability or both, swollen cities, dying traditional village cultures. It is harder to get a handle on the vitality of many Third World countries. You get a sense of that, perhaps, from watching a West African market woman sail regally through the market-day tumult with a fantastic array of things balanced on the tray on her brightly kerchiefed head. Or from the peanuts you buy in India—wrapped in a page covered with quadratic equations, torn from a child's exercise book.

This section deals mostly with the many problems and the sometimes erratic course of Third World history over the two or three decades since most of these countries gained their independence. But it would be well to remember the human lives that compose those histories, the human vitality that in the long run is surely the best hope for all the village peoples of the globe.

PROBLEMS OF DEVELOPING NATIONS

Marshall McLuhan, the media expert, applied the term *global village* to the peoples of the world, linked by television and other media of communication into a single worldwide community. In the last decades of the twentieth century, however, the term seemed equally appropriate for the village peoples of the globe, who despite all cultural differences were united by even more compelling hopes and problems.

The most all-encompassing of these problems is poverty. The poverty of the have-not nations is not simply a lack of cars, television sets, or flush toilets. Poverty in the Third World means shantytowns full of the unemployed—and no work back home in the villages either. It means malaria, cholera, typhoid, sleeping sickness, leprosy, hookworm—all the plagues of the Old Testament still killing children and crippling their elders in our century. It means malnutrition even in a decent year: If the crop is bad or nonexistent in arid India or the Sahel countries south of the Sahara, it means swollen bellies, matchstick arms, death under the blowing dust.

Dealing with such fundamental problems requires meeting such basic needs as enough food, drinkable water, access to some sort of clinic. It means selling birth control to people for whom children are a duty, a source of free labor, and the only available old-age insurance. After these needs, the newer nations must find funds for education, roads, capital investment in industrial or agricultural projects that might give their people hope for a better way of life in the future.

The basic economic problems of the global South are those we have seen evolving for over a century, first in Latin America and then in the colonial world during the period of the New Imperialism. They are problems rooted in the basic inequality of North and South, and in the global division of labor—and wealth—this inequality has fostered.

The traditional way of acquiring money to pay for development was through the export of what Third World countries had to sell: raw materials or agricultural products. The new nations thus joined Latin America as commodity exporters, shipping overseas vast quantities of coffee, tea, sugar, bananas, copra, palm oil, wheat, beef, cotton, rubber, oil, copper, iron, uranium, bauxite.

When the prices for these products of the southern earth were high, as in the 1960s, the South did passably well—and invested commensurately in new projects. When the prices went down in the world markets, as they did in the 1970s and 1980s, the new countries suffered. Commodity prices, furthermore, were frequently determined not by Third World producers, but by speculators in First World countries or by what Second World governments were willing to pay. Desperate for foreign exchange, the countries of the global South often cut back even on subsistence agriculture in order to put more land into export crops—and hence had to import food. The result was a very serious set of export-related problems.

A second major category of difficulty was the sort of dependency syndrome that had afflicted Latin America for so long. Third World countries in general depended on other nations for both manufactured goods and energy—meaning mostly oil. Again, a crucial factor in the economic development of the global South was beyond their control, in the hands of oil sheiks and European or American or Japanese manufacturers.

A third fundamental problem for developing nations followed directly from those of commodity exports and dependency. This was the huge debt that many countries in the South incurred, particularly over the 1970s and 1980s, because the other way to capitalize development projects was to borrow the money. This many Third World countries did, negotiating loans from major European or North American banks and from such international agencies as the World Bank and the International Monetary Fund (IMF). When these loans began to come due, the countries of the South found commodity prices still low, the cost of dependency for oil and essential manufactured goods still high. Many of them could not repay the loans or even make interest payments on them—unless they borrowed more money.

Basic tactics for dealing with global markets, dependency, and debt in the early days of the great liberation often involved centralized, controlled economies, development guided paternalistically by the new Third World governments. Government marketing boards, protective tariffs, fixed prices for export goods, subsidized prices for food staples, and long-range development plans were common approaches. Following the precipitous Third World decline of the 1970s, however, many developing nations pinned more of their hopes on free enterprise and market forces rather than on central planning. Pressured to free up the economy by such powerful aid donors as the IMF, Third World governments risked riots and even rebellions in order to cut subsidies that kept food prices low or permitted foreign investments and foreign imports to rise. They could only hope that these risks and sacrifices would be counterbalanced by economic growth comparable to that of the capitalist West, or of the newly developed nations of the East Asian Pacific rim.

In the 1980s, the downward slide at least slowed. Banks with large outstanding loans to Third World countries preferred to extend these loans—at increased interest, of course—rather than absorb the huge losses of a default. Energy prices settled somewhat as a global petroleum glut developed. But the best the South could expect from such modest improvements was an equally modest easing of the pressure. More new strategies for growth were suggested, such as emphasis on agriculture through land redistribution, free-market prices, and a smorgasbord of policies in between. But the road to renewed economic growth seemed long indeed.

TRADITION VERSUS CHANGE

The rapid pace of social change in the present century gave all cultures "future shock," the jolting confrontation with the unfamiliar and the new. In the Third World, however, the differences between the traditional and the modern, between the way things were done when the older generation was young and the way the new generation wanted to do them, could be infinitely greater than they were in the developed world. Relations between rich and poor, between young and old, between men and women were all affected. So were the special Third World problems of relations between foreigner and native, between Westernization and traditional ways.

Economic differences and dependencies involving the large landholders or wealthy merchants and their less affluent fellow citizens of course existed in the non-European world long before the Europeans arrived. Imperial exploitation sometimes enhanced these differences by making the large landowners or merchant princes even richer. But political liberation after 1945 in most cases did nothing to bridge the gap between the landed magnate and the field hand, the export merchant and the stevedore.

Indeed, independence often added a new elite: the political leaders and party chiefs who had freed their country and felt that, as no less a democrat than Andrew Jackson would have it, "to the victors belong the spoils." There were mitigating factors. In countries where social revolutionaries were in power, as in China and North Vietnam, ideological constraints perhaps limited the wealth of the new rulers. In African countries, the new big men often felt a traditional responsibility to share their wealth with their large extended families in the villages. Nevertheless, many Third World politicians became some of the world's gaudiest grafters, wallowing in flashy suits and big imported cars while their countries sank deeper into poverty.

The conflict of generations was also exacerbated in the slowly modernizing countries of the Third World. A first priority for many new nations was Westernized education that would teach the young the skills they would need to transform their countries in years to come. An unhappy by-product of such educations, however, was to turn young people with education thoroughly against the old life. Preferring the modern material and cultural life to which they felt entitled as their country's new elite, they sometimes turned their backs on their elders and their villages entirely. Compelled to return and do government work in the backwoods, they longed for the city and a return to "civilization."

Women also grew discontented, perhaps for more convincing reasons, in the decades after independence. Traditional societies everywhere had regulated the lives of women even more rigorously than European or American societies had. Women's work—like men's—was clearly defined. In some cultures, as in the Islamic world or Hindu India, many women were largely cut off from male society and from public life generally. In the developing world, furthermore, women were often "the poorest of the poor," traditionally exploited economically by fathers and husbands, often left to feed the family when their men went off to the city to work.[1]

None of these patterns would give ground easily. Some of the new efforts at economic development even made women's lives harder. Aid for African development, for example, frequently went to traditionally male labor. Education, when it was offered in the villages, was normally taken advantage of by men rather than by women.

To these social problems must be added a whole complex of difficulties revolving around the continued economic, technological, and cultural dependency on the nations of the developed North. Foreign technical experts had to stay on in former colonies to keep what Western technology there was running, and to build more. But they were understandably resented. Westernized elites among the indigenous population also created problems—indeed, embodied them in their own persons. A child of the old traditional order, the Westernized non-Westerner was a sometimes tragic figure, torn between the tastes and values

---

[1]Paul Harrison, *Inside the Third World: The Anatomy of Poverty* (New York: Penguin Books, 1979), pp. 438–439.

of the new world he wanted his country to join and the deep roots of his people in an older life.

THE THIRD WORLD CITY

The physical image of the contrast between old and new in the global South in the later twentieth century was the Third World city—and its surrounding shantytown.

Urban migration, the key to the modernization process in Europe and America in the nineteenth century, reached crisis proportions in Asia, Africa, and Latin America in the later twentieth century. Driven by the lack of land and jobs in the rural areas, drawn by dreams of the high life or by a realistic awareness that education, health care, and job opportunities were concentrated in the city, millions of peasants poured into Third World cities every year.

In the downtown city centers, foreign business outlets and domestically owned emporiums glistened with modernity. But the new immigrant from the country would never find his niche in this glittering world of the city center. His world would be the shantytown.

The majority of those who migrated to the city got no jobs, and the few who did worked as manual laborers, street hawkers, or something less respectable. Still, entire families came, finding a square of littered earth to call their own in shantytown, and hanging on, hoping that their streetwise, half-educated children would at least find a toehold in the modern world.

THE CHALLENGE OF THE 1990s

As early as the 1980s, as we have seen, developing nations began to turn away from the government-run state socialist economies of their founders. Facing steep declines in already low standards of living, they turned increasingly to foreign investors and free-market forces as the road to prosperity. The results, although hopeful in the long run, were often disturbing as the early 1990s passed. The numbers went up: production figures, export totals, overall growth rates all improved. But only some segments of the population—business leaders, entrepreneurs, large-scale farmers—profited, and governments came under increasing pressure from the masses who did not.

Visits to even successfully developing countries in the mid nineties revealed a paradoxical combination of new affluence and traditional poverty. Economic growth overlapped with growing social tensions and sometimes bitter conflict. In an Indian village, a new refrigerator might stand in the modest living room of a house without electricity, a "high-tech cupboard" purchased for prestige as much as in hopes of rural electrification to come. Across the subcontinent, meanwhile, the social fall-out of India's free-market boom of the early 1990s included mushrooming indebtedness, higher dowries for brides, and a new surge of peasants flocking to the cities in search of better-paying jobs, which too often were not there.

Modern apartment blocks like this were common in Caracas, Venezuela, capital of one of the most developed of the Third World countries. A short ride away, however, a typical Third World shantytown houses many thousands of country people who have come to the city in search of a better life—and failed to find it. (Monkmeyer Press)

In Africa, drought, fluctuating commodity prices, clan and ethnic feuding, and inefficient dictatorships continued to spread poverty, violence, and death. Yet the modern skyscrapers of cities like Johannesburg and Abidjan stood as symbols of the postliberation potential of the world's second-largest continent. Nelson Mandela's victory in South Africa alone opened up dazzling possibilities of economic growth for the whole southern half of Africa. But the strains of change were felt there too. You could be mugged twice in one day on the streets of downtown Johannesburg, and political campaigns revived anti-white feeling in Zimbabwe. Warring clans in Somalia drove out foreign relief workers and fought for the streets of Mogadishu, while the carnage of Rwanda reminded observers of the end of the world.

In Latin America too, economic revival paradoxically seemed to bring more problems than popular well-being. In Mexico, the signing of the North American Free Trade Agreement and a trend toward free elections seemed to promise better times. In the short run, however, these advances were accompanied by rebellion, political assassination, and a debt crisis that required another American bailout in 1995. Rich South Americans made Miami their playground, while South American Indians chewed *coca* leaves to deaden the cold and hunger and gazed into a future that looked very like their poverty-stricken past.

The challenge of the 1990s, then, was to survive the tumultuous changes taking place across the developing world. Long-term economic growth could bring a marvelous future for all. The problem, for many, was simply to last that long.

SUMMARY

The prosperity, political stability, and high-tech modernity of the global North in the later twentieth century contrasted strikingly with the serious political, economic, and technological problems of the nations of the global South during these same years.

The Third World countries of Asia, Africa, and Latin America covered large tracts of the globe where the agricultural village was still the basic unit of social organization. The South faced such basic problems as lack of adequate food, medical care, and education for exploding populations. In addition, Third World countries felt a strong need to develop economically in order to achieve the urban-industrial prosperity enjoyed by the nations of the North. Efforts to achieve these ends, however, trapped the global South in economic dependency on the North and led to cruel suffering when commodity prices, loans, and foreign aid from the North declined.

Conflicts between the traditional world of the village and the new urban world also threatened Asians, Africans, and Latin Americans with the same sort of painful cultural uprooting that afflicted Western peoples when the Industrial Revolution first spread in the preceding century. And many Third World people who did come up from the villages to join the modern world of the city ended up in shantytowns, the slums that ringed the new metropolises from Caracas to Hong Kong.

The problems were the same, but the patterns of response varied from one region of the Third World to another.

Many of the countries of the South were one-party governments or military dictatorships, and revolutions and coups were common on all three Third World continents. Even China, with its ancient tradition of central government, was shaken by the social experiments of Chairman Mao and other Communist leaders, including such abortive efforts as the Great Leap Forward and the Cultural Revolution. India, under Nehru and his daughter, Indira Gandhi, managed to preserve that nations's democratic institutions while struggling with its immense economic, demographic, and religious problems.

A broad swath of Muslim countries, from Iran to North Africa, developed rapidly on the basis of oil wealth, though the gap between rich and poor remained substantial. Much of Africa south of the Sahara struggled with considerably more limited resources and much greater dependency on world commodity prices, bank loans, and international aid. In Latin America, finally, similar economic problems led to a number of revolutions, from Cuba to Nicaragua, which sought state socialist solutions to the difficulties of development. By the 1990s, however, many Third World leaders were shifting to the free market to bring national prosperity.

SUGGESTED READING

AFSHAR, H., ed. *Women in the Middle East: Perceptions, Realities, and Struggles for Liberation.* New York: St. Martin's Press, 1993. Perceptive studies of women in various parts of the Middle East.

ALI, T. *An Indian Dynasty: The Story of the Nehru-Gandhi Family.* New York: Putnam, 1985. Critical evaluation of the Indian rulers.

BARNET, R. J., and R. E. MULLER. *Global Reach.* New York: Simon and Schuster, 1974. The role of multinational corporations in shaping the economies of developing countries.

BRANDT, T. W. *North–South: A Program for Survival.* Cambridge: MIT Press, 1980. Urges major changes in the distribution of global wealth.

BREESE, G., ed. *The City in Newly Developing Countries.* Englewood Cliffs, N.J.: Prentice Hall, 1972. A number of valuable essays on the problems of rapid urbanization in the underdeveloped world. See also M. P. Todaro, *Internal Migration in Developing Countries* (Geneva: International Labor Office, 1976) for more on causes of country-to-city migration.

BRYDON, L., and S. CHANT. *Women in the Third World:*

Gender Issues in Rural and Urban Areas. New Brunswick, N.J.: Rutgers University Press, 1989. Useful general essays on households, migration, and rural and urban production across the developing world.

CHENERY, H., et al. *Redistribution with Growth.* London: Oxford University Press, 1974. The case for combining social justice with economic development.

DITTMER, L. *China's Continuous Revolution: The Post-Liberation Epoch, 1949–1982.* Berkeley and Los Angeles: University of California Press, 1987. Theoretical analysis of Chinese efforts to maintain the drive for revolutionary change after seizing power in 1949. For subsequent developments, see J. Gittings, *China Changes Face* (London: Oxford University Press, 1990), an experienced reporter's analysis of the conflicts that climaxed with bloodshed in Beijing. Views of militant Chinese youth of two different sorts may be found in G. Yuan's *Born Red: A Chronicle of the Cultural Revolution.* Stanford: (Stanford University Press, 1987) and Li Lu's *Moving the Mountain* (London: Macmillan, 1990), on the student revolt that climaxed in the Tienanmen Square violence.

ELLIOTT, C. *Patterns of Poverty in the Third World.* New York: Praeger, 1975. Survey of the basic problem of the world's newer nations.

FINER, S. E. *The Man on Horseback.* London: Pall Mall Press, 1962. Military takeovers in the Third World. On the political corruption of many civilian governments among the new nations, see J. Nye, "Corruption and Political Development," *American Political Science Review,* vol. 61 (1967), pp. 417–427.

HARRISON, L. E. *Underdevelopment Is a State of Mind: The Latin American Case.* Lanham, Md.: University Press of America, 1985. Controversial contention that the roots of Latin American underdevelopment are to be found in the institutions and attitudes of Latin Americans, rather than in larger economic factors or foreign exploitation.

HARRISON, P. *Inside the Third World,* 2nd ed. Harmondsworth, England: Penguin, 1981. Vivid first-hand reportage by a well-traveled journalist.

HOURANI, A. *The Emergence of the Modern Middle East.* London: Macmillan, 1981. Written by an authority on reform and revolution in this volatile region. See also S. K. Farsoun, ed., *Arab Society: Continuity and Change* (London: Croom Helm, 1985), a collection of essays on society and politics.

LEWIS, O. *Children of Sanchez.* New York: Random House, 1966. Vivid, if controversial, account of the culture of poverty.

MILLER, F. *Latin American Women and the Search for Social Justice.* Hanover, N.H.: University Press of New England, 1991. Historical overview, emphasizing the twentieth century and such ongoing concerns as democracy, revolution, education, and feminism.

MITTER, S. S. *Dharma's Daughters: Contemporary Indian Women and Hindu Culture.* New Brunswick, N.J.: Rutgers University Press, 1991. Modern Indian women come to terms with ancient Indian traditions.

MOGHADAM, V. M. *Modernizing Women: Gender and Social Change in the Middle East.* Boulder, Col.: Lynne Rienner, 1993. Valuable survey of women as agents and objects of social change.

MOWOE, I. J., and R. BJORNSON, eds. *Africa and the West: The Legacies of Empire.* Westport, Conn.: Greenwood Press, 1986. Examines cultural influences and conflicts in the new African nations of the latter part of the twentieth century.

PALMER, I. *Food and the New Agricultural Technology.* Geneva: UN Research Institute for Social Development, 1972. The Green Revolution—and its unintended side effects.

RUTHENBERG, H. *Farming Systems in the Tropics,* 2nd ed. Oxford: Clarendon Press, 1976. Survey and analysis of traditional agricultural methods in many developing nations. On land redistribution to peasant farmers, see the UN Food and Agriculture Organization's *Progress in Land Reform, 6th Report* (New York: United Nations, 1976). On less tractable ecological problems, like deforestation and desertification, see E. Eckholm, *Losing Ground* (New York: W.W. Norton, 1975).

SEITZ, J. L. *The Politics of Development: An Introduction to Global Issues.* New York: Blackwell, 1988. Possibilities and problems of economic development.

STAVRIANOS, L. S. *The Global Rift: The Third World Comes of Age.* New York: William Morrow, 1981. An analysis of the emergence of the developing nations by a leading global historian.

VON LAUE, T. H. *The World Revolution of Westernization: The Twentieth Century in Global Perspective.* New York: Oxford University Press, 1987. Analysis of Western influences on the rest of the world, with emphasis on the West's distinctive political culture.

CHAPTER 48

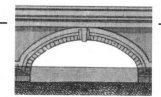

THE BIRTH OF A GLOBAL CULTURE

A DISINTEGRATING WORLDVIEW

THE TRAJECTORY OF TWENTIETH-CENTURY CULTURE

In the twentieth century as in the nineteenth, Western culture had a widespread influence across the non-Western world. Even the collapse of the Western empires in the third quarter of this century did not end this unprecedented spread of the influence of one civilization on all others. From physics to fiction, the impact of the West continued to reshape the life of the mind around the world. This was so even though Western culture was undergoing a deeply disturbing crisis of beliefs and values of its own.

The history of arts and ideas in the twentieth century, then, followed a unique trajectory. From crumbling truths and revolutionary art styles at the beginning of the century, cultural history arched to the beginnings of a uniquely global civilization by the century's end. This chapter will outline aspects of this unprecedented cultural odyssey from a disintegrating Western world view to the brink of a genuinely global culture.

MATERIALISM, SECULARISM, RELATIVISM

Three related intellectual currents contributed centrally to the changing worldview of the twentieth century. These powerful trends were secularism, materialism, and relativism. Born in the West, these new views undermined ancient faiths around the world.

Secularism, seeking to guarantee religious freedom by separating church and government entirely, went back two centuries in Western history. Separation of church and state could be traced to the American Constitution and the French Revolution. In the 1800s, the spread of secularism had undermined the once dominant position of religion in politics, education, and the public sphere generally. After 1917, communist rulers in Eastern Europe sought to eliminate religion entirely. In Western Europe, the spread of secular perspectives led to a sharp drop in church attendance after World War II. Even in the United States, where religious institutions still drew sizable

Sunday crowds, secular humanism found many supporters in the later twentieth century.

Philosophical *materialism* asserted the primacy of matter in the universe, dismissing spiritual or supernatural phenomena as illusions. Nineteenth-century materialism, with its roots in the Enlightenment and the scientific revolution, had a powerful influence on twentieth-century culture. The materialism of Marx and Darwin and Nietzsche's announcement of the death of God found more followers after 1900 than before. Their views added up to a serious challenge to the oldest and most widespread of belief systems—faith in supernatural religion.

Relativism, finally, denied the existence of absolute truths, insisting that no statement could be true except *in relation to* the particular time, place, and circumstances in which it was made. The rise of relativist thinking raised questions about traditional beliefs of all sorts. Some philosophers had always doubted that humans could ever know for sure that their *ideas* about the world corresponded to the *reality* of the world. Specifically, *cultural relativism* developed in the later 1800s as anthropologists found that different sets of beliefs and systems of values suited the needs of different societies. As the century advanced, some scholars began to suggest that *all* human beliefs were determined by the attitudes of particular societies, social classes, and other groups.

Outside the West, these subversive views gained ground somewhat more slowly. Early rulers of liberated colonies, for example, often de-emphasized their own traditional religions and philosophies as irrelevant to the economic and social problems confronting them. In this they were supported by the spread of Western ideologies.

Marxist materialism spread to parts of East and Southeast Asia, where it undercut ancient Confucian and Buddhist systems of belief. Under Mao Zedong, Chinese villagers abandoned their historic reverence for ancestors, while Chinese Red Guards rampaged through the Buddhist temples of Tibet. In Muslim lands, from Egypt to Indonesia, nationalist revolutionaries emphasized the secular state. Liberation leaders concerned centrally with state-building and economic development focused on material improvements in the lives of their peoples. In many parts of Africa and Asia, a traditional village worldview that saw all nature infused with spiritual presences often gave way before secular education and the materialistic temptations of city life.

"This theory that history as it actually was can be disclosed by critical study, can be known as objective truth, and can be stated as such, contains certain . . . assumptions. The first is that history (general or of any period) has existed as an object or series of objects outside the mind of the historian. . . . The second is that the historian can face and know this object or series of objects and can describe it as it objectively existed. The third is that the historian can, at least for the purposes of research and writings, divest himself of all taint of religious, political, philosophical, social, sex, economic, moral, and aesthetic interests, and view this Gegenüber [here, outside world] with strict impartiality, somewhat as the mirror reflects any object to which it is held up. The fourth is that the multitudinous events of history as actuality had some structural organization through inner (perhaps causal) relations, which the impartial historian can grasp by inquiry and observation and accurately reproduce or describe in written history.

Can the human mind discover and state the "objective truth" of history as it actually was? Space does not admit even a brief summation of the voluminous literature dealing with this conception and demonstrating, if not its delusive character, its rejection by scholars and thinkers of high competence in Europe."

◆▶◆◀◆

Charles Beard (1874–1948) was an iconoclastic American historian perhaps best known for his revisionist economic interpretations of the American past. The highly relativistic philosophy of history expressed in this essay on the "noble dream" of objective truth in history has disturbed many twentieth-century historians.

How many of the "assumptions" Beard lists would you accept? If you do not accept them, what would this do to your confidence in the "objective truth" of history? Can history be true in some other sense than as a mirror image of past events?

Charles A. Beard, "That Noble Dream," in Fritz Stern, ed., The Varieties of History from Voltaire to the Present (New York: Meridian Books, 1956), p. 317.

Radical relativism spread more slowly beyond the West than secularism and materialism did. Believers in new Western ideologies like socialism or nationalism were as much "true believers" as the followers of traditional religions—and there were still plenty of those left in the world. Nevertheless, some commentators claimed to detect a genuine crisis of basic beliefs as the end of the century approached.

SCIENCE: FROM ATOMS TO OUTER SPACE

One source of this confusion of fundamental convictions was a transformation of the primarily scientific worldview that the Western world had been cultivating for the preceding three or four centuries. Since the days of Coper-

nicus and Newton in the sixteenth and seventeenth centuries, science had increasingly seemed to educated Western people to provide answers to the riddles of the universe that philosophy and religion had once attempted to explain. Around the turn of the twentieth century, however, scientists began to uncover evidence and to develop theories that brought much of the Newtonian worldview into question. By the 1920s and 1930s, disturbing questions were being asked about the ultimate nature of matter, the validity of natural law, and the very possibility of scientific truth.

The distinctive qualities of matter had been clearly defined since the seventeenth century. Matter possessed mass and extension in space; it was solid, made of tiny concrete particles called atoms. But around 1900, the work called into question during the 1920s. The certainty of mathematics, the standard of truth since Plato's day, had been challenged by the formulation of the first non-Euclidean geometry in the nineteenth century. Pragmatic philosophy, developed in America by William James, declared that truth was a matter of usefulness: that the truth of an idea changed as its use-value changed from one time or situation to another.

The relativity of truth invaded pure science after the turn of the century with Albert Einstein's famous theory of relativity in physics. Einstein demonstrated that both space and time, the absolute givens of Newtonian physics, were in fact always relative rather than absolute. Einstein defined time as a form of perception rather than as something "out there." Time, he declared, was relative to the position of the observer, to his motion through space; he even showed that time passes more slowly the more rapidly the "clock" that measured it moved. Space also was far from fixed and absolute. The size of an object

Marie Curie, the French scientist whose exploration of the properties of radium challenged ancient assumptions about the nature of matter itself. Curie, winner of two Nobel Prizes for science, discovered radium and demonstrated that, in the process of radiation, matter may be transformed into pure energy. (The Bettmann Archive)

of Marie Curie with radium—which disintegrated from matter into pure radiant energy—and the discovery of cosmic rays and X rays caused some scientists to question the solid materiality of all physical phenomena. The researches of H. A. Lorenz and of Ernest Rutherford and Niels Bohr showed that the allegedly solid atom was in fact composed largely of space between subatomic particles orbiting around a nucleus. In time, even these particles were discovered to be composed not of matter, as it had once been defined, but of pure charges of energy.

Natural laws, the linchpins that had held the material world together since Newton, were also reinterpreted in disturbing ways in the decades after 1900. Evidence accumulated that there were exceptions to these allegedly absolute principles. These exceptions might be rare, and they might occur largely at the microscopic level. But they led scientists to think more and more that natural "laws" were statistical probabilities rather than absolute truths.

The very possibility of scientific truth, finally, was

Albert Einstein, the most famous genius of the "Second Scientific Revolution." This was the man whose theory of gravitation upset Newton's and who introduced relativity into the exact sciences. His genial humanity also helped to give science a "human face" just as the increasing abstractness and complexity of the modern physical sciences rendered them almost incomprehensible to most nonspecialists. (The Bettmann Archive)

moving at velocities approaching the speed of light would actually decrease, whereas its mass would increase as the velocity did. Einstein's general theory of relativity redefined the universe as a whole as a four-dimensional continuum in which time and space were relative to each other—and in which the queasy layperson might feel that he or she had nowhere solid left to stand.

Werner Heisenberg put the capstone on the confusion at the end of the 1920s by announcing in his notorious principle of indeterminacy that there were definable limits to human knowledge. Even the introduction of a scientific measuring instrument, Heisenberg asserted, would so alter the reality being measured that the complete truth about the behavior of even an electron could never be known.

Most of these doubts about the nature and validity of human understanding had to do with the far limits of scientific knowledge, with subatomic particles or speeds approximating the velocity of light. But such doubts left the most enlightened Westerners questioning the omniscience of their own scientific gurus.

Yet twentieth-century researchers did not give up the search for scientific truth. In fact, as the century advanced, discoveries came so thick and fast that the later 1800s and the 1900s were increasingly hailed as a "second scientific revolution." Perhaps most sensational and sweeping in their impact were developments in nuclear energy, cosmology, and space technology.

The American atomic bombs over Japan, which brought an end to World War II, launched the world as a whole into what quickly became known as the atomic age. Those relatively primitive bombs based on nuclear fission—the "splitting" of the atom—were soon replaced by much more powerful hydrogen bombs based on nuclear fusion. Nuclear fusion, as it turned out, could also be generated in a controlled fashion, which produced a limitless flow of power for peaceful as well as military uses. In the second half of the twentieth century, then, many nations switched to nuclear power for a large part of the energy they needed.

Even more amazing breakthroughs came in the previously science-fiction realm of space travel. Beginning around 1960, space scientists began to explore the universe beyond the earth's atmosphere. Soviet cosmonauts orbited the earth and spent months in space. The United States sent astronauts to the moon, landed unmanned spacecraft on Mars, and photographed other planets close up.

New theories about the origin, structure, development, and possible future of the universe also emerged in the mid-century decades. In the later 1900s, the so-called "big bang" theory predominated among cosmologists. In this view, all the matter and energy in the universe had at one time been condensed into a single incredibly dense sphere. Then, a few billion years ago, this primal fireball exploded. The result was the cosmos we know—an expanding universe in which galaxies, stars, planets, and smaller fragments propelled by this cosmic explosion continued to fly apart at incredible speeds.

Almost all the behavior of this expanding universe proved to be explainable in terms of three basic forces. These were gravity, redefined as a field of force linking all matter; the electromagnetic force that holds atoms together; and the strong nuclear force that binds the core particles of the atom.

Scientists developed theories about the end of the world as well as its beginning. Some saw the expansion of the universe continuing forever. Others predicted that eventually the force of gravity would reverse the expansion of the cosmos, pulling stars and galaxies back together into a condensed mass similar to that from which they had come.

There was general agreement, however, that by that time the planet earth would long since have been consumed. The sun, following normal stellar evolution, would expand into a red giant star larger than the earth's orbit, incinerating all the inner planets. Neither the history of the world nor that of the cosmos, in short, looked like having a particularly happy ending.

SCIENCE: FROM PSYCHOLOGY TO SOCIOBIOLOGY

The biological sciences also experienced drastic changes during the twentieth century. Even more controversial than the ideas of Einstein and Heisenberg were the theories of human nature proposed by such students of the human mind as Sigmund Freud and Ivan Pavlov. At the same time, new discoveries and theories transformed the life sciences as they did the physical sciences.

The middle decades of the century in particular saw a remarkable series of medical discoveries. Penicillin, discovered in the 1930s, was only the first of a number of "wonder drugs" that curbed infections and cured once fatal diseases. Vaccines were developed that virtually wiped out such plagues as polio. Medical science also developed pills that controlled the psychological tensions and depressions generated by the pressures of modern society. For a time, it looked as if there might be a pill for every ill, with lengthening life spans, health, and happiness a virtual birthright for citizens of an industrializing world.

There were problems, however. The global influenza epidemic that followed World War I killed more millions than the war itself. Late in the century, once "eradicated" diseases began to take a toll once more. And at least one new major plague haunted the world in the 1990s. AIDS—acquired immune deficiency syndrome—was an invariably fatal disease commonly transmitted sexually, for which no cure was known. As the number of those infected grew, the world whistled past the graveyard, ignoring a pestilence that, if not contained, could match the Black Death of the Middle Ages in its consequences.

Early in the century, meanwhile, a number of new theories concerning human psychology also emerged. Sigmund Freud's concept of the human mind emphasized sexuality, childhood, the repression of our basic impulses, and the dominant role of the unconscious mind.

For Freud the human psyche resembled an iceberg. The conscious portion of the mind is only the tip of the iceberg; the unconscious mind, nine-tenths of the whole, is invisible beneath the surface. But it is the drift of that submerged nine-tenths that determines where the visible tip will go. This unconscious mind beneath the surface is driven by what Freud called *libido,* primal psychic energy consisting originally of sexual desire—which thus becomes the central motivating force in human life.

Libidinal energy, Freud believed, is dammed up or repressed in childhood by painful encounters with reality or authority. Repressed desire escapes, however, in socially sanctioned sexual activity, as sublimated creative energy, or as mental illness, the form in which Freudian psychiatrists most frequently encountered it.

Another psychological pioneer was the Russian Ivan Pavlov, the first proponent of the school of behaviorist psychology. Working primarily with animals in his laboratories, Pavlov developed the concept of the conditioned reflex as the central explanation for human as well as other animal behavior. Discovering that animals could be conditioned by positive or negative responses to their behaviors, he argued that accidental or deliberate conditioning in a given social environment determined how all human beings behave.

Behaviorists came to believe that mental phenomena are little more than by-products of environmentally conditioned behavior. Like dogs conditioned—in a famous experiment—to salivate at the sound of a dinner bell, the most complex human behavior patterns were products of material conditioning, and nothing more.

Broader biological theory, meanwhile, also generated some disturbing new ideas. Early in the century, a surge of pseudoscience emphasized racial differences, typically asserting the superiority of caucasoid human beings over negroid, mongoloid, and other subdivisions of the human race. The horrors of Hitler's holocaust of the Jews and general revulsion against racist policies in other countries led most authorities to turn to cultural explanations for human differences. Human culture and social conditioning rather than genetically inherited biological traits, they asserted, determined most behavior. In particular, authorities rejected the view that people of different races or genders were essentially different in character and temperament. Basic human traits, from national character to mother love, were attributed to nurture—how a child was raised—not to "human nature."

In the later twentieth century, however, proponents of the new discipline of sociobiology suggested that a number of human traits, from aggression and territorial defensiveness to altruistic behavior, were to some degree rooted in human genes after all. Some feminist theorists argued for an essential difference between the temperaments of men and women, as opposed to differences produced by different upbringing and education. The 1990s

Jean-Paul Sartre and Simone de Beauvoir, the pre-eminent French intellectuals of the mid-twentieth century, clink glasses in the convivial café setting where they were most at home. In their writings, which ranged from philosophy to fiction, they gave powerful expression to the existential worldview of the Western world after World War II. (AP/Wide World Photos)

even saw the return of nineteenth-century ideas of fundamental racial differences in basic intelligence. A new wave of biological determinism seemed to be rising, with unpredictable but potentially disturbing political consequences.

PHILOSOPHY: FROM EXISTENTIALISM TO DECONSTRUCTION

Like the new scientific worldview, the most striking new philosophies of the twentieth century took shape in Europe and spread slowly to the rest of the world. Existentialism emerged in the first half of the century, structuralism and its spinoffs poststructuralism and deconstruction in the second half. Both streams of thought provided philosophical underpinnings for the increasingly negative view of the human condition that prevailed in much of the world as the century drew near its end.

Existentialists saw the world and human life as simply existing, lacking all higher meaning, significance, or point. Developed by German and French thinkers between the 1930s and the 1960s, this materialistic view declared that all philosophical or religious *explanations* for our existence were mere human inventions. In Jean-Paul Sartre's telling phrases, "the heavens are empty" and "hell is other people."

On the positive side, existentialists claimed the most radical freedom ever asserted—the right to *invent* values, to *impose* meaning upon a meaningless universe. But even existential freedom brought its share of *Angst*, or anguish—the terrifying obligation to make up the meaning of life.

Structuralists were more likely to be students of language, literary critics, or anthropologists than philosophers. Their worldview, far from dismissing theories, seemed to assert that *only* systems of thought and structures of language were real. Structuralist anthropologists like Claude Levi-Strauss studied the *patterns* of myths, not their social or historical references. What mattered about a book, structuralist critics declared, was not its content but the patterns of language it revealed. Structuralist thinkers also expanded the concept of language to include all systems of "signs" or symbols. They insisted that only these systems of meaning mattered—not the "real world" which the words, images, or other symbols claimed to represent.

Poststructuralists often allied themselves with Marxists, feminists, and other proponents of social change. They argued that the establishment brainwashed the public into accepting the status quo by controlling the "discourse," the permissible forms of expression and lines of argument. They rejected the literal meanings of the "text," as they called a book, a picture, a political speech, or a style of clothing. Instead, they sought to expose the real significance of the "subtext" beneath the official text—and to show how this system of signs really functions as a tool of social control.

Deconstructionists sometimes seemed to go even further, suggesting that *only* discourses and systems of signs really existed at all. At the very least, they insisted, we can know nothing about the "things signified"—only about the systems of "signifiers" or symbols we use to discuss the world. In deconstructionist analysis of a book, the author, the author's intent, even the text itself do not exist. Only the *reader's perception* of these things is demonstrably there at all.

THE NEW FUNDAMENTALISM

These multiplying challenges to traditional views and values triggered an impassioned counterattack in the later decades of the twentieth century. Fundamentalist movements in the world's great historic religions vigorously challenged materialism and relativism in the west and secular influences everywhere.

Fundamentalist religion called for a return to the basic principles of ancient faiths—to belief in the literal truth of the Christian Bible, for instance, or to rigorous application of the Muslim Law. Fundamentalists also emphasized traditional practices and customs, from dietary regulations and distinctive costumes to traditional caste or gender roles. They were often aggressively militant, ready to fight for their beliefs. Hindus, Muslims, and Sikhs fought in the streets of northern India; Muslim extremists fought their fellow Palestinians as well as Israelis in the Near East. In the United States, evangelical Christians attacked secular humanism, crusaded against pornography and abortion, and urged prayer in the schools.

In the short run, at least, these movements had considerable success. Fundamentalist Christians in the United States supported political candidates who shared their views and seemed within reach of some of their goals when the conservative Republican Party won big at the end of 1994. Orthodox Christianity revived in Russia following the fall of communism, refurbishing dilapidated churches and crowding religious services once more. Islamic fundamentalists actually seized control of governments in Iran and Sudan and mounted violent campaigns against secular regimes in Egypt, Algeria, and elsewhere. The booming Southeast Asian state of Singapore aggressively encouraged "Confucian values" as a support for capitalism, while various forms of Buddhism began to make converts even in the west.

How successful this fundamentalist counterattack might be in the long run remained in doubt. Western Europe's churches did not seem to be refilling, and Japan continued to celebrate Christmas without Christianity, as a marketing device. Muslim Pakistan twice elected a woman, Benazir Bhutto, prime minister—a distinctively untraditional role for a woman in Muslim lands. And despite the high visibility of fundamentalist Christianity in the United States, most Americans appeared to feel that religion was a private matter, not a requirement for citizenship.

MODERNISM AND REVOLUTIONARY ART, 1890–1945

MODERNIST EXPERIMENTS AND POLITICAL COMMITMENT

Twentieth-century literature and art reflected two basic tendencies around the world. One of these trends was the modernist enthusiasm for literary experiments. The other put art at the service of revolutionary and authoritarian political regimes that promised social change.

Twentieth-century artists and writers produced a good deal of sharp criticism of existing social and economic institutions. Other writers and artists devoted their talents to advancing revolutionary causes or the agendas of ideological regimes. Such politically committed art and literature could celebrate the rediscovery of African or Asian traditions or hail the triumphs of European, Latin American, or Asian revolutions. Political commitment was the lifeblood of this socially relevant writing.

Perhaps even more challenging, however, was the rise of the modernist movement. Modernist artists and writers tore up the rule book on how to produce a well-made play or painting, a well-designed novel or building. The modernists launched a wide-ranging reassessment of all the elements of their various crafts, from pictorial composition and traditional dance steps to plot and character in fiction. They experimented in all forms of literature and art, producing works that left many readers baffled and alienated. Later in the century, their postmodernist successors roused even more hostility by their rejection of the "canon" or standard classics of Western culture, past and present.

Some writers and critics thought these two tendencies—political commitment and modernist experimentalism—contradicted each other. Art-for-art's sake modernists argued that art with a political or social viewpoint was little better than propaganda. Socially concerned artists insisted that "modern art" was decadent and did not serve the cause of social progress. Some of the best twentieth-century writing and art, however, successfully combined experimental artistic techniques with strongly held social commitments.

MODERNISM IN THE ARTS

Early twentieth-century modernism generated a host of new schools and individual experimentation. Modernists operated in an atmosphere of militant manifestos and defiant "little magazines," grubby studios, and bohemian cafes. They shrugged off the censors who found their subject matter obscene and ignored the general public, who could not understand them. For some, popularity itself was evidence of "selling out," pandering to the vulgar taste of the mass market. To all modernists, what mattered was originality and self-expression.

The modernist insurrection in the arts began before the turn of the century in France with painters such as Paul Cézanne, Vincent van Gogh, and Paul Gauguin. These pioneers of modernism painted landscapes and still lifes, peasants, city streets, and South Sea islanders with directness, distortion, and an unacademic lack of realism and finish. Their simple figures and visible brushstrokes struck contemporaries as crude—and impressed most of the art world since as the genius of a new direction in artistic expression. By the early 1900s, painters such as the French *fauves* ("wild beasts") and the German expressionists were daubing their rude figures with bright or off-key colors that stunned generations raised on the perfection of Raphael or Leonardo da Vinci.

Modernism quickly replaced Renaissance naturalism and its close study of anatomy, perspective, and nature with a new passion for pure form. Modern artists gave themselves over wholeheartedly to exploring the formal elements of which all art is made: color, line, shape, volume, texture, movement, tone. They also glorified the quest itself; novelty, exploration, and innovation in the arts became ends in themselves. Originality in art, a cult since the romantics, became the high god of the modernists.

New schools of art thus proliferated during the early decades of the present century. Futurism in Italy and Russia came to terms with the speed and power of modern technology, worshipping at the shrine of the locomotive, the automobile, and the airplane. Cubism in France, led by the expatriate Spaniard Pablo Picasso, broke nature up into its component geometrical shapes and reassembled them in barely recognizable forms on the canvas. Surrealist artists such as Salvador Dalai tried to liberate the Freudian unconscious by painting a dream world of sexually suggestive figures, melting clocks, and technicolor skies. Mavericks such as Paul Klee, Vasily Kandinsky, and Piet Mondrian abandoned subject matter completely, painting purely abstract patterns and brightly colored shapes that were dazzlingly decorative but totally without content.

Modernism raged happily through the arts. Architects such as Frank Lloyd Wright insisted that modern buildings should not imitate traditional Gothic or Greek styles but should follow function and integrate their structure into their natural surroundings. The twelve-tone scale invented by Arnold Schönberg revolutionized modern music, and Igor Stravinsky's *Firebird, Rite of Spring,* and other ballets scandalized Paris with their bizarre themes, staging, and rhythms, and their apparent abandonment of melody and harmony. American dancer and choreographer Martha Graham developed modern dance as an expression both of deep human emotions and of great themes in human life and myth. The Bauhaus artistic community in Germany even revitalized the crafts, promoting a new awareness of modern materials through creations such as glass walls and tubular metal chairs.

Norwegian artist Edvard Munch's "The Scream" is often seen as an expression of the spiritual anguish of the earlier twentieth century. How has the artist achieved this effect, described by one student as "like the sound fingernails screeching across a blackboard"? (Edvard Munch, "The Scream" 1893. Tempera and Casein on cardboard. 36 x 29" [91.3 x 73.7] Nasjonalgalleriet, Oslo)

Pablo Picasso (1881–1973), the king of modern art, was in his heyday between the wars. A lifelong experimenter—he lived into his nineties, changing every decade, sometimes every year—Picasso most disturbed the art world with his development of cubism before, during, and after World War I. Pictures such as *Les Demoiselles d'Avignon* and *Les Trois Musiciens* broke their subjects up into their component shapes, simplified these shapes into geometry, and then rearranged them for artistic effect, much as you might arrange flowers in a vase or rocks in a Japanese garden. Later cubists slapped paint on canvas with gay abandon, pasted on bits of linoleum or newsprint for textural effects, and generally played more freely and happily with reality than Western artists had ever done before.

MODERNISM IN LITERATURE

Western literature went even further during the modernist era, rebelling not only against Western literary traditions but against Western society itself.

This endemic war between twentieth-century Western writers and their world also had its roots in the nineteenth century. It built upon romantic bohemianism, which despised the vulgar philistinism of the middle classes, and on the nineteenth-century belief in art for art's sake. Convinced that artists had a unique vocation, a higher calling than mere moneymaking, and that they must be true above all to their talent, modernist writers took up the cudgels against the twentieth century with an iconoclastic vigor that is hard to find in any other period.

The "best people" and leading institutions of Western society took a savage drubbing. Political corruption, commercial greed, the hollowness of patriotic slogans and organized religion, the emptiness of old-fashioned morality were all exposed to public contempt in the work of experimental writers such as Marcel Proust, James Joyce, Franz Kafka, Eugene O'Neill, and T. S. Eliot, and even by such strong but fairly conventional stylists as Thomas Mann, Aldous Huxley, D. H. Lawrence, and Ernest Hemingway.

Writers also expressed their sense of artistic vocation—and their disinterest in a large readership—by a growing emphasis on self-expression as the point of art. This approach led in turn to a deliberate obscurity cultivated through the use of unfamiliar allusions, private symbols, and even foreign languages and references to details of the author's personal life that no reader would be likely to understand. Thus Eliot, perhaps the most famous Western poet of the century, was able to squeeze three languages and references to an Elizabethan dramatist, a French romantic poet, Dante, and the Hindu Upanishads into half a dozen lines of his poem *The Wasteland*.

The conviction that self-expression—rather than communication—was the point of literature led poets in particular to avoid narrative line, developed argument, or even sentence structure and syntax. The Italian futurist Filippo Marinetti gave poets "entire freedom" to use "disjointed words . . . without the connecting wires of syntax."[1]

Yet wonderful work could come from writers and artists working in these modernist modes. In novels like *To the Lighthouse*, Virginia Woolf pioneered the "stream of consciousness" technique, widely used since, which views events entirely through the eyes, hearts, and minds of characters in the story. James Joyce's notorious novel *Ulysses* follows not a Greek hero but an ordinary Irish advertising solicitor through a single unexceptional day in Dublin, making that day emblematic of the whole of modern culture at its most various and dehumanizing. Franz Kafka's strange and sometimes terrifying parables of modern life, including short stories like "Metamorphosis" and "In the Penal Colony" and such enigmatic

---

[1]David Perkins, *A History of Modern Poetry from the 1890s to the High Modernist Mode* (Cambridge, Mass.: Harvard University Press, 1976), pp. 308–309.

Pablo Picasso's famous painting of an attack on a Spanish town, <u>Guernica</u>, used Cubist techniques of breaking up, simplifying, and re-assembling images to present a deeply disturbing view of modern war. The painting, which was kept in the United States throughout the years of the Franco dictatorship, has been sent to Spain since the restoration of democracy in that country. (Pablo Picasso, <u>Guernica</u> 1937. Oil on canvas, 11′5½″ × 25′5¾″. On extended loan to the Museum of Modern Art, New York, from the estate of the artist.)

novels as *The Trial,* suggested haunting, even horrifying depths beneath the surfaces of modern life.

REVOLUTIONARY ART AND LITERATURE

Two examples of earlier-twentieth-century revolutionary culture will be touched on all too briefly here: the diverse culture flowerings that occurred in Mexico and India.

In Mexico, painting was the predominant art in the remarkable renaissance that followed the revolution there. A militant "Indianism" infused much of this work. As part of their effort to elevate the long-oppressed peasantry, the Mexican revolutionary governments of the 1920s and 1930s celebrated the Native American as the most downtrodden of all prerevolutionary groups. The recent revolution itself, with its potential for Mexican spiritual rebirth, also offered vital subjects for Mexican art and literature. And the broadest human ideals, as epitomized in the rending experience of the revolution, captured the imagination of the new artists.

The most admired builders of Mexico's revolutionary culture between the wars were its internationally known group of mural painters, José Orozco, David Siqueiros, Frieda Kahlo, and above all Diego Rivera. In huge modernistic paintings on the walls or ceilings of public buildings, these artists celebrated the greatness of pre-Columbian Mexican culture and of the revolution, the nobility of the peasant and the factory worker, Mexican patriotism and human achievement. Rivera's poetic,

massively simplified, formally composed murals of *Earth and the Elements,* and *Man in Four Aspects* (laborer, scientist, philosopher, rebel) bring years of training in European modernism to the service of the Mexican Revolution. Earth tones, simplified forms, and sheer monumentality combine to give the ideals of the revolution heroic stature.

On the other side of the world, in India, continuing developments in Hinduism combined with a surge of Indian literary creativity. The result was vigorous cultural support for the nationalistic political movement spearheaded by the Congress party. On the religious side, traditional Hinduism was taught in seclusion by gurus such as Ramana Maharishi, who neither traveled nor wrote but instead instructed disciples at his isolated *ashram* in the south.

On the literary side, the Indian flowering grew through a fertile fusion of Indian and European elements. The influences of Western romanticism and realism contributed to the emergence of the modern novel and short story in India. Romantic and historical subjects persisted, but there was more attention than before to realistic description and modern psychological portraiture. Social problems, ranging from the caste system to the condition of women, became important subjects.

The leading light of this self-confident, self-conscious Indian cultural revival was Rabindranath Tagore, whose Nobel Prize for literature in 1913 earned him worldwide renown. Tagore's poems, plays, stories, and novels were rooted in a deep love of his native Bengal, of the river Ganges that flows through it to the sea, and of the peasant villagers among whom he lived much of his life. His vision had a deep spiritual dimension as well, and he worked for both religious and secular education in India.

Rabindranath Tagore's global lecture tours in later life made him India's best-known man of letters. He embodied the fusion of ancient Hindu beliefs and Western influences that lay at the heart of the whole Indian nationalist movement, the fusion that would create the modern nation of India at mid-century.

TOTALITARIAN ART AND LITERATURE

The forms of totalitarian culture were as diverse as the cultural traditions from which these new and extreme forms of twentieth-century authoritarianism sprang. Yet there were some similarities too.

All totalitarian societies glorified leadership and leaders. All had their elites—even the allegedly egalitarian Communists, for whom the party itself became a vanguard elite. Most had their "chosen people," a class, race, or nationality whose glorious destiny was the object of the exercise. Most had a strong sense also of a great enemy—the capitalists, the communists, the Jews—and of a coming battle between light and darkness. Against this fearful foe, at this critical moment in history, the chosen must stand together as an indestructible collective whole.

Nazi propagandists tirelessly preached the greatness of the *Führer,* the party elite, and the Aryan master race. They condemned Jews and the "Jewish principle" as the great enemy and justified any measure that might be necessary to defeat this foe. Hitler described his "struggle" as this great race war between the German master race and the Semitic "subhumans."

Nazi art attempted to communicate this message with an eclectic array of romantic nineteenth-century and glossy modern imagery. Paintings of Hitler accoutered as a knight in shining armor illustrated his role as defender of his people. The monolithic, square-pillared Nazi public buildings, sometimes described as "totalitarian gothic," projected the sense of monumental power that was central to the Nazi self-image. Nazi regalia itself—the military uniforms, medals, weapons, the death's heads and lightning-shaped SS insignia, the flapping blood-red banners with the hooked-cross swastika emblem—all radiated the barbaric strength the Nazis clung to.

The great party rallies were carefully staged so as to embody all these core qualities of Nazi totalitarianism. One, at least, has been preserved: the Nuremberg rally of 1934, which the gifted film-maker Leni Riefenstahl made into the artistically acclaimed *Triumph of the Will.* It is all there, living still on film: the German Gothic architecture of the old city and the new Leader descending in a shiny modern airplane to his people. The blond, clean-cut Hitler Youth, the packed stadium, and the hooked-cross banner, the *Führer* leaning toward them with his rising off-key rhetoric, his voice shaking with passion, fist slamming the podium. Below him, the rigid military formations greet every chopping point with right arms shooting up, voices rising in the rolling *Sieg heil!*—"Hail, victory!"—of the Nazi salute.

Many talented people were filled with genuine enthusiasm for the Russian Revolution in the early years. The symbolist poet Aleksandr Blok produced an evocative vision of the most violent days of the revolution in *The Twelve,* the lusty, sometimes brutal epic of a Bolshevik platoon—led by the symbolic figure of Christ!

Theatrical reformers such as Vsevolod Meyerhold rejected the well-made plays and meticulously realistic productions for which prerevolutionary Russia had been famous. On bare stages garnished with naked ladders, pulleys, and other gear, they mounted mass proletarian spectacles.

With the rise of Stalin to mastery of the Soviet Union in the thirties, however, the cultural ferment was quickly stilled.

Stalin's own ideas on art were few, but he did encourage one central contribution to the cultural life of Russia—the cult of his own personality. His picture was everywhere, his infallible wisdom trumpeted from party congresses to every schoolchild's "Stalin corner." Glorification of the leader was thus as much a central feature of Soviet as of Nazi totalitarianism.

Naturally, glorification of the working masses, the proletarians and peasants who were the chosen people of the Communist promised land, was another salient aspect of Soviet totalitarianism. And so, finally, was an ideologically unlikely emphasis on Russian nationalism. The need to generate enthusiasm for building up the national economy and preparing for the threatening war with Hitler's Germany accounts for this Communist effort to remind Russians of their past greatness.

The art and literature that embodied these concepts went by the label of *socialist realism.* It was, as the Communist Union of Soviet Writers declared, an art "saturated with the heroic struggle of the world proletariat and with the grandeur of the victory of socialism . . . reflecting the great wisdom and heroism of the Communist Party. . . ."[2]

The socialist realist paintings of those days show brawny factory workers or bronzed farmers toiling for the motherland, Lenin Speaking to the People, or heroic incidents from the Russian past. Formula novels, plays, and films glorified the achievements of "shock workers" (those who exceeded their quotas), the successful completion of great construction projects, and other achievements of the Five-Year Plans. Poetry and history celebrated Stalin, comparing him to past heroes such as Peter the Great, exag-

---

[2]Gleb Struve, *Soviet Russian Literature 1917–1950* (Norman: University of Oklahoma Press, 1951), p. 239.

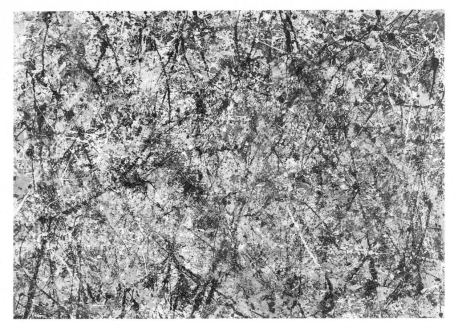

Jackson Pollock's "Number 1, 1950 (Lavender Mist)" is a prime example of the abstract expressionist painting of the New York school. Modernism enjoyed perhaps its last great flowering in the United States after World War II. And Pollock, laughed at in his own day for painting methods like pouring the pigment directly from the can onto a horizontal canvas, was hailed as a giant among the modernists in the later twentieth century. (Jackson Pollack, "Number 1, 1950 [Lavender Mist]." Oil, enamel, and aluminum on canvas. 2.210 × 2.997 [87 × 118 in.] National Gallery of Art, Washington, D.C. Alisa Mellon Bruce Fund 1976)

gerating his part in the Revolution of 1917, and praising his omniscience, activism, and many victories.

Even within this framework, however, some impressive art could be produced. The internationally celebrated films of Sergei Eisenstein, in particular, grappled with the artistic problem of the collective hero posed by Communist doctrine with remarkable success. Eisenstein's masterwork of the 1920s, *Battleship Potemkin,* immortalized the 1905 naval mutiny that Communists saw as a forerunner of their own revolution. Art-film fanciers in the decadent West were soon lining up to revel in Eisenstein's surging crowd scenes and searing montage effects—the shattering cuts from cheering crowds to charging police, and then to the unforgettable close-ups—a baby carriage jolting down the wide cement stairs, a screaming face, broken glasses, blood gushing from an eye.

MODERNISM, POSTMODERNISM, AND CULTURAL CONFLICT, 1945–1995

MODERNISM AROUND THE WORLD

Modernism became the true high-international style of the twentieth century—particularly after World War II. As early as the years between the wars, however, non-European writers such as the Argentine Jorge Luis Borges and the Japanese painter Togo Seiji were producing widely admired work in the modernist vein. In the decades after World War II, the modernist determination to break with Western cultural tradition made the modernist style accessible to peoples around the world.

Modernism's reduction of art to its fundamental formal elements made modernist work uniquely comprehensible as a purely aesthetic experience, as culture-free as art could be. Experimental art, it seemed, was truly free of cultural limitations—and hence it was the ideal international style.

Modernist architecture in particular traveled with ease and appropriateness around the globe during the post-World War II years. Developed especially by European architects such as Mies van der Rohe or le Corbusier, these distinctively twentieth-century styles of building were based on exploiting the possibilities of new building materials and modes of construction: reinforced concrete, glass, steel, plastics, the high-rise block, and the geodesic dome. The result was a vocabulary of basic shapes and sweeping contours that was as free of associations with any particular culture as any art could be.

Modernist techniques and styles were thus applied with equal success to public buildings and business blocks, hotels, and universities in many countries. Chinese-born American architect I. M. Pei could design with equal ease the Mile High Center in Denver and the glass pyramid added to the Louvre art museum in Paris.

Entire national capitals for countries as culturally diverse as Brazil, Arabia, and India were built in the modernist mode. A roughly representational mural on a local theme, a decorative band of Aztec hieroglyphics or Arabic script seems to have been enough to make modernist architecture fit into any tradition around the world.

EUROPEAN LITERATURE BEARS WITNESS

In the later as in the earlier twentieth century, meanwhile, many writers sought to use literature to expose social ills. Many of the new targets, however, were the radical totalitarian regimes that had seemed to offer hope before World War II.

An internationally known example was George Orwell, a British socialist author who vividly depicted the suffering of the masses during the Great Depression before World War II—and then exposed the communist solution to the problem of poverty after the war. Orwell's novels *Animal Farm* and above all *1984* warned of a totalitarian future where some are "more equal" than others and a Stalinist "Big Brother" rules an enslaved population through propaganda and terror.

Survivors of continental totalitarian regimes also testified to the nightmare underside of the century's dream of a brave new world. In West Germany, Günter Grass's *The Tin Drum* forced the German generations who had plunged into two world wars and cheered Adolf Hitler to face their past. In the Soviet Union, Boris Pasternak's *Dr. Zhivago* offered an epic and deeply moving account of the collapse of Russian society during the Revolution. Alexander Solzhenitsyn's writings, especially the brief but powerful *One Day in the Life of Ivan Denisovitch* and his multivolume compilation of prisoners' memoirs, *The Gulag Archipelago,* vividly exposed the brutality of Stalinist labor camps.

NORTH AMERICAN SOCIAL CRITICISM

In the United States as in Europe, writers chipped away throughout the century at American society's faults and failings. Between the wars, the experimental plays of Eugene O'Neill tried virtually everything, from Greek tragedy set in rural New England in *Mourning Becomes Electra* to using voodoo drums to involve us in the decline and fall of a Caribbean dictator in *The Emperor Jones.* William Faulkner crated his own world in the deep south, setting many of his novels and stories in the imaginary Yaknapatawpha county, Mississippi, and novels like *The Sound and the Fury* entirely in the minds of its highly disturbed characters.

After World War II, the writings of such widely admired novelists as Norman Mailer and Saul Bellow seldom presented an orthodox "good guy" hero. Sylvia Plath's poems and autobiographical novel, *The Bell Jar,* revealed the psychological anguish of growing up sensitive and a woman in mid-century America. The plays of Arthur Miller probed deeply into the American psyche, exposing the witch-hunting mentality of the McCarthy years in *The Crucible* and the hollowness at the heart of a typical American family in *Death of a Salesman.* Novels like Ralph Ellison's *Invisible Man* and *Beloved* by Pulitzer Prize winner Toni Morrison drew upon the African-American experience to forge complex and powerful works of art.

The interior of Eero Saarinen's Trans-World Airlines terminal at Kennedy Airport in New York looks appropriately space-age in this photograph. Modern building materials freed modernist architects from pillars, arches, and other structural devices typical of earlier centuries. Glass, steel, and poured concrete created entirely new contours for modernist buildings. (PH Archives)

Both world wars and the Vietnam War triggered floods of antiwar writing. And some young Americans in each generation turned their backs on middle-class society altogether and followed Ernest Hemingway to the bullfights in Spain where *The Sun Also Rises* or Jack Kerouac *On the Road* across America.

LATIN AMERICAN MAGICAL REALISM

Latin America bloomed somewhat later but in an equally dazzling display of literary experimentation and social criticism. Some Latin American writers became leading modernist voices in the earlier 1900s; but it was after 1945 that Latin American "magical realism" began to generate books with a global appeal.

Leaders in the glittering galaxy of Latin American writers included Jorge Luis Borges, Carlos Fuentes, and Gabriel García Marques. Borges, an Argentine writer who spent many years in Europe, became internationally known between the wars for his short fictions, tales that seemed to combine the charm of anecdotes or Arabian nights' entertainments with deeper meanings, philosophical mazes without exits.

Carlos Fuentes, a Mexican author educated in the United States, and the Colombian novelist Gabriel García Marques became leading practitioners of the unique combination of realism and fantasy called *magical realism.* Fuentes's mingling of naturalistic detail and dream-like surrealism won him an international reputation for such novels as his study of the corruption of a Mexican Revolutionary hero, *The Death of Artemio Cruz.* García Marques's worldwide best-seller, *One Hundred Years of Solitude,* carved out his private universe in the jungle-girt Colombian village of Macondo. Whether it is the discovery of ice in the tropics or the arrival of a flying carpet over the rooftops, life is always full of wonders in Macondo. Like Faulkner's county, García Marques's village turned local color into high art.

AFRICA'S SEARCH FOR CULTURAL IDENTITY

Like other regions overrun by Western imperialists in the nineteenth century, liberated twentieth-century Africa faced a problem of cultural identity. African writers and artists inevitably felt the influence of Western, particularly European culture. But they also sought eagerly to recover their precolonial roots in the traditional African past. Out of this mixed heritage and the traumatic experience of the great liberation itself, Africa forged new forms of cultural expression in the second half of the century.

Some of the most widely known African literature was produced in two of the world's international languages, English and French. French-speaking West African poets like the Senegalese Léopold Senghor—later president of his country—celebrated the mysterious essence of Africa in the poetry of *négritude,* or "black-

ness." English-language writers such as Chinua Achebe won global renown for novels like *Things Fall Apart,* dealing with the shattering impact of imperialism, and *A Man of the People,* vividly evoking the chaotic results of liberation. In southern Africa, a galaxy of black and white writers, including Nadine Gordimer and J. M. Coetzee, made the world conscious of the dehumanizing consequences of apartheid.

Other creative spirits used African rather than European languages, among them another major international language, Arabic. The Egyptian writer and critic Taha Hussein knew both Europe and his homeland well despite blindness from an early age. Taha wrote of this own life in two beautiful volumes, *An Egyptian Childhood* and *Stream of Days,* while his later critical writings urged modern Egyptian culture to find its place in a Mediterranean context.

South of the Sahara, excellent writers in languages from Wolof to Zulu gave western and southern Africa rich regional literatures in the postcolonial period. In modern Nigeria, for instance, Yoruba folk opera mingled traditional myths and history in a medley of forms including silent mime and spoken dialogue, song and dance, and powerful African music.

Independent Africa's search for cultural identity has often found vigorous expression in music and dance. Traditional black African music combined polyphony and percussion in complex rhythms that intrigue modern musicologists. Drums, xylophones, and the hand piano, or *mbila,* produced an intricate yet intoxicating outpouring of sound that was distinctively African.

African dances, widely preserved and developed, continued to play a key part in rural African society. Line and round dances were common, and sensational stilt dances never failed to awe visitors. The integration of old and new come home vividly when you see stilt dancers celebrating a ritual occasion in a West African village— and later opening a new supermarket in town.

ASIA'S CONFRONTATION WITH CULTURAL CHANGE

In Asia as in Africa, a variety of peoples confronted social change in the second half of the twentieth century. The impact of Western influences, economic growth, war, and politics brought sweeping changes to established forms of Asian literature and art.

In India, writers in English and in a number of historic Indian literary languages produced fiction that focused on Indian problems yet found an international audience. R. K. Narayan, author of many books about the fictional south Indian village of Malgudi, was particularly well-known and widely read outside his own country. Kamala Markandaya surveyed a broad spectrum of Indian life, from dusty villages to teeming cities, in such novels as her widely admired *A Handful of Rice.* Perhaps the most famous of all "Indian" writers, however, was "Indian" only by ancestry. V. S. Naipaul, born of immigrant parents in the West Indies and a resident of Britain for most of his life, traveled the world to write novels and travel books about the Caribbean (*Guerrillas*), Africa (*A Bend in the River*), the Middle East (*Among the Believers*), and the India from which his ancestors came (*India: A Wounded Civilization*).

In China, student culture had opened wide to Western influences in the earlier decades of the century, welcoming Western lecturers and devouring Western classics. After the triumph of the Communists in 1949, however, the cultural life of the Middle Kingdom was dominated by Mao Zedong's dictum that "Politics Takes Command!" in the arts. As in Soviet Russia under Stalin, literature in Mao's China set out to chronicle the victories of idealized workers and communists over evil capitalists, landlords, and other oppressors. Chinese drama and opera also hailed the achievements of the People's Liberation Army and Chairman Mao, the "great helmsman." Only in the last decades of the century, under the more pragmatic regime of Deng Hsiaoping, did a few writers begin to expose the grimmer side of the Great Leap Forward and the Red Guard era in first-person narratives like Gao Yuan's *Born Red: A Chronical of the Cultural Revolution.*

Japan, as we have seen, absorbed many Western social and cultural influences during the later nineteenth and earlier twentieth centuries. Its military ambitions shattered in World War II, a new Japan rose to the economic heights in the following half-century. Japanese culture vividly expressed the impact of these dramatic changes.

Postwar Japan preserved many of its traditional arts, including print making, calligraphy, and the classic Japanese theater, honoring skilled practitioners of these arts as national treasures. At the same time, however, Japanese architects like Tange Kenzo, designer of the Hiroshima Peace Memorial, won international prestige for building in the modernist style.

Emblematic of these conflicting traditions was the career of Mishima Yukio. Mishima's brilliant postwar novels glorified Japan's traditional past, including samurai militarism, and condemned the new, Westernized Japan— yet combined sensuous Japanese prose with Western psychological analysis. Torn between two traditions, Mishima turned the last volume of his masterpiece, *The Sea of Fertility,* over to his publishers—futilely urged Japanese troops to overthrow their government—and then committed *sepukku,* ritual suicide in the ancient samurai tradition.

POSTMODERN MODES

Hovering behind these cultural problems of the later twentieth century was a new tendency in the arts increasingly labeled *postmodernism.* Like the structuralists, poststructuralists, and deconstructionists considered above, postmodernists challenged even twentieth-century culture to jus-

tify itself. For postmodernists, modernist giants like T. S. Eliot or Frank Lloyd Wright were as much elitist enemies of the new, free art as any earlier classic or academician.

Postmodernism, like modernism, emerged in the West. but it soon found niches in other parts of the world as well.

Postmodernists, like their modernist predecessors, felt betrayed by Western institutions and ideologies. They rejected a society that they believed had plunged arrogantly into the quagmire of the Cold War, ravaged the global environment, and oppressed people of color, women, and young people. They responded with a sardonic tone that took nothing seriously and was at its most effective when debunking the institutions and ideals of the age.

Literary conventions also crumbled once more in the hands of the postmodernists. American novelist John Hawkes firmly declared that "the true enemies of the novel" were "plot, character, setting, and themes."[3] And, again like deconstructionists and poststructuralists in philosophy, postmodernist writers denounced modern society as the artificial creation of its ruling classes. Canadian critic Linda Hutcheon thus declared that the larger goal of postmodernism was to subvert belief in such basic structures as "capitalism, patriarchy, liberal humanism."[4]

Postmodernism erupted first in architecture, where modern tower blocks of glass and concrete were rejected as soulless. Postmodernist architects added bright colors, playful details, and architectural touches borrowed from earlier styles, though the latter were deployed with a knowing wink as joking allusions to the dead past. Postmodernism affected many other aspects of twentieth-century culture too, from journalism, photography, and motion pictures to music, the dance, television videos, and fashion in clothing. Everywhere a tongue-in-cheek sense of playfulness and artificiality dominated the postmodern cultural scene.

Postmodernist modes emerged most importantly in literature. Postmodernist writers rejected realism, emphasized word-play, extravagant or intrusive styles, and story lines that were impossible or outrageous. They claimed no exalted artistic vocation, yet constantly put artists themselves at the center of their "self-reflexive" work. They saw science fiction or detective stories as every bit as "important" as esoteric poems or ponderously obscure novels, reminding their readers that what they were reading was, after all, only a story.

The new approach soon left mere material reality far behind. In *Invisible Cities,* Italy's Italo Calvino offered an incredible travelogue of physically impossible but philosophically intriguing urban complexes as they might have been described by a postmodern Marco Polo to a

---

[3]Quoted in "John Hawkes: An Interview," *Wisconsin Studies in Contemporary Literature*, vol. 6 (1965), p. 143.

[4]Linda Hutcheon, *The Politics of Postmodernism* (London and New York: Routledge, 1989), p. 2.

very gullible Kublai Khan. Postmodern critics followed poststructuralists and deconstructionists in asserting that it was "impossible any longer to see reality as something 'out there,' a fixed order of things which language merely reflected."[5]

POSTMODERNISM BEYOND THE WEST

Outside Europe and North America, postmodern modes gradually infected other late twentieth-century cultures as well. Much Latin American magical realism had a postmodern ring, mixing fact and fantasy in self-conscious artifacts. The same could be said for much African and other art that commingled often gritty realism with supernatural legendry, history with myth. And the most developed of Asian societies produced full-fledged postmodern literature whose medium of expression was at least as important as its message.

Among the writers of Latin America's literary "boom," Manuel Puig produced a series of postmodern novels and plays like *Betrayed by Rita Hayworth* and *Kiss of the Spider Woman.* His work drew heavily on such popular culture icons as mystery stories and romance fiction, glamour magazines, sports, and above all the movies. In works like *Hopscotch,* Julio Cortázar, an Argentine writer based in literary Paris, produced works that read like wrestling matches with language itself.

African writers who aroused interest as postmodernists included Sony Labou Tansi, weaver of intricate webs of "suprareal fiction." Nigerian writer Ben Okri mingled African folk beliefs with the realities of African village and shanty-town life in his prize-winning *The Famished Road.* Here compassionately described characters mingle with hallucinatory, often terrifying creatures out of African legend.

In Asia, Japan's rapid postwar plunge into an affluent consumer society dominated by foreign cultural imports produced some sophisticated postmodern work. Tanaka Yasua's novel, *Somehow, Crystal,* was a plotless adolescent daydream of glittering shops and brand-name products, American or European words, and unrelated feelings. From Bombay came Muslim novelist Salman Rushdie, mixing India's real past with its ancient religions in *Midnight's Children.* Rushdie earned a death sentence from Iran's Ayatollah Khomenei for his blasphemous treatment of the Prophet Muhammad in his international bestseller, *The Satanic Verses.*

Wherever postmodernism spread, it raised disturbing questions about what was real, what was important, and what values ought to dominate our lives. In a world in the grip of surging change, readers in many lands found relief in realms of fantasy and games, pop culture, and radical challenges to the way things were.

[5]Terry Eagleton, *Literary Theory* (Minneapolis: University of Minneapolis Press, 1983), p. 108.

POPULAR ARTS WITH A GLOBAL REACH

FOLK ART GOES COSMOPOLITAN

On the popular level as well as in modernist and postmodernist circles, the arts displayed a tendency toward convergence and the beginnings of some sort of genuinely global taste in the later twentieth century. Both traditional folk art and contemporary popular art exhibited these trends toward common patterns of development.

Traditional arts would seem at first glance the least likely to contain such a global dimension. Artistic traditions, after all, are typically the defining features of separate regional cultures. From patterns on pots to styles of temple building, traditional styles have historically distinguished one culture from another, heightening each people's sense of its own uniqueness. Styles in African masks, the folk dances of various Soviet socialist republics, Andean textiles, Appalachian folk tales—all are cultural products that—it is often suggested—only a native can completely appreciate.

As it happens, however, the present century has seen a steadily growing appreciation for the traditional arts of all peoples. Interest in other peoples' cultural traditions spans an astonishing range today, from arts as demanding as Japanese Kabuki theater to those as accessible as African drumming and Cossack dances.

This international smorgasbord of traditional art has had its limitations and weaknesses. The very popularity of foreign culture could lead to the proliferation of "airport art"—mass-produced copies of authentic village art intended to separate tourists from their travelers checks. Even the most sensitive nonnative, furthermore, is unlikely to grasp the full social and spiritual significance of traditional art removed from its place in a living culture and hung like a trophy on a museum wall.

On the other hand, interest in other peoples' traditional art forms did mark a very considerable broadening of the world's taste. When whole museums were dedicated to "primitive" art, when sophisticates from New York, Paris, Berlin, New Delhi, Tokyo, or Mexico City could look at one another's traditional art with some understanding and with genuine admiration, the world's peoples were clearly closer to mutual respect than they had ever been before.

POPULAR ARTS, FROM MUSIC TO THE MOVIES

Modernism was in a sense *the* first global style, the intercontinental style par excellence. But it was also high culture, an art for elites. People with education, money, and power stayed in modernist hotels, worked in modernist commercial, cultural, or government buildings, read

Toure Kounda and his French West African band excite the crowds in Paris. Colorful African dance troupes like this one found a worldwide audience in the later twentieth century. Costume, razzle-dazzle, and crowd-pleasing verve were undergirded by precision and complexity in both music and dance. (Gamma-Liaison, Inc.)

Borges and Joyce, and covered their livingroom walls with abstract expressionist art. Recent years, however, have seen the birth of an international popular culture as well.

Popular arts having an international appeal were perhaps most noticeably those of music and film. Jazz, blues, and other forms of African-American music had a global appeal between the two world wars, as did such Latin American dances as the samba, the conga, and the rhumba. American rock 'n' roll, West Indian reggae, and the performances of intercontinental superstars such as the British Beatles and Rolling Stones continued this tradition of internationally adored popular music. A group hadn't "arrived" until it had toured Australia, and hotel musicians in Communist Yugoslavia were belting out international favorites such as "Itsy-Bitsy Teeny-Weeny Yellow Polka-dot Bikini" in the depths of the Cold War Years.

Perhaps the most dazzlingly successful form of popular art internationally, however, was the motion picture.

The seemingly indestructable Rolling Stones continued to draw huge audiences around the world from the 1960s to the 1990s. Elaborate staging contributed to the spectacular appeal of such concerts. (AP/Wide World Photos)

The films of Hollywood's dream factories also went back to the interwar years in their popularity, and it was a popularity that continue throughout the second half of the century. Worldwide taste for American television—also a film medium—was overwhelming. Despite the ideological objections of some governments, despite the clucking of people with more sophisticated sensibilities in many countries, mass audiences around the world took enthusiastically to American television series.

The taste for American films and television shows was not a passion for things American so much as for things *modern*. American television had the urban feel and the smell of money, the violence, slickness, professional precision, and glitter of the century itself. Television series such as "Dallas" were the dream of all the world—an unrealistic fantasy of a global Texas symbolized by the gleaming new skyscrapers and fabulous wealth of that quintessentially twentieth-century city.

Over the postwar decades, other nations also developed major motion picture industries. Artistic film-making flourished from France and Italy to India, China, and Japan. But other countries also produced their share of movies intended as popular entertainment. India's film industry evolved from musical comedies to high-velocity adventure films based on American sex-and-violence models. Hong Kong contributed Bruce Lee and the martial-arts movie to the world's menu of popular film fare. And on a Chinese state airliner winging its way toward Tibet, you could watch the latest installment of "The Legend of a Tycoon"—"Dallas" Chinese style.

BUILDING GLOBAL CULTURE

Five centuries ago, the great regional centers of the globe were virtually closed books to one another. China was half mythical to Europeans, all the rest of the earth barbarians to the Chinese. The New World was as unknown to the Old World as Eurasia was to the peoples of the high Andes or the Valley of Mexico. Even one century ago, only a few sons of Asian princes studied in Europe, a handful of Western scholars pored over Sanskrit or Arabic texts, and almost no one cared about preliterate cultures enough to attempt to understand the arts and ideas of the world's preurban populations.

Today's picture, comparatively speaking, is one of massive cultural interaction on all levels. And these exchanges of ideas, images, music, emotional attitudes, and mystical inspirations can scarcely help but draw the peoples of the world closer together. To know an Arab or an American may not be to love him, but it is at least to *know* him better than we ever have before.

Rigid uniformity of outlook or aesthetic expression is probably unlikely—thank goodness, many will say. Complex regional societies, even individual nations, have in the past nourished quite a range of subcultures. Still, some of the widest disparities among the varied cultures of the world do seem to be fading, and some universal tastes and enthusiasms manifesting themselves. The result may well be enough of a harmony of feeling and belief to enable us all to live together on our common planet with a minimum of social discord—somewhere down the road.

SUMMARY

The influence of Western culture on the rest of the world remained great throughout the twentieth century. Yet by the end of that century, a genuine global culture did seem to be emerging.

Western art and thought themselves underwent a serious crisis during this period. Science, philosophy, and religion all faced powerful challenges from the spread of materialism, secularism, and various kinds of relativism. Yet the sciences added greatly to our understanding of the universe we live in. Existentialism, structuralism, and their offshoots transformed the way many people saw their world. And resurgent fundamentalism mobilized some of the world's great religions to reassert their basic values in the world.

In the arts, modernist experimentalism combined with revolutionary political and social commitments to make the

first half of the century a turbulent one for the West and the rest of the world. The cultural history of the second half of the twentieth century continued to reveal strong social and political influences on artists and writers in many lands. The period since 1945 also saw late modernism give way to even more experimental postmodern writing and art.

Popular art in particular, meanwhile, developed a global reach in the course of the twentieth century. Western peoples learned to admire the traditional arts of many cultures. Peoples around the world absorbed and imitated Western, especially American film, television, and music. Though there were still strange and exotic things to be seen in many lands, the makings of a global civilization seemed to be coming together as the year 2000 approached.

SUGGESTED READING

ACHEBE, C. *Things Fall Apart.* New York: Heinemann, 1981. A disturbing novel of the new Africa by a leading African writer.

ARNASON, H. H. *History of Modern Art,* 2nd ed. Englewood Cliffs, N.J.: Prentice-Hall, 1977. Well-illustrated and well-written history of modern art.

BARRETT, W. *Irrational Man: A Study in Existential Philosophy.* Garden City, N.Y.: Doubleday, 1958. Origins and cultural impact of existentialism, from Kierkegaard to Sartre. For selections expertly introduced by a philosopher, see W. Kaufmann, ed., *Existentialism from Dostoyevsky to Sartre* (New York: New American Library, 1956).

BORGES, J. L. *Labyrinths, Selected Stories, and Other Writings.* New York: New Directions, 1969. One of the first of the Latin American writers to win an international reputation with his enigmatic fiction.

CALVINO, I. *Invisible Cities.* Trans. W. Weaver. New York: Harcourt Brace Jovanovich, 1974. Enigmatic vignettes of unreal yet intellectually challenging cityscapes.

DANGAREMBGA, T. *Nervous Condition.* Harare: Zimbabwe Publishing House, 1990. An African girl half-way between village life and a Western-dominated world.

ELIOT, T. S. *The Waste Land and Other Poems.* New York: Harcourt, Brace, 1955. The poems that defined the cultural despair that underlay much of the frivolity of the 1920s.

ELLISON, R. *Invisible Man.* New York: Random House, 1972. Being black in America; a classic.

ELLMAN, R., and C. FEIDELSON. *The Modern Tradition: Backgrounds of Modern Literature.* New York: Oxford University Press, 1965. Valuable collection of position papers on the modernist mode.

FEUER, L. S. *Einstein and the Generations of Science.* New York: Basic books, 1974. A close look at the people and ideas that launched the twentieth-century surge in the sciences.

FREUD, S. *Civilization and Its Discontents,* trans J. Strachey. New York: W. W. Norton, 1961. Psychoanalysis applied to the nature and problems of modern civilization.

GAMOW, G. *Thirty Years That Shook Physics.* Garden City, N.Y.: Anchor Books, 1966. A scientist and scientific popularizer on the "Second Scientific Revolution" of this century.

GARCÍA MÁRQUEZ, G. *One Hundred Years of Solitude,* trans. G. Rabassa. New York: Harper & Row, Pub., 1970. Epic of the Latin American backlands, written in the neosurrealist "magical realist" style of many postwar Latin American writers. On this Latin American literary renaissance, see D. F. Gallagher, *Modern Latin American Literature* (New York: Oxford University Press, 1973).

GRASS, G. *The Tin Drum,* trans. R. Manheim. New York: Random House, 1971. One of the leading postwar German writers looks back scathingly at his country's experience in this century.

GREEN, C. *Cubism and Its Enemies.* New Haven, Conn.: Yale University Press, 1987. Highlights the differences between cubism and other modernist movements, especially surrealism.

HESS, T. B., and J. ASBERRY, eds. *Avant-Garde Art.* London: Macmillan, 1967. Essays on major movements in the arts from the turn of the century to the 1960s.

JOYCE, J. *Ulysses.* New York: Random House, 1967. The archetypal modernist novel, challenging both the ethical and aesthetic values of the time.

KAFKA, F. *The Penal Colony: Stories and Short Pieces, Including The Metamorphosis.* New York: Schocken, 1961. Good selection of the anguished short fictions of this distinctive twentieth-century spirit of the period between the wars.

KUHN, T. *The Structures of Scientific Revolutions.* Chicago: University of Chicago Press, 1962. Valuable insight into the workings of the scientific mind in a century that has learned more about the material world than any other.

LIM, S. C. *Fistful of Colors.* Singapore: EPB Publishers, 1993. Revealing novel of ethnic and generational differences in today's Singapore.

MISHIMA, Y. *The Temple of the Golden Pavilion,* trans. I. Morris. New York: Putnum, 1981. Passionate and profound novel built around the destruction of Kyoto's Golden Pavilion after World War II. For Japan's literary flowering after 1945, see H. Hibbett, ed., *Contemporary Japanese Literature: An Anthology of Fiction, Film, and Other Writing since 1945* (New York: Knopf, 1977).

NARAYAN, R. K. *Under the Banyan Tree.* New York: Viking Press, 1985. Stories of traditional village India.

OKRI, Ben. *The Famished Road.* New York: Doubleday, 1992. An African "spirit child" moves effortlessly from reality to magic.

PUIG, M. *Kiss of the Spider Woman.* Trans. T. Colchie. New York: Knopf, 1979. Postmodernism with a political slant.

RUSHDIE, S. *Midnight's Children.* New York: Knopf, 1981. Postmodern novel of Anglo-Indian cultural disarray.

SENGHOR, L. *The Collected Poetry.* Trans. M. Dixon. Charlottesville: University of Virginia Press, 1991. English versions of the poetry of *négritude.*

TAGORE, R. *A Tagore Reader.* Ed. A. Chakravarty. New York: Macmillan, 1961. Good collection of the Indian master's work.

TANAKA, Y., ed. *Unmapped Territories.* Seattle: Women in Translation, 1991. Stories by Japanese women writers.

WOOLF, V. *To the Lighthouse.* New York: Harcourt Brace Jovanovich, 1964. Masterpiece by one of the giants of the high modernist period between the wars.

CHAPTER 49

THE WORLD AT A TURNING POINT

TOWARD A NEW WORLD ORDER?

A WATERSHED IN HUMAN EVENTS

On at least two levels, the world seemed to be at a turning point as the twentieth century drew to a close. Politically, diplomatically and militarily, the global order that had emerged in the aftermath of World War II did seem to be dissolving at last. From the perspective of statesmen and politicians, this was the moment—an old order crumbling, a new one not yet established—to try to impose a new direction on the course of world history. At the same time, deeper, slower-moving currents, economic, technological, social, and institutional, appeared to be pushing the peoples of the world toward a greater degree of cohesive action and interaction than ever before. Altogether, it looked like a watershed in human events.

There were, however, problems with both these scenarios for a new order of things. Many of the political realities of the 1990s raised serious challenges to the politicians' dream of a new world order. And larger trends toward global cooperation and integration were countered by an equally visible drift toward global disarray and even disaster.

This final chapter will try to outline some of the main currents that seemed to be carrying the world, for better or for worse, toward some sort of major turning point as the year 2000 drew closer.

THE TRIUMPH OF THE WEST

To many, the United States looked like a winner as the 1990s began. The Western alliance as a whole certainly seemed to be riding high.

The Cold War was over. The Soviet satellite empire in Eastern Europe had crumbled, Germany had been reunified within the Western alliance, and Soviet troops had pulled back out of Eastern Europe, abandoning the gains of World War II. The Soviet Union itself had finally fragmented as one-party rule gave way to contested elections, the Soviet planned economy crumbled, and most of its constituent republics seceded from the U.S.S.R.

In the Western alliance, by contrast, forces for integration and advance had never been stronger. Western Europe—"the Twelve" as the members of the European Community called themselves—moved toward greater economic unity than ever before and talked openly of future political union as well. German and other Western business people fanned out over Eastern Europe, signing contracts to rebuild shattered socialist economies, and to make a tidy profit while doing so. From the other side of the Atlantic, the United States rode shotgun on this careering stagecoach of Western success, winning "splendid little wars" in Central America and the Middle East. Sober commentators warned against "triumphalism" in a world still beset with problems, but it was hard not to feel cheered at the end of forty years of tension between the two superpowers and their allies.

In these circumstances, U.S. Presidents George Bush and his successor Bill Clinton began to elaborate plans for a new and better international order.

President Bush's hopes for a new world order focused on a number of traditional American goals. These included democratic governments, free-market economies, free trade, and world peace. Unstated but clearly understood by the rest of the world was America's intention to remain preeminent in world affairs. To achieve these ends, President Bush depended on close personal contacts with the leaders of other nations. These included America's long-time Western European allies in particular, but also former ideological foes in Moscow and Beijing.

President Clinton, more concerned with America's domestic economic problems than with foreign policy, tended to see international affairs in economic terms also. He won congressional ratification of two key international trade treaties, the General Agreement on Tariffs and Trade (GATT) and the North American Free Trade Treaty (NAFTA). He also sought to broker peace agreements in Israel and Ireland and used force or the threat of it to impose democracy on Haiti and peace in Bosnia.

Other Western statesmen had other agendas for the brave new world. French President François Mitterand and German Chancellor Helmut Kohl championed a more unified Europe, economically united, with its own security system and an unprecedented degree of political union as well. International civil servants in the United Nations saw a more active role for that organization in the global future.

Western ways spread around the world in the second half of the twentieth century. Here, the Western alphabet and number system, costume, haircut, and even a Western soft drink are superimposed on East Asian surroundings. (Stock/Boston)

THE PUBLIC MOOD

This confident, aggressive mood, however, did not last. By the mid-1990s, it had given way to a vague yet profound sense of uncertainty, of a post Cold War world without clear rules or established directions. Many found it harder to navigate in these new and uncharted seas beyond the dangerous but familiar shoals and reefs of the post-war decades.

A basic problem was the end of equilibrium, of the dependable balance of a bipolar world. Many nations East and West, North and South, had structured their policies around the balance of power between the U.S.A. and the U.S.S.R. Allies, client states, guerrilla groups seeking aid, and nations locked in private feuds or pursuing ambitions of their own had often exploited the old status quo with great sophistication. Offering their support to one side or the other, warning of danger from one camp if they were not given immediate help by the other, changing sides or flirting with both sides, the weak had often manipulated the strong as much as they had themselves been used.

But the problem was larger than that. It was as if a global tug of war had suddenly come to an end—leaving all participants sprawling in a tangled heap on the ground. Everyone saw opportunities—for freedom, for prosperity, for a peace dividend, for bringing the troops home, for revitalizing international organizations, restructuring institutions, realigning priorities. But the very fact of a world without rules, precedents, guideposts, or certainties contributed to anxieties and fears.

Anxieties, fears—and anger. Peoples everywhere seemed prone to feel betrayed, oppressed, put upon, and mad as hell. Americans whose incomes had scarcely risen in twenty years—but who still had houses and cars—were as angry as Russians whose economy had collapsed entirely. American religious conservatives were bitter over what they perceived as an anything-goes morality, includ-

ing limits on public prayer, publicly funded abortion, and mass media awash in sex and violence. But Muslim fundamentalists were even more violently angry over the simple separation of church and state in their traditionally Islamic countries. Student demonstrators in South Korea, striking labor unions in France, skinhead thugs in Germany, and voters for unlikely protest candidates in many lands—despite their differences—all shared a public mood of ill-contained outrage.

There was no way of telling how long this mood would last. But in the mid-1990s, it seemed to inflame political campaigns and public discourse everywhere. It was a mood that pointed toward an uncertain future.

 # A WORLD IN DISARRAY

ECONOMIC DISLOCATION

Beneath these confusions and resentments seemed to lie a broad spectrum of more general problems. These included economic dislocations, social dysfunctions, and inflamed ideological and religious creeds.

The economic problems of the industrialized states differed significantly from those of the developing countries. A major problem for the world's developed nations was commercial competition. Thus, the trade imbalance between the world's two most dynamic economies, those of United States and Japan, ran heavily in Japan's favor. Seemingly endless negotiations aimed at opening up Japanese markets to American goods strained the vital relationship between the two economic superpowers.

Two related problems were high unemployment and low wages in the industrialized Western nations. Some Western European countries, such as France, faced unemployment levels as high as 12 percent in the 1990s. Other developed countries, like the United States, had unemployment rates only half that high—but many workers were trapped in low-pay, no-benefit service jobs, flipping hamburgers or bagging groceries in supermarkets. Some blamed both unemployment and low-wage jobs on competition from low-paid workers in developing countries. Others thought lack of education excluded many from well-rewarded jobs in increasingly high-tech economies.

The developing nations of the world continued to have their share of economic problems too. These included many difficulties that went back to independence and beyond into the colonial period.

Thus international capital still shied away from the risks of investing in unstable poor countries. Powerful international loan agencies like the International Monetary Fund continued to require recipients to abolish inefficient state enterprises and cut subsidies on food and other basics. These policies cost jobs, raised food prices, and sometimes filled the streets with rioters—which further discouraged international investment in developing countries. Low international prices for the commodities they exported, wretched infrastructure, and ill-educated populations further undercut development in the global South.

SOCIAL DYSFUNCTION

Many social problems also beset both new and developed nations. Migration, for instance, was a problem for rich and poor alike. Rich countries struggled to absorb waves of migrants—from Africa and Asia into Europe, from Latin America into the United States. Poor countries saw an accelerating flow of village people into the shantytowns that ringed the cities. Thus, urban poverty, slum conditions, competition for nonexistent jobs, and other consequences plagued Paris and Johannesburg, Los Angeles and Rio de Janeiro.

Social problems involving youth and age also tormented both rich and poor countries. In the developing world, large families produced rapidly expanding populations, half of whose members were in their teens and twenties. Low-skilled younger generations drifted easily into unemployment, crime, and radical politics. In Western Europe, North America, and the developed East Asian rim, by contrast, populations who raised small families and benefited from modern medicine and high health standards grew older every year. Aging populations collected social security and had more medical expenses, imposing a heavy economic burden on society's working-age generations. Old people also made easy victims: in America, they were often mugged on the streets; in Russia, old people living alone were murdered for their apartments.

Shattered families also contributed to the social pathologies of the late twentieth century. In the United States, girls too young to raise children nevertheless had

them, and unemployed fathers deserted families they could not support. In underdeveloped countries, men left their families in distant villages to find work in the cities, heaping a heavy burden of work and child rearing on their wives. Both worlds tried to deal with the problems of decaying families and a fading sense of family responsibility. The United States considered legislation to deprive unwed mothers of income support. Singapore proposed a "Sue Your Son" law allowing neglected elderly parents to take undutiful sons to court for nonsupport.

IMPASSIONED CREEDS

Among the broader forces for disorder, two that seemed particularly capable of sabotaging all efforts at social harmony were matters of opinion rather than of material circumstance. These were the ancient problems posed by religious militance and the more recent ideological furies generated by modern nationalism.

Islam seemed the most aggressively militant of the world religions in the later twentieth century. Muslims demanded a return to traditional Islamic principles in politics, law, economics, and social relations in many lands, from North Africa to southern Asia. But India, once so tolerant of all faiths, was torn by a Hindu revival movement and threatened by Sikh terrorists as well as by Muslim militants. Some forms of Judaism in Israel, Catholicism and Protestantism in Ireland, and the evangelical Christianity in the United States all served as focuses of discontent, dissent, or demands for often extreme political action. Religious commitment, a force that seemed to have long since accepted the modern secular state, thus appeared to have become a powerfully divisive force in the world again.

Among the modern ideologies, socialism had declined precipitously, its communist variant eclipsing itself even more completely. But modern nationalism, never dormant, flared up even more violently once more. Arabs who knew Saddam Hussein for a bloody tyrant nevertheless cheered him on, as much as a champion of "the Arab nation"—the brotherhood of all Arabs—as because he was a Muslim. Eastern Europe rejected Russian domination more out of nationalistic resentment of foreign rule than out of love of democratic institutions. The resulting welter of conflicting nationalisms in this area as well as in Russia itself fostered oppression of national minorities, disputes over "ancestral lands" claimed by more than one people, and the collapse of political unity from Yugoslavia to the Soviet Union. The countries of Latin America, resentful of U.S. interventions, remained strongly nationalistic. Even in Western Europe, the Basques in Spain, the Irish Republican Army, and other nationalist groups carried on desultory struggles for independence. Nor were great powers immune to the spell: Both the United States and Japan seemed notably imbued with this secular faith in the preeminent importance of their respective nation-states.

THE MODERN WORLD

180°W
150°W
120°W
ARCTIC OCEAN
Alaska (U.S.)
KALÂTDIT NUNAT (DEN.)
ICELAND
60°N
CANADA
UNITED STATES
ATLANTIC OCEAN
30°N
Tropic of Cancer
MEXICO
CUBA
HAITI
DOM. REP.
PUERTO RICO (U.S.)
DOMINICA
ST. LUCIA
BARBADOS
TRINIDAD AND TOBAGO
ST. VINCENT
GRENADA
JAMAICA
HAWAIIAN ISLANDS
BELIZE
GUATEMALA
EL SALVADOR
HONDURAS
NICARAGUA
COSTA RICA
PANAMA
GUYANA
SURINAME
FRENCH GUIANA
VENEZUELA
COLOMBIA
ECUADOR
0°
Equator
KIRIBATI
PACIFIC OCEAN
TUVALU
VANUATU
WESTERN SAMOA
FIJI
TONGA
NEW CALEDONIA
Tropic of Capricorn
PERU
BRAZIL
BOLIVIA
PARAGUAY
CHILE
ARGENTINA
URUGUAY
30°S
NEW ZEALAND
60°S
Antarctic Circle

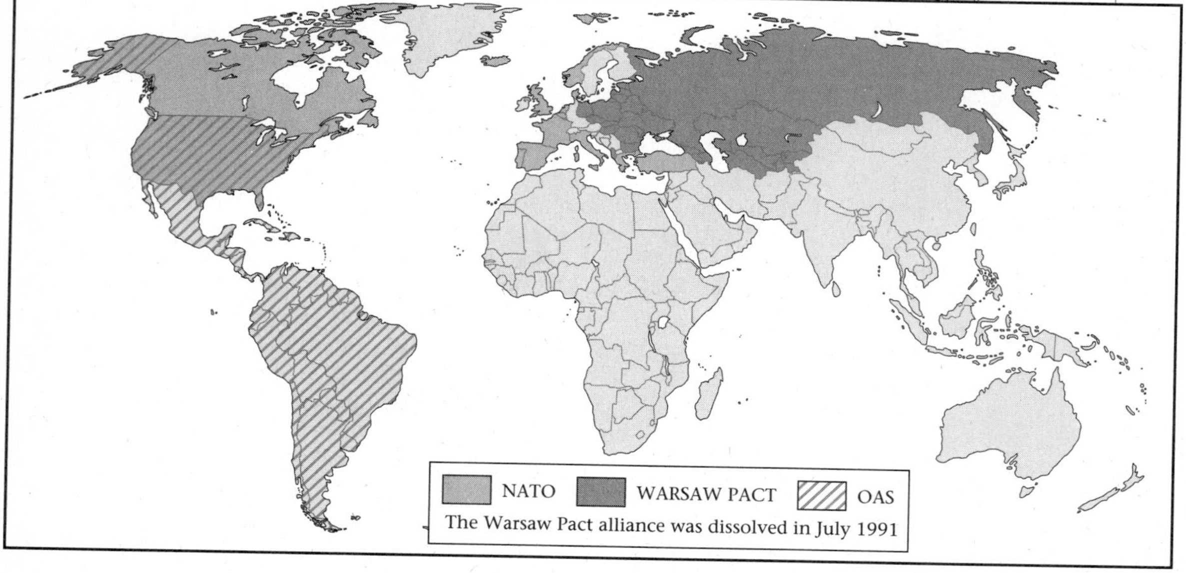

NATO
WARSAW PACT
OAS
The Warsaw Pact alliance was dissolved in July 1991

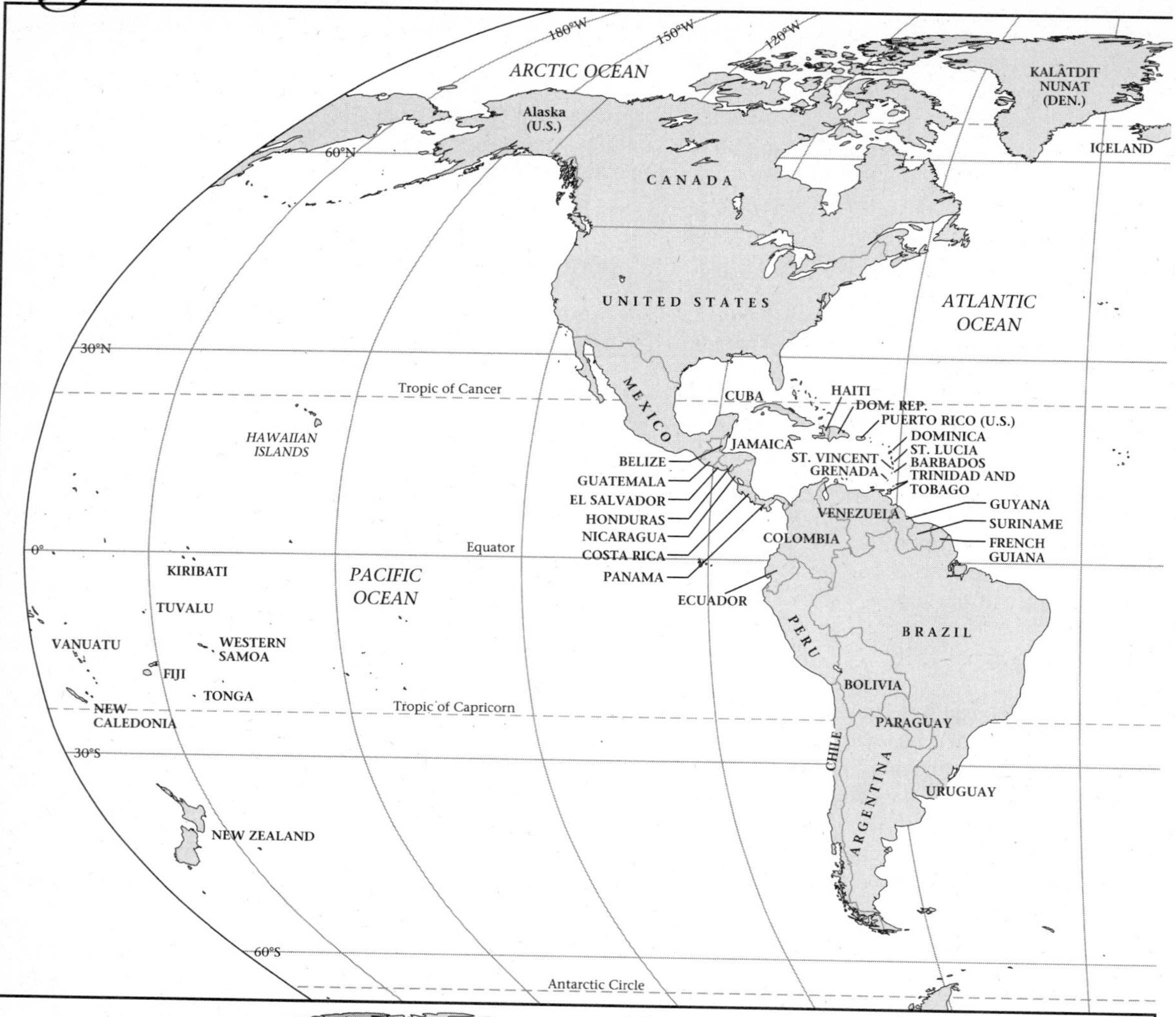

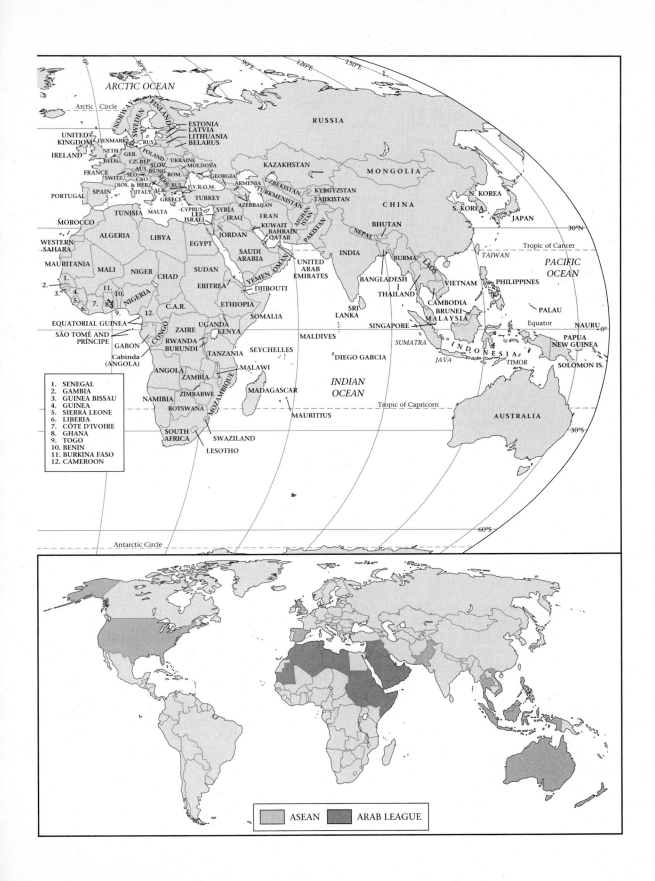

A Planet at Risk

Population and Poverty

Beyond these economic, social, and ideological sources of discord, the world faced some deeper, more long-term problems at the end of the millennium. Population growth and deep poverty, pollution, resource exhaustion, and potential environmental crises loomed.

Human productivity continued its increasingly steep upward curve in the twentieth century. But the multiplying product of the new industrial society also continued to be distributed very unequally. The large majority of the new goods and services were consumed by a small percentage of the world's people living in advanced industrial societies. By sucking resources out of the underdeveloped world for processing in the wealthy West, indeed, modern industrialism sometimes made the lot of the poor nations relatively worse than it had been in earlier times, when material want was more equitably distributed to all the world's peoples.

Accelerating population growth also contributed to the earth's problems. The population explosion, checked in the developed nations, continued to multiply the mouths that needed feeding in Asia, Africa, and Latin America. Scientific agriculture and medical conquest of disease in particular allowed more people in the Third World to live longer. These regions, however, remained the poorest on the globe. Population growth thus added not to human happiness, but to the sum total of human misery. Indeed, the demands of mushrooming populations for food, housing, education, and jobs repeatedly overwhelmed the best efforts of poor countries to improve their standards of living. Political instability, crime, and corruption often followed in the wake of these deteriorating economic conditions.

To many experts, all the mechanisms for a catastrophic Malthusian collision between expanding population and inadequate food supply seemed to be in place. Natural disasters—droughts, floods, earthquakes—repeatedly triggered waves of starvation and disease, particularly in parts of Africa and Asia. Even worse things might lie in the future for the poor nations of the global South as the seemingly inexorable cycle of unequally distributed wealth and uncontrolled population growth continues.

Pollution and Dwindling Resources

Not even the most developed nations, however, were free of serious long-range threats to their prosperity and quality of life. Again, technology, which had made ours the most materially advanced of all civilizations, also seemed to be the potential cause of impending disasters.

Sensitive individuals had been aware of the pollu-

tion of the natural environment from the earliest days of the Industrial Revolution. But things became far worse in the course of the twentieth century. By the later half of the twentieth century, the pollution that had poisoned and darkened the rivers and skies of nineteenth-century industrial towns had spread death to many life forms in rivers, lakes, and seas and filled the skies over great cities with choking smog. And the pollution of the environment as a whole threatened, as we shall see, far worse things to come.

Pollution could, at considerable cost and with great effort, be overcome. However, the inexorable dwindling of the natural resources that had made the Industrial Revolution possible was an irreversible process. Essential minerals and metals, petroleum and related fossil fuels all existed in finite quantities in the earth's crust. Plastics and other synthetic materials, nuclear power and other new energy sources might in time replace some of what was rapidly disappearing. Whether this substitute technology would be as cheap, more dangerous, or more polluting to the environment, however, remained to be seen.

The Environmental Crisis

Even more frightening possibilities, some experts believed, menaced an industrializing world as the year 2000 drew near. The human race, some authorities declared, had dangerously upset the balance of nature. If so, there would be a high price to pay.

Environmental warnings proliferated through the second half of the twentieth century. Pesticides intended to help farmers could poison whole food chains, filling streams with fish floating belly up and bringing "silent springs" when no birds sang. "Acid rain" produced by industrial gases could destroy whole forests. Land reclamation projects could wipe out entire species in wetlands and other specialized environments. Periodic petroleum spills from giant oil tankers visibly decimated wildlife along seacoasts.

Again, technological progress seemed to bring unexpected and terrible by-products in its wake. The widespread cultivation of a limited number of plant and animal species of particular usefulness to the human race, for instance, threatened the valuable diversity of nature. Hence, if a virus or blight should destroy one of these widely cultivated plants or animals, the world would no longer possess the natural variety of species within which substitutes might be found. Our very mastery of the environment thus seemed to be carrying us within range of unprecedented dangers.

Perhaps the worst long-range environmental threats, however, were to the earth's atmosphere. The release of enormous quantities of industrial gases and automobile exhaust fumes into the air and the burning and clearing of primordial rain forests, which produced much of the atmospheric oxygen we breathe, could lead to a genuinely global catastrophe. The "greenhouse effect," in which new layers of gas in the upper atmosphere reflected solar heat back to the earth's surface, as glass does heat in a greenhouse, could produce a slow but vastly destructive "global warming." As temperatures rose around the planet, rich agricultural land could turn into dust bowls, while melting polar ice raised the world's sea levels and flooded the port cities of the world. Holes in the natural ozone layer of the upper air, by contrast, could admit destructive solar radiation formerly excluded by ozone, now a diminishing atmospheric gas.

From oil-polluted recreational beaches to global catastrophe seemed a large leap to skeptics. But not, even the doubters had to admit, an impossible one.

THE DRIFT TOWARD ONE WORLD

GLOBAL TRENDS

Challenging these forces of disorder and disintegration, however, other global trends pointed just the other way, toward unity and global integration. One of the fundamental clichés of the times was that the world grew smaller every year. And one of the great utopian dreams of this blood-soaked century was that we would one day recognize that we were all citizens of the same planet and start trying to live like it.

There were in fact several ways in which the drift toward one world had already gone considerably further than most people realized in the 1990s. Common patterns

of national development, for instance, seemed to some to be producing nations that were more alike politically, socially, and economically than ever before. The development of modern technology had shrunk the world drastically, making all parts of it accessible in hours, information from anywhere available in seconds. The growth of economic interdependence linked our fates, making what a Middle Eastern ruler decided to do of crucial importance to ordinary citizens in America or Japan. In addition, the peoples of the globe became increasingly bound by international agreements and organizations over the past century. And there were already classes of people whose international careers and lifestyles made them genuine world citizens.

These and other evidences of a long drift in the direction of global interdependence and integration will be examined in this section.

PARALLEL PATTERNS OF DEVELOPMENT

One hopeful sign was what appeared to be an emerging pattern of common political, social, and economic structures in the last decades of the twentieth century. It seemed at least possible that the profound differences of preceding decades—between East and West in the cold war and between North and South in the global economic sweepstakes—were giving way to some shared goals and common institutions.

Politically, one-party states, military dictatorships, and other forms of authoritarian government appeared to be on the defensive. After 1989, the Eastern European countries replaced their self-perpetuating communist regimes with competing parties and free elections. Some-

The Peace Corps at work. President Kennedy's attempt to channel the idealism of American youth into a program to help other people help themselves was still going strong more than thirty years later. Here, a Peace Corps volunteer helps schoolchildren in Costa Rica tend their garden. (Monkmeyer Press)

times they re-elected people connected with the old Communist governments—but there was no talk of abrogating democracy again. In Latin America, the military rulers who had dominated politics for so long gave way to elected governments almost everywhere. At the beginning of 1995, only one un-elected ruler—Fidel Castro in Cuba—remained in the western hemisphere.

In Africa, some of the old liberation leaders allowed themselves to be voted out of office. In 1994, South Africa held its first democratic election and chose its first black African president, the remarkable Nelson Mandela. In Asia, freer elections in Korea, Taiwan, and elsewhere added strength to the Indian and Japanese examples of democratic governance.

There were still major exceptions. Deng Hsiaoping's Communist party still ran China, and Boris Yeltsin's Russia was no model democracy. Many other authoritarian governments remained, especially in Africa and Asia. Still, some analysts saw long-term advantages to democracy that made this freer form of government look like the wave of the long-term future. Democratic governments, after all, did do a better job of protecting the rights of the governed. Elections provided periodic opportunities to replace corrupt, tyrannical, or ineffectual leaders. Democracies were also much more flexible than authoritarian regimes—a valuable feature in rapidly changing times.

Socially, there seemed to be general acceptance of the need for at least some sort of welfare safety net and for entitlements financed by taxes and administered by government. Public education, public health, retirement benefits, and some unemployment compensation were widely accepted government responsibilities. Many added aid for mothers with dependent children, job retraining in times of economic change, child care for working parents, and other supports.

There were challenges to this large welfare apparatus. Poor countries could hardly afford such services, yet their people demanded them. European and American governments found their highly developed welfare systems too expensive and began to consider cutbacks. In general, however, citizens of both industrial and less developed states wanted and needed modern welfare nets. And since democracy allowed the people to express their preferences by voting, it seemed unlikely that the world's social welfare programs would really be eliminated anytime soon.

Economically, finally, the 1980s and 1990s saw a widespread turn from state-run economies to free-market capitalism. First in the developing countries of the global South, then in the former communist countries of Eastern Europe and Asia, the economic theories of Adam Smith seemed to be replacing those of Karl Marx. In Russia, China, and many smaller nations, state planners and five-year-plans gave way to entrepreneurs and market forces like the law of supply and demand.

The basic reason for the shift appeared to be the markedly greater productivity of free markets over command economies. Western Europeans enjoyed a much higher standard of living than Eastern Europeans did, while Japan and the East Asian "tigers," from South Korea to Singapore, vastly outproduced Communist China, North Korea, or Vietnam. Third world countries, after decades of following the communist model, decided to take a second look at capitalism—and began to change their ways too.

It also seemed possible that a major economic revival lay ahead. The growth of Third World markets, the trend toward global free trade, and improved economic productivity, some economists declared, could trigger a wave of long-term prosperity, like that of the decades after World War II.

The West and the world as a whole thus seemed to be turning to a single profitable economic system as the century drew to a close.

An American Telephone and Telegraph communications satellite is lofted into space by a NASA rocket. Technology linked all the continents as the twentieth century drew to a close. It also seemed to many to threaten global well-being, devouring resources, polluting the environment, and absorbing energy and funds that, some felt, should be used to help people with more immediate problems, such as poverty and even survival. (A. T. & T. Co., Photo/Graphics Center)

TECHNOLOGY SHRINKS THE WORLD

In the nineteenth century the age of steam and telegraphy strapped continents across with rail lines, bound one continent to another with steamships, and laid down undersea cables that provided almost instantaneous communication around the world. Intercontinental empires flourished as never before. Economic interdependence grew apace. Technological progress thus made a true world order possible for the first time.

Throughout the twentieth century technology continued to make such a global order easier to attain. The supertanker dwarfed the steamships of the turn of the century—which were already ten or twenty times the size of their sail-driven predecessors. Automobiles, buses, trucks, and trains that travel more than 150 miles an hour revolutionized land transport in this century. And the air, penetrated only in dreams by our ancestors, was successfully and massively invaded in the twentieth century. Electronic communications were also updated dramatically by devices ranging from telephones and radio to television, the computer terminal, and the communications satellite.

The result of these improvements in transportation and communication was an immensely expanded number of encounters between peoples. Such international encounters between ordinary citizens of different countries took many forms. We think first perhaps of tourists, traveling easily in Europe or America, or being the first in their group to fly to visit Tibet or Katmandu. But students spent considerably more time studying at universities abroad, and young backpacking travelers wandered the dusty roads everywhere by foot or by bus all through the second half of the century. Business people and military personnel were routinely posted overseas for periods of years, while the former particularly felt as much at home on intercontinental jets as on a commuter train at home. Perhaps most importantly, millions of migrant laborers—"guest workers"—lived for years, sometimes for lifetimes, in foreign countries.

Such close contacts with other peoples dwarfed any previous contacts between the continents. To know your neighbors was not necessarily to love them, of course, and culture shock or resentment of intrusive foreign ways were common early reactions in such people-to-people encounters. But many who were fortunate enough to meet and live with others came to feel that, although their own ways were clearly better, there was something to be learned from the rest of the world too.

GLOBAL INDUSTRIALIZATION

Applied science and technology also made ours "one world" in other important ways. The cultures of all rich nations, and even the urban cultures of less affluent societies, were extremely similar at least in their common dependence on advanced technology. The peoples of many countries thus shared a common technological sophisti-cation, styles of life based on machines, and attitudes of mind inculcated by modern industrial society. The "gentlemen of Japan" who watched Admiral Perry land in the 1850s had almost nothing in common with their American visitors. A century and a half later, descendants of those first American travelers to Japan might buy their automobiles or television sets from that country. They might even find the American factory they work at bought up and reorganized by Japanese business managers.

The cultures of the less developed regions also had more in common, thanks to the worldwide spread of modern industrial technology. Third World people who moved from the more traditional back country into urban areas would find themselves sucked into whole new patterns of life. Machine skills, industrial discipline, and the bright lights downtown would be enough to give a lathe operator in South Africa something very important in common with similarly employed factory workers in Mexico or Scotland.

Even the large number of citizens of the Third World who stayed in their villages would find themselves depending on industrial technology in many ways. From plastic buckets and store-bought clothes to the school bus and the radio, they would feel the impact of a larger world. And that first contact might well set them on the road to still deeper involvement in the larger technological society that girdled the globe.

If we all did move further toward one world, then, industrial technology would have played a key role in bringing it about.

ECONOMIC INTERDEPENDENCE

Money, any cynic or economic historian will tell you, makes the world go round. The economic historian, at least, would probably feel that if the world was moving toward a higher degree of unity, that unity would be fundamentally economic in nature.

The economic dimension of the New Imperialism of the nineteenth century was obvious even to contemporaries. Western needs for raw materials and markets, for investment opportunities and cheap labor, were certainly among the prime causal factors. The first intercontinental political institutions, then, reached their highest development on a foundation of economic relationships.

When the formal political empires crumbled after World War II, as we have seen, the economic ties that underlay them did not crumble as well. In some places, Western investment and exploitation of cheap labor overseas, Western draining of natural resources and dumping of manufactured goods in Third World markets have even accelerated since the great liberation.

In the twentieth as in earlier centuries, furthermore, imperial economic ties worked both ways, making each side increasingly dependent upon the other. If Europeans or Americans bought copper or coffee or oil or jute from a former colony, that commodity-producing people became dependent on European or American markets and on the prices set in those markets far away. At the same time, however, the purchasers became dependent on their sources. Developed economies could sometimes prove extremely vulnerable to oil boycotts or high commodity prices overseas.

When large Western banks offered substantial development loans to Third World governments, those governments and their peoples—whose labor must in the end pay back the loans—mortgaged their future to foreign financial institutions. But the banks also incurred a massive dependency. The default of loans large enough to help whole nations develop could shake the biggest bank, could put the entire financial underpinnings of the Western World in jeopardy.

Awareness of the importance of the international economy led the world's leaders to move toward a global free market more energetically than ever before. The success of Western Europe's Common Market inspired the successful negotiation of NAFTA and a number of other regional agreements freeing up trade, investment, and economic relations generally. Led by President Clinton, leaders of Asia-Pacific powers and the nations of the Americas agreed to work toward complete free trade early in the new century. And GATT, ratified after years of negotiation, provided a global framework for free and productive economic relations between the peoples of the world.

GLOBAL ELITES

At the top of this slowly evolving international order might be detected a new international elite, true citizens of the world whose labors were welding the globe into the "one world" of which idealists sometimes dreamed. Consider, for instance, the following conversation between two businessmen, overheard in a bar in New Delhi:

"How's the wife?"

"Oh, very well. And Sally?"

Pictures of growing children passed from hand to hand. Compliments were exchanged. Another round was ordered.

It was a conversation scarcely worth noticing. Except that one of the two men was American, the other Japanese. They first met in Panama, where their respective firms were engaged in construction projects. They were engineers, experts in earthquake-proof construction, in New Delhi for an international conference on earthquake engineering.

"Please give my regards to your wife."

"And mine to Mrs. Takahira."

The names were not Sally or Takahira, but the rest of the conversation was quite real. And the two men themselves represented a very important group in the world today—the new global elite.

There were a number of such elites, actually. Engi-

One world, seen from space. Keeping the globe intact is the greatest single challenge facing the generations that will carry the human venture into the twenty-first century. (NASA Headquarters)

neers and scientists, managers and business executives, representatives of governments and of international agencies were among the most important. They included such people as the Ford technicians who set up assembly lines in the Soviet Union in the 1930s, the Russian technicians in Cuba in the 1960s, and the Cuban technicians in Africa two decades later. Jet-hopping around the world, rebuilding the world in the image of our century, they contributed enormously to the sense any traveler could feel of one world in the making.

There were also strictly national elites who were cast so thoroughly in an international mold that they constituted a force for international solidarity without ever crossing a national frontier. In their Western-style business suits or their American-style shirt sleeves, sharing a common body of technical training, managerial skills, career-mindedness, greed, or humanitarian dedication, they were much more alike than any of their ancestors could have been.

Likeness did not guarantee harmony among peoples. But contacts and common interests among elites seemed to make international tolerance and understanding that much more likely in the future.

INTERNATIONAL ORGANIZATIONS

Some degree of international organization binding the nation-states on a global scale had emerged even in the nineteenth century. At that time, a series of technical organizations were set up to deal with problems common to many nations, or to provide international institutions

The United Nations headquarters in New York. The second global organization has long outlasted the first and made important contributions to the international community. Its location in New York City reflected America's key global role after 1945. (Monkmeyer Press)

where they were obviously necessary. Such groups included the International Telegraphic Union in 1865, the Universal Postal Union of 1874, and patent, copyright, and other international unions from the 1870s on. Organizations relating to peace and war between nations were also established, notably the International Red Cross in 1864 and the World Court (Permanent Court of Arbitration) set up by the First Hague Conference in 1899.

The twentieth century, and particularly its second half, saw two major attempts at global organization intended to keep the peace and to deal with problems common to a number of peoples. The League of Nations, founded after World War I, and the United Nations, growing out of World War II, represented the most ambitious efforts thus far at global organization. Even the U.N., however, should be seen as only the apex of a pyramid of regional and global institutions that affected all our lives.

As we have seen, Europe established an elaborate structure of regional associations in the later twentieth century—in some cases two such structures, one for Western Europe, one for the east bloc. Besides the two military alliances, NATO and the Warsaw Pact, there were throughout the Cold War decades the Common Market and its Eastern equivalent, COMECON. The West also boasted the European Coal Community, the European Steel Community and EURATOM, the European Atomic Energy Community. These latter were true supranational rather than merely international organizations, since they had some power to control aspects of the policy of their member nations, rather than simply carrying out their wishes.

Other important regional organizations included the Organization of American States, the Central American Common Market, the Latin American Free Trade Association, the Organization of African Unity, the Organization of Petroleum Exporting Countries, as well as the regular meetings of the heads of state of nonaligned countries, the

economic summits that brought together the leaders of the seven most developed Western nations, and so on.

Global organizations associated with or grouped around the United Nations, finally, included the Food and Agricultural Organization, the World Health Organization, the United Nations Educational, Scientific, and Cultural Organization, the World Bank (International Bank for Reconstruction and Development), and the International Monetary Fund, as well as such holdovers from earlier years as the World Court and the International Labor Organization. At the top of this bewildering array of world organizations stood the United Nations, with its Security Council for the great powers and its General Assembly for all the nearly two hundred nations of the world.

The story of these twentieth-century attempts at organizing our world on a scale that transcended the nation-state was one of continual expansion, and of expansion in more ways than one. International associations certainly grew in number, from a handful of multilateral organizations and compacts at the turn of the century to thousands today. Originally centering in Europe, they spread to Asia, Africa, and the Americas, as the names of some of the regional groups listed above indicate. The staffs and activities of such institutions also expanded and become more truly international. From small numbers of administrators, most of them European or American, these staffs grew to thousands and tens of thousands, drawn from all parts of the world and working on all continents.

The world thus had at least an embryonic international bureaucracy in place, attempting to do for international problems what the civil services of the nations did for their own people. These international administrators still depended totally on the nations, particularly the great powers, for the funding and support to do their work. Nevertheless, they might have an important part to play in our common future.

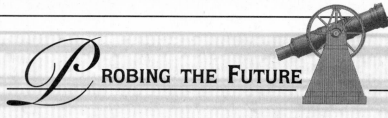

$\mathcal{P}$ROBING THE FUTURE

"*If contemporary history involves global considerations, and if nearly all American and European historians lack a knowledge of Oriental and African languages, how can they possibly be qualified to write this kind of history? Will traditional Western parochialism preclude any true understanding of the processes through which we are living?*

The implicit assumption behind your question—that history will continue to be written from a narrow American or European point of view—is that the only important history that will be written in the next generation will be European or American. There is, in fact, distinguished historical scholarship in the Arab world, in Africa, China, Japan, and Soviet Asia, with its own points of view. It would be very foolish for us to suppose that Western Europeans and Americans will continue to have a monopoly of historical knowledge. From my point of view, it would be even more foolish for us to desire to have such a monopoly. Young countries at last are involved in historical scholarship, and we must begin to accept them on equal terms. After all, is it unreasonable to speculate that these young areas which are going to have such a hand in making the future will also have a large share in writing its history?"

———— ◆◆◆ ————

The questioner here is the well-known European historian Norman F. Cantor, and the response is that of the equally distinguished European and world historian Geoffrey Barraclough. Barraclough, among other achievements, is the editor of the essential Times Atlas of World History.

Do you see ways of overcoming the inherent problems that Western historians may have in writing global history? Do you agree with Barraclough that history by non-Western scholars will become increasingly important in the future? In what ways might a history of the world written by scholars of the nationalities Barraclough mentions differ from that written by an American?

Geoffrey Barraclough, "Contemporary World History," in Norman F. Cantor, ed., Perspectives on the Past: Conversations with Historians, Vol. 2 (New York: Macmillan, 1971), pp. 361–362.

SUMMARY

Hopes for a genuinely new World Order rose in the aftermath of the Cold War. United States President George Bush spoke of a democratic, free-market world at peace, European statesmen of a more unified and prosperous Europe, U.N. leaders of a more potent international organization.

The public mood, however, soon turned sour in a world beset by many problems.

Major forces of disorder included economic dislocation, social problems of all sorts, and passionately held religions and ideologies in conflict.

The planet itself seemed to some to be at serious risk at the end of the twentieth century. Swollen Third World populations, intractable poverty, pollution, and the potential exhaustion of essential natural resources combined with looming environmental crises to add to the world's woes.

Yet there was also a detectable movement toward global unity and integration in the later twentieth century. This drift toward one world, a global community of peoples linked politically, economically, technologically, and in other ways, seemed to accelerate in the later twentieth century. Associations of individuals, compacts between governments, and supranational organizations grew more numerous. Modern means of transportation and communication, increasing economic interdependence, and more and more face-to-face contacts between peoples of diverse cultures all contributed to this trend.

In a world so full of promise, yet so profoundly threatened, the human venture into history had never been more exciting, more dangerous, or more problematical in its outcome than it was as it moved toward the end of its fifth full millennium of the history of civilization.

SUGGESTED READING

ATTALI, J. *Millennium: Winners and Losers in the Coming World Order.* Trans. L. Connors and N. Gardels. New York: Times Books, 1991. International relations in a post-Cold War world. See also C. W. Kegley and E. R. Wittkopf, eds., *The Future of American Foreign Policy* (New York: St. Martin's Press, 1992) for essays on America's place in the new world order.

BARNET, R. J. *Global Reach: The Power of the Multinational Corporations.* New York: Simon & Schuster, 1974. The multinational corporation as a key factor in the world economy.

BUGINCOURT, J. "A New Colonialism," *Development Forum* 5 (1977). Critical treatment of Western tourism in the Third World.

CERVENKA, Z. *The Unfinished Quest for Unity: Africa and the OAU.* London: Friedman, 1977. Good example of a major regional organization with more potential for unity than is commonly assumed. On the original impetus for African togetherness, see I. Geiss, *The Pan-African Movement* (London: Methuen, 1974).

CHAUDHURI, N. *The Continent of Circe.* Bombay: Jaico Pub. Co., 1966. The mind-set of Westernized elites in Third World countries.

CONNELLY, P., and R. PEARLMAN. *The Politics of Scarcity.* New York: Oxford University Press, 1976. Discusses Third World commodity producers' cartels, another important organizing force in the evolving global economy.

DIAZ-ALEJANDRO, C. F. "North–South Relations: The Economic Component," *International Organization,* vol. 29 (Winter 1975), pp. 213–241. The broad picture of this central aspect of the often painful ties that bind developed and underdeveloped countries.

FOSTER, G. M. *Traditional Cultures and the Impact of Technological Change.* New York: Harper & Row, Pub., 1963. The homogenizing impact of modern technology around the world.

HERMAN, B. *The Optimal International Division of Labor.* Geneva: International Labor Organization, 1975. One important form of global interdependence is explored here.

HUNTINGTON, S. P. "The Clash of Civilizations?" *Foreign Affairs* vol. 72, No. 3 (Summer, 1993), pp. 22–49. Widely discussed thesis that after the Cold War clash of ideologies will come conflict between historic civilizations—Western, Islamic, and so on.

JOEKES, S. P. *Women in the World Economy.* New York: Oxford University Press, 1987. Brief cross-cultural survey of women in developed and less developed economies.

LASSERRE-BIGORRY, J. H. *General Survey of Present-Day International Migration for Employment.* Geneva: International Labor Office, 1975. Summary of migrant labor patterns around the world.

LUARD, E. *A History of the United Nations.* London: Macmillan, 1982. Deals with the earlier years of the most promising international political organization to date.

MEAD, M., ed. *Cultural Patterns and Technical Change.* New York: New American Library, 1955. A distinguished and concerned anthropologist gives her view of the impact of modernizing technology on the diversity of cultures.

ROBERTSON, R. *Globalization: Social Theory and Global Culture.* London: Sage Publications, 1992. A leading sociological analyst of the globalization process summarized sociological explanations for the increased interaction between peoples.

ROSTOW, W. W. *The World Economy: History and Prospect.* (Austin: University of Texas Press, 1978.) A well-known developmental economist looks ahead to the global future.

TOBIAS, M. *World War III: Population and the Biosphere at the End of the Millennium.* Santa Fe, NM: Bear and Co., 1994. Massive study of the impact of overpopulation on the environment.

VON LAUE, T. *The World Revolution of Westernization: The Twentieth Century in Global Perspective.* New York: Oxford University Press, 1987. Controversial but stimulating account of the impact of globalism on regional cultures around the world.

WALLERSTEIN, I. *The Capitalist World-Economy.* Cambridge: Cambridge University Press, 1979. Economic predominance as a global force.

INDEX

James II of England, 465
Jamestown, 432
Janissary Corps, 380, 476
Japan
    aggression of, 645
    militarism and, 639-640
    China and, 314-315, 399-406, 646
    fall of, 656
    Meiji restoration, 550
    Mongols and, 325
    New Imperialism and, 550
    in 1900, 569-570
    under Tokugawa shogunate, 482-484, 485-486
    after World War I, 593
    World War I and, 590
    after World War II, 665-666, 707-708
    World War II and, 652, 654-667
Jaruzelski, Wojciech, 674
Java, 296, 297, 448
Jazz Age, 599
Jefferson, Thomas, 523, 525
Jehovah, 7
Jeremiah, 151
Jericho, 18
Jerome, Saint, 231
Jerusalem, 72-75,
    Crusades and, 252
Jesuits, 371, 448
    missionaries to China, 482, 551
Jesus Christ, 75, 169-170
    Islam and, 262
Jiang Jiehi, 615-621, 646
Jiang Qing, 723
Jiangxi Soviet, 619
Jihad, 262-265
    in twentieth century, 693-694
    in West Africa, 489-490
Jinnah, Muhammad Ali, 695
Joan of Arc, 255-256
Johanson, Donald, 8, 9
Johnson, Lyndon, 702-703
Jonson, Ben, 368
Joseph II, Emperor, 463
Joveyni, 322
Joyce, James, 743
Judaism
    Islam and, 262
    origins of, 74-75
    spread of, 230
Judea, 74
    Babylon and, 36
Judges, 72
Julius Caesar, 161
Junkers, 463
Justinian, 251
Justinian, Code of, 251, 256

Kaaba, 262, 263
Kabuki theater, 486
Kahlo, Frieda, 744
Kaifeng, 306, 308
Kali, 95
Kalidasa, 185
Kamakura shogunate, 399
Kangxi emperor, 480-481
Kano, 407
Kano Chronicle, 407
Karakorum, 323
Karanga people, 410
Karli, cave temples of, 179, 183-184
Karnak, 54
Kashmir, 385, 695-697
Kashta, 62
Kassites, 32
Katanga, 691
Katina, 407
Kautilya, 90-93
Kellogg-Briand Pact, 598
Kelly, Joan, 362
Kennan, George, 671, 682
Kennedy, John, 674-675, 677, 695-696
Kennedy, Robert, 703
Kenya, 547, 690-691, 726-727
    liberation of, 690-691
Kenyatta, Jomo, 690-691, 726-727
Kepler, Johannes, 469
Kerensky, Alexander, 610

Kerensky offensive (1917), 583
Khadijah, 262
Khafre, 54
Khajuraho, 295
Khanates, 323
Khartoum, Battle of, 546
Khayyám, Omar, 385
Khmer Empire, 298
Khmer Rouge, 726
Khoisan click languages, 222
Khomeini, Ruhollah, 694-695
Khrushchev, Nikita, 677
Khufu, 54
Kiev, 251
    Mongols and, 323
Kikuyu people, 690-691
Kilwa, 286
Kim Il Sung, 676
King, Martin Luther, Jr., 702, 703
Kipling, Rudyard, 542
Kinship
    in Paleolithic period, 13-14
    political institutions and, 20-21
Kiuprili family, 475-476
Kiva, 334
Kizilbashi, 381
Knights, 240, 243
Knights of Labor, 529
Knossos, 125-127
Kohl, Helmut, 683, 706, 755
Kongfuzi. See Confucius
Kongo, 408-409
Koran, 262, 270
Korea, 303, 313, 550
    China and, 313, 396
    U.S.S.R. and, 671
Korean War, 676
Kounda, Toure, 751
Krishna, 94, 95
Kristalnacht, 635
Krupp, Albert, 511
Krupskaya, Nadezhda, 609
Kshatriyas, 89, 292
Kublai Khan, 323, 327
Ku Klux Klan, 528
Kukulcan. See Quetzalcóatl
Kush, 61-64
    Axum and, 202
    metalworking in, 147-148
Kuwait, 694-695, 724
Kyoto, 314-315

Labé, Louise, 360
Labor movement, 508-509
    in United States, 529
Labour Party, 687, 695, 706
La Cruz, Juana de, 537
Lalibela, 282, 285
"Lament of Lady Qi, The," 306
Land bridges, 11
Land of the Two Rivers. See Mesopotamia
Lan Xang, 298
Laocoön, 137
Laos, 296, 298, 550, 676
Laozi, 112, 151
La Rochefoucauld, 471
Lascaux caves, 15
Last Supper, The (da Vinci), 367
Latifundia, 160
Latin America
    authoritarianism and, 640
    Cold War and, 674-676
    development of, 728-729
    Great Depression and, 603-604
    in 1900, 570-571
    in nineteenth century, 530-536
    preurban cultures of, 432
    Spain and, 447-448, 530-532
Latvia, 651
La Venta, 120
Law
    of accumulation, 509
    in Athens, 132-133
    in Babylon, 34-35
    in Byzantine Empire, 256
    in China, 303
    in England, 247

    in France, 247
    in Hebrew culture, 74
    in Islam, 263, 270
    in Persian Empire, 78
    in Rome, 163
    of supply and demand, 509
Lawrence, T. E. ("of Arabia"), 587
League of Nations, 591
Leaves of Grass, (Whitman), 537
Le dynasty, 396
Lebanon, 693
Lee Kuan Yew, 708
Lee, Robert E., 528
Legalism, 104, 107, 112
Lenin, Vladimir Ilich, 592, 591, 607, 609-612
Leo X, Pope, 369
Leo Africanus, 411-413
Leonardo da Vinci, 366-367
Léon-Portilla, Miguel, 366
Leopold, 548
Lepanto, Battle of, 363, 475
Levi-Strauss, Claude, 741
Lewenhak, Sheila, 597
Lexington, Battle of, 523
Li, 310
Liberalism, 509, 628, 632
    revolutions and, 607-608
Liberation struggle, 687-688
Libido, 740
Li Bo, 311
Libya, 548
    World War II and, 653
Liebknecht, Karl, 633
Life, beginning of, 7
Lincoln, Abraham, 526-528
Linear A/B, 125
Lingam, 182
Ling Mengqi, 400
Lion Hunt Frieze, 40
Li Shimin. See Tang Taizong
Li Si, 107, 112
Literature
    in ancient city-states, 22
    in ancient Greece, 137-139
    in Arabic culture, 273
    in China: under Ming dynasty, 400; under Mongols, 328; under Qin dynasty, 110-111; under Qing dynasty, 485; under Song dynasty, 311; under Tang dynasty, 311
    in Egypt, 53
    in Enlightenment, 471
    in India, 94-95, 177: under Guptas, 185
    in Japan, 316: under samurai, 401; under Tokugawa shogunate, 486
    in medieval Europe, 258-259
    in Mexico, 336
    modernist, 743-744, 747-749
    in Muslim world, 385
    in the Renaissance, 367-368
    in Romantic era, 518
    in Rome, 168-169
    in Sumeria, 38-39
    in United States, 536-537, 747-748
Lithuania, 651
Little Big Horn, Battle of, 573
Liu Bang. See Han Gaozu
Liu Tsung-yuan, 108
Li Yuan, 302-303
Llaneros, 533, 538
Lloyd George, David, 564, 589
    World War I and, 583, 589
Locarno treaties, 598
Locke, John, 470, 509
Logos, 170
Lohans, 312
Longbow, 254
Longfellow, Henry Wadsworth, 537
Long March, 619-620
Lost Generation, 599
Louis IX of France (Saint Louis), 246-247
Louis XI of France, 361-362
Louis XIV of France, 461-462
Louis XV of France, 504
Louis XVI of France, 503-505
Louisiana Purchase, 525
Louis Philippe, 515
Louvois, Marquis de, 462
Lower Egypt, 43-45
Loyola, Ignatius, 371